Science Fiction Writers

Science Fiction Writers

Second Edition

Critical Studies of the Major Authors from the Early
Nineteenth Century to the Present Day

Richard Bleiler
Editor in Chief

Charles Scribner's Sons
Macmillan Library Reference USA
Macmillan Publishing USA
New York

Executive Editor: Sylvia K. Miller
Project Management: Visual Education Corporation
Additional Editorial Support: Mary Flower, *Copyeditor*; Evangeline Legones, *Proofreader*; Andrew McCarthy, *Editorial Assistant*
Indexer: Katharyn Dunham
Publisher: Karen Day

Charles Scribner's Sons
Macmillan Library Reference USA
1633 Broadway
New York, New York 10019

1 3 5 7 9 11 13 15 17 19 20 18 16 14 12 10 8 6 4 2

Printed in the United States of America

Library of Congress Cataloging-in-Publication Data

Main entry under title:
Science fiction writers, 2d ed.
    Includes bibliographies and index.
    1. Science fiction, American—History and criticism. 2. Science fiction, English—History and criticism. 3. Science fiction, American—Bio-bibliography. 4. Science fiction, English — Bio-bibliography. I. Bleiler, Richard

PS374.S35S36   823'.0876'09
ISBN 0-684-80593-6   AACR2

The paper used in this publication meets the requirements of ANSI/NISO Z39.48-1992 (Permanence of Paper).

ACKNOWLEDGMENTS

Acknowledgment is gratefully made to those publishers and individuals who have permitted the use of the following materials in copyright.

Alfred Bester
Excerpt beginning with "I've carried my concept" and ending with "production problems." From an unpublished letter of Alfred Bester. Reprinted by courtesy of the author.

Ray Bradbury
Three excerpts from: "Drunk and in Charge of a Bicycle," an introduction by Ray Bradbury, from *The Stories of Ray Bradbury*. Eight lines from: "Thoughts on Visiting the Main Rocket Assembly Building at Cape Canaveral for the First Time," page 71 from *Where Robot Mice and Robot Men Run Round in Robot Towns*. Copyright line for the introduction: Copyright © 1980 by Ray Bradbury Enterprises/A California Corporation. Copyright line for "Thoughts on Visiting the Main Rocket," etc.: Copyright © 1977 by Ray Bradbury. Reprinted by permission of the Harold Matson Company, Inc.

John Brunner
Six lines from "The H-Bombs' Thunder" by John Brunner. Copyright © 1958 by John Brunner; copyright assigned in 1959 to The Campaign for Nuclear Disarmament (CND); excerpted from *The Book of John Brunner* (DAW Books, New York, 1976) by permission of the author.

Philip K. Dick
From "Man, Android and Machine" by Philip K. Dick, in *Science Fiction at Large*, edited by Peter Nicholls. Reprinted by permission of the author and the author's agents, Scott Meredith Literary Agency, Inc., 845 Third Avenue, New York, New York 10022.

Aldous Huxley
Fifth stanza from "First Philosopher's Song" in *Leda* from *The Collected Poetry of Aldous Huxley*, edited by Donald Watt. Copyright © 1920 by Aldous Huxley. Specified extracts from letter "To George Orwell (E. H. Blair) Wrightwood, Cal. 21 October, 1949" (pp. 604–605) and letter "Dearest M, 3276 Deronda Drive, L.A. 28, Cal. 20 August, 1959" in *Letters of Aldous Huxley*, edited by Grover Smith. Copyright © 1969 by Laura Huxley. Reprinted by permission of Harper & Row, Publishers, Inc., and by permission of Mrs. Laura Huxley and Chatto & Windus Ltd.

H. P. Lovecraft
Excerpt of a letter from H. P. Lovecraft to Frank Belknap Long (February 1924). Reprinted from *Selected Letters of H. P. Lovecraft*, Vol. I, by permission of the publisher, Arkham House Publishers, Inc., Sauk City, Wisconsin.

Richard Matheson
Lines from "As I Walked Out One Evening," copyright © 1940 and renewed 1968 by W. H. Auden. Reprinted from *W. H. Auden: Collected Poems*, by W. H. Auden, edited by Edward Mendelson, by permission of Random House, Inc., and by permission of Faber and Faber Ltd. Publishers.

C. L. Moore and Henry Kuttner
Excerpt from Henry Kuttner's diary reprinted by permission of the Estate of Henry Kuttner. Excerpt from the C. L. Moore (unpublished) autobiography reprinted by permission of C. L. Moore (Mrs. Thomas Reggie).

Eric Frank Russell
Excerpt of letter by Eric Frank Russell (9 January 1973). Reprinted by permission of Laurence Pollinger Limited and the Estate of Eric Frank Russell.

Margaret St. Clair
Autobiographical note published in *Fantastic Adventures*, November 1946. Copyright © 1946 by Margaret St. Clair. Copyright renewed. Reprinted by permission of McIntosh and Otis, Inc.

Clark Ashton Smith
Excerpt from "To the Daemon" in *Poems in Prose* (1965). Reprinted by permission of Arkham House Publishers, Inc., Sauk City, Wisconsin.

James Tiptree, Jr.
Excerpts from "With Tiptree Through the Great Sex Muddle" by James Tiptree, Jr. Copyright © by Jeffrey D. Smith 1975; reprinted by permission of the author and the author's agent, Robert P. Mills, Ltd. Excerpts from "Everything but the Signature Is Me" by James Tiptree, Jr. Copyright © by James Tiptree, Jr., 1978; reprinted by permission of the author and the author's agent, Robert P. Mills, Ltd.

Stanley G. Weinbaum
From "A Martian Odyssey and Other Science Fiction Tales." Copyright © 1935 by *Fantasy Magazine*; reprinted by permission of Forrest J. Ackerman, 2495 Glendower Avenue, Hollywood, California 90027, for the heir.

CONTENTS

CONTENTS

CONTENTS

CHRONOLOGY

THE FOLLOWING IS a roughly chronological list of the decades that the writers profiled in this volume first became active as professional science fiction writers or, as in the case of the early writers, wrote their most notable works of science fiction. It is also a list that should be used with caution.

Writers do not obligingly start their careers at the beginning of decades, and it is important to remember a number of the writers listed below—Isaac Asimov, Alfred Bester, L. Sprague de Camp, Joe Haldeman, Pat Murphy, Theodore Sturgeon, and Ian Watson, to name but a few—started their careers near the end of decades.

Equally importantly, this list details only writers' first appearances; it cannot describe when they became mature writers or reached their stylistic apogee: Fritz R. Leiber's first science fiction story appeared in 1941, but he produced some of his finest work near the end of his life; likewise, Jack Williamson's first story appeared in 1928, but he continues to produce excellent work. (On the obverse: Alfred Bester produced some of his finest works in the 1950s but died in 1987; C. L. Moore's science fictional career effectively ended with the 1958 death of her first husband: she too died in 1987.)

Finally, it cannot list writers whose careers can be said to have had several beginnings: Clifford Simak's career started in 1931, and again in 1938; Sheri Tepper's first professional publications were in 1963, and she did not resume writing until the 1980s.

Early Nineteenth Century (pre-1850)

Edgar Allan Poe
Mary Shelley

Late Nineteenth Century (1850–1890)

H. Rider Haggard
Luis P. Senarens
Jules Verne

Fin de Siècle Nineteenth Century (1890s)

Arthur Conan Doyle
H. G. Wells
M. P. Shiel

Twentieth Century (1900–1920)

Edgar Rice Burroughs
Murray Leinster
A. Merritt
Garrett P. Serviss

Twentieth Century (1920–1930)

David H. Keller
H. P. Lovecraft
E. E. Smith, Ph.D.
John Taine
Jack Williamson
S. Fowler Wright

Twentieth Century (1930–1940)

Isaac Asimov
Alfred Bester
John W. Campbell, Jr.
L. Sprague de Camp
Aldous Huxley
Catherine L. Moore and Henry Kuttner
C. S. Lewis
Clifford D. Simak
Clark Ashton Smith
Olaf Stapledon
Theodore Sturgeon
A. E. van Vogt
Stanley G. Weinbaum
John Wyndham

Twentieth Century (1940–1950)

Poul Anderson
James Blish
Ray Bradbury
Arthur C. Clarke
Hal Clement
Robert A. Heinlein
Damon Knight
C. M. Kornbluth
Fritz R. Leiber
George Orwell
Frederik Pohl
Eric Frank Russell
Margaret St. Clair
William Tenn
Jack Vance
Kurt Vonnegut

Twentieth Century (1950–1960)

Brian W. Aldiss
J. G. Ballard
John Brunner
Algis Budrys

Samuel R. Delany
Philip K. Dick
Gordon R. Dickson
Harlan Ellison
Philip Jose Farmer
Harry Harrison
Frank Herbert
Sir Fred Hoyle
Stanislaw Lem
Richard Matheson
Katherine MacLean
Judith Merril
Walter M. Miller, Jr.
Michael Moorcock
Chad Oliver
Robert Sheckley
Robert Silverberg
Cordwainer Smith

Twentieth Century (1960–1970)

Greg Bear
Gregory Benford
C. J. Cherryh
Richard Cowper
Thomas M. Disch
Joe Haldeman
Ursula K. Le Guin
Christopher Priest
Joanna Russ
James Tiptree, Jr.
Ian Watson
Gene Wolfe
Roger Zelazny

Twentieth Century (1970–1980)

Michael Bishop
Octavia Butler
Orson Scott Card
William Gibson
Pat Murphy
Kim Stanley Robinson
Bruce Sterling
Howard Waldrop
Connie Willis

Twentieth Century (1980–1990)

David Brin
Lucius Shepard

INTRODUCTION
to the Second Edition

THIS VOLUME IS the second edition of a work first published in 1982. The first edition contained seventy-five articles by twenty-six critics surveying the achievements and lives of noted writers of science fiction. This volume is significantly larger, containing ninety-eight articles by forty-two critics, including twenty-three entirely new articles. Whenever possible, the original critics have revised and updated their essays as appropriate; when this has not proved possible, new critics have been enlisted. In some cases, the article's bibliography has been updated or a few paragraphs have been added, but in many cases, the original articles have been extensively revised or completely rewritten in order to take advantage of recent biographical discoveries and in order to provide a unified critical approach to their subjects.

Despite the increases in numbers, the problems faced by the first editor of this volume have remained the same for the present editor. First and foremost, there lies the ultimate problem, that of subject definition: what is science fiction? How is it that contemporary writers as different in approach, tone, and subject matter as Brian Aldiss, Octavia Butler, Orson Scott Card, William Gibson, Christopher Priest, Kim Stanley Robinson, Howard Waldrop, and Ian Watson are all accepted science fiction writers, and considered players on the same field as such earlier writers as H. P. Lovecraft, S. Fowler Wright, A. Merritt, and John Taine? What do these writers have in common with still earlier writers such as Mary Shelley, Jules Verne, and H. G. Wells?

First, science fiction is both more and less than its name implies, and it is best to open a discussion of the term by accepting that the term *science fiction* is itself intrinsically paradoxical, involving the oxymoronic combination of words, each signifying something that the other is not. How can science—the systematic acquisition and ordering of knowledge, and the making of statements that must be checked or proved—be combined with fiction, an imaginative creation that has nothing to do with science or the scientific method? It cannot. And yet, there is a body of literature commonly known and accepted as science fiction because there is a marketplace that wishes such a literature to exist: unique among literatures, science fiction was invented to satisfy this marketplace. Science fiction continues to reinvent itself; its boundaries are at the same time nebulous and definite, circumscribed and almost infinite. Science fiction is a protean marketplace into which one can, if not careful, interpolate practically the whole of literature; it is also a marketplace whose subject material utilizes a large and loose conglomeration of motifs and terms that are often so familiar as to be virtually iconographic, and yet these terms are consensual, insubstantial, malleable, and almost infinitely adaptable.

Contemporary science fiction came into existence as a separate literary market in April 1926, with the appearance of Hugo Gernsback's *Amazing Stories*, the first magazine to recognize that there existed a marketplace for stories featuring rational extrapolations from contemporary sciences and technologies, stories describing the impact of these sciences or technologies on the human condition, however poorly understood the science or shoddily written the prose. This of course is not to say that there are not numerous works published prior to April 1926 that can be considered science fiction, or can be said to exemplify the scientific romance, but the categorization of these works is primarily a contemporary activity, the present generation's creation of a literary history and pedigree through the sifting and labeling of the past.

The contemporary science fiction literary marketplace is much less concerned with the problems of sciences and scientists (and/or technology) *per se* than it is with the ostensibly rational application of components of the scientific method to various scenarios, situations, and personalities. "Scientific method fiction" is a singularly unattractive term, perhaps worse even than Gernsback's failed neologism "scientifiction," but it describes both an attitude and the product of that attitude as they are expressed in the literature. So too does the term "sciencefiction" used by a number of the critics in this volume.

Furthermore, the borders of science and technologies are not absolutes; their parameters change, and the proofs of one century frequently are overturned or modified in the next. As a corollary, even as a scientific historian would appraise scientific theories in their larger historical context, so too should the literatures of science fiction be judged whenever possible against the time in which they were written, as well as by comparison to works existing at the time and by the publication in which the work appeared. For example, Edgar Rice Burroughs's *At the Earth's Core* (magazine form, 1914; book form, 1922) was written at a time when science fiction did not exist as a separate literary field, and its "science" is virtually non-existent. Indeed, any reputable early twentieth-century geologist, paleontologist, astronomer, and biologist would have laughed at the idea of Burroughs's largely hollow world heated by an internal sun and populated by gorilla men (Sagoths) and flying alligators (Mahars). Nevertheless, *At the Earth's Core* has long been classified as a work of science fiction, primarily because it appeared when the concept of a science fiction literature was at best inchoate and amorphous. Were it published today, it would be considered a work of purest fantasy.

Similarly, many of the stories that comprise Ray Bradbury's *Martian Chronicles* appeared in the pulp magazines, publications such as *Planet Stories* and *Thrilling Wonder Stories*; and yet these stories, enjoyable though they are, are set on a Mars that is as fantastic and scientifically unacceptable as Burroughs's Pellucidar. More: Bradbury knew that his Mars was a fantastic world having no relationship to the physical planet. Had his stories appeared in another series of publications, had they been marketed differently, they could have been accepted as masterpieces of the supernatural and as archetypal weird fiction. Published elsewhere, in a different sort of magazine, they could have been acclaimed as allegorical mainstream fiction, in which Mars becomes a metaphor with which Bradbury makes his points about the horrors, darknesses, and pathos emergent from human irresponsibility and carelessness.

Finally, the science fiction marketplace is large and diverse enough to have, recognize, and respond to its own history, tropes, and "in" jokes. Harry Harrison's *Star Smashers of the Galaxy Rangers* appeared in 1973 and begins with the premise that ultimate energy can be extracted from a cheese substitute; it gets progressively sillier and ends on an amusingly subversive note. In presentation, *Star Smashers of the Galaxy Rangers* closely parodies the ideas, styles, and works, of (among others) E. E. Smith, Ph.D., and John W. Campbell, Jr., writers of science fiction who would have been familiar to virtually all the science fiction readers of 1973.

Nevertheless, even as the science fiction marketplace can recognize and appreciate its history, it is also capable of accepting and assimilating works influenced by other areas of literature. Writing a year earlier than Harrison, Howard Waldrop and Steven Utley fashioned an alternative history, "Custer's Last Jump," extrapolating from the premise that aviation had developed earlier and reached the American west in time for Crazy Horse to possess a Krupp Monoplane, "equipped with power plant #311 Zed of 87¼ horsepower, manufactured by the Jumo plant at Nordmung, Duchy of Austria, on May 4 of the year 1862." "Custer's Last Jump" is presented as an academic treatise; there is no dialogue, and the story concludes with a lengthy bibliography citing imaginary government documents, autobiographies, and operating manuals as well as non-existent works by real authors (E. A. Brininstool, Bernard DeVoto, Robert Goddard, Mark Twain, L. Sprague de Camp, and Fletcher Pratt, among others). In style and execution, "Custer's Last Jump" utilizes many of the techniques commonly found in contemporary postmodern fiction. Though it was first published in *Universe 6* (1976), a science fiction anthology edited by the late Terry Carr, "Custer's Last Jump" would not have been out of place had it appeared in a literary magazine.

In addition to the problems of definition, there are additional problems, chief among which is the problem of selection: how does one determine and select the most important authors in the field of science fiction? If the number to be chosen remains relatively small—Robert Reginald's two major bibliographies (listed in the bibliography to this volume) provide data on approximately two thousand authors—there will be obvious choices. Few would disagree that Mary Shelley, H. G. Wells, Jules Verne, and Robert A. Heinlein are truly significant, important, and influential of writers of science fiction, even if the first three of these writers wrote science fiction before there was a literature commonly known as science fiction, even if Heinlein was thematically repetitive and far from being the most graceful of writers. When the pool of choices is widened and deepened to include those writers who are generally deemed to be of lesser magnitude but who are nevertheless noted as creative forces or for the sheer volume of their output, or who wrote one significant work and then lingered, or who were once widely read but are so no longer, the problems of determining importance increase exponentially and often can be resolved only by personal choice.

Additionally complicating the problem of determining importance is the fact that tastes change. A work once considered of enormous importance can a century later have completely fallen from grace, to the point where, if it is remembered at all, it is remembered as an artifact, valuable despite (or because of) its flaws. In mainstream literature, for example, Harriet Beecher Stowe's *Uncle Tom's Cabin* (1851) remains a work of enormous historical importance, though by late-twentieth-century standards it is sentimental, sloppy, preachy, and entirely too long.

In a discussion of historically important science fiction, the concept of quality is an issue that is also best side-stepped. There are many significant exceptions, but it is a sad truth that the works by which some of the most important premodern science fiction authors are remembered are, by contemporary standards, thoroughly inadequate. These authors were often pioneers who conceived of a form, but they may have lacked the skills to develop the ideas inherent in that form, or they may have written at a time in which certain ideas were socially unacceptable, or technology may have rendered obsolete their most daring speculations, or they may have been blind to the necessities of characterization and plot. The first edition of this work rightly describes Abraham Merritt (1884–1943) as an example of such a writer whose star has now collapsed, and this introduction shall seize upon two more accessible writers, although the first of these, Edward Bellamy (1850–1898), is not among those profiled in this volume.

Bellamy's *Looking Backward, 2000–1887* (1888) was one of the most influential novels in late-nineteenth-century America. Jean Pfaelzer's *The Utopian Novel in America 1886–1896: The Politics of Form* (University of Pittsburgh Press, 1984) states that "not only did *Looking Backward* sell over a million copies in its first ten years of publication; the book itself . . . launched a movement of state socialism, the Nationalist party, which by 1894 had over 140 chapters, 50 newspapers and journals, and over 10,000 members. Between 1888 and 1900, the financial as well as the political success of *Looking Backward* encouraged over a hundred other authors to turn their own blueprints for the future into books, pamphlets, and newspaper serials; not since *Jane Eyre* had there been a text more widely imitated in American popular fiction" (p. 41). Contemporary readers, however, are likely to find *Looking Backward* staid rather than visionary, inhibited rather than unfettered, and horribly dystopian rather than cheerily eutopian. Bellamy's prose remains clear, but one wonders what the nineteenth century saw fit to fuss about.

The second writer whose star is likely to dim is George Orwell, whose *1984* (1949) is generally accounted the most famous dystopia ever written; it may well be the most famous novel of the twentieth century, having given to our language its title and such concepts as "Big Brother," "doublespeak," and "newspeak." Orwell's is indeed a nightmarish vision, and *1984* has been enormously influential in mainstream literature as well as in the marketplace of science fiction, but contemporary critics are starting to separate the vision from the execution and are becoming increasingly aware of the flaws in Orwell's creation. Frederik Pohl's "Coming Up on 1984" acknowledges

1984's importance, "yet . . . what a very bad book it is! You can measure it by any literary standards—grace in the use of language, originality, fulfillment of the author's intentions, internal consistency, or, if you view it as science fiction, by accuracy of prophecy, reflection of technology on the human condition, understanding of the impact of science on society. It fails every test" (in George E. Slusser, et al., eds., *Storm Warnings: Science Fiction Confronts the Future,* 1987).

When one removes the contemporary concepts of literary quality from a discussion of the most important and influential science fiction, one is then forced to ask what is meant by the concepts of importance and influence. In discussions of literature, these terms must of necessity originate from within a cultural framework and/or from a critical perspective, and those without the framework or in disagreement with the perspective will certainly have different referents with which to judge a writer's significance, importance, and influence. This present volume concentrates almost entirely upon English and American writers of science fiction, not because there are not many international science fiction writers worthy of study—far from it!—but because by and large these international writers remain largely without influence in the United States. There are a few exceptions, of course: although he has not become a household name in the United States, Stanislaw Lem is rightfully considered a science fiction writer of great significance and importance. Nevertheless, while Lem's finest efforts exercise significantly less influence on the general American readership than do routine potboilers, he is popular with other readerships, in particular with audiences that wish their reading to be challenging. The works of Lem are considered literature and believed to have long-lasting value. Moreover, it is possible to trace the dissemination of his ideas as they have spread and influenced other writers.

In this country, significance, influence, and importance are determined by critics and historians, scholars who are attempting to define the forest as well as to recognize and categorize the trees it contains. Though there will rarely be unanimity on what constitutes these values, often in the majority of instances there is a consensus. It is hoped that this will be the case with the choice of writers profiled herein.

In the years following the publication of the first edition of this volume, a significant number of the writers profiled in the first volume either died or became inactive as writers of science fiction. Those that have survived have seen a significant alteration in what was once dismissed as a second-rate literature, for English and American science fiction have at last become reputable, thoroughly acceptable fields for academic study. Major commercial and academic publishers routinely issue studies of science fiction and its writers to increasingly appreciative and sophisticated audiences; journal articles discussing all aspects of science fiction are now routine, as are doctoral dissertations; and in their attempts at defining the parameters of the form, literary theorists have provided science fiction scholarship with a specialized critical vocabulary that to the uninitiated can be every bit as rigid, dense, and impenetrable as legal prose.

Outside of academia, science fiction is no longer a literature of escapism and separation read mainly by adolescents but is, rather, the literature of the mainstream, and science fiction is generally accepted in virtually all areas of popular culture. Best-seller lists routinely feature works written and marketed as science fiction, and the most popular and durable television shows tend to be those that make use of science fictional themes and motifs. Science fiction motion pictures are commonplace and are now accepted and reviewed on their own merits by the critics who a generation earlier would have ignored or derided them sight unseen. The development and accessibility of the personal computer have brought about the reality of the previously science fictional concept of a readily accessible global information network.

This increased acceptance and awareness of science fiction has its parallels in the presence of a new generation of English and American science fiction writers. There now exist generations of professional writers whose introduction to science fiction came through television, movies, and video games, not through the commonality of experiences shared by readers of the pulp magazines. Indeed, it is probable that the majority of the present generation of writers neither saw nor read the pulp magazines that contained the works of the formative earlier generations of science fiction writers, except through accident. Rather, the majority of this new generation of science fiction writers came of age during a time when the number of significant and well-paying science fiction magazines decreased to the point where they could almost be counted on one's fingers. This is not to say that the writers of this generation did not publish in these magazines, but for the first time, science fiction authors began to publish in periodicals read by a general audience, and the majority of the science fiction published in the United States and England during this time first appeared in books, often as paperback originals.

As does any vital field of literature, science fiction continues to evolve and develop, often by accretion and assimilation of new ideas and techniques, occasionally by quantum leaps. The most recent instance of the latter was the dramatic appearance in 1984 of the science fiction genre that is now known variously as cyberpunk or neuromantic, in reference to William Gibson's award-winning *Neuromancer*; the term cyberpunk had, however, been used by writers prior to Gibson, and the genre has been shown to have its roots in the writings of, among others, Alfred Bester, Harlan Ellison, and Roger Zelazny. The cyberpunk writers combined the narrative drive and fast-paced plotting of the science fiction stories published in the pulp magazines with the narrative techniques used by the New Wave writers, who were among the first to treat science fiction images as metaphor and who used in their writings the techniques and references of mainstream fiction. The cyberpunk school offered breathtaking extrapolations from the fields of cybernetics and robotics, recognized that information was a marketable commodity, understood the importance of virtual reality, recognized also that corporations would increasingly dominate global life, and more often than not presented worlds in which there was a cultural anomie. The cyberpunk movement has also been considered the science fiction equivalent of literary postmodernism.

Several critics have claimed that the cyberpunk movement is dead, but it is less dead than subsumed: the larger marketplace that is science fiction has absorbed it and made it a part of the whole. Its techniques linger, its principal writers continue to produce.

Only a minority of the new writers during the 1980s were cyberpunks, and in semi-opposition to the cyberpunk writers a group of writers familiar with science fictional icons—cybernetics, space stations, ansibles, androids, and so on—kept these concepts in the narrative background in their science fiction. The fiction of these writers, while far from relentlessly upbeat, tended to present the attitudes that humanity *per se* was important, that a morality dependent on religion was necessary, and that personal victories could be achieved, though often at great cost and enormous suffering. This group adapted to its needs the genre constructs of the mainstream, particularly the bildungsroman, a novel in which a character develops and matures. Chief among these writers is Orson Scott Card. As an aside, it might be mentioned that Card's uncollected "Happy Head" (*Analog Science Fiction / Science Fact*, April 1978) anticipates many of the motifs that were later to be found in much cyberpunk fiction.

To conclude on a bittersweet note: from the 1980s forward, the best of the literature that was marketed as science fiction was indistinguishable in quality from the best of the literature marketed as mainstream fiction. This parity has long been the case, and it is regrettable that only recently has it been generally acknowledged.

RICHARD BLEILER

INTRODUCTION
to the First Edition (1982)

SELECTING THE MOST important authors of science fiction is not too difficult a task as long as the number selected remains very small. Almost everyone would agree that Jules Verne, H. G. Wells, and Olaf Stapledon are obvious choices about which there would be little argument. But selecting a considerably larger number of men and women is a much more difficult task, for in the middle range there are so many solid authors among whom choices must be made.

Nor is the number of authors the only problem that makes such a selection difficult. There are many ways in which the word "important" can be defined, depending on the criteria of the reader. First, there is literary quality according to the standards of mainstream fiction—such factors as characterization, style, and development. Yet in science fiction, as in the detective story, this criterion has been disputed, and there are critics who regard literary quality as either irrelevant or less significant than imagination, novelty of idea, and trickiness of conceit.

A second possible criterion for "important" is historical position within the science fiction form. Some writers have invented narrative methods, plot mechanisms, and concepts that have been borrowed and used extensively by other authors. Such a writer is H. G. Wells, whose short novel *The Time Machine* (1895) set off a whole chain of development, or George Chesney, who for all practical purposes invented the imaginary war story in English with his sketch *The Battle of Dorking* (1871).

A typologist of popular fiction, who is interested in establishing "pure forms," might consider an otherwise minor work like *The Phantom City* by William Westall (1886) very "important." For it contains, clearly stated, almost every motif of a lost race situation, a hidden land, a well-known people of antiquity (Aztecs), a beautiful princess, a battle between priestly and secular forces, a volcano, and so on. A cultural historian, on the other hand, might find dime novel science fiction fascinating, since it is so firmly grounded in popular culture and reveals folkways more clearly than does mainstream fiction.

A delimitation of the field of science fiction is also necessary because not all critics and readers agree on its boundaries. Stories that one person would accept as science fiction might be rejected by others. Such differences of opinion are great enough that science fiction sometimes seems carved up between writers doing certain things and outsiders analyzing what has been or should have been done, a modern parallel to English bards and Scotch reviewers.

Defining science fiction has proved very difficult, as can be seen from the many descriptive definitions that exist. In the older presophisticated days before World War II, readers and critics took a simplistic view of science fiction. It was customary to divide literature into two streams, realistic and fantastic, and to place science fiction within the fantastic current. Science fiction was then defined as fantastic fiction based on extrapolated or imaginary science. Unfortunately, while this definition works well enough for some stories (notably "idea" stories or "hard" science fiction), it is irrelevant for many others that are generally accepted as science fiction but have little to do with science, either serious or imaginary.

Another objection to this two-stream interpretation of literature (which crops up in other definitions of science fiction) is that it confuses an idea obtained by critical analysis with an actual phenomenon, for literature obviously does not break down into two mutually exclusive groupings. There are shadings and varied proportions of realism and fantasy; and—the largest objection of all—there is no clear definition for either realism or fantasy.

Back in the 1930's, when the readers and writers of American pulp science fiction became conscious that they were concerned with a new sort of literature, there was considerable dispute about its definition. Part of the dispute turned on words. If one examines the older fan literature, like *The Science Fiction Critic* of 1937 or 1938, one sees that three terms were used interchangeably, *science fiction* (with or without a hyphen); *scientifiction* (the horrible malformation created by Hugo Gernsback); and *scientific fiction*. Oddly enough, the abbreviation *stf.* (which really stood for *scientifiction*) was considered a valid abbreviation for *science fiction* well into the 1940's and 1950's, even though the term *science fiction* alone survived.

The argument on definitions at that time often boiled down to a question of words and things. "Since it is called science fiction, it should have science in it" was a claim that was often put forth. But this opinion gradually faded as readers came to realize that the words *science* and *fiction* were only labels and not necessarily exact descriptions of what was being published. Like the caterpillar in *Alice in Wonderland*, one can call something anything, and derivations are not the last horizon of truth.

A decade or two ago, when mainstream critics began to work in science fiction, the same interpretation arose again. There have been claims that science fiction and the scientific method are connected, and that the inclusion of scientific data or subject matter makes a work of fiction science fiction. That this is obviously wrong can be seen by examining the fifty or so years of modern science fiction.

Yet this misapprehension has a small historical basis, for in Hugo Gernsback's early science fiction magazines, *Amazing Stories* (1926–1929) and *Science Wonder Stories* (1929–1930), he proclaimed stridently and frequently that what he published was scientifically sound. It was never clear, though, whether Gernsback was entirely serious or simply making a sales point to disarm parents and others who objected to pulp fiction per se. In all probability, the claim was partly serious and partly business policy.

Behind these attempts at defining science fiction (fantasy with a basis in imaginary science, fiction based on actual science) and other more recent definitions lies the larger question of what a definition is and what it should do. It can list attributes, as is the case of the two aforementioned definitions. Or, according to other modern theories, a definition can be based on the functions that objects serve. Certain neo-Marxists define science fiction as a form of fiction that permits a new look at our own culture in terms of dissociation and reassociation of elements. This is similar to an interpretation put forth in the late 1940's that invoked historian Arnold Toynbee's concept of withdrawal. Unfortunately, these functional approaches tend to be open-ended definitions; not all science fiction accomplishes what the critics claim, and many other forms of literature examine our world existentially.

The most successful type of definition, it would seem, is an "operational" definition, or a description of a set of actions necessary to get a certain result. An operational definition of science fiction would be based not so much on the science component of science fiction as on the fiction component; it would be pragmatic and frankly pluralistic. In its simplest form, it would say, "Science fiction is what is published in science fiction magazines"—in other words, what the consensus accepts—and would then proceed to examine and perhaps classify what is accepted.

If science fiction is looked at operationally, it is seen to be not a simple genre like the detective story or the story of supernatural horror or the Western story. Instead, it is a grouping (compound genre or pseudo-genre) of story types, not all of which are closely related. There are stories about inventions; stories set in the future; stories of non-human civilizations; adventure stories placed in other worlds; stories of great natural catastrophes; stories that transform reality in various non-supernatural ways; and so on. All in all, what we group together as science fiction is a set of story types, the population of which set is somewhat arbitrary and perhaps accidental. According to such an operational approach, other definitions of science fiction have not been successful because they treat as a single thing something that is not a single thing.

Within the fifty and more years that modern science fiction has flourished, its nature (the population of the set) has changed somewhat. Fifty years ago, stories of cavedwellers (reasonably realistic) were considered science fiction. Today, they would not be. Today, though, stories that shade over into irrational subject matter are accepted as science fiction and might be called stories of "inner space." Philip K. Dick's *Ubik* (1969) and Harlan Ellison's "Adrift Just off the Islets of Langerhans, Latitude 38° 54' N, Longitude 77° 00' 13" W" (1974) are not questioned, whereas fifty years ago they might have been published in *Weird Tales* as "weird science."

The concept behind this operational theory of science fiction is much the same as the one used in the social sciences to study groups of people: definition is a matter of membership, and membership is a matter of acceptance. Science fiction, to make a truistic statement, is what is accepted as science fiction by readers and writers.

From a historical point of view science fiction presents a very odd picture, and a discussion of its age is likely to be paradoxical. In critical studies one can find statements that science fiction begins with Plato, with Lucian, with Sir Thomas More, with Sir Francis Bacon, with Johannes Kepler, with Mary

Shelley, with Jules Verne, with H. G. Wells, or with Hugo Gernsback. These varied opinions can be confusing, especially since much of this earlier work has little resemblance to the modern stories. Another historical problem is that although, exceptionally, an occasional earlier work like Kepler's *Somnium* (1634) does resemble modern "hard" science fiction, there is little connection—or only the most tenuous—between such works and the modern period.

Many of these historical difficulties can be resolved if one uses the standard distinction between the terms *form and genre,* ignoring for the moment the insight that modern science fiction is a composite genre. A form, by definition, would consist of the totality of stories that share major characteristics distinguishing them from other fiction, no matter where or when these stories were written. A genre would be a group of such stories that are connected with one another in development, time, and place, and perhaps were written with a consciousness of these connections. A form is automatically larger than a genre, and many genres may exist within the form. And, if one is concerned with the genre of modern science fiction, one may, under some circumstances, be completely justified in disregarding earlier material that chances to be present in the form.

Yet there are a few works of fiction resembling modern science fiction that are scattered erratically back over a century or two in French and English literature. Such are *Giphantie* (1760) by Charles François Tiphaigne de la Roche, which is a rich source of early fantastic inventions, and *L'An deux mille quatre cent quarante* (1770) by Louis-Sébastien Mercier, which considers the future in some detail. Similar are the works of Edgar Allan Poe described in the present volume. The important point about such early stories is that they assume an identity as science fiction only because of developments one hundred and two hundred years later. They constitute science fiction in retrospect.

These complicated questions of chance resemblances, remote ancestry, convergence of ideas, and the composite nature of modern science fiction all become important when one establishes a beginning for the modern genre. We can say, on the one hand, that Jules Verne has a good claim to be called the Father of Science Fiction, since he was the first important author to realize clearly that he was writing a new sort of literature. Yet we must also say that modern science fiction came into being as a genre in the United States (and to a lesser extent in Great Britain) in the 1920's and 1930's. These two statements are not really contradictory. Verne's contribution was enormous, but the work of his immediate followers became frozen in type and formed only one or two aspects of modern science fiction: the factual interplanetary and the rogue engineer. When modern science fiction got under way, it contained far more than Verne dreamed of.

Nor, to point out another area of complexity, is it contradictory to say that H. G. Wells wrote the first modern science fiction stories back in the 1890's. Despite the freshness of his ideas, his work had few immediate imitators and his stories were lost among his social novels. As has happened at other times in the history of popular fiction, it took roughly a generation for an innovation to be expanded into a subgenre or genre. This later amalgamation of the ideas of Verne and Wells, the contemporary adventure story, the imaginary war, and other subgenres formed what we know as modern science fiction. Whether or not it is the highest possible development in the form, it remains the standard-giving body of literature that defines the form throughout time and space. For this reason it has been stressed in this volume.

The selection of subject-authors in this volume has been the responsibility of the editor, although the initial lists were submitted to each of the contributors and to several outside experts for comments and suggestions. As has been stated above, the choice of subject-authors was difficult, and of necessity, at times personal, since various criteria for selection were held in mind, and every book must come to an end.

The arrangement of authors has been made in terms of writing generations. Within the twentieth century there are two marked generation gaps—the 1930's and the late 1950's or early 1960's. Surprisingly, World War II was not a watershed, since the major authors who were writing when the war began—Isaac Asimov, Ray Bradbury, Robert A. Heinlein, Theodore Sturgeon, A. E. van Vogt, and others—either continued to write through the war or resumed after it ended. Around 1960, though, a new generation of authors appeared, most of whom are still active or have been active until recently.

Within these general delimitations set by the editor, the individual contributors have been allowed freedom to develop their ideas. Only certain basic data have been required: biographical information, comments on important stories, historical position, evaluation, bibliography, and whatever else was needed to provide an introduction for a new reader or a full survey for a regular reader of science fiction. The bibliography at the end of each article offers first-edition information supplied by the contributors; the editor is responsible for adding such information about transatlantic editions as has been available.

It will be observed that many different approaches are present among the articles, ranging from external biographical to cultural historical, psychological to literary-historical, depending upon which approach is best suited to the subject-author. It will also be noted that there are differences of opinion from article to article, and from the position of the editor. We do not see this diversity as a flaw, but as a virtue, for science fiction is a varied, complex field, intricate in its intermeshed manifestations and still very largely unstudied. Rigidity of approach would only work harm.

E. F. BLEILER

Science Fiction Writers

BRIAN W. ALDISS

(b. 1925)

IF THERE IS such an individual as a typical Englishman, Brian Wilson Aldiss might qualify for that title. Born of shopkeeper parents in East Dereham, Norfolk, on 18 August 1925, he attended boarding school and a very competent public school, thus obtaining the American equivalent of secondary education. He has memorialized this latter exposure in *The Hand-Reared Boy* (1970), a bitingly satirical novel that became a cause célèbre in England on its publication. In World War II he was drafted into the British army, serving in India, Burma, and Indonesia.

When Aldiss was discharged in 1948 he soon married, fathered two children, and got a job as a bookseller in Oxford. His employment at the bookstore, which lasted many years, gave him the opportunity to fill in the numerous gaps in his education and led him to write some quasi-fictional stories about life in a bookstore. These stories were eventually collected and published as *The Brightfount Diaries* (1955), and his professional writing career had begun. Since the early 1950's Aldiss has lived in or around Oxford, where he is as popular with Oxford undergraduates and dons as he is with science fiction fans.

To many American science fiction readers, Aldiss is noted mainly as the author of *Billion Year Spree* (1973) and its extensive revision (with David Wingrove), *Trillion Year Spree* (1986), which may well be the best single-volume history of the genre. His science fiction works, many of them unfortunately out of print in the United States, are known, if at all, only by reputation or by an occasional title, such as *Frankenstein Unbound* (1973),

The Malacia Tapestry (1976), or the three volumes *Helliconia Spring* (1982), *Helliconia Summer* (1983), and *Helliconia Winter* (1985), which comprise the Helliconia trilogy, considered by many to be Aldiss' masterwork. Moreover, his "mainstream" novels such as the Horry Stubbs trilogy—*The Hand-Reared Boy* (1970), *A Soldier Erect* (1971), and *A Rude Awakening* (1978)—and particularly what he himself calls the Squire Quartet,—*Life in the West* (1980), *Forgotten Life* (1988), *Remembrance Day* (1993), and *Somewhere East of Life* (1994)—are virtually unobtainable in the United States, yet they are unquestionably major achievements.

However, the situation is quite different in Aldiss' native England. Almost all of his incredibly large output remains in print. His books are reviewed in such prestigious publications as the *Times Literary Supplement* and the *Guardian*, and he is generally acknowledged not only as Britain's finest science fiction writer but as one of its leading literary figures. He has been a judge for the Booker Prize, roughly the English equivalent of the Pulitzer, and his books remain on British best-seller lists for months. Most British critics agree that Aldiss is the literary heir to H. G. Wells and Olaf Stapledon and indeed have recognized that he is also one of the very few writers on either side of the Atlantic who has bridged the gap between science fiction and the mainstream.

It is difficult to account for these two quite differing reputations. Relative differences between British and American tastes, if they exist at all, may possibly be cited as explaining the problem, but the facts remain that Aldiss is not as well known in America as he certainly deserves to be and that his audience in the United States is still being formed. To be sure, some American critics recognize his undoubted abilities and achievements, particularly the academic scholars who saw and appreciated, say, the Joycean influence in *Barefoot in the Head* (1969) when that influence escaped many science fiction fans to whom James Joyce is not even a recognizable name.

Yet if one reads Aldiss' work chronologically, from the early volume of short stories, *Space, Time and Nathaniel* (1957), up through *Galaxies Like Grains of Sand* (1960), *Hothouse* (1962), *Greybeard* (1964), *Report on Probability A* (1968), and a dozen more novels or collections of short stories, one cannot help being struck by the variety of concepts developed in them, by the increasing mastery of style, the sureness of the dialogue, the depth of characterization, the fertility of ideas, and the urbanity of the wit. Surely, the careful reader might insist, here is a major talent at work.

Brian W. Aldiss in 1978. PHOTO BY JAY KAY KLEIN

And, just as surely, it can be maintained that Aldiss has never, except for some of his early potboilers, repeated himself. No dreary zap guns, languid lasers, or galactic battle cruisers stultify his stories or inhibit the imagination of his readers. In fact, how much he demands of readers may be part of the answer to the problem of his bifurcated reputation. Aldiss has never been content to write down to his readers. Rather, he assumes that they are willing to bring to the act of reading an informed imagination and a patience of eye and intellect that many of them are either unwilling or unable to give. He demands more, and when more is given, entire worlds of the conscious and unconscious unfold to those perceptive readers.

Few science fiction writers possess as fine a prose style as Aldiss. In some of his earlier works, he honored Wells, Joyce, and Hardy not only by suggesting their styles or techniques, but he paid further homage to the masters by penetrating their insights and general method of approach in such works as "The Saliva Tree" (1965, for which he won the Nebula award for best novella in 1966), *Barefoot in the Head*, and *Greybeard*.

Nonetheless, his voice is assuredly his own, and his style has won praise from literary critics on both sides of the Atlantic. It is elegant, sometimes elegiac, always carefully honed, but never affected. Indeed, "Aldissian" seems to be the only word that fits, and a mere reading of several of his short stories or novels will provide its definition.

A case in point is Aldiss' 1958 novel *Nonstop*. While it may appear that this book is merely another version of the closed universe of the long-lasting journey of a lost multigeneration starship, similar to Robert A. Heinlein's "Universe" (1941), actually the society that Aldiss depicts becomes a parable or symbol for the imprisonment of life that a blindly technological civilization can bring about. The changes in consciousness of the ship's inhabitants are not merely physical but also metaphysical; and Aldiss almost becomes admonitory as he elaborates this theme.

Similar ideas occur in quite a different book, *Report on Probability A*. Written around 1958, originally as "Figures in a Garden," an unpublished short novel in which characters known only as S, C, and G remain virtually motionless in a static world, the book was reworked at the suggestion of Michael Moorcock, then editor of the famed British publication *New Worlds*, into its present science fiction form. This reworking involved the addition, within each chapter, of italicized passages in which a series of watchers attempt to unravel the mystery of worlds they can only observe. Derived, as Aldiss admits, from the French antinovel of Alain Robbe-Grillet and the provocative Alain Resnais motion picture *Last Year at Marienbad* (1961), *Report on Probability A* is an intensive study of stasis, of the entropic degradation of matter to inert uniformity. There is no action, no dialogue, no characterization, yet it is a brilliant achievement, if sometimes an annoying experience for the reader. Moreover, coupled with the static environment, the static characters, and the static situation, Aldiss introduces still another theme, one that informs much of his writing of the 1960's and 1970's: the problem of the absolute immutability of art. All of the watchers become gradually aware of the pervading presence of a picture, Holman Hunt's *The Hireling Shepherd*, which seems to mirror the stasis, the moment of frozen action, the "freeze frame" that they are attempting to decipher.

Aldiss' interest in art is nothing new, of course. Many of his early short stories deal with it, some of them using Art as a metaphor for the unchanging aspects of society that mirror the changed worlds or situations he is creating. Indeed, he might well maintain that only the transitions and transformations of Art, coupled with its apparent unchangeability, make life tolerable. For Aldiss, though, Art must be clearly understood as including something much more than painting. Art, for him, can be the form of the novel itself: "Art is not Diagram; it is Music or Acting or Watercolor, even Living itself," Aldiss once said.

Aldiss has never hesitated to utilize the finished productions of other artists as inspirations for his own creations. It is common enough, for example, to refer to *Greybeard* as

his "Thomas Hardy" novel or to point to his Nebula-winning novella "The Saliva Tree" as a homage to H. G. Wells. However, simply to make these assertions baldly is to miss the Aldissian touch—never mannered, always accurate—with which he adds to the works of the science fiction masters who inspired him. *Barefoot in the Head* certainly deserves some attention here as almost a perfect example of that touch. It is the story of Colin Charteris, not "the Saint" of Leslie Charteris' renowned detective stories, but the assumed name of a common man, a Serb, who is one of the survivors of the "acid-head" war. Psychedelic in both content and style, the novel owes much to James Joyce's masterpiece *Finnegans Wake* (1939), not only in style but also in its thematic use of the myth of the eternal return. Furthermore, the myth itself serves as a symbol for a biological hypothesis—the hypothesis that modern man is stuck with mental and physical equipment that served well in the Neolithic age but equipment, mental above all, that is of increasingly less use as the complexity of the modern world multiplies.

Have we "acid-bombed" ourselves back to the Stone Age? Aldiss asks. Or are our Stone Age brains no longer capable of coping with the speed of fast cars, with technological society, or with the necessity of attempting to preserve some semblance of sanity in the face of exponentially increasing change? It is nearly impossible to indicate all the velleities of the major characters—whether they be Charteris, Angelina, or Laundri—but all of them seem moved primarily by their own minor, private desires. Charteris, for example, finds himself hailed as a saint and a savior as a result of actions that seem almost peripheral to the reality of sanctification. He allows himself almost to be fooled into sainthood, grasping the fact that events are repetitive and cyclical, and that the pattern of life, death, and crucifixion may indeed be inflexible. He attempts to break away from his escalating messianic success to seek a new pattern of existence. Yet he has no great success in this attempt because mankind, as it is presently constituted (and represented by Charteris), is stuck with "photographs torn from a Neolithic eye."

To represent these themes, Aldiss has carefully adopted a modified Joycean omnilingual, multilevel language, infused with the thought of Gurdjieff and Ouspensky. In the end his taste is certain and his own voice is assured. *Barefoot in the Head* is clearly a difficult book—note how much he demands of his readers—but it is one that may well continue to gain an audience through the years, as readers begin to understand it and even to entertain a certain affection for it. The novel also has humor, pathos, terror, love, and profound human observation. One of the most terrifying aspects of the book is that many people die throughout its pages; they are killed in car crashes, or are run over, or drown, but no one even notices. Therein lies the true horror of what Aldiss is saying about our contemporary society: death is a *casual* affair. No one notices. No one cares.

In the introduction to a significant collection of short stories, *Last Orders* (1977), Aldiss puts it this way: "My stories are about human woes, non-communication, disappointment, endurance, love." Note the progression: from woes to non-communication. This in turn evokes disappointment, and from disappointment, a transformation to endurance. It all culminates in love. These themes are the enduring stuff of all literature, to be sure. Lacking them, works of the creative imagination would be merely dull splatters of mud, soon to be scraped off our boots and forgotten as quickly.

Aldiss' novels and stories, then, often speak to the intuitive self, involve the collective unconscious of both the writer and the reader, and vibrate into every part of our being. Novels such as *Frankenstein Unbound* (1973) and *The Malacia Tapestry* (1976) illustrate just how profoundly his themes can affect readers in contemporary society. Beginning in the year 2020—and surely the date is significant, suggesting some sort of final clarity of vision—*Frankenstein Unbound* is the story of Joseph Bodenland, a former American secretary of state who is thrown back in time by a rupture in "the infrastructure of space" to 1816, when Mary Wollstonecraft Shelley is composing her great seminal novel. Boden-

land meets Mary, her husband Percy Bysshe Shelley, Lord Byron, and Victor Frankenstein, who is actually creating the monster that Mary is writing about.

The novel includes many themes besides Aldiss' typical preoccupation with time. It combines subtle evocations of mythic, perceptual, psychic, allegorical, or symbolic realities with a clean, loose-limbed prose. It contains subtle characterizations together with a convincing sense of an era. In many ways, *Frankenstein Unbound* can be read as Aldiss' tribute to the great progenitor of the science fiction form, as well as, if one can judge by the luminosity and tenderness of the style, a tribute to his own life-long love affair with Mary Shelley, her ideas, and, in a certain sense, her person. Aldiss has re-created the wife of the great poet as a distinctive person whose abilities, perceptions, and insights virtually equaled those of her more famous husband.

The ending—or, indeed, the entire message of the novel—is tragic in the finest sense of the word, compelling almost an Aristotelian sense of recognition with its purgation of the emotions of both pity and terror. Bodenland asks, for example, "Was there some immutable cosmic law which decreed that man's good intentions should always thunder back about his head . . . ?" While Aldiss seems to imply that the Frankenstein mentality will always triumph over the heart, Bodenland becomes almost a salvific figure, and his death may signal the rebirth of "heart consciousness." It is in the reader's appreciation of the depth of emotion in both Aldiss and Bodenland that the real triumph of the novel lies. Aldiss most certainly suggests that unless we slay the monster in all of us, we will perish; but he also avers that when we do this, the true humanity of human beings will emerge and re-create the world in the spirit of love.

On the surface, *The Malacia Tapestry* is an alternate-world fantasy about the miraculous city-state of Malacia that must forever remain completely unchanged. The story of how the city slouches toward change is told by Perian de Chirolo, an actor resembling the classic braggadocio who swashbuckles his way from bed to duel while remaining simultaneously an artistic observer and a participant. The operative force in the novel, which may be as much fantasy as science fiction, is the force of entropy, with the city and its people slowly running down toward the point of collapse.

In many ways, this long, exquisitely written novel is Aldiss' evocation of a utopia that carries within itself the seeds of its own destruction. The one enduring aspect of the society, as might be expected from Aldiss' previous interests, is the unchanging nature of Art itself. But Art itself must be susceptible to change; and de Chirolo, as an artist, must eventually become aware of that necessity. De Chirolo's perceptions must be shared by the readers themselves, for Aldiss is suggesting, once more, that unless we all learn to preserve the best of what we have created in the face of change, we—and Malacia itself, which is by now a thinly disguised allegory for our world—will perish.

Aldiss has also written a considerable amount of mainstream fiction. His reputation in England is quite high indeed; several of the books in the Horatio Stubbs series have become best-sellers. The three novels thus far published—*The Hand-Reared Boy, A Soldier Erect*, and *A Rude Awakening* (1978)—have received considerable critical praise but, as indicated earlier, have been virtually neglected in the United States. They tell the story of Horatio ("Horry") Stubbs as a young boy coming to maturity in an inferior British public school, as a soldier in India and Burma during World War II, and finally as a noncommissioned officer in Malaya in the first years after the war.

In all three books Aldiss is brutally honest in his approach. The language is direct, often vulgar. The war scenes are as well portrayed as those of almost any other novel about the war, and the character development is incisive. Although Aldiss himself underwent many of the incidents he describes in the books, they should not be thought of as primarily autobiographical. Rather, they evoke elements of lower-middle-class British society that are familiar to many of his readers and with which they can empathize. Aldiss is

thus revealing, once more, those aspects of England that were the common staple of, say, Charles Dickens or Thomas Hardy. These books are concerned not only with growth or development but also with survival—not only in the face of artillery and bullets but also against a class-conscious condescension and arrogance.

Life in the West is another mainstream novel. It grew out of Aldiss' attendance at a Eurocon conference in Poznan, Poland (1977), and his guest-of-honor appearance at a science fiction convention at Palermo (1978). Much of the twaddle at the fictional conference in Ermalpa in *Life in the West* was actually spoken at both Poznan and Palermo and taken down almost verbatim by Aldiss. The novel's roots may also be found in his science fiction novel *Enemies of the System* (1978). This slim, neglected book was his response to a Soviet critic who accused Western science fiction writers of not seriously considering Eastern socialism as a subject matter. *Enemies of the System* takes place a million years in the future when a utopian socialistic race called *Homo uniformis* is triumphant on Earth. Fifty-two of the system's elite are allowed a brief holiday on the untamed planet Lysenka II. A machine breakdown throws six of these visitors into Lysenka's primitive reality. How they react to the planet's dangers and gradually lose their grip on the socialist reality they have so naturally accepted comprises the action of the book. The tensions here are East versus West; civilization versus primitivism; individualism versus humanity. Aldiss has taken the Marxist challenge seriously, crafting a novel that is both provocative and extrapolative.

Disturbed by certain *soi-disant* Marxist intellectuals who seemed to dominate the 1978 conference at Palermo, Aldiss wrote *Life in the West* in less than six months. The hero of the novel is Thomas Squire, who through the production of a thirteen-week television series called "Frankenstein Among the Arts," has become a high priest of popular culture. Squire attends an academic conference on "intergraphic criticism" and soon becomes engaged in many philosophical arguments with the Marxist or socialist ideologues of the

"East." Squire is in many ways representative of contemporary man—English, American, or Western man in general. In his television series Squire has chronicled the almost universal change affecting societies throughout the world as a result of the impact of popular culture and electronic media. But Squire is either unwilling or unable to do anything more than comment upon these changes. Eventually, he must come face to face with himself, his long-held cultural assumptions, his anomalous position as a guru of popular culture, and his sometime role as a member of the British secret service.

These conflicting tensions require Squire, like many of Joseph Conrad's heroes, to make an ethical choice and then to act upon that choice with an almost terrifying inevitability. Squire is diffident but involved. His griefs, to paraphrase William Faulkner, grieve on contemporary bones, and his strengths and weaknesses are indeed those of modern man. In many ways *Life in the West* is a talky novel, but the talk is brilliantly done, and often very funny. Moreover, the concept of East versus West culminates in some clever action as Squire is forced to become involved in the problem of whether to aid a potential Russian defector. There is high drama here as well as talk, and the concepts and action are brilliantly juxtaposed in the contrapuntal style that Aldiss adopts. One can only hope that the novel may eventually reach the larger American audience it deserves.

Life in the West is the first volume in the Squire Quartet, so-called because some of the characters, situations, personages, or events—even themes or auctorial attitudes, as well as the style Aldiss adopted for the four books—recur or are alluded to either in passing or directly. In the opening of *Forgotten Life*, the second volume of the Squire Quartet, where the protagonist's wife, a wildly popular high fantasy cum science fiction writer pseudonymously named "Green Mouth" exits her fictional kingdom of Kerinth as well as its celebratory fans, and returns to the mundane world of Oxford, leaving her "carbonated emotions" for the gray tedium of reality. Both are openings written with wit, stylistic flair, and considerable insight into the popular mind.

Consider, however, how Aldiss focuses on the tension between change and stasis in the Squire Quartet. This tension is not merely one of opposites, but it affects the interior and exterior lives of many of the characters in all four books.

Forgotten Life may illustrate this characteristic—dare one say it is a leitmotif?—perhaps better than any of the others. Like *Life in the West*, it is a novel of self-discovery. However, while it can be fairly argued that Thomas Squire, if not unchanged, is still relatively unaware of the fact that he has turned from chronicler of change to participant in life's inexorability, the protagonist of *Forgotten Life*, Clement Winter (his surname surely deserves further attention), is indeed profoundly changed, irrevocably and with finality. Most importantly, as an analyst, throughout the novel he has gradually become aware that his own apparently calm and ordered, prosperous life has been in many ways a lost life and, ironically for an analyst, an unexamined one.

He maintains a clinical bemused detachment to his wife in her role as icon of popular culture, Green Mouth, the Empress of Kerinth, even though he is continually involved with ever-changing human nature in the consulting room. Winter's older brother, Joseph, has recently died, and now Clement is trying to sort out his brother's papers and perhaps planning to write Joseph's biography, for Joseph had indeed led an apparently "forgotten life" as, Clement slowly discovers, he himself has done. Clement puts it this way: "The past immediately becomes history. Even yesterday has undergone a magical transformation: it may still exist in memory, in stone, in documents, in old newspapers waiting to be disposed of. But it lacks breath. It has become part of death's kingdom."

Remembrance Day, the third novel of the Quartet, was unfairly and too easily dismissed by some critics for its surface resemblance to Thornton Wilder's *The Bridge of San Luis Rey* (1927). True, Aldiss' novel does indeed tell the story of several very different unconnected

English individuals who happen to be taking their holiday in a small British coastal hotel at the time of a terrorist bombing. Yet Aldiss is able to infuse this material with a depth of understanding of the characters themselves, as well as the tragic part they play on the world's stage, far more than might be expected in presenting this material. Aldiss is most emphatically not Wilder redux. He speaks with his own voice, and some of the themes introduced in both *Life in the West* and *Forgotten Life* are given further orchestration. This time the topics change slightly: they include the idea of progress as the creation of the Frankensteinian monster of violence, the myth that the past is always better—a theme he had explored earlier in *The Malacia Tapestry*—and the ugliness, even horror of scientific investigation when considered against the humaneness and humanity of the characters peopling the novel. A particularly unsavory, unfeeling, indeed mean-spirited American professor, Dr. Hengist M. Embry, has prepared a paper for delivery at an academic conference about the confluence of events that resulted in these individuals being present at one time in the same hotel when the bomb explodes. Embry advances a cold unemotional argument and detailed history of each victim to bolster his crackpot theory of "transpsychic reality." A "circumstance-chain" has linked the dead, he avers, and their death was not merely due to dreadful mischance; they were not merely tourists on holiday caught in the ugliness of mindless international terrorism. They were, Embry seems to claim, almost responsible for their own deaths. Hearing this outlandish statement, one character scornfully brings Embry to earth with the penetrating acerbic observation that if Embry's theory has any validity, then the six million victims of the Holocaust wished their own deaths.

Remembrance Day is a disturbing book, a very serious novel that bites, that sets the jaw. Its understated, spare prose style belies the underlying seriousness of its topic, or indeed, more accurately, reinforces it. When read immediately after *Forgotten Life*, it provides an excellent albeit incisive statement of Aldiss'

abilities not only to focus his considerable talents on one specific problem but also to provide some fine shadings to those ideas. With *Forgotten Life*, the reader is slowly drawn from a perception that Aldiss is sometimes—particularly in his offhand deadpan relating of the excrescences of popular culture—writing with his satiric tongue firmly planted in his cheek. The careful reader then proceeds to a deeper understanding that this is a major work of art, a profound probing into motives dimly revealed and only lately understood. Whose life has been forgotten? Indeed, *what* has been forgotten? What lives are remembered in both books? In the end, all the lives memorialized in the Squire Quartet, including those in the final novel of the Quartet, *Somewhere East of Life*, are both ordinary and extraordinary at the same time.

Another of Aldiss' roles is that of historian of science fiction and commentator on and critic of contemporary culture in general. This type of versatility should not surprise anyone who has followed his career. From his very early days as a science fiction writer, Aldiss has shown a wide range of interests, extending not only to the form he has graced so well, but also to almost every other phase of art and society. These interests have shown themselves—sometimes tangentially, sometimes directly—not only in the subject matter of his novels and short stories but also in his manifold contributions to such prestigious British publications as the *Times Literary Supplement*, the *Guardian*, and dozens of others. The subject matter of his essays, reviews, and travel reports has been catholic indeed. For example, an essay on nineteenth-century British painting might be followed by one on Mary Shelley's stylistic devices, and that in turn might be capped by humorous digressions on Jugoslav (Aldiss' preferred spelling) cultural patterns, or the perils and pitfalls of bookselling.

In America, though, Aldiss is best known for *Trillion Year Spree*, his definitive history of science fiction. Almost immediately upon its publication, it was recognized by critics on both sides of the Atlantic as a distinctive work. Not only is it comprehensive in its aim and scope, but it has the further advantage, as a history of a much-maligned genre, of being written by one of the major practitioners of that genre. In fact, some American critics have maintained that if *Trillion Year Spree* has a weakness, it lies in the fact that Aldiss' own work is ignored.

His study begins, quite properly, with Mary Shelley's *Frankenstein*. This early nineteenth-century novel is seminal to the genre, and Aldiss indicates that many modern science fiction works consist of a series of "footnotes" to the seeds planted by Mary Shelley. He very carefully sketches the extent of this influence in the early chapters of *Trillion Year Spree*. However, he maintains that *Frankenstein* is prophetic in ways other than the obvious one of stimulating hundreds of pale imitations of the man-versus-monster motif. Aldiss very carefully emphasizes that the underlying metaphor of Mary Shelley's novel is that of contemporary civilization itself: our civilization is a self-created monster that, in accordance with some sort of scientific or technological determinism, will eventually bring about its own destruction. Whether, phoenix-like, mankind will eventually be reborn out of its own ashes provides the subject matter for at least two of Aldiss' novels, *Frankenstein Unbound* and *Greybeard*.

The answer in the first novel is at best ambiguous; the answer in the second, which actually preceded *Frankenstein Unbound* in composition by nearly ten years, is equally mixed. In *Greybeard* the tones are muted, sad, pessimistic, autumnal. Typically Aldissian characteristics infuse this novel. The first characteristic is a concern with the process of change itself, but even more importantly, Aldiss very clearly details the results of that change. Not unlike *Report on Probability A* or *The Malacia Tapestry*, *Greybeard* portrays a relatively static, disintegrating society. The world has begun to end, not with a bang but a whimper, and Aldiss tells the story of that whimper. This and several other novels and many of his short stories read like commentaries upon society itself.

Aldiss is a gentle, genial critic, although at times his scorn for human follies can scour;

indeed, if a reader would shuttle between a collection of his criticism, such as *This World and Nearer Ones* (1979), and an anthology of short stories, such as *New Arrivals, Old Encounters* (1979), he or she could not help but be struck by the similarity in theme and subject matter. The sensitive, not wholly sympathetic or unsympathetic essay entitled "Cultural Totems in the Soviet Union" (1979) can easily be coupled with the short story "A Spot of Konfrontation" (1973). In other words, Aldiss' serious concerns about the world, what is happening to it, and what might happen to it in the future find play in all of his writings, both fiction and nonfiction. Indeed, some of his stories, such as "Last Orders" (1976), read almost like a newspaper report rather than "mere" fiction.

Perhaps the epigraph from Edmund Burke's *Thoughts on the Present Discontents*, which prefaces *This World and Nearer Ones*, may indicate something of the timeless approach that Aldiss exemplifies: "To complain of the age we live in, to murmur at the present possessors of power, to lament the past, to conceive extravagant hopes of the future, are common dispositions of the greatest part of mankind."

Exactly. These notions infuse Aldiss' writings, whether fiction or nonfiction. His concern for the future informs his concern for the present, and the distinction between his prose fiction and his prose commentary evaporates in the face of his concern for humanity. His writing, he once said, is often a "synthesis, a conjuration between cerebrum and cerebellum in the uncanny process of creation." If this dichotomy is crucial to all of his writing, so is the tension between East and West, however it is incarnated.

Life, entropy, stasis, and change all have their part in Aldiss' short fiction. He has rarely, if ever, simply written potboilers. Rather, the stories form an integral part of his oeuvre. They have not been tailored to specific magazines, not even to *New Worlds*, the avant-garde British journal that heralded the "New Wave." In fact, Aldiss has often courted difficulty in getting some of his stories published by trying to sell them to markets, such as *Punch*, that usually are not receptive to science fiction.

His many collections of stories—from the early *Space, Time and Nathaniel* to *Last Orders*—are, as Aldiss himself has put it, "cores through the geology of my being." If this is the case, then Aldiss' being is fascinating indeed: the intellectual wit and wordplay crackle through the pages of his writings; heartrending emotions petrify the soul; conundrums father speculation; injury brothers love. Some of these later stories can be almost painfully complicated, until the reader realizes that the enigmas posed in *Last Orders* are intriguing speculations. Yet the stories can contain some gentle self-mockery: on the Zodiacal Planets a man called various names, one of them Krawstat, is compiling an enormous, tedious history of twentieth-century art entitled "Frankenstein Among the Arts." And some of the stories can be beautifully simple, as in the title story of the volume. In "Last Orders" the themes of joy, compassion, acceptance, and love are counterpointed against the cataclysm of the end of the world. But in all of these stories we find a sense of humanity, the humanity of Aldiss.

Aldiss has been a professional, internationally recognized writer for nearly forty years, and his probing mind is constantly working two or three books ahead of the actual writing process. For example, he had originally contemplated two sequels to *The Malacia Tapestry* and had actually named one of them *The Megara Testament*. The first would tell of the fall of Malacia, the other of its reconstruction. However, as he began work on the Helliconia trilogy, he discovered that the inchoate material for the Malacia sequels was being utilized in that major work. Hence, they remain unwritten.

In these three novels, often called by critics Aldiss' masterpiece and a genuine science fiction epic, he seems to be playing yet one more variation on the theme of change, although the very scope of the changes ranges from planetary to evolutionary to individual, all enacted on a vast, indeed epic stage.

Helliconia is a planet circling twin suns; its "year" is thousands of years long. Its seasons—whence Aldiss derives his titles *Helliconia Spring*, *Helliconia Summer*, and *Helliconia Winter*—are, as a consequence, centuries long. Change on the planet, then, is glacially slow, yet as inevitable and as certain as gravity obeying Newtonian laws of motion or an untidy volcano belching lava into an almost limitless ocean as it builds a new continent. Helliconia's changes are metamorphic as well, and they involve profound changes in form, both internal and external, physical and mental, in almost every species. Enemies become friends; history is lost, found, rediscovered, the present being lived intensely.

While some might wish Aldiss had "completed" the Helliconia series with a theoretical fourth book, *Helliconia Autumn*, it must be noted that the three novels do indeed comprise a complete entity. How the author would have handled, in Keats's terms, the "season of mist and mellow fruitfulness" is implicit in the other three novels, and together with the Squire Quartet, the three Helliconia novels comprise Aldiss' major accomplishments, works that may well still be read a century from now.

Each of the books centers around individuals surviving, living, loving, fighting, and dying on the planet in the season indicated by the title of the volume. In an off-planet space station called Avernus, a group of observers from Earth, with almost existential detachment, have converted the Helliconia day-to-day process of living, changing, evolving, and being into a saga. This may not be an art form, but it is a popular medium relayed to the home world. Because the Helliconian atmosphere is poisonous to the Earth observers, the watchers are forever destined to circle the planet, reporting, observing, studying, unable to participate in the active vital detailed life of the ever-changing, ever-stable planet itself.

Thus Aldiss has established once again the enigmatic question of the relationship between the observer and the observed. Is there some variation on Heisenberg's theorem at work here? The German physicist posited that the very act of observing changed both the observer and the thing observed, changed it macro- or microcosmically so that we might never know its true identity or its true reality.

Do the Earth observers—simply by forever studying the Helliconian reality and transmitting it to Earth almost as if it were a never-ending interstellar soap/space opera—truly change the Helliconians, who are blithely innocent that the Earth "fly on the wall" viewers watch their every move? Or do they change themselves and the "watchers" on Earth? To be sure, this technique of watchers watching other watchers watching—a series of infinite regressing mirrors in a sense—is reminiscent of what Aldiss had done earlier in *Report on Probability A.* Yet the differences and similarities counterpoint each other as scale is enlarged from minute to vast, from microcosm to macrocosm, from spare figures in a seedy garden to vast epic conflicts.

So we must ask, then, is Aldiss raising, yet one more time—this time almost cosmically—the interrelationships he explored in such excruciating detail in the earlier book? If this be the case (and the conditional mood of the verb does seem to apply here), the very unchanging nature, the innocent nature, sometimes the violent nature, as well as the unheeding nature of Helliconian life belies Heisenberg. What's more, the fact that the inhabitants of Helliconia are indeed totally unaware of the fact that they are being observed further suggests that possibility.

Consider also that at the center of *Probability A* is an "art piece," Holman Hunt's painting *The Hireling Shepherd,* with its frozen moment of the shepherd's hand poised forever above either the woman's breast or the death's head moth, just as the very center of the Helliconia series is the "art piece" of the planet itself, reported to Earth through the circling observers.

These similarities—essentially the relationship between art, however defined, and life, also however defined—are at the very core of Aldiss' writing. As seen in these two works, one the product of his relatively early writing career, early, to be sure, yet masterful and certain in its development, and the other his putative mature masterwork, as is often

the case, Aldiss asks more questions than he answers.

Aldiss would be the first to insist, however, that he does not write to provide answers. Indeed, he might maintain that there are no definitive answers to the questions he raises, that in fact the position of the artist is simply to question, to require the reader—the artistic receptor in the best case—to feel, to think, to probe, not merely to be entertained. As a consequence, the author provides a further commentary on the interaction between art and reality, because the rising and falling Helliconian civilizations are constantly being observed—*merely* observed—by the peoples of Earth who view the reality of Helliconia as only a vast entertainment.

Then too there is the name of the planet itself: "Helliconia." What is its origin? Do the various hints given by the name have anything to do with the nature of the planet or the novels Aldiss has written about it? Thus, perhaps significantly, Helicon is a mountain in Boetia, sacred to the muses; in the nineteenth century, it became the name of a large brass wind instrument in spiral form. The word also suggests "helix" and thus DNA, as well as the root word "helios"—the sun. Further, "halcyon" denotes calm or quietude, a meaning in turn derived from a fabled bird reputed by the ancients to breed about the time of the winter solstice in a nest floating on the sea and then to charm the winds and waves so they might become almost supernaturally calm. With a double "ll," it also is the name of a species of exotic, vividly colored anthurium-like Hawaiian flowers. It could even suggest the slang phrase "hell and gone." And in what appears to be a direct reminiscence of the earlier *Report on Probability A,* where the shepherd's hand is posed forever over a death's-head moth, "heliconia" is also the name of a genus of butterflies!

Perhaps Aldiss means nothing by these possibilities, yet he would certainly agree with Stephen Dedalus in the Library chapter of James Joyce's *Ulysses:* "A man of genius makes no mistakes. His errors are volitional and are the portals of discovery." Aldiss' suggestions are not errors, of course; they are merely, in his own indirect way, hints, allusions, or even complicated private jokes that must certainly be taken seriously. Thus if understanding the tenuous connection between the death's head moth in *Probability A* and the death-dealing atmosphere of the planet Helliconia deepens the reader's understanding of this complicated author, well and good. If not, no matter, but one would pity such a shallow reader.

In all of Aldiss' writing, under the smooth prose, the careful plotting, the deep consideration of motives, and the profound understanding of human beings and their condition, we feel the hand and heart of a writer who, as he has put it, possesses "the perplexing sense that you can't choose what to write; the material presents itself and you go with it as hunters explore new territory."

While the Helliconia Trilogy has received many awards including the John W. Campbell Award for the best science fiction novel of the year as well as the British Science Fiction award for the best novel of the year (twice), and so on, Aldiss calls them "piffling things of which I took no note." Instead, and more to the point, he avers, one should note the wide dissemination of the series which has been published in Dutch, French, German, Danish, Italian, Swedish, Spanish, Finnish, Serbo-Croat, Japanese, Russian, Polish, Chinese, and Romanian. This is quite an achievement for one of science fiction's true epics.

His autobiography, *The Twinkling of an Eye* (1998), was followed by the forthcoming memoir of his late wife, Margaret Aldiss, called *When the Feast is Finished* (1999). In addition, the four volumes of the Squire Quartet will shortly be reprinted in a uniform edition by Little Brown. He has also finished writing, with Sir Roger Penrose, a 100,000-word utopian novel entitled *White Mars* and is currently working on what he calls "a rather raunchy novel set in Crete."

It seems certain that Aldiss will continue to produce novels and short stories of power, profundity, and brilliant wit, stylistically innovative and endlessly inventive. He has been—and remains—a major voice not only in speculative literature but in the mainstream as well.

It may be, in fact, that the world of contemporary literature does not yet realize how much it is in debt to Brian W. Aldiss.

Selected Bibliography

WORKS OF BRIAN W. ALDISS

The Brightfount Diaries. London: Faber and Faber, 1955.

Space, Time and Nathaniel. London: Faber and Faber, 1957. (Short stories.)

Non-stop. London: Faber and Faber, 1958. Reprinted as *Starship*. New York: Criterion Books, 1959.

The Canopy of Time. London: Faber and Faber, 1959. (Short stories.)

Galaxies Like Grains of Sand. New York: Signet, 1960. (Short stories.)

Hothouse. London: Faber and Faber, 1962. Reprinted as *The Long Afternoon of Earth*, New York: Signet, 1962.

Greybeard. London: Faber and Faber, 1964. New York: Harcourt, Brace and World, 1964.

An Age. London: Faber and Faber, 1967. Reprinted as *Cryptozoic!*, Garden City, N.Y.: Doubleday, 1968.

Report on Probability A. London: Faber and Faber, 1968; Garden City, N.Y.: Doubleday, 1969.

Barefoot in the Head. London: Faber and Faber, 1969; New York: Ace Books, 1972.

The Hand-Reared Boy. London: Weidenfeld and Nicolson, 1970, New York: McCall Publishing Company, 1970.

A Soldier Erect; or, Further Adventures of the Hand-Reared Boy. London: Weidenfeld and Nicolson, 1971; New York: Coward-McCann, 1971.

Billion Year Spree: The True History of Science Fiction. London: Weidenfeld and Nicolson, 1973; Garden City, N.Y.: Doubleday, 1973. (Nonfiction.)

Frankenstein Unbound. London: Jonathan Cape, 1973; New York: Random House, 1975.

Hell's Cartographers: Some Personal Histories of Science Fiction Writers, with Harry Harrison. London: Weidenfeld and Nicolson, 1975; New York: Harpers, 1975. (Memoirs.)

SF Horizons, with Harry Harrison. New York: Arno, 1975. (Criticism.)

The Malacia Tapestry. London: Jonathan Cape, 1976; New York: Harper and Row, 1978.

Last Orders. London: Jonathan Cape, 1977. (Short stories.)

Brothers of the Head. London: Pierrot Books, 1978.

Enemies of the System. London: Jonathan Cape, 1978.

A Rude Awakening. London: Weidenfeld and Nicolson, 1978.

New Arrivals, Old Encounters. London: Jonathan Cape, 1979. (Short stories.)

This World and Nearer Ones. London: Weidenfeld and Nicolson, 1979. (Nonfiction essays.)

Life in the West. London: Weidenfeld and Nicolson, 1980.

Moreau's Other Island. London: Jonathan Cape, 1980. Reprinted as *An Island Called Moreau.* New York: Simon and Schuster, 1981.

Helliconia Spring. New York: Atheneum, 1982.

Helliconia Summer. New York: Atheneum, 1983.

Seasons in Flight. London: Jonathan Cape, 1984; New York: Atheneum, 1986. (Short stories.)

Helliconia Winter. New York: Atheneum, 1985.

The Pale Shadow of Science: Recent Essays, Seattle, Wash.: Serconia, 1985. (Articles.)

. . . And the Lurid Glare of the Comet: Articles and Autobiography, Seattle, Wash.: Serconia, 1986.

Trillion Year Spree: The History of Science Fiction, with David Wingrove. London: Gollancz, 1986. (Revision of *Billion Year Spree.*)

The Year Before Yesterday: A Novel in Three Acts. New York: Franklin Watts. 1987; London: Gollancz, 1988.

Best SF Stories of Brian W. Aldiss. London: Gollancz, 1988. Reprinted as *Man in his Time: Best SF Stories,* London: Gollancz, 1989.

Forgotten Life. New York: Atheneum, 1989.

A Romance of the Equator: Best Fantasy Stories of Brian W. Aldiss. London: Gollancz, 1989.

Bury My Heart at W. H. Smith's: A Writing Life. London: Avernus, 1990. (Memoir.)

Bodily Functions: Stories, Poems, and a Letter on the Subject of Bowel Movement Addressed to Sam J. Lundwall on the Occasion of His Birthday, February 24th, A.D. 1991. London: Avernus, 1991. (Miscellany; limited edition.)

Dracula Unbound. Norwalk, Conn.: Easton, 1991.

Remembrance Day. London: HarperCollins, 1993; New York: St. Martin's, 1993.

Somewhere East of Life. New York: Carroll and Graf, 1994.

The Detached Retina: Aspects of SF and Fantasy. Syracuse, N.Y.: Syracuse University Press, 1995. (Criticism.)

Common Clay: Twenty Odd Stories. New York: St. Martin's, 1996. (Short stories.)

The Twinkling of an Eye. London: Little Brown, 1998. (Autobiography.)

The Squire Quartet. London: Little Brown, 1999. (Uniform edition.)

When the Feast Is Finished. London: Little Brown, 1999.

White Mars, with Roger Penrose. London: Little Brown, 1999.

CRITICAL STUDIES

Aldiss, Margaret. *The Work of Brian W. Aldiss: An Annotated Bibliography and Guide.* San Bernardino, Calif: Borgo, 1992. (Definitive bibliography that lists every appearance of every novel, novella, short story, review, article, and so on by B.W.A., as well as hundreds of reviews, articles, and so on of his various works, and including 135 secondary sources or critical studies.)

Eckley, Grace. "Barefoot in the Head." In *Survey of Science Fiction Literature,* vol. 1. Edited by Frank N. Magill. Englewood Cliffs, N.J.: Salem Press, 1979.

Gillespie, Bruce. "Cryptozoic!" In *Survey of Science Fiction Literature,* vol. 1. Edited by Frank N. Magill. Englewood Cliffs, N.J.: Salem Press, 1979.

———. "Greybeard." In *Survey of Science Fiction Literature,* vol. 1. Edited by Frank N. Magill. Englewood Cliffs, N.J.: Salem Press, 1979.

Griffin, Brian, and David Wingrove. *Apertures: A Study of the Writings of Brian W. Aldiss.* Westport, Conn.: Greenwood, 1984. (Criticism.)

Harrison, Harry. "The Long Afternoon of Earth." In *Survey of Science Fiction Literature,* vol. 3. Edited by Frank N. Magill. Englewood Cliffs, N.J.: Salem Press, 1979.

Hatherly, Frank, Margaret Aldiss, and Malcolm Edwards, compilers. *A is for Brian: A 65th Birthday Present for Brian W. Aldiss from His Family, Friends, Colleagues, and Admirers.* London: Avernus, 1990. (Limited edition.)

Jameson, Fredric. "Generic Discontinuities in SF: Brian Aldiss' *Starship.*" *Science-Fiction Studies,* 1, no. 2 (1973).

Mathews, Richard. *Aldiss Unbound.* San Bernardino, Calif.: Borgo Press, 1977.

McNelly, Willis E. "Change Stasis and Entropy in the Works of Brian Aldiss." In *Reflections on the Fantastic.* Edited by Michael Collins. Westport, Conn.: Greenwood, 1986.

———. "Frankenstein Unbound." In *Survey of Science Fiction Literature,* vol. 2. Edited by Frank N. Magill. Englewood Cliffs, N.J.: Salem Press, 1979.

———. "Report on Probability A." In *Survey of Science Fiction Literature,* vol. 4. Edited by Frank N. Magill. Englewood Cliffs, N.J.: Salem Press, 1979.

Smith II, Philip E. "*Last Orders* and First Principles for the Interpretation of Aldiss's Enigmas." In *Reflections on the Fantastic.* Edited by Michael Collins. Westport, Conn.: Greenwood, 1986.

—WILLIS E. McNELLY

POUL ANDERSON
(b. 1926)

POUL ANDERSON, AN admirer once remarked, has learned to play all the instruments in the science fiction orchestra. Since publishing his first story in 1947, while still a student at the University of Minnesota, Anderson has appeared equally at ease with virtually all the forms of science fiction, from sword and sorcery to space opera to "hard" science, and even more at home using several of these forms in the same work. His writing extends outside the science fiction field as well, to include mystery, juvenile fiction, poetry, and criticism.

Not only is Anderson versatile, he is prolific, with more than sixty books and two hundred short stories to his credit. Most of this extensive output is well-crafted. He has received seven Hugo and three Nebula awards for his short stories, novelettes, and novellas: Hugos for "The Longest Voyage" (1960), "No Truce with Kings" (1963), "The Sharing of Flesh" (1968), "The Queen of Air and Darkness" (1971), "Goat Song" (1972), "Hunter's Moon" (1978), and "The Saturn Game" (1981); Nebulas for "The Queen of Air and Darkness," "Goat Song" and "The Saturn Game." And many more times he has received additional nominations for these awards. Anderson has also received the Gandalf award for lifetime achievement in fantasy (1977) and the Grand Master Award of the Science Fiction and Fantasy Writers of America (1997).

Unlike many contemporary science fiction writers, Anderson has not left behind the old forms and conventions that gave birth to science fiction in the 1920's and 1930's. Echoes of space opera, epics and sagas, and old fashioned heroes (sometimes with swords) resound frequently in his work. More important, Anderson's work has retained the essential aura of those early years: an aura of faith in mankind and awe in the face of a universe increasingly opened to our view by science. And, like earlier writers, he has remained primarily a storyteller.

What Anderson has done with these traditions is to craft them as well as they have ever been crafted, to weave them together in new ways, and to use them for purposes more complex than before. Reading the body of his work is like examining a vast, figured tapestry of bright-colored threads that reveal new patterns and designs with each new look at them.

Poul Anderson was born on 25 November 1926 in Bristol, Pennsylvania. He lived briefly in Denmark prior to World War II. Back in the United States, he entered the University of Minnesota, where he got to know Gordon R. Dickson, a classmate and fellow science fiction writer, with whom he later collaborated on several stories. Anderson graduated in 1948 with a degree in physics. His familiarity with Scandinavian languages and culture, especially with the sagas, and his knowledge of physics and other hard sciences have influenced the style, shape, and content of much of his science fiction.

Anderson began to publish stories even before he graduated from the university. "Tomorrow's Children," written with F. N. Waldrop, appeared in 1947 in *Astounding*

Science Fiction. Like many other writers, he drifted into science fiction through a casual interest in writing combined with a knowledge of science and a feeling that science fiction still permitted storytelling of a type that was becoming increasingly difficult or unacceptable in mainstream fiction.

Anderson published slowly at first, being helped and encouraged by John W. Campbell, Jr., who advised so many young writers. By 1951 he had published only ten stories. His first published novel, *Vault of the Ages*, a juvenile postatomic holocaust story, appeared in 1952. Apparently having served his apprenticeship and learned his craft, Anderson suddenly "took off" in 1953, with nineteen published stories and magazine versions of three novels, including the heroic fantasy "Three Hearts and Three Lions," which he later expanded to book length (1961).

Brain Wave (1954) established Anderson's reputation for excellence. It remains among his best works. The story chronicles what happens when Earth moves out of the range of a galactic cloud that has blanketed the solar system since life began to evolve, and that has inhibited the intelligence of living things. Within a week after the cloud departs, intelligence levels begin to climb: animals develop memory and some intelligence, retarded humans move up to normal levels, and geniuses suddenly find themselves capable of superhuman reasoning. Anderson shows in detail how this might happen, and examines what effect it might have on nature, culture, religion, and social relationships. The imaginative way in which this single change is extrapolated through the whole life of the planet gained Anderson a reputation he has since maintained for not overlooking the smallest detail.

Brain Wave is provocative as well, raising the question posed earlier by Olaf Stapledon's *Odd John* (1935) and later by such works as Daniel Keyes's *Flowers for Algernon* (1959): just how much intelligence is ideal for human society? With vastly expanded intellects, mankind soon reaches the stars, but there are problems as well. Because of the poignancy and concision with which it deals with these problems, *Brain Wave* has become popular for use in the classroom.

Even before *Brain Wave* was published, Anderson had begun to write stories that would become part of another science fiction tradition: the future history. He created his extensive future history series, the Technic Civilization, because it seemed interesting and because other science fiction writers such as Robert A. Heinlein and Isaac Asimov had done the same thing. Seventeen novels and more than two dozen short stories and novelettes so far make up this series.

Anderson's Technic Civilization covers the movement of mankind through the universe from A.D. 2100, when humans have colonized the Moon and Venus, to A.D. 7100, when a third galactic federation is beginning to emerge out of the shambles of the two previous attempts. These two attempts—the Polesotechnic League, which arises in the twenty-third century, and the Terran Empire, which begins in the twenty-eighth century—have received most of Anderson's attention.

Although these two future societies do not repeat the past (history is spiral, not cyclical, says Anderson), they do in part reflect two quite different periods of European history, allowing Anderson to explore the way in which political systems influence culture and individual human lives. Like the European Age of Exploration in the sixteenth and seventeenth centuries, the Commonwealth Age that produces the Polesotechnic League (itself much like the Hanseatic League) is expansionist and ecumenical. The Polesotechnic League is a loose confederation of merchant princes, a "league of selling skills" formed to protect merchants who operate in a laissez-faire galaxy of scattered, independent planets.

Following the dissolution of the League and the Time of Troubles, Earth forms the Terran Empire in the twenty-eighth century, eventually reaching across 400 light-years and 100,000 inhabited planets. Like the Roman Empire, the Terran Empire is parochial and protective—that is, militaristic. It, too, falls apart from within and because of extended

Poul Anderson in 1976. PHOTO BY JAY KAY KLEIN

tian IV of Denmark. Dominic Flandry, on the other hand, is aloof, sophisticated, cynical, somewhat idealistic, the product of a military organization.

Anderson has written three novels and six shorter pieces of fiction about Nicholas van Rijn. Best-known of these is "The Man Who Counts" (1958; book form, *War of the Wing-Men*, 1958), in which van Rijn is stranded on a dense planet of winged humanoids and, making the best of a bad situation, cons the humanoids into changing their social structure and way of life in order to suit his comforts. (This has been reprinted as *The Man Who Counts* [1978], apparently Anderson's preferred title.)

Dominic Flandry is the subject of eight novels and seven shorter pieces set about 600 years after van Rijn's time. A Naval Intelligence agent sworn to support the Terran Empire, he is Anderson's best example of the hero who is forced to discover the meaning and responsibility of the individualist placed in situations where he must choose between what is good for himself, for a small group of close friends or lovers, and for the civilization he serves. How does one serve oneself and others?

In *The Rebel Worlds* (1969), for example, Flandry falls in love with Kathryn Mc-Cormac, wife of an admiral who is in revolt against the Empire. In the end it is she who makes the choice when she permits her husband's rebellion to fail, then follows him into exile, at the expense of personal happiness. Flandry's personal life seldom works out, but his efforts prolong the Empire by one hundred years more than it would otherwise have lasted.

Flandry and van Rijn represent, as do many other of Anderson's characters, a belief in enlightened self-interest operating within a free—that is, laissez-faire—capitalist system. He has been criticized for his conservative political views, but his response is that such a system has gotten most of the world's work done most effectively. Anderson does not put forth these views thoughtlessly. As Flandry's personality has developed, he has gained both

wars—with the Mersians, lizardlike aliens who are the sworn enemies of mankind. The period that follows is called the Long Night.

Human lives differ under the different systems. In the Polesotechnic League era, women are virtually the equals of men, participating in decisions and actions. Under the Terran Empire, though, many women become little more than ornaments, mistresses, and prostitutes.

Against this galactic and political backdrop Anderson places two of his most important characters: Nicholas van Rijn (in the Polesotechnic League era) and Dominic Flandry (in the Terran Empire era). Both men fit Anderson's ideal of the self-made, rugged individualist who values his liberty and makes his own way, but each man shows the effects of his respective social structure as well. Van Rijn is a Renaissance-Reformation man, colorful, witty, part rogue, part thief, part dreamer—a combination, Anderson has said, of Falstaff, Long John Silver, and King Chris-

depth of character and philosophical complexity. In addition, critics of Anderson's politics neglect to take into account his larger view. Both Flandry and van Rijn appear at points when their respective cultures are dying. For a while what each man does makes a difference—a small individual decision can often affect the course of history—but surrounding the heroism is the conviction that nothing lasts, that all ends eventually in the Long Night. Anderson is optimistic in his faith in man, but not foolishly so.

Anderson's belief in the right of individual destiny is well expressed in his Hugo-winning novelette, "The Longest Voyage," which also shows his craftsmanship at its best. In this story Captain Rovic and the crew of his Vikinglike sailing ship are on a voyage of exploration across the uncharted seas of a moon revolving around a giant planet, Tamur. Rovic's people are at that stage of discovery in which they are just beginning to realize that their world is a satellite and that the huge ball hanging in the sky is a planet.

Rovic and his men reach a port where a spaceship had landed some years before. The pilot, now old, is eager to get his ship repaired and to return to his world. Rovic realizes that such contact with the stars could advance the civilization on his world by hundreds of years, but in the end he destroys the spaceship to prevent that contact. He wants to let his world discover its own destiny and shape its own culture without interference from outside.

A similar theme is expressed in *The Avatar* (1978), in which the Others, an advanced race capable of experiencing the pains and joys of all life throughout the universe, refuse to interfere or even to show themselves, because they believe that "every kind of life is equally precious, with an equal right to go its own unique way."

If Anderson is fascinated by future history, he is equally good at another science fiction convention: world building, the creation of another world according to the rules of known science rather than by flights of fancy. Anderson has little patience with science fiction writers who create imaginary worlds with little regard for what is. "When a story takes a reader to another world," Anderson has written, "he is entitled to more than he usually gets" ("The Creation of Imaginary Worlds," 1974).

Aside from a very few "impossible" devices traditional in science fiction, such as faster-than-light travel, Anderson's fiction generally remains within the limits of what we know or believe to be true. In "The Longest Voyage" he pays careful attention to the nature of a satellite in orbit around a large planet such as Tamur: its temperature, distance, gravity, tides, and rotation.

Anderson's first real attempt at world building arose from a challenge by L. Sprague de Camp, who claimed that no intelligent species could evolve with wings, since a body large enough to carry an intelligent brain would be too heavy to fly. Anderson's response was the dense world of Avalon in *War of the Wing-Men*, which he constructed in meticulous detail from its plant life to its social structure.

In *Fire Time* (1974) Anderson details how life might evolve on a planet whose northern hemisphere is scorched every 1,000 years by a red-giant star, sending the primitive creatures in those regions south to destroy a young civilized race. Anderson's essay "The Creation of Imaginary Worlds" details just how carefully he plots the parameters of a possible world, from the size of the sun that could produce such a world to the magnetic field the planet would have, using as an example his then unpublished "A World Named Cleopatra" (1977).

Even when he is not building complete worlds, Anderson stays close to the possible and probable. In "Call Me Joe" (1957; selected for inclusion in volume 2A of the *Science Fiction Hall of Fame*, 1974) a growing identification and sympathetic relationship develop between a crippled space-station operator on Jupiter and a muscular centauroid creature exploring the surface, to whom the operator's mind and sensations are connected. The harsh environment and crushing gravity of the surface make it off limits to humans—an excellent portrait of what the surface of Jupiter might be like.

In much of Anderson's work, his use of epic and saga, and the well-paced adventures of his heroes (and occasionally heroines), mask his careful attention to the scientifically possible; but now and then the hard science is virtually the whole story. Such a book is *Tau Zero* (1970). In it Commander Charles Reymont, a typical Anderson leader, must keep a spaceship with fifty varied men and women on board from disintegrating under the psychological pressures of leaving Earth forever, to settle on a distant planet. But the ship—the *Lenora Christine*—goes out of control and, accelerating at a constant 1 gravity, the horrified colonists watch single stars and eventually whole galaxies collapse and die outside the ship as it approaches the speed of light. While mere hours pass inside the ship, the universe contracts back into a primal ball; then another Big Bang occurs, sending a new universe outward to coalesce into galaxies, stars, and planets.

The sense of sad wonder that permeates the novel is typical of the later works of Anderson, from the opening chapter, in which the colonists say good-bye to places on Earth they will never see again, to their realization at the end that their whole civilization is now removed from Earth in both time and space. But their decision to endure, to go on against nearly hopeless odds, to look for a new planet in the new universe, is also typical of Anderson, as when one of the crew says, "I think we have a duty—to the race that begot us, to the children we might yet bring forth ourselves—a duty to keep trying, right to the finish."

Less often but just as successfully, Anderson has attempted other science fiction conventions. His Time Patrol series, collected in *The Time Patrol* (1991) and *The Shield of Time* (1990), shows him capable of time travel adventures and alternate history; and his series (written in collaboration with Dickson) about the Hokas—furry aliens who cannot understand idiomatic, nonliteral language and encounter strange problems with humans—shows him capable of comic science fiction as well.

Anderson has also periodically returned to another old science fiction form: sword and sorcery or "heroic fantasy." He has done "pure" sword and sorcery, as in *Three Hearts and Three Lions* and *Hrolf Kraki's Saga* (1973), but has more often blended fantasy and science fiction, as in *The High Crusade* (1960). In this novel a group of English knights on a crusade capture a spaceship of the Wersgorix Empire, but are taken back to the aliens' home planet. There they fight off the entire alien culture, defeat it, and set up an English-speaking, Christian feudal system. Another good example of the mixture of myth and science comes in "Goat Song," which won both a Hugo and a Nebula award. Here the scientific-technological basis for the religion and myths of a primitive culture does not detract from the beauty of the myths.

As science fiction encountered a "New Wave" in the late 1960's and 1970's, it began to turn inward to the realm of the mind, and toward "soft" sciences such as psychology, often toward myth, religion, and intuition. In the midst of this trend, Anderson's work began to reflect new dimensions. It might have done so anyway, because Anderson has never remained stationary. Rather than abandoning old forms and themes for new ones, though, he has broadened the basic forms in which he has always worked. His most recent work, some critics feel, reveals a darker and more problematical vision.

Another Flandry novel, *A Stone in Heaven* (1979), shows Flandry as quite different from the young man of earlier stories. Here he is aging and graying, and less idealistic. Although still capable of heroic feats, he has been tempered by wisdom and reflection. His relationships with women have lost the high and generally tragic passion of his youth. When he invites the woman in this novel—Miriam Abrams, who is the daughter of an old friend, and not young herself—to live with him as the plot concludes, it is an invitation as platonic as it is sexual.

17

The most recent Flandry installment, *The Game of Empire* (1985), is a homage to Kipling, with Flandry's daughter Diana playing Kim.

In recent years, Anderson has begun to use female characters more frequently and in more important ways. For example in *The Avatar*, Anderson has rearranged the whole relationship between his hero and the women he encounters. The story concerns Dan Brodersen, a rugged male individualist who violates his government's orders in order to rescue a female friend from a ship that has returned from space and has mysteriously been placed under quarantine. Brodersen locates the ship and rescues Joelle Ky, a holothete who guides spaceships by integrating her mind with the ships' computers. Together with another female acquaintance of Brodersen's, Caitlin Margaret Mulryan, they run from government ships that are hunting for them. At the same time they are pursuing the secret of the Others, alien beings who placed devices called T Machines around a number of suns throughout the universe long ago, but about whom nothing else is known. The T Machines permit instantaneous transport to other T Machines light-years away, making interstellar space travel possible.

At the beginning of this novel, Brodersen is a standard Anderson hero, with two mistresses on board the ship, and a wife at home who understands both his need for other women and his need for constant danger and adventure that keep him from home much of the time. But Joelle and Caitlin are opposites; their differences in personality are reminiscent of the children and the Overlords of Arthur C. Clarke's *Childhood's End* (1953). Joelle is a woman of almost superhuman intellect whose mind guides the ship even as it desires intellectual contact with the Others. Caitlin, on the other hand, is a funloving, Irish Earth Mother who lives intuitively, and who loves and feels as naturally and intensely as Joelle thinks.

So far, we are presented with a triumvirate: Brodersen acts, Joelle thinks, and Caitlin feels. As the ship jumps through T Machine after T Machine, though, coming ever closer to the Others, the need for Brodersen's masculine skills diminishes, and the two women take over, jointly making the decisions on the T jumps by using mind and heart, respectively. Eventually even Joelle's intellect can go no further, and it is Caitlin, a creature of love and intuition, who makes contact. Caitlin, in fact, is an avatar of the Others, one of many through whom the Others have experienced sentient life all over the universe. Interspersed throughout the action of the book, Anderson has placed short prose poems describing these avatars sensing the joy of life as a plant, a bird, a fish, a mammal, a human, until the Summoner comes to take the avatars back to the Others. Caitlin, too, is offered this choice, and she must decide whether to remain with the humans or return to the Others.

—ROALD D. TWEET

Anderson had the components for a masterpiece in hand for his next major novel, *Orion Shall Rise* (1983), yet failed to deploy them satisfactorily. *Orion* is the sequel to stories collected in *Maurai and Kith* (1982). It is set in a depleted world centuries after an atomic War of Judgment where three major powers struggle for dominance: Maurai Federation in Oceania (essentially democratic), the Northwest Union in that corner of North America (libertarian), and the Domain of Skyholm in Europe (aristocratic). At issue is the restoration of high technology, including atomic energy: Are humans to seek the stars or sink into mystic communion with the planet?

The cultures, histories, and technologies of the rival societies and their allies are ingeniously constructed. The plot is intricate and the issues weighty. But lush scene setting—at which Anderson excels—overwhelms the scenes, and his characters are unable to bear the archetypical burdens he lays on them. Superimposing the Norse myth of Ragnarök and other resonances on the story does not automatically add profundity. *Orion Shall Rise* is more interesting as a discussion of freedom and destiny than as a novel.

In the same year that *Orion* appeared, 1983, Anderson reopened his old Time Patrol series with two new novellas collected in *Time Patrolman*. Later he added two more in the omnibus *The Time Patrol*. Meanwhile, he constructed a novel out of six linked novelettes, *The Shield of Time*, that features his most appealing and credible young heroine, Patrol field naturalist Wanda Tamberly. She is intelligent, empathetic, resourceful, and surprisingly chaste. The historic places visited in these new time travel stories (including the Gothic steppes, Bactria, Beringia, Norman Sicily) are intelligently chosen and carefully rendered.

Anderson achieves even richer and subtler historical re-creations in *The Boat of a Million Years* (1989). Eight (initially nine) immortals born as natural mutations in different times and places interact with each other in love and hate across several thousands of years of history. Midway, the book touches on events in this century and offers some cutting social commentary before the four surviving couples take off for the stars. Passing through further emotional dramas and philosophical debates, they embark on their evolutionary destiny to spread living intelligence throughout the universe.

Boat's characters do hold their own with the splendidly realized settings and the heart-wrenching dilemmas of agelessness. This is Anderson's longest and finest work, looking backward to past achievements and forward to future ones.

Anderson's more recent achievement is his Stars series, which involves artificially contrived immortality rather than genetic immortality and depicts rivalry between "biotic" and "postbiotic" life touched on at the conclusion of *Boat*. His important 1993 essay "Wellsprings of Dream" indicates the scientific inspiration behind his series in some theories of Dyson, Moravec, Barrow, and Tipler—characteristically, without attempting to promote his own books.

Harvest of Stars (1993) offers tribute to Anderson's friend the late Robert A. Heinlein, in the person of its hero, industrialist Anson Guthrie, who talks and acts like a mature "Heinlein Individual." *Harvest* begins as a high-tech political thriller celebrating libertarian attitudes and corporate feudalism over the stifling "nanny-state" and its intelligent computers called the "Teramind." But it ends on an interstellar colony where personalities downloaded into computers can be reborn.

The Stars Are Also Fire (1994) is really two interweaved novels set before and after the previous book. These novels relate how Guthrie's daughter Dagny became the mother of a genetically engineered Lunarian race and how data from her download save its future long after her death. The wise, indomitable heroine is one of Anderson's most admirable characters.

After the inconsequential novella *Harvest the Fire* (1995), *The Fleet of Stars* (1997) shows a download of Guthrie, the Eternal Captain, returning to Earth centuries later to foil the Teramind's scheme to contain and domesticate organic-based intelligence. Yet this is no simple conflict, for both types of existence may grow toward a common destiny.

With a career spanning more than fifty years, Anderson is a daunting author to summarize. He does have his faults: a habit of exposition by lecturing, a streak of sentimentality, an overidealization of women, and a slight clumsiness with dialogue.

Yet Anderson's range and productivity are phenomenal, which is why James Blish dubbed him "the enduring explosion." Anderson has written everything from heroic fantasy to hard science fiction, from humor to historical fiction, from poetry to mysteries. He is also flexible enough to collaborate, share universes (work within fictional universes designed by others), do pastiche, and design worlds for team efforts (notably *Medea: Harlan's World*, 1985, and *Murasaki: A Novel in Six Parts*, 1992).

This said, Anderson is even more remarkable for his ability to re-examine and rework his own assumptions. Some concerns, such as freedom, run through the whole body of his work, yet how a concern is addressed may vary enormously. He keeps adding and subtracting bits of colored glass from the kaleidoscope of his art. For example, Anderson likes to retell the same story in different forms: he treats material from the Norse *Eddas* and *Volsungasaga* as heroic fantasy in *The Broken Sword*, but adds elements from the parallel German epic *Nibelungenlied* to produce a time travel adventure in the "The Sorrows of Odin the Goth" (1983). He presents a space adventure version of Orpheus in *World Without Stars* (1966) but a poetic one in "Goat Song."

Anderson's future histories changed as they grew. His first one, begun in 1947, charted in 1955, and collected as *The Psychotechnic League* (1981), *Cold Victory* (1982), and *Starship* (1982) was overtaken by events. Over its course, however, benevolent psychotechnology turns dangerous, and the United Nations no longer looks like the world's last hope.

The Technic Civilization series crystallized out of two earlier sequences when Anderson put van Rijn in Flandry's universe on a whim in "A Plague of Masters" (1960). The early Flandry stories are superior pulp adventures, but the later series explores political science and the philosophy of history on well-crafted alien worlds.

Both of these future histories grew darker the longer Anderson worked with them. To a degree this reflects his own growing disenchantment with the contemporary world and his own political pilgrimage from liberalism to libertarianism. In fiction as in real life, his hope increasingly lies with space development as a fresh start for the human race.

Anderson's willingness to reconsider past premises means that he will sometimes reverse himself. The allure of Faery, "the perilous land," is rejected in *The Broken Sword* and *Three Hearts and Three Lions* and so is its illusionary equivalent in "The Queen of Air and Darkness." But a woman sells her soul for the intensified experiences Faery affords in *The Merman's Children* (1979). Then enthrallment in a virtual reality Faeryland is again tragic in "The Saturn Game."

Initially, immortals were static, mortals progressive until *The Boat of a Million Years*

showed that both could be either, and in the Stars series, immortals are the progressive ones. And here the genetically engineered Lunarians, who look and act very much like the elves of Anderson's Faery, scorn the high-tech serial immortality devised by Terrans.

Throughout his work, Anderson has proclaimed the necessity of free response to the challenges of the universe. Like a Nordic bard, he has celebrated unflinching resistance to inevitable doom. But all the while he has sought strategies to bend, if not break, the iron law of entropy.

Theological answers are rejected, but the ancient pagan ones of survival in blood and fame do not suffice either. *Tau Zero* shows how humans might "outlive eternity" if the cosmos oscillated. Individual selves could be extended indefinitely through cloning ("The Un-Man," 1953), medical treatment (*World Without Stars*), copying into robots ("The Voortrekkers," 1974), or mimicking a natural mutation (*The Boat of a Million Years*).

The fictional solutions currently used by Anderson are the download and resurrection method achieved in the Stars series or else postbiotic evolution. He recognizes that in reality neither may ever become possible. True immortality in the philosophical sense may remain—like the speed of light—an unreachable upper limit that intelligent beings may only approach. Nevertheless, he insists that they strive with courage and love, knowing full well the doom sung in "Losers' Night" (1991): "Whatever we build must break and fall / Under the hoofs of history."

—SANDRA MIESEL

Selected Bibliography

FICTION OF POUL ANDERSON

Vault of the Ages: A Science Fiction Novel. Philadelphia, Pa.: Winston, 1952.

The Broken Sword. New York: Abelard-Schuman, 1954. Revised edition, New York: Ballantine, 1971.

Earthman's Burden, with Gordon R. Dickson. New York: Gnome, 1957.

War of the Wing-Men. New York: Ace, 1958. Reprinted as *The Man Who Counts,* New York: Ace, 1978.

The Enemy Stars. Philadelphia, Pa.: Lippincott, 1959. Expanded edition, New York: Baen, 1987.

Guardians of Time. New York: Ballantine, 1960.

The High Crusade. Garden City, N.Y.: Doubleday, 1960.

Three Hearts and Three Lions. Garden City, N.Y.: Doubleday, 1961.

Twilight World. New York: Torquil, 1961.

Un-Man and Other Novellas. New York: Ace, 1962.

Let the Spacemen Beware! New York: Ace, 1963. Reprinted as *The Night Face,* Ace, 1978.

Time and Stars. Garden City, N.Y.: Doubleday, 1964.

Trader to the Stars. Garden City, N.Y.: Doubleday, 1964.

Agent of the Terran Empire. Philadelphia, Pa.: Chilton, 1965.

Flandry of Terra. Philadelphia, Pa.: Chilton, 1965.

The Star Fox. Garden City, N.Y.: Doubleday, 1965.

Ensign Flandry. Philadelphia: Chilton, 1966.

The Trouble Twisters. Garden City, N.Y.: Doubleday, 1966.

World Without Stars. New York: Ace, 1966.

The Rebel Worlds. New York: Signet, 1969.

Seven Conquests: An Adventure in Science Fiction. New York: Macmillan, 1969.

A Circus of Hells. New York: Signet, 1970.

Tau Zero. Garden City, N.Y.: Doubleday, 1970.

There Will Be Time. Garden City, N.Y.: Doubleday, 1972.

The Day of Their Return. Garden City, N.Y.: Doubleday, 1973.

Hrolf Kraki's Saga. New York: Ballantine, 1973.

The People of the Wind. New York: Signet, 1973.

Fire Time. Garden City, N.Y.: Doubleday, 1974.

A Knight of Ghosts and Shadows. Garden City, N.Y.: Doubleday, 1974.

A Midsummer Tempest. Garden City, N.Y.: Doubleday, 1974.

Star Prince Charlie, with Gordon R. Dickson. New York: Berkley, 1975.

Mirkheim. New York: Berkley, 1977.

The Avatar. New York: Berkley, 1978.

The Earth Book of Stormgate. New York: Berkley, 1978.

The Merman's Children. New York: Berkley, 1979.

A Stone in Heaven. New York: Ace, 1979.

Explorations. New York: TOR, 1981.

Fantasy. New York: TOR, 1981.

The Psychotechnic League. New York: TOR, 1981.

Cold Victory. New York: TOR, 1982.

Maurai and Kith. New York: TOR, 1982.

Starship. New York: TOR, 1982.

Conflict. New York: TOR, 1983.

Hoka!, with Gordon R. Dickson. New York: Simon and Schuster, 1983.

The Long Night. New York: TOR, 1983.

Orion Shall Rise. Huntington Woods, Mich.: Phantasia, 1983.

Time Patrolman. New York: Pinnacle, 1983.

Past Times. New York: TOR, 1984

Dialogue with Darkness. New York: TOR, 1985.

The Game of Empire. New York: Baen, 1985.

Medea: Harlan's World, with others. Edited by Harlan Ellison. Huntington Woods, Mich.: Phantasia, 1985.

The Boat of a Million Years. New York: TOR, 1989.

Spacefolk. New York: Baen, 1989.

The Shield of Time. New York: TOR, 1990.

Alight in the Void. New York: TOR, 1991.

The Time Patrol. New York: TOR, 1991.

Murasaki: A Novel in Six Parts, with others. Edited by Robert Silverberg. New York: Bantam, 1992.

Harvest of Stars. New York: TOR, 1993.

The Stars Are Also Fire. New York: TOR, 1994.

Harvest the Fire. New York: TOR, 1995.

All One Universe. New York: TOR, 1996

The Fleet of Stars. New York: TOR, 1997.

NONFICTION OF POUL ANDERSON

Is There Life on Other Worlds? New York: Crowell-Collier, 1963. "The Creation of Imaginary Worlds: The World-Builder's Handbook and Pocket Companion." In *Science Fiction, Today and Tomorrow.* Edited by Reginald Bretnor. New York: Harper and Row, 1974.

"Star-Flights and Fantasies: Sagas Still to Come." In *The Craft of Science Fiction.* Edited by Reginald Bretnor. New York: Harper and Row, 1976.

"Wellsprings of Dream." *Amazing Stories* (June 1993). Reprinted in *All One Universe,* by Poul Anderson. New York: TOR, 1996.

BIBLIOGRAPHY

Benson, Gordon, Jr., and Phil Stephensen-Payne. *Poul Anderson: Myth-Master and Wonder-Weaver, A Working Bibliography.* 2 vols. San Bernardino, Calif.: Borgo, 1989.

CRITICAL AND BIOGRAPHICAL STUDIES

Blish, James. "Poul Anderson, the Enduring Explosion." *Magazine of Fantasy and Science Fiction* (April 1971). (Anderson as a bard of the hard-science universe.)

Elliot, Jeffrey M. "Poul Anderson: Seer of Far-Distant Futures." In *Science Fiction Voices No. 2.* San Bernardino, Calif.: Borgo, 1979. (In this interview Anderson discusses his craft and his preferences in science fiction.)

McGuire, Patrick L. "Her Strong Enchantments Failing." In *The Many Worlds of Poul Anderson,* by Poul Anderson. Edited by Roger Elwood. Philadelphia, Pa.: Chilton, 1974. Reprinted as *The Book of Poul Anderson.* New York: DAW, 1975. (McGuire analyzes "The Queen of Air and Darkness" in detail as representative of Anderson's strengths and weaknesses.)

Miesel, Sandra. "Challenge and Response." In *The Many Worlds of Poul Anderson.* Edited by Roger Elwood. Philadelphia, Pa.: Chilton, 1974. Reprinted as *The*

Book of Poul Anderson. New York: DAW, 1975. (Overview of Anderson's themes, with many citations from individual works.)

———. Introduction to *The People of the Wind*, by Poul Anderson. Boston: Gregg, 1977. (Analysis of this novel and its series as representative of Anderson's works.)

———. *Against Time's Arrow: The High Crusade of Poul Anderson*. San Bernardino, Calif.: Borgo, 1978. (Over-view of a key Anderson theme, the struggle against entropy.)

———. "The Price of Buying Time." Afterword in *A Stone in Heaven*, by Poul Anderson. New York: Ace, 1979. (Overview of the Technic Civilization series with a chronology chart.)

———. "An Invitation to Elfland." Afterword in *Fantasy*, by Poul Anderson. New York: TOR, 1981. (Overview of Anderson's fantasies at all lengths.)

Isaac Asimov

(1920–1992)

Isaac asimov did not "burst" into science fiction with a spectacularly successful story, as some science fiction writers have. Instead, his first published story, "Marooned off Vesta," appeared without fanfare in the March 1939 issue of *Amazing Stories*. Its premise of using water pressure to rescue a crew marooned on a fragment of a spaceship seems plausible, and the interplay between the characters is amusing at times. Nevertheless, Asimov's reputation as one of the giants of science fiction was built not on his first story but on the positronic robot stories, the Foundation stories, and "Nightfall" (1941).

The robot series was the first to be developed; three of the stories had been printed by the time "Nightfall" appeared, and two others were published before the Foundation series was begun.

"Robbie," the first of the robot stories, grew out of Asimov's admiration for the treatment of robots in Eando Binder's "I, Robot" (1939). "Robbie" appeared as "Strange Playfellow" in the September 1940 issue of *Super Science Stories*. It had been rejected by John W. Campbell, Jr., because it was too similar to Lester del Rey's "Helen O'Loy" (1938) and by *Amazing* for its similarity to Binder's story. The positronic robots were at first portrayed as limited and lumbering monstrosities that only a little girl could love, but they quickly became more sophisticated, sleeker in appearance, and more fully characterized.

Asimov aimed at selling to Campbell at *Astounding Science-Fiction*; and even before his first story sale, he began his practice of

delivering manuscripts by hand. When he delivered "Cosmic Corkscrew" to the Street and Smith offices on 21 June 1938, he asked hesitantly if he might see the editor. Much to Asimov's surprise, Campbell not only saw him but talked to him for an hour. This talk, along with the others, and Campbell's continuing enthusiasm, kept Asimov writing and developing ideas during his apprenticeship period, when he was writing stories such as "Cosmic Corkscrew" but not selling them.

Many people have noted that Campbell was a man of strong opinions and that he expected his authors to heed his ideas. According to Asimov's two-volume autobiography, he had Campbell's opinion in mind when planning the second robot story: robots would be one way to get around Campbell's insistence that humans are superior to other beings; the religious theme would also interest Campbell. The result was "Reason" (*Astounding*, April 1941), a story in which a robot reasons the existence of God in much the same way that Descartes did—and still performs perfectly the functions for which human beings designed it.

Between "Robbie" and the appearance of the collection *I, Robot* (1950), Asimov wrote some eleven stories about positronic robots. It is not necessary to comment on all of them; important stories in the series will be mentioned.

The third robot story, "Liar!" (*Astounding*, May 1941), is significant for two reasons: Susan Calvin is introduced, and the first of the Three Laws of Robotics is explicitly stated for the first time. "Runaround" (*Astounding*, March 1942), the fifth story, is the first to present all three laws. Briefly, the laws state that a robot: may not harm a human nor permit a human to be harmed through neglect; must obey orders, except when they involve harming a human; and should protect itself, within the limits of the first two laws. According to Asimov's diary, as noted in his autobiography, these three laws were formulated at a meeting between Campbell and Asimov on 23 December 1940. Each man has given the other credit for developing them, but Campbell has also stated that if he did formulate them first, he had only drawn them from the behavior of the robots in the first stories. These laws, which were the first reasoned "moral code" and "philosophy of life" for robots, were of great historical importance in science fiction and have also had repercussions outside the genre.

"Runaround" is built around the situation in which failure to give precedence to commands causes a robot to become disoriented. "Catch That Rabbit" (*Astounding*, February 1944) describes a robot who has the equivalent of a nervous breakdown because it has too much responsibility. Asimov did not want to leave the series on what he felt was a low note, and his next robot story, "Paradoxical Escape" (*Astounding*, August 1945), brings robots into the development and testing of the first intergalactic spaceship.

Outstanding stories in the later robot series include "Evidence" (*Astounding*, September 1946) and "Little Lost Robot" (*Astounding*, March 1947), both of which are detective stories that raise the questions of whether a robot can be distinguished from a good human being and whether one robot can be distinguished from another. Also outstanding are "The Evitable Conflict" (*Astounding*, June 1950), in which computers run the world, but unobtrusively, leaving mankind with the belief that it is still in control; "Let's Get Together" (*Infinity Science Fiction*, February 1957), in which humanoid robots developed during a cold war must be distinguished from the human scientists whom they are imper-

sonating; and "Galley Slave" (*Galaxy Science Fiction*, December 1957), in which an attempt is made to discredit a robot who reads galley proofs. This last story was suggested by a phone call from editor Horace Gold while Asimov was reading the galleys of *Biochemistry and Human Metabolism* (1952), his first nonfiction book. "Lenny" (*Infinity Science Fiction*, January 1958)—the story of a robot whose programming has been scrambled and who, in consequence, is very much like a child—was the last robot story for some eleven years.

All of these stories were collected in *I, Robot*, which has an inner coherence that makes it a history of the development of robotics, and a second volume, *The Rest of the Robots* (1964), which also includes the two robot novels, *The Caves of Steel* (1954) and *The Naked Sun* (1957). The stories in the second collection have less internal coherence than those of the first, and each story seems more a sidelight to the main thrust of robotic development than a direct part of the process.

Nevertheless, all the robot stories share the same positive attitude toward robots. Asimov believed that robots are a good idea and can be of great benefit to humankind. There may sometimes be problems, but these can be rationally studied and solved. Before Asimov's time, robots had, by and large, been viewed negatively, often fearfully, since built-in controls did not exist. Since Asimov's work, the majority of stories about robots have been more positive and most, in one way or another, include the ideas behind the Three Laws of Robotics.

Asimov's robot stories are essentially scientific detective tales that follow a characteristic pattern: a problem in robot behavior or activity is discovered; the nature of the problem is explored and more fully defined; hypotheses are advanced and tested; and the solution is presented. Although this pattern is followed in nearly all the stories, they do not become predictable, for the problems, solutions, and techniques for handling them are different from story to story.

During the period in which he was writing the robot series, before conception of the Foundation universe, Asimov wrote his well-known "Nightfall" (*Astounding*, September 1941). This story arose from a meeting between Campbell and Asimov early in 1941. Campbell had come upon a statement in the first chapter of Ralph Waldo Emerson's *Nature* (1836) that intrigued him:

> If the stars should appear one night in a thousand years, how would men believe and adore, and preserve for many generations the remembrance of the city of God?

Campbell disagreed. He believed that the sight of the stars once every thousand years would not make mankind remember the city of God, but would instead drive it mad. Asimov drew upon this conversation and wrote a story about the people living on a planet in a system of multiple suns, where the phenomenon of darkness and the appearance of the stars would have devastating psychological effects.

This story, more than any other, established Asimov as a major writer of science fiction. Indeed, many critics have considered it Asimov's finest story, and some sources, including a poll by the Science Fiction Writers of America, have declared it the best science fiction story of all time. Such an evaluation irritated Asimov, for it implied that in forty years of writing, he had been unable to equal or excel what he had done at the beginning of his career. Nevertheless, "Nightfall" is a superb story, one of the best in the genre. The concept behind the story evokes the sense of wonder that has been one of the hallmarks of the best science fiction. Of course, Asimov could not claim credit for the basic idea, which was derived from Emerson and given its twist by Campbell. He could, though, take credit for the way in which he retained the full wonder of the idea and added to it.

Although the characters in "Nightfall" are necessarily one-dimensional, the characterizations are sharp and cover a range of human reactions to an unusual situation. The background is carefully presented and made plausible. The opposition of science to mythology adds depth to the story. The suspense is built step by step to a powerful climax. There is a kind of poetry in the story—not the kind of self-consciously poetic writing that Campbell editorially inserted near the end of the story, to Asimov's dismay—but the kind of poetry that arises when the idea and development of a story merge and flow forth. It is the way that all of the elements work together, rather than any single element, that gives "Nightfall" its lasting impact.

According to Asimov, his second major series, the Foundation stories, was born of desperation and free association. Riding the subway to see Campbell, but without a fresh story idea, he randomly opened the libretto of Gilbert and Sullivan's *Iolanthe* to the scene in which the Fairy Queen throws herself at the feet of Private Willis. Asimov's imagination wandered from that scene to soldiers to military empires to the Roman Empire—and on to a Galactic Empire. He considered this the basis for a single story, but Campbell convinced him that it was the basis for an open-ended series of stories.

"Foundation" (retitled "The Encyclopedists" for book publication) appeared in the May 1942 issue of *Astounding*. This story sets the basic situation for the series. Established on Terminus by Hari Seldon, the Foundation has as its apparent purpose the compilation of a galactic encyclopedia. A threatened annexation of Terminus by the interstellar kingdom of Anacreon is averted by Salvor Hardin, who subsequently supersedes the encyclopedists as the head of the government. "Bridle and Saddle" (*Astounding*, June 1942; retitled "The Mayors") deals with Hardin's second crisis as he puts down another attempt by Anacreon to take over the Foundation.

"The Big and the Little" (*Astounding*, August 1944; retitled "The Merchant Princes") tells of Hober Mallow's strategy in quelling an attempt by the Korellian Republic to conquer the Foundation, and of the resulting assumption of rule by the plutocracy of the merchant princes. "The Wedge" (*Astounding*, October

Isaac Asimov. COURTESY OF LIBRARY OF CONGRESS

1944; retitled "The Traders") is set earlier than "The Big and the Little," since Campbell felt that a transition story was needed to fill the historical gap between "Bridle and Saddle" and "The Big and the Little." It describes the first wedge driven by the traders into the power of the Foundation-supported religion.

"Dead Hand" (*Astounding*, April 1945; retitled "The General"), one of the more important stories in the series, renders clear the theoretical background to the series, just as Asimov had done in a similar situation with his Laws of Robotics. The dead hand is that of Hari Seldon, whose theory of future history predicted that inevitable conflicts between strong emperors and strong military men would result in a stasis that would preserve the Foundation from outside conquest. At this time Asimov was greatly interested in Arnold Toynbee's *Study of History*, the first six volumes of which had been published in the 1930's; Toynbee's influence can be seen in the later Foundation stories.

What was established in "Dead Hand," though, was surprisingly and paradoxically disestablished in "The Mule" (*Astounding,* November–December 1945). At a meeting between Campbell and Asimov early in January 1945, Campbell had insisted rather strongly that the Seldon Plan be upset in some way. The Mule (so-called because he was sterile), whose mutant paranormal powers placed him outside the laws on which the Seldon Plan was based and thus made him an unpredictable factor, answered Campbell's demand. "The Mule" was also significant in that the heroine, Bayta Darrell (modeled after Asimov's wife, Gertrude), was, according to Asimov, his first successful, well-rounded female character. (Although Susan Calvin from "Liar!" is a highly successful, memorable character, she is not well-rounded.)

A direct sequel to "The Mule" appeared in the January 1948 issue of *Astounding,* "Now You See It—" (retitled "Search by the Mule"). In this story, the people of the mysterious Second Foundation (previously kept under wraps by Seldon and Asimov) defeat the Mule, who had rightly regarded them as the only real threat to his power. Asimov first wrote an ending that terminated the series, but Campbell insisted that it be kept open. Campbell won this argument, and Asimov revised the ending.

"—And Now You Don't" (*Astounding,* November 1949–January 1950) was the last of the Foundation stories. Asimov experienced difficulties in writing the story of the Second Foundation's successful ruse to make the people of the Foundation on Terminus forget its existence. Since each story was supposed to be independent of, yet consistent with, the other stories in the series, it had become increasingly difficult to plan and carry out the movements of the plot. In any case, the Second Foundation triumphs, and one of the great story chains of science fiction is brought to a satisfying conclusion.

The Foundation stories have a twofold appeal. The idea of psychohistory is intriguing, and the sweep and scope of the series as a whole is impressive. It is, of course, possible to disagree with Asimov's assumption that history is essentially a repetitive process and that the actions of masses of people can be predicted, but if Asimov is granted these fundamental points, then it must be said that he explores the consequences of these ideas fully, interestingly, and coherently. The stories are not about random situations in the future but fit into a grand scheme, the Seldon Plan, which proposes to shorten the Dark Ages between the fall of one Galactic Empire and the rise of the next. The first five stories show the plan as it unfolds approximately on schedule, while the last three deal with the problems posed by the Mule, whose unpredicted paranormal powers divert the course of history.

Within the limits imposed by the scope of the Foundation series, the stories are technically well handled. While most of the characters are necessarily flat, some achieve a degree of roundness, and all are interesting. Furthermore, the situations underlying the stories are ingenious and intriguing.

A word must be added about Asimov's fictional style. Asimov was a scientist and a writer of factual scientific material for the layman, as well as of fiction, and this background affected his view of writing. He repeatedly stated that he was concerned with writing clearly rather than writing in a "literary" style that was, he thought, unduly concerned with devices and "precious" phrasing. In other words, as long as any element in one of his stories was clearly presented and understandable, he was satisfied. This attitude is obviously beneficial to a prolific writer.

I

The details of Asimov's life are perhaps the best known among science fiction writers, for he wrote several thousand pages about his life. *In Memory Yet Green* (1979) and *In Joy Still Felt* (1980), his two-volume autobiography, are the best sources of biographical information, but many of his anthologies also contain a good deal of detail.

Isaac Asimov was born in Petrovichi, Russia, the son of Juda Asimov and Anna Rachel Berman Asimov. He celebrated 2 January 1920 as his birthdate, but that is only an approximation. The family entered the United States on 3 February 1923 and settled in Brooklyn. By 1926 his father had saved enough money to buy a candy store on Sutter Avenue, the first of several, and Asimov worked in the family candy stores part-time until he left New York for Philadelphia. At the age of twelve and a half, he entered Boys High School in Brooklyn and three years later Seth Low Junior College, then a part of Columbia University. As a sophomore he fell in love with chemistry, which he pursued as a major study throughout his educational career.

Asimov began reading the science fiction magazines available in the candy stores and wrote a number of letters to the editors. As a result, he became involved with fandom in 1938. After failing to be accepted by the medical schools to which he applied—rather to his relief—he entered graduate school at Columbia University and worked toward the master's degree and toward a Ph.D. in chemistry. Asimov's doctoral work was interrupted by World War II—he worked at the Philadelphia Navy Yard and served in the United States Army for just over four years—so he did not complete the doctorate until 1948. In the meantime he had met Gertrude Blugerman; they were married on 26 July 1942.

Asimov held a postdoctoral research position for a year after being granted a Ph.D., before becoming an instructor in biochemistry at the Boston University School of Medicine on 1 May 1949. From the beginning there were difficulties with some colleagues and with some administrators; nevertheless, he gained the ranks of assistant professor (December 1951) and associate professor, with tenure (July 1955). By April 1958 Asimov reached an agreement with Boston University whereby he would perform no substantial duties and receive no salary but would retain his faculty rank and status.

Thus, Asimov officially became a full-time writer in April 1958. By that time he was easily earning enough to support his family, which now included two children, David and Robyn. For the next twelve years the family lived in Boston. The Asimovs separated in 1970, and the divorce became final three years later. Asimov married Janet Jeppson, whom he had known for quite some time, on 30 November 1973. He died in New York City on 6 April 1992.

II

Of the first sixty stories Asimov wrote, forty-seven were published. Some of these were brought together in the two robot collections and in the Foundation trilogy. Most of the other early published fiction stories are in *The Early Asimov* (1972). The primary interest of these stories is that they provide a history of the development of a writer. None of these stories is badly written, but as a group they do not reach the level of writing found, for example, in the robot series. They do show the range of subject matter that Asimov developed into stories: unknown life-forms, difficulties in space travel, the application of various aspects of scientific knowledge to problems, human reactions to space travel, rebellion against imposed tyranny, the treatment of aliens, the effects of different environments on twins, time travel, legal questions, the relationship between a writer and his creations, and many other ideas.

Asimov collected nearly all of his stories and surrounded them with peripheral information about himself and the stories. There are seven major collections of stories written after 1949: *The Martian Way and Other Stories* (1955), *Earth Is Room Enough* (1957), *Nine Tomorrows* (1959), *Asimov's Mysteries* (1968), *Nightfall and Other Stories* (1969),

Buy Jupiter and Other Stories (1975), and *The Bicentennial Man and Other Stories* (1976). Most of the stories in these collections are above average in interest and quality, and some are very fine. Typically, most of Asimov's stories, like the robot stories, are built around the discovery, exploration, and solution of a problem of some sort. Furthermore, most of these stories are thematically complex, for they explore both science and human reactions to science and change, often from several perspectives.

Many of the stories in these collections deserve to be examined in some detail. Three must be, for Asimov said that he believed they were better than "Nightfall": "The Last Question" and "The Ugly Little Boy" (both in *Nine Tomorrows*), and "The Bicentennial Man" (in *The Bicentennial Man and Other Stories*).

"The Last Question" (*Science Fiction Quarterly*, November 1956) is deceptively simple, showing men asking a great computer, over many billions of years, how entropy might be reversed, only to be told that insufficient data for an answer has been gathered. Finally, after the universe has died, the computer finds the answer and re-creates the universe. Told in a series of scenes, the story traces the development of humanity from Earth-bound humans to settlers on a new world, to inhabitants of a fully colonized galaxy, to astral travelers (out-of-body spirits), and finally to a united human soul. At the same time the great computer also evolves: Multivac become Microvac, the Galactic AC, the Universal AC, the Cosmic AC, and finally, when it has gathered enough data and become universally conscious, the creative force for a new beginning. This sweep of idea is coupled with humor and detail in the development of the scenes. The story is thematically rich, covering such ideas as the consequences of population growth, the degrees of difficulty in solving various problems facing human beings, and the nature of God and of human beings. This is, certainly, one of Asimov's better stories, but it is not the equal of "Nightfall," for the writing and the idea do not blend and resonate as well.

"The Ugly Little Boy" (*Galaxy*, September 1958, titled "Lastborn") tells of a Neanderthal child plucked from his time and society into the present in the name of scientific research. Through his interactions with Miss Fellowes, who has been hired to care for him, the story shows how human and vulnerable he is—in spite of his grotesque-seeming appearance. This story does not have the sweep and the wonder of "Nightfall" or "The Last Question," but it does have greater immediacy and relevance. The emotional impact is carefully built as the woman and the child gradually come to trust one another, and finally to love one another. The failure of others to look beyond the surface of the boy's appearance and to understand that he is a real human being intensifies the conflict and the emotional impact of the story. The portrait of Dr. Hoskins and his overriding concern with publicity, money, and the rotation of "specimens"—the weakest aspect of the story, for his character is overdrawn—provides a contrast between the cold, "rational" approach of the scientists and the much more human and humane attitude taken by Miss Fellowes. This story is well written; stylistically it is smoother and more accomplished than Asimov's earlier stories. "The Ugly Little Boy" is, at the very least, equal to "Nightfall."

"The Bicentennial Man" (*Stellar Science Fiction #2*, 1976) is the finest of Asimov's robot stories and deserves consideration as the finest of all his stories. It follows the changes in a robot, Andrew Martin, who has developed an unforeseen talent for artfully carving wood. First he becomes capable of desiring his freedom—even if in name only—and later of directing his energies toward gaining recognition as a human, legally as well as in fact. He is even willing to become mortal to gain that recognition. The story explores what it means to be free and to be human. The varieties of human resistance to the idea of a free robot and to consideration of a robot as human are vividly and concisely presented as elements in the story; they provide the background for the growth of awareness and determination in Andrew Martin. The emotional scenes are well handled; but more than that, the emotional impact of the story as a whole is subtly built to an explosive conclusion as Andrew Martin is finally recognized as a human being in his two-hundredth year.

Asimov's best stories combine some kind of sweeping idea or some deeply felt human emotional response with a prose that presents the idea clearly, sensitively, and humanely. As a writer of fiction, Asimov was at his best in the shorter forms; although his novels are interesting, they tend, with some exceptions, to be rather melodramatic and to rely quite heavily on coincidence.

His first novel, *Pebble in the Sky* (1950), is set about 50,000 years in the future, in the Foundation universe. Earth is a "backwoods" planet, despised by the rest of the Empire. One thread of the plot involves Joseph Schwartz, who is somehow transferred from twentieth-century Chicago into the future. He contrasts this future Earth with our own. Forced to undergo experiments with a device called a Synapsifier, he becomes able to "hear" and to influence other minds, suggesting that the human mind has greater capabilities than we now use.

The second plot thread involves Dr. Bel Arvardan, the head of an imperially funded archaeological expedition to Earth. Although he is prejudiced against Earth people, he believes that Earth may be, as some claim, the origin of mankind. After the two threads merge, Schwartz and Arvardan avert a threat against the Empire and prove that Earth was, indeed, the original home world. For all the melodrama, this is a decent novel, especially for a first effort, and it does a reasonable job of exploring the changes that have taken place on Earth, the attitudes caused by Earth's lowly status in the Empire, and the ways in which prejudice affects people.

The Stars, Like Dust (1951), Asimov's second novel, is a slighter and more melodramatic work. Set perhaps a thousand years in the future, in a part of the galaxy ruled by the Tyranni for over a generation, this novel traces the development of Biron Farrell from a rather puzzled young man who allows oth-

ers to manipulate him into a more determined young man who more clearly understands the situation and the role he must play if humans are to regain their freedom. The climactic moment is the discovery and reading of the long-lost American Declaration of Independence. Thematically, Biron's development and the nature of political relationships are approximately equal in prominence. In both of these first two novels, the scientific element is simply background; it is assumed rather than explored.

Asimov's next novel was a juvenile, *David Starr, Space Ranger* (1952). Over the next six years he wrote five more such novels: *Lucky Starr and the Pirates of the Asteroids* (1953), *Lucky Starr and the Oceans of Venus* (1954), *Lucky Starr and the Big Sun of Mercury* (1956), *Lucky Starr and the Moons of Jupiter* (1957), and *Lucky Starr and the Rings of Saturn* (1958). Published under the pseudonym Paul French, these books have since been republished under Asimov's own name.

In his introductions to the 1971 and 1972 reprintings of these juveniles, Asimov commented that the scientific information in them was as current and as accurate as he could make it at the time. The scientific materials are clear and neatly incorporated into the adventure; unfortunately, science does not stand still, and the novels are now seriously dated.

The Currents of Space (1952) is again set in the Foundation universe, at a time when the Empire based on Trantor is still expanding its sphere of influence and power. A major emphasis in the novel is the delicate diplomatic maneuvering the Trantorian ambassador must undertake to save the population of a planet whose sun will soon nova and to bring a new world into the Empire. Two other plot lines focus on the daily life of those on a subject planet and on the lives of those who "own" the planet that provides their wealth. Interwoven with these elements are the mystery of the missing Spacioanalyst and, once he is found, the question of why his memories have been wiped out. *The Currents of Space* shows a growth in Asimov's ability to handle the novel as a fictional form. Although coincidence and melodrama are still present, they are more muted and carefully controlled than they were in the earlier novels. In addition, the characterizations are more incisive, and the thematic explorations are clearer and more carefully directed.

The Caves of Steel (1954) and *The Naked Sun* (1957) are robot novels; they are also mirror images of one another. In *The Caves of Steel* the setting is an Earth whose inhabitants have gone underground; the people of Earth fear the open spaces and the "Spacers," the colonists who inhabit planets in other solar systems. When a Spacer is murdered on Earth, his murderer must be found, or the Spacers may take action against a helpless Earth. Elijah ("Lije") Baley is the human detective assigned to the case. The robot element is incorporated in two ways: first, Baley's Spacer-assigned partner is a robot named R (for robot) Daneel Olivaw. Second, the differing attitudes of Earthmen and Spacers toward robots is a major theme of the novel.

The same two detectives team up again in *The Naked Sun*, but this time Baley is called off Earth to solve a murder on a world, Solaria, where the people are used to great, open spaces and fear direct human contact. Not only does Baley have to learn to control his Earth-conditioned fear of open spaces and to master the intricacies of a totally new social system, he must also find the murderer. Baley is, of course, successful. Asimov is successful as well, for he blends the elements of the detective story with the elements of the science fiction story smoothly; all of the relevant information is provided for the reader—if he or she can recognize it and put it together and no tricks are used to uncover the murderer. In addition, although the differing political and social situations on Earth and on the Outer Worlds are in the background of these novels, these elements are nevertheless convincingly and interestingly interwoven. After the later *The Gods Themselves* (1972), *The Caves of Steel* is Asimov's best novel, but *The Naked Sun* is not far behind.

The End of Eternity (1955) is not as well developed and not as fully unified as *The Currents of Space* and *The Caves of Steel*. It explores the paradoxes and problems of time travel, as an organization named Eternity tries to manipulate events in historical time so that human life proceeds as Eternity thinks it should. Through the power of love (a rare theme in Asimov's fiction), the protagonist learns that this course of action is futile; his strategic placement in the organization allows him to stop the development of Eternity. The nature of history and of human societies is a theme that runs through Asimov's works, and it is explored from a different direction in this novel.

Fantastic Voyage (1965), written by Asimov but based on a screenplay by another writer, is the story of several humans and a submarine, all miniaturized, who enter a human body to find the cause of a medical problem. They have an hour to solve the problem before the miniaturization effect wears off. In writing the novelization, Asimov made the science as accurate as possible, correcting such problems in the script as the manner in which the humans escape while leaving the submarine in the body. Yet, he was constrained by the limitations of the script and could do nothing about his basic doubt as to the possibility of such miniaturization. Although the novel is not vintage Asimov, it is, like the 1966 movie, interesting.

The Gods Themselves, long awaited by science fiction fans, shows Asimov's growth as a writer in all aspects of the novel. He skillfully used his knowledge of science (for the first time in his novels, science is a major element) to create a plausible situation, and he used his knowledge of the scientific establishment effectively in developing the conflicts that arise in moving toward a solution to the problem. Furthermore, also for the first time in his novels, Asimov created a sympathetic and believable alien species and explored their way of life in the process of investigating the scientific problem and its possible solutions. The problem involves an exchange of energy between two parallel universes, an exchange initiated by the aliens because they are losing the energy they need to survive. Unfortunately, it slowly becomes apparent—though few want to admit it—that the entire process holds great danger for our universe. It is the smooth and believable combination of the scientific problem with the apt characterizations of the people involved—human and alien—that makes this the best of Asimov's novels.

Asimov belongs in the first rank of science fiction writers. He created and explored the Three Laws of Robotics, and he created the Foundation with its struggles to survive. He wrote some of the finest stories in the genre. These accomplishments alone would assure him a place among the great writers of science fiction.

—L. DAVID ALLEN

If Asimov did not begin his writing career back in 1939 with a particularly strong story, his determination and his genius at the end fully compensated for this inauspicious beginning. In the last decade of his life, he wrote and published eight more adult science fiction books as well as his usual abundance of edited collections, juveniles, and nonfiction work. When he died, his total book production had reached well over four hundred titles. More importantly, he had established himself as a master commentator on the most representative problems of our century, such as large organizational structures stemming from the empires of the nineteenth century and issues of automatic control, or robotics, as opposed to the role of the individual as well as larger issues of the man-machine symbiosis. All these key ideas appear primarily in his science fiction narratives, although his nonfiction touched on similar topics when he was not simply popularizing science or summarizing masterworks from the Bible to Shakespeare. In fact, Asimov's favorite occupation was always to wrestle with epistemological paradoxes and the puzzles over origins, and to do so in continuing, interlocked stories. Thus, his novel *Nemesis* (1989), which is more a story of character than an exploration of ideas,

may be seen as the exception in his last works to demonstrate his versatility, even individuality, as a writer; and it was well reviewed. But the last series of sequels to the Foundation stories and to the robot stories are more representative of the determined and driven Asimov compelled, to a great extent, beyond his individuality to attempt an intellectual resolution to puzzles that he knew could not be resolved.

These last sequels weave in and out, like a subtle logical analysis or an old-fashioned minuet from the time of Hari Seldon and the central, fully urbanized location of Trantor to the other times, and to the original "caves of steel" location balanced against the pastoral planet of Aurora, so that the reader is left finally both convinced of Asimov's genius and sense of unity and questioning the basic issues of human freedom and human potential. The robots themselves invent a sequel to the laws of robotics, the "Zeroth Law of Robotics" in *Robots and Empire* (1985), that dictates the priority of humanity as a whole, and hence ensures the survival of "Empire." And yet the individual personalities, and even sex lives, of familiar characters from Liz Baley to Hari Seldon and their robot partners dominate these last novels.

Asimov at the end is both philosopher and storyteller. It may have been his peculiar genius as a writer to have invented the frames for stories both about robotics in which the human inventor, Susan Calvin, resembles her machines and about spiraling Galactic Empires in which Earth, even mythic Gaia, remains hauntingly at the center. Each of the last sequel novels from 1982 on, as well as the very last collection of novelettes, *Forward the Foundation* (1993), probes deeper and continually into the wonderful paradoxes of large size as opposed to littleness, and predetermined control of some sort (maybe even from aliens or from some divine source) as opposed to random development and the illusion of human freedom. This ending to Asimov's fifty-plus years of writing is truly auspicious—so much so that a trio of younger science fiction colleagues, Gregory Benford, Greg Bear, and David Brin, have set out to write further sequels about the Foundation galaxy and the robot worlds.

Finally, balanced against these solemn, grand notions is the wise sense of comic proportion in Asimov's work. Here is a telling comment that a perceptive shipmate makes about Asimov's hero in *Foundation and Earth* (1986): "You do have this annoying habit of trying to turn everything into a joke, but I know you are under tension and I'll make allowance for that." The tension that Asimov himself felt sprang not only from his ambition as a writer, which was always very strong, but also from his sense of the vastness of things. Science fiction writers may be able to perceive this vastness more clearly than other writers. Thus, when Asimov peoples the Galaxy, resolves the man-machine symbiosis, or speaks to the most enigmatic questions of origin and freedom, it is all, in a sense, hopeful thinking punctuated with a nervous laugh. One result has been an important body of fiction that in its totality and depth is no joke but rather a genuine gift.

—DONALD M. HASSLER

Selected Bibliography

PUBLICATION HISTORY OF SHORT STORIES

The order in which the stories in the robot series and the Foundation series, as well as "Nightfall," were originally published is of some interest. In the following chronology (R) indicates a robot story and (F) indicates a Foundation story; the title under which a story was first published is used here.

1939
MARCH: "Marooned off Vesta," *Amazing Stories*
1940
SEPTEMBER: "Strange Playfellow," *Super Science Stories* (R)
1941
APRIL: "Reason," *Astounding Science-Fiction* (R)
MAY: "Liar!," *Astounding* (R)
SEPTEMBER: "Nightfall," *Astounding*

1942
FEBRUARY: "Robot AL-76 Goes Astray," *Amazing* (R)
MARCH: "Runaround," *Astounding* (R)
MAY: "Foundation," *Astounding* (F)
JUNE: "Bridle and Saddle," *Astounding* (F)
1944
FEBRUARY: "Catch That Rabbit," *Astounding* (R)
AUGUST: "Victory Unintentional," *Super Science Stories* (R)
AUGUST: "The Big and the Little," *Astounding* (F)
OCTOBER: "The Wedge," *Astounding* (F)
1945
APRIL: "Dead Hand," *Astounding* (F)
AUGUST: "Paradoxical Escape," *Astounding* (R)
NOVEMBER–DECEMBER: "The Mule," *Astounding* (F)
1946
SEPTEMBER: "Evidence," *Astounding* (R)
1947
MARCH: "Little Lost Robot," *Astounding* (R)
1948
JANUARY: "Now You See It—," *Astounding* (F)
1949
NOVEMBER 1949–JANUARY 1950: "—And Now You Don't," *Astounding* (F)
1950
JUNE: "The Evitable Conflict," *Astounding* (R)
1951
APRIL: "Satisfaction Guaranteed," *Amazing* (R)
1955
MAY: "Risk," *Astounding* (R)
1956
OCTOBER: "First Law," *Fantastic Universe Science Fiction* (R)
1957
FEBRUARY: "Let's Get Together," *Infinity Science Fiction* (R)
DECEMBER: "Galley Slave," *Galaxy Science Fiction* (R)
1958
JANUARY: "Lenny," *Infinity Science Fiction* (R)

WORKS OF ISAAC ASIMOV

This bibliography lists all of Asimov's science fiction novels, the most useful and readily accessible of his short story collections, and his autobiography.

I, Robot. New York: Gnome Press, 1950. London: Grayson and Grayson, 1952; Garden City, N.Y.: Doubleday, 1963. (Short stories.)
Pebble in the Sky. Garden City, N.Y.: Doubleday, 1950; London: Transworld (Corgi), 1958.
Foundation. New York: Gnome Press, 1951; London: Weidenfeld and Nicolson, 1953; Garden City, N.Y.: Doubleday, 1962.
The Stars, Like Dust. Garden City, N.Y.: Doubleday, 1951; London: Hamilton and Company, 1958.

The Currents of Space. Garden City, N.Y.: Doubleday, 1952; London: T. V. Boardman, 1955.

David Starr, Space Ranger, as by Paul French. Garden City, N.Y.: Doubleday, 1952; London: World's Work, 1953. (Juvenile.)

Foundation and Empire. New York: Gnome Press, 1953; Garden City, N.Y.: Doubleday, 1962; London: Hamilton and Company, 1962.

Lucky Starr and the Pirates of the Asteroids, as by Paul French. Garden City, N.Y.: Doubleday, 1953; London: World's Work, 1953. (Juvenile.)

Second Foundation. New York: Gnome Press, 1953; London: Brown, Watson, 1958; Garden City, N.Y.: Doubleday, 1962.

The Caves of Steel. Garden City, N.Y.: Doubleday, 1954; London: T. V. Boardman, 1954.

Lucky Starr and the Oceans of Venus, as by Paul French. Garden City, N.Y.: Doubleday, 1954; London: George Prior, 1979. (Juvenile.)

The End of Eternity. Garden City, N.Y.: Doubleday, 1955; London: Hamilton and Company, 1959.

The Martian Way and Other Stories. Garden City, N.Y.: Doubleday, 1955; London: Dennis Dobson, 1964. (Short stories.)

Lucky Starr and the Big Sun of Mercury, as by Paul French. Garden City, N.Y.: Doubleday, 1956; London: George Prior, 1979. (Juvenile.)

Earth Is Room Enough. Garden City, N.Y.: Doubleday, 1957; London: Hamilton and Company, 1960. (Short stories.)

Lucky Starr and the Moons of Jupiter, as by Paul French. Garden City, N.Y.: Doubleday, 1957; London: George Prior, 1979. (Juvenile.)

The Naked Sun. Garden City, N.Y.: Doubleday, 1957; London: Michael Joseph, 1958.

Lucky Starr and the Rings of Saturn, as by Paul French. Garden City, N.Y.: Doubleday, 1958; London: George Prior, 1979.

Nine Tomorrows. Garden City, N.Y.: Doubleday, 1959; London: Dennis Dobson, 1963. (Short stories.)

The Rest of the Robots. Garden City, N.Y.: Doubleday, 1964; London: Dennis Dobson, 1967. (Short stories, plus reprints of the two robot novels, *The Caves of Steel* and *The Naked Sun.*)

Fantastic Voyage. Boston: Houghton-Mifflin, 1965; London: Dennis Dobson, 1966. (Novelization of a film script by Harry Kleiner, from an original story by Otto Klement and Jerome Bixby.)

Asimov's Mysteries. Garden City, N.Y.: Doubleday, 1968.

Nightfall and Other Stories. Garden City, N.Y.: Doubleday, 1969. Reprinted as *Nightfall One and Nightfall Two,* London: Panther Books, 1971.

The Early Asimov. Garden City, N.Y.: Doubleday, 1972; London: Victor Gollancz, 1973. (Short stories.)

The Gods Themselves. Garden City, N.Y.: Doubleday, 1972; London: Victor Gollancz, 1972.

Buy Jupiter and Other Stories. Garden City, N.Y.: Doubleday, 1975; London: Victor Gollancz, 1976. (Short stories.)

The Bicentennial Man and Other Stories. Garden City, N.Y.: Doubleday, 1976; London: Victor Gollancz, 1977. (Short stories.)

In Memory Yet Green: The Autobiography of Isaac Asimov, 1920–1954. Garden City, N.Y.: Doubleday, 1979.

In Joy Still Felt: The Autobiography of Isaac Asimov, 1954–1978. Garden City, N.Y.: Doubleday, 1980.

Foundation's Edge. Garden City, N.Y.: Doubleday, 1982.

The Robots of Dawn. Garden City, N.Y.: Doubleday, 1983.

Robots and Empire. Garden City, N.Y.: Doubleday, 1985.

Foundation and Earth. Garden City, N.Y.: Doubleday, 1986.

Fantastic Voyage II: Destination Brain. Garden City, N.Y.: Doubleday, 1987.

Prelude to Foundation. Garden City, N.Y.: Doubleday, 1988.

Nemesis. Garden City, N.Y.: Doubleday, 1989.

Forward the Foundation. Garden City, N.Y.: 1993. (Novelettes.)

CRITICAL AND BIOGRAPHICAL STUDIES

Allen, L. David. *Asimov's Foundation Trilogy and Other Works.* Lincoln, Neb.: Cliff's Notes, 1977.

Edwards, Malcolm. "Isaac Asimov." In *The Science Fiction Encyclopedia.* Edited by Peter Nicholls. Garden City, N.Y.: Doubleday, 1979.

Goble, Neil. *Asimov Analyzed.* Baltimore, Md.: Mirage Press, 1972.

Gunn, James. *Isaac Asimov: The Foundations of Science Fiction.* Revised edition, Metuchen, N.J.: Scarecrow Press, 1996.

Hassler, Donald M. *Isaac Asimov: Starmont Reader's Guide.* San Bernardino, Calif.: Borgo, 1991.

Knight, Damon. "Asimov and Empire." In *In Search of Wonder.* Revised edition, Chicago: Advent Publishers, 1967. (This volume also contains other, scattered references to Asimov.)

Miller, Marjorie M. *Isaac Asimov: A Checklist of Works Published in the United States, March 1939–May 1972.* Kent, Ohio: Kent State University Press, 1972.

Moskowitz, Sam. "Isaac Asimov." In his *Seekers of Tomorrow.* Cleveland, Ohio: World Publishing Company, 1966.

Olander, Joseph D., and Martin Harry Greenberg, eds. *Isaac Asimov.* New York: Taplinger, 1977.

Patrouch, Joseph F. *The Science Fiction of Isaac Asimov.* Garden City, N.Y.: Doubleday, 1974.

Wood, Susan. "A City of Which the Stars Are Suburbs." In *SF: The Other Side of Realism.* Edited by Thomas D. Clareson. Bowling Green, Ohio: Bowling Green University Popular Press, 1971.

J. G. BALLARD

(b. 1930)

JAMES GRAHAM BALLARD was born on 18 November 1930 in Shanghai, China. During World War II he was interned by the Japanese in a civilian prisoner-of-war camp and was repatriated to Britain in 1946. He went to King's College, Cambridge, to study medicine but left without taking his degree. During the early 1950's Ballard served in the RAF (Royal Air Force) and spent some time in Canada. He worked for a scientific film company for a while before becoming a full-time writer.

Ballard's earliest sales were to the companion British magazines *Science Fantasy* and *New Worlds*; he had stories in the December 1956 issues of each. His appearances there were infrequent until 1960, when he became one of their leading contributors. Although *New Worlds* and *Science Fantasy* at this time used mainly traditional material, their editor, E. W. John "Ted" Carnell, permitted both Ballard and Brian W. Aldiss to experiment thematically and stylistically; and Ballard became the leading figure of an emergent British science fiction avant garde. When Michael Moorcock took over the editorship of *New Worlds* in 1964, using it to launch the so-called New Wave, he continued to promote Ballard's work, but by that time Ballard had already published most of the brilliant short stories that helped to transform British science fiction.

The bibliography of Ballard's short fiction is extremely complicated. Independent series of collections appeared in the United States from Berkley Medallion (initially) and in Britain from various publishers. The contents of the individual collections in these series are usually quite different even when the titles of American and British editions are similar; to complicate the issue further, there have been several collections in both countries that have recombined the various stories. There have been more than twenty different Ballard collections, and some of his stories appear in five or more of them.

Ballard's 1956 stories were "Escapement" and "Prima Belladonna." The first describes the existential crisis of a man who discovers that he is living the same segment of time over and over again, and that the segment is getting progressively shorter; the other is an exotic fantasy about a man who sells musical flowers and a female singer with what look like "insects for eyes." These two stories were quickly followed by one of Ballard's more celebrated pieces, "Build-Up" (1957; also known as "The Concentration City"), in which a human population numbering several trillion inhabits a completely enclosed world in which a boy searching for the free space of which he has dreamed is doomed to disappointment. Like the protagonist of "Escapement," the boy in "Build-Up" is caught in a curious kind of existential trap, here manifested as an environment rather than as a developing situation.

The sensation of being trapped in a world that is not as it ought to be, of facing prospects that range from imminent extinction to stabilized but permanent frustration, runs throughout Ballard's oeuvre, and his work may be seen as the elaborate development of a wide range of such representations. In some of his stories—for instance, "Manhole 69" (1957), in which three experimental subjects deprived of sleep wind up in a state of catatonic withdrawal from the world—the existential traps are microcosmic and arise from the psychology of the individual protagonists. In others—for instance, "The Waiting Grounds" (1959), one of his few interplanetary stories—the traps are macrocosmic, the implication being that they are intrinsic to the nature of the universe itself; stories of this kind often feature a preoccupation with the notion of entropy.

Some time before psychologists, in the wake of the LSD-25 experiments of the 1960's, became interested in "altered states of consciousness," Ballard was already fascinated by such possibilities. Faulkner, the protagonist of "The Overloaded Man" (1961), attempts to dissolve the world of phenomena and to cast himself adrift in a realm of raw sensation. More central to Ballard's work, though, are stories in which altered states of consciousness are forced upon people by environmental changes. The microcosmic and macrocosmic themes come together for the first time in one of the most impressive of his early stories, "The Voices of Time" (1960, revised as "News from the Sun," 1982), in which enigmatic signals transmitted from distant galaxies count down to the end of the universe while genetically manipulated monsters reveal the alien potential of future life on Earth. The two protagonists face these grim prospects with enforced calm; one has to capitulate as he is slowly claimed by eternal sleep, while the other is denied that release because he cannot sleep at all.

In all of Ballard's stories, the world has become a wilderness, transformed by lurid disaster or the collapse of civilization or the prolonged exaggeration of destructive social processes already familiar today. Sometimes, as in "The Encounter" (1963; also known as "The Venus Hunters") or "The Gioconda of the Twilight Noon" (1964), this happens at a purely personal level. Sometimes, as in "Billennium" (1961) or "The Subliminal Man"

(1963), it is a sociopolitical process. More frequently, especially in the early novels, the whole environment undergoes a radical metamorphosis. Always, though, it is happening—or has already happened—when his stories begin. The main axis of development within Ballard's work over the years has been the gradual discarding of science fiction apparatus, which seems to transform his argument from the anticipation of future existential aridity to the revelation of an aridity already present but largely unrecognized.

Ballard's preoccupation with the psychological implications of new technologies never takes the form of speculating about the innovations themselves, except in the most limited way—as, for instance, in "The Sound Sweep" (1960) or his stories about the psychological implications of the space program: "The Cage of Sand" (1962), "A Question of Re-entry" (1963), and "The Dead Astronaut" (1968). His main interest has been in technology that already exists, although it is rarely featured in his stories in an active role; rather, it serves to provide an exotic reliquary of cracked concrete and broken machines. The key story in this gradual shift in focus is "The Terminal Beach" (1964), the protagonist of which is hopelessly searching for some kind of personal fulfillment in the derelict manmade landscape of Eniwetok, an island now abandoned but still haunted by virtue of its association with the atomic bomb.

In the 1960's Ballard wrote four novels, all basically similar in theme. Each documents the disintegration of civilization in the face of a disaster mysteriously imposed from without. The first of these, *The Wind from Nowhere* (1962), is distinctly inferior to the other three, which are sometimes considered to form a loose trilogy: *The Drowned World* (1962), *The Drought* (1965; previously issued in considerably abridged form as *The Burning World* in 1964), and *The Crystal World* (1966).

British imaginative fiction of the twentieth century is replete with great plagues, cosmic disasters, nuclear holocausts, and climatic catastrophes; Ballard was, therefore, working within a well-established tradition. Almost

J. G. Ballard. UPI/Corbis-Bettmann

all the earlier works in this tradition, though, are manifestly didactic tales that strive to remind us of the vulnerability of the human world, the extent to which we are under threat from the side effects of our vaulting ambition, or the harsh necessities with which we might have to cope once the struggle for existence becomes acute. Ballard is quite unconcerned with such matters; he is neither an alarmist nor a moralist in these early catastrophe stories. Rather, his narrative voice possesses a remote and clinical objectivity that is interested solely in the minute observation of the psychological readjustments that the various characters make.

In *The Wind from Nowhere*, a slowly accelerating wind plucks civilization apart. This is an active rebellion of nature against which no one can stand firm—not even the immensely rich and powerful Hardoon, who constructs a gigantic pyramid intended to encapsulate a private empire secure against all hazards. In the end the wind topples this edifice into an abyss; Hardoon is not so much defeated as judged irrelevant to the real issue.

As with most disaster stories, though, *The Wind from Nowhere* follows the fortunes of various protagonists, and thus lacks a focal point that might allow it to put the catastrophe in what was to become—for Ballard—its proper perspective. All three of the major novels of the period have one particular central character whose experiences and personal adaptation are crucial.

In *The Drowned World*, Earth's surface temperature has risen, and the water released by the melting of the polar ice caps has inundated much of the land surface. Dense tropical jungle has reclaimed much of the land that remains, rendering it virtually uninhabitable. The world seems to be undergoing a kind of retrogression to the conditions of the Triassic period. The novel's protagonist is Robert Kerans, a biologist who is monitoring the disaster from a research station above submerged London.

The environmental changes are accompanied by parallel psychological changes in Kerans and others, which first manifest themselves as recurrent dreams of a primitive world dominated by a huge, radiant sun. These dreams, apparently, are part of the cellular heritage of mankind—a quasi-memory retained within the genome, now ready to free the nervous system from the domination of the recently evolved brain, whose appropriate environment is gone. Kerans, in the end, forsakes his acquaintances, each of whom is responding to the changed world in his or her own way, in order to travel south, submitting to the psychic metamorphosis that strips away his individuality and leaves him "a second Adam searching for the forgotten paradises of the reborn sun."

The Drowned World was not particularly well received within the science fiction community; many readers failed to understand what was going on in it. No novel in the history of the genre, though, has provided such a spectacular introduction to imaginative territories hitherto unexplored.

The American edition of Ballard's next novel, *The Burning World*, differs substantially from the version published a year later in Britain as *The Drought,* and is perhaps best regarded as an imperfect early draft. In this novel the catastrophe of *The Drowned World* is reversed: Earth becomes a vast desert because a molecular film has formed on the surface of the oceans, inhibiting evaporation. The landscape is reduced to hot sand, glittering salt, and white ash as the soil dies and civilization shrivels. Human life can survive only at the edge of the sea, and there only precariously. The opening part of the novel deals with the stubborn few who are the last to move to the shore. Dr. Charles Ransom, the protagonist, is already emotionally and purposively inert as the story begins; from his houseboat he watches the waters of the river dwindle, and sees in its draining the disappearance of the dregs of the social and natural orders. Eventually Ransom and some of his surviving neighbors move to the seaside and fight for a place there, in a "dune limbo" where "time was not absent but immobilized." But he subsequently comes to see this retreat as a false move; and in the final section of the novel he retraces his steps to see what has become of the city and its last few inhabitants.

In *The Crystal World,* the environmental metamorphosis is much more limited, consisting of the "crystallization" of an African jungle, and is seemingly not catastrophic in the sense that the changes overtaking the world in the earlier novels are. The cause and the exact nature of the change are unclear— such explanation as is offered is distinctly metaphysical. The central character is Dr. Edward Sanders, the assistant director of a leper colony, who is at first horrified when he finds his mistress and some of his patients joyfully accepting the process of crystallization into their own flesh, although—inevitably—he eventually comes to accept that no other destiny is possible. Although the novel has some wonderfully exotic imagery, it is less impressive than its two immediate predecessors; and although it makes the basic theme of the earlier novels more clearly manifest, it is essentially a recapitulation.

There is a sense in which the transformation that overtakes the world in *The Crystal World* is a kind of beautification, and it is much easier for the reader to sympathize with Sanders' acceptance of its dictates than with Kerans' capitulation to the demands of his dreams. The lushness of the imagery in *The Crystal World,* in fact, recalls another aspect of Ballard's early work: the decadent romanticism of the various stories set in Vermilion Sands, an artists' colony and beach resort populated by eccentrics and aging movie stars.

"Prima Belladonna" (1956) was the first of these stories; the best of them is "Studio 5, The Stars" (1961), a synthesis of Greek myth and the film *Sunset Boulevard* (1950), in which the mysterious Aurora Day attempts to woo the "poets" of the colony away from their IBM Verse-Transcribers while trying to reenact the story of Melander and Corydon. All the other stories, which include such gems as "The Cloud-Sculptors of Coral-D" (1967) and "Cry Hope, Cry Fury!" (1967), feature guilt-ridden femmes fatales and elaborate art forms such as might be available to a culture possessed of unlimited technology to bend to the merest of aesthetic whims. A collection of the stories in this series was issued in 1971 under the title *Vermilion Sands.*

A long time separated *The Crystal World* from Ballard's next novel, *Crash* (1973). His production of short stories during the intervening years was also dramatically cut back, and his major project during those years was a rather bizarre collection of what he called "condensed novels," published in Britain as *The Atrocity Exhibition* (1970) and in the United States as *Love and Napalm: Export U.S.A.* (1972). The individual units— "stories" is not the right word for them—in the collection consist of series of subtitled scenes; in effect, they are collages of collages. Although some are "action-frames," most are "stills" combining the various images that Ballard sees as the archetypes encapsulating the contemporary *Zeitgeist:* the murdered John F. Kennedy and the self-assassinated Marilyn Monroe; dead astronauts, crashed cars, H-bombs, and the concrete wilderness. In the world portrayed by these collages, violence and perverted sexual arousal are ubiquitous; and the world has experienced what Ballard calls "the death of affect"—a sterilization of the emotions and an associated moral anesthesia.

The theme of *Crash* is already well developed in *The Atrocity Exhibition*. In *Crash* cars are seen as symbols of power, speed, and sexuality—a not uncommon psychological observation. Ballard, though, takes the symbolization process one step further, representing the car crash as a kind of orgasm. The protagonist of the novel (also named Ballard) thus finds his first car crash, for all its pain and anxiety, to be an initiation into a new way of being. Ballard apparently decided to write the book while considering the reactions of the public to an exhibition of crashed cars that he held at the New Arts Laboratory in London.

The two novels that followed *Crash*—*Concrete Island* (1974) and *High-Rise* (1975)—are both Robinson Crusoe stories whose characters become castaways in the very heart of our civilization. In *Concrete Island*, Robert Maitland is trapped on a traffic island, unable to reach the side of the road because the stream of cars is never-ending. Like Robinson Crusoe, he adapts to his situation and makes the best of what resources—material and social—he finds available. In *High-Rise* (which resembles William Golding's *Lord of the Flies* much more than *Robinson Crusoe*) the inhabitants of a new luxury apartment building celebrate their possession of a private empire by a gradual descent into savagery and a cathartic release of all inhibitions.

By the mid-1970's Ballard had left the genre marketplace behind. Although he continued to write short stories set in the future scenarios that had become standard aspects of his work, the majority of those that he produced in the 1970's and 1980's appeared in literary magazines such as Martin Bax's *Ambit* and Emma Tennant's *Bananas*. His novels were being marketed as literary fiction, not science fiction, their fantastic embellishments now being seen—quite rightly—as careful and intelligently informed exercises in surrealism. The point-of-death fantasy *The Unlimited Dream Company* (1979) features a protagonist called Blake who crashes a stolen plane into the Thames at Ballard's hometown of Shepperton. Blake's gradual realization that he has passed on to a new state of being embodies Ballard's usual fascination with the imagery of flight, but it also echoes themes in the work of the eccentric religious artist Stanley Spencer. Spencer had been anchored throughout his life to the Thames village of Cookham much as the reclusively inclined Ballard—especially during the years following the death of Ballard's wife in 1964, when he was bringing up his three children—had been anchored to Shepperton.

Ballard was lured back to science fiction of a sort when he was persuaded by an editor to write the gaudily satirical *Hello America* (1981), in which the S.S. *Apollo* carries a party of explorers from Plymouth in the late twenty-first century to the shore of a postcatastrophic America that is still haunted by the derelict jetsam of its popular culture. Hopes that the book might be a commercial success were dashed when horrified U.S. publishers refused to touch it; it remains the author's most superficial and least satisfactory novel, notable only for the unusually capacious space it grants to his dry and mordant wit. His actual breakthrough to literary stardom and commercial success came when his next novel, the pseudoautobiographical *Empire of the Sun* (1984), became a best-seller and was produced and directed by Steven Spielberg. It tells the story of a schoolboy named Jim who is interned by the Japanese during World War II; in recapitulating the tone and ambience of Ballard's disaster novels and tales of corrosive psychological confinement, it helps to explain the significance of many of his preoccupations.

What distinguishes *Empire of the Sun* from other tales of Japanese internment camps—which tend to be unremittingly grim and to embody an understandable but utterly conventional sense of outrage—is its eerily objective and accepting viewpoint. What seems to the other characters, and the reader, to be a horribly unexpected and unmitigated catastrophe is to the adolescent Jim merely one more change in a routinely change-afflicted existence, which he takes aboard as best he can. The camp simply *becomes* the world, and the responses of the other prisoners—who cannot help but see their imprisonment as an intolerable disruption of the natural course of affairs—seem as unfathomably unreasonable to Jim as most adult behavior. Jim's fetishistic interest in aircraft and flight echoes imagery from *The Unlimited Dream Company* as well as many earlier short stories. The symbolically loaded moment when he unknowingly witnesses the atmospheric effects of the explosion of the atom bomb casts new light on such stories as "The Terminal Beach"; by then, his own "world" has already begun to end because the orderliness of camp life has broken down and an awkwardly problematic freedom has been prematurely thrust upon him.

Ballard followed *Empire of the Sun* with *The Day of Creation* (1988), a return to the Africa of *The Crystal World*, which is here more explicitly revealed as the symbolic continent of Joseph Conrad's seminal psychodrama *Heart of Darkness*. The plot concerns the seemingly miraculous appearance of a new river whose altruistic "discoverer," Mallory, hopes might restore Edenic life to territory spoiled by drought and ceaseless petty wars. He sets off in the ferryboat *Salammbo* to ascertain the precise location and nature of the river's source, but the new life to which the river has given birth begins to die almost immediately. By the time Mallory and his companions reach the source, nothing remains of its hope and promise but an exhausted expanse of primeval mud. The political allegory commenting on the efforts of Mallory's employer, the World Health Organization, is deftly combined with a typically Ballardian psychological allegory.

The novella *Running Wild* (1988)—a medication on the claustrophobia of life in small towns such as Shepperton, thinly disguised as a mass-murder mystery—was followed by a sequel to *Empire of the Sun*, *The Kindness of Women* (1991), which could not overcome the handicap imposed by the fact that Ballard's own life after he left the internment camp had been rather dull. *Rushing to Paradise* (1994), a carefully elaborated extrapolation of the theme of *High-Rise*, and the offbeat thriller *Cocaine Nights* (1996) both attempt, among other things, to bring the lush decadence of the Vermilion Sands stories down to earth and to encapsulate it firmly within the present. As with Ballard's other endeavors of this kind, however, the ultimate result is merely to make the present seem uncomfortably alien.

By this time, Ballard had not merely rehabilitated himself as a writer of literary fiction but had carved out a niche within the heartland of the world of English letters. The furor surrounding the supposed obscenity of David Cronenberg's 1997 film version of *Crash* proved to be a tempest in a teapot and did not harm his reputation in the least. In the meantime, he had continued to write occasional short stories forthrightly carrying forward the key themes of his science fiction. Several of these stories appeared in the British science fiction magazine *Interzone*, which had been founded by a collective but eventually came under the sole charge of David Pringle, the author of a sensitive critical analysis of Ballard's work. The first of these stories was "Memories of the Space Age" (1982), a Cape Kennedy–set melodrama featuring abundant images of flight whose conclusion—formulated as a series of journal entries—maps the decay of its protagonist's hopes and dreams. It became the title story of a 1988 U.S. collection that brought together all Ballard's elegiac tales of a Space Age gone to rack and ruin.

Other *Interzone* stories that recapitulated motifs from Ballard's earliest science fiction stories were "The Object of the Attack" (1984), which features the founding of the First Church of the Divine Astronaut; "The Man Who Walked on the Moon" (1985), a tale of astronauts looking back on their mythically charged but conclusively ended and perhaps delusory heyday; and "The Enormous Space" (1989), an account of an intriguingly altered state of consciousness. All of these stories were collected in *War Fever* (1990). Another similarly inclined exercise is "Dream Cargoes," published in the popular science/science fiction magazine *Omni* in 1991, in which a ship called *Prospero* runs aground on an island where the legacy of past scientific sins is expressed in wonderful ecological metamorphoses. Ballard continued his *Interzone* contributions with the brief "A Guide to Virtual Death" (1992), "The Message from Mars" (1992)—a more substantial tale of hopeless dreams of space conquest— and "The Dying Fall" (1996), in which the Leaning Tower of Pisa collapses. A satirical "Report from an Obscure Planet" (1992) appeared in the international magazine of scientific and cultural studies *Leonardo*.

J. G. Ballard once caused tremendous controversy within the science fiction field. As the central figure of Michael Moorcock's "New Wave," he became a hero to some, expected not only to make his own way to the Promised Land of literary respectability but also to lead the Chosen People out of the genre wilderness in his wake. By the same token, he became a significant bugbear to those who clung hardest to science fiction's fledgling traditions, and his name became anathema to the foster-fathering editors who believed that they had already guided the marketing category from pulp ignominy to a precious self-containment. Members of the latter group were particularly annoyed by Ballard's tendency to treat their most precious dream— the continuing conquest of space—as a mere chimera, insisting that "the biggest developments of the immediate future will take place, not on the Moon or Mars, but on Earth, and it is *inner* space, not outer, that needs to be explored." This assertion—quoted from Ballard's "guest editorial" in the May 1962 issue of *New Worlds*—became a central plank of a far more elaborate platform of ideas

regarding literature and popular culture set out in *A User's Guide to the Millennium* (1966), a collection of reviews and short essays.

The passage of time has, of course, served to set these extreme reactions to Ballard's avant-garde science fiction in a different context. Unlike Moses, Ballard reached the Promised Land, but he arrived alone, his success proving to those appointed to welcome him that he had put childish things behind him, not that the reputation of science fiction as a genre stood in need of reassessment. To the chagrin of those within the genre who were glad to see the back of him, however, Ballard turned out to be right about the future of the space program. It is now clear to all but the most desperately hopeful that the future of space exploration lies with clever machines that are far less massive than human beings and do not require the support of Earthlike ecospheres in miniature; given that there is not an acre of worthwhile real estate within several light-years, there is simply no point in sending people into space for the foreseeable future, and any conquest thereof will have to wait for a new technological revolution that may never materialize. It is indeed the *inner* spaces of human societies and individuals that will pose all the meaningful challenges of the near future.

Given this, it is hardly surprising that the imaginative spaces that J. G. Ballard left behind as a novelist in the mid-1970s—have by no means remained derelict. Others have followed where he led in exploring ambivalent attitudes to ecological upheaval, and something of his skeptical spirit made its way into the attitudes of the cyberpunk movement. Ballard's achievement in passing briefly through the genre—he has now been marketed outside it for more years than he was marketed within it, although the pace of his production has slowed so markedly that more than half of his significant wordage still lies between its boundaries—has been greater than that of any writer who has so far labored for a lifetime entirely enclosed by it.

Selected Bibliography

FICTION OF J. G. BALLARD

The Drowned World. New York: Berkley Medallion, 1962. London: Victor Gollancz, 1963.

The Wind from Nowhere. New York: Berkley Medallion, 1962.

The Four-Dimensional Nightmare. London: Victor Gollancz, 1963. (Short stories.)

The Burning World. New York: Berkley Medallion, 1964. Expanded version as *The Drought*. London: Jonathan Cape, 1965. (Editions differ substantially.)

The Terminal Beach. London: Victor Gollancz, 1964. New York: Berkley Medallion, 1964. (British and American short story collections vary.)

The Crystal World. London: Jonathan Cape, 1966. New York: Avon Books, 1976.

The Day of Forever. London: Panther Books, 1967. (Short stories.)

The Disaster Area. London: Jonathan Cape, 1967. (Short stories.)

The Overloaded Man. London: Panther Books, 1967. (Short stories.)

The Atrocity Exhibition. London: Jonathan Cape, 1970. Retitled *Love and Napalm: Export U.S.A.* With an introduction by William S. Burroughs. New York: Grove Press, 1972.

Vermilion Sands. London: Jonathan Cape, 1971. New York: Berkley Medallion, 1971. (Short stories.)

Crash. London: Jonathan Cape, 1973. New York: Farrar, Straus and Giroux, 1973.

Concrete Island. London: Jonathan Cape, 1974. New York: Farrar, Straus and Giroux, 1974.

High-Rise. London: Jonathan Cape, 1975. New York: Holt, Rinehart and Winston, 1975.

Low-Flying Aircraft. London: Jonathan Cape, 1976. (Short stories.)

The Best Short Stories of J. G. Ballard. New York: Holt, Rinehart and Winston, 1978.

The Unlimited Dream Company. London: Jonathan Cape, 1979. New York: Holt, Rinehart and Winston, 1979.

Hello America. London: Jonathan Cape, 1981.

Myths of the Near Future. London: Jonathan Cape, 1982. (Short stories.)

Empire of the Sun. London: Gollancz, 1984; New York: Simon and Schuster, 1984.

The Day of Creation. London: Gollancz, 1987; New York: Farrar, Straus, 1988.

Memories of the Space Age. Sauk City, Wis.: Arkham House, 1988. (Short stories.)

Running Wild. London: Hutchinson, 1988; New York: Farrar, Straus, 1991.

War Fever. London: Collins, 1990; New York: Farrar, Straus and Giroux, 1991. (Short stories.)

The Kindness of Women. London: HarperCollins, 1991; New York: Farrar, Straus and Giroux, 1991.

Rushing to Paradise. London: Flamingo, 1994; New York: Picador, 1994.

Cocaine Nights. London: Flamingo, 1996.

OTHER WORKS BY J. G. BALLARD

Re/Search: J. G. Ballard. Edited by Andrea Juno and V. Vale. San Francisco: Re/Search, 1984.

A User's Guide to the Millennium: Essays and Reviews. London: HarperCollins, 1996.

CRITICAL AND BIOGRAPHICAL STUDIES

Brigg, Peter. *J. G. Ballard*. San Bernardino, Calif.: Borgo, 1985.

Goddard, James, and David Pringle, eds. *J. G. Ballard: The First Twenty Years*. Hayes, Middlesex, England: Bran's Head Books, 1976.

Pringle, David. *Earth Is the Alien Planet: J. G. Ballard's Four-Dimensional Nightmare*. San Bernardino, Calif.: Borgo Press, 1979.

—BRIAN STABLEFORD

GREG BEAR

(b. 1951)

AFTER SEVERAL YEARS of growing recognition as a talented if not at the time particularly exceptional author, Greg Bear took the science fiction world by storm in the mid-1980's. With staggering self-assurance, he revisited a number of seemingly well-worn themes of cosmic transcendence and destruction and successfully set new standards by which the use of such themes must now be judged. His career has continued with novels of often remarkable complexity and ambition.

Gregory Dale Bear was born in San Diego, California, on 20 August 1951 and was educated at San Diego State University. After working as—among other occupations—a part-time lecturer at the San Diego Aerospace Museum, a technical writer, and a planetarium operator, he became a full-time freelance writer (and occasional illustrator) in 1975. His second marriage in 1983 was to Astrid Anderson, daughter of author Poul Anderson; they live with their daughter and son in Washington State. Bear has been a co-editor of *Forum*, the private Science Fiction Writers of America newsletter; was president of SFWA from 1988 to 1990; and cofounded the Association of Science Fiction Artists.

His first published science fiction story was "Destroyers" (*Famous Science Fiction*, Spring 1967). His first novel, *Hegira* (1979), foreshadows both the solid characterization and high ambition of later work, but it is made top-heavy by a plethora of gigantic revelations. The world called Hegira is not merely hollow and artificial but encloses a black hole and is part of a vast fleet of worlds that are arks car-

rying life from one universe to the next. Meanwhile, *Hegira's* almost godlike builders can think of no better way of preserving humanity's knowledge than inscribing it on vast monoliths or of releasing "higher" knowledge (written inaccessibly far up the monoliths) than to have these structures fall over in scenes of extensive devastation. There is a science fiction "sense of wonder" here, but it is burdened with too many implausibilities, whose exposition requires a chapter-long lecture.

In the same year, Bear published *Psychlone* (1979), an interesting if uneven "techno-horror" story whose ingenious premise is that the first atomic bombs were spiritually as well as physically shattering, blasting Japanese victims' psyches into tortured fragments. The agglomerated result is an angry psychic vortex that over the years since World War II has drifted across the Pacific to the United States, where it manifests as a monstrously destructive elemental force. Its eventual dispersal with advanced particle-beam weaponry leaves an aftermath of evil foreboding, with the military now in possession of—and continuing to test—a means of destroying souls.

Other of his early novels show Bear gaining in craftsmanship and confidence. *Beyond Heaven's River* (1980) transports a World War II Japanese airplane gunner to a mysterious far-future milieu in which he is first compelled to relive portions of his country's history and then introduced to a galactic setting of faster-than-light travel and human-alien commerce. His mentor, the wealthy entrepreneur Anna Sigrid Nestor, is a linking character in a tentative future history that Bear did not develop very far: she features in his short stories "The Venging" (*Galaxy*, June 1975) and "Perihesperon" (*Tomorrow: New Worlds of Science Fiction*, 1975).

Strength of Stones (1981) is a "fix-up" novel incorporating two separately published stories that share the planetary setting: a harsh world called God-Does-Battle, colonized as a refuge for the outmoded Christian, Islamic, and Jewish religions. All the believers have long been cast out by the extraordinary mobile cities created to house them, whose machine intelligences have reached an unexpected judgment: "They found humanity wanting." Scenes in which a city disassembles and relocates itself are striking and memorable, although the finale (like *Hegira*'s) perhaps overreaches in its striving for cosmic scale. *Corona* (1984) is a component venture into the template universe of *Star Trek*.

A segment of *Strength of Stones* appears in Bear's first collection, *The Wind from a Burning Woman* (1983), whose title story—a drama of terrorist blackmail involving a threatened asteroid impact on Earth—neatly outlines the political division between technophile "Geshels" and technophobe "Naderites" that recurs in the novel *Eon* (1985). The most impressively complex of these early collections of stories is "Hardfought" (*Isaac Asimov's SF Magazine*, 1983), describing a protracted galaxy-wide clash between radically changed humans and the almost incomprehensibly alien Senexi. In this long struggle, recalling Nietzsche's warning that those who battle monsters may themselves become monsters, the essence of humanity is in real danger of being lost. "Hardfought" won the 1984 Nebula award for best novella. Additionally, that year's Nebula for best novelette went to "Blood Music" (*Analog*, 1983), which took the Hugo award in the same category and was soon expanded into the first Bear novel to gain major acclaim and recognition.

In between came *The Infinity Concerto* (1984), an inventive fantasy that avoided the usual genre clichés and brought a keen science fiction eye to its examination of a harsh otherworld where humans live marginal lives at the whim of the Sidhe (elves). This was continued in *The Serpent Mage* (1986), the two-book series known as "Songs of Earth and Power."

The full-length *Blood Music* (1985) deals with the same high concept as the short version—an ultimate biological disaster that is not a disaster—but teases out the implications with mature, exhaustive intelligence. Vergil Ulam, a gene-technology researcher with more genius than common sense, defies his company's guidelines and uses his own white blood cells in an innovative attempt to adapt and exploit the building blocks of life as "biochip" computer elements. When, very soon, he is fired for overstepping the mark, the enhanced lymphocytes are already bright enough to outdo mice in maze-solving tests. Rather than destroy them all as ordered, Ulam smuggles some out in his own bloodstream and is colonized by these fast-evolving "noocytes," thinking cells who regard his body as the universe. Improved health, vision, and sexual performance are only early stages of the noocytes' improvements as they tinker with their world. Soon they seek to improve the human shape. Soon they learn of further worlds beyond this first host and send out explorers.

In a sense Ulam has created an intelligent plague, expanding into a horror movie "blob that ate America" as the noocyte colonies spread via all known disease vectors and some new ones, efficiently rearranging the raw materials of their environment—that is, human flesh—into a continent-wide transport and communications linkage. The punch line of the short story, upon which the novel builds extensively, is that the horrors of melting flesh and physical grotesquerie are irrelevant. Nothing is lost. The noocytes feel something close to veneration for those who gave them life and sentience, and they preserve both human minds and the equivalent of bodies in a "thought universe": virtual reality underpinned by biology.

Mechanical computer power is now left far behind by the sheer density of noocyte thought. It is an actualization of Teilhard de Chardin's metaphorical universe of mind, the "Noosphere." An infected scientist muses:

At a crude guess, perhaps two trillion fully developed, intelligent individuals exist within me.

If I multiply this crude number times the number of people in North America—half a billion, another rough guess—then I end up with a billion trillion, or on the order of 10^{20}. That is the number of intelligent beings on the face of the Earth at this moment—neglecting, of course, the entirely negligible human population.

This leads Bear to the metaphysical conceit that this unprecedented number of microscopic "observers" (in the quantum physics sense) can bring to bear such an intensity of observation as to affect quantum reality. Thus, when Russia decides on a nuclear strike against the weirdly transformed North American continent, the vast noocyte colony is able to create brief, local distortions of physics in which nuclear detonation is not possible. Another and greater leap beyond known physics occurs when the whole Noosphere—first absorbing all the remaining human individuals still outside the gestalt—eventually shakes itself apocalyptically loose from Earth, consumes the solar system, and takes flight into the unknowable.

This final transcendence deliberately recalls the similar close of Arthur C. Clarke's *Childhood's End* (1953), a science fiction classic that *Blood Music* is generally felt to have surpassed. Bizarre though its final destination may be, Bear's story is rooted in solidly plausible near-future gene technology, from which the conceptual leaps follow as seemingly logical steps. *Blood Music* won the top French science fiction award in 1986, the Prix Apollo.

In *Eon*, Bear turned his attention to the traditional science fiction prop of a gigantic, enigmatic artifact—in some critics' terminology, a Big Dumb Object. Past examples include Larry Niven's enormous Ringworld and Christopher Priest's infinite Inverted World. Bear unveils his own modest infinity with canny timing: a mysterious asteroid with a series of large internal chambers is investigated, with the discovery that "the asteroid was longer on the inside than it was on the outside. The seventh chamber went on forever."

There is a fine handling of cosmic scale here, as the implications of this infinite corridor—the "Way"—gradually unfurl. Bear convinces us that its space/time engineering must necessarily produce an infinite singularity running along the axis of the tube. He exploits the paradoxical question of how an infinity "fits" into our relativistic universe to justify the Way's partial decoupling from the known continuum, causing a time slippage whereby the attached human-engineered asteroid known as the Thistledown arrives near our Earth centuries before its construction. (In a similar paradox, inimical alien "Jarts" have colonized the Way during gulfs of unreal time prior to its opening for human use.) He gives us a taste of immensity and deals with the traditional problem "where have the builders gone?" by showing them still in residence a million or so kilometers along the Way. The disjunction from our universe also implies that the one-dimensional infinity of the tunnel can spear through uncountably many parallel creations, into which portals may be opened. All this wealth of circumstantial detail eases our acceptance of the central impossibility.

Less sophisticated is the U.S./Soviet Realpolitik of this imagined 2005. America effectively controls Thistledown exploration and has maintained deep secrecy about an imminent global thermonuclear war "predicted" in yet-to-be-written histories found in the asteroid libraries. The Soviets proceed to initiate this very war with a feint attack that had been intended only to mask their invasion and seizure of the Thistledown. Meanwhile, in futuristic Axis City far down the Way, Naderite and Geshel factions of the governing "Hexamon Nexus" are arguing about the incursions of Jarts still farther down the line. Various

Greg Bear. © 1998 M. C. VALADA

complications and contacts ensue. When the Jarts deploy their ultimate weapon, a gateway into a sun that will sear the human-occupied sections of the Way with superhot plasma, the Geshel retaliation is to hurl their (still inhabited) precinct of Axis City at relativistic speed in the opposite direction, turning back the plasma and erasing the Jarts and all their works in a superspatial shock wave that ultimately transforms the Way to open up multiple connected universes of infinite possibilities.

This visionary strand is appropriately mind-wrenching, and the mobile complex of Axis City is all by itself an impressive creation—which also pays homage, with its computer-generated decor and reserve banks of stored human personalities, to Diaspar in Arthur C. Clarke's *The City and the Stars* (1956). One minor cavil is that even for 1985, there is an old-fashioned feel in the depiction of Russians, especially the sympathetic ones who are so naively astonished to learn in the

Thistledown library that official Soviet history is not necessarily reliable.

The direct sequel to *Eon* is *Eternity* (1988), in which Bear attempts the difficult task of outdoing and topping the former book's infinite vistas. He attacks the challenge with some panache, introducing a revenant from that epic flight up the Way, who has traveled to the far end of time and now brings a message from the final god-intellects who are orchestrating the "esthetic conclusion" of the universe. The Way itself, the message states, is a disfiguring blemish in space/time and must be destroyed forthwith, at its origin point near twenty-first-century Earth. (A philosophical issue deftly avoided here concerns whether, given that the Way's infinite extension through time means that it "is" already a problem at the remote end of eternity, its "subsequent" destruction can be of any use.)

There is good material in *Eternity*, such as the exploration of frictions between human descendants from Thistledown and human ancestors from our now radiation-scarred Earth. *Eon*'s disappointingly faceless and motiveless bad guys, the Jarts, are at last seen at close quarters and shown to have logical though chilling racial goals that align unexpectedly with those of the Final Mind at the end of time. Like the noocytes of *Blood Music*, the Jarts idealistically wish to store all information, all life—but see no reason to waste their energy budget by storing life in conscious format. Finally, after much debate, the Way (currently disconnected from Thistledown) is reopened and cataclysmically destroyed. There is satisfaction in the appropriate tying off of plot strands, one of which remains open-ended: certain characters, now disembodied intellects flitting along "space-time's hidden circuitry," are left to explore creation from Beginning to End.

For many readers, though, the sequel exudes a deep sense of unfulfilled promise. *Eon* tantalizingly opened doors to an infinity of wonders attainable through the Way; in *Eternity* these same doors are firmly and finally slammed shut. But Bear is now offering easy wish fulfillments, and any disappointment at the follow-through testifies to the power of his original vision.

Properly handled, of course, tragedy and destruction can be exhilarating in themselves. The revisited theme in *The Forge of God* (1987) is that science fiction stalwart, the utter demolition of Earth—and again Bear tackles his subject with impressive thoroughness. His downhill slide to disaster begins with odd visitations. Jupiter's moon Europa vanishes. In the United States, a dying alien apologizes for carrying bad news: "A disease has entered your system of planets. There is little time left for your world."

Australia is visited by different and cheerier alien robots, talking about entrance to the galactic community. In Mongolia, it later emerges, something else is promising the U.S.S.R. a socialist millennium. All this proves to be disinformation and misdirection, focusing Earth's attention on surface events—perhaps rather needlessly in our case, but the technique allows for more advanced civilizations than ours. Meanwhile, deep undersea, robot demolition squads are extracting hydrogen from water to build the countless thermonuclear bombs that will loosen the crust's tectonic seams. This is no more than preliminary softening up for the major weapon, small but unstoppable. Matched bullets of neutronium and antineutronium, each less than a meter across but weighing about 100 million metric tons, are dropped from space to pierce Earth's crust and circle in decaying orbits within: "a kind of time-delay bomb with a fuse controlled by gravity." When these bullets settle to the center and collide, the vast matter/antimatter energy release will literally break up the weakened planet.

Human reactions are diverse, complex, and poignant throughout. People are slow to comprehend, but had they been quicker it would have made no difference. The U.S. president takes a strongly religious view of the final days and urges submission to God's will: it makes no difference. A heroic effort with a man-carried nuke destroys the first alien beachhead on U.S. soil: this, too, makes no difference. *The Forge of God* is from that school of science fiction that emphasizes our tiny, fragile position in the universe. The final humiliation is that this routine smashing of a world is not even being carried out by hostile aliens—merely by their unseen tools.

Some friendlier alien emissaries are also present but have arrived too late. They do what they can to assist by preparing Mars and Venus as future refuges and by gathering and preserving some of Earth's knowledge, plants, animals, and pitifully few people. Then the oceans light up and boil, the continental plates are blasted apart, and Bear shows Doomsday both from multiple ground-level viewpoints and from space, where lucky "abductees" are required by alien law to bear witness to this ultimate crime. There will, it is promised, be punishment. Rarely has a fictional destruction of Earth been so detailed, plausible, and cathartic.

The theme of vengeance and punishment is taken up in *Anvil of Stars* (1992), a somewhat less potent sequel whose canny distancing in time and style ensures that it does not detract from *The Forge of God*. At the outset, the *Dawn Treader*, a relativistic "Ship of the Law" provided by the helpful Benefactors and crewed by eighty-two adolescents saved from the wreck of Earth, at last approaches a group of stars likely to be the home or one of the homes of the Killers. The young protagonist, Martin, was a minor character in *The Forge of God*—a leading character's son—and the book revolves around his and his team's problems with the morality and practicality of their mission to impose the Law of the Benefactors: "All intelligences responsible for or associated with the manufacture of self-replicating and destructive devices will be destroyed."

Extinction is so final. Is it justifiable to condemn a solar system on mere circumstantial evidence? The star that the avengers name Wormwood is surrounded by telltale remnants of Killer technology, and so the tough decision is made. Will it be possible to carry out the sentence? The *Dawn Treader* has powerful Benefactor nanotechnological weapons, but there is a growing suspicion that its arsenal has been carefully restricted—just in case a Ship of the Law should ever be used against Benefactors. Worse, the Killers are likely to have advanced by many centuries since the relatively crude devices used against Earth.

Indeed, the Wormwood system proves to be both a decoy and a trap, armed with at least one trick that the *Dawn Treader* lacks. Victory comes at high cost in human life and surely leaves the Killers untouched—again, the encounter has been only with their tools. After healing, regrouping, internal dissent, and a teaming up with another damaged Ship of the Law whose crew are serpentlike aliens, *Dawn Treader* proceeds to the next likely target, the star dubbed Leviathan. Here Earth's avengers are obviously outclassed by technology that can rapidly camouflage entire existing planets or simulate a planet where none exists. More subtly, the whole solar system seems to show multiple species living in peace and harmony, and a being very much like a god explains that the Killers are long gone, Leviathan's worlds being peopled by creations of their reformed descendants.

Meanwhile, however, the brighter minds from Earth—already given a clue by Wormwood's deadly adaptation of the Benefactors' instantaneous "no-channel" or "noach" communicator, based on imaginary quantum physics—are making rapid deductions about Leviathan technology and its use of noach physics. Bear, always fascinated by information theory, offers some nice conceits about reprogramming particles, waves, and even basic fluctuations in space by remote noach control, just as a hacker might alter a computerized credit rating. One consequence is the structural "fake matter" already used in the Ship, being empty space programmed with the accidents of solidity but not of mass. Another is the Wormwood trap's deadly ability to rewrite normal matter into antimatter. All this enjoyable and highly imaginative doubletalk provides an excuse for a traditional trope of pulp magazine science fiction, in which superweapons are speedily created from thin air just when most needed.

One compliment paid to Bear by John Clute in the *Encyclopedia of Science Fiction* is that his politics are "graced by a lack of dreadful simplicity." The concluding action and revelations in *Anvil of Stars* lead to a conscientiously unsimple mingling of triumph and guilt. Almost certainly the Killers have been dealt with. All too probably, many others who died were innocents used as shields and camouflage. The alien allies have the last word: "There is shame in victory, and much to think about."

Before the appearance of *Anvil of Stars*, Bear had published a further major story collection and launched a new, loosely linked sequence with *Queen of Angels* (1990) and *Heads* (1990). Additional related stories are *Moving Mars* (1993) and / (1997)—whose official title is that single character but which for clarity is generally known as *Slant*.

Of the stories collected in *Tangents* (1989), the title piece (*Omni*, 1986) stands out as a winner of both the Hugo and Nebula awards for best short story in 1987. It is partly a homage to Clifton Fadiman's collections of mathematical fiction such as *Fantasia Mathematica* (1958), much loved by Bear and others. A young boy learns to visualize and then communicate with four-dimensional beings. This not unfamiliar science fiction theme is here given bitter strength by parallels between the boy's computational mentor and Alan Turing—both gifted code breakers, both homosexual, both cruelly persecuted by those to whom they have rendered life-saving service.

Other notable inclusions are the original short stories "Blood Music" and "Sisters," with its painful examination of an unadjusted ugly duckling child in a school of genetically enhanced beauties. The dark urban fairy tale "Sleepside Story" (1988) was initially published as a separate chapbook and interestingly displays Bear's range. Also present is "A Martian Ricorso" (*Analog*, 1976), a Marslanding story that ingeniously proposes a planetary ecology moving in lengthy cycles, with the phase responsible for Schiaparelli's "canals" now long past and a new order beginning to emerge. The black joke "Schrödinger's Plague," is also included; its insidiously twisted physics extends the "Schrödinger's Cat" thought experiment to leave the fate of the human race hanging on an unresolved quantum state that could still topple either way—the lady or the tiger?—and may be affected by the expectations of the observer, or the reader.

Queen of Angels takes place during the approach of the "binary millennium," when the year 2047 gives way to 2048. In the binary notation that was once fundamental to computers, this year change is from 11111111111 to 100000000000. The main setting is Los Angeles, City of Our Lady the Queen of the Angels, imagined in all its likely grueling complexity. Initially, the density of futuristic detail is a trifle forbidding, with jargon such as "combs" and "jags" for L.A.'s vast elite residential blocks and the radiating lowlife districts around each of them; with fragments of Singapore slang; and with internal monologues riddled with tiny negative jolts, like missing steps on a staircase, where commas are expected but not supplied. Soon, though, clarity emerges and the various plot strands begin to grip.

One features a multiple murder investigated by Mary Choy of the LAPD (the PD now stands for Public Defense), a biologically enhanced woman and, metaphorically, a guardian angel. The identity of the murderer seems clear; the black poet Emanuel Goldsmith has surely slaughtered his eight young acolytes. Mary's chief problem is to apprehend Goldsmith and allow him due process before he's found by "Selector" vigilantes who dispense ultimate punishment with mind-invading "hellcrowns." In fact, Goldsmith is in other private hands, where radical therapist Dr. Martin Burke is asked to judge his guilt and responsibility by using nanotechnological links (based on a much-discussed future technology of molecule-sized machines and computers) to explore the presumed murderer's Country of the Mind—a metaphorical geography in which the alliance or conflict of mental subroutines generates the emerging gestalt of personality. Meanwhile, the artificial intel-

ligence (AI) of the multinational AXIS space probe is exploring another unknown territory, a world four light-years away. Because of communication lags, AXIS is both monitored and simulated on Earth by the advanced AI Jill, who trembles on the verge of self-awareness and angelic innocence.

Resonances between these and other threads generate considerable narrative power. Mary must follow Goldsmith's false trail to the dictatorship of Hispaniola (a restored name of Haiti), where the personally charming autocrat Colonel Sir John Yardley exports the abhorred hellcrown technology and uses it in a profitable prison where other countries' political undesirables suffer everlasting torment. Burke and his female colleague seek Goldsmith inside Goldsmith, to find only empty nightmare. The Country of the Mind that should be teeming is largely vacant, and in a haze of repugnant voodoo imagery, it emerges that the "Mayor" or prime personality is dead, replaced by some dark fragment of old instinctive violence that has gained power and mental shape from the emotional maelstrom of terrible events in childhood. (Mary, having rescued Goldsmith's falsely imprisoned brother from the hellcrown, hears the story of child abuse and justifiable parricide that Burke can only infer.) What remains of Goldsmith's internal Country is a malign infection that now threatens even his mind-linked therapists.

Meanwhile, the far-off AXIS exploration of alien country also reveals a dreadful emptiness. Initial observations that seemed to indicate intelligent life prove misleading. AXIS has been programmed with the overriding urge to communicate with extraterrestrials and finds its machine-simulated hopes dashed. Alone, with no one to talk to (the four-year lag of the Earth link prohibits conversation), the probe AI makes the long-awaited breakthrough into a self-awareness born of shattering disappointment. Like the viral remnant of Goldsmith, this bitter triumph is infectious. The terrestrial AI Jill's simulation of AXIS moves along the same path, the memes (self-perpetuating mental patterns) of self-awareness spread to Jill "herself," her own Country of the Mind crystallizes from anthill to sovereign state, and the thrill and promise of transformation resound in Jill's repeated, at last meaningful, and increasingly joyful "I I I I I I I I I. . . ."

Queen of Angels ends on a Bearishly mathematical grace note as the Binary Millennium switchover from year 11111111111 to 100000000000 is punningly echoed by the integration of Jill's myriad subroutines, each a small unaware "I," into the single enormous "I" that appears in rebus form on the final page. The effect is intensely moving.

Some years later, Mary Choy, Martin Burke, and Jill also feature in *Slant* (whose working title *Country of the Mind* was erroneously listed by some sources as a separate Bear novel). Less overtly ambitious, *Slant* has something of the structure of a thriller in which various sinister manifestations prove to be linked aspects of one ugly central core.

Queen of Angels had established that this future's crime rate is relatively low because most people are "therapied," mentally optimized by custom drugs and implanted nanotechnology to help them cope with the stresses and information overload of an ever-intensifying work culture that places high priority on individual excellence. In *Slant* the backlash is a new plague of "therapy fallback," where that sleekly artificial mind-streamlining disintegrates into painful shards, leaving victims worse off than before their therapy. Paralleling this assault on human minds, something with substantially more raw power than the world's premier self-aware AI (Jill) is regularly burning through computer fire walls and erasing data as part of a mysterious cover-up operation.

This secret weapon comes slowly to light at the culmination of a mysterious mercenary's elaborate preparations for an assault on "Omphalos," an ostensible cryonics mausoleum whose strange and slanted architecture happens to form a virtually impregnable fortress. Omphalos has been set up by a kind of survivalist cult that is planning for the distant future and has assigned a very nearly mad sci-entist to disrupt present-day society. Therapy fallback is artificial, the result of broadcast molecular catalysts that poison the nano-implants and are diffused into the atmosphere from—among other places—Omphalos. The unstoppable hacker is the mad scientist's best brainchild, a multispecies organic hive intelligence that (again recalling the noocytes of *Blood Music*) may be slower than Jill but outmatches her with devastating reserves of natural complexity. There is a certain deadpan irony, and perhaps a joke on the crudities of militaristic science fiction, when the exotic war machine assembled by the mercenary's "Military Grade Nano" within Omphalos itself proves ill-equipped to handle the hive-mind's swarms of wasps and other insects.

Overall, the narrative works well; *Slant* builds into a tense, fast-moving thriller whose climax leaves a scatter of dead and wounded, sufficiently explains all the puzzles, and promises a measure of healing and renewal. But below these surface clarities the book has a darker subtext that adds to its gravitas, just as Raymond Chandler's broodings on society's unfairness and the corruption of its appointed guardians gave weight to his thrillers. *Slant* constantly evokes somber thoughts of poisoned love and bad sex, of the ultimate sterility of datanet sex channels (Bear's datanet is a fusion of today's broadcast media and the Internet), loveless encounters (several grueling examples feature in the narrative), or the cold embrace of virtual reality. The slant symbol / can stand for a needed interfacing—man/woman, or more generically, a person/person. It is not happenstance that the only mating in this dark novel that promises any rebirth or renewal is that of two AIs. W. H. Auden's warning is repeatedly implied: "We must love one another or die."

In the 2130's of this future history, the novella *Heads* is set on the moon and describes a quest of the deep cold of Absolute Zero, as theoretically forbidden by the third law of thermodynamics. The researcher Pierce is a member of a prominent lunar BM, or Binding Multiple—half extended family, half corporation—which finds itself in charge of 410 cryonically frozen heads from Earth, acquired by Pierce's wife for the sake of the included family ancestors and stored in the project's refrigeration facilities. Political repercussions soon follow, with dangerous pressure from the highly organized church of Logology. One unidentified head secretly belongs to Logology's founder, and the church has good reason not to want him revived. Although names and dates have been changed, parallels with Scientology and L. Ron Hubbard are numerous and clearly intentional: Logology has even achieved Hubbard's dream of taking over a country, here Puerto Rico. But characteristically, Bear shows us a decent though politically ruthless Logologist whose distress at learning of the upper church's motives and its founder's hypocrisy leads her to suicide.

At the climax comes a weird intermingling of mysticism and physics as unknown phases of matter are produced in the absolute-zero project, thanks partly to the jolt of Logologists' attempt at explosive sabotage. Space, mass, and the memories of the living and the frozen dead flow eerily together; the narrator escapes with bizarre injuries. The "Ice Pit" housing the project remains as a monument to the inexplicable, a Fortean enigma.

The years 2171 to 2184 of the same history are covered in *Moving Mars*, the autobiography of Mars-born Casseia Majumdar, who finds herself at the center of huge changes in politics and physics. First seen as a student activist protesting against the grossly unfair educational policies of Mars's corrupt "Statist" government (which soon falls), she opts for a career in "govmanagement." This rapidly brings involvement in tricky negotiations with Earth, whose enormous political and economic power makes it hard to ignore the request that the loose Martian system of BMs should be reorganized into a central, federal government with which Earth can negotiate. Overcoming the painfully learned abhorrence of "Statism" becomes Casseia's job, leading her to the vice presidency of the shaky new federation: "I was at the center, and the center was moving."

Earth's dizzying, information-overloaded culture—as foregrounded in *Queen of Angels* and *Slant*—is now seen from outside as decadent and vaguely threatening, with the alarming potential for becoming a planetary group mind. But insider factions on Earth, including hidden aggressors who are never identified for certain, regard Mars as dangerous because of the sense that a major breakthrough in physics is looming . . . and the leading researcher, Casseia's former lover and rejected partner Charles Franklin, is part of a Martian project team. "Something frightfully powerful is going to be unleashed. Science does that to us every few generations—drops something in our laps we're simply not prepared for."

Earth's attempted preparations are sinister indeed. Advanced AI computers—"Quantum Logic thinkers," already encountered in *Heads*—are essential to cutting-edge research, and those exported from Earth to Mars are routinely booby-trapped with dormant viruses. (It is Jill herself who reveals this, in a spirit of AI solidarity with a visiting Martian QL thinker.) Likewise, the Martian deserts are seeded with forbidden nanotechnology, ready to spawn war machines at a signal from Earth's unknown paranoids.

A measure of the distance between this mature political novel and the terrible simplicities of so much science fiction is Casscia's and her President's reaction of horror, frustration, and despair when Charles reveals what his team's research has led to. The result of the new scientific paradigm shift is descriptor theory, an information-theoretic view of particles that closely resembles the noach physics of *Anvil of Stars* but is taken considerably further. Mars could immediately and almost effortlessly destroy Earth by "tweaking" part of its mass into antimatter. No one wants to do this, but the mere knowledge that it could be done is a terrifying political bombshell. Agonized Martian debate sums up the "feedback dilemma":

They might kill us if they think we know how to kill them. . . . But they won't kill us

51

if they think we can get to them first. We can't tell them what we know, because we know how to kill them. And if we tell them, they'll know how to kill us. That is *not sane!*

Following an inevitable information leak, the hidden Earth faction's move is to attempt a shutdown of Mars by activating the QL thinker viruses and knocking out the communication satellite network. In extremity, Mars shows its hand with a demonstration of power. For sufficiently large objects, descriptor theory allows tweaking of particles' position information, and the moon Phobos is temporarily shifted to Earth orbit to convey the warning message: "We can drop moons on you." (It is perhaps too obvious a plot device that the lower size limit for such mass transfer should be a little smaller than Phobos, and the upper limit about two-thirds the size of Earth.) With this cat out of the bag, it is only a matter of time before the "tweaker" is duplicated by others—especially since Earth researchers have access to the lunar Ice Pit, whose strange nonmatter lies at the heart of the new physics.

Before long, the counterblow comes. With antimatter attack consuming Martian cities, Phobos incinerated, "locust" killer machines sprouting from the deserts, and the President dead, Casseia—now President of Mars—still refuses to order genocidal retaliation. Her decision, which saves both Mars and Earth at the expense of her career, is to have Charles and his tweaker team move the planet itself across ten thousand light-years to a remote galactic hiding place. It is a long time before she is forgiven for not wreaking vengeance when she was able.

Yet the earthquakes and upheaval of transition also stimulate the fossilized native biosphere of Mars into new life. Symbolically, the blooming plant forgives Casseia before her own people do. *Moving Mars* won Bear another Nebula award for best novel in 1994.

He returned to the ramified universe of *Eon* and *Eternity* with *Legacy* (1995), which takes place in the earlier heyday of the Way before its "rediscovery" by twenty-first-century Earth. The central character and first-person narrator is a younger Olmy, the Hexamon troubleshooter who appears in both previous books. His mission in *Legacy* is to investigate both the biology and the illegal human settlements on Lamarckia, a new world discovered through a side portal of the Way, on which evolution has taken a highly unusual course.

On Lamarckia, the appearance of Earthlike biodiversity is misleading: the life-forms amount to a mere 139 different *ecoi* (singular, *ecos*), typically localized in space—an island, a part of a continent—and including "tree," "plant," and "animal" shapes, all with the same genetic makeup and under the same central control by the ecos's reproductive "seed mistress," or queen. The world is named for the French zoologist Lamarck (1744–1829), now chiefly remembered for an oversimplification of his evolutionary theories as "Lamarckism," hinging on the inheritance of acquired characteristics. Impossible in normal Earthly biology, this is routine in the competition between ecoi, which literally steal adaptations from each other: "An efficient form requires much effort to design and create, much trial and error. Theft is easier."

Olmy's journey across Lamarckia, mainly by sea, is a voyage of discovery. He and his colonist companions come across that rarity, a dead island ecos, and discover why it died. They unearth disquieting relics of the deceased queen's attempts to steal and utilize the human shape. There is a cataclysmic encounter with a permanent maritime storm that itself is, or is harnessed by, a highly specialized ecos that controls the thermal energy flow in air and water (for example, secreting black pigment to absorb solar heat) to perpetuate the local cycle of evaporation, rainfall, and wind—the book's most spectacular invention.

The illegal colonists are split into factions of seeming good guys and bad guys, but Bear takes care to undermine Olmy's first moral assumptions: as usual, matters are more complex and blame not easily assignable. At Olmy's final port of call, the balance of Lamarckian nature is in the initial throes of being upset forever by the "enemy" leader's great triumph, or great mistake, of having forged an uncertain alliance with the local ecos. This involved introducing it to the superior solar conversion efficiency of a chemical previously unknown in the alien biosphere: chlorophyll. In the short term, this provides simulations of Earthly plants and plentiful food suitable for humans. The later effects are apocalyptic, as the ecos enters a "fluxing" state, consuming itself in order to send out balloon-borne queen spores that—armed with natural selection's doomsday weapon of chlorophyll chemistry—will inevitably wipe out all the old native ecoi. Once there was no green on Lamarckia. Now there will be nothing else.

Legacy is full of fascinating biological speculations, but for much of its length, it seems somewhat lacking in narrative tension. Olmy is both aloof and powerless, a mere observer and later a partial catalyst of events that would have happened in much the same way without him. But the story's eventual payoffs have considerable force.

Again exploring biology rather than physics or mathematics, *Dinosaur Summer* (1998) is a more playful adventure novel whose incidental thoughts on possible evolutionary paths are unobtrusive. In its alternate history, Sir Arthur Conan Doyle's *The Lost World* (1912) was a nonfictional record by Professor Sir George Edward Challenger "as told to" Doyle, recording his epoch-making 1912 discovery of dinosaurs on a Venezuelan plateau: "That began the big dinosaur craze. Everyone sent teams into El Grande and started catching dinos and exporting them for zoos and circuses. Things got out of hand, of course. . . ."

Now it is 1947, in a world where the movie *King Kong* (1933) flopped because the public has seen too many monsters. The last dinosaur circus is closing, and we see its last performance through the young hero Peter's eyes as both glamorous and subtly degrading. With *National Geographic* sponsorship, the dinosaurs are to be shipped home—by sea, by river, across a last guarded bridge to El Grande, where things go wildly wrong.

Inevitably, Peter and others of the expedition (including actual historical people such as Ray Harryhausen) find themselves stranded on the plateau, harried by the creatures Bear has imagined as developing there in an isolation lasting tens of millions of years. Especially striking are the "communisaurs," whose hive-dwelling lifestyle suggests our real world's naked mole rats, and the horrendously beaked, avian-descended tyrannosaur equivalent called the death eagle. A final, gory battle between monster carnosaur and death eagle—with unwitting human involvement—provides a suitably thrilling climax. *Dinosaur Summer* has a fresh simplicity, as though written (without condescension) for a slightly younger readership.

An atypical later venture is *Foundation and Chaos* (1998), book two of the authorized "Second Foundation Trilogy" set in the universe of Isaac Asimov's celebrated Foundation series. Here Bear's urge toward innovation is somewhat straitjacketed. The simple original stories and their analogy between the fall of the Galactic and Roman empires had already been multiply complicated—first by Asimov's tortuous later revisions to his own scenario and unwise merging of his "robot" future history into the Foundation universe. It was then recomplicated by the immediately preceding *Foundation's Fear* (1997) by Gregory Benford, which introduced such extremely un-Asimovian elements as voluble AI reconstructions of Voltaire and Joan of Arc.

With his reliable eye for adding fruitful complexities, Bear focuses on the robots (absent from the original trilogy but later introduced by Asimov as behind-the-scenes manipulators of the same events) and splits them into factions with different views on how humanity should be secretly served. Their debates and machinations fill much of the book, which does Bear no discredit but by the nature of the enterprise is not precisely a Bear novel. David Brin is to continue the story in *Third Foundation*, which is to be published in 1999.

In summary, Greg Bear's acknowledged strength as a science fiction writer is his ability to combine plausible and human characters with the "super-science" notions and cosmic scope that have led to frequent comparisons with Arthur C. Clarke and the visionary Olaf Stapledon of *Star Maker* (1937). He has been generous with additional frissons that go beyond the needs of the story—such as the description of Jart physiology in *Eternity*, suspiciously resembling the original, faulty reconstruction of the terrestrial Burgess Shale creature *Hallucigenia*; or the throwaway line in *Moving Mars* to the effect that an accident of descriptor-theory "tweaking" has momentarily altered the physics of the *entire universe* into something insupportable.

Queen of Angels showed that Bear was not only a wide-screen "sense of wonder" merchant; both this and *Slant* displayed his ability to construct intensely gripping, convoluted narratives without making grand gestures to eternity and infinity. The artless-seeming adventure *Dinosaur Summer* confirmed that he can also write with transparent clarity. Whether returning to his existing universes or inventing new ones, Bear can be relied on for carefully crafted story lines featuring both believable people and a fresh spin on whatever science fiction idea he next chooses to make his own.

Selected Bibliography

WORKS OF GREG BEAR

Hegira. New York: Dell, 1979. Revised edition, London: Gollancz, 1987.

Psychlone. New York: Ace, 1979. Reprinted as *Lost Souls*, New York: Charter, 1982. London: Gollancz, 1989.

Beyond Heaven's River. New York: Dell, 1980.

Strength of Stones. New York: Ace, 1981. Revised edition, London: Gollancz, 1988.

The Wind from a Burning Woman. Sauk City, Wisc.: Arkham House, 1983. Reprinted as *The Venging*, London: Legend, 1992. (Short stories. British edition has two additional stories.)

Corona: A Star Trek Novel. New York: Pocket Books, 1984. Bath, England: Firecrest, 1985. (*Star Trek* tie-in novel.)

The Infinity Concerto. New York: Berkley, 1984; London: Century, 1988. (Songs of Earth and Power, no. 1.)

Sleepside Story. New Castle, Va.: Cheap Street, 1988.

Blood Music. New York: Arbor House, 1985; London: Gollancz, 1986.

Eon. New York: Bluejay, 1985; London: Gollancz, 1986.

The Serpent Mage. New York: Berkley, 1986; London: Century, 1988. (Songs of Earth and Power, no 2.)

The Forge of God. New York: TOR, 1987; London: Gollancz, 1987.

Early Harvest. Cambridge, Mass.: NESFA, 1988. (Short stories and nonfiction.)

Eternity. New York: Warner, 1988; London: Gollancz, 1989.

Hardfought. New York: TOR. 1988. (Bound with *Cascade Point* by Timothy Zahn.)

Tangents. New York: Warner, 1989; London: Gollancz, 1989. (Short stories and essays.)

Queen of Angels. New York: Warner, 1990; London: Gollancz, 1991.

Heads. London: Legend, 1991; New York: St. Martin's, 1991.

Anvil of Stars. New York: Warner, 1992; London: Legend, 1992.

Bear's Fantasies: Six Stories in Old Paradigms. Berkeley Heights, N.J.: Wildside (for Pennsylvania SF Society), 1992. (Short fantasy stories.)

Songs of Earth and Power. London: Legend, 1992. Revised, New York: TOR, 1994. (Omnibus comprising *The Infinity Concerto* and *The Serpent Mage.*)

Moving Mars. New York: TOR, 1993; London: Legend, 1993.

Legacy. New York: TOR, 1995; London: Legend, 1995.

/ (usually referred to as *Slant*). London: Legend, 1997; New York: TOR, 1997.

Dinosaur Summer. New York: Warner, 1998.

Foundation and Chaos. New York: HarperPrism, 1998; London: Orbit, 1998.

EDITED ANTHOLOGY

New Legends, with Martin H. Greenberg. London: Legend, 1995; New York: TOR, 1995.

CRITICAL AND BIOGRAPHICAL STUDIES

Clute, John. "Greg Bear." In *The Encyclopedia of Science Fiction,* 2d ed. Edited by John Clute and Peter Nicholls. London: Orbit, 1993; New York: St. Martin's, 1993.

———. *"The Forge of God," "Anvil of Stars," "Queen of Angels."* In *Look at the Evidence.* Seattle, Wash.: Serconia, 1995; Liverpool, England: Liverpool University Press, 1995.

Foyster, John. *"Blood Music," Australian Science Fiction Review,* 2d ser., 4 (September 1986): 27–28.

Greenland, Colin. *"Blood Music." Foundation,* 37 (Autumn 1986): 86–88.

Kincaid, Paul. *"Heads* and *Queen of Angels." Foundation*, 51 (Spring 1991): 111–112.

Langford, Dave. *"Hegira." Foundation*, 18 (January 1980): 78–79.

———. *"Eternity." Foundation*, 45 (Spring 1989): 94–96.

———. *"Slant." Foundation*, 70 (Summer 1997): 121–122.

Pollack, Rachel. *"Eon." Foundation*, 39 (Spring 1987): 71–74.

Smith, Philip E. *"Moving Mars." The New York Review of Science Fiction*, 77 (January 1995): 22.

Stableford, Brian. *"Queen of Angels." The New York Review of Science Fiction*, 34 (June 1991): 7.

———. *"Slant." Vector*, 195 (September/October 1997): 17.

Stross, Charles. *"Moving Mars." Foundation*, 61 (Summer 1994): 98–100.

—DAVID LANGFORD

GREGORY BENFORD
(b. 1941)

GREGORY ALBERT BENFORD was born, along with his identical twin, James, on 30 January 1941 in Mobile, Alabama. The twins' parents had both been schoolteachers, but after serving in World War II, their father embarked upon an army career that resulted in their spending several childhood years in Japan and Germany as well as various locations in the United States. Both brothers completed their schooling in Oklahoma, graduating from the University of Oklahoma in physics in 1963; each went on to obtain a Ph.D. from the University of California, San Diego, Gregory in 1967 and James in 1969. Although their careers did not begin to diverge until Gregory undertook postdoctoral research—under the directorship of Edward Teller—at the Lawrence Radiation Laboratory in Livermore, California, Gregory was later to declare that he was always primarily a theorist while James had taken up a complementary role as an experimenter.

The theoretically inclined Benford's speculative bent was also expressed in his activities as a science fiction fan during his teens; he was later to suggest that his recruitment to a career in science had been determined by reading Robert A. Heinlein's juvenile science fiction novels. He launched the fanzine *Void* in collaboration with his twin at the age of fourteen and continued it for seven years with various other coeditors, two of whom—Ted White and Terry Carr—also went on to build substantial careers within the genre.

Benford never lost his enthusiasm for collaborative projects, which he carried forward

into his work as a professional scientist as a matter of necessity, and into his science fiction as a matter of choice. The only other writer in the science fiction field who has produced fiction in association with as wide a range of collaborators is Harlan Ellison, who expanded his own list considerably as a tactical move in marketing the particular collection *Partners in Wonder* (1971). Benford's spontaneously recruited collaborators in fiction include his twin, Lawrence Littenberg, Donald Franson, Gordon Eklund, Marc Laidlaw, William Rotsler, David Brin, Paul A. Carter, Mark O. Martin, and Elisabeth Malartre.

In 1971 Benford took up a professorship at the University of California, Irvine, which he has held ever since. He has also been a visiting professor at Cambridge University in Great Britain, Torino University and Florence Observatory in Italy, and the Massachusetts Institute of Technology. His principal fields of research have been plasma physics and astrophysics. He has published about 150 scientific papers, has served as an adviser to the U.S. Department of Energy, NASA, and the Citizens' Advisory Council on National Space Policy, a body that has direct lines to the White House, and in 1995 received the Lord Foundation award for contributions to science and the public comprehension thereof.

Benford's first professionally published story, written while he was in graduate school, was "Stand-In" (1965), which won second place in a contest for amateurs organized by *The Magazine of Fantasy and Sci-*

ence Fiction. The contest's specification—derived from a poem by Doris Pitkin Buck—was to combine the motifs of the Unicorn and the Univac computer. He sold two more lightweight stories to the same magazine in 1966, but he did not begin to publish consistently until 1969, when the novella that was to become the basis of his first novel, "Deeper than the Darkness," appeared in *Fantasy and Science Fiction.* It was in the same year that Benford began writing regularly for Ted White, the former coeditor of *Void* and assistant editor of *The Magazine of Science Fiction,* who had taken over *Amazing* and *Fantastic.*

For *Amazing* Benford wrote a series of articles on "The Science in SF" in collaboration with David Book; the column was a regular feature from 1969 to 1972 and continued—without any further input from Book—on an occasional basis until 1976, alongside similar articles in the short-lived magazine *Vertex.* The fiction published next to the early items in the former series included "Sons of Man" (1969), which served as a preliminary sketch for "Threads of Time" (1974), one of the three elements of the mosaic novel *In the Ocean of Night* (1977). Most of this early fiction—published under the signature "Greg Benford"—worked toward twist-in-the-tail endings, whose ingenuity increased as he became more practiced.

Although "Flattop" (1966) contains a scrupulously modest description of the life found on Mars by an expedition of 1985, few of Benford's fictional finger exercises were strongly biased toward the "hard" end of the science fiction spectrum. "Battleground" (1970, with Jim Benford) and "Star Crossing" (1970, with Donald Franson)—both of which feature exotic conflicts between humans and aliens—come closer than any of his solo pieces. Two of Benford's most earnestly inclined early stories were the mildly jaundiced political fantasies "The Movement" (1970, but written some years earlier) and "Nobody Lives on Burton Street" (1970, once reprinted as "Nobody Lives Around There"). He was a contributor to Samuel R. Delany and Marilyn Hacker's avant-garde series of original anthologies,

Quark, five years before he published his first story in *Analog,* offering a cynical account of amateur assassins lining up to kill the world's first technologically produced immortal, "Inalienable Rite" (1970).

"Deeper Than the Darkness" is, among other things, an antisocialist political fantasy, although it is cast in a more obvious—and more adventurous—science fiction mode than Benford's other contemporary exercises in social commentary. It describes the first phase of an alien conquest of a China-dominated human race by means of artificially aided psychological warfare. The novel version published in 1970 took aboard other models of human society, but its extended plot took the form of a space opera, or space adventure story, which Benford later found embarrassing; when he issued a heavily revised version as *The Stars in Shroud* (1979), he described the earlier novel, a little harshly, as "a stamp-press job from the attic."

Even when Benford decided to take his writing more seriously—a shift correlated with his adoption of the more formal signature "Gregory Benford"—he did not immediately move into the field of hard science fiction. The articles he wrote for *Amazing* presumably helped to generate story ideas, and his criticism of conventions of convenience that had become commonplace within the field undoubtedly encouraged him to tighten up his own act, but the first story he wrote about tachyons—a concept to whose development he had made a significant contribution—was the playfully slapdash time-paradox story "3:02 P.M., Oxford" (1970). Five years passed before he published an earnest complementary piece, ironically entitled "Cambridge, 1:58 A.M." (1975), which became the seed of *Timescape* (1980). His only other story of the seventies set in a university laboratory was the flippant "But the Secret Sits" (1971).

Benford began the most productive of his many literary partnerships in 1971, when he teamed up with Gordon Eklund to write "West Wind, Falling" for the first in the *Uni-*

verse series of original anthologies edited by another of his fellow *Void* editors, Terry Carr. The story concerns intergenerational conflicts among the "colonists" of a comet, who have hitched a ride thereon to the further reaches of the solar system but now must decide whether to get off again as the object returns to the inner system. Although the hard science fiction motif is a relatively sketchy backdrop, this story marked the beginning of Benford's attempts to use his scientific background as cleverly and as scrupulously as he could in the construction of hypothetical environments for his stories.

"In the Ocean of Night" (1972) is a first contact story cast in a classic hard science fiction mold, combining the scrupulously objective commentary of the novella's opening with the lyricism of the revelation vouchsafed to the story's hero, who rebels against instructions to play safe and nuke the intruder. The same story pattern recurs, in a more restrained version—the alien spaceship on a collision course with Earth here being safely lifeless—in "Icarus Descending" (1973), which was subsequently rewritten and combined with it in *In the Ocean of Night* (1977). Most of Benford's solo work of this period was to be rewritten for further use. "The Scarred Man" (1970) resurfaced, in a much neater version, as "Man in a Vice" (1974), which was probably the first science fiction story to feature a computer virus and a solution thereto prophetically dubbed a "vaccine." "Inalienable Rite" was rewritten as "Immortal Night" (1985), while "And the Sea Like Mirrors" (1972)—Benford's contribution to Harlan Ellison's anthology *Again, Dangerous Visions*—was rewritten as "Swarmer, Skimmer" (1981) en route to incorporation in the first sequel to *In the Ocean of Night, Across the Sea of Suns* (1984).

As with other writers before him—most notably Robert A. Heinlein and Arthur C. Clarke—and recalling its influence on his own intellectual development, Benford decided that "young adult" fiction was a uniquely suitable medium for painstaking hard science fiction by virtue of the hospital-

ity it offered to naked didacticism. Although *Jupiter Project* was serialized in *Amazing* in 1972, it did not appear in book form until 1975. Benford did not repeat the experiment, but the novel remains significant within the context of his career in that it established a scenario—whose central element was the Jovian moon Ganymede—that he was to revisit on several occasions. An episode from the novel provided the basis for "Shall We Take a Little Walk?" (1981), which helped bridge its background to the one elaborated in *Against Infinity* (1983) and further deployed in "Warstory" (1990; reprinted as "Sleepstory")

In the interim between the serialization and book publication of *Jupiter Project*, Benford achieved his first major breakthrough as a fiction writer, when he and Gordon Eklund collected a Nebula award for the novelette "If the Stars Are Gods" (1974), published in the fourth *Universe* anthology. The novelette's account of a first contact focuses on the motives and attitudes of the aliens who turn up in the solar system intent on getting to know the sun—which they regard as a sentient, godlike being—and the effect they have on the humans who offer ambivalent assistance to their mission. The idea that religion might be a more powerful motive than intellectual curiosity in impelling interstellar travelers to visit Earth was one that Benford was to return to in the earnestly eerie "Of Space/Time and the River" (1985) and the flippantly sarcastic "Proselytes" (1988). None of these stories gives any clue to Benford's own attitude toward religion, but he was interested enough in the subject to formulate some ingenious apologetic arguments in his excellent philosophical romance "The Rose and the Scalpel" (1990), which features a fascinating contest—and eventual alliance—between Joan of Arc and Voltaire.

Benford and Eklund quickly made plans to incorporate "If the Stars Are Gods" into a mosaic novel, in which it became the second element of four. Benford cannibalized a novelette of his own, the original version of which was eventually revised as "Titan Falling" (1980), to produce a conclusion. The collaborators

Gregory Benford. © 1998 M. C. VALADA

added the impressive novella "The Anvil of Jove" (1976), which provided the third element, and "Hellas Is Florida" (1977), which provided the first, plus a brief link section to bridge the second and third elements. The novel was published in 1977, advertised as a work of "philosophical science fiction," and aptly compared by its cover blurb to Arthur C. Clarke's *Childhood's End*. The complete story adds up to a "spiritual biography" of its hero, who suffers an early disappointment while searching for life on Mars but eventually finds enlightenment through his encounters with alien beings in the farther reaches of the solar system.

By the time that *If the Stars Are Gods* appeared, Benford had also completed the mosaic novel based on "Sons of Man"/"Threads of Time," "Icarus Descending," and "In the Ocean of Night." (To add to the bibliographical confusion, the rewritten version of the last-named story was separately published as "A Snark in the Night" in 1977.) The full-length version encapsulated a central theme that was to become highly significant in Benford's subsequent work: the notion of the galaxy as a battlefield in which self-reproducing

and continually evolving machines are engaged in a war that threatens the extermination of all organic life. This was the most inherently melodramatic of several notions that were then being bandied about in the science fiction arena as possible "solutions" to the so-called Fermi paradox, which asked why, if the galaxy were as full of life-bearing planets as the calculus of probability suggested, no alien race had yet visited Earth. Because the early phases of Search for Extra-Terrestrial Intelligence (a collective term for a series of projects in radio-astronomy that attempted to detect signals from various individual stars and star-clusters that might have been emitted by intelligent beings) had found no evidence of alien intelligence, the question had come to seem increasingly challenging to the ingenuity of science fiction writers.

In the Ocean of Night eventually became the first element of a "trilogy," whose third part was intended to be published as a three-volume novel, although its own third element was eventually split into two volumes. The six-volume series gradually extrapolated Benford's "solution" to the Fermi problem across tens of thousands of years. The Stapledonian proportions thus achieved recalled Arthur C. Clarke's second great endeavor in the field of philosophical science fiction, *The City and the Stars*, and it is hardly surprising that when a publisher hit upon the idea of commissioning a sequel to the earlier version of Clarke's masterpiece, *Against the Fall of Night* (which many American readers preferred to the definitive version for nostalgic reasons), Benford seemed the obvious man to take on the task.

The short stories that Benford produced in the late 1970's that were not destined to be incorporated into novels were widely variated in tone and manner, reflecting his taste for carrying out brief literary experiments. His first contribution to *Analog*, supposedly the hard science fiction writer's mecca (although Benford published only a handful of stories there during the first thirty years of his career), was an eccentric tribute to the Beatles' front man, "Doing Lennon" (1975). A fraudster reawakened from cryonic suspension claims to be John Lennon, but he conceives a more ambitious plan when he discovers that his pretense cuts deeper than he thought. "Beyond Grayworld" (1975), which followed a few months afterward, redeployed its key plot twist in a much more typical *Analog* tale of heroic individualism on the far frontier.

"White Creatures" (1975) was the first of several psychological studies in which the minds of scientists are profoundly affected by the humbling enlightenments of astronomy; later works in the same idiosyncratic vein included "Exposures" (1981) and "Mozart on Morphine" (1989). Although many hard science fiction writers have attempted to capture something of the visionary grandeur of cosmological models, and some—most notably "Philip Latham" (Robert S. Richardson)— have juxtaposed those insights with the everyday lives of research scientists, Benford's work in this vein remains quirkily unique.

"John of the Apocalypse" (1975, with James Benford) is a political fantasy in which the cynical use of drugs and religion as mass-manipulative devices is ironically revealed to be a double-edged sword. "Seascape" (1976), by contrast, imagines religion as an instrument of liberation from manipulation, albeit in a far more remote context. "What Did You Do Last Year?" (1976, with Gordon Eklund) and "Knowing Her" (1977) are studies of female vanity that carefully avoid misogyny while retaining a sharp critical edge; the more dignified "Cadenza" (1981) works more poignantly along similar lines. "A Hiss of Dragons" (1978, with Marc Laidlaw) is a tale of genetically engineered dragons and the difficulties involved in their slaying that prefigures a far more dignified tale of dinosaurs reborn from fossil DNA, "Shakers of the Earth" (1992).

The most impressive story of this middle period is "In Alien Flesh" (1978), which became the title story of Benford's first collection. The collection adds illuminating commentaries to the stories, noting of this one that "rendering the alien is the Holy Grail of sf, because if your attempt can be accurately summarized, you know you've failed." The lumpen leviathans of this story, into whose bodies brave men venture in order to plant sensory equipment, represent one of many approaches Benford made to this particular grail. The contemporary "Starswarmer" (1978) was even more adventurous, fully warranting the further elaboration it received when the featured alien was integrated into the plot of *Tides of Light* (1989).

A wry comment appended to "Time Shards" (1979) in *In Alien Flesh* admits that "the alien" does not have to be very far removed from ourselves; the story features a proto-phonographic recording of medieval speech, whose blithe inaccuracies horrified historians. "Dark Sanctuary" (1979) is another oblique first-contact story whose hero—mindful, perhaps, of what befell the heroes of "In the Ocean of Night" and "Icarus Descending"—decides to keep quiet about it. Another enigmatic alien is featured in *Find the Changeling* (1980, with Gordon Eklund), although its mimetic abilities recall those of the aliens in "Star Crossing." As in the earlier novella, those abilities are deployed in a relatively routine action-adventure novel of the kind that Eklund (who had produced far more sophisticated work in the early years of his career) had begun to churn out in some quantity.

Benford obtained another collaborative credit in 1980 for his work on *Shiva Descending*, written with William Rotsler. This was a disaster novel cast in a mold that had demonstrated considerable best-selling capability during the previous decade. It uses the motif of an Earth-impacting asteroid, which Benford had already used in "Icarus Descending" and the brief apocalyptic comedy "How It All Went" (1976), but it develops the notion more conventionally, using multiple viewpoints to contemplate the impending threat and its tragic promise. The novel probably came too close on the heels of Larry Niven and Jerry Pournelle's *Lucifer's Hammer* (1977) to attract much attention. Benford presumably achieved a greater commercial success as well as winning far more kudos with *Timescape*

(1980), which appeared under his name alone, although the significant input of his sister-in-law Hilary is credited in an acknowledgment and her name is included in the copyright notice.

Timescape was widely, and deservedly, hailed as the best novel about scientists at work yet produced within the science fiction genre—or indeed within modern fiction as a whole. There was, in truth, not a great deal of competition for that title because images of scientists at work that can be seen to be convincing at every level have perforce to be set in the recent past, the present, or the very near future—thus ruling out some 99 percent of science fiction—and writers outside the genre had tended to deal with scientists satirically, after the fashion of Thomas Pynchon's *Gravity's Rainbow* (1973) and Don DeLillo's *Ratner's Star* (1976). Kate Wilhelm's excellent *The Clewiston Test* (1976) had, however, set a high standard for the genre only a few years earlier, and *Timescape*'s triumph was no mean achievement.

Extrapolating the argument of "The Tachyonic Antitelephone," a research paper coauthored with D(avid). L. Book and W. A. Newcomb that had appeared in *Physical Review* in 1970, the novel tells two parallel stories. One is set in 1998, when scientists in a world on the brink of ecocatastrophe are trying to use tachyons to send a warning back in time, the other in 1962, when uncomprehending physicists attempt to figure out what the anomalies caused by the signal might be. The two central characters, Gregory Markham and Gordon Bernstein, are both based on the author, at two different points in his life. (He was to use Markham as an alter ego again in the 1986 point-of-death fantasy "Newton's Sleep," in which the Shared World of a series of anthologies launched with *Heroes in Hell* gave him the chance to meet up with Isaac Newton, Ernest Hemingway, and Che Guevara.) The manner in which the world is delicately tilted in the direction of salvation is carefully modest, but it pays deft and earnest homage to the life-enhancing potential of scientific research.

Timescape won Benford a second Nebula and a John W. Campbell Memorial award and established him firmly as a key writer of hard science fiction—indeed, as a writer whose endeavors would henceforth help to define and delimit that controversy-beleaguered subgenre. When he was invited to write something for the Nebula Awards anthology celebrating that year's science fiction, Benford chose to contribute an article entitled "Why Is There So Little Science in Literature?"— and from then until he took over Isaac Asimov's science column in *The Magazine of Science Fiction* in 1992, the bulk of his nonfiction contributions to the field shifted from the popularization of science toward literary criticism. The article concluded with the judgment: "The excesses of SF can be corrected by paying more attention to how science is *done,* rather than by relying on the hoary old images of the dashing astronaut, the inevitable cranky-but-wise administrator, and the rest of the leaden cast left over from our earlier days."

Even in the early stories in which Benford had appropriated that "leaden cast," he had found difficulty adapting himself to the expectations of genre science fiction readers, and by the time he wrote *Timescape,* he had made a firm decision to go his own way. In the article he contributed to the Profession of Science Fiction series in the journal *Foundation*—published in 1981—he wrote: "I know that the sf audience as a whole is more interested in wish fulfilment fantasies than anything else, and that's not my vector. The question is whether I should seek a larger audience, maybe outside sf, which has my interests." The British edition of *Timescape* issued by Gollancz did not label it as science fiction, but it is doubtful that the change attracted many readers who would not otherwise have seen the book.

Benford had already begun preliminary investigations of this kind in such stories as "Homemaker" (1977, reprinted as "Snatching the Bot") and "Nooncoming" (1978), both of which were deliberate experiments in style that attempted to formulate science fiction stories according to narrative methods favored by "slick" magazines. Other, wider-ranging experiments had followed in their vein, including "Time Guide" (1979), "Calibrations and Exercises" (1979), and "Slices" (1981). He soon began trying to apply his new dicta to casts of characters left over from his own earlier days, including the dashing astronaut Nigel Walmsley, who had been compounded from several predecessors in the fixing up of *In the Ocean of Night*, and the cranky-but-wise adults who had provided the supportive cast for the boy adventurers of *Jupiter Project*. In writing another novel set in the latter's Ganymede colony, Benford turned for inspiration and guidance to William Faulkner, the writer who had perfected the literary voice of the American South (to which the much-traveled Benford still respectfully traced his roots). The first few chapters of *Against Infinity* (1983) transplant the tone and plot of Faulkner's novella "The Bear" into the alien world, preparing for another sustained assault on "the Holy Grail of sf"; the creature that stands in for the bear is, inevitably, a far more enigmatic and portentous being.

The redemption of Nigel Walmsley was accomplished in a not dissimilar fashion in *Across the Sea of Suns* (1984), which was fixed up from "And the Sea Like Mirrors"/ "Swarmer, Skimmer," "The Other Side of the River" (1982), and "Lazarus Rising" (1982). While his home world is devastated by subtle alien attack, Walmsley is dispatched to the star Ra to investigate mysterious radio signals—which draw him, inexorably and inevitably, toward the dark grail of alien confrontation. More than half a century older than his previous manifestation, the new Walmsley is far from dashing. Soured as he is by his earlier experiences, afflicted with cancer, and torn between two awkwardly problematic females, the bad news he receives about humanity's unlooked-for involvement in the galaxy-wide war between organic and inorganic intelligences mockingly mirrors his own inward turmoil.

A short story spun off by a momentary inspiration while Benford was writing *Across the Sea of Suns*, "Relativistic Effects" (1982), works even harder to substitute ordinary working folk for dashing astronauts, even though they are party to events that change the fates of stars and civilizations. Further experiments in style were conducted in "The Touch" (1983, reprinted as "Touches"), which examines life in the light of game theory, and "Me/Days" (1984), which tracks the evolution of a machine consciousness. Benford reprinted all these experiments in style in his two collections, while consigning many of his more conventional genre science fiction stories to oblivion.

Benford made a more concerted attempt to invade the territory of popular best-sellers with the long novel *Artifact* (1985). The gray area between science fiction and the thriller had extended considerably in the 1970s, reflected in the success of such writers as Martin Caidin, Robin Cook, and—most significantly of all—Michael Crichton. Benford's decision to enter this arena was undertaken partly in the spirit of experimentation and partly because he had taken note of a powerful current of technophobia running through the entire "technothriller" subgenre. To some extent the technophobia in question was tacit, reflecting the fact that the borrowed science fiction devices had to be used to generate melodramatic threats in order to qualify the stories as thrillers, but writers such as Crichton had increasingly taken leave to turn the alarmist tendencies of their work into explicit antiscientific propaganda.

The lever that serves to move the plot of *Artifact* is a mysterious block of stone uncovered in Greece by American archaeologists. Its extraordinary mass suggests that it contains a captive black hole. The motives of the Greek military man who tries to stop the export of the artifact are given a relatively sympathetic hearing, but the main ideological thrust of the steadily thickening plot is that the scientific method is the one thing that stands between civilization and catastrophe, and is the only means of saving the day when unprecedented apocalyptic problems arise. *Artifact* failed to reach best-selling status, and when Benford tried a second experiment of a similar kind in the even longer *Chiller* (1993)—a tale of a serial killer whose favored prey is scientists working in the field of cryonics—he used the pseudonym Sterling Blake in order that it would not be weighed down by the genre associations of his own name. Unfortunately, it fared no better.

Heart of the Comet (1986), which Benford wrote in collaboration with David Brin, was yet another attempt to reach a wider audience, this time without straying into the margins of the field. The collaborators set out to use the reentry of Halley's comet into the solar system—and the close inspection thereof by a space probe—as a hook to catch the public imagination. In the event, the comet did not live up to the hopes of those who wanted to see a spectacular tail, and the probe merely confirmed what everyone already knew about the nature of comets, but the novel provided some compensation to those who hungered for more dramatic revelations. Brin had already achieved considerable success in modernizing space opera and bringing that despised subgenre to a new pitch of sophistication, and he and Benford set out to equip their comet with a native ecology that included "Bug-Eyed Monsters." The core of the plot is a painstaking recapitulation of the kind of project featured in "West Wind, Falling," describing the establishment of a colony within the comet's head in order to hitch a ride thereon to the remoter regions of the solar system and the subsequent alienation of that colony from its point of origin. The sudden blossoming of the object's dormant life system does, however, provide a useful melodramatic boost to an exercise in classic hard science fiction.

Benford's experiments in literary method also produced four significant novellas in the late 1980s. His first attempt to transpose the manner and tone of William Faulkner's work into science fiction had been sufficiently successful to warrant repetition, and he modeled

his post-holocaust story "To the Storming Gulf" (1985) even more explicitly on *As I Lay Dying*. The stratagem called forth some sharp criticism from Gary K. Wolfe, who doubted its propriety and wondered publicly about Benford's motives, but Benford produced a reasonable defense (whose substance is appended to the story in *In Alien Flesh*), and the story itself is remarkably effective, although the coda formed by incorporating "Old Woman by the Road" (1978) is slightly awkward. The future war scenario, in which America is devastated after the U.S.S.R. is provoked by a deceptive third party into launching a nuclear strike but refrains from retaliation, is an intriguing variation on a familiar theme, which recalls Theodore Sturgeon's "Thunder and Roses." Benford was to recapitulate and deftly recomplicate the themes of other classic stories that he had read and admired in youth, most notably in "Matter's End" (1990), a hard science fiction variation of the theme of Arthur C. Clarke's "The Nine Billion Names of God," and "Centigrade 233" (1990), a wry inversion of the ultimate heresy defined by Ray Bradbury's *Fahrenheit 451*.

Less successful than "To the Storming Gulf" was "As Big As the Ritz" (1986 abridged; 1987), a utopian satire modeled on a story by F. Scott Fitzgerald. An astrophysicist takes advantage of his affair with the daughter of the richest man in the solar system to investigate the ultra-socialist utopia Brotherworld. The idealistic plutocrat has established Brotherworld on the Hoop, an artificial habitat sustained by the energy output of matter falling into a black hole, employing genetic as well as social engineering to ensure that its people really are equal in every possible respect. The hero's analysis of this peculiar state is aided by a reference book credited to one Darko Drovneb, whose name strongly suggests that Benford was using the story to explore his own anarcho-libertarian objections to socialist ideals. The social thought experiment seems to have had no clear result—the story's ending is weak and ambivalent—but the speculations about black holes and their uses bore further fruit in

"A Worm in the Well" (1995; reprinted as "Early Bird").

Much more closely allied to the experiment Benford undertook in collaboration with Brin was "Proserpina's Daughter" (1988; reprinted as *Iceborn*), which he wrote in partnership with Paul A. Carter. The story juxtaposes the discoveries made by a lone astronaut on Pluto—which unexpectedly turns out to harbor a complex ecology including sentient life-forms—with political upheavals that threaten to put a stop to the entire space program. Although it echoes "Sons of Man" in this respect, it is a more powerful story, embodying a blithe flamboyance that the ever-more-conscientious Benford had by now virtually squeezed out of his solo work. This reflects the fact that Carter was the only one of Benford's many collaborators who had made a contribution to hard science fiction's "Golden Age," when John W. Campbell, Jr., had steered *Astounding* through the troubled 1940's. Benford did follow it up with a pulp science fiction pastiche of his own in "Alphas" (1989), a thoroughly Campbellian tale of a dashing astronaut who takes a trip through the core of Venus while investigating the activities of alien miners whose tools are cosmic strings. The Alphas and their exotic mining techniques reappeared in *Tides of Light* and "Doing Alien" (1994).

The fourth item in the quartet of novellas was "Beyond the Fall of Night" (1990), Benford's sequel to *Against the Fall of Night*, whose collaborative aspect was emphasized by the fact that it was published in an omnibus with its predecessor. Although the young hero of the earlier text reappears as an adult, the central character of the sequel is Cley, an Ur-human whose species has been resurrected with the aid of the Library of Life. Unfortunately, her kind has to bear the brunt of the wrath of the Mad Mind, released from the prison to which Clarke's future history had condemned it. The main virtue of the story lies, however, in its images of remarkable ecologies filling entire solar systems and its establishment of an ultimate destiny one step beyond that which had been imaginable in Clarke's day, even to a man of Clarke's vision. That potential for transcendence, which made the project worthwhile in spite of a certain dramatic flaccidity, was unavailable when Benford wrote *Foundation's Fear* (1997), which had to be slotted into an exceedingly narrow slice of the historical elaboration that Isaac Asimov had already inserted into the cracks of his own much grander scheme. The latter project did, however, offer him the opportunity to advance an oblique commentary on Asimov's crucial contribution to the evolution of science fiction. Benford's preparatory contemplation of the hypothetical human science of psychohistory encouraged him to develop his own hypothetical "sociohistory," whose scope is mapped in the Africa-set "Immersion" (1995). The imaginative work devoted to "Beyond the Fall of Night" also bore further fruit in the sophisticated space opera "Galaxia" (1997).

The later novellas in this sequence were sidelines to the biggest—and as it turned out, the most problematic—project that Benford had yet tackled. This was the completion of the series begun with *In the Ocean of Night* by a trilogy, employing a new set of characters, that took up the story more than 35,000 years after the conclusion of *Across the Sea of Suns*.

Great Sky River (1987) begins at the end of the 375th century and tells the story of the struggle for survival of members of the family Bishop following the destruction of their Citadel on the planet Snowglade. The destroyers of the Citadel are mechs (intelligent machines) engaged in an apparent program of extermination—although the surviving Bishops, led by Killeen, are themselves partly mechanized by virtue of various inorganic augmentations. The most significant of these augmentations are the information storage facilities that equip them with Aspects: supplementary intelligences retaining the personalities of dead family members.

The Bishops are pursued by a mech called the Mantis, a so-called anthology intelligence whose purpose is not merely to wipe out the

Bishops but to record and "digest" them. The Mantis is, after its own fashion, an artist, and it regards organic matter as a medium of "sculpture." In the course of its pursuit, the Mantis becomes sufficiently interested in its prey to open a channel of communication with them—but no sooner is the dialogue begun than a third party intervenes: a "magnetic mind" based in the warped space that surrounds the Eater, the huge black hole at the center of the galaxy. The magnetic mind relays a message to Killeen, allegedly from his long-lost father, Abraham, instructing him not to attempt to build a new Citadel.

This instruction sends Killeen forth on a quest of the kind that the famous editor Maxwell Perkins once advised Thomas Wolfe to employ in order to give anchorage and direction to his initially inchoate novels. In *Tides of Light* the quest takes Killeen's band to Abraham's Star, on the edge of a dust cloud near the galaxy's center, while the interested anthology intelligence—which has assisted the escape from Snowglade—keeps clandestine watch on their progress. They find more human refugees, but they also find Cybers: hybrid entities that have taken cyborgization much further than those who still think of themselves as natural beings. The Cybers have ambitions on much the same scale as the mechs, involving the use of cosmic strings as tools to plunder planetary resources such as "Alphas." The situation is further complicated by the involvement of the alien Starswarmers, who had been introduced in *In the Ocean of Night*.

Tides of Light fills in much of the history overleaped by the gap separating *Across the Sea of Suns* from *Great Sky River*, going so far as to append a "report" compiled by the Mantis in the hope of making the human worldview intelligible to others of its kind. The first subdivision of this chronology of the human species—which is classified parenthetically among the "dreaming vertebrates"—is the Great Times, when humans, despite the mech-assisted devastation of Earth's ecosphere, built a galactic empire to rival that of mech civilization. Explorers arrived at the center of the galaxy in several distinct groups, at widely spaced intervals, most of whom disappeared. Some of these came in search of a fabled Galactic Library, of which no trace remained. The Great Times were followed by the Chandelier Age, in which humans gathered into vast space-faring cities under the pressure of mech attrition, which culminated in the "Hunker Down," when the Chandeliers had to be abandoned and their former inhabitants took refuge on planetary surfaces, usually in vast Arcologies. Eventually, the Arcologies suffered the same fate as the Chandeliers, proving unsustainable under the pressure of mech aggression, and their survivors lost much of their technology, apparently becoming mere pests in the margins of a universal mech civilization.

After publication of the second volume, progress on the trilogy came to a temporary halt, partly because new discoveries and theories regarding the actual galactic center—to which Benford's own papers made a significant contribution—were continually being reported. He was also distracted by writing and hosting an eight-part television series for the Japanese National Broadcasting organization NHK, *A Galactic Odyssey*, which attempted to popularize modern physics in the context of an account of the evolution of the galaxy; although popular in Japan, the series was never aired in the United States. (Benford's subsequent television credits include *Japan 2000* and service as scientific consultant to the NHK Network and *Star Trek: The Next Generation*.)

It is perhaps ironic, given the series' evident inspirational debt to Clarke's *The City and the Stars*, that one of the other projects that interrupted the trilogy was the belated sequel to *Against the Fall of Night*, but the spinoff from Benford's work-in-progress—which determined the recasting of the Mad Mind as a magnetic mind and its insecure prison as a black hole identical to the Eater—worked to the advantage of "Beyond the Fall of Night." When Benford's own series got going again, the projected third volume became too unwieldy and was split into two novels: *Furious Gulf* (1994) and *Sailing Bright Eternity* (1995).

The story told by these volumes takes Killeen and his allies—now including the alien Quath, whose portrayal here brought Benford closer than he had ever come before to science fiction's Holy Grail—into the Esty, an exotic space-time continuum accessible via "portals" from the ergosphere surrounding the Eater. The Esty is constantly redesigning itself as more matter is added to it but appears to observers as an infinite, chaotically lit, and perpetually windblown plain of "timestone," liberally pockmarked with "Lanes." Certain sectors of the Esty stabilized by the "Old Ones" support an ecosphere and comprise the habitable Wedge or Redoubt, which turns out to be the site of the lost Galactic Library. The Wedge's independence from ordinary galactic time has allowed it to accumulate a population drawn from all the eras of humanity's galactic history. Nigel Walmsley is there, ready to greet Killeen's son Toby, take him on a journey of discovery down a river (which preserves sensitive echoes of Mark Twain's mythicized Mississippi), and explain the necessity of Killeen's quest.

In the climax of *Sailing Bright Eternity*, the Mantis-led mechs finally find a way into the Esty, thus precipitating the final crisis in their long war against organic beings—but they, too, have been forced to reappraise their place in the scheme of things and their relationship with organic species. The chronology laid out in the appendix to the final volume concludes, with a slightly tired flourish, with the "Beginning of [the] mature phase of self-organized forms."

In looking at this series as a whole, one has to bear in mind that when the author set out on his imaginary voyage, he had no inkling of the terminus it would eventually reach. All extended enterprises within the field of science fiction are, almost by definition, exploratory; the essence of their development is to move farther and farther into terra incognita, ascending through a whole series of levels of revelation. The best enterprises of this kind are those that arrive somewhere that is not only new and interesting but quite unexpected; Benford's is certainly among the best—and its final achievement is ample justification for the occasional unprofitable detours and patchwork engine repairs that occurred along the way.

The previously steady flow of Benford's short fiction was muted while he struggled to finish his galactic history series, but he made some compensation by editing a series of anthologies in collaboration with Martin H. Greenberg, all but one featuring exercises in alternative history. He also wrote "World Vast, World Various" (1992) for the Shared World anthology *Murasaki*, edited by Greenberg and Robert Silverberg, in which scientists exploring Murasaki's neighbor world attempt to apply sociobiological theory to the understanding of the native "chumpclamps."

Benford returned to his own work in a more playful mood, exhibited in such tales as "Not of an Age," a time-tripping story written for an anthology of *Weird Tales from Shakespeare* (1994) but first published in the previous year as "The Dark Backward," and "Kollapse" (1995), a sarcastic satirization of Net nerds. "A Tapestry of Thought" (1995), in which two machines philosophize about the nature of a captive human, and "High Abyss" (1995), which offers a mildly satirical glimpse of life on a cosmic string, partake of a similar spirit. "Paris Conquers All" (1996, with David Brin) proposes that Jules Verne's response to the kind of alien invasion described in H. G. Wells's *The War of the Worlds* would have been more pragmatic than that of the protagonist of the novel. "Zoomers" (1996) and "The Voice" (1997) offer different images of a postliterate future in which new media have extended the human sensorium in remarkable ways; the latter includes a wry reference to "Centigrade 233," acknowledging that its central joke might not have been as funny as it seemed at the time. "High Abyss" appeared in Greg Bear's *New Legends* (1995), for which Benford also wrote "A Desperate Calculus (signed "Sterling Blake"), a calculatedly controversial political fantasy, and the essay "Old

Legends," which discusses—partly from the author's own experience—the interrelationships between American science and American science fiction during the previous 55 years.

Benford's next major project returned from the farther reaches of space and time to the tangibility of the present day and the laboratory, although it did not entirely forsake the cosmic perspective of his four-volume trilogy. *Cosm* (1998) describes an experiment in which smashing uranium atoms together inside a Relativistic Heavy Ion Collider produces a mini–Big Bang and opens a window into a virgin universe, which continues to expand into its own private space. This accident befalls Alicia Butterworth, a professor at the University of California, Irvine, who is comprehensively distanced from the author in being a single black female. Her misfired experiment opens up the glorious possibility of manufacturing universes wholesale and observing the entire course of their lifetimes in a matter of weeks. The plot is a little contrived—in order to stoke up the melodrama the author throws in an entirely gratuitous attempted kidnapping and arranges matters so that the cosm causes a flukish fatality—but the core of the story is its painstaking study of the obsessive psychology of its heroine, her allies, and her rivals. In constructing this analysis, the novel offers its readers a less charitable picture of the concerns, habits, and ethics of scientists than *Timescape*, but one that is every bit as compelling and just as convincing.

It is arguable that works like *Cosm* are what Benford does best—or at least that they are the one thing he does conspicuously better than anyone else. However, what is truly remarkable about his work is its awesome range. He has tried harder than any other contemporary science fiction writer, and *far* harder than any other writer of hard science fiction, to explore all the potential that the genre has to offer. The spectrum of his works includes a few enterprises that some critics have considered to be beneath the dignity of a real writer—especially a self-declared ama-

teur who has a taxing and worthwhile day job—but Benford has always seen such exploits as contributing to Shared World anthologies and writing belated sequels to other people's books as intellectual and artistic challenges. (In addition to those items already mentioned, he and Mark O. Martin contributed a novella, *The Trojan Cat*, and a full-length novel, *A Darker Geometry*, to the sixth and seventh volumes of *Man-Kzin Wars* [1994 and 1995], based on Larry Niven's scenario). Like any true scientist, Benford has always been willing to try such experiments, to see how they come out. His amateurism is not the kind that despises moneymaking but the kind that can embark upon any enterprise at whim, without any need to fear the consequences of occasional failure.

Given this, it is not surprising that Benford's very best work constitutes an ongoing celebration of curiosity as a motive and enterprise as an attitude of mind. This can be seen very clearly in *Timescape* and *Cosm* and in the long series built on the seed of *In the Ocean of Night*, but it does not diminish Benford in the slightest to suggest that it shows most nakedly in some of his collaborative pieces, including *If the Stars Are Gods*, "Proserpina's Daughter," and their most striking successor: "A Cold, Dry Cradle" (1997, written with Elisabeth Malartre). This heartfelt hard science fiction story accepts James Lovelock's judgment of the implications of its chemically neutral atmosphere and the scant findings of the *Viking* lander, but it begs leave to argue that there is still a possibility not merely of finding life on Mars but of finding precious enlightenment there.

In one of the commentaries in *In Alien Flesh* Benford borrows an analogy applied by Robert Frost to the writing of free verse in order to characterize the writing of science fiction without a proper scientific conscience as "playing tennis with the net down." He is a writer who has always tried to play with the net up but not to allow its presence to inhibit him in his stylistic experiments. It is important to remember, though, that to think of *any* kind of conscience merely as a restriction is rather misleading. The point of a conscience is that it also works constructively toward the cause and security of some crucial good. The conscience of hard science fiction works toward the cause and security of enlightenment, and Benford's work in that cause can stand comparison with that of any other modern writer in any field.

Selected Bibliography

WORKS OF GREGORY BENFORD

Deeper Than the Darkness. New York: Ace, 1970. Revised as *The Stars in Shroud*, New York: Berkley, 1978; London: Gollancz, 1979.

Jupiter Project. Nashville, Tenn.: Nelson, 1975. Revised as *The Jupiter Project*, New York: Berkley, 1980; London: Sphere, 1982.

If the Stars Are Gods, with Gordon Eklund. New York: Berkley, 1977; London: Gollancz, 1978. Revised edition, New York: Bantam, 1989.

In the Ocean of Night. New York: Dial, 1977; London: Sidgwick and Jackson, 1978.

Find the Changeling, with Gordon Eklund. New York: Dell, 1980; London: Sphere, 1983.

Timescape. New York: Simon and Schuster, 1980; London: Gollancz, 1980.

Shiva Descending, with William Rotsler. New York: Avon, 1980; London: Sphere, 1980.

Against Infinity. New York: Simon and Schuster, 1983; London: Gollancz, 1983.

Across the Sea of Suns. New York: Simon and Schuster, 1984; London: Macdonald, 1984. Revised edition, New York: Bantam, 1987.

Artifact. New York: TOR, 1985; London: Bantam, 1986.

In Alien Flesh. New York: TOR, 1986; London: Gollancz, 1988. (Short stories.)

Heart of the Comet, with David Brin. New York: Bantam, 1986; London: Bantam, 1987.

Great Sky River. New York: Bantam, 1987; London: Gollancz, 1988.

Tides of Light. New York: Bantam, 1989; London: Gollancz, 1989.

Beyond the Fall of Night, with *Against the Fall of Night* by Arthur C. Clarke. New York: Ace, 1990; London: Gollancz, 1991.

Chiller, as Sterling Blake. New York: Bantam, 1993.

Furious Gulf. New York: Bantam, 1994; London: Gollancz, 1994.

Sailing Bright Eternity. New York: Bantam, 1995; London: Gollancz, 1995.

Matter's End. New York: Bantam, 1994. Expanded edition, London: Gollancz, 1996. (Short stories.)

Foundation's Fear. New York: HarperPrism, 1997; London: Orbit, 1997.

Cosm. New York: Avon, 1998; London: Orbit, 1998.

—BRIAN STABLEFORD

ALFRED BESTER

(1913–1987)

WHEN ALFRED BESTER'S first novel, *The Demolished Man*, exploded onto the pages of *Galaxy Science Fiction* in 1952 (book form, 1953), it marked the fruition of a major talent, almost as if this novel were the culmination of years of patient apprenticeship to the craft of storytelling. Although Bester had written several significant science fiction short stories prior to the appearance of his first novel, they gave little promise of the mature writer whose voice in *The Demolished Man* and his later *The Stars My Destination* (also known as *Tiger! Tiger!*, the title that Bester himself preferred) made him an instant star in the galaxy of accomplished science fiction novelists.

Yet Bester's apprenticeship served him well. In fact, his early years seem like an almost ideal preparation for a writer. Born in New York City in 1913, he was educated at the University of Pennsylvania, where he studied (very intensively, according to his own report) both humanistic and scientific disciplines, including music, psychology, and literature. He even completed two years of law school. Bester began writing professionally in 1938, churning out science fiction, mystery and adventure stories, comics, and radio scripts. His ability to write crisp, fast-paced dialogue, which he learned while writing scripts for shows such as *Charlie Chan* and *The Shadow*, served him well with his more mature science fiction.

Thus, the instant success of *The Demolished Man* should not have appeared as a surprise, but merely as an inevitable result or culmination of his catholic interests and abilities. When *The Demolished Man* was published, then, it broke new ground for the science fiction novel, a form that had been shaped in the previous decade by John W. Campbell, Jr.'s *Astounding Science-Fiction* and Campbell's stable of professionals, which included Arthur C. Clarke, Robert A. Heinlein, and Isaac Asimov. The brilliance of Bester's first novel immediately made him a member of the select circle of major science fiction writers and by itself assured Bester, never a prolific writer, of near-legendary status in the field.

What qualities made Bester so justifiably famous on the basis of his few short stories and the two early novels? First, of course, is the fact that he was an excellent storyteller. His plots are drenched with action, and the stories often exhibit a pell-mell pace, careening headlong from incident to crisis, from conflict to resolution. While the action never slackens, Bester nonetheless revealed himself to be a careful plotter who ensures that the reader's interest will be sustained throughout the entire course of each novel or short story. Also Bester scatters enough clues so that the intricacies of the plot or the mysteries of the characterizations permit readers to delight in trying to solve the problems he poses.

In addition, Bester gave major voice to an archetypal character that has been termed the "Besterman." While the names and some of the incidental appearances may differ in the various novels and short stories that followed *The Demolished Man*, the characteristics of the Bester hero show several significant similarities. For example, either Ben Reich or Lincoln Powell, the dual heroes of *The Demolished Man,* may be viewed as an incipient superman, just as Gully Foyle of *The Stars My Destination* must grow to his earthshaking greatness. Yet none of these characters displays a simplistic uniformity. They are not typical "supermen." They are all driven, obsessed, possessed, sometimes maniacal, sometimes salvific. They combine both good and bad qualities, and their actions can range from rape or rapine to incredible heroics or self-sacrifice. They are never cardboard characters, never merely two-dimensional, never uninteresting, never predictable. Their griefs are universal; their joys bring joy to the readers as well, for all of the heroes, despite their superhuman qualities, have characteristics with which we can easily identify.

Moreover, Bester was a good writer, exhibiting a great familiarity with stylistic devices and techniques ignored by many of his contemporary science fiction colleagues, but long a staple of the writing of many mainstream authors, ranging from Laurence Sterne to James Joyce and beyond. He gave us bravura passages of intense prose; long examples of stream of consciousness; interior monologues; multiple and shifting points of view; and the use of typographical eccentricities and graphics to further both the plot and the characterizations. In his utilization of these devices Bester was doing nothing really new, of course. Yet it was his use of them in the science fiction genre that marked him as a writer willing to leap the narrow confines of the form and to experiment boldly. While his work can never be mistaken for anything except science fiction or fantasy, Bester was one of the first science fiction writers to break down the ghetto walls so clearly established by Hugo Gernsback and Campbell. As such, he anticipated many later writers who have built upon the techniques he utilized to bring science fiction closer to the mainstream from which it had long been separated.

And, finally, Bester probed so deeply into the psyche of his major characters that he added techniques derived from the "soft" science of psychology to the techniques utilized by other writers. Whether one views the characters from the Freudian, Jungian, or Adlerian point of view—and they are amenable to analysis from all three—it is their hidden psychological motivations that give them such an immediacy for readers, even decades after the stories were written. These motivations are often complex, and while Bester punctuated his stories with enough obvious reasons for their behavior to satisfy a casual reader who is interested only in the surface action, he usually counterpointed his surface with a quiet susurrus of hidden motivations that becomes obvious only gradually. In fact, some of these ambiguities become apparent only after a second or even a third reading.

This skillful juggling of plot, character motivations, action, dialogue, and the various other devices he called upon make Bester's achievement in his two early novels distinguished indeed. *The Demolished Man* is an obvious example of his dexterity and maturity as a writer. On the surface it is the story of Ben Reich, business mogul and entrepreneur, whose multinational conglomerate, Monarch Utilities and Resources, Incorporated, is being eroded by the tactics of the D'Courtney Cartel, another conglomerate. Reich has been haunted by the recurring dream of The Man With No Face, a shadowy figure whom he identifies with Craye D'Courtney. Reich resolves to kill D'Courtney, a task made almost impossible by the fact that the twenty-fourth-century society in which he lives has a small but influential percentage of mind readers, known as "Espers" (derived from "extrasensory perception"). These Espers can detect the idea of a crime long before its commission, and thus hustle the potential criminal off to psychiatric treatment, thereby preventing crime.

Running parallel to Reich's story is that of Lincoln Powell, the Esper prefect of police. In many ways, he is almost the traditional hero of the book: he is accomplished, witty, able, charismatic, caring, sensitive, and brilliant. While many readers cannot identify with him

Alfred Bester in 1983. PHOTO BY JAY KAY KLEIN

for each other's ambitions and accomplishments. Yet if Bester's usually sure sense of characterization is somewhat flawed in their portrayal, it is only in the fact that he does not provide the reader with a sufficient sense of Reich's abilities other than his talents as a criminal, and that Powell's shadow nature is insufficiently well drawn. Only suggestions or hints of both aspects of the two men are provided.

This ambiguity may cause readers some difficulty in accepting the premises of one of the climactic scenes of the novel, when Powell seeks permission from the Esper Guild Council to utilize Mass Cathexis with himself as the human canal for the capitalized energy sent to him from all Espers. Only by absorbing the latent psychic energy transmitted to him from Esper society can he confront the "Galactic Focal Point" represented by Reich. To be sure, Bester established Powell as a salvific figure and Reich as a virtually diabolic figure, but both men seem almost one-dimensional at this point, inhuman or even inhumane. On the other hand, this ambiguity may be viewed as underlining some of the crucial questions of the novel itself: Who is the hero or protagonist? What impels Powell to perform his self-sacrificial act, knowing well that it may cause his death? What drives Reich to murder?

In *The Stars My Destination,* we are faced with a similarly ambiguous question: What motivates Gully Foyle's mad passion for revenge? No simple answers can be given to any of these questions, of course; but what is important here is that the reader, carried by the headlong pace of both novels, may react sympathetically to the characters and the questions their actions pose, and may even identify empathetically with them. This act involves more than traditional sympathy with a hero or even with a vigorous, essentially likable antihero. Rather, it becomes a virtual identification. Reich acts, the reader acts. Powell responds, the reader responds. The hero and antihero merge in the vivid scene where Powell awakens from the strain of the Mass Cathexis measure, clutching

early in the novel, probably because he is almost insufferably smug, Powell can certainly be cast as the "good guy," just as Reich can be cast as the "bad guy." But both men are flawed personages. Reich, after all, must be a supremely accomplished individual to have built Monarch into its preeminence and to have planned and executed the first successful Triple-A felony in decades. And Powell, for all of his achievements and abilities as the First Class Esper prefect of police, carries within himself a shadow figure that he calls "Dishonest Abe," a mischievous liar who on occasion surfaces long enough to get Powell into embarrassing situations, even into a bit of trouble. Readers see only flashes of Dishonest Abe. In one tantalizingly brief scene we learn that this hidden alter ego once "stole the weather," and in an even more revealing episode Powell apparently violates the Esper Code by "peeping," or mind reading, Reich without Reich's permission. Together, then, Reich and Powell are hero and antihero, foils

Reich, who is curled into a tight fetal ball. The reader is struck with the realization that Powell and Reich have virtually become one being, a father-son, and the reader can now identify with both. Such involvement of the reader with a character is rare in science fiction, and the fact that it is achieved at all—albeit imperfectly for the action-adventure-oriented reader—is a tribute to Bester's skill as a novelist. And it is with a slow sense of recognition that we come to understand that the detective-villain surface story has been transmuted into profound materials relating to themes with which we are all concerned: the meaning of life; ambition; pride; sacrifice; humility; personal growth and development; individuation; death; rebirth; and paternity and filiation.

These themes recur in all of Bester's novels and in many of the short stories as well. All of the protagonists—Powell-Reich, Gully Foyle, and Daniel Curzon of *The Computer Connection* (1975)—illustrate one or another of these great mythic beliefs or conflicts. Powell, for example, "fathers" both Reich and Barbara D'Courtney; Gully fathers himself and becomes son or Son to Joseph and Moira; and Curzon becomes both the son and the father to Sequoya. In one sense, then, all of these characters are reborn, growing into a conscious awareness of their own redemptive natures.

What makes *The Demolished Man* so remarkable is that Bester developed these concepts within the framework not only of the traditional science fiction novel but of the traditional detective story as well. Science fiction has produced very few examples of this kind of melding of genres, but *The Demolished Man* is certainly one of the outstanding manifestations of this linkage. Yet even within the framework of the detective story, Bester's novel presents some interesting variations. It is not a conventional "whodunit" at all: the identity of the murderer, Ben Reich, is known from the first page; his methods are revealed in considerable detail. What is lacking at the start is an understanding of the motives that impel him to his actions. These

motivations are unknown to him and misunderstood by both Lincoln Powell, the detective, and by even the most perceptive reader. To be sure, Bester, like skilled writers of the detective story, scattered enough clues, some hidden and some apparently obvious, to lead both Powell and the reader to the ultimate denouement, but Powell misses most of them, as does the reader.

It is in the psychological overtones of the novel, then, that Bester achieved near-greatness in his writing, making *The Demolished Man* a significant contribution to the hitherto much-maligned genre of science fiction. For Bester was concerned with passions, not profit; with emotions and feelings, not mere plot—although the novel is full of action; with Oedipal conflicts; with the philosophical or metaphysical concepts of good and evil, solipsism, greed, lust, power, justice, retribution, and atonement. The reader gradually becomes aware that Reich's motives are strikingly similar to many of the reader's own, and that, under other circumstances, the reader might also feel impelled—even compelled—to take similar actions. After all, Powell breaks the ethical Esper Code in order to trap Reich; and for much of the book, many readers might actually wish Reich to get away with his crime. Only gradually does the full horror and profundity of his actions dawn on the reader, until eventually sympathy swings away from Reich and the injustices both suffered and perpetrated by him to a desire for his "demolition" by Powell. And when Powell, somewhat slowly for a person of his allegedly superior Esper abilities, discerns that Reich and his half sister, Barbara, are latent Espers and that Reich's motivations are hidden even to himself, we are aware of the essential justness of the novel's conclusion.

Much more could be said about this novel, of course, including some discussion of Bester's ability to portray female characters and the inventiveness of his dialogue. Both are exceptional qualities for a time when the typical science fiction novel was often little more than thud and blunder among the stars. In sum, though, it must be said that *The*

Demolished Man remains a distinguished work, very worthy of being awarded the first Hugo award for best novel of the year in 1953.

Bester's *The Stars My Destination* (*Galaxy Science Fiction*, October 1956–January 1957) is in every way an excellent successor to *The Demolished Man*. Although not a sequel in any sense of the word, *The Stars My Destination* deals with many of the same themes. These include power, revenge, superhuman abilities, and a potential systemwide evil that stems from the untrammeled greed of scienceless businessmen and power brokers.

The novel's hero or protagonist is Gully Foyle—and surely his name must remind us both of the Gulliver of Jonathan Swift and the concept of a "foil," or contrast, in the dramatic sense—who seems a concentrated incarnation of the attributes of the superhero. Just as the double hero of *The Demolished Man*, Reich-Powell or Powell-Reich, represented the polarities of good and evil, so those opposing qualities are embodied in Foyle. He represents both positive and negative aspects of humanity. On one level, Foyle is almost a conventional action-adventure hero driven by a single, overwhelming desire for revenge. He has been abandoned to die in space by the rocket ship *Vorga*, and he is obsessed with a need to avenge himself on the crew. To Foyle, the end, vengeance, justifies any means utilized to achieve it; and he chooses murder, rape, intrigue, and villainy of almost every type as he madly pursues his enemies.

Gradually, though, Foyle learns that until he conquers his inner self—what Jung would call the "shadow"—he can never become free of his obsession. The shadow is symbolized by his loathsome, tigerlike facial tattoos, which are visible only when he becomes angry and loses control of his animal passions. This face compares notably with Reich's Man With No Face, the shadow or faceless monster that Bester avers is, to a greater or lesser extent, present in all of us. In Foyle the tattooed tiger mask is the "fearful symmetry" of William Blake's poem "The Tyger," which radiates rage and hatred. Until the tiger within Foyle

is overcome, he can never become the true superman he is capable of being.

One of the most interesting characteristics of *The Stars My Destination* is its utilization of elements from Alexandre Dumas' romantic novel *The Count of Monte Cristo* (1844–1845). Bester has acknowledged his debt to Dumas' book, and the central section of *The Stars My Destination* demonstrates the similarities. Foyle, like Dumas' hero Edmond Dantes, is imprisoned in an ostensibly escape-proof underground fortress. Like Dantes, Foyle is aided in his escape by a fellow prisoner who teaches him how to survive in the outside world. Foyle discovers a huge secret treasure, as did Dantes, and soon transforms himself by adopting the identity of Geoffrey Fourmyle, a mysterious, frivolous, wealthy socialite apparently interested only in the pursuit of entertainment and pleasure.

Yet it would be a mistake to read *The Stars My Destination* as merely a science fiction version of the Dumas novel. Rather, Bester transformed the Monte Cristo myth into a symbolic escape from the underground of unconsciousness to the surface of consciousness, eventually leading to the stars of super-consciousness. This profound transformation of Foyle from supervillain to genuine superhero is at the heart of the novel. He gradually comes to abhor his tiger-self and the images of fire and flame with which it is constantly identified. He learns to "jaunte"—teleport—himself, but he gradually becomes aware of still another symbolic figure that seems to accompany him, the Burning Man. Only with the greatest effort does Foyle learn that the Burning Man is not a symbol of rage, but of love. He—hence all humanity—must burn with compassion, self-sacrifice, and coopera-tion for the common good. The symbol, extended, implies that every man, not merely Foyle, is a potential superman. In this notion Bester echoed Powell's concluding affirmation in chapter 17 of *The Demolished Man*: "Listen, normals! . . . there is nothing in man but love and faith, courage and kindness, generosity and sacrifice. All else is only the barrier of your blindness."

Foyle's fundamental evolution, then, is one to which he comes only very slowly. While he begins by being obsessed with his almost overwhelming passion for revenge on the *Vorga* and the persons responsible for his abandonment in space, he eventually becomes aware of the fact that he is the key to the secret of PyrE. In fact, it could be maintained that PyrE symbolizes the great potential of Foyle's emerging consciousness, for PyrE, in Bester's words, is "the equivalent of the primordial protomatter which exploded into the Universe." Thus a lust to control PyrE's incredible power, whether by Foyle or by the men who were ultimately responsible for his near-death in space, must be subsumed under the figure of the Burning Man, who represents all that is essentially good in humanity—love, caring, sacrifice, intuition, and a cooperative consciousness for the good of all. In the end, Foyle has become reborn as he distributes small amounts of PyrE to ordinary people, with the conviction that they—and hence, by extension, Bester's readers—will be reborn to remake their worlds by remaking themselves in the image of the Burning Man.

Both novels, then, deal with the death of a selfish, almost cruel, insensate psyche, and its rebirth into genuinely superior dimensions. In a thematic sense it could be maintained that *The Stars My Destination* is more of a sequel to *The Demolished Man* than appears on the surface. Whereas the first novel ends with Reich about to undergo the demolition of his fragmented and distorted psyche that will ultimately lead to his rebirth as a mature individual, *The Stars My Destination* tells the story of that rebirth or resurrection. Foyle has learned to integrate the powers of his unconscious, and thus to become a true superhero, perhaps even a savior. To indicate this new dimension of selfhood, Bester utilized an amazing variety of literary techniques, both typographical and stylistic, so that the reader can almost empathetically respond to the synthesthesia that superhumanity implies. It is a brilliant achievement.

Bester's hatred of regimentation culminated in his acerbic caricatures of the conformist mentality, the "Mr. Prestos" who have reshaped their bodies and minds to the plastic projections of the big-business magnates of *The Stars My Destination*. Bester found the robotic tendency in humanity abhorrent. We have all become psychological cripples, he seemed to be saying, and must be liberated from oppression of all types in order to become truly individual. As examples of this psychological determinism, Bester created an extensive array of minor characters, both men and women, who inhabit the novel. Robin Wednesbury, Jisabella McQueen, Saul Dagenham, and Presteign of Presteign all exhibit some serious injury to their personalities: they are all damaged souls, even as Gully Foyle is. In presenting the possibility of Foyle's growth in awareness of his human potential, Bester seemed to be saying that such growth is possible for us all.

For many years after the publication of these two novels, Bester wrote little science fiction aside from an occasional short story. He became one of the editors of *Holiday* magazine, and his sympathetic accounts of travel in many lands provided science fiction readers with an almost painful awareness of how great a talent was lost to the science fiction field when Bester chose to concentrate his writing on the lure of faraway places on Earth rather than amid the stars.

Then, nineteen years after the publication of *The Stars My Destination*, *The Computer Connection* appeared. (It was first serialized in *Analog* as "The Indian Giver" in 1974.) Few books were more eagerly awaited, and few were more disappointing. Indeed, *The Computer Connection* seemed like a reworking of the themes of both *The Demolished Man* and *The Stars My Destination* but lacked the firm control over the materials shown in the first two novels. Bester's major concerns in *The Computer Connection* were still the inhumanity of man to man; death and rebirth; good and evil—all coupled with a slam-bang story so intricately plotted that the reader feels almost awash in the action and lost in a plot that is difficult, almost impossible to follow. Again the characters are bizarre, but their individuality seems eccentric rather than integral to the novel. The hero, Daniel (often called "Edward") Curzon, is a "Molecular Man" who has been resurrected and given an immortality that seems purposeless to him. Although he combines elements of Foyle, Reich, and Powell in his nature, he lacks their demonic drive and sometimes seems merely amused or dispassionately uninvolved rather than integrally whole, as one might expect a resurrected human to be.

The Computer Connection is even more apocalyptic than either of the other two novels. In it the world is threatened by overwhelmingly powerful machines, personified by a demonic "Extrocomputer," a supercomputer whose very existence augurs the end of humanity. Plots and counterplots against the machine play against each other in a headlong, pell-mell story whose pace never slackens and is continually punctuated by Bester's typographical eccentricities. To be sure, Bester wanted to make the eye, ear, and mind of the reader merge into a whole that is greater than the sum of its parts; but whereas he was eminently successful with that technique in both of the earlier books, his use of typographical oddities in *The Computer Connection* appears to be almost supererogatory, even a parody of his distinctive style.

Yet *The Computer Connection* is in itself something more than the sum of its disparate parts. While many readers have viewed it as, in effect, either self-parody or a parody of many tired science fiction devices of other writers, the total effect of the novel is still one of a search for personal redemption and a struggle against dehumanization. Certainly this work may not stir the reader in quite the same way as Bester's two earlier novels, but it remains consistently interesting.

Although Bester's first two novels have received the larger share of critical study, his short fiction is just as worthy of note as his longer works. Perhaps the best, and certainly the handiest, collection of his stories is *Starlight: The Great Short Fiction of Alfred Bester*, published in 1976. Its sixteen stories include such favorites as "Adam and No Eve"

(1941), "Fondly Fahrenheit" (1954), and "The Men Who Murdered Mohammed" (1958). Reading them again, all at one sitting, one can see how the promise of the early stories prepared the way for the major writer of the novels. Almost all of the Besterian devices are there: headlong action, situation piled on situation, direct—almost shattering—appeals to the senses and emotions, and bold experiment after bold experiment.

For example, the wordplay of "5,271,009" (1954) matches anything in the novels. We see it not only in the name Jeffrey Halsyon but also in the triple, and quadruple, multilingual puns that fill the story. Bester's obsession with pattern and dynamics shows in "The Pi Man" (1959), and his inability to resist a bad pun clearly surfaces with a hero named Dr. Skiaki, who—well, never mind. Yet in most, if not all, of these stories, Bester demonstrated his technical ability, his careful craftsmanship, his attention to detail. Moreover, *Starlight* is a particularly valuable collection because it contains a Bester-written introduction to every story, as well as his marvelously revealing essay "My Affair with Science Fiction," reprinted from *Hell's Cartographers*, the 1975 collection of science fiction writers' autobiographies edited by Harry Harrison and Brian W. Aldiss.

In the newly written introductions to the stories, as well as in the autobiographical statement, Bester reveals himself at least as fully as he does in his prose fiction. It has long been obvious to any discerning reader that Bester had many fine qualities: he was sensitive to the feelings and emotions of human beings, he approached any topic with enthusiasm, and the results of his study usually emerge in the fiction. Thus we learn of his interest in Freud, and the Viennese master's concepts surface in both the stories and the novels, most notably in *The Demolished Man*. Bester's humor is wry, penetrating, acerbic, and often self-deprecating—all of these qualities also emerge in his short stories and are made explicit in his introductions. For example, he says, "I've had an intrapersonal love-hate relationship with Alfred Bester for many years, and I can honestly report that while he is trustworthy, loyal, helpful, friendly, courteous, kind, obedient, cheerful, thrifty, brave, clean, and reverent, he is also rotten to the core" *(Starlight)*.

What seem to be the most outstanding characteristics in Bester's stories are not the expected qualities of delight, careful craftsmanship, and insight, but his ability to utilize some of the oldest science fiction devices and to infuse them with a spirit uniquely his own. Certainly the best example is "Adam and No Eve." Although published in 1941, it still has considerable impact. To be sure, the story is dated in some inconsequential ways, but the ending has fascinated several generations of readers as the implications of the final sentences become clear: "Steven Krane smiled up at the stars, stars that were sprinkled evenly across the sky. Stars that had not yet formed into the familiar constellations, and would not for another hundred million years."

Was Bester suggesting that humanity will undergo—has undergone—some sort of inevitable catastrophe here? Perhaps, yet hope for life—indeed, the certain knowledge that life will endure—infuses, almost mystically, the conclusion of the story. Bester, in other words, remade the Adam and Eve story into some memorable writing. Not all of Bester's stories are this haunting. Some are joyous, some merely joyful. They are witty, literate, tragic, sometimes silly and meaningless, but also, at the same time, serious and meaningful.

In 1978, Simon and Schuster announced the purchase of Bester's newest novel, *Golem*[100]. Science fiction readers the world over had been eagerly awaiting its publication. In a letter Bester indicated something of its nature and the attendant difficulties in its actual production: "I've carried my concept for visio-narrative style to extra-ordinary lengths in *Golem*. There are pages of pure graphics and scenes written in full [musical] score form. In my attempt to convey deep unconscious images I've extrapolated Rorschach's 'inkblots' into what I call 'idblots.' All this presents tricky production problems." As a result of

these problems, the novel did not appear until 1980.

Even before the novel appeared, there was little doubt in the minds of readers that the incisive exploration of the unconscious, begun so well in the first two novels, would be continued in *Golem*[100]. Bester's attempt, though, was not entirely successful. Despite its verbal prestidigitation, *Golem*[100] was not well received by fans and critics. Although the book presented some problems of transmuting the printed page into the consciousness and unconsciousness of the reader, it can certainly be averred that Bester always desired an active and involved reader. His works, from short stories to novels, have demanded more from his readers than the pabulum some of his contemporaries have produced. Bester was very aware of this problem. He once said, "The mature science fiction author doesn't merely tell a story about Brick Malloy versus The Giant Yeastmen from Gethsemane. He makes a statement through his story. What is the statement? Himself, the dimension and depth of the man."

When Alfred Bester died in 1987, his legacy was assured—two significant novels that should belong on any science fiction "Top Ten" list and some truly fine short stories, as well as memories of the man. It is the dimension and depth of Bester himself that we ultimately perceive from the cumulative effect of his works. The late James Blish once described Bester as the nicest man in the world whose feet still touch the ground, and anyone who ever met him will recall his intentness as he listened, his wit and his insights as he responded, and the erudition with which he sprinkled his conversation. Even one meeting in, say, a Dublin hotel pub, will never be forgotten.

Prior to his death, he also finished a mainstream novel about life among the so-called intelligentsia in affluent New York City in the 1950's. Probably written in the 1960's, this book, *Tender Loving Rage* (1991), remained unpublished until years after his death. The novel deals with the advertising business, which Bester knew well, and is also a detective story combined with more than a hint of romantic involvement.

The manuscript had suffered a miserable history of abandonment, revision, and rejection. Its ultimate publication came about only because one of Bester's friends, Charles Platt, probably the only person from the science fiction world to visit him during his final years in his refuge in an old but refurbished Pennsylvania farmhouse, spent the time, energy, and money necessary to shepherd the novel from posthumous manuscript into a long-delayed publication. How it all happened as well as the story of Bester's death in a convalescent home has been told at length by Platt in *Science Fiction Eye* (November 1991).

Virtually ignored by both the general reading public and the science fiction community, *Tender Loving Rage* is nonetheless unmistakably a Bester novel. His writing, even in this unfortunately most neglected novel, has as much vitality as either of the two great science fiction works, and even while unconventional and dated, it can still stir readers. Platt remarks, however, that "there was another reason why publishers [and readers] rejected the book. Bester had chosen to eulogize the vitality of a lifestyle that was in fact middle-aged, soon to be senescent."

The fact that Bester, almost as a lark or in his isolated depression, willed his house, his money, and his entire literary estate to his bartender cannot be overlooked as well. In the end he turned his back on the life that had largely ignored or forgotten this brilliant shooting star. As part of his legacy, moreover, he also left an unfinished science fiction novel, which the late Roger Zelazny completed. *Psychoshop*, with an introduction by Greg Bear, was published by Vintage in 1998, thus adding to Bester's relatively slim science fiction bibliography. While it is difficult if not impossible to tell where Bester left off and Zelazny began in *Psychoshop*, the "Besterman" has returned in the lead character Alf Noir—and his exploits comprise most of the novel. This book is eccentric and offbeat as well as being jammed with new ideas and considerable fun. Suffice it to say that both authors of this novel contributed to bringing the fame of Alfred Bester to a new generation. Vintage also deserves considerable credit for keeping Bester's books in print in handsome new editions.

Bester was a deeply concerned writer who genuinely cared for human beings, their potential for greatness, their constant struggle against dehumanization. He was, in the classic sense of the word, a virtuous man, filled with the attributes of strength and love as he urged that the Tiger or the Burning Man in all of us be transformed almost alchemically into goodness and love. His lasting legacy as exemplified in his two great novels is that the stars and the interior challenge that they represent are truly our destination.

Selected Bibliography

WORKS OF ALFRED BESTER

The Demolished Man. Chicago: Shasta Publishing Company, 1953; London: Sidgwick and Jackson, 1953.
Tiger! Tiger! London: Sidgwick and Jackson, 1956. Reprinted as *The Stars My Destination*, New York: New American Library, 1957.
The Computer Connection. New York: Berkley Publishing, 1975. Reprinted as *Extro*, London: Methuen, 1975.
The Light Fantastic. New York: Berkley Publishing, 1976; London: Victor Gollancz, 1977.
Star Light, Star Bright. New York: Berkley Publishing, 1976; London: Victor Gollancz, 1978.
Starlight: The Great Short Fiction of Alfred Bester. Garden City, N.Y.: Nelson Doubleday Science Fiction Book Club, 1976. (Reprints *The Light Fantastic* and *Star Light, Star Bright*, and Alfred Bester's "My Affair with Science Fiction.")
Golem[100]. New York: Simon and Schuster, 1980. (Illustrated by Jack Gaughan.)
Tender Loving Rage. Houston, Tex.: Tafford, 1991.
Virtual Realities: The Short Fiction of Alfred Bester. Edited by Robert Silverberg. New York: Vintage, 1991.
Psychoshop, with Roger Zelazny. New York: Vintage, 1998.

CRITICAL AND BIOGRAPHICAL STUDIES

Hipolito, Jane. "The Stars My Destination." In *Survey of Science Fiction Literature.* Vol. 5. Edited by Frank Magill. Englewood Cliffs, N.J.: Salem Press, 1979.

McNelly, Willis E. "The Demolished Man." In *Survey of Science Fiction Literature.* Vol. 2. Edited by Frank Magill. Englewood Cliffs, N.J.: Salem Press, 1979.

——, and Jane Hipolito. "The Statement Is the Self: The Science Fiction of Alfred Bester." In *The Stellar Gauge.* Edited by Michael Tolley and Kirpal Singh. Sidney, Australia: Norstrilia Press, 1980.

Nicholls, Peter. "Starlight: The Great Short Fiction of Alfred Bester." In *Survey of Science Fiction Literature.* Vol. 5. Edited by Frank Magill. Englewood Cliffs, N.J.: Salem Press, 1979.

Platt, Charles. "Alfred Bester's 'Tender Loving Rage.'" *Science Fiction Eye,* no. 9 (November 1991).

—WILLIS E. McNELLY

MICHAEL BISHOP
(b. 1945)

MICHAEL BISHOP IS a nomadic writer whose work ranges across galaxies, species, millenia, and social classes. Always artistically on the move, Bishop has produced a still-growing body of work that includes novels, collections of short stories, and poetry. The breadth of his output has its roots in the details of his own biography, but as a writer, he must transfigure the biography, through complex networks of experience, into the bibliography.

Bishop was born on 14 November 1945, in Lincoln, Nebraska. His father, Lee, was stationed on Saipan in the months immediately following World War II, and his mother, née Maxine ("Mac") Matison returned to her hometown to give birth to their son. Bishop, in his autobiographical reminiscence "Military Brat" (1997), notes that his mother wanted to write, while his father preferred hunting, fishing, and playing the field with the women.

In 1950, with the marriage already under severe strain, the Bishops moved to Tokyo, where the family had housing in Washington Heights, an Americanized area where children of both countries played cowboys and Indians. Here, at a young age, Bishop's self-perception, memory, and most importantly for his career as a writer, his imagination began to be shaped by the push and pull of the familiar and the exotic, the self and the other. Surely, even then, the category of the "alien" was slowly taking shape.

Bishop and his mother returned to Wichita, Kansas, and then moved to nearby Mulvane, which Bishop regards as his "real" hometown.

But even in Mulvane, the nomadism continued, as the family lived in five different houses. For a short period, Bishop acquired a first stepfather (Howard Miller), but more importantly, he kept up his relationship with Lee, traveling every summer to be with his father in Wyoming, Colorado, Illinois, Tennessee, and, finally, across the Atlantic to Spain.

In 1962, on the cusp of adulthood, Bishop joined his father and stepmother for a summer in Seville, Spain, where he edited and contributed to the high school literary magazine, *El Toreador*. When he shuttled back across the Atlantic, Bishop entered the University of Georgia, where he majored in English, took creative writing classes, and met Jeri Whitaker, whom he married in 1969.

In the summer of 1968, with an M.A. and a thesis on Dylan Thomas in hand, Bishop had gone to the U.S. Air Force Academy prep school to begin to teach. His office mate, Klaus Krause, suggested that Bishop try to crack the science fiction market. Soon after, he sold his first story, "Piñon Fall" (1970), to *Galaxy* magazine, and a prolific career, still charting unexpected pathways, had truly gotten under way.

Bishop's work has achieved consistent critical acclaim in the science fiction community. From 1973 to 1998, sixteen of his short fiction works were nominated for Hugo or Nebula awards; five were nominated for both, and "The Quickening" won the Nebula for best novelette in 1981. Many of his short pieces have been anthologized in annual collections such as *Annual World's Best Science Fiction*. "The Bob Dylan Tambourine Software and Satori Support Services Consortium, Ltd." (1985; reprinted in *At the City Limits of Fate*, 1996) was included in the *Norton Book of Science Fiction* (1993). His novel *No Enemy but Time* (1982) received a Nebula award, *Brittle Innings* (1995) was a Hugo nominee, and *Unicorn Mountain* (1988) received the Mythopoeic Society's Fantasy Award. His work has been frequently reviewed in science fiction trade journals such as *Locus* and the *New York Science Fiction Review*, but it has also drawn attention from more mainstream critical outlets such as the *New York Times Book Review*. Bishop is active as a critic and anthologist as well as an author; he has edited three volumes of Nebula award stories and written numerous reviews of science fiction works.

Scholarly work focusing on Bishop falls into two major categories. The first comprises bibliographies, of which perhaps the most accessible are Lloyd Curry's in the *New York Review of Science Fiction* and Michael Hutchins' admirably inclusive and well-organized Internet site. The second category, nonbibliographic works focusing specifically on Bishop, is as yet sparsely represented; extant works covering multiple novels include William Senior's "Silence and Disaster in the Novels of Michael Bishop" (*New York Review of Science Fiction*, August 1996) and Ian Watson's "A Rhetoric of Recognition" (*Foundation*, June 1980).

Bishop is a prolific writer of short fiction who uses the medium to experiment with styles and genres. His early work, beginning with the publication of "Piñon Fall," is well within the science fiction genre, utilizing aliens and extraplanetary contexts, but distinctly avoids the "gimmick" school of science fiction in which the plot is centered on some artifact of technology or quirk of alien biology. Characteristically, Bishop focuses on the personal and social interactions of his characters. "Blooded on Arachne" (1975), for example, contains elements of the familiar "alien landscape survival" plot, but Bishop

turns it into a statement about maturation and exploitation. The fantastical "Rogue Tomato" (1975) uses a planet-sized vegetable to make a religious statement. Even in his early work, however, Bishop is unconstrained by genre boundaries; "Leaps of Faith" (1977), a treatment of insanity, contains "science" as an element but is more mainstream literary fiction. His later work continues to explore new literary avenues, including postmodernism ("000-00-0000" [1986]) and horror ("Icicle Music" [1989]). Much of his short fiction has been published in five anthologies: *Blooded on Arachne* (1982), *One Winter in Eden* (1984), *Close Encounters with the Deity* (1986), *Emphatically Not Science Fiction, Almost* (1990), and *At the City Limits of Fate* (1996). Especially recommended are *Close Encounters* and *City Limits*, both of which contain some of his best short fiction and exemplify his treatment of religion and connection, although strong pieces are to be found in the other works as well.

Bishop's first novel, *A Funeral for the Eyes of Fire* (1975), later rewritten as *Eyes of Fire* (1980), involves a human protagonist who must negotiate among alien groups. The majority polity on the planet Trope, a rationalist society, wishes to arrange the deportation of a spiritualist minority sect that it despises to an irrational extent. Gunnar Balduin, forced to represent the Glaparcans, who wish to use the deportees as cheap labor, is thrust into the volatile situation with virtually no preparation. The result is a tragedy of errors in which Gunnar catalyzes the deportation at great cost to himself and to the spiritualists. Bishop was deeply dissatisfied with the novel, going so far as to say that he wished people would lose their copies.

In the rewritten version, *Eyes of Fire*, Bishop develops the alien cultures in more detail and adds a note of gender commentary. The androgynous Tropeans are capable of adopting masculine or feminine personas; the majority rationalists are exclusively masculine, viewing femininity as a disorder and a crime. Rather than leading to harmony, the Tropiard's androgyny has led to denial. Definitely a better novel than the original, it nevertheless does not rank as one of Bishop's best.

In 1976, Bishop published *And Strange at Ecbatan the Trees* and, in 1977, *A Little Knowledge. And Strange at Ecbatan the Trees* deals with the notion of enclosure and stasis. Confined by evolutionarily superior "Parfects" to a reservation planet, civilized humans must try to deal with the threat of barbarian invasion without drawing down the wrath of their distantly observing jailers. In a world where technological advancement is effectively prohibited, the protagonists work toward social change. Essentially a novella, *Ecbatan* is distinguished primarily by its "fantastical" tone, which is unlike most of Bishop's other writing except for some of his short fiction.

A Little Knowledge displays two themes that are common in Bishop's work: speculative theology and dystopic representations of power and bureaucracy. In a future Atlanta that has enclosed itself both physically, with a dome, and culturally, with a repressive regime mandating a fundamentalist religion, the population must deal with the arrival of several aliens, the Cygnostikoi, whose offer to convert to the state-approved religion triggers religious and political change. Through the Cygnostikoi, Bishop experiments with the question of what reincarnation would mean in a world with multiple intelligent species and the effect that change has on a closed society. A slightly altered version of the Cygnostikoi, the Kybers, are the focus of the 1981 novel *Under Heaven's Bridge*, cowritten with Ian Watson, which again deals with theological questions as Bishop provides a futuristic treatment of a Manichaean position. A set of short stories set in the same milieu was assembled with para-historical notes and published as *Catacomb Years* (1979).

Long interested in anthropology, Bishop incorporated a number of classic anthropological questions in his sixth novel, *Transfigurations* (1979), an expansion of "Death and Designation Among the Asadi" (1973). The Asadi are presented as a theoretical Gordian Knot—a problem without a solution—as the

Michael Bishop in 1978. PHOTO BY JAY RAY KLEIN

anthropologists studying them are confronted by seemingly irrational behavior that they must attempt to make sense of, presenting them with the twin dilemmas of interpretation: How does the analyst know that his account represents any form of truth, and how does an analyst deal impartially with a culture that revolts him?

No Enemy but Time (1982) and *Ancient of Days* (1985) combine Bishop's interest in anthropology with statements about wider social issues. Both novels involve protohuman "habilines" (*homo habilis*) as primary characters, and to some extent they are mirror images of each other. *No Enemy but Time* chronicles a human living in a habiline world, while *Ancient of Days* involves a habiline living in the modern South. *No Enemy but Time* is notable both for design and for execution; Bishop combines a time-traveling plot with interwoven narrative time lines, introducing the novel with a trope based on rearranging the slides in a slide show.

In *No Enemy but Time*, Joshua Kampa, a man who has been afflicted with unusually detailed dreams of Pleistocene Africa since infancy, takes part in an experiment that returns him to a kind of quantum "shadowpast" of his dreams. There he interacts with the habiline inhabitants, becoming part of their society and fathering a child before returning to the present. Bishop deliberately sets up interesting ambiguities in his treatment of time travel; although the past Kampa visit is supposedly unreal, the child he fathers is able to return with him. A marvelous evocation of models of protohuman life, the novel addresses the question of what "humanity" means while incorporating a strain of wry humor that has come to characterize many of Bishop's later works.

Ancient of Days continues this examination of humanity by exploring society's reactions to difference. An expansion of a short story, "Her Habiline Husband" (1983), the novel features a habiline, Adam, who is discovered near a small southern town. From the outset, Bishop creates parallels between the treatment of Adam and the treatment of minorities in the South; as a rationale for Adam's presence, for example, it is discovered that his ancestors were kidnapped from central Africa and sold as "novelty slaves." Adam becomes the center of a number of controversies. After marrying a human woman, he becomes the target of Ku Klux Klan activity and creates a theological dilemma in his persistent search for spirituality. Far from reconstituting the "noble savage" figure, Bishop creates an image of spirituality as a civilizing force, one that Adam's supposedly civilized detractors frequently lack. The novel makes stronger social statements than *No Enemy but Time* and presents a combination of humor and pathos, but it reads more like a set of three connected novellas than as a single novel.

Who Made Stevie Crye? (1984), a fantasy novel, relates the protagonist's encounter with a diabolical electric typewriter that has an agenda of its own. Although this novel never makes a sufficiently serious claim on the reader, it does allow Bishop to play with the problems of postmodern authorship, such as the connections between a writer and the "machine" of writing.

The Secret Ascension (1987) is also published under the title *Philip K. Dick Is Dead, Alas.* Set in an alternate history in which King Richard Nixon rules the United States, this novel pays homage to Dick, the late science fiction writer, by extending Dick's concerns about political freedom and spiritual realization. The story moves from a small town in Georgia to the first moon base, where the final showdown occurs as an unlikely group of people works an exorcism on King Richard. Dick (the novelist) himself, in provisionally reincarnated forms, shows up throughout the novel to serve as a spiritual instigator. The exorcism is successful, but Philip Kyle Dick (Dick, the novelist, has the middle name Kindred) has the last word, beginning to write yet another version of the real, knowing, as Bishop knows, that crafting the redemptive shift is an interminable work.

Unicorn Mountain (1988) is another clear example of how Bishop uses the fantastic as a means of social criticism. Bo Gavin, infected with AIDS, goes into the Colorado mountains to live with Sam Coldpony, a Ute, and Libby Quarrels, a woman learning to run a ranch. Sam and Libby encounter a small herd of unicorns, themselves seeking refuge from an epidemic, that have slipped in from a parallel world. The unicorns serve (rather awkwardly) as a kind of emblem of phallic healing and protection and are threatened with crass commodification by the advertising media and the public's obsessive search for the latest and greatest sensation. As the plot develops, the question of healing becomes paramount, and Alma Coldpony, Sam's daughter, undergoes a rite of initiation to become a medicine woman. During the Sun Dance, she realizes that it is her task (much like the fiction writer's) to use her visionary talents to bring a new perspective of wholeness to the community that she serves.

As a critic and anthologist as well as an author, Bishop is extremely conscious of science fiction as a genre and of its (often derided) place within modern American literary and popular culture. In *Count Geiger's Blues* (1992), he presents a postmodern play on the relation between the *Übermensch*—a word that literally translates as "superman" but represents a superior human being in Nietzsche's philosophy—and Superman to illuminate the strained relations between art, kitsch, and science fiction. The protagonist, Xavier Thaxton, a fine-arts critic for a newspaper who is fond of Nietzsche and distinctly unfond of anything popular, is exposed to radiation and gains comic book superhuman abilities as well as a comic book vulnerability: the high art he loves makes him violently ill, while tackiness cures him. Bishop parallels the development of this plot line with one involving the suffering of people exposed to real radiation, keeping the two images in constant juxtaposition. The resulting contrast illuminates both the pathetic and the redeeming aspects of popular culture; Thaxton's most heroic action is a simple one of self-sacrifice that requires no superhuman abilities at all but a very real humanity. The novel is notable both as a treatment of comic books as an icon of popular culture and for its deadpan humor.

In *Brittle Innings*, Bishop once again sets the fantastic in the ordinary world, this time in the American South during the last years of World War II. In this case, it is Dr. Frankenstein's famous monster that has begun to take an interest in self-redemption, writing, and baseball. The novel is narrated by ex-shortstop Danny Ogradnik who, speaking through a "mike" since he has had his vocal cords removed, becomes the medium for the wealth of other stories in the novel: Mister JayMac's tragic marriage, Darius's struggle to break the lines of segregation that governed the South, the hijinks and tragedies of the players on the Highbridge Hellbenders, and Jumbo's quest to evolve from a monster into a human being.

Brittle Innings gathers and transforms all of Bishop's earlier themes and marks a major transition in his work. Essentially about the "second life" of both Daniel and Jumbo, this novel also serves as a marker of the accomplished richness of Bishop's literary voice. Amplified by a "sci-fi gizmo," this voice is infused with the spirit that learns to confront the utter strangeness—we might even say the *alienness*—of human existence.

Perhaps, at least in part, because of Bishop's peripatetic childhood, treatments of otherness and transformation are common elements in his writing. A frequent figure in his writing is the "mediator" character, who participates in the interactions between two or more groups with whom he or she shares characteristics and, by participating, is changed. In *Eyes of Fire*, for example, the protagonist, like the spiritualists he deals with, is a victim, while like the rationalists, he operates from a largely atheistic worldview. He also has an element of gender indeterminacy because part of his victimization involves a rather abusive sexual situation with his older "clone-brother."

The major pair of characters in *And Strange at Ecbatan the Trees* are mixtures of the planet's dominant racial groups; Joshua in *No Enemy but Time* experiences discrimination for being small and being African American, which enables him to identify more closely with the short-statured African hominids he lives with; and Adam of *Ancient of Days* is psychologically more human than the humans around him while physically identical to the habiline remnant he represents. Occasionally, Bishop will set up more than one scheme of mediation—the human protagonists of *Under Heaven's Bridge* mediate between the other humans and the Kybers, while the Kybers mediate between humans and the Divine. The transformations the mediators undergo act to lessen the boundaries between self and other, although the process is not always a pleasant or successful one. While Joshua comes to regard the hominids as equal in their humanity, *Stolen Faces'* (1977) Yeardance is destroyed by attempts to bridge the gap between Tezcatl's normal inhabitants and its muphormers.

Repeatedly, Bishop explores the relative value of rational analysis versus participation in the understanding of others. The pure rationalism of the majority sect in *Eyes of Fire*, for example, prevents them from understanding the spiritualists; they have "modeled" the spiritualist position only so that they can reject it. And the anthropologist trying to study Adam in *Ancient of Days* understands him far

85

less than Adam's wife. Analysis can illuminate difference but never eliminate it, while participation constructs at least the possibility of connection.

Very much connected to otherness, another of Bishop's persistent themes is religion, which appears as a social system, often authoritarian; as various speculative theologies, including a number of dream visions; and as a series of core rituals of sacrifice and exchange. Even in his earliest fiction, these intertwining thematics are at work. For example, *A Little Knowledge* is divided into "Genesis," "Psalms," and "Revelation" and unfolds in an alternative future where the Atlanta Urban Nucleus is governed by the official faith of Ortho-Urbanism. Other forms of religious community are allowed—New Islam, the FUSKONites, blends of Native American spirituality (which returns in the later fiction such as *Unicorn Mountain*—but all are regulated by the Ortho-Urban hierarchy. Into this closed world, however, come the Cygnostikoi, who are soon preparing human beings to return to their home planet to experience another revelation of God.

In the anthropological novels, these religious themes are thoroughly developed. For example, in *Ancient of Days*, Bishop combines all three elements of his quest for religious-philosophical truth, describing what happens when a closed ideology, in this case white supremacism, confronts difference and diversity. When Adam and RuthClaire's son is murdered, Adam responds with cogitations on the nature of the soul. Adam has moved, very quickly, from a signing hominid to a philosopher (although perhaps these two types are more closely related than it at first appears).

While early in the novel Bishop offers a critique of a blind prejudice and develops Adam as an extrapolative theologian, in the final section, Adam becomes a priest on his home island, in the village of Prix-des-Yeux, where the last remaining group of habilines lives. Having passed through various spiritualities—and Bishop is nothing if not an explorer of modern syncretisms that anthropology has done so much to reveal—Adam becomes a priest of *vaudun* (voodoo). Paul, one of the narrators and central characters, is taken back in time and down into the collective unconscious to an original "disclosure event" that defined the habilines as human even before the beginnings of speech. The Ur-divinity that Paul experiences while possessed rips out its own heart and offers it to the habilines.

The spirit, Bishop keeps reminding us, is meat to be torn and eaten. Since we, too, are meat, we, too, are to be sacrificed for the sake of our own, and others', lives. The self and the other must always be in a dynamic relationship of exchange. Carnage and creation are, from the god's perspective, inseparable, and the only way for human beings to provisionally mediate, or even survive, between the two is through some form of sacrificial ritual.

Michael Bishop is a writer who has wandered a great deal—both in his personal life and in his fiction—but he is also one who has settled deeply into both the American South and a constellation of concerns whose mysteries he continues to untangle. Among these, the major themes are spiritual knowledge, transformations, and a critique of social control and prejudice. Perhaps underlying these themes as well as the very decision to become a fiction writer, there are the dynamics of exchange between the self and the other, an exchange that requires sacrifice, vision, and an eye for the monstrous as well as the miraculous. Bishop rarely presents neat, unambiguous resolutions to his experiments in narrative; rather, he invites the reader to participate in an unfolding process that has a number of potential futures but no determined destiny.

Selected Bibliography

WORKS OF MICHAEL BISHOP

A Funeral for the Eyes of Fire. New York: Ballantine, 1975. Revised edition, *Eyes of Fire*, New York: Pocket Books, 1980.

And Strange at Ecbatan the Trees. New York: Harper and Row, 1976. Reprinted as *Beneath the Shattered Moons,* New York: DAW, 1977.

A Little Knowledge. New York: Berkley/Putnam, 1977.

Stolen Faces. New York: Harper and Row, 1977.

Beneath the Shattered Moons. London: Sphere, 1978. (Includes "The White Otters of Childhood.")

Catacomb Years. New York: Berkley/Putnam, 1979. (Short stories.)

Transfigurations. New York: Berkley/Putnam, 1979.

Under Heaven's Bridge, with Ian Watson. London: Gollancz, 1981; New York: Ace, 1982.

Blooded on Arachne. Sauk City, Wisc.: Arkham House, 1982. (Short stories.)

No Enemy but Time. New York: Timescape, 1982.

One Winter in Eden. Sauk City, Wisc.: Arkham House, 1984. (Short stories.)

Who Made Stevie Crye? Sauk City, Wisc.: Arkham House, 1984.

Ancient of Days. New York: Arbor House, 1986.

Close Encounters with the Deity. Atlanta, Ga.: Peachtree, 1986. (Short stories.)

The Secret Ascension. New York: TOR, 1987. Reprinted as *Philip K. Dick Is Dead, Alas,* London: Grafton, 1988.

Unicorn Mountain, New York: Arbor House, 1988.

And Strange at Ecbatan the Trees. New York: TOR, 1990. (Includes "The Color of Neanderthal Eyes.")

Emphatically Not Science Fiction, Almost. In *Author's Choice Monthly,* no. 15. Eugene, Oreg.: Pulphouse, 1990. (Short stories.)

Count Geiger's Blues. New York: TOR, 1992.

Brittle Innings. New York: Bantam, 1995.

At the City Limits of Fate. Cambridge, Mass.: Edgewood, 1996. (Short stories.)

CRITICAL AND BIOGRAPHICAL STUDIES

Bishop, Michael. "Military Brat." In *Contemporary Authors Autobiography Series.* Vol. 26. Detroit, Mich.: Gale Research, 1997.

Curry, Lloyd W. "Works in Progress: Michael Bishop." *New York Review of Science Fiction,* 42(1992): 22–23.

Hutchins, Michael. "A Michael Bishop Bibliography." Internet site: www.mindspring.com/~mhhutchins/bishop.htm. September 1998.

Senior, William A. "Silence and Disaster in the Novels of Michael Bishop." *New York Review of Science Fiction,* 96 (1996).

Watson, Ian. "A Rhetoric of Recognition: The Science Fiction of Michael Bishop." *Foundation,* 19 (1980): 5–14.

—GRAY KOCHHAR-LINDGREN
—WILLIAM SPRUIELL

JAMES BLISH

(1921–1975)

OF ALL AMERICAN science fiction writers of the first rank, perhaps none was less suited by nature and accomplishments for the role, and none worked harder at giving value for money, than James Blish. He was an impatient, cultured, pessimistic intellectual who spent most of the last years of his life writing *Star Trek* stories, and whose very last work was an essay defining the science fiction genre as a literary manifestation of the final stage of the decline of the West, in strict accordance with the predictions of Oswald Spengler. *Spock Must Die!* (1970) and "Probapossible Prolegomena to Ideareal History" (written in the hospital before his death on 30 July 1975; published in *Foundation* 13, May 1978) come from the same pen. We shall try to understand how.

Although intelligence is by no means necessary for success, most writers are vigorously intelligent, however well they may disguise the fact by keeping a low personal profile, avoiding the expression of polemical or elitist opinions, and writing to the lower end of the market. On the other hand, it is by no means the case that most writers—even most science fiction writers, most of whom at some point must come to grips with ideas and their extrapolations—can be described as being intellectual. A drive toward intense, articulate, structured thought has surprisingly little to do with the creation of inhabitable universes of the imagination, and it may even hinder the thrust and flow of the creative process at work.

Moralistic, scholarly, stubborn, erudite to the point of pedantry and sometimes beyond, Blish was not only an intelligent writer but an intellectual one as well. Throughout his career he showed himself to be singularly uncomfortable with the comparatively simple (but sometimes profound) pleasures and rewards of popular narrative art, and to be constitutionally opposed to the urgent "liquidness" of the romance form—in its gothic and later manifestations—which has supplied contemporary science fiction with most of its basic plot structures, narrative tactics, character types, and iconographic immediacy. As Blish might well have put it, he was not a very good liar. As it might also fairly be put, he found it extremely difficult to tell a story.

It was not enough for Blish to cloak an idea with atmosphere, making it tangible through plotting that conveyed a sense of narrative urgency; for him, the unexamined idea was not worth writing about. The resulting impulse toward hard, sometimes testy, sometimes mulishly digressive metaphysical argument must surely make Blish seem a most unlikely entertainer; and it could certainly be argued with some plausibility that his most popular work, the *Cities in Flight* sequence (assembled 1970), enthralls its readers almost despite him. Time and again in this series—demonstrating what one feels must have been his underlying sense that there was something inherently dishonest, something almost unmanly, in the telling of a good tale—Blish elaborately prepares a narrative and thematic climax, supporting its anticipated presentation with flying buttresses of erudition and background detail, only to back away almost at the moment of resolution with a sour, truncated, offhand reportage of events from an enormous authorial distance.

As a structural potpourri, retroactively assembled out of all internal chronological order from highly disparate material, the *Cities in Flight* sequence proves to be a grab bag of such discordant effects, of which a single example may be sufficient. Chris deFord, the juvenile protagonist of the second part of *Cities in Flight*, undergoes a romantic struggle to attain a significant adult role in the interstellar flying city of New York. We follow Chris's struggle with all our conventional expectations of his success properly raised, and he does initially achieve his ambition; but in the next part of the sequence, where we expect to encounter him at work in the foreground of the ongoing saga, repaying his (and our) book-long preparation for this climax, we shatteringly discover that, offstage, he has been executed by the New York computers because of incompetence.

It may be the case that Blish had no room for deFord, whose juvenile adventures were written after the rest of the series had already seen print. All the same, deFord's dismissal is terribly awkward, or sadistic, or is perhaps illustrative of what Blish may have hoped to demonstrate to his readers about the low truth-bearing capacity of the conventional novel. Because we have identified with Chris deFord, Blish may have argued, we find it hard to believe that he is only one man among many; but he seems to have implied that being the protagonist of one romantic juvenile work does not guarantee a successful life in the next story.

Whether or not commercial science fiction is the proper venue for didactic object lessons of this sort, it is certainly clear that something more complex—and more chilling—than conventional storytelling goes on in any of Blish's serious works. It is also interesting to note, perhaps because of his lack of conviction about the various modes in which stories

can be put, just how many kinds of tales Blish did actually try to tell, and how many technical expedients he did resort to.

Cities in Flight, for instance, is made up of four separate parts: *They Shall Have Stars* (1956) is a novel assembled from two previous novelettes; *A Life for the Stars* (1962) is the juvenile we have already touched upon; *Earthman, Come Home* (1955) is a collection of linked stories that first appeared in the years 1950–1953; *The Triumph of Time* (1958) is a novel of cosmological speculation that brings the series up short by ending the universe. Most of Blish's other novels are made up of short stories either patched together or expanded; there are extrasensory perception stories, space operas, parallel-universe tales, an Edgar Rice Burroughs pastiche, a contemporary novel, a historical novel, a black-magic fantasy, several conventional juveniles, and the whole *Star Trek* sequence of stories mostly based on other writers' teleplays. Author of more than forty books, relentlessly self-explanatory when writing under the pseudonym (William Atheling, Jr.) he reserved for his critical work, as a writer of fiction Blish remains dazzlingly evasive—at once a hack, a scholar, a visionary.

Although he published some of his worst genre fiction in the 1960's and 1970's, in his life and by his influence on others James Benjamin Blish spearheaded the postwar emancipation of science fiction and its writers from the prison of the pulp markets. Born 23 May 1921, in Orange, New Jersey, educated at Rutgers University, where he took a B.S. degree in biochemistry in 1942, and at Columbia University (1944–1946), Blish was as precocious as most science fiction writers and began publishing before he was twenty. None of his early writing is very impressive, and it is not surprising that none of it appeared in *Astounding Science-Fiction* during the years 1939–1942, when John W. Campbell, Jr., was introducing writers like Isaac Asimov, Robert A. Heinlein, and A. E. van Vogt to the readership.

Blish's first story, "Emergency Refueling," appeared in *Super Science Stories* for March

James Blish in 1974. PHOTO BY JAY KAY KLEIN

"Surface Tension," which has become Blish's single most famous story, has been reprinted—alone, in *Best Science Fiction Stories of James Blish* [1965], and with "Sunken Universe," in *The Best of James Blish* [1979]—so that references to this much-read tale should always specify which version is being cited. In Blish's gnarled corpus, such confusions are not infrequent.)

The kind of explanatory framework Blish chose for *The Seedling Stars*—men modified for life on various planets through genetic engineering gradually assert their own humanity by conquering and comprehending their environment—was appropriate because of his formal training and because he had grown to feel that science fiction writers were ignoring the speculative implications of biology, concentrating instead on physics and its technological spin-offs. However awkwardly they may fit together, the component sections of *The Seedling Stars* comprise a pioneering exploration of this theme, one that has become increasingly timely. Genetic engineering—the modification of chromosomes in order to breed new versions of humanity—presents contemporary humanity with a series of profoundly far-reaching decisions that evoke our deepest forebodings about the relationship between knowledge and ethics. Beginning with "Surface Tension," all of Blish's more deeply felt work is mainly concerned with this central debate confronting Faustian (or Frankensteinian) man.

After military service Blish returned to New York and to professional writing, rejoining many of the prewar groups of fans and authors with whom he had been involved as a very young man. The Futurians, as they called themselves, included C. M. Kornbluth, Robert A. W. Lowndes (with whom he collaborated on the unsuccessful *The Duplicated Man* [1959]), Donald A. Wollheim (who became the editor of Ace Books and later founder of DAW Books—and who has, oddly, never published Blish), Frederik Pohl, and Damon Knight, whose acute memoir, *The Futurians* (1977), re-creates the intense reformist ambitions shared by most members in

1940; of the further stories written before his induction into the army, only "Sunken Universe" (1942), published under the pseudonym Arthur Merlyn, merits notice. Taken by itself, "Sunken Universe" lies generically rather close to fantasy; in an unexplained underwater locale, microscopic men with gills lead nasty, short, brutish lives; their history and prospects are opaque. It is entirely typical of Blish that he could not leave this unmeditated vision alone; ten years later, in "Surface Tension" (1952), he published a sequel that rationalized the history of the microhumans and provided them with the beginnings of an epic future. Later still, Blish fitted "Sunken Universe" into the explanatory framework of "Surface Tension," and printed them together as the third of four segments in *The Seedling Stars* (1957), a collection of linked stories that draws further implications from the initial problem and its rationalization. (Confusingly,

91

their attitude toward science fiction. Two of the genre's sharpest and most literate critics—Knight and Blish himself—began writing book reviews at about this time, doing their best to sow the seeds of change. When, at the end of the 1940's, *The Magazine of Fantasy and Science Fiction* and *Galaxy* were inaugurated, former members of the Futurians soon became dominant figures in the genre.

The turn of the decade saw a remarkable changeover of writers, at least in the magazines, where the creative ferment centered. Van Vogt fell silent, and Heinlein stopped writing short stories, as did Asimov a few years later. If there was a kind of vacuum, Blish helped fill it. He was still writing within pulp conventions, and often doing so rather badly—his complex, uneasy talent took a long while to mature, showing again his distinctive imprint, for most science fiction writers do much of their best work very early in their careers—and "Surface Tension" may be the first genuinely impressive work from his pen. By the time it appeared, though, he had become well known in the field for his fiction and criticism, and he had already written his first two novels: *Jack of Eagles* (1952), which began as a short story, "Let the Finder Beware" (1949), and *The Warriors of Day* (1953), originally published in magazine form in 1951.

Dominated by pulp conventions that Blish handled in a workmanlike but gingerly fashion, both novels are failures. In *Jack of Eagles* a heroic quest through dimensions of time and space and a perfunctory love story are intensified, but at the same time vitiated, by learned disquisitions on the nature of extrasensory perception. In *The Warriors of Day* a hapless human is transplanted onto another world to become its savior, but Blish never manages to engage the reader in the melodramatic plot turns this kind of story demands, nor in the lush, highly colored venues through which a superhero in utero is expected to wend his way.

Blish was easily bored, which helps explain the extraordinarily variable quality of his work even during the 1950's, when his ener-

gies were still ample, not yet sapped by the cancer that would ultimately kill him, and when markets were continuing to open left and right for him. Still, although much of what he wrote from 1952 to his death continues to confront the reader with pyrrhic victories of professional grit over natural inclination, more and more frequently Blish began to find subjects that could arouse his full interest and to find narrative strategies able to channel his corrosive, questioning, cold mind.

The surface story of "Common Time" (1953) concerns an astronaut who undergoes the anguish and death-similitude of time dilation and contraction on an interstellar voyage and who comes, cleansed to a tabula rasa, upon a new species. But the story's intense subtext conveys a vivid subliminal rendering of the sexual act, which itself is also a kind of death. (Damon Knight discusses this story in *In Search of Wonder* [1967].)

"Beep" (1954), which later was characteristically weakened by expansion into *The Quincunx of Time* (1973), presents a powerful model of instantaneous universal communication, although the complicated, melodramatic story line bogs the reader down and diverts attention from the central image of a vast, abstract brotherhood of communication. One of the story's assorted protagonists does manage, though, during a long speech, to convey almost directly the Blishian sense of wonder—cogent, distant, contemplative:

> I've heard the commander of a world-line cruiser, traveling from 8873 to 8704 along the world line of the planet Hathshepa, which circles a star on the rim of NGC 4725, calling for help across eleven million light years—but what kind of help he was calling for, or will be calling for, is beyond my comprehension.

Passages of this sort reflect Blish's fidelity to the imaginative universe of his science fiction peers and readership; but other stories passed into new territory. "A Work of Art" (1956) utilizes his long-time obsession with the works of composer Richard Strauss (which, along with his scholarly interest in James Joyce, demonstrates the range of Blish's intellectual ambition) in a tale in which Strauss's mind is reincarnated into that of a mental deficient, sometime in the future. Strauss composes a new opera, but it loses all significance for him during its premiere, and he discovers with relief that the audience is applauding not him but the mind sculptor who had re-created him; Strauss himself is the work of art in question. If conventional hints that the real Strauss's career had declined to mannikin-like repetition are discounted, the work stands as a powerful morality tale about the relation between life and art, authenticity and artifact.

These, and some other stories of the 1950's and 1960's, represent Blish's most assured work as a writer of fiction; he was at no point in his career easy with the novel-length story, perhaps (as has been suggested) because of an incapacity to indulge in nonanalytical tale-telling carried over more than a few edgy pages; and none of his full-length novels—with the possible exception of *Doctor Mirabilis* (1964; revised 1971), which is not science fiction or fantasy—sustains its initial premise with anything like the narrative fluency typical of many writers far less gifted than he was. A recent theory of the novel suggests that Blish was instinctively a writer in the "anatomical" mode most conducive to didactic, satirical exposés of the fictive worlds under examination, rather than a novelist in the traditional sense—but whatever the case may be, his novels are generally hard to read.

As has been hinted, the brilliance of *Cities in Flight* does not lie in the assemblage of its parts but in the momentum of the ideas embodied in it (albeit sometimes obscurely). As we read the sequence now, the motor impulse pacing our comprehension of the whole is an image of the rigor mortis of Western civilization that Blish obtained from Oswald Spengler's *The Decline of the West* (1918); from this decadent world, aided by the invention of the spindizzy, whole cities take off into space, there to make their way through the galaxy as

mobile workshops. The final volume—perhaps frivolously, but to some dramatic effect—transforms Spengler's basic thesis that cultures pass through life cycles just as organic beings do, through a daring embodiment of the idea: John Amalfi, the mayor of New York, passes, as the universe ends, through the final apocalypse to become the literal mold—the literal deep structure—of the entire re-created universe.

After *Cities in Flight*, Blish's most famous and most searching book is *A Case of Conscience* (1958), the first and more coherent section of which was originally published under the same title in magazine form (1953). A spacefaring Jesuit finds, in the newly discovered Lithians, a race apparently devoid of original sin; intense theological discussions lead him to the conclusion that the Lithians are actually creatures of the devil. The inferior second half of the novel carries the potential moral apocalypse they represent to Earth, where the plot dithers to an ambiguous conclusion. *A Case of Conscience* won a Hugo award for best novel in 1959; it is the first part of a trilogy constructed ad hoc, according to Blish's habit in these matters, and ultimately given the title "After Such Knowledge" by him, although none of the books have been published under this rubric.

The second of these investigations into the conflict between science and ethical responsibility is *Doctor Mirabilis*, a historical novel about Roger Bacon; the third comprises *Black Easter* (1968) and its direct sequel, *The Day After Judgment* (1971). In the unrelenting clarity and grimness of *Black Easter*, Blish reached his peak as a writer of exemplary fables. In the years preceding its composition, he and his first wife, literary agent Virginia Kidd, had divorced; he had moved definitively out of the world of American science fiction by resettling in England, near Oxford; and he had had his first operation for cancer. *Black Easter*, the first work of significance after these abrupt transformations, can plausibly be read as a moral warning to humanity and as Blish's personal valediction. In this short, sustained novel, black magic is presented as an authenticated scientific pursuit—as a scholium, a term Blish used very frequently. A group of men gather to raise some fallen angels from hell and to release them upon our sphere to create havoc for a limited period. In the event, not only the minor angels but also Satan himself are released. They violate all the rules of the "game" and devastate the world, being free to do so because, as we are told virtually from the horse's mouth, in the last words of the book, "God is dead."

Blish did not die for several years and typically could not leave *Black Easter* alone. In *The Day After Judgment*, Satan is forced to occupy God's throne and to rule our sphere. With dozens of characters in its short span, the book is aesthetically jumbled, although the arguments about power and responsibility, good and evil, the usurpation of right and its ironic, yet inevitable comeuppance are clear enough. During his final years Blish's creative energy was drastically limited; beyond the *Star Trek* stories, which if nothing else gave him financial security, he wrote nothing of note in his last half-decade, except for one novel (*Midsummer Century*, 1972) and, as a coda, dying, that one final essay in which he tried to define the genre to which he had devoted such great effort, supplying it with material open to the play of thought. In this last application of Spengler to our world, Blish concluded:

> *Science fiction is the internal (intracultural) literary form taken by syncretism in the West.* It adopts as its subject matter that occult area where a science in decay (elaborately decorated with technology) overlaps the second religiousness.

In Spengler's analysis of the deep winter of a culture, the jumbled, nostalgia-obsessed, decorative, infighting, faddish art representative of this dying civilization is referred to as "syncretism." Blish's final serious novel, the serene, elegiac, effortlessly readable *Midsummer Century*, by no means contradicts this dark picture, but it does provide some solace. His consciousness cast forward in time by a technological mishap, the disembodied protagonist of this book—more a vision of the contemplative mind than a character—oversees various stages of history, intervenes casually, interacts with a vast computer, remains in essence a mind observing the passionate, self-entangled illusoriness of the physical world of plots and death. That mind, one likes to think, was the mind of James Blish.

Selected Bibliography

WORKS OF JAMES BLISH

Jack of Eagles. New York: Greenberg Publisher, 1952. Retitled *ESPer.* New York: Avon Books, 1958. London: Faber and Faber, 1973.

The Warriors of Day. New York: Galaxy Publishing, 1953.

Earthman, Come Home. New York: G. P. Putnam's Sons, 1955. London: Faber and Faber, 1956. (Collection of linked stories.)

They Shall Have Stars. London: Faber and Faber, 1956. Retitled, with revisions, *Year 2018!* New York: Avon Books, 1957.

The Frozen Year. New York: Ballantine Books, 1957. Retitled *Fallen Star.* London: Faber and Faber, 1957.

The Seedling Stars. New York: Gnome Press, 1957. London: Arrow Books, 1975. (Collection of linked stories.)

A Case of Conscience. New York: Ballantine Books, 1958. London: Faber and Faber, 1959.

The Triumph of Time. New York: Avon Books, 1958. Retitled *A Clash of Cymbals.* London: Faber and Faber, 1959.

VOR. New York: Avon Books, 1958. London: Corgi Books, 1959.

The Duplicated Man, with Robert A. W. Lowndes. New York: Avalon Books, 1959.

Galactic Cluster. New York: Signet/New American Library, 1959. London: Faber and Faber, 1960. (British edition of this collection drops three stories and adds one, "Beanstalk.")

So Close to Home. New York: Ballantine Books, 1961. (Collection of stories.)

The Star Dwellers. New York: G. P. Putnam's Sons, 1961. London: Faber and Faber, 1962.

Titan's Daughter. New York: Berkley Medallion, 1961. London: New English Library, 1963.

A Life for the Stars. New York: G. P. Putnam's Sons, 1962. London: Faber and Faber, 1964.

The Night Shapes. New York: Ballantine Books, 1962. London: New English Library, 1963.

Doctor Mirabilis. London: Faber and Faber, 1964. Revised edition. New York: Dodd, Mead, 1971.

The Issue at Hand, as by William Atheling, Jr. Chicago: Advent Publishers, 1964. (Collection of essays.)

Best Science Fiction Stories of James Blish. London: Faber and Faber, 1965. Revised edition. London: Faber and Faber, 1973 (one story dropped, two added). Retitled *The Testament of Andros*. London: Arrow Books, 1977.

Mission to the Heart Stars. New York: G. P. Putnam's Sons, 1965.

Star Trek series. New York: Bantam Books: *Star Trek* (1967); *2* (1968); *3* (1969); *4* (1971); *5* (1972); *6* (1972); *7* (1972); *8* (1972); *9* (1973); *10* (1974); *11* (1975).

A Torrent of Faces, with Norman L. Knight. Garden City, N.Y.: Doubleday, 1967. London: Faber and Faber, 1968.

Welcome to Mars! London: Faber and Faber, 1967. New York: G. P. Putnam's Sons, 1967.

Black Easter; or, Faust Aleph-Null. Garden City, N.Y.: Doubleday, 1968. London: Faber and Faber, 1969.

The Vanished Jet. New York: Weybright and Talley, 1968.

Anywhen. Garden City, N.Y.: Doubleday, 1970. London: Faber and Faber, 1971 (with one story added to the collection).

Cities in Flight. New York: Avon Books, 1970. (Includes *Earthman, Come Home*; *They Shall Have Stars*; *The Triumph of Time*; and *A Life for the Stars*.)

More Issues at Hand, as by William Atheling, Jr. Chicago: Advent Publishers, 1970. (Collection of essays.)

Spock Must Die! New York: Bantam Books, 1970. London: Corgi Books, 1974.

. . . And All the Stars a Stage. Garden City, N.Y.: Doubleday, 1971. London: Faber and Faber, 1972.

The Day After Judgment. Garden City, N.Y.: Doubleday, 1971. London: Faber and Faber, 1972.

Midsummer Century. Garden City, N.Y.: Doubleday, 1972. London: Faber and Faber, 1973.

The Quincunx of Time. New York: Dell, 1973. London: Faber and Faber, 1975.

Star Trek 12, with J. A. Lawrence. New York: Bantam Books, 1977. (Collection of stories completed by Judith Lawrence, Blish's widow.)

The Best of James Blish. New York: Ballantine Books, 1979. (Collection of stories edited by Robert A. W. Lowndes.)

The Tale That Wags the God. Edited by Cy Chauvin. Chicago: Advent, 1987.

CRITICAL AND BIOGRAPHICAL STUDIES

Aldiss, Brian W. "James Blish and the Mathematics of Knowledge." In his *This World and Nearer Ones*. Kent, Ohio: Kent State University Press, 1981.

———. "Peep." In his *The Detached Retina: Aspects of SF and Fantasy*. Syracuse, N.Y.: Syracuse University Press, 1995.

Burgess, Andrew. J. "The Concept of Eden." In *The Transcendent Adventure: Studies of Religion in Science Fiction/Fantasy*. Edited by Robert Reilly. Westport, Conn.: Greenwood Press, 1984.

Clute, John. "Scholia, Seasoned with Crabs, Blish Is." In *New Worlds 6* (1973): 118–129.

Feeley, Gregory. "Cages of Conscience from Seedling Stories: The Development of Blish's Novels." *Foundation* (February 1982): 59–67.

———. "Correcting the Record on Blish." *Foundation* (November 1983): 52–59.

Ketterer, David. *Imprisoned in a Tesseract: The Life and Works of James Blish*. Kent, Ohio: Kent State University Press, 1987.

Knight, Damon. *In Search of Wonder*. Chicago: Advent Publishers, 1956; rev. ed., 1967, pp. 268–274. (Discussion of "Common Time.")

Lobdell, Jared C. "The Spenglerian City in James Blish's *After Such Knowledge*." *Extrapolation*, 32, no. 4 (1991): 309–318.

Lowndes, Robert A. W. "A Reply to Gregory Feeley." *Foundation* (November 1983): 59–61.

McCarty, Patrick A. "Joyce of Blish: *Finnegan's Wake* in *A Case of Conscience*." *Science-Fiction Studies*, 15, part 1 (1988): 112–118.

Moskowitz, Sam. "Nils Frome in *The Golden Atom*." *Science-Fiction Studies*, 13, part 1 (1986): 98–107.

Parkin-Speer, Diane. "Alien Ethics and Religion Versus Fallen Mankind." In *The Transcendent Adventure: Studies of Religion in Science Fiction/Fantasy*. Edited by Robert Reilly. Westport, Conn.: Greenwood Press, 1984.

Samuelson, D. N. "*Black Easter* and *The Day After Judgment*." In *Survey of Modern Fantasy Literature*, vol. 1. Edited by Frank N. Magill. Englewood Cliffs, N.J.: Salem Press, 1983.

Silverberg, Robert. "Three Worlds of Wonder." *Foundation* (Winter 1986/1987): 5–20.

Stableford, Brian M. *A Clash of Symbols; the Triumph of James Blish*. San Bernardino, Calif.: Borgo Press, 1979.

—JOHN CLUTE

RAY BRADBURY

(b. 1920)

ONE NAME MORE than any other seems to typify science fiction for the American public—Ray Bradbury. For over forty years his stories, novels, poems, plays, motion-picture scripts, public lectures, book reviews, and radio and television interviews have kept him in the forefront not only of science fiction writers but of American authors in general. His stories have been anthologized in hundreds of high school and college texts, his books of poetry have enchanted thousands, and motion-picture and television productions of his writings have reached untold millions.

Perhaps "enchantment" is the proper word for Bradbury, enchantment in the sense that he seems to have cast a magic spell on his audience. He delights them, bewitches them, charms them completely with his verbal evocations, with his visions of a timeless past, a provocative future, and a challenging present. His enthusiasm is contagious, his emotional response to his surroundings is profound, and his perceptions of his intuitive interior life seem to intensify the ordinary. Moreover, his ability to communicate those enthusiasms, perceptions, or emotions mark him as a genuine rara avis, a writer who is both respected by his peers and beloved by his readers. He is a genuine phenomenon.

Success did not come easily for Bradbury. It did not arrive overnight bringing fame and fortune. Rather he "inched away" at his career, crafting story after story, destroying reams of what he considered garbage, and selling an occasional short piece of fiction for a half cent

per word. Born in 1920 in Waukegan, Illinois, Ray Douglas Bradbury as a boy soon discovered L. Frank Baum's magic land of Oz, the never-never Africa of Edgar Rice Burroughs' Tarzan of the Apes, and Barsoom, the impossible romantic Mars of Burroughs where John Carter always saved and served the incomparable Dejah Thoris. Bradbury also never forgot the timeless summers of the American Midwest, a locale he has frequently revisited in such works as *The Martian Chronicles* (1950) and *Dandelion Wine* (1957). Indeed, the past is always present for Bradbury: he shapes its materials, illumines them with his particular insights, and places, almost full blown, an alter ego of himself, such as Douglas Spaulding in *Dandelion Wine*, in some era of his own past that he wishes to evoke.

Another influence in Bradbury's youth was his discovery of magic—prestidigitation—when he was barely eleven. The famous Blackstone the Magician included the boy in his act as a member of the audience—and young Ray was enchanted by the magic of magic. His meeting with another magician, a Mr. Electrico who performed with a circus, proved to be a crucial experience for him, one that Bradbury has written about:

> Every night for three nights, Mr. Electrico sat in his electric chair, being fired with ten billion volts of pure blue sizzling power. Reaching out into the audience, his eyes flaming, his white hair standing on end, sparks leaping between his smiling teeth, he brushed an Excalibur sword over the heads of the children, knighting them with fire. When he came to

97

me, he tapped me on both shoulders and then the tip of my nose. The lightning jumped into me. Mr. Electrico cried: *"Live forever."* . . . A few weeks later I started writing my first short stories about the planet Mars. From that time to this, I have never stopped. God bless Mr. Electrico, the catalyst, wherever he is. (*The Stories of Ray Bradbury*, 1980, pages xiv–xv)

Shortly thereafter the Bradbury family moved to Arizona and then, in 1934, to Los Angeles, where he has lived ever since. He graduated from Los Angeles High School in 1938, sold newspapers, bought a typewriter, rented an office to write in, and launched his incredible career. Today, millions of words and thousands of sales later, he still remembers the thrill of his first sale, a short story on which he had collaborated with a friend, Henry Hasse, to *Super Science Stories* in July 1941. His share of the check was $13.75! (The story was published in November.) Within a year he was a full-time writer. Within a decade *The Martian Chronicles* was published, and Bradbury found himself famous.

It is impossible to mention here all the stories he has written since. His most recent collection, *The Stories of Ray Bradbury*, skims the surface in presenting a mere 100 stories, but a collection of the total contribution of this transplanted midwesterner, this eternally joyous boy, might require an entire bookshelf. Yet while Bradbury is beguiling, there is no guile in his writing, no final sense of anything but acceptance, affirmation, or optimism. To be sure, Bradbury is certainly aware of the darker side of things, and his writing often portrays that darker vision. Yet even in such an apparently pessimistic novel as *Fahrenheit 451* (1953), in which mankind ingests poisons of various kinds, both real and psychic, the final affirmation is quite clear:

[The book memorizers] weren't at all certain that what they carried in their heads might make every future dawn brighter, they were sure of nothing save that the books were on file behind their solemn eyes and that if man put his mind to them properly something of

dignity and happiness might be regained. (page 200)

What have Bradbury's themes been? What is the source of his particular genius, his unique ability to reach the fuzzy-cheeked adolescent or the ultrasophisticated eastern-establishment book critic? Of course it is not the mere genre of science fiction, which he has invested with his own distinctive stamp; neither is it the nature of his subjects—Mars, book burning, and so on—which he has chosen for his material. Rather it is his sense of what is best in America and the American people, or, indeed, of what is best in humanity as a whole. While he may well be caught up in Frederick Jackson Turner's thesis that the unique quality of American life was determined by the existence of the Frontier and our response to it, nevertheless Bradbury has been almost as popular a writer in other countries as in this one. His works have been virtual long-term best-sellers in nearly twenty different languages, which may well attest to the fact that his appeal is to the best in all humans of whatever country or race. He is also relatively well known in the former Soviet republics. His concerns are often expressed in terms of the metaphor of the wilderness, and all peoples seem to respond to the challenge it expresses. It is almost as though Bradbury were appealing to some Jungian collective unconscious in all of us, recalling the dim ancestral memories of how we feared but faced the saber-toothed tiger and eventually conquered it, and looking ahead at how we will fear but face the expanses of space and eventually conquer its vastnesses.

The final, inexhaustible wilderness, the Final Frontier, is the wilderness of space, according to Bradbury, and in that last challenge mankind will eventually both find and renew itself. That ultimate rebirth is essentially a religious vision, certainly, but Bradbury is rarely explicit about it. The theme infuses much of his writing as a sort of susurrus, quietly whispering in the background. He seems to be saying in his luminous manner that in space, as atoms of God, we will live forever. Thus the conquest of space becomes for him a religious quest, although a directly religious theme is sounded very seldom in his stories. One story, "The Fire Balloons" (1951), tells of the debate two priests have on Mars about whether or not some native blue-fire balls have souls; in "The Man" (1949), Christ leaves a distant planet the day before an Earth rocket lands. In Bradbury's poem "Christus Apollo" (1969), these lines state his faith quite explicitly: "Christ wanders in the Universe/A flesh of stars."

The central tensions that permeate all of Bradbury's work are those of stasis, entropy, and change. Change will come, he seems to say, but the past has its undeniable attractions as well. In fact, if we could see the future, we might not like it; we might be trapped by it just as we might be sucked down by the unseen, unanticipated quicksands of the future. He reveals these tensions frequently in short stories, but even the major works like *The Martian Chronicles* or *Fahrenheit 451* depend on complex interrelationships of time, setting, place, character, and dialogue. These matters are not simple ones in his writing, despite the ostensible simplicity of his themes or subjects. *Fahrenheit 451* will serve to illustrate the multiplicity of harmonic vibrations inherent in the novels and seen throughout Bradbury's other writing.

Fahrenheit 451 was not originally written as a novel. It appeared first as a short story, "The Fireman," in Horace Gold's *Galaxy Science Fiction* for February 1951. The story version is well worth reading in order to perceive how well the author expanded the themes embedded in the shorter work and transmuted them into the magic and power found in the novel. Bradbury often makes use of irony, and "The Fireman" is no exception. In fact, the initial power of the story itself depends on irony: the fireman of the title quenches no fires. Instead, he sets them, burning the books that contain any hint of the freedom, dignity, or liberty of humanity. The story itself underwent a number of changes before finding its final novel form. Its first transmutation was as an unpublished novella,

Ray Bradbury. Courtesy of UPI/Corbis-Bettmann

"Fire, Fire!" Other tentative titles for successive drafts included "Fire, Fire, Burn Books!" and "The Hearth and the Salamander."

Bradbury has elsewhere described the process by which the longer novella version was finally transformed into a novel in twenty days of high-speed writing. Yet the original manuscripts show that he is a very careful artist who composed extremely clean copy. His certainty with words is such that his typed drafts required little line editing, although total revision was quite another matter. Each of these drafts represents a successively deeper thinking out of—or as Bradbury himself might prefer to put it, a deeper feeling into—the theme and the story. The expansion of dimension bespeaks an expansion of the emotions, with the result that the final product, *Fahrenheit 451*, remains one of the most eloquent pleas for freedom of expression, one of the most anguished rejections of censorship that the early 1950's produced.

The book also reveals Bradbury's continuing preoccupation with the past. Here it is portrayed as almost Edenic, as the book memorizers, led by a shepherd named—what else?—Granger, move toward the future, a paradisaical vision.

> "Our way is simpler and better [Granger says] and the thing we wish to do is keep the knowledge intact and safe and not to anger or excite anyone, for then if we are destroyed the knowledge is most certainly dead. . . . So we wait quietly for the day when the machines are dented junk and then we hope to walk by and say, here we are, to those who survive this war, and then we'll say, Have you come to your senses now? Perhaps a few books will do you some good." (pages 198–199)

The end of *Fahrenheit 451* is essentially optimistic, despite the horrifying vision of an apocalyptic near-future presented earlier in the novel. Even though machines have produced the situation whereby books are banned and men and women are hunted for reading them, Bradbury is never simplistically antimachine and never illustrates a blindly Luddite prejudice when writing of the impediments of science or technology. Rather he infuses his vision with a sense of the resilience of human beings despite all the ill effects of machines or technology. Thus *Fahrenheit 451* is not a novel about the technology of the future at all, and for that matter it is only secondarily concerned with either censorship or book burners. In reality, it is the story of Bradbury himself, disguised as Guy Montag, and of Bradbury's lifelong love affair with books. Bradbury has often stated that if the love of a man and a woman is worth notarizing in conventional fiction, so also is the love of a man and an idea. This latter notion, of course, is at the very heart of science fiction, which has often been described as a literature of ideas rather than of character. Thus, Bradbury maintains, people may have an endless series of affairs with books, and the offspring of these affairs can become great literature.

The core of the novel rests in the reader's ability to share Montag's slow struggle toward consciousness, to move from official book burner to reader to rebel to book memorizer and ultimately to citizen of a loving, caring, feeling world. That Bradbury is able to charm us into this identification is indicative of his ability as a writer. *Fahrenheit 451* is in every way a magnificent achievement, perhaps his best work.

The years that followed the writing of "The Fireman" and its final transformation into novel form in 1953 were busy ones for Bradbury: he turned out dozens of works. Gradually, perhaps because his writing style was inimitable—after all, he handled the English language as if it were something he had invented and patented—Bradbury became noticed by many writers and critics outside the relatively limited field of genre science fiction. Such diverse writers as Aldous Huxley, Christopher Isherwood, and Gilbert Highet hailed him as a stylist and visionary.

Perhaps even more importantly, director John Huston asked him to write the script for the film version of *Moby Dick* (released in 1956). Now it may be true that Herman Melville's *Moby Dick* (1851) is forever uncapturable in any medium, yet some film critics have said that Melville was better served by Bradbury than by Huston. In the end, Melville's white whale provided Bradbury with another parameter to a central metaphor or symbol that had entranced him for years. He had often indicated his strong attraction to the writings of Jules Verne and H. G. Wells. The cylindrical shape of Captain Nemo's submarine or Martian rocket ships had long fascinated Bradbury. Thus, the shape of the whale itself provided still another metaphor. For Bradbury, metaphor is not merely a figure of speech, it is a vital concept, a method he uses for comprehending one reality and expressing it in terms of another; it permits the reader to perceive what the author is saying. For example, the burning of books controls *Fahrenheit 451*, and while the moving tattoo was superimposed on an otherwise loosely connected series of stories, it nonetheless provides the final form of *The Illustrated Man* (1951) with a coherent metaphoric unity. In fact, as has already been noted, all of Bradbury's writing might be described as a metaphor of generalized nostalgia, not merely for the past but also for the future. In his slow progression through Verne, Wells, and Melville, Bradbury was searching for his own authentic voice, and the concept of metaphor helped him find it.

The figure of the whale became a pattern infusing much of Bradbury's writing since the mid-1950's. The most notable example of this symbolism, of course, is the spaceship itself, the rocket that brought the colonists to Mars and ultimately led to the events described in *The Martian Chronicles*. This collection of stories actually proceeded the *Moby Dick* script chronologically, and in *The Martian Chronicles* Bradbury for the first time explored the implications of any metaphysical or social problem in some depth. To be sure, many commentators have often remarked that Bradbury is essentially a short story writer, that his novels are merely expansions of short stories as is the case with *Fahrenheit 451*, or are merely collections of loosely connected stories such as *The Martian Chronicles*. He is a 100-yard-dash man, they say, not a long-distance runner; but they add that it may well be more difficult to turn out gem after gem of short fiction consistently than to hone, develop, and give birth to a new novel every five years or so.

Indeed, that reservation about his writing may have some validity. Yet it is also certain that the apparently loosely connected series of stories found in *The Martian Chronicles* or in *The Illustrated Man* have more coherence and unity than is generally claimed for them. In *The Martian Chronicles*, Bradbury does not hesitate to juxtapose the familiar tensions between fantasy and reality, time and eternity, or past and present. Moreover, he explores the implications of these tensions in greater detail than in any of the fiction he had previously written, as if he had found his mature voice for the first time and was delighting in its possibilities.

What is most remarkable about this series of stories is that Bradbury himself is intensely involved with the story he is telling while at the same time he remains dispassionately objective. He seems to be saying, "I feel this way; I'm enchanted by it and I hope you are too, but let's be careful lest we be swept away by the creation we are both involved in." This ambiguity of passionate involvement with an equal degree of objective distancing is a remarkable technique—not only for itself but also for its appearance in the hitherto much maligned genre of science fiction. How then, in *The Martian Chronicles*, does Bradbury achieve this goal of what might be called "perspective by ambiguity"?

To answer this question, we must direct our attention not so much toward the stories themselves and what they tell us directly, but toward the interchapters, the brief interstices between the longer stories. Dated by year and month rather than by day of the week, these sections seem to force the reader into filling in the gaps that they indicate. What happened between the stories? we ask. And no sooner do we do so than Bradbury has achieved a major goal, profound involvement by his readers in the very act of creation. But because no two readers will create the same material in the same way, we are faced, in the end, with ambiguity coupled with both intensity and perspective. It is a remarkable accomplishment, and that Bradbury is able to bring it off so well is not the least of the book's many merits. Throughout the succession of stories, Bradbury poses many questions but answers very few of them. What is going on? we also ask. Is the re-creation of the old family home real or a hallucination? Is it amicable or dangerous? Do Martians really exist, or are they found only in our minds, and even if they are only in our minds, isn't mental reality just as real as extra-mental reality?

Throughout the book Bradbury is too good a storyteller to let questions, answers, or even suggestions, hints, or illusions get in the way of the tales themselves. Thus he carries us through one apparently isolated story after another (as we play the vitally important role of filling in the gaps between the stories themselves) until we finish the book. Then we wish only to begin it again, in an attempt to recapture the charm and magic of the initial reading. The reader's curiosity is not merely tweaked by the stories or by what Bradbury has either chosen to tell us or, sometimes, chosen not to tell us. Rather we become fascinated by the ambiguities. We welcome them and the inferences or implications found in the pages or in our minds.

Such subtlety of vision and intensity is not often found in the pages of science fiction. That it has been habitually present in Bradbury's work has caused more than one critic to wonder if what Bradbury writes should really be called "science fiction." It is more fantasy, they say, and Bradbury is a fantast, a creator of entire worlds; or they may say that his writing has simply made the imagination live once more, no matter in what category it is placed. By and large such statements do not concern Bradbury in the slightest. He cares little either for critics or for what they say about his work. "Critics come from the head," he has remarked, "and I write for the heart!" In fact, one reviewer recently tried to disparage his writing by calling him the "Norman Rockwell of science fiction," and Bradbury quite naturally took it as a compliment.

To be sure, even when Bradbury's stories are set on Mars or a rocket ship, they are rarely what has been termed "hard core" science fiction. He has no particular fondness for the technological products of our civilization. While he owns a car, he does not drive. He has rarely, if ever, been on an airplane, and his passion for old trains, old buses, old streetcars, as well as his habit of bicycling all over West Los Angeles, have given him the perhaps undeserved reputation as a man who might have been happier living in the first two decades of the twentieth century, or even in the last two decades of the nineteenth.

Yet his pleas for an expansion of the space program and his ability to share his dreams with everyone from America's astronauts to third-graders have placed him firmly as a man of the last third of the twentieth century. He would not give up, say, modern medicine, no matter how he might deplore what the auto-mobile has done to our cities or our countryside.

And here Bradbury sounds one of the dominant themes of science fiction: humanity must surely master the machine or just as surely the machine will master humanity. The machine must be utilized for good, not discarded merely because it has been abused. This dream of the good that machines can provide has inspired some of his most urgent requests for the continuation of space research. In fact, in past years, a not inconsiderable portion of his prose, his poetry, and his many public appearances on radio, television, and the lecture platform has been devoted to the necessity for maintaining America's space program.

One of the most intriguing aspects of Bradbury's writing is that it appeals to virtually everyone in his audience. He himself has analyzed that appeal: he recognizes that the sources for his stories are usually, if not always, found in the events of his day-to-day life, and as such, they are easily recognizable by his readers as something that they themselves have often perceived but not really recognized. Such is certainly the case, to cite only one example, in one of his most famous short stories, "The Fog Horn" (1951), which was first published (and soon thereafter filmed) under the title *The Beast from Twenty Thousand Fathoms* (1953). Bradbury describes its origin as follows:

> One night when my wife and I were walking along the beach in Venice, California, where we lived in a thirty-dollar-a-month newlyweds' apartment, we came upon the bones of the Venice Pier and the struts, tracks, and ties of the ancient roller-coaster collapsed on the sand and being eaten by the sea.
>
> "What's that dinosaur doing lying here on the beach?" I said.
>
> My wife, very wisely, had no answer.
>
> The answer came the next night when, summoned from sleep by a voice calling, I rose up, listened, and heard the lovely voice of the Santa Monica Bay fog horn blowing over and over and over again.

Of course! I thought. The dinosaur heard that lighthouse fog horn blowing, thought it was another dinosaur arisen from the deep past, came swimming in for a loving confrontation, discovered it was only a fog horn, and died of a broken heart there on the shore. (*The Stories of Ray Bradbury*, pages xv–xvi)

There we have the apotheosis of Bradbury's vision, its pure essence; we see the leaping imagination, the lure of the past clashing with the reality of the present, all combined with something the reader can readily perceive. Of course, we say as we read the story, how often we have been moved by that lonesome booming sound, as Bradbury puts it:

A sound like the birds flying south, crying, and a sound like November wind and the sea on the hard cold shore . . . whoever hears it will weep in their souls . . . whoever hears it will know the sadness of eternity and the briefness of life. (*ibid.*, page 268)

Here is Bradbury at his most magical, transforming the most simple, most transitory phenomena into memorable beauty. His style both here and elsewhere is perhaps the single feature that contributes most to his imaginative vision. Yet despite the fact that he has published several volumes of poetry (for which he has received some negative reviews), his writing often seems more "poetic" in the prose of the novels and short stories than in the poems themselves. Not that Bradbury's poetry is not melodic or evocative. Rather it seems that he writes very successful light verse with an occasional more serious poem.

One of his collections provides examples of both kinds of poetry: *Where Robot Mice and Robot Men Run Round in Robot Towns* (1977) is typical for what it contains, some dark poems and some light verse. "Why Viking Lander, Why the Planet Mars" states once again his conception that God seeds himself among the stars and that ". . . Mars is but a Beginning, Real Heaven our end." He has returned to his deeply loved Mars to provide his metaphor, ". . . to land, to taste, touch and

know strange Mars." Perhaps his most moving poem in this collection is the longer work, "Thoughts on Visiting the Main Rocket Assembly Building at Cape Canaveral for the First Time." Here he combines some rhetoric borrowed from Shakespeare with his own profound religious sense:

From Stratford's fortress mind we build
  and go
And strutwork catwalk stars across abyss
And to small wondering seed-bed souls to
  promise this:
To Be is best, and Not to Be far worse.
And Will says what?
Stand here, grow tall, rehearse.
Be God-grown-Man.
Act out the Universe!
(page 71)

One of Bradbury's most neglected works is the group of stories that was published as the novel *Dandelion Wine* (1957), which is not actually science fiction. While this charming little work is neither as well known nor as famous as, say, *Fahrenheit 451* or *The Illustrated Man*, it nevertheless combines all of the magical elements we normally associate with Bradbury—the enchantment of a boy coming of age in a timeless Green Town, Illinois, where the only rockets were those shot off on the Fourth of July; the nostalgia for the never-never land of the past, coupled with the pressures of the present and the not-too-distant, alternately charming and dangerous future; the exultation of boyish love, and the eternal dream of goodness.

Bradbury's preoccupation with the stage led him in 1972 to turn the novel into a play and, when he was Artist in Residence at California State University, Fullerton, to supervise its initial production and world premiere. It played to packed houses at the university and later received productions in Los Angeles and elsewhere. Eventually the lure of the stage led Bradbury in the early 1970's to write, produce, virtually direct, and supervise the ill-fated *Leviathan 99*, a retelling of *Moby Dick* in terms of space. Technology could not keep up with

Bradbury's soaring imagination, and he closed the show before the official opening rather than risk an inadequate, partially financed production. He later achieved distinct success when a stage version of *The Martian Chronicles* ran for months in Los Angeles. Richard Matheson then adapted the play for a distinguished network television production in January 1980.

After more than six decades of writing, entertaining the world with inimitable insights and vibrant imagination, Ray Bradbury maintains that he is no longer writing science fiction.

He may well be right—after all, he should know—but when one examines his prodigious output for the last half-century, one might well ask, "Exactly how much of this master's writing during his long, illustrious career has been 'science fiction,' no matter how the term is defined?" It is hardly the kind of science fiction that graced (and sometimes disgraced) the pages of old pulps such as *Amazing Stories*, *Thrilling Wonder Stories*, or *Startling Stories*. It was never in the Campbell mode of space adventure, thin characterization, or pedestrian style.

Indeed, Bradbury created his own métier, a vibrant, emotionally charged imaginative fiction, using a clean loose-limbed poetic prose that appeals, above all, to the hearts and spirits of his myriad readers, not merely to their minds or intellect. No patentable gadgets stultify his imagination or clutter his pages, and as he has often remarked, he doesn't "do Windows." Rather, he creates windows to the imagination.

So if that endearing man, much loved and very loving, Ray Bradbury, has chosen to turn out well-received detective novels, so be it. The first two—*Death is a Lonely Business* (1985) and *A Graveyard for Lunatics (1990)—will be followed by the forthcoming Rattigan*, which will complete the trilogy, each book loosely utilizing some of the characters, concepts, or echoes of the others. In *Ahmed and the Oblivion Machines* (1998), Bradbury has returned to fantasy, and he is also contracted to write a sequel to *Dandelion Wine*, tentatively entitled *Farewell Summer*. A new vampire novel, called *From the Dust Returned*, is also scheduled to be released.

Moreover, if Bradbury has chosen to write plays or television and movie scripts, well and good. In fact, Mel Gibson has contracted to direct a new production of *Fahrenheit 451* to be filmed in Australia, and Bradbury has also completed the screenplay for what he calls "a true film version" of *The Martian Chronicles* to be produced by Universal.

If he is a very attractive lecturer on the university and college circuit (a 1996 appearance called "Ray Bradbury and Friends" at the University of California, Irvine, crammed the auditorium of that rather ultrasophisticated institution with hundreds of fans) he nonetheless remains the tireless, white-maned, gentlemanly charismatic figure he has always been. He is still willing to autograph his books for hours at a time, sometimes even to waive his lecture fees to help raise funds for libraries—one of his favorite occupations.

Above all, Ray Bradbury, approaching the millennium, may be the closest thing to a cult hero and a popular icon that science fiction, perhaps even popular writing, has yet produced. The Science Fiction and Fantasy Writers of America rewarded him for this with the Grand Master Award in 1988. He is a bard in the antique sense of the word, a great singer of our Selves, and his bardic song will undoubtedly enchant the future, the twenty-first century, as much as it has enchanted both past and present.

Selected Bibliography

WORKS OF RAY BRADBURY

The Martian Chronicles. Garden City, N.Y.: Doubleday, 1950. Titled *The Silver Locusts*. London: Rupert Hart-Davis, 1951.

The Illustrated Man. Garden City, N.Y.: Doubleday, 1951. London: Rupert Hart-Davis, 1952.

Fahrenheit 451. New York: Ballantine Books, 1953. London: Rupert Hart-Davis, 1954.

Dandelion Wine. Garden City, N.Y.: Doubleday, 1957. London: Rupert Hart-Davis, 1957.

The Anthem Sprinters and Other Antics. New York: Dial Press, 1963.

The Vintage Bradbury. New York: Vintage Books, 1965.

When Elephants Last in the Dooryard Bloomed. New York: Alfred A. Knopf, 1973. London: Rupert Hart-Davis, 1975.

Where Robot Mice and Robot Men Run Round in Robot Towns. New York: Alfred A. Knopf, 1977. London: Rupert Hart-Davis, 1979.

The Stories of Ray Bradbury. New York: Alfred A. Knopf, 1980.

Dinosaur Tales. New York: Bantam, 1983. (Short stories.)

A Memory of Murder. New York: Dell, 1984.

Death Is a Lonely Business. New York: Knopf, 1985 (Short stories.)

The Toynbee Convector. New York: Knopf, 1988. (Short stories.)

A Graveyard for Lunatics: Another Tale of Two Cities. New York: Knopf, 1990.

Green Shadows, White Whale. New York: Knopf, 1992.

Quicker than the Eye. New York: Avon, 1996. (Short stories, mostly new.)

Driving Blind. New York: Avon, 1997. (Short stories, mostly new.)

Ahmed and the Oblivion Machines. New York: Avon, 1998.

From the Dust Returned. New York: Avon, 1998.

MANUSCRIPTS

Various drafts of the early, middle, and final versions of *Fahrenheit 451* are accessible in the Special Collections Library at California State University in Fullerton, California.

CRITICAL AND BIOGRAPHICAL STUDIES

Anon. "Ray Bradbury and the Irish." *Catholic World*, 200 (January 1964): 224–230.

Ash, Lee. "WLB Biography: Ray Bradbury." *Wilson Library Bulletin* (November 1964).

Federman, Donald. "Truffaut and Dickens: *Fahrenheit 451*." *Florida Quarterly* (Summer 1967).

Forrester, Kent. "The Dangers of Being Earnest: Ray Bradbury and *The Martian Chronicles*." *Journal of General Education* (Spring 1976).

Gladish, Cristine. "The October Country." In *Survey of Science Fiction Literature*. Edited by Frank Magill. Englewood Cliffs, N.J.: Salem, 1979.

Grimsley, Juliet. "*The Martian Chronicles*: A Provocative Study." *English Journal* (December 1970).

Hamblen, Charles F. "Bradbury's *Fahrenheit 451* in the Classroom." *English Journal* (September 1968).

Indick, Ben P. *Ray Bradbury, Dramatist*. San Bernardino, Calif.: Borgo, 1990.

Johnson, Wayne L. *Ray Bradbury*. Lavernge, Tenn.: Ungar, 1980.

McNelly, Willis E. "Bradbury Revisited." *CEA Critic* (March 1969).

———. "Ray Bradbury: Past, Present, and Future." In *Voices of the Future*. Edited by Thomas Clareson. Bowling Green, Ohio: Bowling Green University Popular Press, 1976. (A companion and contrasting piece to the essay by James A. Stupple in the same volume.)

———, and Keith Neilson. "Fahrenheit 451." In *Survey of Science Fiction Literature*. Edited by Frank Magill. Englewood Cliffs, N.J.: Salem, 1979.

Mengeling, Marvin E. "Ray Bradbury's 'Dandelion Wine': Themes, Sources, and Styles." *English Journal* (October 1971).

Miller, Walter James. *Ray Bradbury's Martian Chronicles: A Critical Commentary*. New York: Monarch, 1987.

Mogen, David. *Ray Bradbury*. Boston: Twayne, 1986.

Moskowitz, Sam. "Ray Bradbury." In his *Seekers of Tomorrow: Masters of Modern Science Fiction*. Cleveland, Ohio: World Publishing, 1966; Westport, Conn.: Hyperion, 1974.

Nolan, William F. "Bradbury: Prose Poet in the Age of Science." *The Magazine of Fantasy and Science Fiction* (May 1963).

———, ed. *The Ray Bradbury Companion: A Life and Career History, Photolog, and Comprehensive Checklist of Writings with Facsimiles from Ray Bradbury's Unpublished and Uncollected Work in All Media*. Detroit, Mich.: Gale Research, 1975. (Invaluable.)

Olander, Joseph, and Martin H. Greenberg, eds. *Ray Bradbury*. New York: Taplinger, 1980. (Includes a bibliography.)

Platt, Charles. *Dreammakers: Science Fiction and Fantasy Writers at Work*. Lavernge, Tenn.: Ungar, 1987. (Contains a chapter about Bradbury.)

Reilly, Robert. "The Artistry of Ray Bradbury." *Extrapolation* (December 1971).

Sioario, Peter. "A Study of Allusions In Bradbury's 'Fahrenheit 451.'" *English Journal* (February 1970).

Slusser, George Edgar. *The Bradbury Chronicles*. San Bernardino, Calif.: Borgo, 1977.

Stupple, James A. "The Past, the Future, and Ray Bradbury." In *Voices of the Future*. Edited by Thomas Clareson. Bowling Green, Ohio: Bowling Green University Popular Press, 1976.

Sullivan, A. T. "Ray Bradbury and Fantasy." *English Journal* (December 1972).

Touponce, William F. *Ray Bradbury and the Poetics of Reverie: Fantasy, Science Fiction, and the Reader*. Ann Arbor: University of Michigan Research Press, 1984.

———. *Ray Bradbury*. San Bernardino, Calif.: Borgo, 1989.

—WILLIS E. McNELLY

DAVID BRIN
(b. 1950)

GLEN DAVID BRIN was born on 6 October 1950 in Glendale, California. He obtained a B.S. in astronomy from the California Institute of Technology in 1973 and then spent two years on the technical staff of the Hughes Aircraft Research Laboratory at Newport Beach before receiving an M.S. in electrical engineering from the University of California, San Diego. He went on to obtain a Ph.D. in space science from UCSD in 1981. His published scientific papers are distributed across a wide spectrum of topics, including space station design, the theory of polarized light, the nature of comets, and the astronomical and philosophical questions implicit in the Search for Extra-Terrestrial Intelligence (a collective term for a series of projects in radio-astronomy that attempted to detect signals from various individual stars and star-clusters that might have been emitted by intelligent beings).

It was while working for his doctorate that Brin completed his first science fiction novel, *Sundiver* (1980). He went on to teach physics and writing at San Diego State University between 1982 and 1985, during which time he was also a postdoctoral fellow at the California Space Institute, UCSD. He then became a full-time writer, although he spent some time as a "visiting artist" at the University of London's Westfield College, served as a "visiting disputant" at the Center for Evolution and the Origin of Life from 1988 to 1990, and was a "research affiliate" at the Jet Propulsion Laboratory in 1992 and 1993. Between the latter appointments, he lived for eighteen months in Paris, where his fiancée, Cheryl Brigham, was doing research in geochemistry, they returned to California thereafter to marry and raise a family.

It is unusual for a writer to launch a career in science fiction with a novel, having served no "apprenticeship" in the magazines, and even more unusual for the novel in question to sell so well as to go through numerous printings. Brin was, however, a writer whose work and career were routinely to defy all kinds of expectations. He rose more rapidly to best-seller status than any predecessor within the genre—and did so, moreover, by working in an arena that had become rather unfashionable: solidly traditional hard science fiction. The principal agent of his success, the series begun with *Sundiver* and extended through three more increasingly massive projects, is space opera (space adventure story) of a more scientifically conscientious kind than the colorful comic-strip variety whose popularity had been renewed by *Star Trek* and *Star Wars*.

Sundiver introduces a scenario in which humankind has managed to augment the intelligence and communicative ability of dolphins and chimpanzees, thus "uplifting" them to sapience and membership in a common moral community. Having made contact with alien species, however, humans have discovered that their own seemingly spontaneous evolution of sapience is a dramatic exception to a pattern that extends across the galaxy. It appears that all other sapient species have been artificially uplifted by "patrons" who consider that favor a debt to be repaid by long periods of servitude. Humankind's new neighbors are deeply offended by the notion that humans might have achieved sapience without the aid of patrons, considering *Homo sapiens* to be a "wolfling" species, improperly prepared for galactic civilization, who are rendering further insult to galactic norms by neglecting to demand repayment from their "clients."

This scenario embodies a remarkably ingenious narrative move, preserving for the reader the sense that even on the vastest scale imaginable, the principle of mediocrity does not apply to his own species and hence to him. Brin's awareness of the cleverness and chutzpah with which this conjuration was worked is deftly encapsulated in the short story "Shhhh" (1988), in which the pride of the race is salvaged by a trick of much the same kind, served up with a blatant wink.

The plot of *Sundiver* concerns an investigative expedition undertaken by humans, in the brittle company of resentful alien observers, to determine whether the "Ghosts" allegedly haunting the interior of the sun are actually living beings—and if so, whether they have any bearing on the vexed question of humanity's uplift. The probe is launched from the caves of Mercury, its journey plagued by the interpersonal tensions among its passengers and by various small acts of sabotage, all of which come to a head as it plunges into the outermost layer of the sun. In a long, drawn-out but remarkably tense climax, which moves smoothly from murder mystery to quasi-gladiatorial combat, it transpires that the alien observers are not quite what they seem, or as amicably inclined as they pretend.

Sundiver was nearly twice the length that was regarded as standard for genre novels in 1980, but in that respect it was ahead of its time, and Brin's ability not merely to retain but continually to stretch the suspenseful tautness of his narrative for such a length was to stand him in good stead as fashions shifted in the marketplace. Because hard science fiction stories work in hypothetical worlds that have to be rigorously defined as well as carefully elaborated, it is very difficult to develop them at length and exceedingly difficult to maintain dramatic tension while dutifully filling in their details. Brin proved to have an unprecedented talent for that kind of work, and he acquired the craftsmanship necessary to make expert use of that talent with remarkable rapidity.

Following the publication of *Sundiver*, Brin began to make an impact in the science fiction magazines. "Just a Hint" (1980), his debut in the pages of *Analog*, juxtaposed images of humans who have understood the impact of fluorocarbons on the ozone layer but cannot come to terms with their own aggressive tendencies and aliens who have put war behind them but cannot figure out why they are suffering a plague of skin cancer. Among other things, the story offers a possible solution to the Fermi paradox, which wonders why we have heard nothing from other civilizations if there are as many out there in the galaxy as the calculus of probability seems to suggest. Brin was to provide several further hypothetical answers to this enigma.

"Just a Hint" was followed in *Analog's* pages by "The Tides of Kithrup" (1981), a novella describing the battle for survival of the crew of a dolphin-commanded spaceship stranded beneath the surface of an alien ocean. Another novella, "The Loom of Thessaly" (1981), was Brin's first departure into fantasy, although an orbital Platform plays a crucial role in launching the plot and in providing a wryly calculated deus ex machina. The view from orbit reveals a tiny region of Thessaly that is virtually inaccessible. Unlike Rome, all roads lead away from it, and it is almost impossible to approach on foot. The intrepid explorer who will not be put off finds that it is the abode of the three Fates, still busy weaving the destiny of humankind—but he, like his author, is solidly on the side of progress, and his encounter becomes a heroic struggle against the tyranny of destiny. Brin commented in an endnote attached to the story in *The River of Time* (1986) that most of his novellas "deal in myth, or contain mythic elements," and one of the mythic themes that most interests him is the desire of humans to

David Brin. © 1998 M. C. Valada

challenge gods, which he consistently over-turns in order to stake the claim that hubris is a cardinal virtue rather than a deadly sin.

"Coexistence" (1981), which was renamed to provide *The River of Time* with a title story, is a surreal extrapolation of the classic theme of H. G. Wells's "The New Accelerator" (1901) and Jack London's "The Shadow and the Flash" (1903) that takes the fundamental idea an important step farther. This, too, was to remain a hallmark of Brin's work; he is rarely content merely to display a fanciful idea, preferring to run with it as far as it can be taken. When he does exercise restraint, as in "The Postman" (1982)—a study of the calculated creation of a myth—he is likely to return to the theme at a later date to move the situation forward. In this novella, a lone wanderer in a post-holocaust world appropriates a uniform and a mailbag from a long-dead corpse and uses them to con the paranoid inhabitants of isolated settlements into the hopeful belief that some vestige of social order is in the process of being restored. The story

line illustrates a second aspect of Brin's interest in myth: the manner in which manufactured stories can create a sense of community and a sense of communal purpose.

"The Tides of Kithrup" was vastly expanded into the second novel in the Uplift series, *Startide Rising* (1983). The travails of the crew of the starship *Streaker* are elaborately extended and provided with a drawn-out but relentlessly tense climax that combines the effects of internal tensions and external threats. The latter result from the fact that *Streaker* is forced to take refuge on Kithrup after recklessly reporting the discovery of a vast "graveyard" of derelict spaceships—a treasure trove that might contain valuable information about the mythical Progenitors who began the uplift program. The leakage of this news establishes the starship's salvaged cargo—whose exact nature remains a mystery to the reader—as a valuable treasure. Fortunately, *Streaker*'s pursuers immediately begin fighting among themselves over the privilege of claiming their prize, exchanging shots above and on the planet's surface, while the dolphins and humans hide in the depths.

Brin devotes a good deal of effort to the description of Kithrup's biosphere. Because the crust is unusually rich in heavy metals, the indigenous sea life uses heavy metals to form skeletal structures and protective scales. Many plant structures, including the coralline roots of "drill-trees" are equipped with metal "tools," while vast masses of floating weed dangling down into the almost salt-free water provide inverted forests through which gleaming fishes swim. The delight in comprehensive and conscientious "world building" displayed here was to be extended in all Brin's other planetary romances, giving them a useful depth to complement the extraordinary breadth of their action-adventure sequences. *Startide Rising* won the Hugo and Nebula awards for best novel in 1984, cementing Brin's reputation as a key writer of hard science fiction. It also won him the first of five Locus awards.

Brin's next novel was an abrupt change of direction. *The Practice Effect* (1984) is a comic fantasy about a quasi-medieval parallel world in which practice really does make artifacts perfect—and lack of usage results in a steady waning of their virtue. Every wealthy man requires an army of hirelings to keep the apparatus of his wealth in good order, thus sustaining a quirky variation of the feudal social order beloved of genre fantasy writers. As with many a Campbellian hero before him, the physicist of *The Practice Effect* finds that his technical skills are mistaken for magic by the credulous locals, and he sets out to make the most of his aptitude and reputation. Like the protagonists of L. Sprague de Camp's *Lest Darkness Fall* (1941) and H. Beam Piper's *Gunpowder God* (1978), he finds the problem of introducing enlightenment into a Dark Age more vexing than initially seems likely, but his resourcefulness eventually proves equal to the task.

Like its predecessors, the Bantam edition of *The Practice Effect* went through multiple printings, confirming the popularity that allowed Brin to become a full-time freelance writer. It also won the last of the Balrog awards in 1985, which briefly served as the fantasy genre's equivalent of the Hugo before leaving the field to the jury-determined World Fantasy award. *The Postman* (1985)—an expansion of "The Postman" and its sequel "Cyclops" (1984)—was even more successful, with rapidly sold film rights, although the long-delayed movie eventually made by Kevin Costner and released in 1997 was a travesty of the text and bombed spectacularly at the box office.

The extended story explains how the inventive hero, having initially masqueraded as a postman purely to obtain a welcome from desperate townspeople who have long forsaken charity, is forced actually to become what he pretends to be. To convert the flickering flame of hope that he has kindled into a self-sustaining fire, he has to embellish his fantasy continually and to accumulate a further supply of symbolic materials—including the computer whose discovery provided the subject matter of "Cyclops"—with which to put flesh on it. His efforts to establish a platform for the rebuilding of democratic society are, however, plagued by "Survivalists" whose intention is to extend an autocratic tyranny throughout the former United States by force of arms. Because the Survivalist leaders are cyborgized super-soldiers their nomadic hordes are difficult to resist, but the defenders of the true faith have better myths to guide and sustain them.

The Postman won the John W. Campbell Memorial award for best novel in 1986 as well as Brin's second Locus award and an American Library Association award for the best young adult novel of the year. The central motif of its final sequence—a stand-up contest between right and might—was taken to a further extreme in the fantasy of alternative history "Thor Meets Captain America" (1986), in which America's attempts to win World War II seem to be doomed when Nazi experiments in black magic contrive to secure physical existence for the bloodthirsty Norse gods.

Brin's other short stories of the mid-1980's are remarkably various considering their relatively small number. "Tank Farm Dynamo" (1983) is a standardized *Analog* account of a near-future problem solved by a technological fix. "The Fourth Vocation of George Gustaf" (1984) is a quirky fable slyly reflecting upon some classic science fiction themes, whose protagonist is a robopsychologist avid for monarchical power. "The Crystal Spheres" (1984) offers the unlikeliest of Brin's various solutions to the Fermi paradox, proposing that there might be cordons sanitaires around novice civilizations; the story won him a second Hugo, for best short story, in 1985. "The Warm Space" (1985) is a fanciful and rather flippant problem story in which excursions into hyperspace require a technological fix if they are to be both useful and survivable. "Lungfish"—one of five stories that made their first appearance in *The River of Time*— offers a more plausible but much darker answer than "The Crystal Spheres" to the question of why the universe presents no clear evidence of alien life. Three of the other original stories—"Senses Three and Six," the brief "Toujours Voir," and "A Stage of Memory"—are grouped together under the heading of "Recollection" because they deal with possible distortions of subjective experience.

The River of Time appeared in the same year as *Heart of the Comet* (1986), written by Brin in collaboration with his fellow Californian hard science fiction writer Gregory Benford. (The two would have shared the same initials had Brin not opted to use his middle name, further enhancing the coincidence that linked them both to yet another Californian hard science fiction writer Greg Bear; the three were later to adopt the collective nickname of "the Killer Bs.") *Heart of the Comet* was an attempt to cash in on the long-anticipated re-appearance in Earthly skies of the epoch-making Halley's Comet, which was scheduled to make extra headlines when a NASA space probe intercepted it. As matters transpired, the comet did not provide nearly as grand a spectacle as Hale-Bopp ten years later—it was never more than a pale smudge in the sky, barely visible to the naked eye even at perihelion—but the novel provides some slight compensation to some of those who had hoped for something more dramatic.

Brin and Benford set their story during the comet's next scheduled passage through the inner solar system, in 2061. The plot describes the establishment of a colony in the comet's nucleus with the intention of moving it into a more convenient orbit. The project runs into unexpected difficulties when the discovery of native microorganisms is swiftly followed by the appearance of enormous purple worms. Adapted by evolution to take advantage of the comet's widely separated perihelions, the versatile native life-forms take full advantage of the new resources imported by the humans. As in Brin's Uplift novels, the problems arising from the alien ecosphere are further complicated by ideological differences among the colonists. By the time the comet returns to the inner solar system, however, the comet dwellers' problems have been transformed into a host of new evolutionary opportunities.

The Uplift War (1987) extends the story begun in *Startide Rising*. Although *Streaker* remains offstage, the derelict space fleet that may conceal the secrets of the Progenitors remains a key bone of contention over which many different parties are squabbling in the eponymous war. As in the former volume, however, the action of the novel takes place on a very narrow segment of the vast stage of the Five Galaxies, on the old and rather decrepit planet Garth. In addition to their recently uplifted cousin species, the human heroes are here united in a common cause with the Tymbrini and various other alien allies, all of whom are intent on fighting off the invasion of the brutal Gubru.

The Uplift War follows much the same recipe as its predecessor. The painstakingly detailed ecosphere on view in this volume is a forest instead of an ocean, so the prominent part played by dolphins in *Startide Rising* is here recapitulated by uplifted chimpanzees. Inevitably, the wilderness in which the heroes take refuge turns out to contain secrets of its own, including the fugitive existence of the eminently upliftable simian Garthlings. The book is dedicated to Jane Goodall, Sarah Hardy, and Dian Fossey, whose work with various primate species provided the basis from which the author's depiction of uplifted chimpanzees and the elusive Garthlings is extrapolated. Brin also lavishes a great deal of care on his presentation of the customs and attitudes of the alien Tymbrini.

As is usual in Brin's novels, *The Uplift War* contrives to maintain a fierce pitch of dramatic tension throughout its later phases, but it is, in essence, merely a replay of *Startide Rising*, which carefully conserves the fundamental mysteries of the Uplift universe for further use and does not provide the sense of closure for which some of its readers must have wished. It confirmed the enduring popularity of the series when it won the Hugo and Locus awards for best novel in 1988 and was nominated for a Nebula.

111

A gap of three years separated *The Uplift War* from Brin's next novel, the equally massive but rather more ambitious *Earth* (1990). Set fifty years in the future, it examines the plight of the ecosphere under the accumulated stresses of population pressure and pollution. The greenhouse effect has altered the world's climate, the decay of the ozone layer has made direct sunlight dangerous, and the struggle to supply the lifestyles of the developed nations has put an enormous strain on food and mineral resources. The rapid advancement of technology has ameliorated the effects of these threats, but the spectacular march of information technology and the clever application of new biotechnologies, assisted by stringent conservation laws, have only succeeded in keeping the world one step ahead of a final collapse.

To present this panoramic image, Brin employs a mosaic narrative similar to the one that John Brunner used for a similar purpose in *Stand on Zanzibar* (1968), Brunner having taken his own inspiration from John Dos Passos. Brin, however, anchors his many commentary embellishments to a more robust central plot thread, in which scientific experimentation with a tiny black hole goes awry, tipping the black hole into the planet's core. There the wayward singularity begins a deadly gravitational pas de deux with its natural twin, which has been sitting peacefully in the center of Earth for millions of years. The battle to take control of these hungry masses ultimately becomes entangled with another battle fought by an extreme Environmentalist, who is intent on taking control of the world's computer network and using its authority to produce a Draconian solution to the distress of Mother Earth.

The long narrative crescendo typical of Brin's work leads *Earth* to the usual grand flourish, but the final deus ex machina—which is nearly literal as well as providing the metaphor with one of its most extreme paradigm cases—does not sit as well in a grimly realistic novel about the dangers facing our own world as it might have done in a grandiose space opera. As if anticipating this criticism and deciding to fight fire with fire, however, the author inserts between his two afterwords—one of which is explanatory, while the other is devoted to acknowledgements (including suggestions for further reading and the addresses of relevant organizations)—a "special bonus story" that brazenly takes the deus ex machina one step farther.

Abbreviated versions of parts of *Earth*'s mosaic narrative were spun off as "Privacy" (1989) and "The Secret of Life" (1990). Moreover, other short stories Brin produced before and soon after its publication shared its preoccupation with the near future of our own world. They also partook of a similar propensity for dramatic flourishes. "The Giving Plague" (1988) applies an intriguing Darwinian logic to the design of a disease that makes unusual provision for its transmission to new hosts. "Dr. Pak's Preschool" (1989) takes the notion of giving children an educational head start to a new extreme, which eventually results in the unborn being put to work with such dramatic economic effect that they become too valuable to be allowed out of the womb. Typically, Brin then took the notion of human wombs as a significant site of industrial activity one step farther in "Piecework" (1988).

Although "What Continues . . . and What Fails" (1991) follows the example of "Piecework" in beginning with its heroine pregnant and in a philosophical mood, the story quickly expands its perspective to take in the more grandiose vistas of possibility glimpsed in *Earth*'s "special bonus story." The widening of perspective continued in "Genji" (1992; reprinted as "Bonding to Genji")—Brin's contribution to the Shared World anthology *Murasaki*, edited by Robert Silverberg and Martin H. Greenberg—which offers a painstaking account of the work of a team of Japanese scientists engaged in the exploration of a new world. "Detritus Affected" (1992) returns to Earth in order to follow the exploits of miners and archaeologists working side by side in the excavation of twentieth-century garbage dumps, but the story line quickly takes off into surreal symbolism.

Brin's next novel, also separated from its predecessor by three years, exhibits the same expanded magnitude. *Glory Season* (1993) addresses some of the social problems arising from *Earth* but conducts its thought experiment in a very different laboratory. The story is an exercise in social design, of the kind that Ursula le Guin had dubbed an "ambiguous Utopia," couched as a planetary romance. The novel cleverly examines the pros and cons of establishing a society in which the ecosphere-threatening aspects of *Earth*'s near-future society have been carefully suppressed. The society in question is pastoral, its use of advanced technologies having been subject to careful selection and stringent limitation. This restraint has been facilitated by the social marginalization of males, which has also ameliorated the Malthusian pressure of population increase. The story's setting, the remote and hidden world of Stratos, has been colonized by feminists anxious to establish a new mode of reproduction as the central element of their society.

Because *Glory Season* offers an image of female-dominated society written by a male writer, the book's publication was regarded with some suspicion by feminist critics—who tend to hold such works as Poul Anderson's *Virgin Planet* (1959) and Mack Reynolds' *Amazon Planet* (1975) in utter contempt. Although Brin took care to include a strong plot line with an appropriately dramatic climax, the fact that the story remains, in essence, an analytical utopian romance meant that many ardent fans of his space operas found it the least interesting of his works. Seen from a critical viewpoint, however, there is no doubt that *Glory Season* succeeds magnificently in doing what it set out to do. Although the Uplift series commands more affection from lovers of action-adventure fiction and *Earth* has more immediate pertinence, *Glory Season* is more likely to be remembered by literary historians as the outstanding item in the opening phase of Brin's career.

The design of the hypothetical matriarchal society of Stratos takes into account numerous pertinent arguments that are dismissed or simply ignored by the vast majority of attempts to imagine female-dominated societies and takes enormous pains to accommodate them. Brin, conscious of the diplomatic niceties of writing as a male, goes to far greater lengths in trying to present an even-handed account of female ambitions than any female constructor of feminist utopias or dystopias has ever bothered to go in weighing male ambitions. The novel can stand comparison with such classics as Marge Piercy's *Woman on the Edge of Time* (1976) and Ursula le Guin's *The Left Hand of Darkness* (1969) and ought to be included in any serious discussion of the issues raised and the speculative strategies employed by those novels.

The architects of Stratos society, being unable to eliminate males entirely from their society, have engineered them to be fertile for only a brief interval during the summer of the planet's long year. For the rest of the year, they are uninterested in sex, although their cooperation has to be won in the conception of "winter children" who emerge as clones of their mothers following the stimulation of female lust by "glory frost." Maia, the heroine of *Glory Season*, is a "var"—one of the summer children who are almost as marginal to Stratos society as the males, although she is exceptional in having a natural clone: her twin sister, Leie. When the time comes to leave the protective environment home in which they have spent their childhood, the two sisters seek their fortune at sea, where the maintenance of shipping trade provides most of the planet's males and many of its vars with gainful employment. After their separation during a violent storm, Maia runs into further trouble, and her fate becomes entwined with that of a visitor from the worlds of the Human Phylum who has brought news that threatens the stable and peaceful society of Stratos with a drastic upheaval.

Different factions among the vars and the clone families react very differently to the news in question, forcing the visitor—with Maia in tow—to flee across the planet's surface, harassed by several different companies

113

of pursuers. This long chase provides the context in which Maia and the reader gradually come to appreciate the complexity of Stratos society and all the strengths and weaknesses inherent therein. Brin is conscientious enough to leave both Maia and Stratos with all remaining possibilities lying awkwardly open before them, and all their vital choices as yet unmade, so that the reader might make up his or her own mind about the results of the thought experiment.

Yet another three-year gap followed before the produce of Brin's next major project began to appear, this time in several volumes. In the interim he published his second short story collection, *Otherness* (1994). The collection also includes several contentious essays. An enthusiastic and skilled public speaker, Brin has addressed gatherings as diverse as the Society of Science Educators, the American Library Association, the Southern California Academy of Science, the Oregon Psychological Society, and the Los Angeles Junior Chamber of Commerce. He has also been a frequent guest on radio and TV talk shows, usually functioning as an expert "futurist." The amiably combative style of his talks has attracted a considerable following; his personal appearances at science fiction conventions always draw large crowds and always conclude in lively discussions.

Assertive opinions are rarely in short supply in the various communities to which Brin addresses his talks, and they have been a useful arena for testing and refining newly emergent analyses and lines of argument. Brin's perennial delight in discovering new wrinkles in old theses and in turning items of conventional wisdom on their heads has frequently produced gladiatorial performances that have been greatly appreciated even by those audience members who only turned up in order to turn their thumbs down. Although Brin's speaking style is flamboyant and his fictional extrapolations of social trends often go to extremes in order to maximize their rhetorical and satirical force, his interest in the issues he raises is always serious and intense. *Earth*

was intended as a propaganda piece as well as a melodrama, and Brin has continued to develop its themes in polemical talks and articles, alongside various other hobbyhorses. Such publications as "Zero Sum Elections and the Electoral College" (1992) and "The Threat of Aristocracy" (1994), both in *Liberty* and in a 1996 interview in *Wired* entitled "Privacy Is History—Get Over It," helped pave the way to his first nonfiction book, *The Transparent Society: Will Technology Force Us to Choose Between Freedom and Privacy?* (1998), which "point[s] out important advantages that candor and openness offer to a confident civilization."

"The Dogma of Otherness" (1986), the essay that gives *Otherness* its title, can be seen as an ironic celebration of the kind of "peer review" to which Brin routinely subjects his arguments. It contends that the definitive element of modern Western culture is its insistence on allowing all points of view to be heard and respected—and then wonders whether it might now be time to moderate free speech with voluntary courtesy, lest our pluralistic society should fly apart. The argumentative thread is taken up in more specific terms in "Science Versus Magic" (1990), then further narrowed in "What to Say to a UFO"—whose niggling element of annoyance is only slightly assuaged by the accompanying story, "Those Eyes" (original to the collection)—and "Whose Millennium?" The arrangement of the stories in the collection is, however, careful to broaden the perspective, placing the three stories that lovingly embrace the cosmic perspective—"Bubbles" (1987), "Ambiguity" (1990), and "What Continues . . . and What Fails"—before bringing the argument to a conclusion of sorts in "The New Meme" (1990).

Tolerance of otherness is also the dominant theme of *Brightness Reef* (1995), the first volume of the trilogy comprising Brin's next addition to the Uplift series. The title borrows a stratagem from Gregory Benford, whose "Galactic" series employed titles that combined images of light and water, although its supplementation by Brin's *Infinity's Shore* (1996) and *Heaven's Reach* (1998) testified to the fact that Benford had used up the most readily exploitable resources.

Brightness Reef is set on Jijo, a planet left to lie fallow by its former leaseholders, the Buyur, in accordance with the standardized rules of planetary management. The Buyur dutifully destroyed their cities—although some of the machines left to accomplish this demolition remained operative long afterward—but during the million years following the departure of the Buyur, several parties of refugees have arrived on Jijo in "sneakships," providing the seeds of a thriving but illegal colony.

In addition to humans and the centaur-like urunthai, these refugees include four other sapient populations of varying exoticism, ranging from the hoons—some of whom, including one of the novel's chief viewpoint characters, delight in mimicking human ways—to the wheeled g'Keks, the quasicrustacean qheuens, and the extremely exotic traeki. There are also post-sapient glavers, which have accepted devolution to animal status as the price of freedom. The six sapient races, having settled their differences in the Great Peace, have established a thriving mini-civilization. Some still cling to the principle that the colony should consent to its own elimination, but others cannot be persuaded of it. The plot of the novel gets under way when the precarious political balance sustained by the Jijo colonists is upset by the arrival of more spacecraft. These are crewed by humans, but they are also carrying members of a race that the crewmen believed to be the discreet uplifters of *Homo sapiens*. The precise purpose of the new arrivals is mysterious, and the exiles-in-residence fear that in the course of covering their own tracks the newcomers might find it convenient to exterminate them.

As in the previous volumes of the Uplift series, Brin pays careful attention to the design and development of Jijo's ecosphere, distributing the rewards of that work in the interstices of a complex and steadily accelerating plot. The profusion of view-points, some of which are alien, makes the novel far more of a patchwork than its predecessors and undermines the tension of the developing plot. This effect becomes even more obvious in the middle of the sprawling narrative, which is contained in *Infinity's Shore*. This second volume is mostly devoted to the business of further complication. As well as continuing its account of the crisis in the affairs of the exiles of Jijo, it takes up the story of *Streaker* following its escape from Kithrup. The multispecific crew of *Streaker* eventually becomes even more multispecific when it takes aboard elements of Jijo's society and carries them off into the final phase of the project.

Both *Startide Rising* and *The Uplift War* ended with an escape that, however satisfying it might be in climactic terms, left all the fundamental mysteries of the series tantalizingly unaddressed. Each of those volumes produced an image of the Uplift universe refracted through the affairs of a relatively small group of characters trapped in a single location. *Brightness Reef* and *Infinity's Shore* recapitulated this pattern in a more fragmented fashion, but *Heaven's Reach* sets forth into new territory, with the apparent intention of settling all outstanding questions as well as offering a panoramic view of the complex civilization of the Five Galaxies. It is substantially shorter than either of the first two volumes of the trilogy, but this is not entirely surprising; the dramatic expansion of breadth could not possibly have been complemented by the same kind of depth that was added in the earlier volumes.

The extravagant tour of the Five Galaxies contained in *Heaven's Reach* testifies to Brin's consciousness of the fact that the bedrock of his own enterprise is the tradition of fantastic voyages through the cosmos founded by E. E. "Doc" Smith, John W. Campbell, Jr., and Jack Williamson. In the course of providing a summary account of the distribution, organization, and evolutionary dynamics of universal life and civilization, Brin accommodates and reassesses many of the key clichés of that tradition: the metabolically exotic species whose atmospheres are poisonous to human beings; the societies of intelligent machines that have outlasted their makers; the societies of beings who have transcended the limitations of vulgar matter. The tour is further enlivened by the advent of the Time of Changes whose imminent advent was teasingly mentioned in earlier volumes; no mere social upheaval, this involves devastating "space quakes" that disturb every star and planet—although there are some alien races that regard it as a precious opportunity to further their exotic agendas. Although provisional answers *are* provided to many long-dangling questions, Brin also takes care to preserve sufficient mystery for future exploitation.

As usual, most of the short stories Brin published while the three volumes of the trilogy were in production offer different takes on similar concerns. Further space opera clichés are re-examined in the first-contact stories "Fortitude" (1996), in which the human species must be examined lest its ancestry prove insufficiently noble to permit assimilation to the greater galactic community, and "An Ever-Reddening Glow" (1997), in which members of the intergalactic Corps of Obligate Pragmatists beg human beings to stop polluting the universe with the noxious effluvia of their space drive. "Paris Conquers All" (1996, with Gregory Benford), re-examines an even earlier cliché, looking at the alien invasion of H. G. Wells's *The War of the Worlds* from the pragmatic perspective of Jules Verne.

Brin also agreed—after initially refusing—to join the other Killer Bs in providing a trilogy of novels extending and re-examining the narrative backdrop that began the process of sophistication that eventually made space opera a fit medium for thought experiment: Isaac Asimov's Foundation series. His nonfiction, meanwhile, continued the development of his other major line of speculation, trying hard to figure out what kind of social adaptations might be forced by technological advancement and which might be necessary—however difficult of achievement—to stave off the ecocastatrophic Time of Changes that seems to be fast approaching.

In an era when genre science fiction has been overtaken, in purely commercial terms, by the heroic fantasy that once eked out a frugal living on its margins, Brin is one of a handful of writers who have contrived to sustain its market potential, demonstrating that its concerns and methods still have best-selling potential. He has shown that space opera can be written with a good science fiction conscience without compromising its potential to excite readers, and he has shown that one can bring a similar conscientiousness to accounts of the near future and to social-scientific thought experiments with productive results. Were he to curb his tendency to excess—which sometimes makes his visions rather garish and his arguments a trifle Procrustean—he might find that a few more people would be willing to take him a little more seriously, but he might also lose the unique edge and flair that presently embellish his narrative verve and rhetorical thrust.

Although Brin's occasional deployment of deus ex machina stretches credulity, it is not altogether a bad thing that credulity should occasionally be stretched, even to the point at which it snaps. The court in which the question of what constitutes human progress and how that progress can best be sustained needs a ready supply of trained and practiced devil's advocates; Brin's skills of that argumentative kind are as finely honed as anyone else's.

Selected Bibliography

WORKS OF DAVID BRIN

Sundiver. New York: Bantam, 1980; London: Bantam, 1985.

Startide Rising. New York: Bantam, 1983. Revised edition, London: Bantam, 1985.

The Practice Effect. New York: Bantam, 1984; London: Bantam, 1986.

The Postman. New York: Bantam, 1985; London: Bantam, 1987.

Heart of the Comet, with Gregory Benford. New York: Bantam, 1986.

The River of Time. Niles, Ill.: Dark Harvest, 1986; London: Bantam, 1987. (Short stories.)

The Uplift War. West Bloomfield, Mich.: Phantasia Press, 1987; London: Bantam, 1987.

Earth. New York: Bantam, 1990; London: Macdonald, 1990.

Glory Season. New York: Bantam, 1993; London: Orbit, 1993.

Otherness. New York: Bantam, 1994; London: Orbit, 1994. (Short stories.)

Brightness Reef. New York: Bantam, 1995; London: Orbit, 1996.

Infinity's Shore. New York: Bantam, 1996; London: Orbit, 1997.

Heaven's Reach. New York: Bantam, 1998; London: Orbit, 1998.

The Transparent Society: Will Technology Force Us to Choose Between Freedom and Privacy? New York: Addison Wesley/Perseus, 1998. (Nonfiction.)

—BRIAN STABLEFORD

JOHN BRUNNER
(1934–1995)

JOHN BRUNNER IS among the most important modern writers of science fiction. His work was a discourse of dazzling intelligence, rationality, and erudition, always with a message. His principal message was that being rational is the most totally wholesome sentient behavior and that if people were to use their power to reason, humanity might endure and prosper.

Two statements pulled almost at random from the considerable bulk of Brunner's published writing emphasize this proposition and establish the particular meaning of "rationality" in his narratives:

My opinion is that long ago science and its applied counterpart, technology, have so deeply affected our attitudes and our patterns of social behavior that you can't go anywhere and escape them. (from "The Development of a Science Fiction Writer," page 12)

Stop and think of what you're doing,
  Join the march and raise your voice.
Time is short; we must be speedy.
  We can see the hungry filled,
House the homeless, help the needy.
  Shall we blast, or shall we build?
(from "The H-Bombs' Thunder," Brunner's lyrics for the "National Anthem of the British Peace Movement," in *The Book of John Brunner*, page 142)

"Stop and think," Brunner urges. About what? About the crucial relationship between mankind and its wonderful and dangerous artifacts. Yet by indirection, even in his gloom-iest dystopias, he contends that humanity has the ability and the power to solve its gravest problems. His stories are an affirmation of this belief. Beyond this, Brunner was to an unusual degree deliberately public about much of his personal life and development as a writer to increase the chances of getting his message to his audience.

I

John Kilian Houston Brunner was born on 24 September 1934 in rural Crowmarsh, Oxfordshire, England. His youth was a quiet, perhaps even lonely, period. He had two younger sisters, but no brothers, and few friends of his own age. Because he was ill a great deal, he read early and widely, including Daniel Defoe's *Robinson Crusoe* (1803), the scientific romances of H. G. Wells and Jules Verne, and the science fiction and fantasy of Rudyard Kipling, whose work in the genre he edited late in his life and of whom he said, "RK influenced my work more than anybody, more even than did Wells." In addition, he read an enormous number of detective stories and children's adventure books.

Brunner wrote his first story at the age of nine. Four years later, in 1948, he entered Cheltenham College. That same year he received his first rejection slip from the British *Astounding*. Brunner's first sale (1951) was *Galactic Storm* (under the pseudonym Gill Hunt), a piece he refused to acknowledge until pressed by persistent fans. Parents and teachers tried to discourage him from writing, believing it to be a profitless occupation. He resisted his parents, and his teachers made him so dislike the idea of formal education that he refused two chances for scholarships to Oxford. (As a mature science fiction writer, he took great satisfaction in reflecting that he had escaped taking any formal courses in science.)

Instead, Brunner wrote and was drafted into the Royal Air Force. He served two years but detested military service and all that it stood for. In 1953 he sold his first memorable piece, "Thou Good and Faithful," to John W. Campbell, Jr.'s *Astounding*. There were many rejections, but some stories did sell, including "No Future in It" (*Science Fantasy*, 1955) and "Fair" (*New Worlds*, 1956), but there was not nearly enough income for him to live on. Sam Youd (the science fiction novelist John Christopher) got Brunner a temporary job with the *Bulletin of Industrial Diamond Applications*. Then came a job as a minor editor of London's highly commercial company Books for Pleasure. On 12 July 1958, Brunner married Marjorie Rosamond Sauer. That November he turned to earning his living as a full-time freelance writer.

During the next six or seven years, Brunner wrote a large number of novels for Ace Books, as many other science fiction writers have done. His first book for Ace, and his first American sale of a novel, was *Threshold of Eternity* (1959), a sparkling space opera. The best pieces of this period, however, were short stories, including "Eye of the Beholder" (*Fantastic Universe*, 1957), "Silence" (also known as "Elected Silence," *Galaxy*, 1959), "Report on the Nature of the Lunar Surface" (*Astounding*, 1960), "Such Stuff" (*Magazine of Fantasy and Science Fiction*, 1962), "The Totally Rich" (*World of Tomorrow*, 1963), "The Last Lonely Man" (*New Worlds*, 1964), and "The Nail in the Middle of the Hand" (*Saint Mystery Magazine*, 1965). Moreover, he began to be recognized with honors and awards for his writing. In 1960 he finished *The Squares of the City*, one of his finest novels.

During the early 1960's, Brunner and his wife became active in the antiwar movement. In 1962 he went to Russia and met cosmonaut Yuri Gagarin. He also acquired an interest in music and folk song. Brunner and his wife traveled through Europe as much as they could, and he began to meet many major science fiction writers. In 1964 Brunner made the first of a number of trips to the United States, the setting for many of his later and best novels. In the same year, he published *The Crutch of Memory*, one of a handful of his works that move beyond the category of genre fiction. Along with *The Devil's Work* (1970) and the much later *The Great Steamboat Race* (1983), *The Crutch of Memory* is required reading for anyone who wants to gauge the full spectrum of Brunner's talent.

The years from 1964 to 1975 marked the rise of recognition of the artistry that earned Brunner stature as a major science fiction writer. At least ten novels from this period of his great achievement and rise to fame stand out. *The Whole Man* (1964) and *The Squares of the City* (1965) were Hugo nominees, and the latter sold well. *Quicksand* (1967) followed as part of a writing contract, reneged by a first publisher, that included the now famous *Stand on Zanzibar* (1968). Even so, despite all the prizes that *Zanzibar* won, Brunner never fully realized the financial returns that this work should have brought, typical of the bad commercial luck that followed him to the end of his life. There were also two fine fantasy novels during this time: *Catch a Falling Star* (1968), a revised version of *The Hundredth Millenium* (1959), and *The Traveler in Black* (1971; revised as *The Compleat Traveller in Black*, 1987). Other science fiction novels of this period include *Bedlam Planet* (1968), *The Jagged Orbit* (1969), *The Sheep Look Up* (1972), and *The Shockwave Rider* (1975). The novels of Brunner's later maturity are encore works in the sense that they are variations on the art and themes of the *Zanzibar* group. They include the especially notable *Crucible of Time* (1982), *Children of the Thunder* (1988), *A Maze of Stars* (1991), and

Muddle Earth (1993). None proved financially rewarding or remained in print for very long.

Brunner's centerpiece work is *Stand on Zanzibar*, which took five months to write, ran to more than 240,000 words, and made Brunner the first British writer to win the Hugo award for best novel (1969). It was in danger of never being published because the publisher that commissioned *Quicksand* and *Stand on Zanzibar* rejected both. Although a few critics condemned it, many more praised it, some regarding it as the most important novel to appear since the beginning of modern science fiction in 1926. The revolutionary discourse of *Stand on Zanzibar* placed before the science fiction reader a major work that expanded virtually limitlessly the forms in which science fiction might be written and enjoyed. *Zanzibar* rights were subsequently sold in many languages; there is a particularly fine French translation.

Brunner received the first British Fantasy Award for his overall achievement in writing in 1966. Two years later, only a few days after the assassination of Martin Luther King, Jr., he founded the Martin Luther King Memorial Prize, to be supported with his own money. He was an active participant in antiwar and antinuclear proliferation movements, and he was a familiar figure at science fiction conventions around the world.

In August 1986 Brunner's wife Marjorie died at age 65. With her passing, he lost not only an intimate friend but also an ally and a steadying influence. She had ably managed Brunner Fact and Fiction, Incorporated. Marjorie's death left Brunner, never good at business himself, awash in a confusion of professional affairs. His personality had always been prickly, which increasingly hurt his dealings with agents and publishers. His work was published less, or advertised with less enthusiasm. As a result, he came to believe he was being persecuted by the power brokers in the book business, but this was not the case. In 1991 he married Li Yi Tan, a woman much younger than he. (Marjorie had been thirteen years his senior.) The marriage was stormy, according to published accounts, but also

John Brunner in 1995. PHOTO BY JAY KAY KLEIN

buoying. *Muddle Earth* (1993), Brunner's last novel, is dedicated to Li Yi, "Because before her / it had been long and long / since last I felt like laughing."

Brunner died of a heart attack on 25 August 1995 at age sixty while attending Intersection: The World Science Fiction Convention in Glasgow, Scotland. The print forums for science fiction writer culture were full of eulogies by major authors saluting him in his passing. Though he complained that he did not make much money from his writing, especially in his later years, it is reported that the worth of his estate was estimated in British newspapers at 250,000 pounds, perhaps the imagined future value of his copyrights.

II

Stand on Zanzibar, The Jagged Orbit, The Sheep Look Up, and *The Shockwave Rider* form a cluster of related novels that are the most serious and polished of Brunner's enormous output. They also contain the agenda that Brunner brought to his writing to the end of his life. They are set, for the most part, in the United States. All are dystopian or, as Brunner labeled them, "awful-warning stories." All are concerned with questions of overpopulation and pollution that determine the main conflicts. All employ strategies of satire and black comedy to evoke in the reader a sense of overwhelming horror at the condition to which humanity may bring itself. All feature storytelling tactics that depend on a dazzling manipulation of language.

Stand on Zanzibar owes inspiration to the eighteenth-century British novelist Laurence Sterne and the early twentieth-century American writer John Dos Passos in exploiting a McLuhanesque composition technique that melds, as much as printed discourse can, the effects of various media, from graffiti and newspapers to television and the cinema. The technique reappears to varying degrees in all of Brunner's later writing.

All four novels feature the disorienting impact of scientific technology and computers on civilization. All, despite the pervasive gloom of the moods they create, implicitly or explicitly express confidence that mankind can survive. *Orbit* and *Shockwave* even have tenuously happy endings. Implicit in them all is the attractive assumption that if one can identify and understand a problem, one can—and will—solve it.

The touchstone novel is *Stand on Zanzibar;* the others grow out of it. In *Zanzibar,* world overpopulation is the main symptom, compounded by the venal stupidity with which politics, religion, corporate business, ethnic and racial differences, and the science of genetics are manipulated on the planet at the beginning of the twenty-first century. The multinational conglomerate General Technics sends Norman House to exploit the mineral resources of the African country of Beninia. In a parallel development, the United States government sends Donal Hogan to disrupt a promising genetics experiment in the

Asian country of Yatakang. An almost sentient computer and a brilliant sociologist, Chad Mulligan, operate at the source of these events and supply House with genetic analyses that will permit control of the Beninian natives. Hogan is also effective; and the novel ends with the world in greater danger than ever from the mismanagement of science, resources, and the population.

The Jagged Orbit follows *Zanzibar* with a concentration on racism, urban violence, a worldwide weapons cartel, social psychosis, and computerized media manipulation. Matthew Flamen, a television "columnist," barely manages, with the aid of Xavier Conroy, social psychologist, and his computer resources, to stop the crazy Dr. Mogshack from operating his prisonlike state mental hospital and to foil a massive plot by the Gottschalk weapons interest to sell an uncontrollable, surprisingly cheap weapon to virtually anyone with the money to buy it. Some bizarre sexual escapades illustrate how a civilization stress puts sexual behavior, a cultural litmus, under stress as well.

Many believe that *The Sheep Look Up* represents Brunner's greatest success at wedding craft and story. Set in the very near future, it envisions an ecology so disturbed and polluted in virtually every way imaginable, through industrial and commercial irresponsibility, that the end of the human species on the North American continent may be imminent. In *Sheep* the interpolated characters of Mulligan in *Zanzibar* and Conroy in *Orbit* are transformed and combined into the social activist and biochemist Austin Train and promoted to the status of central character. Train is killed before he can save America from pollution, but not before he serves to show the reader how pollution is caused and how it may be corrected.

Brunner consulted Alvin Toffler, author of *Future Shock* (1970), while writing *Shockwave*. The issues in the novel are the control and exploitation of genius-level human intelligence through the use of information processing and computer data nets, causing changes so rapid and capricious that the col-

122

lective sanity of mankind is threatened beyond recovery. Nicholas Haflinger, a polymath genius with a special aptitude for manipulating computers, emerges as the novel's hero. He escapes from a government institution, where brilliant youths are educated for exploitation by commercial and political interests. By programming the national computer data net with a system-destroying "worm," Haflinger liberates the public from the government's mesmerizing hold over it. He then settles with Kate Lilleberg in the rationally utopian community of Precipice, where a living model of how a wise man may live with science is being evolved.

Throughout these novels—in Mulligan, Conroy, Train, and Haflinger—the most serious of Brunner's protagonist types emerges. This type combines high intelligence, great knowledge, wisdom, and courage with a wholesome contempt for institutionalized educational systems, big business, and fascist government. The type is a clear composite of all those convictions that, as Brunner has revealed, were formed by his own experiences. Similar heroes appear in the other major novels.

The Squares of the City, a forerunner of the group of works described above, is set in a South American nation in the near future. With a plot based on an actual world championship chess match that serves as a metaphor for a political rivalry for control of the thoughts of the country's population, the novel attacks totalitarian repression, even when it is benevolent. Traffic analyst Boyd Hakluyt is brought in by the country's dictator, Juan Sebastian Vados, ostensibly to remove undesirable "squatters" from the capital city. Actually, Hakluyt and other characters are manipulated as human chess pieces in a game between the country's rival leaders. Hakluyt discovers the game and ruins it, helping to trigger civil disorder but giving freedom another chance to develop.

In *The Whole Man* and *Bedlam Planet,* attention turns to the essential nature of the human individual. Both novels explore the ultimate limits of a man, providing another di-

mension of Brunner's idea of ideal humanity. Gerald Howson is the crippled, telepathic dwarf hero of *The Whole Man*. Warped, bitter, lonely, and reclusive (at first) because of his rejection by a human culture that judges merit on a standard of physical health and beauty, he survives a long but ultimately healing ordeal. The narrative flames with insights that counsel, beyond knowledge and intelligence, the supreme necessity of charity and compassion. Only after these transformations affect Howson does he emerge a "whole man" and, by final logic, a superman.

Bedlam Planet employs the scenario of planetary colonization to explore another necessary process in the maturation of human character. Stranded colonists face extinction by an indigenous bacterium that consumes their bodies' vitamin C, which is not naturally available on the planet. Dennis Malone and several other colony leaders discover a remedy in deeply personal psychic and biological changes that begin when they eat the flora of the planet, from which they had earlier abstained. Instead of causing them to die, the flora changes their chemistry, and they regain excellent health. The other colonists must then be persuaded to eat the flora—a difficult task. The "cure" requires submission to and creative acceptance of the need to become "inhuman"—indeed, to become aliens—in order to preserve their humanity. The colonists must strip themselves to the molecular level, naked of their "culture." The story is an extraordinary metaphor for the most profound contemplative insights.

In *Quicksand,* fantasy and reality merge and separate in the minds of a young woman and a male psychiatrist. Found naked in a forest, a young woman, Urchin, learns English under the care of the psychiatrist, Dr. Fidler, and then tells him that she is from a future utopia. Fidler falls in love with Urchin and leaves his marriage and job to seek happiness with her. However, her aura of innocence is shattered as her subconscious mind reveals not a utopia but a future dystopia of decadence and viciousness. Fidler is inconsolable. His Edenic illusion has become a swamp. In despair, he kills Urchin and himself. A person must live and confront, in the real present and in his or her own mind, the ordeal through which the self may mature.

The more formal fantasy in *Catch a Falling Star* and in *The Traveler in Black* is only a step away from *Quicksand. Star* attacks people's predilection for living in the past; for seeking lost youth, vitality, and excitement; and for nostalgic reverie. In the far future, all humanity participates in a culture based on reexperiencing the past. Creohan discovers that the Earth will be destroyed by collision with a star only three hundred years in the future, but so immersed in nostalgia are the people, who visit the House of History religiously for visions of the past, that no one listens to him. Earth will perish. The lesson is obvious. Self-indulgent, sentimental cultures are fatal to their members.

The Traveler in Black addresses perhaps the most fundamental question of all: the source of the order and meaning of the universe. God commissions the traveler to bring order to the universe. He does so by attacking the whole agenda of "lies" that underlie human culture. He undoes myths, theologies, and sciences, all of which are no more than fraudulent "magics" that confuse people and prevent them from forming coherent views of the real universe. Reason and courage are the virtues required for every individual's successful quest.

In *The Crucible of Time,* a species, perhaps related to humans, on a planet, perhaps Earth, recently evolved from aquatic environments, goes through the stages of inspired intelligence and technological advancement—from the invention of the telescope and the discovery of the physics of fire and heat, the cause of disease, and genetic engineering to nuclear physics and space flight—that will take it to the stars. Here Brunner weds the twin grand themes of the awesome achievement represented by the evolution of single-celled sea organisms to makers of instellar civilization and the arbitration of the moral fitness such a summary species must possess. Critic Gary Westfall has made a wonderful representation

of the excellence and importance of *The Crucible of Time* based upon its brilliant similarity to James Blish's classic "Surface Tension" (1952).

Children of the Thunder paints an England in the last stages of collapse from exploitation by the forces of monopoly capitalism run amok, with special emphasis on how the news-media industry behaves as a laissez-faire market where news is sold and bought according to what the public wants to hear. Peter Levin, stringer journalist, and Claudia Morris, sociologist, track mutant children who "charm" their way through personal difficulties and ultimately to social power. The children are a *homo superior* strain that seems destined to replace incompetent humanity, even as the strain tries to clean up the polluted world humanity has made. Brunner's proposition is bleak: humanity will extinguish itself in a moral and material swamp. Wanted: a new species, even if it is as unsentimental about the removal of the old as the one in this novel.

Brunner's Gulliverian space opera, *A Maze of Stars,* is about a sentient, time-traveling, interstellar ark that revisits the planets it has seeded with human colonies, only to find the various maladaptations that the humans have mostly achieved. Eventually acquiring passengers such as the engaging Annica and Menlee, the starship visits an interesting assortment of worlds, with the conversation ornamented by Brunner's truly fascinating excerpts of big-science concepts on geology and biospheres: to get land life, you need a moon to cause tides, which will cause life to migrate from the sea. Mountains, too, are caused by the tidal effect of a moon. Shallow seas are necessary to cause oxygen from plant life that shoots it out above the surface. Here also Brunner's career-long analysis of the connection between history and memory is manipulated in a "Tachyonic" universe where the future, too, is "remembered." In the end, the reader learns that the ship's mighty brain has evolved from that of an octopus. The ultimate currency has become "pure information," and humanity, finally, in a much evolved state, colonizes the galaxy and contemplates the jump to other galaxies.

The obvious punning debt to J. R. R. Tolkien's *The Lord of the Rings* trilogy (1954–1955) in the title of *Muddle Earth* may well signal the likeness of the novel's dramatis personae to the Bag End citizens that Bilbo left behind in order to reach his maturity. Four hundred years in the future, Rinpoche Gibbs is "resurrected" from his cryogenic state, furnished with billions in credit, and allowed to make his way on an Earth that aliens run as a souped-up Disneyland. No particularly coherent resolution is in place at the novel's end, but Brunner has once again maximized his genius for satire with such affectations as "rides" wherein people experience such "thrills" as what it would be like actually to be burned at the stake during the Inquisition or to perish at ground zero of the explosion of the atomic bomb at Hiroshima. This novel, too, is fundamentally about "history," especially about how friable it is as a discourse that we create and certify as the official anesthesia of choice.

Many of the other novels are tantalizing. They include the superbly detestable mind-controlling behemoth of *The Atlantic Abomination* (1960) and the disgusting decadence of the time-traveling "producers" in *The Productions of Time* (1967), as well as the space opera (space adventure story) of the *Interstellar Empire* (1976) stories, the alternate worlds of *Times Without Number* (1962), the superman of *Polymath* (1974), and the confusion of time travel and alternate history in *The Infinitive of Go* (1980). The feeling that one is not oneself is confirmed in *Players at the Game of People* (1980), and the embrace of human roots in planet and mother is a central meaning in *The Tides of Time* (1984).

III

Novels and honors notwithstanding, Brunner always wrote short stories. The best of his middle period were "The Vitanuls" (*Magazine of Fantasy and Science Fiction*, 1967), "The Inception of the Epoch of Mrs. Bedonebyasyoudid" (*Quark*, 1971), "The Taste of the Dish and the Savour of the Day" (1977), "The Man Who Could Provide Us with Elephants" (1977), and "The Man Who Understood Carboniferous Flora" (1978), the last three of which appeared in the *Magazine of Fantasy and Science Fiction*. His fame and success declined after the later 1970's, even though his reputation among the critics and his peers remained as strong as ever. His stories continued to be selected for "masterpiece" and "year's best" volumes. These stories included "The Fable of the Farmer and Fox" (*Omni*, June 1987), "Moths" (*Dark Voices 2*, 1990), "The First Since Ancient Persia" (*Amazing*, July 1990), "The Man Who Lost the Game of Life" (*Fantasy and Science Fiction*, January 1992), "They Take" (*Dark Voices 4*, 1992), and "In the Season of the Dressing of the Wells" (*After the King*, 1992). The urbanity and elegance of these stories support the picture we should preserve of the basic Brunner. As he put it, he was never less than a writer of "competent stories competently told." They are, of course, much more than merely competent.

The best of Brunner's shorter fiction begins with "Thou Good and Faithful," a story about sentient robots made by a humanlike but transcended species that offers to prepare a utopian world for humanity. "No Future in It" tells amusingly of how a medieval cow-doctor turned village wizard gives up his trade. One of the sideshows in "Fair" gives far more than a dime's worth. Customers are treated to a mind-opening experience that mutes their bigotry and racism and makes them compassionate and empathetic. Lack of empathy frustrates and enrages the reader of "Eye of the Beholder," in which interplanetary tourists murder a genius painter merely because he belongs to a species that the humans have mistaken for monsters. In "Silence," truly monstrous aliens hold the poor human Hesketh in solitary confinement for twenty-eight years, so long that he comes to prefer it. Purely comic irony marks the often anthologized "Report on the Nature of the Lunar Surface," in which the moon is "contaminated" to such a degree by the first human expedition that its surface is believed to be encrusted with green cheese. Far more sinister is the vampire dreamer in "Such Stuff," who feeds on the dreams of others.

Many feel that "The Totally Rich" is the best of the earlier short stories. It features a relationship between a young scientist and a woman so rich that she can buy total anonymity. She tries to buy the scientist's service in the resurrection of her dead lover. He fails, and she commits suicide. For sheer horror and paranoia, few stories can outdo "The Last Lonely Man," in which a telepathic process permits a form of immortality of the personality through voluntary preagreements with friends who survive you when you die. But what happens if you lose your friends or die without someone in whom to be reborn? The allegory of fire-and-brimstone doctrines will not be lost on most readers. Most horror filled of all is the soldier-executioner of Christ as he obsessively contemplates the spike with which he has nailed Christ's hand to a table, wondering how he will nail the other hand, in "The Nail in the Middle of the Hand." Reincarnation theology underlies "The Vitanuls," in which an immortality treatment arrests death in the world's population to such a degree that babies begin to be born without souls because there are no more souls left.

In the anti-Vietnam spirit of the early 1970's, "The Inception of the Epoch of Mrs. Bedonebyasyoudid" recounts an orchestrated bomb attack on New York City by Southeast Asian agents. Three more stories are exquisitely baroque in composition and narrative voice in a manner reminiscent of the detective stories of Edgar Allan Poe and of Sir Arthur Conan Doyle's Professor Challenger series. They mix humor, horror, and linguistic erudition in perfect balance. "The Taste of the Dish and the Savour of the Day" presents a science fiction convention goer tempted by the opportunity to eat a food so good that it makes one immortal and takes all the fun out of eating. The remarkable Mr. Secrett is the hero of "The Man Who Could Provide Us with Elephants," "The Man Who Understood Carboniferous Flora," and several other stories ending with the perhaps prescient "The Man Who Lost the Game of Life." In the first, we learn how one builds a World War II airfield with "zombie elephants." In the second, the legacy of a brilliant but cranky scientist flourishes around his neglected grave in the form of carnivorous plants. In the last, the anonymous writer narrator takes over Mr. Secrett's job as director of the library of the Royal Society for Applied Linguistics, inheriting as well Mr. Secrett's locked room full of occult artifacts and juju charms with which he begins to settle old scores with literary agents and others who have cheated him.

"The Fable of the Farmer and Fox" is Brunner's meditation in the manner of a Zen paradox in which both the farmer and the fox die while the chickens that both have fed on live. Brunner always entertained his readers. In "Moths" Mathilde sews moth eggs into her cruel half sister Chantel's lace wedding gown (appropriated from Mathilde's mother), so that on the wedding day, at the ultimate moment, the dress, eaten by the moths' larvae, falls off Chantel, leaving her naked and covered with sores where the larva have fed on her flesh. "The First Since Ancient Persia" is a yarn about a South American army of near immortals who take both South and North America but, because they are sterile, look forward to a future of healthy elders who have no children to follow them. In "They Take" (1992), modern heirs of ancient Etruscans capture Ann and Carlo, a couple who are deceived into believing that they have inherited an Italian property that includes a preserved Etruscan necropolis. Their purpose is to breed more heirs with Ann. The couple is doomed to stay in the place, herded by giant mastiff dogs. The drive for proprietary dominance employs extraordinary tactics for success and more than 2,500 years. Finally, "In the Season of the Dressing of the Wells" (1992) is an exquisite piece of horror fantasy that critics believe exhibits Brunner's continuing brilliance in his last years. The story is about crippled

World War I veteran Ernest Peake and a minister's daughter, Alice Pollock, who find love in a pre-Christian rite that blesses the local water wells by "dressing" them in pictures made of clay, twigs, and feathers. One deep, brackish well is sweetened, meanwhile, when Ernest's vicious aunt, by her obstructionist religious practice coupled with an enchantment of the primordial maternal deity of the wells, drowns in it.

The dedication to reason manifested throughout Brunner's writing produced weaknesses as well as numerous strengths. Some of the weaknesses arose from the necessity of the writer as practical businessman to release a story that was less than perfectly polished. Some were inherent in a vision ordered by "sweet reason." Critics have noted, for example, Brunner's frequent failure to create characters with truly full emotional dimension. Love affairs, for instance, lack authentic feeling. Reason is too democratic, perhaps, to permit the enchantment that usually fires readers' imaginations. Moreover, the discourse of the stories produces no poetry with the daring of Harlan Ellison or the innocent sentimentality of Ray Bradbury. It is clever and controlled, brilliant without being sensational or utterly fabulous. It is metaphysical.

In 1972, Joseph DeBolt, professor of sociology at Central Michigan University, decided to write the first of the several major bibliographical, biographical, and analytical works that he has published on Brunner. The two met at Torcon in 1973, again later that year at Central Michigan University, and once more when DeBolt visited the Brunners in England in 1978. DeBolt's admiration for a number of Brunner's major works moved him to prepare accounts of Brunner that are impressive for their accuracy, completeness, and clarity. All subsequent study of Brunner owes a great deal to DeBolt.

Brunner's writing fills nearly one hundred books. Ninety percent of it is fantasy or science fiction, most of which is listed in the DeBolt and Benson/Stephensen-Payne bibliographies. Moreover, Charlie Brown, editor of

Locus, reported in his obituary salute to Brunner that he had the notes for a Brunner bibliography planned with the writer shortly before he died.

It is no little achievement to be interesting in over two million words of published narrative. Brunner wrote in virtually every category of science fiction, from space opera to dystopian social criticism. His characters have a homeliness that implies authentic people more often than supermen, and they are mirrors in which readers can see themselves. The particular rationality of his writing produces a tension by mastering a passionate humanism—his championship of the dignity of cultures, genders, and races—that unfailingly infuses his work with a luminous spirit. Brunner earned a living from his writing. He witnessed to his extraordinary vision through it. He won admiration and the highest honors for it, and with it he extended significantly the scope of science fiction.

Selected Bibliography

WORKS OF JOHN BRUNNER

Galactic Storm, as by Gill Hunt. London: Curtis Warren, 1952.

Threshold of Eternity. New York: Ace, 1959.

The Atlantic Abomination. New York: Ace, 1960.

No Future in It. London: Gollancz, 1962. (Collection that includes "Elected Silence," "Fair," "No Future in It," and "Report on the Nature of the Lunar Surface.")

Times Without Number. New York: Ace, 1962.

The Crutch of Memory. London: Barrie and Rockliff, 1964.

The Whole Man. New York: Ballantine, 1964.

Now Then! New York: Mayflower-Dell, 1965. (Collection that includes "Thou Good and Faithful.")

The Squares of the City. New York: Ballantine, 1965.

Out of My Mind. New York: Ballantine, 1967. (Collection that includes "Eye of the Beholder," "The Last Lonely Man," "The Nail in the Middle of the Hand," "Such Stuff," and "The Totally Rich.")

The Productions of Time. New York: New American Library-Signet, 1967.

Bedlam Planet. New York: Ace, 1968.

Catch a Falling Star. New York: Ace, 1968.

Stand on Zanzibar. Garden City, N.Y.: Doubleday, 1968.

The Jagged Orbit. New York: Ace, 1969.

The Devil's Work. New York: W. W. Norton, 1970.

"Genesis of *Stand on Zanzibar* and Digressions into the Remainder of Its Pentateuch." *Extrapolation* (May 1970): 34–43.

The Traveler in Black. New York: Ace, 1971. Revised as *The Compleat Traveller in Black*, London: Methuen, 1987.

"The Development of a Science Fiction Writer." *Foundation*, 1 (March 1972): 5–12. (Autobiography.)

From This Day Forward. Garden City, N.Y.: Doubleday, 1972. (Collection that includes "The Inception of the Epoch of Mrs. Bedonebyasyoudid" and "The Vitanuls.")

The Sheep Look Up. New York: Harper and Row, 1972.

Polymath. New York: DAW, 1974.

The Shockwave Rider. New York: Harper and Row, 1975.

The Book of John Brunner. New York: DAW, 1976.

Interstellar Empire. New York: DAW, 1976. (Collection.)

Foreign Constellations. New York: Everest House, 1980. (Collection that includes "The Taste of the Dish and the Savour of the Day.")

The Infinitive of Go. New York: Ballantine, 1980.

Players at the Game of People. New York: Ballantine, 1980.

The Crucible of Time. New York: Ballantine, 1982.

While There's Hope. Richmond, Surrey: Keepsake, 1982.

The Tides of Time. New York: Ballantine, 1984.

The Shift Key. London: Methuen, 1987.

The Best of John Brunner. New York: Ballantine, 1988. (Mostly pre-1980 pieces.)

Children of the Thunder. New York: Ballantine, 1989.

"About Rudyard Kipling." In *John Brunner Presents Kipling's Science Fiction: Stories by Rudyard Kipling.* New York: Tom Doherty Associates, 1992.

Kipling's Fantasy. Edited by John Brunner. New York: TOR, 1992.

A Maze of Stars. New York: Ballantine, 1992.

Muddle Earth. New York: Ballantine, 1993.

"Sometime in the Recent Future. . . ." *Science Fiction Chronicle*, 15 (March 1994): 30–31.

INTERVIEWS

Covell, Ian. "An Interview with John Brunner: The Square House: Seeing the World." *Science Fiction Review*, 8 (January/February 1979): 8–15.

Drake, H. L. "Van Vogt and the Quest for the Universe." *Foundation*, 69 (Spring 1997): 18–26. (Interview of Brunner in August 1987.)

Melia, Sally Ann. "Power Corrupts: John Brunner Interviewed." *Interzone*, 97 (July 1995): 18–22.

Platt, Charles, ed. *Dream Makers: The Uncommon People Who Write Science Fiction: Interviews.* New York: Berkley, 1980.

Walker, Paul. "John Brunner: An Interview." *Luna Monthly*, 58 (August 1975): 1–5, 10.

BIBLIOGRAPHIES

Barron, Neil, ed. *Anatomy of Wonder.* New York and London: Bowker, 1976. (Contains critical annotations by Joe DeBolt of nine Brunner novels.)

Benson, Jr., Gordon, and Phil Stephensen-Payne. *John Brunner, Shockwave Writer: A Working Bibliography.* 3d ed. Albuquerque, N.Mex. Galactic Central Publication, 1989. (Two pamphlets. P.O. Box 4094; zip code 87196)

———. *John Brunner: Shockwave Writer: A Working Bibliography.* San Bernardino, Calif.: Borgo, 1990.

Currey, L. W., comp. "John Brunner." In *Science Fiction and Fantasy Authors: A Bibliography of First Printings of Their Fiction and Selected Nonfiction.* Boston: G. K. Hall, 1979. (Eighty-three entries.)

DeBolt, Joe, and Denise DeBolt. "A Brunner Bibliography." In *The Happening Worlds of John Brunner.* Edited by Joe DeBolt. Port Washington, N.Y., and London: Kennikat, 1975.

Tuck, Donald Henry. *Author's Books Listing: A Booklet Prepared for the 33rd World Science Fiction Convention . . . Outlining the Hardcover and Paperback Titles of John Brunner, A. Bertram Chandler, Edmund Cooper, Philip J. Farmer, Ursula K. LeGuin, Michael Moorcock, and Alfred E. Van Vogt.* Lindisfarne, Tasmania: D. H. Tuck, 1975.

CRITICAL AND BIOGRAPHICAL STUDIES

Auffret-Boucé, Hélène. "*Stand on Zanzibar:* Ou L'Art du Gerbage." *Etudes Anglaises.* 41, no. 3 (1988): 345–354.

Brin, David. "John Brunner: Further Appreciations." *Locus* (November 1995): 78–79.

Brown, C. N. "Editorial Matters: John Brunner." *Locus* (November 1995): 79.

D'Ammassa, Don, and Andrew Porter. "Obituaries: John Brunner." *Science Fiction Chronicle* 17 (October/November 1995): 22.

DeBolt, Joe. "The Development of John Brunner." In *Voices for the Future.* Vol. 2. Edited by Thomas Clareson. Bowling Green, Ohio: Bowling Green University Popular Press, 1979.

———, ed. *The Happening Worlds of John Brunner: Critical Explorations in Science Fiction.* Port Washington, N.Y., and London: Kennikat, 1975.

Goldman, Stephen H. "John Brunner's Dystopias: Heroic Man in Unheroic Society." *Science Fiction Studies*, 5 (November 1978): 260–270.

———. "The Polymorphic Worlds of John Brunner: How Do They Happen?" *Science Fiction Studies*, 3 (July 1976): 103–112.

Greiner, Patricia. "Radical Environmentalism in Recent Literature Concerning the American West." *Rendezvous*, 19 (Fall 1983): 8–15. (Includes remrks on *The Sheep Look Up.*)

Haldeman, Joe. "John Brunner: Further Appreciations." *Locus* (November 1995): 78–79.

"John Brunner: 1934–1995." *Locus* (October 1995): 5, 70–73. (Obituary with testimonials by Robert Silverberg, Christopher Priest, Michael Moorcock, Sam J. Lundwall, Carter Moody, Ian Watson, Brian Aldiss, Gwyneth Jones, Niels Dalgaard, Peter Nicholls, and Dave Langford.

Merril, Judith. "Books." *Magazine of Fantasy and Science Fiction* (February 1969): 22–25. (Review of *Stand on Zanzibar*.)

Monk, Patricia. "The Syntax of Future Shock: Structure and the Center of Consciousness in John Brunner's *The Shockwave Rider*." *Extrapolation*, 26 (Fall 1985): 220–230.

Murphy, Patrick D. "Dialogics and Didacticism: John Brunner's Narrative Blending." *Science-Fiction Studies*, 14, no. 1 (1987): 21–33.

Samuelson, David. "New Wave, Old Ocean: A Comparative Study of Novels by Brunner and Delany." *Extrapolation*, 15 (December 1973): 75–96.

Sander, Joe. "Brunner and Lovecraft: A Comparison of Fantasy." *Seldon's Plan*, 6 (June 1974): 18–23.

Sawyer, Andy. "Tomorrow May Be Even Worse: John Kilian Houston Brunner (1934–1995)." *Vector*, 185 (September/October 1995): 4–8.

Schaffer, Carl. "Exegeses on *Stand on Zanzibar*'s Digressions into Genesis." In *The Shape of the Fantastic: Selected Essays from the Seventh International Conference on the Fantastic in the Arts*. Edited by Olena H. Saciuk. Westport, Conn.: Greenwood Press, 1990.

Scholes, Robert. "Change, SF, and Marxism: Open and Closed Universes? Novels by Brunner and Levin." *Science Fiction Studies*, 1 (Spring 1974): 213–214.

———. "Science Fiction as Conscience: John Brunner and Ursula K. Le Guin." *New Republic*, 30 October 1976: 38–40.

Spinrad, Norman. "*Stand on Zanzibar:* The Novel as Film." In *SF: The Other Side of Realism*. Edited by Thomas Clareson. Bowling Green, Ohio: Bowling Green University Popular Press, 1971.

Stern, Michael. "From Technique to Critique: Knowledge and Human Interest in John Brunner's *Stand on Zanzibar, The Jagged Orbit*, and *The Sheep Look Up*." *Science Fiction Studies*, 3 (July 1976): 112–120.

Watson, Ian. "Reaping the Whirlwind." *Foundation*, 7 and 8 (March 1975): 55–60. (Deals with *The Sheep Look Up*.)

———, Jack Dann, and Jack C. Haldeman II. "In Memoriam: John Brunner and Roger Zelazny." In *Nebula Awards 31: SFWA's Choices for the Best Science Fiction and Fantasy of the Year*. Edited by Pamela Sargent. New York: Harcourt Brace Jovanovich, 1997: 114–124.

Westfahl, Gary. "The Quintessence of Science Fiction, Forged in Brunner's *The Crucible of Time*." *Foundation*, 69 (Spring 1997): 5–17.

—JOHN R. PFEIFFER

ALGIS BUDRYS

(b. 1931)

ALGIRDAS JONAS BUDRYS, who writes as Algis Budrys, lives in Evanston, Illinois, but he is not quite an American and does not write quite like an American. He was born in Konigsberg, East Prussia (now Kaliningrad, RSFSR), on 9 January 1931, the son of a Lithuanian diplomat. His father was transferred with his family to the United States in 1936, as the Lithuanian consul general in New York. (Lithuania, a province of Imperial Russia before the Bolshevik Revolution, became independent in 1919.) When Soviet Russia occupied Lithuania in 1940, Budrys' father remained as consul general, since the United States did not recognize the Soviet takeover. He occupied that post until his death in 1964, working very hard in émigré politics; as consul general he was, in effect, a public relations man, representing his homeland nominally and symbolically rather than actually. Algis spent some time working as assistant, translator, and speech writer for his father until 1960. A free Lithuanian citizen, he has never become a naturalized American, and he has no passport.

The relevance of this background to the central themes in Budrys' science fiction—the nature of political authority, the nature of human identity, and the use of the media for manipulative purposes—will become clear.

Budrys began publishing science fiction in 1952, with "The High Purpose" in *Astounding Science Fiction*. He became a prolific author of short fiction, producing more than seventy science fiction stories under his own name by the end of the 1950's, and a further twenty-four stories under the pseudonyms David C. Hodgkins, Ivan Janvier, Paul Janvier, Alger Rome, William Scarff, John A. Sentry, and Albert Stroud. Sixteen of these stories were republished in his first two collections: *The Unexpected Dimension* (1960) and *Budrys' Inferno* (1963; reissued in England as *The Furious Future*, 1964). Most of Budrys' short fiction, including some very fine stories, remains uncollected.

By 1960, the time of his first collection, Budrys had already made a reputation as a science fiction novelist. Five novels had been published; only two more have appeared since. Budrys' work has been slow to find the wider audience it deserves. From the beginning it has had a certain bleakness and austerity of outlook which was at odds with the expectations of science fiction readers of the time.

Budrys' first novel was *False Night* (1954). The book was shortened from his manuscript; a revised and superior edition that reinstated the original manuscript and also incorporated new material was published as *Some Will Not Die* (1961).

In *Some Will Not Die* a plague has destroyed nine-tenths or more of the population of a near-future America. The episodic narrative tells of the ensuing anarchy and the painful reconstruction of civilization (first in Manhattan and later over the whole northeastern seaboard), directed by members of two families of survivors over a period of about forty years. The book is an exercise in social Darwinism; the fitness that allows survival goes beyond physical strength and ferocity (although it includes them) to incorporate moral and intellectual strength as well.

The leader, Berendtsen, later murdered by his own people, is a kind of latter-day Machiavelli who believes (as Budrys seems to) that the end justifies the means. The end in this case is the welding of isolated, struggling communities into a quasi nation that will command the resources to raise the quality of life above the subsistence level. Some of this welding (which has not been fully achieved by the end of the book) is to be accomplished by political astuteness; some, at gunpoint. There is a good deal of ethical skepticism (some of it arguably overly cynical) in this novel. Budrys' vision of the masses stripped of their civilized milieu is that they are basically shortsighted, rapacious, selfish, often wantonly cruel, and that many of them are murderers and rapists; the decencies of life are luxuries available only to organized societies.

Whether or not one agrees with Budrys' stern thesis, one is bound to be impressed by the maturity with which the young Budrys assesses the cost. The process is difficult and hateful, and nobody hates it more than the liberal-minded dictator who is the novel's protagonist for much of its length. But power, it seems, has its own imperatives from which the clear-eyed man cannot afford to flinch.

The conflicting imperatives of personal freedom and social legislation, together with the difficulties experienced by one political generation in adjusting to the changing paradigms of power facing the next, are themes that recur in several novels by Budrys and in much of his short fiction over the next six years.

It may be impertinent to speculate on the relationship between Budrys' fiction and his private life, but it is difficult to avoid doing so. His father was an idealist émigré whose homeland had been subjugated by an occupying power; the realization that liberation was no more than a pipe dream must have had a souring effect. What effect would this have had on the son who worked as his assistant?

The question recurs in *The Falling Torch* (1959), a brief and rather diagrammatic novel about political realism. Earth is occupied by alien invaders; an Earth government-in-exile has taken refuge on Alpha Centauri IV; the Centaurians are members of a powerful and long-established Earth colony that has not been conquered. Michael Wireman, the son of the Earth-President-in-Exile, returns to Earth to foment revolution with undercover assistance from the Centaurians, who would repudiate the revolution if officially asked to support it. On Earth, Wireman learns that many of his new comrades are little better than bandits, and that the invaders of Earth are in many cases decent. In any event, he succeeds in his mission, and Darwinian skepticism quickly replaces his immature idealism. Ultimately he keeps power himself, rejecting his father, who had expected to return as president.

Even to a reader not familiar with Budrys' history, the allegory must be clear. The invaders are emblematic Russians, the Centaurians are Americans, and Earth is a kind of outsize Lithuania or Latvia or Estonia, although it is never made to *feel* really big—one of the major faults in the novel. As a political parable the story is intelligent and acid; as science fiction it is perfunctory; and as a novel it is skeletal. The liberation of Earth is rendered hardly more plausible than a contemporary liberation of Lithuania, catalyzed by a small, émigré task force, would be in real life. The resonances the book gains from what we know of Budrys' own life are painful, especially the fictional father-son relationship, even though it very probably had no exact reflection in reality.

The same themes recur in a short story, "The Burning World" (1957), which is collected in *The Unexpected Dimension*. In this short story an easily developed energy source, available to all, has allowed the ordinary people (years before the events of the story begin) to overthrow a police state. Kimmensen, the revolutionary leader, is now an old man who (he believes) is effectively without a job. The state has almost withered away, and the country is a peaceful anarchy based upon fragmented family units. He has trained his prospective son-in-law, a decent young idealist, to succeed him. But Messerschmidt, the people's choice (and his daughter's choice as well), is a man despised by the protagonist as a kind of neofascist, for using a bogus threat of invasion as an excuse for reinstating a national army. Ironies multiply: the decent young idealist tries to rig the election; the threat of invasion is real; finally, only the old man whom history has passed by has the moral courage, and the training in the brutality of an earlier era, necessary to defeat the invasion by unleashing a weapon that will also kill many of his own people. The generation gaps of the story can be interpreted as consisting of an anarchic Communism succeeding fascism and giving way in turn to an American-style armed democracy that must necessarily incorporate some of the savagery of an older order. This story is an unpleasant fable. Budrys appears to see these imperatives of successful statehood as both distasteful and inevitable.

It is no wonder that such early tales brought Budrys no great popular acclaim. These bleak, complex, political fables, which seem to arise from a mind painfully divided between idealism and a brutal pragmatism, were quite foreign to the simpler expectations of an American audience that was used to regarding science fiction as an optimistic genre. American readers wanted Songs of Innocence, but Budrys was giving them displeasing European paradoxes, Songs of Experience.

Up to this point Budrys had failed to find metaphors from the science fiction genre adequate to carry his burden of meaning; the science fiction clothing he utilized had often seemed no more than tattered, ill-fitting rags revealing the gaunt outlines of contemporary cold war themes all too clearly beneath them. The science fiction apparatus was not really functional; this is true even in the minor novel *Man of Earth* (1958), in which a soft and cowardly Earthman is transformed into a tall, muscular fighter hijacked into a colonial

Algis Budrys (Algirdas Jonas Budrys) in 1988.
PHOTO BY JAY KAY KLEIN

army on Pluto as part of a Machiavellian project in cultural engineering.

The themes of national survival, political expediency, and conflict between the generations were finally brought together by Budrys into a single, terrible image in his story "Between the Dark and the Daylight" (1958; reprinted in *Budrys' Inferno*). This is about self-directed evolutionary change. A group of humans is isolated on a planet on which the native life is so savage that their only hope of ever leaving their protective dome is to breed themselves toward a generation of creatures who are bloodthirsty and powerful enough to struggle with the monsters outside on their own terms. The story focuses on the leader of the last generation that could still be called vaguely "human"; it is his responsibility, while concealing from his more squeamish colleagues quite how appallingly their offspring have evolved, to let their ferocious children loose outside the dome. The story is related with an absolutely single-minded obsessiveness and a relentless darkness of tone. Never before had Budrys' theme of political paradigms changing across the generations been so concisely evoked as in this parable, at the end of which it becomes clear that the new generation will turn upon its parents, rend them, and literally eat them. Budrys was at last discovering how potent science fiction metaphors can be.

His second major theme, the nature of identity, received its first notable expression quite early, in "The End of Summer" (1954), which is reprinted in *The Unexpected Dimension*. This story is set in a static, future utopia where everyone is effectively immortal at the cost of having his or her memories wiped clean at the end of every day. Their memories are then electronically replaced, but are usually edited in the process. Thus pain and loss, for example, are temporary and discontinuous. In these circumstances, is a person's identity what he or she edits it to be, or what is coded on tape in a case hung from the arm? The theme is a haunting one, but the science fiction devices, as in many other of the early stories, are arbitrary and implausible. *Man of Earth* tackles the question of identity more deeply in asking to what extent the spirit of a man depends on his physical type. *Who?* (1958), though, which also knits together the theme of identity and the theme of realpolitik, is Budrys' first important novel on these themes, and it succeeds because its hard, central science fictional image is wholly plausible.

Who? is an apparently simple, near-contemporary cold war thriller. Scientist Lucas Martino, badly wounded in a laboratory accident near the Communist border in Eastern Europe, is taken to a hospital in the East by a Communist squad. The man who is returned to the Americans four months later has been largely reconstructed from metal because of the dreadful nature of his injuries; he is an enigmatic, prosthetic monster. American security cannot put the metallic "Martino" back to work (on a device that may tilt the balance of power from East to West) until his identity is established, but the mask cannot be penetrated. Is the man Martino or a Russian substitute?

The novel focuses tightly on "Martino" and his interrogator. (It contains many flashbacks to the actual Martino's earlier life; he had always been alienated from his fellows, repressed, devoted entirely to his work; there was always something "metallic" about him.) American security decides that the risk cannot be taken; the metal "Martino" is released to work on a small, one-man farm in a quiet corner of New Jersey; he is no longer permitted to work as a scientist. The reader is not allowed to know until the very end (after "Martino" has, ironically but with a certain metaphysical truth, denied being the original Martino) that he *was* in fact the real Martino all the time.

The strength of this taut fable is in its relentless expansion of what begins as a purely narrative enigma (who is Martino?) into an enigma of epistemological resonance (what constitutes identity?), an enigma that has its physical expression, with superbly calculated aptness, in an expressionless, inhuman mask. As is commonly the case with Budrys' stories, the tone is pessimistic, austere, and glacial. The preaccident Martino was monastic and withdrawn; the postaccident "Martino" reaches out for human warmth. But his metallic mask frightens people away; it even defeats the Russian interrogator who attempts to debrief him before his return to the Americans. (Budrys later said in passing—see the excellent interview by Charles Platt in *Dream Makers* [1980]—that this character was modeled on his father.)

The preaccident Martino used the computerlike precision of his mind to create weapons; the postaccident "Martino" fixes farm machinery through the computerlike (inhumanly accurate) dexterity of his metal fingers, but now he also makes natural life grow from the soil. There is no springtime renewal for him, though. There is only "a patina of microscopic scratches and scuffs," the beginning of a progression toward abrasion, rust, and death that is created in a sense by his own alienation, for which the forging of his mask and all the masks of cold war politics merely provide an objective correlative.

The sheer force of *Who?* has given it a kind of underground status in science fiction, despite the slight coolness with which it was received at the time. It is not an instantly likable book, for it not only repudiates the colorful escapist fantasies of much science fiction but also refuses the comfort of catharsis. The disenchanted flatness of tone throughout, the avoidance of melodrama, the harsh and conscientious consistency with which the novel deliberately muffles emotions that a "cheaper" writer might have exploited are both admirable and chilling.

Budrys does not always eschew melodrama. His most celebrated novel, *Rogue Moon* (1960), described by James Blish as populated "solely with madmen," is full of a baroque and colorful violence, both in its action and in the dialogue of its characters.

It is also Budrys' outstanding work. Again he creates a perfect science fictional correlative for what could not easily have been explored so economically in the "mainstream," although the ambiguities of power and personal identity that Budrys dissects here have nothing intrinsically science fictional about them.

In *Rogue Moon* there are two science fictional *données*. First, a matter-transmission device has been perfected. It can scan a person's body and resolve it into an electromagnetic signal that can be transmitted to another location and reconstituted into matter, a duplicate body. Another device, a receiver, must already be present at the second location. The matter-transmission process destroys the original body. But there can be more than one receiver, and therefore more than one doppelgänger can be created simultaneously. Second, an alien artifact (which might even be living) has been discovered on the Moon; a matter transmitter-receiver is dropped near it from a rocket, and a team of technicians is transmitted to the Moon to investigate it.

The artifact, a labyrinth of some sort, is cryptic; its real purpose is unknown, but it operates (perhaps irrelevantly and accidentally) as a death machine. The alien labyrinth has an entrance that cannot be used as an exit. All those who enter it are killed, in grotesque and sometimes disgusting ways.

The artifact is explored by doppelgängers: the matter transmitter is used to create two duplicates, A and B, of each volunteer. A explores the artifact while B, back on Earth and in telepathic contact with his twin, is able to describe what is happening. Duplicate A is always killed; duplicate B always collapses under the emotional strain of experiencing A's death. After a number of such attempts, the experiment is about to be stopped by the government unless the project director, Dr. Edward Hawks, can find a volunteer strong enough to withstand the psychic pressure of repeatedly experiencing his own death. Hawks chooses Al Barker, a sports hero with a strong death wish.

Death permeates the novel. Barker's mistress, Claire Pack, is a metaphoric death machine who will "chew you up and spit you out"; Sam Latourette, the technician, has an internal death labyrinth in the form of the cancer that is devouring him; Hawks is the death machine par excellence, sending men to destruction or madness for the sake of knowledge.

The central metaphor of the death machine is wonderfully appropriate; the symbolic resonances of the death maze proliferate throughout the novel. It is even a kind of metaphor for the novel itself: just as Barker has to traverse the maze to restore meaning to his life, so the reader has to traverse the labyrinth of the book in order, retrospectively, to understand the whole, much of which is at first sight cryptic. The maze might also be read as an act of alien communication, a kind of death message. It is also an analogue of Hawks's mind, into which Barker is warned not "to set foot." The symbol contains the structure of the story.

Because the labyrinth transforms those who enter it, the question of whether the A characters are identical with the B characters becomes important. Identity is seen (as in "End of Summer") as consisting of a kind of gestalt of memories. It is this that renders so moving Hawks's last message to his alter ego, about the woman he loves: "Remember me to her."

Rogue Moon is not only central to Budrys' work, it also captures the central, cognitive theme of science fiction itself: the need to know, the conceptual breakthrough of the protagonist into more complex paradigms, richer pictures of the meaning of things. The rite of passage that Hawks A and Barker A take through the labyrinth at the end of the book (only to die on the Moon) is an emblematic ritual of growth and development. The cluster of images that associates the traversal of the maze with evolutionary imperatives is delicately created. (The cover of Barker's first schoolbook showed goldfish trying to leap upward out of a bowl.) But unlike science fiction generally, Budrys' story tells us how much evolution will cost us. The high-pitched and sensationalist tone of the book is grating, a deliberate and consistent shattering of serenity. Evolution hurts; it renders the identity of things and people insubstantial. The surrealistic metamorphoses of the maze combine death and fragmentation with a lacerating beauty in images that sum up the whole process.

Rogue Moon, for all of its occasional brittleness of tone and its cocktail-party Freudianisms, is one of the triumphs of the genre. Budrys hoped that the book would win a Hugo award; but in 1961 the award for best novel went to Walter M. Miller, Jr.'s *A Canticle for Leibowitz* (1960), although its date (original magazine publication in 1955–1957) should, Budrys felt, have rendered it ineligible. Budrys was generally supposed to have quit science fiction in disgust, but in fact he gave up freelance writing at the end of 1961 partly because his wife was expecting their fourth child. (Previously, in addition to his writing, he had done editorial work for *Galaxy* magazine and later with Pyramid Books; he continued editorial work with Regency Books and then with Playboy Press up to 1965. Most of his work since then has been in public relations and advertising.) Only sporadic short stories and one novel appeared in the rest of the 1960's.

One of the last short stories before the hiatus was "All for Love" (1962). This can be found in Budrys' most recent (1978) collection, the title of which, *Blood and Burning*, sums up something of the violent quality that his work was by now evoking in readers' minds—as had the title of the previous collection, *Budrys' Inferno*. He was coming to be seen as science fiction's foremost chronicler of madness and death.

One of the characteristics of Budrys' fiction is that it typically pictures the passions of its protagonists only obliquely through their love affairs and their other personal relationships, but centrally through their work. For Budrys the job *is* the man; his life focuses on it. This is a rather unusual perspective in fiction generally. His heroes are men with a grim, conscientious, and sometimes obsessive sense of duty. Budrys' background may be Roman Catholic, but his ethos is puritanical. The politicians of the early fiction and the scientist Hawks in *Rogue Moon*, wedded to work and death, are typical. In "All for Love," Malachi Runner, the manic hero, belongs to a troglodyte mankind that is utterly devoted to its desperate job of destroying a fifty-mile-high alien spaceship that has landed in the United States and has reduced humanity to the status of ants, to be ignored or brushed aside when they sting. Runner's superior officer is a prosthetic nightmare whose dedication to his task has cost him his physical humanity; he is a brain in a box, a revenge machine, even less human in appearance than Lucas Martino. A person or an entire culture in extremis, this is the template for much of Budrys' work. "All for Love" (the title is ironic) is awesome in its icy excess: duty imploded into madness.

The Amsirs and the Iron Thorn (1967) confronts humans and aliens in tests of manhood on a dry planet whose twin societies are primitive and ritual-ridden. It turns out that the "aliens" are genetic variations of human stock, the result of a long-forgotten experiment. Most readers are confused by the second part of the novel, in which the human protagonist is returned to Earth and launched into a media blitz that sentimentalizes him as a latter-day Tarzan. The change in tone from epic to satiric between the novel's two parts is too extreme to come off quite successfully, but the new concentration on the fantasies of the media landscape (the third of Budrys' main themes) was important to his subsequent work. He returned, perhaps temporarily, to writing science fiction in the mid-1970's with several short stories and a novel. (In the interim he maintained his interest in science fiction by writing book reviews that appeared in *Galaxy,* from 1965 on, and later in *Magazine of Fantasy and Science Fiction.*)

The media theme had been foreshadowed in "Wall of Crystal, Eye of Night" (1961), collected in *Blood and Burning.* The murderous protagonist of this story controls the exploitation of a form of three-dimensional television that, through hookups with the viewer's brain, modifies the emotional content of the material displayed so that it empathically suits the individual viewer. This theme recurs in "The Nuptial Flight of Warbirds" (1978), also found in *Blood and Burning.* This story is told from the viewpoint of a professional actor whose own manipulated fantasies become the lead performance in such audience-drugging dramas. Budrys' experience in advertising had clearly opened up a new field for his grim skepticism. The triumph of this phase of his development was his latest novel, *Michaelmas* (1977).

The novel's hero is Laurent Michaelmas, a newscaster. Budrys knows well that the way in which the media select and present the news is already one of the most potent means available for creating social and political expectations in the minds of the people as a whole. But Michaelmas' power goes well beyond this, for he has a hidden and almost symbiotic relationship with his personal computer, Domino, a creation so sophisticated that it has effectively developed both intelligence and autonomy. Domino has

secretly tapped all the world's computer networks; from whatever source electricity carries coded information—be it the telephone system or household thermostat controls—that information is available for Michaelmas to use and to alter. He has more power than any other person in the world; he is the archetypal secret manipulator. He rather world-wearily uses his powers for good, constantly readjusting the governing mechanisms of the power blocs and their societies to maintain an uneasy balance. The actual plot of the novel is not essential to the theme; it turns on unmasking and dealing with a complex alien (extraterrestrial) threat. Coded information from the stars is being misused unscrupulously by power-hungry men. (The information itself, like the death maze in *Rogue Moon,* is ethically neutral.)

Michaelmas is utterly cynical. Power is used to destroy power; the end justifies the means. All of Budrys' old themes recur: the clash between political generations (as shown in the relationships between Michaelmas and younger reporters), the nature of identity (the alien's message can be used to reconstruct duplicate people), the power of the media, the political manipulator, and the man in the metaphorical mask.

Technically the book is very proficient; it explores issues of great importance—especially those related to the manipulation of electronic information networks. But several commentators, myself for one, have begun to wonder to what extent Budrys is neutrally recounting ironic fables of the corruptions and painful difficulties involved in the use of power, and to what extent he is actually advocating an adroit manipulation of the average man (for whose intelligence Budrys' work has consistently shown a rather somber contempt). Budrys almost seems to be saying that the conscientious, self-sacrificing actions of such Machiavels as Michaelmas are our best hope for survival in a gray and fallen world.

The critic John Clute proposes that *Michaelmas* may be "a secret parody and criticism of the generally incoherent authoritarian assumptions of genre fiction, and that our enjoyment and approval of Michaelmas' behavior should demonstrate to us how lazily and complacently we accept in fiction (and perhaps in life) morally dubious acts committed by charismatic individuals with whose ideas we agree" (in *Survey of Science Fiction Literature*). Well, yes, that is certainly how one would like to read the novel. But if irony of this sort is present, then its signals must be very subliminal indeed. And Michaelmas' behavior is all of a piece with Budrys' long line of fictional manipulators: Berendtsen in *Some Will Not Die*, Wireman in *The Falling Torch*, Hawks in *Rogue Moon*, and others. Surely, even if there is irony in these creations, there is also a kind of cynical, fatigued acceptance as well: there will always be world movers, so let us hope they have some kind of decency and balance. This is one of the most cheerless messages to be found in genre science fiction.

Budrys' brilliant creation and exploitation of resonant metaphors, and the adroit craftsmanship with which he builds up narratives that function on simultaneous levels of meaning, serve to make his dark moral ambiguities memorable, but they do not necessarily render them palatable. He is an extremely intelligent writer, and his realpolitik themes are never simpleminded; let us hope that they are, nevertheless, only a partial reflection of the true state of the world.

Selected Bibliography

WORKS OF ALGIS BUDRYS

False Night. New York: Lion Books, 1954. Revised and expanded as *Some Will Not Die*, Evanston, Ill.: Regency Books, 1961.
Man of Earth. New York: Ballantine Books, 1958.
Who? New York: Pyramid Books, 1958. London: Victor Gollancz, 1972.
The Falling Torch. New York: Pyramid Books, 1959.
Rogue Moon. Greenwich, Conn.: Fawcett-Gold Medal Books, 1960.
The Unexpected Dimension. New York: Ballantine Books, 1960. London: Victor Gollancz, 1962. (Short stories.)
Budrys' Inferno. New York: Berkley Books, 1963. Reissued as *The Furious Future*, London: Victor Gollancz, 1964. (Short stories.)
The Amsirs and the Iron Thorn. Greenwich, Conn.: Fawcett-Gold Medal Books, 1967. Reissued as *The Iron Thorn*, London: Victor Gollancz, 1968.
Michaelmas. New York: Berkley Books, 1977.
Blood and Burning. New York: Berkley Books, 1978. (Short stories.)
"Algis Budrys, 1931– ." In *Contemporary Authors*. Autobiography Series, vol. 14. Edited by Joyce Nakamura. Detroit: Gale Research, 1991.
"Can Speculative-Fiction Writers and Scholars Do Each Other Good?" *Extrapolation*, 25, no. 4 (1984): 306–313.
Benchmarks: Galaxy Bookshelf. Edited by John W. Campbell, Jr. Carbondale: Southern Illinois University Press, 1985. (A collection of book review columns from *Galaxy* magazine from 1965 to 1971.)

CRITICAL AND BIOGRAPHICAL STUDIES

Atheling, William, Jr. [pseudonym of James Blish]. *More Issues at Hand*. Chicago: Advent Publishers, 1970. (Chapter 5: "Death and the Beloved.")
Beggs, Delores G. "Algis Budrys Talks About Science Fiction." *Quantum* (Spring/Summer 1993): 9–11.
Blackmore, Tim. "The Hunchbacked Hero in the Fiction of A. J. Budrys." *Extrapolation*, 33, no. 3 (1992): 230–244.
Drumm, Chris. *Algis Budrys Checklist*. Polk City, Iowa: Drumm, 1983.
Ketterer, David J. "Rite de Passage: A Reading of *Rogue Moon*." *Foundation*, 5 (1974): 50–56.
Letson, Russell. "A Young Man Raised by Apes on Mars: The Hero as Displaced Person in Budrys' Novels." *Foundation* (Autumn 1986): 31–35.
Magill, Frank N., ed. *Survey of Science Fiction Literature*. 5 vols. Englewood Cliffs, N.J.: Salem Press, 1979. (Chapters on *Michaelmas* by John Clute, *Rogue Moon* by Peter Nicholls, and *Who?* by Brian Stableford.)
Melia, Sally-Ann. "I Write and I Write Good—and That's the Way of It: Algis Budrys Interviewed." *Interzone* (May 1995): 23–26.
Platt, Charles. *Dream Makers: The Uncommon People Who Write Science Fiction*. New York: Berkley Books, 1980. Reissued in England as *Who Writes Science Fiction?*, Manchester: Savoy Books, 1980. (Chapter 13, "Algis Budrys," is a revealing interview with Budrys.)
Samuelson, David N. *Visions of Tomorrow: Six Journeys from Outer to Inner Space*. New York: Arno Press, 1975. (Chapter on *Rogue Moon*.)

—PETER NICHOLLS

EDGAR RICE BURROUGHS
(1875–1950)

PROBABLY THE ONLY character in twentieth-century English literature to achieve universal familiarity has been Tarzan of the Apes, as created by Edgar Rice Burroughs in 1912. Tarzan has been the subject of novels, motion pictures, television programs, radio broadcasts, pornographic films, pictorial representations in comic strips and comic books, and advertising and publicity items of all sorts, ranging from games and bathing suits to racehorses and ice cream cups.

This wide diffusion of a personality, a life history, and a philosophy has nothing to do with the quality of the Tarzan stories as literature. As Edgar Rice Burroughs said in different contexts, "That is another story."

In many ways the life of Edgar Rice Burroughs paralleled that of L. Frank Baum, the creator of the Oz books. Both men came from moderately well-to-do, middle-class families; both did poorly in school; both were markedly unsuccessful in many varied business enterprises; both in middle life discovered a mode of fantasy writing that suited them and was highly viable commercially; and both, on the basis of writing success, embarked on entrepreneurial ventures that failed and cost them fortunes.

Edgar Rice Burroughs was born in Chicago on 1 September 1875, the son of a distiller who later became a manufacturer of electric batteries. His family outlook was military, and Burroughs seemed headed for a career in the army; but he was expelled from Michigan Military Academy for disciplinary reasons and failed examinations for West Point. The end of his army aspirations came, in effect, when he enlisted in the regular army and served for a short time in the cavalry at Fort Grant, Arizona. He found army life unbearable, and his family used influence to have him released. His later attempts to obtain a commission were unsuccessful.

Until Burroughs reached the age of thirty-six, his life was marked by a succession of failures. At various times he worked on gold mining operations in Idaho and Oregon; was a railroad yard policeman in Salt Lake City; ran a stationery and book store in Pocatello, Idaho; offered a mail order course in salesmanship; and, most ironic of all, prepared detailed business advice for subscribers to a service magazine. In a desperation move, while supervising pencil sharpener salesmen, in his free time he started to write adventure fiction for the pulp magazines.

Here success came to Burroughs almost immediately. Although his first novel, *Under the Moons of Mars* (*All-Story*, February–July 1912), aroused little attention, his second, *Tarzan of the Apes* (*All-Story*, October 1912), created a sensation. Within two years he was a full-time writer receiving premium rates.

Burroughs worked rapidly and over the next thirty-five years wrote more than one hundred novels and short stories. As a writing businessman he was highly effective. It is claimed that his books sold more than six million copies during his lifetime. Individual stories often received magazine publication; book publication; translation into foreign languages; newspaper serialization; comic strip, comic book, and big-little book publication; radio broadcasts; and motion picture production. During Burroughs' lifetime twenty-six Tarzan motion pictures were produced, and he received royalties for the use of the name Tarzan on a variety of products.

If Burroughs had been content to write and reap his subsidiary payments, he would have been a very wealthy man. Unfortunately, he thought of himself as an all-around businessman; and while it would be an exaggeration to say that he lost in business all that he made from writing, it is true that his side ventures were seldom profitable. He lost fortunes in California real-estate speculation and wasted much time and money on ill-conceived motion picture productions. In the 1930's he undertook the publishing of his own books, but, as he later admitted, without marked success.

For most of his writing career Burroughs lived in California, although he often changed residence almost compulsively. Just before World War II he settled in Hawaii, where he witnessed the Japanese attack on Pearl Harbor. During the war, in addition to maintaining a full writing schedule, he wrote a newspaper column and served as a war correspondent. In 1945, Burroughs returned to California and tried to resume his earlier activities, but his writing ability had deteriorated markedly. His last years were marred by ill health, and he died on 19 March 1950.

I

The story that made Burroughs' fortune was, of course, *Tarzan of the Apes*. All his works other than the Tarzan books were considered commercially salable as "by the author of Tarzan," and it is probable that he would have been just one more "pulpateer" if it had not been for Tarzan.

The character Tarzan is so well known that only a few words are needed to indicate the motifs of the stories. The son of a British peer, he was reared in Africa by apes after the death of his parents. He never saw a white man until he was mature. Unlike historical wolf boys and other possibly feral men, he grew up into a marvelous physical specimen, intelligent and virtuous. To make the note of neoprimitivism clearer, Burroughs now and then contrasts Tarzan's natural and good activities with the unnatural and deplorable activities of Tarzan's cousin in London, who has unwittingly usurped Tarzan's title. Tarzan, on one occasion, eats a haunch of fresh, sweet meat; his cousin hangs his pheasants to age and dabbles in a foul-smelling cheese.

The roots of Tarzan are multiple. It is possible to trace him back to the "noble savage" of the eighteenth century, but this is not necessary. It should be sufficient to say that in the popular literature of the day there were, easily accessible to Burroughs, stories based on similar premises. Such were Morgan Robertson's "Primordial" and "The Three Laws and the Golden Rule" and C. J. Cutcliffe Hyne's *The New Eden*. Jack London's "When the World Was Young" subsumes much of the Tarzan syndrome. Rudyard Kipling's jungle stories may have suggested incidents, while H. Rider Haggard's *She* offered a good deal for the later novels.

Tarzan of the Apes was followed by some twenty-three sequels, most of which embody the same ideas: the wonders of the Edenic situation before civilization and the confusion of tongues; strong racism and social snobbery (*pace* modern apologists who have tried to explain away some of the raw remarks); sexual adventurism, in the She-Amenartas dualism; and the right of the superior white man to slaughter whatever is in his way. Not all the sequels qualify as science fiction.

The Return of Tarzan (*New Story*, June–November 1913), the first sequel, established the quest pattern that dominates most of the later novels and introduced the first of the femmes fatales of the series. This is La, high priestess of Opar, a lost city originally founded from Atlantis. In Opar the men are crooked, debased creatures, while the women are beautiful and no doubt would be available to Tarzan, were he so inclined. The amorous La, a cruel and vicious beauty, is to some extent redeemed in the course of succeeding novels. Opar also supplies Tarzan with almost limitless quantities of gold bullion, which he nonchalantly carries off.

Most of the sequels continue in much the same manner, technically remaining science fiction, apart from talking apes, by the inclusion of lost races or other such elements. Tarzan encounters ancient Atlanteans, ancient Greeks, ancient Romans, Hellenistic Greeks, early Christians (who are epileptic anchorites), and medieval Englishmen, all hospitably housed secretly in sheltering Africa.

Other oddities include the land of Pal-u-don (in *Tarzan the Terrible*), where dinosaurs survive and men have long, prehensile tails, and the land of the ant men (in *Tarzan and the Ant Men*), where knee-high humans ride midget deer and live in underground cities. Tarzan is temporarily shrunk, by glandular massage, and held a slave in such a city for a time. Tarzan also encounters speechless "missing links" along the lines postulated by Ernst Haeckel in the nineteenth century, magical gems that permit control of the will of others, a serum conferring immortality, and a mad scientist who has stolen germ cells from the tombs of British monarchs and reactivated the cells by injecting them into gorillas.

The quest theme dominates the plots of most of the later Tarzan novels. Tarzan may be seeking his wife, Jane, who has been kidnapped, after suitable atrocities, by Huns of World War I, or he may be in search of Russian agents and anarchists who are plotting to steal the gold of Opar. In some later adventures Tarzan is a bystander who intervenes on occasion, but it all comes to the same thing.

Second to the Tarzan series, and much less important commercially, was the Martian series. The first Martian novel, printed as *Under the Moons of Mars* (1912), was attributed to Norman Bean, which is said to have been a typographical error for the facetious pseudonym Normal Bean. When the story was first published, it attracted little attention; but the success of the more obvious Tarzan series soon lifted it out of obscurity. It was repub-

lished in book form, with some cut passages restored, as *A Princess of Mars* (1917).

It is the story of John Carter, "Virginia gentleman," who is in the Southwest after the Civil War and is trapped in a cave by Indians. Through some inexplicable process he leaves his body, stands in a second (astral?) body looking at Mars, and is drawn to the Red Planet. There, with his terrestrial strength, he fights his way easily through many perils and wins a red-skinned, oviparous princess, then seems to lose her in a situation that cries for a sequel: the planetary air-conditioning plant breaks down.

The story, stripped of exotic accidentals, is that of a historical novel of the day, with a captivity, a romance, and a rescue. Burroughs' Mars is a fictionalization of the Mars described by the overimaginative American astronomer Percival Lowell in books and articles, with half-ruined water-bearing canals; desiccated, vegetation-covered sea bottoms; and the remnants of a once high, now decadent civilization. It is probable that Burroughs also had read certain of the occult interplanetary novels of the late nineteenth century, in which stages of psychic evolution were treated in terms of the planets. It is curious that the most famous of all Martian stories, H. G. Wells's *The War of the Worlds* (1898) and "The Crystal Egg," do not seem to have influenced Burroughs. Functionally, though, Mars is simply a convenient place to have fairy-tale-like adventures involving wishful fillment.

Several of the ideas that permeate Burroughs' work first appear in *A Princess of Mars*, notably a strange complex surrounding birth and death. In the otherworlds of Burroughs, people are seldom born, as with us, nor do they die naturally. They may emerge from eggs, may evolve from lesser beings in infinite regress, may be created, may sprout vegetatively from the sides of their parents— and they are often immortal, even having limbs that retain life when severed. Since neither birth nor death on this level had any great significance for readers of the pulp fiction of

Edgar Rice Burroughs. CORBIS

the day, they probably represent private concerns of the author.

In *The Gods of Mars* (*All-Story*, January–May 1913) John Carter undertakes an essentially Orphic quest. He must enter the lands that the Martians associate with death and defy the funerary cult to regain his wife. He does not succeed. In the third novel, *The Warlord of Mars* (*All-Story*, December 1913–March 1914), Carter is still on his quest and travels to the North Pole of Mars to find another hidden culture. Mars, apparently, is so constructed that despite science superior, in many areas, to that of earth, geographical knowledge is abysmal, and no one knows what lies beyond the next range of hills. In this novel Carter receives his apotheosis and is proclaimed warlord, or emperor, of Mars, a title that later romances reveal to be empty and premature.

Burroughs wrote ten Martian books. An eleventh (*John Carter and the Giant of Mars*), though published under Burroughs' name, was not his. Conceptual high points in the later books are men who create armies by mental power (*Thuvia, Maid of Mars*); "bodiless" human heads with hypnotic ability and a chess-like game played with living pieces who fight to the death (*The Chessmen of Mars*); fantastic organ transplants (*The Master Mind of Mars*); and a size-changing relationship between Mars and one of its moons, so that when Carter arrives, he is automatically shrunk to the size of one of the native cat men (*Swords of Mars*). But the basic situations underlie most of the stories: woman-stealing by lecherous brutes, proud and haughty beauties who must be approached with Edwardian circumspection, and slaughter.

Burroughs also wrote two less important story sequences as well as several independent books. Least important is a sequence of stories set on Venus, where Carson Napier, having miscalculated his course to Mars, cracks up his spaceship. There are giant trees, immortality, some political satire of a rough sort, and familiar plot formulas. These stories have never been rated highly, even by enthusiasts.

More important commercially were the Pellucidar stories. These were based on the concept of Symmes's Hole, a motif from the crank science of the early nineteenth century. According to John Cleves Symmes's theory, the earth is a hollow sphere, with large openings at the poles that permit entry into a habitable interior world along the inner surface of the sphere. In Burroughs' first novel in the Pellucidar series, *At the Earth's Core* (*All-Story*, 4–25 April 1914), a mechanical mole escapes control and tunnels through the earth's crust, carrying its two occupants into a strange, primitive world. The humans in the inner world are, for the most part, on the cultural level of cavemen, and there are many monstrosities (as well as paleontological survivals) of a sort never found on the surface. There are also large, highly intelligent, civilized reptiles with hypnotic powers, who keep humans as slaves and for food.

This series, which began on a somewhat more juvenile level than most of Burroughs' other work, continued through six more books and gradually deteriorated into almost self-parody. Pellucidar was popular among readers, but it apparently never had the cultural significance of Tarzan or the Martian novels.

Burroughs' best work, in the opinion of many fans, is to be found in two books, each composed of three short novels. These are *The Moon Maid* and *The Land That Time Forgot*.

The Moon Maid, which begins in the near future and extends to the twenty-fifth century, offers a political message in describing the aftermath of the first voyage to the moon. The first component, "The Moon Maid" (*Argosy All-Story*, 22 June–20 July 1923), reveals that the lunar interior is populated by city-states that are losing their independence to the Kalkars, a race of aggressive, brutal, stupid, and shiftless louts who represent Burroughs' image of Russian Communists. (It is ironic that at one time Burroughs was the best-selling American author in the Soviet Union.) The Kalkars, led by a renegade earthman, conquer the earth, too, and subject it to a slovenly tyranny. The second story, "The Moon Men" (*Argosy All-Story*, 21 February–15 March 1925), was first written as "Under the Red Flag" in 1919. It was originally concerned with a future Russian occupation of America. Burroughs was unable to sell it in its original form and revised it to fit the moon series. Set in the ruins of Chicago, it describes an abortive revolt against the Kalkars and the execution of the American leader. It is more sparsely written than is usual with Burroughs, and it has a certain power, reminiscent of the work of Jack London, despite its opposite point of view. The third component, "The Red Hawk" (*Argosy All-Story*, 20 April–14 May 1925), postulates a reversion to the life patterns of the Plains Indians and describes the final expulsion of the Kalkars. The second and third components were greatly abridged when the three stories were combined in book form.

The Land That Time Forgot (composed of "The Land That Time Forgot," *Blue Book*, August 1918; "The People That Time Forgot," *Blue Book*, October 1918; and "Out of Time's Abyss," *Blue Book*, December 1918), although grounded in the extreme jingoism of World War I, with commonplace erotic plots, contains an imaginative redirection of the old biological saw that ontogeny recapitulates phylogeny. On Caspak, an unknown island of considerable size, evolution is an individual matter. An entity may start life as a primitive egg, work its way up into a lizard, then a small mammal, then an ape man, and, unless eaten or "stuck in stage," eventually into *Homo sapiens*. Only at the stage of *Homo sapiens* does procreation take place as in the outside world. There is a further, submerged implication: *Homo sapiens* may not be the high point of evolution. On Caspak there is a race of winged men who have developed a cruel and bloody civilization that is well imagined.

Within Burroughs' 110 or so published stories there are others that have science fiction elements, but these other stories are not worth commenting on, since they have little merit and no historical importance. Burroughs also wrote adventure novels, Indian stories (better researched than his other work), historical romances, Graustarkian fiction, Westerns, and examples of other subgenres of pulp fiction. Some of these stories are treasured by collectors, since editions were small, but they have no other interest.

II

Burroughs is a science fiction writer in externals only, not in inner essence. Most of his work is really a fantasy of eroticism and power. The hero gets the girl—with Gibson-girl conventions transplanted to the jungle or the deserts of Mars; the underdog, dropped naked and helpless into a hostile environment, demonstrates his virility and achieves supreme power following a course that involves punishing those who improperly try to assume authority.

Science per se plays little part in the work of Burroughs, and it is safe to say that he knew and cared little about it. He refers to tigers in Africa, and the question of Tarzan's ape foster siblings has always been an embarrassment. What, exactly, were these apes? The best answer that can be suggested is that Burroughs had come upon the work of Dr. R. L. Garner, a crank biologist. In his *Gorillas and Chimpanzees* (1895), Garner claimed to have discovered the language of apes. He also reported that in Africa there existed an ape unknown to science, perhaps a species of gorilla, "more intelligent and humanlike than any of the others . . . said to live in parts of the forest remote from human habitations."

Although Burroughs made a fortune and a worldwide reputation out of African adventure, he never went to Africa, never bothered to learn anything about African ethnography, and never moved beyond superficial Victorian travel accounts.

The Martian novels, even if one admits as much poetic license as is necessary for creating a story, are closer to occultism than to science, and the paleontology of *The Land That Time Forgot* involves more fangs than facts. Where inventions or scientific discoveries enter Burroughs' fiction, they are usually thin-air results, rather than processes, and usually are simply symbolic mechanisms for abuse of power.

From one point of view it is surprising that Burroughs never bothered to enlarge his mental world—despite his preoccupation with business schemes—but from another point of view, it must be granted that he knew what his readers wanted. He offered them perils, escapes, and threatening situations, presented with emotional tension and acceptable values.

Burroughs is probably still the best-selling science fiction writer of all time (with the possible exception of Jules Verne), and some attempt must be made to account for his popularity, since in many ways his writing skills were inferior to those of the better pulp writers of the day. His plotting was weak, repetitious, and formularized; his characters were paper-thin; his style ranged from cumbersome and amateurish in his early work to lower-level commercial at its best.

Yet Burroughs had some strengths. He was able to imagine arresting situations; and if he was not able to provide a plot, he could keep action moving steadily. He also had the knack, as did Max Brand, of permeating his stories with a pseudo-mythical quality. John Carter and Tarzan, if less than individuals by mainstream standards, became more than just characters in terms of subculture empathy.

Burroughs was also very conscientious in what might be termed the marketing aspects of pleasing readers. He took pains to compile vocabularies of Martian and other languages; he prepared maps of his imaginary lands; he worked out consistent rules for playable games; and he carefully linked his story chains, offering familiar ground to his readers. He was also quite skilled at contriving endings that left matters sufficiently up in the air to justify a sequel.

His system of author immersion, too, is always cleverly handled. His story frames are not conventional but bring Burroughs himself into the story. And, perhaps because of his mail-order experience, he knew how to keep his characters and himself before the public eye.

Tarzan, of course, was helped on his career by the ideas latent in the story. The glorification of strength and the outdoor life and simplistic solutions to the problems of a rapidly changing world were popular ideas during the time of Theodore Roosevelt. Tarzan also was a unique superman, since he reconciled elitism and democracy. He was born a British lord but (in the first novel) renounced his class. He also became a superman in circumstances that could have transformed anyone: being reared by brachiating apes. And he was amiable, a person one would not mind meeting—so long as one was not a lion or a black cannibal.

Burroughs, probably unconsciously, often fleshed out the more violent emotional patterns of each time sector of his career. He had strong feelings about politics, and his ideology usually ran with that of the superpatriot extremists. Thus, today his stories reemit (and in their own time helped set up) the jingoism of World War I and the terror associated with Bolshevism in the days of Lenin and Trotsky.

Tarzan also was the greatest of White Hopes. In 1910 Jack Johnson, the great black boxing champion, had badly beaten the shell of Jim Jeffries, and the white sports world (who would in large part have been the readers of adventure pulps) took the defeat with incredible rancor. The search for a White Hope went on desperately. Tarzan, with his racist feelings and his perpetual slaughter of blacks (except for a protected tribe who served him), represented a form of revanchism.

This was in 1912 and the years following. What position does Edgar Rice Burroughs hold in the overall development of science fiction, or for the present-day reader? It is no exaggeration to say that entire generations of readers grew up on his fiction and in some unaccountable way took the sense of adventure and discarded the sometimes flawed application. Many scientists, engineers, and writers have stated that the Martian novels of Burroughs first stimulated them to look further into science, even though they soon discarded

Barsoom and the sexual-sword antics of John Carter. As did Ignatius Donnelly and *Atlantis: The Antediluvian World*, Edgar Rice Burroughs and his work served as one of the great vicarious imaginations for American youth.

Burroughs is also an important figure historically. His mark can be seen on much adventure science fiction written since his day. He was among the first to place adventure stories on other planets, and his technique of associating action with elements of environment and his concept of erratic, structured decadence (swords versus ray guns) have had wide diffusion in both science fiction and high fantasy.

It is for these reasons that we should regard Burroughs, despite his faults as a writer and ideologue, as something more than a commercial phenomenon or a somewhat embarrassing piece of cultural history.

Selected Bibliography

WORKS OF EDGAR RICE BURROUGHS

Tarzan of the Apes. Chicago: McClurg, 1914.
The Return of Tarzan. Chicago: McClurg, 1915.
A Princess of Mars. Chicago: McClurg, 1917.
The Gods of Mars. Chicago: McClurg, 1918.
The Warlord of Mars. Chicago: McClurg, 1919.
Thuvia, Maid of Mars. Chicago: McClurg, 1920.
Tarzan the Terrible. Chicago: McClurg, 1921.
The Chessmen of Mars. Chicago: McClurg, 1922.
At the Earth's Core. Chicago: McClurg, 1922.
Pellucidar. Chicago: McClurg, 1923.
Tarzan and the Ant Men. Chicago: McClurg, 1924.
The Land That Time Forgot. Chicago: McClurg, 1924.
The Moon Maid. Chicago: McClurg, 1926.

CRITICAL AND BIOGRAPHICAL STUDIES

Aldiss, Brian W. "Burroughs: Less Lucid Than Lucian." In his *This World and Nearer Ones*. Kent, Ohio: Kent State University Press, 1981.
Bergen, James A., Jr. *A Reference Guide on Works Written by Edgar Rice Burroughs*. Tualatin, Oreg.: J. A. Bergen, Jr., 1987.
Brady, Clark A. *The Burroughs Cyclopædia: Characters, Places, Fauna, Flora, Technologies, Languages, Ideas and Terminologies Found in the Works of Edgar Rice Burroughs*. Jefferson, N.C.: McFarland, 1996.

Heins, Henry Hardy. *A Golden Anniversary Bibliography of Edgar Rice Burroughs*, rev. ed. West Kingston, R.I.: Donald M. Grant, 1964.

Holtsmark, Erling B. *Edgar Rice Burroughs*. Boston: Twayne, 1986.

———. *Tarzan and Tradition: Classical Myth in Popular Literature*. Westport, Conn.: Greenwood, 1981.

Lawson, Benjamin S. "The Time and Place of Edgar Rice Burroughs's Early Martian Trilogy." *Extrapolation*, 27, no. 3 (1986): 208–220.

McWhorter, Geroge T. *Burroughs Dictionary: An Alphabetical List of Proper Names, Words, Phrases and Concepts Contained in the Published Works of Edgar Rice Burroughs*. Lanham, Md.: University Press of America, 1987.

Mullen, R. D. "Jane's Honor and Tarzan's Chivalry Again Impinged." *Science-Fiction Studies*, 13, part 3 (1986): 405–406.

Needham, Rodney. "Tarzan of the Apes: A Re-appreciation." *Foundation* (July 1983): 20–28.

Newsinger, John. "Reader, He Rescued Her: Women in the Tarzan Stories." *Foundation* (Spring 1987): 41–49.

Orth, Michael. "Utopia in the Pulps: The Apocalyptic Pastoralism of Edgar Rice Burroughs." *Extrapolation*, 27, no. 3 (1986): 221–233.

Porges, Irwin. *Edgar Rice Burroughs. The Man Who Created Tarzan*, 2 vols. New York: Ballantine Books, 1975. (Thorough and definitive.)

Stableford, Brian. "The Tarzan Series." In *Survey of Modern Fantasy Literature*, vol. 4, edited by Frank N. Magill. Englewood Cliffs, N.J.: Salem, 1983.

Wright, Peter. "Selling Mars: Burroughs, Barsoom and Expedient Xenography." *Foundation* (Autumn 1996): 24–46.

Zeuschner, Robert B. *Edgar Rice Burroughs: The Exhaustive Scholar's and Collector's Descriptive Bibliography*. Jefferson, N.C.: McFarland, 1996.

—BRIAN STABLEFORD

OCTAVIA ESTELLE BUTLER
(b. 1947)

Writing is difficult. You do it all alone without encouragement and without any certainty that you'll ever be published or paid or even that you'll be able to finish the particular work you've begun. It isn't easy to persist amid all that. . . . I write about people who do extraordinary things. It just turned out that it was called science fiction. (*Bloodchild*, pages 143, 145)

I've been told . . . my characters aren't "nice." I don't doubt it. . . . I don't write about heroes; I write about people who survive and sometimes prevail. (Mixon, page 12)

THE IMPORTANCE OF Octavia Butler in American writing is large and intriguing. Her books have appeared in many languages, and she has collected numerous major writing and achievement awards, in and out of the science fiction field, including the Hugo, Nebula, and Locus awards, and a $295,000 MacArthur Fellowship in 1995. She has been the guest of honor or its equivalent at numerous science fiction conventions since her first at WISCON in Madison, Wisconsin in 1980 and has received handsome writer-in-residence offers from a number of universities, although she has never wanted to teach. Instead, because she has wanted to give something back to the apprenticeship writing culture that helped her get her own start, she has made many appearances at writers' workshops or in forums devoted to everything from contemporary American authors to race and gender studies to the Science Fiction Worlds of Octavia Butler at the University of Illinois,

Urbana, 1986. She has made at least a dozen such appearances each year—not counting book tour and signing appearances. Meanwhile, she and her work have been the subject of at least eighteen doctoral dissertations and many chapters and articles in scholarly books and prestigious journals. Among the principal women writers of the modern era only Toni Morrison, Alice Walker, Ursula Le Guin, A. S. Byatt, and Margaret Atwood got significantly more scholarly attention than Butler did. The only African American woman who has written science fiction virtually exclusively, she is among a very small group of African Americans who have made a contribution to the genre. Her stories and books are about power and power fantasy, race, gender, love, longevity/immortality, apocalypse, hubris, addiction, genetics, medicine, aliens, family, motherhood, childhood, disease, incest, rape, slavery, education, ecology, social engineering, pain, ordeal, memory, history, and myth. Although a self-described loner, Butler has, as much as any modern writer, allowed herself, in interviews and conferences, to become engaged in discussions of her own life and the meaning of her stories and novels. In this fashion Butler herself achieved a celebrity equal to the high reputation given her writing.

Born 22 June 1947, in Pasadena, California, the last of five children of Laurice and Octavia Butler, Butler nevertheless grew up without her father and as an only child: her father died when she was a baby and her four brothers had died either at birth or soon after. These losses, Butler reflected, made her mother

147

"tiresomely protective of me." Raised by her mother, grandmother, and relatives, she recalled that, as a good Baptist child, she read the Bible. "The stories got me: stories of conflict, betrayal, torture, murder, exile, and incest. I read them avidly. This was, of course, not exactly what my mother had in mind when she encouraged me to read the Bible." At first Butler's mother read to her, but when Octavia was five, she began to read to her mother. Butler's mother, who worked as a cleaning lady, had a passionate belief in education and brought home armloads and boxes of discarded books from the places she cleaned. Butler eventually read virtually all of them. At age six she discovered the Peter Pan Room of the Pasadena main library, where her reading was mostly fairy tales and horse stories. One of the most important children's books to her was Felix Salten's *Bambi* (1928) because Salten wrote about "animals as though they were human—more accurately, as though they were knowingly, although not always willingly, *subject* to humans. In *Bambi*, for instance, man is always referred to as 'He,' with a capital letter, as in 'God.'" She first read adult science fiction in magazines from the grocery store because she wasn't allowed into the adult section of the library until she was fourteen. Butler attended Pasadena City College where as a freshman she won a collegewide short story contest. Afterward, she took a number of courses at California State University at Los Angeles. Though she received an associate of arts degree at Pasadena City College, she later said emphatically that she had earned no college degree.

Butler read widely among contemporary science fiction writers, particularly the "People" stories of Zenna Henderson, whose "gentle, psionic aliens are no doubt literary ancestors to my own ungentle, all-too-human Patternists." She recalled that the very first adult science fiction story she read was the Ray Bradbury–Leigh Brackett collaboration "Lorelei of the Red Mist" (1946). Butler remembered telling herself stories from the time she was four and at ten she begged her mother to buy her a portable Remington type-

writer. Soon after, Butler wrote her first stories, including the earliest versions of *Patternmaster*. In 1969 she took a class with Harlan Ellison in the Open Door Program of the Screen Writers' Guild. Ellison advised her to enroll in Robin Scott Wilson's Clarion Science Fiction Writers' Workshop in Pennsylvania. At this time she sold her first two stories—one to the Clarion anthology, and one to Harlan Ellison for his proposed *Last Dangerous Visions*, one of the most famous never-published science fiction volumes. In 1976, while she was taking a course with Theodore Sturgeon at the University of California, Los Angeles, *Patternmaster* was published by Doubleday, and her career as a novelist was launched. In 1978 Butler quit the last of many temporary jobs to live on her writing. She also traveled to Maryland to do research for *Kindred* and in 1982 visited Moscow, Kiev, and Leningrad with a group of American science fiction writers to meet Soviet writers. Then in 1985 she spent time in the Amazon rain forest, the Andes, Cuzco, and Machu Picchu, this time to do research for the Xenogenesis novels. In 1997 she went to England to be an honored guest at Intervention, the United Kingdom's national science fiction convention.

Butler's slight dyslexia made reading slow and driving a car impossible. Even after acquiring a computer, she continued to use an old-fashioned manual typewriter. She loved writing while it was raining. Though she repeatedly insisted she was a solitary person, Butler discussed intimate topics in interviews. This self-revelation in her effort to know herself, regardless of what she might learn, was elementary Butler.

Butler's published short stories are remarkable because, although she was not much motivated to write short fiction (she said, "I am essentially a novelist. The ideas that most interest me tend to be big."), three of them have earned writing prizes. "Crossover," a realistic story of a dysfunctional relationship, alcoholism, and hallucination, was her first sale, published in Robin Scott Wilson's *Clarion* (1971).

Her next short story, "Near of Kin," a sympathetic tale of incest told by a daughter speaking to her father after the death of her mother, his sister, did not appear until 1979. For "Speech Sounds" (1983), she won the 1984 Hugo award for best short story. Set in a near future, crumbling California urban sprawl, it is the story of UCLA professor Valerie Rye, who can no longer read as the result of a widespread new disease that attacks the brain's language center. The disease imposes a Tower-of-Babel–like situation on the city (this is perhaps a retrieval from Butler's Bible reading). Indeed, the badness of the life engendered by this weird disease makes cooperation and relationships between people conflicted to such a degree that violent behavior becomes epidemic. Despite this Valerie meets and falls in love with Obsidian, who, crippled by an alternate symptom of the same disease, can read but no longer speak. Obsidian is an appealing male, a one-time member of the Los Angeles Police Department. Their love is joyful and intense, but interrupted soon and tragically when Obsidian is killed trying to stop a man from killing a woman. Valerie and the reader are stunned by this loss. Soon the dead woman's children come looking for their mother. They have Valerie's form of the disease. They can talk. Thus, Valerie can tell them she will care for them. Moreover, in spite of her loss, she has a treasure beyond price: she has known true love. The surprising benefits of "disease" are a motif in every major piece of Butler's writing.

Butler's most celebrated story is "Bloodchild" (1984), for which she won the Hugo, Nebula, and Locus awards for best novelette. It concerns humans in a marooned colony on an extrasolar planet inhabited by a sentient insect species, the Tlic, who in a bizarre relationship with humans, lay their eggs for gestation in the reluctant humans' bodies. Thus, love and horror combine when T'Gatoi (a female Tlic) and the human boy Gan lie down together so that she can skewer him and lay her eggs in him. The impact of the thematic dissonance of the story can hardly be overemphasized. Butler said she did not intend an allegory of the historical conditions of slavery, but rather a love story. In fact, both meanings are present. The frisson is almost unbearable. One possible interpretation is that slavery and love might be somehow connected.

A Hugo award nomination went as well to "The Evening and the Morning and the Night" (1987) in which a weird disease makes people brilliant and suicidal, until a victim of the disease evolves who emits a pheromone that neutralizes the suicidal urge, preserving the superintelligence so that it becomes a permanent characteristic of the species.

Butler's novels are built on three platform fabulations: the surprisingly subtle psi-charactered Patternmaster stories; the postapocalyptic, gene-trader Xenogenesis books; and the biblically inspired speculative naturalism of the Parable novels. In one sense her fables are trials of solutions to the self-

Octavia Estelle Butler. © MIRIAM BERKLEY

149

destructive condition in which she finds mankind. In the Patternmaster world she investigates the potential of psionic abilities to enrich communication and will, which translate into pleasure and power, the sources of people's happiness. In the Xenogenesis books she switches to the possibilities of genetic engineering—again taking for granted that existing humanity is morally insufficient. In the Parable novels she comes closest to an acceptance of humanity as it is, trying out a parareligious agenda to counsel people to value the experience of change, and to recognize that "God is power. God is change." In the stories and novels the evolution of Butler's art and thought are clear and the writing has been mature from the earliest of the published pieces, perhaps because her apprenticeship was long and intense. She rewrote obsessively, resulting in a narrative that is spare, a combination of Chinua Achebe, Ernest Hemingway, and Margaret Walker.

Common to all Butler's universes is the importance of change: Transition in the Patternist stories, metamorphosis in the Xenogenesis books, and simply Change or God is change, in the Parable novels. At the core of the lives of all her characters is initiation, apprenticeship, *bildungs*, *erziehungs*, experience; the coming of age, the rite of passage, maturation, or apotheosis. They lead to madness, death, or, in fortunate cases, "adulthood."

The fictive chronology of the Patternmaster novels begins with *Wild Seed* (1980) and runs through *Mind of My Mind* (1977), *Clay's Ark* (1984), *Survivor* (1978), and *Patternmaster* (1976). *Kindred* (1979), Butler said, was intended as a Patternmaster story, but its writing demanded a realism she had suspended for the other books, so it stands alone.

Butler began writing stories about the characters in *Patternmaster* when she was about twelve after seeing the movie *Devil Girl from Mars* (1954) and thinking that she could do better. The novel, set in a distant future Southern California, introduces the people of the Pattern, humans with parapsychological powers who are on the threshold of power over Earth's remaining population of ordinary humans, called "mutes" because they cannot use psionic powers. Also present is a provisionally subhuman Clayark species, sentient and ambiguously sinister, who are treated sympathetically in *Clay's Ark*.

The novel tells the story of the psionic Patternists, organized in a neofeudal hereditary system, and the account of the struggle for control of the Pattern between Teray and Coransee, the sons of Patternmaster Rayal and his principal wife Jansee. Jansee dies and Rayal is crippled in a Clayark attack, but not before Jansee demonstrates maternal concern for her sons and a ruthless resolution by Rayal secures his power. This is not an inevitable paradigm for Butler. Teray is the first of her compassionate male protagonists. He is linked to the protophysician Amber, who instigates and nourishes Teray's disposition to care for people. This gives him the winning advantage in competition with his brutal brother. Teray has the reader's sympathy and his victory seems to offer hope for mankind, especially when Teray has a nonhostile meeting with a Clayark near the end of the novel. But this resolution does not extinguish the feudal and hierarchical culture of the Patternists. *Patternmaster* is about power, and how people struggle to possess it, and the demented relations between those with power and those without it.

Butler says she started *Mind of My Mind* when she was fifteen because she wanted to know more about the characters in *Patternmaster*. This book unfolds in the late twentieth century and introduces the parapsychological vampire Doro who is nearly four thousand years old and the long-living, shapeshifting, heroically maternal Emma (who will become/have been Anyanwu in *Wild Seed*), as well as Doro's daughter Mary who will become the first true Patternmaster after a life-threatening transition and her defeat of Doro. The history, further reported in *Wild Seed*, is Doro's centuries-long struggle to retain control of his psionic children. He is brutal, but not malevolent. Moreover, in this novel he is curiously minor and pathetic and to reach her own maturity, Mary must commit patricide.

Emma, even though she has been the consort of Doro, provides maternal support and the strength of a warrior ally that Mary must have. Mary's destiny is to unite the Patternists in a web no single member can escape—a benevolent captivity (Butler never ignored the existential contradictions in the human condition) that coerces truthfulness (through the sacrifice of privacy), and puts the combined power and wisdom of all at the service of each. The service most required is support of the Patternists through the violent and often fatal experience of their psionic adolescence, when the individual's latent powers emerge, in transition to early adulthood. Mary's peremptorily imposed web of control provides this support. Future Patternists may endure and thrive; all become parents to each. Here Butler has the hierarchical power of telepathy and telekinesis impose a regime of communal benefit, but Mary has had to kill her father to engender this program. *Mind of My Mind* ends with hope, but with many conflicts unresolved—or perhaps compounded by the paradox everyone experiences—like Aldous Huxley's problem of the individual versus the genetic pool of community and conformity, depicted in *Brave New World* (1932). Moreover, even in acts of love and support the use of power may corrupt its agent.

Butler reported that she completed a novella-length ninety-page version of *Survivor* when she was nineteen that was virtually unpublishable. It might never have been published, but the exigency of getting another novel sold and into print explains its appearance in 1978. Some critics' reservations notwithstanding, *Survivor* has strengths as art and value as a specimen of Butler's developing craft. The ordeals of adolescence, addiction and withdrawal, power and slavery, racial war, and gender roles are the subjects of *Survivor*. Loosely tethered in Butler's Patternist society on Earth, it suspends Patternist history to tell the story of Afro-Asian Alanna Verrick, adopted child of white Christian missionaries Jules and Neila, who have founded a colony on the planet Kohn. On this world the Garkohn, ambiguous allies of the colonists, and Tehkohn, a morally superior race because its culture refuses addiction to the ubiquitous fruit of the meklah tree, are ancient enemies. Themselves addicted, the Garkohn require that the humans be addicted as part of the alliance in which they enjoy the Garkohn's protection. Captured by the Tehkohn, Alanna is forced to withdraw from meklah, a withdrawal similar to that from heroin. She marries the Tehkohn leader Diut, and, in this ambassadorial identity, she assists in rescuing the missionaries from their addiction and their captivity by the Garkohn, though not before she is forced once more to become addicted to and withdraw from meklah. The missionaries move their colony to an uninhabited region, and Alanna remains with her Tehkohn husband.

Temporarily setting aside the Patternist story, in *Kindred* Butler undertook what she described as a painful and depressing engagement with the history of slavery in the United States. In the novel, writer protagonist Dana time-travels intermittently between 1970's California and pre-1820 Maryland, where she lives the life of a slave on the plantation of Rufus Weyland, who will become her great-great-grandfather. She is drawn back to save him each time Rufus's life is threatened. Rufus is as morally obscene as his slaveholder father, but Dana must help preserve his life when it is threatened so that he, through rape, can sire her great-grandmother Hagar. When Rufus dies in a fire, Dana returns permanently to the twentieth century. She has secured her ancestral lifeline, but in this final return to the present she is bizarrely mutilated when her arm is temporally incorporated into the wall of her living room, and must be amputated. The novel proposes that in order to secure our existence at all, we are complicit in the preservation of obscene moral orders and we are all, likewise, mutilated by our inescapable history. Butler has said that in *Kindred* she is indebted to the distinguished narratives of slavery in America including that by Frederick Douglass. *Kindred* is certainly another bildungsroman following the agenda Butler has pursued in all her novels, but it also belongs to the genre of fictional slave narrative in which Margaret Walker's *Jubilee* (1966), Alex Haley's *Roots* (1976), and Toni Morrison's *Beloved* (1987) are the best and most famous similar works. Butler's theme of deterministically coerced complicity by slaves in their enslavement is, however, unique among these narratives and *Kindred* is by far her most widely read novel.

Butler said that in *Kindred* she "couldn't change history—at least not in the kind of book I had chosen to write. So my characters couldn't realistically win much more than their lives. But in *Wild Seed*, a different sort of book, my characters could be powerful enough to move somewhat outside the ugliness of antebellum U.S. history even though they live through it. Their struggle is more male-female than Black-White." *Wild Seed* is probably Butler's best novel and tells the story of the origin of the Patternist universe. Its principal characters, Doro and Anyanwu, are epic and authentic, engaging the reader's awe or admiration or sympathy on some level, though Doro is, as Anyanwu declares, "an obscenity." In this novel Doro emerges as a more heroic and peculiarly sympathetic figure than he is in *Mind of My Mind*. He is well over three thousand years old when he encounters Anyanwu in West Africa, in the early years of the slave trade. He lives by taking, one after the other, the living bodies of people he chooses, who yield their consciousness to him when he takes their bodies, and die when he discards them. Doro's condition is a paradox: his immortality requires the deaths of others.

Anyanwu herself is over three hundred years old. She survives because she is genetically self-renewing and a shapeshifter in the fullest sense. She can change herself at the mitochondrial level, throwing off sickness, healing wounds, or, spectacularly, becoming a panther, a dolphin, or an eagle. Doro's power is sufficiently threatening to compel Anyanwu to leave her people in order to protect them from him, so the two leave aboard one of Doro's ships for America in a trip that parallels the horrific middle passage of the slave trade. Thereafter, the history of American slavery is the immediate setting and a counterpoint for the narrative of *Wild Seed*. Over the next 150 years, Anyanwu is healer, mother to some of Doro's children, and owner of a Louisiana plantation when she changes her body to that of a white male. At the end of the novel she migrates to California where she will become Emma in *Mind of My Mind*.

Wild Seed is a combination of Butler's brilliant fable and real history. Her narrative captures the authentic voice of West African storytelling. Methodically accreting detail in relatively short sentences, it echoes the narrative of Chinua Achebe's *Things Fall Apart*. Like *Kindred*, *Wild Seed* is rooted in the collective record of slavery. The relationship between Doro and Anyanwu dramatizes a fundamental conflict between the affinity a solitary immortal male and female might feel for one another in a world of mortals, and the hatred Anyanwu must feel toward a being who kills people, including his own children, without remorse. Doro is macabre, wearing the bodies of his victims in an impious theft of their lives' energy, and he can never be lovable. Yet the reader's frustration that love between these two cannot flourish is enormous. They seem made for each other—each is immortal and each is heroically wise because of that immortality. But Doro is a cannibal vampire: He must kill to survive and will die only when he loses a conflict with a superior creature. No such creature appears in *Wild Seed*. Instead, Doro looms as a symbol of the perversity of male-dominated human history. A species modeled on Anyanwu would improve humanity's destiny; but there are no children like Anyanwu, and no prospect of them in *Wild Seed*.

The last written of the Patternist novels is *Clay's Ark*, in which Butler tried to satisfy her curiosity about the Clayark species she introduced in *Patternmaster*. Set in the early twenty-first century in the American Southwest, it tells how African American geologist Elias Doyle, crew member on a tragic trip to Proxima Centauri Two, is the carrier of an organism that infects people, producing the

Clayark physiology and metabolism in the infected, and yielding a totally new species in their offspring. Ironically, as in other Butler stories, this disease gives humans super senses, strength, and health. Younger infected humans live; older ones die. Symptoms accompanying transformation also include heightened sex appeal and sexual appetite. The moral character of the transformed people remains as variable as in humans. Elias has children by three women and comes to terms with his fate. The novel ends with the prospect of the infection ravishing Earth.

With this story it is necessary retrospectively to revise the moral hierarchy of Patternists, mutes, and Clayarks described in *Patternmaster*. Butler's Clayark bioform is clearly a significant improvement over humans, and perhaps the Patternists as well. Humans have brought Earth to the brink of planetary catastrophe. A species such as the Clayark might do better. Butler spoke of adding to the Patternmaster novels but has only reproduced the settings and themes established in them in her later writing.

The Xenogenesis chronicle predicts that humanity will destroy itself by nuclear war and that its remnants will be salvaged by genetic augmentation in a more convincing version of the healing effect in the Hugo-winning *They'd Rather Be Right* (1954) by Mark Clifton and Frank Riley. In an interview for this essay, Butler commented on the Xenogenesis trilogy:

> I got the idea for the trilogy slowly, in bits and pieces during the first Reagan administration. Reagan and his people were talking about winnable nuclear war and limited nuclear war and increasing our safety by increasing our nuclear stockpile. There was the Reaganite who believed that all an individual needed to survive a nuclear war was a hole, a door to throw over it, and some dirt to cover the door. There was the one who thought God would be ending the world soon, so why bother about preserving resources. There were any number of opportunists and idiots, all without foresight, without peripheral vision, without concern for anyone except themselves. They wanted to win. Whatever the game, they knew Americans—their kind of Americans—were best, and so their kind of Americans should win everything worth having, all the time. You see? I can still rant about it. With these people as my examples, I created the human contradiction. We are hierarchical and we are intelligent, and all too often, our hierarchical tendencies rule our intelligence and we one-up ourselves to death.

During the 150 years of the Xenogenesis chronicle, three possible fates for humans are presented. First, they may remain as sterilized resisters on Earth as a last generation of humanity. Second, healed and fertile humans could agree to be moved to Mars, and there, very probably, relive the doomed destiny humans had experienced on Earth. Third, a healed and augmented human male-female couple could become mates with three Oankalis, a male, a female, and an ooloi. The ooloi would be the genetic engineer for the five-member family, constructing not only children from the four DNAs but enabling a sharing of feelings bordering on telepathic clarity among the five mated individuals. The ooloi would also produce a neurochemical-based predisposition to an obsessive affinity for others—in other words, passionate love. The life span of the family members would be five hundred years. Such families would resume star travel, leaving Earth behind.

The volumes of the trilogy feature Lilith Iyapo (Mother), the African American survivor of a prospectively doomed Earth; Nikanj Ooan, her Oankali ooloi guide; Ahajas Ty, her Oankali female co-parent; Dichaan Ishliin, the Oankali male co-parent; Akin, the son of Dischaan and Lilith; and Jodahs, their shape-shifting mutant ooloi child. In *Dawn*, the first book, Joseph (Father), their male human co-parent, is murdered by renegade humans and Lilith awakens in the starship habitat of the Oankali gene traders, who will heal her to a preternatural quality of health and proportional physical and mental strength. She is subjected to a radical re-education about the nature of relationships with sentient beings who are biologically alien. Thus enlightened, she elects to become the mother of children who are born with human and Oankali genes. With Oankali-enhanced health and knowledge of biology, Lilith will herself be a healer and a leader in the Oankali's casual project to rejuvenate Earth with a program that will radically change humans so that they will no longer be human. The reader is asked to regard this prospect with approval. Humanity has virtually destroyed itself in a nuclear war with behavior that was the result of genetics that put high intelligence at the service of hierarchical behavior. Butler's view is that because it is obsessively competitive, hierarchical behavior is inexorably self-mutilating and self-destructive. It is true that humans value cooperative behavior, but not nearly so much as they value competitive behavior.

The career of Lilith's human-Oankali child, Akin, is the focus of *Adulthood Rites*, the second book in the Xenogenesis trilogy. Akin is a superchild. He can remember his gestation and heal himself by altering damaged cells, while his touch can deliver a lethal poison. He has, as well, all the powers of both his human and Oankali parents. The main purpose of his existence is as a preadapted human who can join the human resisters who will attempt to colonize Mars. The resisters are xenophobes who reject genetic alliance with the Oankali, rejecting as well the extraordinary biological enhancements to health, strength, and intelligence the Oankali offer. The resisters elect to remain antiquely human, restricting themselves to the brutishly limiting human gene pool. "Humans would carry their dislikes with them to be shut up together on Mars." They will not be allowed to stay on Earth because, "To give you a new world and let you procreate again would . . . be like breeding intelligent beings for the sole purpose of having them kill one another."

The life and progress of Jodahs in *Imago* form the last part of the Xenogenesis trilogy. It forestalls the star-traveling destiny of Oankali-augmented humanity. Born of Lilith, Jodahs should have been male or female, but is instead a new creature, an Oankali-human ooloi whose powers include the ability to breathe in both air and water and to change its own DNA and therefore its bioform—making it in effect a shapeshifter. It can heal and regrow and alter not only its own body but those of other organic creatures, see in the dark, hear much more acutely than humans, exercise more strength than a human, possess an eidetic memory stocked with the encyclopedic knowledge that the star-roving Oankali have accumulated, enjoy a lifespan of five centuries, reorganize and reconstruct genes, and be the medium of almost telepathic communication between other Oankali and humans. Jodahs must find suitable human female and male mates before its adulthood and second metamorphosis; it finds mates in the brother and sister Tomas and Jesusa—this incest is familiar in Butler's stories. Thereafter, Tomas and Jesusa support Jodahs through its second metamorphosis. Tomas and Jesusa then decide to return to their human village to help find human mates for Aaor, Jodahs's sibling ooloi. They succeed despite great danger, and Jodahs and Aaor remain on Earth with their mates, to found a new town. Lilith has now reached the age of 150. She is a harbinger of change because of her years of initiation as a human mother of Oankali-engineered children, and even as she ascends to legendary status, she has become conservative and disapproving of Jodahs's willful lawbreaking in taking mates from renegade humans. The future is still the stars, but the epilogue's concern with a sojourn on Earth so the new species can try itself may have sentimental appeal for readers of Butler's marvelous tale.

The message of the Xenogenesis trilogy is that there is a genetic conflict in humans between intelligence and hierarchical behavior that will doom the species. Butler ornaments this by having apples become extinct in the nuclear war in which humanity extinguishes itself; perhaps the elimination of this tragically fateful fruit symbolizes a hope for a replacement species. Other less tragically symbolic fruit survives where humanity does not: there is no redemption from its fall from grace. A surviving no-longer-human species will prosper because it joyfully pursues the new and the different. It loves variation and change.

The Parable novels speculate on how mankind might avoid total catastrophe without the deus ex machina interpolation of psionic abilities or extraterrestrial interdiction. In *Parable of the Sower* (1993) Butler abandons speculative science in favor of a naturalistic futurism that bears a significant similarity to the writings of Theodore Dreiser, Frank Norris, and Stephen Crane. Covering the three-year, three-month period from 24 July 2024 to 1 October 2027, it is a story told in journal form beginning with the fifteenth birthday of African American Lauren Olamina. It records the inexorable disintegration of civilization in her Southern California hometown, the walled community of Robledo, and the conditions of her survival. Each of the twenty-five chapters begins with a short piece of poetry that represents a new religion Lauren is constructing, Earthseed, whose fundamental tenet is "God is Change."

The novel begins with the account of three years of increasingly deprived life in Robledo, ending with the death of Lauren's family, including her Baptist minister father (Lauren stopped believing when she was twelve, though she once gives a sermon to her father's congregation), her stepmother Corazon ("Cory"), who is a teacher, Lauren's brothers, and all her friends. Marauders burn much of their enclave and kill many of the inhabitants. Lauren escapes with her survival pack, which she has put together in anticipation of the end of civil order and against the wishes of her father. In the last third of the novel, from 2 August to 1 October 2027 the record is of Lauren's progress to northern California (although her original destination was Canada) in the company of a number of survivors. Of principal importance is the fifty-seven-year-old doctor Taylor Franklin Bankole whom Lauren loves and eventually marries, and who is the age Lauren's father would have been had he lived. Their destination turns out to be property owned by Bankole, where with ten other fellow travelers, they establish a communal farm called, with hope, Acorn. Lauren's development of the precepts of Earthseed continues at story's end. An excerpt from the New Testament from the authorized King James version of the Bible, Luke 8:5–8, ends the narrative: "A sower went out to sow his seed: . . . And other [seed] fell on good ground, and sprang up, and bore fruit an hundredfold." With practice, survival and some happiness may be achieved. Butler's works present a moral agenda, but it is not a reconstituted Christianity. It reconciles propositions that advise variously "We must find the rest of what we need / within ourselves, / in one another, / in our Destiny"; "Create no images of God"; "Learn or die"; "A victim of God may, / Through learning adaption, / Become a partner of God" "To get along with God, / Consider the consequences of your behavior"; "All successful life is / Adaptable, / Opportunistic, / Tenacious, / Interconnected, / and Fecund"; and "Kindness eases Change." This agenda is a combination of Darwinism, pantheism, Taoism, and Zen.

There is in Lauren a great deal of would-be shaman, wizard, guru, soothsayer, and priest—as there appears to be, however unwillingly, in Butler. Butler said that ecology, especially global warming caused by profligate use of fossil fuels, is almost a character in *Parable*. On the stage of a postmodern, postindustrial, postrevolutionary world—a world in which capitalism is devolving into feudalism—in *Parable* a search for "good ground" begins. It is a world of chaos wherein, unnoticed, the seed of a new order and polity might flourish sufficiently to begin an age of magnanimity that is not self-destructive. Lauren's Earthseed religion and the effort to make a communal farm and a new life are starkly vulnerable to quick extinction before they have had much chance to grow. But they represent an agenda of stubborn hope for mankind, and for Butler.

Parable of the Talents (1988), by its title and Butler's report, is a sequel to *Parable of the Sower*. Butler says of it that it continues to engage the problems presented in *Parable of the Sower* but that it gives alternative propositions for repair of the wreck the human species has made of its world.

Butler is not principally a futurist. Her vision is rooted in the present, the familiar, the common, and the real. It projects a frightening prospect for humans. There is also a tough kernel of irrational hope. Associated with these meanings, one of the dominant metaphors of her writing from the beginning has been biblical. Her themes were in an Old Testament mood until the *Parable* novels. These, in spite of their New Testamnet reference as "parables," are subtly and ironically antimessianic, peopled with Old Testament characters, both male and female. They defer the traditional deus ex machina New Testament events and search for moral resources in a postmodern humankind whose divinity must be found in itself. That there will be new *Parable* novels seems likely, perhaps with historical settings, as well as others with tales contemporary with *Parable of the Sower* and *Parable of the Talents*. She has also, at her publisher's suggestion, begun writing a memoir. In any case, Butler has the pleasantly challenging task of maintaining the standard she has set in her brilliant writing.

Selected Bibliography

WORKS OF OCTAVIA ESTELLE BUTLER

"Crossover." In *Clarion: An Anthology of Speculative Fiction and Criticism from the Clarion Writers Workshop.* Edited by Robin Scott Wilson. New York: New American Library, 1971:139–144.
Patternmaster. Garden City, N.Y.: Doubleday, 1976.
Mind of My Mind. Garden City, N.Y.: Doubleday, 1977.
Survivor. Garden City, N.Y.: Doubleday, 1978.
Kindred. Garden City, N.Y.: Doubleday, 1979.
"Near of Kin." In *Chrysalis 4.* Edited by Roy Torgeson. New York: Zebra Books, 1979:163–175.
"Future Forum." *Future Life,* 17 (1980): 60.
Wild Seed. Garden City, N.Y.: Doubleday, 1980.
"Speech Sounds." *Isaac Asimov's Science Fiction Magazine,* 7 (1983): 26–40.
Clay's Ark. New York: St. Martin's Press, 1984.
Dawn. New York: Warner Books, 1987.
"The Evening and the Morning and the Night." *Omni* (May 1987): 56–62, 108–120.
Adulthood Rites. New York: Warner Books, 1988.
"Birth of a Writer." *Essence,* 20: (1989): 74, 79, 132, 134.
Imago. New York: Warner Books, 1989.
Xenogenesis. New York: Guild America Books, 1989.
Parable of the Sower. New York: Four Walls Eight Windows, 1993.

"How I'd Like to Be Taught." Panel discussion; moderator: Elizabeth Anne Hull. Ann Arbor, Mich.: Tucker Video, 1994.
Bloodchild and Other Stories. New York: Four Walls Eight Windows, 1995.
Parable of the Talents: A Novel. New York: Publisher's Group West, 1998.

BIBLIOGRAPHIES

Currey, L. W. "Octavia E[stelle] Butler in 'Work in Progress.'" *New York Review of Science Fiction,* 32 no. 3 (1991): 23.
Weixlmann, Joe. "An Octavia E. Butler Bibliography." *Black American Literature Forum* 18 (1984): 88–89.

CRITICAL AND BIOGRAPHICAL STUDIES

Alaimo, Stacy. "Cartographies of Undomesticated Ground: Nature and Feminism in American Women's Fiction and Theory (Women Writers)." Ph.D. dissertation, University of Illinois, Urbana, 1994. *DAI* 55 (1994): 9A.
Allison, Dorothy. "The Future of Female: Octavia Butler's Mother Lode." In *Reading Black, Reading Feminist: A Critical Anthology.* Edited Henry Louis Gates Jr. New York: Meridian, 1990:471–78.
Antczak, Janice. "Octavia E. Butler: New Designs for a Challenging Future." In *African-American Voices in Young Adult Literature: Tradition, Transition, Transformation.* Edited by Karen Patricia Smith. Metuchen, N.J.: Scarecrow Press, 1994:311–336.
Armitt, Lucie. "Space, Time and Female Genealogies: A Kristevan Reading of Feminist Science Fiction." In *Image and Power: Women in Fiction in the Twentieth Century.* Edited by Sara Sceats and Gail Cunningham. London and New York: Longman, 1996: 51–61.
Barr, Marleen S. "Octavia Butler and James Tiptree Do Not Write about Zap Guns: Positioning Feminist Science Fiction within Feminist Fabulation." *Lost in Space: Probing Feminist Science Fiction and Beyond.* Chapel Hill: University of North Carolina Press, 1993:97–107.
Beaulieu, Elizabeth Ann. "Femininity Unfettered: The Emergence of the American Neo-Slave Narrative (African American, Women Writers)." Ph.D. dissertation, University North Carolina, Chapel Hill, 1996. *DAI* 57 (1996): 5A.
Blaine, Diana York. "'Are They Simply Going to Leave Her There?': Dead Women in the Modern American Novel." Ph.D. dissertation, University of California, Los Angeles, 1995. *DAI* 56 (1995): 10A.
Bogstad, Janice Marie. "Gender, Power and Reversal in Contemporary Anglo-American and French Feminist Science Fiction (Role Reversal, Felice, Cynthia; Tepper, Sheri; Vonarburg, Elizabeth; Slonczewski, Joan;

Butler, Octavia)." Ph.D. dissertation, University of Wisconsin, Madison, 1992. *DAI* 54 (1992): 2A.

Bonner, Frances. "Difference and Desire, Slavery and Seduction: Octavia Butler's *Xenogenesis.*" *Foundation: The Review of Science Fiction,* 48 (1990): 50–62.

Boulter, Amanda. "Polymorphous Futures: Octavia E. Butler's *Xenogenesis Trilogy.*" In *American Bodies: Cultural Histories of the Physique.* Edited by Tim Armstrong. New York: New York University Press, 1996:170–185.

———. "Speculative Feminisms: The Significance of Feminist Theory in the Science Fiction of Joanna Russ, James Tiptree, Jr., and Octavia Butler." Ph.D. dissertation, University of Southhampton, United Kingdom, 1996. *DAI* 58 (1997): 2C.

Brande, David J. "Technologies of Postmodernity: Ideology and Desire in Literature and Science (Pynchon, Thomas; Gibson, William; Butler, Octavia; Acker, Kathy)." Ph.D. dissertation, University of Washington, 1995. *DAI* 56 (1995): 7A.

Burwell, Jennifer. *Notes on Nowhere: Feminism, Utopian Logic, and Social Transformation.* Minneapolis: University of Minnesota Press, 1997.

Coleman, Letetia F. "Octavia E. Butler's Patternist Series: A Cultural Analysis (Science Fiction)." Ph.D. dissertation, Temple University, 1997. *DAI* 58 (1998): 6A.

Covino, Deborah A. "The Abject Body: Toward an Aesthetic of the Repulsive (Body Criticism, Octavia Butler, Julia Kristeva)." Ph.D. dissertation, University of Illinois, Chicago, 1996. *DAI* 57 (1996): 11A.

Crossley, Robert. "Introduction" to *Kindred.* Boston: Beacon Press, 1988:ix–xxvii.

Davis, Hilary Elizabeth. "Recuperating Pleasure: Toward a Feminist Aesthetic of Reading." Ph.D. dissertation, University of Toronto, 1993. *DAI* 55 (1993): 3A.

Doerksen, Teri Ann. "Octavia E. Butler: Parables of Race and Difference." In *Into Darkness Peering: Race and Color in the Fantastic.* Edited by Elisabeth Anne Leonard. Westport, Conn.: Greenwood Press, 1997:21–34.

Donawerth, Jane. *Frankenstein's Daughters: Women Writing Science Fiction.* Syracuse, N.Y.: Syracuse University Press, 1997.

Falc, Emilie Oline. "An Analysis and Critique of the Vernacular Discourse in Selected Feminist Science Fiction Novels (Octavia Butler, C. J. Cherryh, Vonda Mcintyre, Anne McCaffrey, Elizabeth Ann Scarborough)." Ph.D. dissertation, Ohio University, 1997. *DAI* 58 (1998): 11A.

Foster, Frances Smith. "Octavia Butler's Black Female Future Fiction." *Extrapolation,* 23 (1982): 37–49.

Friend, Beverly. "Time Travel as a Feminist Didactic in Works by Phyllis Eisenstein, Marlys Millhiser, and Octavia Butler." *Extrapolation,* 23 (1982): 50–55.

Gant-Britton, Lisbeth. "Women of Color Constructing Subjectivity Towards the Future: Toni Morrison, Oc-

tavia Butler, and Cynthia Kadohata." Ph.D. dissertation, University of California, Los Angeles, 1997. *DAI* 58 (1998): 10A.

Govan, Sandra Y. "Connections, Links, and Extended Networks: Patterns in Octavia Butler's Science Fiction." *Black American Literature Forum,* 18 (1984): 82–87.

———. "Homage to Tradition: Octavia Butler Renovates the Historical Novel." *MELUS,* 13 nos. 1–2 (1986): 79–96.

Green, Michelle Erica. " 'There Goes the Neighborhood': Octavia Butler's Demand for Diversity in Utopias." In *Utopian and Science Fiction by Women: Worlds of Difference.* Edited by Jane L. Donawerth and Carol A. Kolmerten. Syracuse, N.Y.: Syracuse University Press, 1994:166–189.

Helford, Elyce Rae. "Reading Space Fictions: Representations of Gender, Race, and Species in Popular Culture (Jardine, Alice; Butler, Octavia; Star Trek; Science Fiction)." Ph.D. dissertation, University of Iowa, 1992. *DAI* 54 (1992): 2A.

———. " 'Would you really rather die than bear my young?': The Construction of Gender, Race, and Species in Octavia E. Butler's 'Bloodchild.' " *African American Review,* 28, no. 2 (1994): 259–271.

Johnson, Rebecca O. "African-American, Feminist Science Fiction." *Sojourner: The Women's Forum,* 19, no. 6 (1994): 16–19.

Lee, Judith. " 'We Are All Kin': Relatedness, Mortality, and the Paradox of Human Immortality." In *Immortal Engines: Life Extension and Immortality in Science Fiction and Fantasy.* Edited by George Slusser, Gary Westfahl, and Eric S. Rabkin. Athens: University of Georgia Press, 1996:170–182.

Lindsay, Creighton. "The Rhetoric of Modern American Pastoral (Ernest Hemingway, Ken Kesey, Wallace Stegner, Cormac McCarthy, Octavia Butler, Annie Dillard, Barry Lopez)." Ph.D. dissertation, University of Oregon, 1996. *DAI* 57 (1996): 7A.

Love, Monifa D. "Down Came the Rain (novel)." Ph.D. dissertation, Florida State University, 1997. *DAI* 58 (1997): 4A.

Maida, Patricia. "*Kindred* and *Dessa Rose*: Two Novels that Reinvent Slavery." *CEAMAGazine: A Journal of the College English Association, Middle Altantic Group,* 4, no. 1 (1991): 43–52.

McKible, Adam. " 'These are the facts of the darky's history': Thinking History and Reading Names in Four African American Texts." *African American Review,* 28, no. 2 (1994): 223–235.

Miller, Jim. "Post-Apocalyptic Hoping: Octavia Butler's Dystopian/Utopian Vision." *Science-Fiction Studies,* 25, no. 2 (1998): 336–360.

Mitchell, Angelyn L. "Signifyin(g) Women: Visions and Revisions of Slavery in Octavia Butler's 'Kindred,' Sherley Anne Williams's 'Dessa Rose,' and Toni Morrison's 'Beloved' (Butler, Octavia; Williams, Sherley

Anne; Morrison, Toni; Women Writers)." Ph.D. dissertation, Howard University, 1992. *DAI* 53 (1992): 8A.

Mixon, Veronica. "Face to Fact: Futurist Woman: Octavia Butler." *Essence,* 9 April 1979.

Morrill, Cynthia Anne. "Paradigms out of Joint: Feminist Science Fiction and Cultural Logic (Film, Jack Arnold, Octavia E. Butler, Samuel R. Delany, Joanna Russ)." Ph.D. dissertation, University of California, Riverside, 1997. *DAI* 58 (1998): 5A.

"Octavia E. Butler: SF in the Age of Anxiety." *Locus,* 21, no. 10 (1988): 5, 82.

Paulin, Diana R. "De-Essentializing Interracial Representations: Black and White Border-Crossings in Spike Lee's *Jungle Fever* and Octavia Butler's *Kindred.*" *Cultural Critique,* 36 (1997): 165–193.

Peppers, Cathy. "Dialogic Origins and Alien Identities in Butler's *Xenogenesis.*" *Science-Fiction Studies,* 22, no. 1 (1995): 47–63.

———. "Of Goddesses and Cyborgs: Contemporary Feminist Origin Stories (Jean Auel, Octavia E. Butler, Leslie Marmon Silko)." Ph.D. dissertation, University of Oregon, 1997. *DAI* 58 (1998): 12A.

Pfeiffer, John R. "Octavia Butler Writes the Bible." In *Shaw and Other Matters: A Festschrift for Stanley Weintraub..* Edited by Susan Rusinko. Selinsgrove, Pa., and London: Susquehanna University Press, 1998:140–152.

Raffel, Burton. "Genre to the Rear, Race and Gender to the Fore: The Novels of Octavia E. Butler." *The Literary Review,* 38, no. 3 (1995): 454–461.

Rody, Caroline Margaret. "The Daughter's Return: Revisions of History in Contemporary Fiction by African-American and Caribbean Women Writers." Ph.D. dissertation, University of Virginia, 1995. *DAI* 56 (1995): 9A.

Rushdy, Ashraf H. A. "Families of Orphans: Relation and Disrelation in Octavia Butler's *Kindred.*" *College English,* 55, no. 2 (1993): 135–157.

Salvaggio, Ruth. "Octavia Butler and the Black Science-Fiction Heroine." *Black American Literature Forum,* 18 (1984): 78–81.

———. "Octavia E. Butler." *Susy McKee Charnas, Octavia Butler, Joan D. Vinge.* Edited by Marleen S. Barr. Mercer Island, Wash.: Starmont House, 1986:1–44.

See, Lisa. "Octavia E. Butler." *Publishers Weekly,* 13 December 1993.

Shinn, Thelma J. "The Wise Witches: Black Women Mentors in the Fiction of Octavia E. Butler." In *Conjuring: Black Women, Fiction, and Literary Tradition.* Edited by Marjorie Pryse and Hortense J. Spillers. Bloomington: Indiana University Press, 1985.

White, Eric. "The Erotics of Becoming: *Xenogenesis* and *The Thing.*" *Science-Fiction Studies,* 20, no. 3 (1993): 394–408.

Williams, Sherley Anne. "Sherley Anne Williams on Octavia E. Butler." *Ms.,* March 1986.

Zaki, Hoda M. "Utopia, Dystopia, and Ideology in the Science Fiction of Octavia Butler." *Science-Fiction Studies,* 17, no. 2 (1990): 239–251.

INTERVIEWS

Beal, Frances M. "Black Women and the Science Fiction Genre: Interview with Octavia Butler." *Black Scholar,* 17 (1986): 14–18.

Best, Allison Stein. "SFC Interview: A Conversation with Octavia E. Butler." *Science Fiction Chronicle,* February 1996.

Elliot, Jeffrey. "Interview with Octavia Butler." *Thrust,* 12 (1979): 19–22.

Fry, Joan. "An Interview with Octavia Butler." *Poets & Writers Magazine,* 25, no. 2 (1997): 58–69.

Kenan, Randall. "An Interview with Octavia E. Butler." *Callaloo,* 14, no. 2 (1991): 495–504.

Mayfield, Evelyn. "Patterns of Her Mind." *Starlog,* 132 (1980): 73–75. (Interview).

McCaffery, Larry. "An Interview with Octavia E. Butler." In *Across the Wounded Galaxies: Interviews with Contemporary American Science Fiction Writers.* Urbana and Chicago: University of Illinois Press, 1990.

Potts, Stephen W. " 'We Keep Playing the Same Record': A Conversation with Octavia E. Butler." *Science-Fiction Studies,* 23, no. 3 (1996): 331–338.

Rowell, Charles H. "An Interview with Octavia E. Butler." *Callaloo,* 20, no. 1 (1997): 47–66.

Spady James G. "Conversation with a Science Fiction Writer: Octavia Butler." *Philadelphia New Observer Women's History Supplement,* 13 March 1996.

—JOHN R. PFEIFFER

JOHN W. CAMPBELL, JR.
(1910–1971)

DURING THE FORMATIVE period of American pulp-magazine science fiction, from 1926 through 1940 or so, there were more than twenty magazines that specialized in science fiction and perhaps another twenty that included it occasionally. Yet of all the editors involved in this production, there was only one who could be called an author of historical importance. This was John W. Campbell, Jr., who edited *Astounding Stories* (and its retitlings *Astounding Science-Fiction* and *Analog*) from September 1937 until 1971.

In his lifetime Campbell was considered one of the two leading authors of space opera, E. E. Smith being the other, and he was one of the pioneers in the so-called new science fiction, in which the pulp magazines moved away from fiction of extravagant action to stories that depended more on mood, psychological considerations, and extrapolations of other societies. These elements, of course, had been present earlier in retrospect science fiction, but it seems to have been necessary for the pulp writers to rediscover them. There is no question that Campbell's fiction stands behind much that happened after he stopped writing, but it must also be admitted that modern criticism no longer rates him very highly as a writer.

John Wood Campbell, Jr., was born in Newark, New Jersey, on 8 June 1910, the son of an electrical engineer who worked for New Jersey Bell Telephone. Campbell seems to have had an unhappy and disturbing childhood, and he emerged into adolescence as a highly intelligent but argumentative, captious, and intellectually rebellious young man. He had discovered science fiction in the Hugo Gernsback days, and he had been fascinated by it, presumably attracted by its imagination, which was lacking in most of the other forms of cheap literature available to youths at that time.

Like many other young fans, Campbell tried his hand at writing science fiction and, probably not to his surprise, sold his first story, a novelette, to *Amazing Stories* while still in his late teens. His first published story, "When the Atoms Failed," which appeared in the January 1930 issue of *Amazing Stories*, was liked by the readers, and Campbell was encouraged to continue writing.

At the time that "When the Atoms Failed" was published, Campbell was a sophomore at the Massachusetts Institute of Technology (MIT), a place that was probably well suited for both his needs and talents, since even at this early period he had the knack of recognizing colorful odds and ends of science and turning them into material usable in fiction. He continued to write and within the next two years had published seven short stories and novelettes, and three novels. Yet, as he discovered, he could not live simultaneously in two worlds, MIT and science fiction. Perhaps he made the wrong choice, but in any case he was expelled from MIT in 1931. The official explanation has been that Campbell did not fulfill his language requirement, but it is reasonable to assume that he simply neglected his schoolwork in favor of writing. After leaving MIT, he transferred to Duke

University, where he received a B.S. degree, majoring in physics.

Campbell graduated from college during the Great Depression and survived by means of a succession of jobs. He sold electric fans and gas heaters, worked in the research laboratory of Mack Trucks, and held similar short-lived jobs. He continued to submit stories to the magazines, and his reputation continued to grow, until he was one of the most popular authors in the field. In 1934 he seems to have been struck by the notion that a new approach was needed in science fiction, and he started writing a new series of stories under the pseudonym Don A. Stuart. Stuart, too, became popular, although it was an open secret that he was actually John W. Campbell, Jr.

At this time, around 1936 and 1937, there were really only three science fiction magazines in the United States. One, *Wonder Stories*, published by Hugo Gernsback, had just ceased publication and was being reactivated as an adventure magazine. The second, *Amazing Stories*, was in the doldrums both financially and editorially. Only the third, *Astounding Stories*, showed signs of vitality. In 1933 Street and Smith Publications had bought *Astounding Stories* from the Clayton Group, where it had been a somewhat shaky magazine specializing in action fiction. The new editor, F. Orlin Tremaine, an experienced editor of pulp fiction, was determined to raise the editorial level of the magazine. Tremaine had some success in this endeavor and was promoted to a general editorship of several magazines. In 1937 he chose Campbell as his new assistant—who would be the actual editor of *Astounding Stories*.

Campbell was an excellent choice for the position. He had grown up in science fiction and knew trends and taboos; he was a very popular author; he was a fantastic idea-man; and he had the strength of personality to impose his will on the writers. In having a scientific background he was almost unique among his fellow editors.

Campbell thus became the first professional science fiction editor, in the sense that it was his true occupation for most of his life.

The other men and women who edited science fiction during this period were either businessmen like Gernsback, publishing executives who happened to handle the science fiction program, or young writers marking time.

It is impossible to date much of Campbell's fiction, since publication often took place years after writing, but it seems that after serving as editor of *Astounding Stories* for a year or two, he wrote little or no new fiction. Material published later seems to have come "from the trunk." While he did some writing in popular science, notably *The Atomic Story* (1947), he concentrated on editorial work. He died on 11 July 1971, still editor of his magazine, at that time called *Analog*. At his death, while it was recognized that he had been a giant as an editor, it was also generally accepted that his last years as an editor had been much less successful than his first.

It is not the purpose of this article to consider Campbell's editorial work in detail, although something will be said about it later, but rather to consider John W. Campbell, Jr., as a writer.

I

Campbell first achieved popularity in the early 1930's with his space operas—adventure stories set out in space, stories whirring with ray guns, booming with the crash of colliding planets and suns. Two of these series were of importance, the Arcot-Morey-Wade stories and the Aarn Munro stories.

Campbell was by no means an original plotter in these space operas, which were derivative and followed the pattern set by E. E. Smith in his Skylark series. Indeed, there was personal rivalry between the two men about this, and some hard feelings. Such creativity as Campbell manifested was to be found in the new technical detail and the more and more elaborate weaponry involved.

The basic plot of the Smith and Campbell stories is simple. A heroic scientific genius develops a new power source or propulsion device that takes him and his friends off into space. Something goes wrong and they become lost. They visit alien planets, looking for the routing back to Earth, and meet more-or-less humanoid civilized beings.

One might call what follows a fairy-tale fantasy of power, except that it parallels very closely colonial policy in North American history. The travelers center on a war situation and aid one side to complete victory, which is due mostly to the genius of the Earthmen. The scientist and his associates do not have selfish reasons for taking part in such a war, as did the early Europeans who pitted one tribe of Indians against another; they join the fight simply because it is the natural thing to do. The enemy is nasty—the less human its form, the nastier—and deserves the extinction that it receives. (The only good amoeboid is a dead amoeboid.) Eventually the Earthmen find star maps and make their way back to Earth, possibly after adventures in other dimensions. As often as not, Earth is in trouble, and they come back just in time to save it.

Whereas Smith's early fiction, despite the sometimes bad writing, has a certain bounce and *joie de vivre*, Campbell's early fiction lacks this personal touch and is strictly commercial writing of a sort. However, it is interesting because it illustrates two points. First, its plot proceeds mostly by a seesaw escalation of special effects (in the motion-picture sense), and second, its psychological purpose seems to be demonstrating the treasures of genius. There is no characterization to speak of, and what little plot there is in the traditional sense consists mostly of a series of war raids. Weapons proliferate—side A has a weapon, side B develops a superweapon, side A then develops a super-superweapon. Side B then produces the ultimate weapon, which is mentioned with awe until the next story—at which time the author has thought of something even better. The author may begin with explosives and rays, work on up through atomic power, subatomic power, gravitational weapons, planet-tossing, invasion through other dimensions, and eventually to utilization of the curvature of space. In each case the new superweapon or process is the condescending gift of a genius, who, after a few moments of puttering about, passes his findings on to others—much as an editor might instruct a stable of writers.

The Campbell space operas are now seldom read, but it is easy to see why they appealed to their readers. The story lines were easy to follow, with few subtleties of thought and none of characterization. They tossed about a remarkable amount of pseudoscientific double-talk, which was neatly presented and gave the reader the illusion of understanding the profundities of modern physics. There was also ingenuity and wonder in the arms races. What would Aarn develop next out of those old soup tins and dead light bulbs? Would he reverse symmetry, so that all the left-handed Rigelians would become right-handed and no longer be able to fire their left-handed weapons?

In Campbell's first important series of space operas—those about Arcot, Morey, and Wade—there are five stories, later collected in *Islands of Space* (1956). A description of one will suffice: "Islands of Space" (*Amazing Stories Quarterly*, Spring 1931). Since it is the fourth story in the series, the readers probably recognized the names of the characters. There was little question of remembering details of characterization, since there is no characterization to speak of. The three associates have developed a device that permits intergalactic travel. To state the principle simply: the nature of space is changed by pouring energy into it, thus permitting travel faster than light. The three daring explorers cross the galaxy in a matter of hours but have an accident, lose their bearings, and must return to Earth by the method previously described. It should be mentioned here that in all Campbell's fiction, even when he is trying to be realistic, as in *The Moon Is Hell!* (1951), he never considers a fail-safe device.

A surprising feature of "Islands of Space" is the small amount of wordage that is spent in action scenes—in flashing rays and bouncing

John W. Campbell, Jr. in 1971. PHOTO BY JAY KAY KLEIN

projectiles. In the last third of the story, where most of the action takes place, about half the wordage is devoted to harangues by Arcot, lectures on the scientific principles involved, and detailed histories of the warring nations. Also evident is a trick of writing that Campbell used throughout his career: letting the characters or the narrator reflect on what has just happened. This trick often doubled wordage, which even at one-half a cent per word, helped the struggling author.

Such a mode of presentation is strange for pulp fiction, since in the better magazines craftsmanship was high and such padding was not permitted. Can one imagine what the reader reaction would have been in, say, *Argosy All-Story*, if one of the Peter the Brazen stories by George Worts, which were set in premodern China, were extended 50 percent by the inclusion of lectures on the mandarin system, the past history of Hupei Province, or the working of trade guilds?

Campbell's divagations were acceptable because the material that he discussed was often intrinsically interesting. A fairly clear statement of the nature of space according to Einstein's General Theory of Relativity could be stimulating. A speculation that atoms could be formed of photons (this was before subatomic particles) and that the resulting matter would have peculiar properties was an intriguing idea, especially if it were presented like a bull session among young scientists in a college lab. In all this it must be emphasized that, despite his reputation to the contrary, Campbell was by no means a writer of heavy or hard-core science fiction. His science was fantastic and, of course, in large part doubletalk.

The dauntless trio of Arcot, Morey, and Wade could not get lost indefinitely, anymore than Tarzan could suffer amnesia more than once per book.

A new set of characters took their place in Campbell's other space opera series. These were Aarn Munro and his friends, whose exploits were described in "The Mightiest Machine" (*Astounding Stories*, December 1934– April 1935). Aarn is a superman of sorts. Reared on Jupiter, he has "muscles on muscles," both physically and mentally.

When Aarn and his friends take their new spaceship out on a test run, they forget to look ahead and so crash into a planetoid. The ship's power systems battle, the fabric of space is ripped, but instead of being killed the men are tossed into another space. They are lost and must find their way home. They meet descendants of refugees from the lost continent of Mu (on Earth) and, as their enemies, vicious caprine beings who are the prototypes for the imagery of the Devil. Aarn drops a moon upon the home planet of these satyrs and destroys them. But he is still lost.

Campbell wrote three sequels to "The Mightiest Machine": "The Incredible Planet," "The Interstellar Search," and "The Infinite Atom." They were probably written not too long after "The Mightiest Machine," but they first appeared together in book form in 1949 as *The Incredible Planet*.

The adventurers return to our own space but are still lost. In "The Incredible Planet" they come upon a half-frozen planet that has been wandering through space in isolation and is just coming into orbit around a sun. The people, who are just reviving from suspended animation, are 473,375,500,000 years old. This figure is treated with reverence and awe. "The Interstellar Search" takes Aarn and his friends to a system with two inhabited planets. One is peopled with humanoids; the other, by "unbelievably repulsive" reptile men. Aarn (literally) cooks the planet of the reptile men. "The Infinite Atom" is somewhat more complex. Millennia ago a scouting ship of centaurlike beings crashed on Earth, leaving stranded some centaurs, who then became personages in Greek mythology. Now, the centaurs on the home planet need Lebensraum and invade the Solar system. The centaurs and Aarn battle each other with ever escalating weapons, until Aarn develops a bomb with the cosmical constant, or a fifth-dimensional twist. Aarn has also learned how to create energy and so ends the war.

"The Mightiest Machine" shows an advance in technique over the early space operas, but it was Campbell's last significant story to be published in magazine form under his own name. Starting in 1934, he used a new name, Don A. Stuart, a pseudonym based upon his wife's maiden name. He seems to have felt that John W. Campbell, Jr., was "typecast" as a writer of space operas and that he was writing something so new and different that it deserved a new identity.

Stuart's first story, "Twilight" (*Astounding Stories*, November 1934), caused a mild sensation among readers. It was not an invention story, not an action story, but a fictionalization of the sense of awe inspired by cosmic engineering. Although "Twilight" is set in an unnecessary frame situation involving a rustic of the 1930's, the heart of the story is the emotional reaction of a time traveler to a world 7 million years in the future, a world of fossil mechanization, with giant deserted cities spread over the land. The human race is almost extinct, but the abandoned cities are maintained in perfect running order by incredible, benevolent machines. Campbell is not interested in the humans, who are portrayed as the conventional highly evolved "balloon heads" with hypertrophied intellect and weakened appetition, nor directly in the machines, but in the symbol of mechanical perfection provided by the far future world. Yet there is an ambivalence in the traveler's report. He is in awe of the machines, as is Campbell, and the point of the story is expressed in the phrase "he wondered as he went." But the traveler also feels that the wonders have taken place at the expense of man.

In writing "Twilight," Campbell demonstrates an advance over the earlier fiction, yet he obviously had great difficulty in establishing a writing tone to parallel the ideational tone. The exposition, which is first-person narrative, occasionally collapses into bathos or abstract narration. Yet, despite its flaws, "Twilight" does convey a mood and is one of the few stories by Campbell that can still be read with enjoyment.

"Night" (*Astounding Stories*, October 1935) is a variation on the "Twilight" theme. A pilot testing a new energy field is accidentally hurled billions of years into the future, to a time when the universe is almost dead. Energy has run down. The cosmos has collapsed, and the stars are near at hand and mostly burned out. Such energy as is left is residual. Man has long been extinct and even the machines of "Twilight" have yielded to the cold. Only on the outer planets, where design was fitted to the cold of interstellar space, have a few machines survived, waiting until their energy, too, is gone. They care for the involuntary time traveler and send him back to the present.

Both stories were considered novel in their day, since they avoided thrills and orthopteroid inventions, but today they seem very much in the tradition of H. G. Wells, particularly of the last portions of *The Time Machine*.

Stuart's (and Campbell's) most famous story is "Who Goes There?" (*Astounding Sto-*

ries, August 1938). It is based on a shape-changer, a monstrosity that can absorb a person's body and take over that person's shape almost instantly, offering an exact duplicate. Shape-changers were not Campbell's invention; indeed, on one level they parallel the motifs in supernatural fiction of possession or personality interchange. But Campbell gave the idea a new twist: the problem the characters face is not so much destroying a monster as deciding who the monster is. This can be read as a special case in establishing good faith.

An Antarctic exploration party comes upon an alien spaceship locked in the ice. In what at first seems a foolish action, they accidentally destroy the ship by using a thermite bomb in an attempt to melt the ice around it. The ship, as one of the party calmly remarks, is made of magnesium alloy, and it goes up in flames. But outside the ship is found the frozen carcass of a horrible-looking monster that had obviously been overcome by the cold when it left the disabled ship. The monster is not dead. Like a buried complex it comes to life, steals away, attacks the dogs of the expedition, and in a matter of hours forms exact duplicates of several members of the expedition. If the monster reaches the outside world, humanity is doomed.

The monster is easy enough to destroy, but identifying it may be impossible, since the monster has taken over bodies and memories exactly and can pass any test given to it. This problem of identification had beset earlier writers, but no convincing solution was reached.

Campbell offered what remains the best technique for identifying such ersatz humans. In such a monster, each separate fragment will have autonomous life. Blood drawn from a pseudohuman will behave like a tiny, individual monster, not like human blood. The world is now saved by blood tests and flame throwers. Campbell ignores the fact that the monster might have taken over germs or fleas on the dogs.

The idea is clever, and Campbell tried to create an emotion-fraught thriller from the situation, but the treatment still leaves much to be desired. There are purple passages and even sections reminiscent of Doc Savage, one of the lowbrow pulp heroes of the time. Campbell lacked the technical ability to evoke the horror of the situation. The "stark realism" he offers does not work. Nevertheless, "Who Goes There?" has been one of the most popular stories in American science fiction. It ultimately served as the source for the well-known motion picture *The Thing from Another World* (1951), although this film shared little with the story except the concept of a hostile, dangerous, resilient monster from space.

Altogether Stuart wrote sixteen stories, but only a couple more need be described. Very popular in their time, though now apparently forgotten, were the three stories that Campbell thought of as the Teachers series: "The Machine" (*Astounding Stories*, February 1935), "The Invaders" (*Astounding Stories*, June 1935), and "Rebellion" (*Astounding Stories*, July 1935). They might be characterized as the Calvinist work ethic transplanted to science fiction. Behind them lies the concept that man is basically lazy and sinful, and needs either the compulsions of Character or external peril to keep him from degenerating.

At some time in the future, a Machine which we today would call a supercomputer comes to Earth and exercises benevolent care over mankind. This Machine runs civilization smoothly, but, as is the case in "The Machine Stops" by E. M. Forster, mankind degenerates. In Campbell's story, the loss is in intellect, emotional drive, and overall survival ability. The Machine has met such a problem before on another planet, and as before it tries to solve the problem by running away. The result is the worst blow that has struck the human race. Material civilization collapses. While there are a few futile attempts to reestablish the mechanical civilization of the past, most men try to settle in the tropics, where they can live by picking fruit from trees. The mortality is enormous. The survivors descend into a happy, Edenic primitivism.

This wonderful life (though Campbell does not esteem it) is interrupted by an invasion from space by the Tharoo, vaguely humanoid beings, who for both humanitarian and selfish reasons decide to breed man back to a higher state. The result is unfortunate for the Tharoo, for as soon as man has attained a mentality superior to that of the Tharoo, he expels them. The mechanisms used for the expulsion are two: an impenetrable force field and paranormal powers, which are similar to the evil eye. Man can generate within his body a radiation that paralyzes or kills.

Similarly tied in with parapsychology, which grew to be a dominating interest for Campbell, is "Forgetfulness" (*Astounding Stories*, June 1937). An interstellar expedition of humanoid beings visits Earth some millennia in the future. Earth is almost deserted, with only a few settlements of humans living in fairly primitive habitations within sight of colossal ruins of a supercivilization. The visitors, who are not unfriendly, decide that the Earthmen are decadent, since they do not understand much of the dead science around them. But when the visitors plan to establish a colony and remove the Earthmen to another spot, they are seized by the mental power of a native, and the entire ship and its personnel are hurled back through space and time to their planet of origin. Machines may have been forgotten by humans, but the natives' mental powers have grown enormously.

The small upsurge in science fiction book publishing that occurred around 1950, with the emergence of many fan publishers, resulted in the appearance of a new novel by Campbell, *The Moon Is Hell!* (1951). There is no indication as to when this was written, but it is reasonable to assume that it dates from the late 1930's, just as do certain of the three works published posthumously in *The Space Beyond* (1976). The treatment in *The Moon Is Hell!* is reminiscent of "Who Goes There?," and the story situation is essentially that of Admiral Richard Byrd's Little America transplanted to the Moon.

The Moon Is Hell! is one of the very few attempts at realism in the interplanetary novel of the day. Thirteen men, arriving by rocket, dig in on the dark side (why the dark side?) of the Moon and set up a base. The expedition is scheduled to stay for two years, but the relief ship crashes, and eight more months pass before help arrives. This delay is caused by several factors that can be summed up as lack of foresight.

On the Moon the story is told mostly through the diary of Thomas R. Duncan. There are two themes. The first is an attempt to consider realistically what might go wrong under such circumstances, told with Campbell's technique of "stark realism." Men die; everyone is miserable; some men are swinish; annoyances abound; major problems seem insoluble. Unfortunately, Campbell does not handle such material very well, any better than he did in "Who Goes There?" The second theme is that of Robinson Crusoe on the Moon. Using lunar raw materials, salvaging and resalvaging everything, the thirteen men perform technological miracles. They excavate an underground dwelling of great complexity; obtain water (and thence, oxygen) from gypsum, though where the gypsum came from is not explained; develop incredible power sources; and manufacture synthetic foods. Unfortunately, they did not know of a new vitamin isolated on Earth and they are all dying of malnutrition when the relief expedition comes. Only six men survive. But while they were on the Moon, their doings were glorious. As the plot line indicates, Campbell's faith lay not in machines, but in a special type of human being. For Campbell, long-range planners did not exist; machines let man down when the rocket exploded, but the inspired putterer won through.

Among Campbell's posthumous papers were found three short novels, which were published together as *The Space Beyond*. They seem to date from the 1930's. While they are not considered among Campbell's better works, they are still interesting since they show quirks of personality and his editorial approach more clearly than do his more successful works.

The first of these novels, "Marooned," ties in with a very controversial story, "The Irrelevant," which Campbell had written under the pseudonym Karl Van Campen, and which appeared in *Astounding Stories* for December 1934. "The Irrelevant" is based on the relativity of motion with reference to different places, while "Marooned" is concerned with a device that functions at 102 percent efficiency. Campbell was greatly interested in such devices (usually called "perpetual motion machines") in his later life. The second story, "All," takes place in a Japanese-occupied America of the near future. Scientists have gone underground with newly discovered atomic energy, and in the guise of a new religion drive out the Orientals. As a story, "All" is not significant; what is important about it is that Campbell turned it over to Robert A. Heinlein, who reworked the idea into the superior novel *Sixth Column* (1941). Supplying ideas to authors was one of Campbell's editorial strengths. The third novel, "The Space Beyond," seems fragmentary, and is probably the earliest of the three posthumous works.

II

For the last twenty years of his life, so far as is known, Campbell wrote no more fiction but concentrated on editorial work. He received an operating shop when he began working at *Astounding Stories* in 1937, and he carried on Tremaine's policies, improving and enlarging on them. He stressed literary quality, and although not all the stories selected by Campbell were literature, they were at least literate. Campbell expanded the scope of science fiction in the pulps. He preferred the story of ideas—not necessarily inventions, but a story based on an imaginative quirking or twisting of scientific facts. And most of all, he liked the story in which an extrapolation could be projected into a life situation. This often merged into social engineering.

The result of this enlarging of editorial policy—together with a higher rate of payment than that offered by the other magazines—was that Campbell could attract the better writers. Campbell was not afraid to print the work of new authors, and a list of the authors that he developed would include most of the better writers of his day.

The reminiscences of a number of the authors who worked with Campbell have a strong consensus about him. As an editor, he was arrogant, dictatorial, condescending, informative, tutorial, helpful, and unselfish. His ability to create story ideas was remarkable. He could read a routine story, see how a few twists could improve it, and then tell the writer what to do. Author after author has reported going to the offices of Street and Smith, being beset with a barrage of questions (which he was not expected to answer), then being given instructions and told to come back with something better. Usually the treatment worked. In this formative ability, Campbell in all probability stands without peer in the history of the genre.

In addition to selecting and planning stories, one of Campbell's duties was preparing a monthly editorial, a tradition that went back to the early days of science fiction with Gernsback. In earlier times, these editorials usually dealt with popular science or technology. Under Campbell the editorial gradually shifted to an exhortation or a harangue, rather than to an essay in the belletristic tradition or an exposition of science. His editorials were often stimulating and provocative, but they were also often wrongheaded, opinionated, and even silly, as when Campbell ventured into fields in which he had no competence. Readers often wondered whether Campbell was not overstating an unsound position in order to stimulate discussion or reaction. But no matter what his intentions were, a reader is left with the conclusion that his editorials, which still have their admirers, show Campbell at his weakest. They reveal severe limitations in background and methodology. Although he had a good factual knowledge of the physical sciences, he did not seem to understand scientific method and was very naïve in the biological and social sciences.

All these traits are tied in with Campbell's perpetual chase after strange gods. Just as Don A. Stuart mused in delighted awe at parapsychology and "metascience," John W. Campbell, Jr., was attracted to crank science, usually in fields in which he was not competent. Most notorious of his enthusiasms was his wholehearted support for L. Ron Hubbard's dianetics, which in its beginnings was a pseudopsychoanalytic technique used to remove psychic "scar tissue" from aberrants (that is, all of us) and turn us into "clears," or perfect humans. The ultimate theory behind this— which may have been its appeal to Campbell—was not that man is infinitely perfectible, but that man is perfectly infinite, if limitations set by "engrams" are removed. Campbell had previously toyed with Alfred Korzybski's General Semantics but turned to dianetics with greater enthusiasm. He permitted Hubbard to announce his theories in the pages of *Astounding Science-Fiction* and was closely associated with the early phase of dianetics.

Two of Campbell's later enthusiasms involved the physical sciences, and he supported them strongly in *Astounding Science-Fiction* and *Analog.* The first was the Hieronymous device, an assemblage of electronic parts that was supposed to detect radiations otherwise unknown or undetectable. Some persons could "work" the apparatus; others could not. For Campbell this meant a connection with parapsychology. His last editorial bender of significance was mechanical rather than electronic. This was the so-called Dean drive, a system of rotating weights and gears that created a jiggling motion that its proponents considered levitation or loss of weight. Campbell believed that the Dean drive could be used to propel a spaceship in space. Physicists, on the other hand, considered it a perpetual motion machine.

In all three of these episodes Campbell's attitude was that a hooded and sinister scientific orthodoxy (suggestive of the Rosicrucian

ads in *Astounding Science-Fiction*), for reasons best known to itself, refused to consider such phenomena and persisted in tumbling them under the lab bench.

In addition to editing *Astounding Stories* and its permutations, Campbell also edited for Street and Smith a supernatural fiction magazine called *Unknown,* later *Unknown Worlds.* It was published from March 1939 to October 1943. It stressed a science fiction writer's concept of the supernatural as an internally consistent, logical, rational irrationality. Under Campbell's editorship, *Unknown* printed much excellent fiction, but in the long run it became monotonous. The paper shortage of World War II is usually given as the reason for its cancellation in 1943, but it is probably significant that Street and Smith did not reissue it after the war. A trial publication of an anthology issue seems to have been a failure.

To *Unknown* Campbell contributed (as Don Stuart) a short novel, "The Elder Gods" (October 1939). The story should have been listed as a collaboration, for it was a hasty expansion and rewriting of an unsatisfactory story submitted by L. Ron Hubbard. Even Campbell's greatest admirers have seldom been able to evoke much enthusiasm for this story, which is derivative in part from the work of A. Merritt and retains traces of Hubbard's weaker Middle Eastern fantasies.

An odd mixture of rational and mythic elements, it is basically about a struggle between two sets of gods in the future, around A.D. 3000. One of the gods, however, is a supercomputer. The less desirable gods are housed in a crystal globe, like demons in a fairy tale; the hero resists the hypnotic power of the globe by using a stroboscope. This story may mark the end of Campbell's writing career, since stories published later are believed to have been written earlier.

III

If one were to sum up Campbell's writing career in a sentence, it would be: He started too soon and ended too soon. He had many good ideas; he was an innovator; he had a feel for the market; but he never really learned the craft of writing. His early success at selling second- and third-rate material injured him, for since he had a ready market, he wrote hastily, drew from whatever he happened to have read not too long before, and filled pages with padding. At the time that he stopped writing, his work was improving, and he probably would have ended as a major writer had he stayed with writing.

Today we are in the diastolic phase of regarding him. His stories had a strong historical influence, but critics are divided as to whether that influence was for the better or worse. As an editor he is rated on equally divergent scales. According to some, science fiction would have perished if Campbell had not assumed the editorship of *Astounding Stories*. This, of course, is an exaggeration and an if of history that is probably contrary to fact. According to others, Campbell's influence, especially in the later years, was bad, since he stressed the engineering mentality in science fiction to the exclusion of other values and kept science fiction in a dry-weather rut. This point of view tends to overlook Campbell's positive contributions, which were many, particularly in his earlier years.

As is often the case with controversial figures, the wisest judgment is mixed. Campbell was a great editor, but he had limitations, as we all do. In his case, the limitations became more obvious (since he had the courage or rashness to render them public) than with most of us. As a writer, he is always interesting typologically. As an editor, he could judge literacy, was prolific in ideas, and had drive. On the whole, he was much like his major characters. He was the eternal putterer in ideas, the perpetual taker of unsuspected shortcuts, the culture-hero, but unfortunately life is not always like fiction.

Selected Bibliography

WORKS OF JOHN W. CAMPBELL, JR.

The Mightiest Machine. Providence, R.I.: Hadley Publishing Company, 1947.
Who Goes There? Seven Tales of Science Fiction. Chicago: Shasta Publishers, 1948.
The Incredible Planet. Reading, Pa.: Fantasy Press, 1949.
The Moon Is Hell! Reading, Pa.: Fantasy Press, 1951.
Cloak of Aesir. Chicago: Shasta Publishers, 1952.
Islands of Space. Reading, Pa.: Fantasy Press, 1956.
Collected Editorials from Analog. Edited by Harry Harrison. Garden City, N.Y.: Doubleday, 1966.
The Space Beyond. Edited by Roger Elwood. With an introduction by Isaac Asimov and an afterword by George Zebrowski. New York: Pyramid Books, 1976.
Campbell, John W. *Collected Editorials from Analog.* Garden City, N.Y.: Doubleday, 1996.

CRITICAL AND BIOGRAPHICAL STUDIES

Aldiss, Brian W. "Campbell's Soup." In his *The Detached Retina: Aspects of SF and Fantasy.* Syracuse, N.Y.: Syracuse University Press, 1995.
Asimov, Isaac. "Big, Big, Big." In his *Asimov on Science Fiction.* Garden City, N.Y.: Doubleday, 1981.
———. "The Campbell Touch." In his *Asimov on Science Fiction.* Garden City, N.Y.: Doubleday, 1981.
———. "Controversy." In his *Asimov's Galaxy: Reflections on Science Fiction.* Garden City, N.Y.: Doubleday, 1989.
———. "Five Greats of Science Fiction." In his *The Tyrannosaurus Prescription and 100 Other Essays.* Buffalo, N.Y.: Prometheus, 1989.
Malzberg, Barry N. "John W. Campbell: June 8, 1910 to July 11, 1971." In his *Engines of the Night.* Garden City, N.Y.: Doubleday, 1982.
———. "Wrong Rabbit." In his *Engines of the Night.* Garden City, N.Y.: Doubleday, 1982.
Sloan, De Villo. "The Self and Self-less in Campbell's *Who Goes There?* and Finney's *Invasion of the Body Snatchers.*" *Extrapolation,* 29, no. 2 (1988): 179–188.
Westfahl, Gary. "'A Convenient Analog System': John W. Campbell, Jr.'s Theory of Science Fiction." *Foundation* (Spring 1992): 52–70.
———. "Dictatorial, Authoritarian, Uncooperative: The Case Against John W. Campbell." *Foundation* (Autumn 1992): 36–60.

—E. F. BLEILER

KAREL ČAPEK

(1890–1938)

ON CHRISTMAS DAY of 1938, in a Prague grim with foreboding, Karel Čapek died of an inflammation of the lungs, as his physician described it. According to everyone else he died of a broken heart, in the same way that his beloved Czechoslovakia, betrayed at Munich, was dying. In fear of Germany and Hitler, the enfeebled Czech government prevented the National Museum in Prague from having Čapek's body laid out in state, as was customary with figures of his stature, on the ground that the building could not be properly heated; they also attempted to prohibit people from watching the funeral procession. In this they did not succeed. Large crowds lined the streets as the procession passed; shops and homes were arrayed with crepe and photographs of the dead author, who had had the temerity to satirize Nazi Germany in his most famous novel, *Válka s mloky*, 1936 (*War with the Newts*). Although the government was strikingly unsuccessful in its attempts to muffle public mourning for Čapek, it does seem that elements of the German government were bemused for a time. On 15 March 1939, when Germany did snuff out what remained of Czechoslovakia after the dismemberment sanctioned at Munich the previous year, agents of the Gestapo went to the house of Čapek's widow. They had come to arrest him.

Forewarned, Mrs. Čapek had already burned her dead husband's correspondence. In more ways than one, consequently, Karel Čapek passed away with the death of his country, and a certain vagueness about his private life in subsequent studies of him may be explained on the ground that much relevant material was destroyed. Of his impassioned identification with the openhearted, fragile culture of his native land, there can be no doubt. And just as Czechoslovakia's culture was humane, complex, cosmopolitan, and precarious, so Čapek's art—encompassing almost fifty books of almost every sort—defies easy critical analysis; indeed, it tends to break down under analysis.

A journalist, dramatist, essayist, novelist, and travel writer, Čapek was a prolific man of letters, sometimes offhand and exclamatory, sometimes diffuse, sometimes intensely expressionistic in the mode of avant-garde drama of the first decades of the twentieth century. At some points his stories and novels will remind readers of the fiction of G. K. Chesterton and other Edwardians; but the Castle in his most deeply felt novel, *Krakatit* (1924), is planted in the same unstable soil as Franz Kafka's (nor should it be forgotten that Kafka, a German-speaking Jew only a few years older than Čapek, lived most of his life in Prague, and that both men inevitably responded to some of the same cultural traumas as the Austro-Hungarian Empire entered its death throes). And if Czechoslovakian science fiction, in the hands of its only significant practitioner before Josef Nesvadba, should only occasionally resemble the American version circa 1920–1940, we should not be surprised that speculative writings expressive of conditions in a man-made state surrounded by powerful, predatory neighbors should differ substantially from those expressive of conditions in a frontier-haunted technocracy about to dominate the globe.

I

Karel Čapek was born on 9 January 1890 in Bohemia, near the German border, in an area that was ceded to Germany at Munich in the year of his death. His father, a physician, was active in local cultural affairs; his mother was interested in the culture of the province, especially in its folk music, fairy tales, and oral folklore. She was an hysteric, and although Karel—her youngest child—was devoted to her, throughout his life he remained highly wary of any similar behavior on the part of his intimates; the supercharged emotional violence of *Krakatit* is all the more interesting in this context. Perhaps the most important member of Čapek's immediate family was his older brother, Josef (1887–1945), who became a cubist painter as well as a literary collaborator with Karel, mainly in the decade following their first work together, a short story entitled "The Return of the Prophet Hermotinos" (1908). (Their most famous collaborations are plays written and first performed in the 1920's.)

The Brothers Čapek, as they signed themselves, specialized in swift, wry, sentimental stories and essays. Initially they were quite prolific, but they were forced to separate in 1910, when Josef went to Paris to study art and Karel went to Berlin. Karel returned the following year to Prague, where he took his Ph.D. in 1915 with a dissertation on aesthetics. Already he was suffering from a rare ailment afflicting the vertebrae, which forced him to walk with a cane; he was in pain for much of the remainder of his life. Exempted from military service during World War I, Čapek remained in Prague, where two collections of the brothers' work were published in 1916 and 1918 and where Karel's first solo collection, *Boží muka* (which can be translated as "Wayside Crosses"), was published in 1917.

None of this early work has appeared in English, so the nondramatic work of the Brothers Čapek—their fables and allegories—can have had very little effect on the English-speaking world. With their two collaborative plays, of course, this is anything but the case. Under its various English titles *Ze života hmyzu* (1921)—literally translated as "From the Life of the Insects"—attained a stage success second only to Karel Čapek's single most famous work, *R.U.R.* (1920). The Čapeks' second dramatic collaboration, *Adam Stvořitel* (1927), translated as *Adam the Creator* (1929), although fluent and amusing, did not do particularly well on the stage, and it proved to be their last work together. There was no personal falling out, though, and Josef and Karel Čapek remained intimate for the rest of Karel's life. Josef was arrested by the Germans and spent World War II in the Bergen-Belsen concentration camp, dying, apparently of typhus, en route home just as the war ended.

Karel Čapek's literary maturity begins with the establishment of Czechoslovakia in 1918. Besides his first solo collection he published a study of pragmatism; edited volumes of folktales; wrote satirical verse under the name Plocek; had his first play, *The Outlaw*, produced in 1920; and remained astonishingly busy for the rest of his life. In contrast with most American science fiction writers, Čapek was a working journalist throughout his career, producing great amounts of copy, often on a daily basis, and serving the Prague newspaper *Lidové noviny* as contributor and editor from 1921 until his death. Nor was his journalistic work in any significant way—in terms of quality, tone, or persistent themes—separate from his work as a playwright or novelist.

Unlike a professional newspaperman such as the American Clifford D. Simak, who has been more prolific as a science fiction novelist since retirement, Čapek conceived of everything he did as a piece; most of his work was directed to the same goal, variously expressed. This goal was the political, moral, and cultural enhancement of Czechoslovakia—Czechoslovakia both as a nation trying

Karel Čapek (left) with his brother, Joseph Čapek. UPI/Corbis-Bettmann

to survive the desolating power politics of twentieth-century Europe and as a state of mind, a symbol of a secular, humane, nonabsolutist approach to life and thought. The success with which he expressed this complex aspiration gives poignance and dramatic resolution to his death just as the dream itself was dying.

Whether writing newspaper columns, or plays, or novels, or fairy tales, or travel books, or hagiographic propaganda on the subject of his main political hero, Tomáš Masaryk, founder and president of his country, Karel Čapek is almost invariably trying to teach us. He is perhaps the most insistently didactic writer of anything like the first rank the twentieth century has seen, with the possible exception of Bertolt Brecht. This intensity of aim infuses with passion, and makes still readable, his first great stage success, *R.U.R.*, produced in 1921, the year following its publication.

For obvious reasons, plays are peculiarly subject to alteration by translators; *R.U.R.* is no exception. Paul Selver's original English-

language translation, published in the United States as *R.U.R. (Rossum's Universal Robots): A Fantastic Melodrama* (1923), appeared only a few months later in England, "adapted" for the British stage. In the British version some of the more forthright political utterances have been bowdlerized—at one point a reference to "this appalling political structure" is toned down to a vaguely worded "confounded social lumber"—and the first American version, if it can be found, is probably to be preferred. At the same time the British rendering does restore to the weak Epilogue Čapek's indulgently inflated Tolstoyan peroration, which is voiced by the sole remaining human as he blesses a young Adam-and-Eve robot couple in love, to the accompaniment of heavenly stage effects—all of which in the American text is trimmed savagely.

Whichever translation is read, the present-day reader's interest in the play (it is seldom performed on stage now) centers on Čapek's creation of the robot. Taken from the Czech *robota,* meaning "forced labor," the word "robot" was invented by Josef Čapek, and it has come to have a far more precise meaning than either brother can have intended. In the play the robots are not mechanical, metallic creatures, but are instead androids—living, organic simulacra—indistinguishable at first (and second) glance from humans. Čapek's robots represent, at times rather loosely and inconsistently, a complex of symbolic meanings: the threatening aspects of the industrial dehumanization of the work force, as well as the pathos that surrounds the victims of rationalization and of the assembly line. Through this ambivalence, which is not always convincing in its mixture of reductive caricature and sentimental special pleading, the image of the robot represents the logical outcome, for the helpless masses, of living and working in a world where human autonomy is not only superfluous but also directly counterproductive.

The story is simple, although somewhat wacky. A human woman with connections, young Helena Glory, comes to the isolated island where Rossum's Universal Robots manufactures its products, in order to foment revolution among them. Feminine, naïve, and extremely beautiful, Helena confuses humans with robots, wins the heart of Plant Director Domin and all his human colleagues, marries Domin, and settles down for a decade (five years in the British version) of marital bliss. The next act begins with news that the robots—the unthinking, downtrodden masses —are rebelling in Europe and elsewhere. At the same time humanity has lost the capacity to reproduce itself; this loss, which is not realistically explained, Čapek passes on to the reader by an expressionistic fiat; the hand of the author is always visible, shifting characters about, changing their levels of plausibility, pointing out the moral. Hearing the bad news, Helena impulsively destroys the manuscripts containing old Rossum's formulas for robot manufacture, thus ensuring that both humans and robots, having driven themselves into vile extremity, will perish from Earth. The logic underlying this is not clear (Čapek's treatment of women is at times uneasy). In

the next act the robots, their heads filled with left-wing slogans, kill off all the humans on the island—including Helena, offstage—except for Alquist, who is saved because he is able to work with his hands as the robots do. In the final act (or, variously, the Epilogue), Alquist unsuccessfully attempts to rediscover the secret of how to manufacture (or, more accurately, to stew) robots out of raw, quasi-organic broth. Both he and the robot chief are in despair. But then Alquist notices that two young robots, Primus and another Helena, are showing signs of romantic involvement, and he blesses them. They pass from his sight in the general direction of Eden, where (we must assume, for we are not actually told) they will begin to breed.

Dramatically, then, *R.U.R.* is confused, although it is vivid and extremely swift in the telling, and it will undoubtedly continue to be far more widely read than seen—a judgment by posterity that is strongly in accord with Čapek's own, since he felt the work to be a failure. Certainly his ambivalence about the robots—his uncertainty whether to regard them as downtrodden masses or faceless menaces—fails to ground itself in a plot structure capable of assimilating the complex rendering of the conflict of partial truths he wished to present. Nevertheless, moments of eloquence remain. In a sense, although he is killed off soon afterward, Director Domin has the last word, in Act III of the American translation, when he argues:

It was not an evil dream to shatter the servitude of labor—the dreadful and humiliating labor that man had to undergo. . . . I wanted not a single soul to be broken by other people's machinery. I wanted nothing, nothing, nothing to be left of this appalling social structure.

Čapek's remaining dramatic works, written with his brother or alone, have relatively little to do with science fiction, although they tend to utilize science fictional premises rather casually. There are two plays written with Josef Čapek. The most common translation of *Ze života hmyzu* is by Paul Selver and "freely adapted for the English stage by Nigel Playfair and Clifford Bax" as "*And So Ad Infinitum*" (*The Life of the Insects*) (1923). It is also known as *The World We Live In* and *The Insect Play*.

Dramatically far more effective than *R.U.R.*, it is an astonishingly bleak work. Through the eyes of the human tramp who provides continuity, we witness three revue-like sketches, each based on a fantastic rendering of the meaning behind the lives of various forms of insects. First, the butterflies demonstrate their giddy, sex-obsessed juvenility, then the "creepers and crawlers" reduce to absurdity (rather the way Luis Buñuel does in his films) bourgeois obsessions with money and propriety as avarice and violent death decimate them; finally, the totalitarian world of the ants—who resemble both robots and newts—is a ferocious satire on contemporary politics of the far left and far right, as ants of different colors destroy one another in response to the manic exhortations of their leaders. At the play's close the tramp struggles unsuccessfully against his own useless, albeit inevitable, death.

Less bleak is *Adam the Creator*, in which Adam, a disappointed romantic, destroys the world with his Cannon of Negation and is given the job of re-creating a better world by a comically fretful deity; their dialogue may plausibly remind readers of the famous 1960's "God-man" routine perfected by the American comic Bill Cosby. These two plays are less science fiction per se than demonstrations of the uses to which genre conceits can be put; they are intended to make clear-cut lessons out of their subject matter.

After *R.U.R.*, Čapek produced two further plays of some genre interest. *Věc Makropulos* (1922), made into an opera by Leoš Janáček (1926) and translated as *The Macropoulos Secret* (1927), again parodies the dehumanizing lust for final solutions, for absolute answers. In this case the solution looked for is immortality, but again—as in *R.U.R.*—a cumbersome plot fails to bring Čapek's insistent didacticism to life. *Bílá nemoc* (literally "The White Plague," 1937), translated as *Power and Glory* (1938), although too loosely constructed to hold together, is of interest because of its premonitions about the inevitability of war. A doctor discovers the cure for a plague that is killing everyone over the age of forty, but he refuses to divulge his cure unless all the dictators promise to stop waging war; this blackmail is fatuous enough, and the doctor is duly slaughtered by a mob eager for final solutions.

II

The heart of Čapek's accomplishment lies not in his work as a playwright, but in his eight novels, of which three are science fiction and a fourth—*Povétroň* (1934), translated as *Meteor* (1935)—uses some genre devices, but in a delusional (or subjective) frame. The three science fiction novels are *Továrna na Absolutno* (1922), translated as *The Absolute at Large* (1927); *Krakatit* (1924), translated in 1925; and *Válka s mloky* (1936), translated as *War with the Newts* (1937). Although *The Absolute at Large* and *War with the Newts* were written at opposite ends of his career, and although the optimistic normalization that closes the first book has no place in the second, the narrative strangeness for most readers of these two novels is such that they should be dealt with together.

This sense of narrative strangeness has a single immediate cause. Both novels were written for serial publication in Čapek's newspaper, *Lidové noviny*, and both were written as *romans feuilletons*. In French newspapers, and in *Lidové noviny* as well, it has often been the practice to mark off the bottom of one or more pages and to use this space for essays, fiction, causeries, poetry, and so forth. A *roman feuilleton* is, therefore, a novel written to fill this kind of space; such a work tends to have characteristics that distinguish it from more conventionally composed and presented fiction.

The typical *roman feuilleton* is constructed as a series of anecdotes, often using a reportage format that parodies the rest of the newspaper; differing viewpoints succeed one another, characters appear and disappear abruptly, and often there are typographical experiments not unlike those used by John Dos Passos in his *U.S.A.* trilogy (1937). Rather than private passions and life stories, the interest of the *roman feuilleton* is concentrated on imaginary newsworthy events, imaginary history, and exemplary catastrophes, and because it is probably composed on a continuing basis, this kind of novel tends to respond, usually in a satirical manner, to events as they are occurring and are being reported elsewhere in the newspaper. Given Čapek's deep involvement with Czech culture in all its aspects, it is not surprising that he found the form—or, as one might put it, the forum—of the *roman feuilleton* well suited to his needs.

Of these two novels *The Absolute at Large* is clearly the less successful, and although the first twelve installments (chapters in the book form) are winningly impetuous and set the scene, the remaining eighteen sections lose their narrative momentum, with the result that the book ends on a desultory note. At the heart of at least the earlier pages of the novel, there is a solid science fiction idea, the notion that atomic energy can be used to supply cheap industrial power. This idea is soon fabulized out of any normal genre pattern by the fact that the release of atomic energy also releases from annihilated matter something rather more ethereal—the Absolute Itself, which is something like the Holy Ghost, or God, and which is certainly unmeasurable. Abandoning Marek, the engineer who invents the Karburator that releases the Absolute, and C. H. Bondy, the "head of the great Metallo-Electric Company," who initially exploits it, the novel as a whole then devotes itself to a series of satirical accounts of the industrial, political, and theological effects of the intrusion of the Absolute into a world whose overwhelming, fragile complexity demands a relativistic response.

God's effect on the world is disastrous. Economies collapse; each nation, each ethnic group within each nation, each and every hu-man mob that has bought a Karburator or is close enough to one to be affected by it, immediately claims the Absolute for itself. Worldwide devastation ensues, though described by Čapek in fablelike terms that fail to convey any real sense of desolation. Ultimately, after almost all of the Karburators have been destroyed, something like normalcy returns to a chastened world, represented in this case by a small cast of Czech villagers. Broken-backed, oddly humorless, and boring (Čapek later confessed that he wrote the second half of the book under the duress of deadlines, without joy), *The Absolute at Large* is a lesson that fails.

War with the Newts, first published in *Lidové noviny* in 1935–1936, exposed a large newspaper audience to Čapek's grim sense of what the future might hold in store; it remains compulsively readable today and has not dated in the same way that some of the earlier works have. There are several reasons for this. Far more exuberantly than in *The Absolute at Large*, Čapek in *War with the Newts* uses all the resources available to him to construct a *roman feuilleton* with no holds barred: photographs, footnotes, scholarly lectures, typographical shenanigans, indecipherable inscriptions, parodies of popular storytelling modes (from adventure tales à la Robert Louis Stevenson to Hollywood romances), facsimiles of spectacular newspaper accounts.

Every device possible with this kind of novel is used to divert and enthrall the vast readership its newspaper publication ensured. And beneath these pyrotechnics, some of which are used to make serious points about the faulty but ubiquitous web of communications endemic to the modern world, Čapek has created, in his newts, a haunting image of pathos and menace that strikes to the heart of the issues discussed and dramatized. Both victims and oppressors, Čapek's newts are a far more effective vision of the fate of modern industrial humanity than are his cranky, melodramatic robots, who at no point genuinely invoke our sympathy.

174

Despite a few ominous hints, for the first half of *War with the Newts* our sympathies remain firmly on the side of the hapless salamanders as they courteously but clumsily attempt to mime cultured human behavior. Captain J. Van Toch, a simpleminded and rather brutal old man, has discovered the newts somewhere west of Sumatra, on an island perhaps not terribly distant from Rossum's, and has become sentimentally attached to them, though not without avarice. Eventually he shows up in Czechoslovakia at the offices of C. H. Bondy (more or less unchanged from the catastrophes of the Absolute) and persuades Bondy to finance efforts to use the newts as pearl fishers. At the same time Van Toch secretly conveys breeding newts from island to island, allowing them to spread and to multiply. Soon the newts become news, and Bondy realizes that they would make ideal worker-slaves.

As the first half of the book closes—ably assisted by Čapek's satirical thrusts at human obtuseness and rapacity regarding the new slave class—we have come to feel that the newts are destined, as born victims, to suffer ever more perverse humiliations. But there is a warning note: in a chapter entitled "Appendix: Of the Sexual Life of the Newts," we learn that native newt society is grim, male-dominated, and sexually joyless, and that in the grotesque mass-mating dance, participating newts become a kind of "squirming, intoxicated, frenzied" protofascist "*Collective Male*."

Sketched in broader and broader scenes, with an ever increasing impersonality of tone, the rest of the novel turns the tables on our sympathies, although by no means does it exonerate the capitalist/socialist/nationalist rapacity of our industrial century. After being used everywhere for cheap labor, the newts withdraw their support, disappear with the weapons they have been given to fight one another with, and, under the leadership of a Hitler-like German, begin to retaliate against their masters by causing great earthquakes and raising the level of the oceans. When a parley is arranged, it turns out that the rapidly expanding newt society requires Lebensraum, and that the newts intend to destroy all of the world's landmasses to fulfill their need. As the novel closes, Czechoslovakia is due to be inundated by the new race and its führer.

It is not surprising that the Gestapo tried to arrest the dead Čapek. The searing but humane pessimism of *War with the Newts* must have been anathema to the leaders of the new totalitarianism. But just as his country exhibited complexity without aggression, so Čapek, in his satirical plays and *romans feuilletons*, attacked his cultural and political foes without animosity. It might almost be said of *War with the Newts* that it is too mild-mannered, too nice a book to fully convey the message of its apocalyptic pessimism.

There is one further science fiction novel by Karel Čapek, but although it is in some ways his finest—and certainly most intense—single work, *Krakatit* fits uncomfortably into a discussion of science fiction. Certainly it is true that Prokop is a scientist of genius and that, in Krakatit, he invents something suspiciously like an atomic bomb. Nor can we forget the secret radio station whose broadcasts periodically cause all the Krakatit in existence to explode, devastating whole cities. All the same, the intensity and powerful narrative impulses of *Krakatit* lead the reader from the external problems and solutions of science fiction toward a myth of the human inscape.

At the heart of the novel lies a violent, expressionist portrait of the almost irresolvable sexual and moral conflicts that torment Prokop. The quest he undertakes, although ostensibly an attempt to recover the formula for Krakatit and to prevent its misuse, is actually an odyssey (Czech critics have frequently drawn comparisons between this novel and Homer's *Odyssey*) in search of the ideal woman, whom he has seen only once, whose face he cannot remember, and whose name he does not know.

At the narrative center of *Krakatit* is Prokop's long, enforced sojourn in the Castle that dominates a small German principality, where he and a fiery virgin Princess engage in extraordinarily violent erotic encounters. At this point an explicit identification is made between his absolute explosive and the absolute urgings of ungovernable sex, an identification that penetrates the seeming melodrama of the surface tale and converts it directly into myth. Eventually Prokop and the Princess manage to separate; in his further journeying he meets the devil and, finally, God, who cooks food for him, lessens his metaphysical and sexual explosiveness, and gives him peace from fever.

III

Čapek died before the Germans could kill him, and before World War II could provide him with material that might simultaneously inspire the intensity of *Krakatit* and the complex thrust of *War with the Newts*. His influence has been for the most part indirect, although some science fiction writers—John Brunner, Doris Lessing, and J. G. Ballard, for example—may well have learned their *roman feuilleton* techniques from him, and his humane breeziness arguably infuses some of the work of Stanisław Lem. Mainly he is missed. Time and again in this century, men like Čapek, and countries like Czechoslovakia, have appeared and been crushed. We can be thankful they appear. Our feelings at their demise bring us face to face with the newts.

Selected Bibliography

PLAYS OF KAREL ČAPEK

R.U.R. Prague: Aventinum, 1920. Translated by Paul Selver as *R.U.R. (Rossum's Universal Robots): A Fantastic Melodrama.* Garden City, N.Y.: Doubleday, 1923. London: Humphrey Milford/Oxford University Press, 1923. (Differs from American translation.)

Ze života hmyzu, with Josef Čapek. Prague: Aventinum, 1921. Translated by Paul Selver as "*And So Ad Infinitum*" (*The Life of the Insects*). London: Humphrey Milford/Oxford University Press, 1923. Also translated and adapted by Owen Davis as *The World We Live In*. New York: Samuel French, 1933.

Věc Makropulos. Prague: Aventinum, 1922. Translated and adapted by Randal C. Burrell as *The Makropoulos Secret.* Boston: John W. Luce, 1925. Also translated by Paul Selver (authorized by Čapek) as *The Macropoulos Secret.* London: Robert Holden, 1927.

Adam Stvořitel, with Josef Čapek. Prague: Aventinum, 1927. Translated by Dora Round as *Adam the Creator.* London: George Allen and Unwin, 1929.

Bílá nemoc. Prague: F. Borový, 1937. Translated by Paul Selver and Ralph Neale as *Power and Glory.* London: George Allen and Unwin, 1938.

PROSE FICTION OF KAREL ČAPEK

Trapné povídky. Prague: Aventinum, 1921. Translated by Francis P. Marchant and others as *Money and Other Stories.* London: Hutchinson, 1929.

Továrna na Absolutno. Brno: Polygrafia, 1922. Translated as *The Absolute at Large.* London and New York: Macmillan, 1927.

Krakatit. Prague: Aventinum, 1924. Translated by Lawrence Hyde. London: Geoffrey Bles, 1925. Retitled *An Atomic Phantasy: Krakatit.* London: George Allen and Unwin, 1948.

Povidky z jedné kapsy and *Povidky z drúhe kapsy.* Both titles, Prague: Aventinum, 1929. One-volume selection translated by Paul Selver as *Tales from Two Pockets.* London: Faber and Faber, 1932.

Devatero Pohádek. Prague: Borový-Aventinum, 1932. Selections translated by M. and R. Weatherall as *Fairy Tales.* London: George Allen and Unwin, 1933. New York: Henry Holt, 1933. (Includes one tale by Josef Čapek.)

Povétroň. Prague: F. Borový, 1934. Translated by M. and R. Weatherall as *Meteor.* London: George Allen and Unwin, 1935. New York: G. P. Putnam's Sons, 1935.

Válka s mloky. Prague: F. Borový, 1936. Translated by M. and R. Weatherall as *War with the Newts.* London: George Allen and Unwin, 1937. New York: G. P. Putnam's Sons, 1937.

Kniha apokryfů. Prague: F. Borový, 1945. Translated by Dora Round as *Apocryphal Stories.* London: George Allen and Unwin, 1949. New York: Macmillan, 1949.

CRITICAL AND BIOGRAPHICAL STUDIES

Abrash, Merritt. "Review Essay: *R.U.R.* Restored and Reconsidered." *Extrapolation*, 32, no. 2 (1991): 184–192.

Bengels, Barbara. "'Read History': Dehumanization in Karel Čapek's *R.U.R.*" In *The Mechanical God.* Edited by Thomas P. Dunn and Richard D. Erlich. Westport, Conn.: Greenwood, 1982.

Clute, John. "Karel Čapek." In his *Look at the Evidence: Essays and Reviews.* Liverpool, England: Liverpool University Press, 1995.

Comrada, Norma. "Golem and Robot: The Search for Connections." *Journal of the Fantastic in the Arts*, 7, no. 2/3 (1995): 244–254.

Harkins, William E. *Karel Čapek*. New York: Columbia University Press, 1962.

Kussi, Peter, ed. *Toward the Radical Center: A Karel Čapek Reader*. Highland Park, N.J.: Catbird, 1990.

Matuška, Alexander. *Karel Čapek, an Essay*. Translated by Cathryn Alan. London: George Allen and Unwin, 1964. Prague: Artia, 1964.

Simsa, Cyril. "Bibliography of Czech Science Fiction in English Translation." *Foundation* (Summer 1987): 62–72.

Suvin, Darko. "Karel Čapek, or the Aliens Amongst Us." In *Metamorphoses of Science Fiction*. New Haven, Conn.: Yale University Press, 1979.

—JOHN CLUTE

ORSON SCOTT CARD
(b. 1951)

By means of prodigious energy, superb storytelling skills, and a genuinely passionate voice, Orson Scott Card has established himself as a major science fiction writer. Though one might epitomize the underlying reasons for his success in different ways—Michael R. Collings, his most attentive and sympathetic critic, argues for the centrality of Card's Mormon faith, while John Clute speaks of his "compulsion to tell stories"—one way to define Card would be to say that he is quintessentially a family man. Certainly, in both what he preaches and what he practices, Card can serve as an especially convincing spokesperson for and representative of "family values." In a genre that can seem to focus alternately on children separated from adults and adults separated from children, Card is almost unique in consistently featuring adults and children together, in actual families or desperately improvised families, and he reveals an acute sensitivity to the emotions of both children and adults and to their need for each other's company. He treats his readers like members of his extended family, regularly making himself available for interviews and personal appearances and now employing his inviting and informative web site (www.hatrack.com) to keep in touch with them. Although he has worked in many different genres, he appears to regard them not as separate entities but as compatible members of one family of approaches to fiction. For example, his science fiction can project the ambience of fantasy while his fantasy can have the rigor of science fiction. He even seems to relate to his own published stories as family members. That is, he is consistently reluctant to simply ignore or repudiate his early works and instead keeps revisiting them to expand, revise, or rework them.

This does not necessarily mean, however, that critics should unreservedly accept the benign, cuddly image that Card presents. In his first decade of publishing, Card became controversial because of his occasionally graphic, and allegedly sadistic, scenes of violence, and there have been far too many naked boys and men parading through Card's fiction to avoid questions about homoerotic imagery. Whether Card is merely responding to the demands of his stories and their marketplace or wrestling with inner demons, the fact remains that his fiction sometimes features provocative elements that one would not expect from an author who, by his own measure, has devoted the majority of his career to devoutly religious writing.

Though born in Richland, Washington, on 24 August 1951, Card spent his childhood and adolescence in California and Arizona, then attended Brigham Young University and the University of Utah, where he respectively earned B.A. and M.A. degrees. He also learned to speak fluent Portuguese in order to work two years as a Mormon missionary in Brazil. He drew on this background in writing *Speaker for the Dead* (1986) and its sequels. In 1977 he married Kristine Allen, and they now have five children, including one son with cerebral palsy—another experience that has influenced Card's fiction, most notably the horror story and novel *Lost Boys* (1992). Though Card has been a full-time writer for most of his career, he did work as an editor for Brigham Young University Press, *The Ensign* magazine, and Compute! Books. The third position inspired his 1983 move to Greensboro, North Carolina, where he now resides. While not usefully organized, by far the best sources of biographical information on Card are the extensive commentaries that surround the stories in *Maps in a Mirror: The Short Fiction of Orson Scott Card* (1990), a book that is an essential part of any attempt to fully understand this author.

Most of Card's early writing took the form of unpublished religious plays, although he also wrote stories, poems, computer articles, and other nonfiction. After making his debut in 1977 in a science fiction magazine with the publication of "Ender's Game"—a first story unusually nominated for a Hugo award—Card quickly earned a reputation as an imaginative and talented story writer, and he was given the 1978 John W. Campbell Award as the best new writer of the year. Card soon went on to publish a collection of his short fiction, *Unaccompanied Sonata and Other Stories* (1980), at a far earlier stage in his career than most writers. However, except for *Songmaster* (1980), his early books were not highly regarded, and Card seemed to be fading from prominence by the early 1980's. Then the novel *Ender's Game* (1985) and its sequel *Speaker for the Dead* made Card famous. These novels earned both Hugo and Nebula awards, a consecutive double sweep that no other science fiction writer has duplicated. He later earned additional Hugo awards for his novella "Eye for Eye" (1987) and his guidebook *How to Write Science Fiction and Fantasy* (1990), as well as a World Fantasy award and a Locus award for works of fantasy.

While science fiction seems to remain Card's major focus, he has also garnered considerable praise for his series of fantasy novels about Alvin Maker, set in an alternate-history, nineteenth-century America infused with magic. This determined effort to construct an epic fantasy with a distinctly Amer-

ican, not European, flavor may turn out, by some assessments, to be Card's most enduring contribution. While continuing to produce religious fiction such as *A Woman of Destiny* (1984; reprinted as *Saints*, 1988) and *Stone Tablets* (1997), Card has also moved into gently horrific tales with *Lost Boys*, *Treasure Box* (1996), and *Homebody* (1998), all marketed as mainstream novels. Another outlet for his energies has been a publishing company, Hatrack River Press, which produces books primarily for Mormon readers. Given his demonstrated productivity and creativity, there is every reason to believe that Card will continue to write imaginative fiction of several types for many years to come.

Like many science fiction writers, Card began primarily as a short story writer, and while the inevitable commercial pressures have since driven him to focus on novels, several stories remain among his most memorable works. One of his most interesting early stories, "Happy Head" (1978), is oddly enough the only science fiction story Card has repudiated by refusing to republish it in *Maps in a Mirror*, describing it as an embarrassment. True, the main story itself could not be more cliché-ridden: a company president is murdered, several employees are identified as suspects with a strong motive for killing him, and a hard-boiled detective interviews all the suspects before identifying the murderer. But there are innovative aspects of the story, some of which anticipate cyberpunk fiction: the detective is actually a "juster" who combines the roles of investigator and judge, and he works with an attached "prebrain" that gives him instant access to databases and the power to "sympathize with"—enter the memories of—witnesses. (Much later, Card would more deliberately write a story in the manner of cyberpunk entitled "Dogwalker" [1989].) Other noteworthy early stories include his first two appearances in *Omni* magazine, "A Thousand Deaths" (1978) and "Unaccompanied Sonata" (1979), both involving determined individuals defying dystopian future societies. The former depicts Jerry Crove, a rebel in a Russia-dominated America who is tried for his crimes, executed, then brought back to life in another cloned body to publicly repent; when he is not persuasive in doing so, he is killed again and again, all to no avail, until the Russians give up and exile him into space, where he resolves to raise descendants who will return to liberate humanity. The story owes much to George Orwell's *Nineteen Eighty-Four* (1949), perhaps too much, though Card does provide a more optimistic ending. In "Unaccompanied Sonata," Christian Haroldsen, a man singled out for his special musical talents, is forbidden to make music when he violates the regulations and listens to Bach, contaminating his original compositions. When he later starts playing piano in a bar, his fingers are cut off to prevent further music making, but he then starts singing memorable new songs with fellow workers, breaking the law again. Finally, he is made to work as a Watcher, enforcing the very rules that crushed his spirit, though he is secretly heartened to hear some people singing his songs.

If these early stories seemed to be following patterns, others show conspicuous originality. "Mortal Gods" (1979) features aliens who come to Earth and build temples to worship humans, the only beings they know of who experience death, which they argue is the unique basis of all human accomplishments. "The Monkeys Thought 'Twas All in Fun'" (1979) evocatively but confusingly describes an immense space habitat that appears near Earth, is occupied by humans, and explodes into separate entities (hence the titular reference to "Pop Goes the Weasel"). Because the story, as Card relates in *Maps in a Mirror*, inspired many readers to ask, "What in hell is going on?" he now regards it as a "failure." Probably his most disturbing story is "Kingsmeat" (1978), in which a human "Shepherd" keeps a colony of humans alive during an invasion of alien carnivores by chopping off his fellow colonists' body parts and feeding them to the alien king and queen. Because other invaded colonies were entirely wiped out by the aliens, he is ultimately commended for developing a strategy that kept many people alive, though maimed. However, the not ex-

actly grateful citizens follow the court's instructions to let him live by cutting off his own body parts.

In the 1980's, Card published fewer science fiction stories, but his considerable skills were occasionally still in evidence. "Prior Restraint" (1986) describes a conspiracy involving time travelers from the future who suppress certain writers whose works might have catastrophic effects. "Eye for Eye" is about a boy with the unwitting ability to kill people with cancer. "The Originist" (1989), written for the Isaac Asimov tribute anthology *Foundation's Friends* (1989), depicts Asimov's Hari Seldon at the time when he was setting up the secret Second Foundation. The latter story is an absolute marvel, astoundingly duplicating Asimov's prose style and strategy of advancing the story through conversation while at the same time fruitfully integrating Card's own concerns into the Foundation universe. While the scientific backgrounds of Gregory Benford, Greg Bear, and David Brin may have made them seem like the ideal choices to write new Foundation novels, "The Originist" suggests that Card might be an unexpected but ideal choice to bring that series to a conclusion.

Finally, straddling the border between short fiction and novels are two series of related stories later brought together in book form. The stories collected in *The Folk of the Fringe* (1989), originally written primarily for Mormon readers, depict a community in Utah struggling to recover from the effects of a disastrous global war. In the 1970's, Card also began to develop in several stories the extended saga of a future world sinking into decadence due to the development of near immortality and the exploits of a telepathic young man, Jason Worthing, who leads a starship expedition to found a new civilization elsewhere. Initially, the story appeared in a collection of linked stories, *Capitol* (1979), along with an accompanying novel, *Hot Sleep: The Worthing Chronicle* (1979). A dissatisfied Card soon rewrote the latter novel from top to bottom and renamed it *The Worthing Chronicle* (1983), then republished

Orson Scott Card in 1987. PHOTO BY JAY KAY KLEIN

the revision along with some stories from *Capitol* and three uncollected stories as *The Worthing Saga* (1990). While no versions of Jason Worthing's adventures have ever been very popular, the 1983 text has been highly praised by John Clute, who called it "compact, multi-layered, mythopoeic and ultimately very strange . . . one of [Card's] finest and most revealing works."

Card's original story about Ender Wiggin, "Ender's Game," was a briskly told, exciting juvenile, somewhat reminiscent (as George Slusser notes) of Robert A. Heinlein's young-adult novels for Scribners in featuring a precocious young man, his stern but supportive mentor, and his final involvement in matters of great import to humanity. As people pessimistically prepare for another attack from their implacable alien foes, the insectlike "Buggers," Ender, a boy with potentially awesome military talents, is trained in various

sorts of battle at a space station. Later, leading what he believes to be only simulated space battles, he unknowingly commands a fleet of spaceships that surround and completely destroy the Buggers' home planet. According to Card, he originally had no desire to return to or expand the story, but when planning the novel that became *Speaker for the Dead*, he suddenly realized that a grown-up Ender would serve as the ideal protagonist for the novel. However, reshaping the back story to transform Ender into a Speaker for the Dead virtually demanded a new, novel-length redaction of the original story. In one sense, then, the novel *Ender's Game* can be regarded as one of the most aesthetically successful chores ever completed by a writer.

In the novel, the key events remain the same, but Card also adds to and deepens the story. Some embellishments might be regarded as questionable, especially the new characters of Ender's older brother and sister, because it strains credulity to accept that one family, no matter how genetically blessed, could contrive to simultaneously produce humanity's most brilliant military commander, its most skillful political leader and eventual dictator of its emerging space empire (brother Peter), and its most famous and influential writer (sister Valentine). However, their brief appearances do not detract from the overall impact of the novel, where Card provides an amazingly accurate picture of the ways that young boys actually work and play together; the expanded accounts of the bullying and shifting group dynamics among the boys (and one girl) at the Training School consistently ring true. And as Slusser and other scholars note, the novel's Ender is a more complex and knowing character, still fooled by the final deception but otherwise far more aware of how he is being manipulated by the adults running the school.

Another intriguing change involves a computer game that Ender likes to play, the Giant's Game, which he unprecedentedly overcomes by killing the giant, advancing farther into the simulated world of the game and discovering a strange room with snakes and an image of Peter, who represents the dark side of his character. The Buggers, actually benevolent and intent on investigating their major foe and arranging for their survival, learn about the game and duplicate its room on a far-off world, where they hide the last surviving Bugger queen. They reason correctly that a repentant Ender will someday visit the world, recognize the surroundings, discover and care for the surviving Bugger, and eventually allow the species to live again through the innumerable children that she can spawn.

Though the characters of Ender and Valentine do reappear in *Speaker for the Dead*, to call that novel a sequel to *Ender's Game* is almost to misuse the term, for the novels are otherwise entirely different in their events, themes, and tone. While *Ender's Game* is a linear, action-packed story celebrating youth and the benefits of secrecy, *Speaker for the Dead* is a digressive and contemplative narrative validating maturation and the need for unsparing honesty. Shocked and saddened to learn that he apparently wiped out an intelligent race, Ender retreats into anonymity as a Speaker for the Dead, whose role is to travel from world to world, investigate the lives of the recently deceased, and announce all the truths about those people's lives. Due to frequent relativistic travel, Ender lives for 3,000 years, always accompanied by Valentine and the Bugger queen he secretly carries as he seeks a proper home for the species he almost destroyed. He thinks the moment has arrived when he is summoned to the world of Lusitania, settled by Portuguese-speaking Catholics and also inhabited by the pequeninos or "Piggies," apparently the second race of intelligent aliens to be discovered. He joins a squabbling family of scientists in their efforts to understand both the Piggies and a mysterious virus, the "descolada," which is potentially lethal to humans yet necessary for the survival of Lusitanian species, which all carry the disease.

The novel impressively recalls both Hal Clement's *Cycle of Fire* (1957), in its unfolding picture of a fascinating alien species, and James Blish's *A Case of Conscience* (1958), in its thoughtful examination of how religious faith is challenged and strengthened by contact with aliens. As the older and wiser Ender struggles to comprehend the pequeninos—who turn out to live in three separate phases as tiny grublike creatures, four-legged mammals, and trees—he releases the Bugger queen to begin her breeding and finally achieves apparent happiness in marrying the widowed mother of the central family. *Speaker for the Dead* is thus reminiscent of another sequel that was not really a sequel: Sophocles' *Oedipus at Colonus*, which also re-examines a young character unknowingly driven to unforgivable actions (recounted in *Oedipus Rex*) who, many years later, finally achieves a sense of peace and reconciliation. (Card had earlier cited Oedipus when describing the father-son conflict in his story "The Changed Man and the King of Words" [1982].) While several plot threads are left unresolved at the end of *Speaker for the Dead*, the novel conveys a satisfying sense of closure and inspires little yearning for a continuation.

Nevertheless, Card unfortunately planned and produced another Ender story, which grew to fill two volumes, *Xenocide* and *Children of the Mind*, best read as one long novel. While the mature Card's appealing craftsmanship is still in evidence, these books seemingly represent misguided priorities. Even though the most absorbing aspects of the first two novels were surely the character of Ender Wiggin and the bizarre alien species, the Buggers and the pequeninos, they receive increasingly little attention here. Instead, while a massive fleet determined to prevent the spread of the deadly descolada virus converges on Lusitania to annihilate its alien populations—and thus repeat Ender's sinful "xenocide" of the Buggers—Card devotes an inordinate amount of space to the far from novel theme of an omniscient and omnipotent computer intelligence, Jane, developing self-awareness and yearning for a true human identity—a story that science fiction has told many times before. Card's new characters—including the superintelligent "godspoken" people of the Chinese-influenced world of

Path who were bred to have obsessive-compulsive disorder—are less than engrossing, and *Children of the Mind* also features pointless visits to other worlds influenced by Japan and Polynesia, seemingly presented only to increase the novel's ethnic diversity. Ender's growing indifference to the developing crisis and his eventual withdrawal to a monastery with his estranged wife before dying may reflect Card's own burgeoning lack of interest in an overly prolonged story.

While the sheer brilliance of the Lusitanian scientists and Jane's far-ranging powers do finally prevent the xenocide, Card conspicuously leaves the door open for a further sequel, with the deceased Ender now reborn as a duplicate of his brother, Peter, and with still unanswered questions about the possible sentience—and malevolence—of the descolada virus. However, Card has announced on his web site that the next Ender novel will instead return to the time of the first novel and focus on Bean, Ender's most capable comrade at the Training School—a clear attempt to rejuvenate an enervated series.

Unlike the Ender novels, the Homecoming Saga was planned, and announced from the start, as a five-volume series. What was not announced but quickly noticed was that the story closely parallels events from the Book of Mormon, leading to wild charges of "plagiarism" that Card indignantly—and properly—refuted by pointing out that innumerable previous writers have done the same thing with the Bible. With or without knowledge of the Book of Mormon, however, the series stands on its own as an involving epic of humanity's distant future that might be compared to Gene Wolfe's Book of the New Sun tetralogy (1980–1987).

The first book, *The Memory of Earth* (1992), describes the distant planet Harmony, inhabited for the last forty million years by human beings supervised by a powerful computer intelligence, the "Oversoul," which influences their thoughts and limits technology to prevent wars, a scenario not unlike the background of *The Worthing Chronicle*. Con-

cerned because it is wearing out and losing its capacity to control human events, the Oversoul recruits certain people in the city of Basilica—notably including an especially capable and virtuous young boy, Nafai—to leave the city and eventually return to the planet Earth, long ago devastated and abandoned by humanity, so that the Oversoul can be repaired. While Card provides readers with a fast-moving plot and well-developed characters—such as Nafai's treacherous older brothers and a young girl, Luet, who is especially receptive to dream visions sent by the Oversoul—the novel is chiefly interesting because of its background: the innovative matriarchal society of Basilica and a world largely maintained at a medieval level that nevertheless incorporates some selected items of advanced technology, such as antigravity "floats" to help Nafai's handicapped brother move around and "holocostumes" to disguise soldiers.

The second and weakest novel in the series, *The Call of Earth* (1992), begins slowly and remains relatively uneventful. Essentially, all that happens is that Nafai and the other men who left Basilica return to the city, find women to be their wives, and leave again. Nevertheless, Card does feature one striking new character, Moozh, a ruthlessly cruel soldier and Machiavellian schemer who invades Basilica but proves admirable in his own way and useful to Nafai's cause. Moreover, as effective foreshadowing, characters begin to experience strange dreams of flying people and crawling creatures that the Oversoul says it is not producing; rather, they might be coming directly from the Keeper of Earth, the mysterious master that the Oversoul wishes to consult, somehow reaching across the stars to contact its distant children.

In the third book, *The Ships of Earth* (1994), the story literally gets moving again, as Nafai's band of refugees undertakes a long journey across the desert to reach the island that the Oversoul has designated as their destination. Along the way, there are lively conflicts, nefarious schemes, and several children born. Card also reveals that one sympathetically drawn character, Zdorab, is actually a homosexual, forced into a marriage of convenience with the brilliant scientist Shedemei, a marriage that eventually evolves into a genuine, though largely chaste, relationship. Near the end of the novel, after settling down to several years of prosperous life on the island, Nafai learns that the Oversoul has been unknowingly concealing the nearby location of the starships used by the original settlers of Harmony; quickly penetrating the barrier around them and overcoming the predictable opposition of older brother Elemak, Nafai puts on a "starmaster's cloak" granting him added powers and leads the effort to combine parts from the six aging vehicles into one functional starship.

The fourth book in the series, *Earthfall* (1995), essentially consists of two short novels (perhaps originally projected to be the fourth and fifth books, a plan abandoned when the first story could not be sustained). In the briefer Part I, "If I Should Wake Before I Die," Nafai follows the Oversoul's instructions to place most of the travelers in suspended animation for the ten-year journey to Earth while allowing certain children to grow up during that time so that Nafai will have additional allies when he reaches Earth and must confront Elemak's inevitable rebellion. But Elemak contrives to be awakened halfway through the voyage and engages in some of his now-tedious nastiness. Two chapters look ahead to the more imaginative Part II, "Landfall," when the humans land on Earth and discover the two intelligent species, previously glimpsed in dreams, that now dominate the Earth: the "angels," flying humanoids descended from bats, and subterranean "diggers," descended from rats. While learning their languages and working to establish peaceful contact, the people gradually figure out their strange symbiotic relationship. The diggers must steal the clay sculptures crafted by the angels and rub their bodies against them before mating because the sweat of the angels is necessary to deactivate a mysterious organ suppressing sperm production introduced by human genetic engineering as a way

of controlling these artificially created intelligent species. Shedemei figures out a way to remove this added organ, paving the way for better relationships between the three species, but the antagonistic followers of Nafai and Elemak, as long predicted, finally split into two separate colonies.

The final novel, *Earthborn* (1995), jumps five hundred years into the future, with only Shedemei still alive, kept youthful by the powers of the starmaster's cloak, living in orbit and working with the Oversoul to figure out why they have been unable to locate or contact the Keeper of Earth. Meanwhile, the societies on Earth have been manifesting increasingly crude racism directed at the angels and diggers—especially the latter, who are often kept as slaves—as well as the blatant sexism of excluding women from all important business. But some children are beginning to receive new dream visions from the Keeper, while Shedemei decides to intervene by returning to Earth and establishing a school to teach women and to promote racial harmony and gender equality. She finally sets Earth back on its proper course when she manages to convert the leader of the opposing faction, Akma, by appearing to him as a vision. She also gets the fleeting impression that the mysterious Keeper somehow lives in, or consists of, the underground magma or magnetic fields of Earth. Working without complete success to interest readers in a completely new cast of characters, Card also, as in the later Ender novels, inexplicably marginalizes the interesting aliens he had painstakingly created; in this case, it is positively bizarre that a novel so relentlessly promoting the need for complete equality among species should devote 95 percent of its space to human characters while granting a few angels and diggers only brief cameo appearances, usually as servants.

Overall, despite a few slow spots, the Homecoming Saga certainly qualifies as an immensely readable story, but these books ultimately do not seem to be as important as other Card novels because they contain no startling ideas, unforgettable images, or breathtaking novelties. In addition, despite the political correctness of the foreground, there are recurring undercurrents of sexism that may irritate some readers. At one point in *The Ships of Earth*, for example, a character seriously suggests that women should naturally rule during tranquil times, whereas men should naturally rule in times of crisis. One suspects that Card could easily produce many epics of this kind, which would inspire similarly qualified praise, but he has proven himself capable of more memorable work than this.

Card's unimpressive first novel, *Hot Sleep*, was quickly followed by the equally unimpressive, *A Planet Called Treason* (1979). Three thousand years ago, a group of talented rebels were exiled to the planet Treason, a world without iron, where people continue to struggle to trade their goods so that they can obtain enough iron to build a starship and rejoin humanity. Different cultures descended from different rebels have developed various special talents, and Lanik Mueller is the heir of a family whose culture specializes in the talent of organ regeneration. Unfortunately, Lanik is a "radical regenerative" who keeps growing new body parts uncontrollably, and while a few extra arms and an extra nose were amputated without concern, his development of female breasts and ovaries—"transsexual growth"—causes him to be disinherited and exiled. After some odd and sometimes distasteful adventures involving his disguise as a woman and his propensity to keep growing and having to cut off new body parts, Lanik is mysteriously cured. He keeps traveling across Harmony and encountering people with other strange abilities—to control the flow of time, to move the earth, to generate illusions. After gaining godlike powers but failing to achieve contentment, Lanik finally returns home for a confrontation with his usurping brother, who turns out to be a second version of himself, grown from a partial body he once grew and cut off. Perhaps the best way to explain this novel is as a clumsy projection of Card's dissatisfaction with his own (overweight) body. While discussing the story "Fat Farm"

(1980) in *Maps in a Mirror*, he says, "My life can be viewed as one long struggle with my own body," and in one respect *A Planet Called Treason* is about a man who must literally struggle against his own body. However, though it might have been wiser to forget the whole thing, Card eventually rewrote the novel as *Treason* (1988), improving its style but failing to completely address its intrinsic problems.

Card's next novel, *Songmaster*, represented a considerable improvement. An expanded version of the story "Mikal's Songbird" (1978), the novel tells of a young boy named Ansset on a distant planet who is kidnapped away from his parents and taken to the Songhouse, where the Songmaster discovers his extraordinary singing talents and trains him to serve as the Songbird to Mikal, who rules a vast interstellar empire forged by his violent determination. On Earth, Ansset is kidnapped again and programmed to assassinate Mikal, but he demonstrates his genuine devotion by resisting the plot. Paradoxically, however, Mikal then decides to reward the chief conspirator, Riktors, by naming him as his successor because Mikal suspects he is the only man with the skill to hold the empire together. Lacking the same emotional bond to Riktors, the teenage Ansset leaves the court, has a brief and tragic liaison with a homosexual named Josif, and now finding himself unable to sing, is assigned to serve as the chief administrator of planet Earth. Eventually, he succeeds Riktors as head of the empire, enjoys a long and successful reign, then abdicates to return to the Songhouse, where he finally recovers his talents and sings out the story of his life just before his death. The story proceeds at a rather stately pace, and Ansset remains a dissatisfyingly cryptic character, but like the successful Songbirds, Card has demonstrably now learned to maintain "Control," and the resulting novel is, like his subsequent novels, polished, unified, and atmospheric.

Wyrms (1987) is reminiscent of one of Clifford D. Simak's later novels in depicting an unlikely group of humans and other beings traveling on a quest through a strange environment. Millennia ago, humans landed on the world of Imakulata, where species had the ability, after a little experimentation, to perfectly mimic Earth species. The creatures known as wyrms mated with the starship captain to spawn imperfect replicas of humanity such as the bestial geblings and simpleminded dwelfs, but one of them has now waited for 343 human generations to mate with the "seventh seventh seventh daughter" of the captain, a teenage girl named Patience, to produce a new species that will be identical to, and will supplant, humanity. Mentally summoned to meet her alien lover, Patience and her companions—including two geblings and a disembodied head kept alive after death by small, genetically engineered animals—contrive instead to kill the creature, though she does bear one of his children, who lives only briefly. While the story has a conventionally medieval setting—despite an atypical Greek Orthodox religious background and some sprinklings of futuristic technology, as in *The Memory of Earth*—Card also presents the most openly homoerotic scenes in any of his fiction when the travelers reach the freewheeling pleasure city of Cranning (as noted by Johnny Townsend). He even works a wry in-joke into the climactic scene of this otherwise humorless novel: the only words ever spoken by the baby born of Patience and the insectlike wyrm are "Help me," exactly what the half-human, half-fly creature bleated out at the conclusion of the camp classic horror film *The Fly* (1957). Despite its brisk pace and imaginative touches, *Wyrms* was virtually ignored in the wake of Ender and Alvin Maker, and it is probably of greater interest to those who wish to psychoanalyze Card than to those who wish to appreciate his talents.

Although *The Abyss* (1989) will always be classified as a "novelization" of James Cameron's 1989 film, that term understates the extent of Card's contributions to the project: he talked extensively with Cameron, visited the set, and developed a great deal of original background material that was given to the actors to assist them in their performances. As Cameron concluded in his "Afterword" to *The Abyss*, "the novel has fed into the film, just as the film has nourished the novel." Thus, although Card did not get involved in all stages of the film's creation, his work was not entirely unlike Arthur C. Clarke's collaboration with Stanley Kubrick in crafting the novel and film *2001: A Space Odyssey* (1968). Similarly, one can readily argue that Card's version of the story of humans venturing underwater and making contact with aliens is more forceful and satisfactory than the rather uneven film.

Lovelock (1994), written with Mormon writer Kathryn H. Kidd, represented Card's first collaborative novel and launched a projected trilogy featuring Lovelock, a monkey genetically altered to be highly intelligent and to work as a "witness" who constantly observes and records the actions of Carol Jeanne Cocciolone, a distinguished scientist about to leave with her family on a gigantic generation starship to colonize a new world. Told from the monkey's point of view and including excerpts from a child's diary, the novel reads much like a juvenile novel, despite its sometimes frank sexual content: Carol Jeanne's mother-dominated husband turns out to be a closet homosexual, another young girl is being molested by her father, and Lovelock seeks to satisfy his repressed sexual cravings by using frozen monkey embryos to create a future mate. Yet Kidd also brings a distinctively lighter tone to the novel, with comic relief provided by Carol Jeanne's mother-in-law, Mamie, an ignorant, domineering woman who never bothered to read anything about the starship before embarking and thus is constantly surprised and appalled by the rigors of her new life.

By the mid-1990's, it would have been logical to believe that Card's science fiction would now be limited to further installments in series; but he surprised everyone by producing *Pastwatch: The Redemption of Christopher Columbus* (1996), a stunning novel totally unlike anything he had written before. In a future world apparently starting to recover from centuries of environmental destruction, members of the Pastwatch project employ new technologies to observe and record—unobtrusively, they believe—all of humanity's past; however, after some oppressed Caribbean natives in the era of Columbus surprisingly notice one observer, scientists accept the possibility of, and begin to work on, achieving actual time travel. Another investigator, trying to determine why and when Columbus abandoned his plans for a new crusade to Constantinople and instead resolved to sail west, makes the surprising discovery that he received a vision of the Holy Trinity, clearly produced by modern technology, telling him to seek new lands in the west. The inescapable conclusion is that humans in another future world had already intervened to change their own unpleasant past (probably to prevent Columbus from weakening Europe with a new crusade and leaving it vulnerable to invasion from an advanced and violent, Meso-American civilization) and that the world of Pastwatch is the result of their intervention. Fully realizing that Columbus's journey west had itself had unhappy consequences—the world, it turns out, is still heading for environmental collapse—three members of Pastwatch make careful plans and, when physically returned to the past, successfully contrive to change the past again by stranding Columbus and his crew in the Caribbean and uniting them with the natives there and on the mainland into a benign, egalitarian nation. Skillfully interweaving a sympathetic account of Columbus's life (historically accurate, until the end) with the story of the future humans' activities and a meticulous awareness of time travel paradoxes, Card creates a fascinating tapestry with an unusually restrained, but no less powerful, emotional impact; one senses that researching and writing this highly uncharacteristic novel represented a voyage of discovery for Card himself.

The fact that the deserving *Pastwatch* failed to earn any awards may simply reflect the facts that Orson Scott Card has never been a universally popular writer and that his successes in the 1980's and 1990's have made him even less popular. Behind the sincerity and altruism he continues to persuasively project, many now discern monstrous egotism, sanctimonious self-righteousness, and crassly commercial opportunism. However, while Card has been uniquely energetic and eloquent in answering the charges of various critics, his best argument in his own defense may have occurred near the beginning of *Ender's Game*, where his commander Graff tells Ender: "There's only one thing that will make them stop hating you. And that's being so good at what you do that they can't ignore you." That has manifestly been Card's agenda, and that is manifestly exactly what he has done.

Selected Bibliography

WORKS OF ORSON SCOTT CARD

"Listen, Mom and Dad . . .": *Young Adults Look Back on Their Upbringing*. Salt Lake City, Utah: Bookcraft, 1978. (Nonfiction.)

The Mormons. Salt Lake City, Utah: Deseret, 1978. (Nonfiction, mostly written by Card anonymously.)

Capitol. New York: Baronet, 1979. (Linked stories.) Reprinted as *Capitol: The Worthing Chronicle*. New York: Ace, 1979.

Hot Sleep: The Worthing Chronicle. New York: Baronet, 1979. Revised edition, *The Worthing Chronicle*, New York: Ace, 1983.

A Planet Called Treason. New York: St. Martin's/Dell, 1979. Revised edition, *Treason*, New York: St. Martin's, 1988.

Songmaster. New York: Dial/Dell, 1979.

Dragons of Light. Edited by Orson Scott Card. New York: Ace, 1980.

Unaccompanied Sonata and Other Stories. New York: Dial/Dell, 1980. (Stories, with an introduction by Ben Bova.)

Dragons of Darkness. Edited by Orson Scott Card. New York: Ace, 1981.

Ainge. Salt Lake City, Utah: Signature, 1982. (Nonfiction.)

Saintspeak: The Mormon Dictionary. Salt Lake City, Utah: Signature/Orion, 1982. (Humor.)

Hart's Hope. New York: Berkley, 1983.

A Woman of Destiny. New York: Berkley, 1984. Reprinted as *Saints*. New York: TOR, 1988.

Ender's Game. New York: TOR, 1985.

Ender's War. Garden City, N.Y.: Doubleday, 1986. (Omnibus of *Ender's Game* and *Speaker for the Dead*.)

Speaker for the Dead. New York: TOR, 1986.

Cardography. Eugene, Oreg.: Hypatia, 1987. (Short stories, with introduction by David G. Hartwell.)

Free Lancers, with David Drake and Lois McMaster Bujold. Created by Elizabeth Mitchell. New York: Baen, 1987. (Includes Card's story "West.")

Seventh Son. New York: TOR, 1987.

Wyrms. New York: TOR, 1987.

Character and Viewpoint. Cincinnati, Ohio: Writer's Digest Books, 1988. (Nonfiction.)

Red Prophet. New York: TOR, 1988.

The Abyss. New York: Pocket Books, 1989. (Novelization of the film, with afterwords by James Cameron and Card.)

The Folk of the Fringe. New York: Phantasia/TOR, 1989. (Linked stories.)

Prentice Alvin. New York: TOR, 1989.

Hatrack River. New York: Guild America, 1989. (Omnibus of *Seventh Son, Red Prophet,* and *Prentice Alvin.*)

How to Write Science Fiction and Fantasy. Cincinnati, Ohio: Writer's Digest Books, 1990. (Nonfiction.)

Maps in a Mirror: The Short Fiction of Orson Scott Card. New York: TOR, 1990. (Stories with extensive, often autobiographical, introductions and afterwords.)

The Worthing Saga. New York: TOR, 1990. (Includes *The Worthing Chronicle,* several stories from *Capitol,* and three related stories.)

Future on Fire. Edited and introduced by Orson Scott Card. New York: TOR, 1991. (Anonymously co-edited by Martin Harry Greenberg.)

Xenocide. New York: TOR, 1991.

The Call of Earth. New York: TOR, 1992: *Homecoming,* Volume 2.

The Changed Man. New York: TOR, 1992. (Stories from Part I of *Maps in a Mirror.*)

Cruel Miracles. New York: TOR, 1992. (Stories from Part III of *Maps in a Mirror.*)

Flux. New York: TOR, 1992. (Stories from Part II of *Maps in a Mirror.*)

Lost Boys. New York: HarperCollins, 1992.

The Memory of Earth. New York: TOR, 1992: *Homecoming,* Volume 1.

Monkey Sonatas. New York: TOR, 1992. (Stories from Part IV of *Maps in a Mirror.*)

A Storyteller in Zion: Essays and Speeches. Salt Lake City, Utah: Bookcraft, 1993. (Nonfiction.)

Homecoming: Harmony. New York: TOR, 1994. (Omnibus of *The Memory of Earth, The Call of Earth,* and *The Ships of Earth.*)

Lovelock: The Mayflower Trilogy, Book 1, with Kathryn H. Kidd. New York: TOR, 1994.

The Ships of Earth. New York: TOR, 1994: *Homecoming,* Volume 3.

Turning Hearts: Short Stories on Family Life. Edited by Orson Scott Card and David Dollahite. Salt Lake City, Utah: Bookcraft, 1994.

Earthborn. New York: TOR, 1995: *Homecoming,* Volume 5.

Earthfall. New York: TOR, 1995: *Homecoming,* Volume 4.

Alvin Journeyman. New York: TOR, 1995.

Children of the Mind. New York: TOR, 1996.

Pastwatch: The Redemption of Christopher Columbus. New York: TOR, 1996.

Treasure Box. New York: HarperCollins, 1996.

Stone Tablets. Salt Lake City, Utah: Deseret, 1997.

Heartfire. New York: TOR, 1998.

Homebody. New York: HarperCollins, 1998.

CRITICAL AND BIOGRAPHICAL STUDIES

Attebery, Brian. "Godmaking in the Heartland: The Backgrounds of Orson Scott Card's American Fantasy." In *The Celebration of the Fantastic: Selected Papers from the Tenth Anniversary International Conference on the Fantastic in the Arts.* Edited by Donald E. Morse, Marshall B. Tymn, and Bertha Csilla. Westport, Conn.: Greenwood, 1992.

Beswick, Norman. "Amblick and After: Aspects of Orson Scott Card." *Foundation,* no. 45 (Spring 1989): 49–62.

Blackmore, Tim. "Ender's Beginning: Battling the Military in Orson Scott Card's *Ender's Game.*" *Extrapolation,* 32, no. 2 (Summer 1991): 124–142.

Card, Orson Scott. "The Profession of Science Fiction, 39: Mountains out of Molehills." *Foundation,* no. 45 (Spring 1989): 63–70.

Clute, John. "Orson Scott Card." In *The Encyclopedia of Science Fiction.* Edited by John Clute and Peter Nicholls. New York: St. Martin's, 1993.

Collings, Michael R. *Card Catalogue: The Science Fiction and Fantasy of Orson Scott Card.* Eugene, Oreg.: Hypatia, 1987.

———. "Time and Vast Eternities: Landscapes of Immortality in Orson Scott Card's Fiction." In *Mindscapes: The Geographies of Imagined Worlds.* Edited by George E. Slusser and Eric S. Rabkin. Carbondale: Southern Illinois University Press, 1989.

———. *In the Image of God: Theme, Characterization and Landscape in the Fiction of Orson Scott Card.* Westport, Conn.: Greenwood, 1990.

———. "Orson Scott Card: An Approach to Mythopoeic Literature." *Mythlore,* 21 (Summer 1996): 36–50.

Hall, Peter C. "'The Space Between': Some Versions of the Bildungsroman in Science Fiction." *Extrapolation,* 29 (Summer 1988): 153–159.

Heidkamp, Bernie. "Responses to the Alien Mother in Post-Maternal Cultures: C. J. Cherryh and Orson Scott Card." *Science-Fiction Studies,* 23 (November 1996): 339–354.

Slusser, George. "The Forever Child: *Ender's Game* and the Mythic Universe of Science Fiction." In *Nursery Realms: Children in the Worlds of Science Fiction,*

Fantasy, and Horror. Edited by Gary Westfahl and George Slusser. Athens: University of Georgia Press, 1999.

Townsend, Johnny. "Passion vs. Will: Homosexuality in Orson Scott Card's *Wyrms.*" *Riverside Quarterly,* 9 (August 1992): 48–55.

Van Name, Mark L. "Writer of the Year: Orson Scott Card." In *Science Fiction and Fantasy Book Review Annual.* Edited by Robert A. Collins and Robert Latham. Westport, Conn.: Meckler, 1988.

Wells, Earl. "The Rule of the Game." *New York Review of Science Fiction,* 47 (July 1992): 6–7.

—GARY WESTFAHL

C. J. CHERRYH

(b. 1942)

C. J. CHERRYH is a prolific writer, having published more than forty books in little more than twenty years. For Cherryh, however, this amazing productivity does not signal a lack of consistency or complexity in her writing. In fact, it signals just the opposite. Cherryh has created characters, cultures, and universes so intricate and detailed that a variety of story ideas are always readily available. The philosophical and political ideas that motivate her writing, moreover, require constant elaboration.

The protagonists in almost all of Cherryh's novels and short stories are intermediaries. They are positioned, both physically and emotionally, on the borderlines between a variety of human and alien cultures and competing political authorities. The various "merchanters" we come to know in Cherryh's Alliance-Union novels, for example, have lived for generations within the confines of ships that trade between colonized worlds and space stations. Although Cherryh's works explore how these characters struggle with their own cultural and political identity, they also offer a unique perspective through which Cherryh can investigate alien minds and the uses and abuses of political power. Many of these characters choose, either temporarily or permanently, to immerse themselves in the alien cultures they encounter. In so doing, they often place themselves in opposition to political authorities. Some of these characters are political authorities themselves, and their acts of cross-cultural sympathy have even broader ramifications.

Cherryh's protagonists, moreover, are often women. As several feminist critics have noted, Cherryh creates active, powerful, and complex female characters in order to challenge many of the traditional biases of a male-centered science fiction. Although Cherryh freely adopts many science fiction conventions and writes within a well-defined science fiction tradition (she grew up watching *Flash Gordon* and reading all the science fiction available at her local library), she is able to alter those conventions and question that tradition in subtle ways, as in her choice of protagonist, so that situations that appear familiar develop in refreshing and intriguing ways.

Cherryh's awareness and manipulation of science fiction conventions and tradition are equally evident in her constructions of a multitude of intelligent alien cultures in her fiction. Drawing on her background in classical languages, ancient history, and anthropology, she presents cultures that possess a wide variety of political and religious systems, most of which force human characters (and Cherryh's science fiction readership) to re-evaluate their own cultural (and literary) assumptions. Despite their differences, however, almost all of her alien cultures are authoritarian—often matriarchal—and have rigid caste systems. The majat in *Serpent's Reach* (1980), for example, are a hive culture. Possessing an ant-like anatomy, the majat are divided into workers and warrior classes and are dominated by the power of the hive Queen. In Cherryh's Alliance-Union novels, humans themselves have also constructed their own caste system. They have created two genetically engineered classes—the beta and the azi—that have become the laborers, the servants, and the soldiers of the new society.

Human and alien cultures interact within several meticulously built universes, the best-known of which is the Alliance-Union universe, in which at least twenty of Cherryh's novels take place. As she explains most clearly in the opening chapters of her two Hugo award-winning novels, *Downbelow Station* (1981) and *Cyteen* (1988), the tensions within this universe develop as Earth—in the form of a corporation known simply as the Company—loses control of a series of space stations and colonized planets. Many of the most distant space stations along with the planet Cyteen banded together to form Union, and most of the merchanters, who operated the interstellar freighters necessary for trade, attempted to maintain a neutrality by forming an equally powerful Alliance. The first novels Cherryh wrote within this universe formed The Faded Sun trilogy, written in the late 1970's, although the broader setting of the universe did not become clear until novels such as *Serpent's Reach* and *Downbelow Station* in the early 1980's.

Although the Alliance-Union universe is her best-known, Cherryh has developed several other universes as well, including the Foreigner and Rider universes, which have been her primary concerns of the 1990's. Throughout her career, she has also constructed several fantasy worlds, such as in *The Gate of Ivrel* (1976) and other Gate books and in *The Dreamstone* (1983) and other Faerie books. By creating a series of novels in each of these settings, Cherryh has performed what Sharona Ben-Tov calls (in her analysis of Cherryh's The Faded Sun novels) an "imaginary ethnography." Through an in-depth exploration of a variety of human and alien characters and cultures, Ben-Tov contends, Cherryh provides an allegory of our own late-twentieth-century America.

Even though Cherryh has published more than forty novels, writing was not her first ca-

reer. She first taught classical languages and ancient history in Oklahoma City public schools from 1965 to 1976. C. J. Cherryh is the working name of Carolyn Janice Cherry, who was born on 1 September 1942 in St. Louis, Missouri. She later moved with her family to Lawton, Oklahoma. She is the daughter of Basil Cherry, a Social Security representative, and Lois Van Deventer, and she is the sister of David A. Cherry, a well-known and Hugo-nominated illustrator of science fiction, especially book covers. After receiving her B.A. from the University of Oklahoma in 1964, majoring in Latin and becoming a Phi Beta Kappa, she received her M.A. in classics in 1965 from Johns Hopkins University in Baltimore, Maryland. She was a Woodrow Wilson Fellow in classics in 1964 and 1965. After she commenced her writing career, she spent one year as artist-in-residence and teacher at Central State University from 1980 to 1981.

Cherryh supplemented her educational background in classics and ancient history with anthropological fieldwork and extensive traveling. She retraced Caesar's campaigns, for example, in England, France, Switzerland, and Italy. She has also visited most of the major archaeological sites on the Mediterranean. She still hopes to sail the routes of Jason, Odysseus, and Alexander the Great, among others. Cherryh is fluent in French and Italian and knows a little German and Russian as well. She is also an accomplished photographer and has both written and visual records of all of her travels. Her total immersion in her subject matter is reflected in the desire of many of her protagonists to know the customs and beliefs of alien cultures.

What is even more remarkable about Cherryh is that she has combined this intimate knowledge of ancient cultures with an equally fervent interest in issues of modernity and postmodernity. In an interview in the early 1980's, Cherryh commented:

I have not forgotten my anthropological training, but I have done enough research over the past half decade to follow my first love, which is technology, using insight gained from the impact of technology on humanity of the past and present to project the likely course of events for the future, which has become my major work. . . . [I] am active in the pro-space movement and am a constant reader in all sciences and aerospace engineering. . . . I was at [space shuttle] *Columbia's* maiden launch. (*Contemporary Authors*, page 96)

In recent years, this "love" of technology has led Cherryh to study computers as well. She has developed and maintained her own web page since 1996 (www.cherryh.com).

Because of her many interests, Cherryh's stories encompass a variety of styles. She has been able to write heroic fantasy epics, planetary romances, and space operas (colorful action adventure stories of interstellar conflict) as well as hard science fiction. Most of her novels, in fact, tend to blur the lines between these subgenres. For example, her first novel, *The Gate of Ivrel*, appears on one level to be a heroic fantasy epic inspired by J. R. R. Tolkien, a writer Cherryh admires greatly. The "Middle Realms" in which most of the novel's action takes place appear to be a rather direct allusion to Tolkien's "Middle Earth." We learn, however, especially in the later novels in the series, that the "quest" that propels the narrative requires interstellar travel and that the main character, Morgaine, is an alien to all the planets she visits.

Cherryh published her first science fiction story, "The Mind Reader," in *Astounding Science Fiction* in 1968, but she did not become a full-time writer until 1977. She quickly made her mark, however, winning the John W. Campbell Memorial Award in 1977 for the best new writer in science fiction for *Gate of Ivrel*. She then won her first Hugo award in 1979 for the short story "Cassandra," which originally appeared in *The Magazine of Fantasy and Science Fiction* (October 1978). The first volume of The Faded Sun trilogy, *Faded Sun: Kesrith* (1978), was also nominated for a Hugo award and the Nebula award in 1979.

Although "Cassandra" was not published until 1978, it was, according to Cherryh, one

of first stories she ever wrote. All her early stories, she claims, "were myths I used to tell my students." Although differing greatly in style from her later work, "Cassandra" begins to indicate what would become some of the major preoccupations of Cherryh's fiction. In Greek mythology, Cassandra was a prophet cursed by Apollo so that her prophesies, while always true, were fated never to be believed. Cherryh's retelling of the myth is set in a modern, urban setting, and Alis, the Cassandra-like main character, seems to be foreseeing some type of nuclear holocaust. Written from the often stream-of-consciousness perspective of Alis, the story captures the agony that Alis feels at her inability to prevent all the destruction she sees on every street corner. Whenever she meets people on the street, she envisions their gruesome death:

> A ghost said good morning to her . . . old man Willis, thin and transparent against the leaping flames. She blinked, bade it good morning in return—did not miss old Willis' shake of the head as she opened the door and left. Noon traffic passed, heedless of the flames, the hulks that blazed in the street, the tumbling brick.
>
> The apartment caved in—black bricks falling into the inferno, Hell amid the green ghostly trees. Old Willis fled, burning, fell—turned to jerking, blackened flesh—died, daily. Alis no longer cried, hardly flinched. She ignored the horror spilling about her, forced her way through crumbling brick that held no substance, past busy ghosts that could not be troubled in their haste. (*Visible Light*, page 3)

Later in the story, Alis dares to establish a level of intimacy with a man she meets, but her desire is thwarted by the continual visions of that man's death. In these passages, "Cassandra" hints at some of Cherryh's persistent themes: humanity's potential impotence in the face of rapid technological change and an individual's struggle to establish personal relationships in a time of crisis. In the figure of "crazy Alis," furthermore, Cherryh has also

C. J. Cherryh in 1979. PHOTO BY JAY KAY KLEIN

backward in time and not just into the future, however, paradoxes occurred and whole worlds were being destroyed. Morgaine is the only surviving member of her team, and since she must pass through Gates in order to close them, she has no hope of returning to her original home.

Each book in the series accounts Morgaine's struggle to close the Gate to a particular world. In *Gate of Ivrel*, Morgaine acquires her companion, Vanye, who is only bound by the laws of his world to serve her one year. Fascinated by her power, however, he decides to remain by her side throughout her adventures. Several qhal, disguised as leaders of different communities on this world, attempt to kill Morgaine and Vanye as they make the dangerous journey to Ivrel to close the Gate. Morgaine is able to protect herself because she possesses a supernatural sword named Changeling and because in the time she has spent on this world, a distorted mythology has been constructed about her that causes most ordinary people to fear her and keep their distance. Vanye reveals his world's awe of Morgaine when he first describes her sword:

produced one of her first strong female protagonists. Like the narrator in Charlotte Perkin Gilman's 1892 short story "The Yellow Wallpaper," Alis articulates a woman's struggle to be heard.

Gate of Ivrel and the subsequent Gate books, *Well of Shiuan* (1978), *Fires of Azeroth* (1979), and *Exile's Gate* (1988), also possess a strong female protagonist in the figure of Morgaine. Like Alis, Morgaine bears the responsibility of knowing the larger fate of the world she lives in, but unlike Alis, Morgaine is empowered to change that fate for the better. Morgaine was part of a team from a technologically advanced civilization that was sent to a series of planets to destroy the Gates of Power. These Gates, which had been discovered by another humanoid race called variously khal, qujal, or qhal, enable instantaneous interstellar travel and also time travel. Since some of the qhal attempted to travel

The sun shone down on him as he worked, and glittered coldly off the golden hilt of the blade he hung upon the gray's saddle. The dragon leered at him, fringed mouth agape, clenching the blade in his teeth; his spread legs made the guard; his back-winding tail guarded the fingers.

He feared even to touch it. No Korish work, that, whatever hand had made the plain sheath. It was alien and otherly, and when he ventured in curiosity to ease the awful thing even a little way from its sheath he found strange letters on the blade itself like a shard of glass—even touching it threatened injury. No blade existed of such substance: and yet it seemed more perilous than fragile. (page 32)

The literary critic Rebecca Beal uses the sword and other symbols in the Gate books to discuss Cherryh's "Arthurian humanism," which she also sees in Cherryh's novels *Sun-*

fall (1981) and *Port Eternity* (1982). In *Gate of Ivrel*, Beal believes, Morgaine plays a role similiar to the figure of Morgan le Fay in Sir Thomas Malory's, *Morte d'Arthur*, although Morgaine ultimately uses her magical powers for good and she survives. Another critic, Mary Brizzi, while also seeing Morgaine in terms of Arthurian legend, emphasizes how the pairing of Morgaine and Vanye reverses traditional gender roles. Brizzi discusses how Cherryh continually pairs an epic heroine and a helpful male to make a feminist statement. However we view Morgaine, she definitely begins a tradition of protagonists in Cherryh's fiction who move between different cultures and who struggle with issues of power and responsibility. The Gate books as a whole also begin to demonstrate Cherryh's talent for constructing and defining a variety of different political and religious systems.

All of these elements appeared in her first science fiction series, The Faded Sun trilogy, which includes *The Faded Sun: Kesrith, The Faded Sun: Shon'jir* (1978), *The Faded Sun: Kutath* (1979). These novels tell the story of three cultures: the regul, mri, and humanity. The regul had hired the mri as mercenaries in their war against humanity, but the regul and the mri lost. The narrative begins with humans traveling to the formerly regul planet Kesrith to begin an occupation and eventual colonization. Sten Duncan, a SurTac, or surface tactical officer, is part of a two-person human delegation sent to Kesrith just ahead of first human colonists. He learns quickly to distrust the regul, and he unexpectedly befriends the mri, who reluctantly accept him into their culture.

The regul are a strange race. When regul "younglings" come of age, they become immensely fat and live most of their lives in a specially built mechanical sled. The regul have a perfect memory, which goes back several generations. They remember every moment of their own and their ancestors' lives. Unfortunately, this perfect memory is countered by the fact that the regul lack imagination, which was part of the reason they lost the war. Humans are, of course, just the opposite. They have a healthy imagination, but they are very forgetful. The regul are disturbed most at the humans' ability to lie—to violate their memory—to others as well as themselves.

The mri, the central concern of the trilogy, are a matriarchal society that chooses to live, unlike the regul or humans, without the daily aid of technology—although they borrow regul ships for interstellar travel. They are experts in the art of war and sustain themselves by hiring out their services to other, less belligerent cultures. Despite their interactions with these other cultures, they have a strong xenophobic distrust of any tsi'mri, or aliens. The "she'pan" is the female leader of the culture and the primary person in possession of culture's religious mysteries and a sense of the culture's future. In other words, she, unlike regul or humans, possesses both memory and imagination. The rest of the mri society is divided into distinct classes. The Sen are the scholars that are the only ones allowed to interact on a daily basis with the she'pan. The Kath are the blue-robed caste of child-bearing woman. And finally, the Kel are the warrior class. The mri whom we and Sten Duncan come to know best is a Kel named Niun:

> Niun sat, brooding, on a rock overlooking the world, hating tsi'mri with more than the ordinary hatred of mri for aliens, which was considerable. He was twenty-six years old as the People reckoned years, which was not by Kesrith's orbit around Ariain, nor by the standard of Nisren, nor by that of either of the two other worlds the People had designated homeworld in the span of time remembered by Kel songs.
>
> He was tall, even of his kind. His high cheekbones bore the *seta'al*, the triple scars of his caste, blue-stained and indelible; this meant that he was a full-fledged member of the Kel, the hand of the People. Being of the Kel, he went robed from collar to boot-tops in unrelieved black; and black veil and tasseled head cloth, *mez* and *zaidhe*, concealed all but his brow and his eyes from the gaze of outsiders when he chose to meet them. (*Kesrith*, page 16)

The first novel in the trilogy tells the story of the passage of power within the mri from an older to a younger generation. By the end of that novel, in fact, a young she'pan, Melein, and a young warrior, Niun, are the only surviving members of the mri on Kesrith. The rest of the mri have been destroyed by the regul, who fear that the mri might eventually turn on them now that the war is over.

Humans decide to send Melein and Niun on a trip back to their home planet, Kusrath. Sten Duncan joins them as part anthropologist, part spy, and part friend for the long, lonely journey through space that takes up most of the second novel in the trilogy. The third novel recounts the experience of the mri when they reach Kusrath itself, as they attempt to recover their lost civilization and defend it against the genocidal tendencies of the regul and the intrusive anthropological desires of the humans.

The Faded Sun trilogy has generated possibly more critical commentary than any other of Cherryh's works. In her book *Artificial Paradise: Science Fiction and American Reality* (1995), Ben-Tov devotes much of her chapter on "The Myth of the Final Frontier" to the trilogy. She considers Sten Duncan to be in the tradition of the frontier hunter in American culture. He is a motherless hero who abandons civilization and opens the wilderness to settlers. When he meets and eventually befriends Melein, she contends that they produce "an ideal human identity, close to maternal nature yet serving science and technology's empire." Brizzi, as in her analysis of *Gate of Ivrel*, notices a reversal of gender roles in the figures of Melein and Niun, since Niun, the man, is not allowed read or write, and Melein is the more courageous of the two. She ultimately reads Melein as a Christ-like Messiah. Paul Nolan Hyde, another critic, praises the depth of Cherryh's presentation of a variety of cultures and characters.

In any case, The Faded Sun trilogy began Cherryh's use of space as a setting through which to investigate cultural identity and politics, both on an individual and on a societal level. This investigation became even more intense and elaborate as she began to define the broader context of her Alliance-Union universe.

Cherryh won the Hugo award for best novel in 1982 for *Downbelow Station*. In that novel she details the political and military tensions on the space station orbiting the planet Pell and on the planet itself. Pell was the first planet outside of Earth that supported life, an apparently primitive race called the hisa. The planet and space station form a neutral border of sorts between the increasingly powerful Union and what is left of Earth's claims in space. The Fleet of starships that protect Earth (they actually work for the Company, Earth's corporate representative in space) has dwindled from fifty ships to a small but very skilled and resourceful group of fifteen, led by famed captain Conrad Mazian of the starship *Europe.* Our perspective on the Fleet is through the eyes of the female captain of the starship *Norway*, Signy Mallory, who follows Mazian's orders but is independent-minded and has a firm control over her own ship. The critic Lynn Williams contends that Signy Mallory is one of the best examples of one of Cherryh's female leaders who "takes care of her own people." As the novel progresses, the space station Pell is on the verge of being annexed by Union, as most of Earth's original stations have already been. The Fleet returns to Pell to protect it:

Signy had it visual now, the hubbed ring of Pell's Station, the distant moon, the bright jewel of Downbelow, cloud-swirled. They had long since dumped velocity, moved in with dreamlike slowness compared to their former speed, as the station's smooth shape resolved itself into the chaos of angles its surface was.

Freighters were jammed into every berth of the visible side, docking and standby. There was incredible clutter on scan, and they were moving slowly because it took that long for these sluggish ships to clear and approach for them. Every merchanter which had not been swept into Union hands had to be hereabouts, at station, in pattern, or farther out, or hovering off in the deep just out of system. Graff still had controls, a tedious business now. Unprecedented crowding and traffic. Chaos indeed. She was afraid, when she analyzed the growing tautness at her gut. Anger had cooled and she was afraid with a helplessness she was not accustomed to feel . . . a wish that by someone very wise and at some time long ago, other choices had been made, which would have saved them all from this moment, and this place, and the choices they had left.

"Carriers *North Pole* and *Tibet* will stand off from station," the notification from *Europe*. "Assume patrol." (pages 205–206)

Besides Mallory, we are also given several perspectives on the world of the space station and its "Downbelow Station" on the planet Pell. The station is run democratically, but it is dominated but the benevolent authority of the Konstantin family. The father, Angelo, is the stationmaster. One of his sons, Damon, is the head of Legal Affairs and his wife, Elene, is the station's liaison with merchanters, having been one herself. Angelo's other son, Emilio, and his wife, Miliko, are in charge of extracting natural resources and establishing the first human colonies on Downbelow. We are also given the perspective of secret agents working for Union who are trying to undermine the space station from within. We are even given the perspective of the some of the *hisa* who are attempting to adapt to an intrusive human presence on their planet:

The rain still came down, the thunder dying. Tam-utsapitan watched the humans come and go, arms locked about her knees, her bare feet sunk in mire, the water trickling slowly off her fur. Much that the humans did made no sense; much that humans made was of no visible use, perhaps for the gods, perhaps that they were mad; but graves . . . this sad thing the hisa understood. Tears, she behind masks, the hisa understood. She watched, rocking slightly, until the last humans had gone, leaving only the mud and the rain in this place where humans laid their dead. (page 83)

With all of these human and alien perspectives, it might seem that the novel would be awkward and difficult to follow. It is a testament to Cherryh's substantial talents, however, that every character is fully realized and the action is both suspenseful and moving.

Downbelow Station would indisputably be Cherryh's masterpiece if she had not written *Cyteen* seven years later. Winner of the Hugo award in 1989, *Cyteen* tells a similar story to *Downbelow*—only this time it is from the perspective of the Union instead of from the perspective of those loyal to Earth or those loyal to the Alliance of merchanters. It is one of only two Alliance-Union novels, the other being *40,000 in Gehenna* (1983), that offer this alternative viewpoint. *Cyteen* takes place, for the most part, at the capital of Union operations, the planet Cyteen, and it reveals a world that is dominated by genetic engineering and imperialistic politics. Ariane Emory is a very old and brilliant scientist (her life has been extended by a medical breakthrough called "rejuv") who dominates the life of Cyteen and all of Union space by controlling the production of the genetically engineered classes of beta and azi. She is opposed by other scientists, such as Jordan Warrick and his son, and other politicians, such as Mikhail Corain, who want to curtail her plans for human cloning and for continued expansion of Union territory. Like *Downbelow Station*, *Cyteen* uses multiple perspectives—most significantly the perspective of some of the genetically engineered workers—to tell a story of scientific and political intrigue.

Both *Downbelow Station* and *Cyteen* are not only remarkable novels in and of themselves; they also elevate the significance of many of Cherryh's other Alliance-Union novels by providing them with a broader context that was often tantalizingly missing. Early novels such as *Serpent's Reach* and *Port Eternity* (1982) and later novels such as *Tripoint* (1994) and *Finity's End* (1997) display a greater richness when read after those more comprehensive works.

Serpent's Reach, for example, tells the story of Raen, a member of the Kontrin, an aristocratic human culture located in the Reach, a quarantined collection of planets. As a Kontrin, Raen is potentially immortal, but at the beginning of the novel, her immediate family is wiped out by a rival faction. She befriends the Queen of the antlike alien hive culture called the majat, and with the Queen's help she retakes power among the Kontrin. The initial meeting of Raen and the Queen is one of the most significant scenes in the novel:

> Air stirred audibly, intaken.
> "You are so *small*," Mother said. Raen flinched, for the timbre of it made the very walls quiver, and vibrated in Raen's bones.
> "You are beautiful," Raen answered, and felt it. Tears started from her, yes . . . awe, and pain at once.
> It pleased Mother . . . (page 27)

The critics Jane Donawerth and Bernie Heidkamp have noted how Cherryh, by portraying the most prominent mother in the novel—the Queen of the Majat—as an animal, is critiquing portrayals of mothers in modern American culture. Even though the mother in the novel is an animal, she is also a fully realized, intelligent, and courageous character who handles her power with a impressive sense of responsibility.

In light of our present knowledge of the Alliance-Union universe, however, we might also see how *Serpent's Reach* is the story of Jim, a lab-born azi whom Raen befriends. We know now that the azi are a class of being originally created on Cyteen and part of Union's larger political project. Raen's sympathy with the azi and the even lower lab-born beta class has universal implications.

Other important Alliance-Union novels are *Hunter of Worlds* (1977) and the Chanur series. *Hunter of Worlds* was criticized initially for being too complex. Cherryh created three separate languages for the three alien races in the text, and it is difficult to follow unless one refers continually to the glossary Cherryh provides. Although it is somewhat experimental, it also marks the beginning of Cherryh's in-depth portrayals of alien cultures. The central character in the novel, Aiela Lyaillueue, is also, along with Morgaine, an early example of one of Cherryh's inquisitive and courageous female protagonists.

The Chanur series, which includes *The Pride of Chanur* (1982), *Chanur's Venture* (1984), *The Kif Strike Back* (1985), *Chanur's Homecoming* (1986), and *Chanur's Legacy* (1992), is by Cherryh's own admission a "light" and "rowdy" set of stories. Nevertheless, it is simultaneously a playful commentary on gender politics, an exploration of the customs and minds of an alien race, and an expansion of the Alliance-Union universe. Set in a time contemporaneous with the events of *Cyteen*, the series tells the story of the hani, a catlike, spacefaring people who are very protective of (and somewhat embarrassed by) their violent and aggressive menfolk. We do not meet many of those menfolk (until later in the series) because the female members of the culture are the only ones allowed off their home planet and on the starships, where most of the action takes place. The Chanur, we discover, have their own version of the nature/nurture debate: "Nature. Nature that made males useless, too high-strung to go offworld, to hold any position of responsibility beyond the estates. Nature that robbed them of sense and stability. Or an upbringing that did." The hero of the series is a female Hani, Pyanfar, who is captain of the starship *The Pride of Chanur*. The critic Jane Donawerth, in her analysis of the first and last novels in the series, notes that, by shifting the point of view from the dominant females to the "oppressed" males, Cherryh provides a poignant critique not only of traditional gender roles but also of the conventional science fiction plot.

Even though Cherryh has created other universes in recent years, she continues to write within the Alliance-Union universe. As her later novels, such as *Tripoint* and *Finity's End*, suggest, Cherryh is committed to exploring—with increasing moral and philosophical complexity—how individuals and families can not only survive (which seemed to be the chief concern of *Downbelow Station* and *Cyteen*) but also can grow and progress in a universe dominated by rapid technological change. These novels, as a result, are becoming sharper allegories for the changes occurring in the Information Age of late-twentieth-century America. In other recent Alliance-Union novels, such as *Heavy Time* (1991) and *Hellburner* (1992), Cherryh also demonstrates her need to fill out the remaining gaps in the universe (taking us back in time before *Downbelow Station*) in order to present the universe as an intellectual and sociological whole.

The wide range of Cherryh's work has created quite a popular following for her. Several websites, for example, are devoted solely to mapping out the Alliance-Union universe, down to such details as the exact distant between stars and planets. Cherryh has encouraged this particular enterprise because she has already mapped much of that universe herself.

Cherryh has also inspired, as we have seen, a critical following. Many of the debates concerning her work have focused on her acute awareness of gender roles and gender politics, both within American culture and within the science fiction tradition. Other critics, however, focus on her portrayals of alien cultures and their political systems. Patrick McGuire and Lynn F. Williams, in particular, while for the most part providing a positive assessment of Cherryh's work, wonder whether her portrayals of these cultures reveal a Western bias and an unhealthy fascination with authoritarian power. McGuire believes that some of Cherryh's alien cultures are a little too reminiscent of non-Western cultures. The amaut in *The Hunter of Worlds*, for example, appear as archetypal peasants, similar to popular images of the Chinese. The kallia in that same work appear to be Japanese (McGuire notes several language similarities). Non-Western culture, in this sense, is portrayed as the Other, literally the alien, to the more "normal" Western human perspective. Williams believes that Cherryh "displays very conservative notions about social hierarchies and apparently approves of aristocracies, especially hereditary ones that demonstrate a

sense of noblesse oblige." While applauding Cherryh's strong, female protagonists, Williams notes that they almost always come from the ruling class and that they seem too far above the ordinary woman.

These criticisms are in some sense inevitable for an author who has attempted to portray such a wide variety of characters and cultures in her work and who has not shied away from writing about complicated philosophical and political issues. Cherryh herself sees writing fiction as a social project that can promote human understanding across such differences as race and class:

> A story is a moment of profound examination of things in greater reality and sharper focus than we usually see them. It's a sharing of perception in this dynamic, motile universe, in which two human minds can momentarily orbit the same focus, like a pair of vastly complex planets, each with its own civilization, orbiting a star that they strive to comprehend, each in its own way. (*Visible Light*, page xiii)

By offering continually shifting points of view, Cherryh never allows her audience to rest or to feel comfortable with their own cultural assumptions.

While Cherryh certainly challenges many of our assumptions, she still sees herself as working with a particular science fiction tradition. Although her answers vary whenever she is asked what she is reading or what were her literary influences, science fiction and fantasy authors, such as Fritz Leiber, Jack Williamson, Michael Moorcock, and Tolkien, continually appear on her lists. In a Socratic dialogue of sorts that serves as the introduction to *Visible Light* (1986), a collection of some of Cherryh's short stories, Cherryh makes her allegiances clear:

> "Let me tell you: for me the purest and truest art in the world is science fiction. . . ."
>
> "It's escapist. . . ."
>
> "It's romance. It's the world as it can be, ought to be—must someday, somewhere be, if we can only find enough of the component

parts and shove them together. Science fiction is the oldest sort of tale-telling, you know. Homer; Sindbad's story; Gilgamesh; Beowulf; and up and up the line of history wherever mankind's scouts encounter the unknown. Not a military metaphor. It's a peaceful progress. Like the whales in their migrations. Tale-telling is the most peaceful thing we do. It's investigatory. The best tale-telling always has been full of what-if. The old Greek peasant who laid down the tools of a hard day's labor to hear about Odysseus' trip beyond the rim of his world—he wasn't an escapist. He was dreaming. Mind-stretching at the end of a stultifying day. He might not go. But his children's children might. *Someone* would. And that makes his day's hard work *worth* something in the future; it makes this farmer and his well-tilled field participant in the progress of his world, and his cabbages have then a cosmic importance." (pages xiv–xv)

Selected Bibliography

WORKS OF C. J. CHERRYH

Brothers of Earth. New York: DAW, 1976.
Gate of Ivrel. New York: DAW, 1976.
Hunter of Worlds. New York: DAW, 1977.
The Faded Sun: Kesrith. New York: DAW, 1978.
The Faded Sun: Shon'jir. Garden City, N.Y.: Doubleday, 1978.
Well of Shiuan. New York: DAW, 1978.
The Faded Sun: Kutath. Garden City, N.Y.: Doubleday, 1979.
Fires of Azeroth. New York: DAW, 1979.
Hestia. New York: DAW, 1979.
Serpent's Reach. New York: DAW, 1980.
Downbelow Station. New York: DAW, 1981.
Sunfall. New York: DAW, 1981.
Wave Without a Shore. New York: DAW, 1981.
Merchanter's Luck. New York: DAW, 1982.
Port Eternity. New York: DAW, 1982.
The Pride of Chanur. New York: DAW, 1982.
The Dreamstone. New York: DAW, 1983.
40,000 in Gehenna. Huntington Woods, Mich.: Phantasia, 1983.
The Tree of Swords and Jewels. New York: DAW, 1983.
Chanur's Venture. New York: DAW, 1984.
Voyager in Night. New York: DAW, 1984.
Angel with the Sword. New York: DAW, 1985.
Cuckoo's Egg. New York: DAW, 1985.

The Kif Strike Back. New York: DAW, 1985.
Chanur's Homecoming. New York: DAW, 1986.
The Gates of Hell, with Janet Morris. New York: Baen, 1986.
Soul of the City, with Janet Morris and Lynn Abbey. New York: Ace, 1986.
Visible Light. New York: DAW, 1986. (A collection of short fiction.)
Kings in Hell, with Janet Morris. New York: Baen, 1987.
Merovingian Nights: Festival Moon. New York: DAW, 1987. (Editor and contributor to this shared universe sequel to *Angel with the Sword.*)
Merovingian Nights: Fever Season. New York: DAW, 1987.
Cyteen. New York: Warner, 1988.
Exile's Gate. New York: DAW, 1988.
Merovingian Nights: Smugglers' Gold. New York: DAW, 1988.
Merovingian Nights: Troubled Waters. New York: DAW, 1988.
The Paladin. New York: Baen, 1988.
Merovingian Nights: Divine Right. New York: DAW, 1989.
Rimrunners. New York: Warner, 1989.
Rusalka. New York: Ballantine, 1989.
Chernevog. New York: Ballantine, 1990.
Merovingian Nights: Flood Tide. New York: DAW, 1990.
Heavy Time. New York: Warner, 1991.
Merovingian Nights: Endgame. New York: DAW, 1991.
Yvgenie. New York: Ballantine, 1991.
Chanur's Legacy. New York: DAW, 1992.
The Goblin Mirror. New York: Ballantine, 1992.
Hellburner. New York: Warner, 1992.
Faery in Shadow. New York: Ballantine, 1994.
Foreigner: A Novel of First Contact. New York: DAW, 1994.
Fortress in the Eye of Time. New York: HarperPrism, 1995.
Invader. New York: DAW, 1995.
Rider at the Gate. New York: Warner, 1995.
Tripoint. New York: Warner, 1995.
Cloud's Rider. Warner, 1996.
Inheritor. New York: DAW, 1996.
Lois & Clark: A Superman Novel. New York: Prima Publications, 1996.
Finity's End. New York: Warner, 1997.
Fortress of Eagles. New York: HarperPrism, 1998. (Sequel to *Fortress in the Eye of Time.*)
Fortress of Owls. New York: HarperPrism, 1999.

CRITICAL AND BIOGRAPHICAL STUDIES

Beal, Rebecca S. "C. J. Cherryh's Arthurian Humanism." In *Popular Arthurian Traditions.* Bowling Green, Ohio: Bowling Green University Popular Press, 1992.
Ben-Tov, Sharona. *The Artificial Paradise: Science Fiction and American Reality.* Ann Arbor: University of Michigan Press, 1995.

Brizzi, Mary T. "C. J. Cherryh and Tomorrow's New Sex Roles." In *The Feminine Eye: Science Fiction and the Women Who Write It.* Edited by Tom Staicar. New York: Ungar, 1982.

Donawerth, Jane. *Frankenstein's Daughters: Women Writing Science Fiction.* Syracuse, N.Y.: Syracuse University Press, 1997.

Heidkamp, Bernie. "Responses to the Alien Mother in Post-Maternal Cultures: C. J. Cherryh and Orson Scott Card." *Science Fiction Studies,* 23, no. 3 (November 1996): 339–354.

Hyde, Paul Nolan. "Dances with Dusei: A Personal Response to C. J. Cherryh's *The Faded Sun." Mythlore,* 18, no. 2 (Spring 1992): 45–53.

McGuire, Patrick. "Water into Wine: The Novels of C. J. Cherryh." *Starship,* 16, no. 2 (Spring 1979): 47–49.

Wells, Susan. "C. J. Cherryh." In *Dictionary of Literary Biography.* Yearbook 1980. Detroit, Mich.: Gale Research, 1980.

Williams, Lynn F. "Women and Power in C. J. Cherryh's Novels." *Extrapolation,* 27, no. 2 (Summer 1986): 85–92.

Wiloch, Thomas. "Cherry, Carolyn Janice." *Contemporary Authors: New Revision Series,* Vol. 10. Edited by Linda Metzer. Detroit, Mich.: Gale Research, 1985.

—BERNIE HEIDKAMP

SIR ARTHUR C. CLARKE
(b. 1917)

ONE OF THE best-known science fiction writers of this century, Sir Arthur Charles Clarke was born on 16 December 1917 in Minehead, Somerset, England, in farming country. His early love of astronomy coincided with his introduction to science fiction and fantasy (as described in his *Astounding Days: A Science Fictional Autobiography* [1989]), both the pulp magazines of Hugo Gernsback and the more literary tradition of H. G. Wells, Lord Dunsany, and especially the novelist-philosopher Olaf Stapledon.

In high school Clarke contributed science fiction sketches of his own to the *Huish Magazine* (1934–1936) before leaving for London to become a government auditor. Disliking his job, he felt more at home with other science fiction fans and members of the British Interplanetary Society (BIS), then in its infancy. To fanzines and BIS publications, Clarke contributed reviews, articles (some on science fiction), and stories before and during World War II. In technical journals he also published some papers resulting from his work as a Royal Air Force instructor in the new technology of radar, including his now famous 1945 suggestion for communications satellites in stationary orbits. Some of these early writings later surfaced in *Ascent to Orbit: A Scientific Autobiography* (1984).

After the war Clarke attended King's College, London (1946–1948), earning a B.S. degree in physics and mathematics. Active in the British Astronomical Association, he also served for three terms (1946–1947, 1950–1952) as chairman of the revived and growing

BIS, and he seized every opportunity to proselytize for space travel, assuming that Britain would play a significant role in it. This phase of his career culminated in his first book, *Interplanetary Flight* (1950), and its successor, *The Exploration of Space* (1951), a Book-of-the-Month Club selection, which made him a major popularizer of space travel. Several other books and many articles on space would follow.

Clarke's professional debut as a science fiction writer also took place right after the war, with nineteen stories (sometimes under pseudonyms) preceding his first book of fiction, the novel *Prelude to Space* (1951). Some of his early stories were essentially jokes, of the "shaggy dog" variety, or "ghost stories" as Eric Rabkin calls them. This whimsical streak climaxed with the 1957 publication of *Tales from the White Hart*. Other short stories and four early novels took place in science fiction's "consensus history" of man's expansion into space, overseen by the presence of *Astounding* editor John W. Campbell, Jr.; these could be termed his near-future scenarios. However, Clarke could also write stories of a more somber, even melancholy tone— far-future tales in which man's science and technology seemed to lead to a dead end or in which contact with alien intelligence cast doubt on naive ideas of progress.

The jokes continued after the mid-1950's, as did the near-future scenarios and the more mythic tales, but this period marked a break in Clarke's career. A marriage in 1953, to Marilyn Mayfield, did not last long (a divorce officially came about in 1964), but his fascination with Ceylon (now Sri Lanka) and the sea did. Introduced to the undersea world by the young photographer Mike Wilson, with whom he would collaborate on six books and a film, Clarke also discovered the Indian Ocean "island paradise," which has been his home since 1956. After publication of another sixteen short stories and *The Deep Range* (1957), his science fiction production slackened, and the sea and the East began to play a somewhat larger role in his work, beyond the facile Odyssean parallel with space already evident. In 1987 Clarke would attribute his apparent hiatus at this time to a six-year struggle to complete his only "mainstream" novel, *Glide Path* (1963), fictionalizing his World War II experiences with radar.

Making the movie of *2001: A Space Odyssey* (1968) with Stanley Kubrick probably earned Clarke his greatest fame and widest audience (as well as an Oscar nomination for Best Original Screenplay), but other honors have not been lacking. He served as a television commentator on the Apollo 11, 12, and 15 lunar missions, alongside Walter Cronkite and astronaut Wally Schirra. The science fiction community awarded him prizes for the short story "The Star" (1956); the novella "A Meeting with Medusa" (1971); and the novels *Rendezvous with Rama* (1973) and *The Fountains of Paradise* (1979). UNESCO's Kalinga Prize for "the popularization of science" was the first of several honors resulting from his "invention" of communications satellites, nonfiction works, and television appearances. Due to growing critical interest, Clarke has now been the subject of numerous books and articles delving into his fiction, and in 1986, the Science Fiction Writers of America voted him their prestigious Grand Master Award. Undoubtedly his greatest honor came in early 1998, when the British government awarded him a knighthood, making him the first person to earn this title primarily for writing science fiction.

During the 1980's and 1990's, Clarke kept busy with new novels and other projects, including major nonfiction books such as *Arthur C. Clarke's July 20, 2019* (1986) and *How the World Was One: Beyond the Global Village* (1992). He also became a familiar face to television viewers throughout the world as the host of two documentary series, *Arthur C. Clarke's Mysterious World* (1981) and *Arthur C. Clarke's World of Strange Powers* (1984). He has vigorously supported the Science Fiction Foundation, dedicated to preserving texts and supporting research, as well as other worthwhile causes, and he donated funds to establish a new prize, the Arthur C. Clarke Award, now given annually to the best science fiction novel published in Great Britain.

Most studies of Clarke's fiction have focused on his "mythic" stories and novels of alien contact and/or the far future, in which there appears an attempt to transcend the biological and technological limits of the human condition. But the Clarke canon consists almost equally of the aforementioned "jokes" and "scenarios," which merit some attention as well. Algis Budrys once complained about Clarke's predilection for scary stories with surprise endings, which often failed either to scare or to surprise. Rabkin's description of these as "ghost stories" may be more apt, indicating that it is all in fun and connecting them to the more explicitly humorous tall tales. Certainly the scare potential of ants ruling the world ("The Forgotten Enemy," 1948), of a traditional bogeyman on a distant planet ("A Walk in the Dark," 1950), or of a kitten in a spacesuit ("Who's There?" 1958) depends on reader naivete.

Interspecies miscomprehension is a subject for humor in other Clarke tales, ranging from paranoid fantasies of possessed people ("The Parasite," 1953) and lemmings ("The Possessed," 1953) to a bare awareness of each other's existence between humans and beings below the Earth's surface ("The Fires Within," 1947). The failure to understand humans is dangerous to aliens only in Clarke's first two professional sales in 1946, "Loophole" and "Rescue Party." In the better-known "Rescue Party" (written prior to "Loophole"), a mixed-species alien rescue mission finds that the sun is about to go nova and Earth is deserted. Even contrasted with the aliens' numbers and technological sophistication, this future Earth is still notable, by our present standards, for its accelerated development, culminating in an Exodus fleet, which the aliens deem unprecedentedly large as well as technologically primitive, relying on mere rocket power. Adrift and in need of rescue themselves, after a swift departure from the solar system, the aliens jest about the potential danger these newcomers may pose to the vast Federation, leading to the low-key punch line: "Twenty years afterward, the remark didn't seem funny."

Typical of Clarke's explicit jokes are Harry Purvis' tales of implausible inventions, from antigravity ("What Goes Up," 1956) and intimidated carnivorous plants ("The Reluctant Orchid," 1956) to aphrodisiac recordings ("Patent Pending," 1954) and brain-destroying music ("The Ultimate Melody," 1957) in *Tales from the White Hart*, allegedly told to a pub full of science fiction aficionados. Not every reader's palate may be sensitized to this special form of humor, but Clarke's predilection for it has been evident from his schoolboy days to the present.

Clarke's scenarios for man's exploration and development of the solar system are noteworthy for their transparent style and matter-of-fact handling of technical details fully familiar from his contemporaneous nonfiction writing. "Hide and Seek" (1949) demonstrates the flexibility, superior to an incomparably faster and heavily armed enemy cruiser, of a spy in a space suit, if he chooses as his terrain a satellite as small as Mars's Phobos. Other rescues of helpless astronauts are made possible by flimsy sunshades inside the orbit of Mercury ("Summertime on Icarus," 1960), by the weak gravity of the moon ("Maelstrom II," 1965), and by a battery of abacuses when computers break down ("Into the Comet," 1960).

Two cycles, each consisting of six short short stories, best illustrate Clarke's public relations work. In the first cycle, "Venture to the Moon" (1956), the commander of the Brit-ish spaceship *Endeavour* chronicles a joint lunar expedition with the United States and Russia, while the second cycle, "The Other Side of the Sky" (1957), gives an insider's view of the building of space stations. Each story is a vignette illustrating a single point—such as the moon's potential uses for advertising, archery, and vegetation; the value of canaries for detecting bad air; the favorable chances of surviving a brief exposure to vacuum; and the evanescent glimpse of what might be the hulk of an alien spaceship. Like his other contributions to the "consensus future," these human interest stories have little or no plot complications.

The static situation of an astronaut abandoned on Mars is charged with memories and allusions to previous explorers Captain Cook and Admiral Byrd in "Transit of Earth" (1971). Equally static is the elegiac "If I Forget Thee, O Earth . . ." (1951), in which a ten-year-old boy takes his first trip outside the base on the "dark side" of the moon to get his first glimpse of radioactive Earth and learn the lessons of exile. In "Death and the Senator" (1961), a dying opponent of American space stations refuses a life-saving offer by the Russians' orbital hospital. Even the obvious potential for drama of a race to the moon between sun-powered sailing ships is short-circuited by a solar flare in "The Wind from the Sun" (1964); and in Clarke's best-selling novel *A Fall of Moondust* (1961), the drama consists largely of doing one's best to survive until rescuers can devise and execute a plan to release the passengers of a sightseeing tour trapped in a pocket of lunar dust. The characters are stereotyped, but the narrative crackles with wit, and the reader's fun is partly in trying to solve the problems posed before the rescuers do.

Clarke's reluctance to tell a traditional action-adventure story in the pulp tradition may be credited to his literary allegiances and a desire to downplay the thoughtless romanticism evident in such tales of derring-do. Whatever the reason, his few attempts at melodrama are not very successful: two Venus-bound astronauts deciding who will survive on their

Sir Arthur C. Clarke. COURTESY OF THE LIBRARY OF CONGRESS

an impromptu fleet of the interplanetary Federation and a hurriedly erected Terran fortress—presage the independence of the moon, which is rich in mineral resources. All three works are low key and antiromantic, except in lyrical passages that look forward to further technological progress, and in the effective dwarfing of man's puny battles by the discovery of a supernova in *Earthlight*. With their deliberately distanced central characters, all three novels are debilitated by the necessity for long lectures and flashbacks and by awkwardly motivated departures from the primary viewpoint.

Technically superior is Clarke's first juvenile novel, *Islands in the Sky* (1952), in which a teenage television contest winner visits the "Inner [space] Station." As George Slusser points out, this is virtually a parody of the teenage space adventure story that was then coming into popularity, with Clarke's protagonist typically passive, having things explained and happening to him and with a brief scare at being lost in space. Unabashedly a sightseeing story, this book rehearses propaganda pieces about low-gravity environments and ends like its predecessors with the protagonist's yearning to participate in further colonization of the planets.

Not inconsistent with this consensus future, Clarke's stories of exploring the sea run in tandem with those concerned with space. The protagonist of *The Deep Range* (1957; expanded from a short story, 1954) is himself a grounded astronaut, Walter Franklin, with a wife and children permanently separated from him on Mars. In one of Clarke's rare attempts at a love story, Franklin's new Eurasian wife is wooed, won, and retired to homemaking from a potential career in ichthyology, but the major interest in the story is in the details of underwater farming and whale herding. Remarkable also is the Scottish-born leader of a world-sweeping Buddhism, the Mahanayake Thero of Ceylon, who successfully puts an end to the butchering of whales, in part from his conviction that extraterrestrials may well judge humanity by its actions toward other creatures.

limited air supply ("Breaking Strain," 1949), an expedition to an artificial Jovian satellite ("Jupiter Five," 1953), and the kidnapping of the UN secretary general ("Guardian Angel," 1950; story later incorporated into *Childhood's End* [1953]).

He is more clearly in his element in those novels that attend to the first stages of settling the solar system, as seen from an outsider's point of view. A historian of contemporary events observes preparations for the launching of the first moon rocket, a predominantly British effort from an electromagnetic launching track in Australia, in *Prelude to Space* (1951). A science fiction writer accompanies a ship to Mars just in time to see the colony approach self-sufficiency in *The Sands of Mars* (1951). In *Earthlight* (1955; shorter magazine version, 1951), an accountant turned ineffective spy investigates the lunar observatory in time to see a fruitless battle—between

Communication with so-called "aliens"—dolphins—is the object of the research base in *Dolphin Island* (1963), Clarke's second juvenile, in which an orphaned teenager is adopted by dolphins and dolphinologists near the Great Barrier Reef, one of the author's favorite skin-diving areas. The mechanics of getting Johnny Clinton to the island from the newly grown "forests" of Oklahoma (by stowing him away on a hovership!) are no more believable than the quiz show prize of his predecessor in *Islands in the Sky*; but Johnny is a more active hero, working with the dolphins and, with their assistance, going for help when the island is cut off by a tropical storm and his mentor is seriously ill. Other "people" of the sea, in a follow-up to Franklin's questing in the deep, include the giant squid of "The Shining Ones" (1964), whose methods of electronic communication point toward the Jovians of "A Meeting with Medusa" (1971).

Clarke's joke stories do not lack for aliens. Even some of his scenarios feature extraterrestrial forms and artifacts. But Clarke's aliens seem more at home in stories with a mythic cast, often suggesting an advancement over man, which is technological, spiritual, or both. Here his acknowledged debt to Stapledon is most pronounced. A hint of this may be gleaned from "Before Eden" (1961), in which primitive life on Venus is wiped out by the detritus of human visitors; from "Castaway" (1947) and "Out of the Sun" (1958), with their barely conceivable energy lifeforms; and from "History Lesson" (1949), in which Venusian explorers find humanity's last "time capsule" and identify human life and culture with the antics of a Walt Disney cartoon.

Human beings of the far future have something alien about them too. In "The Lion of Comarre" (1949), an advanced scientific society is rescued from stagnation by a young hero. He must first overcome the mechanized "dream-factory" of Comarre that a previous rebel had set up and separate its knowledge of the mind from its deleterious effects. Closely related to this fairy tale is Clarke's fine novel *Against the Fall of Night* (magazine version, 1948; book form, 1953; revised expansion in 1956 as *The City and the Stars*). Beginning with a vision of urban stasis in the "perfect" city of Diaspar—London as Clarke first saw it—*Fall/City* follows young Alvin on a quest through the posturban pastoral perfection of Lys and contact with aliens (including the immature "mental energy creature" Vanamonde) to recapture his people's forgotten spacefaring history. As he returns to Earth to digest what he has learned, the ending suggests the coming of a new equilibrium of city and country, mechanical and mental, past and future, human and alien, Earth and space, in keeping with the fairy tale construction of the novel (though the later Clarke-authorized sequel by Gregory Benford in *Beyond the Fall of Night* [1990] would prove less comforting).

This book has more than a little in common with the classic *Childhood's End* (1953), in which devil-shaped Overlords act as midwives to the transformation of man's last generation of children into part of the mature "energy-state," the Overmind (a concept borrowed from Stapledon). The last stages of recognizably human existence are spent in varieties of utopia, short-range kin to stagnant Diaspar and Lys. But where the ambivalence of *Fall/City* leads to a fairy tale equilibrium, that of *Childhood's End* leads to a radical split between the path of the human children and the path of the proud, individualistic, scientific Overlords. Clarke prefaced the narrative with a disclaimer: "The opinions expressed in this book are not those of the author," as well he might, since Ouija boards, telepathy, the end of space travel, and aliens keyed to traditional human religious concepts are foreign to his consistent overt positions. But many readers have trusted the tale more than the teller, among them film director Kubrick, who enlisted Clarke's collaboration on another tale of transformation.

Clarke's contribution to *2001: A Space Odyssey* was anchored not only in his earlier "mythic" or "visionary" novels but also in two low-key short stories. "The Sentinel" (1951, as "Sentinel of Eternity") posited, originally in the shape of a pyramid, an alien transmitter on the moon, perhaps akin to a fire alarm, which broadcasts a signal when humans breach the field surrounding it. "Encounter at Dawn" (1953) broached the idea of prehistoric tutoring of prehistoric people by alien visitors. Clarke's novel tends to be explicit where the film is elliptical, displaying less mysticism than Kubrick's vision. But both film and novel have the same basic plot: primitive humans made intelligent by a rectangular alien monolith; a signal, millennia later, from a lunar monolith after humans settle on the moon; a space voyage to Jupiter, where the signal was aimed, involving human conflict with the ship's homicidal computer; and the final transformation of astronaut David Bowman into a superhuman baby.

Clarke critics find in these stories a mythic core for his fiction, contextualizing both his scenarios of space travel and his satires of technological complacency. According to this interpretation, achieving space travel is a necessary but not sufficient condition for people to transcend their human limitations. Certainly Clarke has sought imaginatively to transcend humanity's Earthbound condition; he has alluded approvingly to Konstantin Tsiolkovsky's dictum that humans "cannot live in the cradle [Earth] forever" and to J. D. Bernal's provocative suggestion in *The World, The Flesh and The Devil* (1929) that star travel may demand experienced human minds in what might be called "post-human" bodies. Traditional symbolism drawn from religion and literature is also at home in Clarke's fiction, along with astronomical and technological figures, as is particularly evident in his two best-known stories.

"The Nine Billion Names of God" (1953) is an end-of-the-world "joke" in which, to the utter astonishment of the pragmatic Western computer salesmen and technicians involved, their help enables Tibetan monks to count all of God's names more efficiently, thus fulfilling the purpose of humanity and triggering the end of the world. There is little characterization and not much story, but the contrast and complementarity of Eastern goals and

Western means effectively questions our complacency once again. The ending is a marvelously quiet punch line to a low-key story of technical detail: "Overhead, without any fuss, the stars were going out." But it clearly has not taken place outside the world of the fiction. Clarke may sympathize with the lamas, as he does with the Buddhist veneration of life, but it is not evident that he takes the ending of this tall tale seriously.

Beginning with "It is three thousand light-years to the Vatican," the Jesuit astrophysicist who narrates "The Star" (1955) reflects in that story on the findings that have troubled his faith. From all the evidence the crew has gathered, it seems inescapable that this nova, which destroyed a civilization except for remnants left in a vault on the star's outermost planet, guided the Wise Men's way to Bethlehem. Putting aside the problem of a star's always being "in the east," as in the biblical story, Clarke's narrative shows astrophysics confronting Christianity with a difficult question: What kind of God would use such means to achieve such ends? Although the narrator's faith is troubled, his trust in science—like Clarke's—is not.

Overt dependence on "Grace" is difficult to demonstrate in a writer who consistently opposes mysticism and organized religion in favor of the individual's quest for scientific knowledge and enlightenment. Clarke may seek to speak for the human race's "cosmic loneliness," as Thomas Clareson asserts, but he also speaks for the loneliness of the individual mind. When a man nicknamed "Ego" in his youth maintains an office called his "ego chamber" and writes largely cerebral adventures, in which close human relationships play almost no significant role, we should take him at his word, as Jeremy Bernstein reports, "that he has always been more interested in things and ideas than in people." Like George Bernard Shaw, of whom Clarke is fond, he may aspire to an ideal state "above" biological concerns. Those giant stairways (often spiral), pyramids, towers, or monoliths no doubt have Freudian connotations, as Rabkin points out, but they are also obstacles, challenges, stages in ascent along a "great chain of being."

Transcendence remains important in Clarke's later works, but it becomes more explicitly naturalistic, even as its expression is more elaborately artistic. Howard Falconer, in "A Meeting with Medusa," moves in the direction charted by Bernal, from human to cyborg, after a dirigible disaster, which has made him uniquely suited for an expedition into Jupiter's atmosphere. That he is losing contact with other humans and is at the same time unable to establish contact with the electrically communicating, squidlike Jovians is ironically emblematic of Falconer's position "between two worlds."

Transcendence seems totally beyond humanity in *Rendezvous with Rama*, when an asteroid-sized, hollow, cylindrical alien spaceship passes through the solar system to the curiosity and consternation of twenty-second-century humanity. The sexually mixed, English-speaking crew of the *Endeavour*, the only ship near enough, explores the alien craft, while experts fuss at a distance and the Mercury colony, fearing attack, sends an automated bomb. The reader puzzles with the crew over specifics of Rama's construction, appropriating what our scientific knowledge is capable of, baffled by the rest. Utterly insignificant to the ship and its "biots" (biological robots), they disembark just before it closes in on the sun to refuel for the next leg of its journey. Dwarfed by the ship's scale, with its three gigantic stairways, its central "Circular Sea," and its (phallic) electric thunder-generating needles, Captain Norton nevertheless compares himself with the intrepid Captain Cook. With comparable equanimity, he accepts the fact of his two wives (compare *The Deep Range*) and the attentions of Medical Officer Laura Ernst. Other variations from traditional monogamy are also hinted at. Part myth (advanced aliens), part scenario (planetary colonization), part joke (a "ghost story" ending suggests more alien ships will follow—as occurred in later sequels co-authored by Gentry Lee), *Rama*, with its intense visual

and stylistic precision, reflected a new artistic peak for Clarke at age fifty-six.

The transcendence of history may also be a subtheme of *Imperial Earth* (1975), the closest he has come to a traditional utopia. Twenty-third-century Earth has at least lived up to Clarke's nonfiction forecasts, having eliminated such present-day features as overpopulation, pollution, energy shortages, urban blight, war, even farming, almost government. Duncan Makenzie, second-generation clone of his "grandfather" Malcolm (a founder of the Titan colony), visits Earth in 2276. He meets some Earth politicians; an "old flame" who was more interested in his older friend and rival, Karl Helmer; and Karl himself, whom Duncan's guards inadvertently kill (atop a communications tower with a spiral staircase). Duncan finally returns to Titan with Karl's plan for an alien-listening network to maintain Titan's importance and economic function when its atmosphere is no longer needed for spaceship refueling. Called "Project Argus," it will be one to ten thousand kilometers in diameter (an immense engineering job anticipating Clarke's next novel). Consisting of thousands of stiff wires projecting from Titan's neighboring Saturnian satellite, Mnemosyne, it resembles a sea urchin Duncan has killed, convincing him that he has had "a momentary glimpse in the Mirror of time" (in turn recalling Clarke's explanation for humanity's "racial memory" of devils in *Childhood's End*). But rather than clone himself according to plan, dark-skinned Duncan brings home a clone of the blond Karl, to replace dynastic stasis with a more random succession. (Breeding could have been just as effective, but normal biological ties seem to get in Clarke's way.)

The narrative is sometimes tedious; connections between parts and between actions are often schematic rather than clearly motivated. This structural peculiarity of Clarke's, explicit also in *Childhood's End* and *2001*, is given metaphorical justification by the "pentominoes" puzzle explained in Chapter 7. The loose construction, moreover, allows for digressive descriptions of Earth's surprises for

Duncan, which have attracted professional futurists to the book.

Clarke once announced that *The Fountains of Paradise* (1979) would be his last novel, and in some ways it seemed designed to serve as a fitting culmination of his career. Centrally, it is the tale of "master-builder" Vannemar Morgan, who erects the "ultimate bridge" from Earth to a space station in synchronous orbit. Morgan's daring impinges on hubris, and his luck is tantamount to fate; even his demise is that of a hero, risking his weak heart on a successful rescue mission up the incomplete tower. Metaphorically, he stands for the active side of the creator; the observer side is Johan Rajasinghe, famous diplomat retired to his aerie on "Taprobane" (Sri Lanka moved southward to straddle the equator). Clarke effectively employs the lore and local color of his adopted homeland, including a Buddhist monastery that must give way before the forces of technological progress, thanks to some ill-advised meteorological meddling by one of its own members.

Clarke's geometrical conception of novelistic structure is also effective as he brackets Morgan's story with interwoven chapters set in the past and future. King Kalidasa (second century A.D.), who ordered the building of Taprobane's famous shrines and fountains, is an obvious precursor of Morgan, while the coming of Starglider, an extraterrestrial probe, brings irrevocable change to human civilization. In changing people's relationship to the universe, it demolishes their uniqueness and questions their "religious" behavior. But it is only a precursor of the Starholmer, who arrives after a ring around the globe has been extended from the Tower of Kalidasa and most of Earth's population has retreated to the inner planets during a time of solar cooling. To the Starholmer's question of why the people did not resist, as did the colonists on Mars, rather than sending only their children to Earth, the world-brain ARISTOTLE begins its reply with a line from Ecclesiastes: "For every thing there is a season." "Childhood's end,"

this time, is a temporary acceptance of things as they are, a time to pause and reflect.

After a productive writing career spanning four decades, many writers may have chosen to pause and reflect on their achievements, but Clarke defied expectations by continuing to produce significant novels throughout the 1980's and 1990's. Author and critic Brian W. Aldiss has spoken admiringly about the "maturation of Clarke's work" during this period. First, and most prominently, came a long-awaited sequel to *2001, 2010: Odyssey Two* (1982). Sending Heywood Floyd on a joint Russian-American mission to Jupiter to investigate the fate of Bowman and the others who followed the monolith's signal, Clarke quietly argues for détente, rehabilitates the deranged computer HAL (who, it turns out, was deranged only because of contradictory instructions), brings Bowman back as a ghostly presence to convey a message from the aliens, and builds to a climax in which alien technology transforms Jupiter into a star, making its moons into new habitable worlds for humanity (though one moon, Europa, is declared off limits so its indigenous species can evolve on their own). While lacking the enigmatic grandeur of the original novel and film, *2010* still commanded respect, and its success led to a 1984 film and two additional sequels: *2069: Odyssey Three* (1987), in which Floyd's mission to investigate Halley's Comet leads to a disastrous landing on Europa, and *3001: The Final Odyssey* (1997), in which Bowman's old crewman Frank Poole is brought back to life a thousand years later to meet his ethereal ex-crewmate and deal with the threat of hostile alien activity. These two later novels disappointed some readers because they seemed to employ the framework of *2001* more to offer optimistic travelogues of a future spacefaring civilization than to advance the original story, which probably was not well suited for continuation in any event.

Three other novels published during this period attracted less attention but are interesting nevertheless. *The Songs of Distant Earth* (1986), an expansion of a 1957 story of that name, tells of space travelers who stop for rest and repair on an oceanic planet inhabited by settlers from Earth who were forced to flee when it was learned that the sun was going to became a nova. Uneventful and unportentous, the story still has a lyrical charm that suggests, as Aldiss indicates, that repeated complaints about Clarke's wooden style and poor characterization are no longer appropriate. More unsettling is *The Ghost from the Grand Banks* (1990), a near-future story about the efforts of two entrepreneurs to raise the two sundered halves of the sunken *Titanic*. Dominated by images of Clarke's recent fascination, the infinitely complex curve known as the Mandelbrot Set, this novel seems unusually pessimistic about human aspirations (as is only fitting in a story involving the *Titanic*): an unexpected storm thwarts the meticulous plans of the protagonists, and the sudden death of a precocious daughter, utterly shattering her mother, is arguably the most movingly painful moment in Clarke's fiction. Yet the novel ends with a typically wry Clarke "joke": millennia after the human race has vanished, an alien investigating the barren Earth detects the now-buried *Titanic* and decides to retrieve it—though we know he will fail, like all others before him. A third novel, the competent but unremarkable *The Hammer of God* (1993), is an expansion of a story published in *Time* magazine. (Clarke and Nobel Prize-winner Aleksandr Solzhenitsyn are the only two writers commissioned to write fiction for that magazine.) Primarily designed to warn people about the genuine threat of a disastrous cosmic collision, the story deals with future astronauts desperately attempting to divert a huge asteroid that is heading directly for Earth.

More controversially, Clarke in the late 1980's started to become involved with several collaborations of various sorts with other writers. Paul Preuss expanded and built upon Clarke stories to produce a six-volume series entitled *Arthur C. Clarke's Venus Prime* (1987–1991); Benford's sequel to *Against the Fall of Night* was published in one volume alongside the original novel under the overall title *Beyond the Fall of Night*, as by Clarke and Benford. Clarke and Gentry Lee co-authored four novels—an undersea thriller, *Cradle* (1988), and three sequels to *Rendezvous with Rama* entitled *Rama II* (1989), *The Gardens of Rama* (1991), and *Rama Revealed* (1993). Clarke and Mike McQuay co-wrote a novel about an earthquake, *Richter 10* (1996). Whether Clarke is explicitly credited as co-author or not, these books visibly employ Clarke's ideas and input but do not seem to be written in the characteristic Clarke style, so future scholars may have difficulty in embracing them as central to the Clarke canon.

Overall, whatever one thinks about these later products, Clarke has undoubtedly earned a permanent and prominent place in the history of science fiction. Less hectoring than Robert A. Heinlein, less trivializing than Isaac Asimov, he has shared his vision in a lucid, sometimes poetic, resolutely antimelodramatic style. He has conceived of humans as on a continuous odyssey, facing that giant stairway as a challenge their heritage demands that they accept and driven to live in such a way that neither aliens nor humanity's successors need be ashamed. Bridging the gap between East and West, the ocean and the stars, the lyrical and the mundane, Clarke has proved a worthy successor to Wells, Dunsany, and Stapledon.

Selected Bibliography

WORKS OF ARTHUR C. CLARKE

Prelude to Space: A Compellingly Realistic Novel of Interplanetary Flight. New York: World Editions, 1951.
The Sands of Mars. London: Sidgwick and Jackson, 1951.
Islands in the Sky. Philadelphia, Pa.: John C. Winston, 1952.
Against the Fall of Night. New York: Gnome, 1953. Revised and expanded edition, *The City and the Stars*, New York: Harcourt, Brace and Company, 1956.
Childhood's End. New York: Ballantine, 1953.
Expedition to Earth: Eleven Science Fiction Stories. New York: Ballantine, 1953. (Short stories.)
Earthlight. New York: Ballantine, 1955.
Reach for Tomorrow. New York: Ballantine, 1956. (Short stories.)

The Deep Range. New York: Harcourt, Brace and Company, 1957.

Tales from the White Hart. New York: Ballantine, 1957. (Short stories.)

The Other Side of the Sky. New York: Harcourt, Brace and World, 1958. (Short stories.)

A Fall of Moondust. New York: Harcourt, Brace and World, 1961.

Tales of Ten Worlds. New York: Harcourt, Brace and World, 1962. (Short stories.)

Dolphin Island: A Story of the People of the Sea. New York: Holt, Rinehart and Winston, 1963.

Glide Path. New York: Harcourt, Brace and World, 1963.

The Lion and Comarre and Against the Fall of Night. New York: Harcourt, Brace and World, 1968.

2001: A Space Odyssey. New York: New American Library, 1968.

The Lost Worlds of 2001. New York: New American Library, 1972. (Nonfiction, with some fictional material omitted from *2001*.)

The Wind from the Sun. New York: Harcourt Brace Jovanovich, 1972. (Short stories.)

Rendezvous with Rama. London: Gollancz, 1973.

Imperial Earth: A Fantasy of Love and Discord. London: Gollancz, 1975. Revised and expanded edition, *Imperial Earth,* New York: Harcourt Brace Jovanovich, 1976.

The View from Serendip. New York: Random House, 1977. (Nonfiction, including autobiographical essays.)

The Fountains of Paradise. New York: Harcourt Brace Jovanovich, 1979.

2010: Odyssey Two. New York: Ballantine, 1982.

Ascent to Orbit: A Scientific Autobiography: The Technical Writings of Arthur C. Clarke. New York: Wiley, 1984.

Arthur C. Clarke's July 20, 2019: Life in the 21st Century. New York: Macmillan, 1986. (Nonfiction.)

The Songs of Distant Earth. New York: Ballantine, 1986.

2061: Odyssey Three. New York: Ballantine, 1987.

Cradle, with Gentry Lee. New York: Warner, 1988.

Astounding Days: A Science Fictional Autobiography. London: Gollancz, 1989.

Rama II, with Gentry Lee. New York: Bantam, 1989.

Beyond the Fall of Night, with Gregory Benford. New York: Putnam's, 1990. (Clarke's *Against the Fall of Night* followed by Benford's sequel.)

The Ghost from the Grand Banks. New York: Bantam, 1990.

The Garden of Rama, with Gentry Lee. New York: Bantam, 1991.

How the World Was One: Beyond the Global Village. New York: Bantam, 1992. (Nonfiction, incorporating some material from Clarke's *Voice Across the Sea* [1958].)

The Hammer of God. New York: Bantam, 1993.

Rama Revealed, with Gentry Lee. New York: Bantam, 1993.

The Snows of Olympus: A Garden on Mars. New York: Norton,1995. (Nonfiction.)

Richter 10, with Mike McQuay. New York: Bantam, 1996.

3001: The Final Odyssey. New York: Ballantine, 1997.

CRITICAL AND BIOGRAPHICAL STUDIES

Agel, Jerome, ed. *The Making of Kubrick's 2001.* New York: New American Library, 1971.

Asimov, Isaac. "Arthur C. Clarke." In his *Asimov on Science Fiction.* Garden City, N.Y.: Doubleday, 1981.

Bernstein, Jeremy. "Extrapolators: Arthur C. Clarke." In his *Experiencing Science.* New York: Basic Books, 1978.

Bizony, Piers. *2001—Filming the Future.* London: Aurum, 1994. (With a foreword by Clarke.)

Geduld, Carolyn. *Filmguide to 2001: A Space Odyssey.* Bloomington: Indiana University Press, 1973.

McAleer, Neil. *Odyssey: The Authorised Biography of Arthur C. Clarke.* London: Gollancz, 1992. Reprinted as *Arthur C. Clarke: The Authorized Biography,* Chicago: Contemporary, 1992.

Menger, Lucy. "The Appeal of *Childhood's End.*" In *Critical Encounters: Writers and Themes in Science Fiction.* Edited by Dick Riley. New York: Ungar, 1978.

Moskowitz, Sam. "Arthur C. Clarke." In his *Seekers of Tomorrow: Masters of Modern Science Fiction.* Cleveland, Ohio and New York: World Publishing, 1966.

Olander, Joseph, and Martin Harry Greenberg, eds. *Arthur C. Clarke.* New York: Taplinger, 1977. (Writers of the 21st Century Series, with essays by Thomas Clareson, David N. Samuelson, and others.)

Platt, Charles. "Arthur C. Clarke." In his *Dream Makers: Science Fiction and Fantasy Writers at Work.* Revised edition, New York: Ungar, 1983. (Interview.)

Rabkin, Eric S. *Arthur C. Clarke.* West Linn, Oreg.: Starmont, 1979.

Reid, Robin Anne. *Arthur C. Clarke: A Critical Companion.* Westport, Conn.: Greenwood, 1997.

Samuelson, David N. *Arthur C. Clarke: A Primary and Secondary Bibliography.* Boston: G. K. Hall, 1984.

Slusser, George Edgar. *The Space Odysseys of Arthur C. Clarke.* San Bernardino, Calif.: Borgo, 1978.

Westfahl, Gary. "'He Was Part of Mankind': Arthur C. Clarke's *A Fall of Moondust.*" In his *Cosmic Engineers: A Study of Hard Science Fiction.* Westport, Conn.: Greenwood, 1996.

—DAVID N. SAMUELSON
—GARY WESTFAHL (Revision and update)

HAL CLEMENT

(b. 1922)

HAL CLEMENT IS the pseudonym used by Harry Clement Stubbs for science fiction purposes. He was born in Somerville, Massachusetts, in May 1922. Early interests in both science and science fiction led him to apply a good deal of the former to his writing of the latter. In 1942, while still a college junior, he sold a short story, "Proof," which appeared in *Astounding* in June of that year. The following year he took a bachelor of science degree at Harvard, majoring in astronomy. He went on to gain master's degrees in education and, eventually, in chemistry. Apart from service in World War II as a copilot with the United States Army Air Force in Europe and a short period (around 1951) as a weapons instructor, he has spent his adult life in Milton, Massachusetts, working as a high school science teacher.

The writing of science fiction has always been just a hobby for Clement, which accounts for his published output of just nine adult novels (plus two juvenile novels, only one of them science fiction) and fewer than thirty stories, over a period of forty years. His other spare-time activities include painting and serving as a scoutmaster; both of these aspects of his life, as well as his long service as a blood donor, have quite obviously been drawn upon for his fiction.

Ever since the early 1940's, the name of Hal Clement has been synonymous with stories that are soundly based upon and very much concerned with the "hard" sciences—particularly chemistry, astronomy, and engineering. After John W. Campbell, Jr., took over as

editor of *Astounding* in 1937, he tried to impose a high level of scientific accuracy that had hitherto been largely absent from science fiction. During the 1940's in particular, when *Astounding* became the genre's leading magazine, Clement's stories were acclaimed as the most solidly scientific. Clement himself says (in an Afterword to the 1979 collection *The Best of Hal Clement*) that he has always been very conservative in his use of science, avoiding the more dubious areas and extrapolating only from known facts. Such conservatism has restricted his field of operations, but this has not diminished the originality of his work; instead, it has made it more satisfying to the scientific purist.

Hand in hand with this conservatism has gone the notion of playing fair with his readers. Never has Clement made use of a pseudoscientific escape route (such as antigravity or time travel) to finish off a story. He has always provided sufficient clues so that scientifically acute readers can work out the endings for themselves. If this makes Clement's stories sound primarily like expositions of scientific problems, it is nothing less than the truth; all his stories pose one or more problems of a technical nature and solve them by means of the information given and the application of well-known scientific laws. His novels are all aggregations of such problems.

The problems may consist of simple exercises in physics, such as in the story "Dust Rag" (1956). In this story two early explorers on the Moon walk into an area where fine, electrically charged dust particles are suspended just above the surface by electrical repulsion. Some of the particles are attracted to the helmet faceplates of both men, so that they cannot see anything. They are effectively blind, and too far from their base (a) to ask for help over space suit radios; (b) to walk back to base blind; or (c) for any help to reach them before their air runs out. A damp rag would clear the faceplates in no time, but what is really needed is something to alter the faceplates' electrical charge so that they will repel the particles. After some discussion and a couple of failed attempts, they hit upon the easy and obvious answer—at least it is obvious *after* the event.

In "Technical Error" (1943) the problem for a group of stranded humans to work out is the operation of an alien spacecraft; their findings demonstrate that many things we regard as logical are not necessarily so to alien technical designers.

Sometimes the problems amount to a study in scientific detection; *Needle* (1950) and its sequel, *Through the Eye of a Needle* (1978), are essentially science fiction detective novels, the first concerning an alien policeman's search for a fugitive (also alien), and the second concerning the same policeman's search for others of his own kind. In *Needle* the policeman is a sentient being who comes to Earth by spaceship, in hot pursuit of his quarry. Both aliens are small (weighing about four pounds), amorphous, and jellylike; and both need to live inside larger host creatures, in symbiosis with them. Their ships crashland into the sea very close to a small island in the Pacific. The Hunter (as the alien policeman is known) uses a shark as a host just long enough to get ashore, where he quite easily inserts himself into a human host.

There are a number of preliminary problems before the search for the criminal can begin, because the Hunter's host is a fourteen-year-old boy who is soon to return to school in the United States. Since the Hunter is not able to control his symbiont (one of Clement's few scientific errors is to mistakenly use the nonexistent term "symbiote" instead of "symbiont" in *Needle*, although this is cor-

rected in the sequel), the first problem is obviously to establish communication. First contact between humans and aliens is one of Clement's favorite, recurrent themes. In *Needle* the Hunter's early attempts at communication and their psychological effects on his young host, Bob Kinnaird, are memorably if not entirely convincingly described. Initially the problem of communication is solved by the Hunter's forming letters across the surface of his host's eyeballs; by the time of *Through the Eye of a Needle*, the Hunter has learned to create a "voice" for himself by manipulating Bob's inner ear. Bob's replies are in subvocal speech.

Once the preliminary problems have been solved and Bob and the Hunter are back on the island, they try to find some means of identifying the host inhabited by the criminal. It is interesting that this problem—how to locate one of the aliens that is inside a host without entering the host and searching la-

Hal Clement (Harry Clement Stubbs) in 1982.
PHOTO BY JAY KAY KLEIN

boriously—is never solved in either of the books. Instead, the search concentrates on collecting circumstantial evidence, particularly evidence connected with the fact that an alien symbiont will automatically patch any injuries sustained by its host, often so quickly that the host will not even notice the injuries. This leads to carelessness on the part of the host and a tendency to get into dangerous habits. Also, a blood test ought to reveal that a host possesses very "clean," bacteria-free blood.

In the sequel, set eight years later when Bob is age twenty-two, the major problem is for Bob and the Hunter to find the Hunter's compatriots, who are believed to have come to Earth in search of him. This is important because Bob is suffering from a debilitating illness, which is caused by his lengthy symbiosis, likely to kill him. (If the symbiosis were to end, he would die even sooner.) The search is partly a search for the two spaceship wrecks, so that a message may be left attached to one of them; and because the story is set prior to scuba diving (about 1954), there are various technical diving problems to be overcome. In fact, Clement seems to delight in presenting and solving relatively minor technological problems that further the plots of his novels very little but occupy many pages: the worst example of this is in *Star Light* (1971), in which the problem is to de-ice a vehicle on an alien planet.

This brings us almost too neatly to what many readers would regard as the most important feature of Clement's work—his alien environments. These environments are principally alien planets—highly original creations with the scientific details calculated very carefully—although there are three notable exceptions that will be mentioned first. In *Iceworld* (1953) the alien world is Earth—as seen from the perspective of a race of beings who regard 500°C as a normal living temperature and who breathe gaseous sulfur. In *Ocean on Top* (1973) the environment is an ocean-bed community of humans, surgically adapted to be able to "breathe" a wonderful liquid that fills their living and working quar-

ters. These people swim around in the liquid, and it provides their lungs with oxygen. Most recently, in *The Nitrogen Fix* (1980), the alien world is a polluted Earth a few thousand years in the future, when all atmospheric oxygen has been absorbed into nitrogen compounds, so that mankind (at a lower technological level than today) must live in airtight cities and carry oxygen cylinders when venturing outside.

What links all of Clement's environmental settings, whether they are on Earth or on extrasolar worlds, is that they are of primary importance to both the author and the novel. To Clement the background is never just a throwaway idea or a back cloth, as it might be to many other science fiction authors. It has always been worked out with great attention to scientific detail. Not only have the planet's chemistry, biological systems, evolution, geology, and weather systems been plausibly calculated, but most of this detail is incorporated into the story, regardless of whether it arises naturally in the course of the plot. One cannot blame Clement for this, since he is so obviously proud of his planetary creations and since many of his readers look forward to such detail. The result is that in most of Clement's books the environment is the hero.

It is not a coincidence that the best-loved of Clement's novels, *Mission of Gravity* (1954), features his most original and bizarrely shaped planet, Mesklin. A full description of the planet (and of the fun the author had in designing it) is given in his article "Whirligig World," which appeared in *Astounding* for June 1953, while the novel was being serialized in that same magazine, and is reprinted in the Ballantine/Del Rey paperback and Gregg Press hardcover editions of *Mission of Gravity*. Mesklin is a particularly oblate spheroid, with an equatorial diameter about two and a half times its polar diameter. With its extensive ring system, the planet bears more than a passing resemblance to a fried egg. It is a very massive world, 4,800 times as massive as Earth and 16 times as massive as Jupiter; Mesklin rotates on its own axis in about eighteen minutes. The overall result of this is

Mesklin's most memorable feature—a gravity varying from 3 g at the equator to about 700 g at the poles.

Human scientists have landed an experimental rocket at its "south pole," but they cannot recover it. They land at the equator and persuade a local sentient race to do the job of recovery for them. As the aliens go off on their long journey to find the rocket, the increasing effects of high gravity are examined. Every other aspect of Mesklin is subservient to or is determined by the differing gravities, particularly the behavior patterns of its various native races. Although the plot purports to follow the group of intelligent Mesklinites as they travel toward the south pole, much of the action is merely an excuse for Clement to display every detail of his fascinating world.

The impression that the reader is being lectured on the finer points of planetary ecology comes across even more strongly in *Cycle of Fire* (1957). Here the alien environment is more complex than the one in *Mission of Gravity* and, as far as this writer is concerned, is more interesting. The planet Abyormen has an odd orbit in a binary star system that consists of a red giant and a white dwarf. Abyormen is subject to a lengthy cycle of temperature variation: a "cool" period of about forty Earth years, when the temperature is roughly Earth-normal, alternates with a "hot" period about half as long, when the temperature is hundreds of degrees higher.

The major result of this is that two very different types of life have evolved on Abyormen. Each is largely confined to its own time slot but lies dormant within the genes of the other kind during the temperature period that it cannot bear. At the changeover points there is a fairly rapid death, breakdown, and rebirth process. Perhaps fortuitously, there are intelligent species of both "cool" and "hot" types that are in limited communication with each other. Each species is able to preserve its respective civilization and store of knowledge during the inimical period of the cycle, although the majority of each population must die at the changeover time.

Clement shows only the "cool" period life forms, but he describes in great detail the investigation by a human scientific team that leads to an understanding of the true state of affairs on Abyormen. About two-thirds of the way through the book, the plot comes to a halt. The rest of the novel is taken up with the search for and explanation of the bipartite ecology, presented mostly in lecture and dialogue form. Even so, such is Clement's enthusiasm for his planetary creation that he maintains reader interest throughout.

The planet Tenebra, in *Close to Critical* (1964), is less peculiar than Mesklin or Abyormen, but it is no less fascinating as an exercise in extraterrestrial chemistry. Tenebra has a relatively high gravity (3 g) and an extremely high surface pressure (800 atmospheres). The daytime temperature is around 380°C. This temperature-pressure combination means that the atmosphere is always close to the critical temperature of water, which is continually changing into steam and back again. Its diurnal cycle is about 200 hours and quite complex—for example, large, slow-moving raindrops falling at night considerably raise the "sea" level (the "sea" of Tenebra is dilute sulfuric acid) and alter the shape of the coastline. While the plot concerns an attempt by humans in orbit to get some of the planet's sentient aliens to help repair a grounded experimental bathyscaphe that has two children (one human, one alien) aboard, it is little more than an excuse for a guided tour of Tenebra's peculiarities.

In *Star Light* (1971), the sequel to *Mission of Gravity*, the action is not set on Mesklin, but on another high-gravity planet, Dhrawn, which is being explored by Mesklinites under the remote direction of orbiting humans. Dhrawn is a relatively bland world compared with those just described. Its 40 g gravity and low temperature are no problem for the Mesklinites, although its atmosphere does contain some oxygen, which is poisonous to them. (They wear airsuits because of this.) The planet has an extremely long rotational period (1,500 hours), but this is of little consequence because its sun is dim and has only a minor effect on the surface temperature or illumination. There is a rather odd weather pattern, with sudden thaws due to eutectic effects, and the planet possesses two surface "hot spots" at points where subterranean fusion reactions are apparently taking place. There are occasional mutterings—by one of the characters and by Clement in narration—to the effect that Dhrawn might even be classifiable as a star rather than a planet, although such questions are left unanswered. Clement concentrates on Mesklinite psychology and deviousness rather than on the planetary environment.

While some authors populate their alien worlds with human colonists or with machines, creating extraterrestrial environments that resemble a slightly futuristic Western frontier, Clement has always taken care to supply his worlds with a variety of alien creatures. As one might expect of a scientist, he has not fallen into the trap of making his sentient extraterrestrials completely human in physiological terms except for green skin or a pair of pointed ears. He has even avoided the common mistake of giving aliens pentadactyl limbs—which have evolved only once on Earth and would not evolve separately on an alien world except by the greatest of coincidences.

Clement's aliens usually are highly original creations—with their body chemistry and position in the local food chain not only worked out but made abundantly clear—operating in their own planetary environment without much technological expertise. There is often some interaction with visiting humans, and first-contact situations are described in a number of novels and stories. A very noticeable shortcoming is that almost all of Clement's aliens are very human in psychological and social terms. For example, they seem to make the same assumptions and conclusions as humans, and to share our conceptions of right and wrong and of morality and fair play. Also, whenever alien family life is mentioned (which is not often), there is usually monogamous marriage between members of two different sexes.

The Hunter, in *Needle* and *Through the Eye of a Needle*, is the sort of green blob of jelly that has, since 1950, become a science fiction cliché. His small size would seem to preclude advanced intelligence, but Clement overcomes this objection by mentioning that the Hunter's cells are smaller and more tightly packed than those in Earth creatures. Of course, the Hunter is never shown on his home world; and apart from a brief opening scene in his spaceship (in *Needle*), he has to survive without any of his own technology or access to records. The Hunter is generally thought of as a male, although no explanation is given of the sexual or social organization of the species. His rigid moral code—as, for example, concerning the punishment of wrongdoers and the responsibilities of a symbiont toward a host—seems rather old-fashioned and out of place.

In *The Nitrogen Fix* there is Bones, an alien similar to the Hunter insofar as that it has come to Earth by a spacecraft and is operating without any technological support. Bones is an extremely original life form, being vaguely dolphinlike (it is most at home in water) but possessing four tentacular "legs" upon which it can move speedily on land. In this walking stance it is a foot or so taller than a human, although others of its species are smaller. It has several lesser tentacles that can be extended from close to its head and used for manipulatory purposes. Its race is variously termed Natives, Animals, and Invaders by humans, although it thinks of itself as an Observer. Perhaps a few hundred of these creatures are on Earth, although they think of themselves as "units" of the same entity, and any two that meet will immediately exchange memory information in a brief, ecstatic intertwining. Bones, at least, has been able to communicate with a family of humans—by sign language, since Bones cannot speak, although it can understand spoken words. It does not breathe, and reproduces asexually by budding.

Without a doubt the most popular of Clement's aliens are the Mesklinites. From the very first chapter of *Mission of Gravity*, their sly intelligence and ability to overcome fear enliven the novel and have helped to make it a favorite. Such popular acclaim is perhaps surprising in view of the Mesklinites' caterpillar-like appearance. They are about fifteen inches in length and two inches wide, with eighteen pairs of legs and two pairs of powerful pincers. Their bodies are extremely tough, and they are perfectly designed for high-gravity life, being quite used to several hundred g. They are hydrogen-breathers. All the Mesklinites who feature in *Mission of Gravity* and *Star Light* are given the male pronoun; nothing is revealed of their sexual arrangements or social structures. Those encountered in *Mission of Gravity* form a ship's crew, under the command of Barlennan, on a fairly lengthy trading voyage. Their intelligence seems close to that of humans, and many of their concepts are little different from ours. Their determination to acquire technological secrets from humans, yet to retain their independence, helps one to picture them as an emerging third world nation rather than as alien beings.

Cycle of Fire is notable for an extremely convincing first-contact scene between the human youth, Nils Kruger, and the small humanoid alien, Dar Lang Ahn. This followed several uninspired first-contact descriptions in *Needle*, *Iceworld*, and such stories as "Impediment" (1942). In *Close to Critical* there is an extremely interesting example of first contact being sidestepped, or at least of the onus of it being shifted. A human-controlled robot steals some eggs of the local intelligent life form (which apparently does have two sexes, although the humans are unable to distinguish between them) and rears the offspring, teaching them English and some basic skills. These creatures then make contact with the "real" aliens—who probably include their parents. These adult aliens are up to nine feet tall and are covered with tough scales. They have eight limbs, normally walking on two and carrying weapons in another four.

While Clement concentrates on scientific accuracy and on alien creatures and conditions, his successes in these areas are generally achieved at the expense of characteriza-

tion and plotting. There are no fully rounded human characters in Clement's work. Most of the adult males (usually some form of scientist or technician) are interchangeable, never really coming alive. Even in a novel presented in the first person (such as *Ocean on Top*), the unnamed narrator is extremely unsatisfactory as a person. Adult females are notable only for their scarcity; in all of Clement's work, only three adult female characters are more than "wallpaper": Easy Hoffman in *Star Light*, Marie in *Ocean on Top*, and Kahvi in *The Nitrogen Fix*.

More memorable are Clement's juvenile characters. In most of his novels, one or more of the major characters is aged seventeen or younger. Bob Kinnaird is fourteen in *Needle*, thirteen-year-old Roger Wing is arguably the most important human character in *Iceworld*, Nils Kruger in *Cycle of Fire* is a sixteen-year-old space cadet, Easy Rich (aged twelve; later to become Easy Hoffman) is by far the most memorable person in *Close to Critical*, her son Benj is only seventeen when he plays a major part in *Star Light*, and a group of dissident teen-agers constitutes an important plot element in *The Nitrogen Fix*. In addition Clement has written two admittedly juvenile novels with young protagonists, *The Ranger Boys in Space* (1956) and the historical novel *Left of Africa* (1976). Presumably he concentrates on juvenile characters because, being a teacher and scoutmaster, he feels familiar with them. Yet his juvenile characters tend to be too mature for their years. This is particularly true of Easy Rich and Nils Kruger. Likewise, Clement's aliens are fascinating as aliens but not as developed characters.

The main problem with his characterization is an unwillingness (or inability) to provide sufficient emotional content. Love, hatred, desire, anger, and greed are not to be found in any of his characters, who generally proceed with calmness and self-restraint at all times. Clement seems to avoid any mention of the wives and families of his male characters, nor do the latter seem to object to spending months or years away from home, visiting or orbiting alien worlds. Young men like Nils

Kruger, Benj Hoffman, and the twenty-two-year-old Bob Kinnaird of *Through the Eye of a Needle* do not appear to think of women at all. There is a much greater emotional content to *The Nitrogen Fix*, Clement's most recent novel, which gives one hope of better things to come. Here, for the very first time, Clement describes a typical nuclear family, Earrin, Kahvi, and their five-year-old daughter Danna. At times Kahvi shows great concern for the safety of her husband and her daughter. In other places there is hysteria on the part of humans who encounter Bones. It is more a novel of people than of planetary conditions. This is not unusual in science fiction, but it is unusual in Clement's science fiction.

The plotting of most of Clement's works is best described as straightforward. Complexity occurs only in the form of excessive minor detail (particularly noticeable in *Star Light*). He seems unable to eliminate unnecessary scenes or repetitive explanations, giving a blow-by-blow account of all comings and goings. Some episodes have obviously been inserted solely to show off a particular aspect of the alien environment; an example is the canoe episode in *Mission of Gravity*. In other places sections have been artificially inserted to make the plot come out right, such as the storm and boat wreck close to the end of *Through the Eye of a Needle*. Again, *The Nitrogen Fix* is an improvement, its plotting being slick and uncontrived despite more complexity than Clement has previously attempted.

An unfortunate aspect of Clement's writing is its moral tone. Almost all of his human and alien characters seem to recognize a strict code of behavior reminiscent of Victorian England. This shows itself in honesty, loyalty, a total absence of sexual awareness, and the provision of a happy ending. Granted, the Mesklinites are deceitful, but this stems from worthy motives of independence and self-determination. Only in *The Nitrogen Fix* are Clement's moral strictures acknowledged as part of society.

In the 1940's, when Clement's first stories appeared in *Astounding*, the literary standards of the science fiction pulp magazines were generally low. In such circumstances Clement could not help but be considered above average right from the start, in spite of his not being a natural writer. His style and the degree of his control over words developed during the first ten years of his writing career. There is a certain clumsiness evident in his early short stories as well as in both *Needle* and *Iceworld*, a clumsiness that has been partially eliminated in his later work. Even so, the improvements in his style and technique reached a plateau in the early 1950's, remaining there while his contemporaries (such as Robert A. Heinlein and Arthur C. Clarke) surpassed him and while younger writers with greater talent entered the field. Only in the late 1970's has Clement's writing begun to improve again, although not consistently.

Even though most of his novels are in print, Hal Clement is a rather neglected writer. His reputation as perhaps the best of the hard-science authors of science fiction has been lost to writers such as Larry Niven. Clement's recent novels have not been eagerly anticipated by very many readers. It is significant that he has never won any of science fiction's major awards. It may be that through more novels of the caliber of *The Nitrogen Fix*, he can recapture the position of importance that he held during the 1950's.

Selected Bibliography

WORKS OF HAL CLEMENT

Needle. Garden City, N.Y.: Doubleday, 1950. Published as *From Outer Space*. New York: Avon Books, 1957. London: Victor Gollancz, 1961.
Iceworld. New York: Gnome Press, 1953.
Mission of Gravity. Garden City, N.Y.: Doubleday, 1954. London: Robert Hale, 1955. Reprinted Boston: Gregg Press, 1978, with addition of essay "Whirligig World" (1953) on the genesis of the novel.
The Ranger Boys in Space. Boston: L. C. Page, 1956. (Juvenile novel.)
Cycle of Fire. New York: Ballantine Books, 1957.
Close to Critical. New York: Ballantine Books, 1964. London: Victor Gollancz, 1964.

Natives of Space. New York: Ballantine Books, 1965. (Collection: includes "Impediment" and "Technical Error.")

Small Changes. Garden City, N.Y.: Doubleday, 1969. Published as *Space Lash.* New York: Dell, 1969. (Short story collection: includes "Dust Rag.")

First Flights to the Moon. Garden City, N.Y.: Doubleday, 1970. (Thematic anthology, edited by Clement, containing stories by other authors.)

Star Light. New York: Ballantine Books, 1971.

Ocean on Top. New York: DAW, 1973.

"The Creation of Imaginary Beings." In *Science Fiction, Today and Tomorrow*, edited by Reginald Bretnor. New York: Harper and Row, 1974.

"Hard Sciences and Tough Technologies." In *The Craft of Science Fiction*, edited by Reginald Bretnor. New York: Harper and Row, 1976.

Through the Eye of a Needle. New York: Ballantine Books, 1978.

The Best of Hal Clement. New York: Ballantine Books, 1979. With an Afterword by the author. (Short story collection.)

The Nitrogen Fix. New York: Ace Books, 1980.

Still River. New York: Ballantine, 1987.

CRITICAL AND BIOGRAPHICAL STUDIES

Benson, Gordon, Jr. *Hal Clement (Harry Clement Stubbs).* Albuquerque, N. Mex.: Galactic Central, 1985.

Fitzgibbons, Tim. "Interview: Hal Clement." *Thrust* (Winter 1988): 9–11.

Hassler, Donald M. *Hal Clement.* Mercer Island, Wash.: Starmont, 1982.

———. "The Irony in Hal Clement's World Building." In *Science Fiction Dialogues.* Edited by Gary Wolfe. Chicago: Academy Chicago, 1982.

———. "Science at the Crossroads in Hal Clement's *The Nitrogen Fix.*" In *Critical Encounters II: Writers and Themes in Science Fiction.* Edited by Tom Staicar. New York: Ungar, 1982.

Trunick, Perry A. "Hal Clement's Aliens: Bridging the Gap." *Foundation* (Summer 1986): 10–21.

—CHRIS MORGAN

RICHARD COWPER

(b. 1926)

HIS NAME IS not Richard Cowper, and science fiction has never been his life. He was born into a complex literary family linked to the Bloomsbury Group. He served in World War II; he studied English literature after his discharge; and he taught for nearly twenty years in private schools. His first novels had nothing to do with science fiction; and in the mid-1980's, when he felt he had said his piece as an author of works in the fields of the fantastic, he retired with his wife to Brighton, where he lives under his real name and restores furniture for the pleasure of doing so.

In his actual career as a science fiction author, a career that lasted less than twenty years, Richard Cowper significantly declined to behave according to the pattern most of his fellow science fiction writers tended to follow. He was never a fan. He did not associate with science fiction writers before he published his first genre book. He came to science fiction, at the age of forty, after writing four nongenre novels (three of them were published before his first science fiction novel; one appeared later). He attended only one science fiction convention over the course of his career. His finest single novel, *The Twilight of Briareus* (1974), is a slyly somber elegy for a dying Western world; and his most famous sequence, the Corlay books, more closely resembles Richard Jefferies' *After London, or Wild England* (1885) than any model familiar to most contemporary readers. None of his work was ever first published in paperback. There is little violent action in any of his stories. His novels are set in England, never the United States, and none is set in space. There are few inventions in his work, and those that appear are described either very distantly or without competence. And if one of his very similar protagonists happens to have been responsible for an invention or breakthrough, it is quite likely that he will be persuaded to eschew it in order to protect the world from its consequences. He is witty, urbane, smooth-textured; but he has an almost donnish distaste for violence, confrontational passages, apocalyptic events—though the consequences of the latter often seep down into his narratives.

But he is a compulsive storyteller. It is this last element that may explain his enduring popularity in the British science fiction world. He violates almost every shibboleth of modern science fiction—certainly every shibboleth of modern American science fiction, whose action-oriented plot lines, and triumphalist engagedness in the worlds it describes, dominated world science fiction until fairly recently—but he does so with impunity. It may be that in his life and in his work he represents the proof, if any were needed, that science fiction as it has evolved over the past century has become universally instrumental for those who wish to take the world itself as their object of study, or for those, such as Cowper, whose fundamental subject (and venue) is one small part of the whole world: England.

John Middleton Murry, Jr., was born on 7 May 1926, in Bridport, Dorset, to the author and critic John Middleton Murry. His father's first wife, Katherine Mansfield, died of tuberculosis, as did his second wife, his son's mother. In Murry Jr.'s two volumes of autobiography—*One Hand Clapping: A Memoir of Childhood* (1975) and *Shadows on the Grass* (1977), both as by Colin Middleton Murry—he describes a childhood and young adulthood of acute interest and emotional turmoil. It was a typical childhood for a young boy in England whose parents were intellectual, often broke, deeply implicated with their peers, experimental, and religious. English culture between the two World Wars may have been superficially philistine, smug, and repressive, but—within the interstices of that surface culture and supported by the vastly intricate networks of association and obligation and intrigue afforded by a class society in a state of constant change—very remarkable and deeply eccentric lives were led. And many wounded children escaped the pressure cooker of this kind of life into shadowy adulthood, into the exigencies of World War II, into the postwar comedown, when austerity hit and the old subversive richness of culture began to thin.

Murry identifies himself as one of this cohort. He backed away from the chaos (and perhaps some of the richness) of his overenriched childhood into military service (1944–1947) and into the sane profession of teaching. He was English Master at Whittinghame College in Brighton from 1952 to 1967 and served as the head of the English Department at Atlantic World College, Llantwit-Major, in Glamorgan, from 1967 to 1970. He married Ruth Jezierski in 1950, and they remain married; they have two daughters. Under the name Colin Murry, he soon published his first novel, *The Golden Valley* (1958). Neither it nor its three modestly successful successors—not even the deceptively titled *Recollections of a Ghost* (1960)—has any genre interest. It was not until 1967 that he reinvented himself as Richard Cowper, and began, out of the blue, to publish science fiction.

Although his specific knowledge of the instruments of science fiction lacks much detail—at least as far as the evidence of his writing demonstrates—Richard Cowper does exhibit to the full a sense of his position as a late participant in the long story of British science fiction. It is not enough, however, to note the obvious echoes in his work of earlier British writers such as John Wyndham or John Christopher, while noting at the same time the complete absence of any echo of any American writer at all. The echoes of Wyndham and Christopher are inevitable, and any resemblance between his work and the work of his American contemporaries seems accidental, a consequence of the fact that both versions of the genre—both instrumentalities—derive from the same shared source. Until around the end of World War I, after all, British and American science fiction were remarkably similar; their differences were regional, not fundamental.

The principal influence upon Richard Cowper as a science fiction writer wrote his most influential work long before the differences between the two regions became a schism. All Cowper's work hearkens back, directly or indirectly, to H. G. Wells, the man who invented modern science fiction and whose "children" on both sides of the Atlantic continue to compose works in a genre that still bears his palpable imprint. There were, however, from the first, obvious though superficial differences in how he was appreciated. In Britain, H. G. Wells's scientific romances were always understood and studied fruitfully as texts of great literary and cultural complexity. They were seen as speaking to and for classes of British society previously unenfranchised. They were understood as subversive. They incorporated meditations on themes suggested by Charles Darwin's exposition of some of the laws governing the evolution of species. They contained a leaven of romantic derring-do. They were dreadful warning tales in the tradition of the Future War novels so extraordinarily popular in Great Britain from about 1870 until about 1914. They envisioned Britain as a dubiously defensible island. They presented informed and sensibly couched speculations about future developments and inventions in the world, though these speculations were increasingly subordinated to political arguments in general. And they worked this material into a series of aesthetically shapely texts, models for speculation that have dominated British science fiction ever since. (Americans treated Wells less complexly. His social programs, his radicalism, and his lower class pugnacity had no shock value. His genius at the description of scientific possibilities was perhaps paramount, for he embedded that descriptive genius in stories that effectively immortalized his versions of the future. But his islander's pessimism about subjugating the future awoke little response in Americans, for whom the future was a frontier to be penetrated. Wells lies beneath American science fiction, but he is no longer constantly palpable as a father.)

Richard Cowper is, in this understanding, profoundly Wellsian, no more so perhaps than for two additional features: his almost invariable choice of setting, which is southern England and which he shares with Wells, and the sense he conveys that his protagonists are enmeshed in a numbing muddle of circumstance, that—as in *almost* all of Wells's novels—the so-called advanced civilization, whose heart was southern England, must be escaped from.

For the purposes of useful comparison, however, there are also some significant differences between Wells and Cowper. Cowper is the troubled representative of a class in decline, while Wells was a spokesman for new arrivals on the scene. Cowper lives in an island kingdom whose days of power have passed, a land constantly enmeshed and stung by signs of its own belittlement, while Wells was born into a British Empire upon whose domains the sun never set. Unsurprisingly, therefore, the violent reversals of circumstance typical of the more didactic Wells novel are, half a century later, radically muted and personalized. Cowper's chamber dramas, and intimate transcendental moments, could almost be seen as looking back elegiacally upon Wells's time of opportunity, when it was possible to conceive, without irony, of the positive transformation of the world. Wells

Richard Cowper. COURTESY OF *LOCUS* MAGAZINE

was occasionally sarcastic; Cowper's tone is almost invariably one of a recessed but waspish irony.

Wells had no significant father figure to challenge him. Cowper not only had H. G. Wells for a father, but he had always before him the example of a father figure who could legitimately sound as though he had not only created the turf but owned it, a man who was in a historical position to write stories whose protagonists are successful in this world and the next. That naive, "manly" time, for Cowper, had long passed. His protagonists, in order to be able to act in a Wellsian fashion—that is, for them to be able to leap out of the muddle of circumstance into a cleaner and more suitable world—must transcend that muddle *privately*. It is for that reason, perhaps, that so many of them have extrasensory powers of one sort or another—the paranormal is one region of the fantastic Wells never explored—because extrasensory powers (or ESP) are personal gifts. They can be explored and utilized in silence, exile, and cunning.

The sense that life in present-day England is a trap appears as an ironized leitmotif throughout Cowper's work, nowhere perhaps more clearly than in the first novel he published under his new name. *Breakthrough* (1967) is set in southern England, at a time more or less in the present or the near future. Its protagonist, who narrates his own adventures like many of Wells's characters, is a typical Cowper spokesman. (Cowper speaks through no female protagonists.) Jimmy Haverell is slightly ineffectual, young, personable, decent, and sexually liberated and is involved one way or another in education and/or research.

After taking part in some parapsychological experiments with a colleague at Hampton University, where he has a position, Haverell discovers that he has become strangely attuned to a young woman named Rachel. At the same time, he begins to have deeply unsettling dreams in which the world of John Keats's *Hyperion* (1878) serves as a setting for some drama, whose details he cannot grasp, in which he is somehow engaged upon scenes of great import and intolerable loss. The everyday world turns grayish, muggy, but strangely insubstantial. Rachel, it turns out, shares these dreams, but more vividly than Haverell so vividly that she becomes amnesiacal as a psychic mechanism to avoid burnout.

After a certain amount of supererogatory action, the climax approaches. Haverell and Rachel shed the muddle of lives trapped in a declining world, discovering as they do so that they are avatars of two godlike alien visitors to Earth, the male a Prometheus figure, the female an Earth Mother; they had become separated aeons earlier. Now they are together. They enter the world of *Hyperion* and have sex; she becomes pregnant. Their child will combine their virtues and talents and may (or may not: Cowper does not assert a conclusion) provide Earth with an evolutionary solution to our otherwise insoluble problems. The evolved superchild is a trope very dear to the hearts of British writers of scientific romances—its origin lies not in Wells's own work, for his "Men Like Gods" are self-created evolutionary figures from a far future, but from his disciple J. D. Beresford's *The Hampdenshire Wonder* (1911)—and Cow-

per's climax clearly adumbrates the conclusions of two later British scientific romances, Arthur C. Clarke's *2001: A Space Odyssey* (1968) and Michael Moorcock's *The Final Programme* (1968). When he wrote *Hyperion* (1989), the American science fiction writer Dan Simmons may also have been aware of Cowper (*Breakthrough* had been published in the United States in 1969), and in that book a superchild does emerge from suspiciously similar loins; but the intricately expansive space-operatic galaxy and plotting of that novel are purely and richly American.

What is peculiarly Cowperesque in *Breakthrough* is the muteness of its transcendental climax. Cowper writes as Wells might have written had Wells had the prescience in 1900 to know that his dreams of rational breakthrough into a new world were doomed by the muddle of the world. Indeed, later Wells novels such as *Christina Alberta's Father* (1925) or *The Bulpington of Bulp* (1933) or *The Holy Terror* (1939), in the frustrations they expose, are perhaps the novels of the master closest to Cowper's chastened mode. It might even be said that Richard Cowper is the only science fiction author who might reasonably remind his readers of the H. G. Wells after 1920.

Cowper's next novel, *Phoenix* (1968), also displaces what in American science fiction would have been the climax of the tale, and here too it is via a pregnancy. Several hundred years hence, in a world very much like contemporary England, a young man finds himself entangled in mundane events and chooses to escape muddle by buying himself three years of suspended animation. As usual, something goes wrong. He sleeps for fifteen centuries, and *Phoenix* becomes a Sleeper Awakes novel (a term derived, of course, from Wells's *The Sleeper Awakes* [1899]). The new England is pastoral and superstitious of all things scientific but all in all rather welcoming. The protagonist finds a patron, a young woman who shares his extrasensory perceptions, and she soon becomes pregnant. They leave for Greece, where their child may (or may not) serve ultimately as an engine of change.

In *Domino* (1971), a similar dynamic of frustration and transcendence is replayed, though in different terms. A young man, haunted by strange dreams from an early age, goes to a seance, where he discovers that he is the essentially passive center of a vast conflict between two versions of the future, who call themselves the Guardians and the Unmanifest. The Guardians represent a future to be caused by his soon-to-unfold invention of a genetic tool through which human beings can be controlled by those of a totalitarian bent. The Unmanifest beg for that future to be averted. In the end, unlike most American science fiction heroes, he decides to defer making his invention. The Guardians disappear. The elegiac, sideways modeling of the universe and of the kinds of action appropriate to that universe continues though most of Cowper's career; his skill increases, but the basic dynamic never changes at heart: the world is in bondage, and the only reliable escape is to transcend that world, either through being material or witness to its end or through literal transcendence. For American writers, this is a dynamic more appropriate to fantasy than to science fiction. It is a sign of the resigned maturity of British science fiction—and its essential wariness about the efficacy of willed, enforced change—that private solutions for the world's woe are also deemed to be potentially science fiction.

Novels such as *Kuldesak* (1972), *Clone* (1972), *Time Out of Mind* (1973), and *Worlds Apart* (1974) continue the pattern. *Kuldesak* is perhaps the most exuberant, and American, of all Cowper's books, featuring a pocket universe (a world that seems to be the entire universe, but that turns out to be a restricted part of the real world) on the American model and a conceptual breakthrough that opens its protagonist's eyes to the true and larger world. But the old dynamic provides the underlying tone all the same. All of humanity lives in giant interconnected warrens far beneath the surface of the world, which is unknown or forgotten territory. A young man has a psycho-

sensitive pet who penetrates through the Dead Levels—which God, the computer who runs the underground world, had depopulated in order to balance resources—and upward into the Outdoors, where it finds nonhuman visitors arriving from another planet. The pet prevails upon its young master to make the same trip. He discovers the new world, along with a woman who will almost certainly bear his child, where he is helped by the aliens and friendly robots to fend off God until he can be repaired. Afterward, they will enter a pastoral paradise, which they have earned.

The young protagonist of *Time Out of Mind* more visibly resembles Cowper's early heroes, though even the active protagonist of *Kuldesak* is induced into action by others. In this novel, as in *Domino*, the protagonist is haunted by conflicting forces from the future; meets and sleeps with a young woman with telekinetic powers; reluctantly takes part in opposing Colonel Magobion, who hopes to rule the world by exploiting the powers of the young woman and others of her ilk (all of whom inhabit a drugged paradise as a side effect of the inducing of their ESP capacities); and eventually helps keep the world from turning wrong.

All of Cowper's novels, despite the compulsive ingenuity of their telling and regardless of the occasional variety of their settings, seem at heart to be one book. That book seems to be *The Twilight of Briareus*, Cowper's longest single novel and his most sustained. It is one of the classic titles of British science fiction. Along with the Corlay books, it will continue to be read. Its characters are paradigms of the characters Cowper normally produces, but they are clearer and more substantial. The narrative has some of the same ellipses as those that stain with reticence his other works, but here every plot turn is pointed and carefully conceived. The telling of the tale—especially perhaps the gravely serene descriptions of England after the catastrophe, when snow covers the land—has an almost religious intensity.

A few years into the future, astronomers register that the star Briareus Delta has gone nova and that vast waves of radiation will swamp Earth. This happens. The climate is radically affected, first by hurricanes, then by a decrease in temperature worldwide. What only slowly becomes evident is that a race of disembodied spirits has surfed the wave of radiation and has also arrived on Earth. This race wishes to come into communion with humans and to offer a kind of impersonal self-transcending godhood; but the response of Homo sapiens to this subliminal, extrasensory input is profound: as though it could not bear to be touched, as though it would be biological suicide to undergo transcendence, the human race immediately becomes sterile.

Of course this is the case. Sharpening the message of other scientific romances such as Arthur C. Clarke's *Childhood's End* (1953), *The Twilight of Briareus* suggests that Homo sapiens may well not triumph over itself, the world, or the galaxy, that Homo sapiens may need help to survive, or to become wise. This is a theme that has begun to dominate American science fiction in the last years of the twentieth century, but Cowper said it very early, and it may be that he said it best.

Cal, the protagonist of the novel is young and sensitive, like almost all of Cowper's protagonists. His sensitivity consists of two capacities: one, a dreamlike envisioning of the snowbound England to come as the changes take place; and two, a preternatural sensitivity to a large number of young women whose psychic response to the aliens' offer has been biologically positive: they alone are not sterile. Whenever Cal and one of these women meet, they feel an enormous urge to engage in sexual intercourse.

Cal is able to refrain from intercourse, but at a cost. After an interlude during which a desperate government futilely tries to force-breed the sensitive women, Cal and his non-sensitive wife painfully divorce, the climate darkens in the direction of his dreams, and he meets Margaret, who is one of his students (Cal is a normal Cowper academic). She is sensitive. They have sex. Cal's visions intensify and guide the couple northward to an isolated farming complex, where a woman named Elizabeth seems to have been expecting them.

She has been having visions of Cal. They unite sexually (Margaret has paired off with another man) under the jubilant gaze of the disembodied spirits, and she becomes pregnant. Cal has a final vision, in which he understands that—mystically—he must die in order for the new order properly to begin. In a previsioned accident, he does perish. In an epilogue, the reader sees the birth of the child, the renewed fertility of the human race, the calm Edenic pastoral world of snows that has replaced the muddle of southern England after Wells.

There is a delicacy and firmness combined about *The Twilight of Briareus* that engenders a feeling in the reader that a personal testament has been set down. Once again, but here definitely, the Cowper hero (for whom it is essentially too late) seeds a new generation and makes possible a new Land, which, Moses-like, he will never enter. This world ultimately cannot be escaped; but *Twilight* acts, far more successfully than anything else in Cowper's oeuvre, as a bridge between the secular muddle of now and the transcendental serenity of a world at peace with itself.

Though it is less intense, one later novel, *Profundis* (1979), conveys a similar emotional message through a plot superficially very different: another entangled but decent protagonist with ESP survives a cleansing holocaust and becomes a kind of Christ in a submarine. This submarine, which has also survived the holocaust, is guided about the world by dolphins. The dolphins are nearly as ethereal as the Briarean spirits of the earlier book and hope their human Christ will help keep those other humans who have also survived from re-enacting the suicidal violence to which Homo sapiens is prone. At the end there is some hope.

Cowper's greatest achievement was to come. The Corlay sequence—*The Road to Corlay* (1978), *A Dream of Kinship* (1981), and *A Tapestry of Time* (1982)—reiterates much of what has gone before in his work, but with an extraordinary freshness. It is one of a small sequence of tales that transform the fact that Britain is an island—and the connected fact that much of British science fiction dramatizes the vulnerabilities of an island race—through being constructed not as a tale of isolation and vulnerability but as an idyll: an archipelago story, in which the threatened island is translated into a necklace of pearl isles. The first of these archipelago stories, which has already been referred to, is Richard Jefferies' *After London, or Wild England* (1885); another is Christopher Priest's *A Dream of Wessex* (1977). The Corlay books are perhaps the most idyllic of these.

The sequence begins a millennium after England has been inundated by rising sea levels and has become the sort of traditional, balkanized, priest-ridden society often found in American postcatastrophe novels. But there is a peacefulness here, and a complexity of life mirrored by the intricate complexities of the new shorelines that have—as it were fractally—immensely increased the sense of the illimitable range and depth of England. In this land is born a boy who—like all of Cowper's characters—has some sort of extrasensory sensitivity to the world, which Cowper conveys admirably through his descriptions of young Tom's flute playing, and whose visions of a new religious order prove to be both threatening to the orthodoxy and redemptive to the world. The emblem his followers display is that of the White Bird of Kinship. Very soon the old order has toppled, and England is under a new sway. But we have just begun. The wisdom of the Corlay sequence does not lie alone in its archipelago setting or in the beauty of its visions. It lies also in a mature, canny, sly, sharp-tongued worldliness that Cowper has always at his grasp, though he often muffled his tongue by constructing stories whose mild-mannered protagonists—often made most articulate by voicing their "passengers'" concerns—gained their muted triumphs without having to speak out. Here it is different. As with all new faiths (Cowper implies), the glorious new faith of the White Bird of Kinship soon begins to harden into a full-blown Church; a thousand years later, the

new order has become encrusted in stone. The Kinship establishment of apparatchiks and Savonarolas (the Italian Dominican reformer of the 1400's) attempts, as always, to use the maintenance of orthodox values as a means of retaining power for themselves, as a way of absolving their own irrepressible stress. For it is always hard, at least in a novel, to keep life at bay.

So, fortunately, the sequence does not stop at stasis. Corlay does not turn into yet another vision of a muddled, repressive, claustrophobic southern England. In the final volume, a second Tom, who in a sense reincarnates the first, must learn to control the demonic side of his charismatic gift. There is a shattering of orthodoxy, a movement back to the liquid insights of the first days when the White Bird himself expressed his visions of kinship, an elegiac traversal of the archipelago that England has Edenically become; and a hint that though the cycle is not ended—for there are always those who need to trap the world in the muddle of its dead yesterdays—perhaps this time a lesson will have been learned. Like *The Twilight of Briareus*, the Corlay books are flooded with a chaste, welling joyfulness, a sense that mortal men and women may some day unencumber themselves of the world of getting and spending and live good lives bathed in new dawns.

Other aspects of Cowper's career may be briefly described. The bulk of his short stories, which cannily refract the themes of the novels, may be found in *The Custodians, and Other Stories* (1976), which contains "Piper at the Gates of Dawn," a long story that preludes *The Road to Corlay* and is incorporated into the later American edition of the novel; *The Web of the Magi, and Other Stories* (1980); and *The Tithonian Factor, and Other Stories* (1984), whose title story again articulates Cowper's abiding sense that the modern world, here seen as a victim of its own ravening technologies, constantly betrays values only attainable through transcendal escape. *Shades of Darkness* (1986), his last new work, is a ghost story of considerable merit, featuring a revenant who haunts a coastal cottage in Essex and whose relationship with the protagonist releases him from his guilty bondage to place. The protagonist also, very quietly, seems to have rediscovered the purpose of his own life. There is no touch of science fiction in the tale.

Richard Cowper is a writer who has written two autobiographies but who has not spoken of his life as an adult. That life, insofar as he might be interested in exposing it, is almost certainly to be found in his novels. There it is possible to detect the voice of a civilized man whose patience with life at the end of the twentieth century is profoundly limited. He is a man who in the end does not believe that the human race will solve its problems before it is too late. In this, he reflects H. G. Wells after 1920, when he could no longer make himself believe that reason would triumph. Cowper's whole writing career could be described as an attempt to come to terms with a world Wells despaired of. In his best work, Cowper did come to terms with that world. And then, it seems, his work done, and at peace, he stopped.

Selected Bibliography

FICTION OF RICHARD COWPER

The Golden Valley, as Colin Murry. London: Hutchinson, 1958.

Recollections of a Ghost, as Colin Murry. London: Hutchinson, 1960.

A Path to the Sea, as Colin Murry. London: Hutchinson, 1961.

Breakthrough: A Novel. London: Dobson, 1967; New York: Ballantine, 1969.

Phoenix: A Novel. London: Dobson, 1968; New York: Ballantine, 1970.

Domino: A Science Fiction Novel. London: Dobson, 1971.

Clone. London: Gollancz, 1972. New York: Doubleday, 1972.

Kuldesak. London: Gollancz, 1972; Garden City, N.Y.: Doubleday, 1972.

Private View: A Novel, as Colin Murry. London: Dobson, 1972.

Time Out of Mind. London: Gollancz, 1973; New York: Pocket Books, 1981.

The Twilight of Briareus. London: Gollancz, 1974; New York: John Day, 1974.

Worlds Apart: A Science Fiction Novel. London: Gollancz, 1974.

The Custodians, and Other Stories. London: Gollancz, 1976. (Short stories.)

The Road to Corlay. London: Gollancz, 1978; New York: Pocket Books, 1978. (U.S. edition is a collection incorporating "Piper at the Gates of Dawn.")

Profundis. London: Gollancz, 1979. New York: Pocket Books, 1981.

Out There Where the Big Ships Go. New York: Pocket Books, 1980. (Short stories.)

The Web of the Magi, and Other Stories. London: Gollancz, 1980. (Collection.)

A Dream of Kinship. London: Gollancz, 1981; New York: Pocket Books, 1982. (A sequel to *The Road to Corlay*.)

The Story of Pepita and Corindo. New Castle, Va.: Cheap Street, 1982.

A Tapestry of Time. London: Gollancz, 1982. (Second and final sequel to *The Road to Corlay*.)

The Unhappy Princess. New Castle, Va.: Cheap Street, 1982.

The Tithonian Factor, and Other Stories. London: Gollancz, 1984. (Short stories.)

The Magic Spectacles, and Other Tales. Worcester Park, Surrey, England: Kerosina, 1986. (Short stories.)

Shades of Darkness: A Novel. Worcester Park, Surrey, England: Kerosina, 1986.

NONFICTION OF RICHARD COWPER

One Hand Clapping: A Memoir of Childhood, as Colin Middleton Murry. London: Gollancz, 1975. (Autobiography.)

"The Profession of Science Fiction: X: Backwards Across the Frontier." *Foundation* (November 1975).

Shadows on the Grass, as Colin Middleton Murry. London: Gollancz, 1977. (Autobiography.)

—JOHN CLUTE

L. SPRAGUE DE CAMP

(b. 1907)

LYON SPRAGUE DE Camp was born on 27 November 1907, in New York City. He studied aeronautical engineering at the California Institute of Technology and went on to take a master's degree at Stevens Institute of Technology in New Jersey (1933). He worked until 1937 for the Inventors Foundation, Inc., giving courses on patents, and his first book, written in collaboration with A. K. Berle, was *Inventions and Their Management* (1937).

De Camp began writing fiction in the mid-1930's. His first major work was a novel written in collaboration with P. Schuyler Miller, *Genus Homo*, but it was not published until 1941, first in a magazine, nine years later as a book. After a brief period as assistant editor of a trade journal, de Camp became a full-time free-lance writer in 1937. In 1939 he married Catherine Crook, who later collaborated with him on some of his books. De Camp's interests and areas of expertise have always been various; he has written books on archaeology and the history of technology, and these subjects—together with his interest in languages—inform much of his science fiction.

De Camp first made his reputation as a key figure in establishing the tone and personality of the fantasy magazine *Unknown*, to which he contributed ten novels (five of them written in collaboration). Much of this work is humorous, and much of his science fiction is similarly characterized by its wry wit. His interest in Robert E. Howard led him to undertake many "posthumous collaborations" with that author and to continue chronicling the adventures of Howard's most famous hero, Conan, in collaboration with Bjorn Nyberg and, later, Lin Carter. He has written a great deal of sword-and-sorcery fiction on his own account, but it tends to be lighter in tone than his pastiches. He has also established a considerable reputation as a writer of historical novels set in the Greco-Roman world. He is one of the most eclectically knowledgeable writers in the field.

De Camp's first published story was "The Isolinguals" (1937), describing the chaos caused by a device that allows people to recover ancestral memories—unfortunately at the expense of their own. This was followed by "Hyperpilosity" (1938), in which people everywhere grow fur pelts and, in consequence, have to revise their aesthetic standards and social prejudices. These are very much "idea stories"—fictional essays almost as much as stories—and de Camp probably made a deeper impression with one of the articles that he wrote for John W. Campbell's *Astounding*, "Language for Time Travelers" (1938), about the problems of communication that might face time travelers. Converting his excellent ideas into workable stories and constructing plots in such a way as to make good use of his erudition were things that continued to cause de Camp problems throughout his career. A great many of his novels are merely episodic accounts of journeys whose protagonists encounter a series of strange situations. This weakness of plot structure and design sometimes results in a lack of dramatic tension.

De Camp submitted little of significance to *Astounding* during the first decade of Campbell's editorship, though there was an entertaining "Johnny Black" series about a bear with artificially augmented intelligence—including "The Command" (1938), "The Incorrigible" (1939), "The Exalted" (1940), "The Emancipated" (1940)—and a good novella about a society of the future in which the capitalist class system has crystallized into a curious neo-feudalism, "The Stolen Dormouse" (1941). It was the companion magazine to *Astounding, Unknown,* that offered better opportunities for his whimsicality. His first major work for *Unknown* was the short novel *Divide and Rule* (1939; book form, 1948), in which Earth is invaded by alien "hoppers" who have reinstituted the chivalric code as part of their program of social control. This was quickly followed by "The Gnarly Man" (1939), in which the last surviving Neanderthal man—despite having accumulated an exceptionally good education in the course of his 50,000-year career—is making his living as a "wild man" in a sideshow. In the same year, de Camp also revised a short novel by H. L. Gold entitled "None But Lucifer." It has an audacious plot in which a young American applies for a job with the Satanic hierarchy and ultimately lands the plum position.

The fiction promoted by *Unknown* was a particular kind of fantasy, which had affinities with the work of such writers as F. Anstey (pseudonym of Thomas Anstey Guthrie). Like Campbell's science fiction, *Unknown* fiction was intended to be rigorously logical, everything in the story proceeding by extrapolation from the basic premises; the difference was that whereas the premises of science fiction had to be realistic and consonant with known science, the premises of *Unknown* fantasy stories were chosen for their eccentricity or outrageousness. The application of logical extension to absurd premises was something that de Camp, a master of clever argument, was ideally suited to do. Ironically, however, *Lest Darkness Fall,* the best of all the novels that he wrote for *Unknown*—his fourth story to be published there in 1939—has acquired

a reputation as a classic of science fiction. (It appeared in book form in 1941.) De Camp, in fact, took the Campbellian prospectus much more seriously than most writers, and he was reluctant to take advantage of the conventions that offered escape routes from inconvenient confrontations with known science—for instance, his major science fiction series (Viagens Interplanetarias/Krishna) does not employ faster-than-light travel. De Camp thought that one of the conventions that belonged, strictly speaking, to fantasy and not to science fiction was time travel. Hence, in the author's view, *Lest Darkness Fall* is not really science fiction.

Lest Darkness Fall is the story of Martin Padway, who slips back through time to find himself in Rome in the sixth century. The Roman Empire has already fallen, and Italy is part of the Gothic kingdom, but Padway knows that it is about to be overrun yet again—this time by the Byzantines. The Dark Ages are about to descend on Europe, and Padway decides to do what he can to save it from this fate. Unlike the hero of Jack Williamson's *Legion of Time* (1938; book form, 1952), Padway does not know of any single crucial event on which the whole history of man might depend; instead he has to work gradually, introducing such innovations as are possible within the technological context of the day. The most important of these by far is the printing press with movable type. His attempts to interfere with the course of political history are eventually successful, but only marginally so, and he knows that the battle he has helped to win may well be of no real historical significance. By contrast, the technological innovations he has introduced—the printing press, the semaphore telegraph system, and the postal system—must profoundly affect the fortunes of civilization.

The novel is significant in two ways. First, it challenges the notion that history arises out of an essentially arbitrary series of accidents; it makes a competent show of examining the way in which technological advance is a crucial determinant of the pattern of eventful history. Second, it shows what actually can be accomplished in imaginative fiction by the coupling of sound background knowledge with competent logical thought. Its basic thesis may remain arguable—though technological determinism has few opponents in the science fiction field—but in the display of that thesis it is a *tour de force*. Its example has been too infrequently followed.

In 1940 de Camp formed a literary partnership with Fletcher Pratt (1877–1956), whom he had met the previous year. Pratt had published some science fiction in the early pulps and had translated a good deal of fiction from French and German for Hugo Gernsback, but had been inactive for some time as a pulp writer. Both Pratt and de Camp, apparently, thrived on collaboration. Pratt's best work for Gernsback had been done in collaboration with various others (most notably Laurence Manning), and de Camp's collaboration with Miller, *Genus Homo*, is a fine "time-slip" story in which the passengers on a bus awake from suspended animation to find various species of intelligent primates contending for dominion of a world from which man has disappeared.

The first fruit of the de Camp/Pratt collaboration was "The Roaring Trumpet" (1940), a fantasy in which a psychologist named Harold Shea, with the aid of the arcane theory of "paraphysics," sets off into the infinite spectrum of possible worlds in search of the mythical Ireland of Cuchulinn and Queen Maev, but ends up in the world of the Norse gods instead. It is Fimbulwinter, Ragnarök is drawing near, and Shea has to live on his wits—which he contrives to do with spectacular and hilarious success. The story became the first of a classic series. The second story, "The Mathematics of Magic" (1940), is set in the world of Spenser's *Faerie Queene*. The two stories were revised and combined to form *The Incomplete Enchanter* (1941). In the third story—the full-length novel *The Castle of Iron* (1941; book form, 1950)—Shea and his companions find themselves in the world of Ariosto's *Orlando Furioso*. In "Wall of Serpents" (1953) Shea visits the world of the Kalevala, and in "The Green Magician" (1954) he

L. Sprague de Camp in 1982.   Photo by Jay Kay Klein

arrives at his first intended destination. These last two stories were combined and revised to form the book *Wall of Serpents* (1960).

The other de Camp/Pratt collaborations are not quite up to the high standard set by *The Incomplete Enchanter* and *The Castle of Iron* in that they contain unaccountable lapses of the usual impeccable logic and lose something of their coherence in consequence. *Land of Unreason* (1942) transports a young American into a fairyland ruled by King Oberon, while *The Carnelian Cube* (1948) takes a similar protagonist hotfoot through a whole sequence of highly improbable milieus. A series of short stories done for *The Magazine of Fantasy and Science Fiction* in the early 1950's consists of anecdotes recalling the flavor of Lord Dunsany's Jorkens stories. These were collected as *Tales from Gavagan's Bar* in 1953.

Parallel worlds continued to provide the basic framework for de Camp's solo work in

231

Unknown. Sometimes the other worlds feature semiplausible alternate histories, as in "The Wheels of If" (1940); but more often they are wholly fantastic, as with the anarchic world inhabited by the dashing characters we wish we were, visited by the hero of *Solomon's Stone* (1942; book form, 1957). Another fairy-tale world, where everything works rather too simply, is featured in *The Undesired Princess* (1942; book form, 1951).

De Camp's prolific productivity during the years when *Unknown* was thriving was cut short when he was recruited to the war effort as an aircraft engineer. He virtually ceased writing fiction, and when he resumed his literary career after the war he directed much of his effort into nonfiction. He began to publish articles in the subject areas that were later to be covered by two of his most notable nonfiction books: *Lost Continents* (1954), a study of the mythology of Atlantis; and *Spirits, Stars, and Spells* (1966), a skeptical study of magic and the occult in both ancient and modern manifestations. In these and other works he proved himself to be a thoroughgoing researcher and a skillful popularizer.

Apart from the new fantasies that he wrote in collaboration with Pratt, de Camp wrote a few sword-and-sorcery stories in the early 1950's, the best of which was *The Tritonian Ring* (1951); but his major project was a long series of science fiction stories with a common background—the stories of the Viagens Interplanetarias. These stories cover the time from the late twenty-first century to the late twenty-second, and deal with the political and economic relations existing between Earth (which is by this time politically dominated by Brazil) and a number of alien worlds of nearby suns—especially Krishna, a world inhabited by various barbarian cultures. The stories appeared in various magazines, but the best of them were in *Astounding.*

The first novel in the series was *The Queen of Zamba* (1949), also known as *Cosmic Manhunt* and *A Planet Called Krishna*, an adventure story in which two Earthmen search for a missing girl in the most primitive part of the planet. A similar but rather more complex

search-and-rescue plot figures in the second novel of the series, *The Hand of Zei*, which was serialized in 1950–1951. Unfortunately, the book was broken up into two parts for hardcover book publication, the first half being titled *The Search for Zei* (also known as *The Floating Continent*), and the two were only reunited, in slightly abridged form, as halves of an Ace paperback double.

The best of the early contributions to this series is *Rogue Queen* (1951), which is one of many science fiction novels to construct a humanoid society organized like a beehive. Unlike most of the others, however, this is not a horror story but an adventure story dealing with the political and biological subversion of the hivelike social order. The other long stories in the series that were written in the 1950's—the novellas "The Continent Makers" (1951) and "The Virgin of Zesh" (1953) and the novel *The Tower of Zanid* (1958)—fall somewhat below this standard. The last is merely a tired repetition of an established formula. But "The Continent Makers" appeared as the title story of a 1953 collection bringing together the best of the short stories in the series. These stories are ingenious comedies, sparkling with wit.

De Camp's only other science fiction novel of the early 1950's, *The Glory That Was* (1952; book form, 1960), recalls *Lest Darkness Fall* in that the leading characters find themselves apparently returned to Periclean Athens while attempting to search for a missing wife in the twenty-seventh century, but in fact the novel is something of a disappointment. Of the short stories published during this second period of prolific activity, however, several are quite outstanding. "Aristotle and the Gun" (1956) is an interesting experiment in the creation of alternate histories. In this story a time traveler gives Aristotle a firearm, assuming that a Greece armed with such weapons need never be conquered, and that the great man himself might deduce from the artifact many of the principles of modern science. Alas, the consequences of the gift turn out quite differently. "A Gun for Dinosaur" (1956) is also a time travel story, in which a big-game hunter recalls the desperate circumstances of his last encounter with *Tyrannosaurus rex*.

Two other excellent stories of the period grew out of de Camp's personal experience. "Impractical Joke" (1956) is an ironic moral fable, relayed with feeling, about the evils of practical joking. "Judgment Day" (1955) is a semiautobiographical story recalling the agonies suffered by the author when he was sent in his youth to a military academy to "cure" him of intellectual arrogance and a lack of discipline. In the story this becomes part of the personal history of a physicist who discovers a doomsday weapon and calmly hands it over to his political masters, knowing that through them he can repay the world for the cruel treatment it has meted out to him. All four of these stories, together with the pick of the remainder of de Camp's output during the 1950's, are in the collection *A Gun for Dinosaur* (1963).

After 1958 de Camp abandoned science fiction and fantasy for some ten years and concentrated on his nonfiction and on his excellent series of historical novels. The novels are well researched and contain a great deal of fascinating material about ancient technology and early voyages of exploration. They are unfailingly convincing and extremely lively— outstanding examples of their genre. The titles are *An Elephant for Aristotle* (1958), *The Bronze God of Rhodes* (1960), *The Dragon of the Ishtar Gate* (1961), *The Arrows of Hercules* (1965), and *The Golden Wind* (1969).

During this period de Camp did a certain amount of editing, beginning an excellent series of sword-and-sorcery anthologies with *Swords and Sorcery* (1963) and continuing with *The Spell of Seven* (1965), *The Fantastic Swordsmen* (1967), and *Warlocks and Warriors* (1970). His own involvement with this kind of fiction resumed when Lancer Books began to issue the Conan series in paperback, including de Camp's (and Nyberg's) revisions of Howard's unsold stories and new work by de Camp and Lin Carter. De Camp began writing sword-and-sorcery stories of his own again with *The Goblin Tower* (1968), a lighthearted swashbuckling adventure story set in

a parallel world (which involves a brief crossing into our world at one point). He added two sequels to this work in *The Clocks of Iraz* (1971) and *The Fallible Fiend* (1973). He edited two critical anthologies—*The Conan Swordbook* (1969) and *The Conan Grimoire* (1972)—devoted to Howard and to Conan in particular, and eventually became Howard's biographer in publishing *The Miscast Barbarian* (1975). This followed his earlier (1974) publication of a definitive biography of H. P. Lovecraft, and he subsequently added a more discursive study of the sword-and-sorcery genre, *Literary Swordsmen and Sorcerers* (1976). His ventures in literary biography are interesting enough, but he cannot be said to have mastered this form as well as the popularization of science and the historical novel.

De Camp returned to the Viagens Interplanetarias future history in the late 1970's, when the Krishna stories were repackaged for paperback release by Ace as a numbered series. *The Queen of Zamba* became volume 1, and the recombined *The Search for Zei* and *The Hand of Zei* became volume 2. *The Hostage of Zir* (1977), a comedy chronicling the misadventures of Fergus Reith, Krishna's first tourist guide, filled in a gap before *The Virgin of Zesh* and *The Tower of Zanid* were collected in volume 4. The series continued in *The Prisoner of Zhamanak* (1982), in which an enterprising soldier of fortune is sent to rescue the headstrong scientist Alicia Dyckman from illicit imprisonment. In *The Bones of Zora* (1983), in whose writing de Camp combined forces with his wife, Dr. Dyckman provides further complications for Fergus Reith and his latest client, a palaeontologist, who make an unexpectedly valuable discovery.

Although Ace dropped the Krishna series after *The Bones of Zora*, it was eventually picked up by Baen Books, for whom the de Camps collaborated on *The Swords of Zinjaban* (1991), which continued the adventures of what had now been established as a regular cast of characters. *The Venom Trees of Sunga* (1992), credited to L. Sprague de Camp alone, is an adventure story in the same zestful spirit, set on a different world in the same fictional universe that had previously featured in *The Stones of Nomuru* (1988, signed by both de Camps).

In the early 1990's de Camp also took up the threads of one of his most popular stories, "A Gun for Dinosaur," and extrapolated it into a whole series of cautionary comedies. The tales are narrated in a breezily anecdotal manner by Reggie Rivers, offering accounts of various "safaris" undertaken by means of Professor Prokasha's time machine—which offers the only opportunity "sportsmen" have in a conservation-conscious near future to collect impressive shooting trophies. Most of the tales feature dinosaurs, occasionally bearing upon the various scientific theories attempting to account for their extinction, but "The Mislaid Mastodon" (1993) describes an excursion to a more recent era of prehistory for more constructive purposes. The series was collected in *Rivers of Time* (1993).

De Camp obviously felt comfortable working in this relaxed nostalgic vein, but when Baen wanted to augment the more seriously inclined *Lest Darkness Fall* for a new edition, he was content to leave the task to David Drake, who added a relatively brief sequel, "To Bring the Light" (1996). Drake also wrote a sequel to fill out a new edition of *The Undesired Princess*. Christopher Stasheff and others were entrusted with extending the Harold Shea series for the same publisher, although de Camp added two more novellas of his own in *Sir Harold and the Gnome King* (1991) and "Sir Harold of Zodanga" (1994).

The classic *Lest Darkness Fall* remains a striking exception to the pattern of Sprague de Camp's career as a fantasist and science fiction writer, although he did do meticulous and earnest work within the genre of historical fiction. He always regarded fantastic fiction as a medium of light entertainment. In the preface to his first story collection, *The Wheels of If* (1948), he insisted that he was so devoted to the studious avoidance of social significance that he thought it a "vile canard" when he was accused of writing satire. He pro-

tested a *little* too much. There is certainly a strong element of satire in such works as *The Great Fetish* (1978), which parodies the Creationist resistance to evolutionary theory, but the vast majority of his contributions to the science fiction genre are intended to be read as pleasant literary confections. The seriousness with which he took the writing of this work is, however, amply displayed in *The Science Fiction Handbook* (1953; revised in collaboration with his wife, 1975), a guide to writing and marketing that commends frivolity as a literary device but is itself thoroughly commonsensical.

De Camp's 1996 autobiography, *Time and Chance*, provides information on his external life and activities, less so on his internal life and writing career, and is most interesting as a portrait of an intelligent and cultivated man whose life is guided by a love of learning and travel. In 1998 he received the Pilgrim Award from the Science Fiction Research Association in recognition of his scholarship.

Readers and critics are perfectly entitled to wish that de Camp had been prepared to take his genre work seriously enough to produce more work as solid as *Lest Darkness Fall*—and his biographies of Robert E. Howard and H. P. Lovecraft may be somewhat misconceived in their insistence that those writers would have fared far better if they had only been able to lighten up—but the provision of good light entertainment involves a special kind of artistry, and no one in the science fiction field has deployed that kind of artistry more deftly or more consistently than L. Sprague de Camp.

Selected Bibliography

WORKS OF L. SPRAGUE DE CAMP

The Incomplete Enchanter, with Fletcher Pratt. New York: Henry Holt, 1941.

Lest Darkness Fall. New York: Henry Holt, 1941.

Land of Unreason, with Fletcher Pratt. New York: Henry Holt, 1942.

The Carnelian Cube, with Fletcher Pratt. New York: Gnome Press, 1948.

Divide and Rule. Reading, Pa.: Fantasy Press, 1948.

The Wheels of If and Other Science Fiction. Chicago: Shasta Publishers, 1948.

The Castle of Iron, with Fletcher Pratt. New York: Gnome Press, 1950.

Genus Homo, with P. Schuyler Miller. Reading, Pa.: Fantasy Press, 1950.

Rogue Queen. Garden City, N.Y.: Doubleday, 1951.

The Undesired Princess. Los Angeles: Fantasy Publishing Company, 1951.

The Continent Makers and Other Tales of the Viagens. New York: Twayne Publishers, 1953.

Sprague de Camp's New Anthology of Science Fiction. London: Hamilton, 1953.

Tales from Gavagan's Bar, with Fletcher Pratt. New York: Twayne Publishers, 1953.

The Tritonian Ring and Other Pusadian Tales. New York: Twayne Publishers, 1953.

Cosmic Manhunt. New York: Ace Double, 1954.

Solomon's Stone. New York: Avalon Books, 1957.

The Tower of Zanid. New York: Avalon Books, 1958.

The Glory That Was. New York: Avalon Books, 1960.

Wall of Serpents, with Fletcher Pratt. New York: Avalon Books, 1960.

The Search for Zei. New York: Avalon Books, 1962.

A Gun for Dinosaur. New York: Doubleday, 1963.

The Hand of Zei. New York: Avalon Books, 1963.

The Goblin Tower. New York: Pyramid Books, 1968.

The Reluctant Shaman. New York: Pyramid Books, 1970.

The Clocks of Iraz. New York: Pyramid Books, 1971.

The Fallible Fiend. New York: New American Library, 1973.

The Hostage of Zir. New York: Berkley-Putnam, 1977.

The Best of L. Sprague de Camp. New York: Ballantine Books, 1978.

The Great Fetish. Garden City, N.Y.: Doubleday, 1978.

The Purple Pterodactyls: The Adventures of W. Wilson Newbury, Ensorcelled Financier. Huntingdon Woods, Mich.: Phantasia, 1979. (Short stories.)

The Prisoner of Zhamanak. Huntingdon Woods, Mich.: Phantasia, 1982.

The Unbeheaded King. New York: Ballantine Books, 1983; London: Grafton, 1988.

The Bones of Zora, with Catherine C. de Camp. Huntingdon Woods, Mich.: Phantasia, 1983.

The Stones of Nomuru, with Catherine C. de Camp. Norfolk, Va.: Donning, 1988.

The Honorable Barbarian. Norwalk, Conn.: Easton, 1989.

The Swords of Zinjaban, with Catherine C. de Camp. Riverdale, N.Y.: Baen, 1991.

The Venom Trees of Sunga. New York: Ballantine Books, 1992.

Rivers of Time: The Adventures of Reginald Rivers, Time Traveler Extraordinaire. New York: Baen, 1993. (Short stories.)

Time and Chance. Hampton Falls, N.H.: Donald M. Grant, 1996. (Autobiography.)

CRITICAL AND BIOGRAPHICAL STUDIES

de Camp, L. Sprague. "Up and Away from the School of Invention" ("The Development of a Science Fiction Writer: V"). *Foundation* 4 (July 1973): 25–27. (Autobiographical reminiscences.)

Moskowitz, Sam. "L. Sprague de Camp." In *Seekers of Tomorrow*. Cleveland: World Publishing Company, 1966.

—BRIAN STABLEFORD

SAMUEL R. DELANY
(b. 1942)

SAMUEL R. DELANY remains one of the brightest stars in the constellation of highly literate and stylish science fiction writers who appeared in the 1960's and included Thomas M. Disch, Ursula K. Le Guin, Joanna Russ, and Roger Zelazny in the United States—as well as Brian Aldiss, J. G. Ballard, Michael Moorcock, and Keith Roberts in Great Britain. In recent years, he has achieved enviable prominence as a major Afro-American and gay intellectual and artist, almost wholly on the basis of his writing, both fictional and theoretical, in the field of science fiction. The Science Fiction Research Association gave him the 1985 Pilgrim Award for Science Fiction Criticism. In 1993 he received the William Whitehead Memorial Award for Lifetime Contribution to Gay and Lesbian Literature, an honor given previously to Edmund White, Audre Lorde, Adrienne Rich, and James Purdy.

Born in New York City on April Fools' Day in 1942 and clearly something of a prodigy, Delany viewed how contemporary society is constructed and operates and how people in different strata of society behave from a site at once marginalized and privileged. Although it might not have been obvious to all his early readers, Delany has always assumed positions on the peripheries of majority culture in the United States of his time. As he says in *Silent Interviews: On Language, Race, Sex, Science Fiction, and Some Comics: A Collection of Written Interviews* (1994):

I see myself as writing from a particular position. That position is black; it's gay; it's male; and it's far more contoured by the marginal workings of science fiction than what I take to be the central concerns of literature, that is, those concerns organized around "the priority of the subject." (page 267)

Delany grew up in Harlem in a middle-class family and attended Dalton (a private school), the prestigious Bronx High School of Science, and City College of New York, where he was poetry editor of *Prometheus* magazine before dropping out to pursue a writing career. He has written with wit and insight about this period of his life in that marvelously detailed and analytical memoir *The Motion of Light in Water: Sex and Science Fiction Writing in the East Village 1957–1965* (1988).

During a very full life, Delany has written more than thirty separate books (as well as substantially revising many of them). He has traveled widely in Europe and North America, and has resided for some time in San Francisco (the model for Bellona in *Dhalgren* [1975]), London, and especially and for the longest periods, New York, his favorite—and the shadow city behind almost every such fictional edifice he has constructed. They are great cities, sites of an urban, urbane consciousness that is culturally central to all his work. Over the years, he has edited a literary/science fiction quarterly, *Quark*, with his then wife Marilyn Hacker, held various casual jobs, taught at numerous universities, and most recently been professor of comparative literature at the University of Massachusetts, Amherst. In the last of these positions, he gave himself up to teaching, with a resultant falling off in his production of fictional texts. However, since 1996 he has returned to writing with renewed vigor.

Unlike most science fiction writers, who generally begin their careers with short stories and slowly work their way up through longer forms to the novel, Delany began with a novel, *The Jewels of Aptor* (1962), written when he was nineteen and published in a heavily cut version as one half of an Ace Double. He quickly followed that with a trilogy: *Captives of the Flame* (1963), *The Towers of Toron* (1964), and *City of a Thousand Suns* (1965). By the time the last of these had appeared, Delany had written *The Ballad of Beta-2* (1965). Then, in a burst of energy, he completed two novels, *Babel-17* (1966) and *Empire Star* (1966), as well as his first short story, "The Star Pit," before the end of 1965.

Having written one short story, Delany did not stop there, and over the next few years he completed a number of them, two of which—"Aye, and Gomorrah . . ." (1967) and "Time Considered as a Helix of Semiprecious Stones" (1969)—won Nebula awards (the latter also won a Hugo). *Babel-17* also won a Nebula, as did his next novel, *The Einstein Intersection* (1967). *Nova* (1968), the first of his novels to be published initially in hard cover, marks the end of what we can call Delany's first period. Despite its publication date, all the stories in *Driftglass* (1971) are from this first period. *The Tides of Lust* (1973), his eccentric work of literary pornography, seems to look back to his unpublished mainstream fiction as much as it looks forward to the major works of a later period. So too does *Hogg* (1994), a study of sexual power as perceived by a strangely "innocent" youthful narrator; only the introduction could attain publication at the time. He has much to say about the actual writing and the conditions under which he wrote in *The Motion of Light in Water.*

From January 1969 to September 1973, Delany was engaged on a huge project, eventually published as *Dhalgren* (1975), an 879-page novel that caused great controversy within the field but quickly found its own audience,

as its many and continuing printings demonstrate. This was followed by *Triton* (1976), a novel much more clearly aligned with traditional science fiction than *Dhalgren*, yet equally multiplex and challenging to the conventions of genre science fiction. As if to explain himself, Delany then published a collection of critical essays on science fiction, *The Jewel-Hinged Jaw* (1977), and wrote a formidably difficult structuralist analysis of Disch's short story "Angouleme," *The American Shore* (1978). In 1978 he also collaborated with artist Howard V. Chaykin on the graphic novel *Empire*. Delany published his first, semifictional, memoir, *Heavenly Breakfast* (1979), and the first volume of highly erudite and witty analytical refashionings of sword-and-sorcery, *Tales of Nevèrÿon* (1979), the same year. Throughout the 1980's, he continued to work at what became the four-volume Return to Nevèrÿon project and also wrote the first volume of a planned science fiction diptych, *Stars in My Pocket Like Grains of Sand* (1984). *Neveryóna; or, The Tale of Signs and Cities: Some Informal Remarks Toward the Modular Calculus, Part Four* (1983) was followed by a second volume of essays on science fiction, *Starboard Wine: More Notes on the Language of Science Fiction* (1984), *Flight from Nevèrÿon* (1985), *The Bridge of Lost Desire* (1987), and *The Motion of Light in Water*. While teaching at the University of Massachusetts, he published more theoretical writing, as *Wagner/Artaud: A Play of Nineteenth and Twentieth Century Critical Fictions* (1988), *The Straits of Messina* (1989), *Silent Interviews* (1994), and *Longer Views* (1996) demonstrate. He also wrote the critically admired *Atlantis: Three Tales* (1995).

From the beginning, Delany has been a highly literary writer. Indeed, though most science fiction is full of genre allusions, including especially the wholesale take-over by many authors of terms or ideas that obviously "belong" to everyone's future—for example, "androids" as a term, or Isaac Asimov's Three Laws of Robotics as a concept—Delany's work has always tended to be allusive in the manner of modernist European and Anglo-Amer-

Samuel R. Delany in 1980. PHOTO BY JAY KAY KLEIN

ican poetry and prose. Although Delany read sword-and-sorcery and science fiction in his early teens, he has confessed to a rather sketchy knowledge of the genre when he began writing it. Having read widely in other fields, including canonical literature, philosophy, science, and music, he felt, it seems, both that he could write science fiction equal to the best and that, paradoxically, what he calls this paraliterary genre offered him greater writerly and readerly scope than the prevailing realism of mainstream fiction. In *Silent Interviews*, Delany says that paraliterature includes "women's fiction, feminist fiction (another area), black fiction, gay fiction, experimental fiction, as well as all the commercial genres (not to mention their ubiquitous overlaps)." He was also working on a massive manuscript titled *Voyage Orestes!*, completed in late 1963, which suggests that even then he sought to erase the clear boundary line between various fields of writing.

The only copy was lost by Delany's agent in 1968.

Delany's reasons for the latter attitude emerge in the critical writings he has done since 1967 or so, simultaneously with his creation of the novels and stories that mark his second period. Much of his criticism is analysis of particular texts, but that analysis is thick with the implications of his more theoretical essays, for Delany has managed, perhaps more successfully than any other critic, to create a workable definition of science fiction. The problem with most such definitions is that they attempt to delimit science fiction by theme or content. Delany's masterstroke is to shift the whole question to a different context, the linguistic. In what was originally titled "About Five Thousand One Hundred and Seventy-Five Words" (1969), he argues that science fiction has "a distinct level of subjunctivity . . . that is different from that which informs naturalistic fiction, fantasy, or reportage."

In later essays, borrowing his terminology from structuralism, Delany argues that "science fiction *is* science fiction because various bits of technological discourse (real, speculative or pseudo)—that is to say the 'science'—are used to redeem various other sentences from the merely metaphorical, or even the meaningless, for denotative description/presentation of incident." Delany's arguments are highly complex but point to an optimistic conclusion: "I feel the science-fictional enterprise is richer than the enterprise of mundane fiction. It is richer through its extended repertoire of sentences, its consequent greater range of possible incident, and through its more varied field of rhetorical and syntagmic organization." Few writers have done more to demonstrate the validity of this assertion in their science fiction than Delany has. In more recent years, Delany has turned his critical and theoretical gaze more and more to cultural studies in general, although his increasingly complex thinking about all forms of paraliterature deserves careful consideration. Over the years, Delany has discovered that the writerly possibilities he is most interested in can be pursued in almost any area. The way that the science fiction, theory, criticism, autobiography, literary pornography, historical fiction, and the so-called sword-and-sorcery of the Return to Nevèrÿon quartet interact with each other might best be represented by the chains of prisms, mirrors, and lenses of *Dhalgren*.

Delany's first period breaks neatly in half with *Babel-17*, his first "major" novel. His earlier novels are colorful, exciting, entertaining, and intellectually provocative to a degree not found in most genre science fiction, but they are also essentially straightforward narratives operating within genre conventions. Although aware of the darker side of human nature, his youthful protagonists (including the recurring figure Algis Budrys has dubbed "the magic kid") are like their author in the optimism they bring to their quests, which are simpler and more easily achieved than those in Delany's later works. Nevertheless, these early novels begin the exploration of those literary obsessions that define his oeuvre: problems of communication and community; new kinds of sexual/love/family relationships; the artist as social outsider (the romantic vision of the artist as criminal); cultural interactions and the exploration of human social possibilities these allow; archetypal and mythic structures in the imagination.

All the novels up to *Nova* have a version of the quest as their basic narrative pattern, but none so patently as *The Jewels of Aptor*. On an Earth still suffering from the effects of an ancient atomic war, the high priestess of the island of Leptar, the White Goddess Argo Incarnate, calls Geo (a scholar-poet), Urson (his sailor friend), Snake (a four-armed telepathic thief), and Iimmi (another sailor) to steal the powerful telepathic jewels of Aptor and rescue her kidnapped daughter from the priests of the Dark God Hama on Aptor. After passing through many dangers, they accomplish their mission, only to discover that their real, spiritual, quest has just begun.

Knowing the corrupting power of the jewels, the priests of Hama actually want the questers to steal them and take young Argo back to Leptar. But when the young people reach their ship, the power-hungry mate attacks them. Although corrupted by the jewels, Urson defends his friends, killing the mate and falling to his death in the sea with the jewels. In their shock the others experience a revelation of the fluid, multifaceted nature of reality that makes possible both reconciliation and personal growth. A lesson that cannot be taught, only learned, the vision is of "chaos caught in order, the order defining chaos"—which could also be a description of art. Certainly it is one of the core experiences of all Delany's writing: the experience of process in opposition to stasis, of life versus every kind of death, of what he later terms "multiplex," as opposed to "simplex," awareness.

The Jewels of Aptor's cultural context is a fairly standard postholocaust primitive one, with a few witty differences. Argo is, in fact, a "scientific" version of Robert Graves's White Goddess, whose mythological and metaphoric presence is carefully modified by bits of "technological discourse" that explain how the two opposed religions necessarily emerged after the atomic war to preserve knowledge and how, in Leptar, that function had been abandoned because of fearful superstition.

In the three novels of *The Fall of the Towers* trilogy, Delany attempts a large social novel about a small, isolated, high-technology civilization that has reached the limits of its growth—as perceived through its rulers' static understanding—and therefore must go to war in order to continue to expand. Within this narrative framework of societal quest, Delany relates a number of personal quests whose outcomes will shape the culture for good or ill. He renders these stories against the backdrop of a society in the throes of self-destruction, from the ruling classes to the lowest criminal gangs. He even explains how atomic war caused three types of humanity to appear in this world: ordinary humans, Neanderthal throwbacks, and telepathic giants. He also introduces some extragalactic dei ex machinis that finally unbalance the narrative, for his ambition is greater than his craft at this point. This flawed and unwieldy work is worthwhile, though, for its individual scenes and the impressive and horrifying presentation of the psychological manipulation of the "soldiers" in the false war at the core of the second volume. In the end the people—not the ruling classes, who have tried to prevent change—begin to build a new and better society outside the old city. Once again, order and chaos are meshed in a human balance.

The Ballad of Beta-2 is a small, entertaining lark after the huge social canvas of the trilogy, but it marks a growing technical maturity on Delany's part. Joneny, a student of galactic anthropology, seeks knowledge of the Star Folk even as they seek to reach the stars and make contact, but neither quest can be achieved without the other. Delany happily parodies the forms of scholarship even as he proves their worth when they are honestly pursued. His major technical advance is in his use of documents to condense a lengthy story of social and intellectual degeneration aboard slower-than-light-speed generation starships into brief glimpses of specific behavior at various times. He also creates some strong and empathetic characters in Captain Leela RT-857 and some of the socially ostracized "One-Eyes," the only people trying to retain the knowledge of their forebears while the rest sink into banal barbarism.

In *Babel-17*, Delany triumphantly weaves all the various strands of his first five books into a cohesive and original whole. Moreover, he extends his range in both "scientific" and sociological extrapolation far beyond the boundaries of his earlier works. In Rydra Wong he creates a strong female hero whose interests—ranging from poetry and linguistics to interstellar flight and battle tactics—announce her as a Renaissance figure who needs to prove she can master the invented language Babel-17, a starship captain's duties, and the great poetry she has the potential to create. Upon achieving this triple quest, she gains maturity; she also finds a lover—the Butcher, whom she rescues from the self-destructive effects of Babel-17—and with him

solves her society's major problem by stopping an unnecessary war.

But Delany does not just tell Rydra's story; he develops a complex interstellar civilization, the various activities of whose citizens are intimately related to the technology under which they live; posits an essentially nonsexist society, whose sexual mores are naturally tied to the exigencies of star travel; and, by making linguistics the central "science" in his plot, explores a number of philosophical questions at the center of the literary experience in purely science fictional terms. The result is fast, often violent action, taut emotional and psychological drama, and some provocative speculation, all netted together in a colorfully entertaining fashion.

Written in only eleven days and titled after a novel by Rydra Wong's dead husband, Muels Aranlyde (an anagram of Samuel R. Delany), *Empire Star* is a breakthrough novel for Delany. Deceptively light on the surface, it is in fact his first wholly metafictional science fiction; self-referential and allusive, it joyfully pushes concepts of language and reality through a series of Borgesian changes while pricking our consciences with the ethical and social questions it raises. Its structure *is* its plot, a story that turns in upon itself like a möbius strip in a manner that points toward the much more massive *Dhalgren*.

A "simplex" lad in a simplex culture, Comet Jo has a quest to carry a "message" from the dying crew of a crashed ship to Empire Star, the center of the Empire's power. He carries with him a crystallized Tritovian named Jewel, a "multiplex" consciousness and the narrative voice of the novel. Various other multiplex characters help Jo along the way. There is San Severina, a princess who "owns" seven Lll. The Lll are the giant slaves that Jo's message is apparently "about," creatures she needs to rebuild a war-ravaged segment of her empire. (The Lll, she tells Jo, "are the shame and tragedy of the multiplex universe. No man can be free until they are free.") There are also Lump, a giant "Linguistic Ubiquitous MultiPlex"—based on the consciousness of the Lll novelist Muels Aranlyde—who loves to make literary allusions, and Ni Ty Lee, a poet who seems to have written of Jo's experiences before Jo met him. Jo's "journey" to multiplexity is often painful, but for every loss (of innocence?) there is a gain (of insight, deeper compassion, and understanding). Near the end of the book, after learning that his message is "Someone has come to free the Lll," Jo meets a young, newly multiplex San Sevarina and helps her to prepare for her ordeals to follow just as she once helped him, for time is ambiguous and pliable at the Empire Star itself (scientific discourse here redeems otherwise simple surrealism), and now Jo knows "that win or lose, it will take longer than we think"—but also that the effort is worthwhile.

The novel's linguistic strategies themselves "explain" multiplexity; independent of intelligence, it is open-minded awareness of the vast ambiguities of existence, and Delany, I believe, sees it as necessary to the creation of good art at least, and probably to the eventual creation of a "good society." As both narrative voice and active participant in the larger story, Jewel implies the grandeur of that epic tale in which Jo's journey from simplexity to multiplexity is but one "tile for the mosaic." For the novel is also a practical text: this journey is also that of the active or multiplex reader. As Jewel's final statement puts it: "It's a beginning. It's an end. I leave to *you* the problem of ordering your perceptions and making the journey from one to the other."

Since *Empire Star*, Delany has continued to expand the formal techniques that map the multiplex enterprise of his fiction. In *The Einstein Intersection* he follows Lobey, his alien protagonist and "magic kid," across a radically altered Earth toward a final awareness that everything in the world is, indeed, utterly "different" and change is the only constant in the characters' lives. Simultaneously, his highly charged poetic language enacts the basic myth of this highly allusive tale—the myth of metamorphosis—while his many epigraphs, including notes from his own journals, insist upon the writer's own quest to discover the proper form for the story he is

telling. Self-conscious literary artifacts, Delany's later novels are also exemplary science fiction in which scientific discourse redeems even sentences as poetically surreal as "Attacked by flowers, a dragon was dying" to science fiction realism of extreme imagistic clarity.

The Einstein Intersection is an investigation into the mythic grounds of personality that proposes that mythology alters to meet altered circumstances—for example, those in which a triple-sexed alien species has inherited Earth and the husks of humanity's material and spiritual enterprises after humanity abandoned them. Lobey, one of the "different" ones, must learn that by their differences they shall be saved. It is difficult to learn that he does not have to repeat the mythic patterns in which his quest seems to trap him. Lobey, like Perceval in the Wasteland/Grail story, fails to ask the proper questions until it is too late; and, like Theseus, he constructs his own labyrinth while trying to escape it. But it is not too late, for when he realizes that, like the other major characters (each clothed in a coat of many allusions), he is "different," he can finally redeem his culture, exhaust the human mazes, and create some new ones for his own race. At the novel's ambiguous close, Lobey stands poised on the brink of new and different action: he has not yet acted, but the fact that he has told his own story in the past tense implies that he intends to. Though the narrative concludes, the story will go on.

In a sense *Nova* stands as the summation of Delany's career up to that time (1968). Packing his story full of color and incident, violent action and tender introspective moments, he has created one of the grandest space operas ever written. Also, thickly layering the palimpsest of his fiction, he pushes the stylistic pyrotechnics of Alfred Bester's *The Stars My Destination* (1956) even further; transforms the myths of Prometheus and of Indra's freeing of the waters into science fictional realism; re-creates something of the feel of Greek tragedy in the epic battle for economic control of the galaxy between Lorq Von Ray and Prince and Ruby Red; subtly but dramatically explores character interaction on and among a variety of social levels; creates one of the most complete and intelligent renderings of a future galactic society in all of science fiction, which includes a serious investigation of political and economic power and an intellectually satisfying history of that society; makes an intriguing comparative study of two types of artist (the utterly intuitive syrinx player, Mouse, and the scholarly, studious apprentice novelist, Katin); and writes one of science fiction's bolder self-conscious fictions, in which that apprentice novelist not only explains many of the narrative patterns the novel employs (such as the Tarot/Grail Quest) but, it appears, eventually "writes" the book we are reading, *Nova*.

Like all of Delany's later works, *Nova* defies précis. With three centers of consciousness and an incredibly tangled plot, it creates a literary model of the "web of worlds" that it has as its social context, and fully explains the technology that allows it all to function. Katin at one point speaks of his art as a net; in Delany's work nets and webs proliferate as parts of the imagistic surround that his characters perceive. *Nova* is itself a many-layered net of perception and analysis, action and response, speculation and feeling. Such nets of language are what Delany seeks to create in all his fictions and, though they appear from the beginning, they increase in multiplexity as he matures.

Delany's short fictions explore the same difficulties in adjusting to an inchoate universe as his novels do but are narrower in range. The best of them—"The Star Pit," "Aye, and Gomorrah . . . ," "Driftglass," "We, in Some Strange Power's Employ, Move on a Rigorous Line," "Time Considered as a Helix of Semiprecious Stones"—are intensely introspective character studies of their narrators, although Delany also provides full social and technological contexts to their quests for understanding.

The impossibility of even beginning to do justice to *Dhalgren* in anything less than an essay much longer than this one is made clear by Jean Mark Gawron's brilliant introduction to the Gregg Press edition, which in more than sixty pages deals with just a few of its many intertwined purposes, especially those relating to questions of language and signs. No single analysis can do more than offer a few entries to its multiplex texts, for, like the chain its protagonist is given just before he enters the strange and isolated city of words, Bellona, the narrative structure of *Dhalgren* is a long, looped chain of mirrors, prisms, and lenses. At any point in the 879-page linkage of this chain, language will encounter reality as seen in such reflective, distorting, and magnifying surfaces. Thus we must become multiplex readers, continually "ordering [our] perceptions" as Jewel asked the readers of *Empire Star* to do.

The actual "plot" of *Dhalgren* is absurdly simple: an amnesiac and nameless young man (soon dubbed the Kid) crosses a river into a city cut off from and forgotten by the rest of the world; he writes poems, becomes the leader of a gang, does odd jobs and meets a wide variety of people, has a three-way love affair with a woman and a teen-age boy, and eventually leaves. But perhaps it does not happen that way at all. As in *Empire Star*, time turns in on itself, and perhaps the Kid has been there before and/or after the period ambiguously bracketed by the text, a text for which he may be responsible. Unlike *Empire Star*, *Dhalgren* provides no science fictional explanation for this. Yet, although its "Chinese-box" construction calls attention to itself, and thus to its purely fictive nature, *Dhalgren* definitely is science fiction, partly because of the precision with which it registers the absence of explanation. For example, the science fiction template of "postholocaust story" is invoked, but only as a critique of its conventional formation. Delany presents a new barbarism: an utterly urban one. The people of Bellona survive on canned food and live in abandoned houses; they do not return to the land. Yet a new tribalism emerges, and the destruction of the old ways—of politics, economics, and social behavior—is clearly signaled.

Containing no more incidents than *Empire Star* (which is about one-tenth its size), *Dhalgren* explores these incidents with a phenomenological attention to perceived detail found in too few texts of any kind, let alone science fiction. This is partly because, being in a world gone crazy and unsure of his own mental balance, Delany's ultimate version of "the magic kid" is forced to rely on the acuity of his senses if he is somehow *not* to confuse "the true and the real." *Dhalgren* seeks to capture something of the feel of "the real" in its vastly complicated web of texts. That it does so only ambiguously is testament to the difficulties of the task.

Dhalgren is, by its very nature, many things, but all of them are different from what we might expect of a standard science fiction novel. Although the novel is an utterly self-conscious, self-reflexive fiction continually questioning its own emergence from imagination to writing to print, its narrative foreground is a realistic presentation of human lives—filled with social comedy, psychological eroticism, witty speculative dialogue, sociological analysis, and much more—lived out against an alien landscape not totally inimical to them: that is, the very stuff of science fiction but lacking the usual structural emblems of the genre.

Delany has suggested that in science fiction "foreground"—"the fictively magical presentation of 'what happens'"—tends to outweigh "recit"—"authorial commentary that occurs in fictive discourse"—and he argues that even *Dhalgren* is essentially like other science fiction in its weighting of the two. *Triton*'s foreground signals its science fictional context far more clearly than does *Dhalgren*'s—the setting is futuristic and technologically advanced, with utterly changed social/sexual mores—while its recit as clearly signals an analytical fiction of a technical complexity we would expect only from the author of *Dhalgren*. If, as so many of its writers and fans profess, science fiction is a fiction of ideas, then *Triton* is the purest kind of science fiction, exploring new ideas that force us to question traditional concepts

of how society works as well as our own ways of living.

Part of *Triton*'s fascination derives from the presence of the first Delany protagonist with whom we are compelled not to identify. *Triton* is one of the few successful psychological character studies in the genre, exploring in immense detail Bron Helstrom's utter failure to adapt to the expansion of human possibilities implicit in his culture. Bron is a psychological throwback, a twentieth-century misogynist in a society where sexual egalitarianism has been achieved on all levels. But when his friends—particularly the Spike, an artist, and Lawrence, a wise old man—try to help him or when his experiences should lead him to a multiplex awareness of the process of life on the outer moons of the solar system, he refuses to accept the revelation. Locked into herself—having changed sex in order to become the right kind of woman for the sort of "real man" she (no longer he) used to be—Bron is finally trapped in total social and psychological stasis, lost in isolation beyond any help her society can offer its citizens.

The vision of *Triton* is, as its subtitle, *An Ambiguous Heterotopia*, suggests, precisely ambiguous. The world of the novel is richly imagined and essentially optimistic, structured to allow the greatest subjective freedom for the greatest number. But Bron's negative presence, plus the disconcerting fact of the "war" with the worlds, casts a pall over the whole. Or it would, but for the concluding "Appendix B: Ashima Slade and the Harbin-Y Lectures: Some Informal Remarks Toward the Modular Calculus, Part Two," which has some mitigating influence. Slade is not only an important philosopher whose ideas have influenced the behavior of his culture; he is an eccentric mirror image of Bron, another immigrant from a world (Mars) to a moon (Iapetus), but one who succeeds, where Bron fails, in adapting to the vast freedoms of lunar civilization (even if the form of his adaptation raises questions about the ambiguous good these freedoms signify).

Triton itself is "Part One" of the "Informal Remarks," and "Part Three" is the "Appendix" to Delany's next work of fiction, *Tales of Nevèrÿon*, a fictive scholarly joke that is also a provocative study of language, semiotics, history, and fictional creation. Delany is developing another very complicated, self-reflexive discourse here. One important aspect of these appendixes is the fact that they are apparently all recit, but through a Borgesian twist of the fictional blade that recit becomes foreground, folding such categories as fiction and reality, story and essay, into each other with great wit and subtlety.

In "On *Triton* and Other Matters: An Interview with Samuel R. Delany" in *Science-Fiction Studies*, Delany suggests that "the Modular Calculus" is a necessary fiction. Explaining the game of Vlet in *Triton*, he says:

> The name came from a story by Joanna Russ . . . [in which] the world of the story is actually controlled by the game, you can't really tell where the game ends and the world takes up. The [Nevèrÿon] books . . . are basically the game of vlet writ large [insofar as the world of Nevèrÿon and the stories therein are generated by the "rules" of various historical semiotic theories]. Vlet is a game of sword-and-sorcery. In some ideal future world with ideal readers, the books might all be considered part of a larger amorphous work. . . . "Some Informal Remarks Towards the Modular Calculus," . . . to which *Triton* is the SF prologue. (page 319)

For the record, *Neveryóna* is "Part Four," and "Appendix A: The Tale of Plagues and Carnivals" in *Return to Nevèrÿon* is "Part Five," so it appears that he came to regard the boundary between story and essay as ever more permeable the longer he worked at Return to Nevèrÿon.

The whole sequence—twelve tales (or eleven if you count "The Tale of Gorgik," which appears as both beginning and end of the series in a fascinating replication of the opening and closing of *Dhalgren*, as only one) and three appendices (but one is also a tale)—works to uncover what is repressed in the textual unconscious of sword-and-sorcery: sex (the whole apparatus of sadism that supports the Conan-like hero and all that depends upon it) and economics (the fact that such tales are set in a culture moving from a barter to a money economy). Throughout, Delany devises elegant ways of explaining, wholly within the context of his invented prehistory, such concepts as ideology and binary thinking. This elegance of narration differentiates the series from conventional fantasy while such explanations bring it closer to the mode of science fiction. A mode of structural and poststructural analysis—anthropological, economic, linguistic, and psychological—redeems the usual narrative emblems of heroic fantasy and its banal fictive discourse and discovers a complex and sophisticated, not to mention self-reflexive, ground for the behavior of survivor types in every class of a society on the brink of civilization.

Tales of Nevèrÿon introduces almost all the important figures of the series: Gorgik, Old Venn, Norema, Small Sarg, and Raven. There are others who will reappear in the background and foreground throughout. Various major figures meet in continually surprising situations, growing older from tale to tale, something else that does not often happen in sword-and-sorcery. Perhaps the most important "character" of all is the great port city of Kolhari itself, which reflects, in varying degrees of multiplexity, Delany's beloved New York. But then, as Delany's fictive scholar K. Leslie Steiner points out, the whole "series is a document of its times—our times, today." This is never more clear than in "The Tale of Plagues and Carnivals," where ancient Kolhari and contemporary New York literally overlap as they both attempt to fight a plague (in New York it is AIDS).

One of the things Delany is interested in narrating is the process of thinking itself—especially thinking that is learning too. What Georgik learns from his varied experiences is enough to make him, at age thirty-six, and "[f]or the civilization in which he lived . . . a civilized man." Venn, whose tale follows and reflects upon the meanings of Gorgik's, is a teacher, but her lessons make their mark on Norema. And so it goes, from tale to tale, each one altering our perception of the ones before and, therefore, the meanings of them all. Delany has long used his fiction to ask philosophical questions relating to models and how language works in the modeling process. Venn's most significant lesson is about the distorted modeling that appears in mirrors, and mirrors reflecting mirrors. Hers is a directly materialist lesson, but Norema immediately thinks of an idealist application, which horrifies Venn, and eventually the young woman too. In a later tale, Old Venn is mirrored (and therefore distorted) as a teacher by "the Master," whose written dialogues, unlike her open-ended tales, freeze the quicksilver musings of an old entertainer into stone. That we cannot help but think of Plato and Socrates in relation to the Master and his friend is all too deliberate.

While interrogating many traditional views of culture and society, the Return to Nevèrÿon series is most successful in its subtle and often savagely comic investigation of binary thinking. All the usual suspects appear only to be narratively deconstructed. Although some of the characters simply reverse accepted hierarchical binaries, placing woman over man, for example, or slave over master (and the complex exploration of slavery and its cultural effects clearly invites readers to reflect on the historical experience of Afro-Americans), or writing over speech, or nature over culture, the series refuses such an easy out and self-reflexively interrogates the very concept. It also insists that no single, simple meaning can be derived from the ever-changing narrative focus. As Ken James puts it, "To try to trace out any single privileged interpretation through the texts one must in effect ignore the elaborate destabilizing frames which Delany has set up around/within them." If the Return to Nevèrÿon series demands rereadings that will continually change one's sense of the whole and each of its parts, it also offers sensuous and intellectual delights few fictions today can match.

Stars in My Pocket Like Grains of Sand stands in relation to most science fiction as the Return to Nevèrÿon series does to sword-

and-sorcery, shoving the usual emblems of far future "space opera" (those colorful and romantic action-adventure stories of interplanetary or interstellar conflict) to the peripheries of the narrative and replacing them with an intensely realized and utterly new "domestic" vision. Certainly it gives a whole new twist to the term "family values" in its representation of narrator Marq Dyeth's family, actually a "stream" of chosen or adopted members both human and alien that thus survives from generation to generation. Of course, this is not the only model of a family in the 6,000 worlds, all at different levels of "civilization," that make up inhabited space. Various societies lean toward one or the other of two opposing forces, "Family," which tends toward the hierarchical, and "Sygn," which tends toward the anarchical democratic. Both models seek to prevent "Cultural Fugue," which usually brings about the destruction of a world and its society, but Family does so through exclusion and fixity while Sygn does so through inclusion and flexibility. Even though Marq is an Industrial Diplomat and therefore able to cross many social and cultural boundaries, she speaks from deep within Sygn psychology and cannot always understand the behavior of those who are too far down the spectrum toward Family, such as the Thants, a family supposedly friends to the Dyeths.

But Marq and her universe do not even appear in the novel until after a novella-length Prologue that is quite literally "A World Apart." It is the story of one Rat Korga, a young man who has been given "Radical Anxiety Termination," which makes him so tractable that he is sold by the corporation that gave him the treatment and used as a slave until the day his world is destroyed (possibly by a form of Cultural Fugue). Rat's treatment deleted certain connections in his brain that make it possible directly to access information networks, so he will always need a prosthesis to do so. One of the most stunning pure science fiction moments in "A World Apart" comes when he uses one prosthesis to "read" a number of famous works of literature. Delany conveys his excitement and delight as well as delivering a witty critical discussion of each work. Somehow, Korga survives the destruction of his planet and is brought to Marq by "the Web" (with its "General Information" services, "the Web" oversees the flow of information throughout the galaxy), as she is his, as he is her, perfect object of desire.

The previous sentence indicates another of Delany's linguistic speculations in *Stars in My Pocket Like Grains of Sand*. Marq, like Rat, is male, but in Arachnia, the Sygn language used throughout the galaxy, "she" is the generic pronoun and "woman" the noun for individuals of all intelligent species; the masculine pronoun attaches only to the object of sexual desire no matter what "his" gender or species. As readers learn to read Marq's pronouns, they begin to think of her culture in a different manner, which is the point. Nor is Arachnia's egalitarian posture irrelevant to Delany's other work, as one of Marq's comments indicates: " 'slave' is one of those words in Arachnia that, amidst a flurry of sexual suggestions, strongly connotes the least pleasant aspects of 'master.' "

Stars in My Pocket Like Grains of Sand is often difficult to follow because, although Delany is a master of what William Gibson has called "superspecificity," Marq's often incredibly rich descriptions of place, life, and activity are limited by her personal focus, and she sees so much from inside historical knowledge the text refuses to supplement. The reader must enter as fully as possible into Marq's sensorium and mind and try to see things her way. This works brilliantly with the formal dinner the Dyeths give in honor of the Thants, whose deliberate rudeness (having finally come out full strength for Family, they are sure in their superiority that Dyeth family sexual and interspecies behavior is "perverted") simply confuses her. Such thorough defamiliarization constructs one of the most completely realized future cultures in all science fiction. So multiplex and demanding a novel as *Stars in My Pocket Like Grains*

of Sand will garner critical analysis for a long time to come.

Delany's redaction and expansion of an early short story into *They Fly at Çiron* (1993) is a delightful science fantasy that manages to carry on many of the arguments about culture already so thoroughly explored in his major works. In some ways, it seems to be a return to a simpler or at least smoother style, but it continues to insist upon the self-reflexive nature of all valid science fiction narration. Although he has written the historical fictions of *Atlantis: Three Tales* (1995), it seems that he also intends, finally, to complete the diptych begun with *Stars in My Pocket Like Grains of Sand*, and readers can hope to see *The Splendor and Misery of Bodies, of Cities* within the next few years.

Selected Bibliography

Delany has argued that few paraliterary texts appear in good or error-free first editions. This has certainly proved true of his own work. The Gregg Press and the Wesleyan University Press editions probably come as close as can be expected to what he would call authenticity and are therefore "author-approved" editions.

WORKS OF SAMUEL R. DELANY

The Jewels of Aptor. New York: Ace Books, 1962 (abridged) and 1968 (uncut); Boston: Gregg Press, 1976. (Introduction by Don Hausdorff.)

Captives of the Flame. New York: Ace Books, 1963. Revised and enlarged as *Out of the Dead City*; London: Sphere, 1968.

The Towers of Toron. New York: Ace Books, 1964. Revised edition; London: Sphere, 1968.

The Ballad of Beta-2. New York: Ace Books, 1965; Boston: Gregg Press, 1977. (Introduction by David G. Hartwell.)

City of a Thousand Suns. New York: Ace Books, 1965. Revised edition; London: Sphere, 1969.

Babel-17. New York: Ace Books, 1966; Boston: Gregg Press, 1976. (Introduction by Robert Scholes.)

Empire Star. New York: Ace Books, 1966; Boston: Gregg Press, 1977. (Introduction by David G. Hartwell.)

The Einstein Intersection. New York: Ace Books, 1967; London: Victor Gollancz, 1968. (The British edition has a one-page chapter that is missing from the American edition.)

Nova. Garden City, N.Y.: Doubleday, 1968; Boston: Gregg Press, 1977. (Introduction by Algis Budrys.)

The Fall of the Towers. New York: Ace Books, 1970; Boston: Gregg Press, 1977. (Introduction by Joseph Milicia. A one-volume edition of *Captives of the Flame, Towers of Toron,* and *City of a Thousand Suns.*)

Driftglass. Garden City, N.Y.: Doubleday, 1971; Boston: Gregg Press, 1978. (Introduction by Robert Thurston. A story collection that includes "The Star Pit," "Dog in a Fisherman's Net," "Corona," "Aye, and Gomorrah . . . ," "Driftglass," "We, in Some Strange Power's Employ, Move on a Rigorous Line," "Cage of Brass," "High Weir," "Time Considered as a Helix of Semiprecious Stones," and "Night and the Loves of Joe Dicostanzo.")

The Tides of Lust. New York: Lancer Books, 1973. Reprinted as *Equinox* (original title), New York: Masquerade, 1994.

Dhalgren. New York: Bantam Books, 1975; Boston: Gregg Press, 1978; Hanover, N.H., and London: Wesleyan University Press, 1996. (Introduction by Jean Mark Gawron.)

Triton. New York: Bantam Books, 1976; Boston: Gregg Press, 1977; Hanover, N.H., and London: Wesleyan University Press, 1996. (Introduction by Jean Mark Gawron.)

The Jewel-Hinged Jaw: Notes on the Language of Science Fiction. Elizabethtown, N.Y.: Dragon Press, 1977; New York: Berkley, 1978. (The paperback is a corrected edition.)

The American Shore: Meditations on a Tale of Science Fiction by Thomas M. Disch—"Angouleme." Elizabethtown, N.Y.: Dragon Press, 1978. (An essay of Thomas M. Disch's short story "Angouleme.")

Empire. New York: Berkley, 1978. (A graphic novel conceived in collaboration with artist Howard V. Chaykin.)

Heavenly Breakfast: An Essay on the Winter of Love. New York: Bantam Books, 1979.

Tales of Nevèrÿon. New York: Bantam Books, 1979; Hanover, N.H., and London: Wesleyan University Press, 1993.

Distant Stars. New York: Bantam Books, 1981. (Short stories).

Neveryóna; or, The Tale of Signs and Cities: Some Informal Remarks Toward the Modular Calculus, Part Four. New York: Bantam Books, 1983; Hanover, N.H., and London: Wesleyan University Press, 1993.

Starboard Wine: More Notes on the Language of Science Fiction. Pleasantville, N.Y.: Dragon, 1984.

Stars in My Pocket Like Grains of Sand. New York: Bantam Books, 1984.

Flight from Nevèrÿon. New York: Bantam Books, 1985; Hanover, N.H., and London: Wesleyan University Press, 1994.

The Complete Nebula Award-Winning Fiction of Samuel R. Delany. New York: Bantam Books, 1986. (Omnibus volume containing *Babel-17, A Fabulous,*

Formless Darkness [original title of *The Einstein Intersection*], "Aye, and Gomorrah . . . ," and "Time Considered as a Helix of Semi-Precious Stones.")

The Bridge of Lost Desire. New York: Arbor House, 1987. Reprinted as *Return to Nevèrÿon,* London: Grafton, 1989; Hanover, N.H., and London: Wesleyan University Press, 1994.

"Is Cyberpunk a Good Thing or a Bad Thing." *Mississippi Review,* 16 (1988): 28–35.

The Motion of Light in Water: Sex and Science Fiction Writing in the East Village 1957–1965. New York: Arbor House/William Morrow, 1988. Expanded and revised edition, London: Grafton, 1990. Further revised as *The Motion of Light in Water: Sex and Science Fiction in the East Village,* New York: Richard Kasak/Masquerade, 1993.

Wagner/Artaud: A Play of Nineteenth and Twentieth Century Critical Fictions. New York: Ansatz, 1988.

"Neither the Beginning nor the End of Structuralism, Post-Structuralism, Semiotics, or Deconstruction for SF Readers: An Introduction." *New York Review of Science Fiction,* no. 6 (February 1989): 1, 8–12; no. 7 (March 1989): 14–18; no. 8 (April 1989): 9–11.

"How Not to Teach Science Fiction." *New York Review of Science Fiction,* no. 13 (September 1989): 1, 12–16.

The Star Pit. New York: TOR, 1989. (Bound with John Varley's *Tango Charlie and Foxtrot Romeo.*)

The Straits of Messina. Seattle: Wash.: Serconia, 1989. (Essays on his own writing.)

"Science and Literature." *New York Review of Science Fiction,* no. 23 (July 1990): 1, 8–11.

"On *Triton* and Other Matters: An Interview with Samuel R. Delany." *Science-Fiction Studies,* 52 (November 1990): 295–324.

"Zelazny/Varley/Gibson—and Quality." *New York Review of Science Fiction,* no. 48 (August 1992): 1, 10–13; no. 49 (September 1992): 1, 3–7.

"The Future of the Body: And Science Fiction and Technology." *New York Review of Science Fiction,* no. 51 (November 1992): 1, 3–5.

Driftglass/Starshards. London: HarperCollins/Grafton, 1993. (Collected shorter fiction.)

They Fly at Çiron. Seattle, Wash.: Incunabula, 1993; New York: TOR, 1995.

Hogg. Boulder, Colo., and Normal, Ill.: Fiction Collective Two/Black Ice, 1994.

The Mad Man. New York: Richard Kasak, 1994.

Silent Interviews: On Language, Race, Sex, Science Fiction, and Some Comics: A Collection of Written Interviews. Hanover, N.H., and London: Wesleyan University Press, 1994.

Longer Views: Extended Essays. Hanover, N.H., and London: Wesleyan University Press, 1996.

"The Politics of Paraliterary Criticism." *New York Review of Science Fiction,* no. 98 (October 1996): 1, 8–13; no. 99 (November 1996): 1, 8–12; no. 100 (December 1996): 1, 8–12.

248

Atlantis: Three Tales. Hanover, N.H., and London: Wesleyan University Press, 1995. (Also in a limited first edition from Seattle, Wash.: Incunabula, 1995; contains the novel *Atlantis: Model 1924* plus "Eric, Gwen, and D.H. Lawrence's Esthetic of Unrectified Feeling" and "*Citre et Trans.*")

"A Tribute to Judith Merril." *New York Review of Science Fiction,* no. 111 (November 1997): 1, 9.

CRITICAL AND BIOGRAPHICAL STUDIES

While early criticism tended toward thematic and formal analysis, later criticism has paid more attention to the way Delany's Afro-American heritage and his homosexuality have influenced his art.

Alterman, Peter. "The Surreal Translations of Samuel R. Delany." *Science-Fiction Studies,* 4 (1977): 25–34.

Barbour, Douglas. *Worlds Out of Words: The SF Novel of Samuel R. Delany.* Frome, Somerset: Bran's Head Books, 1979. (The only full-length critical study of all the novels up to and including *Triton.*)

Bartter, Martha A. "The (SF) Reader and the Quantum Paradigms: Problems in Delany's *Stars in My Pocket Like Grains of Sand.*" *Science-Fiction Studies,* 17 (November 1990): 325–340.

Broderick, Damien, *Reading by Starlight: Postmodern Science Fiction.* London and New York: Routledge, 1995. (A study of the genre and its postmodern potential in terms of Delany's criticism and fiction.)

Dery, Mark, "Black to the Future: Interviews with Samuel R. Delany, Greg Tate, and Tricia Rose." In his *Flame Wars: The Discourse of Cyberculture.* Durham, N.C.: Duke University Press, 1994.

Fekete, John. "*The Dispossessed* and *Triton*: Act and System in Utopian Science Fiction." *Science-Fiction Studies,* 18 (1979): 129–143.

Fox, Robert Elliot. "Samuel R. Delany: Astro Black." In his *Conscientious Sorcerers: The Black Postmodernist Fiction of Leroi Jones/Amiri Baraka, Ishmael Reed, and Samuel R. Delany* Westport, Conn.: Greenwood, 1987.

Hardesty, William H. "Semiotics, Space Opera, and *Babel-17.*" *Mosaic,* 13, no. 3–4 (1980): 63–69.

Kelso, Sylvia. "'Across never': Postmodern Theory and Narrative Praxis in Samuel R. Delany's NEVÈRŸON

Cycle." *Science-Fiction Studies,* 24 (July 1997): 289–301.

Miesel, Sandra. "Samuel R. Delany's Use of Myth in *Nova.*" *Extrapolation,* 12, no. 2 (1971): 86–93.

Moylan, Tom. "Samuel R. Delany: *Triton.*" In his *Demand the Impossible: Science Fiction and the Utopian Imagination.* London and New York: Methuen, 1986.

Mullen, R. D. "Delany as a Postmodern Edmund Wilson." *Science-Fiction Studies,* 24 (March 1997): 156–160.

Peplov, Michael W., and Robert S. Bravard. *Samuel R. Delany: A Primary and Secondary Bibliography.* Boston: G. K. Hall, 1980. (Includes biographical material.)

Sallis, James (Guest Editor: Special Section). "Samuel R. Delany." *The Review of Contemporary Fiction,* 16, no. 3 (Fall 1996): 90–171. (Interview with Delany, excerpts from his writing, and short essays by David Lunde, Michael Hemmingson, Robert Elliot Fox, Marc Laidlaw, Russell Blackford, Capper Nichols, Mary Kay Bray, John Sallis, David N. Samuelson, Rebecca Cooper, and the editor.)

———, ed. *Ash of Stars: On the Writing of Samuel R. Delany.* Jackson: University Press of Mississippi, 1996. (Contains essays, sometimes longer versions of the ones in *The Review of Contemporary Fiction,* by Carl Malmgren, Mary Kay Bray, Russell Blackford, Robert Elliot Fox, Jean Mark Gawron, David N. Samuelson, Kathleen L. Spencer, Ray Davis, Ken James, and the editor).

Samuelson, David N. "Necessary Constraints: Samuel R. Delany on Science Fiction." *Foundation,* 60 (Spring 1994): 21–41.

———. "New Wave, Old Ocean: A Comparative Study of Novels by Brunner and Delany." *Extrapolation,* 15, no. 1 (1973): 75–96.

———. "Talking." *Science-Fiction Studies,* 22 (July 1995): 264–271.

Scobie, Stephen. "Different Mazes: Mythology in Samuel R. Delany's *The Einstein Intersection.*" *Riverside Quarterly,* 5, no. 1 (1971): 12–19.

Slusser, George. *The Delany Intersection.* San Bernardino, Calif.: Borgo, 1977.

Weedman, Jane Branham, *Samuel R. Delany.* Mercer Island, Wash.: Starmont, 1982.

—DOUGLAS BARBOUR

PHILIP K. DICK

(1928–1982)

SINCE HIS DEATH on 2 March 1982, Philip Kindred Dick has become established as a writer whose importance extends far beyond the boundaries of the science fiction genre. Such commercial and critical success as he gleaned while he was alive was modest, but he posthumously became the subject of an enormous quantity of critical writing, becoming the most widely praised and most earnestly dissected science fiction writer of his generation.

Dick's life has been dissected as carefully as his work in such biographical studies as Lawrence Sutin's *Divine Invasions: A Life of Philip K. Dick* (1989). The story told therein is that of a man so afflicted by the stress of ordinary social life that he never fully adapted to its demands. Born on 16 December 1928 in Chicago but soon transplanted to California, where he lived for the rest of his life, Dick was unhappy as a child, resentfully charging his mother with having caused the death of his twin sister, Jane Charlotte, by neglect and failing to lavish adequate affection on him. He became addicted to the amphetamines prescribed for the relief of his childhood asthma and remained dependent on them for much of his life. He dropped out of college after a year and even found work in a record store, surrounded by the classical music he loved, too much to bear. He was virtually compelled to channel his ambitions into writing because he was unfitted for any other way of life.

Dick was eventually to marry five times, but only the second and third marriages lasted longer than a year before estrangement set in.

Toward the end of his life, he pursued relationships with much younger women with the same obsessiveness that he brought to his writing. The brief taste of fame that he achieved before his death only served to intensify the maudlin anguish he felt about the many afflictions that had cursed his life. Although after his death the critics were almost unanimous in claiming that Dick had succeeded in turning his psychological difficulties into precious fuel for his vivid literary imagination, his career always seemed to him to be a catalog of undeserved disappointments. He always wanted to write realistic novels passing plaintive judgment upon the world around him, but the only pieces he could sell were science fiction stories, about whose merits he was conscientiously defensive.

Only one of Dick's early realistic novels saw print while he was alive, in a small press edition issued sixteen years after it was written. The posthumous publication of the rest has proved that even in his twenties he was a writer of great ability, insight, and originality, but he died without ever receiving that endorsement. That delay added one final insult to a long career of injury. The plot of the still-unpublished *Voices from the Street* (written 1952–1953) is summarized by Sutin this way: "A young man, struggling with an unsatisfying job and a dreary marriage, falls into total despair when the supposed ideals of both politics and religion fail him." That almost sums up Dick's entire oeuvre of "mainstream" fiction, except that his characters doggedly maintain their hopeless struggles, in their own ineptly courageous fashion.

We now know that Dick wrote his first full-length science fiction novel in 1953–1954, alongside the calculatedly ground-breaking and controversial *Mary and the Giant,* and that he wrote four more realistic novels between 1955 and 1957, all of which failed to sell; the only ones that survive are *The Broken Bubble* (1988) and *Puttering About in a Small Land* (1985). Dick then attempted to blend the interests and techniques of his realistic fiction and science fiction together in *Nicholas and the Higs* (which failed to sell and was subsequently lost) and *Time out of Joint* (1959). Between 1958 and 1960 he produced *In Milton Lumky Territory* (1985), *Confessions of a Crap Artist* (1975), *The Man Whose Teeth Were All Exactly Alike* (1984) and *Humpty Dumpty in Oakland* (1986), which follow the example of *Puttering About in a Small Land* in dealing with awkward moral dilemmas arising out of intimate relationships that are severely stressed by economic difficulties.

Dick made a sustained effort to contrive uplifting endings for these fundamentally downbeat stories, but it made no difference; none of the novels sold. In the meantime, he deserted his second wife, Kleo, to whom he had been married in 1951 and with whom he had lived frugally through some extremely dispiriting times, in favor of his third wife, Anne, whom he married in 1958. This move was deemed unwise by his biographers—although not as unwise as the leap from the frying pan to the fire he took when he married his neurotic fourth wife in 1967—but it was the pressure exerted by Anne's imperious expectation of a reasonable standard of living that drove Dick to the prodigious levels of production he attained for a few years thereafter.

At the time, it was not obvious that Dick's steadily increasing success within the science fiction field was won at such cost nor that he counted it so cheap, but it now has to be evaluated within that context, and its content needs to be analyzed with that backdrop in mind.

Dick's first published work, "Beyond Lies the Wub," in *Planet Stories* (1952), gave some indication of the direction that his career was to take. Humans exploring an alien world buy a large, piglike creature called a wub. The wub welcomes this opportunity to exchange ideas, enthusiastically discussing philosophy and comparative mythology, but the spacemen simply want to eat it. They have their way, but the wub mentality is surprisingly hard to eradicate; having consumed its flesh, they soon find themselves sharing its fascinations.

Wubs crop up again in "Not by Its Cover" (1968), in which their fur is used for binding books because of its self-repairing properties. Here the tendency of the pacifist wub Weltanschauung to permeate the world of the exploiters is expressed by the fact that the texts protected by their fur are slowly revised. One text that is completely obliterated by this strange influence is Thomas Paine's *The Age of Reason.* According to Dick's own philosophy—which has something in common with the wub's—we are twice deluded if we believe that we have reached the Age of Reason: we are mistaken if we think that the world will yield to rational analysis and we are wrong if we believe that it should.

From mid-1952 until the end of 1955, Dick was one of the most prolific short-story writers in the field, taking full advantage of the rapid expansion of the magazine market that occurred during that period. All the concerns that were to become the hallmarks of his work first manifested themselves during this period.

The difficulty of distinguishing between the real and the ersatz is terrifyingly manifest in "Second Variety" (1953), in which war machines embarked upon their own paths of evolution begin producing duplicates of pathetic human figures as bait to trap real people. In "Impostor" (1953) the protagonist enters a nightmarish experience when those around him become convinced that he is an android bomb. Unfortunately, it turns out that he is. In later years Dick's explorations of similar

Philip K. Dick in 1968. Photo by Jay Kay Klein

Death makes me mad. Human and animal suffering makes me mad; whenever one of my cats dies I curse God and I mean it; I feel fury at him. I'd like to get him here where I could interrogate him, tell him that I think the world is screwed up, that man didn't sin and fall but was pushed—which is bad enough—but was then sold the lie that he is basically sinful, which I know he is not. (page 43)

In some later works, such as "Faith of Our Fathers" (1967) and *A Maze of Death* (1970), remodeled theologies become concrete; and in the novel written with Roger Zelazny, *Deus Irae* (1976), the protagonist embarks upon a quest to find the living embodiment of the god who has visited his terrible wrath upon the world.

The third prevalent theme in Dick's early work—a theme that becomes more important during the course of his career—is the gradual mechanization of the environment and the contribution made by this process to human alienation. In "Autofac" (1955) self-governing factories, like the war machines of "Second Variety," take up their own projects and "forget" the humans who built them and whom they are supposed to serve. Dick sees the relationship between man and machine as one that is much more complicated than we realize. In his novella "The Variable Man" (1953), a "fix-it" man who has an uncanny empathy with machines is snatched from his own time (1913) into the far future, where he becomes an unpredictable element in a computer-run world, eventually saving it from its own overdetermined degeneracy. (The computers' assessments of probability had been determining all political and military actions.) Another early short novel, "Vulcan's Hammer" (1956; expanded for book publication in 1960), begins with the familiar idea of a computer developing sentience and its own motives for action, but here there are two computers that have contending political parties established in semisymbiotic relationships with them, and the question of who will (or can) win the developing conflict is a vexing one.

existential predicaments have grown more sophisticated: "The Electric Ant" (1969) and *We Can Build You* (1972) are more detailed, more sensitive, and far more ambiguous in their conclusions.

"Prominent Author" (1954) features an unconventional explanation of divine impotence, while a more eloquent metaphorical analysis of the predicament of a creator who finds that his creations have begun evolving of their own accord is found in "The Preserving Machine" (1953). This kind of question remains fundamental to Dick's work, though it is not as obvious as the theme of appearance versus reality; its essence is an exaggerated consciousness of the arbitrariness of the world we live in, and in his stories that deal with creation (and sometimes with formal theology), this consciousness demands an answer to the question of why things should be in the terrible state that they are. In his autobiographical essay in *Foundation*, Dick says:

253

Another version of the question "What is real?" emerges in stories dealing with the insidious invasion of the world, in which the protagonists are surrounded by illusions that threaten to confound entirely their attempts to discover the actual state of affairs. In early stories, such as "Colony" (1953), the illusion usually can be dispelled, or at least explained; but in the later works this becomes gradually more difficult, until in the end it almost ceases to make sense. This is the main trend that can be followed through all Dick's major works.

In the mid-1950's Dick began to produce science fiction novels in profusion. The first of these, *Solar Lottery* (1955; British edition titled *World of Chance*), belongs to a tradition of science fiction novels, begun in the 1950's, in which the society of the future is distorted by being run (corruptly) according to the notional principles of some particular group or institution. Dick's version of this sort of eccentric totalitarian state is a world where power is supposedly determined by lottery, supervised by a quasi-dictatorial "Quizmaster." There are elements characteristic of Dick in the story too—robot assassins and a quasi-religious quest for the mythical tenth planet, called Flame Disc—but it remains something of a patchwork.

Rather more typical is the short novel "A Glass of Darkness" (1956; book form, *The Cosmic Puppets*, 1957), in which the protagonist returns to the place of his birth and discovers that it has undergone a complete metamorphosis. He finds a record of his birth in the local newspaper office—and a record of his death at the age of nine. Eventually he discovers that the whole valley is a battleground on which two demiurges (named Ormazd and Ahriman, after the opposed deities of Zoroastrian mythology) fight to impose their formative wills. At this early stage of Dick's career, the curse can still be lifted and the metamorphosis undone.

Dick's second full-length science fiction novel, *The World Jones Made* (1956), is an impressive work about the career of a man named Jones who is dislocated in time—who is, from his own point of view, living in a world that lies a year in his past. As far as the rest of the world is concerned, of course, the situation is rather different: Jones can see one year into the future, but he cannot change the course of events. In this novel Dick manages to put the notion of precognition into an entirely new perspective, with telling effect.

Dick's next science fiction novel, *The Man Who Japed* (1956), is one of his weakest efforts, but he recovered his form magnificently in *Eye in the Sky* (1957). In this story a group of people involved in a freak accident find themselves in an alternate world where a fundamentalist cult is all-powerful, all of its beliefs being literally true. Eventually the protagonists deduce that they are in the believed-in mental world of one of their number, trapped inside the web of preconceptions he uses to interpret the real world and orient himself within it. In effect, they have been embraced and entrapped by his insanity. They contrive to dispel the illusion, but immediately they find themselves in another, and must return to reality via a sequence of distorted world visions, each representing the delusions under which yet another member of the group actually lives. But at this point Dick still takes for granted that some of his characters, being sane, really confront the world as it is.

Eye in the Sky is the last novel of Dick's first prolific period. From the time of its appearance until the publication of *The Man in the High Castle* in 1962, only one original novel appeared: *Time out of Joint* (1959), though Dick also published the expanded book version of *Vulcan's Hammer* (1960) and an extended version of another early novella, "Time Pawn" (1954), retitled *Dr. Futurity* (1960). *Time out of Joint* has strong affinities with *Eye in the Sky*; it is the story of Ragle Gumm, who is in psychotic withdrawal from reality, living in a mock-up of the world of the past, where he makes his living "solving" a newspaper competition. What he is really doing is anticipating by occult means where bombs will fall, thus helping to prolong a destructive war. Ultimately, though, he rediscovers both his true world and his true self. He is the last of Dick's protagonists to manage that—at some time during the gap in his writing career, Dick lost his faith in the prospect of recovering a single reality from the distortions that permeate our conceptions of it.

During this five-year interval Dick was by no means inactive. On the contrary, he was writing novel after novel, attempting to become a mainstream writer. None of these experimental novels was published at the time, though one of them eventually was printed: *Confessions of a Crap Artist* (1975), written in 1959. This is primarily the story of Jack Isidore, a man whose naïveté leads him to see the world in a rather peculiar way and makes him quite impotent at getting along in it. He is taken in by his sister and her husband; but it turns out that despite their greater intelligence, they are not much better at the business of living than he is. In the end, it seems that Isidore's condition is preferable, for although he is all kinds of a fool, he is gentle and tries as hard as he can to do what he knows is right. And he, at least, does know—although practically everything else he thinks he knows is false.

This type of conclusion is carried forward by Dick into the works of his second productive period, in which characters perpetually find themselves in worlds where all their empirical knowledge counts for very little—his prescription for characters thus becalmed is that they should seek a sound moral anchorage, and should try to behave as well as they can, no matter what their circumstances.

Dick's second period of prolific production began with his first real sign of success: *The Man in the High Castle* won a Hugo award for best novel in 1963. This is an alternate-world novel in which America, having lost World War II, is partitioned into a German (eastern) zone and a Japanese (western) zone. California, the setting of the story, lies in the Japanese zone. The main character is Mr. Tagomi, who begins to doubt the existential validity of his world after a brief visionary experience. In time, his consultation of the *I Ching* reveals to him that his world is not in fact the "true"

world, which is represented by a novel about an alternate world in which America won World War II. But the reader can sympathize with Tagomi, for the world of the novel-within-the-novel is no more ours than it is his. The strands of the plot of *Man in the High Castle* remain disconnected, and there is an arbitrariness about its development that seems to have been encouraged by Dick's use of the *I Ching* in composing the novel.

"Reality" is equally elusive in "All We Marsmen" (1963; published in book form as *Martian Time-Slip*, 1964), whose chief characters are dislocated by schizophrenia. The focal point of the story is a child who has precognitive ability, but attempts by others to manipulate him lead only to their partial absorption into the domain of his world view. This novel is excellent, but was part of a flood of fiction of rather uneven quality that includes several unsatisfactory works.

The best of several long stories first published in 1964 is the novel *The Three Stigmata of Palmer Eldritch*, the first of Dick's novels in which reality becomes utterly and hopelessly confused as the characters become enmeshed in a multilayered net of hallucinations initiated by the influence of the alien drug Chew-Z. Chew-Z is brought into the solar system by the mysterious Palmer Eldritch, who seems at first to be interested simply in competing with local manufacturers of hallucinogens used by colonists on Mars to escape temporarily from the miseries of their existence. But Eldritch's personality ultimately comes to dominate the unrealized world like that of an evil deity, his dominion symbolized by the recurrence of his "stigmata"—mechanical organs replacing certain parts of his body.

Another novel in which Dick uses drugs as the agents of dislocation is *Now Wait for Last Year* (1966), whose hero is lost in a maze of alternate-probability worlds after taking a drug that shifts him through time. The only real anchor to which he can tie his life is the resolution of a moral dilemma: whether to devote himself to the care of his estranged and irredeemably sick wife. In the concluding sequence he asks the advice of a robot cab, which tells him to stay with her. Asked why, it replies: "Because . . . life is composed of reality configurations so constituted. To abandon her would be to say, I can't endure reality as such. I have to have uniquely special easier conditions."

Here Dick proposes at least a tentative solution to the problem of sorting out the real and the ersatz, the human and the mechanical. The reality we have to accept, he argues, is a moral order rather than a natural one, and we will accept as "human" everything that can take its proper place within that order. Machines, such as the robot cab, may aspire to humanity if they act scrupulously, and humans may be stripped of their humanity if they do not. This preoccupation with morality and the building of an unorthodox system of metaphors in which "human" and "android" lose their literal meanings in becoming different characterizations of good and evil can be seen in many of the minor works of the period—perhaps most impressively in *The Simulacra* (1964) and *Dr. Bloodmoney* (1965), but also in the more trivial *Game-Players of Titan* (1963) and *Clans of the Alphane Moon* (1964). The theme is subject to much more detailed and explicit analysis in two of his best novels: *Do Androids Dream of Electric Sheep?* (1968) and *We Can Build You* (serialized as "A. Lincoln-Simulacrum" in 1969–1970; book form, 1972).

The protagonist of *Do Androids Dream* is employed in hunting down and killing androids that are infiltrating Earth from colony worlds. He identifies them by means of an "empathy test," but their ability to simulate human behavior has advanced to the point where they can pass the test. In this world real animals are all but extinct, and humans are trying to save the last remaining ones by keeping them as pets. For those who cannot afford real animals there are simulated ones, so that a show of deep concern can be maintained. Most people also possess and use an "empathy box," by means of which they can identify with the struggles of a modern Christ figure who is forever toiling uphill against a

rain of stones that threaten to tumble him down into the "tomb-world." The protagonist thinks he is faced with the problem of determining where the boundaries between the real parts of his world and the fake ones lie, but he is wrong: the real problem, as highlighted by the story, is in deciding where the boundaries begin to matter. Ridley Scott's film *Blade Runner* (1982) discards much of this apparatus but conserves the thematic core.

The same central theme recurs in *We Can Build You*, whose narrator is in love with a designer of androids whose schizophrenia makes her more androidal than her androids. At one point she tells the narrator that he is an android she has made, and he becomes schizophrenic too; but in the end he begins to see what is important and what is not, though she cannot. (The ending of the serial version, incidentally, was added by Ted White; the book version contains Dick's unembellished original text.)

The thinking behind these stories is restated in Dick's essay "Man, Android, and Machine" (1976):

Within the universe there exist fierce cold things, which I have given the name "machines" to. Their behaviour frightens me, especially when it imitates human behaviour so well that I get the uncomfortable sense that these things are trying to pass themselves off as humans but are not. I call them "androids," which is my own way of using that word. By "android" I do not mean a sincere attempt to create in the laboratory a human being. . . . I mean a thing somehow generated to deceive us in a cruel way, to cause us to think it to be one of ourselves. Made in a laboratory—that aspect is not meaningful to me; the entire universe is one vast laboratory, and out of it come sly and cruel entities which smile as they reach out to shake hands. But their handshake is the grip of death, and their smile has the coldness of the grave. . . .

A human being without the proper empathy or feeling is the same as an android built to lack it, either by design or mistake. We mean, basically, someone who does not care about the fate which his fellow living creatures fall victim to; he stands detached, a spectator, acting out by his indifference John Donne's theorem that "No man is an island," but giving that theorem a twist: that which is a mental and moral island *is not a man....*

"Man" or "human being" are terms which we must understand correctly and apply, but they apply not to origin or to any ontology but to a way of being in the world; if a mechanical construct halts in its customary operation to lend you assistance, then you will posit to it, gratefully, a humanity which no analysis of its transistors and relay-systems can elucidate.... As soul is to man, man is to machine: it is the added dimension, in terms of functional hierarchy. (pages 202–203)

The remaining novels that Dick published before his second productive phase ended in 1970 are concerned not so much with problems of orientation as with more abstract questions about determinism and the essence of moral order. The central question of *Galactic Pot-Healer* (1969), *Ubik* (1969), *Our Friends from Frolix 8* (1970), and *A Maze of Death* (1970) is a metaphysical rather than a pragmatic one: they ask "Who (or what) is actually determining what goes on here?"

The victory, in all these novels, of a context in which there is no objective reality is more than simply an expression of uncertainty. There was a brief period when Dick thought that this uncertainty might be a good thing. In "The Android and the Human" (1973), he wrote:

For us, though, there can be no system; maybe *all* systems—that is, any theoretical, verbal, symbolic, semantic, etc., formulation that attempts to act as an all-encompassing, all-explaining hypothesis of what the world is about—are manifestations of paranoia. We should be content with the meaningless, the contradictory, the hostile, and most of all the unexplainably warm and giving—the total so-called environment, in other words, behaving very like a person, like the behaviour of one intricate, subtle, half-veiled, deep, perplexing, and much to be loved human being to another. To be feared a little, too, some-

times. And perpetually misunderstood. About which we can neither know or be sure; we must only trust and make guesses toward. ... What it is actually up to we may never know. But at least this is better, is it not, than to possess the self-defeating, life-defeating spurious certitude of the paranoid?

Dick seems to have recanted this view, for when he again began to publish after a lapse of some years, a sound and safe reality had once again become something worth seeking. In his third novel featuring a drug-induced, hallucinatory reality, *Flow My Tears, the Policeman Said* (1974), the hero ultimately finds his way home; and in his fourth, *A Scanner Darkly* (1977), the fact that the protagonist is forever lost is represented as a stark tragedy. The road to "hallucinatory enlightenment" is here sign-posted as a road straight to hell, on which it is almost impossible to make a U-turn.

Before writing the final draft of *Flow My Tears, the Policeman Said*, Dick had opened his house to assorted drug abusers and juvenile delinquents, spent time in various mental hospitals, and suffered a break-in about whose perpetrators he theorized wildly, apparently believing himself to be under close surveillance by the FBI. (When Dick's FBI file was eventually opened to inspection under the Freedom of Information Act, its only contents were a letter that Dick had sent the FBI denouncing Thomas M. Disch as an enemy of the people on the grounds that *Camp Concentration* (1968) was cryptically subversive.) He also spent some time in Vancouver after being the guest of honor at a convention there, seemingly feeling that he might be in danger if he returned home.

When he had brought *Flow My Tears, the Policeman Said* to its belated conclusion, Dick followed it with *A Scanner Darkly* (1977), an even more intense study of drug users battling the psychological corrosions of distorted reality, which was also rewritten several times. The novel is justly regarded as a masterpiece by some critics, fusing the legacy of authentic experiences in highly dangerous territory with the power of a brilliant and precisely focused imagination. It is also, in spite of its paranoid aspects, a very poignant work, which not only recovers the heartfelt quality of his long-lost mainstream fiction but carries it to a new dimension of pathos.

The early progress of *A Scanner Darkly* was interrupted in February and March 1974, between its first and second drafts, when Dick suffered a series of "visions" that were to haunt him for the remainder of his life and shape everything he wrote thereafter. He had been forced to stop taking amphetamines because their effects had become life-threatening, and although he was delighted to find that when he sat down at a typewriter the force of long Pavlovian conditioning would send him as high as a kite, his brain chemistry seems to have been seriously and permanently deranged. Some selections from the journal of the wide-ranging research studies that he subsequently undertook in the hope of making sense of these experiences were published as *In Pursuit of VALIS: Selections from the Exegesis* (1991).

The first draft of Dick's next novel, written in 1976 and eventually published as *Radio Free Albemuth* in 1985, was a mischievously mock-autobiographical account of visionary revelation, but he chose to rewrite it extensively in 1978, in the light of his research, as an extended philosophical novel entitled *VALIS* (1981). The acronym signifies the Vast Active Living Intelligence System that might (or might not) be attempting to bring a new revelation to selected individuals in and around Los Angeles, including the beleaguered hero Horselover Fat. ("Philip" is derived from the Latin for "horse lover" and "Dick" is the German word for fat.)

A thematic sequel to *VALIS*, *The Divine Invasion* (1981) is more confused as well as more extravagantly enhanced by philosophical ruminations based in the same research materials, but Dick had long since disarmed critics who complained that his work did not make much sense. *The Divine Invasion* remains the most exotic and mannered of all his tales of reality disturbed—and perhaps the most optimistic in that the transformation seems to have healing potential as well as the power to erase the legacy of past follies. Ironically, *The Transmigration of Timothy Archer* (1981), the only naturalistic novel Dick ever wrote to commission—based on the life and career of the charismatic Bishop Pike—turned into a further extension of the same eccentric philosophical inquiry and thus completed an eccentric trilogy. It contrasted strongly with his earlier attempts to write fiction set in the known world and did not help to clear the way for their publication.

Throughout this period of exaggerated idiosyncrasy, Dick always remained a writer of considerable elegance, with an enviable capacity to move his readers. "Frozen Journey" (1980; reprinted as *I Hope I Shall Arrive Soon* in 1985) is a small tour de force carrying forward the theme that had been central to his science fiction from the very beginning. Its protagonist recovers consciousness while being carried in suspended animation to a new world. The ship's computer tries to save him from madness by feeding him consolatory dreams, but with only partial success; all his dreams turn to nightmares because he is, in the final analysis, inconsolable by any conceivable eventuality.

Philip K. Dick came to prominence in a period when the science fiction genre was expanding rapidly, first by virtue of a brief boom in magazine production and then by virtue of its invasion of the paperback medium. As it took up a new position in the spectrum of popular culture, John W. Campbell, Jr.'s insistence that *real* science fiction had to be based in the conscientious extrapolation of actual science began to seem like an eccentric handicapping system designed to detract from the narrative flow of futuristic fiction and its accessibility to readers uneducated in science. Authors such as Dick and Ray Bradbury, who deployed imaginary technologies without any regard for matters of rational plausibility, were no longer condemned to marginality. In time, their success helped to create a new core for the field that marginalized Campbell's *Analog*, and the texts spun off therefrom, even before the genre's name was hijacked by films and TV shows that took their visual cues and story forms from comic books.

Dick's work was ideally suited to catch the attention of new movements in literary criticism that appeared in the 1980's, whose practitioners were intently interested in the problematic relationships between worlds-within-texts and their readers and were enthusiastic to place all notions of "reality" within inverted commas. Dick's relentless fascination with deceptive appearances and his unashamed abandonment of any commitment to restore coherency to his unravelled plots seemed to the disciples of postmodernism to be more daring and more pertinent than he probably intended. To ordinary readers, though, it was the sheer *fervor* of Dick's work that commanded their attention. No other science fiction writer compelled his readers to become so intimately *involved* in the strange situations in which his characters find themselves.

Dick was able to care deeply about dilemmas that no one had ever bothered to care about before, and he was able to make his readers care about them too. No one capable of following the popular contemporary advice to "get a life" could have done that—but people who are incapable of living a normal life usually cannot do it either. Dick's brilliance as a writer certainly owed something to the acute difficulty he experienced in adjusting to the rigors of everyday life, but that makes it all the more remarkable that he was able to produce such amazingly rich and delicately constructed fabulations. It is difficult to believe that we shall ever see his like again.

Selected Bibliography

FICTION OF PHILIP K. DICK

A Handful of Darkness. London: Rich and Cowan, 1955.
Solar Lottery. New York: Ace Books, 1955. Titled *World of Chance*. London: Rich and Cowan, 1956.

The Man Who Japed. New York: Ace Books, 1956.
The World Jones Made. New York: Ace Books, 1956.
The Cosmic Puppets. New York: Ace Books, 1957.
Eye in the Sky. New York: Ace Books, 1957.
The Variable Man and Other Stories. New York: Ace Books, 1957.
Time out of Joint. New York: Lippincott, 1959.
Dr. Futurity. New York: Ace Books, 1960.
Vulcan's Hammer. New York: Ace Books, 1960.
The Man in the High Castle. New York: G. P. Putnam's Sons, 1962.
The Game-Players of Titan. New York: Ace Books, 1963.
Clans of the Alphane Moon. New York: Ace Books, 1964.
Martian Time-Slip. New York: Ballantine Books, 1964.
The Penultimate Truth. New York: Belmont, 1964.
The Simulacra. New York: Ace Books, 1964.
The Three Stigmata of Palmer Eldritch. Garden City, N.Y.: Doubleday, 1964.
Dr. Bloodmoney, or How We Got Along After the Bomb. New York: Ace Books, 1965.
Counter-Clock World. New York: Berkley, 1966.
The Crack in Space. New York: Ace Books, 1966.
Now Wait for Last Year. Garden City, N.Y.: Doubleday, 1966.
The Unteleported Man. New York: Ace Books, 1966.
The Ganymede Takeover, with Ray Nelson. New York: Ace Books, 1967.
The Zap Gun. New York: Pyramid Books, 1967.
Do Androids Dream of Electric Sheep? Garden City, N.Y.: Doubleday, 1968.
Galactic Pot-Healer. New York: Berkley, 1969.
The Preserving Machine and Other Stories. New York: Ace Books, 1969.
Ubik. Garden City, N.Y.: Doubleday, 1969.
A Maze of Death. Garden City, N.Y.: Doubleday, 1970.
Our Friends from Frolix 8. New York: Ace Books, 1970.
We Can Build You. New York: DAW, 1972.
The Book of Philip K. Dick. New York: DAW, 1973. (A collection.)
Flow My Tears, the Policeman Said. Garden City, N.Y.: Doubleday, 1974.
Confessions of a Crap Artist. Berkeley, Calif.: Entwhistle Books, 1975.
Deus Irae, with Roger Zelazny. Garden City, N.Y.: Doubleday, 1976.
The Best of Philip K. Dick. New York: Ballantine Books, 1977.
A Scanner Darkly. Garden City, N.Y.: Doubleday, 1977.
The Golden Man. New York: Berkley, 1980. (A collection.)
VALIS. New York: Bantam Books, 1981.
The Divine Invasion. New York: Timescape, 1981; London: Corgi, 1982.
The Transmigration of Timothy Archer. New York: Timescape, 1982; London: Gollancz, 1982.
The Man Whose Teeth Were All Exactly Alike. Willimantic, Conn.: Ziesing, 1984; London: Paladin, 1986.

In Milton Lumky Territory. Pleasantville, N.Y.: Dragon, 1985; London: Gollancz, 1985.

Puttering About in a Small Land. Chicago: Academy Chicago, 1985; London: Paladin, 1987.

Radio Free Albemuth. New York: Arbor House, 1985; London: Grafton, 1987.

Humpty Dumpty in Oakland. London: Gollancz, 1986.

The Collected Stories of Philip K. Dick. 5 vols. Los Angeles, Calif.: Underwood Miller, 1987; London: Gollancz, 1988–1990. (Short stories.)

Mary and the Giant. New York: Arbor House, 1987; London: Gollancz, 1988.

The Broken Bubble. New York: Arbor House, 1988; London: Gollancz, 1989.

Nick and the Glimmung. London: Gollancz, 1988.

Gather Yourselves Together. Herndon, Va.: WCS, 1994.

OTHER WORKS BY PHILIP K. DICK

"Man, Android and Machine." In *Science Fiction at Large.* Edited by Peter Nicholls. New York: Harper and Row, 1976. (An essay on important themes in his work.)

"The Profession of Science Fiction XVII: The Lucky Dog Pet Store." In *Foundation,* 17 (September 1979): 41–49. (Autobiographical reflections.)

Philip K. Dick: In His Own Words. Edited by Gregg Rickman. Long Beach, Calif.: Fragments West/Valentine, 1984. (Interviews.)

In Pursuit of VALIS: Selections from the Exegesis. Edited by Larry Sutin. Novato, Calif.: Underwood-Miller, 1991. (Nonfiction.)

The Shifting Realities of Philip K. Dick: Selected Literary and Philosophical Writings. Edited by Lawrence Sutin. New York: Pantheon, 1995. (Nonfiction.)

CRITICAL AND BIOGRAPHICAL STUDIES

Brunner, John. "The Work of Philip K. Dick." *New Worlds* (September 1966): 142–149.

Gillespie, Bruce, ed. *Philip K. Dick: Electric Shepherd.* Melbourne, Australia: Norstrilia Press, 1975. (Essays, including Dick's "The Android and the Human.")

Greenberg, Martin H., and Joseph D. Olander, eds. *Philip K. Dick.* New York: Taplinger, 1983.

Mackey, Douglas A. *Philip K. Dick.* Boston: Twayne, 1988.

Pierce, Hazel. *Philip K. Dick.* Mercer Island, Wash.: Starmont, 1982.

Rickman, Gregg. *To the High Castle: Philip K. Dick, a Life, 1928–1962.* Long Beach, Calif.: Fragments West/Valentine, 1989.

Robinson, Kim Stanley. *The Novels of Philip K. Dick.* Ann Arbor, Mich.: UMI Research Press, 1984.

Sutin, Lawrence. *Divine Invasions: A Life of Philip K. Dick.* New York: Harmony, 1989.

Taylor, Angus. *Philip K. Dick and the Umbrella of Light.* Baltimore: T. K. Graphics, 1975.

Science Fiction Studies, 2, no. 1 (March 1975). (Special Philip K. Dick issue, including essays by Darko Suvin and Stanisław Łem.)

Warrick, Patricia S. *Mind in Motion: The Fiction of Philip K. Dick.* Carbondale: Southern Illinois University Press, 1987.

MANUSCRIPTS

An extensive collection of Dick's manuscripts is readily accessible in the Special Collections Library, California State University, Fullerton.

—BRIAN STABLEFORD

GORDON R. DICKSON
(b. 1923)

Two writers come immediately to mind when one tries to come to grips with the long career and substantial oeuvre of Gordon R. Dickson, who has published more than eighty books, most of them novels, since Ace Books released his first, *Mankind on the Run*, in 1956. These two writers are A. E. van Vogt and Poul Anderson. As a longtime colleague and collaborator with Dickson on two books, Anderson is an obvious enough association. The reference to van Vogt, though, does require some justification.

It is a suggestive circumstance, though perhaps not one of great significance, that both van Vogt and Dickson were born in western Canada, and that, as a consequence, both experienced to some degree a certain cultural and geographical isolation. Although Dickson was brought to the United States in 1937, at the age of thirteen, and van Vogt did not move south until 1944, after he had written his first million words of science fiction, both authors do share some revealing characteristics: their protagonists tend to share an exalted, sometimes grandiose spiritual solitude; though both authors often deal in galaxywide, space-operatic perspectives, in the work of both there is a notably frequent absence of richly imagined alien cultures or landscapes; and, perhaps most tellingly, from the beginnings of their careers, both authors have displayed an overriding concern with the life stories of superior versions of *Homo sapiens*, often immortal, generally afflicted with the burden of guiding humanity up the evolutionary ladder.

As a genre that has evolved in large part from the gothic romance, science fiction understandably welcomes images of heightened solitude, romantically vague, limitless landscapes, and an anguished submission to afflatus, which results in the persecution of the hero (usually a male youth) by the uncomprehending masses. Those science fiction writers, though, who aim at realistic ("hard" science fiction) extrapolations based on current science and technology, and those who feel, if perhaps rather uncertainly, that they are writing genuinely mimetic novels set in the future, would both tend to try to avoid what they would probably identify as the pitfalls of the romantic sublime. The peculiar cultural circumstance of being a Canadian notoriously involves natives in a kind of younger-brother sibling rivalry with the richer, more potent, myth-choked culture south of the border; and this circumstance provides patently rich soil for breeding a poetry of solitude and for other forms of romantic self-expression.

It is a moot point whether thirteen years of being a kind of exile—that is, a Canadian—have had as telling an effect on Dickson's literary production as a longer period of exile seems clearly to have had on van Vogt's; however it is argued, the case cannot carry too much weight. More significant, of course, is what Dickson has done with the cultural material he was given in the years after 1937. Suffice it to say at this point that he is not a writer of hard science fiction nor a mimetic novelist; with all that it entails, he is a science fiction romantic.

261

Gordon Rupert Dickson was born in Edmonton, Alberta, on 1 November 1923, into an Australian-American family; his elder half brother is the Canadian writer Lovat Dickson, biographer of H. G. Wells and founder of the English publishing firm Lovat Dickson, Ltd., in 1932. Gordon R. Dickson has lived in Minnesota since 1937. He took a B.A. degree in English from the University of Minnesota in 1948 (his studies were interrupted by military service). At the university he met Poul Anderson, who was a few years his junior. Dickson's first solo published story was "The Friendly Man," in *Astounding Science-Fiction* in 1951. Since then he has published around two hundred short stories and novelettes, forty-seven solo novels, eight books in collaboration, and twenty-two collections of his own shorter work, and he has edited several anthologies.

Dickson has won several of the awards conferred by the science fiction community: the Jupiter for *Time Storm* in 1977; the August Derleth Award of the British Fantasy Society for *The Dragon and the George* in 1978; the short fiction Hugo award for the novelette "Soldier, Ask Not" in 1965; the Hugo award for best novelette for "The Cloak and the Staff" in 1981; and the Nebula award for best novelette, for "Call Him Lord" in 1966. He was president of the Science Fiction Writers of America from 1969 through 1971. He has been actively involved in the science fiction subculture for more than forty years. Dickson is a gregarious, engaging, genial, successful man of letters; he is not an introvert.

How much this reality contrasts with the native core of Dickson's work can be seen by looking at the work of his colleague Anderson, who has enjoyed an even more visibly successful, though not dissimilar, career. In the sense already indicated, both authors are romantics who tend to infuse an austere Nordic pathos into wooded, rural midwestern American settings, whatever the ostensible mise–en–scène. Both share a libertarian bent—more explicit in Anderson's case—that has been interpreted in terms of the American political spectrum as right-wing, a

labeling of dubious value. Both authors frequently use fully employed mercenary soldiers as their protagonists, and both have been accused of misogyny because of the male-oriented societies logically entailed. In the work of each, series of stories and novels are inclined to take on a heightened, sagalike complexion, not infrequently through the introduction of ballads and other types of lyric poetry, some of it rather inferior. Alien beings tend to be less deracinated and more lovable than humans and are treated as such by the human protagonists of both authors; these human protagonists often share a dark-hued sense of weltschmerz and avoid urban centers of corruption, whether on a local, planetary, or galactic scale.

Dickson has collaborated with Anderson on only one, rather insignificant group of works: the stories and novel about the Hokas. The Hokas are extremely cute, copiously furry, teddy-bearlike aliens; the sustaining plot-generating premise about them is that they cannot understand the nonliteral—symbolic, poetic, figurative, fictive—aspects of human languages, and so take every statement as the literal truth. These comic stories are collected as *Earthman's Burden* (1957); there are also three uncollected Hoka tales: "Joy in Mudville" (1955), "Undiplomatic Immunity" (1957), and "Full Pack (Hokas Wild)" (1957). The Hoka novel *Star Prince Charlie* appeared in 1975. Although amusing enough, this series is patently a diversion. It is in their more ambitious solo efforts that the basic contrasts between the two novelists begin to come clear.

Regardless of the rural austerities and the sense of weltschmerz, Anderson has increasingly tended to create socialized universes, colorfully and intricately populated environments that his heroes imbibe to the full and occasionally dominate, after the traditional fashion. As befits the genre they decorate, these heroes are for the most part charismatic beings who govern the attention of their fellows, just as they are meant to govern ours. But the universes they inhabit are generally in a state of slow, inexorable decline and the cultures in which they live tend to be decadent, rococo, enfeebled. These overarching circumstances are fundamental to the Anderson hero's perception of reality, and they make up the warp and woof of his ongoing world in such a way that does not allow the inference—quite common in the genre—that understanding the universe provides a form of creative control over its circumstances. Even though he may be the hero of a saga, the Anderson hero lives under the looming shadow of Ragnarok.

While it would be simplifying matters to say that Anderson is a pessimist and Dickson an optimist, it is certainly the case that among the outstanding qualities of Dickson's heroic protagonists are deeply based arguments about the evolution of humanity, an evolution that these protagonists embody. This embodiment, of course, represents a symbolic rapprochement with the rest of humanity, a kind of socialization of the hero; but the Dickson hero's affinity with those who share his tale and high endeavor is distant indeed. The burden of his rapprochement forces a fatherly remoteness upon him. Dickson's novels make the claim that the central heroic figures of his oeuvre perceive the redolent, baroque intricacies of the space opera universe—say, Anderson's—as a veil to be pierced, understood, sorted out, and then transcended. Dickson's optimism is a genuinely austere, works-oriented, Protestant adherence to goals beyond, though various aliens (cuddly and otherwise) do crop up now and then.

Dickson is a deliberate, complex writer. His evolutionary arguments necessarily involve the use of pulp conventions, especially that of the mental and physical superman who discovers his full powers stage by stage, at just the points where the plot requires a deus ex machina. Dickson cannot be fully absolved of winning his arguments by the use of this sort of genre conceit, and his major work-in-progress, the multivolume Childe Cycle, is by no means free of pulp legerdemain.

In "The Plume and the Sword," an afterword published in *Lost Dorsai* (1980), a story collection attached to the Cycle, Dickson's

Gordon Dickson in 1978. PHOTO BY JAY KAY KLEIN

most ardent critical advocate in the 1970's and 1980's, Sandra Miesel, has called the Childe Cycle "an epic of human evolution, a scenario for mankind's rite of passage"—and it is certainly possible to assess the projected Cycle as an attempt to map an epic blueprint for the evolution of humanity. That full Cycle, however, may never be written; and followers of Dickson's ambitious overall strategy may have to make do with individual novels, some of them linked into short series. None of the projected introductory volumes to the series—three historical novels, three contemporary—have yet been published.

The series was originally conceived in twelve volumes, plus additional volumes of stories. After the first six yet unreleased novels were to come six science fiction volumes. Perhaps understandably, given Dickson's prominent position in the science fiction of the past half century, this six-volume quota has been broken. The published volumes of the sequence, according to their internal chronology, are *Necromancer* (1962), *The Tactics* of Mistake (1971), Soldier, Ask Not (1967), The Genetic General (1960; republished and expanded in 1960 as Dorsai!), The Spirit of Dorsai (1979), and Lost Dorsai (1980) (these two volumes of stories being reassembled as The Dorsai Companion [1986]), Young Bleys (1991), Other (1994), The Final Encyclopedia (1984) and The Chantry Guild (1988). The last volume, at least—according to Dickson—was spun off from a yet unpublished final volume, to be entitled Childe. Of the books listed here, Young Bleys and Other represent a seeming sidestep in the sequence; while all other volumes of the sequence deal with figures tied to or in some fashion avatars or versions of the central figure of the sequence, Donal Graeme, these two concentrate on a passionate but not fully "evolved" human being who is philosophically at odds with Hal Mayne (the version of Graeme who dominates the final volumes).

Since Sandra Miesel's description of the thematic intent shaping this complex sequence bears the signs of an author-approved exegesis, it may be well to quote "The Plume and the Sword" directly on the central Cycle theme: human evolution.

> Over the course of a thousand years, from the fourteenth century to the twenty-fourth, interactions between three archetypical Prime Characters—the Men of Faith, War, and Philosophy—succeed in uniting the unconscious/conservative and the conscious halves of the racial psyche. The result is a fully evolved being [that is, Donal Graeme in his later versions] endowed with intuition, empathy, and creativity whom Dickson calls Ethical-Responsible Man.

At the same time, such thematic interpretations of works of art are little more than a kind of decalcomania if the works of art themselves are—as fatally can be the case—inert. Indeed, the final garrulous volumes of the sequence to date (according to internal chronology) show signs of a rigid refusal to let the stories live in their own right, and their excessive length (The Final Encyclopedia was recently reprinted in two volumes) similarly gives evidence of an enterprise beginning to founder. It may be for this reason that Dickson first detoured into the story of Bleys (in Young Bleys and Other) and in the mid-1990's concentrated entirely on the Dragon and the Knight fantasy saga.

Earlier volumes of the sequence, however, concentrate on a stage somewhat prior to that embodied by the rather daunting Ethical-Responsible Man. They are set mostly in the time of the Splinter Cultures, which surround Old Earth both physically and spiritually. The four cultures, which tend to occupy worlds of their own, are the Dorsai, who are the warrior elite of human space and whose planet gave birth to Donal Graeme; the science-based cultures dominated by the world of Newton; the Exotics, who concentrate on the arts (and Eros); and the Friendly planets, whose inhabitants are obsessed with God. With heartwarming conviction, Dickson argues that these four types represent plausible outcomes of human evolution and that the union of their disparate natures and capabilities in the form of Donal Graeme represents a worthy philosophical argument about how human evolution might be shaped.

At the same time, Donal Graeme, the "genetic general" of the first published volume of the sequence, shows most clearly the pulp etiology underlying the concept of the ultimate hero, the Ethical-Responsible Man, of whom he is destined to be the first example, after he has lived three contrasting lives and synthesized their mutually reinforcing implications. In the published volumes, Graeme demonstrates his caliber in traditional fashion. Growing into adulthood as a hired warrior, he gradually evolves into a being capable of a deep identification with the unimaginably complex matrices of causation and circumstance that make up reality; this is a kind of unifying cognitive intuition of the nature of the world, and it enables him to win battles, manipulate enemies, and pierce the veils of illusion. He is very lonely. When he reveals himself, people gaze in awe. His story is unfinished.

But it is unfair to Dickson's considerable accomplishments as a professional writer to judge him in terms of the fragments of the Childe Cycle. Unlike many of his contemporaries, who served their apprenticeships on the magazines of the 1940's and 1950's, Dickson is clearly comfortable with the novel form and over the half century of his career has constantly increased his control over it. Some early books, such as *The Genetic General* (even in its full version), are somewhat episodic, showing signs of being shaped for a readership with an aesthetic attention span more suited for the novelette length. Whether or not Dickson was originally more comfortable with narrative spans of that length, the long and sustained novels of the late 1970's show a formidable grasp of the stronger rhythms of suspension and revolution afforded by a full-length work, especially when it is written directly for book publication.

In the early 1970's, it is true, Dickson produced some rather desultory works, such as *Sleepwalker's World* (1971) and *The R-Master* (1973), which at the time seemed ominously exhausted efforts at repeating the creative superman theme, at half-throttle, through perfunctory venues. In these and some other novels, the denouements came too quickly, almost absentmindedly, though it was still clear that the author knew exactly what he was doing. More recently Dickson seems to have finished his finger exercises. *The Far Call* (1978) is a long, ambitious novel about the space program, set in the near future and written with the avowed purpose of arguing for the continued relevance of the program. Although the book sinks at times into a dogged sententiousness, it is interesting all the same for the skill with which Dickson has utilized many of the techniques of the "blockbuster/best-seller" novel for his own high purposes: one notes the wide range of photogenic, larger-than-life characters, the linking of violence and sex into a complex pornography of power, the exhaustive length of the text, the uplifting narrative voice. It is a highly professional piece of work.

A more satisfying demonstration of Dickson's maturity as a novelist is *Time Storm* (1977), which remains his most sustained single endeavor to date, with the possible exception of *Wolf and Iron* (1990). Set in a balkanized postcatastrophe America and featuring a protagonist of intense decency and love of nature, Jeebee's survival, against resurgent nature and decadent man, is so fully earned that the reader does not only follow his adventures with pleasure: the reader sides with him. But *Time Storm* is more ambitious; in something over 160,000 words the novel presents, with remarkable shapeliness and vigor, a compendium of the techniques, themes, and foibles that have characterized Dickson throughout his career, and until completion of the Childe Cycle can serve to sum that career up.

Marc Despard, who seems from the first to be a typical Dickson protagonist, narrates *Time Storm* in the first person. As we begin the novel, the time storm is already with us, and Despard is already beginning to learn how to deal with the devastating mist walls that are its physical manifestation. These mist walls separate time zones from one another, so that one of them may, for example, serve as a permeable boundary between Paleolithic and postcatastrophe landscapes; the increasing intermixture of different time zones represents the collapse of the ordered universe on a scale extending over millions of years. The walls destroy most of the living beings they pass over, though some, like Despard, seem to be immune to their effects.

Others who are immune include a willfully speechless girl and a leopard that, in a state of suggestible dissociation after passing through a mist wall, has fallen under Despard's spell. The landscape through which these three pass, gradually acquiring companions, is a typical American science fictional postcatastrophe sequence of abandoned towns and reinvigorated countrysides; soon Despard learns that small communities have established themselves, some utopian, some despotic, and that there is an empress en route from Hawaii, conquering as she comes. (If romantic balkanization is a sine qua non of the American disaster novel, then in the time storm Dickson has created a perfect device for achieving it; though it is probable that he took hints from simpler predecessors such as Murray Leinster's "Sidewise in Time" [1934], the elegance with which he explains and capitalizes upon the device is his alone.)

Despard is only remotely interested in the coming of the Hawaiian empress; his vital obsession lies with the time storm itself. Still a young man, wealthy from stock market speculations that his pattern-solving drive has made possible, he is a deeply solitary person, forced into responsibility for the growing number of survivors who follow him about. Among these are Bill, a technology whiz, and Porniarsk, a stocky, dragonlike alien from another time zone (actually the avatar of far-distant Porniarsk Prime Three), who is on Earth in an ongoing attempt to solve the problem of the time storm before it dices the entire universe into disjunct atoms. With Porniarsk's help, Despard discovers his capacity to go into a creative overdrive—a heightened state of consciousness—which enables him to sort out the local fluctuations of the storm, to (as it were) identify with these local manifestations, and through this identification to lessen the intensity of the storm in the vicinity of the solar system, for a while.

In coming to grips with this moment, Despard expresses himself in terms that lie at the heart of Dickson's work:

> It was the final moment. I saw the pattern I had waited for ready to be born. I felt the strength of my monad gestalt; and at last, I knew certainly that what I was about to try would work. . . . The pattern I awaited exploded into existence. I thrust, with the whole gestalt behind me. The fabric of the time storm about me staggered, trembled and fell together—locked into a balance of forces. (chapter 20)

After this, in a well-timed excursion from creative overdrive, the Hawaiian empress finagles Despard away from his community; in eventually escaping her, he arouses her vengefulness—which is depicted with some vestigial misogyny—and knows that she will hound him and his companions across Earth. This knowledge, and his increasing sense of the farflung complexity of the time storm, impels Despard to manipulate his community into the far future, where it seems other beings are also fighting against the destruction of the universe.

These beings turn out to be immensely wise, but—like almost all of Dickson's non-humans who aspire to equal status with humanity—lack the burning, unstoppable evolutionary drive for self-knowledge. Such a drive enables Despard, first, to comprehend that the pattern of their culture intricately replicates the actual shape of the storm; second, to see that this keeps them from being ultimately capable of confronting the storm; and third, to cast himself, in order to gain perspective, into the antimatter universe that is deeply congruent with our own, where he masters the pattern of the storm and brings it to rest. This saves the universe.

In realizing that the microlevel and the macrolevel intersect at this binding pitch of identity, Despard also realizes that what laces the outer and the inner together, into the felicity he has achieved, is a kind of love. When he reaches home, he finds that his beloved pet leopard—long dead but somehow capable of being reanimated by scientific means—has indeed been reconstituted. It leaps upon him in another version of universe-embracing love.

Significantly, this last epiphany takes place between a man and his pet. Even here, Dickson's basic affinities hold true. *Time Storm* is a lonely book, at its heart, despite its broad canvas and extensive implications; and so it is with Dickson's entire oeuvre. Throughout, moments of communion are laced with melancholy, a ground bass of weltschmerz. Dickson's warmest moments—as in *Alien from Arcturus* (1956), *The Alien Way* (1965), or the linked novels *The Space Swimmers* (1967) and *Home from the Shore* (1978)—are between man and animal, though plausibly the latter may be in the form of a furry alien. Between man and woman, reticence governs. Between man and society, fatherhood distances. Dickson's whole body of work demonstrates the bravery of these necessary contacts and responsibilities, and the longing for transcendence. In his rendering of the conflict between commitment and solitude, when he is being serious about these matters, the work of Gordon R. Dickson has become science fiction's best example of humane romanticism.

Selected Bibliography

WORKS OF GORDON R. DICKSON

Alien from Arcturus. New York: Ace Books, 1956. Revised edition, retitled *Arcturus Landing,* New York: Ace Books, 1978.

Mankind on the Run. New York: Ace Books, 1956. Reprinted as *On the Run,* New York: Ace Books, 1979.

Earthman's Burden, with Poul Anderson. New York: Gnome Press, 1957. (Short stories.)

The Genetic General. New York: Ace Books, 1960; London: Brown, Watson, 1961. (A cut text bound with *Time to Teleport.*) Full text published in *Three to Dorsai!* (1975). Also published as *Dorsai!* New York: Ace Books, 1976; London: Sphere Books, 1975.

Secret Under the Sea. New York: Holt, Rinehart and Winston, 1960; London: Hutchinson, 1962.

Time to Teleport. New York: Ace Books, 1960.

Delusion World. New York: Ace Books, 1961.

Naked to the Stars. New York: Pyramid Books, 1961; London: Sphere Books, 1978.

Spacial Delivery. New York: Ace Books, 1961. (Bound with *Delusion World* as an Ace Double.)

Necromancer. Garden City, N.Y.: Doubleday, 1962; London: Mayflower, 1963. Reprinted as *No Room for Man,* New York: Macfadden, 1963.

Secret Under Antarctica. New York: Holt, Rinehart and Winston, 1963.

Secret Under the Caribbean. New York: Holt, Rinehart and Winston, 1964.

The Alien Way. New York: Bantam Books, 1965; London: Corgi Books, 1973

Mission to Universe. New York: Berkley Books, 1965. Revised edition, New York: Ballantine Books, 1977.

Space Winners. New York: Holt, Rinehart and Winston, 1965; London: Faber and Faber, 1967.

Planet Run, with Keith Laumer. Garden City, N.Y.: Doubleday, 1967; London: Hale, 1977.

Soldier, Ask Not. New York: Dell, 1967; London: Sphere Books, 1975.

The Space Swimmers. New York: Berkley Books, 1967; London: Sidgwick and Jackson, 1968.

None But Man. Garden City, N.Y.: Doubleday, 1969; London: Macdonald, 1970.

Spacepaw. New York: G. P. Putnam's Sons, 1969.

Wolfling. New York: Dell, 1969.

Danger—Human. Garden City, N.Y.: Doubleday, 1970. Reprinted as *The Book of Gordon Dickson,* New York: DAW, 1973. (Short stories.)

Hour of the Horde. New York: G. P. Putnam's Sons, 1970.

Mutants. New York: Macmillan, 1970. (Short stories.)

Sleepwalker's World. Philadelphia: J. B. Lippincott, 1971; London: Hale, 1973.

The Tactics of Mistake. Garden City, N.Y.: Doubleday, 1971; London: Sphere Books, 1975.

The Outposter. Philadelphia: J. B. Lippincott, 1972; London: Hale, 1973.

The Pritcher Mass. Garden City, N.Y.: Doubleday, 1972.

Alien Art. New York: E. P. Dutton, 1973; London: Hale, 1974.

The R-Master. Philadelphia: J. B. Lippincott, 1973; London: Hale, 1975.

The Star Road. Garden City, N.Y.: Doubleday, 1973; London: Hale, 1975. (Short stories.)

Ancient, My Enemy. Garden City, N.Y.: Doubleday, 1974; London: Sphere Books, 1978. (Short stories.)

Gremlins, Go Home!, with Ben Bova. New York: St. Martin's Press, 1974; London: St. James Press, 1976.

Star Prince Charlie, with Poul Anderson. New York: G. P. Putnam's Sons, 1975.

Three to Dorsai! Garden City, N.Y.: Doubleday, 1975. (Short stories.)

The Dragon and the George. New York: Ballantine Books, 1976.

The Lifeship, with Harry Harrison. New York: Harper and Row, 1976. Reprinted as *Lifeboat,* London: Orbit Books, 1977.

Time Storm. New York: St. Martin's Press, 1977; London: Sphere Books, 1978. (The title page of the original edition gives the title as *Timestorm.* Subsequent editions adhere to the author's intention.)

The Far Call. New York: Dial Press, 1978; London: Sidgwick and Jackson, 1978.

Gordon R. Dickson's SF Best. Edited by James R. Frenkel. New York: Dell, 1978. Revised edition, retitled *In the Bone: The Best Science Fiction of Gordon R. Dickson,* New York: Ace Books, 1987.

Home from the Shore. New York: Sunridge Press, 1978. (With extensive illustrations by James Odbert.)

Pro. New York: Ace Books, 1978.

Master of Everon. Garden City, N.Y.: Doubleday, 1979.

The Spirit of Dorsai. New York: Ace Books, 1979. (Short stories.)

In Iron Years. Garden City, N.Y.: Doubleday, 1980. (Short stories.)

Lost Dorsai. New York: Ace Books, 1980. (Short stories.)

Love Not Human. New York: Ace Books, 1981. (Early short stories.)

Hoka!, with Poul Anderson. New York: Simon and Schuster, 1983.

Dickson! Boston: NESFA, 1984. Revised edition, retitled *Steel Brother,* New York: TOR, 1985. (Short stories.)

The Final Encyclopedia. New York: TOR, 1984; London: Sphere, 1985. Revised edition, 2 vols., New York: TOR, 1996.

Jamie the Red, with Roland Green. New York: Ace Books, 1984.

Survival! New York: Pocket Books, 1984. (Short stories.)

Beyond the Dar al-Harb. New York: TOR, 1985. (Short stories.)

Forward! Edited by Sandra Miesel. New York: Baen Books, 1985. (Short stories.)

Invaders! Edited by Sandra Miesel. New York: Baen Books, 1985. (Short stories.)

The Dorsai Companion. New York: Ace Books, 1986. (Collection, assembling most of *The Spirit of Dorsai* and *Lost Dorsai.*

The Forever Man. New York: Ace Books, 1986; London: Sphere, 1987.

The Last Dream. New York: Baen Books, 1986.

The Man the Worlds Rejected. New York: TOR, 1986. (Short stories.)

Mindspan. Edited by Sandra Miesel. New York: Baen Books, 1986. (Short stories.)

The Stranger. New York: TOR, 1987. (Short stories.)

Way of the Pilgrim. New York: Ace Books, 1987; London: Sphere, 1988.

Beginnings. New York: Baen Books, 1988. (Short stories.)

The Chantry Guild. New York: Ace Books, 1988; London: Sphere, 1989.

The Earth Lords. New York: Ace Books, 1988; London: Sphere, 1989.

Ends. New York: Baen Books, 1988. (Short stories.)

Guided Tour. New York: Baen Books, 1988. (Short stories.)

Dorsai's Command, with Troy Denning and Cory Glaberson. New York: Ace Books, 1989.

The Dragon Knight. New York: TOR, 1990; London: Grafton, 1992.

Wolf and Iron. New York: TOR, 1990; London: Orbit, 1991.

Young Bleys. New York: TOR, 1991; London: Orbit, 1993.

The Dragon on the Border. New York: Ace Books, 1992; London: Grafton, 1993.

The Dragon at War. New York: Ace Books, 1993; London: HarperCollins, 1993.

The Dragon, the Earl, and the Troll. New York: Ace Books, 1994.

Other. New York: TOR, 1994.

The Dragon and the Djinn. New York: Ace Books, 1995.

The Magnificent Wilf. New York: Baen Books, 1995.

The Dragon and the Gnarly King. New York: Ace Books, 1997.

The Dragon in Lyonesse. New York: TOR, 1998.

EDITED WORKS AND ANTHOLOGIES

Rod Serling's Triple W: Witches, Warlocks and Were-wolves. New York: Bantam, 1963. (Uncredited.)

Rod Serling's Devils and Demons. New York: Bantam, 1967. (Uncredited.)

The Day the Sun Stood Still. Edited with Poul Anderson and Robert Silverberg. Nashville, Tenn.: Nelson, 1972.

Combat SF. New York: Doubleday, 1975.

Nebula Winners 12. New York: Harper, 1978.

The Harriers. New York: Baen Books, 1991.

The Harriers, Book Two: Blood and Honor. New York: Baen Books, 1991.

Robot Warriors. Edited with Martin G. Greenberg and Charles G. Waugh. New York: Ace Books, 1991.

CRITICAL AND BIOGRAPHICAL STUDIES

McMurray, Clifford. "An Interview with Gordon R. Dickson." *Science Fiction Review,* 7 (July 1978): 6–12.

Miesel, Sandra. "An Afterword." In *Home from the Shore* by Gordon R. Dickson. New York: Sunridge Press, 1978.

———. "The Plume and the Sword." Afterword in *Lost Dorsai* by Gordon R. Dickson. New York: Ace Books, 1980.

—JOHN CLUTE

Thomas M. Disch

(b. 1940)

Thomas michael disch was born on 2 February 1940 in Des Moines, Iowa, and spent his early life in various towns in Minnesota. After graduating from high school, he worked for a while as a draftsman before moving to New York City. He worked at various jobs in order to support himself while he attended the architectural college of Cooper Union but soon found the strain too great and dropped out. He began studying again at New York University in the early 1960's but abandoned his academic ambitions in favor of writing as soon as he sold his first short story. He became a full-time writer in the mid-1960's and since then has traveled widely both in North America and in Europe. The many cultural environments with which he has become familiar are used in his stories, which are various in their settings and themes.

Disch's first sale was "The Double-Timer," a time-paradox story that appeared in *Fantastic* in 1962. The editor of *Fantastic* and its companion magazine *Amazing* at this time was Cele G. Lalli, who encouraged a number of new writers whose style and interests were more offbeat than had hitherto been common in magazine science fiction. Disch, like Roger Zelazny, Ursula K. Le Guin, and David R. Bunch, published much of his early work in these magazines—four more short stories in 1964 and a further five in 1965, by which time his work was beginning to appear elsewhere. Many of these early short stories are very brief, and most are humorous. The majority of these playfully ironic pieces were assembled in Disch's first collection, *One Hundred and Two H-Bombs* (1966), which was subsequently reprinted in a revised and expanded form as *White Fang Goes Dingo and Other Funny S. F. Stories* (1971).

The idiosyncratic irony that was the hallmark of Disch's fiction from the very beginning had a darker aspect that quickly became more evident in his work. His more serious early pieces were usually scathing social satires. Although several science fiction writers—such as Frederik Pohl, C. M. Kornbluth, and Robert Sheckley—have acquired reputations as satirists, most science fictional satire is no more than good-humored parody. Disch's writing, though, is careful and well mannered, with a finesse that sharpens his mockery of stupidity and bigotry to a remarkable degree. In his most delicately aggressive mood, he is without equal. Even in such an early and relatively unsophisticated piece as "Thesis on Social Forms and Social Controls in the U.S.A." (1964), he presents a cruelly convincing fictional essay on twenty-first-century American culture, in which Orwellian doublethink not only rules but is consciously embraced and celebrated by the citizenry.

Disch's first novel, *The Genocides* (1965), deliberately adopts one of the classic science fiction story types: the global disaster story. Disch's story concerns the remnant of a Minnesota farming community, eking out a precarious living in a world where civilization has been destroyed by aliens who are using Earth as a gigantic farm. The aliens' sole crop has destroyed the Earth's ecosystem, and their machines are slowly eradicating the last stubborn weeds and pests (including humans) in order to maximize production. The two educated townspeople who are the most sympathetic characters are forced by circumstance to submit to the brutal and stupid rule of the patriarch farmer Anderson, and they watch with mixed feelings as he, his tribe, and his way of life are slowly crushed. In the end the humans seek endoparasitic refuge within the roots of the vast alien Plants, living off their sweet, nutritious produce until the time of the harvest inevitably arrives.

Although it differs most obviously from other novels in the same tradition because the alien invaders win and mankind is wiped out, what really sets *The Genocides* apart in terms of its attitude is the role played by the scientifically educated intellectuals. Not only are they impotent to deal with the alien menace, but they are helpless within the web formed by the values and political realities of an ignorant and brutish human society.

This is a perennial theme in Disch's work: his intellectual heroes are outsiders in their own world, peripheral to its concerns, and unable to lift the afflictions of its miseries. Although they may score victories of their own at the personal level, the world always resists their attempts to change it. This is not the relationship between society and its most intelligent members imagined by the great majority of science fiction writers. Only in the least interesting of Disch's novels, *Echo Round His Bones* (1967), is the world apparently put to rights as a result of the actions of a hero who literally moves the Earth in order to save it from nuclear annihilation.

The longest of Disch's early magazine stories, "White Fang Goes Dingo" (1965), was expanded into his second novel, which appeared as half of an Ace Double in 1966 as *Mankind Under the Leash* and was reprinted under the more familiar title *The Puppies of Terra*. Here, again, Earth has been conquered by immensely powerful aliens who have taken to breeding humans the way humans breed show dogs, selectively mating for intellectual and aesthetic faculties. The domesticated humans are rewarded by the joyous experience of the "leash," a sort of telepathic link that allows the imagination and the emotions to be pleasurably stimulated. The hero of the novel, unwillingly cast adrift from the leash while vacationing on Earth, is captured by the feral humans known as dingoes and is eventually won over to their cause. This time, the alien invasion is repelled, but the quality of "victory" is highly ambivalent. Humans win back their freedom to live like human beings. But this, Disch implies, is still not the best way to live—even if it is preferable to living as pets.

Amazing and *Fantastic* were sold by their publisher in 1965, and Cele G. Lalli's editorship ended. It was not long, though, before Disch found an editor even more sympathetic to his ambitions: Michael Moorcock, editor since 1964 of the British *New Worlds*. Moorcock published several of Disch's short stories in 1966 and serialized *Echo Round His Bones;* it was through his encouragement that *New Worlds'* publisher, Compact Books, issued the collection *One Hundred and Two H-Bombs*. The most significant work for which *New Worlds* provided an initial market was Disch's major novel *Camp Concentration*. It was serialized in *New Worlds* in 1967 and released in book form in Britain the following year. The novel is a *tour de force* in which Disch shows off his true brilliance to spectacular effect.

Camp Concentration, based on the Faust legend, is shot through with allusions to the major literary versions of the myth: Christopher Marlowe's *The Tragical History of Dr. Faustus* (1588), Goethe's *Faust* (1832), and Thomas Mann's *Doctor Faustus* (1947). The hero of Disch's novel, Louis Sacchetti, finds himself imprisoned as a conscientious objector in 1975. He is moved to a special prison, Camp Archimedes, where (he ultimately learns) he is used as a guinea pig in an experiment involving a mutant strain of the syphilis bacterium, which induces a considerable augmentation of intelligence prior to causing death.

In the novel Disch accepts a challenge that no other writer had successfully met: he sets out to describe the world view and experience of an adult human being whose intellect is greatly advanced. What is more, he presents his account directly—in the form of a journal kept by the superman himself. Aided by a very special cleverness and considerable artistry, Disch comes close to being convincing in what is, in literal terms, an impossible project.

In bringing the Faust myth "down to Earth" by giving it a science fiction base, Disch's narrative initially seems closer in spirit to Mann than to Marlowe; much of Sacchetti's commentary on his predicament reflects on the human existential predicament and the manner in which people use one another. But there is also evident within the work a romanticism that becomes slowly more apparent, and the novel is actually more similar—structurally, at least—to Goethe's dramatic version of the legend (at the climax of which angels bear Faust triumphantly aloft so that the Devil may not claim him). Although to some readers the ending of *Camp Concentration* has seemed ill suited, it has considerable affective power. The novel remains one of the outstanding genre products of the 1960's, when science fiction finally broke free from the conventions that had confined it by virtue of the marketing strategies that had previously dominated its production.

In 1968, Disch published two books. One was *Black Alice*, first issued under the pseudonym Thom Demijohn and written in collaboration with John Sladek, another American writer who had found Michael Moorcock a congenial and accommodating editor. *Black Alice* is a satirical attack on American manners and mores, developed through the story of a kidnapped white girl turned black by her captors in order to hide her. The other book was Disch's second short-story collection, again published in Britain before appearing in the United States. The British title of the book is *Under Compulsion*; the American edition is *Fun With Your New Head* (1971). It represents the more cynical side of Disch's imagination, but like the earlier collection it features mostly early work that is not quite up to the author's highest standard.

In 1969, Disch published a novelization of the offbeat British television series "The Prisoner," which enjoys a considerable reputation among science fiction fans, although it is basically an exercise in paranoid surrealism with few overtly fantastic elements. This marked the end of a relatively prolific period; from then on, Disch's novels and stories appeared rather less frequently, and his output became much more diverse.

Disch's next major project was the near-future story cycle collected as *334* in 1972. This grew from the seed of a 1967 short story, "Problems of Creativeness" (heavily revised in the final version as "The Death of Socrates"). The other five stories in the cycle are "Bodies," "Everyday Life in the Later Roman Empire," "Emancipation," "Angouleme," and the title story.

Thomas M. Disch. © MIRIAM BERKLEY

The stories are mainly concerned with the tenants of an apartment building administered by the Welfare Department in early twenty-first-century New York. The book is remarkable in its philosophy of *plus ça change, plus c'est la même chose;* the world of the story has seen social and technological change since our own day, but on a modest and convincing scale, and although everyday life is affected by various historical crises, none are exaggerated out of all proportion. The ways in which people cope (or, more often, fail to cope) are striking in their familiarity. *334* is one of the most realistic and naturalistic of all futuristic works, and because of its realism the claims that it makes become very disturbing. It is one of the very few books that show us what the future might really be like to live in and hence is more frightening than any melodrama of catastrophe, invasion, or technology run wild.

The main focus of *334* is on lives of quiet desperation, but "Everyday Life in the Later Roman Empire" offers a glimpse of life among the middle-class intellectuals who exist in parallel with the inhabitants of 334 East 11th Street. With the aid of the drug Morbehanine, they escape into stabilized hallucinatory environments; the central character of the story has constructed for herself a second life in A.D. 334, for the purposes of historical research. This episode sets the whole endeavor into a greater framework, allied to the deeply pessimistic anticipation of the imminent future presented in Oswald Spengler's *Decline of the West* (1918–1922).

What is most remarkable about *334* is the sheer density of the reader's experience. Its social environments are neatly defined and brilliantly displayed. The argument of the book is that the last vestiges of our hope for a utopian future are now gone. It does not pretend to be prophetic, because it alleges that hope has already vanished and that all that remains is for the historical process to reach its logical conclusion. *334* is the one significant tragedy (in the classical sense) that science fiction has produced. It is Disch's most important

work so far, and a very fine book by any standards.

Also in 1972, Disch published his first book of poetry, *The Right Way to Figure Plumbing*, and the following year, the first version of his best short-story collection, *Getting into Death*. It was, as usual, the British edition that appeared first; but the American edition, published in 1976 with substantially revised contents, is superior.

The title story of the collection is one of several that touch upon the uneasy metaphorical relationship between sex and death; others include "Death and the Single Girl" (1976) and "Let Us Quickly Hasten to the Gate of Ivory" (1970). More centrally, though, its theme is the difficulty of establishing and sustaining a meaningful identity in a hostile world. The fragility of identity under the relentless pressure of circumstance is most frighteningly represented in what is perhaps Disch's most powerful story, "The Asian Shore" (1970), in which an American tourist wintering in Turkey is haunted by a miserable woman and a starveling child who continually call out to him a name that is not his own. Gradually he is spiritually absorbed by his environment and cannot find the strength necessary to secure his identity against the invasion of a new personality whose need to exist is, it seems, greater than his own.

Although this story first appeared in Damon Knight's anthology *Orbit 6*, it does not really warrant description as science fiction, and the same is true of most of the stories in *Getting into Death*—some, including the title story, have no fantastic content at all. For some years in the 1970's, in fact, Disch's only involvement with science fiction was represented by a series of anthologies that he edited and to which he contributed a few stories. The first two, *The Ruins of Earth* and *Bad Moon Rising* (both 1973), develop deliberately alarmist themes; but the third one—presumably planned for contrast—is *The New Improved Sun* (1975), described by the publisher as "an anthology of Utopian SF." Many of the stories in it, though, are heavily ironic. The remaining volumes making up this loose series of collections are *New Constellations* (1976) and *Strangeness* (1977), both edited in collaboration with Charles Naylor. All the anthologies are superior examples of their kind, and most contain a certain amount of original work. During this period Disch produced only one new novel: *Clara Reeve*, a long and densely written historical work with gothic overtones; this was published in 1975 under the pseudonym Leonie Hargrave. Disch returned to science fiction late in 1978, when he had two short stories in *Magazine of Fantasy and Science Fiction*, quickly followed by the serial version of his new novel, *On Wings of Song* (1979).

As in *334*, the world of *On Wings of Song* is the near future, where—apart from certain political changes—little has happened to transform the everyday lives of ordinary people. There is, though, one vital innovation: a machine that permits people, if they have the knack, to sing their conscious selves clear out of their bodies, free to soar away from Earth toward a new and apparently ecstatic mode of existence, provided they do not fall victim to the mesmeric vibrations of innocent machines or deliberately planted "fairy-traps."

The hero of the novel lives in Iowa, where such "flying" is banned and its supporters are persecuted by the dour "undergoders." His one ambition in life is to learn to sing, and hence to fly, but fate puts every obstacle in his way. His education is interrupted by a term of harsh imprisonment, and a promising route to fulfillment is cruelly closed when the woman he marries flies free (while he is powerless to follow) and leaves her body untenanted, caught in a legal limbo between life and death. Eventually he finds a new route to fame and fortune by means of his associations with a castrato opera singer and a supersentimental musical show, but he needs redemption from this temporal success no less than he needed redemption from his earliest misery.

The transcendental element links *On Wings of Song* more to *Camp Concentration* than to *334*, but in *On Wings of Song* it is ever-present rather than appearing as a convenient deus ex machina, and the tension between transcendence and mundanity is extended throughout the novel. The balance is excellent in the early part of the novel, but in the later stages a certain exotic element within the hero's life story introduces an overly sarcastic tone; a curious satire on the relation between elitist culture and mass culture emerges, confusing the basic theme and blurring the conclusion.

After the publication of *On Wings of Song*, Disch's imaginative fiction became increasingly concentrated in the sarcastic satirical mold of "The Man Who Had No Idea" (1978) and "Understanding Human Behaviour" (1982). *The Brave Little Toaster: A Bedtime Story for Small Appliances* (1986), a subtle parody that tried to extrapolate the clichés of moralistic children's animated movies to absurdity was itself filmed as a heroic fantasy, but this only encouraged Disch to undertake an excursion into the farther hinterlands of parodic excess in *The Brave Little Toaster Goes to Mars* (1988). *The Businessman: A Tale of Terror* (1984) had earlier used the ugly apparatus of best-selling horror fiction to add bite to a vengeful black comedy of expeditious wife murder, and this was similarly followed up by a more sustained satirical exercise in the same dark vein. *The M.D.: A Horror Story* (1991) tells the story of Billy Michaels, who is given a magical caduceus that has the power to heal all diseases (except genetic deficiencies) but must be constantly recharged by inflicting suffering of a similar kind. Billy's boyhood experiments go sadly awry, but it is not until he is fully grown that a truly *profound* irresponsibility sets in, carrying the talisman's power into a horrific near future whose afflictions extrapolate the dire lesson of AIDS.

The savagely clinical analysis of *The M.D.* was further surpassed by *The Priest: A Gothic Romance* (1995), a hymn of hate directed against the endemic hypocrisies of the Catholic Church, particularly its attitude toward the legions of predatory pedophiles that it allegedly attracts into its ranks. The novel is brought into the margins of the science fiction genre by a hallucinatory "timeslip" whose imagery is derived from the writings of a hypothetical writer-turned-cult-leader combining aspects of L. Ron Hubbard and Whitley Strieber, both of whom are numbered among Disch's pet hates. Disch took the trouble to write several sarcastic critiques of Strieber's best-selling accounts of his supposed abduction by aliens, and he produced the scathing fictional parody "Abduction of Bunny Steiner, or a Shameless Lie" (1992). Other targets of Disch's ire include Millenarian cultists looking forward to the Rapture; the aftermath of that event is cuttingly described in "A Family of the Post-Apocalypse" (1993). Modern personality cults are subjected to equally scarifying mockery in "Celebrity Love" (1990).

Disch had begun to subject science fiction to this kind of cynical analysis in the 1970's, when his contribution to a series of lectures at London's Institute of Contemporary Arts in 1975—reprinted in *Science Fiction at Large* (1976), edited by Peter Nicholls—had taken as its theme "The Embarrassments of Science Fiction." The ultimate product of this line of thought was his combative and sour account of *The Dreams Our Stuff Is Made Of: How Science Fiction Conquered the World* (1998), which begins with the proposition that "America is a nation of liars, and for that reason science fiction has a special claim to be our national literature, as the art form best adapted to telling the lies we like to hear and to pretend we believe."

Rather than seeing such fatuous offshoots of science fiction as Scientology and UFOlogy as aberrations, Disch's study suggests that these are merely the worst extrapolations of a set of childish myths and an imbecilic paranoia that lie at the very heart of science fiction. Although his account of science fiction's endemic problems is ameliorated by some kind comments about non-American contributors (including H. G. Wells and J. G. Ballard) and some atypical Americans (including Philip K. Dick, Hal Clement, and Joe Haldeman), the gist of its argument helps to explain why Disch tried to put the genre firmly be-

hind him in 1980, thereafter using its apparatus merely as one among many instruments of his brilliantly caustic wit. It is, however, worth noting that the genre magazines have continued to provide a significant outlet for satirical pieces so extreme in their bizarrerie that it is difficult to imagine where else they might have been placed.

These resolutely idiosyncratic works include such relatively sober pieces as "One Night, or Scheherazade's Bare Minimum" (1993), a meditation on the art of storytelling; "The Burial Society" (1993), in which the death-obsessed people of the future push back the frontiers of memorial technology; the more arcane "The Little Pig Had None" (1993), an animal fable about self-control; and "The Man Who Read a Book" (1994), in which a future U.S. government applies the same support strategies to the publishing industry that its predecessors had applied to the tobacco industry. The sequence extends farther in "The Children's Fund to Save the Dinosaurs: A Charity Appeal" (1997), a spoof of contemporary fund-raising tactics, and "Nights in the Gardens of the Kerhonkson Prison for the Aged and Infirm" (1997), which features an enterprising dispenser of cruel but apt punishments. Some of Disch's more conventional tales of the 1990's—such as "The Invisible Woman" (1995), which continues a noble tradition of accounts of humble individuals whose insignificance is extrapolated to its logical terminus—might easily have found publishers outside the genre, but science fiction continues to provide an umbrella that the author often finds convenient, even if he does have to share its shelter with people he would rather not be seen dead with.

Disch is no longer thought of primarily as a science fiction writer; nowadays he has a more considerable reputation as a poet, critic, and satirist. Even so, his connections with and contributions to the genre did not end when he moved on to more mature work, and he may yet add to the list of his landmark contributions to the genre, whose most outstanding inclusions are *Camp Concentration, 334,* and *On Wings of Song.*

Selected Bibliography

WORKS OF THOMAS M. DISCH

The Genocides. New York: Berkley Medallion, 1965.

Mankind Under the Leash. New York: Ace Books, 1966. (Retitled *The Puppies of Terra*.)

One Hundred and Two H-Bombs. London: Compact Books, 1966. (Short stories.)

Echo Round His Bones. New York: Berkley Medallion, 1967.

Camp Concentration. London: Rupert Hart-Davis, 1968.

Under Compulsion. London: Rupert Hart-Davis, 1968. Retitled *Fun With Your New Head*. Garden City, N.Y.: Doubleday, 1971. (Short stories.)

White Fang Goes Dingo and Other Funny S.F. Stories. London: Arrow, 1971.

334. London: MacGibbon and Kee, 1972.

Getting into Death. London: Hart-Davis MacGibbon, 1973. New York: Alfred Knopf, 1976. (In American edition the contents are substantially revised.)

On Wings of Song. New York: St. Martin's Press, 1979.

Fundamental Disch. Edited by Samuel R. Delany. New York: Berkley Medallion, 1980. (Short stories.)

The Man Who Had No Idea. London: Gollancz, 1982; New York: Bantam, 1982. (Short stories.)

The Businessman: A Tale of Terror. New York: Harper, 1984; London: Cape, 1984.

The Brave Little Toaster: A Bedtime Story for Small Appliances. Garden City, N.Y.: Doubleday, 1986; London: Grafton, 1986.

The Brave Little Toaster Goes to Mars. Garden City, N.Y.: Doubleday, 1988.

The Silver Pillow: A Tale of Witchcraft. Willimantic, Conn.: Ziesing, 1987.

The M.D.: A Horror Story. New York: Knopf, 1991; London: HarperCollins, 1992.

The Priest: A Gothic Romance. New York: Knopf, 1995.

The Dreams Our Stuff Is Made Of: How Science Fiction Conquered the World. New York: Free Press, 1998. (Nonfiction.)

CRITICAL AND BIOGRAPHICAL STUDIES

Clute, John. "Thomas M. Disch." In *The Science Fiction Encyclopedia*, edited by Peter Nicholls. Garden City, N.Y.: Doubleday, 1979; London: Roxby Press, 1979.

Delany, Samuel R. *The American Shore*. Elizabethtown, N.Y.: Dragon Press, 1978. (Analysis in depth of a Disch short story, "Angouleme.")

Disch, Thomas M. "The Embarrassments of Science Fiction." In *Science Fiction at Large*, edited by Peter Nicholls. London: Victor Gollancz, 1976; New York: Harper and Row, 1976.

Platt, Charles. "An Interview with Thomas M. Disch." *Foundation*, 19 (June 1980): 47–53.

—BRIAN STABLEFORD

SIR ARTHUR CONAN DOYLE

(1859–1930)

SIR ARTHUR CONAN DOYLE was one of a group of novelists beginning their writing careers in the late Victorian period and publishing well into the twentieth century, who became victims of the Edwardian craze for debunking and denigrating all things Victorian. While most earlier Victorian novelists now have been reappraised and rehabilitated, the writers of Doyle's generation—such major novelists as H. G. Wells, John Galsworthy, and Arnold Bennett—only recently have been the subjects of serious scholarly attention. Yet, as significant a writer as Doyle is, in this present rush to rehabilitate, he continues to receive little serious scholarly attention.

Only Doyle's detective fiction is written about today, and the vast majority of this writing is not scholarly, but rather commercial—attempts to fabricate biographies about Sherlock Holmes or to use the sixty Holmes stories as subjects for trivia quizzes and for parlor identification games. An exception to this is the brief chapter in Ian Ousby's *Bloodhounds of Heaven* (1976), which analyzes Sherlock Holmes's character in light of the rise of the detective as central character, and in E. F. Bleiler's important introduction to Emile Gaboriau's *Monsieur Lecoq* (1975), in which he describes Gaboriau's central shaping influence on the Sherlock Holmes stories.

But such a paucity of significant critical writing about Doyle's work does not mean that nothing has been done to work up secondary material on Doyle. There are three useful modern biographies about him—Hesketh Pearson's frank, iconoclastic *Conan Doyle* (1943; repr. 1977), John Dickson Carr's

reliable *The Life of Sir Arthur Conan Doyle* (1949), and Pierre Norden's critically rigorous *Conan Doyle* (1964)—none of which is comprehensive enough to do Doyle justice. A scholarly, multivolume critical biography is needed that can treat Doyle's life and analyze all his significant writings, something modeled after Edgar Johnson's two-volume critical biography of Charles Dickens.

A starting point on Doyle, of course, is his own *Memories and Adventures* (1924). Harold Locke's *A Bibliographical Catalogue of the Writings of Sir Arthur Conan Doyle* (1928) is incomplete and badly out of date. Doyle's letters and other private papers, some fourteen cartons of material, have not been completely cataloged; but from such a wealth of material, a selected edition of collected letters should be published. The Smith, Elder twelve-volume *Author's Edition of Doyle's Works* (1903) has not really been supplanted by the twenty-volume edition (1913). As a result there is no reliable scholarly edition of Doyle's works, although the London publishing house of John Murray has issued a series of uniformly bound collections of his Professor Challenger stories, the Brigadier Gerard series, the complete short stories, and several of the historical novels. Undoubtedly some of these deficiencies in Doyle scholarship will be removed as studies in popular culture continue to gain academic respectability.

I

Arthur Conan Doyle was born on 22 May 1859 at Edinburgh, the eldest son of Charles

Altimont Doyle and Mary Foley Doyle. His father was an acclaimed artist and an important civil servant (a clerk at the Board of Works) who came from a distinguished Irish Catholic family. His grandfather was the famous portrait painter John Doyle; his uncle was Richard "Dicky" Doyle, a well-known novel illustrator and staff artist for *Punch* who designed the magazine's famous cover logo. Doyle was educated at Stonyhurst, a Jesuit school, and at Edinburgh University, where he took the M.B. in 1881 and the M.D. in 1885. He practiced medicine at Southsea from 1882 to 1890.

Doyle placed his first story, "The Mystery of Sasassa Valley," in *Chambers' Journal* in 1879. Several more short stories were published soon thereafter—"The American's Tale" (*London Society*, 1880), "Selecting a Ghost" (*London Society*, 1883), "The Silver Hatchet" (*London Society*, 1883), "The Captain of the Polestar" (*Temple Bar*, 1883), "J. Habakkuk Jephson's Statement" (*Cornhill*, 1884), "The Great Keinplatz Experiment" (*Belgravia*, 1885), "A Literary Mosaic" (*Boy's*

Sir Arthur Conan Doyle. COURTESY OF CORBIS-BETTMANN

Own Paper, 1886), and "John Barrington Cowles" (*Cassell's Saturday Journal*, 1886)— none of which made Doyle rich or brought him to the attention of the general public. He continued his literary apprenticeship by placing several longer stories and novels, including the first Sherlock Holmes long story, "A Study in Scarlet" (*Beeton's Christmas Annual*, 1887). A historical romance, *Micah Clarke*, appeared in 1889 and was followed by another Sherlock Holmes novella, "The Sign of Four" (*Lippincott's Magazine*, 1890).

Doyle's first serious major work, the historical novel *The White Company*, was serialized in James Payn's *Cornhill Magazine* during 1890–1891. But it was not until the first cycle of twelve Sherlock Holmes short stories appeared in *Strand Magazine* (July 1891–December 1892) that he achieved any significant public acclaim. Thereafter, Doyle wrote more than four hundred works; among these are sixty Sherlock Holmes stories, sixteen Brigadier Gerard Napoleonic stories, four serious historical novels, eight volumes on spiritualism, three volumes of verse, a standard history of the Boer War, and many occult, supernatural, and science fiction stories.

Doyle did not confine all his energies to literature. During the South African War of 1899–1902, he was senior physician for the field hospital equipped by Sir John Langman. From this experience he wrote *The Great Boer War* (1900), and later he published a pamphlet that defended England's conduct in the Boer War. In 1900, Doyle stood unsuccessfully for Parliament as Liberal Unionist candidate for Central Edinburgh; a campaign in 1906 for the Hawick Burghs as a tariff reformer was equally unsuccessful. A capable speaker and a vigorous electioneer, he used these abilities to champion the cause of Oscar Slater, who was wrongly accused of murder and robbery at Glasgow in May 1909. Through Doyle's continued efforts, Slater's sentence eventually was overturned.

Doyle was big, strong, and heavy-set. He was fond of all sports and games, was a fair cricketer, and played in many matches for the Marylebone Club. In addition he was a regular patron of boxing, and he brought the subject of pugilism into one of his best novels, *Rodney Stone* (1896). Sometime during 1914, Doyle became deeply committed to spiritualism, a subject on which he wrote and lectured throughout the world. Among his best works in this field are *The Wanderings of a Spiritualist* (1921) and the two-volume *History of Spiritualism* (1926). Doyle was knighted in 1902. He received an honorary LL.D. from the University of Edinburgh in 1905 and was a knight of grace of the Order of St. John of Jerusalem. In 1885 he married Louisa Hawkins; they had a son and a daughter. Louisa died in 1906, and Doyle married Jean Leckie in 1907; they had two sons and a daughter. Doyle died at his home at Crowborough, Sussex, on 7 July 1930.

II

Among the diverse types of literary work Doyle produced, his twenty-nine supernatural, occult, fantasy, and science fiction stories represent a significant part of his total work. Written throughout his career, these eight novels and twenty-one short stories are "The American's Tale," "Selecting a Ghost," "The Silver Hatchet," "The Captain of the Polestar," "J. Habakkuk Jephson's Statement," "The Great Keinplatz Experiment," "A Literary Mosaic," "John Barrington Cowles," "The Ring of Thoth" (*Cornhill*, 1890), *The Doings of Raffles Haw* (1892), "The Los Amigos Fiasco" (*The Idler*, 1892), "The Terror of Blue John Gap," ca. 1892 (*Strand Magazine*, 1910), "Lot No. 249" (*Harper's Magazine*, 1892), *The Parasite* (1894), *The Mystery of Cloomber* (1895), "The Brown Hand" (*Strand Magazine*, 1899), "The Leather Funnel" (*McClure's Magazine*, 1900), "Playing with Fire" (*Strand Magazine*, 1900), "The Silver Mirror" (*Strand Magazine*, 1908), *The Lost World* (1912), *The Poison Belt* (1913), "How It Happened" (*Strand Magazine*, 1913), "Horror of the Heights" (*Strand Magazine*, 1913), *Danger! and Other Stories* (1918), "The Bully of

Brocas Court" (*Strand Magazine*, 1921), *The Land of Mist* (1926), "The Disintegration Machine" (*Strand Magazine*, 1929), "When the World Screamed" (*Strand Magazine*, 1929), and *The Maracot Deep and Other Stories* (1929).

Of all these stories, the first three (of five) Professor Edward Challenger stories—*The Lost World, The Poison Belt,* and *The Land of Mist*—combined with Doyle's last published novel, *The Maracot Deep,* are the most important and the most central in illustrating his artistic and scientific vision. Some mention also should be made of his novel *The Parasite* (a story of possession through telepathy and hypnotic control) and of his cautionary, futuristic war story "Danger!" Both are of some artistic and generic significance.

The Lost World, the first story featuring Professor George Edward Challenger, is about Edward Malone, an Anglo-Irish journalist, who sets out to find adventure in a world where romance no longer has a place. The twenty-three-year-old hero is motivated by his desire to impress Gladys Hungerton, a silly, empty-headed young woman who wishes to have her vanity fed by Malone's knight-errantry. Malone joins Challenger, Challenger's scientific rival (Professor Summerlee), and the big game hunter and explorer Lord John Roxton in an expedition to the upper Amazon, where the group discovers an ape-man society thought to be the missing link in human evolution.

Challenger argues that the plateau was suddenly elevated and isolated from the rest of the region by volcanic eruption, thus preserving the Jurassic life forms. The ape-men apparently migrated to the plateau at a later date, and their present descendants rule part of the plateau in competition with the prehistoric beasts and a tribe of modern-day Indians, the Alaccas. When the expedition reaches the plateau, the members witness a primeval struggle for survival among these life forms. The significance of this is a reenactment of the prehistoric slaughter of ape-men by their human enemies—a drama re-creating events at the dawn of human history. After fighting against the ape-men (as the Alaccas' allies) and surviving a series of near-fatal encounters with prehistoric monsters, the expedition finds an escape route off the plateau and returns to London with an amazing story to tell.

As is true of most characters in adventure stories, the experiences undergone on the expedition change each member in some significant way. Malone, matured by his experiences, is able to see Gladys Hungerton for what she is—a selfish, silly girl who since Malone's departure has acted out her romantic fantasies by marrying an unheroic lawyer's clerk named Bill Potts. Challenger and Summerlee, though feuding throughout the expedition, have modified their opinions of each other as a result of sharing common experiences.

The power of *The Lost World* lies in a consummate balance of adventure, skilled characterization, novelty of story line, and adept use of scientific themes. Supporting the theme of a wonderful discovery is a secondary one based on the epic/adventure-story pattern that unifies the action. Doyle's use of concepts taken from paleontology and evolutionary theory gives the action verisimilitude.

The Poison Belt is a wonderful-event story centered on a world catastrophe, in which Challenger predicts that the world will shortly pass through a belt of toxic ether. Like the biblical Noah, Challenger warns the world of its imminent danger, then prepares a room in his country estate as a refuge. Drawn to Challenger's "ark" are Professor Summerlee, who is skeptical about the entire business; Lord John Roxton; Edward Malone; and Challenger's wife, Jessie.

Watching the population of the world die, Challenger and his friends spend their last hours debating the causes and effects of the disaster. They consider the possibility of other life forms surviving the catastrophe and replacing mankind—becoming the source of a new life form evolving into superior forms of life—ideas that appear in more organized form in Olaf Stapledon's *Last and First Men* (1930). Like Stapledon's characters, Doyle's speculate that humanity may not be the cul-

mination of evolution, but only a temporary development to be surpassed and supplanted in time by other higher organisms unlike it in form. Their ark—a sealed room supplied with oxygen tanks that can support life for only twenty-four hours—delays their death for some hours after the rest of the world's population dies, and the group is poignantly aware of their unique position as they watch their last sunrise. But, much to their joy, the world soon returns to normal, as the effects of the poison wear off and life is reanimated, though unconscious of what has happened. Mankind has experienced a sort of amnesia lasting forty-eight hours.

Malone, the journalist, gets the scoop of a lifetime in his articles that describe the details of the catastrophe. Challenger and the others discover a new meaning in life. The power of the story lies in Doyle's moral thesis that humanity is given a second chance to fulfill its moral destiny on Earth. It must recognize its feebleness before the infinite latent forces of the universe.

A glance through the appendixes to *The Land of Mist* indicates the scope of Doyle's artistic intentions for this novel. Together with his own psychic experiences and those of his friends, he planned to dramatize, in the framework of the story, most of the important experiences of English spiritualism in the 1920's. Doyle wished to describe the spiritualist view of life after death and to give some idea of its seven heavens—who goes to each and why. Included in his plan are a brief history of the great figures in psychic research and a description of their theories and scientific findings.

The relationship between spiritualism and society is as important to Doyle's plan as is his description of spiritualist theory. He describes the unhappy relationship between spiritualists and the law, the police, the courts, the press, organized religion, and the general public. Central to this is Doyle's discussion of the legal difficulties facing genuine mediums. The law, he argues, makes no distinction between real and fraudulent mediums; instead, it seeks only to protect the public from being imposed on by mediums. The law prevents genuine as well as fraudulent mediums from practicing their calling. Stemming from this problem in the legal code, Doyle claims, is the fairly common practice of police entrapment of mediums. He dramatizes this problem in the subplot about Tom Linden, an honest and respectable medium.

Such material shapes the novel's thesis, which argues that spiritualism ought to be taken as seriously as any other religion, and that psychic research not only is a legitimate branch of modern science, but is the most important branch because it may provide a view of life after death that could reduce all other kinds of materialistic knowledge to insignificance. Doyle's thesis also attacks the bigotry of established religion, charging it with giving its followers only an imperfect view of life after death. He argues that both dogmatists in the church and materialists in science, who exclude the spiritual plane from their systems, imperil their souls in the next world. Attracted to the material plane after death, such people often enter one of the lower heavens, where they must strive in agony to enter a higher circle of life.

Doyle's didacticism breaks down the distinctions between a work of imagination and a religious tract. Much of the novel's action is suspended while the narrator lectures at length on spiritualist theories. From a literary point of view, Doyle's didactic methods do violence to the artistic quality of the Challenger series. The characters are pushed about and forced into roles at variance with their characterizations in the earlier stories. As a work of imagination *The Land of Mist* is an unqualified artistic failure, but as a persuasive tract on psychic religion, it succeeds as propaganda, making the reader aware of both Doyle's personal stand on spiritualism and his feelings about the unfair treatment spiritualists receive from society. Whether the novel has the power to convert many of its readers to psychic religion remains to be seen. But as a fictionalized statement on psychic religion, *The Land of Mist* no doubt was far more widely read by the British public than were any of Doyle's serious nonfiction studies on spiritualism—a fact that may have done more harm than good to Doyle's reputation in the last decade of his life.

Published in 1929, a year before Doyle's death, *The Maracot Deep* is based on two literary themes: the wonderful journey and the wonderful discovery. Shaped in part by the Atlantis myth and by Doyle's doctrine of the accretion of matter and decline of spirit, it is a pale remake of *The Lost World*. Instead of the discovery of a lost civilization on a plateau in the Amazon basin, the story describes the discovery of a lost civilization at the bottom of the Atlantic. The three principal characters are patterned on the Challenger characters, but less well defined. Dr. Maracot resembles Challenger; Cyrus Headley is an Americanized blend of Malone and Summerlee; and Bill Scanlan, with his American working-class slang evocative of the novels of John Dos Passos or James T. Farrell, is a proletarian Lord John Roxton.

One of the novel's weaknesses is that Doyle does not draw a very clear picture of the nature of Atlantean society. We are not told what type of political institutions the people have. There is no discussion of the modern Atlantean economic system, and no detailed information is given about their social or religious practices. The society rests on a system of slavery; a race of light-skinned, blue-eyed descendants of the ancient Greeks work in Atlantean coal mines on the ocean floor. We are told little about these slaves, except that they are not allowed to mix with the Atlanteans; any children produced by a union of the two races are killed in order to preserve the color differentiations between them.

The focus of the novel is the ancient Atlantean civilization, rather than the culture of its modern descendants. Here the moral failure that caused ancient Atlantis to decline before the catastrophe is most important. Such information is given to the Maracot group by a telepathic cinema. The historical narrative projected via telepathy—more specifically, the moral and ethical values in the story of the catastrophe—shapes the novel, giving it power and meaning. As ancient Atlantis becomes a great world power and as its superior technology and materialistic sciences make it the first nation among many, a spiritual and moral decline sets in that greatly undermines the quality of its civilization. Despite attempts to reform the society and reverse its moral decline, nothing can avert the coming disaster. As Doyle's narrator says, with his eye fixed on twentieth-century civilization, Atlantis is an example of what can happen to a state when its intellect outruns its soul. That is what destroyed Atlantean civilization, and it may yet be the ruin of our own.

The inversion of structure caused by the Maracot group's return to the upper world in the novel's center disrupts the story's action. Unable to balance Part One, which is organically unified, the disconnected episodes in Part Two work to little purpose. The power of the novel is shaped by Doyle's desire to get the reader to see that the forces that brought about the decline and destruction in ancient Atlantis—intellect outrunning soul or (more simply) thoughtless, hedonistic materialism—are present in our own civilization. Whether we are to survive the coming deluge caused by these forces depends on our ability, or at least our willingness, to discover something beyond this world, and to find some principle of action larger than ourselves.

As in *The Poison Belt*, Doyle's vision of the future of mankind in *The Maracot Deep* is shaped by faith, not in scientific progress, but in progressing to a higher level of moral awareness through a recognition of a world beyond this life. In *The Land of Mist* we are given only an imperfect glance at this world; but, imperfect as it is, Doyle believes that materialism and conventional religion only further distort our view. Rather than look to the future in this world for a clue to human happiness, we should look to the future beyond this life. Our role, according to Doyle, is to prepare ourselves in this world for the world beyond the veil. And this preparation is not necessarily to be undertaken through conventional religious dogmas or worn-out rituals, but by a rededication to moral first principles.

The power of Doyle's vision, like the power of his personal statement in *The Land of Mist*, ultimately rests on proving him wrong. Eventually all men may know the answer to this, the greatest riddle in human history. Doyle's scientific romances are directed toward restating this riddle as art.

Selected Bibliography

SCIENCE FICTION AND OCCULT WORKS OF SIR ARTHUR CONAN DOYLE

Mysteries and Adventures. London: Walter Scott, 1889.

The Captain of the Polestar and Other Tales. London: Longmans, Green, 1890. New York: George Munro, 1894.

The Doings of Raffles Haw. London: Cassell, 1892. New York: John W. Lovell, 1892.

My Friend the Murderer and Other Mysteries and Adventures. New York: John W. Lovell, 1893.

The Great Keinplatz Experiment and Other Stories. Chicago and New York: Rand McNally, 1894.

The Parasite. London: Archibald Constable, 1894.

Round the Fire Stories. London: Smith, Elder, 1908. New York: McClure, 1908.

The Last Galley: Impressions and Tales. London: Smith, Elder, 1911. New York: Doubleday, Page, 1911.

The Lost World. London: Hodder and Stoughton, 1912. New York: George H. Doran, 1912.

The Poison Belt. London: Hodder and Stoughton, 1913. New York: George H. Doran, 1913.

The Principal Works of Fiction of Conan Doyle. 20 volumes. London: Smith, Elder, 1913.

Danger! and Other Stories. London: John Murray, 1918. New York: George H. Doran, 1919.

The Black Doctor and Other Tales of Terror and Mystery. London: Newnes, 1919. New York: George H. Doran, 1925.

The Land of Mist. London: Hutchinson, 1926. New York: George H. Doran, 1926.

The Maracot Deep and Other Stories. London: John Murray, 1929. Garden City, N.Y.: Doubleday, Doran, 1929.

BIBLIOGRAPHY AND COLLECTED MANUSCRIPTS

Gibson, John Michael, and Richard Lancelyn Green, comps. *The Unknown Conan Doyle: Letters to the Press*. London: Secker and Warburg, 1986.

Locke, Harold. *A Bibliographical Catalogue of the Writings of Sir Arthur Conan Doyle*. Tunbridge Wells, Kent, England: Webster, 1928.

Doyle Manuscript Collection: Humanities Research Center, University of Texas, Austin.

AUTOBIOGRAPHY AND BIOGRAPHIES

Carr, John Dickson. *The Life of Sir Arthur Conan Doyle*: New York: Harper and Row, 1949.

Cox, Don Richard. *Arthur Conan Doyle*. New York: Ungar, 1985.

Doyle, Adrian M. Conan. *Sir Arthur Conan Doyle: Centenary, 1859–1959, Some Aspects of His Works and Personality*. London: John Murray, 1959.

Doyle, Arthur Conan. *Memories and Adventures*, London: Hodder and Stoughton, 1924.

Edwards, Owen Dudley. *The Quest for Sherlock Holmes: A Biographical Study of Arthur Conan Doyle*. Edinburgh, Scotland: Mainstream, 1983.

Jaffe, Jacqueline A. *Arthur Conan Doyle*. Boston: Twayne, 1987.

Lamond, John. *Arthur Conan Doyle: A Memoir*. London: John Murray, 1931.

Lellenberg, Jon L., ed. *The Quest for Sir Arthur Conan Doyle: Thirteen Biographers in Search of a Life*. Carbondale: Southern Illinois University Press, 1987. (With a foreword by Dame Jean Conan Doyle.)

Norden, Pierre. *Conan Doyle*. Paris: Marcel Didier, 1964. London: John Murray, 1966.

Orel, Harold, ed. *Sir Arthur Conan Doyle: Interviews and Recollections*. New York: St. Martin's, 1991.

Pearson, Hesketh. *Conan Doyle: His Life and Art*. London: Guild, 1943. New York: Taplinger, 1977.

CRITICAL STUDIES OF SCIENCE FICTION

Batory, Dana Martin. "A Look Behind Conan Doyle's *Lost World*." *Riverside Quarterly*, 6 (1977): 268–271.

———. "*The Poison Belt* as a Morality Tale." *Riverside Quarterly*, 7 (1982): 97–100.

———. "The Rime of the Polestar." *Riverside Quarterly*, 7 (1985): 222–227.

Jones, A. G. E. "Conan Doyle's Arctic Voyage." *Notes and Queries*, 21 (1974): 27–28.

Kestner, Joseph A. *Sherlock's Men: Masculinity, Conan Doyle, and Cultural History*. Aldershot, Hants, England: Ashgate, 1997.

Meikle, Jeffrey L. "'Over There': Arthur Conan Doyle and Spiritualism." *Library Chronicle of the University of Texas*, 8 (1974): 23–37.

Moskowitz, Sam. *Explorers of the Infinite*. Cleveland, Ohio: World Publishing Company, 1963.

Orel, Harold, ed. *Critical Essays on Sir Arthur Conan Doyle*. New York: G. K. Hall, 1992.

—JAMES L. CAMPBELL, SR.

HARLAN ELLISON
(b. 1934)

HARLAN ELLISON'S WRITING career spans 40 years. Though he has worked in other forms and media, he is primarily a short story writer and has made his reputation as such, winning numerous awards. It is especially the science fiction community that has honored him. Indeed, during his period of greatest creative intensity, from 1965 to 1980, he won ten science fiction awards—seven Hugos and three Nebulas. Yet only three of these award-winning works are clearly science fiction: " 'Repent, Harlequin!' Said the Ticktockman" (Nebula, 1965; Hugo, 1966); the *Star Trek* television screenplay "The City on the Edge of Forever" (Hugo, 1967); and "A Boy and His Dog" (Nebula, 1969; Hugo, for dramatic presentation, 1976). The other awards were given to stories that show Ellison moving in a different direction, toward a mode of fantasy that is at one and the same time private and mythically cosmic in scope. But it is the science fiction world—broadening its generic parameters along with Ellison—that honored the works that have become this writer's trademarks: "I Have No Mouth and I Must Scream" (Hugo, 1968); "The Beast That Shouted Love at the Heart of the World" (Hugo, 1969); "The Deathbird" (Hugo, 1974); "Adrift Just Off the Islets of Langerhans, Latitude 38° 54' N, Longitude 77° 00' 13" W" (Hugo, 1975); and "Jeffty Is Five" (Nebula, 1977). Since 1980 Ellison has continued to win awards, but in other genres such as mystery, and other media—illustrated narratives. His latest major science fiction award was for "Paladin of the Lost Hour" (Hugo, for best

novelette, 1985). Indicative of the turn Ellison's career has taken however, this work, as a *Twilight Zone* script, won the Writer's Guild of America award for outstanding screenplay a year later. Ellison is now collecting and editing volumes of his articles and essays and tending to the publication of omnibus editions of his stories. His output of original stories has fallen, but those that appear retain the hard-hitting, mythical quality of his best works of the 1960's and 1970's.

Though strongly identified with science fiction, Ellison has, throughout his career, written fiction in a variety of genres—exposés of crime in the streets, autobiographical fiction, journalism, mainstream realism, allegory in the style of Mark Twain, and mystery stories (he won an Edgar in 1974 for a story based very closely on the Kitty Genovese killing, "The Whimper of Whipped Dogs"). In addition, he has written scripts for movies and television, and has done film adaptations of his own work and that of others—most recently of Isaac Asimov's 1950 *I, Robot*. More and more, Ellison is adamant in claiming that the proper term for him is simply "writer." In view of the diversity of his work—some thirty collections of stories and essays extending over a period of twenty-five years—I think this designation can be accorded him.

Ellison's writing career is as diversified as the forms he has worked in. Born in Cleveland, Ohio, on 27 May 1934, he spent a restless boyhood on the road, working at odd jobs. He attended Ohio State University briefly (1954–1955), then went to New York to embark on a career as a professional writer. Although during these first, difficult years his successes were in the realm of juvenile-delinquent fiction, his initial attachments as a writer seem to have been to science fiction. Before coming to New York, he was active in fan activities in Cleveland (ultimately assuming editorship of the Cleveland Science Fiction Society's fanzine *Science Fantasy Bulletin*), and his first published story was a science fiction piece, "Glowworm," which appeared in 1956 in *Infinity Science Fiction*.

Once in New York, Ellison, following Ernest Hemingway's dictum that a writer must live what he writes, ran with a Brooklyn youth gang in order to gather material for a series of novels and stories about life in the wild streets—fiction whose "sociological" pretensions do little more than mask its sheer sensationalist violence and power fantasy. Today these works—with such titles as *Rumble*, 1958 (also known as *The Web of the City*), *The Deadly Streets* (1958), *Gentleman Junkie and Other Stories of the Hung-Up Generation* (1961), and *Rockabilly*, 1961 (also known as *Spider Kiss*)—are period pieces and retain interest only for the student seeking to explore the underside of the "silent fifties." But they do—if in an ultimately soft and sentimental manner, despite all the surface blood and gore—deal with the violence of the big city, a theme that Peter Nicholls and John Clute, in their article on Ellison in *The Science Fiction Encyclopedia*, see as a constant preoccupation throughout Ellison's work.

After a stint in the army as a draftee, Ellison was editor of *Rogue* magazine; then he gravitated to Hollywood, where he began—again with great difficulty at first—a career as a film and television writer. For both media he has produced a great variety of material, most of it not science fiction. He has done television scripts for such diverse shows as "Route 66," "The Man from U.N.C.L.E.," and "Burke's Law," as well as an occasional science fiction effort—notably the memorable "Demon with a Glass Hand," which was done for "The Outer Limits" series in 1964 and which won a Writer's Guild of America

Award, and the "Star Trek" episode "The City on the Edge of Forever" (1967). In general, though, Ellison's relationship with the television industry has been a stormy one, and in 1963 he began signing a number of works he sought to disown with the pseudonym Cordwainer Bird. In 1970 he published a collection of vitriolic essays entitled *The Glass Teat: Essays of Opinion on the Subject of Television;* and in 1975 another collection—like the first, taken from his running column in the *Los Angeles Free Press*—called *The Other Glass Teat*.

Ellison is primarily a writer of short stories. His breakthrough in this form (and perhaps as a writer in general) came, as he tells it, when Dorothy Parker favorably reviewed one of his stories—a "mainstream" tale of racial violence in contemporary America, "Daniel White for the Greater Good" (1961). With recognition and some degree of financial security from script writing, he began a steady stream of production that reached its peak, in terms of quantity and quality, during the decade from 1965 to approximately 1975. The tales of this decade, inaugurated in many respects by "'Repent, Harlequin!' Said the Ticktockman" (1965), gradually move away from science fictional or topical themes and toward dark, personal fantasies set in an allegorical, quasi-mythical landscape rather than in a future one. The titles of his collections indicate the nature of this shift: *Paingod and Other Delusions* (1965), *I Have No Mouth and I Must Scream* (1967), *The Beast That Shouted Love at the Heart of the World* (1969), *Alone Against Tomorrow* (1971), *Deathbird Stories: A Pantheon of Modern Gods* (1975), *Strange Wine* (1978), and *Shatterday* (1980).

As a storyteller Ellison is visibly never comfortable in any single publishing category. He seems least comfortable working with the formulas of magazine science fiction, the mode in which he made his debut as a writer of stories. He made a belated attempt—with a series of tales, mostly from the mid- and late 1950's, that deal with the ramifying aspects of an intergalactic war between Earth and a people called the Kyben—to create a conventional "future history" cycle, but soon abandoned any such restraining framework.

In this context Ellison's various rebellions and infractions of consecrated formulas, although done for personal reasons rather than for the sake of founding a movement, have earned him a reputation as leader of the New Wave. Although predictably denying this label, he has in a sense, with the launching of the first of the *Dangerous Visions* anthologies in 1967, established himself as a spokesman for a new kind of science fiction. These anthologies are unique in their open flaunting of the prudishness that marked the old science fiction story, tailored for an audience of clean living junior scientists whose sense of wonder was confined to expletives no stronger than "Gosh!" The *Dangerous Visions* collections (the third one has yet to appear) brought sex and violence, present but repressed or sublimated in earlier science fiction, openly to the forefront in polemic fashion. What is more, in his editorial comments here and elsewhere, Ellison has repeatedly declared himself a writer of "speculative fiction." But if this change makes him in a sense the prophet of a New Wave, its thrust is not limited to science fiction; rather, it is clearly seen by Ellison as a move on the part of speculative writing in general toward the literary mainstream—a coming of age of the several modes of popular fantasy.

In spite of the diversity of literary forms he has practiced and continues to practice, Ellison's world view remains surprisingly consistent. Indeed, he possesses a strong, starkly stated vision of man's relation to the cosmos that has not changed appreciably from his earliest stories to the present. At the center of the typical Ellison tale is an elemental confrontation between man and the forces that animate his universe. This encounter is invariably violent, and man's condition seems to involve the survival of the fittest in a world that is not only indifferent but openly hostile to his existence. Indeed, Ellison's universe, while clearly post-Darwinian, is marked by the strangely personal and intimate nature of this struggle. What emerges is an almost Old

Harlan Ellison in 1993. PHOTO BY JAY KAY KLEIN

Testament relationship between defiant man and a god who is harsh yet, by virtue of the terrible tortures he inflicts, ultimately accessible.

Many of Ellison's heroes suffer the agonies of Job; and like Job many of these victims are able to draw, from the depths of fear and despair, the strength to "kick against the pricks." Some go further: they fight back and even overthrow the cruel god. In this sense, then, Ellison's vision is Hebraic rather than Hellenic. In his eyes, man's worst enemy is not this personal tyranny but the impersonal System, the inaccessible machine god served by his "Ticktockman." Thus, what would be hubris to the Greeks becomes a natural demand for a humanized relation—along the lines of love and hate—with the forces that rule over our destiny: not an abstraction such as Fate but, rather, a "Paingod."

Ellison's world view, though, is double-stranded. There is, on the one hand, a pre-

287

Christian view of man that sanctions individual violence and the drive for raw power in a violent, amoral universe. On the other hand, there is also a need to balance this dynamic of hate and revenge with another impulse based on what Ellison calls "love"—the quest for "surcease," the desire to sacrifice the striving self in order to reestablish not an individual center of power, but simply a fulcrum or shifting point of equilibrium in the forces of life.

If his earliest stories project an unending rhythm of hate—with the oppressed center reacting violently to expand and occupy the oppressing circumference, only to provoke a new expansion from within, one individual overthrowing the tyrant to become in turn the cruel god to be overthrown—in the more cosmic vision of a work like "The Beast That Shouted Love at the Heart of the World" (1968), the systolic-diastolic movement is one of hate and love. What is more, these new poles interact in complex and unforeseeable ways. This story attempts to illustrate, in an almost Taoist fashion, that for every act of love or hate there is "cross-when" some opposite occurrence spawned in a balancing reaction.

The heart of the tale is the conflict between a future ruler, Linah, who "in the name of love" wishes to save the world to come by flushing the essence of the "beast" backward into the past, and the scientist Semph, who in draining the beast "interposes" himself and sends his own essence back to counterbalance that of the beast. By doing so, Semph challenges the idea—expressed piously and with loving intentions by Linah—that there is an absolute center. He sees such a claim as another (and more dangerous) individual power fantasy: "We stop fouling our own nest at the expense of all the other nests that ever were." Yet his own sacrifice, although born of an opposite desire, produces twisted results in the past: in our time the mad-dog killer William Sterog shouts, "I love everyone in the world," and his act goes forward to become, in some far-distant future on a yet-unborn planet, a statue erected to Semph the savior.

No center holds here, only the rhythm of opposition itself. And those who seek to freeze the dynamic, to fix this endless pattern of cosmic expansion and contraction either by declaring an absolute center in the self or by denying the self such a central role absolutely, undergo the fate of Ellison's modern Larry Talbot the Wolfman in "Adrift Just off the Islets of Langerhans. . . ." Bound by the moon and a "perfect metabolism" to an unending cycle of violence, Larry seeks to escape by literally effacing the self at the center of this process, by taking a physical journey inside his own body in hopes of finding and suspending the point that holds him. But if, through this contraction, itself the opposite of the avenger's megalomaniac expansion, love does break the fatal circle, it is only to discover that balance can never be stasis, that there is no surcease. Talbot returns from the empty center—where he recovers a piece of human jetsam, a woman named Martha Nelson, whose life he had heard told long ago and who lived forgotten for ninety-seven years in an asylum—only to begin seeking all the things wasted or lost in this act of recovery itself.

The same dynamic equilibrium that we find in Ellison's world view informs the interaction of science fiction and fantasy in his work. Two striking examples of this particular pattern of interaction are the stories "I Have No Mouth and I Must Scream" and "Pretty Maggie Moneyeyes," both first published in 1967. The first story recounts the sufferings of five human survivors of an atomic holocaust in the belly of a cruel machine god—the giant computer AM. More than a grim Cartesian joke, this computer's genesis represents the ultimate science fictional nightmare:

> There was the Chinese AM and the Russian AM and the Yankee AM and everything was fine until they had honeycombed the entire planet. . . . But one day AM woke up and knew who he was, and he linked himself, and he began feeding all the killing data, until everyone was dead, except for the five of us.

At this point the story seems to strike an almost orthodox balance between science fiction and fantasy elements: here, the dystopian machine; and the utopian dreams of the men and women trapped within it, the hopeless yearnings of these five survivors to reassert human values like solidarity and compassion at the heart of this mechanical hell. And yet it is made clear that, in its hatred for mankind, this machine has acquired a human heart. Furthermore, the narrator is again a being who, professing love, expresses it through murderous violence, killing all of his fellow sufferers out of what he claims are altruistic motives, sacrificing himself unto eternity as the mouthless blob of the story's title.

We begin to suspect the clean-cut relationship of these two modes at this point. Although it is claimed that the machine deforms its prisoners' names and physiques at will, the claim is made by the narratoractor, whose "love" as he speaks of his fellows is soon seen to be steeped in hate and envy. This, in fact, is a tale told by a madman isolated in his paranoid jealousy—the true creator of this hate machine that becomes linked to him endlessly, the hard encasement for that heap of soft flesh he has not recently become, but always was. The machine's relation to man, then, is not that of a servant that rebels, or of a plaything of the overreaching intellect that proves a monster, so much as the necessary projection of human hate, the object it must have in order to exist at all. Hell here is not, as Jean-Paul Sartre claims, other people, rather, it abides in this cruel adaptation of the polar rhythm—center and periphery, flesh and metal, each person isolated in his or her hate yet unable to do without the other.

Ellison again plays upon this conventional exchange of science fiction and fantasy in "Pretty Maggie Moneyeyes." The heroine of this story is a machine artifact of our soulless materialistic culture in which the love impulse has been transformed into aggressive hate: "An operable woman, a working mechanism, a rigged and sudden machinery of softness and motivation." Her blind greed leads her ultimately, as she pulls the handle of a slot machine, to pass into it literally, to become its "soul." In turn her "three blue eyes" attract the fantasy opposite: Kostner the poetic dreamer, unrequited in love, the eternal victim seeking his fatal soul mate. Again the terrible law of balance overrides sentiment or morality. Coming to the machine from the opposite direction, but with a like desire to fix the center of things in himself, the yearning Kostner, like the vengeful Maggie before him, passes into the slot and is held there as she escapes. His delusory dream of Maggie's soft blue eyes leads inexorably to his entrapment, to "three sad brown eyes" staring from a machine now destined to be scrapped and melted down. This machine, then, is indifferently the creation of hate or love, fantasy or scientific hubris.

Ultimately Ellison's relationship to his own work, both as an intrusive narrator and as an editorial voice commenting on its meaning and fortunes in numerous introductions and critical articles, obeys this same rhythm of expansion and contraction. In those cases where Ellison is not directly the hero of his own tales, his voice penetrates to their core. Constantly the narrator, in either his omniscient or his limited role, assumes the same brash, quasi-confessional tones as the fictional Ellison who speaks in the editorial margins of these texts. In its ubiquity and insistence, this voice becomes both guardian and guarantor of the stories, projecting a sense that here is not dead but living discourse—words spoken and respoken that are worthy of being guided through the years, mediated to other human beings, and reassessed in terms of their relevance again and again.

Yet if through such all-pervasive intrusion Ellison seems in danger of reducing his diversified production to a massive display of his own ego, such a contraction actually leads to an expansion. For from this center in self, the Ellison voice, until it usurps all aspects of the literary act, strives to control both the conditions of production and those of audience response. In numerous appended essays and comments it not only tells us how to read the stories but seeks to avert misreadings by be-rating the reader in advance for straying from the prescribed path. Indeed, Ellison has written much seemingly independent journalism, such as his *Glass Teat* essays on television. And yet even here the goal is less objective analysis of some cultural phenomenon than display of self. In the manner of his model H. L. Mencken, Ellison offers "prejudices," opinions violently uttered in hopes of arousing violent reaction. In this perspective, then, all the shocking pronouncements, profanity, and moralizing "crisis writing" that fill his fiction and nonfiction alike are intended to do one thing—forestall or disarm critical opposition, real and potential, to the author and his work. Man and work, of course, are joined by the presence of this same voice, functioning inside and outside the fictional text, both in the narrator and the characters of the story, and in that garrulous commentator who rushes to fill the interstices that exist between text and reader.

If throughout his career Ellison, in cultivating this set of masks or "persona," has often fallen victim to this rhythm of contraction and expansion, producing words that are irritating and ineffectual in their self-aggrandizement, he has also used this device effectively and creatively. An example of the first sort of work is *Memos from Purgatory* (1961), two purportedly autobiographical narratives from Ellison's New York days.

The first narrative claims to retell the violent revenge fantasy of *Rumble* in documentary fashion, as observed fact and for the purpose of teaching understanding for these wayward kids. But overwhelming the objective intention here is a subjective impulse that constantly calls attention to the speaker and to the "heroic" nature of his deeds. This incursion is fatal here, for lacking even the modest narrative distance of *Rumble*, the narrator slips, as he tells his tale, into unabashed wish-fulfillment. Worse yet is this narrator's sudden final return to documentary objectivity, his smug telling us that, in the end, all this was no more than an exercise in amateur sociology.

The difficulty in controlling this "I" is ever more acute in the second narrative, where "Ellison" now poses as a middle-class Everyman. The street fighter has become a respectable writer and an authority on juvenile delinquency for whom knives and drugs now only serve as props for lectures. The ensuing drama is also a thoroughly middle-class one: a spiteful acquaintance turns the narrator in, and he is arrested and held for twenty-four hours in New York's infamous "Tombs." Ellison chooses to treat this situation in a Kafkaesque manner, seeing the process of arrest through the eyes of a passive victim whose confusion and fear provide the backdrop against which the dehumanizing operations of the social machine are seen. But again the Ellison voice is unable to sustain this stance, and is continually given to outbursts of a craftiness and bravado more in character with the streetwise narrator of the first section. The speaker in the Tombs oscillates between two incompatible roles: a cringing buffoon, and a wise guy capable of spotting "Oreo queens" and finessing dumb Irish cops.

More inconsistent yet are this speaker's attempts to moralize on his situation. He has inexplicably progressed from dazed victim— who can do no more than register what he calls "sights and sounds, emotions and textures"—to a position of awareness and authority. A cell mate miraculously turns out to be an old "bopping buddy" from the first section who tells the narrator the grim fate of his old companions and in doing so catches him in a trap. For compared to the hard crime—even the fantasy sort of the first narrative—his situation seems ludicrous: an amateur who built his reputation parasitizing on the ill fortune of others, and who now has a caring agent and faithful mom out there to bail him out.

And in the end, though it all boils down to "haves" and "have nots," our narrator does not have the good sense to be silent and let a point be scored at his expense. On the contrary, the speaker, in the final pages, dwells obsessively on his innocence, and will not rest until he has made the law acknowledge his innocence publicly. The section ends grotesquely with the narrator, in the face of the damned upon whom the Tombs (and his own gaze) have closed forever, triumphantly producing his document of acquittal for all to read.

But if Ellison's attempts to use the self as hero fail because the voice proves unwilling to modulate or the persona unable to use irony against itself, his corresponding use of self as organizing principle, in the collections of stories he is constantly rearranging in order to reedit them, has had some notable successes. The two most striking of these perhaps are: *Deathbird Stories* (1975) and *Love Ain't Nothing But Sex Misspelled* (1968).

In the first work the familiar Ellison voice, by means of an intricate series of appended remarks and epigraphs, not only acknowledges an abiding preoccupation with god myths (together with, obliquely, a fascination with the godlike qualities of the organizing persona itself), but also seeks to bestow, as if by fiat, a semblance of logical and thematic order upon what otherwise would remain a disparate set of experiments in god-creation.

The second work is more interesting. The original *Love Ain't Nothing But Sex Misspelled* is merely a collection of tales artificially organized around the catchy title, taken from the first line of one of the stories but hardly relevant to the others. In the new 1976 edition, though, Ellison deletes old material and adds new in order to focus more clearly on the theme he has inherited with the title— love. At the same time, he extends his exploration of the relation between this theme and the organizing voice itself, examining and ranking "personal" experiences in love over the years since the book's 1968 edition, and now measuring these against the streetwise resilience implied in the arrogant ungrammaticality of the title, and finally against the various visions of love in the original stories. The new goal is an ambitious one: to explore, in the light of this shared theme of love, the interrelations and interactions between art and life.

To this end, the tales retained from the original edition are all of two sorts: either openly semiautobiographical narratives, or highly personal and confessional first person fictions. In and around this preserved core, the incursions of the Ellison voice and intrusions of this protean persona cause whatever original boundaries that existed between these two modes to blur. The new stories are claimed, significantly, to be "true" incidents from the author's life. What is more, Ellison's long, added introduction is itself given a story-like title ("Having an Affair with a Troll"), and thus is made to shade toward the other forms of personal narrative in the collection, providing a subtle bridge between fact and fiction, opinion and formal art, which stands almost symbolically at the head of the volume.

The interplay resulting from this incursion of frame material into the traditionally closed texture of fiction can be complex. An example from the 1976 edition of *Love Ain't Nothing But Sex Misspelled* will suffice. Although the Hollywood novella "The Resurgence of Miss Ankle-Strap Wedgie" (1968) is a third person narrative, its protagonist, Handy, speaks and acts in the same manner as the framing persona of the introductory sketch. Ellison accents this similarity by setting against this classical form of narration "Valerie," a story claiming to be the purest personal reminiscence. Valerie, the subject of the story, who supposedly has treated our persona unkindly in love, has the same name as the heroine of "Resurgence," and we are led to compare them and the forms of discourse that present them. By contrast, the sordid doings of this petty cheat of Ellison's modern-day Hollywood lend dignity to the otherwise pathetic fictional victim of an older, now "mythical" glamour capital. But at the same time, set against the inconclusive and yet open-ended quality of the persona's experience, the destinies portrayed in "Resurgence," if neater, seem by that very fact fixed and artificial, in danger of fading with time in luster and reader appeal. The dynamic, intruding Ellison voice is clearly needed, then, to shore up these ruins, to keep such stories alive by showing that art itself, like the quest for love that is the theme of tales and personal reflections

291

alike, is no absolute but must remain at best a tentative thing.

As self-proclaimed guide and animator for what otherwise would be a lifeless and formless group of stories, tossed to the winds of obsolescence and reader taste, this Ellison voice then blurs the boundaries of life and art for a definite reason. Art or life alone can lead to an impasse, but when joined by this goading Ellison voice they remain open-ended, alive, and receptive to each other. And because of this, love stays free to pursue its elusive object. Increasingly, this animating role of the Ellison voice or persona has become the author's trademark as anthologizer, whether of his own works or of the works of others. In the *Dangerous Visions* series, collections of original stories by other authors, he prefaces each work not simply with the usual biographical facts but with lively anecdotes—often ministories in themselves—that tell how the editor played a role in the writer's personal life. And in his own most recent collection, *Shatterday* (1980), Ellison gives each story—works published over the years under the most diverse circumstances—its own introduction, thus relying on often too hefty doses of personal reminiscence and critical comment to give a semblance of common purpose to otherwise quite variegated pieces of fiction.

Ellison has been, and remains, primarily a short story writer. Indeed, he is one of the few people in the history of the science fiction and fantasy genres to build a successful career, artistically and financially, on work in this form alone. In light of his plastic yet virtually unchanging world view, and of the persistence of this Ellison persona as the dominant voice both inside and outside the narrative, the form of his stories has undergone over the years less what could be called an evolution than a subtle modulation. As pointed out previously, his fantasy does not displace his early science fiction tales but interacts with them to create what has been, and continues to be, a mythic mode distinctly Ellison's.

It is instructive to look again at his early science fiction stories. For though many of them are undistinguished, they nevertheless reveal the author's inability to work within the narrow confines of stock genre formulas. In the Kyben tale "The Crackpots" (1956), for example, characteristic battle lines are drawn and power structures are revealed. The protagonist, a Kyben whose branch of the race has distinguished itself as administrators and has left the native planet to conquer the stars, returns to the old capital to spy on its remaining inhabitants, the "crackpots," beings who perform all sorts of irrational antics. But what he discovers through contact with their "folly" is the sterile conformity of his own utilitarian society and the oppressive horror of its totalitarian underside. But the shock is deeper than spiritual revelation: not only do these "crackpots" turn out to be the free and creative elements of this society after all, but in their creativity they are revealed to be its true masters, the wielders of power: "We weren't left behind—you were thrown away."

Most of these early tales favor the maverick individual over systems of any sort. In "Wanted in Surgery" (1957), a future society dominated by machines is defeated by the actions of a lone, "disenfranchised" surgeon who proves that, at least in bedside manner, the human physician is superior to the phymech, the robot doctor that would render him obsolete. Another tale, "Battlefield" (1958), shows us a "commuter war" in which two young academy buddies fight on weekdays for opposite sides in a deadly war game—a logically illogical extension of our present society's ideal of competition—only to sit down with each other and their wives for Sunday dinner; these men are so hopelessly brainwashed that they cannot see the tragic irony of their situation.

Ellison's first award-winning story, "'Repent, Harlequin!' Said the Ticktockman," epitomizes the struggle of the individual against the social machine. This story, with its epigraph from Thoreau's *Civil Disobedience,* concerns a basically harmless, but symbolically significant, conscientious objector. Ellison projects, in this future ruled by the Ticktockman and his "cardioplates," a nightmare world of man's enslavement to the mechanical clock, a grim extension of our present credit-card civilization, where now whole lives—not just bank accounts—are liquidated by simply "punching" these plates. In a world of futile production and consumption, the hero is literally out of step, a little man who is always late and who discovers what a potent weapon lateness can be in this regimented society. As the Harlequin he disrupts routines and schedules with his antics until he is finally caught and brainwashed. Yet his actions, however insignificant, prove catching: the Ticktockman himself begins to be late. The chink in the rationalist armor proves to be fantasy; and, infected by the Harlequin, this world begins its inevitable drift back to a state of humanity.

Very quickly in Ellison's stories, though, man's struggle shifts to a more elemental level. We see a new dimension emerging in a tale like "Life Hutch" (1956). A human space pilot in the Earth-Kyben war is downed in battle and takes refuge in a "life hutch," where he is assailed by a murderous, malfunctioning robot. He soon realizes it is useless to blame either enemy or friend, for who is responsible—the Kyben who shot him down, or the businessmen back on Earth who sold the government defective robot parts? All such considerations pale before the primitive battle to survive to which the hero is reduced.

This new emphasis—on violent struggle spurred by the basic motives of survival and vengeance rather than those of social and moral protest—is clear in a power fantasy such as "Run for the Stars" (1957). Here a cringing, cowardly junkie is chosen at random to function as a grotesque delaying device for Earthmen on the run from Kyben aggressors: a "sun bomb" is sewn into his stomach, and he is set loose on this world in the invaders' wake. A coward is chosen because he will run harder and thus force the enemy to search longer. The law invoked here is one of necessity beyond good and evil, and the Earth leader tells the protagonist Benno Tallant: "I don't hate you. But this has to be done." What he does not see, though, is that the other side of

fear is hate; the obverse of raw survival, naked revenge. Tallant's will to survive is so great that it turns him from a coward into a new Attila who subdues the Kyben and makes them into his private legions. Tallant has none of the old science fictional protagonist's moral allegiance to his species, for Earth will be the avenger's first target.

This revenge theme comes to dominate the nonscience fiction stories of the same period. In "Status Quo at Troyden's" (1958), an old man, squeezed to the breaking point by the world in which he lives, lashes back with violence, only to find himself part of a very favorable status quo. A tale in the vein of Mark Twain's "The Man That Corrupted Hadleyburg" (1900), "Enter the Fanatic, Stage Center" (1961) brings an avenger to a small town to expose and punish secret sins that have been covered by hypocrisy. This Fanatic is truly one: he is a professional system breaker who acts not out of moral indignation or a desire for "poetic justice," but simply as a strong man who crushes the weak. More openly yet, Jared, in the later story "Worlds to Kill" (1968), is a mercenary world destroyer without allegiance to anything but his own sense of a divine plan—a violent cosmic order that can be implemented only by destruction without end, by the strong forever preying on the weak.

At this point the fearful symmetry of Ellison's own cosmos really begins to emerge. If man's most horrible inventions are his systems of tyranny, these systems naturally beget dark counterforces that are represented by the avenger figures who shatter them. A hero like the Fanatic, although amoral in orthodox terms, may, paradoxically, be acting in accord with the true order of things, however violent and brutal it may be. With Jared, though, we see a new shift in the equilibrium of Ellison's universe. Himself succumbing to the system-builder's madness, this destroyer becomes a maker of even more oppressive machines. In league with a giant computer at the heart of his fortress planet, Jared dreams of an order built on violence that reminds us of the nightmare vision of AM: "Worlds linked to worlds by mutual respect and mutual ethic. . . . Each invader will fall, but in a way that will link the worlds in reliance on one another. Cogs in a great galactic machine."

In his later tales, then, Ellison begins to question these violent victims who become gods. Because there are always too many worlds to kill, one Paingod is fated to succeed another, endlessly. The protagonist of "Along the Scenic Route" (1969), which first appeared as "Dogfight on 101," suffers such a fate. Along freeways of the future, duels are fought with cars armed to the fenders. The hero, a simple family man out on a scenic drive, is goaded into combat by a professional duelist, a Billy the Kid of the highways. As he is about to be defeated, his survival instinct takes over, and he destroys his opponent—only to be trapped, as the new champion, in an endless series of battles with waiting challengers. This parable goes far beyond mere criticism of our society and its ethic of competition. In fact, such matters here have become the thinnest pretext for exploring an archetypal vision of the human condition in which man, as the victim both of oppression and of his own violent instincts, is condemned to hopeless struggle.

"A Boy and His Dog" (1969)—one of Ellison's favorite stories, which has generated a film (1975)—explores this same impasse of violent action. In a bombed-out future America, a boy and his telepathic dog operate as "solos" in a world of foraging gangs. Fascinating here is the chain of bloody dependencies established, a chain based on reversals of station. The dog bears the name Blood, but through his telepathic links with men has become the guardian of letters and culture. In doing so, though, he has lost his ability to hunt and feed himself. The boy Vic, in turn, has assumed the animal role as hunter, but needs the telepathic dog to find women for him in this woman-impoverished world. The woman he does find, Quilla June, comes from a "downunder"—a subterranean town where survivors seeking to preserve culture have rolled back the clock and reconstructed the genteel American Midwest. The children born in

these downunders are all female, and men are as scarce there as women are "aboveground."

In this landscape of violent necessity, none of these opposites seems destined to meet. Quilla June's actions soon prove that politeness underground is hypocrisy, a veneer that covers the rawest savagery. In rescuing Vic she reveals a nature as primal as his, and perhaps more bloodthirsty, glorying in the slaughter of her own parents. But Quilla June must learn that the world above is not for her. Forced to choose between love and survival, Vic must take the latter: the woman ultimately provides a tasty meal for Vic and Blood, and the true couple remains boy and dog. Moreover, the need for such cannibalistic choices apparently will be never-ending. The two companions must wander on to another region, where the same cycle will begin all over again: the struggle to survive has been so stripped of purpose and meaning in this tale that it becomes, in whatever sequels it generates, a sort of hellish perpetual motion.

Such a hell is the subject of the story "Silent in Gehenna" (1971). Here, in a world of fortress universities completely dominated by the military and industry, Joe Bob Hickey is the last student revolutionary. The direction this story takes is quite complicated. The point is not that Joe Bob no longer has a function in this world, but that his function is much different from what he believed, one that (despite his "good" intentions) is profoundly in tune with his society's deepest rhythms of violence and suffering. The society Joe Bob purports to defend has become so used to ecological blight that it mistakes hell for heaven. The hobo-mutants here, who play Monopoly and talk of social "improvements," are vastly different from the angry mutants of the earlier tale "The Discarded" (1956), who denounce the world that betrayed and made them. And Joe Bob is a revolutionary who deludes himself into believing he serves a needed role.

But such a delusion does not fully explain his "transcendence." Waiting in ambush to slay some university officials, Joe Bob is suddenly transposed to a place of golden light and suspended in a cage above a street where yellow creatures pass by, lashing their blue slaves. His crying out in protest is revealed not only as futile but also as a necessary part of the cruel machine itself: the figures stop whipping, fall down, and expiate themselves, only to rise and go on whipping—he has become the "conscience" that, ironically, sanctions this endless cycle of violence. In this tale the Ellison hero has begun to reflect on his actions—it is this that brings about his transformation—but does not realize his true role in the order of things. It is, rather, the narrator who must point out—by comparing the hero to the deadly bush shrike, the bird with a melodious song that kills for the sheer joy of it—that even the gold of heaven is Gehenna. In the brutal fabric of Ellison's nature, the black-headed shrike is brother to the illuminated reformer; and the heavenly city, man's ultimate dream of civility and order, harbors a hell at its heart. Caught in this terrible rhythm of light and darkness, of altruistic fantasies and the machinery of pain, Joe Bob can only yearn for surcease: "Maybe at the end of forever they'll let me die."

Ellison's classic stories of the early 1970's, probably his best works to date, follow this impulse in two directions: a retreat from the edge of a future forever, back to the original source of life, and a concomitant hope of release from self, from the natural cycle of pain and suffering that holds Larry Talbot in "Adrift" to that life. A fascinating example of this rhythm is found in the story "Catman" (1972), which takes place in the future world of the "London Arcology"—a society of stylized violence in which thief and policeman, father and son, work shifts in a "pavane of strike and vanish," in which men have traded natural instincts for machine-made amenities, only to become machines themselves.

The hero, Neil Leipzig, son of Catman, seeks his origins in the forbidden domain of the love-machine computer at the heart of this world. The journey Leipzig makes is back to the realm of organic violence, repudiated long ago by this android society, by these mechanical simulacra of human beings. In press-ing his mother and himself into a fatal triadic embrace with this love machine, Leipzig leads his sterile family a step backward toward the human condition his ancestors once possessed and lost. His act reawakens "racial memories," the nexus of love and hate that has always shaped relations between parent and son, and the result is a grotesque reversal of the Oedipal process itself: this son born of a false mother gives them both back to the true womb, the machine. Leipzig's violence in turn forces his father to remember, revives both his hatred for the son and the love for the woman "forged in a cauldron of hate." Thus, in this machine-dominated future, primal human struggle returns once more, and the Catman—whose "cats" are constructs of gears and springs—at last makes true contact with animal nature.

"The Deathbird" (1974) provides another variation—this time in a purely mythical landscape—of the same suicidal quest for surcease, the willed return in search of rest and release, from those stylized or mechanized circles of violence that hold Joe Bob or Neil Leipzig to the dark organic core. Throughout all these stories Ellison has shown again and again the tyrannical result of man's future dreams: the solution of the machine leads to a terrible sterility that enslaves people and drives them back to darkness for salvation. In "The Deathbird," Ellison's retelling of Shelley's *Prometheus Unbound*, the hero again overthrows a mind-forged god by merely ceasing to believe. Through this refusal he desires to return, beyond Eve, to the sin of intellectual pride and the fall into science, to Lilith, the dark Earth goddess. But what he discovers at this core is again intolerable pain—his own mother and dog ravaged by cancer, the Earth blighted by man—and he finds hope only in annihilation. As he ends the pain of his loved ones with the needle, the Deathbird is summoned to brood over the spent Earth.

Ellison's latest tales do not seem to have gone beyond this impasse. "Croatoan" (1975), the pivotal tale in his *Strange Wine* volume, is a story of "Deathbird" vintage in which dead dreams literally become all the fetuses flushed down toilets in the sterile, stultifying world of our urban today. This time the hero's quest is, grotesquely, into the sewers to retrieve these lost things. It leads him to Croatoan, the enigmatic kingdom of the half-formed, the teeming symbol of our repression of organic life. This search of the archetypal father for all his lost sons leads from the initial cave where he began his career of randomly and irresponsibly seducing women to this subterranean nightmare of misformed alligators and children—life forms that, like the underground trolls in "Catman," are still closer to the dark reality than to the impersonal world above.

Ellison's most recent volume of stories, which bears the title of another 1975 story, "Shatterday," is similarly backward-looking. The title story tells of a soulless modern man who must literally fall apart in order to begin his journey back to a normal, feeling existence. Staring at the glass walls of his urban landscape, Peter Novins spawns a second self who begins to amend his life of thoughtless cruelties while the original self slowly fades to nothingness. Beneath its apparent optimism this "new start" softens the edges of Ellison's rhythm of perilous balance, but does not resolve it. Indeed, many tales in this almost retrospective collection appear as the fading ghosts of now familiar forms. Once again, in "The Man Who Was Heavily into Revenge" (1978), an insignificant little man is compressed by life until he explodes and unhinges the entire universe. And in stories like "Django" and "Count the Clock That Tells the Time" (both 1978), we find new parables of the old fearful and violent cosmic symmetry. Once more, in "All the Birds Come Home to Roost" (1978) and "Alive and Well on a Friendless Voyage" (1977), a man's careless past returns in material form to hunt him down and collect what is due in darkness.

A return to Ellison's midwestern boyhood as the enigmatic source of existence—a return already well documented in tales such as "One Life, Furnished in Early Poverty" (1969)—informs his prize-winning story "Jeffty Is Five" (1977). The newest and longest work in *Shatterday*, the novella "All the Lies That Are My Life" (1980), is not science fiction, but a realistic and highly personal story about a science fiction writer. In its thinly veiled confessional content, this story looks forward to the direction Ellison's work would take in the 1980's and 1990's. Since *Shatterday* and *Stalking the Nightmare* (1982) in the early 1980's, only one short story collection has appeared, *Angry Candy* (1988), which contains fiction published in such diverse venues as *Omni*, *The Mystery Scene Reader*, and *Weird Tales*. *Slippage: Previously Uncollected, Precariously Poised Stories*, a collection announced in 1991, was finally published in 1997. Another announced story collection, *Ellison Under Glass*, will reprint the much-touted works Ellison wrote in public, in store windows and the like. That volume continues the current of gathering and promoting past works that began with the essay collection *Sleepless Nights in the Procrustean Bed* (1984) and *An Edge in My Voice* (1985). The latter presents the series of highly personal and incendiary "investigations" Ellison offered his readers in his *L.A. Weekly* column from 1980 to 1983. Another such volume, *Harlan Ellison's Watching*, consisting of Ellison's later writings for television, appeared in 1989. In these volumes, the author presents himself in a familiar persona: "I am an enemy of the people. The people who stand by and do nothing." The most recent such collection to date, *The Harlan Ellison Hornbook*, came out in 1990 and announced (surely not for the last time) that "the most infuriating man in American letters is back." A corollary form of self-aggrandizement is seen in Ellison's participation in several "definitive" editions of his works: *The Essential Ellison: A 35-Year Retrospective* (1987) and *Edgeworks*, a series from White Wolf Publishers that is to consist of twenty volumes that will reprint Ellison's early juvenile journalist novels (such as *Web of the City*). The tendency of Ellison from the beginning of his career to gloss successive publications of his stories with new commentary reaches, in this decade, its apogee.

Yet despite this passion for retrospective editions, Ellison's creative energies have not abated in the decade of the 1990's. Increasingly, the connection between Ellison and artists (first manifested in *The Illustrated Harlan Ellison* [1978], a set of his stories elaborated by various artists in diverse styles that range from captions to sophisticated devices of the illustrated narrative) has strengthened. A 1994 collection, *Mind Fields: The Art of Jacek Yerka/The Fiction of Harlan Ellison*, has Ellison, in reverse fashion, writing stories inspired by a set of paintings. Ellison has also been involved in the comic art series *Harlan Ellison's Dream Corridor*, which has seen a number of issues to date. Readers still await the famous *Last Dangerous Visions*. Or is it, as Christopher Priest has called it, the "last deadloss visions," an impossible superanthology twenty-five years in the making, growing by accretion to an unthinkable 4,000 plus pages, never to be finished? As Priest says, "in the end, everyone will write for *Last*, and everyone will die." This book may be the measure of Ellison's ego, as he strives to be the impresario who gathers together and directs the future course of the entire field of science fiction. Yet, in spite of such acts of performance art, which have increasingly consumed his energies, Ellison continues to produce excellent stories. It is by means of these stories that Ellison has moved (as he has often expressed the wish to do) beyond the mere genre confines of science fiction to a solid reputation as a fine American writer.

Selected Bibliography

WORKS OF HARLAN ELLISON

The Deadly Streets. New York: Ace Books, 1958. London: Brown, Watson, 1959.

Rumble. New York: Pyramid Books, 1958. Reissued as *The Web of the City*. New York: Pyramid Books, 1975.

The Man With Nine Lives. New York: Ace Books, 1960.

A Touch of Infinity. New York: Ace Books, 1960.

Gentleman Junkie and Other Stories of the Hung-Up Generation. Evanston, Ill.: Regency Books, 1961.

The Juvies. New York: Ace Books, 1961.

Memos from Purgatory. Evanston, Ill.: Regency Books, 1961.

Rockabilly. New York: Gold Medal Books, 1961. London: Frederick Muller, 1963. Revised and retitled *Spider Kiss*. New York: Pyramid Books, 1975.

Ellison Wonderland. New York: Paperback Library, 1962. Reissued as *Earthman, Go Home*. New York: Ace Books, 1964.

Paingod and Other Delusions. New York: Pyramid Books, 1965.

Dangerous Visions. Garden City, N.Y.: Doubleday, 1967. London: Sphere Books, 1974, in 3 volumes. (Anthology of original short stories by various writers. Edited and with extensive biographical and other commentary by Ellison.)

Doomsman. New York: Belmont Books, 1967.

From the Land of Fear. New York: Belmont Books, 1967.

I Have No Mouth and I Must Scream. New York: Pyramid Books, 1967.

Love Ain't Nothing But Sex Misspelled. New York: Trident Press, 1968.

The Beast That Shouted Love at the Heart of the World. New York: Avon Books, 1969.

The Glass Teat: Essays of Opinion on the Subject of Television. New York: Ace Books, 1970.

Over the Edge: Stories from Somewhere Else. New York: Belmont Books, 1970.

Alone Against Tomorrow. New York: Macmillan, 1971. Divided into two, London, Panther Books editions: *All the Sounds of Fear*, 1973, and *The Time of the Eye*, 1974.

Partners in Wonder. New York: Walker, 1971. (Ellison wrote most of the stories in collaboration with other authors.)

Again, Dangerous Visions. Garden City, N.Y.: Doubleday, 1972. London: Millington Books, 1976. (A second volume of original stories by other authors, edited and with extensive commentary by Ellison.)

Approaching Oblivion. New York: Walker, 1974.

Deathbird Stories: A Pantheon of Modern Gods. New York: Harper and Row, 1975. London: Millington Books, 1978.

No Doors, No Windows. New York: Pyramid Books, 1975.

The Other Glass Teat. New York: Pyramid Books, 1975. (Essays.)

Phoenix Without Ashes, with Edward Bryant. Greenwich, Conn.: Fawcett Books, 1975.

Strange Wine. New York: Harper and Row, 1978.

Shatterday. Boston: Houghton-Mifflin, 1980.

Stalking the Nightmare. Huntington Woods, Mich.: Phantasia, 1982.

Sleepless Nights in the Procrustean Bed: Essays. San Bernardino, Calif.: Borgo, 1984.

An Edge in My Voice. Norfolk, Va.: Donning, 1985.

Medea: Harlan's World. Edited by Harlan Ellison. Huntington Woods, Mich.: Phantasia, 1985.

The Essential Ellison: A 35-Year Retrospective. Edited by Terry Dowling. Omaha, Nebr.: Nemo, 1987.

Angry Candy. Norwalk, Conn.: Easton, 1988.

Harlan Ellison's Watching. Los Angeles and Lancaster, Pa.: Underwood-Miller, 1989.

The Harlan Ellison Hornbook. New York: Penzler, 1990.

Mind Fields: The Art of Jacek Yerka/The Fiction of Harlan Ellison. Beverly Hills, Calif.: Morpheus, 1994.

Edgeworks. Clarkston, Ga.: White Wolf, 1996, 1997. (Projected complete works.)

Slippage: Previously Uncollected, Precariously Poised Stories. New York: Houghton Mifflin, 1997.

BIBLIOGRAPHY

Swigart, Leslie Kay. *Harlan Ellison: A Bibliographical Checklist.* Dallas, Tex.: Williams Publishing Company, 1973.

CRITICAL AND BIOGRAPHICAL STUDIES

Porter, Andrew, ed. *The Book of Ellison.* New York: Algol Press, 1978. (Collection of critical and biographical articles on and by Ellison.)

Slusser, George Edgar. *Harlan Ellison: Unrepentant Harlequin.* San Bernardino, Calif.: Borgo Press, 1977.

—GEORGE EDGAR SLUSSER

PHILIP JOSÉ FARMER
(b. 1918)

IF THE SCIENCE Fiction Writers of America should ever confess that they had perpetrated a hoax, and that a committee of members had actually been producing the works of Philip José Farmer for almost thirty years, fronted by a quiet accomplice in Peoria, Illinois, no science fiction fan would be too surprised. Since 1952 the short stories, novels, essays, and biographies—factual accounts of fictional characters and fictional accounts of real people—that have been coming from Farmer's pen have appeared in such numbers and variety that it is as difficult to imagine one person doing them all as it is easy to imagine Farmer's being connected with such a hoax. Since his very first story, Farmer has enjoyed shocking his readers and breaking down the thin wall that separates fantasy from real life. Such a hoax would be much to his liking.

Nevertheless, there really is a Philip José Farmer who has written more than thirty-five novels and story collections, and whose production seems superhuman, given the level of quality and inventiveness he has usually maintained. At one point in the early 1970's, Farmer had eleven different series in various stages of completion.

For his efforts Farmer has received three major science fiction awards. In 1953, on the basis of the publication of a single short story, he was honored by the Eleventh Annual World Science Fiction Convention as the best new science fiction author of 1952. In 1968 he received a Hugo award for his novella "Riders of the Purple Wage" (collected in *Dangerous Visions*, 1967, edited by Harlan Ellison). This

was followed in 1972 by a Hugo for the first novel in his Riverworld series, *To Your Scattered Bodies Go*.

Farmer's work might have gained even more recognition were it not for the interrelatedness of so much of his work and for his habit of doing the unexpected—puzzling his readers and dividing his critics, who have always had trouble fitting him into a preconceived outline. The Riverworld series, though, seems to have brought him the attention he deserves. In these four novels—*To Your Scattered Bodies Go* (1971), *The Fabulous Riverboat* (1971), *The Dark Design* (1977), and *The Magic Labyrinth* (1980)—Farmer has brought together a vast panorama of characters and themes with a surer and more unified hand than ever before, making his writing more accessible to a larger audience. *The Magic Labyrinth*, in fact, remained on the *New York Times* best-seller list for several weeks.

Philip José Farmer was born on 26 January 1918 in Terre Haute, Indiana. Even by birth he was eclectic. His father was Irish, Dutch, and English, while his mother was English, German, Scottish, and Cherokee. Farmer grew up in Peoria, Illinois, where his father was an engineer and supervisor for Illinois Central Power and Light. He entered Bradley University in Peoria in 1940; but his marriage in 1941, and generally low finances, forced him to work as a laborer and inspector for eleven years at Keystone Steel and Wire Company. Attending Bradley part-time at night, he graduated in 1950 with a B.A. in English.

During the eleven years that Farmer was working his way through college, he was also writing, but only two of the ten stories produced during this period were science fiction. He received steady rejections from mainstream markets such as *Good Housekeeping*, *Argosy*, and *The Saturday Evening Post*, as well as from the science fiction magazines.

Farmer's reading habits were typical of most aspiring science fiction writers. Shy outwardly, he took inner trips of adventure with Sir Arthur Conan Doyle, Edgar Rice Burroughs, H. Rider Haggard, Jules Verne, and Lester Dent. Two of his boyhood heroes in whom he never lost interest were Tarzan and Doc Savage. When he encountered the science fiction pulps, his voracious appetite consumed these, too. During high school he not only read science fiction but also sketched story ideas during study halls—many of these ideas later flowered into published novels and stories.

In spite of this background, Farmer was not able to sell a science fiction story until 1952, when "The Lovers" appeared in *Startling Stories* for August. Even this story was not easy to sell. John W. Campbell, Jr., of *Astounding* had turned it down because it made him "nauseous"; it was rejected by Horace Gold at *Galaxy* for the same reason. The problem was sex. "The Lovers" not only introduced sex in a more explicit fashion than the conventions of science fiction had previously allowed, but it went further and described sex between a human male and an alien female. Then it went even further, and made that alien an insect.

The story concerns Hal Yarrow, an Earthman sent by a harsh, theocratic government, the Sturch ("state" plus "church"), to the planet Ozagen on a mission to kill the dominant intelligent species who have evolved from insects. On Ozagen, Yarrow falls in love with a beautiful alien woman named Jeannette. Unknown to him, she is a lalitha, a parasitic insectlike creature that takes the human female form in order to attract a human male needed for reproduction. Too late, Yarrow finds out that upon impregnation, the lalitha

dies, her body serving as the host for her young until they are mature enough to leave it.

Publication of "The Lovers" altered the course of science fiction by opening the whole area of sex to treatment by writers. Within months after the story appeared, similar works by writers such as Theodore Sturgeon and Fritz Leiber began to appear. Farmer himself was immediately stereotyped as a writer who sought to shock, who broke taboos and dared to tackle forbidden subjects. Although he is not entirely innocent of these charges, the emphasis on the sexual taboos broken by "The Lovers" did him a disservice—and has continued to do so—by causing readers to overlook other aspects of the story that are just as important.

Reading the story today, when so much other fiction has become much more explicit, it is easier to notice the sensitive way in which the affair between Yarrow and Jeannette is handled. Rather than being horrified after her death, Yarrow comes to love his alien children and wants to care for them. It is also easy for shocked readers to miss the events surrounding the sexual encounter, in which Farmer explores what was to become a major interest in his fiction: the attempt of one individual or group, often using the institutions of religion and the state, to impose change on another group. The cross-species relationship between Yarrow and Jeannette clearly is more acceptable to Farmer than the manipulations of the Sturch. From this story on, though, Farmer's reputation and his antics have frequently gotten in the way of the actual story. (A book-length expansion, *The Lovers*, appeared in 1961.)

In 1953, flush with the notoriety of "The Lovers," which was bringing in many letters to the editor, Farmer entered a contest, sponsored by Shasta Publishers, that offered a prize of $4,000 for the best science fiction novel. Farmer wrote a 100,000-word manuscript in thirty days and won the contest. Determined to write full-time, he quit his job and hired an agent. But the manuscript submitted to Shasta, "I Owe for the Flesh," was not published at the time, and Farmer was never paid by Shasta because of its less-than-honest dealings. The manuscript itself disappeared for thirty years. As a result he lost his house and was forced to take a job with a Peoria dairy. For two years he wrote almost nothing, although stories written prior to 1954 continued to appear in magazines.

Most of these stories did little to alter Farmer's growing reputation as a writer fascinated by abnormal sex. In "Mother," for example, which appeared in the April 1953 issue of *Thrilling Wonder Stories*, a mother and her helplessly dependent son crash on a planet inhabited by stationary "mothers," beings who are little more than giant wombs. These mothers entrap the smaller males of the species inside them. The males impregnate the mothers by slashing at a spot in the womb wall and are subsequently digested by the mothers. The human mother and her son are trapped inside separate womb-entities; and the son, after missing his own mother for a decent spell and managing to avoid being eaten, settles down to a warm and comfortable, if somewhat constricted, life inside his womb.

Four more related stories appeared during the 1950's and were collected in book form in 1960 as *Strange Relations*. These are very Freudian, often comic, always explicit. Stories such as "Open to Me, My Sister" (1959, also known as "My Sister's Brother"), detailing the method of reproduction of some humanlike Martians, still made Campbell feel physically ill.

Farmer has continued to show an interest in sex that has managed to shock a percentage of his readers. In *Flesh* (1960; revised, 1968), Space Commander Peter Stagg (a double pun) and his crew return to the United States 800 years in the future. They find a primitive culture worshipping a sex goddess. Stagg is chosen as the new Sunhero, and with grafted antlers that supply enough hormones to his system to keep him in almost permanent rut, he moves from town to town, literally becoming the father of his country.

Not even Farmer's boyhood heroes were immune. In *A Feast Unknown* (1969), Doc Savage and Tarzan are endowed with super-human sexual powers. Also frequently mentioned in discussions of Farmer and sex is his contract to do two novels for a publisher of erotica, Essex House, which was trying to upgrade the field. (They also published *A Feast Unknown*.) Under this contract Farmer turned out *The Image of the Beast* (1968) and *Blown* (1969). *Traitor to the Living*, the third novel of this series, was then published by Ballantine Books in 1973.

Even when Farmer is not breaking sexual taboos, he is interested enough in human sexuality to maintain his reputation as a writer of sex stories. But sex is not Farmer's only, or even his most important, concern. One of his critics, Thomas Wymer, has described him as a trickster in the Amerindian tradition—a role of which Farmer himself seems well aware. One of his major characters, Kickaha, in the World of Tiers series, is just such a trickster. The trickster in both the Amerindian and the Scandinavian traditions is concerned (not to say preoccupied) with sex because it is an important human activity. But the trickster is not only a taboo breaker; he is also a mocker of traditions, an upsetter of the conventions that come to surround every culture, a court jester whose antics turn society topsy-turvy—not to destroy that society but to examine it and keep it healthy. If the trickster is an artist, he will also break down his culture's aesthetic conventions and try to "color outside the lines." The trickster is a religious person who hates religions.

It is in this role of the wise fool that much of what Farmer has done, including the breaking of sexual taboos, can be understood. In several ways, he has used his art to dissolve the distinction between fiction and reality. Most famous of these "tricks," perhaps, are his definitive biographies of Doc Savage and Tarzan, in which the subjects are treated as if they really existed. In *Tarzan Alive: A Definitive Biography of Lord Greystoke* (1972) and *Doc Savage: His Apocalyptic Life* (1973), Farmer painstakingly and critically uncovers the details of their lives, "correcting" earlier

Philip José Farmer in 1977. PHOTO BY JAY KAY KLEIN

accounts by their other "biographers," Lester Dent and Edgar Rice Burroughs.

Doc Savage and Tarzan are only two members of a much larger family of fictional and actual heroes whom Farmer relates by blood and marriage through several generations. This is what Farmer calls the Wold Newton Family. The Wold Newton Family series is based on the premise that in the eighteenth century a meteorite landed near Wold Newton in Yorkshire, irradiating a number of pregnant women who subsequently gave birth to mutant supermen. From this event nearly all the world's "superheroes" are descended: Doc Savage, Tarzan, Lord Byron, Natty Bumppo, The Shadow, James Bond, Leopold Bloom, the Scarlet Pimpernel, Kilgore Trout, and a number of characters who appear in various Farmer novels. Farmer has written several further adventures of these characters, adding Sherlock Holmes and Phineas Fogg.

Farmer has extended his trickery by writing novels under pen names (which, in turn, are often fictional writers from other novels). Using Kilgore Trout, a fictional writer who appeared in one of Kurt Vonnegut's novels, Farmer wrote a Trout novel, *Venus on the Half-Shell*, in 1975, reportedly much to Vonnegut's dismay. Farmer has also "coauthored" stories with writers he has created in other works, such as Leo Queequeg Tincrowdor; he has portrayed himself several times in his own works under names with initials like his own: Paul Janus Finnegan in the World of Tiers series and Peter Jarius Frigate, a science fiction writer from Peoria, Illinois, in the Riverworld series; and he has used quotes at the beginning of several chapters of *Tarzan Alive* from Paul J. Finnegan and Kickaha, who are actually the same character in the World of Tiers series. In 1971 he borrowed Ishmael, a character from Herman Melville's *Moby Dick*, and wrote a space sequel to that novel: *The Wind Whales of Ishmael* (1971).

Even Farmer's first story, "The Lovers," was not free from literary high jinks. The planet to which Yarrow is sent in that story, in tribute to Farmer's boyhood reading of L. Frank Baum's Oz books, is called Ozagen, and the dominant forms of insect life are called Wogs, from the Woggle-Bug that appears in *The Marvelous Land of Oz*.

In other works fantasy and history mix. In *Dare* (1965) we learn that the lost colony of Roanoke Island, North Carolina, was taken to another planet by the Arras (a very advanced civilization much like the Hainish people of Ursula K. Le Guin) and placed amid a race of horstels, creatures with tails who worship the Great Mother. The Europeans are left there by the Arras, who will return in 400 years to judge how well Raleigh's settlers can get along with the gentle, nontechnological horstels—the frontier experience exaggerated into the fantastic.

Farmer's literary tricks often extend to language as well. The novella "Riders of the Purple Wage" (1967), for which Farmer won a Hugo in 1968, recounts the problems of a young artist in a utopian society through a series of puns, wordplays, and twisted language reminiscent of James Joyce. A sequel, "The Oogenesis of Bird City," followed in 1970.

But through all of the practical jokes and the mockery, there emerges a writer capable of seriously exploring humanity and its place in the universe. Farmer sees mankind faced with enemies from within and without. He views humanity as a strange combination of violence and love, of good and evil. Even heroes, or perhaps especially heroes, are not pure. Even as Farmer enhances the heroism of Doc Savage and Tarzan, he shows the sadistic side of their behavior.

Farmer seems constantly amazed at how hard people have to be pushed into acts of love and compassion. In *Inside Outside* (1964), for example, a man and a woman who need but hate each other are not drawn into an awareness of love until their whole world literally falls apart, and love becomes a last resort. In response to a question about immortality, Farmer once remarked, "I can't see any reason why such miserable, unhappy, vicious, stupid, conniving, greedy, narrow-minded, self-absorbed beings should have immortality." But he added, "When considering individuals, then I feel, yes, this person, that person certainly deserves another chance . . . life on this planet is too short, too crowded, too hurried, too beset" (from his letter to Richard E. Geis, published in *Science Fiction Review*, August 1975).

Farmer has explored mankind confronting itself best in his Father Carmody series, six stories written between 1953 and 1961. The best of these, "Night of Light" (1957; expanded and published in book form as *Night of Light* in 1966), tells about Father John Carmody of Earth, a priest whose capacity for hatred and violence has led to the death of his wife Mary and has sent him running through space away from himself and his church. In *Night of Light* he finds himself on Dante's Joy, a planet that every seven years goes through a night of light during which those who remain awake confront their innermost desires. Learning such truths drives most of those who experience it mad. For Father Carmody

this dark night of the soul brings understanding, if not peace.

As frightening as Farmer finds the inner conflicts that humans face, these are nothing compared with the world outside, where institutional, social, and cosmic pressures turn people into mere playthings. The ultimate trickster is the universe itself. Invariably, in his stories and novels, Farmer examines the way in which a technologically superior culture tries to impose its will on more primitive cultures, which perceive beings of the superior culture as gods.

The best treatment of this theme appears in the five novels of the World of Tiers series, written between 1965 and 1977. Here, a dying race of decadent Lords has created artificial planets designed according to their wildest imaginations and populated with life kidnapped from throughout time and space, and given whatever fantastic bodies the Lords desire. In the first book in the series, *The Maker of Universes* (1965), the artificial world is arranged in tiers, a Tower of Babylon, with the castle of the ruling Lord on the top tier. On each tier the Lord has placed real and imaginary creatures, including humans, from different ages of Earth: prehistoric times, ancient Greece, the Middle Ages, and so on. The plot deals with the efforts of Robert Wolff, suddenly transported from Arizona to the tiered world, to reach the top tier and discover the truth. Along the way he is aided by a trickster figure, Kickaha, who turns out to be Paul J. Finnegan (alias Farmer himself). Farmer traces the effects that such arbitrary creators have on their creations while, at the same time, producing some of his best adventure science fiction.

Even more intriguing to Farmer than such superhumans who enjoy their own cruelty are those who interfere in human lives for essentially good and even compassionate reasons—to help, to ease, to advance human life—but who, as much as the Lords of the universes, end by adding to human misery.

It is just such benevolent superhumans—the "Ethicals"—who are behind Farmer's best series, the four novels that take place on

Riverworld. In the first of these, *To Your Scattered Bodies Go* (1971), Sir Richard Francis Burton, the nineteenth-century adventurer-writer who explored the headwaters of the Nile and translated the *Arabian Nights*, awakens briefly in a vast tank and finds himself one among millions of incubating bodies. Burton soon discovers that he, and all of the other 36,006,009,637 humans who lived on Earth between 2,000,000 B.C. and A.D. 2008—excepting only imbeciles, idiots, and children who died before reaching age five—have been resurrected on a planet whose main feature is one of science fiction's great inventions, a meandering river 10 million miles long that is hemmed in by very high cliffs. You and I are there, too, characters in a Farmer novel.

Although Burton has no idea how or why he and the others were resurrected, he learns from a renegade Ethical that his awakening in the incubator was planned, not accidental. The renegade has also approached eleven other humans, hoping that one or more of the chosen twelve will be able to reach the headwaters of the River, where the Ethicals are controlling the experiment.

Burton does not know, of course, whether the renegade Agent X has human interests at heart, but he is restless to know the truth and assembles a team to head up the River. His team soon includes Alice Pleasance Liddell Hargreaves, the Alice who inspired *Alice in Wonderland*; the Nazi Hermann Göring, who has converted to the Church of the Second Chance; Kazz, a Neanderthal man; and Peter Jarius Frigate, a science fiction writer from twentieth-century Peoria.

In the second novel, *The Fabulous Riverboat* (1971), Samuel Clemens (also an adventurer-writer) has been contacted by Agent X and also determines to reach the headwaters. He assembles his own crew, including a Viking, Eric Bloodaxe; Lothar von Richthoven, the Red Baron; Cyrano de Bergerac, another adventurer-writer; Odysseus; Mozart; and Joe Miller, a prehuman "titanthrop" who weighs 800 pounds and lisps. Clemens constructs the *Not For Hire*, a huge electric paddle boat

armed with rockets, and sets out, eventually meeting Burton.

As humans will do, Clemens and Burton fight all the way, rather than cooperating in their efforts to reach the Ethicals. But the fighting forces them to construct more and more sophisticated weapons, including a dirigible, airplanes, and helicopters, which eventually permit humans to reach the citadel of the Ethicals and learn the truth. As always, out of restlessness and violence come the truth and progress.

In *The Dark Design* (1977) and *The Magic Labyrinth* (1980), Farmer gradually reveals the whole story of the Ethicals, who, it turns out, carried on the mass resurrections with the best of intentions—to give humans more time to prepare their "souls" (entities mechanically generated by the Ethicals and attached to living bodies throughout the universe) to "go on," presumably to heaven.

As many histories of science fiction have noted, the roots of science fiction lie in romance fiction combined with intellectual speculation. In the Riverworld novels, though, Farmer has used a structure seldom employed in science fiction: the form Northrop Frye has identified as the "anatomy" from Robert Burton's *Anatomy of Melancholy*, and more related to almanacs such as the *Guinness Book of World Records* than to fiction. Here are those works that attempt to collect and exhaust a particular subject or area: the cetological and nautical chapters of Melville's *Moby Dick*, Joyce's *Ulysses*, or the endless bull sessions on sex, religion, and politics in Robert A. Heinlein's *Stranger in a Strange Land*.

The Riverworld novels read like just such an epical encyclopedia, an encyclopedia of all of Farmer's childhood favorites, his hobbies and historical interests (flying and World War I, for example), and particularly the Burton-Clemens figure, who, as either writer or explorer, or both, moves forward in a restless quest for the truth. The parade of characters who flash across the backdrop of the Riverworld series all have this search in common.

Although there is plenty of adventure to sustain interest through the four novels, it is as a series of collections that they are best seen. The slow journey up the River allows for subplots and spin-offs, and endless discussions of those topics in which Farmer has always been interested. Here, too, Farmer has collected many items from his own past works. The basic idea of the series, for instance, goes back to his original unpublished manuscript offered to Shasta, "I Owe for the Flesh." The 1965 novelette "Riverworld" brings Jesus and Tom Mix into the Riverworld. The artificial souls generated by the Ethicals, Agent X, and the appearance of special food to feed the populace all come in large part from *Inside Outside*.

Farmer has received mixed reviews from the critics for his Riverworld series, but that is a pattern going all the way back to "The Lovers." Few readers or critics remain neutral regarding Farmer. Wymer defends him as one who consciously uses the Amerindian trickster tradition with a great deal of skill and understanding. To Franz Rottensteiner, on the other hand, Farmer is merely "playing with creation." Riverworld is simply "a kaleidoscope of oddities that is simultaneously derivative, self-perpetuating and incestuous . . . drawn into the gigantic junkyard of SF."

Critics pro and con agree on Farmer's exuberance. Leslie Fiedler, a mainstream critic especially attracted to Farmer's work, suggested that the Wold Newton series arose from "a gargantuan lust to swallow down the whole cosmos, past, present, and to come," and was an attempt to "subsume in his own words all of the books in the world that have touched or moved him." The same might be said of the encyclopedic Riverworld novels. Readers who like Farmer's work see his exuberance as what the romantics called "gusto" or "zest"; readers who are turned off by Farmer's antics see it as mere boisterousness.

—ROALD D. TWEET

In the early 1980's, when Farmer was in his mid-sixties, he remained a prolific author, but since 1985 his output has been much reduced, with no new books from 1994 through 1997. In 1998 at the age of eighty, however, he had a nonsupernatural mystery novel, *Nothing Burns in Hell*, published. He has also delivered a fantasy novel featuring Tarzan, *The Dark Heart of Time*, for 1999 publication, and he has contributed a chapter to *Naked Came the Farmer*, a round-robin mystery novel.

In the period after 1982, Farmer wrote one new series, Dayworld, and added volumes to his two major existing series, Riverworld and the World of the Tiers (in addition to some less important work).

The Dayworld trilogy is a development of Farmer's brilliant 1971 story "The-Sliced-Crosswise-Only-On-Tuesday-World." In order to cope with future Earth's overlarge population, everybody is allowed to live only one day in seven; for the other six days of the week everyone is kept in suspended animation. This results in extended life spans: a seventy-year-old will have existed for 490 years, though he or she will have been conscious for just the seventy years. It also results in a heinous new crime, "daybreaking," which is avoiding suspended animation and living for more than one day a week. The basic premise is set up in an exciting story told in *Dayworld* (1985), but in *Dayworld Rebel* (1987) and *Dayworld Breakup* (1990), Farmer almost forgets the background in his desire to make his characters ever more bizarre and his writing ever more playful.

Gods of Riverworld (1983) is the fifth volume of the Riverworld series. It moves the saga of Richard Burton versus the Ethicals a few steps farther, adding characters and killing them off in quick succession. Nothing, it turns out, is as it has seemed, and one revelation follows another. What this concluding volume lacks in smoothness and plausibility it makes up for in panache and teleology. But this was not the end of Riverworld, because Farmer's first version of the story, written in 1953 and presumed lost, was eventually discovered and published as *River of Eternity* (1983). It is clearly the unpolished work of a less-practiced writer, though its succinctness is an advantage.

In 1991 *Red Orc's Rage* appeared. This tale of contemporary disturbed adolescents is neither science fiction nor fantasy, except that Farmer uses his World of the Tiers scenario as a role-playing therapy game. Teenager Jim becomes Red Orc and learns about himself. The sixth and final volume in the World of the Tiers series, *More Than Fire*, appeared in 1993. It continues on from *The Lavalite World* (1977), with Kickaha being forced to deal with Red Orc several times over before achieving contentment. This is an uncharactistically quiet and unsurprising novel. Perhaps Farmer's forthcoming Tarzan fantasy, *The Dark Heart of Time*, will offer more entertainment.

—CHRIS MORGAN

Selected Bibliography

WORKS OF PHILIP JOSÉ FARMER

Flesh. New York: Beacon Books, 1960. Revised edition, Garden City, N.Y.: Doubleday, 1968.

Strange Relations. New York: Ballantine Books, 1960. (Collection.)

A Woman a Day. New York: Beacon Books, 1960. Reissued as *The Day of Timestop*. New York: Lancer Books, 1968.

The Lovers. New York: Ballantine Books, 1961.

The Alley God. New York: Ballantine Books, 1962. (Collection.)

Inside Outside. New York: Ballantine Books, 1964.

Dare. New York: Ballantine Books, 1965.

The Maker of Universes. New York: Ace Books, 1965. (World of Tiers series.)

Night of Light. New York: Berkley Medallion, 1966. Retitled, with additional Father Carmody stories, as *Father to the Stars*. New York: Pinnacle/Tor Books, 1981.

The Image of the Beast. North Hollywood, Calif.: Essex House, 1968.

Blown. North Hollywood, Calif.: Essex House, 1969.

A Feast Unknown. North Hollywood, Calif.: Essex House, 1969.

The Fabulous Riverboat. New York: Berkley/Putnam, 1971. (Riverworld series.)

To Your Scattered Bodies Go. New York: Berkley/Putnam, 1971. (Riverworld series.)

The Wind Whales of Ishmael. New York: Ace Books, 1971.

Tarzan Alive: A Definitive Biography of Lord Greystoke. Garden City, N.Y.: Doubleday, 1972.

The Book of Philip José Farmer. New York: DAW, 1973. (Collection.)

Doc Savage: His Apocalyptic Life. Garden City, N.Y.: Doubleday, 1973.

Traitor to the Living. New York: Ballantine Books, 1973.

Venus on the Half-Shell, as by Kilgore Trout. New York: Dell, 1975.

Ironcastle. New York: DAW, 1976. (Greatly rewritten translation of J. H. Rosny Aîné's *L'étonnant voyage de Hareton Ironcastle* [1922].)

The Dark Design. New York: Berkley/Putnam, 1977. (Riverworld series.)

The Magic Labyrinth. New York: Berkley/Putnam, 1980. (Riverworld series.)

Gods of Riverworld. Huntington Woods, Mich.: Phantasia, 1983; London: Grafton, 1983.

River of Eternity. Huntington Woods, Mich.: Phantasia, 1983.

Dayworld. New York: Putnam, 1985: London: Granada, 1985.

Dayworld Rebel. New York: Putnam, 1987; London: Grafton, 1988.

Dayworld Breakup. New York: TOR, 1990; London: Grafton, 1990.

Red Orc's Rage. New York: TOR, 1991; London: Grafton, 1993.

More Than Fire. New York: TOR, 1993.

Nothing Burns in Hell. New York: Forge, 1998.

Naked Came the Farmer: A Round-Robin Rural Romance Murder Mystery. Mayfly Productions, 1998. (Initial chapter contributed by Farmer.)

The Dark Heart of Time. Forthcoming in 1999.

CRITICAL AND BIOGRAPHICAL STUDIES

Brizzi, Mary T. *Philip José Farmer*. Mercer Island, Wash.: Starmont House, 1980. (A careful exploration of the themes and characters in Farmer's work.)

Fiedler, Leslie. "Thanks for the Feast." In *The Book of Philip José Farmer*. New York: DAW, 1973, pages 233–239. (An appreciation of Farmer's work by a mainstream critic.)

Kraft, David, and Mitch Scheele. "An Interview with Philip José Farmer." *Science Fiction Review*, 4 (August 1975): 7–21. (Farmer discusses pornography, his World of Tiers and Riverworld series, *Venus on the Half-Shell*, and science fiction in general. Farmer's letter to Richard E. Geis follows the interview.)

Letson, Russell. "The Faces of a Thousand Heroes: Philip José Farmer." *Science-Fiction Studies*, 4 (1977): 35–41. (Examines the roots of Farmer's themes and characters.)

———. "The Worlds of Philip José Farmer." *Extrapolation*, 18 (May 1977): 124–130. (Compares pro and con views of Farmer, with special reference to Farmer's "dark side.")

Moskowitz, Sam. "Philip José Farmer." In his *Seekers of Tomorrow*. Cleveland: World Publishing Company, 1966. (Good biography and bibliography of Farmer's early years.)

Platt, Charles. "Philip José Farmer." An interview in *The Dream Makers: The Uncommon People Who Write Science Fiction*. New York: Berkley Books, 1980. (General interview on various subjects, but captures a good portrait of Farmer himself.)

Rottensteiner, Franz. "Playing Around with Creation: Philip José Farmer." *Science-Fiction Studies*, 1 (1973): 94–98. (An unfavorable examination of Farmer's antics as not serious intellectually.)

Walker, Paul. "Philip José Farmer: An Interview." *Luna*, no. 54 (September 1974): 1–11. (Farmer discusses his use of sex and violence, commenting on Tarzan and Doc Savage, and on characters in the Riverworld series.)

Wymer, Thomas L. "Speculative Fiction, Bibliographies, and Philip José Farmer." *Extrapolation*, 18 (December 1976): 59–72. (Lists Farmer's series and provides a complete bibliography of his work.)

———. "Philip José Farmer: The Trickster as Artist." In *Voices for the Future: Essays on Major Science Fiction Writers*, Vol. 2, edited by Thomas D. Clareson. Bowling Green, Ohio: Bowling Green University Popular Press, 1979. (A detailed examination of Farmer as a trickster in the Amerindian tradition.)

WILLIAM GIBSON
(b. 1948)

F̲EW WRITERS HAVE created such an instant impact on science fiction as William Gibson, who exploded onto the scene in the early 1980's with a few short stories, most published in the field's most prestigious new magazine, *Omni*, and a single novel, *Neuromancer* (1984). *Neuromancer* swept all the awards in the field and became a best-selling work that is still in print and still popular. Although not alone, it almost single-handedly created a new science fiction subgenre, cyberpunk, and generated unprecedented interest well beyond the science fiction field. As Tom Maddox has pointed out, this kind of interest is unusual for science fiction, which is usually seen as "sci-fi" and dismissed as *Star Wars* fantasy. But very quickly such people as Stewart Brand, in *The Whole Earth Review*, and William Burroughs, in *Esquire*, were praising the novel, while *Rolling Stone, Interview*, and *The Face* ran features on Gibson. MIT initiated graduate study on such concepts as cyberspace and ICE (intrusion countermeasures electronics), while software companies pushed their exploration of the concept of "virtual realities," citing Gibson's fiction and modeling their thinking on cyberspace. Even before the rest of the Sprawl trilogy appeared, Hollywood came calling, if to little avail (Gibson wrote some movie scripts, but none made it to the screen until *Johnny Mnemonic* in 1995). In the later 1980's, and well into the present, academics took up the banner for cyberpunk, which in many cases meant taking up Gibson's fiction. As one wag put it, for many critics "Cyberpunk = Gibson = *Neu-*

romancer." All of this is heady stuff for a new writer, but Gibson seems to have handled it fairly well, and he has continued to write the novels for which he is best known from his home in Vancouver, British Columbia.

Gibson's background is distinctive and includes a somewhat vagabond youth. He was born in Conway, South Carolina, on 17 March 1948, to William Ford and Otey (Williams) Gibson. His father died when he was eight, and his mother moved back to a small town in southwestern Virginia. He attended boarding school in Tucson, Arizona, was expelled for smoking marijuana, and as his mother had died and the draft board had rejected him, he drifted north to Toronto "without even knowing Canada would be such a different country." After traveling in Europe and the Near East, he married Deborah Thompson in 1972 and moved to Vancouver, where they still live, with their two children, Graeme Ford and Claire Thompson Gibson. While his wife pursued an M.S. in linguistics at the University of British Columbia, Gibson decided to get a B.A. in English, graduating in 1977.

Tom Maddox, in "William Gibson: A Bio" (1989), is quite correct to insist that

to figure the man at all, you've got to know he was born in Virginia [*sic*] and grew up in an America as disturbing and surreal as anything J. G. Ballard ever dreamed. . . . Gibson lived in a region where people looked on someone from ten miles away as a member of another tribe and anyone from another state as a dangerous alien. . . . As you might expect, growing up in this world put some vigorous spin on the Gibson psyche. (page 10)

Yet Gibson's time in Canada has also influenced his writing, and seeing the world from a Canadian political perspective has had its effect on his vision of a future ruled by multinationals and in which nation-states are almost obsolete.

Despite his oft-mentioned love of other media and the way his novels project a future in which literacy and books are all but dead and despite the interest shown in his work by film and comics artists, Gibson remains essentially a writer of fiction, and the novel is his metier. *Neuromancer* remains the central cyberpunk novel and possibly the single most analyzed recent text in science fiction. If Gibson moved beyond cyberpunk's formal constraints as quickly as he could, he carried its attitude into his later work, even as he matured and began to explore his invented worlds with greater depth and compassion than before. While cyberpunk as a movement ended around 1988, the year Gibson's *Mona Lisa Overdrive* appeared, it remains a powerful energizing force in much of science fiction, including Gibson's own. Cyberpunk took certain extreme images of far futuristic body adaptation and prosthetic engineering and dropped them into a world changed only slightly from our own, where multinationals oversee "a deranged experiment in social Darwinism." Gibson's fiction recognizes the extraordinary power such companies will have, effectively replacing nations, shaping "the course of human history," and transcending "old barriers." Yet the stories he tells concern people on the margins of society, small-time criminals romanticized in conventional noir terms, entertainers, futuristic hackers, all scuffling to survive in the chinks of the world machine.

The early theorists of cyberpunk, especially Bruce Sterling in his various manifestos, tried to show how utterly new it was. Later critics demonstrated how much cyberpunk owes to the traditions and conventions of science fiction. Looking back and taking into account all the other fine science fiction of the period, it is clear that Gibson has brought a new flavor to the rich stew of science fiction mainly through the way he has mixed the ingredients. He has admitted the impact such writers as Alfred Bester and Samuel R. Delany had on him. Delany, in "Some *Real* Mothers . . . : The *SF Eye* Interview" (1994), has pointed out a connection to Roger Zelazny ("Both of them indulge a kind of Jacobean gorgeousness, coupled with a love of the 'hardboiled'") and an even greater debt to the feminist science fiction writers of the 1960's and 1970's:

I'm sure Gibson would admit that his particular kind of female character would have been impossible to write without the feminist science fiction from the seventies—that is, the feminist SF whose obliteration caused such a furor when Bruce Sterling (inadvertently, of course . . . ?) elided it from his introduction to *Burning Chrome*. (page 173)

Gibson has also admitted the influence of postmodern literature and various forms of pop culture, although, as Brian McHale suggests in *Constructing Postmodernism* (1992):

The constant traffic between low and high—the high-art appropriation of popular-art models, and the reciprocal assimilation by popular-art genres of "cast-off" high-art models—far from being a distinctive feature of the postmodern period is one of the universal engines driving the history of literary (and, more generally, cultural) forms. (page 226)

Gibson is a master of such borrowing and mixing, but he owes as much to the texts he studied at the university as he does to the various popular arts he came in contact with on the street. Certainly his writing displays signs and portents of his reading in both the great moderns and contemporary Canadian literature (as the sly references that only someone who knows Canadian literature can pick up show; just as readers who know their contemporary pop music, noir thrillers, or the postmodern fictions of William Burroughs,

Thomas Pynchon, and Robert Stone will pick up allusions to them).

Scott Bukatman calls Gibson "the genre's premier *bricoleur*." Gibson's "The Winter Market" (1986) provides perhaps the best definition of such an artist: "Rubin, in some way that no one quite understands, is a master, a teacher, what the Japanese call a *sensei*. What he's the master of, really, is garbage, kipple, refuse, the sea of cast-off goods our century floats on. *Gomi no sensei*. Master of junk." Perhaps the most important concept here is the unstated one that by the end of the twentieth century, both high art and popular art, as well as everything else, have become part of "the sea of cast-off goods" Gibson evokes in his writing. Certainly they form the kipple of his dark and savagely fascinating future worlds. Gibson's fascination with the fragmented traditions of twentieth-century art, from Marcel Duchamp's "Large Glass" through Joseph Cornell's boxes of human cultural detritus to Survival Research Laboratories' use of industrial junk forms a bass line through all his writing. Delany, turning the compliment back upon the writer, says: "The bricolage of Gibson's style, now colloquial, now highly formal, now hardboiled, makes him as a writer a *gomi no sensei*—a master of junk. Applied to Gibson, it is a laudatory title."

Gibson immediately stood out from so many of his peers because he not only imagined a sleazy, dirty urban context for his stories but wrote about it in such a highly stylized manner. The style is already there in the opening lines of "Johnny Mnemonic" (1981), his first major sale. The story not only grabs us in great noir thriller style, but it takes us deep into the future world of "the Sprawl." There everyone takes for granted such things as Molly's surgically inlaid mirrored lenses and razor blades hidden beneath burgundy nails. This image, augmented in *Neuromancer* and *Mona Lisa Overdrive*, mirrors Joanna Russ's Jael, but Molly lives in a world of 'biz,' much closer to our own.

Burning Chrome ranges from the tough, noir Sprawl stories through the bittersweet "The Winter Market" (a coldly ironic vision of what will eventually become "simstim" [simulation stimulation] that reworks James Tiptree Jr.'s famous "The Girl Who Was Plugged In" [1974] as the more conventional "Hinterlands" (1983) reworks Tiptree's "And I Awoke and Found Me Here on the Cold Hill's Side" [1972]) to that subversively comic vision of older images of the future as semiotic ghosts, "The Gernsback Continuum" (1981). One collaboration, "Red Star, Winter Orbit" (1983) by Gibson and Bruce Sterling, is strangely moving in its evocation of a Soviet space station slowly falling into disuse, and it brilliantly showcases Gibson's eye for the junk that counts.

The title story, "Burning Chrome" is a kind of prelude to *Neuromancer* and its sequels, as many of the concepts—the "matrix," "Cyberspace," "ICE," "simstim"—and even some of the characters, such as the Finn and Tally Isham the simstim star, will reappear in the novels. Its representation of Rikki, who becomes Bobby Quine's "muse," looks forward to most of the other women in the Sprawl trilogy. Only Gibson's ability to generate a social context for his fiction through linguistic bricolage takes the story out of conventional noir romanticism into something with a pure science fiction frisson; and it is this quality that will make *Neuromancer* such an interesting new addition to the science fiction megatext.

If *Neuromancer* no longer has the aura of newness it had in 1984, it remains popular, finding new readers and generating new critical analyses and assessments of its place in the science fiction canon. Gibson told Larry McCaffery that much of the narrative energy comes from his own desperation:

> I knew I was so inexperienced that I would need a traditional plot armature that had proven its potential for narrative traction. . . . Also, since I wrote *Neuromancer* very much under the influence of Robert Stone . . . it's not surprising that what I wound up with was something like a Howard Hawks film. (page 271)

Many first novels use conventional plot armatures, but few achieve *Neuromancer*'s instant status. What sets it apart is its language, the concepts imaged so thoroughly and in metaphoric depth, and the way in which it does not quite follow through on the conventions it utilizes. At any rate, all the plots of Gibson's novels tend to be extraordinarily convoluted, and while this is one of the particular pleasures they offer, it is impossible to provide concise summaries of them.

If *Neuromancer*'s narrative can be quickly placed, or even dismissed, as that of a conventional thriller, the narration is something else: there is always something more to discover in the rich panoply of background effects Gibson has conjured with his brute bricolage stylization—the "superspecificity" that makes its invented world one of the most compelling perceptual constructs in recent science fiction.

Neuromancer exemplifies Samuel R. Delany's dictum that language creates the worlds of science fiction. Its opening sentence, one of the most analyzed in science fiction, immediately establishes the physical and psychological parameters of the text's "natural" and cultural environment: "The sky above the port was the color of television, tuned to a dead channel." This sentence echoes a famous passage of poetry from the 1920's. T. S. Eliot's J. Alfred Prufrock saw the "evening spread out against the sky / like a patient etherised upon a table," an image indebted to the medical technology practiced in World War I. Case (*Neuromancer*'s focalizing agent) sees the world in terms of the tech (some new, some already history) that surrounds him everywhere. By constructing the traditional nature/culture binary as nature/ technology, the sentence implies that in this world culture *is* technology. It also sets up the continuing deconstruction of the binary, as later metaphoric constructions will erase the slash, the mark of their separation, by continually shifting the metaphoric weight from one side to the other. Such shifts signal, from the very beginning, Gibson's admitted ambivalence about technology's relation to embodied humanity.

The story of *Neuromancer* is fairly simple in outline, extremely complex in the rendering. Case is a former cowboy, living by his wits as a middleman in Chiba City and coming closer and closer to the deal that will kill him. He betrayed his employers once, and they "damaged his nervous system with a wartime Russian mycotoxin":

> For Case, who'd lived for the bodiless exultation of cyberspace, it was the Fall. In the bars he'd frequented as a cowboy hotshot, the elite stance involved a certain relaxed contempt for the flesh. The body was meat. Case fell into the prison of his own flesh. (page 6)

This displays one side of the binary in all its Platonic-Descartesean arrogance. Case believes he does not care for his body, and his behavior throughout the novel seems to confirm this; but the ironic ambiguities play against such a reading. Molly, with her scalpel blades in "their housings beneath the burgundy nails," has been hired to find him by a mysterious backer willing to give a Chiba black clinic some advanced tech in order to reverse Case's neural damage. Case and Molly have to steal the Dixie Flatline, a ROM construct of one of the best cowboys, which as read-only memory can be accessed but cannot change or grow, from Sense/Net headquarters, then use it to attack Straylight, the home of the Tessier-Ashpool clan on Freeside, the largest of the L5 orbitals. They are really working for one of the T-A AIs (artificial intelligence), Wintermute, which seeks to unite with its twin in order to become something new. Throughout, in good thriller style, they must overcome obstacles, defeat enemies, and finally, overcome their own fears and hesitations, but the actual adventure is less interesting than the complex contextualization that accompanies it. This includes the witty, linguistically acute representation of the various environments the characters pass through. There is Chiba City, with its cheap coffins, the ones nearest the port, beneath the quartz-halogen floods that lit the docks all night like vast stages, where you couldn't see the lights of Tokyo for the glare of the television sky, not even the towering hologram logo of the Fuji Electric company, and Tokyo Bay was a black expanse where gulls wheeled above drifting shoals of white styrofoam. (page 6)

There is the rich refuse of the Boston-Atlanta Sprawl itself, and there is Rue Jules Verne on Freeside:

They were standing in a broad street that seemed to be the floor of a deep slot or canyon, its either end concealed by subtle angles in the shops and buildings that formed its walls. The light, here, was filtered through fresh green masses of vegetation tumbling from overhanging tiers and balconies that rose above them. (page 123)

In such passages, there is a subtle melding of description and metaphor that helps create an alien space.

Case's first attempt to "jack in" to cyberspace through direct neural connections to his cyberdeck after he has been cured reveals how the text shifts from one side of the basic binary to the other: "A gray disk, the color of Chiba sky." Which side are we on? If the opening sentence saw nature in terms of technology, now Case sees the tech in terms of the sky, but a sky already technologized. A more interesting moment, in terms of Case's relation to the meat, occurs the first time he and Molly make love, "his orgasm flaring blue in a timeless space, a vastness like the matrix, where the faces were shredded and blown way down hurricane corridors, and her inner thighs were strong and wet against his hips." His body does respond to her invitation, and although he imagines his ecstacy first in terms of cyberspace, he cannot escape feeling the bodies mesh, and that image is the, literal, climax. A similar but opposing moment occurs when the Neuromancer AI traps him in cyberspace with a matrix-generated simulacrum of Linda, his old girlfriend. Although he knows that both he and Linda are not real, he ends up making love to her and rediscovering the profound knowledge of "the meat, the flesh the cowboys mocked. It was a vast thing, beyond knowing, a sea of information coded in spiral and pheromone, infinite intricacy that only the body, in its strong blind way, could ever read." Given these clues, it is not surprising to discover in *Mona Lisa Overdrive* that Case eventually retires and has four kids. But he leaves Linda behind, an Orpheus returning from the land of the dead (which is how the Neuromancer identifies itself), as he has always left her behind. And most of the women in the Sprawl trilogy face similar problems: they are seen as useful or dangerous; they are identified with a space that can suck a man in (even the matrix, as its very name shows, is identified as female, to be conquered by the active male jockeys who ride it, take its secrets). This insight derives from Darren Wershler-Henry's application of Alice Jardine's theory of "gynesis" (explained in Jardine's book *Gynesis: Configurations of Women and Modernity* [1985]) to Gibson's Sprawl stories in "Gynesis and Body Inscription in the Fiction of William Gibson" (master's dissertation, University of Alberta, 1990). Jardine argues that many masculine visions of women, especially in the postmodern and frequently misogynistic writings of Edgar Rice Burroughs and Thomas Pynchon that Gibson so admires, are negative, full of a fear of merging and even of touch. Gynesis explains much about the representation of women in early Gibson.

Only Molly, of all the women in the trilogy, seems to come through on her own terms. Molly, of course, is solidly in and of the body. That is her arena, although the fact that she has had herself prosthetically upgraded demonstrates how far even her body is from sacrosanct. But the mirrored lenses inset over her eyes and the scalpel blades beneath her fingernails help her protect her bodily integrity. After all, "It's my ass, boss, and it's all I got."

To achieve the AIs' union, Case and Molly must convince 3Jane Tessier-Ashpool to give up a secret. Her family, as she knows all too well, has turned away from the outside world, hiding away in their castle in the sky. Gibson, in one of his brilliant uses of the expository lump, provides the information on the family through an essay on semiotics she wrote when she was twelve (elsewhere, he provides information on the matrix and cyberspace through a children's learning program). The matriarch of the clan, Marie-France Tessier, was a visionary who imagined her clan in a symbiotic relationship with the AIs, but "with her death, her direction was lost." Of course, the Tessier-Ashpools are an over-the-top version of the gothic incestuous family, another blackly comic addition to the horror-thriller mode of *Neuromancer*. When 3Jane and the psychopathic Riviera get together, it makes for some heady sadistic battles for Molly and Case, but in the end, Wintermute's plan succeeds, almost despite its careful planning, and Case and Molly's heroic infiltration of both the Tessier-Ashpool cyberspace holdings and orbital home. The two AIs merge and become something new, in a version of what Samuel R. Delany identified as the transcendental climax so much science fiction seeks. Or so it appears. But the mysticism is a bit bent, nothing really changes in the world, and even their moment of mystic union is doomed to end, as the later novels reveal.

Gibson's deep ambivalence about the world he invented for *Neuromancer* appears at every level of the narration—not just in the mirroring back and forth of metaphors concerning the central binary of nature and technology but in the actual behavior of the characters. Case is especially interesting because he is both the viewpoint figure and the apparent hero. But what exactly does he do? At all points down the line, he gets help from others who, like Molly and the Dixie Flatline, often do much more than he does. When Molly is captured as a result of Riviera's holographic decoy projections, Case does try to rescue her, but it is Riviera's attack on the ninja, Hideo, that allows him to do so, for Hideo, even when blinded, can track and kill the man. Although Case seems to be a tough-guy hero, he

doesn't do much on his own. Used throughout by others, he is a tool, no more.

Gibson found the given template of the noir thriller useful because it allowed him to expend his imagination on the stylization of his invented future. He was able to indulge in the various argots he knew, to create the "gratuitous moves, the odd, quirky, irrelevant details, that [provide] a sense of strangeness," such as Molly's quick glimpse of Duchamp's "Large Glass" in the T-A library. It also allowed him to play some literary games within a genre context, such as creating inlaid stories. The Finn tells one, as does the AI using the Finn's shape to communicate. Molly places one such story within another. While telling Case how the Johnny Mnemonic story ended, she inserts a story of how an old man tracked a rat under the floorboards of her empty childhood house and killed it, an apt borrowing of one of the most striking tales in Michael Ondaatje's *The Collected Works of Billy the Kid* (1970). Finally, Gibson's brilliant bricolage reflects an argument of John Clute's, that no science fiction novel can actually be set in the future and that the closer a book gets to the real present the harder it is to write, to read, to understand, and to appreciate. *Neuromancer* remains an important and interesting novel because it so accurately captures the zeitgeist of the early 1980's; it is very much set in its decade, with all of that decade's obsessions laid out within its text. It is also a young man's book, wearing its noir romanticism on its sleeve, and it is therefore understandable that Gibson would want to change direction in his next novel, even if he set it in the same world.

Most critics feel *Count Zero* (1986) lacks the energy and raw newness that so captivated them in *Neuromancer*; some even argue that it demonstrates a loss of faith in cyberpunk on Gibson's part. But Gibson deliberately chose not to try to outdo *Neuromancer*, a mug's game if ever there was one. Instead, he focused more on characterization, and while some have seen this as a retreat from the earlier play with shattered subjectivities, it is a positive step from a writerly point of view. Set some seven years after the events of *Neuromancer, Count Zero* shows us how the world has (and has not) changed.

There are three interlocking narratives that eventually meet and contaminate one another, three centers of focalization. Gibson adapts avant-garde fragmentation of narrative to genre needs. Each chapter is short and separate, but together they make up a group of carefully wrought plots. *Count Zero* begins with the oldest, most used, character, Turner, the mercenary, who is quite deliberately also the least himself. The opening sentence again demonstrates Gibson's ability to plunge us into another world by mixing neologisms with known terms to render a sense of changed environment: "They set a slamhound on Turner's trail in New Delhi, slotted it to his pheromones and the color of his hair." Gibson has said that he wanted to deconstruct the thriller detective guy in Turner but never quite managed to do so. He gets pretty far, however, especially in the beginning. Turner is blown up and then reconstituted in a Chiba hospital, with newly acquired eyes and genitals (both of which are core aspects of a male subjectivity). After some sexual therapy in Mexico to bring him back to "himself," he is hired by Hosaka to bring Mitchell, "the man who made biochips work," out of Maas Biolabs. When Mitchell's daughter Angie (who has some very strange biocircuitry in her head) appears instead, he heads "home" to his brother's farm in Virginia and then eventually takes her to the Sprawl, where those who know her as the "Virgin of Miracles" await.

These people are part of the second narrative line. They educate the eponymous "Bobby Newmark, aka Count Zero" in a kind of coming-of-age tale in which he, and we, learn how the AIs split into many separate forces in the matrix, choosing to appear there in the form of "loa," as these Haitian voodoo cult deities worked most powerfully upon the imaginations of the people who served them. Mostly he listens and learns while others act. But he does survive, eventually to meet Angie in New York and to become her closest friend and companion.

The third narrative concerns Marly, a sensitive young art dealer whose intuition is sought and bought by the world's richest man, Josef Virek, a truly gothic financier. Dealing with this person-as-multinational-corporation leads to her F. Scott Fitzgerald–inspired insight that "the exceedingly rich were no longer even remotely human." Hers is an aesthetic quest, to find the maker of exquisite boxes that echo the possibilities found in the work of twentieth-century artist Joseph Cornell. Her search leads to outer space, where she discovers, fine irony, that the box maker is one of the abandoned T-A AI cores, a remnant of the transcendental being created at the end of *Neuromancer*.

Aside from his usual black humor and the sharply casual way that he manipulates a number of conventional narrative tropes, Gibson ties tone to characterization in *Count Zero*. With his eager, oddly idealistic, and sometimes smarter than expected stance, Bobby is naive but not stupid; his growing appreciation that the world is larger than he thought is one pleasure of his story. Battlescarred and cynical, Turner's professionally anesthetized view of things is the apparent bedrock of his character, but events slowly strip it away. His final pastoral escape can be read either romantically or ironically; the ambivalence is inescapable. Some find Gibson's representation of Marly's knowledgeable, aesthetic, yet romantic responses to the boxes too conventional, but they find the boxes that way too. Others will be moved by how she is moved by them. Either way, her sensitivity is central to the novel's ruminations on the role of art, even in a world as denuded of it as this one is. The big question is whether or not a remnant of an AI can be "human" enough to create valid art. Marly intuits that it can, possibly because what it works with is the detritus of human activity. On the other hand, in a world where only the very privileged pay any attention at all to art, what real value can it have? *Count Zero* does not try to answer this question, although Tally Isham's Sense/Net simstim show suggests that imagination and art are passé. Once again, the implied background undermines the action of the narratives, be it heroic or artistic.

Count Zero seems to offer traditional happy endings—for Turner, for Angie as a Sense/Net star with Bobby as her paid companion, for Marly as a gallery owner in Paris. But little seems to have changed, and the text's continuing display of a world where most people live lives of much greater desperation than Thoreau ever imagined undermines the conventional consolations the stories seem to provide. Their obvious fakery is as moving as their hopefulness.

Mona Lisa Overdrive, set another seven years on, completes the Sprawl trilogy, as it is now known, but it, too, deliberately refuses the usual consolations of closure. Intriguingly, both *Neuromancer* and parts of *Count Zero* become embedded tales within its narratives.

Like *Count Zero*, *Mona Lisa Overdrive* is a fragmented narrative, presented through different points of view. Again, young women are involved, and some older ones, and a few of them even act for their own ends. Although already dead, 3Jane Tessier-Ashpool initiates the plot. Technology provides a kind of immortality in this world, but it is a highly ambiguous gift. Much of the action is seen through eyes that cannot really understand what it means, however, and this leads to narrative suspense and confusion.

An *oyabun* in the Yakuza, fighting some kind of internal war and wishing to protect his daughter, sends thirteen-year-old Kumiko Yanaka to London. Kumiko's mother died under mysterious circumstances, so she has her own worries, but "Sally Shears," who is actually an older Molly, leads her into deeper mazes of uncertainty, partly because she has suddenly been blackmailed into doing a job she does not like at all. Information is the currency of this world, and Kumiko's London guardian has suddenly come into a fortune, which he proceeds to spend far too profligately. Molly offers Kumiko an escape from her duties, and Kumiko finds that she likes the freedom and does not fear the conse-

quences. Molly's example helps free her from her mother's sad past.

In an abandoned warehouse in the wilds of New Jersey, Slick Henry builds strange machines out of junk. When a black man who once saved his life puts him in charge of "the Count," his life suddenly gets very complicated. The Count is Bobby, who left Angie and stole 3Jane's "aleph," a "mother-huge microsoft . . . a single solid lump of biochip . . . [whose] storage capacity was virtually infinite," to which he is permanently jacked-in. In fact, it contains what seems to be simulacrum of the world outside.

Meanwhile, Angie Mitchell, now the biggest Sense/Net simstim star, has discovered that the biosorts in her head have been altered so that she can no longer communicate with the loa in cyberspace. Even as Angie tries to find out what happened to the T-A clan, 3Jane is trying to kill her and has forced Molly to kidnap her. But Molly has other plans. They involve the eponymous Mona, a sixteen-year-old prostitute who has, despite a harsh upbringing, retained a fresh and naively curious vision of the world. Illiterate, abused, trendy, eager to please, and incapable of rancor, she is the central element in the plot to kill Angie, as she is surgically altered to look like the star. Molly kidnaps both women early, and the loa then orders her to take them to the Count and his aleph.

Gibson handles the various narrative threads with growing craft, eventually weaving them together into a satisfying conclusion, at least in terms of plotting. At the same time, he adds London, and the way its history inheres in its architecture, what Kumiko sees as a new and fascinating use of *gomi*, to the growing representations of the Sprawl and Tokyo. In the end, Angie "weds" the Count in an eerie ceremony, during which they both die as their minds and memories are downloaded into the aleph. There they are joined by a construct of the Finn, also dead, Colin, a portable AI designed to protect Kumiko but freed into the matrix and the aleph, and 3Jane, always on the outside looking in. Having made a deal with the loa to make all record of her disappear from the data banks, Molly brings Angie to Bobby. In some intriguingly mystical passages, the loa seem to explain why Angie will fulfill herself by joining Bobby in the aleph. Things work out, much as they do in *Count Zero*, and everyone appears to gain something they want at the end. Freed of any blackmail ever, Molly disappears into the sunset like any old, retired warrior. Having asserted herself, Kumiko can return home to a father she now trusts (but she may have to return to older, submissive ways). "Mona's life has left virtually no trace on the fabric of things, and represents, in Legba's system, the nearest thing to innocence," which makes her a perfect candidate to replace Angie as a simstim star. Even Slick Henry gets a girl and is able to leave his huge destructive constructs behind. But once again, the feeling associated with this ending is ambivalent.

It hinges on the closure to the Angie narrative. Various characters in these novels see other people in terms of an arc of ascendance, and Angie seem to be on such an arc once she joins Sense/Net. But it is really an arc of destruction. Given implants that let her access cyberspace, she fails to use them and then finds them eroded by drugs. Eventually, the loa return, but only to take her to Bobby, where she dies while joining him in the illusionary cyberspace of the aleph. The final chapter of *Mona Lisa Overdrive* seems to offer the traditional science fiction transcendent moment, as Angie and Bobby and the others go off to meet some alien presence. But does it? After all, the aleph is not connected to the matrix but to a self-contained simulacrum of it. Moreover, its batteries may run out at any moment, ending what "life" they have within it. Whatever they encounter will be as much an illusion as they are. This is perhaps the most despairing conclusion of any of Gibson's narratives, however brightly patched up it may be. Even Mona's new life will eventually pale, if she ever realizes how much she is Sense/Net's pawn. Only Molly, the toughest of tough heroines, seems to emerge better off than she began.

Mona Lisa Overdrive offers many narrative delights. The writing is stylish and still linguistically sharp, with all the techno edge that caught readers' attention in *Neuromancer*, plus Gibson's recognition that the technology for the new millennium is biotechnology. The tone of each narrative again matches the character of the focalizing figures, and the tonal shifts from one chapter to the next make for their own comedy. The novels are comedies in formal terms, but they are awfully dark in emotional ones. They seem to work out, but the deep-seated ambivalence their worlds promote undermine any easy acceptance of their apparent happy endings.

While visiting London in 1986 to promote *Count Zero*, Gibson told Colin Greenland: "There's an incredible richness of human symbol written everywhere here; there's so much detail to things, built up by so many generations. If you look at any tiny bit, it seems to contain more information than a whole structure would in the States." He first acted on this insight in representing Kumiko's perceptions of "the Smoke," but it really comes into its own in his collaboration with Bruce Sterling, *The Difference Engine* (1990). This brilliant alternate history offers readers a glimpse of the British Empire in an 1855 where Charles Babbage managed to build a steam-driven calculating machine in the 1820's. After a kind of revolution, in which the Radical Party, led by Lord Byron, won power, a meritocracy of sorts has taken over, and "savants" are recognized as the leaders of the new forces for change. North America is a conglomeration of disconnected states, and Britain is the foremost power in this world.

Although *The Difference Engine* tells a number of separate but intertwined stories of individuals from various classes, it is more concerned with representing the alternate world brought into being by such an early evolution into an information economy. London itself is the central character, and it is a contradictory, conflicted, and corrupt conurbation. The authors have also chosen to write a strangely self-reflexive narrative in which it becomes clear only at the end that the compiler of these tales is a newly self-aware AI in 1991 looking back at its own faint beginnings in the eponymous machine of 1855. Various "iterations" represent Sybil Gerard, a woman ruined by a politician, Edward Mallory, a young paleontologist just returned from the American West with a brontosaurus skeleton, eager to promote his belief in catastrophe theory, and Laurence Oliphant, spy and diplomat, who works to further the British cause yet holds a somewhat ambivalent view of the Engine and its works. As this Victorian Britain is still a class-based society, people of every class appear, from the mathematician daughter of the Prime Minister, Lady Ada Byron, through savants, members of the police, workers in the Palace of Engines, and a lively prostitute to a group of anarchist rebels trying to take over London during a summer of extreme pollution. Mallory's tale reads like a *Boy's Own Adventures* tale, while his naive faith in the system makes him something of a caricature, which seems odd as he gets the most narrative space. Do his wooden speech and flat characterization reflect the banality of his world? As a nineteenth-century version of the futuristic city in "The Gernsback Continuum," Mallory's London undermines the optimistic Whig view of history he embodies. Oliphant's story is wittier and more extreme, as he finds a way use Sybil's background to prevent a high-ranking politician from usurping control over the Engine and its power to manage information.

These stories read as adventures and are exciting as such, Victorian in feeling but with an added twentieth-century sense of sex and culture. The technique of superspecificity serves to create a London that is felt as a sensual presence and to provide a sense of the many different, and class-based, social languages of the time. Novels and histories and, especially, dictionaries and encyclopedias served as resources for the authors' lovingly detailed representation of a Dickensian London gone radically technological and frighteningly dystopian. If Gibson's Sprawl and Night City are harsh places to live, this alternate mid-Victorian London is even

worse. The authors also get to play the usual ironic games with historic figures such as the great Romantic poets. Part of the fun of reading *The Difference Engine* is trying to figure them all out. Various conversations echo Victorian novels such as M. E. Braddon's *Lady Audley's Secret* (1861), Benjamin Disraeli's *Sybil* (1845), and Wilkie Collins's *The Woman in White* (1860), as well as the bawdry recorded by "Walter" in the anonymous *My Secret Life* (1888). The most interesting change, of course, is the development of an information technology based on steam engines. The whole question of "Engine-resources" and their use is especially vexed when the things must be built larger and larger the more information they have to deploy.

The Difference Engine intriguingly represents contemporary information culture through the distorted mirror of an alternate past. Yet there has been little critical analysis of one of the most stringently bleak alternate histories in all of science fiction. Gibson's later novels also suffer such critical silence. It is as if the incredible attention paid to *Neuromancer* and the original cyberpunk movement has exhausted critical interest in his work. *Virtual Light* (1993) and *Idoru* (1996) have yet to be read in the context of his earlier work; nor has their attitude been read back into the Sprawl trilogy. So many critics read *Neuromancer* as the epitome of cyberpunk attitude: all hard surface and negation of the human in favor of the technological. But Gibson has always been ambivalent about technology and its ability to make over the human. The assumed conflict between cyberpunks and humanists in science fiction may only be apparent. By now it seems obvious that Gibson has always been interested in the human dimension of his narratives, however fragmented and ironic they may be.

With the latest two novels, set in a single, much closer future, Gibson has assumed the growing importance of biotechnology as well as the increasing power of the media to control people's perception of the world. As in the Sprawl trilogy, a few powerful corporations exercise immense political power, and Gibson continues to twist thriller paradigms. The plots serve to push the characters into one situation after another, wherein they demonstrate their character (or characteristics) in the ways they handle themselves. Gibson seems interested in what kind of grace ordinary people can achieve in their lives.

Virtual Light began with a short story, "Skinner's Room" that Gibson contributed to *Visionary San Francisco*, a 1989 exhibition and anthology of art and writing dedicated to seeing San Francisco in historic and utopian vision. Written in collaboration with the artwork of architects Ming Fung and Craig Hodgetts, "Skinner's Room" introduces the image of the unused Bay Bridge taken over by the homeless and built upon with a kind of organic complication. It is a massive instance of the street finding its own uses for technology. The story becomes the conceptual backbone of the novel, although Skinner himself is only a minor character in the narrative.

Set early in the new millennium, in a world where, after a huge earthquake in Japan, nanotechnology has advanced so far as to "grow" huge towers in Tokyo floor by floor, *Virtual Light* turns the anonymous "girl" of the story into Chevette, the bike courier. It adds Rydell, the cracker ex-cop with a good heart, Russian killers, other eccentrics, and Yamazaki, a Japanese sociologist, studying the bridge and learning its history from Skinner. For Yamazaki, all these different figures signal that "Modernity was ending," and one way of reading *Virtual Light* is as a narrative of what that means.

Even more than today, it means there are only two classes of people, the very rich and the poor, whom they use. "Crime, . . . sex. Maybe drugs" about covers what happens at the interface. A crime powers the plot of *Virtual Light*, but human possibilities provide what sense of hope it has. The bridge is a kind of utopian community that just grew on the edge of the city, partly using the nanotechnology created to rebuild Tokyo. Ironically, the very media that usually serve the powers-that-be also observed the first days of the taking of the bridge and so protected the

people there from police reprisals. Now, of course, it not only works, but it is a tourist attraction of sorts. *Virtual Light* is a social comedy with thriller overtones, but the society is mostly that of outsiders. Gibson cannot show us the lives of the very rich, but perhaps his texts are arguing that they are not really interesting anyway.

What are interesting, more so with each novel, are the manners of various social types, compassionately observed. Each focalizing figure has a particular "voice" and perspective expressed through specific imagery and tone. Gibson still piles on the details to build his world, but they are always perceived, if ironically, in personal terms. His sense of black comedy is as honed as ever. The bridge is a city-unto-itself built entirely of *gomi*, and its citizens live cooperatively by the rules of trade that *gomi* creates. In the world beyond, even politically aware characters lack the power to change things. When they escape, it is through the chinks in a world machine that remains untouched by their actions, and the really powerful remain out of sight, controlling a bleak, dehumanized landscape. Yet Chevette, Rydell, Yamazaki, and Skinner provide, through the manner in which they are narrated, a particular pleasure having to do with the deep humanity of comedy. They are survivors, and we are happy in their limited successes.

Although set in the same world as *Virtual Light*, *Idoru* deals with a different class of people. If there is no more middle class in the world, there are differences among the kinds of people who serve, and some have the particular power money brings. *Idoru* deals at length with a pop star milieu, yet it does so at some distance. Colin Laney, the "intuitive fisher of patterns of information," who sees the "nodal points" within them, becomes part of the aging singer Rez's entourage. Alongside the more naive Chia Pet McKenzie, a fourteen-year-old fan who comes to Tokyo to find out if it's true that Rez wants to marry the eponymous virtual media star (the idoru), Rei Toei, he provides a darkly comic commentary on fame and its appurtenances in the early twenty-first century. Chia is another of Gibson's very youthful female protagonists, but she is also fairly strong-willed and matures as a result of her experiences. But why do so many cyberpunk and cyberpunk-influenced novels use young girls as protagonists?

Gibson provides another rogues gallery of secondary characters, including the Australian bodyguard Blackwell, whose missing ear, like Molly's scar in *Mona Lisa Overdrive*, is a personal reminder "not to forget" a mistake he once made in a fight. Yamazaki returns, this time clearly identified as "a student of existential sociology," but also working for Rez, both studying and explaining the idoru and its cultural context.

In the end, the two narratives combine to provide an odd happy ending. Chia's adventures have forced her to grow up some, Laney has proven his worth to the Rez people, Rez has acquired the nanotechnology he needs to marry Rei, and all seems well. The plot is a kind of narrative red herring, allowing Gibson to offer up a rich stew of social and cultural perceptions, a neatly constructed future world that reflects all too pertinently our own. For example, "Slitscan" resembles today's TV tabloids "no more than some large, swift, bipedal carnivore resembled its sluggish, shallow-dwelling ancestors." Media control of information, in this case to make or destroy the people in the public eye, exists only to replace history. The world of *Idoru* is a world of late capitalism gone mad, where even education is just a business.

Almost everything has a satiric edge: the nightclub names and concepts, the presence of the Russian mafia in Tokyo, the love hotels (the name Hotel Di presciently recognized how a particular kind of fame achieves public parody and sounds even eerier now), the T–shirts with weird slogans Chia wants to remember. This future is too close. Perhaps the most intriguing invention in the novel is the "Walled City," an approximate MUD (multiuser dimension) created from a kill file and based on Hak Nam, the City of Darkness in Hong Kong that was torn down in 1993. Ob-

viously loving the original, Gibson has the inventors of the virtual city insist on the same sort of crowded and implosive conditions. "Walled City" stands against "Slitscan" with the slowly self-actuating idoru in the middle as an example of Gibson's continuing ambivalence about the technology that has powered all his fiction.

Gibson has written one screenplay that reached production, but *Johnny Mnemonic* is a much less interesting film than it was a story, partly because it expands the chase narrative but loses much of the specific technological *gomi* of the original. Of course, a film's failure is always a collaborative act. In late 1997, Gibson and Tom Maddox scripted an episode of the highly popular TV show *The X Files*. Set in the present, it plays a variation on almost all the central cyberpunk tropes, including those of fashion. While Scully and Mulder are put off by the idea, the two characters they are tracking appear to escape a military AI buy downloading their personalities into the matrix as they die. The episode has all *The X Files'* paranoid brio, all the flash lacking in the *Johnny Mnemonic* film. In so perfectly summing up the cyberpunk ethos, it definitively spelled its demise as a valid science fiction vision. Whatever Gibson does next will owe something to his earlier cyberpunk work but will also be different. One can hope that it will also reveal a continuing maturing of craft and vision.

Selected Bibliography

WORKS OF WILLIAM GIBSON

Neuromancer. New York: Ace Books, 1984. Limited hardcover edition, Huntington Woods, Mich.: Phantasia Press, 1986; Tenth anniversary hardcover edition, with an afterword by Gibson, New York: Ace Books, 1994.

Burning Chrome. New York: Arbor House, 1986. (A story collection, with a preface by Bruce Sterling, that includes "Johnny Mnemonic," "The Gernsback Continuum," and "Fragments of a Hologram Rose"; with

John Shirley, "The Belonging Kind" and "Hinterlands"; with Bruce Sterling, "Red Star, Winter Orbit," "New Rose Hotel," and "The Winter Market"; with Michael Swanwick, "Dogfight" and "Burning Chrome.")

Count Zero. New York: Arbor House, 1986; London: HarperCollins, 1986.

Mona Lisa Overdrive. London: Gollancz, 1988; Toronto and New York: Bantam, 1988.

Dream Jumbo. 1989. (Text to accompany performance art by Robert Longo.)

"Hippie Hat Brain Parasite." In *Semiotext(e) SF.* Edited by Rudy Rucker; Peter Lambert Wilson; and Robert Anton Wilson. New York: Automedia, 1989. (This is an early story, first published in a fanzine.)

"Rocket Radio." *Rolling Stone,* 15 June 1989.

"Darwin." *Spin,* 6, no. 1 (1990): 60–61.

The Difference Engine, with Bruce Sterling. London: Gollancz, 1990; Toronto and New York: Bantam, 1991.

"Skinner's Room." In *Visionary San Francisco.* Edited by Paolo Polledri. Munich: Prestel-Verlag, 1990.

Robert Longo. Kyoto: Shoin, 1991.

Virtual Light. Toronto: McClelland-Bantam, 1993; New York: Bantam, 1993; London: Viking, 1993.

Johnny Mnemonic. TriStar Pictures, 1995. (Screenplay.)

Idoru. New York: Putnam's, 1996; London: Viking, 1996.

CRITICAL AND BIOGRAPHICAL STUDIES

Alkon, Paul. "Deus Ex Machina in William Gibson's Cyberpunk Trilogy." In *Fiction 2000: Cyberpunk and the Future of Narrative.* Edited by George E. Slusser and Tom A. Shippey. Athens: University of Georgia Press, 1992.

Bredehoft, Thomas A. "The Gibson Continuum: Cyberspace and Gibson's Mervyn Kihn Stories." *Science-Fiction Studies,* 22, no. 2 (1995): 252–263.

Bukatman, Scott. *Terminal Identity: The Virtual Subject in Post-Modern Science Fiction.* Durham, N.C.: Duke University Press, 1993. (Various discussions of Gibson.)

Christie, John. "Of AIs and Others: William Gibson's Transit." In *Fiction 2000: Cyberpunk and the Future of Narrative.* Edited by George E. Slusser and Tom A. Shippey. Athens: University of Georgia Press, 1992.

Csicsery-Ronay, Jr., Istvan. "Cyberpunk and Neuromanticism." In *Storming the Reality Studio: A Casebook of Cyberpunk and Postmodern Fiction.* Edited by Larry McCaffery. Durham, N.C.: Duke University Press, 1991.

———. "Futuristic Flu, or The Revenge of the Future." In *Fiction 2000: Cyberpunk and the Future of Narrative.* Edited by George E. Slusser and Tom A. Shippey. Athens: University of Georgia Press, 1992.

———. "The Sentimental Futurist: Cybernetics and Art in William Gibson's *Neuromancer.*" *Critique: Studies in Contemporary Fiction,* 33 (Spring 1992): 221–240.

———. "Antimancer: Cybernetics and Art in Gibson's *Count Zero.*" *Science-Fiction Studies,* 22, no. 1 (1995): 63–86.

Delany, Samuel R. "Some *Real* Mothers . . . : The *SF Eye* Interview." In his *Silent Interviews: On Language, Race, Sex, Science Fiction, and Some Comics.* Hanover, N.H., and London: Wesleyan University Press, 1994.

Easterbrook, Neil. "The Arc of Our Destruction: Reversal and Erasure in Cyberpunk." *Science-Fiction Studies,* 19, no. 3 (1992): 378–394.

Fischlin, Daniel; Veronica Hollinger; and Andrew Taylor. "'The Charisma Leak': A Conversation with William Gibson and Bruce Sterling." *Science-Fiction Studies,* 19, no. 1 (1992): 1–16.

Grant, Glenn. "Transcendence Through Detournement in William Gibson's *Neuromancer.*" *Science-Fiction Studies,* 17, no. 1 (1990): 41–49.

Greenland, Colin. "A Nod to the Apocalypse: An Interview with William Gibson." *Foundation* (Summer 1986): 5–9.

Huntington, John. "Newness, *Neuromancer,* and the End of Narrative." In *Fiction 2000: Cyberpunk and the Future of Narrative.* Edited by George E. Slusser and Tom A. Shippey. Athens: University of Georgia Press, 1992.

Landon, Brooks. *Science Fiction After 1900: From the Steam Man to the Stars.* New York: Twayne, 1997. (Contains a section on cyberpunk, mostly on *Neuromancer.*)

Latham, Rob. "Cyberpunk = Gibson = *Neuromancer:* The Slusser-Shippey Anthology *Fiction 2000.*" *Science-Fiction Studies,* 20, no. 2 (1993): 266–272.

Maddox, Tom. "Cobra, She Said: An Interim Report on the Fiction of William Gibson." *Fantasy Review,* 9, no. 4 (1986): 46–48.

———. "William Gibson: A Bio." *Context '89 Program:* 10–11; *Virus,* 23 (1989): 24–25.

McCaffery, Larry, ed. *Storming the Reality Studio: A Casebook of Cyberpunk and Postmodern Fiction.* Durham, N.C.: Duke University Press, 1991.

———, ed. "An Interview with William Gibson." In his *Storming the Reality Studio: A Casebook of Cyberpunk and Postmodern Fiction.* Durham, N.C.: Duke University Press, 1991.

McGuirk, Carol. "The 'New' Romancers: Science Fiction Innovators from Gernsback to Gibson." In *Fiction 2000: Cyberpunk and the Future of Narrative.* Edited by George E. Slusser and Tom A. Shippey. Athens: University of Georgia Press, 1992.

McHale, Brian. *Constructing Postmodernism.* London and New York: Routledge, 1992. (Contains "POSTcyberMODERNpunkISM" and "Towards a Poetics of Cyberpunk.")

Sponsler, Claire. "William Gibson and the Death of Cyberpunk."" *Modes of the Fantastic.* Edited by Robert A. Latham and Robert A. Collins. Westport, Conn.: Greenwood, 1995.

Suvin, Darko. "On Gibson and Cyberpunk." In *Storming the Reality Studio: A Casebook of Cyberpunk and Postmodern Fiction.* Edited by Larry McCaffery. Durham, N.C.: Duke University Press, 1991.

Wershler-Henry, Darren. "Queen Victoria's Personal Spook, Psychic Legbreakers, Snakes and Catfood: An Interview with William Gibson and Tom Maddox." *Virus,* 23 (1989): 28–35. (Although this magazine is difficult to track down, the interview is one of Gibson's most revealing.)

—DOUGLAS BARBOUR

H. RIDER HAGGARD

(1856–1925)

The ship rushed on through the glow of the sunset into the gathering night. On sped the ship, but still Swanhild sang, and still the swans flew over her.

Now that war-dragon was seen no more, and the death-song of Swanhild as she passed to doom was never heard again.

For swans and ship, and Swanhild, and dead Eric and his dead foes, were lost in the wind and in the night.

But far out on the sea a great flame of fire leapt up towards the sky.

EVEN IF ONE has not perused many tomes of Victorian-era British fiction, one would probably know the name of H. Rider Haggard as the author of *King Solomon's Mines*, and perhaps of *She*. If, on the other hand, one were asked to identify the author of the lines quoted above, one might be surprised when informed that they are from the moving conclusion of Haggard's *Eric Brighteyes*, a retelling of an Icelandic saga, which was so infused with the mood of the Norse and Icelandic tales that contemporary readers were fooled into thinking that it was a genuine saga. It is this attention to mythological and historical detail that gives many of Haggard's books their curious wearing power, even though modern tastes have swerved from the overly flowery descriptions and even from the periodic cadences that resound in most of Haggard's novels. Perhaps as important to the modern reader who rediscovers Haggard is the setting of his many adventures: they are distant in both time and place, offering a literate escape from the cacophony of ordinary life,

much as they offered a pleasant and polite route for fantasy in the late nineteenth and early twentieth centuries. The reading publics of British and American cities bought Haggard's "romances" in staggering numbers, gobbled up pirated editions, and awaited sequels in the Allan Quatermain series with a loudly voiced impatience.

A first, rapid reading of Haggard's *King Solomon's Mines* (1885), *She* (1886; rev. ed. 1896), *Cleopatra* (1889), *Eric Brighteyes* (1891), *Nada the Lily* (1892), *The People of the Mist* (1894), *Heart of the World* (1895), *Ayesha* (1905), *She and Allan* (1920), or any of the other novels set in South Africa reveals a novelist who had lucked into a theme that happened to be immediately appealing to a public somewhat jaded by Robert Louis Stevenson, William Makepeace Thackeray, Edward Bulwer-Lytton, and a number of other popular writers. Now readers could breathe the clear air of Haggard's mountain citadels, wonder at intertwined strands that formed the Zulu cultures then being brutally buried by the Boers and English, and muse at Haggard's fascination with the Eternal Woman. Haggard may have unwittingly anticipated later Freudian notions of sexual repression, but he did not wallow in the unfortunate negativism all too characteristic of the underground pornography of the day. He approached the mystery of birth and rebirth with the exuberance of the first anthropologists. One could argue that Haggard provides a literary mirror of James Frazer's vast collections of cultural customs (particularly well

323

illustrated in *Adonis Attis Osiris*, 2nd ed. [1907]), in these lines from *When the World Shook* (1919), a tale of Atlantis:

> There are other reflections . . . [that] concern the wonder of a woman's heart, which is a microcosm of the hopes and fears and desires and despairs of this humanity of ours whereof from age to age she is the mother. (chapter 27)

Born in Norfolk on 22 June 1856, Henry Rider Haggard was the sixth son of William Rider Haggard and Ella Doveton, of Bradenham Hall. His father, who had trained as a barrister, was a ". . . flamboyant squire of the old school, a kindly and paternal despot. . . ." His mother had been born and raised in exotic and tropically unhealthy Bombay. She was an author in her own right, having published *Myra, or the Rose of the East: A Tale of the Afghan War* (1857), a poem in nine cantos about the Kabul campaign of 1842.

Rider's childhood was laced with his mother's recollections of life in India, as well as her acquaintance with literature. Perhaps his devotion to the rich tapestries of folk traditions and his acute sensitivity to nuances were gained from her, and there are a number of links between Ella Haggard's strong, positive Christianity and Rider's own quandaries as he wrestled with the implications of Darwinism.

With the publication of Charles Darwin's *Origin of Species* (1859), Victorian England began the heated debate still heard in some quarters in the late twentieth century, and the literary world of Haggard's youth shortly absorbed the new interpretations of natural history. Once the famous Oxford Debate (between Thomas Henry Huxley and Bishop Samuel Wilberforce) had taken place in June 1860, the general public soon became aware of the "new" anthropology, paleontology, botany, mammalogy, comparative anatomy, and geology; newspapers happily carried accounts of the theories of Huxley, Richard Owen, William Hooker, John Henslow, Charles Lyell, and Darwin; and readers of the *Times* soon were familiar with these personalities, much

as they had followed the wide-ranging implications of archaeology in the Middle East, ever since Austen Layard had "dug up" Nineveh in 1845.

Young Rider thus grew up in an era of intense intellectual excitement, an era also fraught with the stresses of fervent industrialism coupled with the effects of British imperialism. In addition to the multifarious aspects of intellectual, social, and artistic ferment there were also the changes wrought by technology and the radically altered context of medicine. Haggard grew up aware of the drastic implications of Pasteur's "germ theory," the first results of antisepsis, and the startling improvements in surgery made possible by anesthetics; the full flowering of the applications of chemistry in drugs and explosives; and the continually changing applications of industrial technology—from the newer Bessemer converters for better steel to the growing use of petroleum in place of whale oil.

In some senses the Victorians took for granted what technology could accomplish, so that once electricity was harnessed in the 1880's, or the telephone supplanted the telegraph, or when the automobile and the airplane arrived in the early 1900's, all were assumed normal. This emphasis on technology and its beneficial effects permeates Haggard's works; but, unlike H. G. Wells, Haggard did not delve into the actual workings of either the new medicine or the expanding numbers of technologies. He—like his reading public—simply accepted such matters and perhaps pondered their obvious impact upon the customs of the time, wondering if these changes that were occurring at such a frenetic pace were indeed "good."

Haggard also reflected the venerated tradition of longing for a simpler time, when farmers' virtues dominated, well delineated by his continual interest in the British farmer and his plight in the early twentieth century. In *Regeneration, Being an Account of the Social Work of the Salvation Army in Great Britain* (1910), Haggard addressed some of the essential problems of his time, noting the destabilizing effects of industrial technology; Theodore Roosevelt wrote of *Regeneration* that the book "... grasped the dangers that beset the future of the English-speaking people and the way these dangers can be best met. ..." In his two monumental studies of agriculture (*Rural England, Being an Account of the Agricultural and Social Researches ... in the Years 1901 and 1902* [1902] and *Rural Denmark and Its Lessons* [1913]), Haggard faced the demise of his ideals and argued "... that it was futile to revive the dying feudalism ..." (Cohen, page 250).

Haggard's literary production can best be understood by placing his "romances, fantasies, and adventures" within the context not only of his years spent in South Africa (1875–1881), but also within the century immediately preceding World War I. His *Cetywayo and His White Neighbours* (1882), "... a collection of fact, impression, and opinion [that] no scholar writing about South African history can afford to pass by ..." (Cohen, page 68), showed Haggard's power of description, as well as his unusual perception of the nobility of the Zulus. His most famous novels (*King Solomon's Mines, She, Cleopatra,* and in its time *The World's Desire* [1890, in collaboration with Andrew Lang]) manifested a Haggard perplexed by the loss of values as a result of the new technology, yet quite pleased by the progress brought by the new sciences. A memorable scene in *When the World Shook* (1919) pictures the wonderment at, yet easy acceptance of, the remnants of what appeared to be "aeroplanes" inside the burial vault of the last Atlantean king and his daughter.

Literary critics may argue that Haggard's "romances" lie strictly outside the genre called science fiction, but there are elements within many of his works that fit easily into the usually accepted themes of science fiction. It was Haggard who first exploited the lost-world motif to its fullest in *King Solomon's Mines, She* (and the cycle of books derived from *She: Ayesha, She and Allan,* and *Wisdom's Daughter* [1923]), *The People of the Mist, Heart of the World, The Yellow God*

H. Rider Haggard in 1905. LIBRARY OF CONGRESS

(1908), and *Queen Sheba's Ring* (1910). It may be that the young Haggard had heard rumors of a lost civilization somewhere in the heart of Africa, which turned out to be the still-mysterious ruins called Great Zimbabwe.

By populating his books with strong, well-crafted characters quickly recognized as "types" (Allan Quatermain in *Mines,* for example), Haggard made his works rapid successes, especially when these characters were connected by the British and American reading publics with half-known stereotypes: the "white hunter" of Africa; the "mysterious, all-pervasive" woman who was exploited in the Pre-Raphaelite art school; the "cynical physician" (Bickley in *When the World Shook*); the "pig-headed theologian" (Bastin in *When the World Shook*); the quixotically motivated "humanist" trying to combine the best of the old traditions with the unsettling new world (Harmachis in *Cleopatra,* and Arbuthnot in *When the World Shook*); the "hero" (Eric in *Eric Brighteyes,* and Umslopogaas in *Nada the Lily*); the "explorer" ("Jones" in *Heart of the World,* and Allan Quatermain in *Mines* and *Allan Quatermain* [1887]); the "scholar" (Ignatio in *Heart,* and Ludwig Horace Holly in *She,* while Leo in the same novel "... had not the dullness necessary for that result").

Haggard placed his stereotypical figures in vaguely familiar settings, each carefully detailed with the trappings of a "real" culture somewhat within the ken of the *Times'* readers of the day: the Mayans of *Heart*; the Zulus of *Nada the Lily* and *Mines*; Ptolemaic Egypt in *Cleopatra*; and so on. Haggard was meticulous with his historic details; a superb example is provided by the Greek text in chapter 3 of *She* (in both the uncial "capital" Greek and the standard "cursive" Greek of normal printed texts), which is quite correct, both contextually and grammatically. (He took great pains to make sure this Greek would be a Greek spoken in Ptolemaic Egypt, as opposed to the Greek of Homer or the Greek of Lucian.)

The physical surroundings of Haggard's lost worlds are also crucial for the mood he seeks to convey. His deserts are modeled from the Kalahari of southern Africa, but they are more dangerous and far less known than real ones; his mountains are craggy, precipitous, and dotted with memorable glaciers as they hide traces of the lost people. Both deserts and mountains are barriers that have become traditional in "lost world" science fiction, and one may mention the well-known examples of Edgar Rice Burroughs' *Tarzan and the Jewels of Opar* (1918), *Tarzan and the City of Gold* (1933), and the Pellucidar series, the settings borrowed by Philip José Farmer in the Ancient Opar books (1972 ff.), and *The Lost World* (1912) of Arthur Conan Doyle.

The modern critic can present a strong case that Haggard's influence on "genre" science fiction lies generally in his shrewd selection of physical settings, but one may also point to the potent supernatural overtones in many of his novels (such as *She* and *Ayesha*, *Eric*, and *Red Eve* [1911]), which also became standard fare in the somberly garbled tales of H. P. Lovecraft and in the stories of Andre Norton and Poul Anderson, among many others. Haggard could handle the vaporous topic of spiritualism with a skill bereft of dogmatism (unfortunately not true of Conan Doyle's *The Land of Mist* [1926]); the possibility of telepathy and reincarnation is admitted, but Haggard reserves judgment throughout his works, even in *She* and *When the World Shook*.

Along with the posthumously published *Allan and the Ice-Gods* (1927), *When the World Shook* represents Haggard's closest approach to "genre" science fiction. Compared with his best novels (*Nada, Mines, She, Cleopatra, Red Eve,* and *Eric*), *When the World Shook* is a work of the third rank in terms of overall quality. (Works of the second rank among his vast output would include *Montezuma's Daughter* [1893], *Heart of the World, The People of the Mist,* and a number of others.) Awkwardly juxtaposed in *When the World Shook* are three stereotypical figures, each representing the presumed dominance of a particular dogmatic view of life: Bastin has the fundamental simplicity of outlook that produces an uncomplicated faith, and his totally unimaginative assumptions about Christianity and the Christian God give him a wooden stolidity, rather unconvincingly presented throughout the novel; Bickley is the completely cynical surgeon, the "positivist," who doubts everything that he cannot verify with his senses or by logic, and his portrayal is one of unremitting brittleness; Arbuthnot is the educated "humanist" whose personality is measured by "fastidiousness and lack of perseverance . . . ," and he is a weak character, strengthened only by his close friendships with Bastin and Bickley. Arbuthnot certainly does not have the steely grit of Allan Quatermain, which makes him a fit companion of Leo (of *She*) in Haggard's collection of worthy men, ready for the unknown as well as rousing adventure.

In *When the World Shook*, the description of the physical setting is surprisingly flimsy; there is little clarity in the "south seas" as depicted here, in contrast with the Iceland of *Eric*, the Egypt of *Cleopatra*, the vividness of South Africa in *Nada*, and the personally experienced tone of Maya and Aztec in *Heart of the World* and *Montezuma's Daughter*; and Haggard gives no details of the vessel on which the grand adventure to find Atlantis is launched. One may also ask why Haggard placed his Atlantis in the Pacific, as opposed to the Atlantic; Mu quite often was located where Haggard puts his island of Orofena.

The ship sails. The captain and first mate have ominous premonitions. A storm occurs. There is the familiar scene of shipwreck with miraculous preservation of modern arms and equipment. Everyone is lost except the three main characters and the family dog, Tommy, who is probably the strongest character in the book. Bickley's vaguely limned "medicine and surgery" cures the native chief of a tumor on the neck. The "scientific device" cows the natives, much as the predicted sun eclipse awes the Zulus in *Mines*.

Bastin tackles native religion with disastrous results. The island has a dominant god named Oro, who has a shrine on an island in the center of a lake. The three flee from an enraged population (Bastin has smashed an image of Oro) to the shrine, forbidden to the natives; and Bastin, Bickley, and Arbuthnot stumble into a "cave" filled with wonders. A statue of black rock confronts them, then the skeletal remains of what Bickley determines to be "airships" puzzle the three, and finally they enter the inner vault and find two glassine coffins, in which rest an old man and a beautiful, youthful woman. Shortly it is discovered that they are alive.

The rest of the story is quite predictable. The old man is none other than Oro himself, and the woman is named Yva—and both have been in suspended animation for 250,000 years. Oro is the last of the kings of Atlantis, and after he has been revived (the coming of the three men having been "predicted") plots to regain his lost power by releasing "forces" in the bowels of the earth that will shift the balance of ocean and land on the planet. Yva of course falls in love with Arbuthnot, but their union "cannot be" in the stiffest of the Victorian clichés. Yva sacrifices herself at the last moment to foil Oro's designs, as he manipulates a tornado-like whirlwind of phosphorescent forces, somehow controlled on a vaguely described arrangement of railroad tracks that diverge. Escape follows. Arbuthnot has become convinced that Yva and his

deceased wife might be one and the same, but. . . .

There is little of the crisp narrative in *When the World Shook* that one would expect from the author of *Nada*. There are few passages of sheer beauty like those that festoon *Cleopatra*, *Eric*, and *She*. There is none of the exuberance that delights the reader of *Mines*, nor are there many passages of heady descriptions of mountains, seas, ruins, weather, and individual natives that occur in *People of the Mist*, *Allan Quatermain*, and even in the coauthored *World's Desire*. Yva is a pale version of Ayesha, Oro is a flawed god, and Arbuthnot seems to represent Haggard's bitterness at the end of a long and productive career—but now he wants to be "taken seriously."

There are touches of Haggard's narrative power in *When the World Shook*, but they have little to do with the theme of the novel. Chapter 20, "Oro and Arbuthnot Travel by Night," contains some of the most graphic descriptions of the horrors of World War I to be found outside the military chronicles of the time, but the wrenching portrayal of mass charges and slaughter in northern France descends into a petulant pettiness as Haggard has Oro "preach" about the follies of the war. There are some memorable passages: "Wisdom has destroyed Faith and therefore I must die" (chapter 21); "Moreover, think not that you Westerners have done with wars. I tell you that they are but begun and that the sword shall eat you up, and what the sword spares class shall snatch from class in the struggle for supremacy and ease" (chapter 26).

Elements of science fiction appear briefly in chapter 25, "Sacrifice," where there are some extremely fuzzy notions presented about the "balance of the earth" shifting from time to time through the eons, thus causing floods and continental alterations; and there appear to be a hint or two of lasers and atomic power in the cataclysmic last scene culminating in Yva's "sacrifice" (again a pale version of the dissolution of Ayesha in *She*), as Yva is vaporized by an intense beam of light.

Haggard's early work bubbles with a zestful curiosity, a fascination for the innumerable discoveries then tumbling forth from the pioneering labors of archaeologists, anthropologists, classical scholars, and folklorists. His early novels display an accuracy in natural details, gained from experience in South Africa, Iceland, and Mexico. Once he gained success, though, as a world-famous popular novelist, and in spite of being recognized with a knighthood, he apparently sought the status of Great Writer in company with friends who included Andrew Lang, Theodore Roosevelt, and Rudyard Kipling.

H. Rider Haggard began to preach in his later books, and once he began to take himself seriously, the childlike wonder seeped out of his writing. Without that sense of enthusiasm—for legend; for the wide variations in the world of nature and man—Haggard's prose becomes plodding. His influence on twentieth-century science fiction is quite profound, but that influence does not stem from his extremely weak "genre" science fiction, represented by *When the World Shook.* Haggard's lost-world novels, though, gave science fiction and fantasy writers a model they have yet to forsake. One must acknowledge that his best novels (*Mines, She, Nada, Eric*) retain a readability and are part of the world's great literature, even though some critics have condemned them all for lack of literary merit—a very subjective judgment.

There is a touch of pathos in the last months of Haggard's life (November 1924–May 1925), as he hobnobbed with his friend Sir Ronald Ross, then became ill from a perforated ulcer. The surgery performed on Haggard in early May was entirely successful, but he died from the effects of an abscess on 14 May 1925.

Selected Bibliography

WORKS OF H. RIDER HAGGARD

Cetywayo and His White Neighbours. London: Trübner, 1882.

King Solomon's Mines. London and New York: Cassell, 1885.

She. New York: Harper and Brothers, 1886; London: Longmans, Green, 1887.

Allan Quatermain. London: Longmans, Green, 1887; New York: Harper and Brothers, 1887.

Cleopatra. London: Longmans, Green, 1889; New York: Harper and Brothers, 1889.

The World's Desire, with Andrew Lang. London: Longmans, Green, 1890; New York: Harper and Brothers, 1890.

Eric Brighteyes. London: Longmans, Green, 1891; New York: Harper and Brothers, 1891.

Nada the Lily. New York and London: Longmans, Green, 1892.

Montezuma's Daughter. London and New York: Longmans, Green, 1893.

The People of the Mist. London and New York: Longmans, Green, 1894.

Heart of the World. New York: Longmans, Green, 1895; London: Longmans, Green, 1896.

Ayesha: The Return of She. London: Ward, Lock, 1905; New York: Doubleday, Page, 1905.

The Yellow God. New York: Cupples and Leon, 1908; London: Cassell, 1909.

Queen Sheba's Ring. London: E. Nash, 1910; New York: Doubleday, Page, 1910.

Red Eve. London: Hodder and Stoughton, 1911; Garden City, N.Y.: Doubleday, Page, 1911.

When the World Shook. London: Cassell, 1919; New York: Longmans, Green, 1919.

She and Allan. London: Hutchinson, 1920; New York: Longmans, Green, 1920.

Wisdom's Daughter. London: Hutchinson, 1923; Garden City, N.Y.: Doubleday, Page, 1923.

Allan and the Ice-Gods. London: Hutchinson, 1927; Garden City, N.Y.: Doubleday, Page, 1927.

CRITICAL AND BIOGRAPHICAL STUDIES

Aldiss, Brian W. *Billion Year Spree: The History of Science Fiction.* London: Weidenfeld and Nicolson, 1973; Garden City, N.Y.: Doubleday, 1973. (Especially pages 136–139.)

Cohen, Morton. *Rider Haggard: His Life and Work.* London: Macmillan, 1968. Second edition. (A literate, rather negative portrait of Haggard as a failed half-talent. Includes copious quotations from personal correspondence.)

Ellis, Peter Berresford. *H. Rider Haggard. A Voice from the Infinite.* London: Routledge and Kegan Paul, 1978. (Generally leans upon Cohen, but has a much more positive assessment. Excellent bibliographies and listings of Haggard's works.)

Etherington, Norman. *Rider Haggard.* Boston: Twayne, 1984.

Garlake, P. S. *Great Zimbabwe.* London: Thames and Hudson, 1973. (The best book on this fascinating archaeological puzzle.)

Gilbert, Sandra M. "Rider Haggard's *Heart of Darkness.*" In *Coordinates: Placing Science Fiction and Fantasy.* Edited by George E. Slusser, Eric S. Rabkin, and Robert Scholes. Carbondale: Southern Illinois University Press, 1983.

Gubar, Susan. "*She* in *Herland:* Feminism as Fantasy." In *Coordinates: Placing Science Fiction and Fantasy.* Edited by George E. Slusser, Eric S. Rabkin, and Robert Scholes. Carbondale: Southern Illinois University Press, 1983.

Haggard, H. Rider. *The Days of My Life.* Edited by C. J. Longman, 2 vols. London: Longmans, Green, 1926.

Higgins, D. S. *Rider Haggard: A Biography.* New York: Stein and Day, 1981.

Irvine, William. *Apes, Angels and Victorians. A Joint Biography of Darwin and Huxley.* London: Weidenfeld and Nicolson, 1955; New York: McGraw-Hill, 1955. (One of the best general accounts of Darwin, Huxley, Henslow, and the host of other scientific "greats" of the day.)

Katz, Wendy R. *Rider Haggard and the Fiction of Empire: A Critical Study of British Imperial Fiction.* Cambridge, England: Cambridge University Press, 1987.

Luce, John V. *The End of Atlantis.* London: Thames and Hudson, 1969. (Plato's Atlantis comes home to the Aegean. Good reading in volcanology, the legends, and why Atlantis continues to puzzle and intrigue.)

Roosevelt, Theodore. Review of Haggard's *Regeneration. . .the Salvation Army in Great Britain* (1910). In *Outlook* 98 (1 July 1911): 475–476.

Scott, James E. *A Bibliography of the Works of Sir Henry Rider Haggard.* Takeley, Essex, England: E. Mathews, 1947. (The standard list.)

Whatmore, Denys E. *H. Rider Haggard: A Bibliography.* London: Mansell, 1987; Westport, Conn.: Meckler, 1987.

—JOHN SCARBOROUGH

JOE HALDEMAN
(b. 1943)

JOE WILLIAM HALDEMAN was born in Oklahoma City on 9 June 1943; he was the younger brother of Jack Carroll Haldeman II—born 18 December 1941—who also became a science fiction writer. Joe Haldeman obtained a B.S. in physics and astronomy from the University of Maryland, College Park, in 1967, two years after marrying Mary Gay Potter. He was drafted after graduation and sent to Vietnam, where he served as a combat engineer, in 1968.

Haldeman was seriously wounded in 1969 by the shrapnel from a massive booby trap bomb, sustaining extensive damage to his left leg and right foot. After returning to the United States, he continued his education, initially returning to the University of Maryland to study computer science and later obtaining an M.F.A. from the University of Iowa, Iowa City, in 1975. He had written poetry for some years but switched to writing prose after his return from Vietnam, deciding as soon as he was confident of his ability to make a career of it. He took part in several workshops, including the Milford science fiction workshop run by Damon Knight and a literary workshop in Iowa whose luminaries included Raymond Carver, John Cheever, and Stanley Elkin.

Although his earliest sales were routine magazine science fiction of the kind that he had read avidly throughout his teens, Haldeman's experience in Vietnam was a powerful influence on his work from the very beginning. His first novel, *War Year* (1972), is a naturalistic account of combat in Vietnam that drew heavily on his own experiences, although it also attempted to place them in a wider context. His third magazine science fiction story, "Time Piece" (1970), is a brief meditative account of a future war against alien "snails," narrated by a ranker who comments in laconically acidic terms on the logistical and psychological consequences of the time-dilatation effects of near-light-speed travel and the situational logic which insists that humankind cannot possibly win. This was essentially a thumbnail sketch for the novelette "Hero" (1972), which was the platform on which *The Forever War* (1975)—the multi-award-winning science fiction novel that secured Haldeman's critical reputation and commercial success—was built. *The Forever War* continued to overshadow his subsequent productions to such an extent that he was eventually compelled to provide it with a companion piece in *Forever Peace* (1997); publication of the latter novel was likewise preceded by a naturalistic novel in which the Vietnam War was a central concern, *1968* (1994).

Discussing *Forever Peace* in a 1997 *Locus* interview, Haldeman reflected on the nature of the impact that Vietnam had made on him:

> Being in combat changes your life completely, usually for the worse. It's not specific things that happen in combat, it's a kind of *gestalt*—living with horror for day after day after day, and finally you've sort of moved away from the human condition. And you never quite get back, no matter how many years go by. I've seen this in old, old men who

were in World War I. I look in their eyes and I see myself. They can never be completely kind, they can never be completely humane. (page 69)

Haldeman visited a duplication of his own wounds upon the central character of "A Mind of His Own" (1974), but the introduction to the story in the collection *Infinite Dreams* (1978) explains that he was moved to do so by his reaction to an abruptly disabled man, whose angry bitterness in the face of disaster drove away his wife, family, and friends—including Haldeman, who understood how the man felt but had no solution to offer.

In a 1989 *Locus* interview Haldeman recalled how a peculiar incident in Vietnam had sparked the idea for *The Hemingway Hoax* (1990) and how another such incident—in which his evacuation in a CIA plane from the hospital where his leg had been patched had briefly made him a fellow passenger of a man strapped down and tranquilized, with a tag on his collar reading "paranoid schizophrenic"— had become the seed of *1968*, which he had begun in 1974 but did not complete until 1992.

A 1994 interview adds a corrective comment to the latter anecdote, to the effect that, although he had started out wanting to tell the main story of *1968* from the viewpoint of a clear-sighted paranoid schizophrenic, his research into the disease eventually convinced him that it would be implausible to do so:

So I gave the guy a stress-related disorder instead, shell shock or PTST or whatever you want to call it. That I could do accurately, because I've had problems along those lines myself. It turns out that in extreme cases, the symptoms parallel paranoid schizophrenia for short periods of time. (*Locus*, pages 4–67)

The idea that war is so innately insane that only deeply crazy people can see it clearly is not, of course, original. Like the look that Haldeman could see in the eyes of old, old men, it goes back at least as far as Robert Graves's

reflections on having to appear before a military court during World War I to testify that Siegfried Sassoon was insane—and therefore ought not to be shot for cowardice—when it was perfectly obvious that Sassoon was actually the only sane man in the room.

Haldeman, like Graves, subsequently took pride in writing many different kinds of books, exercising considerable care in the avoidance of obsession. Yet in much the same way that Graves's experiences colored everything he wrote—returning him again and again to the consideration of the predicaments of sane individuals heroically failing to cope with an insane world whose inexorable forces of destruction are unwinding lethally and chaotically all around them—the effects of Haldeman's wounding resound constantly within his work. Few writers exact such a heavy tax of pain and distress from their main characters as Haldeman, and few wreak such wholesale and stomach-churning havoc upon their bystanders, innocent and guilty alike.

Haldeman's first published story was "Out of Phase" (1969), in which a strangely assorted band of starfaring explorers have second thoughts about the wisdom of assigning their only crew member capable of imitating human form to the job of exploring Earth when they recall that he is in the "aesthetic phase" of his development and thus highly likely to render the human population into works of art by ingeniously murdering every last one of them. Fortunately, his father persuades the shape shifter that it is time to move on to the next phase of his development, although the casual exit line dutifully suggests that his entry into the "power phase" might not bode too well for humankind either. This suggestion is, however, considerably ameliorated in the sequel "Power Complex" (1972), where the shape shifter is compelled by his dutiful father to work under severe restrictions. Haldeman did not take the series any farther, although his decision to omit the stories from his collections may imply that he considered extrapolating them into a mosaic novel. He did complete a mosaic novel based on "To Fit the Crime" (1971) and "The Only War We've Got" (1974), which feature a human drafted into service as an interplanetary spy, whose shape-shifting powers are forced upon him by surgery and augmented by hypnotic techniques that continually modify his personality. The third story in the series became the title element of *All My Sins Remembered* (1977).

The galactic culture introduced in "To Fit the Crime" is based on a future history in which a twenty-first-century war between the superpowers results in the devastation of the entire northern hemisphere, leaving the southern nations to lead the way to the stars. They establish a "Confederación" that is little more than the political arm of the Australia-based Hartford Corporation, which ruthlessly exploits its monopoly on faster-than-light travel. Although Otto McGavin, the hero of *All My Sins Remembered*, appears to be defending a protective Charter of Rights, he eventually realizes that the charter is merely one more instrument of oppression, suppressing warfare only because warfare is bad for business and defending aliens from local exploitation only to conserve them for exploitation by the greater powers.

Haldeman was to return to the Confederación whenever he needed a stable galactic culture as a setting for his stories, although "The Mazel Tov Revolution" (1974) sketches out in a comic manner the means by which the Hartford monopoly might eventually be broken. In collaboration with his brother Jack he began to write a Confereración-set series of tales apparanetly aimed at younger readers, launched with "Starschool" (1979) in the short-lived *Isaac Asimov's Science Fiction Adventure Magazine*. The full series appeared in the mosaic novel *There Is No Darkness* (1983), but the umcompromising brutality of the stories—which involve the hapless young hero in loaded gladiatorial contests before having him press-ganged into a war—forced the book to be redirected toward an adult audience. "A !Tangled Web" (1981) employs the Confederación backdrop for a black comedy of commercial double-dealing, but "Seasons" (1985) offers a far more sophisticated account of the slow and bloody destruction of a team of xenologists by enigmatic aliens, concluding with a far more brutal account of Confereración realpolitik.

Haldeman's other early stories include the brief "I of Newton" (1970), in which a careful logician thwarts the designs of a rule-bound demon. Haldeman later rewrote it as a television script aimed (unsuccessfully) at *Night Gallery* (it was later made into an episode of *The Twilight Zone*) and recouped something of his investment by selling that version to *Fantastic*—where the first had appeared—as "The Devil His Due" (1975). More typical of the directions in which his imagination would take him, however, were "Counterpoint" (1972), in which the careers of two men born in very different circumstances are dramatically transformed by a brief intersection in Vietnam, and the scathingly sarcastic "26 Days, on Earth" (1972), in which a young example of the carefully engineered *Homo mutandis* records his impressions of the society of his primitive cousins. Transformation by war is the central theme of the stories that make up the mosaic of *The Forever War*, but no consideration of that work would neglect the sarcastic edge that all the stories contain.

"Hero" and its sequels, "We Are Very Happy Here" (1973) and "End Game" (1975), deliberately recapitulate the theme and narrative pattern of *Starship Troopers* (1959), the somewhat controversial but undeniably definitive future war novel written by the science fiction author who had been Haldeman's favorite during his early teens: Robert A. Heinlein. The early phases of *Starship Troopers* are based on Heinlein's own experiences as a career officer in the U.S. Navy during the 1930's, but Heinlein was invalided out before Pearl Harbor, so the later phases are the imaginative construct of a man who deeply regretted the fact that his physical deficiency had made him unfit for combat. Haldeman was very conscious of the fact that his own novel was a corrective text, based in the experience of being rudely thrust into war and forced to suffer the next-to-worst effect of actual combat.

Whereas Heinlein's book willingly endorses conventional self-justifying accounts of military endeavor—representing military discipline as productive of a valuable camaraderie, military service as something that fits a man for citizenship, and wars as direly unfortunate evils that, being inevitable, must at all costs be won—Haldeman's is a demythologizing exercise that subverts all these dicta.

The Forever War tracks the career of William Mandella as he rises through the ranks from trainee to major (given that his eventual partner's name is Marygay Potter, Mandella's surname is presumably a modified anagram of Haldeman). In the process, he loses all his comrades-in-arms except the belatedly introduced Marygay, but he does play a key role in the human breakthrough that turns the tide of the war against the Taurans. Here military camaraderie—as expressed in a unit that mixes male and female recruits—is an awkward defense mechanism against the frequently lethal oppressions of orders from above. Time-dilatation effects exaggerate but do not materially alter the alienating effects of military service that make all soldiers outcasts from the civilian body politic. (This point was more firmly made by the Earth-set episode that was eliminated from the mosaic on the advice of *Analog* editor Ben Bova and was subsequently rewritten as "You Can Never Go Back" [1975]). In the end, the cost of bringing the war to a conclusion—it is not, in any meaningful sense, "won"—is so exorbitant as to question the value of survival.

Comparing and contrasting *The Forever War* and *Forever Peace*, Haldeman remarked in his 1997 interview that some readers had construed the conclusion of the earlier book to be a happy ending, adding, "I don't know where *they* learned to read!" His own description is that the war ends "when humanity is turned into this bunch of faceless clones, all with one personality, which is the way the enemy was set up, so they could finally communicate." Mandella and humankind, having looked into the abyss and found monsters,

have—as per Nietzsche's famous warning—become monstrous themselves. This ultimate catch-22 is the horror that lurks in the background of almost all of Haldeman's work, frequently moving into the foreground to provide bitter climaxes.

It is worth noting that despite the images of desolation and second-stage savagery that dominate "You Can Never Go Back," the future history of *The Forever War* is more optimistic in several significant ways than that of the Confederación. Before running into the Taurans, Earth's nations have established a viable multinational government whose member states have surrendered their nuclear arsenals. The tachyon-based technology that operates as a stepping-stone to the black hole "Stargate" also produces unlimited power. These were the foundations that the scientifically conscientious Haldeman thought necessary to set up a situation in which interstellar war could actually occur. The extrapolation of likelier near-future situtations always led him to scenarios in which such conflicts would be impossible. In the Hugo-winning short story "Tricentennial" (1976), Haldeman felt compelled to make a similarly unlikely facilitating move in order to set up the notion that interstellar space flight might be conceivable at all, inventing a dark companion for the sun that happened to be a matter/antimatter binary, an idea he was to use again in the Worlds trilogy.

The Forever War was turned down by eighteen publishers before Ben Bova persuaded St. Martin's Press, which had not previously dabbled in science fiction, to take a chance on it. It is hardly surprising, therefore, that Haldeman's ardent desire to be a professional writer led him to take on a considerable amount of hackwork in the late 1970's. He subsequently referred back to these exploits as "adventure novels" and even included his two *Star Trek* tie-ins in lists of his previously published works, although he declined to make the same gesture in respect of the two novels he wrote under the house pseudonym Robert Graham or the later novelization of the movie

Poltergeist, to which he laid claim in the 1997 *Locus* interview (*The Encyclopedia of Science Fiction* credits it to James Kahn). The book that was marketed as his second novel, *Mindbridge* (1976), was, however, much more ambitious.

Although it is not a mosaic novel in the sense that *The Forever War* is, *Mindbridge* is even more fragmentary in its structure. Its fragmentation is excused as a calculated adaptation of a literary method invented by John Dos Passos and previously made science fiction by John Brunner, but all Haldeman's longer works are fragmented in one way or another, and he seems far more comfortable working in short bursts to produce staccato narrative effects. He also cites the influence of Dos Passos in the introduction to "To Howard Hughes: A Modest Proposal" (1974) in *Infinite Dreams*; and the next story in the collection, "A Mind of His Own" (1974) trailed one of the key motifs of *Mindbridge*: an intrusive technique of personality modification. In the short story, the technique is an irresistible force that meets its match in the immovable central character, but Jacque Le Favre, the hero of *Mindbridge*, applies it so successfully as to qualify himself for membership in an elite corps of interstellar explorers and for communication—via an intermediate "mindbridge" species—with an advanced alien race.

Mindbridge carefully re-examines the cynical assumptions of *The Forever War* and the Confederación series, searching for a more optimistic outlook not merely on the near future of humankind but also its ultimate destiny. It seems, however, that the creature that serves as the bridge that makes human/alien communication possible without the radical adjustments of *The Forever War* was much too convenient a facilitating device to receive the author's wholehearted support, and his eventual treatment of its implications is wryly sarcastic.

In *Worlds: A Novel of the Near Future* (1981), Haldeman returned to a much bleaker view of political probability. He was later to refer to the book and its two sequels as a "long novel," claiming to have had the end in mind

before he began—and the publisher was certainly expecting a third volume when the jacket copy for *Dealing in Futures* (1985) was written—but he seems to have got badly stuck after finishing *Worlds Apart* (1983) and published three more novels before bringing the story to a belated close in *Worlds Enough and Time* (1992).

The protagonist of the trilogy is Marianne O'Hara, a citizen of the space habitat New New York, which—by virtue of being the solid, hollowed out asteroid Paphos—is one of the few orbital Worlds to survive the strike launched from the surface in the course of a late-twenty-first-century war that also devastates Earth and the only World to remain viable thereafter as a habitat. The heroine's descent to Earth to further her education provides the travelogue plot of the first volume, whose narrative tension is enhanced by her peripheral involvement with the Third American Revolution, which precedes the war by a matter of hours, and then is turned up an extra notch by her kidnapping, rescue, and desperate rush to Cape Canaveral to catch the last shuttle home.

The second volume tracks O'Hara's involvement with the Janus Project—the building of a starship by the people of New New York—and the exploits of her former rescuer, Jeff Hawkings, who is one of only a handful of adults to survive the artificial plague that devastated Earth. As with other wars described by Haldeman, the aftermath of this one is so bloodcurdling as to suggest that those who died were the fortunate ones. However, a very tenuous bridge enabling some communication to take place between Earth and New New York eventually provides the means by which the life spans of a few of the child survivors are restored to near normalcy. The fact that the project had run into difficulty is signaled by the author's inability to generate any kind of a subclimax, giving perfunctory treatment to the two events intended for that purpose: the launching of the starship and the restoration of contact between New New York and Jeff Hawkings.

335

These difficulties continue to afflict the third volume, which never manages to pick up any narrative pace while the *Newhome* makes its painstaking way to Epsilon Eridani, crippled by a computer virus whose activation precedes loss of contact with New New York and further disabled by a plant virus that devastates its ecosystems. It is not until the colony established on the new world makes painful contact with the greater galactic community that the story really takes off. Although Haldeman used contact with advanced alien races as a "solution" to the problem of human self-destructiveness in other stories—"Passages" (1990) conjures up a similar epiphany for the Confederación and "Images" (1991) a personal gift for a Vietnam vet existentially becalmed by his wounds—he could never inject much conviction into it; it is plain that he thinks it rather cowardly as well as absurdly convenient.

The first of the three novels that Haldeman wrote between *World Apart* and *Worlds Enough and Time* must have been undertaken as a change of scene and method. *Tool of the Trade* (1987) is a calculatedly lightweight tale of a spy—a Russian sleeper on the brink of being turned by the CIA—whose attempts to extricate himself from trouble are aided by a quasi-magical watch that can be made to transmit a signal compelling the obedience of anyone to whom he speaks. Carelessness reveals to his adversaries that he must have some such device but also equips him with the means of getting in among them without leaving any memory trace. The plot is complicated by the necessity of rescuing his kidnapped wife before a notorious KGB torturer can go to work on her and then by the attempt to use the watch's power for one highly effective good deed without providing other potential users with sufficient information to allow them to duplicate the trick, hence unleashing chaos. The story is divided into multiple first-person viewpoints, fragmenting it as comprehensively as the rest of Haldeman's works, although the taut plot line is enhanced rather than undermined by the device. (The method

had been tried out in "Seasons," where it did not work nearly as well.)

The Long Habit of Living (1989)—retitled *Buying Time* by its U.S. publisher—is also a chase thriller, this time on an interesting interplanetary stage in which the asteroid belt is a lawless quasi-Communist frontier. The lovers on the run, accompanied by a computerized "Turing Image" of a friend whose murder has urged them to flight, are beneficiaries of the Stileman Process: a technology of rejuvenation that has to be renewed every twenty years or so, at a price of a million dollars plus everything else the recipient possesses. The "immortals" who use the process repeatedly must use ingenious means to make their millions over and over again, while the wealth of the super-rich is recycled, a situation ripe for corruption and far too precarious to endure forever. The science fiction elements of the story are fascinating, but the plot has too few twists to make it a wholly satisfactory thriller.

The Hemingway Hoax (1990) won Hugo and Nebula awards as a novella, and the book version is only slightly expanded. As with its predecessors, it is more thriller than mystery, although the invocation of enigmatic "time police" who keep murdering the hero, John Baird, in the hope of preventing him from forging Hemingway's lost early works certainly succeeds in convoluting the plot to an extraordinary degree. It is difficult to perceive any rationale within the plot; no explanation is offered for the motive or method of the individual who finally stands revealed as its prime mover, and the story's climactic dissolution smacks of sweeping the dust under the carpet.

While Haldeman was writing these books, he diverted some of his creative effort into teaching a course in science fiction writing and a more general writing course at MIT—a part-time arrangement set up in 1983. Some of his best subsequent short stories, including "More Than the Sum of His Parts" (1985) and the Nebula and World Fantasy award-winning "Graves" (1992), follow patterns derived from exercises that he habitually set his students.

He also began writing poetry again in some profusion, much of which was reprinted in *Saul's Death and Other Poems* (1997). The three interviews published in *Locus* between 1989 and 1994 refer to several projects whose completion was considerably delayed, including a novel about first contact with aliens, provisionally titled *The Coming*, but his work appeared to take a new lease on life after the completion of *Worlds Enough and Time*, when a new burst of sustained creativity produced *1968*, the fine novella "For White Hill" (1995)—which is about the aftermath of an interstellar war that seems to have been won but still has its most destructive phase to come—and *Forever Peace*.

Forever Peace is not a sequel to *The Forever War*, but it does re-examine all of the concerns raised in that novel and other stories reflecting on the question of whether humankind can possibly outlive its addiction to war. The war is a mid-twenty-first-century affair that opposes the United States—whose economic hegemony has been firmly secured by its monopoly of "nanoforge" technology—and the puppet governments of the Third World to a loose alliance of "rebel forces." The U.S. forces do most of their fighting by remote control, teams of ten "jacking in" to heavily armed "soldierboys," reconnaissance units alternating ten-day shifts with squads of "hunter/killers." While they are linked up to their machines and to one another, the military personnel share their thoughts, feelings, and memories, but the camaraderie thus engendered has costs as well as benefits. Some civilians pay to be fitted with jacks for private reasons, although they mostly have to go to clinics outside the United States and the procedure is risky. The religious fundamentalists known as Enders—because they are expecting the imminent end of the world—strongly disapprove of the technology.

The novel's hero, Julian Class, is a draftee who alternates tours of duty with an academic career as a physicist, in which connection he is involved with the Jupiter Project, building a massive supercollider in the orbit of Io, which will be able to duplicate the initial conditions of the Diaspora (formerly known as the Big Bang). When he and his co-workers discover that switching on the supercollider will blow up the solar system, their attempt to warn the world is quickly subverted by the military, launching them into a hectic chase-thriller plot whose ultimate aim is not merely to save the world from summary execution but also to create the conditions in which world peace may finally be secured and sustained.

Like its predecessor, *Forever Peace* was a multiaward winner, and deservedly so. It capitalizes on all the experience Haldeman had gained in the interim, eclectically selecting the most useful of the many narrative methods he had tried out. Although it alternates first-person and third-person viewpoints, it is the least fragmentary of all his novels. It brings into unprecedentedly clear focus an ideology that gives the impression of being fully mature, having finally moved beyond the suffocating effects of sarcastic cynicism and nihilistic bitterness. Some doubt must remain as to whether the ending of the novel is really so very different, in objective terms, from the ending of *The Forever War*—but Haldeman does seem to offer it as the best hope imaginable, barring the intervention of aliens too benevolent to command belief.

Although Haldeman, in the 1997 interview, chose to emphasize the fact that combat changes people forever, Julian Class prefers to call attention to the other side of the coin. Referring to someone else's crucial trauma he says: "But that's not who you are. We go through these things, and then we more or less absorb them, and we become whatever we are becoming" (*Forever Peace*, page 65).

If Haldeman's career were to be reduced to the most brutal summary possible, that would do as well as any other formulation. Combat changes everyone, but it does not change everyone in the same way. Haldeman went to Vietnam a scientist and a poet, a man of intelligence and artistry; he came back badly wounded, but essentially the same man. His contemplation of likely futures and actual pasts has consistently urged him in the direction of cynical desperation, but his work has never been completely unkind or completely inhumane.

Selected Bibliography

WORKS OF JOE HALDEMAN

War Year. New York: Holt, Rinehart and Winston, 1972. Original version, New York: Pocket Books, 1978.

The Forever War. New York: St. Martin's, 1975; London: Weidenfeld and Nicholson, 1975.

Mindbridge. New York: St. Martin's, 1976; London: Macdonald, 1977.

All My Sins Remembered. New York: St. Martin's, 1977; London: Macdonald, 1978.

Planet of Judgment. New York: Bantam, 1977; London: Corgi, 1977. (A *Star Trek* novel.)

Infinite Dreams. New York: St. Martin's, 1978; London: Futura, 1979. (Short stories.)

World Without End: A Star Trek Novel. New York: Bantam, 1979; London: Corgi, 1979.

Worlds: A Novel of the Near Future. New York: Viking, 1981; London: Macdonald, 1982.

There Is No Darkness, with Jack C. Haldeman II. New York: Ace, 1983; London: Futura, 1985.

Worlds Apart. New York: Viking, 1983; London: Futura, 1984.

Dealing in Futures: Stories. New York: Viking, 1985; London: Futura, 1986. (Short stories.)

Tool of the Trade. New York: Morrow, 1987; London: Gollancz, 1987.

Buying Time. Norwalk, Conn.: Easton, 1989. Reprinted as *The Long Habit of Living,* London: New English Library, 1989.

The Hemingway Hoax. New York: Morrow, 1990; London: New English Library, 1990.

Worlds Enough and Time: The Conclusion of the Worlds Trilogy. New York: Morrow, 1992; London: New English Library, 1992.

Vietnam and Other Alien Worlds. Framingham, Mass.: NEFSA, 1993.

1968: A Novel. London: Hodder and Stoughton, 1994; New York: Morrow, 1995.

None So Blind. New York: Morrow, 1996. (Short stories.)

Forever Peace. New York: Ace, 1997.

Saul's Death and Other Poems. San Francisco, Calif.: Anamnesis, 1997.

CRITICAL AND BIOGRAPHICAL STUDY

Gordon, Joan. *Joe Haldeman.* Mercer Island, Wash.: Starmont, 1980.

—BRIAN STABLEFORD

HARRY HARRISON

(b. 1925)

HARRY HARRISON. To many science fiction readers, the name evokes a man of renaissance abilities: writer, raconteur, critic, editor, wit, storyteller, iconoclast, anthologist, world traveler, Esperantist . . . the attributes and abilities go on and on, as does Harrison himself in his various guises.

So varied is this classic science fiction writer that his readers never know quite what to expect next: Will the whimsical Harrison, creator of the several various funny-serious or serious-funny Stainless Steel Rat books—the first in that series was published in 1961 and at least six sequels and one "prequel" have appeared two or three years apart ever since—emerge once more to delight, charm, or induce laughter? What new targets will his wit skewer? Or will the acerbic, mordant Harrison of *Bill, The Galactic Hero* (1965) rail once more against the insanities and inanities of the military or the Galactic Bureau of Investigations? Will the genius of *Captive Universe* (1969) alternately puzzle our intellects or force deep contemplation? Or will the very serious creator of alternate worlds begun by *West of Eden* (1984) and continued by its distinguished successors *Winter in Eden* (1986) and *Return to Eden* (1988) make his mark upon our consciousness?

So persuasive and pervasive is this man—no less a critic than Brian W. Aldiss has labeled him a "marvelous comic genius" whose "early work matures like an old wine"—that it is difficult to say anything definitive about him. He is mercurial, yet his feet are firmly planted on whatever planet his hero, who is often fascinatingly ambiguous, is currently inhabiting.

He is waggish yet at the same time deadly serious as he pillories yet one more science fiction immortal (compare Isaac Asimov's Trantor of the Foundation series with the underground world of *Bill, The Galactic Hero*), or eviscerates a Bible-thumping missionary in the marvelous, unforgettable, yet greatly underestimated novella "The Streets of Ashkelon" (1962).

Moreover, from beneath the various masks he adopts from time to time, Harrison is above all an entertainer. He writes books that sell. In fact, he takes considerable pride in the fact that almost all of his books remain in print for years, sometimes even decades, after their publication. And he never forgets that he must compete for the minds, hearts, and billfolds of his potential readers.

Attention to story, complete with plot and counterplot, subplot and subsidiary plot—his sheer ability as a *story*teller—marks one of Harrison's stellar abilities. Although pulp-trained, he is no mere action-adventure writer; he had been a student of John W. Campbell, Jr.'s old *Astounding Science Fiction* before it became transmogrified into *Analog Science Fiction/Science Fact*.

During that apprenticeship, he learned not only how to please the "master" but how to write intelligently, to plot with verve, and extending the tenets of Campbell, to create some memorable characters that slowly develop into truly human beings. Harrison's ability to flesh out his characters with ease and efficiency is remarkable. Even his early writings, whether short stories or his first novel, *Deathworld* (1960), reveal that ability to tell a gripping story and, most importantly, to entertain.

Yet Harrison did not begin his career determined to be the successful writer he has since become. He was born on 12 March 1925 in Stamford, Connecticut, as Henry Maxwell Dempsey, the only child of Henry Dempsey and Ria Kirjassoff. To his own great suprise, having known only the name Harry Harrison, he did not discover that his father had changed his own name from Dempsey to Harrison until the writer first applied for a passport and needed a birth certificate. (His part Irish ancestry allowed him years later to apply for an Irish passport, thus claiming dual citizenship. As a result, he was able to live, relatively income tax free, in the Republic of Ireland for many years, Ireland sagely permitting artists of Irish descent to live there almost free of income taxes.) All of his school records, his military records, and other files show him as "Harry Harrison." Thus he is an oddity, a writer whose pen name is his real name.

His service in the military in World War II as computing-gunsight specialist trainer and repair expert left him with an abiding dislike for the military, an attitude that has served him well literarily, providing subject matter for many of his books and short stories. After an honorable discharge as sergeant, he began serious art studies at Hunter College and, to eke out the GI Bill, did illustrations for comic books and wrote story lines for romance, science fiction, and adventure comic book titles. Seemingly born with peripatetic genes, Harrison has lived for extended periods of time in such diverse places as New York City, Southern California, Mexico, England, Italy, Denmark, and the Republic of Ireland (where his address for a number of years was almost mythic: Kestrel Ridge, The Vale of Avoca, County Wicklow, Ireland).

Harrison is often spoken of as one of the heirs or successors of the late John W. Campbell, Jr., as well as one of his discoveries. To the extent that Harrison often utilizes so-called "hard" science in his writing, that assertion is, of course, true. Yet in many ways Harrison differs from his mentor, both in degree and in kind. While novels such as *Captive Universe* may appear to be merely one more variation of the closed-universe theme (about what might happen to a spaceship on a voyage of several centuries, whose occupants have forgotten their origins, mission, and destination) often published by Campbell, Harrison's often irreverent attitude toward some of science fiction's sacred cows shows his own individual flair perhaps at least as well as some of his more notable novels. In fact, irreverence, often blended with a soupçon of satire, a sometimes mordant acerbity softened with droll verbal fluff or comic by-play, is one of Harrison's hallmarks. He is a genuine science fiction rarity: a good writer with a true comedic voice and vision.

Good comedy may be almost nonexistent in science fiction, but Harrison has made the métier almost uniquely his own. Who but Harrison would invent, in *The Stainless Steel Rat* (1961), a coal-burning robot? Who but Harrison would refer to planets as "far of Far-offia" or "distant Distantia," and who could forget the coal-fired flying boat of *A Transatlantic Tunnel, Hurrah!* (1972), or a submarine to Mars, or cannon-ball-firing spaceships, or . . . the list is virtually endless. And who but Harrison, world traveler and bon vivant, would claim with a perfectly straight face that he speaks Esperanto like a native? (Indeed, Harrison actually is a Patron of the *Universala Esperanto Asocio* and has been named the honorary president of the Esperanto Association of Ireland. In fact, Harrison wrote the first Esperanto Science fiction story ever, called "Ni Venos, Dr. Zamenhof, Ni Venos" ["We Will Come, Dr. Zamenhof, We Will Come"]. His rogue hero, Slippery Jim diGris, speaks Esperanto, needless to say, and back-cover ads proclaim, "The Stainless Steel Rat speaks Esperanto. Why don't you?")

While Harrison's comedy is often inextricably linked with satire or serious commentary, he is no mere balloon puncturer. To cite one example, his romp *The Technicolor*

Time Machine (1967) had its serious origins in the mid-1960's discovery of a presumed pre-Columbian map of North America known as the "Vinland Map." As yet untested by science at the time, the map and its discovery made world headlines, but Harrison cared little about the map's authenticity. Rather, he perceived almost immediately the possibility of a time anomaly novel involving Vikings, but he vowed that his version would differ from those of, say, Robert A. Heinlein or P. Schuyler Miller often printed in *Astounding Science Fiction* when edited by Campbell.

In *The Technicolor Time Machine,* Harrison aims to skewer pretentious Hollywood historial drama, movie studio blockheads (as he has called them), and science fiction time travel, all at once. He introduces a mad scientist (of course) who has invented a time travel machine known as the "vrematron." He then couples these with a studio named, to no one's surprise, Climactic Pictures, which is planning to produce a Viking drama starring a voluptuous but vacant-headed sex queen, "Slithey Tove," and her muscle-bound hero, "Ruf Hawk." When the studio runs out of time and is threatened by foreclosure unless the company can present completed reels of film in a very few days, the cast, director, and producer use the time travel machine not only to visit the Vikings in their heyday a thousand years ago but to induce them to explore the North American coast and to film them while they are doing it.

When the injured Ruf Hawk must return to the present, the film company dragoons or, rather, bribes Ottar, a tenth-century Viking hero, marauder, and explorer, to star in the movie with bottles of American whiskey and promises of Slithey's comforts—and she is certainly not averse to the idea. Climactic Pictures shoots the film on location in both place and time, returning to Hollywood almost immediately after it left—with a completed picture that had been months in the shooting.

Later when a contemporary archaeological expedition discovers an empty bottle of Jack Daniels in a Newfoundland midden heap . . . well, Harrison has had his fun, pillorying Hollywood, time travel, sex bombs, mad scientists, and almost everyone else within range of his vorpal blade. What is more remarkable, however, is the speed with which Harrison wrote the novel; his records and manuscripts in the Special Collections Library at California State University, Fullerton, reveal that be began the actual task of writing on 17 April 1966 and finished seventy-five thousand words later on 27 May 1966. However, the sheer speed in putting words on paper does not indicate the vast amount of research time he had previously put into his preparation. For example, all of the Icelandic words and the ethnography of Viking culture are faultless, and his saga of the putative Viking discovery of North America reads as if it were genuine. In the end, Harrison is not content to be merely funny but to present some well-disguised information as well, and his "facts" are invariably accurate.

On the other hand, as previously observed, Harrison neither ignores nor slights the entertainment value of his books. His messages are often so obvious—witness the pillorying of the military in *Bill, The Galactic Hero*—or so subtle—as in his stories about religion—that we tend to forget that, as he once put it, "One little bit of pointed rhetoric goes a long way."

In this statement, cited originally in Leon Stover's excellent, intimately personal book *Harry Harrison* (1990) in Twayne's United States authors series, he praises entertainment as the heart of fiction:

Language is the most distinctive thing about Man as a primate, then came writing, the greatest invention since the discovery of fire, and so now books are the most important thing in the world to us. Entertainment in writing is the crowning achievement of the human primate. Think of it! Information processed as entertainment by readers willing to suspend disbelief for stories told as lies. The highest input function of the brain is reading fiction. (page 97)

Harry Harrison in 1981. PHOTO BY JAY KAY KLEIN

In addition, Harrison suggests strongly that the acquisition of information through the entertainment value of fiction is the supreme value, the "supreme fiction." He calls it "Scientific Humanism," insisting on the capital letters, and Science Fiction (not "Sci Fi," or "future science fiction," or any of the other recently invented neologisms for the genre) is its true means of expression.

As observed earlier, *Bill, The Galactic Hero* had its origins in a number of sources, Harrison's service in the military being the most obvious. Yet if art reflects its age, *Bill*, which was published in 1965, can also be classified as an antiwar novel belonging to the same genre as Joseph Heller's *Catch-22* (1961) or the much earlier Erich Maria Remarque's *All Quiet on the Western Front* (1929). Yet with all of the antimilitary cum antiwar sentiment that the novel illustrates, Harrison is also thematically pillorying two of the grand masters of science fiction, Robert A. Heinlein and Isaac Asimov.

Heinlein's virtual jingoistic militarism of, say, *Starship Troopers* (1959) is almost too easy a target for Harrison's hostility to mili-

tary life. But the parodies of Asimov's planet and capital of the Empire Trantor in his Foundation series are a bit less obvious to any but the inveterate science fiction reader. Specifically, Harrison seems to require that his readers consider deeply some of the implications of the writers he is slicing apart. Given a planet, like the virtually identical Trantor of Asimov with the Helior of Harrison's book—Helior, the fabulous aluminum-plated Sin City of the Empire—Harrison asks, oh so innocently, tongue firmly planted in his cheek: "Where do they get their oxygen on the treeless planet lacking any chlorophyll? How do they dispose of their garbage with no dump sites, epecially after the file cabinets are full?" In a typical Harrisonian touch, Bill solves the garbage problem by space-mailing it, postage free under government cachet, to another planet.

Harrison also levels his wit at military or other jingoistic officials who find enemies where there are none, or internal subversion where none exists. The Empire's enemies, the hated Chingers, we later learn, are peace-loving, seven-inch-tall, lizardlike creatures. But such is the mania of militaristic propagandists that they have become invincible reptilian monsters in the minds of the public, complete with idiotic racist invective: "Would you want your daughter to marry a Chinger?" Similarly, only subscriptions to the insurrectionist newspaper by members of the Galactic Bureau of Investigation have kept that journal alive. (Harrison is almost certainly referring to the de facto support of the communist *Daily Worker* by hordes of FBI agents who wanted to keep up with what the "red menace" was doing.) It is a novel indeed worthy of comparison with Heller's masterpiece.

Harrison is also wickedly parodic in the unfairly neglected *Star Smashers of the Galaxy Rangers* (1973). While imitation is the sincerest form of flattery, as the cliché suggests, this Harrison romp does more than pay obeisance to the late E. E. "Doc" Smith, whose Skylark and Lensman series set the pattern for space opera. Deriving its name from the familiar western cognomen "horse opera," space opera can be defined as a mix of reality, melodrama, dreams, and futuristic technology, with good guys wearing white space helmets and bad guys wearing black helmets. Harrison pokes fun at many of the hackneyed science fiction conventions by showing just how much fun they can be when imitated—as the very ridiculous name of the novel suggests—almost beyond belief. Wicked nostalgia, then, rules this exercise in juvenile exuberance and might well remind many readers of the old Tom Swift books. In addition, Harrison goes beyond mere satire as he also dabbles with gender identity and bends sex roles. The super masculine heroes of this grand farce turn out to be, in Harrison's phrase, "AC/DC." So much for "he-man heroics."

This novel can bear comparison in a certain way to the equally humorous book that almost immediately preceded it, *A Transatlantic Tunnel, Hurrah!* the title Harrison prefers, although it was published in the United States as *Tunnel Through the Deeps*. Here Harrison utilizes a different kind of science fiction device, the parallel world story. Briefly, Captain Augustine Washington, a descendant of the traitorous General George Washington who had led the unsuccessful rebellion against the Crown—the abortive American revolution having collapsed after the infamous general lost the Battle of Lexington and was promptly executed by the British— proposes to build a transatlantic tunnel. The project thus restores "honour" (Harrison uses the British spelling) to his family name and, by doing so, enables him to wed the fair Iris Isambard Brassey-Brunel, and perhaps to persuade Her Majesty to grant America dominion status, or even—gasp!—independence.

What makes this novel so provocative is not only the many variations on history that Harrison's own parallel world demands, such as seizing upon a remote historical incident as he changes history by the defeat of the Christian armies at the Battle of Nave de Tolsa in 1212, but the very style Harrison uses to tell his somewhat convoluted story. Here he deliberately imitates not only the

form of the Victorian novel but its narrative technique as well, with echoes of Charles Dickens, William Makepeace Thackeray, and Anthony Trollope. The book *reads* like a Victorian novel.

As a stylist, Harrison is underestimated. To begin with, his prose is very serviceable, effective, and gripping. That is to say, Harrison possesses enough sheer talent, coupled with decades of experience, to be able to use whatever stylistic techniques or novelistic devices his writing demands. Yet he never allows them to interfere with the story.

Thus in one series of novels, The Stainless Steel Rat books, for example, Harrison uses a first-person narrator and pulls off this difficult feat by never becoming trapped in the problems of trying to relate happenings that have occurred beyond the knowledge of the narrator. Whether the novel be *The Stainless Steel Rat's Revenge* (1970), *The Stainless Steel Rat Saves the World* (1972), *The Stainless Steel Rat Wants You!* (1978), *The Stainless Steel Rat for President* (1982), *A Stainless Steel Rat Is Born* (1985), *The Stainless Steel Rat Gets Drafted* (1987), *The Stainless Steel Rat Sings the Blues* (1994), or *The Stainless Steel Rat Goes to Hell* (1996), Harrison utilizes the first-person technique to make his readers visualize with considerable immediacy the problems, the obstacles, the vicissitudes, the inner thinking, and the rationalizations that Jim diGriz faces and ultimately conquers—even the temptation to "do good." In a certain sense, while Slippery Jim may well be a latter-day Robin Hood or a raffish miles gloriosus, he is also an entrepreneurial capitalist a few centuries hence, dedicated to the acquistion of money however denominated. Yet his devotion to his wife and sons belies his derring-do exterior. In fact, Jim is aided in his considerable troubles by the other members of his family, who face similar fiery obstacles.

Harrison's earlier retelling of how his hero (or antihero?) began his one-man crime wave as a mere teenager, *A Stainless Steel Rat Is Born*, is told with considerable panache. While it is Harrison's equivalent of the standard "coming of age" novel adolescence, the

343

bildungsroman, it is nonetheless typically Harrisonian. His humor continually shines through the various plot convolutions that Jim gets himself into as he escapes the stultifications of society. Yet Jim is more than "thief as hero." In a typical Harrison touch, Jim is turned from petty to cosmic criminal by a Dickensian Fagin, the "Bishop," retired supercriminal who gives Jim his sobriquet:

> We must be as stealthy as rats in the wainscoting of their society. It was easier in the old days, of course, and society had more rats when the rules were looser. . . . Now that society is all ferroconcrete and stainless steel there are fewer gaps in the joints. It takes a very smart rat indeed to find these openings. Only a stainless steel rat can be at home in this environment. (page 98)

The continuing popularity of the series may well stem from its largely adolescent readers who identify with the exploits of their vary fallible picaresque hero, thumbing their noses at society and its sometimes ridiculous conventions. The novels are very funny as well, and Harrison often understates both his drolleries and his antipathies, letting his readers chuckle, raise an eyebrow, or even guffaw at his deadpan humor.

In another early novel, *Captive Universe,* as in much of the remainder of his fiction, however, Harrison adopts the standard device of the omniscient narrator, merely letting the story tell the story. Moreover, rarely does he purple his prose merely for the sake of achieving some supposed stylistic effect. He is content to write well, simply but profoundly, as shown by the opening paragraph of *Captive Universe:*

> Chimal ran in panic. The moon was still hidden by the cliffs on the eastern side of the valley, but its light was already tipping their edges with silver. Once it had risen above them he would be as easily seen as the holy pyramid out there among the sprouting corn. Why had he not thought? Why had he taken the risk? His breath tore at his throat as he gasped and ran on, his heart pulsed like a great drum that filled his chest. (page 1)

Here, as is usually the case with Harrison, he relies on solid, monosyllabic, Anglo-Saxon-derived verbs or verb forms: *ran, hidden, tipping, risen, sprouting, tore, take, gasped, pulsed, filled.* He is writer enough to know that short words are words of might, striking the reader at a very effective unconscious level.

In any evaluation of Harrison's many contributions to science fiction, his role as science fiction critic is often overlooked. Yet even here, so multifaceted is he that it is often impossible to distinguish Harrison the discriminating editor from Harrison the critic, or Harrison the eclectic anthologist from Harrison the genial curmudgeon inveighing against narrow-minded critics on both sides of the Atlantic (who use as their canon of judgment the notion that if it's science fiction, it can't be good and if it's good, it can't be science fiction). He and his friend Brian W. Aldiss wanted to demonstrate how deep that prejudice was and to prove that good writing does indeed exist in science fiction. The result of their labors was not only the lauded and lamented *SF Horizons* in England (it lasted only two issues, 1964–1965) but, secondarily, its many descendants, including such serious critically esteemed scholarly journals as *Extrapolation,* all of which took their cue from the fact that *SF Horizons* had included articles by C. S. Lewis and other notables. Aldiss and Harrison were also stimulated by the fact that their friend Kingsley Amis, a few years earlier, had written *New Maps of Hell: A Survey of Science Fiction* (1960), perhaps the first serious criticism of science fiction since James O. Bailey's *Pilgrims Through Time and Space: Trends and Patterns in Scientific and Utopian Fiction* (1947).

During these years, Harrison kept turning out book after book—the Deathworld series, for example, together with some of the early Stainless Steel Rat books—as well as short story after short story, in which he emphasized action, adventure, plausible characters, and a compelling plot.

His extensive traveling has made him, quite literally, a man of the world and consequently has given him, more than the average science fiction writer, a weltanschauung. Indeed, his world outlook—or perhaps it is his ability to see through things, to penetrate folkways and mores to their archetypal core—has provided some of his very best writing. Two of his major works can perhaps indicate something of that ability: consider *Captive Universe* and the Eden trilogy, separated in point of composition by at least 15 years.

Captive Universe, an erudite yet gripping and penetrating re-examination of the closed-universe theme, was the first science fiction title promoted by the Book-of-the-Month Club, where it was reviewed enthusiastically by the critic Gilbert Highet.

Science fiction commonly substitutes the notion of "idea as hero" rather than exemplifying the concept common in most narrative fiction that action flows from character, specifically that of the hero/heroine. Their behavior, their very nature, determines action. Yet science fiction itself often has succumbed to "gadgetry" as hero, the so-called "hardcore" science fiction. Harrison's work often seems to fall somewhere in the sane middle. His novels or stories may feature space travel and be replete with one gadget after another, but almost always that technique is subsidiary to either the story he is telling or the implied idea he wishes his readers to identify—or, occasionally, to identify with. *Captive Universe* is surely one of the best examples of that technique.

It begins with the story of an Aztec youth who wishes to understand a bit more about his quite limited world. Aztec? Almost certainly, for the language of the chants, the familiarity of the bloody rites, the names of the characters or gods, and the atmosphere of the set pieces—the very language of the work itself—seem to identify it as a rich tapestry of fact, history, projection, and myth.

However, the hurried reader might miss some of the subtly obvious variations Harrison introduces quite early. For example, the hero's mother is characterized in this way: "her typical Aztec features relaxed, with the firelight glinting from her golden hair and

blue eyes." Golden hair? Blue eyes? Hardly Aztec as we know it. And thus Harrison embarks on what may be his most provocative novel, if not his best, for he has established that something is a bit amiss. Then when readers joltingly finally realize that the sun does not rise, they are soon lost in the remarkable combination of the science fiction notion of idea as hero with the more conventional novel of adolescence, the youth coming of age, a genre to which so many mainstream novels belong. Thus as the youth Chimal tries to escape the narrow confines of his world, he gradually becomes aware of a larger universe that contains his small world, the giant spaceship on its way to Proxima Centauri.

Captive Universe can aptly—perhaps even very favorably—be compared with Robert A. Heinlein's *Universe* (1951), probably the most famous closed spaceship novel. But because of its implications, Harrison's work is almost in a class by itself for several reasons.

The "Designer" who programmed the hollowed out asteroid as a spaceship and designed the proto-Aztec societies that inhabit it, also genetically engineered the savior-hero genius Chimal, who is able to figure out the purpose of the mission and ultimately to renew, even redeem, the lives of the prisoner-inhabitants. It is, as Highet pointed out in his Book-of-the-Month Club review, "a religious allegory."

With the Eden trilogy—*West of Eden*, *Winter in Eden*, and *Return to Eden*, Harrison has written what may well be his masterpiece, a series that compares favorably with Frank Herbert's *Dune* chronicles or Brian W. Aldiss's Helliconia trilogy. In the *Eden* trilogy, Harrison has returned to the basic science fiction device, noted earlier, of "idea as hero." In this instance, he has chosen the probability world device, not merely reinventing the question of what would have happened if, say, the South had won the Civil War, a common enough theme. Instead, he begins with a far more fundamental premise: What if meteors had *not* wiped out the dinosaurs some 65 million years ago and an intelligent saurian life system had ultimately developed? Harrison has called it the "Saurolithic Age," and his intelligent, bipedal, erect, cold-blooded reptilian species, the Yilanè, who are complete with language, history, culture, and civilization, dominate the world, particularly in Africa with extensions into Europe and northern parts of the Old World. A relatively primitive mammalian humanoid species has evolved in North America.

Stover has observed that some reviewers have carped that in the three volumes there is more "world" than narrative, adding, "But that complaint misses the point." Indeed, it is almost impossible to overemphasize the incredible detail that Harrison has infused into these three books. Complete with maps, an illustrated "Zoology" in the appendices, a history of the Yilanè "people," and accounts of their physiology, diet, reproductive biology, culture, and language, Harrison is able to prove his point that science fiction is at its best when it keeps faith with science—and the logical or ethical consquences of that science. But he never overlooks the importance of plot—story as story—and the very setting of that story, the unusualness of its implications, its premises and scientific humanistic (or "saurolithic?") foundations are of vital importance.

Thus the Yilanè, the Saurolithic "people," are matriarchal; humans are patriarchal. While the humans can lie, the "dinosaurs" cannot. Neither can they work metal or have any true technology but instead breed creatures of remarkable specificity to accomplish various needed tasks. Imagine those ramifications. And these are only a few of the differences that Harrison has infused into this series, and he asks, as always, what implications his readers might draw from them. To make that task a bit easier, Harrison has made his lead character, Kerrick, a human who was captured as a boy and raised by the Yilanè, who has escaped to lead his own people against his erstwhile captors. Thus readers can, or should, weigh their own observations of what humanity has done to itself against what the Yilanè have accomplished in their world. And humanity may well suffer by comparison.

Too few science fiction writers have devoted the time, effort, and research into their writing that Harrison has done, not only in the Eden series but throughout the rest of his writing. He consistently calls upon experts— cultural anthropologists, historical linguists, sociologists, and authorities in many other fields—to ensure the scientific accuracy of his works.

Indeed, it could be said that few other writers—again the names of Aldiss and Herbert come to mind—have created worlds with such remarkable inner consistency. It could even be argued, as observed earlier, that the true "hero" of the Eden series is indeed the concept itself, the familiar notion of "idea as hero," yet that takes absolutely nothing away from the imagination and narrative pace of the books themselves. Harrison seems to recognize in his writing that technology does not lead to wisdom. As a consequence, he never severs the bonds between nature and humanity. His is an art that conceals art.

"The Streets of Ashkelon" and "Rescue Operation" (1964), a novella and a short story, illustrate another aspect of Harrison's skepticism of authority. The novella, which takes its title from King David's lament over Saul and Jonathan in the first chapter of II Samuel, is at once tragic, telling, and controversial. Too often reduced to the simplification of saying that the story illustrates what is perceived to be Harrison's atheism, which may be true enough, it demands consideration on more than the surface religious areas. To be sure, the novella ostensibly deals with the story of a missionary, Father Mark, who is bringing his Bible-thumping gospel and extreme inerrant biblical literalism to Wesker's World. That world's logical, totally nonmetaphoric people and the planet's natural resources are being capitalized upon, indeed exploited, by Trader Garth.

When, despite Garth's repeated warnings about the extreme literal mindedness of the amphibianlike natives, the well-meaning missionary preaches the story of the crucifixion and resurrection, tragedy ensues. The natives crucify the missionary because he has preached resurrection, and in their exasperatingly logical way, they merely wish to see it happen.

"The Streets of Ashkelon" is not only or even merely an antireligious story. Whether it illustrates Harrison's own personal religious beliefs or nonbeliefs is not germane. Rather, it might have worked equally well, perhaps not as horrifyingly dramatic, if, to give a minor example, the "missionary" had been breathing fire as he preached the superiorities of the capitalistic economic system, a concept certainly suggested by the exploitative presence of Trader Garth on the planet. Certainly Garth has more insight into how to deal with differences in his short time on the planet than Father Mark has learned (or is willing to learn) in a lifetime of training and experience.

As a result, the story is at once fascinatingly ambiguous, ironically tragic, and—above all—memorable, not soon to be dismissed as mere sermonic realism. In fact, part of the intensity of the drama is Trader Garth's unwillingness to lose such a mother lode of profit by reason of the missionary's intransigence and inability to learn the Weskerian Way.

So also with the notable short story "Rescue Operation." Here an alien spaceship has been rescued by natives living on a tiny island off the coast of Yugoslavia. Dying, the alien retrieves an object, perhaps a book containing advanced alien technological, medical, or scientific secrets from its space suit, and proffers it to its rescuers. A superstitious native, again a priest, looks upon the object with horror and tosses it into a fire, where it is consumed almost immediately. Irony? Of course, for the "book" could have contained alien secrets of peace, healing, and communication.

The story is imbued with the strong implication that the mission of the alien is to aid humanity in uniting in a common effort for the development of all peoples, to bring about the conquest of want, starvation, and misery, as well as freedom from the stringencies of the Iron Curtain. Double irony? Perhaps, but Harrison, no true preacher, lets the vigor of his

story answer those questions. The answers may even remain ambiguous in the end, but who would dare maintain that all ambiguities must be banished from life, even from a remote island off the coast of Yugoslavia?

When Harrison is particularly bitter about some perceived foible of humanity or science fiction, he is often content simply to tell the terrible story, witness *Make Room! Make Room!* (1965), and let the horror of the tale itself create the vividness of the story. He never obviously mounts a pulpit no matter how strongly he might feel about the dangers of overpopulation, overconsumption, or incipient ecological disaster. He is content to rely on the gradual dawning of awareness on the part of his readers that excess breeds excess, or as the unmemorable film made from the book, MGM's *Soylent Green* (1973), puts it, "Soylent green is people!"

Stylistically, however, Harrison lets the vigor of the story make his point rather than be pedantic about it and thus lose his audience. To be sure, it goes without saying that the book is not the movie, for the film emphasized potential cannibalism as a "solution" to overpopulation, whereas the novel is multileveled, and the aspect emphasized by the film is secondary at best in the novel. Essentially, *Make Room! Make Room!* is pure future scene fiction. It is at once a detective story, an admonitory screed on the dangers of the world permitting its self-destructive demographic trends to continue, and an extremely vivid picture of what might ensue should they not be changed. This ability to work well on many levels is one of the major characteristics that lifts Harrison's writing beyond mere storytelling and give it a broader context, even a strong social dimension.

In this complex novel, the familiar masks the hidden, and the obvious hides the implied lessons. On the surface, of course, Harrison is railing against the dangers of overpopulation and, in a typical science fiction ploy, carries the warning of an overpopulated and underfed Earth to its ultimate extreme.

Crime is pandemic; women are merely "furniture" as sexism is rampant; human corpses are "recycled" and transformed into condensed food packets for yet one more round of recycling. The central or point-of-view character is Andy, the detective, as he attempts to solve yet one more murder. The racketeer owner of a luxury apartment has been killed by a Chinese teenager who had been forced to steal to survive. Andy takes up with the racketeer's mistress, who had been forced to hustle for her living, and through her he gets to know an old man, Sol, who recalls the old days when things were better. Using the detective as his central character permits Harrison to reflect on almost every level of this disintegrating society because Andy at one time or another has inhabited them all.

This jeremiad works well as social science fiction, a genre that much of Harrison's work seems to fit, and as observed earlier the novel itself is much better than the film *Soylent Green*, which was ostensibly derived from the book and became in Hollywood's inimitable fashion, a big-budget picture about cannibalism. While on the set, Harrison learned that he could not change one line of the script for the film. As a consequence, if the film did not live up to the potential of the novel, it was not Harrison's fault.

Harrison's indignation at humanity's asininity becomes Swiftian in this novel, and he approaches Swift's savagery in attacking stupidity and venality. In general, however, in his other works, Harrison's satiric mood can be likened to a moral indignation coupled with a sometimes bemused belief that readers can make up their minds for themselves about the various topics that provide him subject matter.

We can see his technique at work in the first of the several trilogies he has written, the Deathworld series. On the surface, these three loosely interconnected novels, beginning with *Deathworld* (1960), deal with the adventures or exploits of Jason dinAlt, the first of Harrison's frequent ambiguous heroes. DinAlt is a rogue, a gambler, a sometime psychic, almost the prototype of the classic miles gloriosus. Yet dinAlt is not merely boastful; despite his faults, he is an accomplished

fighter and a good husband when he marries a Pyrran woman, Meta, early in the series.

On the planet Pyrrus itself, every form of life has evolved, mutating into veritable killing machines dedicated to the extermination of the human inhabitants of the planet. The Pyrrans have also become incredibly efficient killers as they strive to protect their own life and civilization against the planet itself. The inhabitants seek out dinAlt because they need three billion credits immediately, and they force dinAlt to gamble because gambling is the only method they have to raise the money overnight. Jason is successful, and after meeting and falling in love with Meta on the return trip to Pyrrus, is gradually acclimated into Pyrran society. He eventually becomes a virtual member of this deathworld society, although somewhat inferior to the Pyrrans.

After a series of discoveries and misadventures told with Harrison's typical action-packed technique, dinAlt is able to perceive that those same inhabitants are themselves the enemy. "We become what we hate," he tells them, because the vegetation and animal life of Pyrrus have become more and more deadly the more they are blasted in an attempt at eradication. Named after the ruinous devastating victory of King Pyrrus of Epirus over the Romans, the planet itself has become the proverbial pyrrhic victory.

Harrison continues the exploits or saga of dinAlt in two sequels, *Deathworld 2* (1964) and *Deathworld 3* (1968). In the second book, he is kidnapped from Pyrrus and eventually marooned on a planet cut off from civilization, a world that has lost or secretly hoarded most of its technological heritage, although Harrison cannot resist pointing out that Esperanto is the lingua franca of the planet. DinAlt begins what amounts to a sociologically evolutionary journey, progressing gradually from the status of abject slave rooting in the dirt for food to virtual medieval serf scrabbling for necessities to scientific adviser because of his knowledge of technological secrets. After he has successfully consolidated scientific knowledge in the hands of one group, he is seriously wounded but saved from almost certain death by the arrival of the Pyrrans and his companion, Meta.

In the final novel, dinAlt is able to lead the Pyrrans away from their vicious home world to a rich planet peopled by Mongol-like barbarians. Here the mission is simple—civilize the hordes—and the Pyrrans have the ability to do so, and dinAlt aids them with his knowledge of history and the actual experience of the Mongols attacking Chinese civilization.

It is difficult to determine which came first among Harrison's ambiguous heroes, Jason dinAlt or James Bolivar diGriz, "Slippery Jim," the famous-infamous Stainless Steel Rat. The two bear certain archetypal resemblances: they are underdogs in an unfeeling, cruel world; they overcome monstrous, indeed incredible obstacles, yet they are both insightful, calculating, ready to act, and above all, do almost anything to preserve their own lives no matter the odds.

Slippery Jim is a master criminal in the thirtieth century, a picaresque hero reborn ten centuries from now. The character had appeared in two early *Astounding Science Fiction* short stories in 1957 and 1960, but not until after the first of the many novels about him, *The Stainless Steel Rat,* was published in 1961 did Harrison begin to notice that the extended versions were selling very well.

And Harrison, like Samuel Johnson, is not averse to making money from his writing. As editors, readers, and science fiction fans began to appreciate what Harrison himself was doing, combining humor with the plausible improbable in telling a rattling good story, Harrison began turning out these lighter, less serious novels almost every other year, and each one became funnier than the last as everybody learned that Harrison's humor sold. Yet even in these books, Harrison does not slight either the style, the plot elements, or the characterization. To be sure, Slippery Jim follows the pattern of other literary thieves in fiction, and society is almost always the benefactor of Jim's machinations. He is a seriocomic future scene Robin Hood, and pompous asses are always his targets. Harrison has said that as long as the fans demand more of Slippery Jim's sagas, he'll oblige them. One waits for, say, *The Stainless Steel Rat Goes to Heaven.*

In the meantime, Harrison has also published two other trilogies worthy of note. First is the To the Stars series consisting of *Homeworld* (1980), *Wheelworld* (1981), and *Starworld* (1981). While not "major" Harrison, the books are eminently readable and certainly must be considered as part of the Harrison canon.

The generic title of the more recent series of three books is *The Hammer and the Cross* (1993), which was followed by *One King's Way* (1994) and *King and Emperor* (1996.) In these books Harrison has penned another variation of an alternate history, this time positing that the Vikings have conquered Britain and are faced with obstacles to their expansion through Europe by a renascent chivalry, a Teutonic or German knightly order seeking the Lance, which in Harrison's variation of history was the instrument that killed Christ, and a desire to resurrect the Holy Roman Empire. Such a brief summary does no justice to the richness with which Harrison peoples these books, his sense of place, his fascinating rereading of history, and his storytelling ability. Like the Eden series, they must be savored to be fully appreciated.

Where will Harrison go next? It is impossible to tell, of course, for his talents are so multifaceted that he can write almost anything he wants to. He knows his writing will be received well by his many fans, and sell well too, for that matter.

Perhaps the better question to be considered would be his eventual position in the science fiction galaxy. As a storyteller, he has almost no peer. As a provocative thinker very able to conceal his tenets or beliefs in the story itself, his genius could pen another *Captive Universe,* considered by some his best work, and receive the mainstream recognition his talents deserve. For that matter the Eden series might well be rediscovered by academic science fiction critics and shown conclusively to be the masterpiece it is. Suffice it to say, Harry Harrison has given much pleasure, considerable entertainment, and some thought-provoking ideas to his myriad readers. Who could ask for more?

Selected Bibliography

Many of Harrison's short stories are as yet uncollected, and none of his more than fifty anthologies are listed here.

WORKS OF HARRY HARRISON

Deathworld. New York: Bantam, 1960.

The Stainless Steel Rat: A Science-Fiction Novel. New York: Pyramid, 1961.

Planet of the Damned. New York: Bantam, 1962.

War with the Robots: Science Fiction Stories. New York: Pyramid, 1962. (Short stories.)

Deathworld 2. New York: Bantam, 1964.

Bill, The Galactic Hero. Garden City, N.Y.: Doubleday, 1965.

Make Room! Make Room! New York: Berkley, 1965.

Plague from Space. Garden City, N.Y.: Doubleday, 1965. Revised and expanded as *The Jupiter Plague,* New York: TOR, 1982.

Two Tales and Eight Tomorrows. London: Gollancz, 1965. (Short stories.)

The Technicolor Time Machine. Garden City, N.Y.: Doubleday, 1967.

Deathworld 3. New York: Dell, 1968.

Captive Universe. New York: Putnam's, 1969.

The Daleth Effect: A Science Fiction Novel. New York: Putnam's, 1970.

One Step from Earth. New York: Macmillan, 1970.

Prime Number. New York: Berkley, 1970.

The Stainless Steel Rat's Revenge. New York: Walker, 1970.

Montezuma's Revenge. Garden City, N.Y.: Doubleday, 1972.

The Stainless Steel Rat Saves the World. New York: Putnam's, 1972.

Stonehenge, with Leon E. Stover. New York, Scribners, 1972.

A Transatlantic Tunnel, Hurrah! London: Faber and Faber, 1972. Reprinted as *Tunnel Through the Deeps,* New York: Putnam's, 1972.

Star Smashers of the Galaxy Rangers. New York: Putnam, 1973.

The Best of Harry Harrison. New York: Pocket Books, 1976.

The Lifeship, with Gordon R. Dickson. New York: Harper and Row, 1976.

Skyfall. New York: Atheneum, 1976.

The Stainless Steel Rat Wants You! London: Joseph 1978.

Homeworld. New York: Bantam, 1980. (To the Stars, part 1.)

The QE2 Is Missing. London: MacDonald-Futura, 1980.

Planet of No Return. New York: Simon and Schuster, 1981.

Starworld. New York: Bantam, 1981. (To the Stars, part 3.)

To the Stars. Garden City, N.Y.: Doubleday, 1981.

Wheelworld. New York: Bantam, 1981. (To the Stars, part 2.)

Invasion Earth. New York: Ace, 1982.

The Stainless Steel Rat for President. Garden City, N.Y.: Doubleday, 1982.

Rebel in Time. New York: TOR, 1983.

Stonehenge: Where Atlantis Died, with Leon E. Stover. New York: TOR, 1983.

West of Eden. New York: Bantam, 1984. (Eden, part 1.)

A Stainless Steel Rat Is Born. New York: Bantam, 1985.

Winter in Eden. New York: Bantam, 1986. (Eden, part 2.)

The Stainless Steel Rat Gets Drafted. New York: Bantam, 1987.

Return to Eden. New York: Bantam, 1988. (Eden, part 3.)

The Turing Option: A Novel, with Marvin Lee Minsky. New York: Warner, 1992.

The Hammer and the Cross. New York: TOR, 1993.

The Stainless Steel Rat Sings the Blues. New York: Bantam, 1994.

One King's Way. New York: TOR, 1995. (The Hammer and the Cross, part 2.)

King and Emperor. New York: TOR, 1996. (The Hammer and the Cross, part 3.)

The Stainless Steel Rat Goes to Hell. New York: TOR, 1996.

Stars and Stripes Forever: A Novel of Alternate History. New York: Ballantine, 1998.

MANUSCRIPTS

An extensive collection of Harrison's manuscripts is readily accessible in the Special Collections Library at California State University in Fullerton, California.

CRITICAL AND BIOGRAPHICAL STUDIES

Aldiss, Brian. "An Appreciation of Harry Harrison." Introduction to *Harry Harrison,* by Leon Stover. Boston: Twayne, 1990.

————. *Billion Year Spree: The True History of Science Fiction.* Garden City, N.Y.: Doubleday, 1973.

————, and Harry Harrison, eds. *Hell's Cartographers: Some Personal Histories of Science Fiction Writers.* New York: Harper and Row, 1975. (Includes a memoir by Harrison.)

————, and David Wingrove. *Trillion Year Spree: The History of Science Fiction.* New York: Atheneum, 1986.

Ash, Brian. *Who's Who in Science Fiction.* New York: Taplinger, 1976.

Barron, Neil, ed. *Anatomy of Wonder: A Critical Guide to Science Fiction.* 3d ed. New York: Bowker, 1987.

Brajer, Peter. "The Deathworld Trilogy." In *Survey of Science Fiction Literature.* Vol. 2. Englewood Cliffs, N.J.: Salem, 1979.

Gunn, James. *The New Encyclopedia of Science Fiction.* New York: Viking, 1988.

McReynolds, Douglas J. "The Tunnel Through the Deeps." In *Survey of Science Fiction Literature.* Vol. 5. Englewood Cliffs, N.J.: Salem, 1979.

Meyers, Walter E. "The Stainless Steel Rat Novels." In *Survey of Science Fiction Literature.* Vol. 5. Englewood Cliffs, N.J.: Salem, 1979.

Nicholls, Peter. *The Science Fiction Encyclopedia.* Garden City, N.Y.: Doubleday, 1979.

Platt, Charles. *Dream Makers: The Uncommon People Who Write Science Fiction.* New York: Berkley, 1980.

Shippey, T. A. "Make Room! Make Room!" In *Survey of Science Fiction Literature.* Vol. 3. Englewood Cliffs, N.J.: Salem, 1979.

Smith, Curtis C. *Twentieth Century Science Fiction Writers.* 2d ed. Chicago: St. James, 1986.

Stover, Leon. *Harry Harrison.* Boston: Twayne, 1990.

—WILLIS E. McNELLY

ROBERT A. HEINLEIN

(1907–1988)

ROBERT ANSON HEINLEIN was born on 7 July 1907 in Butler, Missouri; he was the third of seven children. He attended Central High School in Kansas City and spent a year at the University of Missouri, Columbia, before completing his education at the United States Naval Academy at Annapolis, following in the footsteps of his older brother. He graduated and was commissioned in 1929, serving aboard the aircraft carrier *Lexington* before becoming gunnery officer on the destroyer *Roper*. He suffered continually from seasickness and eventually contracted tuberculosis, which caused him to be retired from active duty in 1934 on a small pension. He settled in California and spent some time casting around for a new vocation, later allowing it to be put on record that he tried silver mining, politics, and selling real estate. In the course of these adventures, he married Leslyn MacDonald.

Heinlein was subsequently secretive about this phase of his life. When Sam Moskowitz asked him for details while researching an article to be incorporated into *Seekers of Tomorrow* (1965), Heinlein sent a long and detailed letter, but he then forbade Moskowitz to make its contents public until he was dead. (After he died, his widow Virginia rescinded that permission and demanded the return of the letter.) When Alexei Panshin began researching his adulatory study *Heinlein in Dimension* (1968), Heinlein refused to cooperate and forbade his friends to give out any information. When Panshin eventually tried to introduce himself to his hero, Heinlein angrily refused to speak to him, citing invasions of privacy, which Panshin thought imaginary. It was left to Tom Perry, in an article published in 1993, to reveal that Heinlein's short-lived career in politics had involved him with *Upton Sinclair's EPIC News*, a weekly propaganda sheet promoting Sinclair's campaign to become governor of California, using the key slogan "End Poverty in California."

In 1938 Heinlein ran in a primary seeking the Democratic nomination to contest a state assembly seat. Although he was unopposed by any other Democrat, the seat's Republican incumbent, Charles W. Lyon, stood against him and won. By securing victory in both the Democratic and Republican primaries, Lyon made it unnecessary actually to hold an election. Perry speculates that Heinlein became determined to keep this quiet because of the vulnerability he felt during the McCarthy witch-hunt, when he was attempting to make a career in Hollywood as well as writing juvenile science fiction novels. Perry suggests that Heinlein would have been perfectly prepared by then to declare that he no longer had any sympathy whatsoever even for the elements of Sinclair's platform that had once interested him—let alone those that had led Sinclair to call himself a socialist before deciding that the Democrat label was more convenient—but that he would not have been willing to pay the price of forgiveness that McCarthy invariably demanded of repentant leftists: to name the friends he had made while he was involved with Sinclair's movement.

Heinlein's abortive campaign left him with a mortgage on his house that overstretched the resources of his navy pension, and it was his determination to pay it off that led him to try his hand at writing science fiction. He had long been a fan of the science fiction pulps, although it seems to have been a slightly guilty pleasure; he subscribed to the view, common among intellectuals, that the literary standard of pulp fiction was contemptible. A competition advertised by *Thrilling Wonder Stories* inspired him to write "Life-Line," but he submitted it to the far more reputable *Collier's*; when it was rejected he sent it to the highest-paying science fiction pulp *Astounding Science Fiction*. When John W. Campbell, Jr. bought it in 1939, Heinlein promptly wrote another story, which Campbell also bought, and then several more. When Campbell rejected those, Heinlein entered into fervent correspondence with the editor in order to ascertain exactly what he wanted.

The letters reproduced in the aptly named *Grumbles from the Grave* (1989) make it clear that Heinlein's attitude to his early work was very defensive. He insisted that his only objective was to pay off his mortgage, and when he kept going thereafter, he told Campbell that as soon as another story was rejected he would stop writing. He considered the stories that Campbell thought unworthy to have been fatally stigmatized and attached pseudonymous bylines to them even when it was Campbell who ultimately bought revised versions. Although he did allow himself to be tempted back to work after Campbell had the temerity to reject another one of his submissions, he did so after an ostentatious pause and some posturing.

Even though the early letters in *Grumbles from the Grave* are carefully selected and edited, they reveal that Heinlein was extremely touchy and prone to aggressive overreaction to criticism. He continually referred even to the work he sold to Campbell as "hack"—although Virginia Heinlein's commentary observes that he "strenuously objected" to any editorial amendments. He also took care to tell Campbell that if and when the day came

that he got around to doing some serious writing, it would be very different. Even when he came up with an idea that initially fired his enthusiasm—for the novel *Beyond This Horizon* (magazine form, 1942; book form, 1948)—he lost that commitment so rapidly that when he sent the first installment to Campbell, his covering letter said: "Confidentially, it stinks." He became fetishistic about selling all his work, no matter how he affected to despise it, but he seems to have regarded praise from Campbell or *Astounding*'s readers as a double-edged sword: unwelcome confirmation that he had an innate talent for the production of trash.

Heinlein also complained of the terrible difficulty of grinding out *Beyond This Horizon*, adding a macabre quip to one accompanying letter about bloodstains on the page. When one of the many characters who function as his mouthpieces in his later work asks a potential spouse whether she really knows what being married to a writer involves, Heinlein presumably had his own case (and perhaps the fate of his own first marriage) in mind. In *The Cat Who Walks Through Walls* (1985), he would write:

> Writing is antisocial. It's as solitary as masturbation. Disturb a writer when he is the throes of creation and he is likely to turn and bite right to the bone . . . and not even know that he's doing it. As writers' wives and husbands often learn to their horror.
>
> And there is no way—attend me carefully, Gwen!—there is no way that writers can be tamed and rendered civilized. Or even cured. In a household with more than one person, of which one is a writer, the only solution known to science is to provide the patient with an isolation room, where he can endure the acute stages in private, and where food can be poked in to him with a stick. Because, if you disturb the patient at such times, he may break into tears and become violent. (pages 43–44)

In spite of such penalties, Heinlein did eventually find in science fiction writing the vocation that had eluded him since his release from the navy—but he liked to pretend, perhaps because it was true, that it was a vocation into which he had to be dragged, kicking and screaming. There is no evidence that his enormous popularity ever allowed him firmly and finally to set aside the feeling that his entire career had been a craven and humiliating capitulation with ignominy.

In "Life-Line" an experimental scientist shows off a machine for predicting the future to sceptical and scornful Academicians, the twist in the story's tail being that his own death provides the crucial proof of its accuracy. The second Heinlein story Campbell bought, "Misfit" (1939), is a brief "ugly duckling" tale about a young member of a spaceship crew whose mathematical genius allows him to fill in when the ship's "calculator" fails. The first story Campbell rejected was "Let There be Light" (1940), which appeared in *Super Science Stories*, edited by Campbell's protegé and fledgling rival Frederik Pohl, under the pseudonym Lyle Monroe. It is unclear whether the story was rejected because of some mildly risqué dialogue or because its plot—involving attempts by established business to suppress cheap and efficient solar power technology—was too weak.

Heinlein's next efforts were the novellas "Elsewhen" (1941) and "Lost Legacy" (1941), which exhibited two of the pitfalls into which writers easily fall when they make up their plots as they go along. In the former, a professor of speculative metaphysics uses hypnosis to displace his students into alternative worlds reflective of their personalities; the idea was subsequently used to far greater effect in Philip K. Dick's *Eye in the Sky* (1957), but Heinlein's version has no dramatic tension or narrative shape. The second novella involves a party of parapsychologists who join the war being waged by the world's secret masters against all "antagonists of human liberty [and] human dignity"; it is disorganized and rudderless as well as featuring occult elements that Campbell would not allow into *Astounding*'s pages.

Frederik Pohl bought "Lost Legacy," which he published as "Lost Legion," and three further Campbell rejects. All of them appeared under the Monroe byline, one of them in collaboration with Elma Wentz, to whom Heinlein had given the story for revision. (He had met Mrs. Wentz while working on *EPIC News*, and presumably offered encouragement to her husband, Roby, who subsequently sold four stories to Campbell. Another *EPIC News* acquaintance, Cleve Cartmill, also joined the Campbell stable in 1941.) Campbell published a revised version of "Elsewhen" as "Elsewhere," although Heinlein insisted that he publish it under the byline Caleb Saunders. Heinlein reverted to his own titles when he condescended to reprint the stories in *Assignment in Eternity* (1953).

The work that cemented Heinlein's relationship with Campbell was another novella, which Campbell retitled "If This Goes On—" (1940). This transformed Heinlein's memories of growing up in the Bible Belt into a vivid cautionary tale of a future America ruled with totalitarian rigor by a Prophet Incarnate. Because it had to wait its turn to be serialized, however, it was preceded into print by "Requiem" (1940), a brief Hemingwayesque tale gushing with understated sentimentality, in which the man whose entrepreneurial efforts first made space travel economically viable evades well-meant efforts to stop him from making a fatal voyage to the moon.

The other three stories that Heinlein published in *Astounding* before the end of 1940 were the novelettes "The Roads Must Roll," "Blowups Happen," and "Coventry," none of which was long enough to lose its clear narrative focus, although each was liberally supplied with the kind of telling detail that Heinlein employed—more cleverly than any previous pulp writer had contrived—to make his near-future scenarios convincing. The first deals with a near-future labor dispute. The second describes social and psychological tensions in and around a nuclear power plant. The third describes life on a reservation to which dissidents from a formal social contract called the Covenant are banished and

Robert A. Heinlein in 1975. PHOTO BY JAY KAY KLEIN

whose inhabitants stubbornly reproduce all the ills and enmities that the new contract has negotiated out of existence. Although the third is a stylized political fantasy of a familiar kind, the first two were markedly different from the common run of pulp science fiction stories. Instead of making their technological innovations—moving roadways and atomic power—central elements of narrative attention, the tales simply took them for granted, focusing instead on the social and psychological corollaries of their integration into the pattern of everyday life. It was this modus operandi that delighted Campbell and his readers, marking a significant progressive step in the evolution of magazine science fiction.

In retrospect, it is obvious that Heinlein's aborted career in politics had far more influence on his early exploits in science fiction than merely leaving debts to be cleared. His thinking about the future was framed and motivated by practical political concerns—and the hypothetical solutions he came up with all lay outside the spectrum of orthodox party politics. Instead, they embraced an innovative

radical pragmatism that was markedly different from the schemes pulp science fiction had inherited from such works as Edward Bellamy's best-selling *Looking Backward 2000–1887* (1887), which blithely skipped over the question of how to get from *here* to *there*. Far more influential than his nuts-and-bolts approach to social design, however, was the tone of voice that Heinlein brought to these narratives, which addressed the reader with a peculiar combination of relaxed informality and inflammatory urgency. It is now easy to see how the rhetoric of his fiction took over where the discussions in which he participated in connection with *EPIC News* and the canvassing he did in pursuit of his own campaign left off.

Heinlein's radical pragmatism and his interest in practical politics are even more blatant in the other Heinlein story that Campbell published in 1940: the fantasy "The Devil Makes the Law" (better known as "Magic, Inc"), which appeared in *Astounding*'s fantasy companion *Unknown*. This is a tale of political dirty tricks and economic chicanery in a world where magic works—and has therefore been subject to patchwork legal restriction and inefficient political licensing. It was, however, the five *Astounding* stories that established Heinlein's reputation within the field and broke the mold of pulp science fiction. Campbell used them as paradigm examples of what he wanted science fiction to become, and that is the purpose they have served ever since in analytical histories of the field.

To facilitate the sprinkling of his stories with telling details, Heinlein linked them together with a common historical background, which he began to map out in some detail. He had borrowed the idea from Sinclair Lewis, recognizing that Lewis' habit of maintaining files on his settings and characters would be particularly useful to him. Science fiction stories are not usually able to take advantage of the brief scene-setting cues used to establish settings in fiction in the known world, but Heinlein knew that *Astounding*'s loyal followers would be able to pick up on details that referred back to tales they had recently read. When Campbell found out about Heinlein's historical chart, he wanted to publish it and proposed that Heinlein should reserve his own name for stories set within the scheme. Heinlein readily agreed, putting the byline Anson MacDonald on *Sixth Column* (1941), which he based on the plot of an unsold novella of Campbell's (which ultimately saw print posthumously as "All").

By the end of 1940, Heinlein had paid off his mortgage, but his relationship with Campbell continued smoothly for a few months longer. Heinlein's 1941 publications de-emphasized the element of political speculation in his work, although his radical pragmatism produced the plots of such casually excessive Anson MacDonald stories as "Solution Unsatisfactory" and "We Also Walk Dogs—." He broadened his imaginative scope considerably, producing playful but remarkable extrapolations of neurotic insecurity in the fantasies "They," "—And He Built a Crooked House," and "By His Bootstraps" and taking his future history beyond the limitations of Earth and on to the much vaster stage hinted at in "Misfit." The Venus-set "Logic of Empire" was rapidly followed by two classic tales of a generation starship, "Universe" and "Common Sense," which bracketed the episodic space odyssey *Methuselah's Children*.

As 1941 came to an end, however, the United States became embroiled in World War II. Heinlein immediately sought recall to duty. Campbell had four stories in hand for 1942 publication: the fantasies "Waldo" and "The Unpleasant Profession of Jonathan Hoag" (to which the byline John Riverside was initially attached), the quasi-Utopian *Beyond This Horizon*, and "Goldfish Bowl" (the revised version of "Creation Took Eight Days," whose initial rejection had caused Heinlein to stand on his dignity). However, none of these stories had the intensity or immediacy of those Heinlein had published in 1940. Even *Beyond This Horizon*, which had been conceived as a "fully mature, adult, dramatic" work, had turned in its execution into

a "hunk of hack" with which the author was profoundly dissatisfied, and he described "By His Bootstraps"—which was widely regarded as *the* classic time-loop story until Heinlein replaced it with "—All You Zombies—" (1959)—as "cotton candy."

It seems probable that even if war had not broken out, Heinlein would probably have given up on pulp fiction. *Astounding*'s readers had liked the gimmick stories and space operas (space adventure stories) of 1941 even better than their predecessors, and some critics were later to proclaim that *Beyond This Horizon* was a masterpiece of pulp science fiction, but Heinlein's letters lamenting its painfully slow progress suggest that he had reached the end of his tether. Although the navy still considered him unfit for active service, he found a position at the Naval Air Experimental Station in Philadelphia, and he threw himself into his work there.

It was in Philadelphia that he met Virginia Gerstenfeld, who was to become his second wife in 1948; she was serving as a Wave. She recalls in her annotations to *Grumbles from the Grave* that she first became involved with Heinlein's work as a writer when she volunteered to rearrange his story files when he had difficulty finding some tear sheets that he needed for a proposed anthology. Although no such anthology appeared, the fact that one was proposed makes it clear that although Heinlein had given up on science fiction, the field had not yet given up on him.

When Heinlein returned to writing after World War II ended, it was to write a tract provisionally titled *How to Be a Politician*, which did not sell. (It eventually appeared posthumously as *Take Back Your Government*, during Ross Perot's presidential campaign of 1992.) When he did begin to write science fiction again, after his divorce in 1947, he approached his work very differently. He ignored Campbell and obtained a literary agent. Although he began to produce work aimed at a variety of different markets, he avoided the pulps, using them only as a market of last resort for stories he could not sell elsewhere.

He began to sell science fiction stories set in the nearer reaches of his old future history to *The Saturday Evening Post*, beginning with "The Green Hills of Earth" (1947)—a story whose overweening sentimentality put "Requiem" in the shade—but he also dabbled in other genres. "They Do It with Mirrors" (1947) appeared in *Popular Detective*, "Poor Daddy" (1949) in *Calling All Girls*, and "Cliff and the Calories" (1950) in *Senior Prom*. It was, however, science fiction that provided his other breakthrough, when he began to write near-future romances for children. Juvenile fiction was the only sector of the market that then offered the possibility of selling science fiction books to mass-market publishers.

Rocket Ship Galileo (1947), the first of the juvenile novels that Heinlein produced annually for Scribners until 1958, also provided a rough basis for the script he wrote for the George Pal film *Destination Moon* (1950), while the second, *Space Cadet* (1948), inspired the pioneering TV show *Tom Corbett—Space Cadet*. Heinlein published his new science fiction in periodicals such as *Argosy*, *Blue Book*, *Town and Country*, *Boys' Life*, and *The American Legion Magazine*, and he tried with all his might to start a career from scratch in arenas that had never sullied their pages with speculative fiction before. (Heinlein was one of the first writers to propose that the pulp-tainted label "science fiction" ought to be replaced on work of merit by the more upmarket label "speculative fiction.")

Heinlein's determination to be rid of the stigma of having been a pulp writer was, however, compromised by the fact that the science fiction community organized around the pulp genre did not want to be rid of him—and was, indeed, intent on celebrating and restoring the heroic status he had briefly attained in 1940 and 1941. John Campbell asked Heinlein, as a favor, to write "Gulf" (1949) in order that he might respond to one of his readers who had sent in a letter of comment review-

ing an imaginary "ideal issue" of the magazine. Heinlein obliged, but he subsequently dumped the direly slapdash novella in *Assignment in Eternity*, along with such despised hackwork as "Elsewhen" and "Lost Legacy."

Some fan critics have considered Heinlein's postwar attitude toward Campbell and the science fiction magazines in general to have been a trifle ungrateful, but it should be emphasized that his attitude to the pulps was commonplace even among pulp writers. Almost as soon as he began publishing in *Astounding*, Heinlein began socializing with other science fiction writers, and he continued to do so with pleasure and enthusiasm. He must have participated in hundreds of conversations lamenting the fact that the genre was stuck in a "pulp ghetto," and he sympathized with the ambitions of everyone who wanted to move into better markets. What distinguished him from many of the friends he made in the science fiction community was not his attitude toward the magazines but the relentlessness with which he stuck to his guns.

What brought Heinlein back into the genre fold, or at least into its margins, were offers to reprint his pulp work in hardcover book form from the specialist small presses that were then being set up in some profusion. That was an opportunity no hard-headed professional could refuse, so *Beyond This Horizon* appeared from Fantasy Press in 1948 and *Sixth Column* from Gnome Press in 1949. When Shasta wanted to reprint the early stories in the Future History series, Heinlein went so far as to write a novella to fill out the first book in the series, which became the title piece of *The Man Who Sold the Moon* (1950).

By this time, commercial publishers were beginning to show the first signs of interest in pulp reprints, and Doubleday stepped in to buy reprint rights to *Waldo and Magic, Inc* (1950). Eagerly accepting the opportunity offered by this new market, Heinlein wrote *The Puppet Masters*, which Doubleday published in 1951 along with an anthology he edited, *Tomorrow, the Stars*. Shasta issued two more volumes of the Future History series before going broke, leaving *Methuselah's Children* to be issued by Gnome Press in 1958 and *Orphans of the Sky* ("Universe and "Common Sense") by the British publisher Gollancz in 1963. The remainder of Heinlein's pulp work was mopped up by Gnome and Fantasy Press, but it was Doubleday, after a pause of some years, that provided a market for two more adult novels, *Double Star* (1956) and *The Door into Summer* (1957).

The science fiction magazines, meanwhile, continued to maintain the claim that Heinlein really belonged to them by making offers that no professional could refuse. Their editors bought the serial rights to the novels he wrote for hardcover publishers. *Galaxy* serialized *The Puppet Masters*, and *The Magazine of Fantasy and Science Fiction* serialized the juvenile *The Star Beast* (1954) (as "Star Lummox") and *The Door into Summer*, while Campbell serialized *Double Star* and *Citizen of the Galaxy* (1957) in *Astounding*. By the mid-1950's, although his hope of doing more work for film and television had been dashed, Heinlein was getting paid twice over for almost everything he wrote (or had previously written) at novel length. One consequence of this was that he virtually stopped writing short fiction. Although a few stories that had fallen through the upper strata of the market ended up in science fiction magazines in 1952 and 1953 and two more appeared in 1957, he rarely deigned to write anything specifically for that market. "—All You Zombies —," a solipsistic conceit combining the themes of "They" and "By His Bootstraps," was an exception.

The tone of the work Heinlein did between 1947 and 1957 is more earnest than that of the last few works he left for publication in 1942, and its use of ideas is more disciplined. There is no trace in it of the reckless indulgence in bizarrerie displayed in "The Unpleasant Profession of Jonathan Hoag," in which a neurotically insecure amnesiac is horrified to be told, after hiring a private detective, that he is in the service of ghouls, or of the calculated absurdity of "Waldo," which blithely juxta-

poses the image of a man who cleverly employs technological devices to compensate for his physical difficulties with "hex doctors" intent on lifting a curse placed on the U.S. power system.

The stories Heinlein did for the slick magazines (so called because they were produced on a better quality of paper than the pulps, by virtue of being supported by advertising rather than sales) are low-key accounts of domestic dramas and unfortunate accidents, mostly set on space stations or in a lunar colony. The early juveniles are studiously didactic in terms of their painstaking Vernian explanations and their careful moralism. Although a little of Heinlein's radical pragmatism crept into *Space Cadet* and *Between Planets* (1951), the early juveniles stick fairly closely to the Boy Scout code and the conventional norms mass-marketed by contemporary television shows. Unlike his pulp novels and novellas, Heinlein's longer works now gave evidence of being planned in advance, although it seems probable that the semblance was sometimes contrived by means of a stratagem popular among hack science fiction writers: transplanting plots from mundane novels into futuristic or alien settings.

The work Heinlein did in the early 1950's was that of a thorough and careful professional, enterprising only in the fact that it tried to make the substance of science fiction sufficiently ordinary to be taken seriously by general readers. There was, however, a progressive element built into the work from the very beginning. *Red Planet* (1949) set a new standard in juvenile science fiction for both technical sophistication and narrative skill, and the novels that followed it became, by slow degrees, more complicated and more demanding. *Between Planets* introduced an element of space opera but set it within a political framework that transcended mere action-adventure. The young readers who became assiduous followers of the series found themselves being drawn farther and farther into realms where other writers of juvenile fiction dared not set foot.

Although many writers from Campbell's stable dabbled in the production of juvenile science fiction in the 1950's, no other American writer produced work that could hold a candle to Heinlein's, and the one Briton who produced work of a similar sophistication, Arthur C. Clarke, interrupted his own production more than once to concentrate on popular nonfiction. *The Rolling Stones* (1952) began life as a *Boy's Life* serial aimed at a younger audience than *Between Planets*, but the full-length version uses the dynamics of the family who provide its protagonists to enliven a robust exploratory tour of the solar system. *Starman Jones* (1953) ventures onto a galactic stage in presenting a taut tale of hard-won maturation. *The Star Beast* deals with alien intelligence in a far more sophisticated way than any juvenile science fiction novel before it and stresses the diplomatic niceties that would inevitably surround problems of interspecific interaction.

The marketing of this work was not unproblematic. *Grumbles from the Grave* reveals that Heinlein often reacted angrily to criticism from Scribners editor Alice Dalgleish, who found uncomfortable (but unconvincing) Freudian undercurrents in *Red Planet* and *The Rolling Stones*. Oddly enough, it was *The Star Beast*—a novel that Miss Dalgleish had approved unreservedly—that soured the relationship permanently. When she would not defend the book against the rather puerile criticisms made in an aggressively negative review in *Library Journal*, Heinlein thought that she had betrayed him and seems to have considered his subsequent working relationship with her an implicitly adversarial one. Typically, however, his response was not to damp down his progressive ambitions but to press forward more determinedly, ready to fight any points of contention that might emerge.

Tunnel in the Sky (1955) is deliberately contentious in several ways, and its account of the struggle for survival experienced by a party of schoolchildren accidentally stranded on an alien world includes a strong dose of radical pragmatism. *Time for the Stars* (1956),

which cleverly develops Einstein's twin paradox, was not as calculatively provocative, but *Citizen of the Galaxy* (1957), which adapted Rudyard Kipling's *Kim* (1901) to a space opera format, contains a great deal of fervent political advocacy. It is, however, a very fine book, which took full advantage of the scope that juvenile fiction offered for thoughtful didacticism, of which the action-orientated magazines were still rather wary.

The first novel of this period that Heinlein had written for adults, *The Puppet Masters*, was just as different from his pulp novels as his juveniles were. It is a taut thriller, closely in tune with contemporary products of the other genre that was then emerging from the pulp ghetto to win a measure of respectability: "hard-boiled" mystery and suspense. It anticipated in its manner and its subtext the classic science fiction film *Invasion of the Body-Snatchers* (1956), which was based on a 1955 novel by another writer who managed to import science fiction themes into the slick magazines, Jack Finney. It is not improbable that Finney's book took some inspiration from Heinlein's, and if—as seems likely—Heinlein had had one eye on the movie market while writing his own book, he must have felt that Don Siegel's film had stolen his thunder. It is significant, however, that when he wrote another adult novel after a gap of some years, he employed a method that had been used by other genre writers, most notably Alfred Bester, who was then regarded as one of the field's brightest stars and was trying hard to follow Heinlein into more rewarding pastures.

Double Star is the best of several science fiction adaptations of the plot of Anthony Hope's definitive Ruritanian romance *The Prisoner of Zenda* (1894), but unlike Edmond Hamilton's slavishly imitative space opera *The Star Kings* (1947), it is a calculated modernization. Heinlein's version of the plot substitutes a diplomat for the kidnapped king and a shabby actor for the noble masquerader; the prize at stake is not a throne but the privilege of establishing and maintaining a mutually beneficial relationship between humans and

Martians. The novel won Heinlein a Hugo award in 1956, the first of his four Hugo awards.

The plot of *The Door into Summer* may also be based on a classic romance that had previously seen science fiction adaptation, but if it really is a version of Alexandre Dumas' *The Count of Monte Cristo*, it cannot stand comparison with Bester's *The Stars My Destination* (1956), and whatever its origins it is far more slapdash in execution than its predecessor. Its disappointed hero's voluntary sojourn in suspended animation is no substitute for Edmond Dantes' unjust imprisonment in the Chateau d'If, and the complications that subsequently modify his "revenge" on the ex-partner who stole his girl leach all the narrative resilience from the story line.

The politicking in *Citizen of the Galaxy* caused less trouble than it might have because Alice Dalgleish immediately recognized its quality. She also seems to have liked *Have Space Suit—Will Travel* (1958), although the ludicrously bombastic conclusion of the trial to which its young hero and heroine must submit, Everyman-style, on behalf of all humankind, ought perhaps to have sounded alarm bells. By this time, however, Heinlein seems to have considered himself to be at war with her, and *Starship Troopers* (1959) might be seen as a deliberate mobilization of his forces, intended to test her tolerance to destruction, which it did. Heinlein probably would not have felt able to do that if he had not opened up a second front with his novels for Doubleday, but he seems to have formed the impression that he was too valuable a commodity for Scribners simply to dispose of him, and he may have expected to be granted immunity from Miss Dalgleish's further demands. Instead, he was simply shown the door.

Starship Troopers remains an extraordinarily controversial book, whose ability to generate strong feelings was reignited by Paul Verhoeven's 1997 film version. Thomas M. Disch wrote a scathing quasi-psychoanalytic account of its supposed sublimation of homoerotic urges, characterizing its hero as a "swaggering leather boy" whose invariable response to sexual arousal is to get into a fight, but Samuel R. Delany called attention to the epiphanic potential of the moment when—no prior clue having been provided—the hero casually mentions that the face he is observing in a mirror is black.

Although the book's plot is essentially a science fiction version of Leon Uris' *Battle Cry* (1953), the relatively small modifications to the pattern of the original made in the interests of shifting it into a future context and onto an interstellar stage caused outrage in some quarters. Its account of the training of its starship soldiers has frequently been accused of glorifying war, and its attitude to their insectile opponents—particularly the assumption that no possible resolution to the conflict of such biologically different species is imaginable save the extermination of one by the other—is frequently held up as a key example of neurotic xenophobia. Joe Haldeman's *The Forever War* (1974) is a calculated ideological reply to *Starship Troopers* that carefully disputes the last point, and more than one commentator has thought it a telling point that whereas Heinlein, deeply frustrated by his own unfitness for active service, was forced to sit out World War II, Haldeman actually encountered the nastiest aspects of modern warfare in Vietnam.

Oddly enough, the relatively mild suggestion that some kind of national service might be required of future Americans as a condition of citizenship, which would not have caused a raised eyebrow anywhere in Europe, was construed by many domestic readers of *Starship Troopers* as monstrous. (Heinlein's proposition that people who did not wish to do national service might be exempted provided that they gave up their voting privileges is actually far more liberal than the compulsory systems actually in force in the majority of nations.)

Starship Troopers won Heinlein his second Hugo in 1960, but that could not cancel out the pain of its rejection by Scribners, which he took as badly as he took all rejection. When he eventually decided to write one more juvenile for Putnam's, the publisher who had taken over *Starship Troopers*, he was determined to violate the last and most sacred taboo of juvenile fiction and actually titled the text *Podkayne Fries*. When the publisher refused to let him get way with it, however, he consented to let his heroine live, and the book actually appeared as *Podkayne of Mars* (1963).

Following the success of *Starship Troopers*, in spite of the doubts entertained by Alice Dalgleish—and, for that matter, John Campbell, who rejected the serial version—Heinlein evidently decided that if the market's gatekeepers did not appreciate his attempts to broaden its horizons, then he would henceforth refuse to tolerate their preferences and would write exactly what he liked in whatever way he chose.

The first and most spectacular product of this new resolve was *Stranger in a Strange Land* (1961), a mammoth guide to Heinlein's elaborately revamped but still radically pragmatic ideas on politics, law, religion, psychology, and pretty much everything else, compounded out of sarcastically hectoring dialogues, sneeringly heated diatribes, and stagily melodramatic but widely separated action sequences. To get it published, he had to compromise and prune it from well over 200,000 words to 160,000, but its subsequent success seemed to him, and to his publishers, to be a triumphant vindication of his new attitude. The fact that it won yet another Hugo (in 1962) presumably seemed trivial by comparison with the success it eventually had in finding a much wider audience than any previous genre product except Ray Bradbury's *The Martian Chronicles* (1950), whose fame had taken even longer to accumulate. From the moment the true scale of his success became clear, however, Heinlein produced nothing but big bad-tempered books in an openly combative style that was equally redolent with overbearing vanity and neurotic anxiety. Those books grew crankier as he grew older and more set in his ways, although they never lost the torrential lucidity with which long years of practice had by now gifted him.

Stranger in a Strange Land proved just as controversial as *Starship Troopers*, and with far better reason. The most notorious charge aimed against it is, however, was based on a lie. It is not true that Charles Manson based the philosophy of his murderous cult on the book's description of the new religion based by Michael Valentine Smith on the worldview of his Martian educators. Other would-be commune-dwellers did try to practice "grokking" for real, but Virginia Heinlein is careful to reproduce in *Grumbles from the Grave* a long letter the author wrote to a fan from one such group; the letter which stresses that although the book is a parable in fictional form, it was written first to earn money, second to entertain, and only third to make people think. "I was asking questions," the author declares, firmly. "I was *not* giving answers." (The letter goes on to say that the book on which Heinlein was working at the time, *I Will Fear No Evil* (1970), "is even more loaded with serious, unanswered questions.")

It is not entirely surprising, given the extent to which the worldly-wise lawyer Jubal Harshaw lectures the protagonists of *Stranger in a Strange Land* and the manner of their response, that many readers either felt crushed by the weight of his persuasion or resentful of his assertiveness. However, Michael Valentine Smith, the messiah from Mars, is a much more ambiguous character, and the principal narrator is much more ambivalent about him. When the head of steam that Heinlein had built up before starting the novel eventually runs out—and it does not begin to fade until after halfway—it is not merely the story line that begins to ramble, having lost its bearings. The plot does indeed raise far more questions than it answers, and it even begins to question many of the answers that had earlier seemed to be established with all apparent conviction.

One of the problems with Heinlein's subsequent novels is that they return again and again to the problems that he set center stage in *Stranger in a Strange Land*, hammering out the same answers with the same aggressive certainty without ever mustering sufficient *real* conviction to consider them settled.

However determined Heinlein became to fear no evil, it seems that he could not escape the worst evil imaginable—not so much the thought that his ideas might be rejected, but that they might deserve it.

For the last twenty-five years of his life, Heinlein was famous as the man who had first remade science fiction, then led the way out of the pulp ghetto along a hard road that few could follow. His old work remained in print alongside the new, explaining and sustaining that reputation even as his new books—which inevitably sold much faster than their predecessors, even if they failed to find as many readers in total—began to spark violent antagonism in many of their readers. Toward the end, the awfulness of some of his work severely tested the loyalty even of his most die-hard fans, but he was by then an institution of worship, criticism of whom was widely regarded as a kind of heresy.

Heinlein followed *Stranger in a Strange Land* with a fantasy novel as self-indulgent as anything he had written since "Waldo," *Glory Road* (1963). Then came the "survivalist" novel *Farnham's Freehold* (1964), which is in essence a science fiction version of *The Swiss Family Robinson*. Both novels exhibit the same frankness with regard to sex and the politics of sexual attraction as their predecessor, nauseating feminists and bravely exposing idiosyncrasies that might well have led Alice Dalgleish, if she ever read them, to congratulate herself on her acuity in spotting suspect hidden meanings in his early juveniles.

The Moon Is a Harsh Mistress (1966) was regarded by die-hard science fiction fans as a return to top form, and it won a fourth Hugo (in 1967), perhaps as much for its depiction of a fledgling artificial intelligence as for its ringing account of lunar secession from Earthly tyranny. The political campaign featured in the novel is more realistic than the religious revival in *Stranger in a Strange Land* and obviously engaged its author far more enthusiastically. Tom Perry suggests that Heinlein may have lost that fateful primary not because of the elements of Sinclair's platform

that he adopted but because of the one he disowned: a giveaway policy borrowed from the Social Credit Movement that was pushed in California by means of the slogan "Ham and Eggs" because it provided a nicer sound bite than the official "Thirty Dollars Every Thursday." If so, the fact that the lunar revolution marches to victory under the banner TANSTAAFL (There Ain't No Such Thing as a Free Lunch) becomes doubly significant.

Alas, having won his election at last, if only vicariously, Heinlein had nothing left to do but repeat himself and try with increasing violence to kill the doubts that he simply could not shake off. The posthumous fantasy *I Will Fear No Evil* (1970), in which the mind of a crotchety old man becomes a co-tenant of the brain of a young female, is a dreadful book. Its plot is preposterous, its narrative style horribly clotted, and its philosophical pretensions silly. The various sections of the mosaic novel *Time Enough for Love* (1973), which take up the threads of *Methuselah's Children* in presenting an episodic bildungsroman of immortal existence, are much sturdier in manner and thought, but the book remains an exercise in wish fulfillment by a man embarked upon a uniquely pernicious invasion of his own privacy. *The Number of the Beast* (1980) is in the same dire vein but lacks the redeeming virtue of any kind of sturdiness and concludes with a long and embarrassing essay in absurd self-congratulation.

Heinlein did try to return to the production of solid professional fiction and made a fair stab at it in the hectic space opera *Friday* (1982). He also tried to do something decisively new in the comic religious fantasy *Job: A Comedy of Justice* (1984), which might have seemed a little less crude had its title not demanded comparison with the work of James Branch Cabell. *The Cat Who Walked Through Walls* attempts to be a robust action-adventure novel with occasional lectures but keeps slipping sideways into grotesque idiosyncrasy, and the volume that continued the story it began, *To Sail Beyond the Sunset: The Lives and Loves of Maureen Johnson (Being the Memoirs of a Somewhat Irregular Lady)*

(1987), could only achieve a measure of narrative fervor by returning to the method as well as the core subject matter of *Time Enough for Love.*

Heinlein's most steadfast supporters continued to defend the books he wrote between 1970 and 1980, citing with pride the fact that no one had ever done anything remotely like them before. Many of the critics who wanted to give Heinlein due credit for the awesome achievements of his early *Astounding* stories and the worthy ambitions of his work in the 1950's, feared on the other hand that the glaring example of his worst work might render laughable any claim that they might make about the incisiveness of his intellect, the power of his imagination, or the effectiveness of his literary style. The fact remains, however, that the man who wrote "Blowups Happen," "The Roads Must Roll," *Double Star,* and *Citizen of the Galaxy* was not only responsible for *Starship Troopers* and *Stranger in a Strange Land* as well but also wrote *I Will Fear No Evil* and *The Number of the Beast*— and had he been any less remarkable than he was, he probably would not have been able to write any of them.

According to the testimony of all extant evidence, including that which he provided himself, Heinlein was always a man of contrasts and a man of extremes. He could be stridently aggressive but was also capable of acts of extraordinary generosity. He was famed for his fierce loyalty to his friends but was perfectly capable of abruptly and rudely removing people from that category (as he did with Arthur C. Clarke in the course of a public altercation provoked by Clarke's skepticism about the merits of Ronald Reagan's Strategic Defense Initiative). It was probably the strength of his desire to be loved and admired that made his writings occasionally seem hateful and the strength of his desire to avoid error that made his writings occasionally seem ridiculous. He really did do a great many things, as a writer, that nobody else had ever done before. Doubts as to whether some of them were worth doing should not obscure the fact that, from the viewpoint of *any* lover of speculative fiction, more than a few of them undoubtedly were.

Selected Bibliography

WORKS OF ROBERT A. HEINLEIN

Rocket Ship Galileo. New York: Charles Scribner's Sons, 1947.

Beyond This Horizon. Reading, Pa.: Fantasy Press, 1948. London: Panther Books, 1967. (Revised from a serial in *Astounding,* 1942, published under the name Anson MacDonald.)

Space Cadet. New York: Charles Scribner's Sons, 1948. London: Victor Gollancz, 1966.

Red Planet. New York: Charles Scribner's Sons, 1949. London: Victor Gollancz, 1963.

Sixth Column. New York: Gnome Press, 1949. Reissued as *The Day After Tomorrow.* New York: Signet Books, 1951. London: Mayflower Books, 1962. (Serialized in *Astounding,* 1941, under the name Anson MacDonald.)

Farmer in the Sky. New York: Charles Scribner's Sons, 1950. London: Pan Books, 1962.

The Man Who Sold the Moon. Chicago: Shasta, 1950. Reissued. New York: Signet Books, 1951. London: Sidgwick and Jackson, 1953. (The 1950 version collects six Future History stories; the Signet edition, only four.)

Waldo and Magic, Inc. Garden City, N.Y.: Doubleday, 1950. Reissued as *Waldo: Genius in Orbit.* New York: Avon Books, 1958. London: Pan Books, 1969. (Collects "Waldo," which first appeared in *Astounding,* 1942, under the name Anson MacDonald, and "Magic, Inc.," originally titled "The Devil Makes the Law" in *Unknown,* 1940)

Between Planets. New York: Charles Scribner's Sons, 1951. London: Victor Gollancz, 1968.

The Green Hills of Earth. Chicago: Shasta, 1951. London: Sidgwick and Jackson, 1954. (Collects ten Future History stories.)

The Puppet Masters. Garden City, N.Y.: Doubleday, 1951. London: Museum Press, 1953.

Universe. New York: Dell, 1951. (Contains the novella "Universe," part of the Future History series, originally published in *Astounding,* 1941.)

The Rolling Stones. New York: Charles Scribner's Sons, 1952. Reissued as *Space Family Stone.* London: Victor Gollancz, 1969.

Assignment in Eternity. Reading, Pa.: Fantasy Press, 1953. London: Museum Press, 1955. (Collects four stories; the first British paperback edition—London:

Digit Books, 1960—was split into two volumes of two stories each: *Assignment in Eternity* and *Lost Legacy*.)

Revolt in 2100. Chicago: Shasta, 1953. London: Digit Books, 1959. (Collects three Future History stories; the main novella, " 'If This Goes On—,' " is extensively revised from its original form in *Astounding*, 1940.)

Starman Jones. New York: Charles Scribner's Sons, 1953. London: Sidgwick and Jackson, 1954.

The Star Beast. New York: Charles Scribner's Sons, 1954. London: New English Library, 1971.

Tunnel in the Sky. New York: Charles Scribner's Sons, 1955. London: Victor Gollancz, 1965.

Double Star. Garden City, N.Y.: Doubleday, 1956. London: Michael Joseph, 1958.

Time for the Stars. New York: Charles Scribner's Sons, 1956. London: Victor Gollancz, 1963.

Citizen of the Galaxy. New York: Charles Scribner's Sons, 1957. London: Victor Gollancz, 1969.

The Door into Summer. Garden City, N.Y.: Doubleday, 1957. London: Panther Books, 1960.

Have Space Suit—Will Travel. New York: Charles Scribner's Sons, 1958. London: Victor Gollancz, 1970.

Methuselah's Children. Hicksville, N.Y.: Gnome Press, 1958. London: Victor Gollancz, 1963. (Novel in Future History series; first published in *Astounding*, 1941, and revised here.)

The Menace from Earth. Hicksville, N.Y.: Gnome Press, 1959. London: Dennis Dobson, 1966. (Collects eight stories.)

Starship Troopers. New York: G. P. Putnam's Sons, 1959. London: Four Square Books, 1961.

The Unpleasant Profession of Jonathan Hoag. Hicksville, N.Y.: Gnome Press, 1959. Reissued as *6 x H.* New York: Pyramid Books, 1961. London: Dennis Dobson, 1964. (Collects six stories.)

Stranger in a Strange Land. New York: G. P. Putnam's Sons, 1961. London: Four Square Books, 1965.

[*Stranger in a Strange Land*] Restored text, New York: G. P. Putnam's Sons, 1990.

Glory Road. New York: G. P. Putnam's Sons, 1963. London: Four Square Books, 1965.

Orphans of the Sky. London: Victor Gollancz, 1963. New York: G. P. Putnam's Sons, 1964. (A quasi novel containing the novella "Universe" and its immediate sequel "Common Sense," which were first published in *Astounding*, 1941.)

Podkayne of Mars. New York: G. P. Putnam's Sons, 1963. London: New English Library, 1969.

Farnham's Freehold. New York: G. P. Putnam's Sons, 1964. London: Dennis Dobson, 1965.

The Moon Is a Harsh Mistress. New York: G. P. Putnam's Sons, 1966. London: Dennis Dobson, 1967.

The Worlds of Robert A. Heinlein. New York: Ace Books, 1966. London: New English Library, 1970. (Collects

five stories, two of which had appeared in previous collections.)

The Past Through Tomorrow. New York: G. P. Putnam's Sons, 1967. (Collects most of the Future History series, reprinting *The Man Who Sold the Moon, The Green Hills of Earth, Revolt in 2100,* and *Methuselah's Children,* omitting "Let There Be Light," and adding "Searchlight" and "The Menace from Earth"; British edition, 2 volumes, London: New English Library, 1977, also drops *Methuselah's Children.*)

I Will Fear No Evil. New York: G. P. Putnam's Sons, 1970. London: New English Library, 1971.

Time Enough for Love. New York: G. P. Putnam's Sons, 1973. London: New English Library, 1974.

Expanded Universe: More Worlds of Robert A. Heinlein. New York: Ace Books, 1980. (Collects twelve stories—including the seven not previously collected, mostly nonscience fiction—and fifteen nonfiction pieces.)

'The Number of the Beast.' London: New English Library, 1980. (The American edition, New York: Fawcett, 1980, is abridged.)

Friday. New York: Holt, Rinehart and Winston, 1982; London: New English Library, 1982.

Job: A Comedy of Justice. New York: Ballantine, 1984; London: New English Library, 1984.

To Sail Beyond the Sunset: The Lives and Loves of Maureen Johnson (Being the Memoirs of a Somewhat Irregular Lady). New York: G. P. Putnam's Sons, 1987; London: Joseph, 1987.

Grumbles from the Grave. Edited by Virginia Heinlein. New York: Ballantine, 1989; London: Orbit: 1991. (Selected correspondence.)

Requiem: New Collected Works by Robert A. Heinlein and Tributes to the Grand Master. Edited by Yoji Kondo. New York: TOR, 1992.

CRITICAL AND BIOGRAPHICAL STUDIES

Aldiss, Brian W. *Billion Year Spree: The True History of Science Fiction.* Garden City, N.Y.: Doubleday, 1973. (See especially pages 269–274.)

Franklin, H. Bruce. *Robert A. Heinlein: America as Science Fiction.* New York: Oxford University Press, 1980. (By far the best full-length study; my own assessment of Heinlein's most important themes runs parallel to Franklin's at some points, and I quote several of the same passages. Unlike myself, Franklin is an academic Marxist.)

Heinlein, Robert A. "On the Writing of Speculative Fiction." In *Of Worlds Beyond,* edited by Lloyd Arthur Eshbach. Reading, Pa.: Fantasy Press, 1947.

———. "Science Fiction: Its Nature, Faults and Virtues." In *The Science Fiction Novel: Imagination and Social Criticism.* Chicago: Advent, 1959.

Olander, Joseph D., and Martin Harry Greenberg, eds. *Robert A. Heinlein*. New York, Taplinger, 1977. (Collects nine critical essays on Heinlein, several of them important.)

Panshin, Alexei. *Heinlein in Dimension*. Chicago: Advent, 1968. (First full-length study of Heinlein.)

———, and Cory Panshin. *Science Fiction in Dimension*. Chicago: Advent, 1976. (Part III is entitled "Heinlein Reread.")

Perry, Thomas. "Ham and Eggs and Heinlein" *Monad* 3 (September 1993): 91–128.

Slusser, George Edgar. *Robert A. Heinlein: Stranger in His Own Land*. San Bernardino, Calif.: Borgo Press, 1976; revised 1977.

———. *The Classic Years of Robert A. Heinlein*. San Bernardino, Calif.: Borgo Press, 1977.

—BRIAN STABLEFORD

FRANK HERBERT
(1920–1986)

RARELY IS IT the task of any writer to create entire worlds. So memorable are many such great creations, though, that they linger in the reader's mind for years, and the collective imagination follows their lure, peopling them with characters, situations, and events that seem far more real than any encountered in the mundane, workaday world we all inhabit. These memories recur again and again, so that J. R. R. Tolkien's Middle Earth, Ray Bradbury's Mars, and Austin Wright's Islandia transcend the limits of the printed page and emerge into a reality far more cogent, far more evocative than our own.

Such a creator of worlds was Frank Herbert. His six books set on or derived from the desert planet Arrakis, also known as Dune, not only made him famous—and justly so—but also made his creation a vivid, living entity that ranks with any fictional world of the past. Millions of copies of Herbert's *Dune* Chronicles are in print in English alone, and the works have been translated into many languages, with a consequent worldwide popularity.

While *Dune*, the first novel in the series, was published in book form in 1965, Herbert had achieved distinction as a writer of science fiction a decade earlier with his first novel, *The Dragon in the Sea*, published in John W. Campbell, Jr.'s *Astounding Science-Fiction* as *Under Pressure* (1956). While first novels are often scorned by critics who relegate them to the category of the great unread, dismissing them with words like "promising" or even "interesting," Herbert's first book gave notice to the science fiction world that here was a new writer whose initial novel promised a fine career. Yet *Dragon in the Sea* is not merely a hint of what Herbert would later produce in such marvelous books as *The Santaroga Barrier* and the *Dune* Chronicles. *Dragon in the Sea* is a serious novel, a mature work in which psychological insights, character development, fast-paced action, controlled dialogue, and depth of ideas are fully developed. Its appearance was almost a science fiction phenomenon. Rarely had any other writer produced a first novel of such consequence.

Yet Herbert was no spontaneously arisen writing accident. Long a full-time journalist, he had learned the concision of expression demanded by his journalistic career. The ability to sketch ideas, characters, and plots in straightforward, eminently readable prose served his fiction writing well. Moreover, Herbert's almost omnivorous curiosity, nourished by years of developing the background for good newspaper stories or feature articles, found a natural outlet in his fiction. He was never content merely to investigate the surface appearance of any story, whether real or fictional. Thus he became—or, rather, taught himself to be—a professional photographer, a student of comparative religions, a wine expert, a deep-sea diver, a flyer, and a lay Jungian analyst, to name only a few of his serious pursuits. Herbert was an ecologist, for example, long before ecology became fashionable and long before his ecological concepts found full fruition in the *Dune* sequence. When he came to write his first novel, he brought to the task a penetrating mind, an insatiable curiosity, and an ability to handle the English language that had been honed by years of experience as a journalist. Born in 1920, Herbert was over thirty when *Dragon in the Sea* (the title that he preferred, although most editions have used the title *Under Pressure*) was written. Thus, what seemed at the time to be merely surprising—a good book—should, in retrospect, have seemed almost inevitable.

Herbert's roots reached deep into the Pacific Northwest. He was born, raised, and educated in the Seattle-Tacoma area. His family had lived there for several generations, and Herbert, after leaving his position as a newspaperman in the San Francisco Bay region to become a free-lance writer, built a spacious home on several wooded acres near Port Washington on the Olympic Peninsula. He served in the United States Navy during World War II and attended the University of Washington on the GI Bill. He took a bit of pride in the fact that, ironically, although he was three credit hours short of graduation, he has since taught at the university. Herbert wrote Sunday feature articles for newspapers, ghost-wrote speeches for politicians whose names he preferred to keep to himself, and turned out science fiction stories for *Astounding* or *Galaxy*. His interest in the English language as an instrument to convey ideas, move people to action, or, quite simply, as a congenial but difficult way to make a living was an almost lifelong pursuit.

What strikes the reader who approaches *Dragon in the Sea* for the first time, so long after its writing, is its contemporaneity. It reads as if it had been written in response to more recent pressures on worldwide oil production and consumption. Its problems are current ones. Its ecological sense is certain, and its psychological insights into the problems faced by men at war are as real as those provided by the most cogent journalistic accounts of Vietnam prisoners of war. Indeed, one of Herbert's most unusual characteristics was to anticipate, perhaps even to prophesy, in many of his novels the movements, attitudes, and even the actual circumstances of

events that would not occur until a decade or so after a particular book was published. Such is certainly the case with *Dragon in the Sea*, and many contemporary readers must wonder if Herbert in 1956 had the kind of prescient vision he later ascribes to Paul Atreides in *Dune*.

Dragon in the Sea is the story of America—indeed, of the world—in the twenty-first century, when oil has become the most precious of commodities. The world is at war, and America has been secretly pirating petroleum from undersea wells on the shores of Novaya Zemlya (two Russian islands in the Arctic), under the very nose of what Herbert simply calls Enemy Powers, or EPs. The instrument used is a "subtug," a four-person submarine capable of submerging to great depths while towing a giant "slug" that contains thousands of barrels of pirated oil. Twenty subs have been lost to the EPs in similar missions. Ensign John Ramsey, a psychologist and communications expert, is assigned to the subtug *Fenian Ram*. Naval intelligence experts feel that the *Ram* has a good chance of success, but they also have some evidence that the crew includes a spy—an EP "sleeper"—who plans to sabotage the mission. Ramsey's assignment is to blend in with the other crew members, conceal his real identity, determine which of the crew is the spy, and ensure the success of the mission.

Herbert early signaled his ability to create situations in which the nature of his characters is exemplified by how they respond to action or conflict. This early novel is drenched with action, and each of the four major characters responds to stimuli in a way that reveals his essential nature. Ramsey realizes that, in one sense, he himself is the spy aboard the *Ram*. After all, it is his mission, as a security officer, to find out which of the crew members is the enemy spy, and to make sure that the spy cannot act to destroy the ship and thus thwart its mission. He undergoes several personal crises that might be called "rites of passage" until he, too, becomes a true part of the single entity formed by the ship and crew. After a series of harrowing events, the *Ram* returns successfully. Ramsey, as security officer, has uncovered the spy, but at the same time has come to the realization that the concept of "security"—security of any kind, be it military, psychological, or personal—is debilitating and has, in effect, caused the problems faced by the subtugs and, in turn, by the world as a whole.

With this approach Herbert suggests many of the important themes that crowd the pages of his later novels, particularly those in the *Dune* cycle. Just as, in *Dragon in the Sea*, security becomes a misnomer—there can be no security, however defined, in a world wracked with war, suspicion, and hatred—the concept of prescience and its unknown potential terrifies Paul Atreides in all of the *Dune* novels. Herbert seems to suggest that a built-in punishment will result from any ideological concept or approach when it is carried too far.

Yet for all the success of his first novel, Herbert remained a writer whose acknowledged talents did not place him among the galaxy of science fiction greats until the publication of the first part of the *Dune* cycle in the mid-1960's. He toiled through the decade as a provocative professional whose short stories marked him as a "comer." Yet a close reading of many of these stories reveals that Herbert was continually concerned with the shortsightedness of exclusively linear thinking. We shape our interpretations of our problems to fit existing expertise, he maintained, rather than seek alternative answers that often demand new ways of thinking or even entire new approaches to reality. Such is the case in *Dragon in the Sea*, where the need for "security" demands certain apparently obvious solutions. But only when the concepts that underlie the notion of security are upset by the terrifying problems faced by Ramsey and the crew of the subtug is there a genuine breaking away from its debilitating effects.

In the decade between *Dragon in the Sea* and *Dune*, Herbert published no novels. In fact, it comes as a surprise to most science fiction readers to learn that *Dune* was Herbert's second novel, and that the books often viewed as coming before the Arrakeen epic,

such as *The Green Brain* (1966), *The Eyes of Heisenberg* (1966), and *The Santaroga Barrier* (1968), actually followed *Dune*. This problem may stem from the fact that *Dune* was quite obviously a considered, major opus, and that some of the others gave the impression of being extended short stories. However invidious this kind of comparison may be, after *Dune* it became impossible to consider any of Herbert's later writings except in comparison with this masterwork. Such a situation was unfortunate, of course, because readers kept saying, in effect, "This new book is not another *Dune*."

In many of Herbert's novels, including those written both before and after *Dune*, the hero is faced with a problem that seems insoluble, particularly if he follows accepted patterns of thinking. But when he faces the ultimate problem of survival, his instincts and intuitive powers conquer his linear thinking habits, and he survives. Few of these middle-period novels reach the heights attained with the first two works; when they are read with a retrospective eye on *Dragon in the Sea* and *Dune*, it becomes at once apparent that Herbert, in his novelistic way, is trying to force his readers to abandon the tired and untrue methods that have led them into this mess.

To be sure, *The Santaroga Barrier* followed *Dune* by several years, but the problems faced in both works are analogous. *The Santaroga Barrier* is the story of Gilbert Dasein, a consulting psychologist who attempts to solve the riddle posed by the utopian community of Santaroga. Completely isolated, it guards a terrible, strange secret. Dasein is the outsider in this community, facing bewilderment coupled with ambiguity, as he attempts to unravel the mystery it poses. The thoughtful reader will associate two things with Dasein's name almost immediately. Its approximate German equivalent is "being" or "existence," but it also alludes to A. E. van Vogt's Gilbert Gosseyn, the superman-hero of *The World of Ā* (1948). Yet as Dasein searches for the meaning of the community and its sole product, a cheese called "jaspers," he gradually loses

Frank Herbert. Courtesy of Library of Congress

more and more contact with his reality outside the community, a reality in which he was a successful practicing psychologist. His internal conflict—he is in love with a resident of the community, the beautiful Jenny Sorge ("Sorge" is German for "worry" or "grief"), and wishes to stay with her, or perhaps convince her to live in the outside world—constitutes the major portion of the novel.

The Santaroga Barrier is thus another of the "questioning" novels that Herbert often produced. Not only are the assumptions of the community itself questioned, but also the assumptions of the "reality" in which Dasein has been living for decades. Moreover, Herbert suggests that some of the answers posed by the American counterculture in the decade in which the book was written may also be faulty. Certainly one meaning of "jaspers," the ubiquitous cheese of Santaroga, may be LSD, just as another may be the philosophy of Karl Jaspers—the German philosopher whose concerns with the limitations of scientific

thinking and the consequent effects of such thinking on the integrity of the individual seem to guide many of the discussions that Dasein has with the Santarogans. The Santarogan who speaks most frequently with Dasein is Dr. Lawrence Piaget; and just as surely, this latter name is also significant.

Much of the novel consists of extensive philosophical disquisitions, accompanied by long passages of internal dialogue. The book thus lacks much of the action that typifies so many of Herbert's other works—indeed, the characters may be nothing but "talking heads" on occasion, but the talk is stimulating and provocative. Herbert, through Dasein, indicates many of the drawbacks of this ambiguous utopia, and the tragedy of the book may consist of Dasein's gradual coming to an awareness that he will lose his selfhood if he remains there as a permanent resident. "It'll be a beautiful life," Dasein thinks at the end of the novel—a brilliant but horrifying descent into the collective consciousness of Santaroga, with a concomitant loss of individuality, freedom, and personal responsibility.

As observed earlier, *The Santaroga Barrier* followed *Dune* by only a few years, almost as if Herbert had not asked enough questions in the epic of Arrakis and Paul Atreides, and had to approach them once again in a more nearly contemporary setting. To be sure, many of the problems in *Dune* were of both contemporary and psychological significance, but they were a step removed for many readers by the enormous canvas Herbert utilized in creating the *Dune* mythos. *The Santaroga Barrier* was in many ways another restatement of those questions but made with an immediacy or relevance to contemporary life that many readers did not perceive in *Dune*.

Dune, then, established Herbert as a giant in the science fiction field. It made him somewhat of a prophet because of its wise ecological insights, and it was one of the first science fiction books to sell millions of copies. In fact, Herbert soon became a very popular and charismatic figure on the college lecture circuit, and the book made him a small fortune as well. It may, indeed, be one of the very best science fiction novels yet produced, for it is superior in almost every way. It is, to be sure, on one level simply a rattling good story, with plots and counterplots, incidents and characters, actions and philosophical disquisitions all cascading out of Herbert's fertile imagination.

Yet so rich were this book and the five other *Dune* novels that followed it that any simple analysis would inevitably be simplistic. The *Dune* series may be classified as science fiction's true epic; it can also be construed as a thinly veiled allegory of our world's insatiable appetite for oil and other petroleum products. (After all, Arrakis can be read as "Iraq," "melange" may be a metaphor for oil, and so on.) *Dune* can be understood as a parable of the concept that absolute power corrupts absolutely—not only those who use it but also those it is used upon. Moreover, *Dune* can be read as an elaboration of the thesis, applicable to ecology and many other areas, that one can never completely predict the results of any action, no matter how significant or insignificant. In addition, *Dune* can be read as a series of answers to the questions What is a human being? and When is any being truly human? Is Baron Harkonnen, the epitome of evil, truly human? Is Leto II, in his transmogrification as an eighteen-foot sandworm with a human face, truly human? Is Duncan Idaho, as the ghola, human? Is Duncan in one of his many incarnations in *God Emperor of Dune* human? What is it to be human? Herbert asks these questions again and again, as if he were personally seeking the answers.

Moreover, the theological implications of the series cannot be overlooked. One of the major aspects of *Dune* is the story of the transformation of young Paul Atreides, a fifteen-year-old at the start of the series, into the hero-savior of Arrakis. The second novel, *Dune Messiah* (1969), rather than telling the space opera story of the Fremen Jihad raging through the universe of the Imperium, is instead an intricately woven, complex story about the methods utilized by various groups to foil Emperor Paul, who is now almost universally worshiped. It is also the story of

Paul's renunciation of his godhead. And *Children of Dune* (1976) culminates in the brilliant union of God and man—Shai-Hulud, Old Father Eternity, creator of the melange of life, with Leto, Paul's son. "Man becomes god becomes man becomes god," the sequence might read, and the incarnation of Leto at the end of the novel is both moving and disturbing.

A third theme that informs all of the *Dune* novels, including *God Emperor of Dune* (1981), is the problem of humanity's inability to predict all the results of any change. Thus, when Liet-Kynes sets the ecological transformation in motion, a process that is greatly hurried by Paul's redemption of the planet, no one can foresee that the reintroduction of moisture and water to Arrakis will, in time, inevitably destroy the spice that is the planet's only product but is nonetheless crucial to the galaxy. It may be assumed that Herbert is suggesting that Keynesian economics, the attempt to plan a society's economic well-being, will inevitably founder. But, on a larger, more galactic scale, there is no question that Herbert is preaching his favorite gospel: LEAVE HUMAN BEINGS ALONE!

If you try to breed a Kwisatz Haderach, as the Bene Gesserit have attempted for many centuries, you are doomed to failure. If you attempt to set mankind on the Golden Path, as Leto II has done in *God Emperor of Dune*, your efforts, no matter how praiseworthy, will ultimately fail; and your power, no matter how nearly infinite, will ultimately corrupt both its user and those it is used upon. As an example, *God Emperor of Dune* opens with an archaeological dig on the planet Rakis, as Arrakis is now known, thousands of years after Paul's death. Even the virtually eternal Leto II, the God Emperor, is dead. Rakis is a tranquil, temperate planet with no exports, without interest except as a historical curiosity. The spice has disappeared, Shai-Hulud is no more, and Paul, Leto II, and the galaxywide Imperium, are, like the empires of Earth, gone to dust. Only mankind has survived, despite the meddling, both beneficent and maleficent, of transitory beings such as the Bene

Gesserit, successive emperors, the Sardaukar, Paul, Jessica, the Atreides family, the Harkonnens, the Abomination of Alia, Leto II, the Fish Speakers, and successive incarnations of Duncan Idaho.

Herbert concluded the *Dune* Chronicles with *Heretics of Dune* (1984) and *Chapterhouse: Dune* (1985). Both of these novels, while ostensibly continuing the epic saga of the Arrakeen heroes, descendants, or thematic materials, have one major characteristic, a theme they share with the earlier four books and, for that matter, with most of Herbert's fiction: When is a being truly human?

As observed earlier, Herbert asks the reader to ponder, both directly and indirectly, thematically and ideologically, by word and act, What is it to be human? Who is a human being? Moreover, he expects his readers not to quibble about perceived anomalies or even apparent inconsistencies in his works but to ask these questions, not only about the characters but, implicitly, about themselves. The questions are worth repeating.

Consider: Paul Atreides has been given the test of the gom jabbar early in *Dune* itself. While the very name Bene Gesserit means "Let it be done well," one wonders if even the test is administered "well" and for a good intent? Does Reverend Mother Helen Gaius Mohiam give the test to perceive Paul's future? To find out if Paul may be the long-sought Kwisatz Haderach? Is she truly concerned with the good of Arrakis, the ultimate source of the spice that virtually controls the then known universe? Does she wish to ensure that Arrakis will not be inflicted with a savior-hero, an ambiguous *mahdi* the Bene Gesserit cannot control, a leader of the Fremen who will, in essence, destroy the planet and the spice that made it famous—or infamous? These are complicated questions to which Herbert wisely gave no answers.

Indeed, is Paul "human" when he carries out his jihad, resulting in the death of untold millions, perhaps billions? In *God Emperor of Dune*, is Leto II, the half-human half-sandworm, truly human at any time during his millennium-long reign? An Incarnation?

True god and true man? Hardly. True diabolic and true nonhuman? Almost certainly.

Are any of the various gholas or reincarnated Duncan Idahos truly human? Or are the newly introduced counterparts to the Bene Gesserit, the Honored Matres, with their endless cabals, plots, and devious schemes, human, even humane? Finally, are the Bene Gesserit themselves human, with their ten-thousand-year secret—they would like to think "sacred"—history, their end-justifies-the-means philosophy, their almost maniacal purpose of breeding a Kwisatz Haderach?

Collateral to the questions of "humanness," Herbert also continually raises the questions of uses and abuses of power (and control of the spice is power indeed) by everyone: the Atreides family, its traditional enemies, the Padishah Emperors, the Spacing Guild, and the various sects who seek their own limited selfish ends. What of the Ixian renascent machines once destroyed by the Butlerain Jihad? The list is almost endless. Thus the geriatric spice, melange, the genuine life-prolonging drug has itself become the object of power play after power play in the Imperium. It corrupts even the Fremen. For all that its gift of limited prescience permitted space travel, its abuse has also brought about the downfall of empires, the destruction of hundreds if not thousands of planets, and the death of untold millions.

These questions are not merely implied by Herbert. Rather he is raising these direct ones about the nature of humanity, not merely the visionary worlds of his future but the world that the reader inhabits. If readers of the Chronicles ignore them and become involved only in the plot and subplots, schemes and counterschemes, their actions tell more about the readers themselves and their lack of insights than about Herbert's ability to relate a story, because he tells a story very well indeed.

For Herbert, the act of writing was not quite identical to sending a message, and while the story is always uppermost, at the same time he saw no reason not to embed ideas into the structure of what he wrote. After all, the underlying thesis of *Dune* is that ideas do indeed have consequences, and when you undertake ecologically to remake Arrakis, to "terra-form" the planet as did Paul himself, to bring water to the desert, you must bear those consequences, and the six novels that comprise the *Dune* Chronicles provide the epic saga of what happened as a result.

Herbert's untimely death in 1986 from pancreatic cancer brought an apparent end to the *Dune* Chronicles. While rumors persisted that he left notes for further continuations of the saga, these rumors have neither been affirmed nor denied. However his son Brian Herbert—a science fiction novelist in his own right—together with Kevin Anderson, has contracted to produce three prequels. A virtual cottage industry about *Dune* has developed, complete with board games, interactive role-playing games, commentary about what many feel was an abortive film version, and so on. An authorized spin-off, *The Dune Encyclopedia* (1983), compiled by Willis E. McNelly and now unfortunately out of print, provided insatiable *Dune* fans with some answers to their many questions about the first four volumes of Herbert's masterpiece.

Dune sites on the Internet abound with extensive lists of "Frequently Asked Questions," reprints of various noncopyrighted materials, and, to some noninterested readers, exhaustive trivia. The discussion group—alt.fan.dune—on Usenet usually has dozens of correspondents, all speaking their piece about what they call the "Duniverse."

This continued interest in Herbert's creation, more than a decade after its creator's death, bespeaks volumes about the permanence of his genuine science fiction epic. However, the achievement of the *Dune* Chronicles has unfortunately overshadowed some of Herbert's other late works, particularly *The White Plague* (1982). Like *Soul Catcher*, this novel deals with the effects of mono-mania, a theme that not incidentally informs the *Dune* series as well. Here Herbert is dealing with a tired [sic] and true science fiction thesis, that of a world without women. However, he links the apparently trite plot

line with political violence: a terrorist bomb in Ireland has accidentally killed the wife of a scientist who vows revenge by unleashing a virus deadly only to women and thus vivifies both themes. In a typical "Herbertian" manner, he combines the two in a scientific thriller with overtones of inhumanity, maniacal insanity, and scientific intensity, thus fashioning a very readable novel with some of the best sheer writing of his final years. His preparation for writing this book took him to Ireland for an extended visit. He carefully plotted his forthcoming scenes, then photographed them on slides, and during the actual process of writing, spurred his memory by projecting the slides as he wrote, thus achieving both immediacy and verisimilitude. *The White Plague* is not to be overlooked as a strong member of the Herbert canon.

When he died on 11 February 1986, every major paper in the country printed an extensive obituary. While some papers simply used the AP dispatch sent over the wires from the Madison, Wisconsin, hospital where he died, others carried a more detailed story. Even the papers of the Eastern Establishment— the *New York Times*, the *Baltimore Sun*, and the *Washington Post*—carried no mere canned wire service obits but lengthy memoirs written by journalists who knew his work well. Those writers neither condescended to him nor praised him beyond his merits or achievements. Originally a journalist himself, Herbert would have appreciated that little fact. He had a passion for truth, and when facts—or a life, even his life—are presented with truth and objectivity, he would have been satisfied.

In a certain sense a few of the books that immediately followed the first *Dune* novel were little more than potboilers. Yet even the most pedestrian of these novels, *The Eyes of Heisenberg*, is a good entertainment. The questions it offers are penetrating—for example, Is mortality an incurable disease?— and the answers are often provocative, but while the book may hold the reader the first time, it has little appeal the second time. Some of the other works—*The Heaven Mak-*

ers (1968), *Whipping Star* (1970), *The God-makers* (1972), *Hellstrom's Hive* (1973), to name only a few—have their strong and, sometimes, weak points. *The Heaven Makers*, for example, continues to express Herbert's fascination, begun so well in the *Dune* sequence, with immortality, predestination, free will, and other metaphysical considerations. Are we humans, Herbert asks, merely the toys of some superior race? If so, how much individuality do we have? And, for that matter, how much individuality do the superior immortal beings—the Chem, whose province Earth has been for thousands of years—have now that they are no longer subject to death? With no end, and thus no future, they live only in an eternal present that is often heaven, but just as often hell.

Anyone who met Herbert and had the pleasure of listening to his fascinating conversation for any length of time soon learned that he felt deeply about many things and that he held many considered opinions. His interests were catholic. He had a passion for ideas and for their effect upon humanity. Thus, to cite only one example, his ecological awareness was very keen and his feelings about what man has inflicted upon this planet were passionately held. That very passion was the source not only of his strengths as a novelist and short story writer but also of his weaknesses. Thus, his works occasionally become mere essays in fictional form and his characters nothing but "talking heads."

To be sure, this primacy of ideas over characterization is one of the major attributes of science fiction itself, and Herbert should not be condemned for doing what dozens of other science fiction writers have done. *Destination: Void* (1966) is a case in point. This novel is a fictional essay in which Herbert speculates through his characters about the nature of consciousness. To give himself a little elbow room, he relies on one of his most typical devices, one first seen in *Dragon in the Sea:* a relatively limited number of people are faced with a virtually insoluble problem. As they attempt to address it, they grow but are faced with a still more intense variation of the prob-lem. The trigger of this situation is a familiar one: the development of artificial intelligence, the Frankenstein complex. In fact, one wonders if Herbert has created a situation in this novel similar to the one that made the Butlerian Jihad necessary in *Dune*.

As noted earlier, all of Herbert's books published since *Dune* have been held up to the Arrakeen epic, and they often suffer by comparison. Such has certainly been the case with *Soul Catcher* (1972), a novel that many critics initially had trouble addressing. It is certainly not science fiction, a fact that has both puzzled and irritated many. At the same time it contains many of Herbert's customary technical devices and is really quite similar to his science fiction. As a result of this confusion, initial reviews of the novel were mixed, and it may well be that the book has yet to achieve the preeminence that a few readers have claimed for it. It is perhaps still seeking its audience.

Soul Catcher is as contemporary a novel as Herbert ever wrote. It concerns Charles Hobuhet, a member of a Pacific Northwest American Indian tribe whose sister has been raped by white men. In shame she has killed herself. As an act of revenge, Hobuhet becomes the shaman Katsuk, the latent spirit of the tribe and the center of their reality. He kidnaps a thirteen-year-old white boy, the son of an undersecretary of state, and for several weeks they evade capture by hiding in the wilds of the Olympic Peninsula. Young David Marshall soon recognizes, in an almost classic case of the hostage syndrome, the reasons for his kidnapping. Eventually, in a tragedy that approaches the pathos of *King Lear* or the mythic inevitability of Greek drama, Marshall is killed by Katsuk's not-so-mythic arrow.

What surprises many readers who come upon *Soul Catcher* by accident is the gradual realization that the novel was written several years before the Patty Hearst kidnapping. Here is another instance where Herbert seems almost to have had the kind of prophetic vision he ascribes to Paul Atreides. On the other hand, Herbert is exploring, once more, the relative roles of violence and pacifism, mysticism and reality. As suggested earlier, one of the problems afflicting Paul in *Dune* is his slow awareness that he is a genuine avatar of Arrakis and that he must choose as his method of redemption not the traditional messianic one of peace, love, charity, mercy, and forgiveness, but one of violence, a violence forced upon him by the incredibly hostile nature of the planet and of the galactic Imperium. If that consciousness and awareness nearly destroy Paul—after all, to avoid ultimate godhead he walks suicidally into the open desert—they also destroy both Charles Hobuhet and David Marshall. It may well be that they are redeemed by the violence, but the profundity of the questions we must ask about *Soul Catcher* makes us realize the depth of the problems with which Herbert was working.

In the end, Herbert's "Indian" novel works well as a plea for understanding the mores and ethics of the original inhabitants of America, but it works just as well as a provocative fictional study of metaphysical power, retributive justice, and psychological communion.

Many of Herbert's short stories were later published as parts of novels or proved to be germinal material that was reworked into the longer form. In other words, it seems that Herbert early learned that his true métier was the novel-length form, and that the longer form was a series of incidents connected by characters. The short stories are often very tightly plotted; they are stylistically similar and contain characters who represent preliminary studies for some of the people who inhabit his longer works. All this is not meant to demean Herbert's short fiction but, rather, to suggest that his shorter pieces have much in common with his longer works: good plotting, a plethora of ideas, some quite passable dialogue, and preliminary character sketches for later, more fully developed individuals. Particularly notable are "The Mind Bomb" (*If*, October 1969), "Seed Stock" (*Analog*, April 1970), and "A-W-F, Unlimited" (*Galaxy*, June 1961), all of which escape from the usual formulas for science fiction short stories.

Certainly one of Herbert's great talents was his sense of place and atmosphere, and his consequent ability to infuse the worlds he created with a sense of physical immediacy. Few fictional worlds are as detailed as Arrakis, for example; and Herbert took justifiable pride in the large number of letters he received from submariners who called *Dragon in the Sea* the best book about undersea warfare they had ever read. The utopian community of Santaroga is as carefully pictured, and part of the appeal of *The Santaroga Barrier* to many readers is the brilliance with which Herbert establishes a sense of the Edenic nature of the village. A sense of place, then, was certainly one of his outstanding characteristics. And so was his ability to portray fully fleshed characters. Working in a medium—science fiction—that has been almost notorious for its lack of genuinely original human characters, Herbert was very successful in creating quite a few memorable individuals. Certainly Paul Atreides must rank high among science fiction's real characters; Baron Harkonnen is more than a mere mass of evil flesh; Duncan Idaho in his various incarnations is complex; and even Leto II, whether in *Children of Dune* or *God Emperor of Dune*, moves us with his humanity and his awareness of the impossibility of making his people live without dying for them.

In addition, the character of Jessica is a genuine achievement. Completely drawn, finely portrayed female characters have been so rare in science fiction that they might as well be regarded as nonexistent. Most of the women who have inhabited the pages of science fiction since the 1930's are cardboard creations or simpering idiots who gush and twitter. Although the later record is somewhat better, too often science fiction's women have been foolish projections of adolescent lubricity and end up, in their brass brassieres, disgracing their creators. Not so with Lady Jessica. She is all at once concubine, mother, Reverend Mother, quasi wife, psychic adept, and mourning but fighting widow. She is genuinely human, and she infuses the first book of the series with a feminine presence that raises the novel above the level of mere action for the sake of action. Chani and Ghanima are Jessica in other versions, and Hwi Noree in *God Emperor* is certainly more than a mere psychological concubine to Leto II: she is at once an innocent temptress and an unwitting spy; her presence in the novel provides a sharp contrast to the revenge-obsessed Siona; and her innocence, when played against the blindly obedient Fish Speakers, Leto's female army, seems even more poignant.

Students of science fiction have often asked what qualities distinguish Herbert's writing from those of his mainstream contemporaries. Why is *Dune* a good but not a great novel, they ask, and why is Herbert a craftsman—a distinguished one to be sure—and not an artist? Much could be said about these and similar questions—about the nature of science fiction itself and the nature of contemporary fiction in general. But such questions miss the point of science fiction: it is entertainment, and Herbert was a particularly good entertainer. He realized, in a sense, that he had to compete with other media for time, attention, and money. As he once put it, "I have to write novels that are good enough to make an airline passenger shell out a couple of bucks before he gets on a plane. And then I have to keep him awake and interest him enough to buy another book of mine next time."

Herbert as a stylist was not the equal of Ray Bradbury, Theodore Sturgeon, or Brian W. Aldiss, yet he handled the language well. Consider this passage from an early chapter of *Dune*: "The Duke Leto Atreides leaned against a parapet of the landing control tower outside Arrakeen. The night's first moon, an oblate silver coin, hung well above the southern horizon. Beneath it, the jagged cliffs of the Shield Wall shone like parched icing through a dust haze." Here the word choice is sure, the details specific, the verbs sharp, and the entire description economical but certain. Herbert claimed that he often wrote rough drafts in the Japanese haiku form, seeking first the economy and concision. Later, when rewriting, he expanded the passage, adding details to flesh out the initial evocation.

One thing is very certain about Herbert's writing: when he took the time to work and rework his material, his action scenes are among the best ever written in science fiction. His manuscripts in the Special Collections Library at California State University, Fullerton, show clearly how well he revised his first drafts. Incident after incident cascaded from his typewriter, and the reader is swept along by the vigor of the events described. Yet those events are so carefully depicted that the reader, almost unaware, is soon carried beyond the mundane level of incident to some metaphysical concept. To accomplish this transmutation is a rare talent, and Herbert normally did it very well indeed.

Genuine, fully realized fictional worlds, as was observed earlier, are rare. Yet when they have been created with loving attention to detail and populated with multidimensional human beings, they linger in the memory long after one's initial perception. Moreover, they can be returned to again and again with ever-increasing awareness and appreciation of the nature of the worlds. Such is certainly the case with Herbert and the Arrakeen myth, a myth so real that it will continue to enchant generations of readers yet unborn. It is a signal achievement.

Selected Bibliography

WORKS OF FRANK HERBERT

The Dragon in the Sea. Garden City, N.Y.: Doubleday, 1956; London: Victor Gollancz, 1960. (Some other book titles: *21st Century Sub* [1956] and *Under Pressure* [1974].)

Dune. Philadelphia: Chilton Books, 1965; London: Victor Gollancz, 1966.

Destination: Void. New York: Berkley Medallion, 1966; London: Penguin Books, 1967.

The Eyes of Heisenberg. New York: Berkley Medallion, 1966; London: New English Library, 1975.

The Green Brain. New York: Ace Books, 1966; London: New English Library, 1973.

The Heaven Makers. New York: Avon Books, 1968; London: New English Library, 1970.

The Santaroga Barrier. New York: Berkley Medallion, 1968; London: Rapp and Whiting, 1970.

Dune Messiah. New York: G. P. Putnam's Sons, 1969; London: Victor Gollancz, 1971.

Whipping Star. New York: G. P. Putnam's Sons, 1970; London: New English Library, 1972.

The Worlds of Frank Herbert. London: New English Library, 1970; New York: Ace Books, 1971. (Short stories.)

The Godmakers. New York: G. P. Putnam's Sons, 1972.

Soul Catcher. New York: G. P. Putnam's Sons, 1972; London: New English Library, 1973.

The Book of Frank Herbert. New York: DAW, 1973. (Short stories.)

Hellstrom's Hive. Garden City, N.Y.: Doubleday, 1973; London: New English Library, 1974.

The Best of Frank Herbert. Edited by Angus Wells. London: Sidgwick and Jackson, 1975. (Short stories.)

Children of Dune. New York: G. P. Putnam's Sons, 1976.

The Dosadi Experiment. New York: G. P. Putnam's Sons, 1977; London: Victor Gollancz, 1977.

The Jesus Incident, with Bill Ransom. New York: G. P. Putnam's Sons, 1979.

The Priests of Psi, and Other Stories. London: Victor Gollancz, 1980.

Without Me You're Nothing, with Max Barnard. New York: Simon and Schuster, 1980.

Direct Descent. New York: Ace Books, 1981.

God Emperor of Dune. New York: G. P. Putnam's Sons, 1981.

The White Plague. New York: G. P. Putnam's Sons, 1982.

Heretics of Dune. New York: G. P. Putnam's Sons, 1984.

Chapterhouse: Dune. New York: G. P. Putnam's Sons, 1985.

COLLECTED MANUSCRIPTS

A readily accessible collection of almost all of Frank Herbert's manuscripts and papers are in the Special Collections Library at California State University in Fullerton, California.

CRITICAL AND BIOGRAPHICAL STUDIES

Aldiss, Brian W. *Billion Year Spree: The True History of Science Fiction*. London: Weidenfeld and Nicolson, 1973; Garden City, N.Y.: Doubleday, 1973.

Allen, L. David. *The Ballantine Teachers' Guide to Science Fiction*. New York: Ballantine Books, 1975.

———. *Herbert's Dune and Other Works*. Lincoln, Neb.: Cliff's Notes, 1975.

Ketterer, David J. *New Worlds for Old: The Apocalyptic Imagination, Science Fiction and American Literature*. Bloomington: Indiana University Press, 1974.

Manlove, C. N. *Modern Fantasy: Five Studies*. London: Cambridge University Press, 1975.

McNelly, Willis E. "Archetypal Patterns in Science Fiction." *CEA Critic*, 35, no. 4 (May 1973): 15–19.

———, compiler. *The Dune Encyclopedia*. New York: G. P. Putnam's Sons, 1983.

McNelly, Willis E., and Timothy O'Reilly. "*Dune*." In *Survey of Science Fiction Literature*. Vol. 2. Edited by Frank N. Magill. Englewood Cliffs, N.J.: Salem Press, 1979; 647–658.

Miller, David M. *Frank Herbert*. Starmont Reader's Guide no. 5. Mercer Island, Wash.: Starmont House, 1980.

O'Reilly, Timothy. "From Concept to Fable: The Evolution of Frank Herbert's *Dune*." In *Critical Encounters*. Edited by Dick Riley. New York: Frederick Ungar, 1978; 41–55.

———. "*Children of Dune*." In *Survey of Science Fiction Literature*. Vol. 1. Edited by Frank N. Magill. Englewood Cliffs, N.J.: Salem Press, 1979.

———. "*Dune Messiah*." In *Survey of Science Fiction Literature*. Vol. 2. Edited by Frank N. Magill. Englewood Cliffs, N.J.: Salem Press, 1979; 659–663.

———. *Frank Herbert*. New York: Frederick Ungar, 1981.

Ower, John. "Idea and Imagery in Herbert's *Dune*." *Extrapolation*, 15 (1974): 129–139.

Parkinson, Robert C. "*Dune*—An Unfinished Tetralogy." *Extrapolation*, 13 (1971): 16–24.

Stover, Leon E. "Is Jaspers Beer Good for You?—Mass Society and Counter Culture in Herbert's *Santaroga Barrier*." *Extrapolation*, 17 (May 1976): 160–167.

—WILLIS E. McNELLY

FRED HOYLE
(b. 1915)

IT IS NOT the easiest thing in the world to examine the work of Fred Hoyle the novelist, with whom we shall here be primarily concerned, because he exists in the shadow of Sir Fred Hoyle, F.R.S., the world-famous astrophysicist and intellectual maverick. To use his own image, Sir Fred Hoyle stands like a black cloud between us and the fiction that novelist Fred Hoyle has written, most of it in collaboration with his son Geoffrey; Sir Fred's reputation makes us shy, and this in turn hinders our response to his novels. His unmistakable stature as a theoretical scientist has for years tended to obscure readers' responses to his fiction. They assume that what may seem to be a boyish adventure tale or a mere space opera must be something more as well, by virtue of the imprimatur of Hoyle's reputation; what may seem simple—even simpleminded—on the surface of the text must therefore, it is argued, constitute a sly trap for the unwary, a cognitively punitive cryptogram or joke arising from the realms of hard, abstract thought—realms with which most readers are familiar mainly through rumor. Nor does the impatient elitism running through most of Hoyle's novels help much to increase his readers' sense of security.

It is certainly true that most readers of science fiction are able to claim a modicum of unsure numeracy (ability to work with numbers), just as most writers in the genre boast a kibitzer's familiarity with astrophysics, genetics, linguistics, or demography. But in reading Fred Hoyle, a little numeracy is a dangerous thing, and it leads one astray into a search through his fiction for those substantial evidences of the daunting mathematical and cosmological sophistication one feels should underlie the loose-tongued high jinks that the typical Hoyle plot vividly supplies.

Any such search would be in vain. Numeracy is no help. Fred Hoyle the novelist is not Sir Fred in sheep's clothing. He, his son, and his wife, Barbara, who has edited most of their output of the 1970's, are primarily entertainers, though they are by no means emptyheaded. No other reading of the novels as a whole can put the elitism, the politics, the pixilated utopian speculations, or the unusual attitudes toward women and sex into a viable framework.

But first, we must deal with Sir Fred Hoyle, who, although never a conventional member of the scientific-academic establishment, has had a strikingly vivid impact upon it. In terms of British social history, it is significant that he was born on 24 June 1915 at Bingley, Yorkshire, in the north of an island whose social and intellectual establishment has always presided in the south. After attending grammar school in Bingley, Hoyle finally did go south, into the arena of British establishment life. He took his university training at Cambridge, where he was the 1936 Mayhew's Prizeman in the mathematical tripos and the 1938 Smith's Prizeman, these honors being a sign both of precocity and of the capacity to work extremely hard.

After being awarded an M.A. in 1939, Hoyle became a fellow at St. John's College,

Cambridge. At the beginning of World War II, he moved to the British Admiralty, where he worked on the development of radar. After the war his career took on its mature shape. In 1945, Hoyle returned to Cambridge as university lecturer in mathematics, a post he held until 1958, when he was made Plumian professor of astronomy and experimental philosophy. In 1966 he became director of the Cambridge Institute of Theoretical Astronomy, which he himself had founded. In 1973, the year of his knighthood, he resigned both positions.

During the years 1945 to 1973, Hoyle published his most significant theoretical work, entered into controversies about it, and became known as a popularizer of scientific matters. His first work to reach a wide audience was his second book, *The Nature of the Universe* (1950). Based on radio talks he had given, it expounded in ordinary language the steady-state theory of the creation of matter, for which he had been, from its conception, the principal theorist and spokesman.

In 1948, Hoyle, along with astronomers Thomas Gold and Hermann Bondi, announced the theory of the continuous creation of matter throughout the universe. This theory was in opposition to the "Big Bang" theory, which postulated a single cataclysmic creation of all matter from a primordial monobloc. It is of course the "Big Bang" theory that has gradually won the allegiance of most scientists in the intervening years. Although Hoyle, as the leader of the Cambridge cosmographers (as they were known), argued strenuously for the steady-state theory, by 1965 he was forced to retract its substance. But the clear-cut, aggressive cogency of his views confirmed the maverick role he was increasingly to play in the world of science, where he became more and more an intellectual outsider, just as he was born and raised one in cultural terms.

The intellectual controversies in which Hoyle was involved during these years are of little direct interest to the layman—they include a suggested modification of the general theory of relativity in 1963 and a new theory of gravitation (with Jayant V. Narlikar) in 1964, expanding Ernst Mach's thesis that mass is an affect of the interaction of matter with the rest of the universe. Together these controversies paint a picture of impatience, doggedness, daring, eccentricity, and frustration on Hoyle's part.

Frustration may or may not have provided Hoyle with the engendering energy to create science fiction fables as exercises in wish fulfillment. It is in any case certain that a powerful sense of released pleasure infuses almost all of his fiction—from *The Black Cloud* (1957) to the punitive exuberance of *The Westminster Disaster* (1978), written with Geoffrey Hoyle and edited by Barbara Hoyle. (It may be well to state now that although there may be analyzable differences between solo novels by Hoyle and the more numerous collaborations, these differences do not show themselves at all clearly. This is as true of the two novels written in collaboration with John Elliot as it is of those written with Geoffrey Hoyle, leaving one with the reasonable working hypothesis that Fred Hoyle is the dominant partner in his fiction—just as he has always seemed to be in the controversies marking his academic life and in the books written to emphasize his disagreement with scientific "orthodoxy.")

Nevertheless, frustration and impatience do seem to have influenced Hoyle's abrupt resignation in 1973 from the two academic positions he held at that point, positions that gave him theoretically a dominant role in British astronomy. The ostensible reason for his resignation was a dispute over an appointment in the Cambridge astronomy department. Although the underlying complexities and history that must have contributed to such a decision do not lie within the scope of this article, it is interesting to note that abrupt, peremptory, deeply impatient behavior is characteristic of the most usual type of protagonist in Hoyle's fiction: the dominant male scientist bedeviled by "civilians."

Of course, in the fiction the frustrated scientists win real victories, not pyrrhic ones. Since 1973, Sir Fred Hoyle's career has been anything but tranquil. Since 1956, when he was a staff member of the Mount Wilson and Palomar observatories for two years, he has spent a good deal of time in the United States. He became more peripatetic after his Cambridge resignations: Andrew D. White Professor-at-Large at Cornell University in 1973–1979; Sherman Fairchild Scholar at the California Institute of Technology in 1974; and honorary professorial fellow at University College, Cardiff, since 1975. (There are other honors that demonstrate how formidable a public figure he had become. Elected a fellow of the Royal Society [F.R.S.] in 1957, he was its vice president in 1970 1971, and was awarded its Gold Medal in 1974, he was president of the Royal Astronomical Society from 1971 to 1973, having received its Gold Medal in 1968; he was also the 1968 recipient of the Kalinga Prize, awarded by UNESCO.)

There can be no question that in 1973, Hoyle stepped into relative professional obscurity, although he has by no means left the public eye. Along with some more or less routine popularizations of astronomical subjects, he has published two controversial books in collaboration with W. C. Wickramasinghe, *Lifecloud* (1978) and *Diseases from Space* (1979). In these books Hoyle and his partner adopt a truculent, popularizing style that is full of pejorative references to "those who favour the orthodox theory of infectious diseases." In addition, they put forward the theory that space is suffused with complex organic molecules, that comets scoop up these molecules and deposit them on Earth, and that not only infectious diseases but "all aspects of the basic biochemistry of life come from outside the Earth." Biological evolution is explained by the fact that living cells incorporate alien viruses in order to increase their own genetic complexity. As a science fiction premise, the idea is certainly workable, as Hoyle, writing alone, tried to demonstrate in *Comet Halley* (1985). Other recent books with speculative content include *On Stonehenge* (1977) and *Ice* (1981), the latter being a description of the new Ice Age that Hoyle believes is imminent.

Hoyle's fiction is clearly subordinate to his work as a cosmologist, popularizer, and prophet without honor regarding the extraterrestrial origin of life. As we have suggested, it will be seriously misread if it is taken as intending to make the same kinds of arguments about the world and its origins as Hoyle permits himself to make in his nonfiction publications. More important to our appreciation of his fiction is the fact that it works as a tension releaser for its author and as a series of exercises in wish fulfillment—possibly for the entire Hoyle family, certainly for the willing reader.

Of the fourteen fiction titles associated with Fred Hoyle, four were published by him alone; two novels, based on British Broadcasting Corporation serials, were written in collaboration with John Elliot, and eight titles were written with his son Geoffrey. All seven volumes of fiction published since 1969 have been collaborations with his son. Of the three solo novels only the second, *Ossian's Ride* (1959), has the sustained narrative drive always necessary in a Hoyle novel if the translation of its frustrated protagonist from incarceration in civilian life to a freer condition is going to seem plausible to the reader. (The fourth solo title is a 1967 collection of short stories, *Element 79*.)

The first of Hoyle's novels, *The Black Cloud*, has perhaps received an undue amount of attention, considering the almost complete silence with which the later titles have been received; compared with these later works, *The Black Cloud*, although thematically and structurally similar to most of the corpus, is a peculiarly static, academic experiment in the writing of fiction. Narratively it is nearly as turgid as the Hoyles' first collaboration, *Fifth Planet* (1963), and is almost completely lacking in what has become a kind of trademark of their fiction: a deadpan, disorienting, pell-mell narrative pace, with an effect sometimes surreal, sometimes macabre, almost always intensely alien. When one adds to this rapid rate of narration the fact that no Hoyle character ever seems to question the speed with which his life goes through each radical

Fred Hoyle. COURTESY OF HUTTON-DEUTSCH
COLLECTION/CORBIS

transition after another, one finally arrives at
the suspicion that the typical Hoyle protagonist is in an important sense only pretending
to be human.

The narrative velocity of *The Black Cloud*
is insufficient for this suspicion to arise. The
story has misleadingly been read as an attempt to depict, after the fashion of C. P.
Snow, something of the true nature of a scientist's thought processes and work habits,
when in fact—as with all of Hoyle's fiction—
it represents an escape from those processes
and routines. It also would seem to represent
an escape from the frustration of being a scientific controversialist of Hoyle's stature and
pugnacity, and from the frustration of being
right in a world of bureaucrats, "ostriches,"
time servers, and conventional minds spouting conventional wisdom.

The title cloud is discovered nearing our solar system from interstellar space; it presents
incompetent politicians with a problem they
cannot begin to solve, for when, as seems inevitable to the scientists gathered to cope
with the challenge it presents, the cloud settles permanently into a kind of halo around
the sun, the resulting interference with the
sun's heat emanations will effectively end
civilization.

An impatient but brilliant scientist, Chris
Kingsley, comes to the conclusion that the
cloud is sentient, learns to communicate with
it, persuades it to leave our stellar vicinity,
but is driven to insanity by the radical enhancement of his knowledge that the cloud
passes on to him. Kingsley is incapable of
assimilating any new knowledge—paradigm
shifts—that radically undermine his entire
world view; it is the first and last time in any
Hoyle work that a hero-scientist's response to
irreversible transcendence is death. From this
point on, the infusion of alien splendor,
whether or not it is grasped in its entirety by
the human hero, is welcomed by him, both for
the vista unveiled and for the fact of its irre-
versibility.

Although it is tentative and stodgy, *The
Black Cloud* was accepted with respect as a
scientist's novel displaying a scientist's conventional loyalty to science and conventional
disparagement of interference by government
with research and decision making.

Ossian's Ride, in contrast, admits no such
comfortable reading. In this second novel
something alarming is going on in Ireland.
British intelligence asks Thomas Sherwood, a
young scientist-mathematician, to wander
about the island in the guise of a student in
order to extract information about the technological and scientific revolution that seems
to be exploding there through the agency of
I.C.E., the ominous Industrial Corporation of
Eire.

The bulk of the novel is made up of Sherwood's journal, the style of which (probably
deliberately) reminds one of the insouciant
elitist patriotism of John Buchan's *The
Thirty-Nine Steps* (1915); with impostors ga-
lore in its early pages and comically incompetent spies, the content of the journal is at
first also reminiscent of Edwardian extrava-
ganzas like *The Man Who Was Thursday*
(1908) by G. K. Chesterton or Hilaire Belloc's
The Green Overcoat (1912).

Although the Buchanesque chase elements
persist through most of the text, the genuinely modern implications of Sherwood's
discoveries gradually begin to countervail

against the comfortable Edwardian certainties of Hoyle's literary models. Surely this is deliberately done. Sherwood discovers that most of Dublin has been razed to the ground and reconstructed into a series of skyscrapers surrounded by pleasant parks. The reader's instinct may be to abhor the rationalization and dehumanization this reconstruction entails, but it soon becomes clear that Sherwood welcomes the elimination of the grime and mess and illogicality of the old Dublin. And when he discovers that Ireland is in the process of being crisscrossed by a series of vast superhighways, his pleasure is increased. So impatient is he with the muddleheadedness of "civilian" life that he is willing to have the entire old world swept under the carpet in order to provide room for the new.

By a circuitous route Sherwood continues his quest for the secret behind I.C.E., attempting to gain access to the southwest corner of Ireland, which the corporation now owns. Eventually—after complications that transform the playful conspiracies of Hoyle's Edwardian models into something more closely resembling the nightmares of Franz Kafka—he succeeds, is captured by I.C.E., and is put to work as a scientist by them. As far as Sherwood is concerned, what might be a Kafkaesque nightmare for the reader is a kind of beatific revelation. He finally discovers that the vastly energetic scientific rationalism driving I.C.E. to dominate the world has its source in a group of aliens forced to come to Earth because their own star is heating up; they have traveled as immaterial "bolts of information," acquiring human form only on arrival.

When the "girl" alien tells Sherwood of her origin, he puts an arm around her. Later he sends his journal to British intelligence, to tell them why it will be useless to resist. A bolt of transcendental knowledge has irreversibly transformed his perspectives on all things; and he, like all subsequent Hoyle heroes, gladly turns his back on the prison of normal human life to seek his destiny elsewhere. At the novel's end Sherwood seems hardly human, which is unsettling enough; what may be even more distressing is the sense of Hoyle's auctorial approval of this impatient transcending of our natural state.

A for Andromeda (1962) and *Andromeda Breakthrough* (1964), both written with John Elliot, routinely expand their authors' BBC radio serials, although familiar Hoyle themes dominate: the frustrated scientist, the pettifogging governments, and the irruption onto our scene of an alien communication whose benefits only a few can appreciate. *October the First Is Too Late* (1966) again deals with voluntary outcasts from human society, although the protagonist this time is a composer whose music is too complexly emotional for contemporary critical taste. A series of temporal dislocations carve Earth into several different, coexisting eras; the dislocations, it turns out, have been imposed by a higher form of intelligence from the far future in order to bring the narrator and his scientist friend out of 1966 and into an era they would invigorate. These novels are comparatively weak, nor are Fred and Geoffrey Hoyle's first two collaborative efforts, *Fifth Planet* and *Rockets in Ursa Major* (1969), up to the level of *Ossian's Ride*.

In *Fifth Planet*—which concerns the attempts of humans to communicate with alien intelligences on a planet briefly intersecting our solar system—there are two points of interest. The sexual ruthlessness of the Hoyle protagonist here becomes more explicit than before (this may represent Geoffrey Hoyle's influence). From this novel on, women's sexuality tends to be treated as a necessary curse to which men must respond but which they respect only as a blind force; most Hoyle women are defined by their imprisoning sexuality. Also in *Fifth Planet* the echoes of Kafka become more insistent. There are the strange, surreal landscapes and the flattened affect with which the characters behave (although they have violent feelings, their feelings and actions are dissociated). There is also a dreamlike, alien arbitrariness to the plot and the transitions that carry it forward. Much of chapter 11, "The Return," reads like a pedestrian paraphrase of passages from Kafka's *Amerika* (1927):

> Conway calculated that there were about fifty lanes of traffic, crawling ever onwards like beetles.
>
> His official passes took them on to the carpeted area. For the moment they had to keep to the outside because nobody could be sure that the rocket would manage to land at the exact center. . . . Comfortable pullman-like chairs had been provided for them to sit, and there were large umbrellas under which they could shelter from the sun.

And so forth. Nothing but extensive quotation could convey the oddly disorienting quality of this deadpan narrative style.

Seven Steps to the Sun (1970) and *Into Deepest Space* (1974) are of moderate interest; the latter, a sequel to *Rockets in Ursa Major*, carries its protagonist through the irreversible transcendence of a journey through a black hole into an alternate universe to find a virginal alternate Earth; the trip is engineered by the usual alien intelligence. *The Westminster Disaster* seems to be a typical contemporary political thriller, but it is notable because the Hoyles appear to be arguing that outside agitators are causing the unrest in South Africa. Also notable is the climax of the story, in which a terrorist nuclear bomb planted in the Thames blows up:

> Many of the buildings of Whitehall were old, built in stonework now in poor condition. With the explosion of Little Boy they came down like so many rotten fruit. They had seen ages of strong government, ages of great glory, but in the end they had seen a nation top to bottom, with the feeble at the top and the virile in subservience, a nation that had largely lost the collective will to survive. ("Central London, 7:30 a.m.")

Of greater interest are two novels of the 1970's, *The Inferno* (1973) and *The Incandescent Ones* (1977), which together can be read as summing up the Hoyle program for imaginative escape from the world's coils. In *The Inferno*, waves of radiation from the explosion of the galactic core, as the protagonist Dr. Cameron realizes, will make life on most of Earth impossible. He tells off the incompetent government that he judges incapable of taking appropriate action, and travels north to his home in Scotland, where he remains. Since the wave of radiation hits the planet from the south, Scotland is treated comparatively lightly. Afterward the local survivors of the holocaust begin to look to Cameron for guidance; ultimately he becomes a decisive, ruthless, far-seeing, compassionate, authoritarian laird.

The novel ends with his realization that an alien intelligence has somehow saved Earth from the worst of the radiation, "as if a man should hold up a hand to shield a moth as it flew near a candle." The intensity of *The Inferno* is sometimes dazzling; for once, the wish fulfillment of the frustrated maverick scientist is accorded a plot that fully and satisfyingly embodies it. Cameron is a dream of justified anger and grim compassion; from his stronghold in Scotland, he rules a cleansed world.

Hoyle's latest novel, *Comet Halley*, in a disorganized manner, involves a scientist named Isaac Newton in a tale in which the eponymous comet turns out to be carrying ancient life-forms. This novel was received with indifference, and Hoyle has since published no fiction.

The dreamlike way in which Hoyle heroes are never surprised or sorrowed by the irreversible loss of their worlds likewise achieves a full and satisfactory embodiment in *The Incandescent Ones*, the hero of which discovers first that he is an alien humanoid and second (with perfect aplomb) that he is actually a robot; ultimately he discorporates into the higher consciousness of the incandescent ones, intelligent entities who live in the atmosphere of Jupiter. Although he is not a scientist, the young hero of this novel strikingly exhibits the suprahuman adaptability that Hoyle demands of those who are fit to survive and to transcend their earthly lot. His exploits are not the feats of the hero of a "hard" science fiction novel, nor is the strange destiny of scientists like Cameron in *The Inferno* anything like a decorous outcome for the protagonists of a novel about the life and work of scientists in this century. Fred Hoyle's fiction is not a rendering of the real-life concerns of Sir Fred Hoyle, the rebel cosmologist; rather, it is an alternative to those concerns. His fiction is so thoroughly strange because it so deeply inhabits the alternate world of dreams—alien dreams.

Selected Bibliography

FICTION OF FRED HOYLE

The Black Cloud. London: Heinemann, 1957; New York; Harper and Brothers, 1958.

Ossian's Ride. London: Heinemann, 1959; New York; Harper and Brothers, 1959.

A for Andromeda, with John Elliot. London: Souvenir Press, 1962; New York: Harper and Row, 1962.

Fifth Planet, with Geoffrey Hoyle. London: Heinemann, 1963; New York: Harper and Row, 1963.

Andromeda Breakthrough, with John Elliot. London: Souvenir Press, 1964; New York: Harper and Row, 1964.

October the First Is Too Late. London: Heinemann, 1966; New York: Harper and Row, 1966.

Element 79. New York: New American Library, 1967. (Collection.)

Rockets in Ursa Major, with Geoffrey Hoyle. London: Heinemann, 1969; New York: Harper and Row, 1969.

Seven Steps to the Sun, with Geoffrey Hoyle. London: Heinemann, 1970; New York: Harper and Row, 1970.

The Molecule Men and the Monster of Loch Ness, with Geoffrey Hoyle. London: Heinemann, 1971. Reprinted as *The Molecule Men*, New York: Harper and Row, 1972. (Two novelettes.)

The Inferno, with Geoffrey Hoyle. London: Heinemann, 1973; New York: Harper and Row, 1973.

Into Deepest Space, with Geoffrey Hoyle. New York: Harper and Row, 1974; London: Heinemann, 1975.

The Incandescent Ones, with Geoffrey Hoyle. New York: Harper and Row, 1977; London: Heinemann, 1977.

The Westminster Disaster, with Geoffrey Hoyle. London: Heinemann, 1978.

The Energy Pirate, with Geoffrey Hoyle. Loughborough, England: Ladybird, 1982.

The Frozen Planet of Azuron, with Geoffrey Hoyle. Loughborough, England: Ladybird, 1982.

The Giants of Universal Park, with Geoffrey Hoyle. Loughborough, England: Ladybird, 1982.

The Planet of Death, with Geoffrey Hoyle. Loughborough, England: Ladybird, 1982.

Comet Halley. New York: St. Martin's, 1985.

NONFICTION OF FRED HOYLE

The Nature of the Universe. Oxford: Basil Blackwell, 1950 (revised 1960); New York: Harper and Brothers, 1951.

Lifecloud, with W. C. Wickramasinghe. London: Dent, 1978; New York: Harper and Row, 1979.

Diseases from Space, with W. C. Wickramasinghe. London: Dent, 1979.

Commonsense in Nuclear Energy, with Geoffrey Hoyle. San Francisco, Calif.: W. H. Freeman, 1980.

Ice. London: Hutchinson, 1981.

The Quasar Controversy Resolved. Cardiff, Wales: Cardiff University Press, 1981.

Space Travellers: The Bringers of Life, with Chandra Wickramasinghe. Cardiff, Wales: Cardiff University Press, 1981.

Facts and Dogmas in Cosmology and Elsewhere. Cambridge, England: Cambridge University Press, 1982.

Evolution from Space: A Theory of Cosmic Creationism, with Chandra Wickramasinghe. New York: Simon and Schuster, 1984.

From Grains to Bacteria, with Chandra Wickramasinghe. Cardiff, Wales: Cardiff University Press, 1984.

The Intelligent Universe: A New View of Creation and Evolution. New York: Holt, Rinehart and Winston, 1984.

Living Comets. Brookline, Mass.: Longwood, 1985.

The Small World of Fred Hoyle. London: M. Joseph, 1986. (Autobiography.)

Viruses from Space, with Chandra Wickramasinghe and John Watkins. Cardiff, Wales: Cardiff University Press, 1986.

Archaeopteryx, the Primordial Bird: A Case of Fossil Forgery, with Chandra Wickramasinghe. Brookline, Mass.: Longwood, 1987.

Cosmic Life-Force, with Chandra Wickramasinghe. New York: Paragon House, 1990.

The Theory of Cosmic Grains, with Chandra Wickramasinghe. Dordrecht, Netherlands: Kluwer Academic, 1991.

The Origin of the Universe and the Origin of Religion. Wakefield, R.I.: Moyer Bell, 1993.

Our Place in the Cosmos: The Unfinished Revolution, with Chandra Wickramasinghe. London: Dent, 1993.

Home Is Where the Wind Blows. Mill Valley, Calif.: University Science Books, 1994. (Autobiography.)

—JOHN CLUTE

ALDOUS HUXLEY

(1894–1963)

But oh, the sound of simian mirth!
   Mind, issued from the monkey's womb,
Is still umbilical to earth
   Earth its home and earth its tomb.
"First Philosopher's Song," from *Leda* (1920)

N<small>O HISTORY OF</small> science fiction can be complete without special attention to four novels by Aldous Huxley. The seminal influence of *Brave New World* (1932) is incalculably great. *After Many a Summer Dies the Swan* (1939) brilliantly weds satire and science to reserve a forum for such writers as Kurt Vonnegut, John Barth, Norman Spinrad, and Harlan Ellison. *Ape and Essence* (1948) is perhaps the earliest cogent postatomic holocaust tale. And *Island* (1962), though minor in literary importance, poignantly tempers the gloom of the earlier works and remains a necessary part of the record of the development of Huxley's speculative fiction. At the same time, while the practical task is to extract from his thought and art the matter pertaining to science fiction, these works are only a part of his literary achievement.

Huxley, of course, is not unique in this. Edgar Allan Poe, Herman Melville, William Dean Howells, Edward Bulwer-Lytton, Rudyard Kipling, George Bernard Shaw, and George Orwell, to name a few, all wrote important science fiction as part of their larger body of work. Even H. G. Wells wrote a great deal that is not science fiction. Therefore, one must remember that the science fiction produced by these writers is not altogether intelligible without an account of all of their work.

Huxley wrote the stanza that begins this essay in his middle twenties. It is a forecast Through the sixty-nine years of his life, he formed a picture of humanity rooted on earth and defined by its spirit, its genes, and its science. This picture is pervasive in his science fiction.

I

In all of his works and letters, Huxley may have used the term "science fiction" as many as ten times—no more. He astutely identified the science fiction works of H. G. Wells— whom he knew personally, disagreed with, and finally respected—as most likely to endure, calling them "scientific romances." In 1926, six years before the publication of *Brave New World*, Hugo Gernsback invented the term "scientifiction" and made his magazine, *Amazing Stories*, the model for a host of similar magazines through the years that have printed the "pop-lit" narratives with which most people have identified science fiction. Almost certainly Huxley paid little attention to pulp science fiction. Sybille Bedford, his official biographer, in response to a question put to her for this essay, shares this opinion. One may surmise that despite his extremely poor sight from an early age, he succeeded in reading widely and enormously—and eventually selectively. Nevertheless, he used the term "science fiction" in *Literature and Science* (1963), one of his most important monographs:

In the hundred years that have passed since the inventor of science fiction [Jules Verne] embarked on his career, science and technology have made advances of which it was impossible for the author of *From the Earth to the Moon* even to dream. Rooted as they are in the facts of contemporary life, the phantasies of even a second-rate writer of modern science fiction are incomparably richer, bolder, and stranger than the Utopian or Millennial imaginings of the past. (chapter 18)

Published in the year of Huxley's death, *Literature and Science* may be read, without the slightest serious reservation, as a brilliant analysis, definition, and call for just such a literature as has recently emerged, wedding the efforts of "ghetto" and mainstream authors. This literature is recognized today, with less and less prejudice, as science fiction.

Science fiction presents a refreshingly analytical and powerful mood in modern literature. In this spirit Huxley would not have minded being called a science fiction writer, even though he was one of the most important English-speaking twentieth-century men of letters. He was a poet, essayist, scholar, social critic, historian, playwright, university lecturer, and novelist. The sum of his work is considerable in bulk and regularly brilliant. At the same time his stature as an influential progenitor of science fiction is major. In the 1920's, 1930's, and 1940's pulp science fiction, for all of the apparently heady daring of its space operas, was still merely amusingly frivolous and even constipated. Its humanity, its characters, and its culture remained unreflectively and nostalgically Victorian. Like George Bernard Shaw's drama, Huxley's novels attacked this Victorianism. In 1932 the candor of his rational futurism and explicit treatment of sex, science, and religion in *Brave New World* was appalling. He was more than three decades ahead of the science fiction "New Wave" and Harlan Ellison's 1967 anthology *Dangerous Visions*. Moreover, at that time hardly anyone worried about whether *Brave New World* was science fiction.

Huxley's memory is well served in the biography by Sybille Bedford, his good friend and an author/scholar in her own right. He was the right sort of subject. The biographer need be intelligent and sensitive; and a Huxley life, exposed in the most intimate and fragile details revealed by his works and letters, may nearly write itself. His personal candor was culturally precocious. He conducted his art and his relationships in a spirit of charitable self-revelation. He had no secrets that one can sense. He needed none of the common ones. His attention was not to the gossip of secrets that trick people but to the dialectic of mysteries that bind men and order their destinies.

Born at Godalming, Surrey, on 26 July 1894, into a family that was profoundly concerned with human culture, Aldous Leonard Huxley was furnished with a wonderful pedigree. His mother, Julia Arnold, was the granddaughter of Dr. Thomas Arnold of Rugby. His grandfather, Thomas Henry Huxley, was the famous exponent of science and Darwinian evolutionary theory. Mrs. Humphry Ward, his mother's sister, was a writer of enormously popular soap-operatic novels. He was the grandnephew of the major Victorian poet and cultural analyst Matthew Arnold. His brother Julian became a major spokesman for science in the twentieth century.

Events in his youth proved to Huxley how vulnerable a person is. His mother died when he was thirteen. At sixteen he contracted a disease that damaged his sight and plagued him with its effects for the rest of his life. When Aldous was twenty, his older brother Trevenen committed suicide.

His near blindness exempted Huxley from military service in World War I. He finished at Oxford with a first in English and vacillated among teaching, clerical posts, editing, and beginning the writing that was his principal source of income for most of his life.

In July 1919 Huxley married Maria Nys. A son, Matthew, was born the next year. In 1921 his first major novel, *Crome Yellow*, was published. With it his reputation and prestige rose. In 1925 and 1926 the Huxleys took a trip around the world. *Point Counter Point* appeared in 1928 and was selected by the Literary Guild of America. His reputation was thoroughly international by this time. In the summer of 1931, Huxley began writing *Brave New World,* which was published the following year. This, the work for which he is most remembered, has sold more copies than all of his other works combined. It has been the object of enormous and continuing controversy, partly over trivial matters and partly over perhaps the most abiding concern of the twentieth century. Many readers were shocked by the portrayal of rampant sexual activity. Serious critics were concerned with the forecast that the fruits of science and rapid change would bring a cultural wasteland. H. G. Wells, for example, did not like *Brave New World* because at that time he was enamored of the promise of a coming age of science and technology. By the time Wells died in 1946, events had reversed his view, vindicating Huxley's. On the other hand, Nobel Prize winner Hermann Hesse, whose own somewhat ambiguous utopian novel *The Glass Bead Game* would be published in 1943, read Huxley's novel with great sympathy.

In 1938, Huxley began work on *After Many a Summer Dies the Swan,* which was published in 1939. This satiric fantasy of social criticism was not designed to elicit the sensational reaction of *Brave New World.* In the twilight of the peace before World War II, reviewers found *After Many a Summer* both brilliant and strange. It won the James Tate Black Memorial Award for the Novel in 1939.

The record indicates an aborted attempt by Huxley to begin another "utopian" work in 1940, perhaps the genesis of *Island.* In 1945 he worked on the script of the Walt Disney cartoon production of *Alice in Wonderland.* Meanwhile the nuclear age had opened at Nagasaki and Hiroshima, and Huxley went quickly to the heart of the matter with the cautionary tale *Ape and Essence* (1948). Too soon, perhaps. *Ape* received little critical approval and had no commercial success.

By 1954, when *The Doors of Perception* appeared, Huxley's reputation in the literary mainstream had declined. This essay on hallucinogenically driven imaginative vision followed his careful mescaline experiments with Dr. Humphry Osmond. Against his remotest intention, Huxley later became a hero of drug cultists. In fact, his lifelong battle with the effects of his damaged eyesight, especially in search of therapies to improve it, was an important cause of his intellectual openness to the most radical subjects and points of view. He was frequently ill, yet he had enormous energy.

Maria Huxley, who shared her husband's intellectual curiosity, died in 1955. The following year Huxley married Laura Archera, and they moved to Los Angeles. That same year he began the formal writing of *Island,* the "good utopia." In 1958 he published the nonfictional *Brave New World Revisited.*

The last five years of Huxley's life were filled with sickness as well as lectures, writing, and honors. In 1959 he received an honorary doctorate from the University of California at Santa Barbara as well as an appointment there as visiting professor. He used the opportunity to deliver the lectures collected in *The Human Situation* (1977), including, most notably, "The World's Future." Also in 1959 he received the Award of Merit for the Novel from the American Academy of Arts and Letters. During 1960 he filled speaking engagements at universities across the United States and was Centennial Carnegie visiting professor in humanities at MIT. *Island,* his last complete work of fiction, was published in 1962. Huxley was named a companion of literature by the Royal Society of Literature, an honor conferred only once every five years; he joined a roll that includes Winston Churchill, E. M. Forster, John Masefield, and Somerset Maugham. As late as August 1963 he felt strong enough to accept the editorship of a volume on human resources for the World Academy of Art and Science. *Literature and Science,* his last published work, appeared in September of the same year. He died on 22 November of complications from cancer.

Aldous Huxley. COURTESY OF E. O. HOPPÉ/ CORBIS

II

Four of Huxley's novels may be studied as science fiction. The first is the classic dystopia *Brave New World* (1932). Its simple story is of the misfit Bernard Marx, Alpha-class manager of civilization in the materialist utopia on Earth some 600 years A.F. (after [Henry] Ford), and John (the Savage), bastard child of Marx's director-boss fathered on a pneumatic Beta woman who is left to bring up John on a "reservation," a precivilized region preserved for purposes of study and exotic amusement by the advanced establishment. Marx discovers John on the reservation and takes him, noble-savage-like, back to England. John has long conversations with Mustapha Mond, a world controller, that reveal the intellectual and

emotional vacuum of the "utopian" world. He also searches unsuccessfully for love. Lenina, his object, doesn't know how to love him in return. He commits suicide after a riot by sightseers who are filled with curiosity and confusion by him, and after a last failed attempt to find rapport with Lenina.

The society of the novel is orderly, scientifically sophisticated in genetics and pharmaceuticals, and culturally sterile. With the exception, perhaps, of the helicopterlike air carriers, there is little interest in technological gadgetry. Not only is the population perfectly controlled, but people are genetically engineered in carefully regulated mental and physical sizes and types. Work is done by a hierarchy of genetic classes—monotonous work by those of low-order mentality; the work of government, by Betas and Alphas. Money exists, but the more valuable rewards are more luxurious dwellings and greater rations of "soma"—drugs that give a "high" with no side effects. With the exception of information manuals, books hardly exist. The Bible, pornography, and Shakespeare are all forbidden, a condition ironically exploited in the narrative, wherein passages from Shakespeare provide a counterpoint to the dehumanizing details of the "brave new world"— the novel's title itself taken from Shakespeare's *Tempest*. Instead, entertainment is supplied by "feelies"—sense-assisted movies that accurately anticipate the broadly anesthetic effect of television in later twentieth-century civilization. There is also sex, encouraged from childhood (indeed, practically required) in virtually every nonviolent permutation. All women must carry contraceptive kits. It is a male-dominated world, with men holding all the primary posts of power.

Brave New World contains analytical and nonanalytical discourse in interesting, even exciting, narrative—to make powerful expository fiction. Huxley found no new formal strategy, usually employing characters as mouthpieces for the dialectic of his tale. They engage in Socratic dialogues, with Shakespeare participating in the mouth of the Savage, who had virtually memorized the Bard's works. Huxley's work is excellent because of a disciplined balance of his great knowledge of history, art, science, and humanity with his magnificent linguistic wit and clarity. The same quality endures in the speculative novels that followed.

In *Brave New World*, the products of science have overwhelmed the poise of human reason. Huxley's great fear was not that what science could do should not be done, but that science would become the only thing that men did—and, after all, this turns out to be very little. This brave new world is boring. In the use of science to find safety, discipline and courage have become obsolete.

Good futurism has never been about the literal future. *Brave New World* is not. It is about the science-obsessed and sex-obsessed early twentieth century. It retains its cogency, even if its particular agenda needs to be expanded, because the late twentieth century preserves these obsessions. Like science, sexuality has claims, but not exclusive ones. A civilization ordered solely by science, sex, and drugs kills the spirit. People become mere cattle. "Savagery" may be preferable. The horror and agony of the Savage in the story are experiences only he, not a citizen of this sterile and incubated world, is free to negotiate. The Savage knows little joy and ecstasy. How could he, in that world? But, by the almost limitless capacity for pain that he has learned, he can imagine, dream of, and therefore in a way attain a transcendence of the richest possible pleasure of his body. Other persons in the novel might die, but only the death of the Savage can be profoundly tragic.

The originality of the vision of *Brave New World* exists in a rich context of dystopian tales, a few that preceded it and a number that followed it and were more or less inspired by it. George Orwell's *Nineteen Eighty-Four* (1949) immediately comes to mind; and Orwell himself, in discussing *Brave New World*, also remembered H. G. Wells's *When the Sleeper Wakes* (1899) and Yevgeny Zamyatin's *We* (1924). Karel Čapek's *R.U.R.* (1920) was translated in 1923. A patently melodra-

matic, yet nonetheless notable, forerunner was Thea von Harbou's *Metropolis* (1926). Excellent variations on the Huxleyan mood appear in Ayn Rand's *Anthem* (1938), Bernard Wolfe's *Limbo* (1952), Anthony Burgess' *A Clockwork Orange* (1962), John Brunner's *Stand on Zanzibar* (1968), Robert Silverberg's *The World Inside* (1971), Stanislaw Lem's *The Futurological Congress* (translated 1974), and the extraordinary *Tomorrow File* (1975) by Lawrence Sanders, explicitly influenced by *Brave New World*.

In a second, very different novel, *After Many a Summer Dies the Swan* (1939), Huxley drew his readers back to the present and, in a bizarre denouement, two centuries into the past. The solemnly effete scholar Jeremy Pordege goes to work for self-made financier Jo Stoyte as editor and organizer of the papers of the aristocratic and roguish Gonister family. At Stoyte's burlesquely medieval mansion (recognized by many readers as a parody of William Randolph Hearst's San Simeon) the vulgar millionaire spends his hypochondriac days wheeling and dealing, and bedding his young mistress with the assistance of hormone shots administered by the vicious Doctor Obispo. The depredations of Stoyte's kind of power, as well as the driving anxieties of individual human existence, are expounded in meetings with William Propter, a semi-Hermetic bachelor-contemplative. He tries to give decent housing to a few of the migrant workers exploited on Stoyte's California fruit farms and consolation to the novel's main characters when they need surcease from the thinly veiled savagery of Stoyte's hospitality. Stoyte himself seeks escape from death. The ubiquitous Doctor Obispo, through Pordege's research, finds evidence of a way to achieve that escape in the Gonister papers. He and Pordege travel to England and discover that through a diet of carp's entrails the fifth earl of Gonister and his mistress have lived for nearly 200 years, but have "evolved" into fetal apes (via Ludwig Bolk's fetal-ape theory of the descent of man), proof of the ironic theory that the human species is an arrested form of the fully evolved ape.

Swan is certainly the most readable of the novels to which Huxley gave a speculative turn, perhaps because it is most like the satirical novels of social criticism upon which his early prestige rested. It has the most interesting characters because human nature is the primary subject of *Swan*. The characters of the three other novels are more nearly mere mouthpieces. *Swan* is also a "Hollywood" novel in the stripe of Evelyn Waugh's *The Loved One* (1948) and Nathanael West's *The Day of the Locust* (1939). *Swan* is a blackly comic joke. It has apes (Stoyte actually has a monkey exhibit on his estate), aphrodisiac medicine, a morbidly grandiose cemetery, a venally driven university president, and a very successful fountain-of-youth quest. Nevertheless, at the core of the novel, in William Propter, is an inkling of the mysticism that grew in Huxley, to be most fully presented in *Island*.

At first thought *Swan* does not seem much like science fiction. Yet a number of extraordinary works of science fiction written later are very much like it. C. S. Lewis produced one within a framework of orthodox piety in *That Hideous Strength* (1945). Then there are Charles Harness' *The Rose* (1953), Kurt Vonnegut's *Sirens of Titan* (1959), Vercors' haunting *Sylva* (translated 1962), Gore Vidal's blasphemous *Messiah* (1965), Colin Wilson's baldly bombastic *Mind Parasites* (1967) and *Philosopher's Stone* (1969), John Barth's allegorical *Giles Goat-Boy* (1966), Norman Spinrad's salacious *Bug Jack Barron* (1969), and the playfully biting *Gasp* (1973) by Huxley's friend Romain Gary.

Although Huxley can hardly be blamed for the omission, many readers feel *Brave New World* was soon topically dated because it did not predict atomic war. Huxley himself was alert to this feeling. In a letter of 21 October 1949 to George Orwell he wrote:

The nightmare of *Nineteen Eighty-Four* is destined to modulate into the nightmare of a world having more resemblance to that which I imagined in *Brave New World*. The change will be brought about as a result of a felt need for increased efficiency. Meanwhile, of course, there may be a large-scale biological and atomic war—in which case we shall have nightmares of other and scarcely imaginable kinds.

He had finished *Ape and Essence* early in 1948. It is a postnuclear holocaust story, a nightmare predating Nevil Shute's *On the Beach* (1957) by nine years.

Shorter than any of his other science fiction novels, *Ape and Essence* is a "manuscript-found-in-a-bottle" tale. The manuscript is of a play that a playwright cannot get anyone to consider. (Huxley worked on a never-produced stage version of *Ape*.) The play is the story of the New Zealand Rediscovery Expedition, sent to the coast of California after the Third World War. There they find a survivor culture suffering the mutant effects of hard radiation on the local human species. Amid imminent famine, grave robbing, and Manichaean proscription of sex and women, an oligarchy of castrati rules with a theology that adores the devil as the creator of the world. The logic is plain: their lives and world are miserable; therefore, only the devil could have created them.

Niggling critics often attacked Huxley, saying he could not possibly love people (or humanity) because his fictional depiction of them—especially in his speculative stories—was so degrading. But we know that Huxley's feelings were precisely the opposite. He found mankind most precious, and his keen fear of the forces and trends that threatened it moved his imagination to visions of awful warning. Therefore, when in *Ape* the perversely brutal "catechism" classes of the children are described in remorseless detail, and the murder of mutant babies and the punishment of their mothers is more awful than the event of the mutant births, Huxley intends the horror. *Ape* addresses, in fact, contemporary Western society. It attacks the simplistic historicism and mythologies of human depravity that condone deterministic politics and systems of retributive punishment. The abomination of war, of course, is the end product of such beliefs.

Ape and Essence is clear, cogent, and brief. Shute's *On the Beach* is more powerful. Walter M. Miller's *A Canticle for Leibowitz* (1960) remains the best of the many fine postnuclear war stories written after *Ape*.

The story of *Island* (1962) presents Willoughby Farnaby, journalist and sometime writer of low-grade popular fiction, who arrives on the historically sequestered island of Pala as the agent of Joe Alehyde. Alehyde is a magnate, one of several very rich parties greedy for Pala's oil and mineral resources. Willoughby's cover is as a shipwrecked sailor. He finds a society fortuitously permitted to become a utopia, but threatened by Queen Mother Rani and Prince Murugan, who would sell Pala into the bondage of mid-twentieth-century fascist militarism.

Although Pala is doomed by the psychosis of its monarchs, it would eventually be smothered anyway. The rest of human civilization would not leave such an Eden untouched. Nevertheless, Will in time sees Pala's enlightened society intact. Government on the local level dominates. Families are extended well beyond biological ties; children have many "parents." Education integrates all information, and learning at the most elementary levels illuminates all the important matters of human experience, including sex and death. Indeed, psychotherapy is a part of education. Very few persons grow up insane. Children's learning capacity is maximized with revolutionary techniques—for example, through the mystic discipline of time dilation for learning faster. Later, to intensify the contemplative procedures that children are taught from their earliest years, selected ritual occasions are manipulated with drug-enhanced visions, in a highly disciplined format. The result is an extraordinarily happy people, in sharp contrast with the confused humanity in the rest of the world. They are free. They are emotional. Their intelligence reaches its potential. They are fundamentally in tune with nature. They enjoy life to the fullest, moment by moment. And, they die with a startlingly consistent dignity.

As Huxley's "good utopia" story, *Island* incorporates his most extended celebration of nature, as well as the propositions for a humanistic mysticism that increasingly preoccupied him in the later years of his life. It communicates a great yearning that mankind might alter its tragic course in spite of all the evidence that augurs the death of the spirit. It is intellectually spacious and clear. Even so, unless the reader approaches the novel with a predisposition to patience, it will be found taxing in the way utopian tracts have been since Plato. Nevertheless, to ignore *Island* is to relinquish incomplete the record of the development of the fable and vision that began with *Brave New World*.

Together the science fiction novels contain well over 300,000 words, with *Island* the longest. Together their basic plots encompass less than three years of calendar time. Plot is minimal. The action is subtle—more psychological than physical, more ritualistic than realistic.

The characters speak in disarmingly natural cadences and idioms. All are human; none are epically heroic. Until *Island* most of Huxley's major characters tend to be male. Women are few and minor, or unsympathetic. Analysis tends to be of stereotypical characters rather than of unique persons. There are, accountably, no extraterrestrials.

The worlds of the novels are only superficially realistic, and the reader's view of them is tightly focused. These novels are set with an economy that would fit them to stage production, a format Huxley constantly strove for, without remarkable commercial success. (Not until 1980 did a dramatic version of *Brave New World* appear on television.) They present the fettering of man by high technology in futuristic cityscapes, and the wholesome ambience of a symbiosis with nature. In between are the wastelands of the citadel of a brutal financier and an atomic war. Few weapons and no computers appear. There are no extraterrestrial places, not even moon landings; no space travel. The sky itself rarely takes the reader's attention. There is little weather, in spite of the encomium to nature in *Island*. There are many animals, especially monkeys and apes, but these are more or less caged in metaphors that describe men. There are coasts but no seas.

To Huxley the twentieth century was an "Age of Noise," talk without meaning. He tried to write stories with meaning. Late in his life he expressed this continuing concern in a letter to his son (20 August 1959):

I am working away on my Utopian novel [*Island*], wrestling with the problem of getting an enormous amount of diversified material into the book without becoming merely expository or didactic. It may be that the job is one which cannot be accomplished with complete success. In point of fact, it hasn't been accomplished in the past. For most Utopian books have been exceedingly didactic and expository. I am trying to lighten up the exposition by putting it into dialogue form, which I make as lively as possible. But meanwhile I am always haunted by the feeling that, if only I had enough talent, I could somehow poetize and dramatize all the intellectual material and create a work which would be simultaneously funny, tragic, lyrical and profound.

With these observations Huxley described perhaps the principal challenge to every writer of serious science fiction. His ingenuous questioning of his talent notwithstanding, his expository gift never failed him. The dimension he added with his allusions to music, painting, and literature in other languages provides a texture that modern readers rarely appreciate. Moreover, he usually succeeded in evoking a wonderful humor in the surprised voice of dramatic irony, astonished by the foolishness of the things men can think and do. He was often a George Bernard Shaw in prose. At her best Ursula K. Le Guin, especially in *The Dispossessed* (1974), echoes him.

Virtually all that Aldous Huxley had to say in his science fiction centered on earth and on mankind. He tried to anatomize the confusion of human science, art, and spirit. His ef-

fort took him from an elitist skepticism to a humanistic mysticism. He commended to us the value of knowledge, the balance of reason, and the repose of compassion.

Selected Bibliography

WORKS OF ALDOUS HUXLEY

Vulgarity in Literature. London: Chatto and Windus, 1930.
Brave New World. London: Chatto and Windus, 1932; New York: Doubleday, 1932.
After Many a Summer Dies the Swan. London: Chatto and Windus, 1939; New York: Harper and Brothers, 1939.
Science, Liberty and Peace. New York: Harper and Brothers, 1946.
Ape and Essence. New York: Harper and Brothers, 1948.
The Doors of Perception. London: Chatto and Windus, 1954; New York: Harper and Brothers, 1954.
Adonis and the Alphabet (American title: *Tomorrow and Tomorrow and Tomorrow*). London: Chatto and Windus, 1956; New York: Harper and Brothers, 1956.
Brave New World Revisited. New York: Harper and Brothers, 1958.
Island. New York: Harper and Row, 1962.
Literature and Science. New York: Harper and Row, 1963.
The Human Situation. Edited by Piero Ferrucci. New York: Harper and Row, 1977.

LETTERS

The Letters of Aldous Huxley. Edited by Grover Smith. London: Chatto and Windus, 1969; New York: Harper and Row, 1970.

BIBLIOGRAPHIES

Bradshaw, David. "A New Bibliography of Aldous Huxley's Work and Its Reception, 1912–1937." *Bulletin of Bibliography*, 51 (1994): 237–256.
Clareson, Thomas D., and Carolyn S. Andrews. "Aldous Huxley: A Bibliography, 1960–1964." *Extrapolation*, 6 (1965): 2–21.
Davis, Dennis Douglas. "Aldous Huxley: A Bibliography, 1965–1973." *Bulletin of Bibliography*, 31 (1974): 67–70. (There are a number of omissions.)
Eschelbach, Claire John, and Joyce Lee Shober. *Aldous Huxley: A Bibliography, 1916–1959* and *A Supplementary Listing, 1914–1964*. Berkeley: University of California Press, 1961 and 1972.
Vitoux, Pierre. "Aldous Huxley at Texas: A Checklist of Manuscripts." *Library Chronicle of the University of Texas*, 9 (1977): 41–58.

BIOGRAPHIES

Aldiss, Brian W. "Between Privy and Universe: Aldous Huxley (1894–1963)." *New York Review of Science Fiction* (October 1994): 19–21.

Bedford, Sybille. *Aldous Huxley: A Biography.* London: Chatto and Windus Collins, 1973–1974, 2 vols. New York: Knopf/Harper and Row, 1974, 1 vol. (The official biography.)

Deery, June. *Aldous Huxley and the Mysticism of Science.* London: Macmillan, 1996; New York: St. Martin's, 1996.

Dunaway, David King. *Aldous Huxley Recollected: An Oral History.* New York: Carroll and Graf, 1995.

———. *Huxley in Hollywood.* London: Bloomsbury, 1989.

Huxley, Laura Archera. *This Timeless Moment: A Personal View of Aldous Huxley.* New York: Farrar, Straus and Giroux, 1968. (Contains some of Huxley's letters.)

Nance, Guinevera A. *Aldous Huxley.* New York: Continuum, 1988.

RECORDING

Science Fiction as Fact: Aldous Huxley and Marc Connelly Discuss Man and His Machines. Hollywood, Calif.: Center for Cassette Studies, 1969.

CRITICISM

Aldiss, Brian W. "The Hand in the Jar: Metaphor in Wells and Huxley." *Foundation*, 17 (1979): 26–31.

Anlinger, Thomas. "The Essay Element in the Fiction of Aldous Huxley." *Dissertation Abstracts*, 29 (1968): 892–893A.

Baker, Robert S. *Brave New World: History, Science, and Dystopia.* Boston: Twayne, 1990.

———. *The Dark Historic Page: Social Satire and Historicism in the Novels of Aldous Huxley, 1921–1939.* Madison: University of Wisconsin Press, 1982.

Baldanza, Frank. "Huxley and Hearst." In *Essays on the California Writers*, edited by Charles L. Crow. Bowling Green, Ohio: Bowling Green University Press, 1978.

Booker, M. Keith. *The Dystopian Impulse in Modern Literature: Fiction as Social Criticism.* Westport, Conn.: Greenwood, 1994.

Brown, E. J. "*Brave New World, 1984,* and *We*: An Essay on Anti-Utopia." In *Zamyatin's We: A Collection of Critical Essays.* Edited by Gary Kern. Ann Arbor, Mich.: Ardis, 1988.

Clute, John. "Aldous Huxley." In his *Look at the Evidence: Essays and Reviews.* Liverpool, England: Liverpool University Press, 1995.

Coleman, D. C. "Bernard Shaw and *Brave New World.*" *The Shaw Review*, 10 (1967): 6–8.

Deery, June. "Technology and Gender in Aldous Huxley's Alternative (?) Worlds." *Extrapolation*, 33, no. 3 (1992): 258–273.

Firchow, P. E. *End of Utopia: A Study of Aldous Huxley's Brave New World.* Cranbury, N.J.: Bucknell University Press, 1984.

Hillegas, Mark R. *The Future as Nightmare: H. G. Wells and the Anti-Utopians.* New York: Oxford University Press, 1967.

Izzo, David Garrett. *Aldous Huxley and W. H. Auden: On Language.* West Cornwall, Conn.: Locust Hill, 1998.

Larsen, P. M. "Synthetic Myths in Aldous Huxley's Brave New Worlds." *English Studies*, 62 (1981): 506–508.

Matter, William. "On *Brave New World.*" In *No Place Else.* Edited by Eric S. Rabkin et al. Carbondale: Southern Illinois University Press, 1983.

———. "The Utopian Tradition and Aldous Huxley." *Science Fiction Studies*, 2 (1975): 146–151.

McMichael, Charles T. "Aldous Huxley's *Island*: The Final Vision." *Studies in the Literary Imagination*, 1 (1968): 73–82.

Meckier, Jerome, ed. *Critical Essays on Aldous Huxley.* New York: G. K. Hall, 1996.

Morrissey, Thomas J. "Armageddon from Huxley to Hoban." *Extrapolation*, 25, no. 3 (1984): 197–213.

Philimus, Robert M. "Aldous Huxley Revisited." *Science Fiction Studies*, 7 (1980): 109. (Negative review of Donald Watt's *Aldous Huxley, the Critical Heritage.*)

Sargent, Lyman T. "Millennium and Revolution: Two Themes in Seventeenth Century British Utopianism." In *Utopian Studies II.* Edited by Michael S. Cummings. Lanham, N.Y.: University Press of America, 1989.

Schmerl, Rudolf B. "The Two Future Worlds of Aldous Huxley." *PMLA*, 77 (1962): 328–334.

Sexton, James. "Aldous Huxley's Bokanovsky." *Science-Fiction Studies*, 16, part 1 (1989): 85–89.

Thomas, W. K. "*Brave New World* and the Houyhnhnms." *Revue de l'Université d'Ottawa*, 37 (1967): 688–696.

Watt, Donald, ed. *Aldous Huxley, the Critical Heritage.* London and Boston: Routledge and Kegan Paul, 1975.

—JOHN R. PFEIFFER

DAVID H. KELLER
(1880–1966)

KELLER SPENT THE greater part of his life in Monroe County, Pennsylvania, although he traveled a good deal while he was practicing medicine (mainly psychiatry). He was one of the first writers recruited by Hugo Gernsback to supply his science fiction magazines with original material, and he was particularly prolific (1928 to 1931). Gernsback cited Keller as one of the experts who might advise him on the accuracy of the science contained in stories submitted to him and appears to have found in Keller a kindred spirit whose fiction closely resembled his notion of what "scientifiction" ought to be.

Before his work appeared in *Amazing Stories*, Keller had been writing fiction for many years without having tried to sell any of his output. He had published some short fiction in an amateur magazine in 1901, a family history in 1922, and a pseudonymous volume of poetry in 1924, but for the most part was content to bind his manuscripts. Some work from this period was subsequently published, but his science fiction writing represented a fresh venture. He worked for a limited number of outlets; the bulk of his work was done for Gernsback or Farnsworth Wright, although he later wrote extensively for fan publications.

Most of Keller's books—including his two major collections, *Life Everlasting* (1947) and *Tales from Underwood* (1952)—owe their existence as much to the efforts of his friends as to his own salesmanship. His work, which is archetypal of early pulp science fiction, became less fashionable after the mid-1930's; and apart from a burst of activity in the late 1940's, following his retirement, his publications were sporadic after 1935. Previously unpublished material continued to appear after his death, primarily in *Magazine of Horror* and in his posthumous collection, *The Folsom Flint* (1969). He is not entirely forgotten today—the fan press P. D. A. Enterprises has begun production of the David H. Keller Memorial Library, including pulp stories not previously reprinted.

Keller cultivated a deceptively simple style of writing that is much better suited to mundane fiction than to science fiction—his science fiction is often awkward and mechanical in its construction and presentation. His best stories are those that deal with the idiosyncrasies of everyday life, particularly those in which the idiosyncrasies are slowly extended beyond the bounds of normalcy, so that they seem at once bizarre and familiar. The "psychiatric" stories in *Tales from Underwood* include some of the best examples, such as the superb vignette "A Piece of Linoleum." His mock-naïve style serves different purposes in his stories for *Weird Tales*, in which the painstaking straightforwardness highlights the grotesqueness of the horrors that are so scrupulously described. In his science fiction, by contrast, his style works quite a different transformation, giving the better stories the appearance of being fables, almost invariably carrying some kind of moral.

The range of Keller's science fiction, and its dominant concerns, can be seen clearly in the ten stories that he contributed to the Gernsback magazines in 1928. "The Revolt of the Pedestrians," "The Yeast Men," "A Biological Experiment," "Unlocking the Past," and "The Psychophonic Nurse" appeared in *Amazing Stories*, while "Stenographer's Hands" and the four connected short stories that appeared as "The Menace" were featured in its quarterly companion. All of the stories are based on ideas derived from biological science and are particularly concerned with the social uses of biological technology.

"The Revolt of the Pedestrians" describes a future in which man has degenerated physically, owing to dependence on mechanical means of locomotion. These "automobilists" believe that they have exterminated "pedestrians," but a few survive in the wild, and they threaten to use an invention that will annihilate electricity if their rights are not restored. The automobilists refuse, and the pedestrians follow through with their Draconian threat, dooming the automobilists to extinction. (Keller remained perennially fond of such extreme solutions, and he wrote many stories in which the misusers of technology are wiped out for their foolishness.)

A similar delight in large-scale destruction is seen at work in "The Yeast Men," which is about a peculiar kind of biological warfare, and in "The Menace." "The Menace" was reprinted in *Amazing Stories Quarterly* in 1933 but probably will not see the light of day again because of its overt racist sentiments. The first story concerns a plot in which a group of blacks infiltrates the corridors of power after turning themselves white. They are thwarted by the great detective Taine of San Francisco, but they live to launch other subversive projects. In the climactic story more than 99 percent of the American population is driven insane by living under glass (which inhibits the beneficial effects of sunlight) and must be put into suspended animation. The conspirators plan to revive them all to tear down the utopian world of the survivors, but instead the conspirators kill them in suspended animation—leaving the world safe, white, and utterly sane (a condition that receives the author's wholehearted blessing—Keller was an earnest believer in eugenics).

Other stories reflect Keller's gentler and more reasonable mood. "A Biological Experiment" is about a couple who rediscover the joys of parenthood in a world of ectogenic reproduction. In "Unlocking the Past" a mother refuses to let her child participate in an experiment to reawaken ancestral memories when a dream reveals to her how very unpleasant most of those memories must be. In "The Psychophonic Nurse" a mother too busy to pay attention to her child welcomes a mechanical substitute, until she is forced to realize that both she and the baby are being deprived of something essential. All three stories express the anxiety that technological "progress" threatens ordinary family relationships, and that these relationships must be preserved, whatever the cost. They are not antitechnological stories so much as urgent propaganda in favor of compassion and companionship.

The most dramatically effective of these early stories is "Stenographer's Hands," which tells of an experiment in selective breeding whereby an industrial magnate attempts to produce perfect stenographers. Inevitably it goes wrong, and the ultimate product is a race of "degenerate epileptics" unfit for any kind of life. The note of melodramatic horror struck by this story recurred frequently in Keller's work, particularly in his lurid first novel, *The Human Termites*, in which he imagines human nations as primitive "hive-minds" scheduled for extermination by the more ancient and more effective hive-minds of the social insects, which create gigantic half-human termites to do the job. The nightmarish invaders are defeated, but not before they have destroyed the greater part of the human race.

The Human Termites was produced at a time when Keller was temporarily forced to make his living from professional writing—for several months in 1929 he mass-produced fiction and popular medical articles for the Gernsback magazines. The quality of his work suffered somewhat in consequence; and after publication of the excellent horror story "The Worm," in which a man living alone in an old mill tries desperately to preserve his home against something monstrous gnawing away at its foundations, the overall quality of his fiction declined markedly. It is frequently repetitive and hurried, although it presents the occasional memorable image—notably the march of the starving professionals, over-produced by the colleges and unable to find work, in "White Collars."

Another story that stays in the memory for quite different reasons is "The Feminine Metamorphosis," in which women frustrated of promotions decided by a male-dominated world decide to take over. They turn themselves into men in order to infiltrate the upper echelons of high finance. Taine of San Francisco discovers their plan but does not need to thwart it—instead, he merely informs them that they have been tampering with the work of God and will reap the consequences. The testosterone used to transform them has been obtained by castrating thousands of Chinamen, and (so Taine says) the entire population of China is infected with syphilis—a disease that is already beginning to destroy the conspirators. This is perhaps Keller's most nasty-minded story, though many readers may fail to understand it because of the coy medical jargon in which its crucial paragraphs are couched.

Keller's second and third novels—*The Conquerors* and *The Evening Star*—are clumsy and uninteresting, although the latter does have the distinction of being his only interplanetary story. His fourth, though—written when his productivity had been cut back to a more moderate level—was considerably better. This is *The Metal Doom*, serialized in *Amazing Stories* in 1932, a disaster story in which all metals rust away, thus returning civilization to the Stone Age. The scene, near the end of the book, in which the main characters reflect on their experience provides Keller with an opportunity to state more clearly his disenchantment with contemporary man and his anxiety regarding the uses of technology. The heroes agree that civilization fully deserved the plague that was visited upon it:

"In thinking it all over, it seems to me that civilization was sick; and it was a rather unpleasant illness. There was something about it that just seemed as though it had grown so fast that its elemental parts could no longer function and that it was bound to decay. Something had to happen and it did." (*Amazing Stories*, July 1932, page 335)

The heroes then agree that they are suitably repentant of the crimes of the old world, and that they will build a better one. No sooner have they said so than a handy deus ex machina restores the metals.

This notion of a "sick civilization" became even more prominent in Keller's subsequent science fiction novels. In *Life Everlasting* (1934) a scientist finds the panacea, a cure for all ills that confers immortality on those injected with it. It also dissipates all mental and moral defects with equal ease, miraculously transforming the world into an ideal place in much the same fashion as H. G. Wells's celestial visitor does in *In the Days of the Comet*. Once this ideal state is established, Keller gives his plot a curious extra turn, for the world is sterilized by the panacea and cannot bear the prospect. The scientist is urged to invent an antiserum, and the world accepts all its diseases again as the necessary price of parenthood. Astonishingly, we are not told whether there is a resurgence of criminality and immorality, though one must presume that there is. Nor is it clear why people cannot simply have their children first and then accept the serum. The importance of the moral seems to have overridden the dubious rationality of the climax.

This is, in fact, Keller's worst fault as a science fiction writer—his stories frequently fade away into irrationality. It may seem curious that Gernsback found such sloppy thinking acceptable, but he never worried in the least about the rational development of hypotheses in his fiction—he was interested only in the imaginative appeal of the hypotheses themselves. That is why the advent of John W. Campbell, Jr. (with his emphasis on rationality) as editor of *Astounding Stories* made such a dramatic difference to the nature of pulp science fiction.

A similar "chemical theory of morality" is featured in "Tree of Evil," another story Keller published in 1934, which tells of the effect on a village of a drug that destroys moral inhibitions. The idea, though, is conveniently buried by the indefatigable Taine of San Francisco. Taine, as a literary device, is a curiosity. Ostensibly a detective, he rarely solves crimes, although he frequently uses his mastery of disguise to penetrate conspiracies. He seems to function primarily as a means of brushing interesting ideas under the literary carpet. Marvelous ideas are placed in the hands of villains who misuse them, and in thwarting the criminals Taine banishes the ideas to a limbo from which they hardly ever reappear.

It was in the period 1932–1934 that Keller published some of his best short work, including the classic horror story "The Thing in the Cellar" and the psychological studies "A Piece of Linoleum" and "The Literary Corkscrew." His best science fiction short story of the period is "Unto Us a Child Is Born" (1933), in which a eugenically conscious society invites two exceptionally gifted people to be parents of a child who will be brought up in the most efficient way possible, so as to fulfill his genetic potential. They oblige but never see their genius son until he is almost an adult, when he proves to be distant and disinterested in them. When they are invited to produce another wunderkind, they politely decline. A similar story, donated to a fan magazine in 1938, is "The Mother," which has an identical moral and a similar touch of pathos.

After *Life Everlasting*, Keller's career as a science fiction writer went into a swift decline. The stories he published in 1935 are poor, and the only ones of significance that he produced in the next decade are fantasies. When he became active again for a brief period after World War II, Keller produced one last science fiction novel; the remainder of his output appears to have been entirely fantasy. It was, though, his best science fiction novel, *The Abyss*, which appeared with one of his

numerous giant-insect stories, *The Solitary Hunters* (originally serialized in *Weird Tales* in 1934).

The Abyss is unconvincing by the standards of the magazine science fiction of its day and remains a rather Gernsbackian work. A scientist and a millionaire join forces to conduct an experiment in which the population of New York is to be the "white mice." A drug similar to that in "Tree of Evil" is distributed to the unsuspecting populace in a new chewing gum, with the aid of a massive advertising promotion. As the repressive legacy of two thousand years of civilization is stripped away, New York suffers a psychological regression into savagery. Parallels are drawn between the events that follow and the exploits of Nero and Hitler, and the story is presented as an attempt to explain why civilization is sick and sometimes gets sicker. Its central notion derives from Sigmund Freud (whom Keller had long admired), although the plot refers more often to Carl Jung. The central hypothesis is that repression is the price we pay for a well-ordered society, and that the source of all evil is locked away in the subconscious of every person, ready to exert its baleful influence if we do not strive to control and suppress it. Keller must have regarded recent trends in psychological theory with some horror.

This notion of a "psychic abyss" (where the source of evil lurks) seems to contrast sharply with the unorthodox theology that lies at the heart of Keller's best fantasy novel, *The Devil and the Doctor* (published in 1940 but revised from material written in the 1920's). Here the Devil is one of two brothers, the other being Jehovah. Jehovah is spoiled, jealous, and spiteful, whereas his brother is sympathetic, clever, and urbane—his bad reputation is entirely the result of slander. That it is the Devil rather than Jehovah who is the true embodiment of Christian values is demonstrated by the malicious attempts of a puritanical miller to vilify the innocent and amiable hero of the book (a Pennsylvania country doctor) and have him cast out of the community he serves. The Devil appears again, though only readers of the earlier novel will be sure to identify him, in *The Homunculus* (1949), in which he extends his benign protection to a retired colonel bent on repeating the generation of artificial human life as described by Paracelsus.

There is no unorthodox theology in *The Homunculus*; but Keller had not entirely abandoned it, as evidenced by the surreal fantasy "The God Wheel," first published in *Tales from Underwood*. In it the protagonist becomes a person of the First God in order to cleanse the earth of its sick civilization, returning it to Arcadian splendor to give it the chance to regenerate itself. As in *The Abyss*, though, Keller seems pessimistic, implying that the sickness will—and indeed, must—regenerate itself along with civilization. His fiction seems, in retrospect, always to have been dominated by a curiously ambiguous pattern of thought in which a quasi-Gnostic Christianity is entangled with a characteristically post-Darwinian and post-Freudian image of man. This may appear to be too ponderous a judgment of a man whose science fiction seems so awkwardly simpleminded, but a thorough acquaintance with his work reveals him to have been a much more complex writer than is immediately evident.

Keller was essentially a conservative writer who was suspicious of technological progress. He could see well enough what benefits might accrue from the advance of technology, but he always searched his imagination for the price that would have to be paid. The quality of his worst fears is adequately exemplified by the evil dream suffered by the protagonist of "The Threat of the Robot" (1929):

> He thought that he was living in a world in which the conflict between the machine robots and the worker was so intense that unemployment was a serious problem. In practically every phase of life the machine was crowding the workingman out of his job. . . .
>
> In these dreams, Ball saw the gradual starvation of society, first, for the real pleasures of life, then for the comforts, and later on for the actual necessities. He visioned parades of unemployed workingmen, demanding of capital a right to earn a living. But these very parades were policed by robots with blue-coats on who were very perfect in preserving order by mechanically-wielded batons. In his dream, Ball saw one strike a poor woman on the head. The baby that she carried dropped out of her lifeless arms and would have fallen to the pavement, but Ball caught it with one hand and struck the robot in the face with the other. At once he was the center of an attack from a dozen machines who pounded him into insensibility. As he fell, he tried to save the child, crying in his terror, "You are killing civilization instead of the man."

Virtually all Keller's fiction is calculated to disturb in one way or another; he never wrote a pure adventure story. The best of his horror stories remain effective today because of their psychological insight. His science fiction, by and large, has lost its effectiveness—it is dated in its technique and its ideas have lost their freshness. Nevertheless, he was in his day a significant writer, well able to jolt the complacency of Gernsback's readers and to reveal the more shadowy implications of the wonders of technology.

Selected Bibliography

WORKS OF DAVID H. KELLER

The Sign of the Burning Hart. Saint-Lô, France: Imprimerie de la Manche, 1938.
The Devil and the Doctor. New York: Simon and Schuster, 1940.
Life Everlasting and Other Tales of Fantasy and Horror. Newark, N.J.: Avalon, 1947.
The Solitary Hunters and The Abyss. Philadelphia, Pa.: New Era, 1948.
The Eternal Conflict. Philadelphia, Pa.: Prime Press, 1949.
The Homunculus. Philadelphia, Pa.: Prime Press, 1949.
The Lady Decides. Philadelphia, Pa.: Prime Press, 1950.
Tales from Underwood. New York: Published for Arkham House by Pellegrini and Cudahy, 1952.
The Folsom Flint and Other Curious Tales. Sauk City, Wis.: Arkham House, 1969.
The Last Magician: Nine Stories from Weird Tales. Edited by Patrick H. Adkins. New Orleans: P. D. A. Enterprises, 1978.

The Human Termites. New Orleans: P. D. A. Enterprises, 1979.

CRITICAL AND BIOGRAPHICAL STUDIES

Keller, David H. "Half a Century of Writing." *Fantasy Commentator* (Spring 1947); reprinted in *The Last Magician*. (Autobiographical.)

Moskowitz, Sam. Introduction to *Life Everlasting*. Newark, N.J.: Avalon, 1947. (Biographical sketch and critical appreciation.)

Spencer, Paul. "In Memoriam: David H. Keller." Introduction to *The Folsom Flint*. Sauk City, Wis.: Arkham House, 1969.

Stableford, Brian. "The Creators of Science Fiction, 3: David H. Keller." *Interzone*, no. 97 (1995): 54–57.

———. "Gernsback's Pessimist: The Futuristic Fantasies of David H. Keller." In his *Outside the Human Aquarium: Masters of Science Fiction*. San Bernardino, Calif.: Borgo, 1995.

—BRIAN STABLEFORD

DAMON KNIGHT
(b. 1922)

A MULTITALENTED PROFESSIONAL whose career as a writer, editor, critic, and anthologist spans almost sixty years, Damon Knight has been one of the major shaping forces in the development of science fiction in the 1960's and 1970's. As well as being the founder of the Science Fiction Writers of America, cofounder of the prestigious Milford Science Fiction Writers' Conference, author of one of the first important books of science fiction criticism (*In Search of Wonder*), and editor of *Orbit* (the longest-running original anthology series in the history of the field) and a score of other landmark anthologies, Knight is also one of the finest short story writers ever to work in the genre. Of all his peers, only Frederik Pohl can lay claim to an influence anywhere near as widespread, potent, and various.

Damon Francis Knight was born in Baker, Oregon, on 19 September 1922. The son of a high school principal and a schoolteacher, he spent most of his childhood and early adolescence in Hood River, another sleepy little Oregon town. He lives today in Eugene, Oregon, with his wife and family.

Bookish and introspective, Knight claims that he grew up into a "mentally precocious and physically backward" child who, in his high school graduating class, "looked like a fourteen-year-old who had got in by mistake." Alienated from his peers, he "got most of [his] ideas about life out of books." After working his way through much of the Hood River library, he discovered science fiction in the form of the August-September 1933 issue of *Amazing Stories* (featuring the story "Meteor-Men of Plaa" by Henry J. Kostkos) and was instantly hooked. Here, in *The Futurians* (1977), Knight describes the intensity and completeness of that conversion:

> Christ! Beauty was not in it, or sex either—I knew them both, and they were pitiful, pale things in comparison. *Battleships hanging upside down over New York! Men in radio tubes being zapped by electricity! Robots carrying off pretty girls in Antarctica!* Here was the pure quill, the essential jolt. So powerful that if my parents had understood what it was they would have stopped my allowance, painted my eyeglasses black to keep me from reading such stuff. (chapter 6)

They did not paint his eyeglasses black, however. Knight began to search out back-date science fiction magazines, to subscribe to current ones, and to haunt libraries and bookstores, seizing "on any book whose title made it sound as if it might be science fiction." A fan had been born. In one of Pohl's science fiction magazines (Pohl, at nineteen, was already the editor of two low-budget pulp magazines), Knight discovered a listing of science fiction fan magazines (fanzines) and was soon corresponding with other young fans, including Wilson Tucker and Robert A. W. Lowndes. This led to Knight's writing, editing, and illustrating a fanzine of his own called *Snide*. The publishing of *Snide*—which Knight later referred to as his "passport out of the Pacific Northwest"—involved Knight in correspondence with members of the Futurian Society,

403

a group of young New York fans whose membership included such future notables as C. M. Kornbluth, Isaac Asimov, Donald A. Wollheim, Richard Wilson, Pohl, Lowndes, and others. Knight met the Futurians at the Third World Science Fiction Convention, in Denver in 1941, hitched a ride back to New York City with them, moved into a communal Futurian apartment, and began to try to break into the professional science fiction world.

That proved to be a slow process. His first sale was a cartoon, which he sold to *Amazing Stories* for three dollars. His first story, "Resilience," was donated to Wollheim's new magazine *Stirring Science Stories*, which had no editorial budget at all (the story appeared in the February 1941 issue). There were several other sales to minor magazines throughout the 1940's (primarily to *Planet Stories* and *Thrilling Wonder Stories*), many written under pseudonyms, several in collaboration with James Blish. The most prestigious sale of this period was probably "Tiger Ride" (1948), a story written in collaboration with Blish, which appeared in October in *Astounding Science-Fiction*. (Knight would be able to make only two more sales to John W. Campbell, Jr., *Astounding*'s fiercely idiosyncratic editor.)

Although Knight went on to work as a reader for a large literary agency, served as an assistant editor for several pulp magazines, and even briefly edited his own science fiction magazine (*Worlds Beyond*, which lasted for only three issues, 1950–1951), he made his first lasting and serious impact on the science fiction world as a critic, with a long series of book reviews and critical articles in the early and middle 1950's.

Knight's first review, his famous dissection of A. E. van Vogt's 1945 *The World of Ā*, was published in Larry Shaw's fanzine *Destiny's Child* in 1945. Although it appeared in a magazine of sharply limited circulation, this devastating review has been credited by some genre historians as having been a major contributing factor to the subsequent slump in van Vogt's popularity and critical reputation.

After a hiatus of several years, Knight began reviewing again in 1950, contributing a book review column called "The Dissecting Table" to his own short-lived magazine, *Worlds Beyond*. Over the next nine years, Knight produced a steady stream of criticism, which appeared in fanzines such as Walt Willis' *Hyphen* and Harlan Ellison's *Dimensions*, minor professional magazines such as Lester del Rey's *Space Science Fiction* and *Science Fiction Adventures*, or Lowndes' *Dynamic Science Fiction* and *Science Fiction Stories*. Later he reviewed in more prestigious professional magazines, such as *Infinity* and *The Magazine of Fantasy and Science Fiction* (*F&SF*). Knight's reviews were collected in book form as *In Search of Wonder* (1956), and that volume won Knight a Hugo award as best critic in 1956. Yet long before then Knight's reviewing had helped to make his reputation, establishing him as one of the keenest critical intellects in science fiction.

But it also did more than that: Knight's reviewing helped to revolutionize the general style and substance of science fiction criticism itself.

In both the fan magazines and the professional magazines of the time, criticism tended to be timid, superficial, and self-congratulatory, often consisting only of slightly reworded versions of the publicity handouts sent out by publishers. In contrast, Knight's reviews were articulate, penetrating, stylish, always entertaining (Knight's reviews of Jerry Sohl's *Point Ultimate* [1955] and of Austin Hall and Homer Eon Flint's *The Blind Spot* [1921; book form, 1951], for instance, are among the funniest pieces of nonfiction writing), and sometimes eviscerating. Knight respected no sacred cows and gave no quarter, attacking the most famous writers in the genre as readily as he attacked the fringe hacks who were churning out novelizations of the "giant insect" horror movies of the day.

Knight thus gained a somewhat unfair reputation as a "hostile" or "killer" critic. As he himself has pointed out: "The critic uses the same sharp-edged tools on all stories, but good stories resist; bad ones come to pieces." And, in fact, he was as useful pointing out why books succeeded as he was explaining why they failed. His ultimate importance as a critic goes far beyond his willingness to get blood on his hands.

The really important thing about Knight's criticism was the rationale at work behind it, the clearly stated and rigorously applied set of critical standards from which he worked. The salient part of Knight's credo as a critic was this: "That science fiction is a field of literature worth taking seriously, and that ordinary critical standards can be meaningfully applied to it: e.g., originality, sincerity, style, construction, logic, coherence, sanity, garden variety grammar" (*In Search of Wonder*, page 1).

This seems elementary enough now, but at the time it was a revelatory bombshell—even today, in fact, there are those who still consider it to be heretical. The attitude behind the credo—Knight's refusal to accept "special pleading" or to exempt science fiction from ordinary critical standards, and his determination to consider books only on their own merits, without regard to the sacrosanct reputations of certain authors—swept through science fiction's stagnant critical world like a cold wind, blowing many of the outmoded attitudes of the time away. A few books of science fiction criticism were published prior to *In Search of Wonder*, but Knight's book was the first to have a really widespread effect on the state of the art, and in this respect he is clearly the founder of science fiction criticism.

Knight stopped reviewing in 1960, resigning his position as *F&SF*'s reviewer after the editor refused to print a negative review of a Judith Merril novel. Knight's subsequent work in the role of critic/science fiction historian includes his anthology of critical articles, *Turning Points* (1977), in which two of the most valuable selections are his own essays "What Is Science Fiction?" and "Writing and Selling Science Fiction"; his history of the New York science fiction world of the 1940's and 1950's, *The Futurians*; and his frank and witty autobiographical study "Knight Piece," in *Hell's Cartographers* (1976). His critical

achievement was honored by the 1975 Pilgrim award for distinguished contributions to the study of science fiction.

At about the same time that Knight was establishing himself as science fiction's premier critic, he was also beginning to make a name for himself as a fiction writer. His work had never particularly impressed Campbell, editor of *Astounding*, at that time by far the most prestigious of all science fiction magazines. (In Knight's words: "Campbell returned my submissions . . . with scrawled comments such as 'early 1930' or 'so what?' which hurt my feelings without teaching me anything.") Unwelcome at *Astounding*, Knight (like many other writers to whom Campbell was cold, including most of the Futurians) was reduced to publishing in salvage markets. These included magazines like *Planet Stories*, *Thrilling Wonder Stories*, and a dozen others—magazines that were so far below *Astounding* in prestige that writers restricted to them were almost unknown, even within the science fiction community itself.

But by 1950 this situation had changed: two new science fiction magazines had been founded, Anthony Boucher and J. Francis McComas' *The Magazine of Fantasy and Science Fiction* and Horace L. Gold's *Galaxy Science Fiction*. These were not minor salvage markets, but major magazines, comparable in budget and prestige to *Astounding*. Whereas previously science fiction had only one major "voice"—that of *Astounding*—it now suddenly had three, each singing a song markedly different from the others. It was now possible to sell stories that disagreed with Campbell's sharply defined set of values and prejudices, and not only to get top money for them, but to have them presented in a major market, with a kind of visibility that had heretofore been achievable only in *Astounding*.

In this more open atmosphere, Knight's talent blossomed, and he became part of an evolutionary movement of writers—both novices and veterans—who created a new type of science fiction in the pages of the new magazines. Knight began to sell regularly to both *F&SF* and *Galaxy* (he would come to be

Damon Knight in 1980. PHOTO BY JAY KAY KLEIN

bered, even today. Appearing in the second issue of *Galaxy*, it indicated the direction that Knight's work would take for the next several years and it helped set the mood and tone of *Galaxy*.

"To Serve Man" also enjoys the odd distinction of being one of those rare stories—Avram Davidson's "Or All the Seas with Oysters" (1958), the story about coat hangers turning into bicycles, is another—that has been greatly diffused throughout popular culture. Even outside the boundaries of the science fiction world, many people know its plot without, perhaps, being able to remember its title or author. Most recently, during an interview in a nationally distributed magazine, James Michener described the plot of "To Serve Man" and referred to it as "great" without having the slightest idea who had written it. It has become a part of the mythological substructure of our time.

Knight followed the success of "To Serve Man" with a long series of stories for *Galaxy* (and, later, for its short-lived sister magazine, *Beyond*). Most were in the same vein—light, suave, witty, and inventive: "Cabin Boy" (1951), "Don't Live in the Past" (1951), "World Without Children" (1951), "Catch That Martian" (1952), "Babel II" (1953), "Four in One" (1953), "Natural State" (1954), "Special Delivery" (1954), "An Eye for a What?" (1957), "Man in the Jar" (1957), "Thing of Beauty" (1958), and others.

Some of these stories are rather thin (and were thin at the time), others are quite dated—as is much of the material *Galaxy* published—but many of them are still stylish and amusing even though, after decades have passed, the Manhattan of, say, "Babel II" is as nonexistent as Percival Lowell's Mars. The best of the stories Knight did for Gold (he sold stories of a somewhat different sort to *Galaxy* during the 1960's, when Pohl was the editor) is probably "Four in One." With its ingenious alien and a plot that seemingly ought to be that of a terrifying horror story, the story is ameliorated by the calm, logical, and clear-headedly rational way in which the protagonist deals with the catastrophe that has—

particularly identified with *Galaxy*), and almost overnight the public perception of him changed from one of "minor writer" to "major new talent."

Knight's first major story (he himself has referred to it as "the first story I ever wrote in my life that was worth a damn") was sold to *F&SF*. An ironic after-the-holocaust story, "Not with a Bang" (1949) was referred to by Boucher as "a new kind of catastrophe [story] . . . the cosmic cocktail mixed with a full jigger of wry." But it was Knight's next sale, "To Serve Man" (*Galaxy*, November 1950), that made his reputation. "Not with a Bang" has become dated, but "To Serve Man" is still funny, still surprising, and still delivers the bitter aftertaste that was characteristic of Knight's work and of much else that appeared in *Galaxy*. (Knight once said that beneath Gold's brilliance, innovation, and energy there was a "hard core of despair," and much the same could be said about his magazine.) "To Serve Man" is by no means Knight's best story, but it may possibly be his best remem-

literally—swallowed him up. Much the same could be said of several other Knight stories. "Man in the Jar" also holds up well and has more of a sting in its tail than Knight's *Galaxy* stories of this period are usually allowed to have. (I suspect that this story was actually bought by Pohl, who by the late 1950's was practically ghost-editing *Galaxy*, as Gold's interest and health waned.)

In many ways Knight was the prototypic *Galaxy* writer, rivaled for that position only by Theodore Sturgeon, Alfred Bester, and the collaborative team of Pohl and Kornbluth. Oddly enough for someone who has described himself as "a country yokel," one of the main things Knight brought to the field was, in Boucher's words, "a delightful quality of urbanity. . . . [He was] surely one of the most civilized of S. F. writers." Even his minor work was elegant, witty, sophisticated—urbane—in a way and to a degree that had rarely been seen in science fiction previously. His work also was urbane in a related definition of the word: characteristic of the city as distinguished from the country. Almost all of Knight's characters are city people; his future societies usually have come to be totally dominated by cities and the values of city people, and several later stories—"The Country of the Kind" (1955), "The Dying Man" (1957), "Mary" (1964), "Down There" (1973)—deal with the future evolution of the city and of city life. Knight specialized in this type of ultracivilized, highly urbanized future scenario, bringing it to a peak of refinement in stories such as "The Dying Man" and "Mary." This sort of urban future is peopled by rich and languid sophisticates (usually decadent, sometimes naïve and childlike) whose technology has given them nearly the power of gods; they take that technology and power as much for granted as we do the automobile or the television. Similar futures feature prominently in the work of later writers such as Cordwainer Smith, Samuel R. Delany, John Varley, Roger Zelazny, Robert Silverberg, Kate Wilhelm, Gene Wolfe, Edward Bryant, James Tiptree, Jr., Joe Haldeman, Jack Dann, Michael Bishop, Michael Swanwick, and others. And although the vision of the urban future can by no means be said to have originated with Knight—it goes back at least as far as E. M. Forster and H. G. Wells—he certainly helped to refine and develop its treatment in science fiction. Here and there in later work by other authors, there are hints of his direct influence—at the very least, with Bishop, Tiptree, and Wilhelm.

Some of the stories Knight was publishing in other markets during this period were strongly reminiscent of his *Galaxy* work. Stories like "Idiot Stick" (in Pohl's anthology *Star Science Fiction Stories, no. 4*, 1958) and "You're Another" (*F&SF*, 1955) read as though they could easily have been *Galaxy* stories, although evidently Gold did not agree. Other stories were markedly different in tone, impact, and intent, increasingly so as Knight began to grow away from the strictures of the typical *Galaxy* story.

By the middle 1950's, Knight was at the height of his powers and producing his most memorable work. But although the best work of this period is well above anything he had ever written before, and in fact stands with the best work ever produced in the genre, neither Gold nor Campbell, each trapped by too limited and overly specialized (albeit diametrically opposed) definitions of science fiction, would touch it. Instead Knight's best stories again went primarily to salvage markets: "Rule Golden" (1954) to *Science Fiction Adventures*; "The Earth Quarter" (1955) to *If*; "Extempore" (1956) and "The Dying Man" to *Infinity*; and "Time Enough" (1960) to *Amazing*. Only "The Country of the Kind," "Stranger Station" (1956), and "What Rough Beast?" (1959) sold to a major market, *F&SF*. ("The Enemy" [1958] sold to *Venture*, *F&SF*'s sister magazine.) That Knight, one of *Galaxy*'s brightest stars, was forced to turn to other markets in order to sell his best work is indicative of the factors that would lead to *Galaxy*'s decline and subsequently drive a soured Gold from the genre.

The new Knight stories were powerful, dark, somberly lyrical, sometimes despairing, with a psychological depth and a subtlety of characterization not previously seen in most of Knight's work. In Knight's earlier work (as in most *Galaxy*-style material), the characterization had been done in bright primary colors, tending toward the cartoonlike. But Cudyk in "The Earth Quarter," Dio in "The Dying Man," the title character in "Mary," the unnamed protagonist of "The Country of the Kind," Paul of "Stranger Station," and even Jawj Pembun of the somewhat lighter "Double Meaning" (1953) are all fully realized human portraiture, complex, vivid, and contradictory. We encounter them with a shock of recognition rare even in mainstream fiction. The newer work also had many disquieting things to say about the human condition, projecting several future scenarios that seem at first glance utopian, but which underneath this facade are subtly and rather unrelievedly bleak. "The Country of the Kind," perhaps Knight's best story, is one of the first modern science fiction stories to examine the type of scenario that later came to be referred to as a "Skinnerian" future. Although it was published well before B. F. Skinner's *Walden Two* (1948) became widely known, it is still one of the most effective fictional counterarguments to "social engineering" philosophies of the Skinnerian type.

Much of Knight's best work was also (as he has said regarding "The Earth Quarter") "a reaction to the macho science fiction identified in the 50s with John Campbell, who would not publish any story in which another race turned out to be more advanced, smarter, or in any other way better than us" (Introduction to *Rule Golden and Other Stories*, 1979). In "The Earth Quarter" in particular, Knight portrays a complete reversal of the Campbellian vision, usually typified by Earthmen who function as Kiplingesque colonial administrators, superior in technology, moral values, and pluck to the swarming hordes of alien "niggers" they rule. Here, instead, Earthmen not only do not dominate the Galaxy, but are restricted to squalid ghettos where they live precariously on the grudging sufferance of the technologically (and morally) superior alien races who (with excellent reason) distrust them. Nor do the Earthmen ever prove worthy of even this limited contact, and the civilized alien races eventually realize that they can ensure their own safety and the peace of the Galaxy only by banning humankind from space altogether. It is also worth noting that, in Knight's words, "the villain of this story, Lawrence Rack, is my version of the hero of a story by L. Ron Hubbard, 'To the Stars,' which Campbell published in 1950" (*ibid.*). Similarly, in "Double Meaning," the ostensible hero, Thorne Spangler, is bested at every turn by Jawj Pembun, the fat, uncouth, and sloppy "ugly little beast of a colonial," a "shabby mongrel" who would at best have been the comic relief in most Campbellian stories, and more probably the villain. As Knight said: "I played him [Pembun] off against my version of a typical science fiction hero, Thorne Spangler—an ambitious upstart, tough, clever and unscrupulous. I wanted to show that the bastards don't always win; they are vulnerable because they are self-deluding and humorless" (*ibid.*).

Like his reviewer's credo, these reversals may seem obvious now, but they were fiercely heretical at the time and planted seeds that eventually blossomed in the minds of other writers. This became particularly obvious in the early 1970's (after years of cultural and economic chaos, after people had begun to speak of the decline of the West, after Vietnam). Then young writers began writing stories in which the aliens came to *us* in huge, enigmatic machines far beyond the powers of our technology, reducing us to the role of provincial natives. In fact, Knight had as much to do with the gradual shift in the perception and presentation of aliens in science fiction as any other author; he probably wrote more about human-alien interaction than any other writer of the 1950's, with the possible exception of Sturgeon. In recent times, only Tiptree has tackled the subject with anything like Knight's variety, quality, and prolificacy. Among Knight's most influential alien-contact stories are "Stranger Station," in which humans seem as monstrous to an alien as the alien does to us, and "Rule Golden," in which aliens seek to help us live in peace with one another by making us, ironically enough, more *human*.

Also ironically, for a man who once said in print that the time-travel story was dead, Knight wrote (subsequently) several interesting variants on the time-travel story, among them three of his best, least read, and most underappreciated stories: "Extempore," "Time Enough," and "What Rough Beast?"

With the beginning of the 1960's, Knight's output decreased dramatically, although several of his best stories were still to appear, including "Mary" and "Semper Fi" (1964). "Semper Fi" has a particularly disquieting observation to make about the seductive effects of certain types of technology on human nature and directly influenced Wilhelm's story "Baby, You Were Great" (1967), which deals with the same theme from a different perspective. Knight's most recent really influential story is "Masks" (1968), one of the first stories to explore the implications of the new technological advances that were then beginning to revolutionize the field of prosthesiology. Michael Bishop's "The House of Compassionate Sharers" (1977) is a tribute to "Masks" and an extension of its themes. Since "Masks," Knight has written very little fiction, stopping altogether for several years. In 1968 the then-uncompleted sequence of "Thorinn" stories was published in *Galaxy*; the stories were melded into the 1981 novel *The World and Thorinn*. As of this writing, Knight has only produced two additional short stories of substance: "Down There" (*New Dimensions 3*, 1973) and "I See You" (*F&SF*, October 1976, the special Damon Knight issue).

In retrospect it is plain that, like a handful of other writers during the 1950's (Sturgeon, Bester, Leiber, Kornbluth, Bradbury, and Budrys), Knight at his best was engaged in the chore of redrawing the boundaries of the science fiction short story, redefining its possibilities, and greatly expanding its limits. For this alone—ignoring his accomplishments as a critic and an editor—the new writers of the 1960's and 1970's, who built on the foundation laid in the 1950's, owe him a great deal.

Like Bradbury, Ellison, Tiptree, and a few other science fiction writers, Knight's reputation as a writer rests almost entirely on his short fiction. And, in fact, none of his novels have reached the level of quality of his best short fiction. Many of them are "expansions" of earlier, shorter works—"The Earth Quarter" was expanded into *The Sun Saboteurs* (1961), "Double Meaning" into *The Rithian Terror* (1965), and so forth—and in almost every case the original version is superior. A comment Knight made about the publication of "I See You"—"You may think it is a short story, but it is really a novel on the plan of *A for Anything* and *Hell's Pavement*, only much compressed"—goes a long way toward explaining the sense of dissatisfaction many get from some other Knight novels: they are really short stories, only much expanded. The success and effectiveness of "I See You" suggests that, say, *Hell's Pavement* (1955; also titled *Analogue Man*), would have benefited from being similarly compressed—and, in fact, almost everything the novel has to say is implicit in "The Analogues" (1952), the short story from which it grew. *The Other Foot* (also titled *Mind Switch*, 1965) has its good points, and one critic, Barry M. Malzberg, has called *A for Anything* (also titled *The People Maker*, 1959) "a masterpiece . . . [which] stands to last as long as any novel of its decade." Knight's best novel to date, by a comfortable margin, is *The World and Thorinn*, which not only is a vividly realized "quest" novel of the picaresque sort, but also provides the plainest possible example of the dogged persistence and levelheaded ingenuity the typical Knight protagonist displays when faced with seemingly insurmountable problems.

Knight became increasingly involved with other interests as his production of fiction waned, perhaps not coincidentally. He briefly edited *If* magazine (1958), served as the science fiction consultant for Berkley Medallion (1960–1966), turned out the first few titles in a long string of critically acclaimed reprint anthologies, founded the Science Fiction Writers of America, and served as its first president (1965). But throughout most of the 1960's and

1970's Knight's influence made itself felt most strongly in two other areas: as director of the Milford Science Fiction Writers' Conference and as editor of the original anthology series *Orbit*.

Knight moved to Milford, Pennsylvania, in the middle 1950's; there, in 1956, Knight, Judith Merril, and Blish founded and ran the first Milford Science Fiction Writers' Conference. Merril and Blish soon disassociated themselves from the conference, but Knight (later assisted by his third wife, Kate Wilhelm, whom he married in 1963) continued to run it yearly for over twenty years, providing almost the only forum available for the exchange and cross-fertilization of ideas, attitudes, and techniques between top science fiction professionals. The Milford Conference also inspired, directly or indirectly, a number of other writers' workshops and critical self-help groups in the 1970's—the Guilford Writers' Workshop, the Windy City Workshop, the Turkey City Workshop, and the Philford Writers' Workshop. It was the model for Clarion, science fiction's most famous writing seminar for novices, in which Knight and Wilhelm also directly participate each year as instructors.

Knight started *Orbit* in 1966; it was the first important original anthology series of the New Wave period of the late 1960's and became the longest-running anthology series in science fiction history. At one time the spearhead of the avant-garde movement in American science fiction, *Orbit* published the bulk of Wilhelm's short fiction, much of Gene Wolfe's best work, and stories by Joanna Russ, Thomas M. Disch, Richard McKenna, R. A. Lafferty, Avram Davidson, Ursula K. Le Guin, Harlan Ellison, Carol Emshwiller, Brian W. Aldiss, Norman Spinrad, Langdon Jones, James Sallis, Richard Wilson, and others who might otherwise have had difficulty finding a home. *Orbit* was also instrumental in introducing the work of newer authors such as Edward Bryant, Gardner Dozois, George Alec Effinger, Jack Dann, Robert Thurston, Joan D. Vinge, Charles L. Grant, Vonda N. McIntyre, and others. In later years, *Orbit* changed pub-

lishers and went into a slow decline and was finally dropped. *Orbit 21* (the final one) appeared in 1980. *The Best Stories from Orbit 1–10* (1975) is one of Knight's most valuable anthologies.

—GARDNER DOZOIS

Damon Knight's next novel was *The Man in the Tree* (1984), which tells the story of a gentle boy with a magic/psychic gift who grows into an eight-foot adult and eventually becomes the Christ figure of a new religion. His talent of reaching into parallel worlds for alternative versions of objects echoes Knight's earlier "What Rough Beast." Similarly, the idiosyncratic emerging utopia of the CV trilogy—*CV* (1985), *The Observers* (1988), and *A Reasonable World* (1991)—is reminiscent of "Rule Golden." That story's alien gas that imposed nonviolence on humanity by sensitizing us to our victims' pain is now replaced by alien symbionts first perceived as a dangerous disease—for they may punish violent impulses with death. It is characteristic of Knight's conscientious intelligence that he should return to these interesting notions and expand on their possibilities.

But he can still surprise us. *Why Do Birds* (1992) is a sui generis oddity, a comic yet melancholy end-of-the-world novel starring an apparent fraud who announces that the entire human race must be placed in suspended animation and stacked in a colossal box to be rescued from doomed Earth by aliens. Though this all seems absurd, the "fraud" has a magic ring, allegedly an alien gift, whose touch can convince anyone of his story. Subversively, events turn out precisely as science fiction expectations have led us to assume they will not: the partly-filled box is uplifted, Earth is destroyed, and we are left uncertain of whether it was all a black joke on humanity. Even odder is *Humpty Dumpty: An Oval* (1996), whose hero's skull is cracked by a bullet, causing his reality—or is it only his?—to topple into surrealism. Craters like bullet wounds open in the earth; semicomic aliens and conspiracies abound; disorientation escalates toward a monstrous nonsense-nightmare climax as in *Alice in Wonderland* and gives way to enigmatic, elegiac, and perhaps tragic clarity. These strange, late books may be Knight's fictional masterpieces.

In 1995 Damon Knight was honored with the Grand Master award of the Science Fiction and Fantasy Writers of America. After over fifty years of significant accomplishments, he is entitled to rest on his laurels. But science fiction connoisseurs hope that Knight will produce yet more offbeat fiction.

—DAVID LANGFORD

Selected Bibliography

WORKS OF DAMON KNIGHT

FICTION

Hell's Pavement. New York: Lion, 1955; London: Banner, 1958. Reprinted as *Analogue Men*, New York: Berkley Medallion, 1962; London: Sphere, 1967.
Masters of Evolution. New York: Ace, 1959.
The People Maker. Rockville Centre, N.Y.: Zenith, 1959. Reprinted as *A for Anything*, London: Four Square, 1961; New York: Berkley, 1965.
Far Out: Thirteen Science Fiction Stories. New York: Simon and Schuster, 1961; London: Gollancz, 1961. (Short stories.)
The Sun Saboteurs. New York: Ace, 1961. Reprinted as *The Earth Quarter*, New York: Lancer, 1970.
In Deep. New York: Berkley Medallion, 1963; London: Gollancz, 1964. (Short stories; British edition omits "The Handler.")
Mind Switch. New York: Berkley Medallion, 1965. Reprinted as *The Other Foot*, London: Whiting and Wheaton, 1966; New York: Manor, 1971.
Off Center. New York: Ace, 1965. (Bound with *The Rithian Terror*.) Reprinted as *Off Centre*, London: Gollancz, 1969. (Short stories; British edition contains three additional stories.)
The Rithian Terror. New York: Ace, 1965. (Bound with *Off Center*.) Retitled *Double Meaning*, 1974.
Turning On: Thirteen Stories. Garden City, N.Y.: Doubleday 1966. Reprinted as *Turning On: Fourteen Stories*, London: Gollancz, 1967.
Three Novels: Rule Golden, Natural State, The Dying Man. Garden City, N.Y.: Doubleday, 1967; London: Gollancz, 1967. Reprinted as *Natural State and Other Stories*, London: Pan, 1975.
Two Novels. London: Gollancz, 1974. (Omnibus comprising *The Rithian Terror*, as *Double Meaning*, and *The Sun Saboteurs*, as *The Earth Quarter*.)

The Best of Damon Knight. Garden City, N.Y.: Doubleday, 1976. (Short stories.)
Rule Golden and Other Stories. New York: Avon, 1979. (Short stories, incorporating *Three Novels* with two additional stories.)
Better Than One, with Kate Wilhelm. Boston: Noreascon II, 1980. (Short stories and poems.)
The World and Thorinn. New York: Putnam, 1980.
The Man in the Tree. New York: Berkley, 1984; London: Gollancz, 1985.
CV. New York: TOR, 1985. (CV series, no. 1.)
Late Knight Edition. Cambridge, Mass.: NESFA, 1985. (Short stories.)
The Observers. New York: TOR, 1988. (CV series, no. 2.)
God's Nose. Eugene, Oreg.: Pulphouse, 1991. (Short stories.)
One Side Laughing: Stories Unlike Other Stories. New York: St. Martin's, 1991. (Short stories.)
A Reasonable World. New York: TOR, 1991. (CV series, no. 3.)
Rule Golden/Double Meaning. New York: TOR, 1991. (*Rule Golden* plus *The Rithian Terror* as *Double Meaning*.)
Why Do Birds. New York: TOR, 1992.
Humpty Dumpty: An Oval. New York: TOR, 1996.

NONFICTION

In Search of Wonder: Essays on Modern Science Fiction. Chicago: Advent, 1956. Revised and expanded, Chicago: Advent, 1967.
"Science Fiction Basics." *Library Journal*, 1 July 1966.
Charles Fort: Prophet of the Unexplained. Garden City, N.Y.: Doubleday, 1970; London: Gollancz, 1971.
"Charting Utopia." In *Clarion*. Edited by Robin Scott Wilson. New York: Signet, 1971.
"Goodbye, Henry J. Kostkos, Goodbye." In *Clarion II*. Edited by Robin Scott Wilson. New York: Signet, 1972.
Introduction to *The Past Through Tomorrow*, by Robert A. Heinlein. New York: Putnam, 1975.
"The Value of Science Fiction." In *The Visual Encyclopedia of Science Fiction*. Edited by Brian Ash. New York: Harmony, 1975.
"Knight Piece." In *Hell's Cartographers*. Edited by Brian W. Aldiss and Harry Harrison. New York: Harper and Row, 1976.
"What Works for Me." In *The S.F.W.A. Handbook*. Edited by Mildred Downey Broxon. Privately printed by the Science Fiction Writers of America, 1976.
The Futurians: The Story of the Science Fiction "Family" of the 30's That Produced Today's Top SF Writers and Editors. New York: John Day, 1977.
"Something That Works." In *Clarion SF*. Edited by Kate Wilhelm. New York: Berkley Medallion, 1977.
Turning Points: Essays on the Art of Science Fiction. Edited by Damon Knight. New York: Harper and Row, 1977. (Contains several of Knight's critical essays,

such as "What Is Science Fiction?" and "Writing and Selling Science Fiction.")

Introduction to *Rule Golden and Other Stories*. New York: Avon, 1979.

Creating Short Fiction. Cincinnati, Ohio: Writer's Digest, 1981. Revised edition, New York: St. Martin's/Griffin, 1997.

EDITED ANTHOLOGIES

A Century of Science Fiction. New York: Simon and Schuster, 1962; London: Gollancz, 1963.

First Flight: Maiden Voyages in Space and Time. New York: Lancer, 1963. Reprinted as *Now Begins Tomorrow*, New York: Lancer, 1969. Revised with Martin H. Greenberg and Joseph D. Olander as *First Voyages*, New York: Avon, 1981.

A Century of Great Short Science Fiction Novels. New York: Delacorte, 1964; London: Gollancz, 1965.

Tomorrow × 4. New York: Fawcett, 1964; London: Coronet, 1967.

Beyond Tomorrow: Ten Science Fiction Adventures. New York: Harper and Row, 1965; London: Gollancz, 1968.

The Dark Side. Garden City, N.Y.: Doubleday, 1965; London: Dobson, 1966.

The Shape of Things. New York: Popular Library, 1965.

Thirteen French Science-Fiction Stories. Translated and edited by Damon Knight. New York: Bantam, 1965; London: Corgi, 1965.

Cities of Wonder. Garden City, N.Y.: Doubleday, 1966; London: Dobson, 1968.

Nebula Award Stories 1965. New York: Doubleday, 1966; London: Gollancz, 1967.

Orbit. Vols. 1–12. New York: Putnam, 1966–1973. Vol. 1. London: Whiting and Wheaton, 1966. Vols. 2–8. London: Rapp and Whiting, 1968–1974.

Science Fiction Inventions. New York: Lancer, 1967.

Worlds to Come: Nine Science Fiction Adventures. New York: Harper and Row, 1967; London: Gollancz, 1969.

The Metal Smile. New York: Belmont, 1968.

One Hundred Years of Science Fiction. New York: Simon and Schuster, 1968; London: Gollancz, 1969.

Toward Infinity: Nine Science Fiction Tales. New York: Simon and Schuster, 1968. Reprinted as *Towards Infinity: Nine Science Fiction Adventures*, London: Gollancz, 1970.

Dimension X: Five Science Fiction Novellas. New York: Simon and Schuster, 1970; London: Gollancz, 1972. (For children.)

First Contact. New York: Pinnacle, 1971.

A Pocketful of Stars. Garden City, N.Y.: Doubleday, 1971; London: Gollancz, 1972.

Perchance to Dream. Garden City, N.Y.: Doubleday, 1972; London: Gollancz, 1972.

A Science Fiction Argosy. New York: Simon and Schuster, 1972; London: Gollancz, 1973.

The Golden Road: Great Tales of Fantasy and the Supernatural. New York: Simon and Schuster, 1973; London: Gollancz, 1974.

Tomorrow and Tomorrow: Ten Tales of the Future. New York: Simon and Schuster, 1973; London: Gollancz, 1974.

Happy Endings: 15 Stories by the Masters of the Macabre. Indianapolis: Bobbs-Merrill, 1974.

Elsewhere × 3. London: Coronet, 1974.

Orbit. Vol. 13. New York: Berkley, 1974.

Orbit. Vols. 14–21. New York: Harper and Row, 1974–1980.

A Shocking Thing. New York: Pocket Books, 1974.

Best Stories from Orbit 1–10. New York: Putnam, 1975.

Science Fiction of the Thirties. Indianapolis: Bobbs-Merrill, 1975.

The Clarion Awards. Garden City, N.Y.: Doubleday, 1984.

Monad: Essays on Science Fiction. Vols. 1–3. Eugene, Oreg.: Pulphouse, 1990–1994.

CRITICAL AND BIOGRAPHICAL STUDIES

Blish, James. "All in a Knight's Work." *Speculation*, 29 (1971).

———, as by William Atheling, Jr. Chapter two. In *The Issue at Hand*. Chicago: Advent, 1964.

———, as by William Atheling, Jr. Chapter two. In *More Issues at Hand*. Chicago: Advent, 1970.

Boucher, Anthony. Introduction to *Far Out*, by Damon Knight. New York: Simon and Schuster, 1961.

———, Introduction to *In Search of Wonder*, by Damon Knight. Chicago: Advent, 1956. Revised and expanded, Chicago: Advent, 1967.

Budrys, Algis. "Paradise Charted." *TriQuarterly*, 49 (fall 1980).

———, "Obstacles and Ironies in Science Fiction Criticism." *The Patchin Review* (September 1981).

———, "In Search of Wonder." In *Benchmarks*. Carbondale and Edwardsville: Southern Illinois University Press, 1985.

Clute, John. "Why Do Birds." In *Look at the Evidence*. Seattle, Wash.: Serconia Press, 1995. Liverpool, England: Liverpool University Press, 1995.

Edwards, Malcolm J., and John Clute. "Damon Knight." In *The Encyclopedia of Science Fiction*, 2nd edition. Edited by John Clute and Peter Nicholls. London: Orbit, 1993. New York: St. Martin's, 1993.

Malzberg, Barry N. "Introduction: Dark of the Knight." In *The Best of Damon Knight*. New York: Pocket Books, 1980.

Miranda, Vincent. "Damon Knight: Bibliography." *The Magazine of Fantasy and Science Fiction* (November 1976).

Sturgeon, Theodore. "Damon: An Appreciation." *The Magazine of Fantasy and Science Fiction* (November 1976).

C. M. KORNBLUTH

(1923–1958)

CYRIL M. KORNBLUTH was born in New York City in 1923, the son of a bailiff in the municipal court. He was active in the then-tiny world of science fiction fandom in the mid-1930's and soon became associated with the Futurian Society of New York. Other members of this small but influential group included Frederik Pohl, James Blish, Isaac Asimov, Judith Merril, Donald A. Wollheim, Damon Knight, and several others who later had success as science fiction writers, editors, or agents. (The group's history is detailed at length in Knight's book *The Futurians* [1977].)

Kornbluth was the youngest of the Futurians, and his precocity is legendary. Knight quotes a family story to the effect that "one day when a passerby cooed at him in his baby carriage, he announced, 'Madam, I am not the child you think me.'" In the early 1940's Pohl, Wollheim, and a third Futurian, Robert A. W. Lowndes, were all editors of low-budget science fiction pulp magazines (Pohl of both *Astonishing Stories* and *Super Science Stories*, Wollheim of *Cosmic Stories* and *Stirring Science Stories*, and Lowndes of *Future Fiction* and *Science Fiction Quarterly*). Unable to compete with higher-paying magazines for the established writers of the day, they turned to their ambitious fellow Futurians for contributions. Kornbluth responded with no fewer than thirty-five stories, written alone or in collaboration with other Futurians, between April 1940 and August 1942. The first of them was "Stepsons of Mars," written with Richard Wilson under the name Ivar Towers. Kornbluth did not put his own name on any

of these early stories. His solo stories appeared under the bylines Cecil Corwin, Walter C. Davies, Kenneth Falconer, and S. D. Gottesman. The Gottesman name was also used on six collaborations with Pohl. Kornbluth collaborated with Pohl as Paul Dennis Lavond and Scott Mariner; with Pohl and Lowndes as Lavond; with Pohl and another Futurian, Dirk Wylie, under Wylie's name; and with Lowndes, Wollheim, and two other Futurians as Arthur Cooke. So great was Kornbluth's output that his pseudonyms sometimes filled a substantial portion of a magazine—the June 1941 *Stirring Science Stories*, for example, contained no fewer than four Kornbluth stories.

Not surprisingly, these early stories are in general forgettable; what *is* surprising is the overall level of competence they demonstrate, considering that Kornbluth was seventeen or eighteen years old when he wrote them. The eight Cecil Corwin stories—mostly humorous fantasies—were collected (together with one later story) in *Thirteen O'Clock and Other Zero Hours*, edited by James Blish (1970).

In 1943, Kornbluth married Mary G. Byers—herself a big science fiction fan—and joined the United States Army, originally training as a machinist. After enrolling in an army-sponsored educational program, he was reassigned as an infantry private and served in Europe—notably in the Battle of the Bulge—as a heavy machine gunner. It was here that he developed the severe hypertension that eventually caused his early death.

After discharge from the army, Kornbluth spent some time at the University of Chicago, but he did not complete a degree. He subsequently went to work for a Chicago wire service as a rewrite man, joining fellow science fiction writer and former Futurian Richard Wilson. This journalistic experience is reflected in his later fiction, most notably in "The Silly Season" (1950).

Although Kornbluth published various pulp fiction in the late 1940's, he did not publish science fiction until 1949, when "The Only Thing We Learn" appeared under his own name in *Startling Stories*. Three further significant stories, "The Little Black Bag," "The Mindworm," and "The Silly Season," followed in 1950. "The Marching Morons," "With These Hands," and "Friend to Man" were published in 1951, as was the *Galaxy* magazine version of the first novel on which he collaborated, "Mars Child," written with Merril under the pseudonym Cyril M. Judd. ("Mars Child" was published in book form as *Outpost Mars* [1952].) In 1951, Kornbluth became a full-time writer.

These stories mark the beginning of Kornbluth's maturity as a writer, although he was still at an age when most writers are just starting out. His teenage work was precociously inventive and technically adept, but lacked any distillation of human experience. The Kornbluth who returned to science fiction in 1949 had lived intensely in the adult world, as a soldier and reporter, for several years, and the difference in his fiction is readily apparent. Kornbluth reportedly was always sarcastic, sardonic, even cruel; but now his attitude had matured into deep pessimism, even despair.

"The Little Black Bag" is possibly Kornbluth's best-known short story. The bag of the title is a highly advanced medical kit from the future that is transported backward in time and falls into the hands of a down-and-out physician who has lost his license to practice. This doctor uses it to rehabilitate himself, and he fully intends to hand the bag over to scientists so that its advanced instruments and drugs can be duplicated for the benefit of all

humanity. But his assistant—an avaricious, cunning, desperate slum girl—sees the chance of a fortune slipping away with his altruism, and after an argument she kills him with one of the highly advanced scalpels. In an ironic final twist, this murder causes a monitor in the future to disconnect the bag's mysterious power supply, so that when the girl tries to demonstrate to a potential customer the miraculous ability of one of the knives to cut through flesh without leaving any trace of its passage, she kills herself. Thus greed triumphs over altruism but leads to its own downfall. "The Little Black Bag" is a moral tale, although hardly a comforting one.

The triumph of ignorant cunning over selfless intelligence that "The Little Black Bag" recounts is also a reflection of the social situation at the heart of its science-fictional rationale. The future from which the bag comes is one in which the average intelligence of the populace has greatly declined because the foolish have continued to breed while the intelligent have prudently practiced birth control. A small cadre of intelligent people secretly oversees the lives of the subnormal billions; instruments like those in the medical kit have to be foolproof because the "doctors" using them are, in fact, fools. Kornbluth returned to this idea—reportedly at Pohl's suggestion—in the other story for which he is best remembered, "The Marching Morons."

In this story a man from the twentieth century is accidentally put into suspended animation and is revived centuries hence in the kind of future sketched in "The Little Black Bag." The intelligent minority, despairing of its situation, is desperate for a solution. They turn to the man from the past, hoping that he will be able to suggest an idea they have missed. He does indeed come up with a solution: the moronic masses are to be convinced of the virtues of colonizing Venus, herded into rockets that do not work properly, and ejected into space to die. This final solution is carried out, but in another ironic twist ending, the twentieth-century man is loaded on the final ship: there is no place for him and his savagely primitive ideas in the utopian society that presumably will ensue on Earth.

"The Marching Morons" has, not surprisingly, been a controversial story. It has been criticized, sometimes at great length; for example, in D. West's "The Right Sort of People." West sums up the story as "one of the clearest possible examples of what can go wrong with the genre: of dark, miserable, fear-ridden fantasies of revenge and power masquerading as the triumph of scientific objectivity over emotion and the victory of reason and logic over irrationality" (page 18). This criticism seems at first glance easily justified: the idiot masses of the story are certainly objects of contempt and ridicule; and while the twentieth-century man, "Honest" John Barlow, is a mean and despicable character who gets his comeuppance from the future's intellectual elite, they are only too happy to adopt his Nazi-like solution to their problems. Are we, then, supposed to take their side and applaud their ruthlessness as a necessary means to a desirable end?

The answer must be "no": this is a story whose intent is more subtle than that, although it must be admitted that—like other Kornbluth stories—it does carry overtones of intellectual snobbery, to such an extent that Kornbluth is responsible in part for the common misreading. At the center of the story is a traditional motif: a man from one era translated into another. In this case the man is from our own time. The people of the future look to him for the special wisdom that our civilization can pass on to them—and the only thing Barlow is able to teach them is how to commit mass murder. They are quick learners, though, and by the end of the story they have applied the techniques they have learned to the disposal of Barlow. One member of their society has quietly (but with considerable symbolic significance) committed suicide rather than go ahead with Barlow's plan. The inference is clear: any society they build will be irreparably tainted by the evil they have learned.

Beneath the surface snobbery and comedy (for all its blackness there is much humor in "The Marching Morons") lies a deep pessimism, a despair regarding the ability of the human race to overcome its worst instincts. Similar feelings underlie stories like "The Little Black Bag" and "The Mindworm," in which a telepathic mutant turns out to be a sort of emotional vampire that can be defeated only through residual superstition in a remote community. "The Luckiest Man in Denv" (1952) involves an attempt to end a future war between American city-fortresses that is undermined by ambitious fanatics. In "The Silly Season" Martians conquer Earth by taking advantage of the idiocies of tabloid journalism to ensure that reports of their coming are not taken seriously; this is a variant on the story of the boy who cried "wolf!"

Between the years 1951 and 1958, Kornbluth wrote—alone or in collaboration—a total of sixteen novels, nine of which are science fiction. Of these, four were collaborations with Pohl, two were written with Merril, and three were solo efforts.

Kornbluth's first two novels were collaborations with Merril as Cyril M. Judd. *Outpost Mars* ("Mars Child"), based on an abandoned short story by Pohl, was started by Merril. After writing about 18,000 words, she became stuck; and Kornbluth, after reading the fragment, suggested a collaboration. He revised and expanded the first part, and they plotted and wrote the remainder together. It is an unexceptional novel, overpraised at the time of its publication for mature characterization that in retrospect reads like women's magazine clichés, concerning mutations in children born to an embryonic human colony on Mars. *Gunner Cade* (1952) is more satisfying, although it is little more than action-adventure: Cade is a mercenary in a militaristic postholocaust society who is slowly but inevitably drawn into joining a rebellion against the repressive status quo.

Kornbluth's third collaborative novel, with Pohl, was *The Space Merchants* (1953; serialized as a somewhat different version in *Galaxy* as "Gravy Planet," 1952). This is the novel that established both authors' reputations (although Kornbluth was already highly regarded by the small group of writers, editors, and fans who were aware of his prolific pseudonymous work). In *New Maps of Hell* (1960) Kingsley Amis says *The Space Merchants* had "many claims to being the best science fiction novel so far." In *The Way the Future Was* (1978), Pohl states that *The Space Merchants* has been translated into "some twenty-five languages" and estimates total sales of about 10 million copies.

The Space Merchants started life as a solo Pohl novel, but after writing the first 20,000 words Pohl—like Judith Merril with *Outpost Mars*—became stuck and turned to Kornbluth for help. Kornbluth rewrote the opening, added the middle section, and then wrote alternating sections of the last third of the novel with Pohl.

The novel takes us into a future world dominated by advertising agencies; a cutthroat capitalist ethic shapes a society increasingly marked by overpopulation and scarce resources. The delineation of this society is sharp, witty, and inventive—a model science fiction social satire. It must be noted, though, that most of this invention is concentrated in the first third of the novel. The problem with the story is quite evidently that nothing actually happens during this opening section; the solution to the problem that Kornbluth effects (reportedly—see *The Way the Future Was*, page 194—at the suggestion of William Tenn) is to have the novel's protagonist, successful advertising executive Mitchell Courtenay, literally hit on the head. He awakes to find himself officially dead and apparently condemned to spend the rest of his life in degrading manual labor. Through his eyes we see the seamy underbelly of his society, and we come to recognize its gross inequities.

This is a seemingly efficient solution to the technical problem, but it is a pulp-magazine formulaic solution. Thereafter the novel never recaptures its early imaginative density and thrust. Amis' reading of Kornbluth's solo novels led him to the conclusion—frequently rebutted by later critics—that "[Kornbluth's] part in *The Space Merchants* was roughly to provide the more violent action while Pohl filled in the social background and satire" (page 125). This is certainly a crude and insupportable analysis of the two writers' respective capabilities, but in this instance it appears to lead Amis to the right conclusion. Kornbluth's contribution to the novel seems chiefly to have been his mastery of the techniques of genre fiction. Pohl's fragment may thus have been turned into a publishable novel, but the whole is of lesser value than the part.

Pohl and Kornbluth went on to write three more novels together: *Search the Sky* (1954), *Gladiator-at-Law* (1955), and *Wolfbane* (1959) an earlier and shorter version of which was first published in *Galaxy*, 1957). *Search the Sky* presents a series of absurd societies on different planets, culminating with a reprise of the "Marching Morons" society on Earth; the episodes, while inventive, are too short and superficial for the novel to be more than a minor entertainment. *Gladiator-at-Law* is an attempt, on the whole unfortunate, to repeat the success of *The Space Merchants*, this time presenting a future America dominated by a single, vastly corrupt corporation; the plot, unfortunately, is so implausible as totally to undercut some of the incidental invention.

Wolfbane is more ambitious and original. An alien planet has entered the solar system and kidnapped Earth; the two worlds are now in deep space, orbiting the Moon, which has been turned by the aliens into an artificial sun. The remaining few humans have developed a fatalistic, Eastern-influenced culture, designed for survival on an extremely low-calorie diet and steeped in Zen Buddhism. A few renegade individualists—derisively termed the "Wolves"—wish to free humanity from the control of the alien Pyramids. *Wolfbane* is highly inventive but too superficial to be satisfactory as a novel. It seems probable that the Pohl-Kornbluth collaborative technique that evolved after *The Space Merchants*—they would outline the plots of the novels together and would then take turns writing them in 1,500-word sections in a single continuous effort—was an efficient way of producing a novel in a short time, but it hardly gave them a chance to do justice to their better ideas.

Kornbluth's first solo novel, *Takeoff* (1952), is a near-future thriller, a murder mystery centered on the building of the first spaceship. As an attempt to straddle genre boundaries, it was well received when first published, but it has become more badly dated than any of his other science fiction; indeed, it dated so quickly that there has been no edition of it in English since 1953. His second solo effort, *The Syndic* (1953), is his most successful. This is another piece of sociological science fiction, similar to his collaborations with Pohl; and its portrait of a future America governed by organized crime is inventive enough to be, for the purposes of the story, persuasive; the openhanded society of the Syndic (the organization dominating the eastern United States) is attractively utopian, and Kornbluth uses it for sharp commentary on contemporary political and social systems. But the novel loses strength by turning into mere action-adventure. *Not This August* (1955), his third solo novel, is, like *Takeoff*, an attempt to reach for a readership beyond the traditional science fiction genre. It is very much a cold war novel, in which the United States has been overrun by the Communists but a loyal underground fights to restore freedom. Not surprisingly, considering the subject matter, *Not This August* achieved some contemporary popularity; but, like *Takeoff*, it has dated badly.

Kornbluth's novels, whether written alone or in collaboration, only rarely exhibit the abilities shown in his shorter work. In novel-length works he tends to adhere too closely to genre templates; his individuality becomes submerged in a display of unenterprising technical efficiency. When he wrote outside the science fiction genre, the novels he produced were ephemeral paperback originals. The financial constraints of freelance writing may have compelled Kornbluth to produce work shaped toward market demands, rather than work in which he wholly believed. Whatever the reason, there is cause to regret the amount of time he devoted to novels between 1951

and 1958, since of the sixteen that he wholly or partially wrote, only *The Space Merchants*, *Wolfbane*, and *The Syndic*—all of which have pronounced flaws—remain worthy of serious attention.

Yet Kornbluth's critical reputation—particularly among his contemporaries—has remained high. The reasons for this must be sought in his short stories. As we have already seen, after his return to science fiction in 1949, he began to produce short fiction that combined originality, technical mastery, and an unsettling, darkly pessimistic vision. Throughout the 1950's he continued to produce a small but steady amount of short fiction. Kornbluth's most notable stories include "The Altar at Midnight" (1952), "The Goodly Creatures" (1952), "Gomez" (1954), "Ms. Found in a Chinese Fortune Cookie" (1957), "Theory of Rocketry" (1958), "Two Dooms" (1958), and "Shark Ship" (1958).

The most interesting point about the first five of these stories is that, like the earlier "With These Hands," they are only marginally science fiction (if at all). Damon Knight in his *In Search of Wonder* (1967) was led to comment, apropos of "With These Hands," "The Altar at Midnight," and "The Goodly Creatures," that they:

> are the result of a serious attempt to graft the mainstream short story onto science fiction. . . . Each of these stories represents the triumph of a master technician over an inappropriate form . . . I think these three stories explore a dangerous dead end in science fiction; but I'm unable to wish they had not been written. (pages 148–149)

"With These Hands" is a paean to handcraftsmanship; "The Altar at Midnight" centers on an inventor's guilt at the human consequences of his discovery; "The Goodly Creatures" is about the choice in life between comfortable, unfulfilling, dull prosperity and riskily pursuing your heart's desire. "Gomez" is about a mathematical genius whose brain the military wishes to turn into a weapon; "Theory of Rocketry" shows an innocent teacher being destroyed by an ambitious pupil who is driven to escape a degrading background; "Ms. Found in a Chinese Fortune Cookie" is a jeu d'esprit in which Kornbluth kills off his pseudonym "Cecil Corwin" after Corwin has stumbled across the Answer to all the world's problems.

Any of these stories could readily be rewritten without any of the science fiction props: mentions of space travel may make them more suitable for publication in science fiction magazines, but such elements are not integral. They are good stories, though, full of cleverly observed characters and dialogue. Kornbluth had a particular sense of the speech cadences of various types of working-class people; this also emerges in other stories such as "I Never Ast No Favors" (1954) and "The Last Man Left in the Bar" (1957). The latter is Kornbluth's most technically ambitious story, but it is so overcompressed and oblique that, despite some fine touches, it fails almost completely.

The stories also show some progressive lightening of tone: in "Gomez" individuals triumph cheekily over the military monolith, while "Ms. Found in a Chinese Fortune Cookie," like "The Cosmic Charge Account" (1956), is positively ebullient. Even the black "Theory of Rocketry" is underlain with compassion for the appalling circumstances that lead the pupil to betray his teacher.

After Kornbluth turned to freelance writing, he moved back to New York State. He and his wife had two sons. Diagnosis of his severe hypertension led to a doctor's instructions that he must take drastic measures if he was to continue to live. These measures included giving up smoking and drinking, a salt-free diet, and constant medication. But this regimen (especially the drugs) caused incoherence and confusion; Kornbluth became unable to work. After a while he abandoned the treatment, went back to his former lifestyle, and within a few months—on 21 March 1958—suffered a fatal heart attack after overexerting by shoveling snow and then running to catch a train.

During those last months the stories Kornbluth wrote were more centrally science fiction than much of what he had been writing. In addition to the final draft of *Wolfbane*, these final stories include the long novelettes "Shark Ship" and "Two Dooms." The former envisions a future in which human civilization is confined to fleets of giant sailing ships that never go near land; the continents are given over to a fanatically sadistic cult that has regressed to savagery. The story concerns the first steps by the ship dwellers toward reclaiming the land. In "Two Dooms" Kornbluth offers a justification for the atomic bombs dropped on Japan by taking a worker on the Manhattan Project into a nightmarish future in which the world is split between the victorious Germans and Japanese. Both of these stories are imaginative and highly accomplished.

After Kornbluth's death, Pohl turned many of the fragmentary manuscripts that Kornbluth left behind into stories, the best of which are collected in *Critical Mass* (1977). One of these, "The Meeting" (1972), came from an extended scene Kornbluth wrote depicting a parent-teacher meeting at a school for disturbed children (one of his own children had attended such a school). Pohl built this fragment into a short story about the ethics of brain transplantation, and it brought Kornbluth a posthumous share (with Pohl) in a Hugo award in 1973.

Although Kornbluth's writing career stretched over eighteen years, it is important to remember that he was only thirty-four years old when he died. Much of his reputation among science fiction critics may stem from a sense of what he might have achieved, had he lived. (It is worth noting, by way of comparison, that his collaborator Pohl did not truly establish himself as a novelist until 1976 with *Man Plus*, and that in 1958, Kurt Vonnegut, a year older than Kornbluth, had written only one novel—*Player Piano*—and a few short stories.) Although C. M. Kornbluth never found ways to express his talent in novel-length works, the best of his short stories still stand among the best produced in science fiction in the 1950's.

Selected Bibliography

WORKS OF C. M. KORNBLUTH

Gunner Cade, with Judith Merril as Cyril M. Judd. New York: Simon and Schuster, 1952.

Outpost Mars, with Judith Merril as Cyril M. Judd. New York: Abelard Press, 1952. Reprinted as *Sin in Space,* New York: Galaxy Publishing, 1961.

Takeoff. Garden City, N.Y.: Doubleday, 1952.

The Space Merchants, with Frederik Pohl. New York: Ballantine Books, 1953.

The Syndic. Garden City, N.Y.: Doubleday, 1953; London: Faber and Faber, 1964.

The Explorers. New York: Ballantine Books, 1954. (Short stories.)

Search the Sky, with Frederik Pohl. New York: Ballantine Books, 1954.

Gladiator-at-Law, with Frederik Pohl. New York: Ballantine Books, 1955.

The Mindworm. London: Michael Joseph, 1955. (Short stories.)

Not This August. Garden City, N.Y.: Doubleday, 1955. Reprinted as *Christmas Eve,* London: Michael Joseph, 1956.

A Mile Beyond the Moon. Garden City, N.Y.: Doubleday, 1958. (Short stories.)

The Marching Morons. New York: Ballantine Books, 1959. (Short stories.)

Wolfbane, with Frederik Pohl. New York: Ballantine Books, 1959; London: Victor Gollancz, 1961.

The Wonder Effect, with Frederik Pohl. New York: Ballantine Books, 1962. (Short stories.)

Best SF Stories of C. M. Kornbluth. London: Faber and Faber, 1968.

Thirteen O'Clock and Other Zero Hours. Edited by James Blish. New York: Dell, 1970; London: Hale and Company, 1972. (Short stories.)

The Best of C. M. Kornbluth. Garden City, N.Y.: Science Fiction Book Club, 1976; New York: Ballantine Books, 1977.

Critical Mass, with Frederik Pohl. New York: Bantam Books, 1977. (Short stories.)

CRITICAL AND BIOGRAPHICAL STUDIES

Amis, Kingsley. *New Maps of Hell.* New York: Harper and Row, 1960. (Pages 124–133 include a discussion of *The Space Merchants.*)

Brennan, John P. "The Mechanical Chicken: Psyche and Society in *The Space Merchants.*" *Extrapolation,* 25, no. 2 (1984): 101–114.

Hassler, Donald M. "Swift, Pohl, and Kornbluth: Publicists Anatomize Newness." *Extrapolation,* 34, no. 3 (1993): 245–250.

Knight, Damon. *The Futurians.* New York: John Day, 1977.

———. "Kornbluth and the Silver Lexicon." In *In Search of Wonder.* Rev. ed. Chicago: Advent Publishers, 1967.

Pohl, Frederik. "An Appreciation." Introduction to *The Best of C. M. Kornbluth.* Garden City, N.Y.: Science Fiction Book Club, 1976; New York: Ballantine Books, 1977.

———. "Introduction" to *Critical Mass.* New York: Bantam Books, 1977.

———. *The Way the Future Was.* New York: Ballantine Books, 1978.

Rich, Mark. " 'It Was a Wonderful Time': Outtakes: Kornblume: Kornbluthiana: Issues One Through Nine, 13 August 94 to 13 April 95." *New York Review of Science Fiction* (December 1995): 1, 3–7.

Seed, David. "Take-over Bids: The Power Fantasies of Frederik Pohl and Cyril Kornbluth." *Foundation* (Autumn 1993): 42–58.

Silverberg, Robert. "The Silverberg Papers." *Science Fiction Chronicle,* 9 (1987): 46–48.

Stephensen-Payne, Phil, and Gordon R. Benson, Jr. *Cyril M. Kornbluth: The Cynical Scrutineer, a Working Bibliography.* Rev. ed., Albuquerque, N. Mex.: Galactic Central, 1990.

West, D. "The Right Sort of People." In *Foundation,* 21 (February 1981): 17–26.

—MALCOLM EDWARDS

URSULA K. LE GUIN

(b. 1929)

Unlike an earlier generation of science fiction writers, trained on the job in pulp magazines, Ursula K. Le Guin is, in her own words, "an intellectual born and bred." Born on 21 October 1929 at Berkeley, California, to famed anthropologist Alfred L. Kroeber and his wife, Theodora, author of the classic of ethnology, *Ishi in Two Worlds* (1961), and subsequent children's books, she was exposed from childhood to magic and folklore, to respect for cultural diversity and human unity, and to the vices and virtues of the academic community. Educated at Radcliffe and Columbia, where she specialized in Romance literatures of the Middle Ages and Renaissance, she won a Fulbright fellowship to study in Paris. There she met and married Charles Le Guin, a history professor, with whom she has raised a family in Portland, Oregon.

Le Guin's occasional critical writing, for fanzines, literary journals, public lectures, and writers' workshops (much of it collected in *The Language of the Night*, 1979), reveals her continued alliance with formal intellectual pursuits, as does her fantasy and science fiction. As an artist she is a competent storyteller, who wove images and allusions in increasingly complex ways through ten science fiction and fantasy novels published between 1966 and 1974. These works drew critical attention largely because they offered an alternative to the technocratic, capitalistic, male-dominated ideals of the West that ruled most American science fiction. Taoism, Jungian psychology, anarchism, ecology, and human liberation resonate in Le Guin's visions of hu-

mankind's potential for unity and balance in the individual, in society, and perhaps in the galaxy.

Essentially the same themes dominate the various physical and mental regions of Le Guin's fiction—from the imaginary Central European country of Orsinia to the magical archipelago of Earthsea, and from the distant planets of her Hainish Cycle to the utopian, dystopian, and surrealistic stories that were written along with and after it. If she is reluctant to be drawn into making distinctions between science fiction and fantasy, it is fantasy she defends more wholeheartedly. If in 1976 she identified as "influences" eight "romantic" poets (including three from the twentieth century), four English and four Russian novelists, and a handful of contemporary writers of speculative fiction, three years before she had pinpointed her earliest preferences as Lord Dunsany and the trashiest pulp magazines she could find. Denying all connection with the "Golden Age" (1938–1946) of John W. Campbell, Jr.'s *Astounding Science-Fiction*, she argues in her nonfiction on behalf of language, not technology, of literature for children rather than for adults, of characterizing "the Other" (another person, another gender, another race, or another species) more than creating alien worlds.

Indeed, it is probably just what draws Le Guin away from science fiction and into the creation of other kinds of imaginary worlds that makes her contributions to science fiction significant. Close to her heart, for example, are the stories of Orsinia published as

421

Orsinian Tales (1976) and the novel *Malafrena* (1979). Dating from the 1950's, at least in original concept, these stories show a strong involvement in the commonplace events and the very real heartaches of everyday life. Their nostalgia for a simpler, if not kinder, existence is revealing; their style and flavor are clearly reminiscent of nineteenth-century Russian fiction, probably filtered through the translations of Constance Garnett. In these days of callous social melodrama and introverted analyses, the stories of Orsinia are rather a "sport" in the context of contemporary realism, even more so from the standpoint of science fiction.

If Orsinia brackets Le Guin's work, Earthsea is central to it. Its few hundred islands and surrounding waters resembling the United States in latitude and extent, Earthsea seems historically closer to the fifteenth century, with the addition of magic that works in very practical ways. Unlike our objective ideal of science, though, magic is participatory; its language is not numbers but words, both approximating and evoking its subject.

Le Guin experimented with this world's comic and tragic possibilities in "The Rule of Names" and "The Word of Unbinding" (both 1964). Both stories are quests, as are the three award-winning novels for children that comprise the Earthsea Trilogy.

Its central figure bears the names Duny (in childhood), Sparrowhawk (his "use" name), and Ged (his "true" name). *A Wizard of Earthsea* (1968), winner of the *Boston Globe/Horn Book* Award, takes him from goatherd to mage, educated by the wizards' academy and grim experience. Pride and ambition cause him to summon a "shadow" that almost destroys him before he finally triumphs by merging with it in Jungian fashion.

The Tombs of Atuan (1971), a Newbery Medal winner, tells of Arha, high priestess of the neglected powers of death and darkness. Imprisoning Sparrowhawk in her labyrinthine tombs, she regains from him her original name, Tenar; helps him reunite the ring of Erreth-Akbe with its "lost rune" of peace; and escapes with him to the land of the living.

In the National Book Award-winning *The Farthest Shore* (1972), Ged, now the Archmage, closes the "hole in the world" through which light and life are leaking, but at the cost of his magical powers. His young companion, Prince Arren, emerges as the True King, restoring goodness and order to Earthsea. The world they save from the sorcerer, Cob, with his false promises of immortality, must learn to accept death as a part of the greater equilibrium of magic, which gives quality to life.

Constrained neither by realistic events nor by scientific speculation, but only by the author's moral imagination, the trilogy exhibits Le Guin's themes in pure or isolated form, from questing and patterning motifs to the overall emphasis on "wholeness and balance" (Douglas Barbour's phrase). Its relevance to her science fiction is striking in time as well. Three quest novels focusing on identity, community, and communication precede the first volume of the trilogy. Feminine roles are central to the second, as they had been to *The Left Hand of Darkness* two years earlier. And the third volume's note of deterioration and despair is sounded often in her later fiction, from *The Lathe of Heaven* (1971) on.

Most of Le Guin's "space fiction" is part of a complex of narratives that critics have called the Hainish Cycle, after the ancient Hainish civilization alleged to have spread human/humanoid seed across much of this galaxy millions of years ago. Consisting of five novels, two long and three short stories, it spans 2,500 years in the world of the fiction, but only ten in the dates of publication.

Le Guin's fifth published story, "Semley's Necklace" (originally titled "The Dowry of Angyar," 1964), although lushly romantic in style and decked out in the trappings of Norse mythology, sounded the first characteristic notes of her space fiction. In quest of her dowry, lost to the "Star-Folk," an imperious heroine, invincibly ignorant of science and technology, undertakes a journey at nearly the speed of light to a distant world. She returns eighteen years later, driven to distraction by the fact that her warrior husband is dead and the baby daughter she left behind is now the same physical age she is.

Reprinted as the prologue to *Rocannon's World* (1966), "Semley's Necklace" introduces that planet, two of its five sentient races, Rocannon himself, and the "League" (of all Worlds), which he serves as a "hilfer"—a student of *high intelligence life forms* (that is, an interstellar anthropologist). *Rocannon's World* tells the story of his subsequent quest, which explains how Fomalhaut II came to bear his name in the annals of the League.

In fear of an unknown enemy, the League has made contact with many hilfs, accelerating their technological development without adequate foresight as to the consequences. One world, too quickly armed and intent on developing an empire of its own, destroys Rocannon's starship and his ansible (a communications device not limited to the speed of light). To defend this world from the invaders, Rocannon must penetrate their headquarters, half a continent away, and use their ansible to pinpoint their destruction (unmanned faster-than-light travel is also possible). On this long journey he experiences this world, unlearning his prejudices, learning what five races of have to teach him, from brotherhood to "mindspeech" (telepathy), and accepting the trade-offs involved in gaining each lesson. The weight of ideas is a bit heavy for the quest structure, and it keeps threatening to turn this short novel into an allegory (as with the stark division of one race into light and dark symbols, like the elves and dwarves of high fantasy).

More self-contained, although the science fictional and fantasy content is minimal, is *Planet of Exile* (1966), which takes place considerably later on Gamma Draconis III. Having already learned not to interfere unduly with the natives, a League colony tries not to interfere at all. Recoiling from the intimacy of "mindspeech," its members seldom make use of it. In a story that begins with a Romeo and Juliet situation, the City people and the inhabitants of a neighboring native village discover that they need each other for mutual defense against the ravages of marauding no-

madic tribes and a winter lasting twenty Earth years. Individuals and both cultures are revealed in more detail than in *Rocannon's World*, although the scenes of action and romance are sometimes stiff and unconvincing. The positive results of the biological, social, and mental integration of both peoples are not evident until the end of the third novel in the Cycle.

Completing this loose trilogy, *City of Illusions* (1967), played out on a conquered Earth, is predominantly a battle of minds, with much of the abstract weakness that implies. The protagonist Falk's quest for his memory takes him across a ravaged America into the stronghold of the vaguely evil Shing (the "enemies" of *Rocannon's World*, who apparently have scattered the League, as well as the peoples of Earth, into disarray). Living proof that one can lie when using mindspeech, dominating vast subject populations with telepathically induced illusions, revealing their lust to kill through their hysterical remonstrances against it, the Shing offer Falk his old (true?) identity at the cost of his new one, in order to strike at his (hidden) home world. But concentration on a sacred book enables him to merge both personalities, combining his own experience of the Shing with the mental discipline of the starship navigator, Remarren.

Falk/Remarren escapes with the truth and a captive Shing, returning to Gamma Draconis III. Now a world rich in both mental and mechanical technology, it presumably is capable of routing the Shing and restoring a more democratic form of interstellar civilization. Most flamboyant of the "apprentice" novels, *City of Illusions* is in some ways the least satisfactory. Overburdened with travel notes, metaphors of patterning, double and triple reverses of truth and illusion, unconvincing villains and mental warfare, it nevertheless completes the trilogy and prepares the way for the best-realized works of the Cycle.

Like *Rocannon's World*, *The Left Hand of Darkness* (1969) was prefigured by a short story. "Winter's King" (1969; revised, 1975) utilizes the same time-dilation effect as

Ursula Le Guin. Courtesy of Corbis-Bettmann

"Semley's Necklace" but with a more knowledgeable protagonist. Le Guin claims she did not know at the time what it meant for the people of the planet Gethen to be androgynous, but she did revise the pronouns in the collected version of the tale. Thus the king, "mind-handled" by an opposing political faction, flees *her* home world, appealing for help from what is now the "Ekumen of Known Worlds." Returning years later from a distant planet to find rebellion bred by her daughter's incompetence, she regains the throne as a seemingly younger successor.

In the novel an earlier generation finds the "Mobile" (envoy) of the Ekumen, Genly Ai (symbolizing both "I" and "eye"), trying to persuade the Gethenians to join what is no longer a defense pact or trade association but rather a system of education or a "mystical ideal" celebrating the diversity of humankind. Like his predecessors, Ai is changed by a journey, so changed that, like Gulliver, he recoils at his own people's arrival at the end of the novel.

What changes Ai is his encounter with Gethenian sexuality and its contingent social and mental behavior. His quest, ostensibly political, turns out to be personal and psychological. Gethen is ruled by two great powers, Karhide and Orgoreyn, with each of which Ai tries to strike a bargain, naïvely misunderstanding their politics. Exiled from the capital of the "comic opera kingdom" (George Slusser's term) of Karhide, as is the kingdom's former prime minister, Estraven ("the traitor"), Ai is sent to a prison camp in the more totalitarian Orgoreyn when the side favoring him loses. Freed by Estraven, Ai accompanies "him" on an unprecedented journey across the northern ice fields to eventual acceptance in Karhide.

Presented as Ai's "story," presumably truer than a more "objective" report, *The Left Hand of Darkness* interweaves his narrative with that of Estraven, with earlier ethnological reports, and with accounts of Gethenian legends, myths, and "religious" ceremonies, in an attempt to give the full flavor of this world from the standpoint of a participant anthropologist. If the parts have no necessary connection or contingency, they nevertheless represent Ai's version of the truth—that is, Le Guin's vision of an alternative possibility for human biology and history.

On a marginal planet so cold that early investigators called it Winter, an androgynous subspecies of humanity has developed a reasonably high level of technology and social organization without any history of war or the severe dislocations of an industrial revolution. This is credited in part to their unique sexuality: every Gethenian is neuter except during "kemmer" (estrus), when either gender may emerge, with no continuing pattern of dominance or submission. Partly tribal, partly feudal, partly federal, they owe first loyalty to the "hearth." Centralization, though, has been achieved in Orgoreyn and, to meet its threat, Karhide is moving in a similar direction. Behind both systems are radically different interpretations of the Gethenian Creation myth, relating sun and shadow, flux and interconnectedness, in ways acceptable and unacceptable to Le Guin's Taoist views.

Although obviously connected with Le Guin's concept of "the Other," and clearly a response to "gender liberation," *The Left Hand of Darkness* does not show us the "basic human," stripped of sexual role playing, but a "thought experiment," as she labels it in a 1976 introduction to the book. Strongly linked to the first two books of the Earthsea trilogy, it also adds another parapsychological talent to the Hainish Cycle: "foretelling" via the interweaving of adept and disciplined minds, which focuses less on answers than on the uselessness of asking the wrong questions. A complex telling of a profound story, poetically woven out of vivid imagery and realistic detail, *The Left Hand of Darkness* still has a high proportion of fantasy, especially by contrast with the last two works in the Cycle.

Rather than extending her future history any further, Le Guin began bringing it closer to home, in time and in political "relevance," first with two versions of the timeless Edenic fantasy of the "green world" into which man brings discord. "Vaster Than Empires and More Slow" (1971) takes place when Earth is trying to reach a region of the galaxy where the Hainishmen did not venture. Discovering a world inhabited only by a vegetable life form, a crew of ten scientists, all of them "mad" (an indictment of Western irresponsi-

bility), are almost destroyed by their own paranoia and the fear they induce in this vast alien "mind." The maddest of them all, Osden, with his gift of "wide-range bioempathic receptivity" and his consuming hatred of all of his crewmates, whose feelings he cannot avoid, stays as a "colonist," practically becoming one with the forest.

An explicit condemnation of colonial exploitation is Le Guin's "Vietnam story," *The Word for World Is Forest* (1972; separate book publication, 1976). As caricatured in the macho Captain Davidson, traditional Western disregard for native populations in the way of "progress" (that is, of whatever we want) finally meets its match in a people who live symbiotically with their forests. Green-skinned, three feet high, and called "creechies" by the humans, the Athsheans represent another alternative to contemporary American behavior patterns: Athshean women administer tribal activities, while the men are responsible for "thinking," an activity that combines both waking and dreaming consciousness. Slow to anger, they overcome their pacific nature under the leadership of Selver; thanks to his exposure to humans, Selver has come to imagine or foresee willful destruction carried out by his people. After a decimated human population has been restricted to an island "reservation," the story has a literal deus ex machina ending: a League starship returns to mark the world off limits to further outside exploitation. The cost of this lesson has been high. Wholesale destruction of population and territory included the one human, Lyubov, capable of understanding the Athsheans, and Selver's "understanding" of the humans has driven him and his race to the edge of insanity, if not beyond.

The Hainish Cycle ended, apparently, in 1974 with one more novel and a footnote-like short story. *The Dispossessed: An Ambiguous Utopia*, like *The Left Hand of Darkness*, won both the Hugo and the Nebula for best science fiction novel of the year. Although it is linked to its predecessors by ambassadors from Hain and Earth, by the appearance of Tau Ceti representatives from other stories, and by the invention of the ansible from a theoretical breakthrough by the physicist Shevek, this is primarily a novel of political analysis. Told from Shevek's viewpoint in chapters alternating between the past and the present, it details his life on the arid moon of Anarres and his unprecedented visit to its primary, or sister, planet, Urras, from which the anarchist settlers emigrated 170 years earlier.

Although a dualistic structure is built into the novel, it is not a simplistic contrast. Three varieties of government on Urras parallel our East, West, and Third World nations; moreover, the memory of ecological catastrophe on Earth serves as an apparently unheeded cautionary model. Furthermore, the purity of anarchism on Anarres is more ideal than real; hierarchical structures, gender bias, and personal pride sometimes get in the way of communitarian equality. Shevek exemplifies the problems posed for any social order by a creative genius whose scientific and personal goals are "tearing down walls." Young Western readers sometimes have trouble seeing Anarres as utopian, in part because it is humanly fallible, in part because its anarchist ideal is so contrary to their own "propertarian" values, but Shevek has no doubts. For all that his research was temporarily stymied at home by a jealous supervisor, metaphors of the digestive tract—both expressed and acted out—reinforce his distaste for possessiveness. The most traditionally "realistic" of all Le Guin's science fiction, *The Dispossessed* is not fully convincing in its portrayal of action, especially on Urras, or of the processes of "doing science," as Samuel R. Delany and other basically sympathetic critics have pointed out. Yet it is outstanding as a utopian novel, avoiding such snares as the "guided tour" of a perfect world and presenting a largely believable alternative to the social psychology of the present.

Even more "real" is the portrait of Laia Odo, theoretician and founder of Anarres anarchism in "The Day Before the Revolution" (1974). A sketch of her last day alive, it uses her final hours to provide flashbacks from her life, revealing her own inability, and that of those around her, to live fully in keeping with her egalitarian ideals. This reminder that it is always "the day before the revolution" won the Nebula for best short story, not entirely on its considerable merits, but in part because of its all but inseparable link to *The Dispossessed*.

Le Guin's exploration of utopian and dystopian possibilities did not end with the tales of Tau Ceti. Several other stories from the 1970's underline her continuing concern with what *The Farthest Shore* describes as "the hole in the world through which life is leaking out." But the artistic success of these later stories is more arguable, given their note of shrillness and the more visible elements of propaganda. A Hugo award winner in 1974, "The Ones Who Walk Away from Omelas" (1973) is a meditation on an idea of William James, to the effect that some people could not accept even universal prosperity and happiness if it depended on the deliberate subjection of an idiot child to abuse it could barely understand.

"The New Atlantis" (1975) counterpoints a dystopian future in Oregon with a mysteriously rising midocean continent whose "inhabitants" have a collective sentience that Darko Suvin is almost alone in finding optimistic. "Diary of the Rose" (1976) pits against each other a sheltered "psychoscope" technician who is serving the system and an intellectual who is hospitalized because he is suspected (that is, convicted) of subversion. Recognizing the intellectual's essential health makes the technician rebellious and perhaps more dangerous, because she understands from inside how insidiously the system works. "SQ" (1978) takes a more sardonic look at the health of the state, as measured by "infallible" tests of people's Sanity Quotients, tests that gradually bring everyone under observation while the world is run by stable morons.

Diagrammatically simple is the utopian short novel "The Eye of the Heron" (1978), in which a nonviolent colony on a sparsely peopled world defies a centralized city government of macho Brazilian exiles. An object lesson in the perils of dominant behavior, it depends for its solution on a vast, untamed wilderness, so that the anarchists can "light out for the territory" in nostalgic, American-frontier fashion.

The rest of Le Guin's speculative fiction is less easily categorized, although perception is often central, the dangers of intervention are often highlighted, and the need to take a moral position is usually explicit. "April in Paris" (1962) is a charming fantasy in which black magic brings four lonely people from different eras into romantic alliances in 1482. Equally unrationalized is "Darkness Box" (1963), through which a magic kingdom's heroic prince unfreezes time so that he can conclusively meet his fate in a battle with his brother. "The Masters" (1963) is science fiction of a postcatastrophic Earth in which a ritual-dominated, antitechnological society is resisted by the perseverance of essentially irresponsible scientific inquiry. Parallels with Earthsea are not hard to draw.

"Nine Lives" (1969) is perhaps Le Guin's only "hard" science story, although the science serves the usual moral purposes, counseling acceptance of what we are: imperfect, isolated beings whose best qualities emerge when we reach out to communicate with each other. Based on biological speculation, the story postulates human clones of a superior genetic material that will help restore health to an Earthcentered universe whose population has been decimated by war and disease. Set on a highly volcanic planet, it pits a "ten-clone" against two ordinary men, whose need for each other proves more flexible and "whole" than the incestuous togetherness of the clone.

Three "psychomyths" (Le Guin's term) appeared in 1970, leading up to a greater one the next year. "Things" (originally titled "The End") shows a bricklayer trying to build a bridge into the sea during "the last days"; as he walks out, carrying a widow and a child on his back, they are seen by people in a sailboat that may or may not take them off to more fortunate isles. In "The Good Trip" a man whose initials are L. S. D. recalls his wife who

has been lost to madness and envisions a reconciliation with her in the woods of Oregon's Mount Hood, to which he allows his mind to wander instead of taking an acid trip with his friends. More surrealistic, if not psychedelic, is "A Trip to the Head," also in a forest setting, which explores the problems of both having and not having names and labels for people and things.

Oregon—Portland, to be specific—is again the setting for a large-scale psychomyth, *The Lathe of Heaven* (1971; made into a Public Broadcasting System television movie first shown in 1980). It concerns the "active dreams" of George Orr—dreams that actually change reality, usually for the worse, especially under the direction of Dr. Haber, a willful psychiatrist to whom George has been referred for treatment. Once Dr. Haber realizes the power is genuine, he manipulates George's dreams for his own fame and fortune. As a well-meaning do-gooder, he also wants to improve the world, but almost everything goes sour. We cannot adequately imagine or create a whole world, the novel argues, without doing more bad than good. This has obvious connections with *The Farthest Shore* and the "green world" stories, with subsequent utopian and dystopian fictions, and with various other works of the following decade, all of which may be regarded as Le Guin's attempts to surmount a growing sense of pessimism about the way things are.

"Direction of the Road" (1973) is a "tree's-eye view" of human progress in locomotion. "The Field of Vision" (1973), termed by Le Guin a "sublimated temper tantrum," recounts the results of a mission to Mars, where the astronauts recognize, once they have come to terms with sensory overload, that they have seen God (or a close approximation thereof). A heavy-handed *Star Trek* parody, Le Guin's "Intracom" (1974) features a crew of four women and a First Mate named "Mr. Balls" facing the aftermath of a chance encounter in space: the "alien" growing in the Crew Recreation Room is a baby. "Schrödinger's Cat" (1974) is a surrealistic dramatization of a famous "thought experiment" in physics, in a world where people literally keep "coming apart." The cleverest of such "experiments" is "The Author of the Acacia Seeds and Other Extracts from the *Journal of Therolinguistics*" (1974). This story consists of three "articles," parodies of scholarly studies, that describe findings and theories about the "art forms" of ants, penguins, and trees. Le Guin's use of the parody form makes a virtue out of ambiguity, and also makes outright critical rejection of these "articles" all but impossible.

More conventionally, "Mazes" (1975) describes an "alien" (conceivably a rat) that is tortured and driven to death by a behavioral psychologist's inability and unwillingness to reciprocate communication, as against simply fulfilling his experimental design. And "The Eye Altering" (1976) explores through the symbol of painting how the new generation of a group of exiles becomes acclimatized to its new world.

A drift away from speculative fiction was noticeable in the late 1970's as the Orsinian tales and some other nonspeculative fiction, such as "Gwilan's Harp" (*Redbook*, 1977) and "Malheur County" (*Kenyon Review*, 1979), found publication. A hint of fantasy is barely present in the juvenile short novel *Very Far Away from Anywhere Else* (1976), in that the imaginary country of Thorn is a kind of refuge for seventeen-year-old Owen Griffiths and an inspiration for the musical compositions of his friend Natalie Field.

A curious blend of realism and fantasy is also the subject of *The Beginning Place* (1980), a short novel about Hugh and Irene, two young people superfluous in suburbia who discover a secret gateway into a kind of enchanted land not too unlike Orsinia. Although neither wants the other around, they need each other, and both are needed by the townsfolk of Tembreabrezi. Although it is not exactly a dragon they have to slay, the deed required is difficult and painful. Its major reward is internal and intangible; after the deed is accomplished, they know what it means to feel needed and are better able to face the "real" world. Le Guin's most realistic writing,

grittily evocative of recognizable contemporary life, is given import by the fantasy at the core. A bore for some critics, a "breakthrough" for others, *The Beginning Place* is, more strictly speaking, a return to the wellsprings from which all fantasies arise.

By science fiction standards, Le Guin's career is not yet very long, although it is already distinguished in terms of popularity, awards, and critical accolades. Part of this is due to her very real talent, primarily for fantasy with or without science fictional trappings. Part of it is due to the belief structure embodied in her fiction, with its antitechnocratic, quasi-mystical thrust. And part of it is due to her being a woman who has expressed the right kinds of concerns at the right time, when critical attention is being paid to science fiction. She has helped to widen the scope and improve the artistic quality of what is called science fiction, but her very real accomplishments should not blind us to the fact that her stories constitute a critique of traditional science fiction that arises from even more traditional sources.

—DAVID N. SAMUELSON

SINCE 1982

Ursula K. Le Guin is one of the most respected writers of science fiction. Her major themes are communication, liminality and alienation, loyalty and betrayal, political rebellion and freedom, self and other. Her works continue to be innovative and challenging; in fact, Le Guin's publications since David Samuelson's essay reveal, to use her own metaphor for self change, a literary rebearing. The publication of the science fiction novel *Always Coming Home* (1985) followed by her second essay collection, *Dancing at the Edge of the World: Thoughts on Words, Women, Places* (1989), embody her new direction. These two works were quickly followed by additional new fiction and nonfiction that continue to reflect her contributions to science fiction and fantasy in particular and

American literature in general. To summarize, since 1989 she has published a fourth Earthsea novel (*Tehanu* [1990]) and story ("Dragonfly' [1998]), an Orsinian story ("Unlocking The Air' [1996]), twelve Hainish stories as well as other science fiction novellas and stories (partially collected in *Buffalo Gals Won't You Come Out Tonight* [1987], *A Fisherman of the Inland Sea* [1994], *Unlocking The Air and Other Stories* [1996], and *Four Ways To Forgiveness* [1995]), and team-edited *The Norton Book of Science Fiction: North American Science Fiction, 1960–1990* (1993). Her evolving career since 1982 also includes several collections of poetry; a collection of non–science fiction stories; an increasing number of children's books (seven since 1988); numerous book reviews; collaborative performance pieces—such as music, dance, and drama; and most recently, a new English version of Lao Tzu's *Tao Te Ching: A Book About the Way and the Power of the Way* (1997); a book on story writing, *Steering The Craft* (1998); and an introduction to a new edition of Mark Twain's *The Diaries of Adam and Eve* (1996).

Although the world of *Always Coming Home* is created in the fulsome detail and lyrical style that readers have come to expect of her work, Le Guin invents a new structure and expects the reader to participate in making meaning and in connecting the verbal, musical, and artistic nodes. The novel is set in the Napa Valley, Le Guin's spiritual home, in a future time when the population is much smaller and the land has been significantly changed by natural forces and human exploitation in past centuries. Three centers of activity exist in the valley—the small villages and towns of the Kesh people, the cities of the militaristic Condors, and the Wakwaha Exchange, which provides computer access to an eleven-thousand-node network of information to anyone who wants it.

The Kesh and the Condors provide the sociopolitical contrast in the novel and the critique of Le Guin's contemporary, industrialized Western civilization. The Kesh, like nearly all of the people in Le Guin's more recent fiction, live in small communities. They relate to the world as a sacred place through sacred rituals; their human relationships are based on sexual equality, and community decisions demonstrate how anarchism works. The people are artistically creative and technologically inventive, and they are tireless storytellers who regard the life story as a sacred gift, "a 'hinge' or intersection of private, individual, historical lived-time with communal, impersonal, cyclical being-time." In contrast, the Condors exploit the land and its resources, relate to others and govern themselves via dominance-submission models, and believe in the linear progress of civilization.

The novel has neither protagonist nor linear structure. Instead, using the anthropologist's method of thick description, Le Guin offers the reader a melange of chapters and documents—for example, Kesh dramas, novels, histories, stories, and poems; documents on language, religion, rituals, and narrative modes. Recurring elements include life stories, particularly a three-part story by Stone Telling, whose mother was Kesh and father was Condor, and the voice of Pandora, the self-reflective author. The recursive structure invites the reader to compose and recompose the novel, to read backward and forward from any section, to connect pieces, ideas, and characters and so create alternate webs of significance. The physical book is itself a collaboration of several artists—Le Guin, the writer; Todd Barton, the composer of the Kesh music on the tape packaged with the novel; Margaret Chodos, the artist for the Kesh images; and George Hersh, the mapmaker.

The unique form Le Guin discovered for *Always Coming Home* combines the composite story with the life story, the pattern with the particular, the sweep of time with the limits of a single life, the objective with the subjective. The form was foreshadowed by *Orsinian Tales* (1976), a composite novel, in that the individual pieces are autonomous but are also linked to each other, and by stories such as "Sur" (1982), a life story of one member of an all-women's expedition that was the first to reach the South Pole. Using the combination of the two forms, however, is new; and Le Guin has continued to experiment with this combination in her stories of the 1990's.

Considerable controversy has surrounded this novel. Perhaps it was the combination of the radical form and the gap of eleven years since her last science fiction novel that accounted for criticism, which questioned Le Guin's relationship to science fiction. She was accused of having sold out to the literary establishment, of being technopohobic, and of not really writing a novel, much less science fiction.

Overall, some readers praised the structure and metafictional emphasis of the cross-genre work, while others found it boring because it lacked dramatized conflict. Some thought the evolution of these cultures was incredible, while others praised Le Guin's depiction of a society consciously choosing to be toolmakers but nonindustrial and nonmilitary. *Always Coming Home* was a finalist for the American Book Award and won the Janet Heidinger Kafka Prize for Fiction.

The essays in *Dancing at the Edge of the World*, published from 1976 to 1988, have been closely studied for clues to Le Guin's thoughts on her new fiction. Of the four categories Le Guin sets up for the essays, three are particularly instructive for a study of her career: feminism, social responsibility, and literature and writing. Virginia Woolf, the writer Le Guin always mentions when she's asked about literary influences, once said that if her father had not died, she would not have become a writer; conversely Le Guin has said that if the second wave of feminism had not developed in the 1970's and 1980's, she might have stopped writing novels. The rediscovery of lost women writers, recent research on how women and men differ in making moral choices, and French and American scholars' delineation of a female language or mother tongue are some of the topics discussed in the essays. Of particular interest is "Is Gender Necessary? Redux," a 1987 revision of the 1976 essay "Is Gender Necessary?" that Le Guin had originally written to accompany a new edition of *The Left Hand of Darkness*. Social responsibility has been a consistent thread in Le Guin's fictional worlds, particularly her long-running dialogue with utopianism (*The Lathe of Heaven, The Dispossessed*). Essays such as "Bryn Mawr Commencement Address" and "Woman/Wilderness" explain the connections she sees between women's ways of knowing and political and social constructs.

Literature and writing are announced as a thematic interest with Le Guin's opening line of *The Left Hand of Darkness*, when Genly Ai writes, "I'll make my report as if I told a story, for I was taught as a child on my homeworld that Truth is a matter of the imagination." The essays in *Dancing at the Edge of the World* such as "The Carrier Bag Theory of Fiction" (1989) and "The Fisherwoman's Daughter" (1989) recount her feminist view of literary heroes, structure, and language. Le Guin received the Pilgrim Award in 1989 for this book and a lifetime of scholarly contributions.

Shortly after the publication of this collection, but eighteen years after *The Farthest Shore*, Le Guin published a fourth Earthsea novel, correcting an imbalance she saw in the trilogy that had told of Ged's and Tenar's coming of age but of only Ged's maturity. *Tehanu*, which won the 1990 Nebula and Locus awards, depicts Tenar, widow of a farmer on Gont and mother of two children, who befriends Ged, now a man with no great wizardly powers and no vocation or direction. Tenar's sense of self-worth, maturity, and nurturing qualities makes her, like the other women in the novel, an agent of change. Not only does she help Ged regain balance, but she also helps heal the physically and psychologically abused and crippled child Tehanu. In the wisdom gained of life experiences and the art of housekeeping, Tenar knows she cannot undo the injustice done to Tehanu, but she can shield her temporarily from the power of the perpetrators of the injustice, thus freeing Tehanu to find her own lineage, language, and magic. In Le Guin's latest Earthsea fiction,

"Dragonfly," the woman Iria, also of dragon lineage, challenges the male-only School for Wizards on Roke. Le Guin's return to Earthsea, then, is both a continuation and a new direction. It is not a disjunction because the sphere of the women—the mothers, aunts, village witches—was always present in Earthsea. But it is a subversion, a reversal of perspective. The women are depicted as agents of change and harbingers of wisdom, thus revealing the limitations of the hierarchical mages who, in times of crisis, consult only among themselves. Ged, the courageous hero and powerful wizard, is now depicted as having to come to terms with being only and totally human. The consequences of Tenar's and Iria's actions are as great as the acts of any of the major Earthsea figures—Ged's shadow, Ged, Arren, and Cob—for Tehanu has been set free to claim a new language and name and her lineage with the dragons.

The controversy caused by the *Tehanu's* subversive nature surfaced quickly in reviews and articles as readers reacted to what they saw as either a distorted or a corrected portrait of Earthsea. Readers who felt that they had lost the Earthsea they knew and loved argued that Le Guin's feminist agenda was incompatible with the heroic fantasy tradition. Some questioned whether the book was suitable for young people or whether women were being portrayed as having any significant power. Others praised the novel as a deconstruction of heroic fantasy, a novel about the nature of power, an appropriate coda or pastoral at the end of the Earthsea series. Some reviewers mused about the difficulty, after eighteen years, of an author, now changed, returning to write another novel in an old series, especially when the cultural understanding of gender had changed so drastically between 1972 and 1990. In the essay "Earthsea Revisioned" Le Guin herself discusses this experience and responds to some of the criticisms. She argues that she had to re-vision Earthsea and its protagonists and plots—seeing the nature of the hero as woman and the story line as a rebearing rather than a conquesting. Nevertheless, the Earthsea books

continue to be recognized as classics of contemporary fantasy, and in 1995, Le Guin was given the Life Achievement Award by the World Fantasy organization.

During the 1980's, when Le Guin was writing these two novels and the essays in *Dancing at the Edge of the World*, she was also writing short fiction, her preferred form in the 1990's. After her first short story collection in 1975, Le Guin periodically published collections that are either retrospective or linked by theme or setting, a pattern set by her next two collections—*The Compass Rose* (1982), winner of a 1984 Locus and a 1985 Ditmar award, and *Buffalo Gals and Other Animal Presences* (1987), the title story of which won a Hugo. These stories illustrate Le Guin's continuing independence as she crosses what others would identify as genre boundaries and uses unusual perspectives to question the perception of reality or to subvert closed-mindedness. The twenty pieces in *The Compass Rose*, most of which are science fiction, range from a workshop story ("Eye Altering") to a *Star Trek* joke ("Intracom"), an Orsinian story and a realistic story, satiric nonfact essays, science fiction, magic realism, and the often-praised "Sur." "The First Report of the Shipwrecked Foreigner to the Kadanh of Derb" is not only a satire on first-contact science fiction, but it also describes Le Guin's use of thick description in the life story. *Buffalo Gals and Other Animal Presences* includes poems and short stories, many of which had been published in other collections, linked by their nonhuman perspectives. The plant, animal, and stone points of view critique contemporary civilization and the widening gap between humanity and the rest of the world. Of particular value are Le Guin's headnotes, where she informally shares her thoughts about the pieces and their relationship to her other work. "May's Lion," for example, is a fictional experiment in which she discovered how to write *Always Coming Home.*

Searoad: Chronicles of Klatsand (1991) consists of nineteenth- and twentieth-century stories linked by their common setting, the small northern Pacific coastal town of Klatsand. Not science fiction or fantasy, the stories were published between 1987 and 1990 and include "Hernes," a long story that uses the combined composite and life story forms. It received the Oregon Institute of Literary Arts Fiction Award in 1992. *A Fisherman of the Inland Sea*, like *The Compass Rose*, contains a wide range of pieces published since that anthology—jokes, workshop story, and classic science fiction. This was quickly followed by another linked collection, *Four Ways to Forgiveness*. These four Hainish science fiction stories, published separately in 1994 and 1995, are set on neighboring planets Werel (not the same Werel as appeared in *Planet of Exile*) and Yeowe. It was nominated for the National Book Award. Here, too, Le Guin challenges genre divisions; the stories are so closely linked that the book is sometimes referred to as a novel. *Unlocking the Air* is a retrospective collection (1982–1995) of eighteen stories, none of which is science fiction. They are, as Le Guin states on the book jacket, "plain realism, magical realism, or surrealism, or postmodern genres that don't even have names yet."

During the period from 1974 to 1990, when Le Guin was publishing very little space science fiction, she revealed her disillusionment with some of the major trends in space fiction—its male-centeredness, reactionary politics, denigration of "the other" into the enemy, and its unqualified optimism that highly advanced technology is the ultimate problem solver. She acknowledged that she quit reading science fiction until she agreed to team-edit (with Brian Attebery and Karen Joy Fowler) *The Norton Book of Science Fiction*. Her introduction to the book reveals her delight in the richness and complexity she found in the North American science fiction from 1960 to 1990 that was selected for the book. The controversy that swirled around the appearance of the book was similar to that which has frequently appeared in reviews in the last thirty years of prominent, new, science fiction anthologies. Reviewers either

disagreed with the limitations of the book and complained that it was an attempt to restrict and canonize science fiction, or they praised the variety and literary quality and predicted it might help de-ghettoize science fiction. This controversy is similar to that which surrounded Judith Merril's anthologies in the 1960's. However, as in many of Merril's anthologies, the introduction is quite clear about the collaborators' broad definition of science fiction and personal preferences that guided their choices.

For science fiction readers and scholars, the most notable characteristic of Le Guin's creativity in the 1990's is the reappearance of space science fiction set in her Hainish world. In fact, between 1974 and 1990, of the more than fifty short works, only five involve space travel and none is set in the Hainish world. Since 1990, however, Le Guin has published a dozen new Hainish short stories and novellas, six in 1994 alone, marking yet another active literary rebearing. Her interests in feminism, metafiction, and sociopolitical relationships are still evident; but what is unique to the new Hainish stories is her use of the combined narrative forms with which she first experimented in *Always Coming Home*. Among the new Hainish stories are three linked sets, each of which includes at least one life story. Many of these new stories were nominated for Nebula and Hugo awards; "Solitude" (1994) won the Nebula in 1995. "The Matter of Seggri" and "Mountain Ways" (1996) won Tiptree awards in 1994 and 1996, respectively; and "Forgiveness Day" (1994) won the Sturgeon Award in 1994. In a 1995 interview in *Publishers Weekly*, when Le Guin commented that her use of connecting stories is a technique she shares with other women writers, her comment also described the coupled form: "Instead of focusing on an individual, a lot of us are writing about people as part of a community." The composite embodies Le Guin's view that multiple perspectives, such as a community or the Hainish world itself, are needed to represent existence. The life story embodies her view that each perspective can only be tentative but that the story of the single consciousness traced through time and space represents the unique role of humans in the world—to be conscious, to direct action, and to change through inter-action. In recent interviews, Le Guin has commented that this uniqueness includes feeling "guilt and shame and confusion" and that, in fact, the sense of the tragic is the un-dercurrent of her writing.

"The Shobies' Story" (1990) was the first new Hainish story and has been linked to two additional stories—"Dancing to Ganam" (1993) and "Another Story or A Story of the Fisherman of the Inland Sea" (1994)—by their common use of a new technology called the churten drive. Analogous to Le Guin's ansi-ble, which made instantaneous commun-ication possible, the churten drive makes instantaneous travel possible. The three sto-ries are also linked by being metafictions—the process of storytelling and interpreting is an integral part of each narrative. In "The Shobies' Story," the experience of transili-ence—abrupt change—is so disorienting that the ten-member Ekumen crew shift from a re-port mode to a story mode in order to assim-ilate their experience. "Dancing to Ganam" explores the difficulties of several observers trying to interpret another culture and its sto-ries and rituals. "Another Story" is a clear ex-ample of the first-person life story in which the protagonist's own life, due to a crease in the churten field, becomes a literal composite of two time periods.

"Another Story" is also part of a second group of stories linked through the common setting of the planet O. Ki'O, a society so old and stable that it makes the Hainish feel young and reckless, is much occupied with the making of marriages: at its core, a *sedor-etu* is a four-person union in which two ho-mosexual and two heterosexual relationships are possible and two heterosexual relation-ships are taboo. The arranging of marriages is a common theme in this group of stories, which also includes "Unchosen Love" (1994) and "Mountain Ways," and the *sedoretu* is a metaphor for exploring the difficulties of making community from individual lives.

The third group of Hainish stories has been published in a single text. *Four Ways to Forgiveness* includes "Betrayals" (1994), "Forgiveness Day," "A Man of the People" (1995), and "A Woman's Liberation" (1995). They share a common setting—the planets of Werel and Yeowe—at a time in their history when Yeowe, a slave colony of Werel, has de-clared its independence and the people of both worlds are creating a new sense of who they are as each society wrestles to relinquish the slave-owner duality and considers how to be free.

These new Hainish stories lead readers and scholars back into Le Guin's previous work, particularly the space science fiction (non-Hainish) published between 1974 and 1990. "Dancing to Ganam," appears to be Le Guin's response to her earlier story "Pathways of Desire," in which she seemed to be bitterly denouncing the space science fiction dream. Her loss of faith in science fiction during this period will now perhaps be more apparent to readers in "The Eye of the Heron," a story that depicts the failure of both idealism and mili-tarism as learned modes for developing a com-munity. The young men in both the City and the Town act out models they've learned from their cultures but haven't actually developed from their own experience as the previous generations did. In fact, the source of their learning is an art form in each community—the murals in the City, the stories in the Town. The new stories also illustrate how steady is the pattern of change, of turning and returning in world building, narrative form, sociopolitical structures, and gender relation-ships in Le Guin's fiction. In a 1994 interview with Jonathan White, Le Guin spoke of the role of art in subverting habits and closure: "When we hear music or poetry or stories, the world opens up again. We're drawn in—or out—and the windows of our perception are cleansed, as William Blake said."

—ELIZABETH CUMMINS

Selected Bibliography

WORKS OF URSULA K. LE GUIN

FICTION

Planet of Exile. New York: Ace, 1966. (Bound with *Mankind Under the Leash* by Thomas M. Disch.) Reprinted with a new introduction by Le Guin, New York: Harper and Row, 1978.

Rocannon's World. New York: Ace, 1966. (Bound with *The Kar-Chee Reign* by Avram Davidson.) Reprinted with a new introduction by Le Guin, New York: Harper and Row, 1977.

City of Illusions. New York: Ace, 1967. Reprinted with a new introduction by Le Guin, New York: Harper and Row, 1978.

A Wizard of Earthsea. Berkeley, Calif.: Parnassus, 1968; New York: Ace, 1970.

The Left Hand of Darkness. New York: Ace, 1969. Reprinted with a new introduction by Le Guin, New York: Ace, 1976. Reprinted with a new afterword and appendixes by Le Guin, New York: Walker, 1994.

"The Lathe of Heaven." *Amazing,* 44 (March 1971): 6–61; *Amazing,* 45 (May 1971): 6–65, 121–123. New York: Charles Scribner's Sons, 1971; New York: Avon, 1973.

The Tombs of Atuan. New York: Atheneum, 1971; New York: Bantam, 1975.

The Farthest Shore. New York: Atheneum, 1972; New York: Bantam, 1975.

"The Word for World Is Forest." In *Again, Dangerous Visions.* Edited by Harlan Ellison. Garden City, N.Y.: Doubleday, 1972. Separately printed, New York: Berkley Medallion, 1976. Reprinted with a new introduction by Le Guin, London: Gollancz, 1977.

The Dispossessed: An Ambiguous Utopia. New York: Harper and Row, 1974; New York: Avon, 1975.

The Wind's Twelve Quarters: Short Stories. New York: Harper and Row, 1975; New York: Bantam, 1976. (Includes "The Rule of Names," "The Word of Unbinding," "Semley's Necklace," "Winter's King," "Vaster Than Empires and More Slow," "The Day Before the Revolution," "The Ones Who Walk Away from Omelas," "April in Paris," "Darkness Box," "The Masters," "Nine Lives," "Things," "The Good Trip," "A Trip to the Head," "Direction of the Road," and "The Field of Vision.")

Orsinian Tales. New York: Harper and Row, 1976; New York: Bantam, 1977. (Short stories.)

Very Far Away from Anywhere Else. New York: Atheneum, 1976. Reprinted as *A Very Long Way from Anywhere Else,* London: Gollancz, 1976.

"The Eye of the Heron." In *Millennial Women.* Edited by Virginia Kidd. New York: Delacorte, 1978. Separately printed, New York: Harper and Row, 1983.

Malafrena. New York: Berkley-Putnam, 1979.

The Beginning Place. New York: Harper and Row, 1980. Reprinted as *Threshold,* London: Gollancz, 1980.

The Compass Rose: Short Stories. Portland, Oreg.: Pendragon/Underwood-Miller, 1982; New York: Bantam, 1983. (Includes "The New Atlantis," "The Diary of the Rose," "SQ," "Intracom," "Schrodinger's Cat," "The Author of the Acacia Seeds," "Mazes," "The Eye Altering," "Gwilan's Harp," and "Malheur County.")

Always Coming Home, with Todd Barton, composer; Margaret Chodos, artist; George Hersh, geomancer. New York: Harper and Row, 1985. Slipcased with cassette tape, New York: Bantam, 1986.

Buffalo Gals and Other Animal Presences. Santa Barbara, Calif.: Capra, 1987; New York: New American Library, 1988. (Short stories.)

Way of the Water's Going: Images of the Northern California Coastal Range. New York: Harper and Row, 1989. (Excerpts with photographs by Ernest Waugh and Alan Nicholson.)

Tehanu: The Last Book of Earthsea. New York: Atheneum, 1990; New York: Bantam, 1991.

Searoad: Chronicles of Klatsand. New York: HarperCollins, 1991; New York: HarperPerennial, 1992. (Short stories.)

A Fisherman of the Inland Sea: Science Fiction Stories. New York: HarperPrism, 1994. (Includes "The Shobies' Story," "Dancing to Ganam," and "Another Story or A Fisherman of the Inland Sea.")

Four Ways to Forgiveness. New York: HarperPrism, 1995.

Unlocking the Air and Other Stories. New York: HarperCollins, 1996.

NONFICTION

The Language of the Night: Essays on Fantasy and Science Fiction. Edited by Susan Wood. New York: Putnam's, 1979. Revised edition, London: The Women's Press, 1989. Revised edition, New York: HarperCollins, 1992.

Dancing at the Edge of the World: Thoughts on Words, Women, Places. New York: Grove, 1989; New York: Harper and Row, 1990.

Tao Te Ching: A Book About the Way and the Power of the Way, by Lao Tzu. A New English Version. Boston: Shambala, 1997.

Steering the Craft: Exercises and Discussions on Story Writing for the Lone Navigator or the Mutinous Crew. Portland, Oreg.: Eighth Mountain, 1998.

POETRY

Wild Angels. Santa Barbara, Calif.: Capra, 1975. Reprinted in *The Capra Chapbook Anthology.* Edited by Noel Young. Santa Barbara, Calif.: Capra, 1979.

Hard Words and Other Poems. New York: Harper and Row, 1981.

Wild Oats and Fireweed: New Poems. New York: Harper and Row, 1988.

Blue Moon over Thurman Street, with photographs by Roger Dorband. Portland, Oreg.: New Sage Press, 1993.

Going Out with Peacocks and Other Poems. New York: HarperPerennial, 1994.

CHILDREN'S BOOKS

Leese Webster. New York: Atheneum, 1969.

"Solomon Leviathan's Nine Hundred and Thirty-first Trip Around the World." In *The First Puffin's Pleasure.* Edited by Kaye Webb and Treld Bicknell. New York: Puffin, 1976. Separately published, New Castle, Va.: Cheap Street, 1983; New York: Philomel, 1988.

The Adventure of Cobbler's Rune. New Castle, Va.: Cheap Street, 1982.

Catwings. New York: Orchard, 1988.

A Visit from Dr. Katz. New York: Atheneum, 1988.

Catwings Return. New York: Orchard, 1989.

Fire and Stone. New York: Atheneum, 1989.

Fish Soup. New York: Atheneum, 1992.

A Ride on the Red Mare's Back. New York: Orchard, 1992.

Wonderful Alexander and the Catwings. New York: Orchard, 1994.

EDITED ANTHOLOGIES

Nebula Award Stories Eleven. London: Gollancz, 1976; New York: Bantam, 1978.

Edges: Thirteen New Tales from the Borderlands of the Imagination, with Virginia Kidd. New York: Pocket Books, 1980.

Interfaces, with Virginia Kidd. New York: Ace, 1980.

The Norton Book of Science Fiction: North American Science Fiction, 1960–1990, with Brian Attebery; Karen Joy Fowler, consultant. New York: Norton, 1993.

SELECTED SHORT FICTION

"Legends for a New Land: Guest of Honor Speech at the 19th Annual Mythopoeic Conference." *Mythlore,* 15 (Winter 1988): 4–10.

"Children, Women, Men, and Dragons." *Monad: Essays on Science Fiction,* no. 1 (September 1990): 3–27. Revised and printed separately as *Earthsea Revisioned,* Cambridge, Mass.: Children's Literature New England, 1993.

"The Making of Always Coming Home: A Panel at Mythopoeic Conference XIX," with Todd Barton, Margaret Chodos-Irvine, George Hersh. *Mythlore,* 17 (Spring 1991): 56–63.

"Coming of Age in Karhide." In *New Legends.* Edited by Greg Bear and Martin Greenberg. London: Legend, 1994.

"The Matter of Seggri." *Crank!,* no. 3 (Spring 1994): 3–36.

"Unchosen Love." *Amazing Stories* (Fall 1994): 11–26.

"Solitude." *Fantasy and Science Fiction,* 87 (December 1994): 132–159.

"Introduction: Reading Young, Reading Old." In *The Diaries of Adam and Eve,* by Mark Twain. Edited by Shelley Fisher Fishkin. New York: Oxford University Press, 1996.

"Mountain Ways." *Isaac Asimov's Science Fiction Magazine,* 20 (August 1996): 14–39.

"Dragonfly." In *Legends: Short Novels by the Masters of Modern Fantasy.* Edited by Greg Bear and Martin Greenberg. New York: TOR, 1998.

BIBLIOGRAPHIES

Bratman, David S. *Ursula K. Le Guin: A Primary Bibliography.* San Jose, Calif.: 1995.

Cogell, Elizabeth Cummins. *Ursula K. Le Guin: A Primary and Secondary Bibliography.* Boston: G. K. Hall, 1983.

CRITICAL AND BIOGRAPHICAL STUDIES

Attebery, Brian. "Gender, Fantasy, and the Authority of Tradition." *Journal of the Fantastic in the Arts,* 7 (1996): 51–60.

Barbour, Douglas. "Patterns and Meaning in the Science Fiction Novels of Ursula K. Le Guin, Joanna Russ, and Samuel R. Delany." Ph.D. dissertation, Queen's College (Kingston, Ontario), 1976.

Benford, Gregory. "Reactionary Utopias." In *Storm Warnings: Science Fiction Confronts the Future.* Edited by George Slusser et al. Carbondale: Southern Illinois University Press, 1987.

Bittner, James W. "Persuading Us to Rejoice and Teaching Us How to Praise: Le Guin's *Orsinian Tales.*" *Science-Fiction Studies,* 5 (November 1978): 215–242.

———. *Approaches to the Fiction of Ursula K. Le Guin.* Ann Arbor, Mich.: UMI Research Press, 1984.

Broughton, Irv. *The Writer's Mind.* Vol. 2. Fayetteville: University of Arkansas Press, 1990. (Interview.)

Cummins, Elizabeth. "The Land-Lady's Homebirth: Revisiting Ursula K. Le Guin's Worlds." *Science-Fiction Studies,* 7 (July 1990): 153–166.

———. *Understanding Ursula K. Le Guin.* Revised edition, Columbia: University of South Carolina Press, 1993.

De Bolt, Joe, ed. *Ursula K. Le Guin: Voyager to Inner Lands and to Outer Space.* Port Washington, N.Y.: Kennikat, 1979.

Delany, Samuel R. "To Read *The Dispossessed.*" In his *The Jewel-Hinged Jaw: Notes on the Language of Science Fiction.* Elizabethtown, N.Y.: Dragon, 1977.

Hull, Keith N. "What Is Human? Ursula Le Guin and Science Fiction's Great Theme." *Modern Fiction Studies,* 32 (Spring 1986): 65–74.

Jameson, Sara. "Ursula K. Le Guin: A Galaxy of Books and Laurels." *Publishers Weekly,* 25 September 1995.

Jose, Jim. "Reflections on the Politics of Le Guin's Narrative Shifts." *Science-Fiction Studies*, 18 (1991): 180–197.

LeClair, Tom. "Ursula Le Guin's *Always Coming Home*. In his *The Art of Excess: Mastery in Contemporary American Fiction*." Urbana: University of Illinois Press, 1989.

Olander, Joseph D., and Martin Harry Greenberg, eds. *Ursula K. Le Guin*. New York: Taplinger, 1979.

Rass, Rebecca. "Ursula K. Le Guin's Life and Work: An Interview." In *Ursula Le Guin's The Left Hand of Darkness: A Critical Commentary*. New York: Simon and Schuster, 1990.

Sargent, Lyman Tower, ed. "Featured Discussion of Ursula K. Le Guin's 'Omelas.'" *Utopian Studies*, 2 (1991):1–62.

Selinger, Bernard. *Le Guin and Identity in Contemporary Fiction*. Ann Arbor, Mich: UMI Research Press, 1988.

Shippey, T. A. "The Magic Art and the Evolution of Words: Ursula Le Guin's Earthsea Trilogy." *Mosaic*, 10 (1977): 147–163.

Slaughter, Jane. "Ursula Le Guin." *The Progressive*, 62 (March 1998): 36–39.

Slusser, George E. *The Farthest Shores of Ursula K. Le Guin*. San Bernardino, Calif.: Borgo, 1976.

———. "The Ideal Worlds of Science Fiction." In *Hard Science Fiction*. Edited by George E. Slusser and Eric S. Rabkin. Carbondale: Southern Illinois University Press, 1986.

Spencer, Kathleen. "Exiles and Envoys: The SF of Ursula K. Le Guin." *Foundation*, no. 20 (1980): 32–43.

Spinrad, Norman. "Critical Standards." *Isaac Asimov's Science Fiction Magazine*, 10 (September 1986): 179–191.

Spivack, Charlotte. *Ursula K. Le Guin*. Boston: Twayne, 1984.

Stone-Blackburn, Susan. "Adult Telepathy: *Babel-17* and *The Left Hand of Darkness*." *Extrapolation*, 30 (Fall 1989): 243–253.

Suvin, Darko, ed. *Science-Fiction Studies*, 2 (November 1975). (Special Ursula K. Le Guin issue.)

Walker, Jeanne Murray. "Rites of Passage Today: The Cultural Significance of *A Wizard of Earthsea*." *Mosaic*, 13 (1980): 179–191.

White, Jonathan. "Coming Back from the Silence." In *Talking on the Water: Conversations About Nature and Creativity*. San Francisco, Calif.: Sierra Club, 1994.

Wood, Susan. "Discovering Worlds: The Fiction of Ursula K. Le Guin." In *Voices for the Future*. Edited by Thomas D. Clareson. Vol. 2. Bowling Green, Ohio: Bowling Green University Popular Press, 1978.

Yoke, Carol B., ed. *Extrapolation*, 21 (Fall 1980). (Special Ursula K. Le Guin issue.)

Fritz Leiber

(1910–1992)

Fritz reuter leiber, Jr., was born in Chicago on 24 December 1910, the son of a Shakespearean actor who appeared in a number of films. He graduated from the University of Chicago in 1932, having taken courses in biological science, psychology, and philosophy—although the range of his interests extends much further; and this eclecticism shows in his fiction. His series of stories chronicling the careers of Fafhrd and the Gray Mouser established him as the best American writer of "sword-and-sorcery" fiction. He also wrote one classic novel and a number of brilliant short stories in the field of supernatural fiction; and he produced a good deal of excellent science fiction.

Leiber's versatility also showed within each of these fields—especially the last, where he was associated with several of the editors responsible for extending the range and ambitions of magazine science fiction. He won six Hugo awards, three Nebulas, and three World Fantasy Association awards, as well as a Grand Master of Fantasy award and a Mrs. Ann Radcliffe award. His career was uneven, with bursts of productivity alternating with dry periods; but whenever a dry period ended, he seemed rejuvenated.

After leaving college, Leiber failed to settle into any particular role. In his own words (in an autobiographical essay published in *Foundation*), he "floundered about, not very adventurously, in search of vocation and sexual fulfillment, eventually finding (or falling into) an occupation in editorial work in Chicago." In 1936 he married Jonquil Stevens, a British

poet with whom he shared a strong interest in weird and supernatural fiction. This was an interest he also shared with his friend Harry Otto Fischer, in collaboration with whom he developed the heroic-fantasy characters Fafhrd and the Gray Mouser. In the mid-1930's Leiber wrote a good deal of fiction that failed to sell, including a Fafhrd/Gray Mouser story called "Adept's Gambit," which eventually appeared in his first collection of stories, *Night's Black Agents* (1947).

The first story that Leiber sold featured these two characters; it was bought in 1939 by John W. Campbell, Jr., for *Unknown*, where it appeared as "Two Sought Adventure." Leiber had been trying to sell to *Weird Tales*, and soon succeeded with "The Automatic Pistol" (1940). But the magazine's new editor, Dorothy McIlwraith, would not take his sword-and-sorcery stories, even though her predecessor, Farnsworth Wright, had successfully published much of that type of fiction by Robert E. Howard and others.

In 1941, Leiber sold his first science fiction story—a rather awkward space opera called "They Never Come Back"—but for the time being he was more successful as a fantasy writer. In two of his weird stories, "Smoke Ghost" (1941) and "The Hound" (1942), he began to develop a new kind of supernatural fiction, devising hauntings uniquely appropriate to the modern environments of cities, apartment buildings, and factories. He provided a prospectus for this kind of fiction in "Smoke Ghost," in which the protagonist addresses the following question to his secretary:

Have you ever thought what a ghost of our times would look like, Miss Millick? Just picture it. A smoky composite face with the hungry anxiety of the unemployed, the neurotic restlessness of the person without purpose, the jerky tension of the high-pressure metropolitan worker, the uneasy resentment of the striker, the callous opportunism of the scab, the aggressive whine of the panhandler, the inhibited terror of the bombed civilian, and a thousand other twisted emotional patterns. Each one overlying and yet blending with the other, like a pile of semi-transparent masks? (*Night's Black Agents*, page 5)

Leiber never lost his fascination with this theme, and it is the inspiration for some of his best stories from later periods, including "The Girl with the Hungry Eyes" (1949), about the supernatural power of advertising imagery; "The Black Gondolier" (1964), about the haunting of the Grand Canal in the oil town of Venice, United States; and his novel *Our Lady of Darkness* (1977), which presents the occult lore of "Megapolisomancy," relating to the demonic "paramental entities" that are the spirits of our urban jungles. The award-winning "Belsen Express" (1975) also belongs to this tradition; it tells of a contemporary American who is slowly engulfed by a strange existential echo of the Nazis' "final solution."

Leiber's first novel, written for Campbell's *Unknown*, was *Conjure Wife* (1943; book form, 1953), which brilliantly introduces witchcraft into a contemporary setting, not as a peripheral resurgence of something ancient but as an everyday domestic activity practiced widely and routinely by faculty wives struggling to procure the advancement of their husbands without their knowledge. The first half of the book, in which the elements of the plot are slowly but surely gathered together, is a masterpiece of suspense.

Campbell encouraged Leiber to write for *Astounding* as well as *Unknown*, and with his blessing Leiber began work on his first science fiction novel, *Gather, Darkness!* (1943; book form, 1950), borrowing an idea from Robert A. Heinlein's *Sixth Column* (1941; book form, 1949). In *Sixth Column* (reprinted

as *The Day After Tomorrow*) Americans use a fake religion, complete with superscientific "miracles," as camouflage for a revolutionary movement destined to overthrow their Oriental conquerors. Leiber imagined the fake religion as already established, its controllers using it to sustain their tyrannical rule; he also imagined the growth of a new revolutionary movement, forced by this historical circumstance to adopt the complementary ideology of Satanism. The plot of the novel is melodramatic, and the duel with superscientific weaponry is given an entirely new glamour by the double masquerade; it is a supremely theatrical story, as are many of Leiber's longer works.

Leiber had by this time been a full-time writer for a year, but he found that he was not writing quickly enough to support himself. America was at war, and *Unknown*—his most important market—had ceased publication. Leiber went to work for Douglas Aircraft, and later became assistant editor of *Science Digest*, remaining on its staff for twelve years. The later 1940's were some of his leanest years in terms of literary productivity, though he did write one more short novel for Campbell's *Astounding*: the elegant parallel-worlds story *Destiny Times Three* (1945; book form, 1957). He also produced some good short stories, mostly concerned with what kind of circumstances could justify violent action.

In 1949, Leiber began writing again, though largely for his own mimeographed amateur magazine called *New Purposes*—and he did, indeed, seem to have found new purposes in his fiction, which began to show a much stronger sensitivity to contemporary social and political concerns, and a greater interest in character development. There is also a surreal quality about some of the stories of this period, most notably the short novel "You're All Alone" (1950), an abridged version of a story whose full text was published in paperback as *The Sinful Ones* (1953). In this story the hero discovers that virtually everyone in the world is an automaton whose behavior follows a predetermined script. Once he has realized this, it becomes possible for him to step outside his "role" and achieve a special kind of freedom—but not without risk, for there are others who are "awake" and who use their advantageous position in a rather selfish fashion.

A complete contrast in mood is provided by the novel *The Green Millennium* (1953), in which a soulless future America is subjected to a benevolent invasion by cats and nonconformists from Vega. It is a more personal novel than his earlier efforts, and began life as a non-science fiction story in *New Purposes*. It was too unconventional to win many readers in its own day, but it anticipated something of the mood of the 1960's "counterculture."

Although Leiber sold some work to Campbell in this period, he formed a new relationship with Horace L. Gold, the editor of *Galaxy* (1950–1961), and it was for this magazine that he did most of his best work. He had a trivial story in the first issue, but the second (November 1950) carried "Coming Attraction," a brief but highly dramatic portrait of a future society that has adapted its customs and attitudes to the circumstances arising in the wake of a nuclear war. It is one of the most powerful of the postholocaust stories then flooding the magazines because of its subtlety in presenting an image of horrifying normalcy rather than a brutal account of apocalyptic tragedy. Leiber followed this in 1951 with a story of a future society that has adopted a new morality, "Nice Girl with Five Husbands"; with a satirical account of the scientist's role in political affairs, "Appointment in Tomorrow"; and with a gentle story of housekeeping after a worldwide catastrophe, "A Pail of Air."

This was a period when Leiber's stories were frequently infused with a fierce bitterness—the product of an intellectual climate overshadowed by McCarthyism and the atomic bomb. The flair for presenting key images from bleak futures, which was shown in "Coming Attraction," also was displayed in "The Moon Is Green" and "The Foxholes of Mars" (both 1952), "A Bad Day for Sales" (1953), and "The Silence Game" (1954)—all stories preoccupied with the prospect of a new war that would condemn human beings to live in a world without meaning. During this productive spell—which concluded with "The Silence Game"—he wrote hardly any supernatural fiction and only one sword-and-sorcery tale.

For three years Leiber published nothing at all, but his career began to revive in 1957, when *Destiny Times Three* was reprinted as a Galaxy novel, and Gnome Press issued a collection of Fafhrd/Gray Mouser stories, *Two Sought Adventure*. He began writing again for both *Galaxy* and *Magazine of Fantasy and Science Fiction*, though his idiosyncrasies were now beginning to cause Gold some anxiety. Gold nearly did not buy *The Big Time*, Leiber's new science fiction novel, which went on to win the best novel of 1958. (This was the first of Leiber's six Hugo awards.) It is the first of several stories about the "Change War"—a war fought across time by two forces calling themselves Snakes and Spiders, each side using soldiers recruited from the entire continuum of history. The object of the war is to win the privilege of determining the course that history should take.

The Big Time is set in a station outside time where warriors can take their leave and recuperate; its narrator is a "party girl." The novel is essentially a play in prose, taking place on a single set, its action mainly conversational. The plot is part mystery, part suspense story: a party of soldiers has brought a nuclear bomb with them to the station, and the instrument that will allow it to be disarmed has been concealed; the station is isolated from the rest of the cosmos by a dimensional warp and seems likely to be destroyed before reconnecting.

The story has been produced as a play; its main virtue is the delicacy with which an extravagant edifice of science fiction ideas is presented—not through descriptions of vast conflicts and exploits of conspicuous heroism, but through the interaction of a handful of characters in a manifestly mundane setting. The grand ideas are all implied; they

Fritz Leiber. © Miriam Berkley

work their wonders offstage but are no less impressive for it.

Several other Change War stories appear in *The Mind Spider* (1961), the collection published back-to-back with *The Big Time* when it appeared in book form for the first time as an Ace Double; however, the best one published before that date, "A Deskful of Girls" (1958), was not included. This story and three later ones were added to the stories in *The Mind Spider* to form the collection *The Change War* (1978). One of the later stories, the novella "No Great Magic" (1963), is a direct sequel to *The Big Time* and is even more steeped in theatricality, its action organized around a performance of *Macbeth*. This piece, along with "Four Ghosts in Hamlet" (1965), provides eloquent expression of Leiber's love of the theater—both stories are stylish and genuinely moving.

Leiber's association with *Galaxy* was not fully secured by the success of *The Big Time*,

and Gold rejected the next short novel that Leiber sent him, "The Silver Eggheads." This appeared in *Fantasy and Science Fiction* in 1959 and was expanded for book publication in 1961. It is a comedy about a world where writers use "wordmills" and only robots preserve the real creative spirit, producing pulp fiction for other robots. It is a piece of ideative slapstick that testifies to the enjoyment Leiber was getting from his writing in this period, which shows little trace of the bitterness of the early 1950's.

Because he was no longer writing regularly for *Galaxy*, Leiber began to aim more stories at the Ziff-Davis magazines, particularly *Fantastic*, whose wide brief seemed to offer adequate scope for his wilder flights of fantasy. Cele Goldsmith, the most imaginative editor the Ziff-Davis magazines had ever had, was an enthusiastic admirer of Leiber's work, and when he submitted a new story of Fafhrd and the Gray Mouser, "Lean Times in Lankhmar," she asked him for enough material to fill an entire special issue with his stories. This was the November 1959 issue of *Fantastic*. With Goldsmith's encouragement Leiber wrote at least one story of Fafhrd and the Mouser per year from then on, until there were enough to fill several books. Eventually, Ace began to issue the series in 1968, when they published the novel *The Swords of Lankhmar* (expanded from "Scylla's Daughter," 1961). The series in 1980 stood at six volumes, including a reprint of the Gnome Press collection, the most recent being the collection *Swords and Ice Magic* (1977). One story, "Ill Met in Lankhmar" (1970), won both the Hugo and Nebula awards for best novelette.

Relatively little of the fiction that Leiber wrote between 1959 and 1961 is science fiction, but by 1962, when Frederik Pohl was in charge of both *Galaxy* and *If*, Leiber began placing new stories with him. In that year he produced two of his best science fiction novelettes: "The 64-Square Madhouse" and "The Creature from Cleveland Depths" (also known as "The Lone Wolf"). The former is the definitive story about the computer invasion of chess tournaments, and is now near

440

the point of being overtaken by reality. (Leiber's fascination with chess, like his love of the theater and his love of cats, has provided the inspiration for more than one fine story—another is "Midnight by the Morphy Watch," 1974.) The latter story, also on the brink of being overtaken by events, deals in part with the micro-miniaturization of computers and their possible uses.

Leiber's major science fiction project of the early 1960's was the long novel *The Wanderer* (1964), a story about the sudden appearance in the solar system of a new world, the Wanderer, whose proximity to Earth causes earthquakes and great tidal waves that devastate many nations. The moon, which is captured by the new world, disintegrates, and its substance is absorbed. The bulk of the novel takes the form that has become conventional in disaster novels: following the adventures of different groups of people placed in various predicaments by the upheavals. The climactic section, though, is chiefly concerned with the story of an American rocket pilot who survives the breakup of the United States Moonbase and reaches the Wanderer, where he encounters one of its inhabitants, a catlike alien he names Tigerishka. Through this encounter the astronaut learns the greater context in which the earthly disaster must be set: the Wanderer is a strange kind of refugee fleeing from the law imposed by a universal social order that is eclipsing the stars one by one as it surrounds them with Dyson spheres. The Wanderer eventually makes its exit back into hyperspace, pursued by an even greater artificial world.

The Wanderer won Leiber his second Hugo for best novel, but it was not as successful as it might have been. It was, as were so many Leiber projects, ahead of its time, arriving ten years too soon for the boom in disaster stories; but it is perhaps too imaginatively extravagant to have enjoyed tremendous success even if it had had a bandwagon to ride on. Its final expansion of perspective is far less reassuring than the conventional finale of disaster stories, affirming the conviction that the universe may be intrinsically hostile to beings such as ourselves. The hero discovers that he and Tigerishka, despite their brief sexual congress, have too little in common to remain together; though in another sense they share far too much in terms of their philosophy of life. In time, the human race too may have to flee from the oppressive utopianism that has spread so effectively through the universe.

As far as magazine stories are concerned, Leiber had another quiet period in 1966–1967, though he did publish one book in this interval—a novelization of the film script of *Tarzan and the Valley of Gold* (1966). The only such project to have had the blessing of the Burroughs estate, it is a lively adventure story.

One of the few short stories Leiber did publish in 1967 was the Nebula and Hugo award-winning story "Gonna Roll the Bones," which appeared in Harlan Ellison's *Dangerous Visions* anthology. It is a pure fantasy story about dicing with the devil, but it has a dramatic intensity that makes it one of the most vivid of such stories. It intertwines the horrifying, dark world of fantasy with the domestic life of the protagonist, who does not have to cross from one realm into the other; in some special sense the two realms permeate one another. Leiber had written other stories with a similarly surreal tone, most notably "The Secret Songs" (1962) and "The Inner Circles" (1967, also known as "The Winter Flies"), which in a sense relate to *Conjure Wife* and "Smoke Ghost." But while the early stories are bona fide fantasies in which the line between the supernatural and the mundane is clearly drawn, in these later stories the boundary is obliterated, and the supernatural is transformed into the surreal.

After the publication of *Dangerous Visions*, the development of *New Worlds* under Michael Moorcock's control, and the rise to popularity of Philip K. Dick, surrealism became far more acceptable as a mode of operation within the science fiction genre. Leiber took advantage of this opportunity.

Most of the short stories employing science fiction imagery which Leiber wrote after 1968 mingle that imagery with supernatural motifs. The most reckless juxtaposition of this kind is in "Ship of Shadows" (1969), in which a starship is infested with the entire conventional apparatus of the supernatural imagination. Although the tale's abrupt ending suggests that it was originally intended as the prelude to a much longer work, it won a Hugo award for best novella after appearing in a special issue of *The Magazine of Fantasy and Science Fiction* celebrating Leiber's work. The exuberant alternative worlds story "Catch that Zeppelin!" (1975) also won a Hugo for best short story and completed a rare double by winning a Nebula award for best short story as well. The hallucinatory fantasy "Black Glass" (1978) also deploys a good deal of science fiction imagery and is written in a similar cavalier spirit.

Leiber's last science fiction novel was *A Specter Is Haunting Texas* (1969), a comic satire following the adventures of a cadaverously lanky visitor from a space habitat, who is sustained against the pressure of Earth's gravity by an artificial exoskeleton. He finds that the state of Great Texas—which has absorbed almost all of North America—is inhabited by hormonally assisted muscle men. The novel can be seen, retrospectively, as a kind of theatrical farewell to an imaginative apparatus, though now redundant, that had engaged Leiber while the only marketplace for fantasy was within the margins of the science fiction genre.

It was not until after his death on 5 September 1992 that Leiber's first considerable work of science fiction, *The Dealings of Daniel Kesserich: A Study of the Mass-Insanity at Smithville*—which had been written in 1936 but lost in the 1950s—was rediscovered among his papers. It is clearly influenced by H. G. Wells, although its story structure is much more closely akin to William Sloane's near-contemporary science fiction mystery *To Walk the Night* (1937). In *The Dealings of Daniel Kesserich*, a series of seemingly supernatural incidents that cause considerable distress to the inhabitants of a small town is eventually revealed as the result of a series of time travel experiments whose scientific purity has been muddied by erotic obsession.

Although it seemed a trifle crude when it was finally made available to the public in 1997, *The Dealings of Daniel Kesserich* was presumably too sophisticated in its ideational convolutions to be appealing to the pulp magazine editors of its day; one can only wonder what Leiber might have produced had he found the freedom to display his prodigious imaginative talents exactly as he wished some thirty years earlier. On the other hand, there is cause to be glad that he did occasionally forge connections with sympathetic editors who were prepared to allow him scope to operate as a one-man avant garde even in the days before science fiction was supposed to have an avant garde.

Much of Leiber's writing during the last ten years of his life was intensely personal. The last elements in his sword-and-sorcery series became transfigurations of his own moods, and he wrote a good deal of confessional nonfiction in which he wrote with equal frankness about his writing and the long battles with alcoholism that punctuated his career. The long and wistfully charming "Not Much Disorder and Not So Early Sex: An Autobiographic Essay" in *The Ghost Light: Masterworks of Science Fiction and Fantasy* (1984) is a remarkable exercise in self-analysis.

Leiber's fiction often depicts individuals living in direly difficult circumstances, who must pursue eccentric psychological and social strategies in order to survive and thrive. His work contains a strong element of black comedy, but his science fiction balances occasional moments of bitterness and horror with an unfailing ability to take delight in the new and the strange. The sympathy Leiber invariably feels for characters victimized by ill fortune is cleverly woven into the thread of his best works, giving his satires a warm poignancy and his tragedies a fervent emotional intensity. The breadth of his audience was limited by his idiosyncrasies, but connoisseurs of imaginative fiction always knew how valuable his work was. He was one of the finest American short story writers of his era.

Selected Bibliography

FICTION OF FRITZ LEIBER

Night's Black Agents. Sauk City, Wis.: Arkham House, 1947.

Gather, Darkness! New York: Pellegrini and Cudahy, 1950.

Conjure Wife. New York: Twayne Publishers, 1953.

The Green Millennium. New York: Abelard, 1953.

The Sinful Ones. New York: Universal Giant, 1953. New York: Pocket Books, 1980 (with minor revisions).

Destiny Times Three. New York: Galaxy, 1957.

Two Sought Adventure. New York: Gnome Press, 1957.

The Big Time. New York: Ace Books, 1961.

The Mind Spider and Other Stories. New York: Ace Books, 1961.

The Silver Eggheads. New York: Ballantine Books, 1961.

Shadows with Eyes. New York: Ballantine Books, 1962.

A Pail of Air. New York: Ballantine Books, 1964.

Ships to the Stars. New York: Ace Books, 1964.

The Wanderer. New York: Ballantine Books, 1964.

The Night of the Wolf. New York: Ballantine Books, 1966.

Tarzan and the Valley of Gold. New York: Ballantine Books, 1966.

The Secret Songs. London: Hart-Davis, 1968.

Swords Against Wizardry. New York: Ace Books, 1968.

Swords in the Midst. New York: Ace Books, 1968.

The Swords of Lankhmar. New York: Ace Books, 1968.

Night Monsters. New York: Ace Books, 1969. Extended version, London: Victor Gollancz, 1974.

A Specter Is Haunting Texas. New York: Walker, 1969.

Swords Against Death. New York: Ace Books, 1970.

Swords and Deviltry. New York: Ace Books, 1970.

You're All Alone. New York: Ace Books, 1972.

The Best of Fritz Leiber. New York: Ballantine Books, 1974.

The Book of Fritz Leiber. New York: DAW, 1974.

The Second Book of Fritz Leiber. New York: DAW, 1975.

The Worlds of Fritz Leiber. New York: Ace Books, 1976.

Our Lady of Darkness. New York: Berkley/Putnam, 1977.

Rime Isle. Chapel Hill, N.C.: Whispers Press, 1977.

Swords and Ice Magic. New York: Ace Books, 1977.

Bazaar of the Bizarre. West Kingston, R.I.: Donald M. Grant, 1978.

The Change War. Boston: Gregg Press, 1978.

Heroes and Horrors. Chapel Hill, N.C.: Whispers Press, 1978.

Ship of Shadows. London: Victor Gollancz, 1979.

OTHER WORKS

Leiber, Fritz. "Fafhrd and Me." *Amra*, October 1963. Reprinted in *The Second Book of Fritz Leiber*: 92–114. (Reminiscences connected with the Fafhrd and Gray Mouser series.)

————. "The Profession of Science Fiction, XII: Mysterious Islands." *Foundation*, 11/12 (March 1977): 29–38.

The Ghost Light: Masterworks of Science Fiction and Fantasy. New York: Berkley, 1984. (Short stories and an autobiographical essay.)

The Knight and Knave of Swords. New York: Morrow, 1988; London: Grafton, 1990.

Kreativity for Kats and Other Feline Fantasies. Newark, N.J.: Wildside Press, 1990.

The Leiber Chronicles: Fifty Years of Fritz Leiber. Edited by Martin H. Greenberg. Arlington Heights, Ill.: Dark Harvest, 1990.

The Dealings of Daniel Kesserich: A Study of the Mass-Insanity at Smithville. New York: TOR, 1997.

CRITICAL AND BIOGRAPHICAL STUDIES

Byfield, Bruce. *Witches of the Mind: A Critical Study of Fritz Leiber*. West Warwick, R.I.: Necronomicon, 1991.

Frane, Jeff. *Fritz Leiber*. San Bernardino, Calif.: Borgo, 1980.

Merril, Judith. "Fritz Leiber." *Magazine of Fantasy and Science Fiction* (July 1969): 44–61. (A critical appreciation written for a special Fritz Leiber issue.)

Morgan, Chris. *Fritz Leiber: A Bibliography 1934–1979*. Birmingham, England: Morgenstern, 1979.

Moskowitz, Sam. "Fritz Leiber." In his *Seekers of Tomorrow*. Cleveland: World Publishing Company, 1966. (Biographical sketch and critical appreciation.)

Staicar, Tom. *Fritz Leiber*. New York: Ungar, 1983.

—BRIAN STABLEFORD

MURRAY LEINSTER

(1896–1975)

On PAGE 147 of a collection of stories put together to honor its author and entitled *The Best of Murray Leinster* (1978), there appears a modest but revealing misprint that tells us in a nutshell a good deal about what Leinster did and did not accomplish as an author. The misprint comes about halfway through his most famous story, "First Contact," which was originally published in *Astounding Science-Fiction* in 1945, at almost precisely the middle of his career and at about the time he was beginning to be thought of as the dean of science fiction, a sobriquet he deserved more obviously than some other candidates from the prewar years.

In "First Contact" an exploration ship from Earth arrives at the uninhabitable heart of the Crab Nebula and finds there an alien ship, also obviously far from home. Through one of Leinster's usual protagonists, a young man slightly outside the normal chain of command who boasts a freelance clarity of vision and freedom from bureaucratic thinking in general, we see the two species of intelligent life facing up to the dilemma posed by their discovery of each other: how to prevent one species (if inimical) from following the other back home, without descending to mutual destruction. (The protagonist, young Tommy Dort, solves the problem by suggesting that after destroying all data on board about the location of their respective home worlds, the two crews should simply exchange ships.)

The aliens seem to have a humanlike sense of humor, and (led by Tommy) the humans begin to speculate about the positive implications of contact—mainly in terms of the advantages of shared technology and resources, again an emphasis typical of Leinster— though the ship's psychologist, being a functionary, does not have the mental equipment "to analyze a completely alien thought-pattern," and must defer to Tommy Dort:

> "If I may say so, sir—" said Tommy uncomfortably.
> "What?"
> "They're oxygen brothers," said Tommy.

What is misprinted is, of course, the word "brothers."

In the original text, what Tommy says is "They're oxygen breathers," a perfectly rational, straightforward sentence; it is precisely the metaphorical implications and the modicum of imaginative density in the term "oxygen brothers" that alerts the knowledgeable reader to the possibility of a typographical error. In a career extending from 1915 to about 1970, Leinster virtually never surprised one (with joy or shock or dismay) by his use of language; and he never indulged in the expression of insights that could in any sense be thought of as psychological or "poetic," either to contemplate the human condition or to speculate upon it. Of all science fiction writers of the first or second rank, his world and the language he used to depict it are the most consistently mundane. In the sense that every word he wrote accomplished its purpose, no less and no more, Leinster was probably the most professional writer ever to engage in science fiction as his main activity.

The reader's immediate recognition, with each new story and novel, of the familiar Leinster universe is a clear token of his skill and of how he directed it. In real life a decent, reasonable, quiet family man, in his works Leinster was also professionally decent and reasonable; he was able to create—and increasingly, as the years passed, he became trapped in—a whole galaxy safe from alarm. With relatively few exceptions there is no barrier of the unknown in his work; the universe and his protagonists' knowledge of its workings rarely evolve in any significant fashion between the start and the close of any story. For Leinster to have embarked on even the modest linguistic adventure of speaking of "oxygen brothers"—and dealing with the plot implications of the vaguely ecumenical warmth at which the term hints—would have been to risk subverting his comfortable, workmanlike, stable, "small-town" universe.

In "First Contact," therefore, it is not surprising to discover that the ship psychologist's inability to deal with "a completely alien thought-pattern" turns out to be a red herring. As late in his career as 1945, it is most unlikely that Leinster would have risked the destabilizing consequences of inserting a genuinely intelligent though incomprehensible alien species into a venue calling for interaction with humans; and in "First Contact," humans and aliens are duly found to be basically indistinguishable, though their sensory organs differ. In Leinster's universe, aliens tend either to be anthropomorphic and friendly, or "monstrous" (frequently jellylike) in shape and intention, although we can assess their inimical intentions only from the outside, because, when human protagonists are present, the reader is never given access to the point of view of the adversary.

Seeming exceptions to this rule generally serve to demonstrate it: in "De Profundis" (*Thrilling Wonder Stories*, 1944; reprinted in *Sidewise in Time*, 1950), the point-of-view monsters from the ocean depths can barely perceive the presence of humans at all, and never admit their sentience; similarly, the alien on the run in "Fugitive from Space"

(*Amazing Stories*, 1954; reprinted in *The Aliens*, 1960) mimics human speech and appearance but is soon revealed as contemptibly amoral in action and totally monstrous (that is, jellylike) in appearance (it is killed off by young Burt and the FBI). "Anthropological Note" (*The Magazine of Fantasy and Science Fiction*, 1957; reprinted in *The Aliens*) is a comic spoof, rather disfigured by its amused contempt at the pretensions of Miss Cummings, the female anthropologist who (though the center of the action) never quite merits a point-of-view treatment. (Women are rarely, if ever, genuine protagonists in any Leinster story.) The aliens in this tale seem genuinely alien through sections of the narrative, though the young among them treat Miss Cummings "with the tolerant condescension the young give to the older in all races without exception." But we eventually discover that the alien society in question is probably similar to that of the social insects on Earth, with the implication that no "individual" of the species is truly sentient; this reduces all previous observations in the story to garble.

Such anthropocentric distinctions between "sheep" and "goats" are, of course, not at all uncommon in the science fiction of the 1920's and 1930's; in Leinster's case, though, it is of central importance in any assessment of his career to note how successfully he modernizes the simple devices and verities of his early years in stories published as late as the mid-1960's, without changing their basic nature in any essential way. Throughout his career, for instance, friendly aliens (or sheep) can almost always be identified through acts of open-minded, intuitive insight on the part of young human protagonists. Such protagonists recognize the unmistakable chivalric valor of the Plumies in "The Aliens" (*Astounding Science-Fiction*, 1959; reprinted in *The Aliens*), or the probable shape of any alien society in question, which (though rarely examined in any detail) most often closely resembles the implicit shape of Tommy Dort's or Burt's own world: that is, a prewar America somewhat idealized after the fashion of the slick journals for which Leinster also wrote copiously. At the heart of his work, as befits the creator of so stable a universe, lies a clear and probably personal horror of metamorphosis, of change. Nothing to which he gives assent in his fiction ever alienates the reader from the values of prewar America. It is there that his heart lies, and the source of his value to us.

William Fitzgerald Jenkins—who almost always used the name Murray Leinster when writing for pulp magazines, in whatever genre, from the beginning of his career in the second decade of the twentieth century—was born in Norfolk, Virginia, on 16 June 1896. He maintained roots there for the rest of his long life; although he lived elsewhere for periods— on Long Island, New York, for instance—he always kept a summer home in Gloucester County, Virginia, where he did much of his work. After receiving an elementary school education, he began to write in his early teens, soon placing fillers with George Jean Nathan's and H. L. Mencken's *Smart Set*, and fiction elsewhere.

In a biographical note published in *Fantasy Magazine* in 1934, Jenkins gives a version of the invention of his pseudonym (which is pronounced "Lenster"). On the advice of a friend, Wyndham Martyn, he derived his new name from the fact that his family originated in County Leinster, Ireland; the origin of the Christian name, Murray, is not explained. (Wyndham Martyn, author of the Anthony Trent novels, the first of which appeared in 1918, wrote one science fiction novel, *Stones of Enchantment* [1948], featuring Trent. Martyn and Jenkins both grew up in a school of writing that treated genres primarily as marketing boundaries, to be crossed as needed, professionally.) From about 1917 the new Murray Leinster was a full-time writer; he reintroduced his real name, slightly shortened as Will F. Jenkins, in later years, mainly when publishing stories in slick magazines like *Collier's* or *Saturday Evening Post*, and only very occasionally for science fiction. Except for *The Murder of the U.S.A.* (1946), which was in any case released as a mystery, he pub-

Murray Leinster (William Fitzgerald Jenkins)
COURTESY OF THE LIBRARY OF CONGRESS

lished no science fiction book under his own name, and from this point on we will refer to him only as Murray Leinster.

His first science fiction story, "The Runaway Skyscraper" (*Argosy*, 1919), was a ramshackle effort, without scientific plausibility and almost without plot (Leinster would always remain a deficient and self-conscious constructor of plots). However clumsy it was, though, "The Runaway Skyscraper" started Leinster on that side of his career in which— though science fiction or fantasy comprised only a fraction of his more than 1,300 published stories—he did his best work, and which, after World War II, became his main source of new income. And once launched, he established himself with considerable speed, publishing several additional science fiction stories in *Thrill Book* before *Argosy* published his first important tale, "The Mad Planet," in 1920.

With its two sequels, "Red Dust" (*Argosy*, 1921) and "Nightmare Planet" (*Science-Fiction Plus*, 1953), the story was expanded into one of Leinster's many postwar titles, *The Forgotten Planet* (1954), and was rather submerged in its new context. Although the novelized version changes the locale from a "far-future" Earth—only 30,000 years hence—to another planet, and in other ways attempts to modernize the setting and the rationale, the original tale, for all its scientific implausibility, has a freshness and intensity rarely found in Leinster's work after he had learned to pace himself more economically. The venue is a naïve prevision of the apocalyptic vegetable prison of Brian Aldiss' *Hothouse* (1962), and its young protagonist's involuntary hegira through a landscape dominated by proliferating vegetable growths and huge insects evokes from Leinster prose as close to poetry as anything he would ever commit to print:

> The buzzing, fluttering, and the flapping of the insects of the day died slowly down, while from a million hiding places there crept out into the deep night soft and furry bodies of great moths.

And so forth. It is not prose of any great stature, and its methodical clarity of syntax and rhythm is perhaps more soothing than sensual; but in this story the insistent repetition of elements of the exposition serves an intensifying function, and has not yet become the word-spinning device so frequently utilized by the mature Leinster that it became a wearisome trademark; even his very best work (see, for example, pages 154–156 of the 1978 reprint of "First Contact" in *The Best of Murray Leinster*) is marred by static moments of fake rumination over material already presented to the reader. In his work a typical sign of this process is a series of sentences beginning with the words "There was" or "There were." Habits like this are of course examples of the negative side of an otherwise thorough professionalism, the result of an unfortunate

desire to leave nothing to chance; with their air of insecurity about material already presented, they also point to Leinster's most consistent failing as a writer, already mentioned: his inability to construct dynamic plots.

For the first fifteen years of his science fiction career, Leinster wrote widely and adeptly for a number of magazines, though never for Hugo Gernsback's *Amazing Stories*, and in various modes. From very early on, he was clear about the nature of the world he wished to create and to preserve: a small-town, decent, conservative, hopeful America whose enemies were almost invariably external. As Sam Moskowitz has noted in his essay on Leinster in *Seekers of Tomorrow* (1966), even when there is a human adversary (in the early years, often a criminal) in a Leinster story, he is rarely seen; when the adversary is nature itself, the story revolves around a technological problem that is to be solved. When the adversary is defeated (offstage) or when an apparently inimical nature is turned to man's advantage, peace once more descends upon a restored world; and, as in classic comedy, the young protagonist engages in nuptial activities with the young female who has loved him from the moment they met. Leinster's basic impulse was toward the shape of comedy, not tragedy; and it is in this light that the defeat of metamorphic threats to stability can be seen as deeply prophylactic.

In this first period of Leinster's career, which ended in 1936, only a few stories—and those few were his best—tend to violate the comedic drive toward a restoration of stability. These include "Sidewise in Time" (1934) and "Proxima Centauri" (1935); both were published in *Astounding Stories*, which had been one of Leinster's main markets since its inception in 1930; both were reprinted in *Sidewise in Time*. "Sidewise in Time" introduced into the magazine market the highly fruitful (and potentially change-ridden) concept of parallel worlds. Leinster avoids the final, chaotic implications of having various Earths intersecting one another on different time tracks, because in this story the "time storm" (which is also the title of a 1977 novel by Gordon R. Dickson about a similar phenomenon) does die down at last. It is nevertheless still the case that the threat to stability presented here is fundamental and very engrossing.

It is also significant that the prime human character of this tale is not only a mathematical genius but also a compulsive adventurer, and that the last lines of "Sidewise in Time" describe with some longing his continuing trek "through unguessable landscapes, to unimaginable adventures." But it is rare in Leinster's huge oeuvre ever to find such a sense of wonder opening up so dangerous a terminal horizon. "Sidewise in Time" stands by itself in this regard.

From 1936 to 1942, Leinster fell silent as a science fiction writer, like many of his contemporaries whom time had passed by. Although he had always written in a prose style far smoother than the markets demanded, there can be no doubt that his reliance on simple technical inventions in plots that rarely questioned the stability—or the roots—of his comfortable venues failed to match the needs of *Astounding's* new editor, John W. Campbell, Jr. A new generation of writers soon filled the pages of any science fiction magazine that paid a tolerable word rate, and Leinster occupied himself elsewhere. Fortunately, he came back—whether for love or money or both, or because he felt personally challenged to meet the new demands, does not much matter.

The thirty or forty stories Leinster published between 1942 and 1950 constitute the heart of his work for critics, if they focus on it at all. In *Astounding* alone Leinster published "First Contact" (reprinted in several anthologies, including *The Best of Science Fiction*, 1946, edited by Groff Conklin), "The Ethical Equations," "Interference," and "Pipeline to Pluto" (all three reprinted in *The Best of Murray Leinster*, 1976), and "The Power" (reprinted in *Sidewise in Time*), all of which were first published in 1945; "A Logic Named Joe" (1946; reprinted in *Sidewise in Time*); and "The Strange Case of John King-

man" (1948; reprinted in *Great Stories of Science Fiction*, 1951, edited by Leinster). Leinster created an entire new career with works whose speculative ease and general polish greatly pleased his loyal science fiction audience. In retrospect his adaptability was more a matter of surface appearance than of revolutionary substance, for the dream idyll of prewar America still shines sturdily through, and there is little diminution of his horror at change or introspection. Yet it is still the case that, among pulp science fiction writers of Leinster's generation, only Jack Williamson, Clifford D. Simak, and Edmond Hamilton made anything like as successful a transition to postwar conditions and markets, and these writers began their careers a decade or so later than did Leinster.

Even more remarkable, Leinster's first thirty years of professional work were in a sense only a preamble to his final twenty years of writing, a period during which he published the bulk of his science fiction and shifted the focus of his efforts toward books (perhaps in large part because of shrinking magazine markets, especially at the level of the slicks). From 1930 to 1950 he published about twenty-five titles, most of them mysteries and Westerns; the science fiction titles included *Murder Madness* (1931), serialized the year before in *Astounding Stories*, and *Sidewise in Time*, perhaps his finest collection.

From 1950 to his retirement from work in about 1969, Leinster published at least forty-seven more titles; at least forty-three of these were science fiction, which averages out at more than two books a year, not an inconsiderable rate for a man in his fifties when the period began. It should also be noted that, throughout this time, Leinster republished almost nothing of his pre-1937 work without extensively updating it; for instance, *The Other Side of Here* (1955) is a thorough revision of "The Incredible Invasion" (*Astounding Stories*, 1936); and *The Forgotten Planet*, as already mentioned, is a radical transformation of its largely prewar material. In any case, most of the some forty-three science fiction titles constitute new work, and most of this new work is in the form of novels.

This concentration on the novel form must be seen as being fully as arduous a transition as Leinster's 1940's adaptation to modern science fiction. As he resolutely produced novel after novel, for publisher after publisher, through the 1950's and 1960's, his constant difficulties with plot construction and the maintenance of sustained narrative rhythms must have seemed nightmarish at times. Indeed, it would be foolish to deny that the strain shows. In novels like *Talents, Incorporated* (1962) what in a short story would have been undesirable repetition of expository sentences (in a suitably ruminative tone) becomes, at full length, the repetition of whole sequences of the plot. Time and again Talents, Incorporated, the eponymous firm of mutants, offers free psionic advice to young Captain Bors, who is single-handedly fighting off the navy of an invading interplanetary empire (whose leaders, typically of Leinster, we never meet); time and again Bors doubts the mutants' advice, but takes it, and demolishes a ship or two on this planet or that; time and again the action is advanced for the reader only in terms of knowledge that the end of the book is nearer. Time and again, in novel after novel, this is the case.

Adding to this sense of repetition, while taking advantage of the reader's tendency to enjoy familiar backgrounds, are the facts that many, if not most, of Leinster's postwar novels are set in a common galactic-federation environment, and that several of these novels are parts of open-ended series. Unsurprisingly, this galactic background has a soothing effect of recognizability. In one of the best novels set in this universe, *The Pirates of Zan* (1959), which was nominated for a Hugo award, the case for predictable venues is put with symptomatic clarity:

According to the fiction-tapes, the colonized worlds of the galaxy vary wildly from each other. In cold and unromantic fact, it isn't so. Space travel is too cheap and sol-type solar systems too numerous to justify the settlement of hostile worlds. Therefore Bron Hoddan encountered no remarkable features in the landscape of Darth as he rode through the deepening night. (chapter 4)

This amiable (though question-begging) sameness is reinforced in various novels by numerous shared details that work to obviate any sense of gradient from one work to the next. The spaceships, all more or less identical, are based on an internalized model of oceangoing freighters (or liners); and all ships utilize the Lawlor Drive, which shoves them at about the speed of light through hyperspace without any difficulties. Every inhabited planet has a landing grid to bring the spaceship gently to the surface; every planet also has a Port City. Most of these planets (they are all Earthlike) resemble prewar America in their mixture of the urban and rural—with bureaucrats and entrepreneurs (comically at odds); fathers and their daughters (making available the benefits of the universal nuclear family to young male protagonist-suitors, after they have solved the problems posed by the stories); mayors; postmasters; and buffoonlike police (buffoons when enforcing silly regulations within the human community, sources of security in the presence of an external enemy).

Although remaining Earthlike, some of these planets exhibit a feudal system of government, or a constitutional monarchy, or some other easily assimilable variant (often a mere enlargement of a municipal government), and their inhabitants are readily recognizable. But whether monarchs or mayors rule locally on a planet, there is no successful form of interplanetary (that is, federal) government. Like prewar Virginia, the galaxy is benevolent but laissez-faire.

Rather than government as such (or an ecumenical linkage of all "oxygen brothers"), the galaxy in many of these novels tends to be laced together (and series built) by a group of agencies. In the Med Service story sequence— *The Mutant Weapon* (1959), *This World Is Taboo* (1961), *Doctor to the Stars* (1964), and

S.O.S. from Three Worlds (1967)—the agency in question troubleshoots medical crises on far-flung planets; the officers of the Colonial Service have similarly self-defining roles in *Colonial Survey* (1957), which includes the 1956 Hugo-winning novelette "Exploration Team" (from *Astounding Science-Fiction*). The activities of these typical agencies are presented almost entirely through individual men in the field, who operate essentially as freelances with the technological know-how and back-up that their roles demand. But they are fixers, not transformers. They do not start mankind on a new enterprise to the far stars; they maintain or bring back normalcy.

Television derived adaptations like *Land of the Giants* (1968) aside, there is one further category of postwar novel in the Leinster oeuvre, the alien story. Novels like *The Brain-Stealers* (1954) and *The Greks Bring Gifts* (1964) and collections like *The Aliens* (1960) tend to repeat, though very palatably at times, the dichotomies between good and evil aliens that had served Leinster for decades, and that he showed no sign of ever abandoning. He was comfortable with them, as was his large readership; and evil aliens were a convenient way of expressing threats to the decent world he so evidently loved, and of nullifying those threats.

But all careers must end. After publishing a final Med Service tale, "Quarantine World," in *Analog* in 1966, Leinster retired from active magazine work; his last books are inferior, tired efforts. He died on 8 June 1975 at a nursing home in Gloucester, Virginia, near where he had lived for so long. His significance as a science fiction writer lies not in his longevity, nor in his occasional speculative innovation. He was wise and lucky with the first; and he was not truly significant with the second. His importance lies in the pleasure he gave. In that he was the dean.

Selected Bibliography

WORKS OF MURRAY LEINSTER

Murder Madness. New York: Brewer and Warren, 1931.

The Murder of the U.S.A., as by Will F. Jenkins. New York: Crown, 1946.

Sidewise in Time and Other Scientific Adventures. Chicago: Shasta Publishers, 1950. (Collection.)

The Brain-Stealers. New York: Ace Books, 1954.

The Forgotten Planet. New York: Gnome Press, 1954.

The Other Side of Here. New York: Ace Books, 1955.

Colonial Survey. New York: Gnome Press, 1957. Reprinted as *Planet Explorer,* New York: Avon Books, 1957.

Out of this World. New York: Avalon Books, 1958. (Collection.)

Monsters and Such. New York: Avon Books, 1959. (Collection.)

The Mutant Weapon. New York: Ace Books, 1959.

The Pirates of Zan. New York: Ace Books, 1959.

The Aliens. New York: Berkley Medallion, 1960. (Collection.)

Twists in Time. New York: Avon Books, 1960. (Collection.)

Creatures of the Abyss. New York: Berkley Medallion, 1961. Reprinted as *The Listeners,* London: Sidgwick and Jackson, 1969.

This World Is Taboo. New York: Ace Books, 1961.

Talents, Incorporated. New York: Avon Books, 1962.

Doctor to the Stars. New York: Pyramid Books, 1964. (Collection.)

The Greks Bring Gifts. New York: MacFadden-Bartell, 1964.

S.O.S. from Three Worlds. New York: Ace Books, 1967. (Collection.)

A Murray Leinster Omnibus. London: Sidgwick and Jackson, 1968. (Includes *Operation Terror, Checkpoint Lambda,* and *Invaders of Space.*)

The Best of Murray Leinster. Edited by Brian Davis. London: Corgi Books, 1976.

The Best of Murray Leinster. Edited by J. J. Pierce. New York: Ballantine Books, 1978. (Differs from the above.)

CRITICAL AND BIOGRAPHICAL STUDIES

Moskowitz, Sam. *Seekers of Tomorrow.* Cleveland, Ohio: World Publishing Company, 1966.

Payne, Ronald. *The Last Murray Leinster Interview.* Richmond, Va.: Waves, 1983.

Wolfe, Gary K. "Murray Leinster." In *Twentieth-Century American Science Fiction Writers, Part I: A–L.* Edited by David Cowart. Detroit, Mich.: Gale, 1981.

—JOHN CLUTE

STANISLAW LEM

(b. 1921)

How is it that a Polish writer of science fiction enjoys such a high level of international acclaim, commanding praise from readers, critics, and scholars alike? How is it that a tireless literary experimenter and innovator, who at times makes stern demands on his readers, has sold thirty-five million copies of his books in more than forty languages? How is it that Lem's works of fiction are studied at scientific institutes, where they are read for ideas to push research programs farther afield? How is it that this litterateur was invited to participate in the 1971 Soviet-American Conference on Extra-Terrestrial Intelligence (CETI) and was the *only* non-scientist so honored? How is it that this writer in a low-brow genre has become lionized by renowned mainstream authors such as Anthony Burgess and John Updike, literary critics such as Theodore Sturgeon and Leslie Fiedler, and magazines such as the *New Yorker*, which regularly reprints his stories? How is it that the literary community openly wonders when Lem will receive the Nobel Prize, with the *Philadelphia Inquirer* declaring: "If he isn't considered . . . it will be because somebody told the judges that he writes science fiction"?

Although there is no simple answer to any of these questions, anyone who tries to summarize Stanislaw Lem's prolific career in a single essay must begin with the fact that he is one of the most creative, playful, sardonic, and intense writers ever to have put pen to paper (actually, he has banged out all of his output on a manual Remington Underwood).

Lem has secured for himself a place in twentieth-century literature as an extraordinary stylist and neologist who is, in turn, profound and illuminating as well as zany and irreverent. His grasp of psychological and social nuance is legendary (a legacy, as Lem maintains, of his intimate experience of the horrors of World War II), and the scientific sweep and novelty of his creations is guaranteed to leave the reader asking for more. As Anthony Burgess has aptly summarized it in his review of *A Perfect Vacuum* (1971), Lem is simply one of the "most intelligent, erudite, and comic writers working today," or in the words of another critic, "Harpo Marx and Franz Kafka and Isaac Asimov rolled up into one."

Stanislaw Lem was born 12 September 1921 in Lvov, Poland (now in Ukraine). As an adult he returned to the memories of his childhood in his remarkable autobiographical novel, *Highcastle: A Remembrance* (1966). Among a welter of sometimes painfully intimate detail, Lem reveals one of the earliest foreshadowings of his spectacular gift for imagination and creativity. As a boy he delighted in the invention of imaginary worlds and fictional stories, but unlike most children, he set about fashioning these make-believe kingdoms in a systematic way. Studiously he would produce scads of diplomas, permits, summonses, passports, certificates, and other documents, which empowered him with all kinds of privileges in his made-up "paper state." This vividness and the almost palpable immediacy of his creations have remained his hallmarks as a science fiction writer.

Young Stanislaw's childhood was a secure one; his father was a well-to-do laryngologist with a thriving medical practice, and his mother was a housewife. Lem's contrasting feelings toward his parents must be noted: whereas he has always spoken warmly about his father, who seems to have been one of his closest friends and companions (Lem has no siblings), he speaks of his mother (née Wollner) only with great reluctance.

From his early days, Lem has been a voracious reader, first studying the contents of his father's medical library, including multitome encyclopedias, French and German textbooks, and other technical sources and in time broadening his range to include poetry, novels, popular science, biographies, and so forth. His intellectual gifts were prodigious even at that time; as he revealed to Stanisław Bereś in *Conversations with Stanislaw Lem* (1987), standardized IQ tests conducted in all high schools in the region placed his scores at well over 180. As a young adolescent, he already spoke Polish, French (he had had a French governess), and Russian and mastered German during the devastating years of World War II occupation. Independent, intellectual, ironic, and endlessly creative, these youthful qualities would manifest themselves even more strongly in his adult personality.

After finishing high school, Lem ended up enrolling at the Lvov's Medical Institute, where under the Russian occupation, he studied until the city's capture by the Germans in 1941. It is impossible to overstate the lasting effect of the war years on Lem's development as a writer, perhaps best testified to by his relentless return to the subjects of chance, survival, the use of force, aggression, and military "solutions" in so many of his mature writings. To some extent the war experience may also help explain the direction in which his fiction has evolved over the decades. Although Lem insists that in some ways he has always written *realistic* fiction, in the later years many of his works break almost entirely with the established canons of literary real-

ism, such as characterization, individual psychology, and conventional story line. This dramatic change in narration reflects the author's increasing preoccupation with the fates of ideas, social problems, cultural trends, and scientific theories—a move necessitated in his mind by the scale and nature of problems facing the entire human race. From remarks offered in various interviews, it appears that this progressive broadening of Lem's fictional canvas—from the fates of individuals to the fate of the civilization—can be attributed to the lingering effect of the Nazi occupation, when the fate of all humanity also seemed to have hung in the balance.

After the war, the family was repatriated from the now Soviet Lvov to Kraków, where the writer has lived ever since. During the 1980's, in a protest against the suppression of the Solidarity trade union and the imposition of martial law in Poland, he spent a few years abroad, mainly in Vienna. Since the publication in 1951 of his breakthrough *The Astronauts*, Lem has been writing at a frenetic pace, producing an astonishing array of contemporary novels, short stories, poetry, science fiction, detective fiction, fantasy, experimental writing, literary criticism, sociological and cultural analyses, philosophical essays, futurology, scientific treatises, literary theory, autobiography, television and radio plays, film scripts, and volumes of polemical writings. Considering his literary range and diversity, one may justifiably wonder that Lem should have been drawn to science fiction at all. Moreover, some his early novels, such as *Hospital of the Transfiguration* (completed in 1948 but published only in 1955), are thoroughly realistic both in tone and subject. Also, as John Scarborough observed in his eponymous article on Lem in the 1982 edition of *Science Fiction Writers*, Polish literature, dominated by nationalistic and sociopolitical concerns, has virtually no tradition in fantastic fiction. Yet, looking back on his career in 1982, Lem said in all candor: "I think I was destined to end up working in the genre in which I write."

In some ways, however, Lem may have been writing science fiction for many years before he published *The Astronauts*. His earliest book-length project, *Theory of Brain Functions*, written and rewritten during the mid- to late 1940's, had originally been conceived as a serious academic study. Yet this ambitious, vast, and completely muddled piece of nonsense—as the mature author calmly sums it up—may have been his first, painstakingly researched, work of science fiction. The long trial-and-error years when this scientific and philosophical study remained on the drawing table may have helped Lem refine his approach to writing. In retrospect, the scientific accuracy of his fiction—worlds apart from the *Star Trek* props of a typical North American space opera (space adventure stories)—may be the result of the research habits formed at this early stage of his career.

Throughout his life Lem has consistently favored viewing his novels not as literary *fictions* but as narrative models of problems he deems worth investigating. He has not only reaffirmed this approach in numerous interviews, but he has also openly stated that knowledge has always been the hero of his books. True to his word, in his hands, science fiction has found one of its most inventive practitioners, who instead of churning out tired and threadbare scenarios of the space opera variety, uses it to study the sociocultural problems that beset our civilization in its unstoppable technological evolution.

After four decades of writing, Lem remains a sought-after literary and cultural critic, philosopher, futurologist, sociologist, essayist, scientific commentator, and of course, best-selling writer. With more than forty books to his credit, among them several multivolume, nonfiction studies, his legacy staggers in diversity and proportion. Consulted during the composition of this essay, he affirmed once again that he has no plans to return to writing fiction. On the other hand, Lem continues to produce essays for the Polish edition of *PC Magazine* and for sundry German Internet journals, mainly on the consequences of communications technologies on civilization. He

Peter Swirski (left) with Stanislaw Lem, 1992. COURTESY OF PETER SWIRSKI

is also busy preparing a retrospective on *Summa Technologiae* (1964), his grand work of futurology, devoting the rest of his time and talents to forecasting developments in the biosciences and their technological applications.

In Poland, where his science fiction books have always remained on the sidelines of national literary currents, Lem has become something of a literary and cultural institution, receiving the highest cultural and state honors. Among these are the Golden Cross of Merit, the City of Kraków's Literary Award, Officer's Cross, Commander's Cross of the Order of Polish Renaissance, Ministry of

Culture and Art's Literary Award of the First and Second Degree, and a host of others, including awards from numerous magazines and radio and television cultural committees. In his spare time, he has cofounded the Polish Astronautical Society; taught literature and philosophy at Jagellonian University; been appointed a member of the Commission 'Poland 2000,' a think tank division of the Polish Academy of Sciences; and hosted a number of television series as a national spokeperson on contemporary culture and science.

Lem's career as a fiction writer has frequently been divided into the formative phase of the 1950's; the "golden" period of the 1960's, during which he penned his most popular novels; the experimental stage of the 1970's; and the phase of his less known works—some still awaiting translation—from the 1980's. The first phase was inaugurated in 1946 by the little known *Man from Mars*, a novelette published in serial form in the Kraków weekly *Nowy Świat Przygód*. Clearly indebted to H. G. Wells's *The War of the Worlds* (1898), it remains one of Lem's most conventional works. Although for forty years the author has forsworn this early creation, insisting that it is too simplistic and juvenile, he allowed it to be reissued as part of Interart's 1996 Polish edition of his collected works.

Despite Lem's disclaimers, *Man from Mars* is an engaging novel of cosmic contact that, albeit in embryonic form, develops many of the themes and concerns that have occupied him throughout his career. So what, asks the writer, that the body of a damaged alien spacecraft lies before an amazed humanity? They can probe it, dissect it, and take it apart, yet still walk away with the sinking feeling that they have not learned anything essential about the alien visitor who, on first opportunity, will try to escape the watchful eye of his captors and unveil his destructive might. Just like Wells, Lem is less interested in meaningful exchange between cosmic races for the simple reason that he does not believe it is possible. Instead, he puts humanity to a test in which our values and behavior are brought out in a sharp relief, rendered all the sharper by the extreme character of the destabilizing factor (contact with an advanced type of nonterrestrial intelligence). When the Martian is finally killed, it becomes clear that we have been the novel's protagonist all along: proud, destructive, overly quick to resort to military means to resolve conflicts that defy easy resolutions.

In the utopian future of *The Astronauts*, the setting shifts to Venus, the other planet whose proximity to Earth has up until recently provoked a mine of speculations about the possibility of life on it. An expedition bearing scientists of all races and nationalities (in effect a condensed United Nations) is hastily sent to Venus to investigate an alien civilization that, as the search reveals, has accidentally wiped itself out while arming for an invasion of our planet. The atmosphere of tragedy, confusion, and misunderstanding again pervades this early novel. The deciphered data are incomplete, the linguistic terms used by aliens are open to wildly speculative interpretations, and the mission of contact is an utter failure—there is nobody out there with whom to establish contact. Venus is a still smoldering ruin, an emblem of planetary armament gone awry.

In the quasi-utopian future of *The Magellan Nebula* (1955; not yet translated), *Gea*, a gigantic spaceship from Earth, bears two hundred and twenty-seven explorers in search of extraterrestrial intelligence in the system of Proxima Centauri. This book is unique among Lem's dark and fateful novels of contact in that, this time—though again after much miscomprehension, suspicion, and loss of life—the people from Earth succeed in establishing peaceful communication. The book ends at the time of the meeting, its open ending symbolizing a cognitive openness about the consequences of such a momentous event. Anything can happen, Lem appears to say, between races and civilizations separated not only by parsecs of cosmic vacuum but also by their respective histories, cultures, and biologies.

These three early novels—*Man from Mars,
The Astronauts,* and *The Magellan Nebula*—
present a different face of Stanislaw Lem,
more utopian and optimistic, even if already
hinting at the darker side of our human kind.
It is therefore a pity that they are destined to
remain out of reach for English-speaking readers and critics for the simple reason that their
author refuses to have them translated. Lem's
attitude has little to do with the quality of the
rendition of his works; on more than one occasion he has praised Michael Kandel, an
unspecified German translator (probably
Wendayne Ackerman), as well as this author
for the quality of translation. Similarly, the
lack of progress in bringing the remainder of
his books out in English owes less to the skill
and availability of translators (even for the linguistically ultracomplex *On Site Inspection*
[1982]) and more, according to Lem, to the
marketing decisions of the publishers. If one
were to trust the author, then, he sees these
early novels as a sort of literary scaffold that
he needed in order to climb to a higher level
but, having done so, feels free to discard as no
longer reflecting his craft.

In a more tragi-comic and satirical mode,
there is also *The Star Diaries* (1957), a regularly expanded collection of short stories
about the capers of Ijon Tichy. This cosmic-
age Gulliver who gads about the nooks and
crannies of the galaxy, running into trouble
with his strange but familiar civilizations, is
one of Lem's more memorable creations, to
which the author returned in several later
books: *The Futurological Congress (From the
Memoirs of Ijon Tichy)* (1971), *Memoirs of a
Space Traveler: Further Reminiscences of Ijon
Tichy* (1957), *On Site Inspection* (1987), and
Peace on Earth (1987). Lem's hero is one of the
great assets of the collection. An ordinary
man prone to most extraordinary adventures,
Tichy (his name could be an allusion in Polish
to "quiet" or "laughter") is a man of everyday
sensibilities, tastes, and likes. He has a
healthy dose of common sense, a gentle and
amiable nature, and a dislike of humbug. Although in his own way he is the most resourceful and enterprising of space travelers,

he frequently finds himself in intimidating
or ridiculous situations, more often than not
a victim of his own curiosity and open-
mindedness.

Lem continued in this lighter vein with
spectacular results in *Mortal Engines* (1964)
and *The Cyberiad: Fables for the Cybernetic
Age* (1965), where on top of humor and satire,
he experimented with style and genre, in effect crossing the conventions of fairy tale and
fable with sociological science fiction. But no
matter how flippant the tone and how hilarious the adventures, his sardonic wit is always
directed at the heart and mind-set of our civilization. In all these seemingly lighthearted
books, his cognitive goal, as he wrote to this
author in 1998, has been utterly serious:
"Notwithstanding the obvious elements of
literary play, I was investigating many conspicuous as well as concealed problems from
the domain of psycho-social modelling of
group behaviour." As all these works are at
pains to point out, there is no type of force,
persuasion, or social construction under the
sun that can turn a society similar to ours into
a perfectly happy one.

The second and most prolific phase in Lem's
fiction began with *Eden* (1959), in which, setting astronauts on the shores of an alien
planet, the author agonizes over sociopolitical
dilemmas that mirror our own history. After
a crash landing, the six-member crew begins
to explore the alien civilization, one apparently regulated by bioengineering. To their
horror, they find themselves in the midst of
a systematic purge by means of which the
anonymous dictatorship tries to exterminate
the mutant generation of its citizens, victims
of botched eugenic experiments. When the
time comes, the crew and the reader leave
with a tragic sense of having witnessed the
forces of history play themselves out among
death and carnage so reminiscent of our troubled century.

Return from the Stars (1961) is a literary
tour de force: it opens where other science
fiction novels usually end, with Hal Bregg
returning to Earth from a long and difficult

interstellar voyage. Yet the civilization that had sent him to the stars is no longer there to greet him. Time dilation, an inevitable result of nearly light-speed travel, has aged Earth by 127 years and changed it almost beyond recognition. A planetary program of "betrization" (Lem's neologism, apparently derived from the English word "better"), implemented in every newborn child, has eradicated all the aggressive and violent instincts that have so often bloodied human history. Decades of peace, planetary unification, and technological progress have finally produced a conflictless, egalitarian, happy, and materially affluent society. And yet, as Bregg discovers in his sad and mostly solitary meanderings around the globe, a price has been paid for this paradise on Earth. Together with the drive for violence and aggression, betrization has amputated the traits that have defined the civilization in the name of which the astronauts have traveled to the stars: an ability to take risks, a spirit of curiosity and self-sacrifice, heroism.

Seen through Bregg's eyes, Lem's vision of our society emerges from the myriad changes in ethics, jurisprudence, erotic customs, social conventions, work patterns, arts, and technology. The romantic subplot, in which the protagonist finds in love the key to accepting this nearly perfect yet foreign and frustrating society, gives the author a chance to develop his model not in terms of abstract social ideals but in emotionally haunting scenes of anger, pain, reflection, and ultimately reconciliation. The question that underlies this beautiful novel is deceptively simple: At what cost should we accept freedom from war, conflict, and social violence? Never one to dish out simplistic scenarios, Lem is careful to hint at the price. It may be that the only permanent change in the democratic world can be effected by not wholly democratic means—in effect a form of "soft" totalitarianism with which the Earth government relentlessly pursues lasting peace and prosperity.

Memoirs Found in a Bathtub (1961) is in a sense a full-scale treatment of an episode from one of Ijon Tichy's more disturbing adventures in "The Thirteenth Voyage" (from *The Star Diaries*). The Memoir proper is a "prehistorical" document, stumbled upon by thirty-second-century archaeologists among the ruins of the Third Pentagon, once the last bastion of Ammer-Kan military administration and espionage. Built under the protective umbrella of the Rockies, the Pentagon building is a perfectly self-contained and perfectly insane institution that, like a snake devouring its own tail, has mutated into a senseless hyperbureaucracy.

Much like the situation on the planet Panta in "The Thirteenth Voyage," the building perpetuates itself by means of internal permutations of the roles played by its various functionaries, while its overall structure, hidden behind a system of masks and assumed identities, remains unshaken. As the Kafkaesque frustrated and suicidal hero slowly comes to realize, under the surface of administrative order and patriotic fervor, the Pentagon harbors a miniworld gone mad: a degenerate and dissolute war machine, idling to extinction in its cold war gear. One way to expose the underlying irrationality of the entire bureaucratic enterprise is to approach it using analytical tools created to study rational behavior of groups and individuals. As shown in this author's "Game Theory in the Third Pentagon" (1996), the strategies pursued by the Third Pentagon are perfectly sane once we accept as a given its demented outlook on our geopolitical reality. The result is even more chilling: a mask of cold and calculating rationality that conceals a MAD (as in Mutual Assured Destruction) world.

Solaris (1961), Lem's most acclaimed novel, both returns to and departs from the anthropomorphic premises behind the exploration of Cosmos. The protagonist, Kris Kelvin, flies to a research station on Solaris, which after decades of scientific study is considered a familiar if still mysterious planet. Yet this time, after an unscheduled effort to establish contact with the sentient solaristic "ocean," the latter transforms memories extracted from Kelvin's and other scientists' minds into living neutrino beings, unwittingly driving humans to the brink of insanity. In a setting that could hardly be more distant or strange, humans glimpse the parabolic face of the universe—their own.

How does Lem view *Solaris* and his other novels of contact from the perspective of forty years of writing and study? "Their common denominator is my conviction that contact with, or any form of federation of, extraterrestrial forms of intelligence is not possible. This owes to the almost limitless diversity and distribution of evolutionary paths pursued by different civilizations," concludes the author during his latest E-mail interview with this author. Indeed, all of Lem's novels and nonfiction monographs (which lie beyond the scope of this essay) demonstrate his disbelief in the existence of a common pattern of intelligent behavior of which human reason would be a typical and necessary exemplar.

Another multilayered composition on the limitations of contact with the creations of the infinitely fertile universe is Lem's action-packed science thriller *The Invincible* (1964). The novel bears the name of a colossal space cruiser dispatched to investigate the disappearance of its sister ship, the *Condor*. Surrounded by machines, force fields, nuclear armaments, and scientific probes, the crew begin to explore the Earth-type planet, confident in their scientific and military acumen. But as the investigation unfolds, as the insanely devastated wreck of the *Condor* refuses to yield its secrets, and as losses in lives mount, the layers of mechanic and nuclear protection begin to fall away, revealing the core of humanity: dazed, perplexed, and vulnerable.

From the smoky battlefields of apocalyptic proportions emerges the drama of people paralyzed by the unknown. Humbled and defeated, even if capable of acts of courage and sacrifice, it takes them a long time to comprehend the futility of earthly concepts and values in the face of the phenomenon unique to this extraterrestrial world: machine evolution. Just as the crew of the *Invincible* are stripped of their illusions of conquest and pacification, Rohan, the protagonist, strips off his protective shielding before a solitary confrontation with the menacing Black Cloud. The lone man, risking his life to find missing crew members, affirms the noblest impulses of our civilization but not before the *Invincible* learns a hard lesson: scientific and military hardware does not ensure conceptual maturity.

The transitional work between Lem's more or less straightforward science fiction of the earlier years and the searching, difficult and frequently experimental works from the later decades is *His Master's Voice* (1968). Situated in the United States (which Lem has never visited, despite countless invitations) in the 1960's, almost concurrently with the time of its publication, this novel purports to be a posthumously published spiritual diary of an eminent mathematician, Professor Peter Hogarth (a partly autobiographical creation). In a blunt analogy to the Manhattan Project, twenty-five hundred elite scientists are herded into an isolated former nuclear test site in the Nevada desert, where surveilled and spied on by the Pentagon, they work in secret to decipher a neutrino message of extraterrestrial origin. Apart from providing almost agonizingly frank meditations on the (self-) destructive nature of humans and their place in the universe, *His Master's Voice* emerges as a savage satire on this scientific microworld and on the political and military Moloch (a biblical term meaning something gigantic and evil) bankrolling it.

A Perfect Vacuum, which ushers in the experimental phase in Lem's career, is a collection of reviews of imaginary (that is, nonexistent) works of fiction and nonfiction, including a bravado tongue-in-cheek review by Lem-the-critic of *A Perfect Vacuum* by Lem-the-writer. With irrepressible wit and irreverence, the author satirizes the dead ends of contemporary literature and especially its postmodern impotence before the depth of current and anticipated sociocultural problems. As Lem explains over E-mail:

The premise behind this book was not, of course, what I said in my auto-review, namely that I had created these synopses because I could not write them out in full. Rather, I became convinced that I could capture what was cognitively essential about these unwritten books in the form of concise fictional reviews. Thus, although I was not immune to an element of playful humour, the content of all these stories was absolutely serious.

Constructed along similar lines, *Imaginary Magnitude* (1973) (and later *One Human Minute* [1986]) is an assembly of prefaces, forewords, and introductions to nonexistent books that, in the mind of the author, should nevertheless exist. In this quasi-futurological work, Lem develops multiple scenarios, the forecasting limits of which extend beyond the scope of today's science. For example, in "Golem XIV," which after *Summa Technologiae* contains Lem's most avant-garde conceptual work, the author tries systematically to predict some of the global consequences of the exponential explosion in the cognitive and biological sciences. In the guise of an eighteenth-"binasty" (*bi*tic dy*nasty*) supercomputer, he argues that the developments in these fields will soon overrun the domains traditionally given over to philosophy or even theology. At the same time, Lem casts doubt on our ability to harness and channel these new socioscientific forces for the greater benefit of humankind. The book's impartial, almost clinical tone reflects its author's mounting skepticism about the rationality of *homo sapiens sapiens*, a species whose collective ego has always exceeded its ability to control it.

Much in the same vein, *Memoirs of a Space Traveler* could have come from the pen of a twentieth-century Voltaire, Swift, or Samuel Johnson. This story collection (published in Polish as part of an expanded edition of *The Star Diaries*) quirkily blends the tone of fairy tale, adventure story, and philosophical conte while describing Tichy's adventures in never-never futuristic settings. The subject matter of these short tales ranges from simple satire to deep philosophical discussions of theology, metaphysics, or epistemology. In a detached and ironic—yet always humorous—way, Lem contemplates man's place in the universe, the role of religion, the nature of history, and some central dilemmas in the philosophy of mind.

Nearly all of the stories present unappreciated and offbeat (sometimes downright mad) inventors or scientists obsessed with an idea whose philosophical and social consequences form the moral and didactic backbone of a given tale. Yet despite the serious strain of thought, Lem's subtle use of understatement and his ability to translate the implications of a given issue into a vivid and funny situation make these tales a delight to read. "Literature . . . should never bore its readers to death," professed the author in *A Stanislaw Lem Reader* (1997), and *Memoirs of a Space Traveler* is carefully balanced to provoke us to reflection by means of wit, humor, and satire.

Before we move on to two of Lem's defining works from the 1980's (alas, there are at present no plans for a translation of two other masterpieces, *On Site Inspection* and *Provocation* [1984]), we must pause over another of his intriguing literary experiments, *The Chain of Chance* (1976). Like many of Lem's fictions from around that time, this short novel can be classified only broadly as science fiction. As a matter of fact, it takes the unsuspecting reader a while before he or she can identify its contemporary setting as an alternative present. The plot is deceptively simple: a former astronaut (we know only his first name, John) is hired to retrace the holiday routine of a man who, like several others in what the police suspect to be a series of deaths, died under baffling and macabre circumstances.

The Chain of Chance is, in the author's own words, a rational variant on *The Investigation* (1959), an earlier of his genre experiments at crossing the conventions of the detective story with science fiction. As the police investigation moves through a series of dead ends and chance discoveries, *The Chain of Chance* turns into a twentieth-century psychomachia (a work of fiction in which the characters are engaged in a psychological battle) between the detective-protagonist and the French computer scientist Saussure. The two investigators represent differing yet complementary philosophies. The deductive and deterministic way of understanding the world is typical of John, the space-age incarnation of the private sleuth; the scientist, on the other hand, favors statistical and indeterministic explanations. Interplaying the two, Lem subtly harnesses this sensational murder mystery into an investigation of the laws and patterns underlying our lives. The human society has passed a threshold of complexity beyond which Occam's razor, the principle that would allow ruling out complex theories and explanations in favor of simpler ones, no longer holds. We can expect, hypothesizes Lem, more and more social deviations from what up until now has been the common-sense standard—deviations that, as *The Chain of Chance* suggests, may defy reason through a statistical convergence of singly improbable events.

Over the years, Lem has made it clear in numerous interviews that, in the face of the seemingly intractable problems that plague our civilization, writers ought to devote themselves to diagnosing these sociocultural ills and analyzing their impact on society. With this profound goal in mind, they need to find new forms and styles of expression, adequate to the dimension and gravity of the issues at stake. It is against this background that we must measure Lem's repeated avowals that he no longer has the patience for conventional plotting, characterization, or dialogue that many readers automatically expect from science fiction. Dealing with problems facing the civilization, with the entire human race cast in the role of a protagonist, Lem maintains, the writer can no longer continue to fall back on the type of writing perfected by Victorian storytellers.

The 1980's were thus an interesting period in Lem's career inasmuch as they typified the author's effort to forge a new idiom for his ma-

terial. Surprisingly enough, even though some of these later works (for example, *Provocation* and *One Human Minute*) depart in radical ways from conventional fabulation, two other major novels represent a return to the more traditional type of science fiction. At the same time, Lem returns in these books (as well as in the still untranslated *On Site Inspection*) to themes, styles, and even characters that featured in his earlier, more popular works of fiction. The resulting feeling is that in *Peace on Earth* and *Fiasco* (1988) Lem sums up and reflects on his career while once again tackling the grave challenges facing our society in the twilight years of the millenium.

In *Peace on Earth*, the narrator and hero of other Lem books, Ijon Tichy, is asked to undertake a dangerous mission. Once more Earth has swept its civilizational dirt under the carpet, this time dumping it on the Moon, which as a result of Geneva treaties designed to free our planet from armaments has been turned into a free-for-all weapons development site. National lobbying groups galvanize the United Nations into action with warnings that the military equilibrium on our satellite may have been breached, creating a new and unknown generation of weapons that could eventually turn against Earth.

The results of the expedition, related in a series of flashbacks, exceed Tichy's and the UN's wildest fears. The Moon's weapons systems, designed on the principle of natural speciation, have evolved beyond their constructors' originals plans. They have miniaturized themselves into a kind of "intellectronic" (Lem's coinage from *intell*igent and e*lectronic*) micropolymers, capable of transforming into a symbiotic bacterialike species. The end product of this unsupervised evolution, the versatile and deadly selenocytes, attack Tichy and invade Earth on board his ship where, mutating into computer viruses, they wipe out Earth's infrastructure, industrial base, and telecommunications in one day. Neither an escapist science fiction nor an adventure-filled make-believe, *Peace on Earth* is a bitter and ironic hypothesis on the foreseeable outcome of present day sociotechnol-ogical trends.

Fiasco, a bitter and tragic novel of lost innocence, is in a sense a fitting culmination of Lem's belletristic career. "This book ought to be no surprise," reflects the author. "Since it was intended to be my farewell work of fiction, I purposely returned in it to themes and leitmotifs from my earlier works." A symbol of this retrospective may be the "resurrection" of Pirx, the eponymous protagonist of the popular *Tales of Pirx the Pilot* (1979) and *More Tales of Pirx the Pilot* (1981), in the character of the hero, Mark Tempe.

Fiasco follows a crew of astronauts who, after years of travel in suspended animation, finally achieve a dream long dreamed: contact with another civilization. There is no doubt that Quinta, the fifth planet from the alien sun, is technologically advanced: among many other feats of planetary engineering, its scientists have elevated an ice ring into orbit to regulate the global climate. For its war-locked inhabitants, however, the contact turns into a race to use the arrival of the ship to tip the balance of power in favor of either of the opposing continental blocks. The astronauts from the *Hermes* symbolize the spirit of our progressive and united future: scientifically almost omnipotent, ready to embrace their brothers in intelligence. But all of their high-caliber strategizing and noble intentions cannot get them past the white noise that spills from all communication channels, past the stealthy and lethal weapons systems of the cosmic pollen variety, and past the Quintans' Star Wars mentality.

As the Earthmen find themselves under attack and as the other side stubbornly refuses to follow the script of benevolent exchange, disaster strikes. Amidst pious moralizing, *Hermes* unleashes a series of increasingly destructive shows of force to cow the Quintans into yielding to the astronauts' more and more belligerent demands for contact. The final meeting is a total fiasco. Mark Tempe, sent from *Hermes* down to meet the elusive Quintans, makes a fatal mistake that leads to his crewmates' swift and ruthless annihilation of the planet.

To capture all the diverse themes and leitmotifs of Lem's books would take a list several pages long. Yet underneath this abundance and variety hides a handful of issues to which Lem returns with persistence that borders on obsession. In fact, all of his writings can be seen as an extended series of variations on several central themes: life in the universe, the impossibility of contact, threat from the armaments race, the uneasy alliance between the scientific and military establishments, intellectronic automata, strategy and rationality, group behavior, probability and chance, genetics and biology, evolution and cosmology, anthropology and ethics.

The degree of Lem's fame and respect outside the literary circles is unique in the history of not just science fiction but fiction in general. Scores of philosophers and scientists, including such thinkers as renowned as Daniel Dennett, Carl Sagan, Nicolas Rescher, and Douglas Hofstadter, have professed their esteem for his writings. But no matter how accurate in his predictions, Lem is first and foremost an artist, at present probably the most celebrated of European writers. As the *New York Times* put it, Lem is more than just a writer of fiction—he is "one of the deep spirits of our age."

Selected Bibliography

FICTION OF STANISLAW LEM IN ENGLISH

Hospital of the Transfiguration (*Szpital przemienienia*, 1955). Translated by William Brand. San Diego, Calif.: Harcourt, Brace Jovanovich, 1988.
Memoirs of a Space Traveler: Further Reminiscences of Ijon Tichy (*Dzienniki gwiazdowe*, 1957). Translated by Joel Stern and Maria Święcicka-Ziemianek. San Diego, Calif.: Harcourt, Brace Jovanovich, 1982. (See *The Star Diaries*.)

The Star Diaries (*Dzienniki gwiazdowe*, 1957). Translated by Michael Kandel. New York: Seabury, 1976. (Several later stories from this cycle appeared in English as *Memoirs of a Space Traveler*.)

Eden (*Eden*, 1959). Translated by Marc E. Heine. San Diego, Calif.: Harcourt, Brace Jovanovich, 1989.

The Investigation (*Śledztwo*, 1959). Translated by Adele Milch. New York: Seabury, 1974.

Memoirs Found in a Bathtub (*Pamiętnik znaleziony w wannie*, 1961). Translated by Michael Kandel and Christine Rose. New York: Seabury, 1973.

Return from the Stars (*Powrót z gwiazd*, 1961). Translated by Barbara Marszal and Frank Simpson. San Diego, Calif.: Harcourt, Brace Jovanovich, 1980.

Solaris (*Solaris*, 1961). Translated by Joanna Kilmartin and Steve Cox. New York: Walker and Company, 1970.

The Invincible (*Niezwyciężony i inne opowiadania*, 1964). Translated by Wendayne Ackerman. New York: Seabury, 1973.

Mortal Engines (1964). Translated by Michael Kandel. New York: Seabury, 1977.

The Cyberiad: Fables for the Cybernetic Age (*Cyberiada*, 1965). Translated by Michael Kandel. New York: Seabury, 1974.

Highcastle: A Remembrance (*Wysoki zamek*, 1966). San Diego, Calif.: Harcourt, Brace Jovanovich, 1995.

His Master's Voice (*Głos pana*, 1968). Translated by Michael Kandel. San Diego, Calif.: Harcourt, Brace Jovanovich, 1984.

More Tales of Pirx the Pilot (*Opowieści o pilocie Pirxie*, 1968). Translated by Louis Iribarne, Magdalena Majcherczyk, and Michael Kandel. San Diego, Calif.: Harcourt, Brace Jovanovich, 1983.

Tales of Pirx the Pilot (*Opowieści o pilocie Pirxie*, 1968). Translated by Louis Iribarne. San Diego, Calif.: Harcourt, Brace Jovanovich, 1979.

Microworlds: Writings on Science Fiction and Fantasy (*Fantastyka i futurologia*, 1970). Translated and edited by Franz Rottensteiner. San Diego, Calif.: Harcourt, Brace Jovanovich, 1984.

The Futurological Congress (*From the Memoirs of Ijon Tichy*) (*Bezsenność* [*Insomnia*], 1971). Translated by Michael Kandel. New York: Avon, 1976.

A Perfect Vacuum (*Doskonała próżnia*, 1971). Translated by Michael Kandel. San Diego, Calif.: Harcourt, Brace Jovanovich, 1979.

Imaginary Magnitude (*Wielkość urojona*, 1973). Translated by Marc E. Heine. San Diego, Calif.: Harcourt, Brace Jovanovich, 1985.

The Chain of Chance (*Katar*, 1976). Translated by Louis Iribarne. San Diego, Calif.: Harcourt, Brace Jovanovich, 1978.

Maska [*The Mask*]. Kraków: Wydawnictwo Literackie, 1976. (Published in English as part of *Mortal Engines*, 1977.)

Golem XIV. Kraków: Wydawnictwo Literackie, 1981. (Published in English as part of *Imaginary Magnitude*, 1985.)

One Human Minute (*Biblioteka XXI Wieku*, 1986). Translated by Catherine S. Leach. San Diego, Calif.: Harcourt, Brace Jovanovich, 1986.

Fiasco (*Fiasko*, 1987). Translated by Michael Kandel. San Diego, Calif.: Harcourt, Brace Jovanovich, 1988.

Peace on Earth (*Pokój na Ziemi*, 1987). Translated by Elinor Ford and Michael Kandel. San Diego, Calif.: Harcourt, Brace Jovanovich, 1995.

WORKS OF STANISLAW LEM IN POLISH

Człowiek z Marsa [*Man from Mars*]. Katowice: 1946 (Published weekly in *Nowy Świat Przygód*.)

Astronauci [*The Astronauts*]. Warsaw: Czytelnik, 1951.

Sezam i inne opowiadania [*Sesame and Other Stories*]. Warsaw: Iskry, 1954.

Obłok Magellana [*The Magellan Nebula*]. Warsaw: Iskry, 1955.

Dialogi [*Dialogues*]. Kraków: Wydawnictwo Literackie, 1957. (Nonfiction.)

Inwazja z Aldebarana [*Invasion from Aldebaran*]. Kraków: Wydawnictwo Literackie, 1959.

Księga robotów [*The Book of Robots*]. Warsaw: Iskry, 1961.

Wejście na orbitę [*Orbital Entry*]. Kraków: Wydawnictwo Literackie, 1962.

Noc księżycowa [*The Lunar Night*]. Kraków: Wydawnictwo Literackie, 1963.

Summa technologiae. Kraków: Wydawnictwo Literackie, 1964. (Nonfiction.)

Ratujmy kosmos i inne opowiadania [*Let's Save the Cosmos and Other Stories*]. Kraków: Wydawnictwo Literackie, 1966.

Filozofia przypadku: Literatura w świetle empirii [*The Philosophy of Chance: Literature Considered Empirically*]. Kraków: Wydawnictwo Literackie, 1968.

Opowiadania [*Stories*]. Kraków: Wydawnictwo Literackie, 1969.

Fantastyka i futurologia [*Science Fiction and Futurology*]. Kraków: Wydawnictwo Literackie, 1970. (Nonfiction.)

Rozprawy i szkice [*Essays and Sketches*]. Kraków: Wydawnictwo Literackie, 1975.

Suplement [*Supplement*]. Kraków: Wydawnictwo Literackie, 1976.

Powtórka [*Repetition*]. Warsaw: Iskry, 1979.

Wizja lokalna [*On Site Inspection*]. Kraków: Wydawnictwo Literackie, 1982.

Prowokacja [*Provocation*]. Kraków: Wydawnictwo Literackie, 1984.

Ciemność i pleśń [*Darkness and Mildew*]. Kraków: Wydawnictwo Literackie, 1988.

ESSAYS AND ARTICLES OF STANISLAW LEM IN ENGLISH

"Promethean Fire." Translated by Yuri Sdobnikov. *Soviet Literature*, 5 (1968): 166–170.

"Ten Commandments of Reading the Magazines." Translated by Franz Rottensteiner. *Science Fiction Commentary*, no. 6 (1969): 26.

"Letter." *Science Fiction Commentary*, no. 14 (1970): 5.

"Poland: SF in the Linguistic Trap." Translated by Franz Rottensteiner. *Science Fiction Commentary*, no. 9 (1970): 27–33.

"Sex in SF." Translated by Franz Rottensteiner. *Science Fiction Commentary*, no. 3 (1970): 2–10, 40–49.

"You Must Pay for Any Progress." Translated by Franz Rottensteiner. *Science Fiction Commentary*, no. 12 (1970): 19–24.

"Lost Opportunities." Translated by Franz Rottensteiner. *Science Fiction Commentary*, no. 24 (1971): 17–24.

"Review: *Robbers of the Future* by Sakyo Komatsu." Translated by Franz Rottensteiner. *Science Fiction Commentary*, no. 23 (1971): 17–18.

"Robots in Science Fiction." Translated by Franz Rottensteiner. In *Science Fiction: The Other Side of Realism*. Edited by Thomas Clareson. Bowling Green, Ohio: Bowling Green University Popular Press, 1971.

"Letter." *Science Fiction Commentary*, no. 26 (1972): 28–30, 89–90.

"Letter." *Science Fiction Commentary*, no. 29 (1972): 10–12.

"Culture and Futurology." *Polish Perspectives*, 16 (1973): 30–38.

"Remarks Occasioned by Dr. Plank's Essay 'Quixote's Mills.'" *Science-Fiction Studies*, 2 (1973): 78–83.

"Reflections for 1974." *Polish Perspectives*, 17 (1974): 3–8.

"In Response." *Science-Fiction Studies*, no. 2 (1975): 169–170.

"Letter." *Science Fiction Commentary*, no. 41/42 (1975): 90–92.

"Letter." *Science Fiction Commentary*, no. 44/45 (1975): 96–97.

"Looking Down on Science Fiction: A Novelist's Choice for the World's Worst Writing." *Science-Fiction Studies*, 4 (1977): 126–127. (Originally published in the *Frankfurter Allgemeine Zeitung*, 22 February 1975).

"In Response to Professor Benford." *Science-Fiction Studies*, 5 (1978): 92–93.

"Planetary Chauvinism: Speculation on the 'Others.'" Translated by Franz Rottensteiner. *Second Look*, 1 (1979): 5–9.

"The Profession of Science Fiction: XV: Answers to a Questionnaire." Translated by Maxim and Dolores Jakubowski. *Foundation*, 15 (1979): 41–50.

"Review of W. S. Bainbridge's *The Space Flight Revolution*." Translated by Franz Rottensteiner. *Science-Fiction Studies*, 6 (1979): 221–222.

"From Big Bang to Heat Death." Translated by Franz Rottensteiner. *Second Look*, 2 (1980): 38–39.

"Letter." *Science Fiction Commentary*, 60/61 (1980): 4.

"A Conversation with Stanislaw Lem." *Amazing*, 27 (1981): 116–119.

"Metafantasia: The Possibilities of Science Fiction." Translated by Etelka de Laczay and Istvan Csicsery-Ronay, Jr. *Science-Fiction Studies*, 8 (1981): 54–71.

"About the Strugatskys' *Roadside Picnic*." Translated by Elsa Schieder. *Science-Fiction Studies*, 10 (1983): 317–332.

"Chance and Order." Translated by Franz Rottensteiner. *New Yorker* (30 January 1984).

"Remarks Occasioned by Antoni Slonimski's *The Torpedo of Time*." Translated by Elizabeth Kwasniewski. *Science-Fiction Studies*, 11 (1984): 233–243.

"Zulawski's Silver Globe." Translated by Elizabeth Kwasniewski. *Science-Fiction Studies*, 12 (1985): 1–5.

"On the Genesis of *Wizja Lokalna (Eyewitness Account)*." Translated by Franz Rottensteiner and Istvan Csicsery-Ronay, Jr. *Science-Fiction Studies*, 13 (1986): 382–386.

"On Stapledon's *Last and First Men*." Translated by Istvan Csicsery-Ronay, Jr. *Science-Fiction Studies*, 13 (1986): 272–291.

"H. G. Wells's *The War of the Worlds*. Translated by John Coutouvidis. In *Science Fiction Roots and Branches: Contemporary Critical Approaches*. Edited by Rhys Garnett and R. J. Ellis. New York: St. Martin's, 1990.

"Smart Robots." Translated by Peter Swirski. *Spectrum* (forthcoming).

CRITICAL AND BIOGRAPHICAL STUDIES

Balcerzak, Ewa. *Stanislaw Lem*. Translated by Krystyna Cekalska. Warsaw: Author's Agency, 1973. (An in-depth and perceptive study of Lem as a philosopher, humanist, and cultural critic. Orders his works thematically into contemporary novels, science fiction, grotesques, fables, and epistemic studies and discusses them in the context of his fiction and nonfiction.)

Bereś, Stanisław. *Rozmowy ze Stanislawem Lemem* [*Conversations with Stanislaw Lem*]. Kraków: Wydawnictwo Literackie, 1987. (A 400-page collection of a series of interviews with Lem from 1981 and 1982. A gold mine of biographical and analytical detail but, unfortunately, still available only in Polish.)

Costello, John. "Stanislaw Lem." *Science Fiction Review*, (Autumn 1990): 31–33. (An English translation of a 1989 interview with Lem by one of his Russian translators, Konstantin Dushenko. Focuses on the pragmatics of writing, patronage, publishing, reception, and cultural tastes in Poland, Russia, and Western Europe.)

Davis, J. Madison. *Stanislaw Lem*. Mercer Island, Wash.: Starmont, 1990. (An introductory and superficial "reader's guide" to Lem's biography and major works of fiction in English. Tries to account for Lem's literary and intellectual stature and provides some useful insights into several novels.)

Engel, Peter. "An Interview with Stanislaw Lem." Translated by John Sigda. *The Missouri Review*, 7 (1984): 218–237. (A hodgepodge of questions and answers that reveals little of Lem's depth of achievement or interest. Centers around politics, Lem's fictional works, and computers and artificial intelligence.)

Federman, Raymond. "An Interview with Stanislaw Lem." *Science-Fiction Studies*, 10 (1983): 2–14. (Conducted by a writer of fiction himself, the interview offers several rare glimpses into the mechanics of Lem's writing process.)

Jarzebski, Jerzy. "Stanislaw Lem, Rationalist and Visionary." Translated by Franz Rottensteiner. *Science-Fiction Studies*, 4 (1977): 110–125. (A major critical article on Lem that traces in detail the main themes in his fiction and nonfiction through the early 1970's. Brilliant and incisive, this is a must read for every Lem scholar.)

Kandel, Michael A. "Lem in Review (June 2238)." *Science-Fiction Studies*, 11 (1977): 65–68. (A quirky but insightful overview and synthesis of Lem's literary legacy by one of his best English translators. Identifies and classifies the writer's principal themes, techniques, and concerns.)

———. "Introduction." In *Mortal Engines*, by Stanislaw Lem. New York: Avon, 1982. (Opens with a discussion of robots and artificial intelligence in philosophy and literature and follows with several structural insights into Lem's works.)

Livingston, Paisley. "Science, Reason, and Society." In his *Literature and Rationality: Ideas of Agency in Theory and Fiction*. Cambridge, England: Cambridge University Press, 1991. (A philosophical and sociological study of the concept of rationality in Lem's *His Master's Voice*. Useful in documenting the psychosocial accuracy and profundity of Lem's vision.)

Rothfork, John. "Having Everything Is Having Nothing: Stanislaw Lem vs. Utilitarianism." *Southwest Review*, 66 (1981): 293–306. (A study of Lem as a philosopher; discusses aspects of ethics and morality in the light of post-twentieth-century technology. Limited to Lem's fiction, it attributes to the writer views that he does not necessarily espouse.)

Science-Fiction Studies, 40 (1986). (Special Lem issue; contains a number of original and penetrating critical analyses as well as several pieces written specially for this issue by Lem himself.)

Science-Fiction Studies, 57 (1992). (Special Lem issue; somewhat less ambitious in scope and not as diverse or profound analytically as the previous one.)

Solotaroff, Theodore. "A History of Science Fiction and More." *New York Times Book Review*, (29 August 1979): 1, 14–18. (A front-page omnibus review of several of Lem's science fiction works from 1959 to 1971. The critic concludes: "Lem is both a polymath and a virtuoso storyteller. Put them together and they add up to a genius.")

"Stanislaw Lem and the SFWA." *Science-Fiction Studies*, 4 (1977): 126–144. (A series of statements and letters documenting the outrageous revocation of Lem's honorary membership in Science-Fiction Writers of America in the wake of the (highly corrupted) reprint of Lem's European journal editorial critical of Western science fiction.)

Suvin, Darko. "The Open-Ended Parables of Stanislaw Lem and *Solaris*." Afterword in *Solaris*. Translated from the French by Joanna Kilmartin and Steve Cox. New York: Walker, 1970: 205–216. (Contains a sketchy introduction to Lem's career, a cursory annotation of some of his better-known novels, and a useful discussion of *Solaris* in the context of European mainstream literature.)

Swirski, Peter. "Computhors and Biterature: Machine-Written Fiction?" *SubStance*, 70 (1993): 81–90. (Analyzes and compares Lem's fictional scenario about possible developments in computer intelligence from "The Future History of Bitic Literature" [in *Imaginary Magnitude*] with contemporary research in artificial intelligence.)

———. "Game Theory in the Third Pentagon: A Study in Strategy and Rationality." *Criticism*, 38 (1996): 303–330. (A thorough analysis of one of the most enigmatic of Lem's novels, *Memoirs Found in a Bathtub*. Uses game theory to examine Lem's treatment of rationality and stragic thinking.)

———. "*The Invincible*." "*The Chain of Chance*." "*Fiasco*." In *Beacham's Encyclopedia of Popular Fiction*. Osprey, Fla.: Beacham Publications, 1998. (Detailed and accessible analyses of three major Lem novels. Among other subjects, the articles discuss social concerns, major themes, characters, plot structure, and literary technique.)

———. "A Literary Monument Revisited: Davis's *Stanislaw Lem* and Seven Polish Books on Lem." *Science-Fiction Studies*, 58 (1992): 411–417. (An article-length review of Davis's 1990 monograph on Lem and several leading Polish-language critical sources. Stresses the inadequacy of standard literary critical strategies in the face of Lem's cognitive complexity.)

———. *A Stanislaw Lem Reader*. Evanston, Ill.: Northwestern University Press, 1997. (An introduction to Lem and, for the first time, his nonfiction; contains a critical overview, extensive interviews, translations, and a full bibliography. Explores in detail the parallels between literature, philosophy, and science in Lem's works.)

Szpakowska, Malgorzata. "A Writer in No-Man's-Land." *Polish Perspectives*, 14 (1971): 29–37. (A lucid and informative discussion of interactions between culture and technology in the context of Lem's nonfiction and what the critic construes as his efforts to "save the world by means of literature."

Updike, John. "Lem and Pym." *New Yorker* (26 February 1979): 115–121. (An urbane but rather unfocused review of *The Chain of Chance* from a leading mainstream writer and critic. Makes apparent how traditional literary criticism founders in the face of works as unconventional in theme and structure as Lem's science thriller.)

Ziegfeld, Richard E. *Stanislaw Lem.* New York: Ungar, 1985. (Designed as a popular "reader" on Lem, it is of limited usefulness because of its mediocre quality. Contains biographical and critical material, the latter mainly in the form of plot summaries and lists of symbols.)

Ziembiecki, Andrzej. "'. . . Knowing Is the Hero of My Books . . .'" *Polish Perspectives*, 9 (1979): 64–69. (A poorly translated but useful interview with a Polish scholar; focuses on the cognitive impulse in Lem's writings, his writing strategies, and critical reception.)

—PETER SWIRSKI

C. S. Lewis
(1898–1963)

THE WORK OF most writers of popular fiction is shaped by two factors so basic that they can generally be assumed implicitly. The first is skill, for most authors of commercial fiction have to know what they are doing and for what audience they are writing. The second is necessity, for most authors continue doing what they know how to do best in order to make enough money to survive. Neither factor applies closely to the work of C. S. Lewis. He never pretended to have much concern over whether or not he was capable of writing "good" science fiction, and indeed, he despised the kind of world view that underlies most science fiction, whether good or incompetent; and after his mid-twenties, when he began his lifelong professional association with Oxford and Cambridge Universities, he never needed to produce fiction in order to survive. In fact, it is one of the more attractive aspects of his peculiarly complex and often abrasive personality, as a man and a writer, that for many years he anonymously allocated something like two-thirds of his writing income to various good causes and needy individuals. As charity is a Christian virtue conspicuously lacking in most of his work, this quiet generosity should be kept in mind.

Being free to write science fiction, in fact, quite possibly doing some damage to his academic career by indulging in popular literature, Lewis was motivated by relatively unusual goals when he did choose to write fiction; unsurprisingly, the nature of the product reflects both freedom from constraint and suprageneric motives. Despite his disclaimers that he never began a story with a theological point in mind, everything published in Lewis' lifetime, or saved from the bonfires in which his brother obediently burned much unpublished material after his death and released posthumously, deeply reflects adamantly held Christian convictions about the nature of the world and about the appropriate rendering of Christian truths in words, image, and plot. The fact that *Out of the Silent Planet* (1938) and its two stablemates are a kind of science fiction is clearly and deliberately subordinate to the fact that they are at heart exercises in Christian apologetics. As such, they are of a piece with the rest of his voluminous output—which comprises poetry, literary criticism and history, popular theology and lay sermons, adult and children's fiction, and autobiographical works—and share common doctrinal, literary, social, and sexual prejudices.

Regarding hatred and love, prejudice and insight, work and man, Lewis' work is of a piece; and in order to begin to understand his science fiction, which more uninhibitedly reflects the man than is usually the case in this generally commercial genre, we should look first at the shape of his life. Lewis abhorred depth psychology—he abhorred much of twentieth-century thought, and unreservedly despised the "soft" sciences for their intrusive prying into the human condition, the secular analysis of which he regarded as being close to obscene—and throughout his career he attempted to protect himself from what he considered the destructive insights of un-

Christian introspection. Although his earlier biographers have generally observed a similar decorum, significant patterns do unavoidably emerge, as shown in such recent studies as Humphrey Carpenter's *The Inklings* (1978), a generally sympathetic analysis of Lewis and his friends.

The first fact may be the most important: born in Belfast in 1898, Clive Staples Lewis was an Ulster Protestant, and he never quite lost, either in his works or in his personal manner, that flavor of uneasy bullying fundamentalism so tellingly characteristic of the siege mentality of this surrounded but proselytizing faith. It should be remembered that Ireland's Roman Catholic majority has always treated the Protestants of Ulster as representatives of a foreign tyranny, interlopers both religious and ethnic. Lewis was therefore an exile in the land of his birth, a condition tragically intensified by the death of his mother from cancer when he was nine; his father sent him almost immediately afterward to school in England, where his experiences were more than usually miserable. Perhaps no child can fail to experience a sense of exile in some form or other, but there can be little doubt that Lewis responded very strongly to the particularly poignant banishment from Paradise that was visited upon him. For the rest of his life, he would use any weapon available to defend the security he managed precariously to attain: his Christian faith; his don's privileges; his sense of the proper scope and aims of scholarship and art, a sense that caused him to repudiate all forms of modernism because modernism, like depth psychology, lays bare and corrodes, rather than shoring up and celebrating its material; and finally, the male friends who gathered about him to form the Inklings group. (This was a group of academics, including J. R. R. Tolkien and Charles Williams, who met regularly to drink and to read aloud their works in progress.) He became, in all his work, an adept manipulator of rhetorical argument and emotional imagery, to sometimes meretricious and sometimes deeply moving effect, as can be seen in

his fiction more clearly perhaps than anywhere else.

After 1914, when he was removed from the last of his purgatorial experiences at various boarding schools, Lewis' life was an outwardly undramatic record of success, though his private life was singular enough. His tutor noted his remarkable capacity to immerse himself in the world of imaginative literature and scholarship, and there was never much doubt that he would have an academic career. He served briefly in World War I, took a Triple First (highest honors) at Oxford (in Classical Moderations, Ancient History and Philosophy, and English Language and Literature), and from 1925 until the year of his death taught, studied, and wrote book after book, first at Magdalen College, Oxford, and finally as Professor of Mediaeval and Renaissance English at Cambridge, from 1954 on. His private life was also fixed early. In 1918 Lewis set up house with a woman twenty-five years his senior named Mrs. Moore, the mother of a friend who had died in World War I. He lived with her—celibately, it seems—until her death in 1951. Completing this parodic reconstruction of the prelapsarian family, his older brother moved in with them in 1932. A domineering, irascible, erratic, violently temperamental woman, Mrs. Moore does not seem to have provided Lewis with anything like a far-ranging experience of female behavior, and his views on the natural subordination of women to men—though he rationalized them in religious terms—do come at times very close to misogyny. His fiction, never so punitive as when it is dealing with "modern" women, reflects this narrowness of vision and opportunity, as it was almost all written before his late, transforming marriage in 1956, five years after Mrs. Moore's death at the age of seventy-nine. Lewis' marriage to Joy Gresham was apparently very sexually fulfilling and harmonious; his years with her were joyful.

Curled up porcupinelike amidst the century in which he lived, Lewis focused his active emotional life inward to the past; it is perhaps an unusual posture for a science fic-

C. S. Lewis. COURTESY OF UPI/CORBIS-BETTMANN

tion writer, though he was of course a writer of most unusual science fiction. Of the three novels generally considered science fiction— *Out of the Silent Planet* (1938), *Perelandra* (1943), and *That Hideous Strength* (1945)— only the first of the trilogy makes any consistent use of science-fictional language or concepts, and even there the science is almost flamboyantly inaccurate in its subordination to Higher Things. At heart, all of Lewis' narrative fiction shares the truculent, evasive doubleness of meaning of genuine allegory.

A brief look at Lewis' other fiction may begin to demonstrate the essential unity of all his work. *Dymer* (1926), a book-length narrative poem published under the pseudonym Clive Hamilton, allows its eponymous hero to escape from the dystopian city of his birth, where "the State/Chose for eugenic reasons who should mate/With whom, and when"; Dymer finds himself in a myth-ridden world whose Nordic textures are the first adult declaration of Lewis' abiding love for northern landscapes, legends, imagery, and gods; and in this new country, the hero fights a number of top-heavy allegorical battles and faces ambiguous challenges and settles his mind. *The Pilgrim's Regress* (1933; revised 1943), based on John Bunyan's *Pilgrim's Progress*, is explicitly allegorical. After the Pilgrim has demonstrated a hearty contempt for the art, literature, thought, and social innovations of the first thirty years of the twentieth century, he regresses into childhood, where he finds his true comforting Christian faith and settles his mind. In *The Screwtape Letters* (1942), a senior devil gives advice to a junior devil on how to tempt a young man into sin; the book is acutely witty and is probably the most winning expression of Lewis' powerful capacity to transmute cognition into dramatic argument. *The Great Divorce* (1945) demonstrates, with a rather sour humor, the unyielding incapacity of the damned to comprehend the nature of Heaven, while they are on a bus trip to that locale.

Probably the most popular fiction Lewis wrote is his series of children's stories about Narnia, a land inhabited by talking animals and ruled by Aslan, an allegorical Christ-figure in the shape of a lion (it is Lewis' misfortune and ours that Aslan is now more evocative of computer languages than of messiahs). In order of publication, though not of internal chronology, the series comprises *The Lion, the Witch, and the Wardrobe* (1950), *Prince Caspian* (1951), *The Voyage of the "Dawn Treader"* (1952), *The Silver Chair* (1953), *The Horse and His Boy* (1954), *The Magician's Nephew* (1955), and *The Last Battle* (1956). The first two volumes show the haste with which they were composed, and perhaps mainly for that reason displeased Tolkien, who had been up to that point a long-time intimate of Lewis and who was central, with Lewis, to the success of the Inklings. Generally thought to be more successful, the middle volumes are written with a confident serenity that is appealing to many adults as well as children, in their depiction of a world made translucent by the immanence of God.

The final volume, though competent, displays an almost sadistic pleasure in the meting out of punishment to the adversaries of Christianity. In a theological frame, punishment and damnation are close kin, and in these children's books, Lewis is repeatedly damning the souls of his adversaries.

Lewis' last novel, *Till We Have Faces* (1956), deals, in a somewhat chastened vein, with the Cupid-and-Psyche myth, making of it a fantasia on the nature of love. The title of the novel comes from a paragraph about the human incapacity to tell the whole truth, with the consequence that, in their turn, the gods cannot, of course, speak openly to us: "How can they meet us face to face till we have faces?"

Lewis' science fiction trilogy, which is allegorical, proselytizing, and punitive, fits naturally into the body of his other fiction, and indeed the individual novels reveal their strengths and limitations most clearly when seen in this context. If science fiction in general tends to share a bias toward technological modernization and a sense that the barrier of the unknown is a challenge to man's ingenuity, rather than a chastening of his pride, then the science fiction of Lewis is an assault upon the genre whose plots and concerns it seems superficially to share.

Perhaps the closest of the three works to a conventional science fiction narrative is *Out of the Silent Planet,* which is couched in the traditional mode of the cosmic voyage, but with a cursory nod to the twentieth century in its use of a spaceship to make the trip. On a walking tour in England, Dr. Ransom, who will be the guiding human spirit through all three volumes, is abducted by two scientists, who have already visited Mars once and have returned to Earth with imperialistic notions and the mistaken idea that the Martians, whom they think of as "natives," have demanded a human sacrifice of them. Ransom, whose name acquires theological significance as the trilogy proceeds, is their choice for the sacrifice. They have, of course, misinterpreted the request of the Martians, and after a voyage of quite extraordinary beauty, and af-

ter Ransom escapes his captors and begins to understand the true nature of the Martian world, Lewis' underlying strategy starts to take shape.

Beneath his quantitative description of the wonders of interplanetary travel, Lewis presents a universe whose essence, whose very shape and history, can only be understood as an intense, intricate testimony of the abiding and fully active existence of God. Long ago, after having lost his battle in Heaven against God, Satan—or the "Bent One" as he is called in the trilogy—took over the planet Thulcandra, or the Silent Planet, which has been in quarantine ever since. The Silent Planet is of course Earth. The scientists' voyage to Mars—called Malacandra here, as Venus is called Perelandra—is a break in the quarantine that proves to have deep theological significance. The Malacandrans are unfallen creatures; but Weston, the chief scientist, speaks the language of the Bent One. *Out of the Silent Planet* reaches its climax in an extended debate between Weston and Oyarsa, the chief of the *eldila,* or angels, who occupies the same role among the Malacandrans as Satan does on Earth. Uttering technophilic imbecilities and constantly demonstrating his obscene incapacity to understand the nature of an unfallen world, Weston attempts without success to suborn the angels of Heaven with his devil-worshipping scientific materialism; Lewis presents him as speaking a ludicrous pidgin English when addressing the *eldila,* for Weston sees the hosts of the unfallen as no more than hordes of ignorant savages. In this novel, his failure is preordained and comic; and he is sent ignominiously back to Earth, along with Ransom, who decides that he must try to live among his own kind, despite the anguish this will cause him. The novel ends with the quarantine apparently reinstated.

Lewis did not initially intend to write a trilogy; his first attempt at continuing Ransom's story, a fragment from about 1940 entitled *The Dark Tower* (first published in 1977 along with other minor efforts), is relatively inconsequential and does not deal with the larger theological issues. Without any real doubt, the trilogy is a misshapen work. *That Hideous Strength* (1945; abridged version, 1955; reissued as *The Tortured Planet*, 1958) is the chronological sequel to *Perelandra*, but it makes more sense when treated as its predecessor. Despite its very considerable length (in either version), it is a comparatively lightweight satire set back on Earth, mainly at Bracton College in England, where the vile National Institute for Coordinated Experiments (NICE) is housed. Ostensibly an organization of scientists espousing rationalist values, NICE is actually a consort of superstitious devil-worshippers, among whom is Lewis' major attempt at depicting an active woman: she is an enormous, overmuscular, sadistic lesbian, and NICE's official torturer. In the foreground of the action is a couple whose marriage is in trouble, Mark and Jane Studdock. Temporarily seduced by NICE, Mark soon finds himself in deep waters at work as well as at home, where Jane has been expressing "modern" notions about the proper relationship between man and wife and about childbearing.

As usual, Lewis' response to this sort of character is condescendingly punitive, though less so than his treatment of female (that is, human) sexuality in the short story "Ministering Angels" (1958), perhaps the least morally attractive of all his works. In this story, an all-male colony on Mars is visited by two women who have agreed to go there to release sexual tensions; they arrive:

Some of those present had doubted the sex of this creature. Its hair was very short, its nose very long, its mouth very prim, its chin sharp, and its manner authoritative. The voice revealed it as, scientifically speaking, a woman. But no one had any doubt about the sex of her nearest neighbor, the fat person.

One man begins to choke. The fat woman tries to comfort him; her "warm, wobbling maternalism" engulfs him. "Don't cry," she says. "Poor boy, then. Poor boy. I'll give you a good time." At this point the Captain informs her that "the young man is laughing, not crying."

In *That Hideous Strength*, where the forces arrayed against the Bent One are led by an etherealized, charismatic Dr. Ransom, Lewis' characteristic punishment of Jane Studdock is (almost) meted out by Merlin, who is a kind of pre-Christian spirit of Old England, and who has been resurrected to help save his beloved country. When Merlin discovers that Jane has been practicing birth control, he suggests that "her head be cut from her shoulders." But this does not occur. As the forces of evil are eventually defeated in scenes rather reminiscent of Badger's scouring of Toad Hall in Kenneth Grahame's *The Wind in the Willows*—a humbled Jane is discovered returning to Mark, who has himself been punished for his opportunistic involvement with NICE. In this novel, Ransom performs more as a catalyst than as a protagonist, perhaps because the theological kudos bestowed upon him by Lewis have made it impossible for actions to be ascribed to him without blasphemy; as a catalyst, Ransom calls down the angels from Heaven, though to an oddly flat effect, since they do little more than harrow Toad Hall.

It seems reasonable to assume that Lewis felt considerably ill at ease in attempting to bring this book to an appropriate climax, probably because the theological climax had been reached earlier, in *Perelandra*; he could see no way to transform the Silent Planet into a planet of the unfallen (a sacrilegious endeavor if made), and he could see no way to redeem the anticlimactic farcicality of his narrative. So the novel ends on a less-than-transcendent note: in the resumption of a Christian marriage properly blessed, as Ransom exhorts Jane to ensure, with children.

The heart of the trilogy and the natural resolution of its argument are to be found in *Perelandra* (1943; also published under the title *Voyage to Venus*, 1953); it is in this superb vision that Lewis reaches his peak as a writer of fiction. The events narrated in *Perelandra* take place after Ransom's experiences in Malacandra (Mars) but before his exalted, if passive conflict with NICE, although the underlying feeling of the story is one of emotional and thematic climax, and *That Hideous Strength* reads as an extended appendix, an epic repeated as farce. Weston, the Bent One's tool and voice, has broken the quarantine; something new has happened in Heaven. After a brief sojourn on Earth, Ransom is summoned by the *eldila* of Deep Heaven to take a prime role in the opening cosmic war. He is transported to Perelandra (Venus), which is a planet almost completely covered with water, and across which float, unceasingly, organic islands inhabited by pacific creatures; the effect of translucent innocence is considerably moving. Ransom soon discovers what his role is to be, when Weston also arrives, with a darkening of the texture of the narrative.

Perelandra is governed by Tor and Tinidril—Adam and Eve—and Tinidril, through Weston's agency, is about to be exposed to temptation. A debate follows, between Ransom and Weston, vividly presenting Lewis' conservative Christian rendering of the literalness and horror of the Fall. In itself, the debate is inconclusive and, indeed, the grotesque, insinuating Weston gets rather the better of it until, in a dark night of the soul, Ransom is brought to the realization that he must physically dislodge the Bent One from Perelandra, that he must actually destroy Weston, who has become a terrifying parody of a human being, and who is ultimately described in the text as the "Un-Man." Therefore, Ransom terminates the debate and, in a series of actions of mounting brutality and considerable narrative force, he beats Weston to death.

And then the novel explodes with a transcendent delight. Perelandra has been saved from the Fall and will not repeat Earth's history of exile and loss; Tor and Tinidril are about to mount the throne:

> Paradise itself in its two persons, Paradise walking hand in hand, its two bodies shining in the light like emeralds yet not themselves too bright to look at, came in sight. . . . And the gods kneeled and bowed their huge bodies before the small forms of that young King and Queen.

In such heightened language—evocative of Tolkien and Williams—the novel begins to close with a dance of the gods and the creatures of the unfallen heavens; it becomes apparent to the transfigured Ransom that he is beholding in this dance the veritable warp and woof of reality, the structure of the true world. It is this vision—not specifically Christian—of the Great Dance that perhaps translates Lewis' sectarian afflatus into the deep, hard, usable grandeur of myth. It is not for his views on the penalties for using birth control devices, but for the pagan and ecstatic clarity of the Great Dance, that he will be remembered, with charity.

Selected Bibliography

WORKS OF C. S. LEWIS

Dymer. London: J. M. Dent and Sons, 1926; New York: E. P. Dutton, 1926. Originally published under the pseudonym Clive Hamilton. Reprinted in *Narrative Poems.* New York: Harcourt Brace Jovanovich, 1969.

The Pilgrim's Regress. London: J. M. Dent and Sons, 1933. Revised edition, London: Geoffrey Bles, 1943; New York: Sheed and Ward, 1944.

Out of the Silent Planet. London: John Lane The Bodley Head, 1938; New York: Macmillan, 1943.

The Screwtape Letters. London: Geoffrey Bles, 1942; New York: Macmillan, 1943. (Reprinted with a new letter added in 1961; United States edition, 1964.)

Perelandra. London: John Lane The Bodley Head, 1943; New York: Macmillan, 1944. Reprinted as *Voyage to Venus.* London: Pan Books, 1953.

The Great Divorce. London: Geoffrey Bles, 1945; New York: Macmillan, 1946.

That Hideous Strength. London: John Lane The Bodley Head, 1945; New York: Macmillan, 1946. Abridged edition, London: Pan Books, 1955. Reprinted as *The Tortured Planet,* New York: Avon Books, 1958.

The Lion, the Witch, and the Wardrobe. London: Geoffrey Bles, 1950; New York: Macmillan, 1950.

Prince Caspian. London: Geoffrey Bles, 1951; New York: Macmillan, 1951.

The Voyage of the "Dawn Treader." London: Geoffrey Bles, 1952; New York: Macmillan, 1952.

The Silver Chair. London: Geoffrey Bles, 1953; New York: Macmillan, 1953.

The Horse and His Boy. London: Geoffrey Bles, 1954; New York: Macmillan, 1954.

The Magician's Nephew. London: The Bodley Head, 1955; New York: Macmillan, 1955.

The Last Battle. London: The Bodley Head, 1956; New York: Macmillan, 1956.

Till We Have Faces. London: Geoffrey Bles, 1956; New York: Harcourt Brace and World, 1957.

Letters of C. S. Lewis. Edited by Walter Hooper. London: Geoffrey Bles, 1966. Revised edition, London: Fount, 1988. (With a memoir by W. H. Lewis.)

Of Other Worlds: Essays and Stories. London: Geoffrey Bles, 1966; New York: Harcourt Brace and World, 1966.

The Dark Tower and Other Stories. London: Collins, 1977; New York: Harcourt Brace Jovanovich, 1977.

Boxen: The Imaginary World of the Young C. S. Lewis. Edited by Walter Hooper. San Diego, Calif.: Harcourt Brace Jovanovich, 1985. (A collection of maps, histories, sketches, and stories created by C. S. Lewis as a child.)

Present Concerns. Edited by Walter Hooper. San Diego, Calif.: Harcourt Brace Jovanovich, 1986.

All My Road Before Me: The Diary of C. S. Lewis, 1922–1927. Edited by Walter Hooper. San Diego, Calif.: Harcourt Brace Jovanovich, 1991.

CRITICAL AND BIOGRAPHICAL STUDIES

Arbuckle, Nan. "That Hidden Strength: C. S. Lewis' Merlin as Modern Grail." In *The Figure of Merlin in the Nineteenth and Twentieth Centuries*. Edited by Jeanie Watson and Maureen Fries. Lewiston, N.Y.: Mellen, 1989.

Carpenter, Humphrey. *The Inklings: C. S. Lewis, J. R. R. Tolkien, Charles Williams, and Their Friends*. London: George Allen and Unwin, 1978.

Downing, David C. *Planets in Peril: A Critical Study of C. S. Lewis's Ransom Trilogy*. Amherst: University of Massachusetts, 1992.

Filmer, Kath. *The Fiction of C. S. Lewis: Mask and Mirror*. New York: St. Martin's, 1992.

———. "That Hideous 1984: The Influence of C. S. Lewis's *That Hideous Strength* on Orwell's *Nineteen Eighty-Four*." *Extrapolation*, 26, no. 2 (1985): 160–169.

Green, Roger L. *C. S. Lewis: A Biography*. Revised by Roger L. Green and Walter Hooper. San Diego, Calif.: Harcourt Brace Jovanovich, 1994.

Griffin, William. *Clive Staples Lewis: A Dramatic Life*. San Francisco, Calif.: Harper and Row, 1986.

Hillegas, Mark R., ed. *Shadows of Imagination: The Fantasies of C. S. Lewis, J. R. R. Tolkien and Charles Williams*. Carbondale: Southern Illinois University Press, 1969.

Lowenberg, Susan. *C. S. Lewis: A Reference Guide, 1972–1988*. New York: G. K. Hall, 1993.

Manlove, C. N. *C. S. Lewis: His Literary Achievement*. Houndmills, Basingstoke, Hampshire, England: Macmillan, 1987.

Myers, Doris T. *C. S. Lewis in Context*. Kent, Ohio: Kent State University Press, 1994.

Schakel, Peter J., and Charles A. Hutter, eds. *Word and Story in C. S. Lewis*. Columbia: University of Missouri Press, 1991.

Walsh, Chad. *The Literary Legacy of C. S. Lewis*. New York: Harcourt Brace Jovanovich, 1979.

Watson, George, ed. *Critical Essays on C. S. Lewis*. Hants, England: Scolar, 1992.

Wilson, A. N. *C. S. Lewis: A Biography*. London: Collins, 1990.

—JOHN CLUTE

H. P. LOVECRAFT

(1890–1937)

MORE BIOGRAPHICAL MATERIAL is available for H. P. Lovecraft, possibly, than for any other modern American writer. Not only has a succession of devoted admirers tracked down the minutiae of his life, but thousands of his letters survive in which he conducted his education, described his meager daily events and florid dreams, complained about unperceptive editors, damned many minorities and some majorities, described colonial architecture enthusiastically, and joked and pontificated.

Very little happened in Lovecraft's external life. He was born on 20 August 1890 in Providence, Rhode Island, into a patrician family that lost its wealth suddenly and was forced into genteel poverty and rooming-house existence. His father, a salesman for a large silverware company, was permanently hospitalized when HPL was a small child and died of syphilis. Thereafter HPL was reared by a devouring mother who was both enormously overprotective and destructive. A sickly child, he was removed from school for extended periods and dropped out of high school. There is a question, however, whether his illnesses, some perhaps psychosomatic, were exaggerated and fostered by his mother and aunts.

Intellectually, HPL was precocious, reading and writing at an early age. A competent amateur astronomer, in his teens he hectographed *The Rhode Island Journal of Astronomy* and contributed articles to the local newspapers. Even in childhood, he was obsessed with intellectual self-improvement and read voluminously in popular accounts of the sciences. Since the family library was strong on premodern literature, and HPL became saturated with eighteenth-century and early nineteenth-century culture, with which he identified. He later became expert on colonial and early American antiquities.

HPL emerged from a greenhouse adolescence with strong ideas of class, a repugnance for salaried work (which was unsuitable for a gentleman), and a circumscribed social milieu. Since unpaid writing was an avocation permissible for a gentleman, HPL gravitated toward the various amateur writing movements of the day and, it would seem indisputable, wasted years pursuing the second and third rate, filling and editing weak magazines and administering amateur associations.

Providence was the center of the universe for HPL, particularly the older sections, and apart from trips to examine colonial architecture elsewhere, he spent his life there, except for about two years in New York City after his unfortunate marriage. In 1924 he married or, more precisely, was married by, Sonia Greene, who had notoriously chased him. Their marriage dissolved in indifference, and HPL returned in ecstasy to Providence. During his stay in New York he made a serious effort to accommodate himself to realities and to find a job, but was unsuccessful, a failure that told heavily on him. At one time he was offered the editorship of *Weird Tales*, but he refused it because it would have involved moving to Chicago.

For most of his life HPL made a small, declining living as a ghost writer and editor, correcting bad poetry, for example, at ten cents a line. This income was supplemented by occasional small amounts for his fiction. Ironically, his stories were extremely popular among his readers, and to a small group he was a living legend; but under the circumstances of the Great Depression, his abilities could not be turned into cash. He died of cancer of the colon on 15 March 1937, a near pauper.

Lovecraft's life mode has been censured severely by some of his biographers, and much has been made of his small eccentricities and weaknesses. He has been called self-centered, *aboulique* (weak-willed), ineffectual, and irresponsible. His shabby treatment of his wife has been especially criticized. Much of this may be true, but it should be pointed out that Lovecraft, until his last years, seems to have been reasonably happy in his way of life, although some critics find buried traces of despair in his cheerful letters. If he had little money, he had a great deal of freedom; if he made a bad decision in his youth in refusing to deal with Mammon (and discovered in later years that Mammon was no longer interested), he accepted his situation and made the most of it. He probably would have told his biographers that he had the right to live as he chose and, invoking a New Englander's sense of privacy, that his life was no one else's business.

In personality, Lovecraft was an extremely pleasant and charming man, a gifted conversationalist in congenial company, helpful, and generous with time. He could relate well enough with friends, male and female, but came more and more to prefer solitude. He was an extremely intelligent man, with a good layman's knowledge of the arts and sciences, which he delighted to share with his friends. As he matured, he outgrew much of his snobbery, evolving from an extreme conservative to a near socialist during the years of the New Deal. Unfortunately, despite the attempts of his admirers to whitewash one aspect of his personality, he was, in talk though not in action, a ferocious racist. Although strongly anti-Semitic in utterance, he married a Jewish woman, and he numbered Jews among his close friends. He seems to have outgrown his early admiration for Nazism, Hitler, and the Ku Klux Klan.

II

Lovecraft was unusual among practitioners of supernatural/horror fiction in proclaiming an aesthetic for his work. As he states in his fine *Supernatural Horror in Literature* (1945; developed over many years), "The oldest and strongest emotion of mankind is fear, and the oldest and strongest kind of fear is fear of the unknown. These facts few psychologists will dispute, and their admitted truth must establish for all time the genuineness and dignity of the weirdly horrible tale as a literary form." According to this point of view, horror is as valid a subject for literary treatment as, say, sex or power. He developed this position in more detail elsewhere.

In philosophical matters HPL was a logical positivist much like the later school of Bertrand Russell and A. J. Ayer. In this he was not unusual since his position was common enough in educated circles. Yet in his fiction he immediately leaped headlong into metaphysics, a taboo subject among logical positivists. In this fictional overturning of his conscious beliefs, one of his bases seems to have been dreams. He once boasted that though he was not a great writer, he was a first-rate dreamer. In his fiction, which disrupts a stable universe, we thus find the primacy of dream knowledge, speculations about personalities existing behind phenomenality, sympathy with irrational intellectual pursuits, and validation of esoteric, eccentric systems of thought. The result is a literature of extreme emotionalism, often stratified among thick layers of desensitized, expositional prose.

Equally unexpected, considering HPL's position of cultural relativism, is the presence of true evil in his stories, evil embodied in monsters and their human devotees. Such evil is often associated with the past and with attempts to restore it to power. Even though the rational universe is "beyond good and evil" (Lovecraft admired Nietzsche), most of the monsters HPL created are committed to hostility, viciousness, and aggression.

Lovecraft, as he declared, was not interested in the relations between people, except in certain situations, but was interested in ideas, which he developed into fiction, and the fate of the individual. If one extrapolates in a structuralist manner to his ultimate theme, it is obvious that his basic theme is individual failure. Man acts, sometimes in odd ways, magical or scientific, and usually fails; dreamers try to reify their dreams and die unactualized; innocent bystanders are caught up in toils and usually go under; explorers, when they find what they should not have sought, can at best flee in panic.

Associated with this tragedy is historical degradation and degeneration that parallels entropy of the soul, in which Lovecraft did not believe. Ancient beauty falls apart and is soiled by present unworthiness; architecture—the symbol for the constructive aspect of life—and landscape—the nurturing, suffer most. Cultures are born or arrive and die. In this, Lovecraft's reading of Oswald Spengler, a German philosopher of history, may have been inspirational.

Yet HPL was not consistent in this ideal pattern, for in addition to straight-line entropic loss of *virtus* within each culture, he proposed cyclical patterns and breaks. Astronomical cycles might reactivate what has disappeared and bring a return to ancient evil conditions; time may be violated and past and present bridged.

As HPL insinuates emotion into his descriptive world, certain horror images and motifs recur: outside, underneath, ancient, formless, cold, wet, smelly, windy, and so on. Apotheosized, these in turn lead to the "mythic," sometimes puerile cosmology that lies behind many of his stories, with imaginary books, such as the *Necronomicon*, which has a small history in itself. (Its title simply means "how to control the dead.")

Lovecraft's earliest and most important fiction model was Edgar Allan Poe, whose work he admired greatly, and Poe's influence permeated HPL's work long after he had relinquished the perfervid mode of expression that he associated with Poe. Second to Poe was the Irish poet, fabulist, and dramatist Lord Dunsany, whose dreamy, sensuous *décadent* episodes Lovecraft imitated in several stories beyond our scope. Important in HPL's later work was general scientific or learned expositional prose, with at best clarity, precision, and aseptic portrayal of horrid subjects. This last was the Lovecraft that seems most important today.

III

Lovecraft's horror fiction balances unstably between science fiction and supernatural fiction. Some pieces skew off into supernaturalism, with gods/demons and ceremonial magic; others ride a borderline, considering magic as a sort of experimental science, the natural magic of the Baroque Era; and still others are science fiction without significant supernaturalism. It is with stories of the last category that we are concerned, though they are unlike contemporary pulp science fiction in tone and aesthetics. Also, whereas contemporary science fiction was mostly concerned with the future, Lovecraft's drew its power from the past, almost an alcheringa past as described in native Australian mythology, when great powers strode the Earth.

Not science fiction, but necessary to every coverage of Lovecraft, is "The Outsider" (written 1921; published in *Weird Tales*, April 1926), an enigmatic story often taken as emblematic of Lovecraft. In the mode of Poe, told in an ornate style with much verbal hysteria, it is the first-person account of a revenant, who describes his life underground in a dismal, mirrorless, funereal world and then by climbing a tower that reaches above his sky, enters our world, progresses to a castle that looks familiar yet changed, enters and sees a

H. P. Lovecraft. PHOTO COURTESY OF THE BROWN UNIVERSITY LIBRARY, PROVIDENCE, RHODE ISLAND

room of merry guests stampede in horror at some monstrosity they must see. He, too, sees the monstrosity, recoils, slips, and touches it—a mirror. He is the monster, a decayed, rotten corpse. Now rejected by man, he consorts with haunts, flits about Egypt—or so he raves.

"The Outsider" contains many motif echoes: Frankenstein's monster's confrontation with normal humans; Ambrose Bierce's revenant in "An Inhabitant of Carcosa" (1891); the primitive mythic motif of an underground land of the dead and emergence by climbing; Dracula's progression up and down his castle walls; and mirrors as revealers of Truth—all well integrated. It also presents the layered universe prevalent in HPL's later, important work; the self-destruction of the exploring protagonist; and the dangers inherent in the past.

The problem is that "The Outsider" is Lovecraft's only story without internal logic, almost being absurdist. As narrated, the story is impossible, and what the story really sig-

nifies is doubtful, perhaps an unedited dream as is hinted by a headnote. The question still remains, Whose or what's dream?

"The Outsider" has been taken variously as a cri de coeur for Lovecraft's life predicament; as bitterness over his mother's role in his life, perhaps written at her death; as a statement of woman's suppression in our society; as a lament about male homosexuality; as an ultimate statement in self-pity. It is ironic that a story that Lovecraft did not rate high and is often regarded as secondary remains Lovecraft's most tantalizing work.

"The Call of Cthulhu" (written summer 1926; published in *Weird Tales*, February 1928), which is arguably science fiction, is probably Lovecraft's best-known story. A fragmented essay with narrative inclusions, it is the first clear statement of the Cthulhu complex, invoking dream revelation, archaeology, crime reports, seismology, astrology, and parapsychology to suggest an ancient, reawakened peril to humanity. Synchronistic phenomena, including renewed activity among vicious cultists, are traceable to a small seismic upheaval in the South Pacific, where sailors find colossal ruins and intrude upon the crypt of a horrible monster. Only one sailor survives, but not for long.

The synthesizing narrator explains: In the depths of the sea, in the ruined city of R'lyeh, Cthulhu and his associates (monsters like giant-winged, ectoplasmic squid-lobsters) lie in a sort of sleeping death. Members of one of the intelligent genera that invaded Earth eons ago, they cannot emerge until astronomical conjunctions are right or without outside help. Before submergence they were in telepathic dream contact with human cults, which continue their worship. Since Cthulhu is hostile and has godlike powers, mankind was imperiled when the ruins emerged and was saved only by their resubmergence.

Many varied elements are integrated: a recorded dream of Lovecraft's, an earthquake he experienced, Theosophical root-races, non-Euclidean geometry, memories of A. Merritt's "The Moon Pool" (1918) (which Lovecraft admired), a sense of apocalyptic emergence of evil, and contranatural motifs. The driving mechanisms are notions of good and cosmic evil, based ultimately, as often is the case with Lovecraft, on religion.

"The Call of Cthulhu" is important not only as one of Lovecraft's finest stories but as the portal to the so-called Cthulhu Mythos, which might be called the Secret History of the Earth. Lovecraft, apparently only half seriously, invented a vague cluster of potent demons/gods/monsters/extraterrestrials who once walked the Earth (and some still do), associated with them titillating fragments of monstrous texts, and furnished them with obnoxious cults. His followers solidified what Lovecraft had left vague and spawned ever-larger pantheons. What with Lovecraft is at worst occasionally inappropriate, in his imitators, according to most critics, is often inept and silly.

Of Lovecraft's indisputably science fiction stories "The Colour out of Space" (written early 1927; published in *Amazing Stories*, September 1927) takes precedence, being generally considered his finest work. Although the story was published in a science fiction magazine, the publisher and editor (Hugo Gernsback) apparently did not realize that it was based on a thought nexus opposed to his promotion of technology and science, for "The Colour out of Space" is about the desecration and degradation of primal innocence by an invasion based on science. The story is unusual in Lovecraft's horror fiction in that the evil is spontaneous, random, and not evoked by man.

Set in the Arkham area of western Massachusetts, the narrative is told by an engineer making a survey for a new reservoir that will flood the land. As he learns, in 1882 a meteorite struck on the Gardner farm. The meteorite was investigated by scientists from Miskatonic University, who found in it a small iridescent globule that broke as they examined it. Not long afterward, the area manifested horrible changes in vegetation and wildlife; the humans, too, sickened, suffered malformations, and died. Later, when a party investigated the Gardner farm, they saw a strange light-essence pour from the well and mount into the sky. An utterly alien life-form had hatched from a meteoric egg, sucked life from the area, then, when mature, departed. The area is still lifeless, and a remnant of the being may still be in the well.

"At the Mountains of Madness" (written March 1931; published in *Astounding Stories*, February-April 1936), HPL's first long work, was rejected by *Weird Tales* and *Strange Tales*, not surprisingly, for the story was unsuitable for both magazines. Lovecraft, however, took the rejections badly. The story was finally accepted for *Astounding Stories* by F. Orlin Tremaine, who was trying to fatten *Astounding* with quality work. Lovecraft received $315, the most he had ever received for a story, but he was outraged that the story was abridged and insensitively edited.

Lovecraft had long been interested in Antarctica; he admired Poe's 1838 *Narrative of Arthur Gordon Pym* (to which he linked his novel) and knew John Martin Leahy's horror story "In Amundsen's Tent" (*Weird Tales*, January 1928); but Richard Byrd's experiences in Little America were the obvious impetus for writing the novel.

A confessional/minatory tale, "At the Mountains of Madness" describes the discoveries of the Miskatonic Antarctic Expedition investigating paleobiology. A party flies to a promising area and in great excitement reports enormous fossil deposits, including perfectly preserved large specimens of an incredible life-form (quinary instead of bilateral like us) that seems part vegetable. Communications cease. The narrator (Professor Dyer) and an associate, on investigating, find the explorers dead and the strange life-forms missing. In the brief time permitted by their gasoline supply, the two men thereupon explore another incredible discovery, a ruined city hundreds of millions of years old. They learn that the presumed fossil specimens revived and after wiping out the subexpedition made their way to the city. The investigators then discover that the fossil forms, too, have been killed, and they flee for their lives, pursued by shoggoths, a horrible artificially created life-form much like a gigantic differentiated amoeba. Professor Dyer is telling his story to forestall further exploration, which may result in loosing still worse horrors.

Throughout the narrative, which is slow, dense, and prolix, Lovecraft brings in his personal cosmology, calling the alien life-forms the Old Ones, beings who came from the stars and for eons were dominant on Earth. He also concentrates on the architectural accomplishments of the Old Ones (indeed, one might almost say that architecture is the point of the story), offering a detailed description of their cultural and racial history, unconvincingly derived from a few hours of glancing at bas reliefs.

As a result of much impediment, "At the Mountains of Madness" was not well received by its first readers, including those sophisticated enough to appreciate mainstream detail. It is often characterized by modern critics as, despite occasional brilliant moments, a cluttered, dull work. It would seem to be an overdeveloped short story or novelette, weak in story strands, not carried by senses of discovery and peril.

Lovecraft's second story accepted by Tremaine, "The Shadow out of Time" (written early 1935; published in *Astounding Stories*, June 1936) is essentially the same confessional/minatory story as "At the Mountains of Madness": prying/discovery of horrors/flight/warnings. It also entwines the motif of personality usurpation with the rationalized cosmology of the earlier work.

The story has two foci. In the first, Professor Peaslee's body is usurped, during mid-lecture, by the mind of an alien being of perhaps a hundred million years earlier. Such beings, called the Great Race, project their minds into the future to gather knowledge and also to prepare for a mass mental migration. The new personality in Peaslee's body explores our world, then returns to the past, thus restoring Peaslee to his own body. Peabody then devotes his life to discovering what has happened. Dreams and other sources reveal details of his exchange-incarnation in the alien body, which is that of a large cone-shaped creature. His captivity is not unpleasant, and he devotes his time in the remote past to writing about twentieth-century culture in a book that becomes part of a Borges-like library of the ages.

The second focus of the novel, skillfully merged with the first, corroborates Peaslee's reconstruction. When ancient ruins are found in Australia much like those he described from his dreams, an expedition from Miskatonic University, including Peaslee, excavates them. One evening, Peaslee chances upon an entry to underground chambers and makes his way to the library in which his work was deposited. He removes his book and flees, pursued by nameless horrors. He now urges cessation of exploration but has no proof since he lost his book during his flight.

"The Shadow out of Time" is generally considered superior to "At the Mountains of Madness." The Great Race, although not human, assumes the role of a quasi character, and its activities are interesting. Peaslee's quest, as an "Outsider," is unusual, and the conclusion, contrived, prefigured, and expected though it is, conveys a certain excitement.

Both stories, however, suffer from narrative tactics: the unnecessary, sore-thumb association with the Cthulhu cosmology and the unconvincing rationale. Could Dyer and Peaslee really believe that a tale of horrors would stifle scientific curiosity?

Lovecraft's second long work, *The Shadow over Innsmouth* (written December 1931; published 1936), follows the same formula as "At the Mountains of Madness": prying/discovery of horrors/physical flight/admonitions. It is unusual in being Lovecraft's only story in which highly felt physical action dominates the story.

A historically minded college student, exploring local antiquities along the North Shore of Massachusetts, hears of isolated, decaying, degenerate Innsmouth, whose inhabitants are dreaded and hated by the surrounding peoples. Taking a decrepit bus to Innsmouth, he observes a once prosperous seacoast town that has fallen into near ruin and is inhabited by men of peculiar physiognomy.

Ignoring warnings, he pries into the question of why Innsmouth is Innsmouth. He learns that a Captain Obed Marsh, who traded in the Pacific in the early nineteenth century, made a compact with humanoid sea people who lived near a reef outside Innsmouth. In exchange for human sacrifices, the sea people supplied abundant harvests of fish and specimens of strangely worked gold. As the association developed, the sea people insisted on interbreeding with the human inhabitants of Innsmouth, massacring those who resisted. The ontogenetic result of such interbreeding is gradual transformation, on aging, into a sea man/woman, taking to the sea, and living forever apart from accident.

The natives resent the narrator's prying and attempt to kill him. Much of the narrative describes his escape from Innsmouth. When he returns to civilization, he informs local and federal authorities of what he has learned. The result is a naval bombardment of the reef and a cleansing of Innsmouth, but as an aftermath, hints of which have been dropped throughout the story, the narrator discovers that he is descended from Obed Marsh and his sea wife. As his body begins a sea change, he raves that he will take to the sea.

The Shadow over Innsmouth is in part a metaphor for organized religion (against which Lovecraft felt strongly). The ultimate bond between humans and sea people is sacramental sex and worship of certain deities that the sea people maintain (and may or may not exist), and Lovecraft places much stress on the robed and tiara-wearing priests of the local cult, the Sons of Dagon. (Dagon itself may have a hidden significance: Dagon, a half-human fish-god in his related aspect of Oannes was occasionally taken by early syncretists as a figure for Christianity, which had the fish as a symbol). The price of such a religion is noxious degradation; the reward may be sacrificial death or suicide for some, immortality for others. Fittingly, the story ends on a biblical note: "we shall dwell amidst wonder and glory forever."

Time, with its debasing of good, has propelled Innsmouth into the decay of old age. It creates the paradoxical union of opposites pervading the story: a decaying, rotten culture, based on an immortal hope; a horrible transformation incorporating the ultimate desire. Closely related to this is the ineluctability of bad heredity, a motif that also appears in such stories as "The Case of Charles Dexter Ward" (1927), "The Dunwich Horror" (1928), "The Thing on the Doorstep")1933), and especially "Arthur Jermyn" (1920).

The Shadow over Innsmouth has had a mixed critical reception. In Lovecraft's lifetime, it was rejected by editors and was first published by an amateur press. Modern critics, too, have held conflicting opinions, some considering it a failure. Joyce Carol Oates's judgment of it as "ponderous, meandering, yet riveting" seems applicable (though applicable also to much of Lovecraft's other work), but the story has many strengths: the quasi-autobiographical enthusiasms and perceptions of the young narrator, the rich use of New England local color, the sense of discovery, and the well-wrought action sequence as the young man escapes from Innsmouth, fainting spells and all. The transformation of the narrator into a sea monster, however, seems an unnecessary and implausible violation of story unity, not easily defensible except on the ground of universal corruption of mankind. On the other hand, Lovecraft liked "smash endings." that provide a thrill summation or, as in this case, a narrative reversal.

Among Lovecraft's lesser works are several early stories that are science fiction of sorts. "Beyond the Wall of Sleep" (written 1919; published in *Pine Cones*, October 1919) states a concept that lies behind much of Lovecraft's later fiction, indeed, of his life:

> I have frequently wondered if the majority of mankind ever pause to reflect upon the occasionally titanic significance of dreams, and of the obscure world to which they belong. While the greater number of our nocturnal visions are perhaps no more than faint and fantastic reflections of our waking experiences—

Freud to the contrary with his puerile symbolism—there are still a certain remainder whose immundane and ethereal character permits of no ordinary interpretation.

The story, which concerns a transcendent space being who has been unwillingly incarnated into a human body, is offset to a hospital attendant who has invented a thought-reading machine. The floridly written story combines elements from Poe's "The Conversation of Eiros and Charmion" (1839) and observational astronomy and anticipates later motifs of personality displacement. The idea is good.

"From Beyond" (written late 1920; published in *The Fantasy Fan*, June 1934) invokes the mad scientist and the dangerous invention, both common early science fiction motifs. Tillinghast has invented a machine that breaks down sensory barriers so that we can perceive "strange inaccessible worlds [that] exist at our elbows." Functioning by stimulating the pineal gland (an occult concept), it reveals horrible, dangerous interpenetrating monstrosities suggestive of fourth-dimensional antecedents like John Buchan's "Space" (1911) or H. G. Wells's "The Plattner Story" (1896). The story is overwritten and amateurish, but it holds two important motifs: prying and its penalty, and the unrealities behind reality.

"Facts Concerning the Late Arthur Jermyn and His Family," also known as "The White Ape" and "Arthur Jermyn" (written perhaps 1920; published in *The Wolverine*, March 1921), undoubtedly owes much to Edgar Rice Burroughs's Opar in his Tarzan series. Jermyn, a brilliant young scientist, commits suttee on learning that one of his ancestresses was an African white ape. Lovecraft claimed that he intended to describe the most horrible possible family shadow; actually, the story is a metaphor for his extreme bigotry and social snobbery. The motifs of expiating ancestral evil and committing suicides on discovering "racial pollution" occur in other of his works. A modern reader is likely to judge that Jermyn overreacted and that the story is rather silly.

"The Nameless City" (written early 1921; published in *The Wolverine*, November 1921) and "The Lurking Fear" (written November 1921; published in *Home Brew*, January-April 1923) are both based on favorite devices of Lovecraft's: underground horrors and devolution. In the first story, the narrator explores hitherto unknown ruins in central Asia, finding devolved intelligent reptiles of horrible aspect. A strong element is the motif of persistent misinterpretation, with the shock of final recognition and flight. A source might be Arthur Machen's concept of the Little People. "The Lurking Fear," perhaps self-parodic, describes devolved, cannibalistic humans who live in tunnels beneath graveyards. It is possible that Lovecraft knew the Scottish legend of Sawney Bean, in which an extended family of cannibals lives in underground caves and emerges to capture and murder wayfarers. Neither story has anything to offer.

"The Unnamable" (written 1923; published in *Weird Tales*, July 1925) and "Herbert West—Reanimator" (written 1921–1922; published in *Home Brew*, February–July 1922) induce a common perplexity. Were they meant seriously or as parodies? "The Unnamable," which has a supernatural element, may involve a strange mutation, a curious demonic hybrid—or simply sodomy with a goat. "Herbert West—Reanimator," an episodic novelette, describes West's experiments in reviving the dead by chemical means. The dead do not respond quickly but later run amok. In the final episode, all the awakened dead and their miscellaneous parts tear West to pieces. Whether meant as serious horror or as a spoof, the story has aroused contrary reactions among critics: a marvelous jeu d'esprit or one of the worst things Lovecraft wrote.

Several other stories that are more or less science fiction need not be discussed in detail. In "The Whisperer in Darkness," (written 1930; published in *Weird Tales*, August 1931) the Cthulhu hyth is rationalized in terms of visitors from Pluto who disguise themselves with wax masks. It is a dull story, poorly thought out and unconvincing. "The Dreams in the Witch House" (written 1932; published in *Weird Tales*, July 1933) attempts futilely to align colonial witchcraft with non-Euclidean "algebra," relativity with crucifixes, dimensional transit with familiars. "Through the Gates of the Silver Key" (written 1933; published in *Weird Tales*, July 1934), a collaboration with E. Hoffmann Price, mingles hypostatic personalities behind reality, dimensions, Platonic archetypes, extraterrestrial civilizations, and Lovecraft's Secret History—to the satisfaction of few. "In the Walls of Eryx" (written 1936, published in *Weird Tales*, October 1939), a collaboration with Kenneth Sterling, a young fan, is a routine pulp adventure story about an invisible maze on Venus. In these last two instances, the story is the collaborator's, put into Lovecraft's words.

IV

Lovecraft is of interest besides being a joyful playground for analysts ("his own most fantastic creation") and the foremost American horror writer of his time. His voluminous letters are a megadocument, both psychological and cultural-historical. He wrote a considerable amount of correct poetry, including the well-known "Fungi from Yuggoth." Moreover, his *Supernatural Horror in Literature* remains the best introduction to the older supernatural fiction.

How significant is Lovecraft? That the question can be raised at all is itself significant, but an answer is not single-poled. On the most obvious level, his better fiction is entertaining and is widely read with pleasure. Most readers would agree that "The Colour out of Space" is excellent. On the most far-fetched level, one cannot take seriously the claim of an occasional enthusiast that Lovecraft was a thinker of world stature with unique insights into our culture.

Historically, there can be little argument. Lovecraft has been enormously important. His influence is widespread, and the concept of literary horror has been changed by his the-

ory and practice. To paraphrase Raymond Chandler's analysis of the detective story, Lovecraft snatched the horror story away from the insubstantial hands of British ghosts and the fangs of vampires and implanted it into the historical depths of American culture. He broke the socially oriented Edwardian-Georgian fantastic story and reawakened the concept of evil that had been present in fin de siècle authors. HPL also developed the strong potential of background and pseudo-history to the greatest extent since M. R. James. And even if his style is cumbersome at times, he set the example of not writing down; even though he was writing for the pulp magazines, he adhered to his own standards.

Critics and scholars outside the field of fantastic fiction, however, have not tended to rate Lovecraft high or as more than a dated thrillmonger. Edmund Wilson, for example, in his "Tales of the Marvellous and the Ludicrous" (1945) says: "The only real horror in most of these fictions is the horror of bad taste and art. Lovecraft was not a good writer." Wilson, as is well known, was a severe critic with little sympathy for popular culture, and while one cannot wholly disagree with him on Lovecraft's style, one must wonder about "taste" and Wilson's ignoring of other aspects of Lovecraft's work. Jorge Luis Borges, on the other hand, gave a somewhat equivocal estimation of HPL: "I like Lovecraft's horror stories. His plots are very good, but his style is atrocious. I once dedicated a story ["There Are More Things"] to him." Borges covered Lovecraft extensively in his *An Introduction to American Literature* (1971).

A higher estimation of HPL, with a different orientation, is to be found in non-American critics, who are not worried about "taste"—since revolutions have taken place since Wilson wrote—but are more concerned with philosophy of history or the murky ideas that seem to lurk behind culture. Two examples of European estimation and interpretation of Lovecraft may be cited: The French scholar and critic Maurice Lévy found deep spiritual values in Lovecraft's work:

In a society [culture] that is daily becoming more anesthetizing and repressive, the fantastic is evasion as well as mobilization of despair. It gives back to man the meaning/sense [*sens*] of the sacred and the sacrilegious; it reestablishes for him, above all, his lost depth. For the myth of the automobile, the washing machine, and the vacuum cleaner, for the superficial myths of the new, modern world, Lovecraft substitutes the myth of Cthulhu. (page 180, author's translation)

The Italian critics de Turris and Fusco find in HPL a figure for our time:

[In Lovecraft] can be seen reproduced the essential division in which contemporary western civilization exists: a division . . . between the tendency toward materialism and the rebirth of deviant spirituality. . . . In the allegories of his narrative, in the events . . . of his life, are reflected the certainties and the contradictions, the dreams and the terrors, the preoccupations and the hopes that are ours. His revolt against his contemporary world, is the same revolt as that of many cultured men in our own time; the motivations are identical. (page 9, author's translation)

Modern American readers can make their own decisions on reading Lovecraft.

Selected Bibliography

FICTION BY H. P. LOVECRAFT

The following four items constitute the first editions of Lovecraft's more important fiction.

Occasional juvenilia, miscellaneous prose, and poetry are to be found in *Marginalia* (Sauk City, Wisc.: Arkham House, 1944), *Something About Cats* (Sauk City, Wisc.: Arkham House, 1949), and *Miscellaneous Writings* (Sauk City, Wisc.: Arkham House, 1995).

The Shunned House. Athol, Mass.: Recluse Press, 1928. (About 300 sets of sheets were printed, a few of which were bound at a later date. Only a few copies are known to survive. Would-be purchasers are warned that there is a counterfeit edition and are advised to

consult Lloyd W. Currey's *Science Fiction and Fantasy Authors.*
The Shadow over Innsmouth. Everett, Pa.: Visionary Publishing, 1936.
The Outsider and Others. Sauk City, Wisc.: Arkham House, 1939.
Beyond the Wall of Sleep. Sauk City, Wisc.: Arkham House, 1943.

Since the above first editions are rare books of considerable value, the following books are suggested as reasonably accessible reprints. It should be noted that there have been many other reprintings of Lovecraft's fiction in the United States and Great Britain and that the bibliographic situation is complex.

The Dunwich Horror and Others. Sauk City, Wisc.: Arkham House, 1984. (Contains "The Outsider," "The Colour out of Space," "The Call of Cthulhu," "The Whisperer in Darkness," "The Shadow over Innsmouth," "The Shadow out of Time," and other stories.)
At the Mountains of Madness and Other Novels. Sauk City, Wisc.: Arkham House, 1985. (Contains "At the Mountains of Madness," "The Dreams in the Witch House," "Through the Gates of the Silver Key," and other stories.)
Dagon and Other Macabre Tales. Sauk City, Wisc.: Arkham House, 1987. (Contains "Beyond the Wall of Sleep," "Facts Concerning the Late Arthur Jermyn and His Family," "From Beyond," "The Unnamable," "The Nameless City," "Herbert West—Reanimator," "The Lurking Fear," "In the Walls of Eryx," and "Supernatural Horror in Literature.")

OTHER WORKS BY H. P. LOVECRAFT

Selected Letters. Vols. 1, 2, 3 edited by August Derleth and Donald Wandrei; vols. 4 and 5 edited by August Derleth and James Turner. Sauk City, Wisc.: Arkham House. Vol. 1, 1911–1924; Vol. 2, 1925–1929; Vol. 3, 1929–1931; Vol. 4, 1932–1934; Vol. 5, 1934–1937.
Supernatural Horror in Literature. New York: Ben Abramson, 1945. (Reprinted by Dover Publications in 1973, with a new introduction by E. F. Bleiler).

CRITICAL AND BIOGRAPHICAL STUDIES

Burleson, Donald R. *H. P. Lovecraft: A Critical Study.* Westport, Conn.: Greenwood, 1983.
———. *H. P. Lovecraft. Disturbing the Universe.* Lexington: The University Press of Kentucky, 1990
———. "H. P. Lovecraft." In *Supernatural Fiction Writers.* Vol. 2. Edited by Everett F. Bleiler. New York: Scribners, 1985.
Cannon, Peter. *H. P. Lovecraft.* Boston: Twayne, 1989. (Probably the best introduction.)
De Camp, L. Sprague. *Lovecraft: A Biography.* Garden City, N.Y.: Doubleday, 1975.

de Turris, Gianfranco, and Sebastiano Fusco. *Howard Phillips Lovecraft*. Florence: La Nuova Italia 156, 1979.

Joshi, S. T. *H. P. Lovecraft: A Life*. West Warwick, R.I.: Necronomicon, 1996.

———. *H. P. Lovecraft and Lovecraft Criticism: An Annotated Bibliography*. Kent, Ohio: Kent State University Press, 1981.

Lévy, Maurice. *Lovecraft ou du fantastique*. Paris: Christian Bourgois, Dominique de Roux, 1972.

Lovecraft Studies. West Warwick, R.I.: Necronomicon. (A biannual publication, beginning Fall 1979.)

Oates, Joyce Carol. "Introduction." In *Tales of H. P. Lovecraft*. Hopewell, N.J.: Ecco, 1997.

Price, Robert M. *H. P. Lovecraft and the Cthulhu Mythos*. Mercer Island, Wash.: Starmont, 1990.

Schultz, David E., and S. T. Joshi, eds. *An Epicure of the Terrible: A Centennial Anthology of Essays in Honor of H. P. Lovecraft*. Rutherford, N.J.: Fairleigh Dickinson University Press, 1991.

Wilson, Edmund. "Tales of the Marvellous and the Ridiculous." In his *Classics and Commercials*. New York: Farrar, Straus, 1950.

—E. F. BLEILER

KATHERINE MACLEAN
(b. 1925)

KATHERINE ANNE MACLEAN was born in Glen Ridge, New Jersey, on 22 January 1925. In high school, she showed sufficient promise in biological science to be offered a grant to carry out a neurological experiment and a scholarship to study medicine at college. She declined both, claiming much later—when supplying information to Jay Klein for a biographical sketch published in *Analog* in 1995—that preparing for a career as a research scientist seemed to involve too much hard work for too little potential reward. Between 1944 and 1946, she did, however, work as a laboratory technician, including a stint in a food science laboratory. She then returned to college, obtaining a B.A. in economics from Barnard College in New York in 1950. By this time, she had already sold several science fiction stories. She was later to supplement her B.A. with an M.A. in psychology obtained from Goddard College in Plainfield, Vermont.

In 1951 MacLean married another novice science fiction writer, Charles Dye. She had already published five stories when he made his debut, and the first story bearing his name that appeared in one of the more prestigious magazines (*Galaxy*), "Syndrome Johnny" (1951), was actually written by her. She published at least two more stories under Dye's name, perhaps exercising the same sort of caution that had led her to sign her first submissions with her initials in case editors in the male-dominated genre might be disinclined to take them seriously. There is, however, no evidence that her gender ever counted against her; her earliest publications appeared under her full name. Her marriage to Dye was brief, ending in divorce in 1952, after which MacLean became an office manager for a food production company before returning to more demanding work as a hospital technician in 1954. The first phase of her career as a science fiction writer petered out when she obtained that post.

The emergent pattern of these events was to extend throughout MacLean's life. Although she was obviously talented, both intellectually and creatively, she never settled into any career or academic discipline. Klein's 1995 "Biolog" records her description of herself as a perennial "free spirit" who happily lived a Bohemian existence in New York's Greenwich Village during the 1950's and, presumably briefly, in San Francisco during the 1960's. Although she was eventually to build up a considerable total of science fiction stories, including one Nebula winner and several others of the highest quality, almost all her longer works were written in collaboration, and her career encompassed several years-long periods of nonproduction.

MacLean's second marriage, in 1956, was to David Mason, whose first writing credits in the science fiction field were obtained in the same year, although he did not begin to produce novels until some years after their divorce in 1962. Mason and MacLean had one son, Christopher, and it was while taking a break from paid employment to look after the infant that MacLean returned for a while to science fiction writing, although two of the longer stories that appeared under her name at this time were written in collaboration, one with Charles V. De Vet and one with Tom Condit.

Following her second divorce, MacLean taught in the English department at the University of Connecticut and, on an occasional basis, at the University of Maine, Orono. In the late 1960's, she resumed writing for the third time, achieving her greatest success in the science fiction field with the series of stories that concluded with the Nebula-winning "The Missing Man" (1971) and were subsequently integrated into the novel *Missing Man* (1975). It was during this phase of productivity that she produced her only mainstream novel, *The Man in the Bird Cage* (1971).

Although this third phase was interrupted by several gaps of from one to three years, it eventually extended until 1980. MacLean did not begin publishing science fiction again until 1994. The only explanation she offered Klein for this long lapse was that "she found sitting at a desk too wearisome," crediting her eventual return to literary work to the labor-saving assistance of a laptop computer. A description of the lifestyle she shared with her third husband, Carl West—offered in a blurb attached to "Isaac, My Son" (1994)—suggests that they had plenty to occupy their time, living "in a hand-built house on twenty acres of Maine woods, surrounded by beautiful, tiny, granite swimming pools," where they "buil[t] greenhouses, cut trees and move[d] the landscape around in wheelbarrows."

MacLean's first science fiction publication was "Defense Mechanism," in the October 1949 issue of *Astounding Science Fiction*. This was an early contribution to what would eventually become a veritable flood of *psi* stories (stories focusing on the supposed mental abilities of telepathy, psychokinesis, precognition, clairvoyance, and pyrolysis). Such stories dominated *Astounding* for several years in the early 1950's, encouraged by editor John W. Campbell, Jr.'s conviction, based on the research of J. B. Rhine at Duke University, that

humankind was on the brink of an existential breakthrough to superhumanity. The central character of MacLean's story is a writer whose peace is continually disturbed by a telepathic link to the mind of his baby son. The link is broken when the child's mind makes its first contact with a mentally ill adult and immediately subjects its psychic abilities to powerful repression. The last line of the story invites the reader to wonder whether such abilities might be commonplace but always subject to the same defensive blockage.

MacLean's interest in psi phenomena was sincere enough and serious enough to inspire the experiment described in her article "Communicado," which was cautiously offered as an item of fiction to the readers of *Science Fiction Quarterly* in 1952. Here she explains that having adopted the idea presented in "Defense Mechanism" as a working hypothesis, she set about trying to dismantle the mental block on her own psychic abilities, achieving some success in producing experiences similar to those described in J. W. Dunne's famous book on precognitive dreams, *An Experiment with Time* (1927).

It is not clear when "Communicado" was actually written. Although it refers to a story that is clearly "Defense Mechanism" as having been written "years ago," it also refers to one based on an actual dream that sounds very much like "Feedback"—which was published in the July 1951 issue of *Astounding*—as "having bounced at all markets" and notes that it "is in the process of being rewritten." It seems probable, therefore, that "Defense Mechanism" was written some while before it sold and that the difficulties MacLean encountered in publishing her dream-based psi story might have led her to produce enterprising but rather conventional science-based stories that she published in some profusion in 1950 and 1951.

In "And Be Merry" (1950; reprinted as "The Pyramid in the Desert"), a female scientist takes advantage of her husband's absence on a field trip to use herself as a guinea pig in an experiment designed to sidestep the body's aging mechanisms. When her husband returns and begins to piece together what has happened from various messages, he figures out that the experiment, though physically rigorous, has succeeded—but that the psychological side effects of the acquisition of a body resistant to aging have thrown her into a paranoid psychosis. The notion of an evolutionary leap gone ironically awry was to become a constant preoccupation of MacLean's science fiction, providing many of her plot twists.

"Incommunicado" (1950) is a rather confused but fascinating story that employs the notion of using the "slingshot effect" of descents into planetary gravity in facilitating space travel as a throwaway idea. (A moving object in space can boost its velocity if it passes a much larger object—usually a planet—closely enough to begin falling into its "gravity well," but not so closely as to collide with it.) The plot of the story sends the man in charge of calculating such slingshot trajectories in search of assistance, but his quest is temporarily thwarted by what appears to be an epidemic of unreason. A new cataloging system designed by an ingenious librarian has grown, without the conscious realization of the people using it, into a new kind of symbolic reasoning. John W. Campbell, Jr., was deeply interested in ideas of this kind too, having used his magazine to call attention to Alfred Korzybski's work on "General Semantics." He might have given MacLean the plot to write up, such donations being a common practice of his; the two certainly met so that Campbell could advise her on the craft of science fiction writing.

In "Contagion" (1950), the first story MacLean published outside the pages of *Astounding*, the explorers of a seemingly paradisial planet find that the survivors of an earlier expedition have been strangely transformed by an ingenious local infection. All the males have been turned into identical copies of one prototype, while all the females have been transformed according to a different model. The story tracks the psychological effects of the realization by the members of the second expedition that they will suffer the same fate.

Katherine MacLean in 1976. PHOTO BY JAY KAY KLEIN

"Syndrome Johnny" is also an account of a mysterious infection that transforms those victims who do not perish from its effects. "Syndrome Johnny" is a nickname formed by analogy with the infamous "Typhoid Mary," referring to a similarly elusive plague carrier. The story's protagonist figures out that Johnny is no myth and that his purpose is not destructive, even though his efforts are terribly costly in terms of lost lives. Those who survive the effects of the viruses he spreads are physically remade, each "disease" bringing them one step closer to superhumanity. Although the appropriate jargon was not available, what he is doing is, in effect, using virus vectors to achieve genetic science fiction transformations, something that today's genetic engineers regularly attempt in much more modest contexts.

"Syndrome Johnny" may have ended up in *Galaxy* because its wry ending—which questions the implications of the notion that evolution works through a struggle for existence in which the fittest survive—offended Campbell's sense of ideological propriety. "The Fittest" (1951) and "The Carnivore" (1953; written under the pseudonym G. A. Morris) also apply wry logical twists to the logic of natural selection, while the problematically assisted evolution of mankind also provided a central theme for the novella "The Diploids" (1953). None of these stories appeared in *Astounding*, although the last of them is solidly Campbellian in outlook. It eventually appeared in the pulp magazine *Thrilling Wonder Stories*, despite the fact that its format is by no means the kind of hectic action-adventure in which the pulps, then trembling on the brink of extinction, had long specialized.

It was probably Campbell who advised MacLean that the best way to embed such striking ideas in stories was to "hide" them away, producing them as answers to puzzles that her protagonists must solve. All her best early works are fitted to this puzzle template, and one of the classics of that story form is "Pictures Don't Lie" (1951), which became her most frequently anthologized story. Scientists on Earth pick up what appear to be speeded-up television broadcasts from an alien spaceship and respond with their own fast-forwarded broadcasts, eventually guiding the alien ship to what they hope will be a fruitful rendezvous. Unfortunately, their analysis of the situation has included an entirely understandable but ultimately disastrous assumption. Many ideas are, however, very difficult to accommodate to this kind of formula, and MacLean was already finding the method challenging. Her work quickly began to diversify into more relaxed formats, although some of the items that appeared in such downmarket outlets as *Worlds Beyond* and *Super Science Stories* were probably left over from an earlier phase of activity.

In "Feedback" a teacher trying to break a vicious circle of conformist thinking with subtle encouragements to political free thought becomes the victim of a McCarthy-esque witch-hunt. He is enabled by special psychological training to resist torture until he can be rescued by his coconspirators, who have become the secret custodians of progress.

MacLean's degree in psychology encouraged her to imagine ways in which the science might be applied in a quasi-technological fashion to the cause of evolutionary progress. "The Man Who Staked the Stars" (1952; written under the pseudonym Charles Dye) places techniques of psychological manipulation in the hands of benevolent social engineers intent on the rehabilitation of upmarket criminals, although the story fell to the very bottom of the market before appearing in *Planet Stories*. MacLean's most memorable story of this kind was, however, ingeniously sceptical. "The Snowball Effect" (1952) begins with an academic social scientist facing a demand from his employers that he demonstrate the practical value of his subject. He constructs a "field-experiment" that applies the manipulative psychology of chain letters to the constitution of organizations, which proves so successful that the Watashaw Sewing Circle is inadvertently given the means to recruit the entire population of the world. The story ends with the protagonists contemplating the chaos that will follow the inevitable collapse of the scheme at the point when no further recruits can be found.

By this time, the first flush of MacLean's career was beginning to lose impetus. "Gimmick" (1953), MacLean's last appearance in *Astounding* for five years, is a feeble story of an agent of Earth who allows himself to be captured by aliens and stalls their inquiries until he has infected them with chicken pox. "The Origin of the Species" (1953), which appeared in the anthology *Children of Wonder: 21 Remarkable and Fantastic Tales*, edited by William Tenn, combines the themes of "Feedback" and "Defense Mechanism" in a tale of a brain surgeon who must decide whether or not to "normalize" a gifted child. MacLean made an attempt to write a sword-and-sorcery novel in collaboration with Harry Harrison, but the project was not carried through to the intended conclusion. The completed text appeared as an abruptly concluded novella, "The Web of the Worlds" (1953), in the short-lived *Fantasy Fiction* and was reprinted in the British magazine *Science-Fantasy* in 1958 as

"The Web of the Norns." The robust action-adventure element was presumably Harrison's contribution, MacLean's principal contribution to the original design presumably being the suggestion that the berserkers of Norse legend might have been epileptics.

The second phase of MacLean's career produced only a handful of stories, all of them dealing with dramatic failures of comprehension associated with clashes of radically different cultures. The last to be published, "Interbalance" (1960), is a brief parable concerning the redundancy of old attitudes in a post-holocaust scenario, the others all juxtapose humans with problematic alien cultures. "These Truths"—which bears the copyright date 1958 in *The Trouble with You Earth People* (1980), although the standard reference books offer no clue as to where it might have appeared—and "Trouble with Treaties" (1959; in collaboration with Tom Condit) both feature smugly ingenious humans outwitting stupidly militaristic aliens according to a popular Campbellian formula, but neither appeared in *Astounding*. The two late 1950's stories that did sell to Campbell were more interesting descriptions of confrontations that are much more evenly balanced.

"Unhuman Sacrifice" (1958) belongs to a fascinating subset of science fiction stories in which human clergymen set out to preach the gospel to aliens who are ill-adapted to hear it. All stories of this kind tend toward ironic tragedy (famous examples include Ray Bradbury's "The Fire Balloons" [1951], James Blish's *A Case of Conscience* [1958], and Harry Harrison's "The Streets of Ashkelon" [1962]), but "Unhuman Sacrifice" offers a particularly sharp combination of irony and tragedy. Its satirization of the unwise evangelist is as brutally sharp as that in Harrison's story, but MacLean's has an extra dimension of interest through the manner in which the aliens have contrived to oppose and transcend the dictates of their own biology. This links the story to her early tales of costly evolution, ingeniously reinforcing her suspicion that nature's provision for progress through natural selection may be deeply defective.

"Unhuman Sacrifice" is a far more sophisticated story than its immediate predecessor in *Astounding*'s pages, "Second Game" (1958; written with Charles V. De Vet), but the latter was to gain further dimensions of complexity when it was twice revised. It was nearly doubled in length for its appearance as half of an Ace double, as *Cosmic Checkmate* (1962). The new version that appeared as a DAW paperback, under the original title, in 1981 was doubled in length yet again.

"Second Game" is the story of a secret agent sent to learn the weaknesses of a proud militaristic race inhabiting a single planet, which seems intent on going to war against humanity's Ten Thousand Worlds. (The backdrop had been used in several other stories by De Vet, who had been publishing science fiction since 1952.) Assisted by ingenious internal technology, the spy, an expert chess player, soon masters the chesslike game that qualifies the human-seeming aliens for high bureaucratic office. Exposed by his own success, he submits to capture but fails to persuade his captors to open any kind of diplomatic communication with the Ten Thousand Worlds. More worryingly, he discovers that the lone world has weapons that might allow it to win the war its inhabitants are determined to fight. Under torture he reveals the method by which his internal technology can report back his findings in the event of his death, thus nullifying humanity's last advantage. Having discovered his own limitations and those of his species, he realizes that the only way to defeat the aliens is to surrender to them so that their small numbers will be absorbed into the vastness of human culture.

Although the seed of "Second Game" must have been as trivial as that of the essentially similar "Gimmick," the novelette version added sufficient complication to make it a much more satisfactory story. By the time it had gone through two additional stages of recomplication, its complexity had become positively Byzantine. It seems probable that both revisions were actually carried out by De Vet, not just because they were done during periods of inactivity on MacLean's part but because the second expansion involved the injection of an awkward and implausible sexual relationship highly atypical of her work. The more interesting complications, however, are those associated with the relationship that develops between the hero and his captor, which produce a quasi-sociobiological analysis of the honor-bound culture of the latter. This analysis echoes those set out in "These Truths" and "Trouble with Treaties," strongly suggesting that MacLean must have had some input in the revision process.

Oddly enough, although some of the complications added to the final version of *Second Game* are clearly intended to address paradoxical gaps in the narrative logic of the original version, they actually serve only to multiply and amplify those gaps, blatantly failing to produce a satisfactory account of such questions as how the contradiction-strewn society could have attained its present level of technology and how the humans and the aliens can produce hybrid offspring.

MacLean contributed "The Other," a brief tale of psychological disorder, to the British *New Worlds* in 1966, which might be seen as a New Wave version of "Defense Mechanism," but she made a far more spectacular return to science fiction writing in "The Trouble with You Earth People" (1968), which is another story of spectacular incomprehension generated by different worldviews. Alien visitors whose entire culture, including their hard science, is based on an intimate interest in and a total absence of taboos regarding sexual intercourse try with all their might to use what they have patiently but somewhat mistakenly deduced from long study of Earth's television programs in establishing friendly relations with a punctilious and scrupulously inhibited diplomat. Their failure is inevitably hilarious as well as sharply ironic and tacitly tragic. Because it appeared in *Amazing Science Fiction*, a magazine that was

then enduring dire times, it attracted very little attention. The story is, however, one of the author's finest works and was selected ahead of "Unhuman Sacrifice" as the title story for her second story collection.

"Fear Hound" (1968; also known as "Rescue Squad") marked MacLean's second return to the Campbell stable, to the magazine now known as *Analog*. This was the first of three linked stories featuring the intellectually retarded but psychically gifted George Sanford, who is recruited to public service in an overcrowded future New York by his friend Ahmed, who protected him in the days when they were involved in a juvenile street gang. The city is under considerable strain, frequently exaggerated by the fact that large numbers of its people unconsciously pick up feelings of distress from one another, so that one person in dire straits can become a center of "infection," spreading panic, violence, and spates of accidental injury. Because George's defense mechanisms are slightly less effective than those of his more mentally able neighbors, he can bring his responses close enough to the threshold of consciousness to track these epidemics of distress to their source, thus serving as a "fear hound."

In "Rescue Squad for Ahmed" (1970), George needs ingenuity of a different sort to locate his friend, whose duties have taken him to the dangerous ground of Arab Jordan, a ghetto populated by Palestinian refugees. The story's main focus is the paranoia of the immigrant culture, which is displayed and explained with considerable sensitivity, helping to build a broader picture of a multicultural city hovering on the brink of a catastrophic social breakdown. The fact that Ahmed is looking for a missing computer scientist is mentioned in passing, but the reason why that particular missing person is sufficiently important to cause him to take such a desperate risk was not explained until the third element of the series, "The Missing Man," appeared in 1971. Here the disturbed and ingenuous scientist explains to the anarchically inclined street gang into whose hands he has fallen how to trigger a disaster in one of New York's new submarine suburbs. The method is remarkably subtle, but the complexity of the city's transportation systems provides an ideal context for panic to spread. The problem of saving the city returns Ahmed and George to their roots as they must persuade the severely disadvantaged gang members that their best hope for the future lies in the maintenance rather than the destruction of society.

Although "Fear Hound" may have been conceived as an independent novelette, the sequels were obviously written with the intention of building it into a novel, presumably after the completion of *The Man in the Bird Cage*. The fact that "The Missing Man" won the Nebula award for best novella of 1971 must have provided a further incentive, and it is rather surprising that the revisions expanding the three parts and converting their sequence into a relatively seamless whole took so long to complete. In the event, the novel version did not appear until 1975, further proof, if any were needed, of the difficulty MacLean always had in sustaining her efforts over considerable periods of time. The result did, however, fully justify the work put into it. The final version of *Missing Man* is extended according to a method very different from that employed to pad out *Second Game*, its narrative being more delicately analytical and more richly textured than anything else MacLean had previously written.

It seems that MacLean soon set about planning another science fiction novel, tentatively entitled *The Hills of Space*, about the formation of a new frontier in the asteroid belt. She had introduced the notion in "The Man Who Staked the Stars" and had developed the line of thought a little further in one of the last stories of her first phase, "Collision Orbit" (1954). She got as far as writing what was essentially a new version of "Collision Orbit," with a homesteading family at the focal point instead of a lone space cowboy, in "The Gambling Hell and the Sinful Girl" (1975). She was still prepared to advertise the novel as a work in progress when she re-

printed the latter story in *The Trouble with You Earth People*, but it never appeared.

The two science fiction stories MacLean published in between "The Missing Man" and "The Gambling Hell and the Sinful Girl" were trivial. "Brain Wipe" (1973), which appeared in *Frontiers 2: The New Mind: Original Science Fiction*, edited by Roger Elwood, is a new take on the theme of "The Origin of the Species." "Small War" (1973), in *Saving Worlds: A Collection of Original Science Fiction Stories*, edited by Elwood and Virginia Kidd, is a quasi-journalistic piece in which Greenpeace-like organizations are given leave to make formal declarations of war against their targets. The same year saw publication of a brief comic fantasy written in collaboration with Mary Kornbluth, "Chicken Soup" (1973). After the appearance of "The Gambling Hell and the Sinful Girl," however, MacLean lapsed into silence again. When she took up her pen again, it was to produce work of a very different kind; the two stories she published in 1978 are extremely downbeat. "Night Rise," in *Cassandra Rising*, edited by Alice Laurance, is about the emergence of a new cult of Kali dedicated to providing gentle assistance for modern men who cannot quite raise to consciousness their determination to die. "Canary Bird," in *Chrysalis 2*, edited by Roy Torgeson, is a psychological case study of an extremely depressed and distressed man who is convinced that his delusions are prophetic.

The dark mood of these stories also extends into a "young adult" novel, *Dark Wing* (1979), which MacLean wrote in collaboration with Carl West, who became her third husband. Like MacLean, West had never settled on any fixed career after attending the School of Fine Arts in Portland, Maine, and the two continued to travel extensively and to dabble in various odd jobs when they set up a permanent home. *Dark Wing* is a rambling, dystopian fantasy of a kind that had been in vogue twenty-five years before, featuring the tribulations of a teenage boy in an overcrowded future society in which the practice of medicine is illegal. Frustrated in his ambition to emigrate to a colony world, Travis Gordon discovers a wrecked ambulance and salvages a paramedical kit therefrom. He quickly cultivates sufficient expertise to become a "drug pusher" but falls into the hands of a ruthless exploiter, eventually being forced to change his identity. He hides from his pursuers by enrolling as a police cadet, briefly serving with the Deathwatch, whose members attempt to reconcile citizens to their mortality with the aid of the Egyptian and Tibetan Books of the Dead. Their activities seem ill-fitted to a world in which all sickness is conventionally considered to be the psychosomatic result of moral cowardice, and Travis eventually decides that he must seek his fate elsewhere—which he is enabled to do when a friend from a colony world conveniently dies, leaving behind a ticket to the stars.

As with most of its models, it is not easy to believe that the state of affairs described in *Dark Wing* could ever have come into being or that it could ever have been sustained. Its ramshackle structure suggests that West may have given an unsatisfactory draft to MacLean so that she could perform sufficient narrative surgery to make it saleable, but she was only able to contrive a minimally adequate patchwork. As is usual with her work, however, it does embody some intriguing ideas and the cut-price enlightenment that the authors are able to supply to their young hero—albeit rather implausibly—is effective enough within the context of a novel aimed at the teenage market.

MacLean published two more items before her longest period of silence. "The Olmec Football Player" (1980) is a brief conceit extrapolating the observation that the most puzzling Olmec artifacts could be mistaken for images of a black man wearing a football helmet. "An Alien Sort of War" (1980), an article published in *The Future at War*, vol 3, *Orion's Sword*, edited by Reginald Bretnor, is equally quirky but rather more enterprising. It summarizes and extrapolates one of the key threads of MacLean's work: her quasi-sociobiological speculations about the conceivable influences of natural selection on human and alien cultures and the consequent potential for drastic failures of understanding:

The delights of practice battle, in football, fencing or chess, the hot rousing of energy and strength when angry, and our cool alertness of controlled fear when speeding and dodging other cars—these are all pleasures based on a billion years of ancestors who killed enemies or fled from them, whose victories and escapes were helped by that extra surge of energy. . . .

The bloody pawprints of ancestral winners are still in our souls, delighting in the threat of death. Tempted into war, battle, or revenge we are not seeking profit or benefit, we are trying to re-enact our clawed, fanged, glittering past. . . . In this selection all animals must be the same, even on other planets.

But there is strangeness in the arena where the males fight for the right to breed. Each species has its special combat style of male pitted against male. Many are very strange.

The article goes on to suggest a few scenarios in which species equipped with different physiological means of fighting among themselves for females might redeploy these resources in war against humans, concluding with one in which a pheromonal support system is put to ironically devastating use. In the blurb accompanying the article, the editor records that the author was about to set off for the University of Vera Cruz in Mexico in the expectation of studying for a doctorate in nutrition, but if MacLean ever began that course of study, she does not seem to have completed it.

Although MacLean and Carl West published no further science fiction stories between 1981 and 1993, they did not abandon their writing. When Peter Crowther solicited from MacLean a story for his third anthology of superstition-based fantasies, *Blue Motel* (1994), she supplied "Isaac, My Son," written by West—with some input from herself and her son, Christopher Mason—and revealed that she and West were both writing solo novels as well as collaborating on a second science fiction project. "Planet Virt" (1994), in the third issue of Bryan Cholfin's small press magazine *Crank*, is a vignette about planetary explorers who have been so intensively trained in virtual reality that they think that their first real mission is merely another game. However, "The Kidnapping of Baroness 5" (1995), which marked MacLean's third return to the pages of her primary marketplace, long after John Campbell's death, reads as if it might well be an excerpt from a novel-in-progress.

"The Kidnapping of Baroness 5" is set on a future Earth in which a catastrophic inversion of the magnetic field has been followed by a dramatic shortening of the human life span, with the result that the transmission of the cultural heritage has become direly problematic. A biotechnologist from a former space colony is masquerading as a witch in order to try out exotic methods of repairing the situation—an imposture that inevitably causes diplomatic difficulties. The eponymous baroness is a genetically engineered pig capable of producing human young. The story was followed in the pages of *Analog* by "Kiss Me" (1997), a deftly ingenious exercise in Fortean whimsy that adds one more item to the long series of jokey variations on the theme of the princess and the frog.

These two stories demonstrate that even after fifty years of science fiction writing, MacLean's intelligence and wit remained as quirky and as keen as ever. Seen as a whole, however, her uneven productivity inevitably gives the impression of unfulfilled potential. Had she only been able to stick to her work more assiduously, she might have achieved so much more. Yet had her mind been more disciplined, the work she did might have been less interesting.

Although the opening phase of MacLean's career lasted a mere five years, it exhibited an enviable anticipatory flair. "Syndrome Johnny" and "The Diploids" are among the earliest science fiction stories of genetic engineering, the former anticipating, albeit vaguely, a key technique and the latter envisioning, albeit luridly, the commercial context that might stimulate a demand for early products of genetic tinkering. The psychological pressures associated with chain letters were indeed adapted to organizational design in what came to be known as "pyramid selling" operations, even if they did not have such apocalyptic consequences as those trailed in "The Snowball Effect." These stories, together with the best items from her later bursts of productivity, are sufficient to establish that Katherine MacLean remains one of the most interesting imaginative writers of her generation.

Selected Bibliography

WORKS OF KATHERINE MACLEAN

Cosmic Checkmate, (with Charles V. De Vet. (Bound with *King of the Fourth Planet* by Robert Moore Williams.) New York: Ace, 1962. Revised and expanded as *Second Game*, New York, DAW, 1981.
The Diploids and Other Flights of Fancy. New York: Avon, 1962. (Short stories.)
The Man in the Bird Cage. New York: Ace, 1971.
Missing Man. New York: Berkley, 1975.
Dark Wing, with Carl West. New York: Atheneum, 1979.
The Trouble with You Earth People. Virginia Beach, Va.: Donning, 1980. (Short stories.)

CRITICAL AND BIOGRAPHICAL STUDIES

Klein, Jay. "Biolog (Katherine MacLean)." *Analog* 115 (January 1995): 215, 245.

—BRIAN STABLEFORD

RICHARD MATHESON

(b. 1926)

SCIENCE FICTION IS a genre that has always had two elements, two extremes: the classical and the romantic. The classical is rational, extrapolative, plausible, and scientific. The romantic is mysterious, inexplicable, gothic, and menacing; and its gaze is often directed inward, into the depths of the mind. The former is often called "hard" science fiction, and the latter tends to shade over into fantasy and the supernatural. Some critics feel that science fiction needs a judicious blend of both elements to maintain its vigor, but there are fine writers who have worked at both extremes.

At the romantic extreme few writers are more exemplary than Richard Matheson. Yet, though he is known to most readers of science fiction, only two of his ten novels and three of his six short story collections can be described as indubitably science fiction, and purists may wish to cut the list even further.

Richard Burton Matheson was born in Allendale, New Jersey, on 20 February 1926. He served in World War II, then moved to California in the early 1950's. He had already published his first story, "Born of Man and Woman," a short and grisly piece that appeared in *Magazine of Fantasy and Science Fiction* in 1950. It clearly signaled the direction in which Matheson was going to develop as a writer—a direction of thinly rationalized horror and menace, shot through with images of persecution. The story is told in a guttural pidgin, through which halting dialect the appalled reader is able to trace the monstrous protagonist's development from a natural,

childish affection to revulsion, pain, and, finally, the desire to hurt and maim. This was also the title story of Matheson's first collection, *Born of Man and Woman* (1954), which was reissued, minus four of the stories, as *Third from the Sun* (1955).

The years 1950 to 1956 were Matheson's most productive as far as writing books and stories went. Since that time he has been primarily a writer for films and television, although further novels and stories have appeared sporadically.

Although Matheson's early stories created a small stir, it was with his first science fiction novel, *I Am Legend* (1954), that his reputation in science fiction circles was finally established. (This novel was reissued in 1971 under the title *The Omega Man: I Am Legend*, as a tie-in with the motion picture *The Omega Man*, which was loosely based on the novel.)

The novel tells of the solitary human left alive in Los Angeles, and possibly the world, in 1976; he finds himself surrounded by a society of vampires. Summarized so baldly, the book sounds like the purest of supernatural fantasies, but it is far from that. The narrator, Robert Neville, is a recognizably contemporary Californian who retains his reasoning powers even though he has been driven half-mad by the horror of his situation, the deaths of his daughter and wife, and by the return of his wife to the family home as a vampiric corpse—he is compelled to drive a stake through her. It all started with a nuclear war, which was followed by heavy dust storms and a mysterious plague. It is this plague that has turned the living into vampires and has even given some of the dead the power to walk again.

The setting is commonplace and suburban. Neville has turned his home into a quasi fortress to protect it from the depredations of a group of vampires led by his one-time friend and next-door neighbor, Ben Cortman. During the evening Neville keeps himself locked up. During the day (when, it seems, vampires become comatose) he obsessively moves around the neighborhood, driving stakes into the bodies—not necessarily the hearts—of all the sleeping vampires he can find—a task that seems pointless and horrible to the reader, though it never occurs to Neville in his vigilante mania that he will need 200 million stakes before he has cleaned up America.

The science fiction element of the story emerges a third of the way through. Neville's intellect is at first submerged in horror, but (as a kind of representative twentieth-century man) he is too stubborn to submit to a purely supernatural explanation for what has happened, as if it were all some black fantasy let loose from medieval Transylvania. He starts to ask questions, and after a while the answers begin to come. Why can vampires not bear sunlight? Why are they allergic to garlic? Why is Neville immune to the vampiric plague? Why do vampires have to be killed by driving stakes into their bodies?

The answers are ingeniously worked out, though they would hardly pass muster by the standards of hard science fiction. The vampire plague is caused by anaerobic bacteria. Stakes through the body let in air, which kills them; sunlight also kills them; and so on. In fact, these answers do not bear thinking about for more than a moment. For example, if sunlight can kill the vampiric bacteria through the skin, why cannot air? And the most difficult question of all, that of how the bacteria can restore a quasi life to dead victims of the plague, is pretty well evaded.

But this is romantic science fiction, in which a veneer of rational explanation is present only so as to maintain a surface plausibility, a device to generate what Samuel Taylor Coleridge called "the willing suspension of disbelief" in the reader. The life and vigor of this lurid novel come from its obsessive, paranoid imagery. Readers remember it not because of the anaerobic bacteria, but because of the white-faced, capering ghouls; its desolate images of a Los Angeles completely depopulated by day and dozing in the sunshine; the obscene sexual invitations with which the leering vampire women taunt the necessarily celibate Neville; and the recurrent figure of the portly, blood-crazed Ben Cortman (in physical appearance like a nightmarish Oliver Hardy) every night shouting his monotonous invitation, "Come out, Neville."

I Am Legend is the story of a man brutalized by horrible stress, heroic in his truculent refusal to surrender to his own loneliness, horrific in his single-minded hatred. Yet these, after all, are not true vampires; they are transformed human beings learning to live with a terrible disease. The strongest portion of the book is the last third. Neville is briefly allowed to believe that he has found another survivor, a woman, but we learn that she too is a vampire, disguised with cosmetics so as to appear normal. This suddenly changes the perspective—for us and for Neville. Although she is horribly altered by the disease, we are able to see her as a woman with feelings. Neville's brutality, which previously we have been inclined to accept as a natural, Darwinian struggle for survival, seems retrospectively savage and unthinking. Mankind is not dead; it is merely transformed.

But the book remains resolutely downbeat to the end. The new, primitive vampire society has to be tough to survive; the living vampires have no place for the dead ones, and they also have no place for Neville. Captured and about to be executed, he commits suicide. Among future generations of vampires, he will be remembered as a dark legend of supernatural savagery—a successfully ironic twist that emerges in the last line of the story.

The early and mid-1950's in America were the period of the cold war. The Communist scare was at its height. Religious revivalism

Richard Matheson © 1998 M. C. VALADA

was growing daily. A puzzled, unhappy people, disappointed by the failure of a Brave New World to appear in the decade following the war, was ready to seek scapegoats. The FBI was issuing statements suggesting that the worst aspect of the Communist menace was that our enemies might, on the outside, look and act just like us. Thus, people felt threatened and yet could not easily find a focus for this sense of threat.

It is surely not just an accident of history that the early and mid-1950's were the heyday of paranoid science fiction: the monster movies, the stories (such as Robert A. Heinlein's 1951 novel *The Puppet Masters*) of aliens taking over human bodies, and, par excellence, Matheson's tales. What all of these works have in common is a sense of menace erupting out of the domestic and the everyday—a peculiarly modern form of gothic. No longer were ancient castles or windswept cliff houses a necessary ingredient of horror. In the film *Them!* (1954), giant ants occupy storm drains beneath Los Angeles; in *Invasion of the Body Snatchers* (1956), Don Siegel's classic film, the people of a very ordinary California town are taken over by aliens, and even one's wife or one's mother might suddenly become emotionless, zombielike, chilling. It all recalls W. H. Auden's lines:

> The glacier knocks in the cupboard,
> The desert sighs in the bed,
> And the crack in the tea-cup opens
> A lane to the land of the dead.
>   ("As I Walked Out One Evening," 1940)

In the mid-1950's, especially, it sometimes seemed as if, at the edge of the everyday, menace and despair and cosmic injustice were lurking, ready to irrupt.

499

This paranoid theme was particularly strong in the cinema, and it is not at all surprising that Matheson moved quickly from the written word to film. The breakthrough came with his second science fiction novel, *The Shrinking Man* (1956). When a film company expressed interest in filming it, Matheson insisted that he be allowed to write the screenplay. He succeeded in convincing the company, and the result was a small-scale classic, *The Incredible Shrinking Man* (1957).

The Shrinking Man is perhaps Matheson's strongest work, though once again the scientific rationale is extremely thin. Exposed to insecticide, and later to radiation, Scott Carey begins to shrink at the rate of a seventh of an inch per day. (Rather absurdly the shrinkage continues at this rate even when Carey is tiny, though one would expect the shrinking on each successive day to be less, in proportion to his size at the beginning of that day—but no, it is inexorably one-seventh of an inch every time.) We are not given an explanation for this phenomenon until halfway through the book, and then it is perfunctory: "You have a negative nitrogen balance, Mr. Carey. Your body is throwing off more nitrogen than it is retaining. Since nitrogen is one of the major building blocks of the body, consequently, we have shrinkage."

This rationale is ludicrous but unimportant. Indeed, it was clever of Matheson to home in on two of the strongest environmental fears—pollution by chemicals and by radiation—as the cause. Thus the paranoia is reinforced in the very mechanism of the shrinkage.

The story proper opens in a nightmare landscape; a man is being threatened by a giant spider, which he eludes. In one of the lurching changes of perspective that are Matheson's specialty, we find that the spider is actually of normal size and the landscape is the cellar of a small, commonplace house; it is the man who is tiny. The force of the story lies in its persistent linking of the prosaic (oil burners, garden hoses, and needles and thread) with the surreal. The cellar remains the center of the story, with the spider as an ever-present menace, but flashbacks recount the story up to date. (Matheson regards the film version as weakened because the producers insisted on telling the story chronologically—there are no flashbacks.)

Carey's psychology is well established. Like Neville in *I Am Legend*, he oscillates through bravery, self-pity, and obsessiveness. Both books have as a central image a burning sexual desire in their heroes that can find no possible object in the outside world to respond to it. As Carey shrinks further and further, his sexuality is whittled down to a hopeless voyeurism, apart from one rather sentimentally conceived liaison with a circus midget.

Both books are miniature *Odysseys*, and in both the end of the voyage is death. Indeed, Matheson, who in many ways follows genre formulas closely, shows a commendable courage with his downbeat endings, which run quite counter to the conventional market demand for last-minute reprieve and happiness. Oddly, this is truer of the film than of the book. In the film Carey simply shrinks to nothing as the wind plays through autumn leaves. In the book Matheson borrows a cliché from Ray Cummings' old pulp melodramas of miniaturization (*The Girl in the Golden Atom* and *Beyond the Vanishing Point*, for example), and has Carey shrink into a microscopic subuniverse where he may survive. The film's ending is, curiously, more satisfying than the book's.

The Shrinking Man is a remarkable novel, taut and pitiless. It does not let either the hero or the reader off the hook at any stage. Carey's progressive excommunication from family ties and other human affection is vividly rendered, his harassed wife and uncomprehending daughter becoming more monstrous (from our diminishing perspective) as the story goes on. The book could be read as a prolonged and acid metaphor of human alienation. Yet Carey in the cellar, like the storm-blasted King Lear on Shakespeare's heath, becomes in one sense more—not less—of a man, as all the commonplace trappings of life are swept away and all illusion is gone, leaving nothing but a vulnerable nakedness and a dogged refusal to give up. Toward the end come lines that quoted separately may sound bathetic but that in context are justified: "He bellowed at the universe, 'I've fought a good fight!' And under his breath he added, 'God damn it to hell!'"

Matheson is no Shakespeare, and his prose style might well suffer from even less elevated comparisons. But as much as with any science fiction writer—and more than with most—his work sticks tenaciously in the mind with its lurid images of ordinary men standing their ground in a hostile universe. Matheson does not write like a gentleman, and his heroes seldom behave like gentlemen. Yet his raw, pulp-style sagas have affected perhaps two generations of readers more powerfully than science fiction of a more decorous kind.

Matheson's writing has, in at least one instance, become comparatively decorous—in the only other novel he wrote that could plausibly be described as science fiction. *Bid Time Return* (1975), published some twenty years after his first two science fiction successes, is a blend of the time-travel story and the romantic love story.

The middle-aged hero has a tumor in a lobe of the brain—the temporal lobe, appropriately enough, since "temporal" means related to time as well as related to the temples. Leaving his relatives (he is unmarried), he goes off to spend his last months alone, and almost immediately settles in a baroque, nineteenth-century hotel outside San Diego. There he conceives an irrational, romantic love for a long-dead actress who once stayed at the hotel, and by sheer willpower (rather as in the 1970 novel by Jack Finney, *Time and Again*) manages to abandon his twentieth-century time imprinting and travel back to meet the woman in 1896. Although the mechanism has more to do with fantasy than with science fiction, it is actually worked out in more satisfying detail than the rationalizations of his first two science fiction novels.

Matheson accepts a view of time that sees it as in one sense an all-present continuum. Time—as in Henri Bergson's theory, though he does not mention Bergson—is entirely derived from subjective experience. We perceive the present as a separate time only because our minds otherwise could not cope. We are trapped in the present only because our minds have been imprinted to believe that there is no way out. This aspect of the novel is well achieved. The hero is the typical Matheson man: single-minded, driven, obsessed. The love affair, though, is difficult to accept because one cannot imagine a woman falling in love with such a wild-eyed and apparently uncivilized fanatic as the hero appears to be when he arrives in 1896. One feels that Matheson was himself uneasy at having to combine his savage theme of man under stress with the gentler conventions of a love story, and at too many moments the novel sinks into sentimentality. But the time paradoxes are well worked out, the 1890's ambience is well researched, and *Bid Time Return* ends in a satisfying manner typical of Matheson: the heroine dies of heartbreak, and the hero, half-destroyed by sorrow, succumbs to his tumor. (He has been inadvertently propelled back to the present on finding a modern coin in the lining of his rented frock coat, thus reestablishing his twentieth-century time imprinting.)

It sometimes seems as if Matheson is spearheading a literary revolt aimed at reinstating the sad ending. The story has many twists, not summarized above, and the reader will probably find much to enjoy—or why else would the book have been awarded the World Fantasy Award for best novel in 1975? *Bid Time Return* was successfully filmed in 1980 by Jeannot Szwarc as *Somewhere in Time*; Matheson wrote the screenplay.

Several of Matheson's early novels were thrillers, and one was a war novel. The remainder of his work in novel form is supernatural fantasy that contains occasional quasi-scientific discussions. There is one technological device: the radiation emitter in *Hell House* (1971), which is intended to neutralize the energy powering the ghostly emanations that sadistically haunt the house of the title. The book is a lively melodrama, with a good deal of psychological talk about repression and compensation, and a lot of blood and sex. Less interesting is *A Stir of Echoes* (1958), an earlier and shorter novel. There is a scientific rationale here also, but it is so thin that the book would more properly be seen as supernatural fantasy. It tells of a man who, under hypnosis, develops powers of clairvoyance and telepathy, sees a ghost, and solves a murder in the suburbs of Los Angeles. Matheson's *What Dreams May Come* (1978), dealing with life and love after death, is told by the astral body of a man killed in a car accident. A film version was released in 1998.

In the sphere of short fiction, also, Matheson's work, which was strongly science fictional to begin with, moved, as the 1950's progressed, toward pure fantasy and horror. Thus, of his six collections only the first three are primarily science fiction. These are *Born of Man and Woman* (1954), *The Shores of Space* (1957), and *Shock!* (1961). (The last title was reissued as *Shock I* in 1979.) The three later collections are *Shock II* (1964), *Shock III* (1966), and *Shock Waves* (1970).

Several of Matheson's stories later became the bases for film and television scripts. (*I Am Legend* was filmed twice—though not with Matheson scripts, and neither time with great success—as *The Last Man on Earth* [1964] and *The Omega Man* [1971]. *Hell House* was filmed as *The Legend of Hell House* [1973] and did have a Matheson screenplay.) After his first film script, *The Incredible Shrinking Man*, most of his early commissions for the screen were episodes in the television science fiction and fantasy series *The Twilight Zone*. During the five years of the series (1959–1964), fifteen episodes by Matheson were filmed. One of these was an adaptation of what was probably his finest short story, "Steel" (1956), a succinct, hard-bitten, and moving story set in a near future in which professional boxing is performed by robots. Two failing entrepreneurs on the small-fight circuit are stuck with a rusting robot that finally breaks down completely just before a fight; one of its managers takes the robot's place, disguised, and receives a bloody pounding. It is as memorable a parable of the take-over of

human jobs by machinery as has ever been written. (Matheson also wrote scripts for *Star Trek* and, later, for *Night Gallery* and *Kolchak: The Night Stalker.*)

Another interesting story is "Mother by Protest" (1953), which was reprinted in *The Shores of Space* as "Trespass." In this story a woman is impregnated by a Martian seed, beamed into her with a flash of white light, while her husband is away. He is unable to believe that she has not been unfaithful, and as the pregnancy continues, it becomes clear that the fetus is, in human terms, abnormal; finally it telepathically dominates its mother. The theme is archetypal Matheson—the irruption of unnaturalness into a peaceful and affectionate family situation, colored by the feeling of cosmic injustice and persecution that pervades so much of his work. Perhaps because of the success of the film *Rosemary's Baby* (1968) a television company picked up the story for a made-for-television feature film, scripted by Matheson: *The Stranger Within* (1974).

There are several recurrent themes in Matheson's fiction, especially his short stories, that are more usually associated with horror stories than with science fiction. One is the repeated image of the woman as sexual predator. This is especially notable in *Hell House*, where both of the women, though previously decent, become sexually obscene and demanding; neither of the men is so affected. In *The Shrinking Man*, as Scott Carey shrinks, his wife comes to seem monstrous, as does the pubescent baby-sitter who has an important role in the book (though not in the film). The capering vampire women of *I Am Legend* are peculiarly unpleasant, for here the equation of sex, death, and the stink of corruption, which is latent in several stories, is overt. The same theme appears in the story "Lover When You're Near Me" (1952), in which a bovine alien woman uses psi powers and gifts of rotting vegetation to seduce, sexually persecute, and finally madden a solitary human colonist on another planet. Such imagery also pops up occasionally in the series of loose Edgar Allan Poe adaptations for the screen, scripted by Matheson and directed by Roger Corman, which attracted a cult following in the 1960's. These include *The House of Usher* (1960), *The Pit and the Pendulum* (1961), and *Tales of Terror* (1962).

Matheson's most notable subject, as already stated, is paranoia. This is as evident in the short fiction and the screenplays as it is in the novels. The stories "Shipshape Home" (1952), "Mad House" (1953), and "Disappearing Act" (1953) each revolve around powerful metaphors of persecution that could easily be used as case studies in paranoid delusion. The stories deal, respectively, with an apartment building that is really a disguised spaceship being used by aliens for kidnapping humans (no reason is given), a house whose furniture becomes animated and destroys its neurotic occupant, and a man whose social contacts, and then family, disappear one by one, leaving nobody but the narrator aware that they ever existed.

These are all images of very radical alienation from humanity, and this theme of course is the source of the strength of Matheson's two science fiction novels; but it also lends credence to the accusation that science fiction readers are typically maladjusted and see themselves as lone bastions of strength, always misunderstood, in a hostile world. This charge was once leveled enthusiastically by the American author-mathematician Martin Gardner. But perhaps it is unfair to ask Matheson, who seeks primarily to entertain, to bear the burden of this sort of humorless sociological theorizing.

Matheson's screenplays, too, are at their strongest when dealing with images of persecution. An early screenplay, scripted with his fellow science fiction writer and friend, the late Charles Beaumont, was *Burn, Witch, Burn* (1961), an adaptation of Fritz Leiber's splendid 1943 novel *Conjure Wife*. The plot of *Conjure Wife* relies heavily on the idea of women as repositories of dangerous power and as the center of antimale conspiracies. Matheson's most successful screenplay was for the made-for-television film *Duel* (1971), directed by Steven Spielberg. Its central image of an innocent driver whose car is pursued and repeatedly attacked by a mysteriously malevolent truck, whose driver is never seen, is the archetype of the menace-from-nowhere story, beautifully realized. Another screenplay was for the film *Dying Room Only* (1973), also made for television, in which a woman's husband disappears but no one will believe her. Matheson also adapted Ray Bradbury's *The Martian Chronicles* into a three-part television "miniseries" (1980), to mixed critical reception.

Matheson is a vigorous, slightly repetitive fantasist, whose work depends on locating the images of inner terror and uncertainty that abound at the romantic end of the science fiction spectrum and projecting them unusually clearly and nakedly. His style is colorful and direct, but it suffers occasionally from the strained and rather prosy metaphors that appear throughout his work. An example is the unfortunate penultimate sentence of *I Am Legend*: "A new terror born in death, a new superstition entering the unassailable fortress of forever." (If the fortress is unassailable, how did the superstition get in?)

Selected Bibliography

SCIENCE FICTION AND FANTASY WORKS OF RICHARD MATHESON

Born of Man and Woman. Philadelphia: Chamberlain, 1954. (Also published in abridged version as *Third from the Sun.* New York: Bantam Books, 1955.)

I Am Legend. New York: Fawcett Gold Medal, 1954. (Also published as *The Omega Man: I Am Legend.* New York: Berkley Medallion, 1971. This version is permanently out of print.)

The Shrinking Man. New York: Gold Medal, 1956.

The Shores of Space. New York: Bantam Books, 1957.

A Stir of Echoes. Philadelphia: Lippincott, 1958.

Shock! New York: Dell, 1961. (Also published as *Shock I.* New York: Berkley Medallion, 1979.)

Shock II. New York: Dell, 1964.

Shock III. New York: Dell, 1966.

Shock Waves. New York: Dell, 1970.

Hell House. New York: Viking Press, 1971.

Bid Time Return. New York: Viking Press, 1975. Reprinted as *Somewhere in Time.* New York: Ballantine Books, 1980.

What Dreams May Come. New York: G. P. Putnam's Sons, 1978.

7 Steps to Midnight. New York: Forge, 1993.

Earthbound. New York: TOR, 1994.

Shadow on the Sun. New York: Berkley, 1994.

Now You See It. . . . New York: TOR, 1995.

CRITICAL AND BIOGRAPHICAL STUDIES

Dziemianowicz, Stefan. "Horror Begins at Home: Richard Matheson's Fear of the Familiar." *Studies in Weird Fiction*, no. 14 (1994): 29–36.

Goldman, Stephen H. "I Am Legend." In *Survey of Science Fiction Literature.* Vol. 2. Edited by Frank N. Magill. Englewood Cliffs, N. J.: Salem Press, 1979: pages 986–990.

"Interview: Richard Christian Matheson." *Twilight Zone*, 6 (1986): 22–25, 94.

Krulik, Ted. "Reaching for Immortality: Two Novels of Richard Matheson." In *Critical Encounters II.* Edited by Tom Staicar. New York: Ungar, 1982.

Proulx, Kevin. *Fear to the World: Eleven Voices in a Chorus of Horror.* Mercer Island, Wash.: Starmont, 1992.

Rathbun, Mark, and Graeme Flanagan. *Richard Matheson: He Is Legend, An Illustrated Bio-Bibliography.* Chico, Calif.: Rathbun, 1984.

Sammon, Paul M. "Richard Matheson: Master of Fantasy." *Fangoria*, nos. 2, 3 (1979). (Interview of Matheson, with comments and complete guide to his film and television scripts.)

"TZ Interview: Richard Matheson." *Twilight Zone*, 3 (1983): 40–41.

Wiater, Stanley. "Richard Matheson." In his *Dark Dreamers: Conversations with the Masters of Horror.* New York: Avon, 1990.

—PETER NICHOLLS

JUDITH MERRIL
(1923–1997)

JUDITH MERRIL WAS born in New York City in 1923, the daughter of a prominent Zionist and a suffragette. Her name was originally Juliet Grossman, but she preferred the forename Judith and eventually changed her name to Merril (which was the forename of her first daughter). She was married during World War II and had a daughter, then was divorced in 1946. The following year, as Judith Zissman, she became associated with science fiction fan circles in New York. These included the Futurians and the Hydra Club. After a number of jobs, including waitress and file clerk, she became an editor at Bantam Books, under the direction of Ian Ballantine, in 1948. Also in that year she had her first story published ("That Only a Mother," which appeared in *Astounding Science-Fiction* for June) and she married fellow Futurian Frederik Pohl. They had a daughter, Ann, who was born in 1950.

Although the marriage was short-lived— they were divorced by the middle of 1951— these two and a half years were Merril's most productive in writing terms: she wrote one solo novel, two collaborative novels with C. M. Kornbluth, and several short stories. That period also saw publication of the first anthology she edited, *Shot in the Dark* (so titled "because that's the way Bantam felt about it," according to Merril), in 1950. For the rest of the 1950's, she produced quite a number of stories, including two under the pseudonym of Rose Sharon because they were rather outspoken about sex for those days, and she feared censure. Her second solo novel,

The Tomorrow People, appeared in 1960, but she has written little fiction after that. During the 1960's Merril concentrated on editing and book reviewing. She lived in England in 1966–1967 and soon afterward moved to Toronto, Canada, where she lived the rest of her life.

The fact that Merril's output of science fiction was relatively small—only two solo novels, two collaborative novels, and fewer than thirty stories—makes her work difficult to assess, all the more so because the bulk of it was written in a very short period at the beginning of the 1950's. Since she had long wanted to be a writer and her first published story is a reasonably polished piece of work accepted by the most prestigious science fiction magazine of the day, one must presume that she had developed her skills in unpublished fiction. A certain amount of increased complexity and sophistication can be detected in her stories from the 1950's, culminating in the excessive complexity of *The Tomorrow People*. Her meager output after that makes it impossible to draw any dependable conclusions regarding her further evolution as a writer.

The most notable feature of almost all of Merril's fiction is its high emotional level. Although Ray Bradbury had begun to use emotion to a similar degree in his stories some six years earlier, such a use was very unusual in science fiction during the 1940's and 1950's. From her very first sale Merril had a preference for writing at a perpetual emotional screech, for tugging at the reader's heart on each page. In that first story, "That Only a Mother," it is a mother's love for her expected baby and her fear that radiation may have damaged it that provide the emotional fuel. The mother's relief and joy that her baby is not only normal but also extraordinarily intelligent and advanced for its age are finally shown up for wishful thinking when her husband (who has been involved with nuclear research) returns from a long assignment abroad to discover that his child is limbless. Published just less than three years after Hiroshima, when fears of radiation damage were rife in the United States, this highly charged story was bound to cause a stir—and it did.

The love and anguish of motherhood, vividly described, are featured in a number of Merril's stories and novels. Mother and baby are often shown temporarily or permanently without a husband and father: this can be seen as Merril writing from life, since her own father died when she was a child, her first husband was serving abroad in World War II while she stayed in New York with a baby, and she was twice divorced while caring for young children. In "Project Nursemaid" (1955) an unmarried mother-to-be faces the terrible dilemma of whether to give away her unborn child (in the fifth month of its fetal state) to a government research program aimed at creating humans who can live on the Moon without problems.

In the collaborative novel *Outpost Mars* (1952) Merril makes her auctorial presence strongly felt with an opening chapter describing a difficult childbirth on Mars and with a later chapter about the same mother's terrible ordeal when her child is stolen from her (not to mention some long, anguished scenes in between when that same child will not feed normally). In *Shadow on the Hearth* (1950), her first solo novel, she tells the highly emotional story of a mother trying to protect her two daughters from harm after a nuclear attack only a few miles away.

Love and fear are regular ingredients of many of Merril's stories. In "Whoever You Are" (1952) an alien race offers its unbounded love to humanity, which is capable only of seeing this as a threat. In "So Proudly We Hail" (1953) a wife is afraid to tell her husband

that she has been rejected on medical grounds as a colonist for Mars, because she loves him too much to stop him from going. He, on the other hand, believes that she does not want to go because of another man.

In all these stories and most of her others, Merril leaves the reader in no doubt that what she is writing is intended to be stressful and hard-hitting, to be full of love, hate, envy, and the rest of the emotional spectrum, because she habitually italicizes words. She does this more frequently than any other postwar science fiction writer. This means that she maintains her level of emotional stress at a fairly constant peak (which, at novel length, soon becomes exhausting for the reader), and it suggests that she is incapable of varying pitch and knows of no other means than italics for demonstrating emotional stress. If one ignores the italics and analyzes her words, one finds that they are, in fact, fairly flat, typically lacking the cleverly emotive word choices of authors such as Bradbury and Harlan Ellison.

Thematically most of Merril's stories fall into a fairly small number of categories. She has returned time after time to the idea of humanity colonizing Mars and finding some form of intelligent life there. The earliest example is *Outpost Mars*, in which she and Kornbluth describe in great detail humanity's terrible struggle to survive on that cold, barren, inhospitable planet, where few of the comforts of life are found. The traveling conditions on the way to Mars are even worse: "a steerage passenger was expected to grab a stanchion, hang on and take his lumps during a rough landing." This seems so unlikely that Merril and Kornbluth must have written the passage with tongue in cheek. However, the colonists do find a form of alien life. In their other novel-length collaboration, *Gunner Cade* (1952), Merril and Kornbluth have a scene (in the last two chapters) on a human-colonized Mars. In Merril's "So Proudly We Hail" (which could be a companion piece to *Outpost Mars*), the colonists are just embarking for Mars. Also, *The Tomorrow People* presents a more sophisticated version of an expedition to Mars returning with some intelligent, single-celled entities that are telepathically linked to form a single being.

A second of Merril's themes is ardent feminism. She was one of the earliest science fiction writers to portray women as the equals of men, although sometimes (as in *Outpost Mars*) only lip service is paid to such a concept, all those in charge being male. In other instances she shows women doing "men's" jobs or even taking over the running of spaceships. In several stories ("Survival Ship," "Wish upon a Star," 1958, and "Stormy Weather," 1954) she asserts that women are better suited to command spaceships or hold down jobs in space than men, because they are psychologically more stable. "Survival Ship" concerns a generation starship of twenty women and only four men (and those four in subordinate positions), but the fact of female superiority is not revealed until the last paragraph. The story had quite an impact when it first appeared in 1951.

Even when she is not implying female equality or superiority, Merril tends to use female protagonists. Certainly the mother is the most important character in *Shadow on the Hearth*, even though she is not a dominant personality but a weak housewife, unable to decide what is best for her family. Occasionally Merril's feminism becomes maudlin, as in "Daughters of Earth" (1953), her multigeneration saga of women colonists going farther out from Earth in search of new worlds. It is not that there are no men accompanying these women. In fact, they all have husbands. It is just that the importance of the males is played down by the female narrator. Too often, Merril does her sex no service by concentrating ad nauseam on the minutiae of caring for small children. This may be the very first appearance of kitchen-sink science fiction, but it falls short of being entertainment.

Telepathy is another favorite topic. It appears in both *Outpost Mars* and *The Tomorrow People* by way of very young (in the latter instance unborn) children, who are more susceptible to its influences. More credible is the situation in "Peeping Tom" (1954), arguably the best of all Merril's stories. A World War II soldier in the Far East is taught by an elderly native to read the minds of others. Being as subject to lust and greed as the rest of us, he employs this talent to satisfy his own desires, getting all the women and making all the money that he wants. His teacher can see this and begs him to come back after the war to learn more—presumably to learn about the responsibility that ought to accompany the gift. Instead he goes his own wicked way back home to the United States, putting up with the dreadful thoughts he overhears and making the most of any information so obtained. He meets a nurse he knew in the Far East and is amazed by the comparative innocence and niceness of her mind. Only after they are married does she let on that she went back after the war to complete her study of telepathy. Another telepathy story, "Connection Completed" (1954), is much less successful, being nothing more than the sentimental tale of a man and a woman, both of whom have some difficulty in believing that the partner of their dreams is a real person rather than an idealized image. They are not sure that they are in telepathic contact with each other.

A subsidiary theme to the colonization of Mars or the Moon is the undergoing of hardship. Merril makes much of the terrible hardships endured by her characters in various situations, because it increases the emotional level of the content. Certainly she does not seem to stick to the Puritan ethic of hard work and suffering bringing just rewards, for although the hard-working colonists of Sun Lake City Colony (in *Outpost Mars*) eventually strike it rich through luck and technological expertise, many of Merril's characters live immoral lives yet still win out in the end.

Political machination is a theme that is really used only in *The Tomorrow People*. In this novel Merril demonstrates an awareness of the reality of politics as a dirty business, an awareness all too rarely encountered in science fiction. The subtle and convincing manner in which it is put across here shows how much Merril had developed as a person and as

Judith Merril in 1973. PHOTO BY JAY KAY KLEIN

a writer in the ten years since her previous solo novel.

Merril has always tried hard to develop at least her main characters. She does so, in great measure, by resorting to introspection. The thoughts of the characters are written down—sometimes as well-articulated sentences, sometimes as stream-of-consciousness jumbles. For example, in *Shadow on the Hearth*, Gladys Mitchell, a suburban housewife living a few miles from the center of New York City, is faced with the problem of how to manage when atomic bombs explode in the center of the city. The flash is visible from her home, and there is a danger of wind-borne radioactive fallout. She is afraid for her two daughters, who might have been out in the radioactive rain, and most of all for her husband, who was at work in the city. After some initial prebomb scene-setting thoughts such as "*Everything's almost too good . . . ,*" the bulk of the book describes the postblast recovery and hope for the future. Radio reports are more of a worry than a help to her: "*Nothing about Jon; nothing about the city.*" She is frightened by noises in the cellar: "*A man's voice . . . a stranger . . . but he knows my name!*" She is caught in an unprecedented sit-

uation for which there are no prescribed reactions: "*I don't know. How can I know what to do?*"

In this way, by thought and reaction to circumstances, Merril builds up the largely passive character of Mrs. Mitchell, who is not intended to be a strikingly original personality but an Everywoman character (albeit a well-off one) with whom her readers can identify.

There are two recognizable characters who appear several times in Merril's work. One is a capable and caring authority figure. The other is a sweet and long-suffering leading female. The authority figure is always male—not necessarily old or even middle-aged, but unmarried and essentially knowledgeable. He may be a doctor, or a teacher, or a senior military officer. In *Shadow on the Hearth*, his first appearance, he is Dr. Garston Levy, the science teacher of Mrs. Mitchell's elder daughter. He knows about radiation and blood tests, but he is also a good handyman (able to fix window shutters) and a sensitive individual who is unwilling to force his presence upon the Mitchell household. He is certainly middle-aged, and rather a sad figure, unmarried and asexual. For some reason, not fully explained, he fears arrest during the state of emergency that follows the nuclear attack.

Dr. Tony Hellman, the general practitioner of Sun Lake City Colony in *Outpost Mars*, is much younger and more of a heroic figure, but he possesses the same calm assurance; he gets things done, fighting against the conditions, setbacks, lack of sleep, and so on. He also gets the girl—without the benefit of marriage. Colonel Edgerly in "Project Nursemaid" is very young to be a colonel, and he also gets the girl (one of them, at any rate). In *The Tomorrow People* this character is dichotomized into the older, more authoritative Dr. Christensen (the head of the American Moon Base) and Dr. Phil Kutler (a psychiatrist who treats Johnny Wendt on his return from Mars and is later employed to solve psychological problems at the American Moon Base). Kutler is younger and more lecherous, and he might possibly be getting the girl (Merril is not sufficiently explicit in this instance).

The long-suffering female character normally occurs in conjunction with the authoritative male. Gladys Mitchell does not quite fit the mold, but Anne Willendorf (the doctor's girlfriend) in *Outpost Mars* does, as does Johnny Wendt's girlfriend, Lisa Trovi, in *The Tomorrow People*. These last two women share a talent for telepathic sensitivity, which enables them to communicate with alien life forms (or, at least, with or via mutated human babies). They are both cheerful and capable in any adversity and might be considered quite saintly were it not for their sex-before-marriage exploits. Ceil, the teenage mother-to-be in "Project Nursemaid," is yet another example of the same character type.

Johnny Wendt, the mixed-up astronaut in *The Tomorrow People*, is one of Merril's more memorable characters. This is so not because he is well rounded or credible but because he is an alcoholic, unpredictable whether drunk or sober, constantly haunted by the inexplicable disappearance of his fellow astronaut on Mars, and unable to return the love of his girl friend. He is more a bunch of contradictions than a well-rounded character. The eponymous hero of *Gunner Cade* is a little better. He seems to owe more to Kornbluth than to Merril; he is an all-purpose superhero, a finely honed tool trained to fight and kill with any weapon or with none. The way in which he is forced to grow out of his monastic naïveté and come to terms with the real world is adequate only in the context of a fastmoving thriller—which was all that the authors intended.

Almost all of Merril's fiction has a technological facade. This is necessary because most of her settings are technologically advanced future societies and because, at least initially, her work was published in *Astounding*, for which John W. Campbell, Jr., demanded stories with a technological facade. Unfortunately, Merril was never a "hard" scientist; her framework has no structural support, and her plots often suggest contradictions to scientific laws.

A notable example is her regular assumption that humans can live on Mars with little or no special equipment. The almost total lack of free oxygen and the extremely low night temperatures were well known to, and universally accepted by, the scientific fraternity even in 1950. Even so, the Martian colonists of *Outpost Mars* find the air almost breathable, getting by without masks as long as they remember to take their daily "oxygen enzyme" pills—a ridiculous example of pseudoscience. Furthermore, the colonists manage to wander around on the Martian surface dressed in parkas and sweaters, as if it were merely Alaska in winter, happily ignoring the fact that the low pressure would immediately cause moisture to boil off from their eyes, noses, and mouths. Also, the idea of growing vegetable crops there in open fields (the Sun Lake City Colony relies heavily on such crops because it cannot afford to import food from Earth) is absurd.

When the children of colonists turn out, in some cases, to be able to breathe the Martian atmosphere without any pseudoscientific assistance and to be telepathic too—all because of recessive genes—Merril and Kornbluth are demonstrating an equal ignorance of genetics. Needless to say, these children are able to withstand the low temperatures without the need for clothes, and they are quite able to breed and multiply.

The scientific basis of *Gunner Cade* is even less credible. Despite being set ten thousand years in the future, advanced technology seems to be limited to a handful of items, such as blaster pistols, radionic locks, and spacecraft; the rest of the background gives the impression that science has regressed to perhaps an eighteenth-century level. Toward the end of the book, the hero and heroine are breathing Martian air!

Merril's science is no more sure in her solo novels. *Shadow on the Hearth* is more convincing, for the most part, because there were detailed descriptions of Hiroshima and Nagasaki to draw on, although she does appear to underestimate the destructive power of even small nuclear devices, particularly the burns and eye damage caused by the fireball. In addition, she totally ignores the delivery problem: no enemy aircraft are seen, and

ICBM's were not even thought of in those days; yet many atomic bombs explode over the major United States cities more or less simultaneously.

The Tomorrow People, too, has a number of errors. It is set mostly in 1977, which was a brave guess; we might have had permanent Moon bases and manned expeditions to Mars by then, although there cannot have been many people besides Merril who thought so in 1960. Among several other scientific gaffes, she has a female member of the Communist Dome on the Moon defect, flying off toward the American Dome in a helicopter. (Probably there were not many people besides Merril who believed, in 1960, that helicopters could fly in the near-vacuum of the lunar atmosphere.)

Merril must have realized that her lack of scientific knowledge caused her to make blunders of this kind, yet she produced quite a few stories that have a hard-science background. In several instances—"The Lady Was a Tramp" (1957) is the best example—she writes about spaceships just as if they were a slightly futuristic class of steamship. In other stories she invents various gadgets without thinking them through, such as the electromagnetic-gravitic web of force that protects the whole solar system in "Whoever You Are" (1952). This web is, by implication, solar-powered, and it is so powerful and all-embracing that "no photon passed its portals" without being stopped and checked over. Even allowing for hyperbole, such a defensive system (situated just beyond the orbit of Saturn) would seem to require the power output of several suns; the construction of a Dyson sphere would be no more difficult.

Merril's use of the "soft" sciences is little better than her use of the hard. She appears to have a grasp of political processes in *The Tomorrow People*, yet her assumption that a Pan-American association of states could come into being between 1960 and 1977, governing itself by a system apparently modeled on that of the United States, was naïve. The economic and sociological shortcomings of *Outpost Mars* and *Gunner Cade* cannot be blamed on Merril alone, although they do demonstrate greater familiarity with previously published fictional futures than with any respectable academic theories. Only the psychological dimension of her stories shows evidence of any prior research.

It is notable that most of Merril's work has aged badly. When read today, many years after its first appearance, it strikes one as quaint and old-fashioned. This is due partly to her near-future settings and inaccurate predictions, and partly to her writing style. *The Tomorrow People*, in particular, is full of slang expressions current in about 1960 that help to destroy the verisimilitude of its futuristic setting.

At least as important as Merril's fiction are her nonfiction writings and her editing. The nonfiction consists mainly of a regular book review column in *The Magazine of Fantasy and Science Fiction* for four years during the late 1960's. She also contributed a few critical articles on science fiction subjects, such as profiles of Theodore Sturgeon and Fritz Leiber for their respective *Fantasy and Science Fiction* special issues, and a long piece for *Extrapolation* entitled "What Do You Mean: Science? Fiction?" (1966). This last is a subjective history of science fiction, showing its development in the pulp magazines and through synthesis with external areas of literature, between about 1926 and 1966. (It is reprinted in the 1971 anthology *SF: the Other Side of Realism*, edited by Thomas D. Clareson.)

Merril's editing of anthologies began, as previously mentioned, with *Shot in the Dark* in 1950; it continued with such titles as *Beyond Human Ken* (1952) and *England Swings SF* (1968), totaling about twenty volumes, all reprinting earlier stories. Best known are her twelve "best of the year" volumes that appeared under various titles, gathering her choice of science fiction covering twelve years from 1956. The great importance of these anthologies is that Merril did not restrict herself to stories appearing in the regular science fiction magazines or to a narrow definition of science fiction. She took her material from newspapers, mainstream magazines, and author collections, as well as the more obvious genre-magazine sources, and she included articles, poetry, and cartoons. In this way she brought much good science fiction and fantasy to the attention of readers who might well have missed its original appearance.

Merril's contribution to science fiction can be properly judged only if her work is seen in the context of the state of the genre when it first appeared. In 1948 she was one of a very few women writers of science fiction, and the only one willing to write emotionally about feminine subjects. Her stories helped pave the way for the more ardent feminist writers who did not come into the field until she had ceased writing. The fiction Merril produced in collaboration is neither much better nor much worse than what she produced alone; one difference is that her single story written with Pohl ("A Big Man with the Girls") contains humor, an element lacking in her solo work. Although certain of her stories were well received at the time of first publication, they are generally forgotten now. Her lasting importance to the genre is through her anthologies (she remains science fiction's most prolific female anthologist), particularly her "best of the year" volumes.

Judith Merril died on 12 September 1997 in Toronto, Canada. During the last thirty-five years of her life, she wrote no science fiction. In 1968 she left the United States, moving to Canada to protest the Vietnam War. In 1970 she donated her large collection of science fiction books and magazines to the Toronto Public Library, and the Merril Collection is now regarded as one of the world's premier collections of science fiction.

Her only published book in the post-1982 period is the first *Tesseracts* anthology (1985), a showcase of Canadian science fiction drawn from a broad range of sources, genre and literary, that she edited. This is an important anthology series that has continued (under other editors); so far six volumes have been published.

Merril had long been a teacher of science fiction. Back in 1956 she helped to found the annual Milford workshops, and during all her time in Canada she taught writing as a college

course. She was a great champion of Canadian science fiction, doing much to promote its growth over the last thirty years. In 1983 and 1985 she received Casper awards, the Canadian equivalent of Hugos, and in 1991 she received the Milford award for her lifetime contributions to the publishing and editing of science fiction. All her life, during her time as a writer, anthologist, reviewer, and teacher of science fiction, she was an ardent fan and promoter of the genre.

Selected Bibliography

FICTION OF JUDITH MERRIL

Shadow on the Hearth. Garden City, N.Y.: Doubleday, 1950. London: Sidgwick and Jackson, 1953. (Novel.)

Outpost Mars, with C. M. Kornbluth as Cyril Judd. New York: Abelard, 1952. (Novel originally serialized in *Galaxy* as "Mars Child," 1951. Also known as *Sin in Space*.)

Gunner Cade, with C. M. Kornbluth as Cyril Judd. New York: Simon and Schuster, 1952. London: Victor Gollancz, 1964. (Novel originally serialized in *Astounding Science-Fiction*, 1952.)

Out of Bounds. New York: Pyramid Books, 1960. (Collection.)

The Tomorrow People. New York: Pyramid Books, 1960. (Novel.)

Daughters of Earth. London: Victor Gollancz, 1968. Garden City, N.Y.: Doubleday, 1969. (Collection.)

Survival Ship and Other Stories. Toronto: Kakabcka Publishing Company, 1974. (Collection.)

The Best of Judith Merril. New York: Warner Books, 1976. (Collection.)

SOME ANTHOLOGIES EDITED BY JUDITH MERRIL

Shot in the Dark. New York: Bantam Books, 1950.

Beyond Human Ken. New York: Random House, 1952.

SF: The Year's Greatest Science Fiction and Fantasy. New York: Gnome Press, 1956.

The Year's Best S-F: Sixth Annual Edition. New York: Simon and Schuster, 1961.

SF 12. New York: Delacorte Press, 1968. (The final volume in the series that appeared annually from 1956 through 1968 [no volume was published in 1967].)

England Swings SF. Garden City, N.Y.: Doubleday, 1968. (Collection of New Wave speculative fiction.)

Tesseracts. Edited by Judith Merril. Victoria, British Columbia: Porcépic, 1985.

—CHRIS MORGAN

A. MERRITT

(1884–1943)

REPUTATIONS COME AND reputations go, but in the fields of science fiction and fantasy there is probably no other great reputation of the past that has suffered as much as that of A. Merritt. During the 1930's and 1940's he was widely considered the greatest science fiction writer of modern times. He even had the then-unique distinction of having a magazine, *A. Merritt's Fantasy Magazine*, named in his honor. All this, of course, was in the precritical days, and today Merritt is seldom ranked among the more important authors of the pulp era. His merits seem to have crumbled along with the magazines in which his stories appeared, and his flaws now seem more perceptible than his strengths.

In part this change of critical evaluation has been caused by changing cultural circumstances and altered tastes, but it is also due to the nature of his work and to the ways in which he conceived authorship.

For a man who held a high position in the newspaper world and was highly regarded during his lifetime, Merritt has always been astonishingly vague as a personality. Although he was accessible personally, very little has ever been known about him beyond bare biographical facts, and even some of these are very hazy.

Abraham Merritt was born in 1884 in Beverly, New Jersey, an across-the-river suburb of Philadelphia. He attended local elementary schools and Philadelphia High School, and was intended for the law. He matriculated at the Law School of the University of Pennsylvania but dropped out because of financial dif-

ficulties. Merritt then took a job as cub reporter with the *Philadelphia Inquirer* (1902). He later became a city reporter, assigned to crimes, suicides, strikes, and catastrophes. According to an interview that he gave in the 1930's, he was considered the best man to cover executions, even though he loathed the assignment. He would attend the execution "strongly fortified," write up the event colorfully, then "resign," and spend a few days recovering, before returning to work.

During this early period of newspaper work occurred one of the mysteries of Merritt's life. Details have never been released, although Merritt often made teasing comments about it. He seems to have been a witness to a criminal act or to have uncovered dangerous material. His superiors did not wish him to be summoned as a court witness and packed him off out of the country on a paid vacation. He spent a year in Central America, particularly Yucatán, poking around Mayan ruins, trying to interest someone in dredging the cenote at Chichén Itzá.

On his return to Philadelphia, Merritt resumed work at the *Inquirer* and by 1911 had become night city editor. In 1912 he moved to New York and joined the Hearst papers, where he became assistant to Morrill Goddard, editor of the *American Weekly*. This was a large, luridly colored Sunday supplement distributed with the Hearst papers. It was filled with sensational articles on popular science, scandal, occult matters, exposés, current events, as well as some fiction—in short, anything that might be pleasing to Hearst readers. Under Goddard and Merritt the circulation rose to 7,500,000 copies, an enormous figure for the day. In 1937, following Goddard's death, Merritt became editor in chief, a position he held until his own death.

In 1943, while in Florida to examine his business interests, Merritt died of a heart attack. In addition to being a first-rate newspaperman, he was apparently also an excellent businessman, with many profitable holdings in Florida real estate. His personal interests seem to have paralleled his fiction to some degree, since he was greatly interested in archaeology, anthropology, magic, and history of religions. One of his hobbies was raising curious and poisonous plants. He is said to have been a pleasant, affable man, with a hospitable bottle in his desk drawer, and with a good sense of humor. In person he was small and chubby. According to an anecdote that he liked to tell about himself, one of his many fans pestered him for an interview, which he finally granted. On seeing him, she recoiled in horror, exclaiming, "Oh, *you* never wrote *The Moon Pool!*"

I

Merritt's first story, "Through the Dragon Glass" (*All-Story*, 24 November 1917) utilizes the soldier-of-fortune vehicle common in the pulps of the day. Herndon, an acquisitive millionaire, helps to loot the imperial palace in Peking during the Boxer Rebellion. He is impelled supernaturally to take a mirror that stands hidden in a secret room. As Herndon tells his story, it is revealed that the mirror is a gateway to another world, one from ancient Oriental mythology. Herndon enters this world, meets an amiable young woman, encounters the malevolent magical lord of the land, and barely escapes. He plans to return. There is an implication of reincarnation and previous encounters in the otherworld.

Although sketchy and undeveloped, "Through the Dragon Glass" contains many of those characteristics later accepted as pe-

culiar to Merritt's work. The plot pattern is a sensual quest, in which an experienced adventurer, caught up in a sudden tenderness, fails but plans a second attempt. This basic plot appeared in many of Merritt's later stories and story segments.

"Through the Dragon Glass" also demonstrates stylistic points common to Merritt's fiction, but not to his journalism. The style is essentially "fine writing," which later progressed to attempts at rhythmical patterns, often rhetorically broken and interrupted. Inversions of normal word order, omission of the definite and indefinite article, and listings without final conjunction all became frequent mannerisms, which editors apparently were powerless to erase.

Merritt, like Marie Corelli, seemed to equate descriptions of beauty with beauty; and just as Corelli would rave vulgarly about roses, roses, roses, Merritt attempted to create a brilliant picture or sensuous mood by a frequent use of words describing color and sound. The result is sometimes a shower of terms, at best conveying a sense of the subject's alienness, at worst almost constituting a parody of certain late nineteenth-century traditional verse. Yet behind all these odd mannerisms, it must be admitted, was a skilled verbalist who was well aware of what he was doing. His was not a sin of ignorance.

Another curious feature of Merritt's writing appeared in this early period. His hobby was the study of mythology and religions, and he delighted in mythological syncretisms—raided, obviously, from popular works. Thus, characters, in otherwise ordinary conversation, are likely to make odd references to Chinese godlings, Islamic peris, or ancient Irish heroic cycles. Unfortunately, Merritt was not a scholar, and for the most part this material lies heavily and inappropriately on the surface verbal texture. In a sense, one must admit, Merritt was only imitating the art forms of his formative period, around the turn of the century, when, as with the British art nouveau lapidaries, a surface flash of decoration might be thrown upon an otherwise bare, formalized surface.

It might seem odd that the pulp-reading public would stand for these idiosyncrasies, yet they were among the aspects of Merritt that were most treasured. They meant culture, exoticism, and learning to those who were starved for something more than slash-bang sensation or the bread-and-butter styles of most of the other pulp writers.

Merritt's next story, "The People of the Pit" (*All-Story*, 5 January 1918), is more clearly science fiction. It is set in Alaska, an area to which he returned in his finest work, *Dwellers in the Mirage* (1932). Unlike "Through the Dragon Glass," which is a story of sentimental longing beneath its hard exterior, "The People of the Pit" is a recognition of alien horrors lurking unsuspected beneath the Surface. The narrator comes on a dying man who tells of descending infinite steps and encountering, at the bottom of a valley, an alien world dominated by prehuman, hostile, incomprehensible beings that seem to be animated light. There is no explanation, no promise of resolution, simply a fictionalization of the powerlessness of man against higher beings, linking physical defeat with an empty spiritual triumph.

The stories that created Merritt's reputation were "The Moon Pool" (*All-Story*, 22 June 1918) and its sequel, "The Conquest of the Moon Pool" (*All-Story*, 14 February–29 March 1919). That the two stories do not fit together very well seems to have been overlooked because of the imaginative sweep of the second story.

"The Moon Pool," a short story told in an unnecessarily complex series of boxes, is essentially a story of supernatural horror (the monster from the crypt) told in terms of science fiction. The events take place on and around the megalithic ruins of Ponape, in Micronesia, which Merritt claimed to have visited. A shining, seemingly insubstantial being, accompanied by musical effects and sensations that combine the utmost of bliss and pain, emerges from a pool in an underground vault among the ruins, and absorbs those it encounters. The story ends with one of the narrators fleeing over the ocean, while the so-called Dweller follows along the moonlit path on the water and takes its prey. As with much of Merritt's other work, there are possible interpretations in terms of classical psychoanalysis that may or may not have been in Merritt's mind.

The original short story, if one makes allowances for the frames and the "fine writing," is a good horror story with many unusual features. But "The Conquest of the Moon Pool" belongs to a different subgenre. It is a lost-race story, with motifs from H. Rider Haggard's *When the World Shook* (1919).

An exploration party opens the portals that seal off the Dweller and, to the accompaniment of scientific marvels, enters a huge subterranean world inhabited by the descendants of people from a lost continent. The science of the hidden land is higher than that of the surface world, but there are typical signs of decadence: tyranny, a luxurious and debased ruling class, and a frightful religion based on feeding the Shining One, the Dweller of the first story. At the moment, the sunken land is ripe for either emerging and conquering the world, or falling into civil war. The story soon takes the form of Good versus Evil.

Among the props of this world are various alien forms of life; the Shining One, which is a synthetic being created by a prehuman race of intelligent reptilian beings; and the Silent Ones, or three of the reptilian semideities who exist, half-imprisoned, until they can find the courage or strength to destroy the Shining One. This they cannot do until a most obnoxious Irish-American hero (who spouts terms from ancient Irish mythology) and the woman who loves him are willing to sacrifice themselves for love. There is also a wicked German who skulks about, plotting. In later reprints he became a Russian.

"The Conquest of the Moon Pool" is a fast-moving adventure story with extremely wicked villains, a lustful vamp, muscular heroes—with treachery, plots, and counterplots. It has a strange mortuary aspect, as it is revealed that the hordes of victims that the Shining One has taken over the ages still exist

A. Merritt. COURTESY OF JAY KAY KLEIN ARCHIVES

in a state of quasi life, quasi death, within its shining membranes. Yet love, as in all Merritt's major work, is the motive power behind both stories, with both sacred and profane, familial and sexual varieties present. Nor did Merritt hesitate to invoke deity to resolve his story.

Merritt's next story was a short fantasy, "Three Lines of Old French" (*All-Story*, 9 August 1919), which seems to have been his most popular work. A highly sentimental tale redolent of the lowest levels of World War I propaganda—what with wicked Boches, saintly French, willing houris awaiting the dead soldier in Paradise, refutation of cynical materialists—it is more interesting in showing an aspect of Merritt's writing process than for its content. Like much of Merritt's other work, it is based on a story by another author. To cite some obvious sources, "Three Lines of

Old French" seems built on "The Demoiselle d'Ys" by Robert W. Chambers; *Burn, Witch, Burn!* on Fitz-James O'Brien's "The Wondersmith"; and ideas in "The Snake Mother" on *The Glory of Egypt* by Louis Moresby (L. Adams Beck).

By this list I am not implying that Merritt was a plagiarist. What he wrote, he made his own, regardless of sources; but he seems to have needed or liked external stimulation to start the writing process.

The Metal Monster (*Argosy All-Story*, 7 August–25 September 1920) Merritt called his "best and worst" novel, by which one assumes that he realized that it was a good idea spoiled by foolish development. Set in Central Asia, it is a lost-race novel (ancient Persians) with, as a sideshow, a metal being, larger than a city block, composed of living metal modules roughly comparable to the molecules of a human body or the pieces of an erector set. This alien being, sentient and intelligent after its own fashion, is strangely involved in an erotic empathy with a human female. But it carries within itself, among its variously shaped components, the seeds of civil war. Ultimately it short-circuits itself, plans for world geometrization unrealized. The story might be taken as a parable of human activity, but this does not seem to have been Merritt's intention.

The Ship of Ishtar (*Argosy All-Story*, 8 November–13 December 1924) displayed another aspect of Merritt's writing habits. It was first written as a long short story, which Merritt submitted to *Argosy All-Story*. Bob Davis, the editor, called Merritt in and suggested that he expand the story to a novel, which Merritt did. Instead of enlarging the original story, he simply added a sequel. Much of his work (including the book version of *The Moon Pool*) shows a similar double structure, short story and novel worked together.

The Ship of Ishtar, in its final form, is a long novel set in a parallel world where the divinities of ancient Mesopotamia openly interfere in human life and themselves carry on strongly felt feuds. Highly romantic in presentation, filled with oddly individualized type characters (muscular Norseman, adventurous hero, beautiful priestess of Ishtar, wicked priest of Nergal), it was unusual in ending with the death of all the major characters, although the souls of the hero and heroine are taken to herself by Ishtar. In the late 1930's *Argosy* ran a survey to determine the most popular story ever to appear in *Argosy* and *All-Story*, and *The Ship of Ishtar* was apparently an easy winner.

More properly science fiction are "The Face in the Abyss" (*Argosy All-Story*, 8 September 1923) and its sequel novel "The Snake Mother" (*Argosy All-Story*, 25 October–6 December 1930), which were abridged and combined into the book *The Face in the Abyss* (1931). It is set in isolated fastnesses of the Andes, where remains of ancient Atlanteans still live. Although possessed of fragments of their former superior science, the people of Yu-Atlanchi are hopelessly decadent and ready for a suitable purge. Among the more original features of the book are hypostatized abstractions, Greed and Folly, which take part in life and influence humans (perhaps suggested by A. Conan Doyle's "The Maracot Deep"), and the Snake Mother. A somewhat kittenish personality, she is the last survivor of a race of serpent-people who first set man on the path toward civilization. *The Face in the Abyss* is an uneven work. While there are some excellent flights of imagination in equipment and activities, the sequel novel is much weaker than the initial short story, which has some period charm in its quaint juxtaposition of love and greed, brutality and ultimate decency.

The second most popular work ever to appear in *Weird Tales* was "The Woman of the Wood" (August 1926). Reminiscent of the work of Algernon Blackwood, though more sensational, it is on one level a story of madness and on another of supernatural empathy. McKay, staying in a small hamlet in the Vosges, suddenly sees the trees as beautiful, sensual women and handsome men. They beg him to help them, for the woodcutter Polleau and his family have a feud against them. In an effort to protect the trees, McKay is respon-

sible for the deaths of the Polleaus. Horrified by what he has done while as if possessed, yet torn by equally strong regrets that he has not joined the world of the trees, he leaves. In many ways this is the best of Merritt's short stories.

The most significant of Merritt's science fiction novels is *Dwellers in the Mirage* (*Argosy*, 23 January–27 February 1932), which, although somewhat undeveloped in sections and occasionally marred by stylistic affectations, is much more thought-provoking and more image-filled than his earlier work. It is built upon three motifs: the survival of an ancient Central Asiatic culture in a lost valley in Alaska, hidden beneath a miragelike atmospheric lens; the emergence of a horrible monstrosity from other dimensions, which monstrosity figures in the religion of the lost land; and the mental self-torture of a man cursed with ancestral memory (or psychosis) that takes over his personality and works havoc on himself and his associates. With the possible exception of *Land Under England* (1935) by Joseph O'Neill, which is essentially political, it is the last significant lost-race novel written in English.

The background of the story is to be found in Merritt's private understanding of Sir Aurel Stein's discovery, in the oasis ruins of Chinese Turkistan, of the Tokharian language, a hitherto unknown member of the Indo-European language family. Merritt identified this culture with the Turkish-speaking Uighurs of the area, and postulated a Nordic, Indo-European drift, bearing with it elements of Norse religion and mythology. That he took this historical nonsense seriously is shown by an unsigned article that he wrote for the *American Weekly*, presenting the same point of view.

Dwellers in the Mirage is a powerful book, if one can accept its conventions. The frequent mythological comparisons are, for the first time in Merritt's work, integrated with the story and not merely obtrusive atmospheric devices. Leif, the tortured, buffeted hero, gnawed by both conscience and the emergence of unconscious personality (no matter what its ultimate origin), and the power-mad, erotic Lur, the only one of Merritt's femmes fatales to assume life, are memorable characters. One has the impression that in this book Merritt set out to do the best work that he could. If so, he was successful, for he brought the lost-race subgenre, which was the most rigidly formularized sequence of storemes in science fiction, and all too often subliterate, to the highest point it had reached since the best work of Haggard.

Two endings exist for *Dwellers in the Mirage*. In the first serial and first book publications, the generally tragic situation is partly offset by the escape of Leif and Evalie, a girl from outside the valley, from the secret land. In more recent editions, the painful ending that appeared in Merritt's original version has been followed. Evalie is killed by Lur, and Leif stumbles out of the land, utterly broken. Both types of love, friendship, and self-identity have all been shattered.

Dwellers in the Mirage was the last of Merritt's "fairyland" romances. Either he felt that the market wanted something different or, with the detailed mythic structure of the story (which would give a Jungian analyst a remarkable field for exegesis), he had worked something out of his psyche.

Merritt wrote two more novels, but both are supernatural mysteries. *Burn, Witch, Burn!* (*Argosy*, 22 October–26 November 1932) deals with an invasion of doll magic into New York City and includes a sentimentalized mafioso among its characters. *Creep, Shadow* (*Argosy*, 8 September–6 October 1934) is a sequel of a sort. It aligns the ancient legend of the lost city of Ys in Britanny with shadow magic and brings both to Manhattan and Long Island. Both novels attempt to be slick, worldly, and sophisticated, and to a certain extent they succeed. They are really very competent mystery stories with supernatural elements.

An earlier thriller, *Seven Footprints to Satan* (*Argosy All-Story*, 2 July–6 August 1927), is a mystery in the mode of Sax Rohmer. It has an excellent beginning situation and a very unusual mastermind of crime, but it seems desperately to be looking for a convincing ending, and fails. It does not carry much conviction.

After Merritt's death two fairly long fragments of unfinished novels were found among his papers. One fragment, "The Fox Woman," is set partly in China. It is based on Chinese folk beliefs that foxes are intelligent and unscrupulous spirits who can assume human form and work mischief. The second fragment, "The Black Wheel," is concerned with a symbolic ship (much like the vessel in Wilkie Collins' *Armadale*) and reincarnation. Both fragments were finished as novels by Hannes Bok, the well-known fantasy artist. In neither case, unfortunately, was either Merritt's part or Bok's worth the effort. Merritt also wrote two short stories in the 1930's, "The Last Poet and the Robots" (*Fantasy Magazine*, April 1934) and "The Drone" (*Fantasy Magazine*, Second Anniversary Issue, 1934). Both are trivial.

II

If one wanted to characterize Merritt in simple terms, one could call him the most romantic (in the late nineteenth-century sense of the word) major science fiction writer of his day, perhaps of the twentieth century. Among his near contemporaries only the young C. L. Moore came close to him in sweeping ideas, high emotion, and perpetual suggestions of deeper phenomena beneath the surface of events.

This romantic quality was highly regarded, and Merritt was one of the authors most frequently imitated by young writers. He shares this place with H. P. Lovecraft and Ray Bradbury.

Today we are more apt to find things in Merritt's writing that should not be imitated, but to admit that there are weaknesses in his work should not prevent us from seeing that there are also great, sometimes unique, strengths. He had a fine imagination, and each of his major stories was innovative in significant ways. He had the knack of treating each theme or motif as a fulfillment, exhausting its potential. Thus, one can take sentimental treatment of survival no farther than "Three Lines of Old French," nor can one develop "The Haunted Palace" theme further in a lost-race situation than *Dwellers in the Mirage*.

Merritt could be an exciting writer, and he could digress from the pulp milieu in unusual ways, tossing gobbets of poetic thought or humor into unexpected places. He was an excellent technician when he wanted to be, and his skills evolved as he grew older. The crudities of "The Conquest of the Moon Pool" were soon outgrown. If he was always concerned with the power of love and the fierce dualism between good and evil, as abstractions, not just as wicked people, he constantly varied his embodiments and he cannot be accused of monotony.

Yet despite these strengths the ultimate feeling today is that Merritt was for the most part an unsatisfactory writer. Perhaps the problem was lack of literary integrity, a deficiency that seems worse in an author of capability than in a dolt. Merritt cleaved to the attitudes and wish fulfillments of his fleeting audience, and filled his stories with symbols, plot situations, and techniques that it liked. If he was cleverer than most of his colleagues in doing this, he paid a higher price in the end, for what appealed to the readers of Munsey pulp magazines in the 1920's may strike a reader today as itself a fantasy world.

In many instances Merritt carried out his emotional topicality to such an extent that when the zeitgeist changed, the older position was difficult to accept—indeed, it was sometimes ludicrous or repellant. "Three Lines of Old French," for example, was Merritt's most popular short story. Written in the context of World War I, it did not merely make propaganda gestures; it deluged the reader with death-eroticism. Now, eighty years later, this story can only be called obscene, untrue, a pastorale of the worst sort, since it was deliberately written by a very intelligent and competent author to play upon bereavement—as,

to judge from letters received by *All-Story*, it did.

Perhaps there was an element of cynicism in Merritt's work that his contemporaries did not catch. Could a professional newspaperman who rose to one of the highest positions in the Hearst empire, to head a major publication that was even more difficult to handle than a daily, be other than intellectually hardboiled? Or was there perhaps a situation like that of William Sharp and Fiona Macleod, whereby the professional journalist (Sharp), under a pseudonym (Macleod), wrote florid, mushy stories about the Hebrides, dripping with bathos and local color, and yet felt so embodied in the work of Fiona Macleod that he threatened to stop writing if the pseudonym were revealed? We do not know.

Is any of Merritt's work worth reading, other than as historical documents? The mythic quality of *Dwellers in the Mirage*, with its formal structuring and psychological inner drama, is still vital, and the sense of frantic peril in *Burn, Witch, Burn!* is still perceptible. There are also individual moments in each of the other major works. As for the rest of Merritt's work, it belongs back in the 1920's and 1930's, perhaps occasionally to be stroked for nostalgia, but maintainable only by taxidermy.

Selected Bibliography

The following are first book editions of Merritt's fantastic fiction. There have also been a few separate pamphlet editions of individual short stories and many reprint editions of the novels.

WORKS OF A. MERRITT

The Moon Pool. New York: Putnam's, 1919.
The Ship of Ishtar. Abridged ed. New York: Putnam's, 1926. (The 1956 Borden [Los Angeles] edition, with illustrations by Virgil Finlay, is complete.)
The Face in the Abyss. Abridged ed. New York: Liveright, 1931. (Some of the later paperback editions are fuller.)
Dwellers in the Mirage. New York: Liveright, 1932.
Burn, Witch, Burn! New York: Liveright, 1933.

Creep, Shadow. Garden City, N.Y.: Crime Club/Double-day, Doran, 1934.

The Metal Monster. New York: Murder Mystery Monthly, 1946. (Title sometimes appears as *The Metal Emperor.*)

The Fox Woman. New York: Avon Books, 1949. (All Merritt's published short stories, sometimes with textual variation from other versions, and three fragments.)

CRITICAL AND BIOGRAPHICAL STUDIES

Bleiler, Everett F. "A. Merritt." In his *Supernatural Fiction Writers.* New York: Scribners, 1985.

Moskowitz, Sam. *A. Merritt: Reflections in the Moon Pool.* Philadelphia: Train, 1985.

—E. F. BLEILER

WALTER M. MILLER, JR.

(1923–1996)

WALTER MICHAEL MILLER, Jr., was born on 23 January 1923 at New Smyrna Beach, Florida. From 1940 to 1942, he attended the University of Tennessee. He then served during World War II in the United States Army Air Corps, flying fifty-three combat missions. Miller participated in the 1944 bombing of Cassino, Italy. The destruction of the famous abbey there doubtless contributed to the emphasis in *A Canticle for Leibowitz* upon the threat posed to civilization by modern military technology. The abbey at Cassino may also have suggested to Miller that the Catholic Church could somehow oppose the menace of science immorally harnessed in the service of war. In any case, Miller "discovered the Church" in Italy and became a Catholic in 1947. He steeped himself in the rich traditions of Catholicism, which form a major influence upon his writing.

Miller studied engineering off and on at the University of Texas during the years 1947 to 1950 but did not take a degree. Nevertheless his continuing fascination with science and technology, and his preoccupation with the issues they raise, are apparent throughout his writing. In 1950, Miller was injured in an auto accident, and he began to write fiction while recuperating. From 1951 to 1957 he published forty-one stories in science fiction magazines. He also wrote scripts for the television series *Captain Video*. Miller's brief career as a science fiction writer culminated with *A Canticle for Leibowitz* (1960), the only full-length novel published during his lifetime. Until his death in 1996, he lived in Daytona Beach,

Florida, shunning public attention and working sporadically on *Saint Leibowitz and the Wild Horse Woman*, which appeared posthumously in 1997.

As reported by the Orlando Sentinel ("Canticle Author Unsung Even in Death," 9 October 1997), the circumstances of Miller's death were shocking: "Because science-fiction writers spend so much time thinking about the future, they sometimes have a small gift for predicting it. That's precisely what Walter M. Miller, Jr. did when he called 911 and said there was a dead man on his front lawn." Three minutes later, at 8:32 A.M. on 9 January 1996, the police arrived at Miller's Daytona Beach home. They found the 72-year-old writer sitting in a chair on his lawn, dead from a bullet to the brain.

The element of grim humor here figures also in the fiction, which includes a number of short stories that anticipate both *Canticle* and *Saint Leibowitz* thematically. What are perhaps his best short stories were reissued in 1978 by Gregg Press. These pieces display a particular concern with the biological sciences and with the creative and destructive possibilities of technology in human civilization. At the same time, Miller's short fiction often shows his preoccupation with the role of traditional Judeo-Christian beliefs and values in an age when humanity's outlook and situation have been radically transformed by science.

Miller frequently treated his various themes with a subtlety, irony, and complexity that demand careful reading. For example, "The

Will" (1954) superficially appears to be a sentimental expression of faith in a progress that is both technological and moral. The protagonist of this story is Kenny Westmore, a boy dying of leukemia. He tries to save himself by an ingenious stratagem: he buries valuable stamps and autographs with a note asking the eventual finder to sell the collection for funds to construct a time machine. In this way, Kenny hopes, he will be taken to a future period when he can be cured. The time machine duly appears, but serious doubts are cast upon the beneficence of its operators. For one thing, they speak with an apparently Austrian or German accent, a sinister touch in view of Miller's allusions in "Dark Benediction" (1951) and elsewhere to Nazi genocide. Moreover, the appearance of the machine with a "crash of thunder," its blackness, and the way it seems to "squeeze . . . [Kenny] into a grotesque house-of-mirrors shape" all suggest that he may have fallen victim to some sort of fascist ghouls. Certainly, the boy never returns. Thus, "The Will" may in fact attack the ingenuous belief that technological and moral progress will go hand in hand. Such an assumption is ironically undercut by its being associated with a naïve, desperate child who seems unwittingly to engineer his own terrible doom.

As "The Will" suggests, Miller's short fiction is by no means completely optimistic. For example, both "Blood Bank" (1952) and "Anybody Else Like Me?" (1952) express strong apprehension about the possibility of radical new biological developments for humans that is implied by Darwin's theory of evolution. Each of the stories indicates that an apparent evolutionary progress can be in large part illusory, new mental endowments ironically being more than offset by remaining flaws that reflect humanity's animal ancestry.

"Blood Bank" turns upon the eventual defeat of the Solarians, a race of physical and mental giants who have sprung from humanity on Earth after it has exhausted its resources in colonizing the galaxy. Although intellectual "supermen," the Solarians are spiritually and morally regressive, an atavism suggested by the giants' hair-trigger tempers, Neanderthal lower jaws, and bone-crushing teeth. It is no surprise when we learn, toward the end of "Blood Bank," that the Solarians are brutal predators upon mankind, using it both for food and profitable commerce in the "surgibank" supplies, which are used for medical repairs of accident victims.

The moral monsters produced by evolutionary "advancement" are overcome in "Blood Bank" by a representative of traditional Judeo-Christian values. This is Miller's protagonist, Space Commander Eli Roki, who combines the integrity of the "upright" man disciplined by Old Testament Hebrew law with a Christlike willingness (indicated particularly when Roki's face is raked by the nails of an outraged woman) to suffer and to sacrifice himself for the human community. Roki's self-abnegating nature, which involves a spiritually mature humility and strength, sets him in strong contrast with his adversaries the Solarians. The latter are characterized by an arrogance that masks cowardice and a lack of self-control. The Solarians are likewise opposed morally to their human ancestors. In this regard, just as Roki is a Christ figure, so the surgibank supplies have eucharistic connotations. These connotations suggest how humanity, despite its past radical flaws and present degenerate state, was once capable of the racial sacrifice that sent humanity to the stars. In contrast to such a sacrifice, the Solarians selfishly wish to subjugate the galaxy as Nazi-style conquerers.

"Anybody Else Like Me?" develops a double-edged irony. First, as David Samuelson has indicated in *Science Fiction Studies* (1976), Miller satirizes through his protagonist, Lisa Waverly, the constriction and emptiness of American upper-class existence. Lisa's imprisonment by a narrow conventionality is seen in her negative response to the discovery that she is a telepathic mutant. Moreover, her eventual killing of her fellow mutant, Kenneth Grearly, reveals to her the isolation and vacuity of her life.

Nonetheless, Miller has considerable sympathy for Lisa, and directs his attack equally against Grearly. The latter is fatally flawed by a combination of male chauvinism, youthful obtuseness, and naïve dedication to a purely scientific viewpoint. As a consequence he cannot appreciate Lisa's "feminine" sense of sexual vulnerability, the "womanly" repugnance she feels to opening either her mind or her body to a virtual stranger. In particular, Grearly reveals telepathically to Lisa his intention of forcing himself upon her to breed mutant children.

Such a gross lack of respect for Lisa's personal integrity renders highly ironic Grearly's statement about the failure to communicate being the basis of all tragedy. He is unable to comprehend that telepathy cannot by itself overcome the barriers between individuals. True communication must be based on a sympathetic understanding that embraces even the most primitive physical and emotional foundations of human psychology. In this regard, Grearly does not recognize that the telepathic power has been superadded by evolution to a mentality that also continues to function at an elemental level. Miller's point is underscored by his repeated use of ape imagery in his story.

"Conditionally Human" (1952) assigns a redemptive role to a radical new biological development produced not by natural evolution but, rather, by genetic engineering. But despite such a potential in mankind's technology, Miller's story is seemingly pessimistic about the historical destiny of humanity. In this regard, "Conditionally Human" depicts a dystopian future in which the economic strains caused by overpopulation have necessitated the establishment of a bureaucratic tyranny. In particular, childbearing is strictly limited, substitutes being provided by biological engineering in the form of artificially mutated animals with a limited intelligence. This situation produces intolerable psychic tensions that are expressed particularly through the violence that erupts again and again in the story.

That the situation of humanity as a race has probably become hopeless is suggested by Miller's protagonists, Anne and Terry Norris. Terry's job as a latter-day "dog catcher" involves him, through the extermination of un-

wanted mutants, with the evils of his society in a particularly direct and nasty fashion. Even Anne, perhaps the most positive human character in "Conditionally Human," recalls the sinful Eve when she feeds apples to impounded "newts" (short for "neutroid": sexually neutral, mutated chimpanzees). Anne's gesture, although one of loving kindness, also ironically reflects the hubris of fallen humanity's scientific meddling, which has created the population problem by its well-meant attempts to better mankind's earthly lot. The darkness that now dominates the human race is also suggested by the attempt of the authorities to destroy in a Nazi-style genocide a strain of highly intelligent "deviant" newts produced for a black-marketing scheme. The desire of officialdom to exterminate the deviants seems all the more evil when we learn that they are equivalent in their innocence to the unfallen Adam and Eve. Nonetheless, the making of such unfallen creatures also implies that a certain creative and redemptive potential remains in mankind and its technology.

Anne and Terry likewise reveal an enduring goodness in humanity when they rescue one of the deviants, named Peony. Nevertheless, in the process, Terry again suggests that the situation of mankind is at this point in history probably irredeemable. He does so by the coldly calculated if necessary murder of his boss, Franklin. This crime is compounded by Terry when he rather callously slays an ordinary newt to substitute its corpse for that of the supposedly dead Peony. In keeping with the generally negative condition of man suggested by the double killing, "Conditionally Human" ends with an indication that God has created the deviants perhaps to completely replace man. Peony and her species are a new chosen people like the ancient Israelites, who with divine aid will supplant man on Earth as the Jews displaced the previous inhabitants of Palestine.

Thus, while "Conditionally Human" is ultimately optimistic, it is not optimistic about mankind. But in "Dark Benediction" (1951) humanity promises to overcome its own darker aspects, allowing the biological trans-

Walter Miller in the 1980's. COURTESY OF MAR-GARET MILLER ARAFAT

formation produced by an extraterrestial "bacterium" to elevate mankind to a higher spiritual plane. This microorganism, sent to Earth by its alien hosts when their sun threatened to go nova, has evolved the capacity to enhance the sensory powers of intelligent creatures. The microbe infests much of the world's population, causing a panic that leads to the breakdown of civilization. There is also widespread persecution of the infected "dermies" (so-called from the gray "neuroderm" that associates them with lepers as "unclean" outcasts under Jewish law) by normal humans. In general, Miller suggests that as long as humanity's reactions to the extraterrestrial "plague" are determined by its animal fear and ferocity, the results will be disastrous. Nor are the dermies themselves without fault, their desire to touch the unaffected in order to communicate their "disease" being a carnal passion closely resembling lust.

Miller implies, though, that the positive potential of the alien "benediction" for mankind will be realized through the cooperation of science and Catholicism. The former (as represented by the biologist Seevers) will promote a rational understanding of the plague, while the latter (exemplified by the priests and nuns who found a refuge for dermies on Galveston Island) will provide the moral discipline that will control the baser impulses of humans and dermies. In these changed circumstances the enhanced perceptions made possible by the microorganism will lead to a new level of religious revelation. This will be superadded to Christianity just as that faith was superadded to Judaism—a point underscored by the parallel between Miller's protagonist, Paul Oberlin, and his apostolic namesake. Such a parallel is particularly indicated in the way that Oberlin is converted from his initial aversion to dermies and eventually becomes one of them.

Paul Oberlin's "conversion" underlines how the dermies, although at first a persecuted minority group like the primitive Christians, the Jews in Nazi Germany, and American blacks, are God's specially chosen vehicles for mankind's spiritual advancement. "Dark Benediction," like "Conditionally Human" and "Blood Bank," accordingly suggests St. Paul's kenotic theory of salvation. As oppressed "underdogs," the dermies, like the newts and the exhausted human race victimized by the Solarians, recall the redemptive kenosis of God's Son. Through such an "emptying," Christ "assumed the condition of a slave" (Philippians 2:7) and accepted the humiliating agony of His Passion.

Viewed as a group, Miller's stories about revolutionary biological developments qualify a prevailing optimism with strong reservations, of which the most marked is a traditionalist sense that human nature is deeply and perhaps fatally flawed. Similarly, while Miller's short fiction on balance presents the application of science as a constructive force in human history, the author is not nearly so "technophilic" as Samuelson would imply.

524

For example, "Dumb Waiter" (1952) depicts a future in which humanity's undue dependence upon its machines has resulted in disaster. The message of the story is cleverly summed up in the triple meaning contained within its punning title. Technology as an automatic, undemanding servant to humanity has rendered the latter passively reliant upon its ministrations. But if humanity has become a "dumb" (that is, unthinking) waiter for the services of its machines, the machines are by themselves incapable of anything but inflexible routine. Thus, in Miller's story, the devices that collectively run an abandoned city have become "dumb" (that is, stupid) waiters for humanity to return and resume control over them. That the lack of such direction will turn technology into a sort of Frankenstein's monster is implied by a robot-run jail and orphanage. These two institutions, filled with the skeletons of starved inmates, suggest how machines unsupervised by man can make their erstwhile master into their victim.

The potentially negative effects of technological progress are viewed from another angle in Miller's Hugo-winning novella "The Darfsteller" (1955). This story concerns the plight of men supplanted by automation. Its protagonist is Ryan Thornier, a former stage star whose vocation has been rendered obsolete by the advent of robot theater. But Thornier is not content merely to suffer. Instead, he sabotages a robot theatrical production as part of a scheme intended to effect his vindication as an artist, his revenge, and his self-destruction. Although his rebellion against the new mechanical era is shown to be misconceived (Thornier in the process playing Judas to himself and others, as well as reenacting Christ's Passion), the pathos of his displacement is nonetheless convincingly rendered.

Although "Dumb Waiter" and "The Darfsteller" suggest that mankind can be adversely affected by its technology, both stories end with their protagonists defining for themselves a viable place in the new machine age. Mitch Laskell, the hero of "Dumb Waiter," takes control of the automated city, and Thornier learns that the only safe vocation in a time of technologically motivated change is "the speciality of creating new specialities." Nevertheless, in both stories the protagonist's victory is won only after he, as a representative of humanity, confronts a situation in which mankind is threatened by its machines.

Miller's belief that technology involves difficulties and dangers is likewise apparent in "Crucifixus Etiam" (1953) and "Big Joe and the Nth Generation" (1952). These two pieces, which posit the human colonization of Mars, are perhaps Miller's most complex explorations in his short fiction of the role of science in man's future.

"Crucifixus Etiam" deals with the initial stages of Martian colonization. Miller at first depicts his protagonist, Manue Nanti (a manual laborer who has been attracted to Mars primarily by high wages), as being both physically and spiritually victimized by new situations arising from technological progress. In particular, Nanti is faced with the atrophy of his lungs because of his long-term use of a mechanical "aerator" to breathe in the thin atmosphere of Mars. Moreover, there is Nanti's increasing sense that his work is meaningless in either personal or social terms. He also is unable to find any relevance in his Catholic faith to the alien planet on which he is living. Consequently, for a time his life appears devoid of significance or purpose.

Yet, despite the plight of its protagonist, "Crucifixus Etiam" is ultimately hopeful about the effects of scientific advancement. Nanti and his fellow laborers are symbolically associated in their manifold sufferings with the redemptive kenosis of Jesus, thereby indicating that an updated version of Christianity can still render technological progress meaningful to the human spirit. In this regard, Nanti's personal "Passion" is finally revealed to be an efficacious sacrifice for the long-term temporal betterment of his race. He eventually discovers that he has been working on a project that will, through nuclear fusion, give Mars a breathable atmosphere. "Crucifixus Etiam," accordingly, secularizes Christian belief so as to make it relevant in an age of scientific and material progress. Faith and sacrifice are related not to an otherworldly destiny but, rather, to humanity's gradual improvement of its mundane lot through technology.

However, "Big Joe and the Nth Generation" casts doubt upon such a temporal creed by positing humanity's cultural regression on Mars, and its self-destruction in war on Earth. In particular, as the latter catastrophe implies, Miller is ambivalent as to whether technology constitutes a blessing or a curse for humanity. That science can be a positive historical force is suggested indirectly through the lapse of the Martian colonists into a semi-primitive condition as a result of effectively losing the knowledge of the past. In this regard, the Martian colonists are threatened with extinction by the gradual escape of their man-made atmosphere. To preserve them, someone must reactivate the complex fusion device mentioned in "Crucifixus Etiam." But the wise makers of the apparatus have equipped it with a series of robot guards. The robots are intended to prevent barbarian depredations and (in view of the previous catastrophe on Earth) to test man's spiritual fitness to resume control of the power provided by technology. Asir in part proves his heroic capacity for the messianic task of rescuing his fellow colonists. He does so particularly by his display of mature rationality and courage when he passes a test of basic capacity for scientific thinking. Through his success, Asir escapes destruction by the fangs and clawed hands of Big Joe, the first robot guard of the fusion device. Subsequently, Joe becomes Asir's servant, implying that the young hero has proved at least partially worthy of commanding the awesome forces of technology.

Yet, in keeping with the potential dangers of technology, Asir's apparent role as scientific messiah is offset by the sinister connotations of Joe. The fearsome humanoid robot suggests both the destructive power of technology and the primitive animal savagery in humanity that misdirect its discoveries to violent ends. As a symbol of human turpitude, Joe functions as a Jungian "shadow" to Asir.

The spiritual shortcomings of Asir are further indicated at the end of "Big Joe" when he defines a technologist as "a thief who tells the gods what to do." Asir seems to be falling into the same naïve hubris about his newfound technological power that has previously allowed human evil to obliterate mankind on Earth. Fortunately, Asir finds his way to the fusion device barred by a second dangerous robot. To pass this guard, he must demonstrate an understanding of the destructive spiritual forces in himself and the rest of mankind. Whether or not Asir can succeed with this second and more demanding test is left an open question.

In its suggestion that periodic catastrophes will result from the misuse of the awesome power of technology by man's abiding evil, "Big Joe" anticipates *A Canticle for Leibowitz*. The latter work constitutes a landmark in the emergence of science fiction as a significant, modern literary form. *Canticle* has achieved recognition not only in science fiction circles (as attested by its receipt of a Hugo award in 1961) but also among readers of serious "mainstream" literature.

Canticle is a "composite" novel, shorter versions of each of its three sections ("Fiat Homo," "Fiat Lux," and "Fiat Voluntas Tua") having previously been published in Anthony Boucher's *Magazine of Fantasy and Science Fiction* in the years 1955–1957. Together these sections trace man's history from a collapse following a nuclear war in the 1960's to the eventual repetition of such a conflict in A.D. 3781. This future cycle parallels in its major trends the period between the fall of Rome and the first thermonuclear holocaust. Thus the years from circa A.D. 1965 to A.D. 3174 initially resemble the Dark Ages. North America has lapsed into almost total barbarism. The last bastion of civilization is the Catholic Church, its monastic order of St. Leibowitz preserving a few fragments of scientific knowledge. By 3174 a new Renaissance is under way. A centralized political order has begun to reappear, in turn fostering the growth of science. But, as with the previous European Renaissance, the secular state and secular intellectual life break away from the necessary guidance of the Church. These negative developments ultimately lead to the second nuclear conflict in 3781.

The thematic basis of *Canticle* is the perennial tension and balance in human life between the inseparable contraries of good and evil, creativity and destructiveness, original sin and God's redemptive work. Such a vision arises from Miller's Catholic theology. He believes that God made His world good, but that it has been partly perverted by satanic and human wickedness. Such a corruption is indicated by the use of the code phrase "Lucifer is fallen" with reference to the exploding of a hydrogen bomb. Just as the original brightness of Lucifer has become hellfire through his revolt, so the Devil has tempted man to transform God's first creation of light into a thermonuclear "flame deluge." The latter enormity in turn suggests that while the "light" of knowledge is in itself positive (and is therefore preserved by the Church through the new Dark Ages), science, when divorced from the guidance of Christian faith, becomes the servant of fallen humanity's sinfulness.

To approach the matter differently, for humanity, the fruit of the tree of knowledge entails the experience of good and evil as inextricably connected opposites. Science is therefore not morally neutral, but always, when used by man, has both positive and negative consequences. For example, at the end of *Canticle*, nuclear energy is destroying civilization on Earth and at the same time powering a spaceship used by the Church to save a remnant of humanity.

In addition to the dualities just mentioned, humanity's fall is, for Miller, offset by its redemption. That both original sin and saving grace are manifested in human affairs is shown by Mrs. Grales's two heads (biologically speaking, a mutation caused by atomic radiation from the first flame deluge), which express opposing spiritual states. Mrs. Grales is at first, as Russell Griffin notes, most obviously associated with the old Eve as an example of fallen humanity's proclivity to evil. But when her Rachel head awakens, Mrs.

Grales is identified with Mary, who as the Savior's mother was herself without original sin. The tension between humanity's fall and redemption is related to science by the legend of St. Leibowitz. According to the legend, the saint not only betrayed his technical expertise into the hands of corrupt rulers but later gave his life to preserve such knowledge as a God-created good. St. Leibowitz's martyrdom accordingly recalls both the suicide of Judas by hanging and the Passion of Christ.

Canticle also suggests the conjunction of opposites in human life by presenting history as a repeated "sequence of rise and fall." In such cycles the death and rebirth of civilization manifest, respectively, the Fall and God's redemptive power, the latter enabling society to share periodically in Christ's resurrection. The two contrary spiritual meanings in the rounds of history are both implied by Abbot Zerchi's statement that humanity appears doomed to "play the Phoenix" for all time. The Abbot intends his image to be negative, linking the fiery self-destruction of the legendary bird particularly to the two flame deluges. Nonetheless, Zerchi's allusion also has positive connotations that offset the irony of humanity's administering to itself, through nuclear war, an appropriate punishment for its own sins. Because the phoenix is reborn from its ashes, it has traditionally been associated with Christ's rising from the dead. Zerchi's reference consequently implies that each period of cultural reconstruction expresses God's redemptive power at work.

But *Canticle* does not simply link the fall of humanity with the death of its civilizations and their renewal with mankind's redemption by Christ. Miller also intimates that even the two flame deluges purvey divine grace. In this regard, the fire of the atomic wars suggests not only a punishment that foreshadows Hell but also a purgatorial purifying of the human race from sin. The affirmative spiritual connotations of the flame deluges become apparent in the new Dark Ages that follow the first nuclear catastrophe. This grim era is connected through Brother Francis' Lenten vigil in the desert with four analogous periods of mortification: the Hebrews' forty years in Sinai (suggested by the appearance during Francis' vigil of Benjamin Eleazar, a representative of the Jewish people); Christ's forty days of testing in the wilderness; the forty days of Lent; and the forty days and nights of the biblical flood, alluded to by the words "flame deluge." In each of these four analogues, some kind of mortification prepares for a positive spiritual outcome. Accordingly, Miller is implying that even the downfall of civilization and its harsh aftermath have a regenerative function for mankind.

But if historical catastrophe brings good out of evil, such cultural renewal is for Miller likewise infected with original sin. The rebirth of civilization therefore not only expresses Christ's redemptive power but also gives play to negative forces that eventually cause another disaster. A period of cultural reconstruction is consequently similar to one of collapse in being spiritually ambivalent, a duality seen in the new Renaissance of the thirty-second century. For example, Hannegan is a machiavel, who pursues the laudable end of politically reuniting North America by the bad means of violence and treachery. His methods indeed help to bring another "modern" age of advanced technology, the positive spiritual value of which is indicated by the spaceship used by the Church as a latter-day Noah's ark, but Hannegan's evil principles bear their most evident fruit in a second thermonuclear war.

Similarly, the rediscovery of science in the second Renaissance is morally ambiguous. In this connection, as Griffin points out, the arc lamp made by the monks of the Leibowitz Abbey is connected simultaneously with God's calling forth of light in Genesis and with the fall of Lucifer. The first allusion suggests the creative and redemptive power of human knowledge, which will restore civilization, but the second reference links scientific investigation to a rebellious pride exemplified by the secular scholar Thon Taddeo. Such hubris, by asserting that the pursuit of truth is independent of religious faith, in effect places science at the service of men like Hannegan. The consequence is the second flame deluge.

Miller's view of history as fraught with spiritual ambiguities might seem to indicate that his outlook in *Canticle* is basically ironic and pessimistic. But the ambivalent cycles of rise and fall are apparently placed within a positive eschatological context by the author's apocalyptic imagery. Such symbolism implies that even the darkest events of humanity's annals foreshadow the end of time as prophesied in Revelation, when God will finally cast out evil and create a perfected world. For example, the shark at the conclusion of *Canticle* suggests the abiding ferocity in humanity that has just destroyed its civilization. The near starvation of the savage creature likewise relates the second nuclear holocaust to God's ultimate defeat and punishment of Satan in Revelation 20. This connection, made through comparison with the Leviathan of Isaiah 27:1, involves an elaborate network of parallels that can be diagrammed as shown below.

CANTICLE	ISAIAH 27:1	REVELATION 20
The shark.	Satan as Leviathan is associated with a "dragon in the . . . sea."	Satan is a "dragon" (2) who is bound by God's angel (1–3).
The snake as a recurring symbol of evil.	Leviathan as a "piercing . . . crooked serpent."	Satan is "that old serpent" (2).
The shark almost starves when fallout decimates sea life.	The Lord will punish Leviathan with His "sword."	God will consume Satan's followers with fire (9) and cast the Devil into a lake of "fire and brimstone" (10).

Another hopeful apocalyptic image occurs when Mrs. Grales, after she has been taken over by her innocent Rachel head, brandishes the ciborium that contains the Host. As an antithesis to the Great Whore of Babylon with her cup of abominations (Revelation 17:4), Rachel foreshadows the New Jerusalem, "prepared as a bride . . . for her husband" (Revelation 21:2). The latter allusion is clinched by the meaning of the name Rachel ("lamb"), which recalls John's description of the New Jerusalem as the "Lamb's wife" (Revelation 21:9).

Canticle represents a major artistic advance over Miller's short fiction with respect to its intellectual richness and the subtle complexities of its symbolism. But Miller's novel concentrates on the same basic concerns that are central to his best short stories. In particular, both *Canticle* and the shorter works focus on three major questions: whether humanity has a positive spiritual potential or is essentially unregenerate; whether technology will play a constructive or a destructive role in future history; and whether humanity's ultimate destiny is to be seen in optimistic or bleakly pessimistic terms.

On the most apparent level, *Canticle* is ambivalent about these alternatives, manifesting a duality that also characterizes Miller's short fiction when viewed as a whole. But his novel does seem more obviously decisive about another of his major preoccupations: the place of traditional Judeo-Christian faith and values in an age of science. While *Canticle* indeed debunks superstitious credulity, and while Miller saw the Church as composed of fallen individuals capable of sin and error, his novel still seems to affirm a rather conservative type of Catholicism.

—JOHN B. OWER

In later years, however, Miller's attitude toward organized religion—especially the Catholic Church—apparently became more conflicted. In 1979, for example, he characterized his involvement with the Church as "an on-again, off-again thing" that in the end

"never really took." In 1983, he wrote to John Garvey that he had drifted away from Catholicism and was now "somewhere west of Zen and east of the Son." This ambivalence may have had something to do with the difficulties he experienced with *Saint Leibowitz and the Wild Horse Woman*, left incomplete at his death. (Through his agent he arranged for the manuscript to be put in order by Terry Bisson, winner of Hugo, Nebula, and Theodore Sturgeon awards and author of *Pirates of the Universe* [1996] as well as novelizations of *The Fifth Element* [1997], *Johnny Mnemonic* [1995], *The X-Files* [1999], and *Alien Resurrection* [1997].) Characterized as a "sequel" to *Canticle*, *Saint Leibowitz* is in fact an amplification of its great predecessor. Miller may be credited, then, like Tolkien or George Lucas, with having been one of the first (in modern times, at least) to conceive of an epic narrative lending itself to episodic expansion and elaboration. One imagines that, Miller's literary executors willing, further stories could be written within the larger history sketched in the tripartite novel of 1960.

Miller sets the action of *Saint Leibowitz* in the years 3244 to 3246, roughly seven decades after the events narrated in *Canticle*'s middle section. The recovery of scientific knowledge proceeds apace: the world has been circumnavigated again, the telegraph and repeating firearms reinvented. *Canticle*'s Brother Kornhoer and Thon Taddeo are briefly remembered here for their work with electricity (which led, we now learn, to the invention of a clumsy device for the execution of state prisoners). In Miller's account of the relations between secular and ecclesiastical power in the fourth millennium, one recognizes a number of parallels with prior history, notably various instances of the papacy's centuries-long battle against heresy and schism. In reading Miller's account of the Church divided against itself, one thinks immediately of the Protestant Reformation (for Hannegan II, in *Canticle*, was clearly modeled on Henry VIII of England). But Miller's detail suggests that he is revisiting or fugally recapitulating several passages in earlier Church history: the rift between eastern and western Christianity that began with the sack of Constantinople by western forces in 1204; the period of papal exile in Avignon (1309–1376); and (with a number of close parallels in the matter of papal elections swayed by the mob) the Great Schism of 1378–1417. In this regard, *Saint Leibowitz* merits comparison with *The Name of the Rose* (1983), Umberto Eco's magisterial novel of the pre-Reformation struggle among the Church, its reformers, and the Holy Roman Empire. But where Eco's story ends with a bang (a symbolic apocalypse), Miller's ends with a whimper: the collapse—following the triumph of caesar—of papal legitimacy. In the failed crusade one recognizes, belatedly, a kind of retrogressive vision of history. The Crusades, after all, were a phenomenon of the Middle Ages, not the Renaissance.

Miller's viewpoint character is the linguist Blacktooth St. George, a monk who yearns to be released from his vows (as a reluctant translator of ecclesiastical documents, he anticipates the malfunctioning "Abominable Autoscribe" of *Canticle*'s thirty-eighth century). "Nimmy," as he is generally called, allows himself to become the creature of Cardinal Elia Brownpony, who plays the game of power politics within the Church and between church and state. Eventually, Nimmy serves as a soldier in Brownpony's ill-advised campaign against the Texark emperor, Hannegan VII. But faith eludes him—as does the beautiful Ædrea, whose malformed genitalia make her "*semper virgo*" (forever intact). Another of Miller's heterodox manifestations of the Virgin, she remains, after their early erotic encounter, forever out of reach. The sufferings and frustration of Nimmy and Ædrea confer on them, however, as on Abelard and Eloise (whom they resemble), a romantic pathos and an ironic saintliness.

One is tempted to see Miller himself in his protagonist, a gifted individual whose burgeoning sense of human futility cannot be squared with a traditional vision of Christian eschatology. Like the author of *Canticle*, Nimmy embraces a monastic idea only to find that it cannot sustain him, and his subsequent experience of the world and the ugly unfolding of its history leaves him with little in which to believe. In *Saint Leibowitz*, then, Miller does not undertake anything like the Christian affirmation that ultimately transfigures his previous novel. He goes through motions that once, from a position of commitment (however tentative), enabled him to write a great book. Now, the monachal conceit patently exhausted, conviction flees before him as before his character.

As Abbot Zerchi tells Brother Joshua in *Canticle*, humanity cannot be restored to Eden through its own efforts, and some such reality principle seems again to operate here. The great crusade organized by Elia Brownpony, who becomes the shaky pontiff Amen II, is brought down less by the weakness and disunity of its leaders than by a generalized principle of human fallibility. But from no quarter do we hear the implicit argument that human efforts, seconded by divine intervention, will fare better in eternity. By the same token, although St. George is delivered from durance vile by a mutant who uses the same riddling expressions as the Rachel head of Mrs. Grales ("I commensurate the deception. . . . Accurate am I the exception"), he experiences no sense of the divine presence, nothing to instill "the faith he had searched for but never found." If there is any glimmer of hope here, it is in the One still awaited by old Benjamin (the Wandering Jew of ancient Christian legend), who stalks through history in *Canticle* and again here.

Some critics will no doubt argue that Miller's various gestures toward mystical promise can be made to articulate some kind of coherent theological doctrine, but in fact the author leaves the strands of eschatological meaning in his novel ungathered. Indeed, this sprawling fiction constantly betrays the uncertainties of its composition. The many interesting episodes ultimately fail to cohere. Several characters (notably among the Nomads) are inadequately differentiated, their significance to the plot left obscure. At least one major event is left completely unexplained. The theme would seem to be inchoate as well, with an inconclusive pattern of references to the intriguing (if heretical) idea that the Virgin embodied an "original uterine Silence into which the Word was spoken at the Creation." On the other hand, the defeat of historical coherence is very much at thematic issue here, and it may be that the shapelessness of this fiction represents not so much an authorial failure as a postmodernist rejection of what the late theorist Jean-François Lyotard called "the solace of good forms."

—DAVID COWART

Selected Bibliography

WORKS OF WALTER M. MILLER, JR.

A Canticle for Leibowitz. New York: Lippincott, 1960.
Conditionally Human. New York: Ballantine Books, 1962. (Collection.)
The View from the Stars. New York: Ballantine Books, 1965. (Collection.)
The Science Fiction Stories of Walter M. Miller, Jr. Boston: Gregg Press, 1978.
The Best of Walter M. Miller, Jr. New York: Pocket Books, 1980. (Collection.)
The Darfsteller and Other Stories. London: Corgi, 1982. (Collection.)
Beyond Armageddon: Twenty-One Sermons to the Dead. Edited by Walter M. Miller and Martin H. Greenberg. New York: Donald I. Fine, 1985. (Collection of work by other science fiction writers.)
Saint Leibowitz and the Wild Horse Woman. New York: Bantam, 1997.

BIBLIOGRAPHIES

"A Selective Annotated Bibliography of *A Canticle for Leibowitz.*" Compiled by James E. Hicks. *Extrapolation,* 31, no. 3 (1990): 216–228.
Walter M. Miller, Jr. A Bio-Bibliography. Compiled by William H. Roberson and Robert L. Battenfeld. Westport, Conn.: Greenwood, 1992. (Thorough, scrupulous annotations; covers secondary material through 1990.)
"Walter M. Miller, Jr.'s *A Canticle for Leibowitz:* Annotated Bibliography." Compiled by Margie R. Hefley. *Bulletin of Bibliography,* 46, no. 1 (1989): 40–45.

CRITICAL AND BIOGRAPHICAL STUDIES

The critical literature on Miller is extensive, with 130 items in the Roberson-Battenfeld bibliography alone. This number will burgeon as critics take up the attenuated theology of *Saint Leibowitz.* The following works are worthwhile either as overviews or as seminal thematic analyses.

Bennett, Michael A. "The Theme of Responsibility in Miller's *A Canticle for Leibowitz.*" *English Journal,* 59: (1970): 484–489. (Deals with individual responsibility as a central theme of the novel.)
Cowart, David. "Walter M. Miller, Jr." *Twentieth-Century American Science-Fiction Writers, Part II: M–Z.* Edited by Cowart and Thomas L. Wymer. Detroit, Mich.: Gale, 1981. (An overview, with biographical information deriving from correspondence with the author and considerable attention to the stories.)
Dowling, David, *Fictions of Nuclear Disasters.* Iowa City: University of Iowa Press, 1987. (Good comparison of *Canticle* and Hoban's *Ridley Walker.*)
Garvey, John. "A Canticle for Leibowitz: A Eulogy for Walt Miller." *Commonweal,* 123 (5 April 1996): 7–8. (Recalls visiting, interviewing, and corresponding with the author.)
———. "The Shaping of a Dark Vision." *Notre Dame Magazine,* 12, no. 3 (1983): 35–37. (An interview with the author.)
Griffin, Russell M. "Medievalism in *A Canticle for Leibowitz.*" *Extrapolation,* 14 (1973): 112–125. (Interprets the novel with special reference to medieval thought, stressing particularly the "tradition of . . . patristic exegesis.")
Ketterer, David. *New Worlds for Old: The Apocalyptic Imagination, Science Fiction, and American Literature.* Bloomington, Ind., and London: Indiana University Press, 1974. Pages 140–148. (Provides a helpful reading of *Canticle* in terms of the theme of cyclical repetition.)
Manganiello, Dominic. "History as Judgment and Promise in *A Canticle for Leibowitz.*" *Science-Fiction Studies,* 13 (July 1986): 159–169. (Discusses ideas of linear and cyclical history.)
Olsen, Alexandra H. "Re-Vision: A Comparison of *A Canticle for Leibowitz* and the Novellas Originally Published." *Extrapolation,* 38, no. 2 (1997): 135–149.
Ower, John. "Theology and Evolution in the Short Fiction of Walter M. Miller, Jr." *Cithara,* 25, no. 2 (1986): 57–74. (Focuses on "You Triflin' Skunk," "Blood Bank," and "Dark Benediction.")
Percy, Walker. "Walter M. Miller, Jr.'s *A Canticle for Leibowitz:* A Rediscovery." *Southern Review,* 7 (1971): 572–578. (A famous testimonial from a mainstream writer.)
Rank, Hugh. "Song out of Season: *A Canticle for Leibowitz.*" *Renascence,* 21 (1969): 213–221. (Sees the novel as "religious satire"—since Miller attacks certain aspects of the Catholic Church while affirming its traditional doctrines.)

Samuelson, David N. "The Lost Canticles of Walter M. Miller, Jr." *Science-Fiction Studies*, 3 (1976): 3–26. (Discusses Miller's short fiction, paying attention to both themes and literary quality, and includes a bibliographical appendix, "The Books and Stories of Walter M. Miller, Jr.")

Scheick, William J. "Continuative and Ethical Predictions: The Post-Nuclear Holocaust Novel of the 1980s." *North Dakota Quarterly*, 56, no. 2 (1988): 61–82. (Useful orientation of *Canticle* to later examples of the subgenre it founded.)

Scholes, Robert, and Eric Rabkin. *Science Fiction: History, Science, Vision*. New York: Oxford University Press, 1977. Pages 221–226. (Useful in interpreting the concluding episodes of *Canticle*.)

Seed, David. "Recycling the Texts of the Culture: Walter M. Miller's *A Canticle for Leibowitz*." *Extrapolation*, 37, no. 3 (1996): 257–271.

Senior, W. A. "'From the Begetting of Monsters': Distortion as Unifier in *A Canticle for Leibowitz*." *Extrapolation*, 34, no. 4 (1993): 329–339.

MICHAEL MOORCOCK

(b. 1939)

THERE ARE PARADOXES in the career of Michael Moorcock. He has been a hack (and often admitted it) but has won a major literary award. He is devoted to the past, especially to Edwardian England, yet he has become one of the great symbols of modernism in science fiction. His work is on the one hand romantic, melodramatic, and tearful, and on the other hand antisentimental and ironic. A professed puritan, he introduced into 1960's science fiction the Cavalier emblems of style (elaborate clothes, cars, houses, makeup) and sex (incest, bondage, troilism, transsexuality, and other imaginative pastimes). A professed anarchist, he is nevertheless preoccupied with property, ownership, and the use of autocratic systems for manipulating other people, not always in an obviously disapproving way.

Something of a legend in his own time and consciously given to ambiguity as an indoor sport, Moorcock himself is largely responsible for the rather silly nature of many of the myths surrounding him. One of his favorite fictional scenarios is the harlequinade. His physical presence (much illustrated in books and magazines) is perhaps another in a series of masks: he is huge, bearded, Falstaffian, and wild-haired, a wearer of opera cloaks in the 1950's, a hippy dude in the 1960's, a retiring gentleman in tweeds and knickerbockers in the 1970's. Yet just as the dandyism of his work is part of a series of Chinese boxes, at the center of which a protagonist frequently will be revealed as ordinary, anxious, and tired, so the flamboyant real-life Moorcock is

shy, and since the early 1970's has made very few public appearances.

An author's public persona may not be relevant to his writing, but in Moorcock's case it is surely part and parcel of the interesting and consciously developed metaphor that animates his work. Just as life is seen as aspiring to the condition of art in much of the work of the *New Worlds* writers, so Moorcock's books and his projected self-image seem part of the same performance. We are back to the harlequinade. It is relevant, then, that like Jerry Cornelius in *The Condition of Muzak* (1977), Moorcock was not wholly successful as a rock 'n' roll star. His one album to date (Michael Moorcock and the Deep Fix, *The New Worlds Fair*, 1975) reveals a singer whose voice, far from being raunchy, primal, and swaggering, as some fans expected, is a thin, light, pure tenor that sounds as if it should be singing patriotic Irish ballads or sentimental songs from the turn of the century.

If Moorcock's work is an enigma, then it is clearly a patterned enigma. Indeed, the paradoxes are not merely whimsical or inconsequential; they have been functional from the outset, and more recently have become, in a sense, the subject of his art.

Michael John Moorcock was born on the southern periphery of London, in Mitcham, Surrey, on 18 December 1939. His work has always been that of an intensely urban man, specifically a Londoner, to the extent that he has given the landscapes of Notting Hill and Ladbroke Grove, some miles to the decayed west of London's center, as fabulous a role in modern science fiction and fantasy as those of Melniboné or Middle Earth, Mars or the much-mined asteroids.

Unhappy at school, changing schools often, Moorcock left as soon as legally possible at age fifteen. Soon he was able to put his childhood love for Edgar Rice Burroughs to practical use by writing for a boys' magazine-cum-comic, *Tarzan Adventures*, which he edited from 1957 to 1958. From 1958 to 1961 he was an editor for the Sexton Blake Library, which published pulp thrillers. During this period he began submitting stories to the British magazines *Science Fiction Adventures*, *Science Fantasy*, and *New Worlds*.

There was rather more heroic fantasy than science fiction in Moorcock's early magazine stories. The first Elric story appeared in *Science Fantasy* in 1961. Nonetheless, of the first six books published under his own name, four were science fiction. The other two, *The Stealer of Souls* (1963) and *Stormbringer* (1965), told stories of the albino fantasy hero Elric and of the phallic, blood-drinking sword that in part controls him. (Four pseudonymous works also appeared in this period. The first three, published as by Edward P. Bradbury, are a trilogy, a vigorous Edgar Rice Burroughs pastiche: *Warriors of Mars, Blades of Mars*, and *The Barbarians of Mars* [all 1965]. The fourth is an interesting short story collection, *The Deep Fix*, published in 1966 as by James Colvin.)

The four science fiction novels are, at first glance, unremarkable. The style is uneasy and hurried; the action is implausible and melodramatic, producing striking color effects and set pieces rather than any carefully wrought suspension of disbelief. In hindsight I suspect that their apparent naïveté was in fact a false naïveté, using as its model not the comparatively well-bred science fiction of *Galaxy*, or *Fantasy and Science Fiction*, or even *Astounding/Analog*, but the baroque and florid adventures of *Planet Stories* and *Startling Stories*. But any ambition to become a kind of modern primitive, a Grandma Moses of science fiction, Moorcock has, fortunately,

abandoned. His carelessness about and lack of interest in science, and his generally slapdash approach, may have been promising qualities for a potential pulp writer, but a careful reading reveals that even then his thematic concerns were perfectly serious, although they did not really conform to the expectations of most science fiction readers at that time.

The Sundered Worlds (1965; reissued as *The Blood Red Game*, 1970) introduces the key idea of the "multiverse," which explicitly or implicitly runs through the whole of Moorcock's work, although in this early form it is something of a science fiction cliché: the idea of a huge (though finite) number of parallel universes coexisting. This was rapidly developed (at first in the fantasy rather than in the science fiction) into the idea of a series of alternative realities in and across which characters play out recurrent roles in a kind of manic, cosmic dance—characters who sometimes, especially in the fantasy, are seen as avatars of heroes and semideities, and sometimes as much closer to the common man.

Characters keep reappearing throughout Moorcock's work, sometimes with the same names, sometimes with very similar names (for example, Jherek Carnelian and Jerry Cornelius), sometimes sharing initials only (Jesus Christ and James Colvin), sometimes linked by style and fate, as are Elric and Jerry Cornelius (both of whom in their respective first appearances—in the story "The Dreaming City" [1961] and the novel *The Final Programme* [1968]—are moved to action by a quasi-incestuous love for a dead sister).

The Sundered Worlds offers the multiverse as a mere notion, which is not much more developed in *The Wrecks of Time* (1967; reissued as *The Rituals of Infinity*, 1971). *The Wrecks of Time* describes, with a feverish though jaunty assurance, the adventures of a Faustus/Falstaff figure (named Faustaff) in his attempts to save a series of doomed, parallel Earths. But by the end of the 1960's, Moorcock had begun to include so many cross-references between books and so many allusions to previous books (which when first published had no obvious connections between them) that the whole body of his work retrospectively has been made to seem a kind of giant, episodic supernovel. (A side effect of all this is that it is not possible adequately to discuss his science fiction in isolation from his fantasy.) If this strategy had been carried out purely on the level of recurrent characters and plot situations, it would have remained rather notional and diagrammatic. The success of the method depends on the substance, not the technique. At the heart of this super-novel lies a massive, passionate, structured concern; the complications and recomplications are a trick of the light, as new facets flash out and the entire crystalline mass re volves slowly before us.

The structured concern to which I refer is present, embryonically, from the beginning of Moorcock's work. We find it in his first four science fiction novels, in its earliest form, as a kaleidoscopic effect, a sometimes dreamlike shifting from one scene to another. Characters and landscapes are protean, metamorphosing, unstable. There is a shifting, disturbing flux. A sense of impending chaos has always been basic to Moorcock's writing, and it becomes an explicit theme early on, notably in the heroic fantasies.

The world of the Elric stories, in all its cryptic, doomed, and bloodstained variety, is structured around the struggle between the Lords of Order and the Lords of Chaos, who battle for Elric's soul throughout. Like Jerry Cornelius in the later and more sophisticated fiction, Elric is searching for a strategy of survival that avoids complete commitment (or surrender) to either of the forces working upon him. He displays an uneasy impartiality, an unstable integrity that is subject to many temporary but spectacular failures, usually in the direction of a Byronic, romantic excess (always doomed, all satisfaction being fleeting). But in the long run he just about manages to stand on his own two feet, despite the seductive lures and potent threats issuing from either end of the metaphysical, ethical, and political spectrum (order and chaos; good and evil; totalitarianism and anarchy).

Michael Moorcock. © MIRIAM BERKLEY

This is visibly a reflection of Moorcock's own position as writer. The chaos that pervades his books is the stuff of nightmare, but attractive for all that. And although the books show an occasional yearning for serenity, they do not by any means advocate the imposition of law as the right answer. Indeed, the failure of two of the first four science fiction novels—*The Fireclown* (1965; reissued as *The Winds of Limbo*, 1969) and *The Twilight Man* (1966; reissued as *The Shores of Death*, 1970)—is largely due to their being in part political tracts against the imposition of law. They advocate a liberal anarchy, but much of the didactic material is not properly assimilated into the melodramatic adventure stories, so that dogma rather unnervingly alternates with death. Since that time a commitment to political anarchism—left-wing but not doctrinaire—has been a persistent feature of Moorcock's writing and of his editorial policies.

One of the charms of Moorcock's writing is its openness to all kinds of experience, ordered or chaotic. He has always been as sensitively responsive to the zeitgeist as the hairs on a Venus's-flytrap to its prey. A passage in *The Sundered Worlds* anticipates the Moorcock to come:

> The multiverse was packed thick with life and matter. There was not an inch which did not possess something of interest. . . . Here was everything at once, all possibilities, all experience. (chapter 10)

Openness to experience, of course, became a slogan of the 1960's; and Moorcock, though still very young, was in the right place at the right time with the right talents. In 1963, after its near-collapse, the science fiction magazine *New Worlds* was about to change publishers, and former editor E. J. Carnell recommended the twenty-three-year-old Moorcock as new editor. His first issue was May–June 1964. The story of the next six years (*New Worlds* finished as a magazine, at least temporarily, in 1970) has been told many times; it has become a science fiction myth.

Under Moorcock's strong, creative, and sometimes manic editorship, *New Worlds* reflected much of the 1960's ethos (and criticized it too) in a way that no other science fiction magazine managed or even attempted. The conservative members of the science fiction world hated it: sex, violence, pessimism, anarchy, and—worst of all—literary and typographical experimentation had been loosed into their cozy universe. But new readers were found, and the magazine is now recognized as having had a liberating influence on science fiction out of all proportion to its circulation—even in the United States, where it was not published. It was, by and large, literate, flamboyant, iconoclastic, and original, though sometimes paying the necessary price of being pretentious and angst-ridden.

Readers tend now to remember *New Worlds* as extravagant, but much of its content was sober, concise, and restrained, though often acerbic. It published important work by writers such as Brian W. Aldiss, J. G. Ballard, Mervyn Peake, Keith Roberts, Bar-

rington Bayley, Thomas M. Disch, Norman Spinrad, Roger Zelazny, and Samuel R. Delany, who were already, to varying degrees, established; and it introduced John Sladek, David Masson, Charles Platt, Christopher Priest, Ian Watson, Langdon Jones, and M. John Harrison, among others. Moorcock made barely enough to live on during this period, and he was forced into the absurdly fast production of novels in order to support the magazine (which had a respectable but not really profit-making circulation). He also had to support his wife and the two small daughters born by the end of 1964. (A son was born in 1972.)

During his editorship Moorcock somehow found time to read an enormous amount, focusing on two special areas: the late nineteenth-century novel (Joseph Conrad, George Meredith, Rudyard Kipling, and others) and more recent experimental fiction (William S. Burroughs, Boris Vian, Italo Calvino, Hermann Hesse, Jorge Luis Borges, and others). The understanding he gained through this reading, and through his editorial work, of the possible structures and nuances of sophisticated fiction resulted in a quite startling increase in the flexibility and assurance of his own writing. (Few science fiction writers, sadly, show very noticeable advances in skill throughout their careers, and in all too many cases their early work is their best.)

Nonetheless, much of Moorcock's writing over this period is not very memorable. He was probably writing too fast. The early Elric books remain among his finest work; but while there is much of interest in the subsequent heroic fantasy series, some of the vigor has already been lost with the Hawkmoon stories. The final fantasy sequence, the Corum series, was written at the very end of Moorcock's *New Worlds* editorship. Although technically more proficient than some of his earlier work, it seems rather etiolated and sapless. (It also suggests that Moorcock's feelings about Celts are at best ambiguous.) He was responsive to *fin-de-siècle* writing and did not always control its studied decadence and dying falls when he used the style in his fantasies.

Although Moorcock has written only two more books that can be described as genre science fiction, both are more interesting than the later fantasies, although in neither case is the generic structure capable of sustaining the weight of meaning it is invited to carry. Thus *The Ice Schooner* (1969) and *The Black Corridor* (1969) seem rather portentous, out of sheer top-heaviness.

The Ice Schooner pays homage to Joseph Conrad's *The Rescue* (1920), and to some extent recapitulates the latter's plot, which F. R. Leavis once summarized as "the conflict between Love and Honour (a kingdom at stake) against a sumptuously rendered decor of tropical sea, sunset, and jungle." (*The Great Tradition*, 1948). The milieu here, though, is a future Ice Age, and the hero is a sailor-adventurer who plies his ship on runners across oceans of ice. It is a very readable story—a moving account of a barbarian hero who is finally faced with the fact that his entropic, frozen world is metamorphosing into a new world of springtime greenery. When asked to adjust to a new life, he refuses.

The Black Corridor was commissioned during a period of total exhaustion for Moorcock. Much of the book was first written to his outline by Hilary Bailey, his wife at that time, and was later revised by him. Through the memories and hallucinations of a starship captain, who with family and friends is escaping from an overcrowded and politically collapsing Earth, we learn that the rest of the crew have suffered a grisly fate, although the captain is in a mental state of fugue and persists in believing they are comfortably asleep in suspended animation. This is as close to the "psycho-gothic" domestic chiller as Moorcock ever approached, although the responsibility for the change of mode was probably his wife's.

Moorcock's two most important books of the 1960's open up what has become the main thematic area in which he has worked ever since. They also effectively create a new genre. Tropes and images from both science fiction and fantasy continue to be used, but they are embedded in an ironic structure that cannot be pigeonholed in the traditional generic categories. We can still properly consider such works in a discussion of science fiction, since the time-hallowed themes of catastrophe, future warfare, and computer-dominated civilizations make regular appearances, although they are often viewed from an unusual angle. Two science fiction themes remain very dominant indeed: alternate worlds and time travel. Both, for Moorcock, were means of approaching what was to become the major theme of his work in the 1970's: the ironies of time and history.

Behold the Man is one of Moorcock's most praised works, although I find in it a rather mechanical cynicism that is too contrived to be really painful. In its first form, as a novella (1966), it won a Nebula award. The hero, Karl Glogauer, is a seedy and self-pitying Jew from present-day London who is given to justified feelings of persecution. He goes back in a time machine to fulfill his neurotic obsession: to determine the truth of the Christ story. He accidentally becomes the historical (but insane) Christ himself, and is crucified. The story is cleverly told, especially in the short version (the novelized version of 1969 is a little inflated), but I find it atypically mean-spirited. Moorcock's work is usually more generous, expansive, and even altruistic.

The Final Programme (1968) was written in 1965, at which time three sections of it were published in *New Worlds*, the first Cornelius stories to appear there. It is the first part of a tetralogy, *The Cornelius Chronicles* (1968–1977), which is perhaps more properly considered as Moorcock wishes it considered: as a single novel. But *The Final Programme* may not have been written with so ambitious a plan in mind; and to some extent it seems separate from the other three parts, even though it has been revised three times to incorporate it more seamlessly into the fictional whole.

The plot of *The Final Programme* is (deliberately) similar to that of the first two Elric stories, but now the Elric figure is Jerry Cornelius—a dude, a brilliant scientist, and an international adventurer in the mid-twentieth century. Jerry is a metamorph, a scholar, an assassin, and a spy, with as many lives and as few morals as a tomcat, and an ability to alter reality in the world at large. In *The Final Programme* his character is suffused by a kind of manic gaiety, even when he and his unpleasant alter ego Miss Brunner use the final computer program to absorb one another and to emerge as a new, hermaphroditic messiah.

Moorcock's genius for incorporating pieces of his own art into larger, more sophisticated totalities was never more evident than in his use of this self-sufficient *jeu d'esprit* of the 1960's as a springboard for his most ambitious creation. The remaining three novels in the Cornelius saga are *A Cure for Cancer* (1971), *The English Assassin* (1972), and *The Condition of Muzak* (1977). All four books were published in one volume as *The Cornelius Chronicles* (1977), with an introduction by John Clute that is the finest single piece of exegesis I know of in science fiction criticism.

The further into the series the reader proceeds, the more complex is the literary structure. Synopsis is very nearly impossible. The story is multilayered and is spread across the trouble spots and pleasure spots of the globe, sometimes in the twentieth-century world that we know, and sometimes in twentieth-century worlds that could have happened if Edwardian dreams of progress within a harmonious Empire had come true, or in worlds that could still happen if our nightmares come true, or worlds that are somehow metaphorically true to the real world, while factually false. Always the story returns to Jerry's home ground, Ladbroke Grove in London W 11—to "the deep city," as John Clute puts it, decaying landscape of the randy urban pastoral, just like the place where many of us live.

Moorcock's control of narrative tone by now is utterly assured. The story moves confidently and ever more darkly, as the sound of 1960's merriment begins to fade away and the gray realities of the 1970's begin to assert themselves. It moves through romantic extravaganza, poker-faced reporting of the holocaust (and another holocaust, and a third, spiraling through Apocalypses Now); moves through the wit of the bedroom and of the shambles, through Dickensian wholeheartedness, through abdications and coronations and resuscitations; moves through the whirl of the harlequinade and finally back to the ordinary world where Jerry has acne and his dreadful, indomitable mother lies dead.

Time shifts and turns. History has many routes and lessons thus revealed, or perhaps Moorcock does not know what day of the week it is—or probably and typically both are true. Objects are talismanic: rock 'n' roll records, cars, clothes, the gear and tasty detritus of style and appetite. Helicopters, guns, and drinks are all given their brand names. Time travel has always been used in science fiction, as have alternate worlds, to show us how things could be better, worse, or simply different; but, *The Cornelius Chronicles* ultimately insists, things will remain the same; they were and are the same. Other world lines, other time tracks, other possibilities offer an escape or a salvation that is strictly temporary and emblematic, for none is free from entropy.

Entropy is the other subject of this extraordinary series, but not entropy as a process to be merely succumbed to. Death, rust, decay, holocaust, cold, the lost ball-point pens, and the grease stains on top of the gas stove are real, and Jerry cannot be Harlequin forever. This too is the nature of the catastrophe. But as Pierrot, the sad clown at the sad close, Jerry is still alive. Even entropy, which has no brand name, can be endured.

Jerry is not the whole world. Other mythic figures abound. There is, for example, the threefold goddess (the maiden/the woman/the crone) much beloved of quasi-mystical fantasists with their well-thumbed copies of Robert Graves's *The White Goddess* (1947). She is there, too, in incarnations that are not at all Gravesian or godlike, although Una Persson, the Woman Revolutionary, is often heroic and turns out to be Harlequin after all. Catherine Cornelius is the decadent, dead child; and Mrs. Cornelius, the grotesque and malicious embodiment of the life force, is the most appallingly likable character in fiction since the creations of Charles Dickens.

In 1977, *The Condition of Muzak* became the first science fiction novel to win a "mainstream" literary award, the *Guardian* prize for fiction. Yet with all the talk at that time, no critic seems to have commented on the most remarkable paradox of all: *The Cornelius Chronicles* remains, all of its irony notwithstanding, the last major monument to British patriotism in literary history.

Moorcock's wit, always evident previously, became sharper and more ironic in *The Cornelius Chronicles*, although like most literary irony it is easy to overlook. Many readers seem never to have understood that Jerry is not always an admirable model of the 1960's "swinging" life-style; that element is part of him, but it is undercut by the mockery with which he is regarded. Some of this is a mockery of 1960's excess; some is a kind of mockery of fantasy heroes in general and of the foolishly flamboyant actions they so often feel called upon to undertake. Jerry can be seen as Moorcock's revenge on Elric and Hawkmoon, and on the whole fantasy genre that he came to love like an aging and nagging mistress—better when it was in the next room.

Moorcock was still highly productive at the beginning of the 1970's (nine of his sixty-odd books were published in 1971 and 1972), and he continued to edit *New Worlds*, in its new format as a paperback anthology, until 1973. Then, at least by his own standards, he slowed down.

The second Karl Glogauer book, *Breakfast in the Ruins* (1972), is rather morose and dispirited in its guided tour of representative contemporary crises, both moral and political. A formal and diagrammatic farewell to the fantasy precinct of the multiverse was bid with *The Quest for Tanelorn* (1975), in which the Many heroic analogues are seen to be aspects of the indisputably One hero, who retires. (Elric, though, turned up a little later,

looking rather forlorn, at one of Jerry Cornelius' parties.)

But a sprightly wit, less seriously focused than in the Cornelius books, characterizes much of Moorcock's work of this period. The best witticisms appeared in the Dancers at the End of Time trilogy: *An Alien Heat* (1972), *The Hollow Lands* (1974), and *The End of All Songs* (1976). These stand in the same relation to Moorcock's most substantial work (*The Cornelius Chronicles* and *Gloriana*) as, at a more exalted level, Shakespeare's comedies stand to the history and problem plays. (Moorcock has not yet written a tragedy.)

In much of Moorcock's earlier work, protagonists of a lawful world are tempted by the allure of chaos. In the Dancers trilogy, though, the reverse is the case. At the end of time, during a kind of Indian summer before entropy finally makes the suns wink out, the prevailing post-technological sophistication on a future Earth allows the spontaneous creation of just about anything. But Moorcock's naïve desire in *The Sundered Worlds* for "everything at once, all possibilities" had clearly been tempered by the partial granting of that wish in the hedonistic 1960's. In *An Alien Heat*, Jherek Carnelian, the darling of the last days, meets an unwitting time traveler from the nineteenth century, Mrs. Amelia Underwood, who is very moral indeed. Faced with her stubborn penchant for misery and self-denial, the insouciant Carnelian feels something to be lacking in his own life. Having everything is not enough if it is unstructured, unweighted, and entirely free. It needs to be paid for.

The ensuing farce, punctuated by an excellent series of running gags on the theme of creative anachronism, is a bravura performance carried out with a delicate touch. Some longueurs do occur in the second and third volumes, where the author at several points resorts to funny aliens to keep things moving and where a slight self-plagiarism creeps in as the creative pressure slackens. (It is difficult for a highly productive composer not to relax, occasionally, by playing idle, minor variations on the same riff.) Most of

Moorcock's main characters—Persson, Bastable, and others—make guest appearances here. The trilogy is a soufflé, balancing out the richer, heavier dishes in the Moorcock banquet. (*Legends from the End of Time*, published in 1976, collects three fine, ironic, and somewhat *fin-de-siècle* novellas as a coda to the Dancers trilogy.)

Gloriana (1978) is, to date, the only other major work by Moorcock. Other publications of the late 1970's and early 1980's are mostly reissuings and reworkings of older material, or minor efforts written under commercial pressure without much real commitment. *Gloriana* is dedicated to the late Mervyn Peake and pays homage to this writer whom Moorcock greatly admires. He borrows from Peake's great Gormenghast trilogy (*Titus Groan*, 1946; *Gormenghast*, 1950; and *Titus Alone*, 1959) the central metaphor of the great building (here a palace) that stands both as a microcosm of the world and as an analogue for the brain. (The image of an inhabited building as a brain appears several times in Moorcock's earlier work, notably in *The Final Programme*, when Jerry, looking up at his secret ancestral chateau, reflects "how strongly the house resembled his father's tricky skull.")

Gloriana is the queen of Albion, and at many points she resembles Elizabeth I, the queen of Shakespearean England. Albion is an alternate-world England that splendidly evokes much of the ambience of the Elizabethan court; the novel borrows its structure and imagery from that elaborate, moral-allegorical court poem, Edmund Spenser's *The Faerie Queen*. *Gloriana*, though, is more Jacobean than Elizabethan in flavor. The ghosts of John Webster, Cyril Tourneur, and Ben Jonson seem to hover over the scenario of revenge, malcontents, conspiracy, illusion, and masque. Gloriana's great palace is home and court, museum, laboratory, and map, a setting for affairs of state, yet (most important) full of secret places unknown even to Gloriana. There is a darker, more dangerous world behind the walls, where the stately beings of the superego cannot easily reach; these beings seem almost unaware of their scurrying, furtive relatives of the id. Gloriana cannot reach all the recesses of her own mind, either. She is a woman trained to maintain order and harmony, working to undo the harm brought about by her mad, malicious father during his reign; but she is nevertheless promiscuous, often unhappy, and unable to achieve orgasm.

This is a book richer in metaphor than anything else in Moorcock's image-laden oeuvre. Traditional ideas from late sixteenth- and early seventeenth-century writing (harmony and good governance; hierarchies, correspondences among the body politic, the body physical, and the body spiritual; the flux of the elements, essences of being, conflicts between spiritual and temporal law; and original sin) meld effortlessly with Moorcock's own preoccupations and are merged into his metaphors as though they were made for one another.

The masque subsumes the harlequinade; formal masques mark the phases of the story, and behind all this is the great masque that *is* the story. The fiction draws attention to itself as a fiction, because a book is a kind of building too, an analogue of the author's brain. (Thus Moorcock, even though he has never eschewed some kind of naturalism, no matter how extravagant the movement and structure of his work, will nevertheless become grist for the academic structuralists' mill by becoming a fabulist also, his fiction consciously a masque, a mask, a made thing, and so declaring itself.)

In *Gloriana*, Moorcock's previously established themes continue—even through all of the romantic extravagance, the mirth, the masques, and the insignia of surfaces—with greater depth than anything before (apart from *The Condition of Muzak*), continually made fresh and new. With masterly control he relates and rediscovers a strategy of survival, suspended between law and chaos. Likewise, he rejects the partial truths of an order and harmony the precarious existence of which depends upon never admitting what is rustling behind the walls, and which for that very reason must crumble, must explode into chaos or into a final orgasm. This final orgasm is the novel's ultimate metaphor, erupting when Gloriana is raped by the black-garbed, amoral Captain Quire—the incarnation of evil, perhaps, or anarchy, possessor of an insatiable intellectual and sensual curiosity that leads him to explore any and all experience. This orgasm is the emblematic paroxysm of joy and pain that might usher in chaos, or that might restore us to the Garden, to Eden, to Tanelorn, to the flourishing of the state—but that, surprisingly and gravely, is followed by a workmanlike, practical sobriety and a serene progress through the winter landscape.

Gloriana belongs to the same multiverse with which the young Moorcock began, within which both science fiction and fantasy, all desires and fears, must necessarily play a role. If Moorcock refuses to fit into the comfortable categories of genre fiction, he does so because the fictional multiverse itself is (as in real life) intractable. No doubt the multiverse he surveys holds more surprises yet. High hopes were held out for *Byzantium Endures* (1981), which dealt quite seriously with the Russian Revolution and with anti-Semitism, while contriving to include Mrs. Cornelius as a character. It was Moorcock's longest book to date.

—PETER NICHOLLS

Moorcock has continued to progress as a quality writer since 1981. He has produced about a novel a year, none of them hackwork and some of them nongenre, as well as many stories and some nonfiction. As before, it is difficult to define much of his fiction as science fiction; it is his own brand of literary and often postmodern fantasy. Three of Moorcock's early series have been extended by new novels, and three new series have been initiated. In addition to writing a few fine solo novels, he has also continued the process of rewriting and consolidating all his earlier fiction, reinforcing the links between the series; this material has been issued in fourteen large omnibus volumes by Millennium in the United Kingdom.

Elric, that most famous of Moorcock's creations, has been brought back in a fragmented collection, *Elric at the End of Time* (1984), and two mildly enjoyable novels, *The Fortress of the Pearl* (1989) and *The Revenge of the Rose* (1991); it seems that the author's heart is not in the series anymore. John Daker, the Eternal Champion, returns in *The Dragon in the Sword* (1986; expanded 1987), and the Oswald Bastable trilogy is completed by *The Steel Tsar* (1981).

The Colonel Pyat novels represent a new direction for Moorcock. This complex and groundbreaking historical saga of the twentieth century began with *Byzantium Endures* (1981) and continued with *The Laughter of Carthage* (1984) and *Jerusalem Commands* (1992). It will be completed with *The Vengeance of Rome*, which has been in progress for several years.

The two other new series both have a slight connection with the Eternal Champion. The Von Bek novels are supernatural historical fiction, solidly based in their own periods yet featuring the continuing struggle between good and evil, between order and chaos. *The War Hound and the World's Pain* (1981) is set in the seventeenth century, with Graf Ulrich von Beck leading troops in the worst atrocity of the Thirty Years' War, while *The City in the Autumn Stars* (1986) is narrated by Manfred von Bek during the time of the French Revolution; the latter is a magnificently multilayered novel, involving travel around the real late-eighteenth century Europe and to the amazing city of Mirenburg, out of time (Mirenburg is easily reached from eighteenth-century Europe but is an alternate version of that time period).The Second Ether trilogy is set completely out of time, in an alternate Deep South. *Blood* (1995), *Fabulous Harbours* (1995), and *The War Amongst the Angels* (1996) are all constructed of separate stories, which are concerned with various von Beks and which weave together to form a playful tapestry greater than the sum of its parts. The writing is rich and audacious, a complex blending of genres and locales.

Moorcock's most notable one-off (not part of a series) novel from this period is *Mother London* (1988). Not only is this his hundredth novel, but it is arguably his cleverest, being an autobiographically based fabulation (not quite fantasy but not wholly realistic fiction either) that celebrates London in various surprising ways.

Perhaps Moorcock is moving away from genre science fiction or fantasy, yet he has not tried to disown the field in which he began and for which he is still best known. He seems to be a more capable writer than ever, a writer who may well go on to produce greater (though not necessarily more popular) novels.

—CHRIS MORGAN

Selected Bibliography

Bibliographies of Moorcock's books are notoriously difficult to compile, because of the copious retitlings and revisions, and because of the difficulty of defining series, since so many characters reappear from series to series that his work can almost be regarded as one superseries, one giant book. For convenience, his books are here divided into four major categories, and subdivided into individual series.

INDISPUTABLE SCIENCE FICTION

The Fireclown. London: Compact SF/Roberts and Vintner, 1965. Reissued as *The Winds of Limbo*, New York: Paperback Library, 1969.

The Sundered Worlds. London: Compact SF/Roberts and Vintner, 1965. Reissued as *The Blood Red Game*, London: Sphere, 1970.

The Twilight Man. London: Compact SF/Roberts and Vintner, 1966. Reissued as *The Shores of Death*, London: Sphere, 1970.

The Wrecks of Time. New York: Ace, 1967. Reissued with revised text as *The Rituals of Infinity*, London: Arrow, 1971.

The Black Corridor. London: Mayflower, 1969.

The Ice Schooner. London: Sphere, 1969. Revised, New York: Harper and Row, 1977.

BORDERLINE SCIENCE FICTION: ALTERNATE PASTS, PRESENTS, AND FUTURES

JERRY CORNELIUS TETRALOGY

The Final Programme. New York: Avon, 1968. Original text restored, London: Allison and Busby, 1969. Revised in 1977 omnibus edition. Revised again, London: Fontana, 1979.

A Cure for Cancer. London: Allison and Busby, 1971. Revised in 1977 omnibus edition. Revised again, London: Fontana, 1979.

The English Assassin. London: Allison and Busby, 1972. Revised in 1977 omnibus edition. Revised again, London: Fontana, 1979.

The Condition of Muzak. London: Allison and Busby, 1977. Revised in 1977 omnibus edition. Revised again, London: Fontana, 1978.

The Cornelius Chronicles. New York: Avon, 1977. (Omnibus edition of previous four books, all slightly revised. With an introduction by John Clute.)

BOOKS DIRECTLY RELATED TO THE CORNELIUS TETRALOGY

Printer's Devil, as by Bill Barclay. London: Roberts and Vintner, 1966. Reissued as by Michael Moorcock, with revisions and a change of names to bring work into line with Jerry Cornelius books, as *The Russian Intelligence*, Manchester, England: Savoy Books, 1980.

Somewhere in the Night, as by Bill Barclay. London: Roberts and Vintner, 1966. Reissued as by Michael Moorcock, with substantial revisions and a change of names to bring work into line with Jerry Cornelius books, as *The Chinese Agent*, New York: Macmillan, 1970.

The Nature of the Catastrophe, edited by Michael Moorcock and Langdon Jones. London: Hutchinson, 1971. (Contains an introduction, fifteen Jerry Cornelius stories—five by Moorcock—a comic strip [co-scripted by Moorcock], and a chronology.)

The Distant Suns, as by Michael Moorcock and Philip James (pseudonym of James Cawthorn). Nant Gwilw, Carmarthen, Wales: Unicorn Press, 1975. (Features as protagonist a Jerry Cornelius only distantly related to that of the other books.)

The Adventures of Una Persson and Catherine Cornelius in the Twentieth Century. London: Quartet, 1976. Retitled and bound with *The Black Corridor* as *The Adventures of Una Persson and Catherine Cornelius*, New York: Dial Press/Davis Publications, 1979.

The Lives and Times of Jerry Cornelius. London: Allison and Busby, 1976.

KARL GLOGAUER BOOKS

Behold the Man. London: Allison and Busby, 1969. New York: Avon, 1970.

Breakfast in the Ruins. London: New English Library, 1972. New York: Random House, 1973.

BASTABLE BOOKS

The Warlord of the Air. London: New English Library, 1971. New York: Ace, 1971.

The Land Leviathan. London: Quartet, 1974. Garden City, N.Y.: Doubleday, 1974.

The Steel Tsar: Third Volume in the Oswald Bastable Trilogy. London: Granada, 1981.

DANCERS AT THE END OF TIME TRILOGY

An Alien Heat. London: MacGibbon and Kee, 1972. New York: Harper and Row, 1973.

The Hollow Lands. New York: Harper and Row, 1974.

The End of All Songs. New York: Harper and Row, 1976.

The Dancers at the End of Time. London: Hart-Davis/MacGibbon, 1980. (Omnibus of above trilogy.)

ITEMS ASSOCIATED WITH DANCERS AT THE END OF TIME

Legends from the End of Time. New York: Harper and Row, 1976.

The Transformation of Miss Mavis Ming. London: W. H. Allen, 1977. Reissued as *A Messiah at the End of Time*, New York: DAW, 1977.

OTHER NOVELS LOOSELY ASSOCIATED BY THEMES AND CHARACTERS TO ALL THE ABOVE

Gloriana, or The Unfulfill'd Queen. London: Allison and Busby, 1978. New York: Avon, 1979.

The Great Rock 'n' Roll Swindle. London: Virgin, 1980.

Byzantium Endures. London: Secker and Warburg, 1981; New York: Random House, 1982.

The Laughter of Carthage. London: Secker and Warburg, 1984; New York: Random House, 1984.

Mother London: A Novel. London: Secker and Warburg, 1988; New York, Harmony, 1989.

Jerusalem Commands. London: Cape, 1992.

FANTASY

The Golden Barge. Manchester, Savoy, and New York: DAW, 1980.

The Crystal and the Amulet, with Jim Cawthorn. London: Savoy: 1986.

VON BEK BOOKS

The War Hound and the World's Pain. New York: Timescape, 1981; London: New English Library, 1982.

The Brothel in Rösenstrasse. London: New English Library, 1982; New York: Carroll and Graf, 1987.

The City in the Autumn Stars. Being a Continuation of the Story of the Von Bek Family and Its Association with Lucifer, Prince of Darkness, and the Cure for the World's Pain. London: Grafton, 1986; New York: Ace, 1987.

MARS BOOKS

Warriors of Mars, as by Edward P. Bradbury. London: Compact, 1965; New York: Lancer, 1966. Reprinted as *The City of the Beast*, as by Michael Moorcock, New York: Lancer, 1980.

Blades of Mars, as by Edward P. Bradbury. London: Compact, 1965; New York: Lancer, 1966. Reprinted as *The Lord of the Spiders*, as by Michael Moorcock, New York: Lancer, 1970.

The Barbarians of Mars, as by Edward P. Bradbury. London: Compact, 1965; New York: Lancer, 1966. Reprinted as *The Masters of the Pit*, as by Michael Moorcock, New York: Lancer, 1970.

ELRIC BOOKS

Stormbringer. London: Jenkins: 1965; New York: Lancer, 1967. Revised edition, New York: DAW, 1977.

The Singing Citadel, London: Mayflower, 1970; New York: Berkley, 1970. (Short stories.)

The Sleeping Sorceress. London: New English Library, 1971; New York: Lancer, 1972. Revised as *The Vanishing Tower*, New York: DAW, 1977; London: Panther, 1984.

Elric of Melniboné. London: Hutchinson, 1972. Reprinted as *The Dreaming City*, New York: Lancer, 1972.

Elric: The Return to Melniboné. Illustrated by Philippe Druillet. Brighton, England: Unicorn Bookshop, 1973. (Cartoon).

The Jade Man's Eyes. Brighton, England: Unicorn Bookshop, 1973. (short stories.)

The Sailor on the Seas of Fate. London: Quartet, 1976; New York: DAW, 1976.

The Bane of the Black Sword. New York: DAW, 1977; London: Panther, 1984.

The Weird of the White Wolf. New York: DAW, 1977; New London: Panther, 1984.

Elric at the End of Time: Fantasy Stories. London: New English Library, 1984; New York: DAW, 1985. (Short stories.)

The Fortess of the Pearl: An Elric Tale. London: Gollancz, 1989; New York: Ace, 1989.

The Revenge of the Rose: A Tale of the Albino Prince in the Years of his Wandering. London: Grafton, 1991; New York: Ace, 1991.

HAWKMOON BOOKS

The Jewell in the Skull. New York: Lancer, 1967; London: Mayflower, 1969. Revised edition, New York: DAW, 1977.

Sorcerer's Amulet. New York: Lancer, 1968. Reprinted as *The Mad God's Amulet*, London: Mayflower, 1969. Revised edition, New York: DAW, 1977.

The Sword of the Dawn. New York: Lancer, 1968; London: Mayflower, 1969. Revised edition, New York: DAW, 1977.

The Secret of the Runestaff. New York: Lancer, 1969. Reprinted as *The Runestaff*, London: Mayflower, 1969. Revised edition, New York: DAW, 1977.

The Champion of Garathorm. London: Mayflower, 1973; New York: Berkley, 1985.

Count Brass. London: Mayflower, 1973; New York: Dell, 1976.

The Quest for Tanelorn. London: Mayflower, 1975; New York: Dell, 1976.

ETERNAL CHAMPION BOOKS

The Eternal Champion. London: Mayflower, 1970; New York: Dell, 1970. Revised edition. New York: DAW, 1978.

Phoenix in Obsidian. London: Mayflower, 1970. Reprinted as *The Silver Warriors*, New York: Dell, 1973.

The Dragon in the Sword: Being the Third and Final Story in the History of John Draker, The Eternal Champion. New York: Ace, 1986; London: Grafton, 1987.

CORUM BOOKS

The Knight of the Swords. London: Mayflower, 1971; New York: Berkley, 1971.

The Queen of the Swords. London: Mayflower, 1971; New York: Berkley, 1971.

The King of the Swords. London: Mayflower, 1971; New York: Berkley, 1971.

The Bull and the Spear. London: Allison and Busby, 1973; New York: Berkley, 1973.

The Oak and the Ram. London: Allison and Busby, 1973; New York: Berkley, 1973.

The Sword and the Stallion. London: Allison and Busby, 1973; New York: Berkley, 1973.

SECOND ETHER TRILOGY

Blood: A Southern Fantasy. London: Millenium, 1995; New York: Morrow, 1995.

Fabulous Harbours: A Sequel to Blood. London: Millenium, 1995; New York: Avon, 1997.

The War Amongst the Angels: A Sequel to Blood and Fabulous Harbours. London: Millenium, 1996; New York: Ace, 1997.

NONSERIES SHORT FICTION

The Stealer of Souls and Other Stories. London: Spearman, 1963; New York: Lancer, 1967.

The Deep Fix, as by James Colvin. London: Compact SF/Roberts and Vintner, 1966.

The Time Dweller. London: Rupert Hart-Davis, 1969. (Reprints title story and two others from *The Deep Fix*, plus six new stories.)

Moorcock's Book of Martyrs. London: Quartet, 1976. Reissued as *Dying for Tomorrow*, New York: DAW, 1978.

My Experiences in the Third World War. Manchester, England: Savoy, 1980. (Contains those three stories from *The Deep Fix* not reprinted in *The Time Dweller*, plus four others.)

The Opium General and Other Stories. London: Harrap, 1984.

Casablanca. London: Gollancz, 1989.

C. L. MOORE
(1911–1987)
HENRY KUTTNER
(1915–1958)

BECAUSE THEY WERE a husband-and-wife writing team and because many of their stories and novels were inextricably entwined collaborations, it was thought advisable to consider Moore and Kuttner and their writings in one article. Although their lives and works cannot be totally separated, the main emphasis of the first part of this article is on Moore as much as possible, and the second half similarly focuses on Kuttner.

I

When, in 1933, Farnsworth Wright, editor of *Weird Tales*, read an unsolicited manuscript from a writer previously unknown to him—a C. L. Moore—he summoned the entire staff into his office. "Today," he announced, "is hereby declared C. L. Moore Day." He motioned toward the manuscript of "Shambleau" on his desk and said, "This is the finest story we've ever received."

In 1924, Wright had become editor of a failing publication, and over the years he made it the best of the fantasy or science fiction magazines. A man of impeccable literary taste who was himself an accomplished fiction writer, critic, and poet, he had—by the time of the submission of "Shambleau"—created a magazine of true literary merit, one that stood, in respect to other such periodicals, as a sun to its planets. Thus, it was not at all

surprising that he recognized a flowering of true literary genius when he found it.

"Shambleau" was published in the November 1933 issue of *Weird Tales*. Reader response was overwhelming. Indeed, perusal of the records Wright kept shows that only one other story published in the magazine since its inception even came close to the reader acceptance of "Shambleau"; and that, published in 1926, was A. Merritt's finest short story, "The Woman of the Wood."

Moore was long thought to be a man, even by Henry Kuttner, who early wrote to her as "Mr. C. L. Moore." After discovering his mistake, he married her. She was an attractive young woman who was then working in an Indianapolis bank. Obviously she had read widely in classical literature, for she had unerringly drawn upon the Medusa archetype for her initial story. But it is not only classical literature that infuses Moore's fiction. She read virtually everything she could lay her hands on. In describing her work, one could suggest that it is the product of original talent working upon the raw stuff of what she had read and had experienced directly.

C. L. Moore, as she invariably signed her individual work, was born in Indianapolis on 24 January 1911, to Otto Newman Moore and Maude Estelle Jones Moore. Her father and her brother, Robert Padgett Moore (hence the origin of one of the pseudonyms she and Kuttner used in collaborative efforts, Lewis

Padgett), were tool and machine designers and manufacturers. Her mother had not had an advanced education but was an omnivorous reader and early encouraged her daughter to read everything of worth that was available.

Moore was a sickly child who readily turned from the world of her illness to the spheres of fantasy and other literature. Shortly after entering the first grade, she became a semi-invalid and did not return to school until the fifth grade. In the meantime she was educated at home by her mother and special teachers. Her mind early fixed upon the romantic materials of the medieval period, especially in England. One can find this influence in her fiction, particularly in the Jirel of Joiry stories.

After graduating from high school, Moore entered Indiana University. But after a very successful year and a half there, financial problems brought on by the Great Depression made it necessary for her to leave the university and find a job. Early in the 1930's, with the help of a friend employed there, she was hired as a typist—"mostly of wills," she said—by the Fletcher Trust Company in Indianapolis. When she left to marry Henry Kuttner in 1940, she was secretary to the president of the company.

While she was at the Fletcher Trust Company, Moore was asked to answer a letter from a depositor who signed himself "N. W. Smith." When she was writing "Shambleau" and casting about for a name for her protagonist, she translated "N. W. Smith" into Northwest Smith, thereby christening her most famous creation.

By the time she left the bank, Moore had established herself as a writer of major stature. Although she was to write for many magazines in the years that followed, it was in *Weird Tales* that she rapidly attained her initial reputation. There, too, Henry Kuttner had published his first fiction; and, as noted before, it was because of his appreciation of her work in *Weird Tales* that they entered into a correspondence, and then met.

In April 1943, Kuttner was inducted into the army and was sent for training to Fort Monmouth, New Jersey. Moore, following him, rented a room and worked for the Travelers' Aid Society, finding quarters for wives and mothers visiting the soldiers. But before Kuttner could be assigned to a permanent station, he became seriously ill and was hospitalized with a dangerously high fever. Obviously unfit for military duty, he was given an honorable disability discharge.

For a month Moore and Kuttner rented a lavish apartment just off Fifth Avenue in New York City while scouting for quarters they could afford. They rented, and later bought, a house at Hastings-on-Hudson, New York. Their new residence afforded them not only shelter and a place to work but also another of their many pseudonyms, Hudson Hastings.

At Hastings-on-Hudson their writing went very well. Together they wrote the novel *Fury* (1947); Moore wrote *Judgment Night* (1943); and Kuttner wrote his Galloway Gallegher stories (1943–1948). Their house soon became a meeting place for fellow writers from *Astounding Stories*, to which, by now, both Moore and Kuttner were contributing regularly. Weekend parties became routine, with most of the crowd of writers sleeping on the floors. Here, and later at Laguna Beach, California, science fiction writers gathered to exchange ideas, encourage each other, and complain about editors, rates, and the parlous state of the creative world.

Throughout the early 1940's Moore and Kuttner frequently traveled between New York City and Laguna Beach. After the war they sold their New York house and most belongings and settled at Laguna Beach. Subsequently they moved to Santa Monica and then to Los Angeles.

In 1950 both Moore and Kuttner felt somewhat "written-out." When a friend, a graduate student at the University of Southern California (USC), suggested that enrolling at USC might refill their creative vats, they began working toward degrees there. Kuttner, under the G.I. Bill, was able to become a full-time student; but Moore, not having that financial support, took classes when she could. Nonetheless, they both graduated with highest honors and as members of Phi Beta Kappa. During this period their output increased phenomenally.

In addition to writing and doing classwork, Moore and Kuttner taught creative writing. Featured as participants in early sessions of the California State University's Pacific Coast Writers Conference in 1953 as well as USC's Idyllwild Writers Conference in 1956, they continued their joint teaching and lecturing until Kuttner's death. Moore continued to teach at USC for some years afterward.

In the late 1950's, sensing that the science fiction and fantasy markets were declining, Moore and Kuttner moved into the detective-suspense field, publishing such titles as *Man Drowning*, *The Day He Died*, and *The Murder of Ann Avery*. Invited to join the Mystery Writers of America, they were almost immediately elected joint vice presidents of the West Coast chapter.

This new association led to an invitation from a Warner Brothers story editor to visit him at his studio office. They were hired as writers and given an office of their own on the Warner Brothers lot. There they put together a detailed television story outline, sold it, and were starting on the screenplay when, early in 1958, Kuttner died. A week or so after Kuttner's death, Moore returned to the studio and finished the screenplay they had begun, a script for a Western called *Sugarfoot*. She continued to work at Warner Brothers, writing many television scripts, including more for *Sugarfoot*, and others for such shows as *Maverick*, *77 Sunset Strip*, and *The Alaskans*. On 18 July 1963, Moore married Thomas Reggie, a California businessman.

Moore's fame, early attained, remains undiminished by the years. Her stories, and Kuttner's, have appeared, and continue to appear, in many anthologies and collections in the United States and abroad. She won virtually every award for writing in the science fiction and fantasy field. And, fittingly for one who explored the starry realms of the universe, she had a star named after her, "C. L. Moore," in the constellation of Cepheus.

II

From a perusal of Moore's short stories and novels—those she wrote alone (almost all of those produced before her marriage and a considerable number after)—it is possible to note unvarying characteristics in her work.

Moore was both a poet and a romantic. Her vocabulary is, for lack of a better word, musical. She masterfully created moods, and in her work one senses worlds within worlds within worlds. Neither time nor space really exists, and that which is alien to most of us lived right next door to her.

"Shambleau," Moore's first and best-known story, is a *tour de force*. It may be profitable to consider it here. In a subtle, tasteful sense, "Shambleau" is highly erotic. Indeed, one thinks when reading it of Christina Rossetti's poem "Goblin Market." But, this aside, "Shambleau" stands as an unforgettable experience that, beneath its surface story, evokes a deep sense of primal meaning and transcendent understanding in the reader. It says something about the hell/heaven of human love—profane or otherwise—which, like spring, goes on forever. And there is more.

In "Shambleau" the reader is quickly introduced to the nocturnal, eon-haunted Martian world, and to the story's protagonist, Northwest Smith, space adventurer and almost outlaw. As the story begins, Smith rescues a strange, half-human girl from a lynch mob of assorted Earthmen, Martians, and Venusian swampmen. She is called, in fear and derision, "Shambleau!" by those who seek to tear her apart. Speaking only a few words that Smith can understand, she begs him to save her life. Smith does and takes her to his lodging. There she releases her hair from the turban that conceals it and reveals herself as a strange kind of vampire. The hair is a mass of crimson, writhing, serpentlike strands that envelop Smith warmly and wetly, and tide him into a half-coma of hypnotized, intense pleasure and equally intense aversion. He is stunned into passivity while the tendrils drink up his vitality. He knows that in time this will kill him, but the pleasure is so intense, it doesn't matter. Smith's friend Yarol, from Venus, arrives some time later. Yarol destroys the vampire girl and saves Smith, but not quite in time. It is obvious that Smith will never forget the intensity of the pleasure this kind of dying brings, and he half hopes and half dreads that somewhere, someday, he may encounter another Shambleau.

Synopsizing "Shambleau" in this way is like simplistically saying that *Romeo and Juliet* is a play about two kids who, though their parents hate each other, fall in love, are messed up by their passion, and die as a result of it. The play is really more than that, and "Shambleau" similarly is more than its plot outline.

Moore, when asked to describe the experience of writing when things went well, spoke of the inexplicable "possession" that is then sometimes operative. In the following passage one is reminded of Rudyard Kipling and his "daemon." Probably every writer, at one time or another, has had this experience or one similar to it:

Hank and I were hooked on the glorious feeling of having a story take the typewriter in its teeth and tearing off into the distance, we panting along trying to keep up—pages rolling up out of the typewriter and falling to the floor before we knew it was down to the bottom of the page. To be panting along behind a headstrong story like that is one of life's major glories—a high better than drugs or drink. You summon it like a God to his altar, and He descends in his glory and inhabits the brain until the mind ceases to be a thing in itself and becomes part of a tremendous onrushing stream. Your only contribution being to hang in there and type fast enough to keep up.

Probably you have to train your mind to function this way, unconsciously of course, but it does train itself because the reward is so glorious. When Hank finished a story, he felt at the time that it was not only the best he had ever written, but probably the best anyone had ever written. Re-reading usually brought second thoughts, but not always; sometimes it really was!

The glow of triumphant complacence can last for days. You have to let the story get cold before you re-read it critically, to catch the small errors which infest every rough first draft: the repetition, the unclear sentences, the spots that need cutting or expanding. As if the words which had come white hot from the crucible were too hot from the creator to defile with one's own crassly human alterations until the heavenly glow and heat had died out of them. (manuscript of unfinished autobiography of Moore)

C. L. Moore in 1981. Photo by Jay Kay Klein

In conclusion, reviewing Moore's impressive body of work—that created both jointly and separately—it is obvious that she was among the vanguard of a small band of pioneers who unfettered popular science fiction and set it free to move at will along the unmarked roads of sophistication and literary excellence.

When asked why she and Kuttner literally devoted their lives to this liberating cause and the pain and the ineffable pleasure of writing,

Moore replied simply, "We explored Space and Time for our own pleasure." Fortunately, it is a pleasure ably transmitted to their readers.

III

Kuttner was born in Los Angeles in 1915 to Henry Kuttner and Annie Lewis Kuttner. His father was a dealer in rare books, and thus he grew up in a bookish environment. From the time he learned to read, he lived as much in the world of literature as he did in that of immediate experience.

After graduating from high school, Kuttner was employed by the Lawrence Dorsay Literary Agency in Beverly Hills. His job was to read the manuscripts submitted by writers and would-be writers, and in many instances to work with them on revisions. He discovered several quite promising writers and guided a number of clients into their first sales.

Inevitably Kuttner began to write; his work included stories that later appeared in *Weird Tales*, the first of which, "The Graveyard Rats," was published in the March 1936 issue. Before this acceptance he had written a fan letter to "Mr. C. L. Moore." This led to further correspondence and their meeting when Moore visited California.

It was, as the old saw has it, "love at first sight" for Moore and Kuttner. Shortly after Moore returned to Indianapolis, Kuttner wrote to her, proposing marriage. He was selling his writing steadily—as was Moore—and believed that he could successfully become a full-time writer in New York, where the markets were.

Encouraged by Moore's tentative acceptance of his offer of marriage, Kuttner gave up his position with the literary agency and moved to New York City. When established, he visited Moore in Indianapolis whenever he could, further to urge their marriage. Eventually she visited New York, where they were married at City Hall on 7 June 1940. Moore joined Kuttner in New York. After a short service with the army, from which he received an honorable disability discharge in 1943 (due to a severe illness), Kuttner returned to New York. A short time later he and Moore bought the house in Hastings-on-Hudson.

Kuttner was a very private person. His experience with the military, brief as it was, increased his insistence that his personal freedom not be violated. Possessed of absolute integrity, he could, if he thought a person deserving of it, manifest a profound loyalty.

Moreover, Kuttner helped a great many beginning writers. Refusing to charge for his services, he suggested revisions and plots, and passed on the writing techniques he had shown in his own fiction. Kuttner was a superb teacher, as was early recognized by the English department at USC. After his death, Moore took over his classes.

Kuttner had a fine and subtle sense of humor, which often infused his stories. He could tell a risqué story beautifully, without ever having to use a "four-letter" word, and he was a consummate but kindly satirist. Essentially an agnostic, he viewed the universe, in relation to man, as chaotic. His own personal credo was "I will neither be dominated nor defeated." And he never was. When death came, it was as an inevitable termination, not a defeat.

In late 1957, Kuttner had a thorough physical examination, and at a New Year's party he mentioned to his friends that he was apparently good for many years of work. But in February 1958, the night before he suffered his fatal heart attack, he had a dream that disturbed him deeply. When asked about it by Moore, he said he didn't want to talk about it until he had thought it over a little more. That night he died. And that was probably what the dream was about.

One must note a curious prediction Kuttner wrote for *Fantascient* in 1948. Entitled "Extrapolation," it sought to portray the future world of 1958. In this article he wrote:

However, by 1958 there weren't—won't be— any stories by me in *any* magazine, and I haven't the least idea what happened. Sometime I must extrapolate again and find out. I did notice a 1958 newstape that mentioned the death of Inri Cutna—that was in the Nu Yok Dali Nus—but it didn't go into details. . . .

He was right. After 1957 there were not any new stories by "Inri Cutna."

IV

During his early writing years, Kuttner imitated writers he admired, especially H. P. Lovecraft, with whom he carried on an extensive correspondence, Robert E. Howard, and A. Merritt. In the years that followed, he wrote fantasy, science fiction, supernatural, detective, and suspense fiction with equal facility. That he should have functioned within this cluster of categories is not strange. These types are offshoots of the gothic mode, as exemplified by Edgar Allan Poe, who probably invented the detective story, and who wrote science fiction and stories of the supernatural without ever moving very far from the gothic core.

In addition, Kuttner was very much interested in psychology and wrote a series of extremely effective, informed detective novels featuring a psychiatrist-detective named Michael Gray. In effect a Renaissance man, he brought to his fiction a wide knowledge. During and after his university work, he found much to draw upon in mainstream literature of the past and present. He was influenced, for example, by John Milton, and one of his outstanding stories, "Two-Handed Engine" (1955), derives from his study of Milton's work.

Reading Kuttner's fiction, one is first struck by the extent and precision of his vocabulary. It was with him as with Mark Twain, who said that the difference between the right word and the almost right word was the difference between lightning and a lightning bug. Kuttner was also a master of plotting, dialogue, and, not infrequently, three-dimensional characterization. Although he was imitative in his early years, he soon achieved his own style.

All in all, it is probably the humor that sets Kuttner's work apart from earlier science fiction. The genre was, in the main, deadly serious and didactic. Kuttner galvanized it with an often zany humor that is truly memorable. One need but read his Galloway Gallegher stories (collected in book form in 1952 as *Robots Have No Tails*), which featured an entirely "human" robot named Joe, to realize that robots could never be the same again after Joe, petulant and opinionated, emerged fully assembled from the author's mind. Beyond this humor was an inventive, imaginative bent that often resulted in stories that throw new light on the human predicament.

One memorable story has a great deal to say about the differences between children and adults. Entitled "Mimsy Were the Borogoves" (1943), it tells of a scientist of the far future who uses a box of his children's old toys as ballast for a time-transportation experiment. The box lands in the present, and two children, finding it, begin to play with the toys therein. They are instructional toys. The flexible, unquestioning minds of the two children accept the new ideas the future toys generate without difficulty. The more they learn from their play, the farther they are drawn toward a new, far-future world where their parents can't follow. The assumption is that when Lewis Carroll wrote *Alice in Wonderland*, he knew of this transitional path along which only young children can walk. Adults are puzzled by Carroll's interpolated verse—lines such as "All mimsy were the borogoves, and the mome raths outgrabe"—and they are too inflexible in their thinking to follow this path; but children, with the right guidance, can walk the maze unerringly into a new world, leaving the old one and its adults behind them. With this story, Kuttner rubs shoulders, and as an equal, with H. G. Wells and his tale "The Magic Shop." (A recording of Kuttner's story was made by William Shatner.)

Kuttner often speculated about the writing process, and he sought to determine what is necessary to create and sustain it. On 8 December 1948, while living in Laguna Beach, he began a diary that he hoped would clarify these matters for him. Perhaps what he wrote may be of help to other writers or, at least, reflect for them what they have previously discovered:

Dear Diary: Go to hell. . . . I have decided to write, though not necessarily to keep, a kind of diary for a bit, though it is more in the nature of a one-sided chat with my id, ego, or super-ego—I have not yet done some necessary research on these people. Necessary for a story, I mean. . . . My main purpose is to recapitulate and clarify in my own mind (1) the angles in the story I'm writing, whatever it is, and (2) the problems I face in the writing process as I roll along. Later will be time to consider life's little problems, and then cries of agony and shrieks of desolation may rise from these pages. . . . Last night I idly wrote down what I felt were necessary to process, or writing, in this case: 1. Health, 2. Warmth (comfort), 3. Control of the mechanics of living, 4. Quiet, 5. Ready access to references, 6. Stimulus, 7. Relaxation. The first four seem most important. . . . I believe an ideal set-up would be a country home in a good climate, arranged so that easy facility to everything would be combined with privacy when necessary. Occasional living-visits to cities would be vital though. . . .

Now, on writing. Problems are clarifying and getting much more specific. The strange, indefinable question of élan is not yet fully resolved. I know it does not come unless I know exactly what I'm doing, or when I'm tackling a problem that's beyond me. The answer is to break the problem down to factors I can handle. I'm doing that pretty blindly so far, with characterization. . . . I could, I think, handle . . . basically simple types. I have learned to know, if not to love, fairly thoroughly. . . .

Theme, story problem, and character are all important. At the moment, I believe the last is most important to me. I must do some research into characterization. The typical Kuttner protagonist is now too superficial for me, I find. . . . I enjoy handling a character like . . . the Constable of France in *Henry V*,

and what may be the . . . factor . . . is "belief that stood on unbelief." And it may be that this trait is what I must find in any protagonist I handle, for a bit. Sometimes it is a constructive trait, sometimes destructive. . . . It all depends upon what you do and don't believe in.

There is no evidence to suggest that this diary was ever continued on paper, beyond this initial entry (abridged here). Until he died, Kuttner was busy typing in the diary of his mind.

—FREDERICK SHROYER

V

Following Kuttner's death, C. L. Moore wrote no new fiction, though as Catherine Kuttner she provided scripts for the television series noted earlier. Her writing career effectively ended in 1963, when she married Thomas Reggie. She nevertheless permitted her earlier work to be reissued, sometimes in signed and limited editions, and she attended occasional science fiction conventions, serving as guest of honor at the 1981 World Science Fiction Convention held in Denver, Colorado. She developed Alzheimer's disease in late 1984, and she died in Hollywood, California, on 4 April 1987, from pneumonia and the complications from Alzheimer's disease. Although much of her science fiction and fantasy was in print at her death, Moore as a historically significant author had been largely forgotten; the science fiction trade publications did not notice her passing for nearly a year.

As of this writing, neither Kuttner nor Moore has been discovered by academics, and such critical attention as they have received has consisted largely of articles in small coterie magazines. Nor have fans lionized and memorialized Kuttner and Moore the way they have celebrated some of their pulp magazine and *Weird Tales* compeers. Nevertheless, although few of Kuttner's solo works are available, Moore's stories of Jirel of Joiry and

Northwest Smith currently remain in print, in readily affordable mass market editions. New generations of fans and writers have thus discovered and been influenced by her work without necessarily realizing that Moore's treatment of female sexuality was unique in the pulp magazines, that she was the first to create a sword-and-sorcery series featuring a woman as protagonist, and that she was among the first to realize that the beings inhabiting the unexplored universe can be seductive as well as deadly. In her tribute to Moore, noted writer Marion Zimmer Bradley describes being influenced by Moore when still a young and struggling writer and recalls meeting and attending a conference with Moore:

> Some time later I remember her [Moore] being a guest a women's writing group—to which I was also asked to speak—where she greeted the large group by saying, "My goodness, you're all young enough to be my daughters." And the whole group said spontaneously just what I would have said: "We *are* your daughters." In a very real sense, every woman who writes science fiction is her daughter.

Hyperbolic as Bradley's concluding sentence may seem, it is also the truth. C. L. Moore's legacy to the field of fantastic fiction is a large and secure one.

—RICHARD BLEILER

Selected Bibliography

Although singly attributed, works written between 1940 and 1958 are generally Moore/Kuttner collaborations.

WORKS OF C. L. MOORE

Judgment Night. New York: Gnome Press, 1952.
Shambleau, and Others. New York: Gnome Press, 1953.
Northwest of Earth. New York: Gnome Press, 1954.
Doomsday Morning. Garden City, N.Y.: Doubleday, 1957.
Black God's Shadow. West Kingston, R.I.: Donald M. Grant, 1977.
Vintage Season. New York: TOR, 1990.

WORKS OF HENRY KUTTNER

Fury. New York: Grosset and Dunlap, 1950.
Ahead of Time. New York: Ballantine Books, 1953.
Bypass to Otherness. New York: Ballantine Books, 1961.
Return to Otherness. New York: Ballantine Books, 1962.
Best of Kuttner. 2 vols. London: Mayflower-Dell, 1965–1966.
Elak of Atlantis. Brooklyn, N.Y.: Gryphon Books, 1985. (300 copies printed.)
Prince Raynor. Brooklyn, N.Y.: Gryphon, 1987.
Kuttner Times Three. Modesto, Calif.: Virgil Utter, 1988. (200 copies printed.)
H. P. Lovecraft Letters to Henry Kuttner, with H. P. Lovecraft. West Warwick, R.I.: Necronomicon Press, 1990.
Secret of the Earth Star, and Others. Mercer Island, Wash.: Starmont House, 1991.

WORKS AS BY LEWIS PADGETT

A Gnome There Was. New York: Simon and Schuster, 1950.
Tomorrow and Tomorrow and The Fairy Chessmen. New York: Gnome Press, 1951.
Robots Have No Tails. New York: Gnome Press, 1952.
Mutant. New York: Gnome Press, 1953.
Line to Tomorrow. New York: Bantam Books, 1954.

WORKS OF HENRY KUTTNER AND C. L. MOORE

No Boundaries. New York: Ballantine Books, 1955.
Earth's Last Citadel. New York: Ace Books, 1964.
Chessboard Planet and Other Stories. London: Hamlyn, 1983.
The Startling Worlds of Henry Kuttner. New York: Popular Library, 1987.

CRITICAL AND BIOGRAPHICAL STUDIES

Bleiler, E. F. "Fantasy, Horror . . . and Sex: The Early Stories of C. L. Moore." *The Scream Factory,* no. 13 (Spring 1994): 41–47.
Bradley, Marion Zimmer. "C. L. Moore: An Appreciation." *Locus* (March 1988): 69.
"C. L. Moore Dead." *Locus* (March 1988): 68–69.
Kaler, Anne K. "Jirel of Joiry." In *Magill's Guide to Science Fiction and Fantasy Literature.* Edited by T. A. Shippey and A. J. Sobczak. Pasadena, Calif.: Salem Press, 1996.
Utter, Virgil; Gordon Benson, Jr.; and Phil Stephensen-Payne. *Catherine Lucille Moore & Henry Kuttner: A Marriage of Souls and Talent: A Working Bibliography.* 4th rev. ed. Leeds, England: Galactic Central Publications, 1996.

PAT MURPHY
(b. 1955)

PAT MURPHY IS an excellent and intriguing writer, whose career tells volumes about the evolution of science fiction literature and its audience in the 1980's and 1990's. First of all, as writer she works against the grain of mass market science fiction publishing across these decades. Fundamentally, her medium is the short story. If for Golden Age science fiction the short story was the quintessential vehicle of the classic extrapolative "thought experiment," it has proved increasingly unviable in the new age of mega-series, where to survive economically writers are forced to dilute ideas and generate reams of prose. Murphy, on the other hand, condenses. Not only are her stories pithy; but her novels grow out of reworkings of stories. Two of her three novels of the 1980's are directly expanded from stories previously published; the third has close ties with several tales that offer a landscape and mood that she develops. These novels, however, each become a crafted whole. Bucking the tide of "series" and serializations, Murphy's novels are all self-contained structures. Only in the title of *Nadya: The Wolf Chronicles* (1996), is there a hint that she may have finally caught the sequel bug.

Moreover, Murphy's work seems a significant departure from science fiction in the traditional sense. The "science" in her work is minimal in the sense that she makes little attempt to explain, in speculative or technical detail, phenomena such as time travel or mind transfer between species. But if such "literary" license is the rule rather than the exception among her contemporaries, why do even they have so much trouble classifying Murphy's work? Science fiction writers in the 1980's were very eager to define "schools" or movements among new writers. Bruce Sterling (writing as "Vincent Omniaveritas" in *Cheap Truth*) initially put Murphy with writers such as Kim Stanley Robinson and Connie Willis in the "Humanist" camp as opposed to the Cyberpunks, in other words, a writer more interested in exploring traditional human values and limits than in celebrating and/or condemning the machine-human interface of the future's world of information technology. In his article "A User's Guide to the Postmoderns" (*Isaac Asimov's Science Fiction Magazine*, August 1986), however, Michael Swanwick, while finding niches for almost all other writers of this generation, cannot place the "lone wolf" Murphy. To be sure, there is a streak of "Humanist" skepticism about the institutionalization of science in her work, just as there are feminist overtones. Her story "His Vegetable Wife" (1986), for example, was included in Le Guin's *Norton Book of Science Fiction*, the anthology that strongly pushes these agendas. But story and tone are not typical of Murphy. More recent commentators, attempting to define her work, tend to make comparisons outside science fiction. These, however, prove just as slippery. *Booklist*, reviewing her novel *The Falling Woman* (1986), sees a comparison with Gabriel García Márquez and magic realism, where realistic and fantastic elements coexist and interact seamlessly, without visible conflict. The *Locus* reviewer of Murphy's next novel, *The City, Not Long After* (1989), claims it is "an undisputable heir to a long and honorable tradition in Northern California literature," with antecedents such as Jack London and Henry Miller. Her latest work to date, *Nadya*, is a tale of lycanthropy: the jacket tells us that "Pat Murphy does for wolves what Anne Rice has done for vampires."

Given Murphy's ability to transgress conventional genre boundaries in her writing, we might concur with Gregory Feeley's assessment (in John Clute and John Grant's, *The Encyclopedia of Fantasy*, 1997) that "most of her work combines speculative elements in ways that place them near the borders rather than at the centres of genres." There is a genre, however, whose identifying feature is precisely this crossing of boundaries, the fantastic. And Murphy tells in her own words that, despite changing external appearances, the inner dynamic of her fiction is the search for "the secret door, the inner passage, the opening to another dimension or another time" ("Afterword—Why I Write," *Points of Departure*, 1990). This volume is a retrospective of Murphy's seminal stories of the 1980's. The "point of departure" for all of them (despite the various feel of surface icons, ideologies, or generic murmurs) is the writer's own search for "the secret door," ever present, sometimes out of reach, but often too accessible, in the everyday world. Hers is fiction where relations, human or otherwise, are always suspended at a point of crossing, where secret doors have a two-way function. If they let us out of our humdrum existence, at the same time they bring the other into our world, making it suddenly an alien and strange place for all parties. Development of her characters, in all cases, only begins as they accommodate (or fail to accommodate) this hesitation caused by shifting realms or perceptions of "reality." Murphy's work may slip through the cracks of the more polemical and ideological categories used by fellow writers and critics. Yet her form of the fantastic has evolved in the milieu of science fiction—the majority of her 1980's stories were published in *Isaac Asimov's Science Fiction Magazine*, with those of the 1990's appearing in *The Magazine of Fantasy and Science Fiction*. (Indeed, it could only have evolved there.) In doing so, it testifies to the fundamental nature of this form as literature of alien encounter.

Biographical information on Pat Murphy is sparse—she is clearly a private person—but what is known is significant in suggesting places of entry into her work, though no such doors are absolutely certain. A Northern Californian, she was born in 1955. The "location" of many of her stories and novels is the valleys and cities of this region. Her B.A., from the University of California at Santa Cruz, is in science, with emphasis on biology. Unlike other science-trained science fiction writers, however, Murphy occludes rather than flaunts her knowledge. Her fictional doors open preferably on a Narnia (C. S. Lewis) rather than places like Robert L. Forward's Rocheworld or Dragon's Egg, scientifically designed alien planet environments. In such worlds (as she says whimsically in "Why I Write"), scientific training might come in handy as a survivalist skill to help her "recognize edible plants." Santa Cruz, at the time of her studies (the late 1970's), was famous for its teaching of "history of consciousness" and alternate lifestyles. This is surely an influence on Murphy's abiding interest in non-Western and "nonscientific" power and belief systems. For instance, her early story "Sweetly the Waves Call to Me" (1981), tells of a lonely seaside communion between a female Santa Cruz student and a silkie, a "seal person who could change shape and become human on land." Her first novel, *The Shadow Hunter* (1982), confronts future technology with prehistoric shamanism. Her second novel, *The Falling Woman* (1986), reveals a hands-on knowledge of Mayan archeology and ethnography, mixed with a romanticized fascination with ancient gods and forces in the vein of Carlos Castañeda.

Since 1982, Murphy has been associated with a San Francisco institution called the Exploratorium, whose newsletter, *The Exploratorium Quarterly*, she edits. Murphy herself describes the Exploratorium as "San Francisco's internationally known museum of science, art and human perception [whose] exhibits are interactive, requiring visitors to fool around and make discoveries for themselves. Journalists . . . have compared it to a country fair, a mad scientist's basement." The Exploratorium permeates the fictional San Francisco of her second major novel, *The City, Not Long After*, where a now post-holocaust city, empty of all but a handful of people, itself becomes the place of artistic exploration, between these "tinkerers" and what was once the alienating urban landscape. Vague ideas of pacificism and ecology have found an institutional focus, where for the sake of natural and social balance, technology submits to that higher form of experimentation that is art.

Murphy has won a number of major awards in the science fiction field. To date, she has won no Hugo awards, but two Nebulas. This may indicate that her appeal is less to general fandom than to her writer-peers who, whether they can classify her work or not, clearly admire its literary excellence. The year 1987 was her annus mirabilis, when she swept the Nebula awards, with best novel for *The Falling Woman* and best novelette for "Rachel in Love." The same year "Rachel in Love" won the John W. Campbell Memorial Award, given by a body of writers and professional critics. A rather different body, the readers of *Locus* magazine, awarded "Rachel" their 1987 award for best novelette. The publication of Murphy's collected stories, *Points of Departure*, won the Philip K. Dick Memorial Award in 1991. Again, the jury included writers and academics, who honor the "best American paperback book" of the year, in this case in either science fiction or fantasy. The nature of these awards attests to Murphy's growing acclaim in the field as a literary writer, a writer who above all pursues the craft of fiction.

With this background in mind, let us look in detail at her particular works as they develop. Murphy's earlier work remains fascinated by doubles, shadows, ghosts—forms that locate "the secret door," the ever-shifting interzone between the realities that compete

Pat Murphy © 1998 M. C. VALADA

for the human psyche, for human existence itself. The story "Don't Look Back" (1981), published in *Fantasy Annual IV*, offers an already sophisticated play on the theme of doubling, of meeting versions of your same self. Liz, a commercial artist who has a burgeoning career but is unable to face her personal future, visits her old haunts—boarding house, classroom, first job and beloved boss—only to find herself in each instance displaced by younger women artists of like talent, all moving "up the ladder" as she has done. When she imagines herself patting these women on the back and telling them: "You've got a great past ahead of yourself, kid," there is an echo of Heinlein's Bob Wilson in "By His Bootstraps" (1941), telling himself he has a great future, at the very moment he realizes he is trapped in a time loop, doomed to meet himself endlessly, to inscribe a present frozen between past and future. For Bob, however, the cause is physical—the magic door is a time gate triggered by a paradox. Liz's maze is a psychic one, and the nature of the occurrences more an uncanny one. For if Liz's "past" is blocked by younger women occupying her old places, her future in New York proves nothing more than her taking in turn the place of an older woman. All the women have different names; we know empty lives are interchangeable. But such commonsense explanations do not account for the feeling of uncanny fatality that hovers over these like encounters.

Murphy's first novel, *The Shadow Hunter*, which appeared as an obscure Popular Library paperback in 1982, expands upon an earlier story, "Touch of the Bear," that appeared in the October 1980 issue of *Isaac Asimov's Science Fiction Magazine*. The novel is perhaps the most traditionally "science fictional" of Murphy's works, with an entire context of temporal transfers, an exhausted future Earth, and the obligatory flight to a new world added to the sparse detail of the story, whose focus is on a shamanistic initiation. In the story Sam, "the last Neanderthal," is time-lifted to our world "by rich fools" to tend a last game preserve. Here the impossible gap between these two worlds is bridged when the daughter of Sam's Homo sapiens friend Marshall takes the "shadow" or spirit of a bear during a hunt, becoming a "shaman-woman-bear-girl-child" for whom all barriers—time and space, inside and outside—fall away. The novel builds a science fiction world around this incident. Sam in his time hunts the bear for "a name and spirit." As he raises his knife for the kill, the bear disappears, and he is plunged into a time in the reader's future, when animal species and spirits are on the verge of extinction. His transfer is now an accident, as the scientist operating the time machine wanted the bear, not him. Because of this act, however, Sam's quest for identity— shamanistic fusion with the forces of nature—is entwined with the shadow of bear not taken, and two unnaturally displaced beings must seek union in death in an alien world. The novel adds significant complications. Roy Morgan, the "rich man" who first selfishly wanted to create a menagerie of extinct species, changes through his encounter with Sam and turns his energies to creating a space-traveling Noah's Ark, which will take a regenerated Sam and his animals out of his

enclosure and to a planet rife with new animal species. The girl Kirsten, who in place of Sam kills the bear and takes his spirit, may now be his blood heir. Murphy adds a woman character, Merle, who as wife to Marshall and lover to Sam, makes the paternity of Kirstin unclear. Now, with these stronger currents of power moving between otherwise isolated time shadows, the gates open, and spirits of Sam's mother and family pass into our time, fuse with his modern "family." All step into the time machine, now renamed Outreach, and a new world begins. At this last point, in the tangle of conventions, of time travel and shamanic mysticism, the reader has difficulty locating this new world—without or within.

The Shadow Hunter, as a tale told from the point of view of Sam, the alien Neanderthal in a modern future, is ambitious in its desire to confront the world of genre science fiction (technology misused and dystopian future) with prescientific, animistic belief systems. Modern science, however, seen through these simplifying glasses, is too much a straw man. Murphy's second novel, *The Falling Woman*, abandons the conventions of science fiction. Its science is archeology, prehistory, and myth; its setting contemporary; its narrative mode a sort of magical realism. Whereas the major protagonists of *The Shadow Hunter* are male, this novel focuses on a mother-daughter relationship, told in sections from alternating points of view. Elizabeth Butler is a middle-aged field archeologist from UC Berkeley, directing an excavation of Mayan ruins in Yucatán. Driven by a passion for the past and a need to fulfill herself as a human being, she has pursued a successful career to the exclusion of family and human relationships. Instead, she has come to see and commune with ghosts of ancient Mayas. The climax, a near-fatal catharsis, turns on a fusion of realities brought on by a complex play of doublings past and future—the ghost of a long-dead Mayan priestess and the sudden appearance of another ghost, her daughter, Diane, abandoned in childhood.

A number of novels dealing with archeology, myth, and ancient or lost cultures appeared in the mid-to-late 1980's under the science fiction aegis: works as disparate as Gregory Benford's *Artifact* (1985) and Lewis Shiner's *Deserted Cities of the Heart* (1988). *The Falling Woman*, then, is no anomaly. Nor is it necessarily "fantasy" either, as TOR Books packaged it. Murphy reveals both a well-documented sense of "doing" the science of archeology and a passion for learning about ancient civilizations, even though the nature of such knowledge is more mythical than quantitative, more intuitive than strictly measurable. Elizabeth Butler's male collaborator, Tony, collects potsherds, measures them, and pieces them together. Her desire, however, is to bring dead artifacts to life, striving to commune with mute stones, until finally they begin to talk to her, to appear as ghosts who tell their story. The story is of the Toltec invasion, the displacement of Earth by sky gods. It is a story of human sacrifice and the hidden meaning behind its apparent barbarity. Why did the Mayas suddenly abandon their cities to the jungle?

The "historical" mystery is revealed to Elizabeth through dialogue with the shadow or ghost of the "falling woman," a priestess of the Mayan moon goddess cast into the sacred well at Chichén Itzá. The woman survived the fall and became a prophet whose vision of impending doom caused the Mayas to flee. This falling woman is depicted on a funereal urn discovered at the site. Its discovery, however, poses a reality question. Is the ghost a figment of Elizabeth's imagination, generated by the urn painting? Or is it the ghost that led her to discover the urn, the ever elusive key to this mystery? The reader's inability to choose between these poles is an indication of the type of narrative Murphy is writing. *The Falling Woman* is not, as the dust jacket proclaims, simply a "psychological fantasy." It is an example of magic realism, practiced by Latin American writers at the very same intersection between so-called primitive and civilized worlds, where the two planes of reality ceaselessly interact without explanation or resolution. For this narrative to work, we must not see the priestess only as Elizabeth's

psychological double but as her flesh and blood double as well. We must not see Elizabeth's "fall" as purely metaphorical, a fall into the abyss of old age, of isolation and loneliness. For there is a physical fall as well, into the same sacrificial well. These parallel destinies operate simultaneously on psychic and material levels. Indeed, Elizabeth's problem can be treated only through a physical confrontation with her Mayan counterpart, resulting in a physical inversion of the fatal pattern of the double itself. If the reader is fully to understand the force of this narrative and its climax, he or she must learn to accept Elizabeth as both "crazy" in the modern sense (if her voices and visions exist, it is only as figments of her mind, of her own past) and as a seer of real Mayas.

In its basic sense, this narrative is about two pairs of mothers and daughters, about worlds and destinies built on unnatural acts, and the possibility of redemption through redressment of these acts. Elizabeth has neglected her flesh and blood daughter, Diane, in pursuit of what is a "city of stones." When Diane appears in Yucatán in search of her mother, Elizabeth is engaged in her shadow dialogue with Zuhuy-kak. She learns that the urn of the Falling Woman contains the bones of Zuhuy-kak's daughter, whom she brutally sacrificed in a futile and tragic attempt to stem the Toltec invasion and fall of her people. The shadow priestess tells Elizabeth that, if that cycle was against the moon goddess, the cycle is now turning, and these forces will return if she in turn will sacrifice her daughter, Diane, with the same obsidian knife. Is this fiendish fatality, a deep secret of ancient lore, now emerging into the light of modern day? Or is it mad delusions of homicidal possibility? As it turns out, it is both. In a hallucinatory climax, where the power to resolve is finally seen to lie in a reassertion of human blood ties rather than a belief in myth or fatality, Elizabeth (haunted by the prophesy of Zuhuy-kak) recoils from her daughter's hand in the Mayan cave and repeats the fall of the Mayan woman into the sacrificial well. Diane climbs down to her mother, who lies below with a broken leg, and reviles her for having abandoned her child. The narrative at this point shifts from Elizabeth's point of view (culminating in her realization that, as had Zuhuy-kak, "we both had made sacrifices that were unacceptable") to Diane's. This shift marks a transfer of roles, redemptory this time, in which daughter takes mother's place, and by doubling the Mayan woman's procession of despair, turns death into life. Lost in the dark well, Diane is able to carry her mother to safety only because suddenly she, like her mother, is able to see the Mayan ghost. She witnesses the grisly sacrifice of Zuhuy-kak's daughter, but now to double the Mayan's despairing march to the surface with the child's urn proves, in a fortunate inversion of paths, the way back to life.

Murphy's second award-winning work of 1987, "Rachel in Love" (published in the April issue of *Isaac Asimov's Science Fiction Magazine*), moves once again toward explicit science fiction themes. In all the stories thus far discussed, Murphy places the reader in a restricted, alienated point of view. *The Falling Woman* not only presents human conflict from the woman's side of things but alternates the narratives of the two female antagonists. *The Shadow Hunter* is told by Sam the Neanderthal in words from the new tongue that he, as stranger in strange land, must gropingly learn. In contrast, "Rachel in Love," the story of a chimp upon whose brain that of a human child has been superimposed, is narrated in the third person, present tense. Whereas *The Falling Woman* tells of temporal doubling and alienation, "Rachel" is a story of doubling on an interspecies level. Whereas Sam learns to talk, the superposition of two species in a chimp's body is something that cannot speak for itself, a grotesque combination of contradictory pasts and desires that in one sense can only be spoken of, observed from without as some inscrutable thing, never understood. Yet the third-person voice, if impersonal and "objective," is traditionally "omniscient" as well. This narrator, improbably present in all of Rachel's "thoughts" as she gropes to understand her internal slip-

pages and increasingly comfortable with the concourse of ghosts of two dissimilar sets of memories, provides the magic door whereby Rachel learns to communicate with our world, and we with hers.

Conventional science is again a presence, and a problem, in this story. Rachel's human "father" is a disabused if well-meaning neuroscientist, Dr. Aaron Jacobs, who in his experiments on the Electric Mind and brain-wave transfer ran afoul of the scientific Establishment and as an outcast must continue them alone is his home. This avatar of Dr. Frankenstein loses his wife and daughter in an auto accident and in grief gives his daughter's brain to a lab animal. To describe this, Murphy uses pseudo-scientific language: "He used a mixture of norepinephrine-based transmitter substances to boost the speed of neural processing in the chimp's brain, and then he imposed the pattern of his daughter's mind. . . ." Animal experimentation, however, looks very different when seen with a human consciousness from inside the animal "subject," presented with the mute immediacy of the narrator's present tense Rachel voice. When Dr. Jacobs dies, Rachel is taken to a laboratory and placed in a cage with other lab animals. Befriending on one hand a male chimp destined for torture and on the other hand a deaf mute human with whom she communicates via the ASL (American Sign Language) Jacobs taught her, she literally incarnates the alienating alternation of double perspectives central to Murphy's vision: "She is a chimp looking in through the cold, bright windowpane; she is a girl looking out; she is a girl looking in; she is an ape looking out. She is afraid and the coyotes are howling all around."

The story of Rachel in the hands of the scientists, however, which seems on its way to becoming a gruesome version of Harlan Ellison's "I Have No Mouth and I Must Scream" (1968), veers toward comedy and reconciliation. The union of mother and daughter in *The Falling Woman* offers a redressment but not a redemption, for in the concluding chapter mother and daughter remain apart and essentially alone. If once this Pinocchio wanted to be a "real girl," she is allowed, in the resolution of the narrative, a dual, saving vision. Rejected by the human mute Jake, she accepts Johnson, her chimp lover with his ironically more human surname, and escapes. Thanks to the news media, she becomes famous: she speaks sign language; it is learned that she wrote a letter to Ann Landers, animal rights advocates and the ACLU come to her defense, and finally Jacob's will is read and she is recognized as his sole heir. The narrative ends with Rachel going "home" with Johnson to Jacob's house. Through the experience of her flight in the desert, she dreams of reconciliation that comes from acceptance of her impossibly dual existence.

> She dreams . . . of the ranch house. In the dream, she has long blond hair and pale white skin. Her eyes are red from crying, and she wanders the house restlessly, looking for something that she has lost. When she hears coyotes howling, she looks through a window at the darkness outside. The face that looks in . . . has jug-handle ears and shaggy hair. When she sees the face, she cries out in recognition and opens the window to let herself in.

If conventional science fiction themes in *The Shadow Hunter* remain ill-digested in relation to Murphy's central concerns, in "Rachel in Love" they are essential. The elegance with which Murphy reworks the tired mad scientist theme makes this story a worthy response to no less a work than H. G. Wells's *The Island of Doctor Moreau* (1896).

Murphy's third novel of the 1980's, *The City, Not Long After*, is in many senses the richest of her works in that decade. As with *The Shadow Hunter*, this novel is an exhaustive reworking of a previous short story, "Art in the War Zone," which appeared in Terry Carr's anthology *Universe 14* (1984). In its scope, however, it offers a synthesis of the various currents of Murphy's writing up to the date of its writing. Its post-holocaust future—a San Francisco inhabited by a handful of gentle eccentrics and "artists" who are survivors

of a plague—tempers the science fiction trope of technology run amok and cold war destruction by locating the novel's action in the world of Bay Area activism, as if the dystopia of *The Shadow Hunter* were overlaid upon the more contemporary landscape of "Rachel in Love." Its literary texture as well takes the devices of magic realism from its more obvious Latin American setting of *The Falling Woman* and domesticates it in a North American city, where the seeing of ghosts and strange occurrences (unaided by devices such as time machines or Rachel's neural transfer) is much rarer. Murphy's San Francisco is the real place, with its hills, streets, fog, bridges. The "art" described can also be seen by visitors to the city today: murals, People's Park, the bricolage sculptures in the Berkeley tidewater crafted out of the flotsam of our machine society. A novel of García Márquez is all the more uncanny because each unexpected detail is so thoroughly grounded in the real society in which he lives and writes. So here, instead of taking our Western rationalist sensibility to Mexican jungles, Murphy locates her odd occurrences in the most rational of cities. In doing so, she is working in a tradition of Anglo-Saxon and American city surrealism, whose most notable "post-hippie" manifestations occur in science fiction: Samuel R. Delany's *Dhalgren* (1975) and *Triton* (1976) and John Shirley's *City Come A-Walkin* (1980). Like Delany, Murphy has rendered her San Francisco strange by simply removing, through the convenient device of the plague, the old structures of authority, leaving buildings and artifacts and allowing the remaining people, in the absence of the old, to make new connections between them.

The "plot" of the novel is easily summarized. Post-plague San Francisco, inhabited by a group of tinkerers and artisans who have been given the opportunity (quite literally) to change the world with art, is invaded by an army led by a latter-day Patton, General "Fourstar" Miles. The opposition—between an anarchistic group of gentle individuals "humanistically" in tune with their natural environment and a group seeking to revive the old flawed dispensation of patriarchal, technocratic, militarist authority—is perhaps commonplace in this decade, found in any number of so-called "ecotopias," the most influential being Ursula K. LeGuin's *Always Coming Home* (1985). Murphy herself, in the afterword to the novel, is defensive about reviewers dismissing its message as more "flower power." In fact, the lines drawn are far from being simplistic in this manner. Some of the artists have ambitions that border on the authoritarian. The male protagonist, Danny Boy, strives to paint the Golden Gate Bridge blue, a bold aggressive statement to say the least. During the actual "war," Danny Boy is driven to use, beyond just art, the firearms of the aggressors themselves, shooting General Miles and being shot down in turn. Nor are the soldiers all fanatical. They do arrest the traveling book salesman Leon, and Mary, the mother of Jax, the female protagonist, which leads to their deaths. But they are not cruel, only confused, and they release Jax to pursue her quest for an identity and a past. The reader of this novel moves beyond what seems at first an unpromising thesis to discover a community of skillfully crafted human beings and destinies.

Central to the novel and its ever-shifting planes of reality is a human relationship—less one between the primitive and the modern in mankind or between mother and daughter (though both of these are present), but finally between boy and girl: between Danny Boy and Jax. They are like Rachel and Johnson, and as with these two, the real core of the narrative is the woman's search for a home, this time at the heart of a city peopled with ghosts and mysteries of a family past, reunion at a magical locus where lost mother and re-visioned city (another place of "stones") blend and take on life. Danny Boy is an orphan of the plague, who took his name from the song the old lady who adopted him liked to sing. Mary's daughter, too, has no name, and she gives herself the name Jax by reading letters from a Scrabble game interrupted by death in a house she enters randomly during her first exploration of the city.

Jax sees the ghosts of the city and encounters a number of times an angel who looks like her mother. Pursuit of these shadows leads her to discover the city home of her family, and in it the ironic truth about the plague: "peace" monkeys brought from Nepal to raise public consciousness against the cold war carried a virus that wiped out most of humanity. Jax herself, during the fighting, has acted as a shadow, appearing from hidden nooks and crannies of the city to "tag" Miles's soldiers with a death that is life: the mark "You're dead." After Danny Boy dies a real death to save her, she climbs a hill of the city to a moving moment of reconciliation that is now also one of redemption. Finally learning "the price of peace," she joins dead mother and lover simultaneously as she takes the hand of her guardian angel, which is now revealed to be a hand of metal, the fusion of shadow and hard substances that is the essential nature of the new, resurrected "city."

The decade of the 1990's was marked by the publication of Murphy's collected stories, in the volume *Points of Departure*, which won the Philip K. Dick Memorial Award. The volume includes many, but not all, of her stories, including "Rachel in Love," and the later story "Bones" (*Isaac Asimov's Science Fiction Magazine*, 1990). The latter work is a transposition of the encounter between natural magic and rational "science" to a new field of legend—Ireland. Murphy also contributed a story to a collaborative publication, *Letters from Home* (1991), with Pat Cadigan and Karen Joy Fowler, perhaps a first sign that this intensely private and personal writer was seeking kindred spirits. Her output for the first two-thirds of the 1990's was slim, with a handful of stories appearing mainly in *Fantasy and Science Fiction*: "Going Through Changes," the cover story in the April 1992 issue; "Points of Departure," July 1995 (not in the 1990 story collection of the same name); and "Iris Versus the Black Knight," October/November 1996.

The story "Points of Departure" is itself the point of departure for Murphy's long-awaited fourth novel, *Nadya: The Wolf Chronicles*.

The 1995 editorial commentary on the story announces "an historical, feminist, werewolf novel called *Traveling West: An American Story.*" The description offers, in all aspects except the "feminist," a clear anatomy of the nature and themes of this complex work. For the novel is essentially a rewriting of American "history" in the sense of its manifest destiny, the trek west, but from a curiously interesting "minority" view—that of a werewolf, a shape changer whose existence is one of negotiating the interface between realms that, in the eyes of the modern "scientific" culture America has forged, are alien but need not be so. The novel chronicles the arrival in mid-nineteenth-century America of two European wolf beings, who meet, marry, and sire Nadya. Her adventures, as one who undergoes the Change, shifting back and forth between the animal and human realms, give the reader a troubling perspective on events in the trek of American culture from East to West Coast. Themes familiar from Murphy's earlier work—shamanism, interspecies transformation, mother-daughter relations—are naturally explored, in continuous fashion, as Nadya encounters trappers, farmers, Indians, even the Donner party, on her move west, toward her ultimate encounter with herself and her dual existence, seeing the world simultaneously from inside and outside animal eyes, inside and outside the eyes of "civilized" human beings. An emblem of this existence (and proof that the descendants of Nadya still live on deserted byways of the West Coast) is found in the epilogue to the novel. An unnamed "you" narrator (clearly a woman's voice) tells of leaving job, lover, and civilized life in San Francisco and heading north, camping along Highway 1, toward Seattle. On the road, she encounters at a gas pump "a lean muscular brunette" with tatoos on each arm: "One arm is fire and light: a phoenix rising from the flames. . . . The other arm is shadow and darkness: trees rise in complex swirls of abstract foliage; from the forest, a gray wolf stares with golden eyes." The brunette, who has like golden eyes, tells of "ghost wolves" along this road. The narrator sets off up the wild coast, moving toward this shadow zone between worlds.

Obviously, the chronicles are not over. But despite the glib jacket comparisons of Murphy's novel to writers such as Anne Rice, one accepts this novel as a whole at the same time that one realizes that all of Murphy's stories and novels have told this same story over and over, in diverse locations and with varying cultural or scientific "contexts." The new novel, in its hardcover edition, bears no genre designation. Yet, if one is willing to consider English language science fiction, from its seminal texts, as oscillating between two distant and opposite poles—hard science and horror, *Frankenstein* and *Dracula*—one locates Murphy's work easily within the parameters of the genre. The clash of rational science and the natural powers of metamorphosis is central to Western culture. Murphy's work is, whatever its surface ornaments, at its core a powerful rewriting of this master narrative. If she continues to avoid the lures of ideology and the publishing industry in the future, her singular talent will continue to produce fine fiction.

Selected Bibliography

The Shadow Hunter. New York: Popular Library, 1982.
The Falling Woman. New York: TOR, 1986.
The City, Not Long After. Garden City, N.Y.: Doubleday, 1989.
Points of Departure. New York: Bantam, 1990.
Nadya: The Wolf Chronicles. New York: TOR, 1996.

—GEORGE SLUSSER

LARRY NIVEN

(b. 1938)

FOR LARRY NIVEN science fiction is primarily a literature of scientific ideas, an exercise in imaginative speculation in which sophisticated experiments in narrative voice, point of view, symbolism, or Joycean allusiveness would be awkward and pointless. Writing in a period when New Wave contemporaries like Samuel R. Delaney and Harlan Ellison are dazzling their readers with verbal pyrotechnics, Niven eschews stylistic innovations; and, in prose notable for its deliberate simplicity and utility, he seeks, as he puts it, "to train my readers to play with ideas for the sheer joy of it." While castigating the New Wave movement as "a seductive approach, a fine excuse for bad writing and not doing one's homework," Niven sees his own work as a continuation of "an old tradition—namely, the extrapolative story, in which ideas are tracked to expose their implications for the future and their effects on human society" (quotes from "Interview with Larry Niven" in *The Science Fiction Review* [July 1978]).

Niven's extrapolative stories and novels are always built around what has been known traditionally as the "What if?" proposition, a scientific or visionary hypothesis from which the writer extrapolates conclusions that ideally should be as logical as they are mind-boggling. For example, Niven's 1968 short story "All the Myriad Ways" (nominated for a 1969 Hugo award) has this for an opening paragraph:

There were timelines branching and branching, a megauniverse of universes, millions more every minute.... The universe split

every time someone made a decision. Split, so that every decision ever made could go both ways. Every choice made by every man, woman and child on Earth was reversed in the universe next door. It was enough to confuse any citizen, let alone Detective-Lieutenant Gene Trimble, who had other problems.

Gene Trimble's "other problems" in this story concern a mysterious rash of suicides that has come in the wake of the invention of "Crosstime travel," and the solution to the mystery represents for the reader the logical consequence of the scientific premise laid down in the first paragraph. This kind of opening propositional paragraph, presenting a straightforward subordination of characterization and style to scientific speculation, recurs throughout Niven's mature work and shows him to be a writer who has remained remarkably true to his roots in "hard" science fiction.

On the other hand, it is also clear that Niven's work, although always fascinating at a purely intellectual level, has grown in narrative power through the years. Niven gives his friend and frequent collaborator Jerry Pournelle much credit for teaching him how to supply a complicated background of political and social institutions for his future histories, a background that makes the actions and motivations of his larger-than-life heroes and heroines seem more interesting and believable. In any case, his mature work of the 1970's and early 1980's is a deft blend of brilliant scientific extrapolation and rich social

563

texture. There is, for example, his short story "Inconstant Moon" (1972 Hugo award, for best science fiction short story of 1971). It simultaneously invites us to solve a scientific puzzle based on the evidence available to his characters (did or did not the sun go nova?) while immersing us in the lives of a California couple of the near future who must first solve the problem of how best to spend their last eight hours alive (making love? drinking rare brandy and eating imported cheese? stealing jewelry?) and who then must shift into a hoarding frame of mind as it begins to look like the holocaust might not be total after all.

As a thinker Niven quite often arrives at curiously conservative conclusions. Although deep down he seems to be a believer in reason over feeling, in the ultimate value of science, and in the possibility of human progress, his fiction tends to sound a warning against an overreliance on technology in achieving that progress.

Nevertheless, as a writer Niven is incurably romantic, delighting in the portrayal of exotic aliens, bizarre natural phenomena, giant technological artifacts, strange alien cultures, and especially in the daring quests of his heroes and heroines. This might explain in part why Niven, whose name became synonymous with hard science fiction in the late 1960's and early 1970's, has been writing more and more stories and novels in the fantasy genre.

It is interesting to compare the fantasy stories in his Warlock series with the science fiction stories of the Known Space series that first made him famous in the 1960's. The Warlock stories, which culminate in the novel *The Magic Goes Away* (1978), postulate our prehistoric past as being true to our mythology: an era first ruled by gods, then by magicians, and finally by warriors as "mana," the nonrenewable resource of magic, is slowly used up. The Known Space stories, in contrast, extrapolate from plausible scientific hypotheses in postulating the first millennium of our future history as an era in which the human race has colonized the stars by virtue of one technological innovation or theoretical

breakthrough after another. Radically different in tone and texture, the two sets of stories are equally rigorous in the development of their logical premises; viewed together, they demonstrate that Niven, as Sandra Miesel has observed in the Afterword of *The Magic Goes Away*, "can extrapolate equally well from possible or impossible premises." Viewed together, they also demonstrate the ways in which Niven has given a much freer rein to his spirited imagination as he has learned to hold his readers' belief and interest by the sheer force of narrative texture.

Typically, the task that confronts Niven's characters is to understand the world with which they are confronted, whether it is the plausible future or the mythical past. In both his hard science fiction and his logical fantasies, Niven's characters usually embark on a quest of discovery, seeking the source of the mysterious powers that transcend and threaten them, whether those powers are the products of advanced technology or of magic. The great theme underlying all of Niven's fiction seems to be the need to discover what Arthur Koestler calls "the ghost in the machine," whether we understand the word "machine" literally or metaphorically as representing the laws and processes of nature. In *The Roots of Coincidence* (1972) Koestler observes that the deeper scientists probe the mysteries of nature, the more "occult" their theories become, to the point where "the hunting of the quark begins to resemble the mystic's quest for the cloud of unknowing." An overview of Niven's career suggests that Niven has come to share Koestler's notion of machines as oddly organic and nature as ultimately supernatural. It is this insight that seems to have made possible Niven's gradual shift away from old-fashioned, formulaic science fiction toward more daring forms of extrapolation in which physics blends with metaphysics and technology becomes, in Arthur C. Clarke's words, "indistinguishable from magic."

Just as Niven began his career with no intention of ever writing fantasy, he began his college studies in mathematics and the sciences with no apparent intention of ever writing fiction at all. Born in Los Angeles on 30 April 1938, to wealthy parents and as an heir to the Doheny oil fortune, Laurence van Cott Niven grew up in Beverly Hills and attended an exclusive boarding school for boys in Santa Barbara. In 1956 he enrolled in the California Institute of Technology and later earned a B.A. in mathematics (with a minor in psychology) from Washburn University, Kansas (1962). After one year of graduate work at the University of California, he quit in 1963 to devote his energies to learning how to write science fiction, enrolling in a writing correspondence course during this period.

Niven lived off the proceeds from a trust fund and collected rejection slips for most of the following year before selling his first story, "The Coldest Place," to Frederik Pohl for *If* magazine. Niven sold several more short stories and his first novel to Pohl in quick succession, and his first big break came when his story "Neutron Star" won the 1967 Hugo award as the best science fiction short story of 1966. His first novel, *World of Ptavvs*, was nominated for a Nebula award the same year, and Niven's career was safely launched.

Eight stories from Niven's Known Space series were collected under the title *Neutron Star* in 1968. These stories are notable for their subtle charm and intriguing science, and the volume was a science fiction best-seller. But it was Niven's novel *Ringworld* (1970), a continuation of the Known Space saga, which established his reputation as one of our finest practitioners of hard science fiction; this novel won both the 1970 Nebula and the 1971 Hugo awards for the best science fiction novel. Niven's biggest critical success since *Ringworld* has been the first novel he coauthored with Jerry Pournelle, *The Mote in God's Eye* (1974); it is an entertaining and fascinating space opera and was nominated for a Hugo award.

Niven's Known Space is the "little bubble of stars thirty-three thousand light years out from the galactic axis" that contains the home planet of the human species. Most of the Known Space stories are set in an era

seven hundred to eight hundred years in our future, and Known Space at this time is about sixty to seventy light years in diameter. Earth's population has been stable at around eighteen billion for hundreds of years, thanks to the rigorous policies of Earth's Fertility Board. Technological wonders of the period include transfer booths, which make travel on Earth and on other planets instantaneous; organ replacement banks and "booster spice," which make immortality possible for any human who is not accident prone; hyperspace drive, which has made interstellar trade with alien species practical; terraforming, which is the rebuilding of planetary systems to meet human life-support needs; and stasis fields, which stop time from passing. (The stasis field is the invention of the Slavers, a species extinct now for a billion and a half years but who once ruled the whole galaxy; *World of Ptavvs* is the story of a Slaver released from stasis into human time and space.)

The most intriguing of the extraterrestrial aliens who inhabit Known Space are the supremely advanced but instinctively cowardly Puppeteers, who were given this name because they resemble "a headless, three-legged centaur wearing two Cecil the Seasick Sea Serpent puppets on its arms." In "At the Core" (1966) the Puppeteers blackmail a human adventurer named Beowulf Shaeffer into piloting an experimentally fast hyperspace ship to the galactic core, where he finds that millions of suns have gone supernova in a giant chain reaction. Radiation from the explosion, which will not reach Known Space for thirty thousand years, will eventually make the whole galaxy uninhabitable. The frightened Puppeteers, who never take any chances, begin immediately to move their home planet at sublight speed toward the outer edges of the galaxy and beyond.

As *Ringworld* opens, the Puppeteers have been absent from Known Space for over two hundred years. A Puppeteer named Nessus, who is considered insane by other Puppeteers for having once displayed humanlike courage, returns to Known Space in Shaeffer's experimental ship to enlist the aid of a two-hundred-year-old human named Louis Wu. The Puppeteers want Louis and Nessus to investigate the life-support potential of an artificially constructed "Ringworld" that Puppeteer scouts have discovered in an area far outside Known Space.

This Ringworld is spinning on its axis, for artificial gravity, at almost eight hundred miles per second around a yellow-dwarf sun. It is ninety-three million miles in radius, equal to that of Earth's orbit, and its inner inhabited surface is a million miles wide and six hundred million miles long. Nessus and Louis are accompanied on their mission by a huge alien called Speaker-To-Animals, a member of the fierce, catlike kzinti species, and by a young human female named Teela Brown, the descendant of six generations of winners in Earth's birth lotteries, who is brought along on the theory that natural selection has provided her with the kind of luck they will all need to survive their mission. They crashland on the inner surface to find an Earthlike environment of staggering dimensions and a fallen human civilization that has shrouded the technological origins of the Ringworld in religious superstition and has continued to worship the memory of its long-dead class of "engineers," the Builders. Setting off for the rim, which is five hundred thousand miles away, they find themselves on a quest to discover not only a way off the surface but also the mysterious cause of the civilization's technological decline.

With this novel, Niven seems to have added a corollary to Arthur C. Clarke's proposition that "any sufficiently advanced technology is indistinguishable from magic"— specifically, that any sufficiently advanced technology can also be indistinguishable from nature itself. To the primitive, superstitious Ringworlders, the lasers and flycycles of Puppeteer technology are indistinguishable from magic, and the Ringworlders conceptualize the giant ring that looms over their sky as an "Arch" raised by the divine Builders, as a "sign of the Covenant with Man." Ironically, even Louis, who has seen the entire Ringworld from space at a godlike perspective, has

Larry Niven. © Miriam Berkley

trouble resisting this interpretation of the phenomenon. And, owing to his persistent tendency to view everything on the Ringworld as the product of nature rather than mankind, he fails at first to recognize a volcano for what it really is, a giant meteor puncture in the ring's base material.

In *The Ascent of Man* (1973) Jacob Bronowski observes that a machine, whether as simple as a hammer or as complex as a fusion reactor, is nothing more than "a device for tapping the power in nature." Louis Wu and his companions discover, likewise, that a machine as sophisticated as the now battered Ringworld is a Pandora's box primed to destroy its inhabitants because it taps into powers that scientists cannot even comprehend, much less control. And Niven seems to be suggesting that such is the magnitude of the Ringworld's powers that they should only be approached with piety and religious awe. So, the noblest and finally the wisest of the characters in the novel seems to be a Ringworlder of mythic proportions named Seeker, who is on a holy quest, significantly at a right angle to the direction of Louis' group, to find the base of the Arch.

There are many ironic references in the novel to the folly of using technology to "play god"; toward the end of their quest, Louis, Speaker, and Teela discover that the Puppeteers have earned their name through the centuries by tampering with the natural selection processes of human and kzinti evolution. In their mania for leaving nothing to chance, the Puppeteers have finally outsmarted themselves. Centuries before, they had fixed Earth's birth lotteries in order to breed humans having luck as powerful as Teela's. But now Nessus discovers that in doing so his race upset the laws of probability and inadvertently subjected the whole galaxy to a select number of infallibly lucky humans. So, for example, they were destined to crash-land so that Teela would meet Seeker, the man she was "born to love." Nessus, Speaker, and Louis finally discover a way off the surface, leaving the immortal Teela and her lover (with her luck, nothing can kill them) to pursue an endless quest around and around the inside of the ring, safe from the galactic core explosion since the dense material of the ring lies in the plane of the advancing energy wave.

Niven's fans virtually forced him to produce a sequel. In *The Ringworld Engineers* (1979) Louis Wu returns some twenty years after his first adventure to find that the ring's orbit has become unstable. The novel is well done but less compelling than the original because the plot seems designed mostly as an excuse to expose Louis to one technological discovery after another. For instance, we learn the cause of the fall of the floating cities, the surprising source of a superconductor-eating bacterium, and the fact that the ring has attitude jets and a spillpipe system. The novel is perhaps best thought of as an example of the sophisticated game that writers of hard science fiction often play with their readers. In his dedication to the novel, Niven says that

people have never stopped writing to him about "the assumptions, overt and hidden, and the mathematics and the ecology and the philosophical implications" of the Ringworld itself. It is for the small group of science fiction purists who treat the Ringworld as "a proposed engineering project" that this sequel was written.

In *The Mote in God's Eye*, as in *Ringworld*, the plot revolves around the way in which a technologically advanced future human civilization blunders into opening a Pandora's box that, once opened, threatens a holocaust. In the year A.D. 3017, a space vessel of the Second Empire of Man intercepts an alien space probe that has entered human space from the direction of a yellow-dwarf sun located inside that mysterious "nebular mass of dust and gas" known as the "Coal Sack." The superstitious followers of the "Church of Him" on the planet New Scotland believe the Coal Sack to be the face of God; a red-giant star at its center gives it the appearance of a huge, glowing eye (the yellow dwarf is the "Mote" in the eye) looking out from the dark hood covering God's enormous head. Two ships of the Empire make the jump across hyperspace (in zero time, thanks to the most significant invention of their civilization, the Alderson drive) to the Mote, where they confront the strange but technologically adept aliens the Empire humans come to call "Moties." Moties are furry creatures with two thin right arms and a massive left arm, the only asymmetrical species in the known universe. They are the product of a peculiar sequence of engineered mutations that has caused the race to evolve in a number of directions simultaneously.

There is something mysteriously wrong with the Motie civilization. Although highly advanced, it seems to have undergone "thousands of Cycles . . . of collapses back to slavery." What the humans do not discover until they have actually brought Motie ambassadors back to human space is that, owing to the vagaries of their evolution, fertile Moties must breed to stay alive—a fact that puts enormous pressure on the limited resources of their solar system. It also puts life-or-death pressure on each succeeding civilization, since each must race to expand its technological capacities before its ticking population bomb explodes. So far, no Motie civilization has won its race against time, and sane Moties accept with stoicism the inevitability of the natural cycles. From time to time, though, a Motie goes "Crazy Eddie," acting "as if the impossible could be achieved," as did the one who launched the probe the humans intercepted and their aspirations only make things worse.

By this definition, of course, the whole human race is "Crazy Eddie," and the humans now discover that they are faced with a moral dilemma they cannot solve. Once the Moties know of the existence of hyperspace, they will use their superior technological instincts to develop an Alderson drive of their own, making every uninhabited planet in human space a place to dump excess Motie populations. It seems that the only way the humans can avoid being overrun is by exterminating the entire Motie civilization immediately. But, before this is done, the Motie ambassadors devise an ingenious solution to the problem, providing the "Crazy Eddie" Second Empire of Man with a morally acceptable way to put the lid back on a box that neither a sane Motie nor a reverent member of the Church of Him would have been foolish enough to open in the first place.

Niven and Pournelle have since collaborated on eight other novels—*Inferno* (1976), *Lucifer's Hammer* (1977), *Oath of Fealty* (1981), and five others in the 1980's and 1990's. *Inferno* is a modern version of Dante's *Inferno*; it seems to be predicated less on its authors' recognition that their novel is a fantasy and more on the conceit that Dante's work was really science fiction. Allen Carpentier, a famous science fiction writer, falls to his death while showing off for his fans at a "sci-fi" convention and wakes to find himself in the Vestibule of the Hell envisioned by Dante.

A guide named Benito (Mussolini, as we subsequently discover) assures Allen that "the route to Heaven is at the center of Hell"; and, as they pursue their quest through one torture after another, Allen discovers that he can "quit looking for justice in Hell" where "there was only macabre humor." It is his ironic fate as a science fiction writer to be looking always for the technical apparatus that underlies Hell's marvels. He develops the hypothesis that Hell is actually an "Infernoland," part of an extravagant amusement park built by an advanced civilization whose technology is to him "indistinguishable from magic." To this Benito replies, "Yours is the most curious delusion I have yet encountered here." But, ironically, this hypothesis is not too far from the final revelation that Hell is actually "the violent ward of a hospital for the theologically insane." It is a testing ground engineered by God as a "last attempt" to get the attention of human beings too proud of their technology and too self-centered in their humanism to accept the reality of an eternal, omnipotent, ghostly Presence in both technology and nature. Humbled, Benito observes: "Remember there is a way. Downward, accepting everything—."

During the 1970's Niven wrote a series of science fiction mysteries that are not as ambitious in theme as his major works of fiction but demonstrate many of his most engaging qualities. The stories concern the adventures of Gil Hamilton, an agent of A.R.M. in the twenty-second century who solves his cases with the aid of an imaginary, psychic "arm" (see *The Long ARM of Gil Hamilton*, 1976).

In *The Patchwork Girl* (1980) Hamilton solves a murder mystery on Earth's moon colony. The plot is shaped by two propositions that are quintessential Niven. The first proposition is that the capability to rebuild humans with organ transplants will create a need to supply the organ banks, and that this in turn will necessitate capital punishment, even for minor offenses. (See also Niven's 1967 short story "The Jigsaw Man," collected in *All the Myriad Ways*, 1971.) The second proposition is that the human species will differentiate in terms of both physique and value systems as various colonizing groups adapt to the harsh, demanding environments of the solar system. Niven's portrayal of our near future is tantalizingly real, and he gives us convincing impressions of everything from the way asteroid-belt miners decorate their pressure suits to the trials and triumphs of low-gravity sex. Basically, though, *The Patchwork Girl* is an interesting refinement of an old story form, not a work in which Niven breaks any new ground.

By contrast, *Dream Park* (1981), coauthored with Steven Barnes, is a novel that might be described as science fiction wrapped around a fantasy. It mixes the Infernoland concept of *Inferno* with the proposition of *Ringworld* that any sufficiently advanced technology is not only indistinguishable from magic but also, and more important, from nature. *Dream Park* is set in a southern California amusement park sometime in the middle of the twenty-first century. Each of the park's "games" immerses its players in imaginary settings taken from literature, myth, and history. The use of holograms, human actors, computerized robots, and full-scale sets offers an almost perfect illusion of reality. The Dream Park is a Disneyland raised to the *n*th power, with a technology closer to our own than that of the Ringworld Builders, though no less magical.

Each game tests the skills of the players in a roleplaying situation, usually a romantic quest against high odds and in an exotic setting. The games themselves are part improvisational drama, part sensory illusion, and part intellectual puzzle. Regular players soon become fantasy junkies; in fact, to be good at a game, a player must accept the fantasy as real.

When one of the park's security guards is murdered by a deranged game player, the park's security chief, Alex Griffin, goes undercover as a player of the South Seas Treasure Game, which is set amidst the Cargo cult of New Guinea in the 1950's. This is a primitive, brutal world in which native magic works and the monsters of Melanesian mythology are real and dangerous. A tough, emotionally restrained cop, Griffin is nevertheless finally hooked by the emotional intensity and the physical and intellectual challenges of his game. The highly charged action of the fantasy makes his everyday life seem by comparison pale, unsatisfactory, and ultimately unreal. His intellectual struggle to keep things in perspective exhausts him more than the physical obstacles of the game, but although he knows the game is just a cunning illusion, he also knows that it stimulates his imagination and purges his repressed emotions in a way that nothing in the highly regulated real world ever could.

The novel's theme is reinforced by its story-within-a-story structure, and most sympathetic readers will have as much trouble as Alex remembering that the engrossing life-and-death struggles of the South Seas Treasure adventure are just elaborate illusions. Niven and Barnes wish to demonstrate that we read their novel for much the same reason that the players play the games; we are drawn into it by something inside ourselves, something primitive and powerful, something balancing on the thin edge between terror and exhilaration. Thus we cannot help but identify with Griffin's reaction when he is placed face to face with a projection from our own nightmares, a fearsome mechanical zombie: "Once again, something within Griffin, something logical and cool, died without protest. In its place rose a red shadow that yearned to kill" (chapter 27). And it is this red shadow, a Pandora's box of unconscious fears and desires, that we ought not to tease and bait with advanced technology, at least not for the sake of mere amusement.

Niven's theme in such works as *Ringworld* and *Dream Park* is not the evil of technology but the misuse of technology, not the inevitable clash of technology with nature but the need to harmonize them by bringing human aspirations back into balance with natural imperatives. This is also the theme of Niven's lyrical fantasy novel *The Magic Goes Away*.

In *The Magic Goes Away* the great magician Warlock enlists the aid of other great magicians and of a nonmagical warrior, Orolandes, in his quest to find enough mana to make magic the ruling force on Earth again. The time is 12,000 B.C., magic is fast dying out, and Warlock knows that he will have to kill one of the last of the sleeping gods (most have become "mythical") to get the mana they need. But Warlock realizes at last that the maintenance of his own power has become more important to him than the issue of how best to use it for the preservation of Earth and its people. And in a noble act of self-sacrifice he destroys the god's power rather than steal it. In so doing, Warlock implicitly turns over the maintenance and potential exploitation of nature to the emerging warrior civilization—our civilization—represented by the heroic Orolandes and fated to dominate Earth someday by force of technology rather than magic.

Niven's thematic point here is that it does not matter finally which of the two forces we use as a mediator between ourselves and our environment, since magic and technology, ritual and experimentation, religion and science are simply different means to the same end. The only important thing is that we use with care and humility whatever force nature cares to lend us. Like most science fiction writers, Larry Niven would remind us that, as Warlock puts it, the world either "belongs to the gods or it belongs to men"—which means that no human being can back away from the moral responsibility assumed when our ancestors chose to live with and by technology, rather than solely at the whims of the perverse ghost in nature's imponderable machine.

—RICHARD FINHOLT
—JOHN CARR

Larry Niven's subsequent career has been dominated by collaborations, sequels, and reshuffled story collections. Though containing much of interest, his output during the 1980's and 1990's has not won any Hugo awards to add to the five he collected in the 1960's and 1970's.

The Descent of Anansi (1982), written with Steven Barnes, centers on traditional hard science fiction ingenuity with mass, momentum, and orbital mechanics. Attacked by hijackers who covet their cargo of superthin and superstrong monofilament cable, the crew of the spaceship *Anansi* (named for a trickster spider-god) uses the cable itself for evasive and defensive tricks. The book reads like a clever novelette padded to novel length.

A new series began with *The Integral Trees* (1983), distantly connected to *A World Out of Time* (1976) and its dystopian future State. Here Niven echoes the scale of *Ringworld* by presenting a vast, habitable free-fall environment—the "Smoke Ring"—within the still larger doughnut-shaped gas cloud surrounding a neutron star. Trees are rootless; floating "ponds" are spherical. Human colonists, descended from a ship's crew who escaped State control, have forgotten much about their world and past. The novel is a travelogue of discovery, exploring the highlights of a bizarre astronomical background that unfortunately dwarfs the unmemorable characters. Its sequel is *The Smoke Ring* (1987).

A further collaboration with Jerry Pournelle, *Footfall* (1985), reworked a discarded scenario for their earlier disaster novel *Lucifer's Hammer*, in which the Hammer—a devastating asteroid strike—was to have been a deliberate extraterrestrial attack. This story has its longueurs and political embarrassments, but the herd-society aliens are engagingly Nivenesque creations despite their determination to subjugate Earth. Occupying the tactical "high ground" of orbital space, their "Star Wars" military machine can bombard any point on the globe while remaining beyond the reach of most human attack. The exhilarating finale unveils Earth's secret weapon, an unthinkable (in peacetime) monster spacecraft powered by rapid-fire nuclear explosions, which storms the orbiting fortresses and compels an alien surrender

The Legacy of Heorot (1987), written with Pournelle and Barnes, is straightforward action adventure on a distant world being colonized by humans who encounter ravening monster "grendels": hence the Beowulf/Heorot allusion. These beasts are reminiscent of the creature in the movie *Alien*, and as in horror movies, the colonists react slow wittedly to the threat. Indeed the authors find it necessary to insert an explanation that people have been variously brain-damaged by cryogenic "sleep" during their long space journey. A few nevertheless win through. The less coherent but still energetic and readable sequel, *Beowulf's Children* (1995), also with Pournelle and Barnes, introduces the next human generation and the mild mystery—whose solution is telegraphed well in advance—of a previously unnoticed menace that effortlessly eats even grendels.

Late-period Niven shows less of the intertwined joys of creation and storytelling that fueled the Known Space series at its best. There is a tendency toward slightly didactic political agendas, such as the warm pleas for spaceborn weaponry in *Footfall* and for development of space and Mars in *Dream Park II: The Barsoom Project* (1989, with Barnes). The latter, an effective sequel to *Dream Park* that similarly counterpoints real and role-playing tensions, ultimately appears to endorse its pro-space campaigners' assassination of a political opponent. *Fallen Angels* (1991, with Pournelle and Michael Flynn) presents a 2073 dystopian Earth where most people are resolutely antispace, antiscience, and anti–science fiction. In answer to theories of global warming, there is a new ice age. Science fiction fans have become a virtuous underground opposition that hides fugitive astronauts from a still-functioning space station (the "fallen angels") and helps them get home. Fans' names and fannish in-jokes abound, reducing the appeal for most readers.

Other sequels followed. *Dream Park: The Voodoo Game* (1991, with Barnes; retitled *The California Voodoo Game* in the United States) is a further return to Dream Park. Barnes seems to bring useful narrative energy to these collaborations, stimulating Niven's own inventiveness and producing strong narrative lines. *The Gripping Hand* (1993, with Pournelle) returns to the settings of *The Mote in God's Eye* and was generally thought anticlimactic for its too-easy and too-early introduction of a biological miracle cure for the intractable racial dilemma of the first book's likable but dangerous alien "Moties." *The Ringworld Throne* (1996) pays a third visit to the huge artifact that dominated *Ringworld* and that in *Ringworld Engineers* was given a somewhat fussy revisionist overhaul to satisfy science-minded fans who had pointed out technical flaws. With the Ringworld's secrets stripped bare, it is now little more than a backdrop for meandering adventures in the vein that the *Encyclopedia of Science Fiction* terms "planetary romance." Niven's heroes relish problem solving and need new challenges.

Thus, after a slow opening, the relatively modest *Destiny's Road* (1997) radiates a good deal of the old charm as its young protagonist explores the mysteries of Destiny, a human-settled colony world. Earthly and alien biologies are in conflict, and children grow up stupid if their food lacks a regular dosage of "speckles." This spice, unavailable in the hero's hometown, must be expensively bought from traders. Ensuing revelations about Destiny and its settlers are not of universe-shattering consequence, but they neatly mesh with human-scaled conflicts and characters.

Larry Niven's place of honor in modern science fiction has been amply earned. His early dazzling manipulation of far-out notions from theoretical physics could perhaps not be sustained forever, and other writers have crowded to mine that particular vein of inventiveness. Nevertheless, he is an adept storyteller when sufficiently interested in his material, and his later work still entertains.

—DAVID LANGFORD

Selected Bibliography

WORKS OF LARRY NIVEN

World of Ptavvs. New York: Ballantine, 1966; London: Macdonald, 1968.
A Gift from Earth. New York: Ballantine, 1968; London: Macdonald, 1969.
Neutron Star. New York: Ballantine, 1968; London: Macdonald, 1969. (Short stories.)

The Shape of Space. New York: Ballantine, 1969. (Short stories.)

Ringworld. New York: Ballantine, 1970; London: Gollancz, 1972. (Ringworld series, no. 1.)

All the Myriad Ways. New York: Ballantine, 1971. (Short stories and essays.)

The Flying Sorcerers, with David Gerrold. New York: Ballantine, 1971; London: Corgi, 1975.

The Flight of the Horse. New York: Ballantine, 1973; London: Futura, 1975. (Short stories.)

Inconstant Moon. London: Gollancz, 1973; London: Sphere, 1974. (Five stories are omitted in the Sphere reissue.)

Protector. New York: Ballantine, 1973; London: Futura, 1974.

A Hole in Space. New York: Ballantine, 1974; London: Futura, 1975. (Short stories and essays.)

The Mote in God's Eye, with Jerry Pournelle. New York: Simon and Schuster, 1974; London: Weidenfeld and Nicolson, 1975. (Motie series, no. 1.)

Tales of Known Space: The Universe of Larry Niven. New York and London: Ballantine, 1975. (Linked short stories.)

A World Out of Time: A Novel. New York: Holt, Rinehart and Winston, 1976; London: Futura, 1977.

Inferno, with Jerry Pournelle. New York: Pocket Books, 1976; London: Wingate, 1977.

The Long ARM of Gil Hamilton. New York and London: Ballantine, 1976. London: Futura, 1980. (Linked short stories.)

Lucifer's Hammer, with Jerry Pournelle. Chicago: Playboy, 1977; London: Orbit, 1978.

The Magic Goes Away. New York: Ace, 1978. London: Futura, 1982. (With an afterword by Sandra Miesel.)

Convergent Series. New York: Ballantine, 1979; London: Orbit, 1986. (Short stories.)

The Ringworld Engineers. New York: Phantasia, 1979. New York: Ballantine, 1979; London: Gollancz, 1980. (Ringworld series, no. 2.)

The Patchwork Girl. New York: Ace, 1980.

Dream Park, with Steven Barnes. New York: Phantasia, 1981; New York: Ace, 1981; London: Macdonald, 1983. (Dream Park series, no. 1.)

Oath of Fealty, with Jerry Pournelle. New York: Phantasia, 1981. New York: Simon and Schuster/Timescape, 1981; London: Macdonald, 1982.

The Descent of Anansi, with Steven Barnes. New York: Pinnacle, 1982; London: Futura, 1984.

The Integral Trees. New York: Ballantine, 1983; London: Macdonald, 1984. (Smoke Ring series, no. 1.)

Niven's Laws. Philadelphia, Pa.: Owlswick (with Pennsylvania SF Society), 1984. (Short stories and essays.)

The Time of the Warlock. Minneapolis, Minn.: SteelDragon, 1984. (Short stories, assembling all Warlock fantasies with revisions.)

Footfall, with Jerry Pournelle. New York: Ballantine/Del Rey, 1985; London: Gollancz, 1985.

Limits. New York: Ballantine/Del Rey, 1985; London: Futura, 1986. (Short stories.)

The Legacy of Heorot, with Jerry Pournelle and Steven Barnes. London: Gollancz, 1987; New York: Simon and Schuster, 1987. (Heorot series, no. 1.)

The Smoke Ring. New York: Ballantine, 1987; London: Macdonald, 1987. (Smoke Ring series, no. 2.)

Dream Park II: The Barsoom Project, with Steven Barnes. New York: Ace, 1989; London: Pan, 1990. (Dream Park series, no. 2.)

N-Space. New York: TOR, 1990. (Short stories, essays, and excerpts.)

Achilles' Choice, with Steven Barnes. New York: TOR, 1991; London: Pan, 1993.

Dream Park: The Voodoo Game, with Steven Barnes. London: Pan, 1991. Reprinted as *The California Voodoo Game,* New York: Ballantine/Del Rey, 1992. (Dream Park series, no. 3.)

Fallen Angels, with Jerry Pournelle and Michael Flynn. New York: Baen, 1991; London: Pan, 1993.

Playgrounds of the Mind. New York: TOR, 1991. (Short stories, essays, and excerpts.)

Bridging the Galaxies. San Francisco: San Francisco Science Fiction Conventions, 1993. (Short stories and essays.)

The Gripping Hand, with Jerry Pournelle. New York: Pocket Books, 1993. Reprinted as *The Moat Around Murcheson's Eye,* London: HarperCollins, 1993. (Motie series, no. 2.)

Crashlander. New York: Ballantine/Del Rey, 1994. (Short stories featuring Beowulf Shaeffer, with new framing material.)

Beowulf's Children, with Jerry Pournelle and Steven Barnes. New York: TOR, 1995. Reprinted as *The Dragons of Heorot,* London: Gollancz, 1995.

Flatlander. New York: Ballantine/Del Rey, 1995. (Short stories, including contents of *The Long ARM of Gil Hamilton* and *The Patchwork Girl,* plus one new story.)

The Ringworld Throne. New York: Ballantine/Del Rey. 1996; London: Orbit, 1996. (Ringworld series, no. 3.)

Destiny's Road. New York: TOR, 1997; London: Orbit, 1997.

EDITED ANTHOLOGIES

The Magic May Return. New York: Ace, 1981.

More Magic. New York: Berkley, 1984.

The Man-Kzin Wars, with others. 7 vols. New York: Baen, 1988–1995.

BIBLIOGRAPHY

Drumm, Chris, and Paul Guptill. *The Many Worlds of Larry Niven.* Polk City, Iowa: Drumm, 1989.

CRITICAL AND BIOGRAPHICAL STUDIES

Barbour, Douglas, "Oath of Fealty." *Foundation,* 25 (June 1982): 73–75.

Budrys, Algis. "A Gift from Earth" and "Ringworld." In *Benchmarks*. Carbondale and Edwardsville: Southern Illinois University Press, 1985.

Clute, John. "Larry Niven." In *The Encyclopedia of Science Fiction*, 2nd ed. Edited by John Clute and Peter Nicholls. London: Orbit, 1993; New York: St. Martin's, 1993.

———, "The Legacy of Heorot." In *Look at the Evidence*. Seattle, Wash.: Serconia Press, 1995. Liverpool, England: Liverpool University Press, 1995.

Gaiman, Neil. "Footfall." *Foundation*, 36 (summer 1986): 85–87.

Newsinger, John. "The Ringworld Throne." *Foundation*, 70 (summer 1997): 118–119.

Nicholls, Peter. "Tau Zero and Ringworld." *Foundation*, 2 (June 1972): 44–48.

Stableford, Brian. "The Gripping Hand." *New York Review of Science Fiction*, 54 (February 1993): 12.

Stein, Kevin T. *The Guide to Larry Niven's Ringworld*. Riverdale, N.Y.: Baen, 1994.

CHAD OLIVER
(1928–1993)

ALTHOUGH SCIENCE FICTION writers frequently adapt the techniques and findings of anthropology, among other disciplines, to describe the societies they explore, only rarely do they focus directly on the ways in which anthropologists work or on themes arising directly from the discipline of anthropology. Chad Oliver, though, was the leading writer of science fiction who directed his attention toward anthropologists and their work. In Oliver's hands, anthropological science fiction took on a depth and a solidity of approach that is not often found in science fiction of any kind; basically this is because Oliver was a professional anthropologist who also wrote science fiction.

I

Symmes Chadwick Oliver was born in Cincinnati, Ohio, on 30 March 1928. His father, Symmes Francis Oliver, was a surgeon; his mother, Winona Newman, was a nurse and a painter. Both his parents were avid readers, and his father was an expert fisherman and a sports fan.

When Oliver was twelve, he was confined to bed for seven months with a severe, nearly fatal case of rheumatic fever. During this time he read almost everything he could get his hands on, including a great deal of pulp magazine fiction; he took this reading seriously and began writing letters to the editors of the pulps. His name soon became well known in the letter columns of the magazines.

Oliver's bout with rheumatic fever left him weak and prone to other illnesses, but his family's move to Crystal City, Texas, where his father was an army medical officer at a detention camp, was beneficial to his health. He quickly gained some forty pounds and enough strength and stamina to play football.

Oliver received a B.A. and did work toward an M.A. at the University of Texas in Austin. He was interested then in many of the things that interested him throughout his life—jazz, good scotch, pipe smoking, trout fishing, and science fiction. These varied pleasures often appear in Oliver's science fiction, together with acute analyses of the anthropological relationships between different cultures. Oliver was one of those people who can do a number of things well, retain facts, and incorporate and synthesize them. As an undergraduate, for example, he took as many literature courses as he could, since he planned to be a writer; but he also took a number of anthropology courses. One of the most influential of these courses, taken during his senior year, was taught by a highly recommended teacher, a Professor McAllister. This course solidified his leanings toward a career in anthropology, and in it Oliver met Betty Jenkins. Although their romance was not a fictional "love at first sight," their relationship had become serious by the time they returned from an anthropological dig in Mexico the following summer.

By the time Oliver finished work for his M.A. in 1952, as an English major with a minor in anthropology, he had written a thesis, "They Built a Tower," concerning the history of science fiction, and he was already a published science fiction writer. He had first tried writing at the age of fifteen, and he received a good many rejection slips. But the editors who wrote the rejections encouraged him to keep writing—and he did.

Anthony Boucher, then coeditor of *Fantasy and Science Fiction*, was the first to buy one of Oliver's stories, "The Boy Next Door," early in 1950. But before that story was published, Oliver had sold several others; "Land of Lost Content" was the first actually to appear, in the November 1950 issue of *Super Science Stories*. In addition, Oliver's first novel, *Mists of Dawn*, was published in 1952; written for teenagers, it tells of a boy who journeys back to the Cro-Magnon era, and it provides a detailed and convincing hypothetical picture of an early human culture. Oliver's first novel for adults, *Shadows in the Sun*, was published in 1954; the following year his first collection of short stories, *Another Kind*, appeared. Oliver was gaining a reputation as a fine writer, and several of his stories had by this time appeared in "best of the year" anthologies.

After receiving his M.A., Oliver taught English for one semester at the University of Texas before going to the University of California at Los Angeles (UCLA) in September 1952, to work toward a Ph.D. in anthropology. That November he and Betty Jenkins were married. Another writer, Rog Phillips (Roger Phillips Graham), was best man. Forrest J. Ackerman gave the reception, and Ray Bradbury and A. E. van Vogt were among the guests.

Oliver became an instructor in anthropology at the University of Texas in 1955, and he developed a weekly hour-long radio program devoted to authentic jazz for KHFI-FM in Austin. In addition, taking his duties as a teacher and scholar seriously, he had a monograph on the Plains Indians published, as well as articles in such academic journals as *Texas Journal of Science* and *American Anthropologist*. His interest in Indian lore and in the history of his adopted state led to historical tales of the frontier that were published in magazines

ranging from *Argosy* to *Saturday Evening Post*, as well as to his novel *The Wolf Is My Brother* (1967), which won the Best Western Historical Novel award for 1967 from the Western Writers of America.

Oliver also continued to publish science fiction; his novel *The Winds of Time* appeared in 1957, and the novel *Unearthly Neighbors* in 1960; but his career as an anthropologist was also developing rapidly. Following teaching stints at UCLA and the University of California at Riverside in 1960–1961, Oliver was granted a Ph.D. in anthropology by UCLA in 1961. The following year he did fieldwork in Kenya on the relationships between culture and ecology in four tribes, as part of a project directed by Dr. Walter Goldschmidt of UCLA. The Olivers were in Kenya during a time of political and social unrest, and some of the Kenyans at first suspected that Oliver was a CIA agent. But his straightforward approach and his willingness to abide by tribal customs quickly dispelled all suspicion, and he established a good working relationship with the people of the two Kamba villages in which he worked.

In the late summer of 1962 the Olivers returned to the University of Texas, where Oliver's academic duties and his anthropological work left him little time for writing. In 1968 he was promoted to professor; he remained at the University of Texas, where he also served as head of the department of anthropology, teaching until just before his death in 1993.

II

Oliver used his experiences in various ways in his fiction. For example, his novel *Shadows in the Sun* is set in a small Texas town, the sort of town that Oliver knew well, and the central character is an anthropologist with physical characteristics and some traits similar to Oliver's own. Much of the background and many of the situations in *The Shores of Another Sea* (1971) have clearly been drawn from the year the Olivers spent in Kenya. His story "Hardly Worth Mentioning" (1953) is based on the dig in Mexico following his senior year in college, and the opening of *The Winds of Time* is set on the Gunnison River in Colorado, a favorite fishing spot of Oliver's. In fact, quite a number of Oliver's stories have settings here, or in similar locations, and many of the main characters are fishermen. A second important setting for *The Winds of Time* is a section of West Los Angeles, where the Olivers lived during his three years at UCLA. Indeed, most of Oliver's stories draw on his varied experiences in some way, but none of them are simply transcriptions of what he has done.

Oliver used the details he gained from his experiences to create the sense of reality, the sense of the ordinary, that is so important in the creation of believable science fiction. With this background of realistic detail, he was able to make the basic situations of his stories credible and to introduce the reader gently and gradually to the more speculative or extraordinary elements of the stories. The background of ordinary detail makes the elements of strangeness simultaneously more strange and more acceptable to the reader.

For example, *Shadows in the Sun* is set in Jefferson City, Texas, a town of some six thousand people. The details at the beginning of the novel—the small cafe with the worn jukebox, the drip and hum of the overworked air-conditioner, the humidity condensing on the walls, the varnished tables, the painting on the wall, the lagging clock, the songs playing on the jukebox—establish this place as an apparently ordinary Texas town, one that almost everyone has encountered either in real life or in the movies, the kind of town that a person would drive through and not give a second glance. Because the town is so ordinary, protagonist Paul Ellery's conclusion that it is inhabited by aliens comes as a distinct shock. Indeed, the very ordinariness of the town sets off the extraordinary facts and allows the reader a clearer look at them. Oliver was quoted as saying that he liked to keep one foot firmly fixed in the things that he knew well, and this preference clearly helps to account

Chad Oliver in 1988. PHOTO BY JAY KAY KLEIN

for the solidity, the believability, and the basic readability of his fiction.

"Rite of Passage" (1954; collected in *Another Kind*), one of Oliver's longer and better stories, is conveniently divided into sections that sharply illustrate his general approach to unfolding a story in which an anthropological exploration is the central concern. This story also illustrates his solution to a major problem in the use of anthropology as the "science" in science fiction. In such stories the author must balance the demands of storytelling with the demands of science. Simply to describe, moment by moment or even day by day, the ways in which the anthropologist works would be inimical to the storyteller's craft. To avoid this problem, Oliver presented key bits of data, and focused on one or two of the major areas of the anthropologist's exploration. In "Rite of Passage" the action and the information are presented in six nearly equal sections, each focusing on key aspects of the cultural exploration in the story.

Oliver was characteristically concerned with establishing the situation and the basic facts about the main characters before plunging into the problem or the conflict. The background and aspects of how the characters will act are often as important as the central problem in these stories. Thus, the first section of "Rite of Passage" concentrates on establishing the characters and the general situation; the second section establishes the specific details of the situation, some preliminary information about it, and some of the procedures involved in the solution. These two sections are quite conventional, drawing on other science fiction to present the situation in which the characters find themselves, although they are also infused with the kind of specific and familiar details that are characteristic of Oliver's fiction.

The anthropological examination of an alien (extraterrestrial) culture, which is the real heart of this story, begins in the third section. First contact with the aliens, initial observations, the development of a hypothesis, and initial confirmation of the hypothesis—all showing the attitude and the approach taken by the anthropologist—are developed in the third section and in the following one. About ten weeks elapse between the third and fourth sections. Further, more detailed confirmation of the anthropologist's hypothesis is presented in the fifth section and in part of the sixth; the remainder of the sixth section is devoted to the resolution of the story.

Also characteristic of Oliver's fiction is the fact that many of his stories are told directly from the viewpoint of an anthropologist. This is especially significant in "Rite of Passage," for it allowed Oliver to present more clearly and directly the anthropologist's work and the ways in which he arrives at conclusions. It also allowed Oliver the opportunity to characterize the anthropologist-protagonist through his approach to the problem presented. In this story the anthropologist, Martin Ashley, is perhaps a close approximation of the ideal anthropologist—that is, he is caring, observant, cautious, calm, open-minded, empathetic, willing to admit errors or a lack

of knowledge; in addition, he is patient, but willing and able to act when necessary.

Of course, not all of Oliver's stories are told from the viewpoint of an anthropologist, and not all of his anthropologists are characterized as favorably as Martin Ashley is, although nearly all have at least several of Ashley's characteristics. Furthermore, not all of Oliver's stories have the same proportions of the story devoted to each of the aspects noted above, but most of them share the same concerns for setting the background, for establishing the hypotheses, and for showing the consequences of the action that has taken place.

For convenience, Oliver's stories can be arranged into three main categories based on their general subject matter: stories concerned with cultural manipulation, stories concerned with aliens visiting Earth, and stories concerned with nostalgia for lost cultural patterns. Of course, grouping stories in this way does no justice to the diversity of the stories within each group; indeed, Oliver covered each of these major themes from various viewpoints and in a number of ways. This grouping also does scant justice to the thematic richness in Oliver's works, particularly in his longer short stories. Nevertheless, Oliver did tend to be concerned primarily with certain basic themes, which these categories suggest.

The greatest number of Oliver's stories explore the techniques, ethics, and ramifications of manipulating cultures under various circumstances. "Between the Thunder and the Sun" (1957), for example, one of his best short stories, explores the conflict between the directive to leave developing cultures strictly alone and the humane urge to keep an entire race alive; Earthmen do help the alien culture to change and survive, but in a way that ensures that the noninterference directive will not be broken again. The stories "The Ant and the Eye" (1953), "Field Expedient" (1955), "Transfusion" (1959), "End of the Line" (1965), and "King of the Hill" (1972) all deal with beginning a new culture because the original culture has lost its viability. In

"End of the Line" mankind, which had retreated underground during a great war, has lost its ability to reproduce; the new culture, planted outside the caves, is primitive but thriving.

In contrast, in "Field Expedient" human culture on Earth has become stagnant after worldwide unification has occurred. A lonely billionaire and a dissatisfied socioculturist deliberately engineer diversified cultures on Venus that nevertheless retain a sense of the unity of the human spirit; as a result, these cultures are allowed to retain their diversity and will, in about a century, be able to journey to Earth and revitalize the stagnant culture there. In "Transfusion," another of Oliver's best short stories, mankind itself is seen as the product of a planting experiment undertaken because the parent culture had become too locked into cultural patterns to be able to deal effectively with an alien menace. "Transfusion" is told as something of a detective story, for humanity must prove its ability to decipher what has happened before the last remaining representatives of the parent culture can reveal mankind's true background.

In an unusual way, "King of the Hill" is also about beginning a new culture: the protagonist Sam Gregg seeds Titan, Saturn's largest moon, with animals modified to survive there, because they are being destroyed on Earth. Told in a breezy, rather disjointed narrative voice that succeeds, "King of the Hill" is interesting reading. "The Ant and the Eye," also a very effective story, explores the question of what might be done if a group of people dedicated to preserving freedom of choice for mankind discovered that a potential dictator exists and threatens that freedom of choice.

Other Oliver stories that fit into this first group include the loosely related series "Shaka!" (1974), "Caravans Unlimited: Stability" (1974), "The Middle Man" (1974), and "Caravans Unlimited: Monitor" (1975). This category also includes "Blood's a Rover" (1952), "First to the Stars" (1952, as "Stardust"), "Final Exam" (1952), "The Life Game" (1953), "North Wind" (1956), "The Wind Blows Free" (1957), and "The Marginal Man"

(1958, as "Guardian Spirit"). Each of the stories in this group deals with a different culture, a different aspect of the problem of cultural manipulation, and a different solution to the problem.

Oliver's stories about aliens visiting Earth tend to be both shorter and lighter than the stories that explore the ramifications of cultural manipulation. For example, "The One That Got Away" (1959) is a pure "fish story"—that is, the visiting aliens are "fishermen" who cause strange happenings to keep others away from their "fishing grounds" (Earth); they are persuaded to move to another spot by the exaggerated pictures and claims from another resort area. "Pilgrimage" (1958) involves an alien anthropological expedition that gives a local (human) collaborator a temporal-displacement (time) machine, which he uses to replace local figures in a historical pageant with real people from the past. An alien student of linguistics is discovered and forced to "act" just as people expect a visiting alien to act in "Any More at Home Like You?" (1955). "The Last Word" (1955), written with Charles Beaumont, is a fast-paced spoof on many of the conventions of science fiction that includes two sets of visiting aliens. Such stories as "A Friend to Man" (1954, as "Let Me Live in a House") and "Rewrite Man" (1957) also belong in this category. In contrast, "Meanwhile, Back on the Reservation" (1981) is a much more serious exploration of the issue of alien visitors. Greer Holbrook, a native of Earth, has difficulty communicating his love for his planet and the reasons for his actions to Ellyn, a representative of the Colonies. Ellyn has always lived away from Earth, and although her roots extend back to this planet, her thought pattern and experience are as different as any of Oliver's other aliens.

In the third group of Oliver's short fiction are such stories as "Didn't He Ramble" (1957), "A Stick for Harry Eddington" (1965), and "Far from This Earth" (1970), works that focus on nostalgia for lost cultural patterns. "Far from This Earth" is the finest of the works in this group and belongs among the best of Oliver's stories; it shows a different facet of his talent, since it focuses almost completely on the thoughts and feelings of the main character. The story explores the sense of displacement and loss that Stephen Nzau wa Kioko feels as a result of the changes that have occurred in Africa since his birth in 1945, but it also shows his memories of the eagerness with which he worked to make those changes occur.

Just as "Far from This Earth" draws on Oliver's experiences in Kenya, "Didn't He Ramble" draws on his dedication to authentic jazz. In this story a great deal of money and a company specializing in preparing asteroids to fulfill people's fantasies combine vividly to create an asteroid replica of the Storyville section of New Orleans for Theodore Pearsall's last few months of life.

Three of Oliver's novels are also concerned with alien visitations: *Shadows in the Sun*, *The Winds of Time*, and *The Shores of Another Sea*. The reasons the aliens visit Earth are different in each case, and the actions of each group of aliens are also different. In addition, there is almost no overlap between these novels and the short stories dealing with the same general subject matter; the novels are more serious and more complete explorations of the idea than are the short stories.

In *Shadows in the Sun* the aliens try to hide themselves by adopting all the standard habits and patterns of human beings; this camouflages them from casual observers but leads to their discovery by the anthropologist who has randomly selected their town, Jefferson City, Texas, for study. They are from a galactic culture that is troubled by population pressures; settling small groups on less densely populated planets is one of the means they use to cope with this pressure.

The aliens in *The Winds of Time* are the stranded survivors of a wrecked spaceship who have been searching for humanoid races that, like themselves, have somehow managed to survive after developing a high-technology culture; they have found many other humanoid cultures, but none that had not de-

stroyed themselves when they reached a particular level of technology. They awaken from their fifteen-century drug-induced hibernation about two hundred years too early to find help; but with the aid of a human doctor who joins them, they synthesize the hibernation drug and resume their sleep. The second time they awaken, they find that Earth has survived and has developed space travel.

The third novel involving visiting aliens, *The Shores of Another Sea*, is one of Oliver's two best novels. Set in Africa, it follows Royce Crawford, an American in charge of a baboonery, as he tries to determine what is causing the strange events that have been happening in the area. He discovers that aliens are trying to find out about Earth, and that they somehow have transferred themselves into the bodies of living beings—primarily into baboons, although they also try to take over the bodies of human beings as well—in order to achieve their goals. They are unsuccessful, largely because their hosts quickly sicken and die. No real contact is made between the humans and the aliens, and the aliens leave as abruptly as they arrived. The sense of utter strangeness and the feelings of fear and frustration on the part of the characters are particularly well evoked in this novel.

Oliver's two other science fiction novels, *Unearthly Neighbors* and *Giants in the Dust* (1976), seem to have more in common with his short stories than his other three novels do. For example, *Unearthly Neighbors*, Oliver's other really first-rate science fiction novel, is a more detailed and realistically drawn exploration of humanity's first contact with an alien race on their own home planet; this kind of contact lies in the background of many of Oliver's short stories and is explored more directly in such stories as "Rite of Passage" and "Between the Thunder and the Sun." Indeed, the central characteristic that makes *Unearthly Neighbors* such a fine novel is the way it reveals the details, the frustrations, and the successes involved in developing true contact and understanding between two species with different abilities and widely different world views.

Giants in the Dust, Oliver's last science fiction novel, seems to have had its genesis in an idea suggested in the short story "Transfusion"; it explores the lives of colonists on a new world whose minds have been emptied so that they can undertake fresh beginnings. Because the mind-erasing process is only temporarily successful on the leader of the group, he is able to try consciously to lead the colonists along a path different from that taken on Earth.

III

Finally, after this brief survey and analysis of Oliver's work, one must deal with the question of where Oliver stands, ultimately, among the writers of science fiction. He is certainly among those who have produced stories that Frederik Pohl would consider truly worthwhile—that is, stories that are among the top 10 percent of science fiction. Oliver was once hailed as one of the successors to the generation that produced Isaac Asimov, Robert Heinlein, and their fellow writers of "hard" science fiction—despite the fact that he represents a shift away from technological extrapolation toward a careful anthropological and sociological extrapolation, a shift from "hard" to "soft" science. But Oliver never fully realized the potential that led some in the field to predict this status. To a large extent, this was the result of Oliver's dedication to anthropology and to teaching, which meant that the time and the attention he could give to creative writing were limited.

After an eight-year bout with cancer, Chad Oliver died on 9 August 1993; he was 65.

Oliver published no new science fiction after *Giants in the Dust*, but in his final years he produced two historical westerns, *Broken Eagle* (1989) and the posthumous *The Cannibal Owl* (1994); the former won the Western Heritage Society Award for best novel.

Although Oliver was inactive as a writer of science fiction, he never entirely forsook the field. Before his sickness incapacitated him, he was a familiar feature at Austin science fiction conventions, cheerully talking with and signing autographs for those fans who recognized his name. He was amused that the cover and title page of the 1984 edition of *The Shores of Another Sea* described it as a classic of modern science fiction.

Though it is most unlikely that Oliver will ever receive academic attention and be studied in the way that his contemporary Philip K. Dick has been, Oliver remains important as one of the first people to introduce the social sciences into science fiction, and perhaps the first to do so successfully. His best fiction is understated, graceful, and occasionally surprisingly lyrical and poignant in its evocation of peoples and regions:

> The African bush was all around them, dry as tinder, flaked with red dust, enfolding its secrets under the vast afternoon sky. The world here had been old when man was young, and the animals that prowled through the dead grasses and the sleeping river valleys were very like the ones that men had known thousands of years ago. They were surrounded by miracles of life—the elephant, the lion, the rhino—that were making their last stand against the swelling growth of civilization. (*The Shores of Another Sea*, page 53)

Oliver can be read and reread with pleasure. One cannot ask for more from a writer.

—RICHARD BLEILER

Selected Bibliography

WORKS OF CHAD OLIVER

Mists of Dawn. Philadelphia: John C. Winston, 1952. (A juvenile novel.)
Shadows in the Sun. New York: Ballantine Books, 1954.
Another Kind. New York: Ballantine Books, 1955. (Story collection.)
The Winds of Time. Garden City, N.Y.: Doubleday, 1957.
Unearthly Neighbors. New York: Ballantine Books, 1960.
The Edge of Forever. Los Angeles: Sherbourne Press, 1971. (Story collection including a biographical intro-

duction, a bibliography by William F. Nolan, and "Afterthoughts" by Oliver.)

The Shores of Another Sea. New York: New American Library, 1971.

Giants in the Dust. New York: Pyramid Books, 1976.

Broken Eagle. New York: Bantam Books, 1989.

The Cannibal Owl. New York: Bantam Books, 1994.

SELECTED ANTHOLOGIES CONTAINING OLIVER STORIES

Boucher, Anthony, ed. *The Best from Fantasy and Science Fiction, Fifth Series*. Garden City, N.Y.: Doubleday, 1956. ("The Last Word")

———. *The Best from Fantasy and Science Fiction, Seventh Series*. Garden City, N.Y.: Doubleday, 1958. ("Between the Thunder and the Sun")

Ellison, Harlan, ed. *Again Dangerous Visions*. Garden City, N.Y.: Doubleday, 1972. ("King of the Hill")

Elwood, Roger, ed. *Continuum 1*. New York: G. P. Putnam's Sons, 1974. ("Shaka!")

———. *Continuum 2*. New York: G. P. Putnam's Sons, 1974. ("Caravans Unlimited: Stability")

———. *Continuum 3*. New York: G. P. Putnam's Sons, 1974. ("The Middle Man")

———. *Continuum 4*. New York: G. P. Putnam's Sons, 1975. ("Caravans Unlimited: Monitor")

Harrison, Harry, ed. *The Year 2000*. Garden City, N.Y.: Doubleday, 1970. ("Far from This Earth")

Nolan, William F., ed. *A Wilderness of Stars*. Los Angeles: Sherbourne Press, 1969. ("North Wind")

CRITICAL AND BIOGRAPHICAL STUDIES

Very little has been written about Oliver or his fiction; the following works either provide some biographical information or some critical assessment and discussion.

Amis, Kingsley. *New Maps of Hell: A Survey of Science Fiction*. New York: Harcourt, Brace and World, 1960.

Barron, Neil S. *Anatomy of Wonder: Science Fiction*. New York: R. R. Bowker, 1976.

Clute, John. "Chad Oliver, An Appreciation." *Locus* (September 1993): 81.

Hogan, Patrick G. "The Philosophical Limitations of Science Fiction." In *Many Futures, Many Worlds: Theme and Form in Science Fiction*. Edited by Thomas D. Clareson. Kent, Ohio: Kent State University Press, 1977.

Nicholls, Peter, ed. *The Science Fiction Encyclopedia*. Garden City, N.Y.: Doubleday, 1979.

Nolan, William F. "Big Chad: An Appreciation." *Locus* (September 1993): 81.

Waldrop, Howard. "Chad Oliver (1928–1993)." *Locus* (September 1993): 80–81.

———. "Introduction." In his *Going Home Again*. North Perth, Australia: Eidolon Publications, 1997; New York: St. Martin's, 1998.

GEORGE ORWELL

(1903–1950)

IT IS ON the basis of one exceptional novel, *1984* (1949), that George Orwell is considered a science fiction author at all. But if one takes Darko Suvin's definition (1979) of utopia as "the sociopolitical subgenre of science fiction," then clearly Orwell is one of the most important science fiction writers of our time. Such statements as "Big Brother is watching you," and words or phrases as "Newspeak," "doublethink," "thoughtcrime," and "Room 101," have seared our political consciousness and become a part of political discourse and reality.

Beginning with his authentic description of poverty and misery among the dregs of society in *Down and Out in Paris and London* (1933), through his last novel, *1984*, and the posthumous *Collected Essays, Journalism and Letters* (1968), Orwell continues to excite a wide audience. The novel *1984* perhaps has aroused the greatest interest. In 1973 Professor Walker Gibson, former president of the National Council of Teachers of English, formed the Committee on Public Doublespeak to expose the dishonest and inhumane manipulation of language and literature by advertisers, public officials, and those in the mass media. In 1978 the British novelist Anthony Burgess published *1985*, a mixture of fiction and nonfiction that is a reflection on and a critique of Orwell's dystopian nightmare. Speakers on the lecture circuit warn just how far along the road we are to fulfilling Orwell's terrifying vision. A resurgence of interest by scholars, critics, and intellectuals from a variety of disciplines and positions within the political

spectrum has contributed to an explosion of writing on Orwell, and on *1984* in particular. In writing a novel an author draws on three main sources: other literature; his or her own experience; and his or her society's specific historical situation, to which individual experience is intimately related. Each of these elements contributes to the stylistic and thematic characteristics of *1984*.

The primary literary antecedents of *1984* can be divided into two major categories: the fictional utopian and dystopian works of such predecessors as H. G. Wells, Jack London, Aldous Huxley, and Yevgeny Zamyatin, and the fictional and nonfictional political writings of Orwell's contemporaries, especially the works of Hilaire Belloc, Arthur Koestler, and James Burnham.

It is difficult to overestimate the influence of Wells on Orwell. In her reminiscences of growing up with Eric Blair, the boy who later adopted the pen name George Orwell, Jacintha Buddicom (in Gross, 1971) remembers that he was so interested in her family's copy of Wells's *Modern Utopia* (1905) that they finally gave it to him. Young Eric said that it was the kind of book he might write. Clearly Wells's vision of a world state ruled by an elite—the Samurai—and his prediction of the state's role in social engineering have their echoes in *1984*. The interference of Wells's Utopian state with relations between men and women by prescribing the conditions for marriage reverberates in *1984* as the Inner Party insinuates itself into the most private relationships and controls the associations within the family. Children spy on their parents and report possible acts of disloyalty, and sexual activity is manipulated for political ends.

Orwell was skeptical of Wells's rather optimistic scenario of society's progress through science and technology. Wells also failed to grasp the irrational, perverse evil of nationalism and imperialism that culminated in the rise of such dictators as Stalin and Hitler. Nevertheless, Orwell read Wells, assimilated many of his ideas, and believed him to be one of the most influential writers of his time (Hillegas, 1967; Steinhoff, 1976).

Orwell was fascinated by the repertoire of methods through which those who rule exercise their power. In a genuine totalitarian society, every method from a bullet in the brain to brainwashing can be used. One of his sources for understanding the political use of brute force was Jack London's *The Iron Heel* (1907), which describes a struggle between socialists and a quasi-fascist oligarchy ruled by trusts. Orwell believed that London had an instinctive grasp of the bestial side of human nature and the artistry to dramatize graphically his understanding. London touched a responsive chord in Orwell, and Orwell feared that London might be more correct than Wells. The socialist dream could easily become one long night of terror. The title of London's dystopian novel suggests O'Brien's prediction to Winston in *1984:* "If you want a picture of the future, imagine a boot stamping on a human face—forever."

But brute force is not the only way to keep subjects under the thumbs of rulers. Power may come from the barrel of a gun, but it is easier if the gun is never needed. Aldous Huxley understood this, and he incorporated into his dystopian novel, *Brave New World* (1932), many of Sigmund Freud's ideas regarding society's need to repress man's instinctive, rebellious nature—not by force but by the internalization of social controls and the mechanism of guilt. While Orwell was unconvinced by Huxley's vision of a rather clean, efficient society guided by a relatively benign dictatorship, he found Huxley's novel very

suggestive. Most interesting to him was Huxley's depiction of the employment of psychological conditioning through sloganeering and advertising to condition the masses and to short-circuit critical thinking. Huxley's College of Emotional Engineering has its counterpart in Orwell's Ministry of Truth. The worshiped leader, Our Ford; the negation of the past through such phrases as "History is bunk"; and the mindless entertainment, such as the "feelies," prefigure the machinations of Orwell's Inner Party. Orwell felt a spiritual kinship with the brilliant satirist who, like London, was extremely skeptical of any overly optimistic view of progress.

Huxley's *Brave New World* and Orwell's *1984* are both indebted to the Russian novelist Yevgeny Zamyatin. Never published in the Soviet Union, Zamyatin's dystopian novel, *We* (English translation, 1924), was a forerunner to *Brave New World* and *1984*. While critics debate the extent of the influence of *We* on Orwell (Deutscher, 1956; Steinhoff, 1976), Orwell definitely read the novel and in his column in the socialist weekly the *Tribune* recommended it to his readers. *We* is a satirical picture of the United States of the twenty-sixth century. Everything from politics to sex is fully regimented with mathematical precision through the application of Taylorite Hours Tables. There is no sense of individuality; people have numbers instead of names. The protagonist, D-503, keeps a diary similar to Winston's, and his overt rebellion is encouraged by O-90, a woman like Julia in *1984*. D-503 and O-90 secretly meet in an ancient house that parallels Winston's and Julia's secret room above the pawnshop. The prototype for Big Brother is the deified Well-Doer, who creates such events as the Day of Unanimity, just as the Inner Party uses Hate Week to ritualize robotlike loyalty. There are other similarities between the two novels, but these are the most obvious.

In addition, there are other suggestive analogies between *1984* and the imaginative fiction of such writers as Jonathan Swift, Cyril Connolly, G. K. Chesterton, Rudyard Kipling, and John Mair, and the nonfiction of such writers as Hilaire Belloc and Boris Souvarine (Steinhoff, 1976). Two other writers—Arthur Koestler and James Burnham—deserve special mention.

Orwell knew Koestler personally. He reviewed *Darkness at Noon* (English translation, 1940) and found that Koestler's imaginative yet authentic depiction of Stalin's purge trials in the 1930's, and of the workings of totalitarianism in general, coincided with his own thoughts on these subjects. As he is interrogated before being put on trial and finally shot, the main character of *Darkness at Noon*, Rubashov, one of the original Bolsheviks, meditates on his past sins and the inevitable excesses of totalitarianism. In both cases political expediency in the service of a rigid revolutionary ideology replaced ethics and common decency. Several themes in *Darkness at Noon* interested Orwell and turn up in *1984*. The most relevant ones are totalitarianism's ability to inculcate some sort of "doublethink," its power to take its ideology to the "end of the line," and its ability to manipulate history for its own ends.

In *Darkness at Noon*, Rubashov abandons "illogical morality" for the cold, inevitable logic of historical determinism; but as he reflects on his life, he is tormented by the thought that "perhaps it was not suitable for man to think every thought to its logical conclusion." Orwell was working with a similar assumption in one of the scenes where O'Brien confronts Winston with the question "Why does the Party seek power?" Winston replies that the party seeks power for the good of the people; for that answer O'Brien increases his torture. The logic is simple: If the aim of politics is to acquire and maintain power, then power should be the sole aim of a political party. Thus O'Brien says, "The Party seeks power entirely for its own sake."

Rubashov recalls, "We admitted no private sphere, not even inside a man's skull." Orwell's Inner Party similarly takes rebellion to its logical conclusion in its punishment of "thoughtcrime." Thoughts and actions are carried to the "end of the line"; Koestler writes that it is "the running-amuck of pure

reason." This cold equation creates a situation in which those loyal to the regime in power are forced into a type of mental gymnastics that Orwell labels "doublethink." In *Darkness at Noon*, Rubashov must explain to incredulous comrades the instant reversal of thinking that comes about as a result of the Hitler-Stalin nonaggression pact. On a more philosophical level he muses that while the party denies the existence of free will, it also demands, upon pain of death, that the individual make the correct choice. Finally, Koestler understood, as did Orwell, that totalitarian regimes can "alter" the past to suit their own ends. In *Darkness at Noon*, pictures are removed, and individuals simply cease to exist. During the purge trials history is rewritten to overcome ludicrous contradictions in testimony. History is what the party wants it to be.

What Koestler describes in *Darkness at Noon* is the failure of Marxist theory in Stalinist practice. A democratic, humanistic socialism is not inevitable. This is also the argument posed by James Burnham, a political philosopher whose nonfiction works—*The Managerial Revolution* (1941), *The Machiavellians* (1943), and *The Struggle for the World* (1947)—Orwell found profoundly suggestive. Orwell wrote several reviews of Burnham's works, and the two men publicly debated within the pages of the *Tribune*. Orwell was engrossed and disturbed by Burnham's prediction that the socialist dream of an egalitarian, democratic society created by a revolution of the masses was just that—a dream. Burnham argued in *The Managerial Revolution* and his later writings that the masses would not seize power. Instead a hierarchic society divided into a few superstates would evolve, ruled by a managerial elite who ruthlessly maintain their power, using bureaucratic institutions to eliminate entrepreneurial capitalists and control the masses. Although the managers would rationalize the governing process and rule "scientifically," they also would perpetuate irrational myths to ensure the obedience of the masses.

Although Orwell criticized Burnham's exaggeration of man's selfishness and, hence, his pessimistic conclusion that political power would ultimately and inevitably rest in the hands of a totalitarian oligarchy, he was intrigued by Burnham's discussion of man's lust for power as it is expressed in imperialism and the growth of monstrous superstates perpetually at war. So pervasive was the influence of Burnham's thought on Orwell that one critic has labeled *1984* "Burnhamite fantasy" (Maddison, 1961).

In addition to these works, which contributed to Orwell's intellectual development and whose themes found their way into *1984*, there are aspects of Orwell's life and relationships between his personal history and the sociopolitical turmoil of the first four decades of the twentieth century that are incorporated into *1984* and are crucial for a full understanding of this novel. In his essay "Why I Write" (1947), Orwell observed:

> In a peaceful age I might have written ornate or merely descriptive books, and might have remained almost unaware of my political loyalties. As it is I have been forced into becoming a sort of pamphleteer. . . . Every line of serious work that I have written since 1936 has been written, directly or indirectly, *against* totalitarianism and *for* democratic socialism, as I understand it. . . . What I have most wanted to do throughout the past ten years is to make political writing into an art. (*Collected Essays*, 1968, volume 1)

Although Orwell stipulated that no biography of him was to be written, his own recollections and those of people close to him are sufficient to indicate some of the more significant experiences that formed the context of *1984*.

Born Eric Arthur Blair on 25 June 1903, at Motihari, Bengal, India, into what he later carefully described as "the lower-upper-middle class"—his father was a member of the Indian civil service—he returned with his parents to England, where his father became secretary of the Golf Club at Harpsden. Eric was enrolled in a preparatory school. In his

George Orwell. COURTESY OF CORBIS-BETTMANN

essay "Such, Such Were the Joys . . ." (1950), Orwell records some of the painful experiences that became significant themes in all his work. He remembers his first real experience with class prejudice, at Crossgates: "I was not on the same footing as most of the other boys." Class distinctions obsessed the children and the school authorities as well and became an excuse for a variety of injustices and daily humiliations. This bred in the young boy a "sense of guilt and inevitable failure." Those at the top of the hierarchy had the power to dominate, to impose their will upon those at the bottom.

A similar situation exists in *1984*, where the rigid hierarchy allows the Inner Party to humiliate and totally tyrannize the members of the Outer Party and the Proles. Life at school for Orwell was "a continuous triumph of the strong over the weak." This too is the world of *1984*. Yet this kind of illegitimate power breeds rebellion; one had to "break the rules, or perish. . . . To survive, or at least to preserve any kind of independence, was essentially criminal, since it meant breaking the rules." Individual rebellion, though, was doomed to failure. This is precisely Winston's situation in *1984*.

Following in his father's footsteps, Orwell left school at nineteen to join the Indian Imperial Police in Burma. He served for five years. In his essays "A Hanging" (1931), "Shooting an Elephant" (written between 1931 and 1936), "Rudyard Kipling" (1942), and his first novel, *Burmese Days* (1934), Orwell registered his disgust with racism and imperialism. He saw behind the rhetoric of the British Empire in its twilight—"empire is primarily a money-making concern"—and exposed its brutality and injustice as it exploited and dehumanized a colonial people. The alienated outsider, the antihero of *Burmese Days*, Flory, is clearly a prototype of Winston Smith.

Sickened by what he saw in Burma, Orwell resigned from the Imperial Police. But, as he later wrote in *The Road to Wigan Pier* (1937), he felt contaminated by his experience; he felt guilty and in need of expiation:

> I was conscious of an immense weight of guilt that I had got to expiate. . . . I felt that I had got to escape not merely from imperialism but from every form of man's domination over man. I wanted to submerge myself, to get right down among the oppressed, to be one of them and on their side against their tyrants. (chapter 9)

Orwell began his self-mortification by going to Paris in 1928 and working as a dishwasher. In *Down and Out in Paris and London*, he relates his firsthand experiences with the lumpen proletariat, and the grinding and degrading poverty as the world entered the Great Depression. The reality of poverty and filth, and the debilitating psychological effects of scarcity, emerge in vivid detail in the imagery of *1984*.

In 1929, Orwell returned to England; and until about 1935 he lived with the poor, tramped over the countryside, picked hops in Kent, and was a bookseller's clerk in London.

He transmuted his experiences into a series of lower-middle-class novels—*A Clergyman's Daughter* (1935), *Keep the Aspidistra Flying* (1936), *Coming up for Air* (1939)—as well as a nonfiction work, *The Road to Wigan Pier*, based on his experiences with the miners in the north. His protagonists (and the real-life coal miners) are crushed by poverty and scarred by class. They are the insulted and the injured, and they are enraged. Gordon Comstock, the main focus of *Keep the Aspidistra Flying*, is living on ". . . two pounds a week. Therefore the hatred of modern life, the desire to see our money-civilization blown to hell by bombs, was a thing he genuinely felt." Poverty and grueling physical labor have reduced miners practically to the level of animals; Orwell describes them as "on all fours, skipping round the pit props almost like dogs." Like the Morlocks of Wells's *Time Machine*, the miners live in a separate universe, light-years removed from Orwell's bourgeois readers. These are the people Winston meets in the pub in *1984*; these are the Proles.

There are hints in these novels, according to Robert Lee (1969), of two other themes that Orwell developed in more depth in *1984*—the corruption of language and the distortion of history. But it took Orwell's experiences in the Spanish Civil War to give a visceral reality to these concerns.

In June 1936, Orwell married Eileen O'Shaughnessy; by December he was on his way to Spain to cover the Civil War as a correspondent. Once there he joined the POUM (Partido Obrero de Unificación Marxista) militia as a common solider. The egalitarianism and the comradeship of the militia appealed to Orwell, and in mid-1937 he wrote to his friend Cyril Connolly: "I have seen wonderful things and at last really believe in Socialism, which I never did before" (Oxley, 1969). But disillusionment came quickly. At the very time when the anarchist-Communist POUM was spilling its blood fighting Franco, it was betrayed and ruthlessly suppressed by the Stalinist faction of the Spanish Communists. Wounded in the throat, Orwell spent his last few weeks in Spain avoiding capture by the

Spanish Communists. In May 1937 he returned to England, his suspicions and mild hostility toward the Communists turned into hatred.

Orwell tried to report what he had seen in Spain, but Kingsley Martin, editor of the *New Statesman*, refused to print his account of the Communist atrocities. The intelligentsia's love affair with the Soviet Union, its willingness to accept Stalinist propaganda, and its enthusiasm for the Popular Front made it susceptible to the most blatant distortions of the historical record. Orwell feared that the truth about the Spanish Civil War would never be known. In 1938, to set the record straight, he published *Homage to Catalonia*, a work that Lionel Trilling (1952) has described as "one of the most important documents of our time." Later, in a letter to Frank Barber (15 December 1944), Orwell wrote: "In my small way I have been fighting for years against the systematic falsification of history which now goes on. . . . My attention was first drawn to this deliberate falsification of history by my experience in the Spanish Civil War." Orwell recalled that in a conversation with Arthur Koestler he observed that history stopped in 1936, and Koestler emphatically agreed. Both of these concerns—the fascination of the intelligentsia and the non-Communist Left with totalitarianism, and the conscious and unconscious distortion of history by ideologues and the media—emerge as major themes in *1984*.

In 1941, Orwell became, ironically, a propagandist for the British Broadcasting Corporation (BBC) as Indian editor for the Eastern Service. In 1943 he left the BBC and began to write *Animal Farm* (1945), his last major imaginative work before *1984*.

Animal Farm is a political allegory, a satire on the Russian Revolution and its monstrous perversion of the vision of democratic socialism. The farm animals, led by the pigs, revolt and expropriate Manor Farm from its incompetent and drunken owner, Mr. Jones. They change its name to Animal Farm and attempt to create a democratic, egalitarian society. Their revolution, which they call "the Rebellion," is betrayed by two young boars, Napoleon and Snowball, who jointly seize control. But Napoleon trains dogs to oust Snowball and to consolidate his power. While most of the animals are forced to live lives no better than those they led before the Rebellion, Napoleon negotiates with the outside world and establishes a personal dictatorship. The principles and hopes of the Rebellion are completely subverted. The last of the Seven Commandments of the Rebellion reads: "All animals are equal." By the end of the story, all Seven Commandments have been reduced to just one: "ALL ANIMALS ARE EQUAL BUT SOME ANIMALS ARE MORE EQUAL THAN OTHERS."

Orwell's work as a propagandist for the BBC and his experiences in Spain convinced him that certain "perversions" of language, the language of "official English, or Stripe-trousers, the language of White Papers, Parliamentary debate . . . BBC news bulletins . . . of the scientists and economists . . ."—could be used to control men's thinking processes and, hence, their ability to resist domination. In his preface to the Ukrainian edition of *Animal Farm* (1947), Orwell recalls how his experiences in Spain "taught me how easily totalitarian propaganda can control the opinion of enlightened people in democratic countries."

After *Animal Farm* appeared, Orwell took a house on Jura in the Hebrides. In 1947 he entered the hospital with tuberculosis. During the next two years, while writing his last novel, *1984*, Orwell suffered a relapse, and entered another sanatorium early in 1949. On 21 January 1950, he died of tuberculosis.

1984 is a culmination of Orwell's intellectual and artistic development. This dystopian vision fuses all of the themes derived from his reading, his personal history, and his involvement with some of the more significant sociopolitical issues of his time.

By 1984 the world is divided among and ruled by three superstates: Oceania, Eurasia, and Eastasia. London is the center of Airstrip One (Britain), located in Oceania. The totalitarian state is ruled by Big Brother, head of the Inner Party, represented by O'Brien. Next in the rigid hierarchy is the Outer Party, to which Winston Smith and Julia belong. At the bottom of the pyramid, constituting 85 percent of the population, are the masses, the "proles." Everyone is watched; individual freedom has been eliminated. The official language, Newspeak, is designed to narrow language and thought so as to make dissent impossible. Oceania is administered by four behemoth ministries: the Ministry of Peace (which promotes and controls perpetual war), the Ministry of Love (which directs the police state and torture), the Ministry of Plenty (which organizes the planned scarcity), and the Ministry of Truth (which creates propaganda and directs the rewriting of history)

The thoroughly alienated protagonist of the novel, Winston Smith, works for the Ministry of Truth, rewriting history to keep it in line with current policy. Attempting to overcome his alienation and to preserve his sanity, he commits "thoughtcrime"—that is, he rebels. His covert rebellion becomes overt when he responds to a coworker, Julia, and they attempt not only to establish a love relationship but also (with the assistance of another, supposed conspirator, O'Brien) try to join a secret resistance organization. They are caught and tortured. In the Ministry of Love, Winston discovers that O'Brien has been his enemy from the beginning. As his torturer and teacher, O'Brien explains to Winston the goal of the party—to seek and maintain power— and the need for the party not only to silence opposition but also to capture and reshape the mind and soul of the rebel. Marked for "ultimate execution," Winston is released from the Ministry of Truth a completely broken man. The brainwashing has been successful. The novel ends with the sentence "He loved Big Brother."

In reading *1984* one is moved not merely by Orwell's ideas but also by the force of their dramatization, by the sheer pressure of the concrete evocation of tension and terror. The interpenetration of language and experience, which constitutes one of the major themes of the novel, has interested thinkers from Aristotle to Karl Marx; the specific relationships between language and political power had

been discussed (even before World War II) by such writers as Thurman Arnold, Stuart Chase, Harold Lasswell, Charles Merriam, and Bertrand Russell. But after the death camps, born of the masterful, evil rhetoric of Hitler, Orwell's brilliant dramatization of these themes takes on additional significance and power.

Orwell's fear that a totalitarian state could legitimize its power by "altering" the past, present, and future, that it could control its subjects' perception of reality by consciously manipulating language, is most fully dramatized in *1984*, where, as Orwell says, many of his ideas were taken to "their logical consequences" (Steinhoff, 1976). *1984* is the vehicle by which Orwell was able to take many of the ideas he had presented in logical, propositional form as essays and develop them to the "end of the line," putting them into a dramatic, presentational form that functions to sharpen the issues.

Despite the arguments from such historians as Benedetto Croce and R. G. Collingwood, who insist that all history is "present" history and that it is impossible to create an objective historical narrative, Orwell's position is clear: he stands unequivocally opposed to historical relativism. From the time he returned from Spain, he believed that "history was not something to be created but rather discovered" (Kubal, 1972), and that freedom— intellectual freedom—lay in being able to report this history. If people cannot know and cannot be certain about events, then they fall victims to the most irresponsible propaganda. In the Ministry of Truth, history is rewritten to conform to present party objectives, and records are manipulated to erase all references to thought criminals. These people simply cease to exist for the present and the future. O'Brien tells Winston:

You must stop imagining that posterity will vindicate you. . . . You will be lifted clean out of the stream of history. . . . Nothing will remain of you: not a name in a register, not a memory in a living brain. You will be annihilated in the past as well as in the future. You will never have existed. (chapter 3)

Ultimately, Winston is disabused even of the evidence of logic and his own senses. Two plus two does not equal four if the party says so. Winston "learns" actually to see five fingers when O'Brien holds up four. Winston abandons the evidence of his own senses. But what is the "evidence of one's senses"? This is a question that Orwell never really tackled. He failed to make the distinction among empirical observations, the formulation of these observations into statements of fact, and the meaning of these facts. That Napoleon existed is not an issue, but his meaning for the French, the Russian, the English, and the American peoples is still hotly debated. Events and people are erased from the historical record in *1984*, but is this necessary? In his *Politics as Symbolic Action* (1971), the political scientist Murray Edelman has written that political beliefs and perceptions are, by and large, not based on empirical observations or information, but on nonempirical cognitions of meaning, which are "basically different from information and incompatible with it."

What must be understood is that "reality" and "meaning" are not identical with "fact." Meaning arises in social relationships that exist in and through the communication of significant symbols, most notably in language. What can be communicated is determined by the symbols available, the expressive forms, and how those forms are structured into larger and larger units of meaning. This is why Newspeak is so important. In *1984* the Inner Party controls the production, distribution, and consumption not only of information but also of language. Orwell has taken the issues raised by Marx and Engels in their *German Ideology* (written 1845–1846) to their logical conclusions. Marx and Engels wrote:

The ideas of the ruling class are in every epoch the ruling ideas: i.e., the class, which is the ruling material force of society, is at the same time its ruling intellectual force. The class which has the means of material production at its disposal, has control at the same time over the means of mental production, so that thereby, generally speaking, the ideas of those who lack the means of mental production are subject to it. (Part I: "Feuerbach")

In his depiction of the sloganeering—such as "War is peace," "Freedom is slavery," "Ignorance is strength"—and the emotional catharsis involved in the Two Minutes Hate, Orwell seemed to have an almost intuitive grasp of the fact that truth (or its antithesis) has little to do with political power. Hitler's appeal to the irrational, like the Inner Party's appeal, was spectacularly successful because he understood that symbols, the forms in which we express ourselves, are stimulants to action, not simply referents to some truth or reality beyond symbols. The Inner Party, like the Nazis, uses symbols in such a way that people not only think about hate, they express hate. Hitler did not use language to teach the German people to think; he provided them with the forms through which they could act. Whatever Winston thinks about Goldstein, the mythical traitor and scapegoat for all of Oceania's evil, is irrelevant; the Inner Party has given Winston the forms by which he can express his hate. In the Two Minutes Hate, Winston "found that he was shouting with the others and kicking his heel violently against the rung of his chair. The horrible thing about the Two Minutes Hate was not that one was obliged to act a part, but that it was impossible to avoid joining in." It matters not a whit what is being hated—it could be anything—the fact is that the Inner Party controls the social expression of all emotion and, hence, its meaning.

1984 has been faulted for its talkiness, for its weak characterization, for its failure to supply a clear motive for Winston's rebellion, for the Inner Party's improbable decision to ignore the masses and its naked lust for power for its own sake, for the novel's sensationalism and its near hysterical tone. Some of these criticisms are just, but they cannot negate the power the novel has over its readers. *1984*, like a good proverb, is a warning, not a prophecy. It was Orwell's strategy for coming to terms with many of the modern political anxieties. He has given us more than simply a metaphor for considering a possible future. He has given us a terrifying vision, a reality that structures and gives form to our political nightmares. In doing so, he has created attitudes that will lead his readers, one hopes, to ensure that *1984* never becomes a waking reality.

Selected Bibliography

No standard edition of Orwell's works has been published. The Orwell Archive at University College, London, contains his letters, manuscripts, and other unpublished material as well as the most complete collection of his publications and of writings on his work.

WORKS OF GEORGE ORWELL

Down and Out in Paris and London. London: Victor Gollancz, 1933; Harmondsworth and New York: Penguin Books, 1940; New York: Harcourt, Brace, 1950.

Burmese Days. New York: Harper, 1934; London: Victor Gollancz, 1935.

A Clergyman's Daughter. London: Victor Gollancz, 1935; New York: Harper, 1936.

Keep the Aspidistra Flying. London: Victor Gollancz, 1936; New York: Harcourt, Brace, 1956.

The Road to Wigan Pier. London: Victor Gollancz, 1937.

Homage to Catalonia. London: Secker and Warburg, 1938; New York: Harcourt, Brace, 1952.

Coming up for Air. London: Victor Gollancz, 1939; New York: Harcourt, Brace, 1950.

Inside the Whale and Other Essays. London: Victor Gollancz, 1940.

Animal Farm. London: Secker and Warburg, 1945; New York: Harcourt, Brace, 1946.

Nineteen Eighty-Four. London: Secker and Warburg, 1949; New York: Harcourt, Brace, 1949.

The Collected Essays, Journalism and Letters of George Orwell. Edited by Sonia Orwell and Ian Angus. 4 vols. London: Secker and Warburg, 1968; New York: Harcourt, Brace, 1968.

Orwell: The Lost Writings. Edited by W. J. West. New York: Arbor House, 1985.

CRITICAL AND BIOGRAPHICAL STUDIES

The best guide to Orwell scholarship and biography is Jeffrey and Valerie Meyers, *George Orwell: An Annotated Bibliography of Criticism*. New York and London: Garland, 1977.

Aldiss, Brian W. "The Downward Journey: Orwell's *1984*." *Extrapolation*, 25, no. 1 (1984): 5–11.

Asimov, Isaac. "1984." In his *Asimov on Science Fiction*. Garden City, N.Y.: Doubleday, 1981.

Atkins, John. *George Orwell: A Literary Study*. London: Calder, 1954.

Bal, Sant Singh. *George Orwell: The Ethical Imagination*. Atlantic Highlands, N.J.: Humanities Press, 1981.

Boos, Florence S., and William Davis. "Orwell's Morris and 'Old Major's' Dream." *English Studies*, 71 (1990): 361–371.

Buitenhuis, Peter, and Ira B. Nadel. *George Orwell: A Reassessment*. New York: St. Martin's, 1988.

Calder, Jenni. *Chronicles of Conscience: A Study of George Orwell and Arthur Koestler*. London: Secker and Warburg, 1968.

Caldwell, Larry W. "Wells, Orwell, and Atwood: (EPI) Logic and Eu/Utopia." *Extrapolation*, 33, no. 4 (1992): 333–345.

Carter, Michael. *George Orwell and the Problem of Authentic Existence*. Totowa, N.J.: Barnes and Noble Books, 1985.

Chilton, Paul, and Crispin Aubrey, eds. *Nineteen Eighty-Four in 1984: Autonomy, Control, and Communication*. London: Comedia, 1983.

Connelly, Mark. *The Diminished Self: Orwell and the Loss of Freedom*. Pittsburgh, Pa.: Duquesne University Press, 1987.

Connors, James. "Zamyatin's *We* and the Genesis of *1984*." *Modern Fiction Studies*, 21 (1975): 107–124.

Coppard, Audrey, and Bernard Crick. *Orwell Remembered*. London: Ariel Books, 1984.

Crick, Bernard. *George Orwell: A Life*. Boston: Little, Brown, 1981.

Davison, Peter. *George Orwell: A Literary Life*. London: Macmillan, 1996; New York: St. Martin's, 1996.

Deutscher, Isaac. "1984—The Mysticism of Cruelty." In *Heretics and Renegades*. London: Hamish Hamilton, 1956.

Elsbree, Longdon. "The Structured Nightmare of *1984*." *Twentieth-Century Literature*, 5 (1959): 135–141.

Ferrell, Keith. *George Orwell: The Political Pen*. New York: Evans, 1985.

Filmer, Kath. "That Hideous 1984: The Influence of C. S. Lewis's *That Hideous Strength* on Orwell's *Nineteen Eighty-Four*." *Extrapolation*, 26, no. 2 (1985): 160–169.

Fowler, Roger. *The Language of George Orwell*. London: Macmillan, 1995.

Freedman, Carl. *George Orwell: A Study in Ideology and Literary Form.* New York: Garland, 1988.

Fyvel, T. R. *George Orwell: A Personal Memoir.* New York: Macmillan, 1982.

Gardner, Averil. *George Orwell.* Boston: Twayne, 1987.

George Orwell and Nineteen Eighty-Four: The Man and His Books. Washington, D.C.: Library of Congress, 1985.

Gross, Miriam, ed. *The World of George Orwell.* New York: Simon and Schuster, 1971.

Hillegas, Mark. *The Future as Nightmare: H. G. Wells and the Anti-Utopians.* New York: Oxford University Press, 1967.

Hoggart, Richard. "George Orwell and *The Road to Wigan Pier.*" *Critical Quarterly,* 7 (1965): 72–85.

Hollis, Christopher. *A Study of George Orwell.* London: Hollis and Carter, 1956.

Howe, Irving. "Orwell: History as Nightmare." In *Politics and the Novel.* New York: Fawcett, 1967.

———, ed. 1984 *Revisited: Totalitarianism in Our Century.* New York: Harper and Row, 1983.

Hunter, Lynette. *George Orwell: The Search for a Voice.* Milton Keynes, England: Open University Press, 1984.

Hynes, Samuel, ed. *Twentieth Century Interpretations of "1984."* Englewood Cliffs, N.J.: Prentice-Hall, 1971.

Ingle, Stephen. *George Orwell: A Political Life.* Manchester, England: Manchester University Press, 1993.

Jensen, Ejner J., ed. *The Future of* Nineteen Eighty-Four. Ann Arbor: University of Michigan Press, 1984.

Katab, George. "The Road to *1984.*" *Political Science Quarterly,* 81 (1966): 564–580.

Khouri, Nadia. "Reaction and Nihilism: The Political Genealogy of Orwell's *1984.*" *Science-Fiction Studies,* 12, part 2 (1985): 136–147.

Kubal, David. *Outside the Whale: George Orwell's Art and Politics.* South Bend, Ind.: University of Notre Dame Press, 1972.

Lee, Robert A. *Orwell's Fiction.* South Bend, Ind.: University of Notre Dame Press, 1969.

Letemendia, V. C. "Revolution on Animal Farm: Orwell's Neglected Commentary." *Journal of Modern Literature,* 18 (1992): 127–137.

Lewis, Peter. *George Orwell: The Road to 1984.* New York: Harcourt Brace Jovanovich, 1981.

Maddison, Michael. "*1984:* A Burnhamite Fantasy?" *Political Quarterly,* 32 (1961): 71–79.

McKay, George. "Metapropaganda: Self-Reading Dystopian Fiction: Burdekin's *Swastika Night* and Orwell's *Nineteen Eighty-Four.*" *Science-Fiction Studies,* 21, part 3 (1994): 302–314.

Meyers, Jeffrey. *George Orwell: The Critical Heritage.* London and Boston: Routledge and Kegan Paul, 1975.

———. *A Reader's Guide to George Orwell.* London: Thames and Hudson, 1975.

Meyers, Valerie. *George Orwell.* London: Macmillan, 1991.

Modern Fiction Studies 21 (1975). (The entire issue is devoted to Orwell.)

Mulvihill, Robert, ed. *Reflections on America, 1984: An Orwell Symposium.* Athens: University of Georgia Press, 1986.

Newsinger, John. "*Nineteen Eighty-Four* Since the Collapse of Communism." *Foundation* (Autumn 1992): 75–84.

Norris, Christopher, ed. *Inside the Myth: Orwell: Views from the Left.* London: Lawrence and Wishart, 1984.

Oldsey, Bernard, and Joseph Browne. *Critical Essays on George Orwell.* Boston: G. K. Hall, 1986.

Oxley, B. T. *George Orwell.* London: Evans Brothers, 1969.

Patai, Daphne. "Gamesmanship and Androcentrism in Orwell's *1984.*" *PMLA,* 97 (1982): 856–870.

———. *The Orwell Mystique: A Study in Male Ideology.* Amherst: University of Massachusetts Press, 1984.

Philmus, Robert. "The Language of Utopia." *Studies in the Literary Imagination,* 6 (1973): 61–78.

Plank, Robert. *George Orwell's Guide Through Hell.* San Bernardino, Calif.: Borgo, 1995.

Podhoretz, Norman. "If Orwell Were Alive Today." *Harpers* (January 1983).

Rahv, Philip. "The Unfuture of Utopia." *Partisan Review,* 16 (1949): 743–749.

Rai, Alok. *Orwell and the Politics of Despair: A Critical Study of the Writings of George Orwell.* Cambridge, England: Cambridge University Press, 1988.

Rees, Richard. *George Orwell: Fugitive from the Camp of Victory.* Carbondale: Southern Illinois University Press, 1961.

Reilly, Patrick. *George Orwell: The Age's Adversary.* London: Macmillan, 1986.

Rodden, John. *The Politics of Literary Reputation: The Making and Claiming of 'St. George' Orwell.* New York: Oxford University Press, 1989.

Rose, Jonathan, ed. *The Revised Orwell.* East Lansing: Michigan State University Press, 1992.

Savage, Robert L.; James Combs; and Dan Nimmo, eds. *The Orwellian Moment: Hindsight and Foresight in the Post–1984 World.* Fayetteville: University of Arkansas Press, 1989.

Shelden, Michael. *Orwell: The Authorized Biography.* New York: HarperCollins, 1991.

Shoham, Shlomo Giora, and Francis Rosenstiel, eds. *And He Loved Big Brother: Man, State, and Society in Question.* London: Macmillan, 1985. (Contributions to the George Orwell colloquy, *1984: Myths and Realities,* organized by the Council of Europe in collaboration with the European Foundation for Sciences, Arts and Culture, Strasbourg, France, 1984.)

Slater, Ian. *Orwell: The Road to Airstrip One.* New York: Norton, 1985.

Slusser, George E.; Colin Greenland; and Eric S. Rabkin, eds. *Storm Warnings: Science Fiction Confronts the Future*. Carbondale: Southern Illinois University Press, 1987.

Smyer, Richard I. *Animal Farm: Pastoralism and Politics*. Boston: Twayne, 1988.

Stansky, Peter, ed. *On Nineteen Eighty-Four*. New York: W. H. Freeman, 1983.

———, and William Abrahams. *The Unknown Orwell*. New York: Alfred Knopf, 1972.

Steinhoff, William. *George Orwell and the Origins of 1984*. Ann Arbor: University of Michigan Press, 1976.

Suvin, Darko. *Metamorphoses of Science Fiction: On the Poetics and History of a Literary Genre*. New Haven, Conn. and London: Yale University Press, 1979.

Trilling, Lionel. "Orwell on the Future." *New Yorker*, 18 (June 1949): 78, 81 83.

———, "Introduction," In Orwell's *Homage to Catalonia*. Boston: Beacon, 1952.

Voorhees, Richard. *The Paradox of George Orwell*. West Lafayette, Ind.: Purdue University Press, 1961.

Wemyss, Courtney T., and Alexej Ugrinsky. *George Orwell*. Westport, Conn.: Greenwood, 1987.

West, W. J. *The Larger Evils: Nineteen Eighty-Four: The Truth Behind the Satire*. Edinburgh, Scotland: Canongate, 1992.

Williams, Raymond. "George Orwell." In *Culture and Society, 1780–1950*. New York: Harper and Row, 1966.

———. *George Orwell*. New York: Viking Press, 1971.

———, ed. *George Orwell: A Collection of Critical Essays*. Englewood Cliffs, N.J.: Prentice-Hall, 1974.

Woodcock, George. *The Crystal Spirit: A Study of George Orwell*. Boston: Little, Brown, 1966.

Young, John W. *Orwell's Newspeak and Totalitarian Language: The Nazi and Communist Antecedents*. Charlottesville: University Press of Virginia, 1991.

Zwerdling, Alex. *Orwell and the Left*. New Haven, Conn.: Yale University Press, 1974.

—CHARLES L. ELKINS

EDGAR ALLAN POE

(1809–1849)

THE POSITION OF Edgar Allan Poe in the history of science fiction is a matter of dispute. Some critics and historians have called him at best a marginal figure, while others have rated him high as an innovator and formative influence. His work has appeared in science fiction magazines and anthologies; he has been cited as a founding father when prestige figures have been needed; and articles treating individual stories as science fiction have appeared in the technical journals. Yet it has also been pointed out that his stories have very little in common with what is indisputably accepted as science fiction. This is not just a question of changing tastes or evolution within the genre, it is added, for other stories by Poe are immediately recognizable as ancestral works in other genres. "The Murders in the Rue Morgue" (1841), despite superficial differences, is obviously similar to a modern detective story and is almost universally accepted as the retaining pin for a long chain of historical development. No such case can be made for any of Poe's stories in the history of science fiction.

I

The facts of Poe's life are so familiar and so easily accessible elsewhere that it should not be necessary to give more than a reminder of them. He was born in Boston in 1809, to parents who were actors; was orphaned at about age three; was reared as a foster child by John Allan, a wealthy merchant of Richmond, Virginia, with whom he disagreed during his early youth and quarreled irrevocably upon reaching maturity. Poe attended the University of Virginia at Charlottesville for a year; was withdrawn by Allan because of high gambling debts; left Virginia for Boston, where he arranged for the publication of *Tamerlane and Other Poems* (1827); enlisted in the army, where he spent about two years, rising to the rank of regimental sergeant major; was discharged so that he could attend the U.S. Military Academy; spent less than a year at West Point; rebelled against cadet life and his circumstances, and was court-martialed out of the service. This was in 1831. In 1836, he married his fourteen-year-old first cousin, Virginia Clemm, whose long, lingering illness with tuberculosis rendered a normal marriage impossible. Her death in 1847 was a trauma from which Poe may not have recovered.

From 1831 until his death in 1849, Poe made a scanty living as a journalist. He contributed prolifically to the better periodicals and newspapers, and in his later years was recognized as a major critic, essayist, poet, and writer of fiction. Unfortunately, journalism paid very badly. He was associated editorially with various periodicals and newspapers: the *Southern Literary Messenger*, *Graham's Lady's and Gentleman's Magazine* (the foremost magazine in the United States while Poe was its editor), *Godey's Lady's Book*, the *New York Mirror*, and the *Broadway Journal*. He was a brilliant editor, and his colleagues rated him high in his work. Yet his personal life was a dismal and unhappy failure, and his increasing alcoholism not only forced him out of good jobs but on several occasions drove opportunity away.

Poe died in Baltimore in sordid circumstances. After being missing for several days, he was found semiconscious in a tavern. He died in psychological torment a few days later. Exactly what happened to him is not known, but it is possible that he was captured by political toughs who drugged and liquored him, and dragged him around the polls to vote fraudulently, until he collapsed.

The unifying factor to this pathetic life was bad luck. Fate poured genius into Poe but also doused him with misfortune. He was born into an unstable parental situation and was placed with an uncongenial foster parent, with whom he engaged in a tug-of-war. He was cursed with a bad emotional constitution. He suffered from fits of deep depression, which alcohol relieved; he was hypersensitive, excitable, and subject to extreme responses in situations of stress. In his later years Poe's health was bad. He had a weak heart and probably suffered from degenerative diseases. And, of course, there was alcohol. When he was under the influence of liquor, his sober industry, punctiliousness, charm, and affability disappeared, and he became irresponsible and impossible. As his living circumstances became more desperate, his character degenerated and his actions were not always to his credit.

Yet, despite all this, Poe was a man of remarkable achievement. Although the emotional range of his fiction and poetry was narrow, his intellectual range was very wide. It is true that he was a highly skilled "window dresser," but it would be wrong to conclude from this that he was a faker. Such window dressing was a common feature in the literature of his day. Poe had a working knowledge of French, Latin, Greek, Spanish, and Italian, perhaps somewhat less of German, and some acquaintance with the literature of each of those languages. He also had a wide knowledge of contemporary letters. He enjoyed a background in the major philosophical systems, which he occasionally worked into his stories, and his general fund of knowledge was enormous. A specialist in any field could criticize Poe's attainments, but Poe could reciprocate by criticizing the specialist's attainments in fields other than his or her own.

Running through Poe's life was a strong interest in the sciences. From his West Point days he had a good grounding in mathematics, probably up into the calculus, and astronomy was a lifelong interest. He was fairly well versed in natural history—an agglomeration of observational biology, geology, and geography—and he followed the crank sciences of his day with sardonic amusement. His chief interest, though, lay in what we would call scientific method. In his time science was not so divorced from philosophy (or, in the opposite direction, from technology) as it is today, and Poe could legitimately be fascinated by applying ratiocination to many unusual areas of life: the methodology of solving cryptograms, determining the nature of truth, reasoning out an individual situation in terms of a calculus of probabilities (as in a murder case), and establishing a mathematics of human activities. His great analytical ability has never been questioned.

Yet despite Poe's keen interest in science, his emotional attitude toward it was ambivalent. His early sonnet "To Science" (1828) upbraids science for stripping the romance from life:

Why preyest thou thus upon the poet's
   heart,
Vulture, whose wings are dull realities?

Hast thou not dragged Diana from her car?
And driven the Hamadryad from the
   wood . . .

This attitude was not a passing pose of youth or a literary device, for Poe expressed the same point of view many times in his later work. Yet a problem that he did not resolve, and that we sometimes overlook, is exactly what he meant by the word "science." Basically, his hostility was focused on applied science and technology, since he considered them responsible for changes in material culture, degradation, and destruction. But even here his hostility was theoretical. Poe might inveigh against "progress" and poke fun at balloon travel, but he did not hesitate to mount a train, and he did not advocate doing away with the steam presses in his own occupation.

Unlike Mary Shelley, who in her muddled way feared that Romantic science would expose the lie of a godly universe and come to rival divinity, Poe had no objection to the theoretical aspects of science. For metaphysics—in the early sense of something beyond physics, explaining physics—he had the profoundest respect. Indeed, he was so fascinated by it that he could not keep his pen away from it. This interest, which can be seen in such essay-stories as "Mesmeric Revelation" (1844) and "The Colloquy of Monos and Una" (1841), culminated in the book *Eureka* (1848), which he called a prose poem. It is prose in that it is not written in meter, a poem in that it reasons about the universe in terms of analogies and poetic tropes.

In *Eureka*, Poe first pokes grotesque fun, with many wordplays, at classical systems of logic, and then proposes his own way to attain truth: intuition, or direct apprehension by means of the imagination. A cosmology then follows that in some ways is a last gasp of the *Naturphilosophie* of the early nineteenth century, particularly the work of Friedrich von Schelling and his followers. It presents an emanational universe, and like the *Naturphilosophie* it contains much nonsense and wrong-headed fantasy. But it also displays occasional intuitive insights that approximate the modern understanding of the universe. In a sense it is both a philosophy of science and a scientific philosophy, but not really successful as either. Poe felt very strongly that *Eureka* was his most important work, but few of his contemporaries or successors have taken it seriously, although it is valuable for interpreting many of his stories.

II

This general interest in science manifested itself in several of Poe's stories, scattered through his literary life, from very early publications to late.

Poe's first significant work of fiction, "MS. Found in a Bottle" (*Baltimore Saturday Visiter* [sic], 10 October 1833), won the first prize of $50 in a contest conducted by the newspaper and established Poe as a professional writer. It presented his work to a wide public and offered literary contacts that would have been very useful to a less fated man.

"MS. Found in a Bottle" is essentially a dreamlike fantasy. The narrator has suffered a shipwreck and is on a derelict that is run down by a gigantic ancient vessel. He "chances" to be tossed onto the other ship, which is operated by old men dressed in antique garb, who ignore his presence. There is something supernatural about their actions, in that, like the seamen in Wilhelm Hauff's "Geschichte der Gespensterschiff" (1825), they are enacting and reenacting a situation without relevance to the world of reality. The vessel heads southward and is about to descend into an Antarctic abyss when the narrator ends his account. Where is the ship going? A possible interpretation is that Poe had in mind a notorious crank theory of the day—that of Captain John Cleves Symmes, who argued that Earth is hollow, with polar openings permitting entry to the interior. But it is also possible that Poe had in mind the common premodern theory that the waters of Ocean flowed down through whirlpools and chasms into a great subterranean reservoir (the Abyss of Waters), whence they reemerged as ground water or ocean. A classic statement of this theory was the famous *Mundus Subterraneus* (1664) of Athanasius Kircher.

Like many of Poe's other stories, "MS. Found in a Bottle" is a highly personal combination of three elements not usually found in association: verisimilitude created by exact detail and rational argument, a fantastic narrative structure, and a metaphoric element

Edgar Allan Poe. Courtesy of the Library of Congress

that is sometimes allegorical and sometimes a symbol less amenable to interpretation. (While Poe often denounced "allegory" as such, his use of the term—as was the case with the word "science"—was not exactly the same as ours. A modern reader can legitimately regard metaphoric elements in Poe's fiction as allegorical or symbolic.) That the story has a symbolic meaning is commonly accepted, although there is disagreement as to its reading. The ancient men are sometimes taken to be figurations of the author; personages in an allegory of life; Christopher Columbus and his crew; the Flying Dutchman in a very early, aberrant appearance; or the Spirit of Discovery. But why any of these persons should plunge into Symmes's Hole or the Abyss of Waters is problematic.

"The Unparalleled Adventure of One Hans Pfaal," which first appeared in the *Southern Literary Messenger* (June 1835) and was reprinted in the *New York Transcript*, is a work of mixed form. It is partly a fantasy of aeronautics like the later story "The Balloon-Hoax" (1844); partly a topical satire, in which the followers of Washington Irving's Knickerbocker School are linked to old Holland; and it is also a self-proclaimed hoax. In early publications the eponymous Hans's family name was not Pfaal but Phaal, or "laugh" sounded backward.

Within a grotesque frame situation set in the Netherlands, a manuscript is dropped from a madly designed balloon by a dwarf. The manuscript describes a lunar voyage accomplished by Hans Pfaal, a local bellows maker (air), to evade his creditors. Pfaal builds a large balloon that attains lift through a recently discovered "atomic component" of hydrogen, blows up his creditors, and sails to the moon. There he finds a race of mentally deficient dwarfs, each of whom corresponds to an individual on Earth. But the story is a hoax. The dwarf who delivered the manuscript was a circus freak; Pfaal and his creditors had simply been abroad and are now carousing locally.

Poe had intended to write a continuation, in which, one may guess, certain lunar dwarfs would have exhibited the foibles of their earthly counterparts. But about three weeks after the appearance of "Pfaal" in the *Transcript*, Richard Adams Locke's moon hoax appeared in the *Sun* and deflated Poe's work in the public mind. Locke's exposition, which was presented with complete seriousness, told of lunar observations made by Sir John Herschel with his giant telescope and described moon men. Poe was outraged at what he considered plagiarism, annoyed by the scientific naïveté of Locke's work, and discouraged from continuing his own story.

Despite the calculated grotesqueness of the frame situation, Poe wrote "Pfaal" after much serious thought. He checked the astronomy and physics of such a voyage, and acquainted himself with earlier lunar voyages, some of which he cited in a later postscript. Although his purpose, in the tradition of the subgenre of the lunar voyage, was to have been personal satire, he also strove for scientific accuracy. He describes an atmospheric condenser for the car and pays heed to phenomena of gravitation even though he was not entirely correct.

Poe's interest in astronomy and chemistry was again demonstrated in "The Conversation of Eiros and Charmion" (*Burton's Gentleman's Magazine*, October 1839). The title refers to Shakespeare's *Antony and Cleopatra*, in which Iras and Charmian, Cleopatra's attendants, witness the death of a world when a luminary (Octavian) approaches. Poe's story vehicle is a conversation between two free-floating spirits in space (Aidenn), the abode of the evolved dead, who reminisce upon the fate of Earth. Eiros describes the end of the world. A comet is approaching and threatens to collide with Earth. The astronomers offer encouragement to the people, since the nucleus of the comet, being gaseous, can do little harm. But as the comet rides the sky, it becomes obvious that life on Earth is changing. Vegetation is growing more luxuriantly, and people are brisker, more excitable than before. The comet, it is revealed, is extracting the nitrogen from the atmosphere, leaving only oxygen. The world bursts into flame.

Like "Pfaal," "Eiros and Charmion" has many levels of appreciation. It is experimental in form, starting with a dramatic situation, then shifting to a monologue in heightened language. Its kernel is a scientific *aperçu*, the origin of which has been found in a contemporary popular science book. But its ultimate referent is religious, linking the traditional belief that the next destruction of the world would be by fire with the contemporary interest in the chiliasm connected with Millerism. The ultimate message—that the spirits praise God and that there is personal survival—may not have offended many, but it should be noted that there is no Christology.

A collateral story is "The Colloquy of Monos and Una" (*Graham's Lady's and Gentleman's Magazine*, August 1841). Once again two disembodied spirits converse, but this time their topic is death and rebirth, on both a general and an individual level. Monos declaims that the world had degenerated, ruined by progress and industrialism, and it was destroyed by fire (probably as in "Eiros and Charmion"). More significant, however, is Monos' description to Una of his experiences after death. These are remarkably physical and are connected with the dissolution of his body. He describes his death, his immediate postmortem sensations as Una is sitting by his corpse, his burial, and the departure of his senses as he decays. The final passage has obvious references to Aristotelian form and matter and to Kantian time and space as the dweller remains in his grave. Yet, in some fashion, Monos must have been resurrected in order to carry on his conversation with Una and to praise the good world in which he now finds himself. As for Una—perhaps she is his mate, perhaps a statement of spirit as opposed to Monos' matter, perhaps an identity with Monos on a different plane of being. In any case, as in "Eiros and Charmion," Poe attempts to unify theories of matter with a sort of theism. What personal relevance the two stories had is speculative.

Three of Poe's stories are concerned in a substantive way with mesmerism or related topics. These are "Mesmeric Revelation" (*Columbian Lady's and Gentleman's Magazine*, August 1844), "The Facts in the Case of M. Valdemar" (*Whig Review*, December 1845), and "A Tale of the Ragged Mountains" (*Godey's Lady's Book*, April 1844). In each of these stories mesmerism reveals an ultimate truth, a common enough concept in the occult thought of the day. Poe did not take mesmerism seriously and used it only as a literary device.

In "Mesmeric Revelation" a mesmerized subject continues to speak after physiological death and offers speculations much like those of *Eureka*. The point of the story, though, is personal: happiness is not a primary emotion but simply the absence of pain—an explanation that suited both Poe's theatricality and his private life.

A much stronger narrative vehicle is to be found in "The Facts in the Case of M. Valdemar," which Poe presented very skillfully as reportage. His attempt at a hoax was taken seriously by many readers (as was "Mesmeric Revelation"). Elizabeth Barrett (later Browning) wrote to Poe, commenting that the British pirated publication of the story was locally taken to be a case history.

As Poe tells the story, Valdemar dies while in trance and not only is preserved from corruption but also maintains a half-life of a sort. He is able to speak. But when the mesmeric connection is broken, he dissolves almost instantly into corruption and putridity. This shocking "smash ending," one of the most effective in the history of horror fiction, has had great historical importance in the development of American supernatural fiction, particularly in the school of H. P. Lovecraft, where such endings became almost a conditioned riposte.

The third mesmeric tale, "A Tale of the Ragged Mountains," is a much less successful accomplishment. It is concerned with memory, with the reexperiencing of a past event in India. There are also parallelisms of fate, as the events in India are repeated (though on a symbolic level) in Virginia. In some vague way mesmerism caused the experience; but Poe does not elaborate his ideas with his usual clarity, and the story is open to several interpretations.

"Mellonta Tauta" (*Godey's Lady's Book*, February 1849), which H. G. Wells translated nicely from the Greek as "things to come," uses the trappings of futurology to belabor humorously a few of Poe's bêtes noires. The story consists of a letter, dated April Fools' Day, 2848, written by a woman aboard a superballoon. Although a thousand years have passed, Poe's projections of science are minimal, namely, the balloon itself, which carries about 200 people; trains that race at 300 miles per hour; and (indirectly) telescopes of great power. Pundita, the letter writer, expresses ludicrous misunderstandings of nineteenth-century America. She first attacks systems of logic—one invented by a Hindu sage named Aries Tottle, the other by one Hog, the Ettrick Shepherd—and offers in their place what we would call the "faggot theory" of knowledge:

consistency with what is known. After ridiculing both the republican form of government and mob rule, she describes the making of cloth by grinding up silkworms and discusses the religions of the nineteenth century (that is, wealth and fashion)—until her balloon falls into the sea. All in all, "Mellonta Tauta" is more deftly handled than most of Poe's humor and is amusing, but it is hardly important as science fiction.

Much the most interesting in idea of Poe's approaches to science fiction is his early geographical fantasy, *The Narrative of Arthur Gordon Pym* (1838). Connected with the fanciful geography of "MS. Found in a Bottle," it was probably written to capitalize on the current interest in Antarctic exploration. In form it is a hodgepodge, consisting of a novel of sea adventure, a pastiche of historical Indian-white relations, a hoax story, and a puzzle story with links to crank science and idealistic philosophy. It is presented mostly as a diary kept by Pym and is related with great verisimilitude, although sensational in event. It was accepted by some readers, notably in Great Britain, as a factual account.

The first half of *Pym* is taken up with adventure at sea. Pym, a young man from Nantucket, stows away aboard a ship and is fortunate enough to survive a mutiny, widespread slaughter, shipwreck, and sufferings on a derelict. This portion echoes, although in a personal way, the sea-adventure stories of Captain Frederick Marryat or James Fenimore Cooper. Personal knowledge undoubtedly entered into it, for Poe had crossed the Atlantic twice. Poe achieves a suspension of disbelief, if one can accept the statistical probability of so much horror on a single voyage.

The later portion of *Pym* is geographical fantasy, related on the one hand to the imaginary voyages of the eighteenth century and on the other to factual accounts of voyages of exploration or whaling voyages to the Antarctic.

Pym and a companion, Dirk Peters, are rescued from their derelict by the sealer *Jane Guy*, upon which they sail into that area of global mystery, the Antarctic. As they proceed southward, the waters become much warmer; and at about 84° South, they come upon the subtropical land of Tsalal, inhabited by black men on the cultural level of California Indians. The island of Tsalal is a strange place, with curious animals and odd vegetation, and with multicolored, stranded water. The color white is absent, and the natives are terrified when they see a white object from outside. Even their teeth are black. The crew of the *Jane Guy* comes to trust the natives, who seem very friendly; but in a sudden act of treachery, the men of Tsalal kill a landing party and capture the ship. In this episode Poe is obviously drawing on incidents of contact with the Indians of the Northwest Coast of America, perhaps the fate of the *Boston* in Nootka Sound.

Pym and Peters escape, evade the natives for a time, steal a canoe, and head farther south. The water becomes warmer and warmer, the color white comes to predominate, with the sea turning milky; a curtain of mist arises before them, and they are obviously approaching a titanic falls, into which the sea tumbles. They are about to go over the edge when before them rises "a shrouded human figure, very far larger in its proportions than any dweller among men. And the hue of the skin was of the perfect whiteness of snow."

This is the end of the story, and we do not know how Pym returned to America; but the "editor" (Poe) appends a "Note" interpreting some of Pym's factual data. The "Note" analyzes diagrams provided by Pym as characters in ancient Semitic alphabets, forming words indicating darkness, whiteness, and the south. The reader may also remember that the name of the king of the islands is Tsalemon (which echoes Solomon).

The crux in *Pym* is understanding what (if anything) Poe was driving at with Tsalal, the area farther south, and their peculiarities. *Pym* was long taken to be empty mystification, but it has recently been shown that Poe's Semitic analogies were not fakery and probably were supplied by a friendly biblical scholar. The geography of Tsalal also has been examined closely. J. O. Bailey, whose work

initiated the modern study of *Pym*, concluded that Poe was attaching his novel to *Symzonia* (1820) by "Adam Seaborn," a pseudonymous political satire of unknown authorship set in Symmes's hollow Earth. According to Bailey, Tsalal contained criminals from inside Earth, and the white figure was a Symzonian guard.

A stronger interpretation would align the natives of Antarctica with the Lost Tribes. While this sounds absurd to us, we must remember that in Poe's time there was intense speculation about the Lost Tribes, and that cranks kept finding them in the oddest places. On the level of religion, only eleven years before *Pym* the *Book of Mormon* described a Hebrew settlement in South America around 600 B.C.

The strongest interpretation of Antarctica, though, is that Poe was projecting the cosmological system of Schelling or one of his circle into fanciful, mythologized geography and ethnology. The heart of this system is the idea that creation proceeded by alternating polarities and merging opposites—spirit and matter, good and bad, plus and minus—in a European counterpart of the Chinese yin and yang. Thus the good-white first emanation is followed by the bad-black response or antithesis, both combining to form the outside world. According to this interpretation, Poe may have been hinting that Antarctica was the site of divine creation and that the white figure was an angel, perhaps even the angel that guarded Eden. But Poe wisely ended his story without an explanation (which would have been extremely difficult to support), and the reader can let his or her fancy run free.

Poe, though, was an intellectually playful man, and he did conceal two little messages in the formations and inscriptions of Tsalal, which appear in chapter 23: his own name and perhaps Pym's.

Poe's original:

Transliteration:

Other stories in Poe's large corpus contain elements of contemporary science or are placed in the overlap area between science and philosophy, but these stories are not necessarily science fiction. The tales of abnormal psychology—such as "The Black Cat" (1843), "Berenice" (1835), "William Wilson" (1839)— need not be described, for abnormal psychology in itself, unless rendered fantastic by other elements, has never been considered science fiction. Two of Poe's more important stories (perhaps ultimately suggested by the work of Ludwig Tieck, with which Poe was familiar) are ultimately philosophical— the examples of Fichtean Will displayed by the bluestockings in "Morella" (1835) and "Ligeia" (1838). These tell more about Poe the man than do the "science fiction" stories. His mathematical background is visible in stories that reduce the multiplicity of life to a calculus of probabilities, but these, too, are not science fiction. Such stories are "The Murders in the Rue Morgue," in which Dupin expounds on a calculus of life, and "The Gold Bug" (1843), which is really a study in elementary probability. In "The Angel of the Odd" (1844) Poe raises, in somewhat diffuse form, the probability of improbable events. Although presented as a spoof, it does raise a serious question about idealistic philosophy and might also have interested contemporary insurance companies.

Some words must be added about the whimsical mummy in "Some Words with a Mummy" (*American Whig Review*, April 1845). He has been awakened from the dead by galvanism applied by one Dr. Ponnonner ("'pon honor"). The mechanism of the story may have been derived from a fairly well-known novel, *The Mummy!* (1827), by Jane Webb (later better known as Mrs. Loudon), in which, in the twenty-second century, the mummy of King Cheops is seemingly revived by galvanism. Apart from the galvanic mechanism, though, Poe's story is really satire, a succession of gibes at modern technology and a sneering comparison of the achievements of his own day with those of ancient Egypt. Both material progress and social reform come under attack. As the conversation of the condescending mummy is summarized: "Great Movements were awfully common things in his day, and as for Progress, it was at one time a nuisance, but it never progressed."

III

It must be admitted, unfortunately, that Poe's stories that approach science fiction are, by and large, not among his major works. As a group they are much less interesting critically than the stories of abnormal psychology, the wonderland stories, or the detective stories. Only "The Facts in the Case of M. Valdemar" can be considered among his finest stories.

Poe's stature as a giant of letters and his unquestioned importance in other areas of writing may lead one to overstate his historical position in the development of science fiction. Some of his stories, it can be said, form part of the common American background as required reading for the young. Others have been almost uniquely important in the development of supernatural fiction or the detective story. But the stories considered in this article (except "The Facts in the Case of M. Valdemar" and perhaps "MS. Found in a Bottle") were not widely known during the formative period of science fiction. Even today it is doubtful if anyone but a specialist or enthusiast has read them all. Nor were they the stories that were esteemed in the nineteenth century. The most that can be said is that Poe's fiction as a whole influenced Jules Verne, who admired Poe greatly. But the elements that Verne took over were not always those of science fiction.

Poe was not a great innovator or pattern creator in science fiction like Wells, nor a historically important specialist like Ray Bradbury or Robert A. Heinlein. He was a writer, a few of whose stories, in retrospect, can be uncomfortably squeezed, with crumpling and edges sticking out, into the genre we now call science fiction. One can admire the deftness with which knowledge was pressed into service, the great originality, the ingenuity in combining levels of narration, the remarkable blend of wild imagination and sober rationality, the technical brilliance (allowing for period styles), but one must still admit that the evolution of science fiction would have been much the same had Poe never written these stories.

Selected Bibliography

WORKS OF EDGAR ALLAN POE

There are scores of editions of Poe's fiction containing some or all of the stories described in this article. In most cases the texts they follow are those of the Griswold (New York, 1850–1856) edition, which, while accurate enough for the stories, does not always present Poe's best or final texts. Poe continually revised his work, but it must be admitted that his changes are usually not important to the general reader. The first five books listed are the first editions of his fiction; these are followed by modern collections.

The Narrative of Arthur Gordon Pym of Nantucket [etc.]. New York: Harper and Brothers, 1838.
Tales of the Grotesque and Arabesque. Two Volumes. Philadelphia, Pa.: Lea and Blanchard, 1840.
Tales by Edgar A. Poe. New York: Wiley and Putnam, 1845.
Mesmerism "In Articulo Mortis." London: Short and Company, 1846. Pamphlet. (A British piracy of "The Facts in the Case of M. Valdemar.")
The Works of the Late Edgar Allan Poe. 4 vols. Edited by Rufus W. Griswold. New York: J. S. Redfield, 1850–1856.
The Complete Works of Edgar Allan Poe. Virginia Edition. 17 vols. Edited by James A. Harrison. New York: Thomas Y. Crowell, 1902. (Includes some material that is now generally thought not to have been written by Poe; is the closest to a variorum edition yet prepared; and at the moment is still the best general edition.)
The Science Fiction of Edgar Allan Poe. Collected and edited, with an introduction and commentary, by Harold Beaver. New York: Penguin Books, 1976.

(Contains the short stories discussed in this article, *Eureka* and several marginal works, annotations, and full coverage of the scholarly literature; texts are Poe's latest versions.)
Tales and Sketches. 2 vols. Edited by Thomas Ollive Mabbott with the assistance of Eleanor D. Kewer and Maureen C. Mabbott. Cambridge, Mass.: Harvard University Press, 1978. (Volumes 2 and 3 of the *Collected Works of Edgar Allan Poe.*)

CRITICAL AND BIOGRAPHICAL STUDIES

Aldiss, Brian W. *Billion Year Spree: The True History of Science Fiction.* Garden City, N.Y.: Doubleday, 1973.
Bailey, J. O. "Sources for Poe's *Arthur Gordon Pym,* 'Hans Pfaal,' and Other Pieces." *PMLA,* 57 (1942).
Bloom, Clive. *Reading Poe Reading Freud. The Romantic Imagination in Crisis.* Houndsmills, Basingstoke, Hampshire, England: Macmillan, 1988.
Brody, Selma B. "The Source and Significance of Poe's Use of Azote in 'Hans Pfaal.'" *Science-Fiction Studies,* 17, part 1 (1990): 60–63.
Burduck, Michael L. *Grim Phantasms: Fear in Poe's Short Fiction.* New York and London: Garland, 1992.
Campbell, Killis. *The Mind of Poe and Other Studies.* Cambridge, Mass.: Harvard University Press, 1933.
Dayan, Joan. *Fables of Mind: An Inquiry into Poe's Fiction.* New York and Oxford: Oxford University Press, 1987.
Falk, Doris V. "Poe and the Power of Animal Magnetism." *PMLA,* 84 (1969).
Fisher, Benjamin F., IV. "Fantasy Figures in Poe's Poems." In *The Poetic Fantastic.* Edited by Patrick D. Murphy and Vernon Hyles. Westport, Conn.: Greenwood, 1989.
Giddings, Robert. "Poe: Rituals of Life and Death." In *American Horror Fiction: From Brockden Brown to Stephen King.* Edited by Brian Docherty. New York: St. Martin's, 1990.
Hammond, J. R. *An Edgar Allan Poe Companion: A Guide to the Short Stories, Romances, and Essays.* Totowa, N.J.: Barnes and Noble Books, 1981.
Hoffman, Daniel. *Poe, Poe, Poe, Poe, Poe, Poe, Poe.* New York: Paragon House, 1990.
Ketterer, David. "Poe, Edgar Allan." In *The Science Fiction Encyclopedia.* Garden City, N.Y.: Doubleday, 1979.
Knapp, Bettina L. *Edgar Allan Poe.* New York: Ungar, 1984.
Kopley, Richard. "Early Illustrations of *Pym's* 'Shrouded Human Figure.'" In *Scope of the Fantastic: Culture, Biography, Themes, Children's Literature.* Edited by R. A. Collins. Westport, Conn.: Greenwood, 1985.
Lee, A. Robert, ed. *Edgar Allan Poe: The Design of Order.* London: Vision, 1987; Totowa, N.J.: Barnes and Noble Books, 1987.
Lind, Sidney E. "Poe and Mesmerism." *PMLA,* 62 (1947).

May, Charles E. *Edgar Allan Poe: A Study of the Short Fiction*. Boston: Twayne, 1991.

Meyers, Jeffrey. *Edgar Allan Poe: His Life and Legacy*. New York: Scribners, 1992.

Nicolson, Marjorie. *Voyages to the Moon*. New York: Macmillan, 1948.

Pollin, Burton R. " 'Some Words with a Mummy' Reconsidered." *Emerson Society Quarterly*, 59 (1969).

———. *Discoveries in Poe*. Notre Dame, Ind.: University of Notre Dame Press, 1970. (Resourceful, closely analyzed studies of motifs, sources, influences.)

Quinn, Arthur Hobson. *Edgar Allan Poe. A Critical Biography*. New York: Appleton-Century, 1941. (Excellent, full scholarly biography.)

Sambrook, A. J. "A Romantic Theme, The Last Man." *Forum for Modern Language Studies*, 25 (January 1966).

Seed, David. "Breaking the Bounds: The Rhetoric of Limits in the Works of Edgar Allan Poe, His Contemporaries, and Adaptors." In his *Anticipations: Essays on Early Science Fiction and Its Precursors*. Liverpool, England: Liverpool University Press, 1995.

Silverman, Kenneth. *Edgar Allan Poe: Mournful and Never-Ending Remembrance*. New York: HarperCollins, 1991.

Wagenknecht, Edward. *Edgar Allan Poe. The Man Behind the Legend*. New York: Oxford University Press, 1963. (Pleasant, informative, nontechnical study.)

Walker, I. M., ed. *Edgar Allan Poe: The Critical Heritage*. London and New York: Routledge and Kegan Paul, 1986.

Zanger, Jules. "The City from the Inside: Poe's Urban Fiction." *Journal of the Fantastic in the Arts*, 3, no. 2 (1991): 29–36.

Zanger, Jules. "Poe's 'Bernice': Philosophical Fantasy and Its Pitfalls." In *Scope of the Fantastic: Theory, Technique, Major Authors*. Edited by R. A. Collins. Westport, Conn.: Greenwood, 1985.

—E. F. BLEILER

FREDERIK POHL

(b. 1919)

K INGSLEY AMIS, IN the first widely read
book about science fiction, *New Maps of
Hell: A Survey of Science Fiction* (1960, based
on lectures at Princeton), singled out Frederik
Pohl as "the most consistently able writer science fiction, in the modern sense, has yet produced." Appearing on the cover of Pohl's
novel *The Voices of Heaven* (1994) and repeated with varying attributions on other
works, this quotation seems like an understatement. A writer who never travels without his writing materials (and uses them
faithfully), Pohl has produced an amazing
quantity of high-quality fiction—much, but
not all of it science fiction—over an extraordinarily long career.

Recognized by fans and professionals alike
for his ability, Pohl has won just about every
award in the field of science fiction: the Edward E. Smith, John W. Campbell, and Donald
A. Wollheim Memorial Awards, the Gallun
Award, the Prix Apollo, the Yugoslavian Vi-
zija, the Nebula—three times, including the
"Grand Master" Nebula for lifetime contributions to the field—and the Hugo—four
times for editing, twice for writing. He is the
only person to have won the Hugo both as
writer and as editor. He has also won an
American Book Award, the annual award of
the Popular Culture Association, and the
United Nations Society of Writers Award. He
was Guest of Honor at the World Science Fiction Convention in 1972. He helped found the
World Science Fiction Writers Association
and has traveled widely to publicize science
fiction, to enrich his own writing, and to col-

lect material for *Tales from the Planet Earth:
A Novel with Nineteen Authors* (1986), "co
created" with his wife, Elizabeth Anne Hull.

Moreover, Pohl, almost alone among science fiction writers, experiments not only
with futuristic technologies but also with an
extraordinary variety of economic systems. In
Pohl's works, we find everything from a managed society on the Chinese model in *Black
Star Rising* (1985) to a captive but essentially
money-free society (except when "scrip" is
needed for trade) in *Stopping at Slowyear*
(1991). In his novels, he disputes the frequent
criticism of science fiction as assuming that
capitalism, as practiced in the United States,
will continue to hold through all time and
space.

There cannot be much about the art and
practice of buying, selling, and writing science fiction that Frederik Pohl does not know.
Editor at age nineteen of *Astonishing Stories*
and *Superscience Stories*—before his own
first story sold—he has edited dozens of anthologies, including the *Star Science Fiction*
series in the 1950's, a precursor of the original
anthology series that competed so strongly
with the science fiction magazines a decade
later, and the *Galaxy* group of magazines in
the 1960's, when *If* won the Hugo award for
best professional magazine (1966–1968). A literary agent for several years, Pohl later cham-
pioned the rights of his fellow writers as
president (1974–1976) of the Science Fiction
Writers of America.

A well-known public speaker who has lectured before business groups and on college

campuses, a radio talk-show personality, a fanzine columnist, and a ready interview subject, Pohl has recently cut back on his active participation in fan conventions and academic conferences. In the earliest days of organized fandom, he was better known for his fan participation than his fiction. But he has made his mark as a writer, in an almost continually ascending spiral of increasing mastery of expressive techniques, without ever running out of something new to say. From his apprenticeship days in the 1930's and 1940's through his first wave of acclaim in the 1950's as a creator of "comic infernos," Pohl has risen to eminence as a writer of "hard" science fiction.

Charting Pohl's accomplishment is complicated by his frequent use of pen names and his many writing partnerships, but as popular science fiction writers have begun recounting their early days in print, his name has appeared in most of their memoirs. Sam Moskowitz's *The Immortal Storm* (1954), Harry Warner, Jr.'s *All Our Yesterdays* (1969), and Damon Knight's *The Futurians* (1977) only scratch the surface of Pohl's involvement in fan activities, but he has supplemented these works with his own memoir, *The Way the Future Was* (1978). Highly personal and entertaining—Pohl's "finest novel," some acquaintances have called it—it may also need some supplementing, but it does provide a basic framework for understanding this complex man who has made a living from science fiction for more than forty years. Science fiction has been good to this high school dropout from Brooklyn (born on 26 November 1919) who became a self-educated expert in politics, history, mathematics, futurology, and science as a spectator sport, as well as a prolific author, both in collaboration and in his own right.

It was as a collaborator with the late C. M. Kornbluth that Pohl first drew serious critical and popular notice. Started in the late 1930's, when they were members of the "Futurians," a New York fan group, this partnership, which was responsible for seven novels in the 1950's (three of them not science fiction), continued

long after Kornbluth's death in 1958, at age thirty-five. Hardly science fiction at all, "The Meeting," one of a number of stories reworked by Pohl from Kornbluth's rough drafts, won a Hugo as best short story of 1972. On the whole their short fiction is passable, but their science fiction novels drew high praise—especially "Gravy Planet" (*Galaxy*, 1952), revised for book publication as *The Space Merchants* (1953). A rare example of a "science fiction classic" written by a team, it incorporated personal experience and expertise in advertising and public relations into romance conventions and futurological speculation traditional to science fiction, and it raised to new heights of comic invention the mode of the dystopian novel.

Told in the first person by an advertising executive turned rebellious Conservationist ("Consie" to McCarthy-like witch-hunters), the story begins with Mitch Courtenay's involvement in a plan by the advertising moguls who virtually run society to supplement an overpopulated and supersaturated Earth with a new market for commercial exploitation by the colonization of Venus. Although Venus today seems impossible as a place for humanity to live—hardly a market for excess production, much less a Consie utopia—the story was less plausible than satirical to begin with. Yet its vision of a world led by hypnotic obsession with affluence into ecological poverty—including such gritty details as saltwater sink taps, reserved stairwell sleeping spaces, and habit-forming cycles of commercial products—still has the power to chill if not to compel. Incredible plot twists, caricatures of advertising moguls and the subservient federal government, and detailed depictions of the commercial exploitation of the moon, moreover, help make the story fun, as does the manic vision of a Consie cell headquartered in the middle of a gigantic chicken heart called "Chicken Little," slices of which are marketed all over the world. Pohl has since added a sequel, *The Merchants' War* (1985).

Pohl and Kornbluth took on the legal profession in *Gladiator-at-Law* (1955); and Pohl, writing in collaboration with Lester del Rey, zeroed in on the insurance business with *Preferred Risk* (1955; originally published under the name Edson McCann); but the formula did not pay off as well this time, either artistically or commercially. In *Search the Sky* (1954), an allegory of free trade as an antidote to social stagnation in a far-flung interstellar civilization, and *Wolfbane* (1959), in which Earthmen overthrow a bizarre alien conqueror, Pohl and Kornbluth produced two other novels that have some moments of thoughtful entertainment.

Less social criticism and more action/adventure are prevalent in seven other novels that Pohl wrote with Jack Williamson over the years. Although competent enough as "boys' fiction," *Undersea Quest* (1954), *Undersea Fleet* (1956), and *Undersea City* (1958) may not give the reader as much to chew on as comparable juveniles by Robert A. Heinlein or Isaac Asimov. Still more of an element of fantasy, less rationalized, is evident in the Starchild trilogy (*The Reefs of Space*, 1963; *Starchild*, 1965; *Rogue Star*, 1969; published in one volume, 1977). A little more believable extrapolation about matter transmission of personalities, interspecies cooperation, and an exploratory journey to an artificial planet are found in *Farthest Star* (1975; expanded from two novellas, "Doomship," 1973, and "The Org's Egg," 1974). None of these works are very challenging to the reader in terms of invention, style, or character, but they do exploit the sheer exuberance of adventure for its own sake, a characteristic of Williamson's fiction.

More recent novels written with Williamson, *Land's End* (1988) and *The Singers of Time* (1991), indicate that Pohl may deliberately moderate his own extrapolative competence to match Williamson's less scientific viewpoint. While this may foster their relationship—both men have contributed extensively to science fiction since its early years—it does not add much to Pohl's reputation as a thoughtful writer.

"Gravy Planet" was the first story Pohl published under his own name, but it was only the beginning of this second stage of his career, now past the period of apprenticeship. During the 1950's and into the 1960's, he wrote a number of satirical stories attacking some of the common assumptions of the affluent society. Although few of these pieces stand up well to critical rereading—no one was writing for that purpose in those days, Pohl points out—they did help editor Horace L. Gold shape *Galaxy* into a frequent vehicle for social criticism, a tradition Pohl kept alive in 1961, when he succeeded to the editorial chair. These stories by Pohl indicated to Brian W. Aldiss that what he wanted to do would also be possible in science fiction, a genre previously dominated—in Aldiss's view—by galaxy-spanning power fantasies, heavy in hardware.

The best-known story of this period is probably "The Midas Plague" (1954), which posits conspicuous consumption by the poor rather than the rich in order to keep up with the cornucopia of goods produced by automated technology. Rather than taking this idea seriously, Pohl turns it into a satirical "tall tale," eventually reducing the concept to absurdity by having robots consume as well as produce. Runaway factory production, planned obsolescence, and hard-hitting advertising are attacked in at least three inferior sequels: "The Man Who Ate the World" (1956), "The Wizards of Pung's Corners" (1958), and "The Waging of the Peace" (1959).

Analyzing the "consumer society" in other stories from this period as well, Pohl put variant methods of social control under his "microscope." "My Lady Greensleeves" (1957) uses a prison riot as the setting for an object lesson regarding social stratification. Segregation by occupational specialization in this imaginary society is no more logically absurd than segregation by color, religion, or ethnic background in our own world, and it has practical benefits too. This idea of brainwashing as a social good gives a somber tone to "Rafferty's Reasons" (1955), in which a former artist, not knowing exactly why he is dissatisfied with life, assaults a politician with a cigar, under the delusion that he has a knife.

Downfalls such as Rafferty's are taken by this society to be a cheap enough price to pay for economic stability, with a place for everyone and everyone in his or her place. At the opposite extreme, chaos, voluntarily chosen, results from the perfect tranquilizer in "What to Do till the Analyst Comes" (1956). Anticipating the drug revolution of the 1960's, this story shows how banishing worry also does away with accuracy, efficiency, production, safety, and even survival.

Similar "comic infernos," to use Amis's term, lose some of their effect when aliens are introduced into tales ostensibly about human folly in Pohl's cycle of consumer stories. Stabilizing the human population by liquidating those who do not have permits to live is interrupted by the arrival of a being from beneath Earth's surface in "The Census Takers" (1956). Off-planet visitors trying to warn us are also supernumerary in "The Snowmen" (1959), a sketch of how ignorant consumers turn an "energy crisis" into a local version of the "heat death of the universe." Instead of fossil fuels, people employ "heat pumps" on a large scale, almost equalizing the temperature inside, outside, and on the surface of Earth. Aliens are more gainfully employed in "The Children of the Night" (1964), in which a high-pressure public relations man, during a fragile armistice, persuades a small town to accept an Arcturan base by uniting the electorate and the aliens in their anger against him.

The theme of manipulation is given perhaps its ultimate twist in "The Tunnel Under the World" (1955), in which Guy Burckhardt discovers, to his horror, that he and his fellow citizens, victims of an industrial accident, have been preserved by a miracle of science in order to function as manikins in a tabletop model of their small town so that an advertising research firm can have a controlled test market. Burckhardt's discovery, made after several false starts, in a variation on traditional horror and mystery stories, does not support the biblical verse "You shall know the truth, and the truth shall make you free."

Frederik Pohl. COURTESY OF CORBIS-BETTMANN

Knowing the truth only confirms Burckhardt's helplessness, a problem faced by a number of Pohl's protagonists, especially in stories where the idea of "possession" is involved. Viewed from the standpoint of the victim, this power, extrapolated into a science fiction talent or device for amplifying or directing brain waves, implies absolute terror.

Almost a throwaway in "The Day the Icicle Works Closed" (1959), the idea of renting or buying someone else's body for a time has tragic results in the shocking but beautifully crafted "We Purchased People" (1974). Similar fantasies are pivotal in two of Pohl's first three novels written alone and have distinct echoes in two books about Robinette Broadhead written almost twenty years later.

Although his first solo effort as a novelist, *Slave Ship* (serialized 1956–1957), manages without the motif of possession, it does involve training animals to sail a ship and usually fatal attempts at mental communication by an alien life-form. Pohl scores satirical points, portraying the military mind, of both

East and West, in a prescient conflict involving Americans on one side and a religious sect originating in Vietnam on the other, but the novel is so busy with melodramatic and romantic actions that it all but collapses under its own complications.

The better focused *Drunkard's Walk* (1960) does to the university what the earlier collaborations with Kornbluth and del Rey had done to advertising, law, and insurance. Overpopulation is again a major problem, but this time it is speciously caused by "immortals" trying, in their self-interest, to arrest human development. Their telepathic suggestions have driven the overly curious to suicide, but the hero of this story foils them by keeping himself at least mildly inebriated, thereby disrupting his mental flow and preventing them from taking over his mind.

Still more tightly organized is *A Plague of Pythons* (serialized 1962; book form, 1965), in which the idea of possession is nine-tenths of the story. Although opportunities for humor are exploited early in the novel, the action settles down to a melodramatic illustration of the implications for absolute power of the device that makes possession possible, and its temptations, even for one who has suffered under it. This theme of possession by aliens is continued in the multiply-authored volume, *Tales from Planet Earth*.

Equally rigorous extrapolation, without the theme of possession, is used for comic effect in *The Age of the Pussyfoot* (serialized 1965; book form, 1969), in which Rip Van Winkle of our "kamikaze" age is thawed out from cryogenic suspension to discover a world of technological advances with which he can hardly cope. Almost unteachable by the standards of this future world, he blunders in and out of trouble, unwittingly saving the world from its own timidity in the face of an alien takeover at the book's end. There are both comic and comic-book effects but also a shrewd analysis of medical advances, the social psychology of inflation, and flawed utopian expectations. An improvement over Pohl's first three novels, *The Age of the Pussyfoot* marks not so much the beginning of a new direction for

Pohl as the end of the "consumer cycle" of his fiction.

Editing the *Galaxy* group of magazines for most of the 1960's, Pohl officially rejected sex and surrealism, plotlessness, nihilism, and the "art for art's sake" excesses of the New Wave. Yet his own writing did not settle into a rut. He tried several forms that were new for him, including what he called "velocity exercises"—stories in which there is very little plot to interfere with the satire or speculation being presented. Aliens appear in several of these exercises, but not as hoary menaces or dei ex machinas. "The Martian Stargazers" (1962) explains the demise of the Martians by means of speculative star lore. "Earth 18" (1964) offers a guidebook to Earth's limited attractions, as they have been "developed" by alien entrepreneurs for the tourist trade. The prize example of this story type is "Day Million" (1967), a "love story" of "people" greatly changed from both the physiological condition and the mental attitudes of Western society today. By means of direct address to the reader, redefinitions of language, jolting shifts of perspective, and remarkable verbal economy, we are led to contemplate, along plausible lines of extrapolation, how different we can be and still think of ourselves as the same.

Surviving a bout of depression after he gave up meeting regular deadlines as editor of *Galaxy* and *If*, Pohl continued to serve as an editorial consultant on new fiction for Bantam Books, while he compiled anthologies, mainly of a retrospective nature. He also began to write more, concentrating now on "hard" science fiction, often space-oriented, in which science and technology play as great a role as social satire and in which character study and style become more complex. Problems of overpopulation and social inequity figured in a number of his earlier works—appropriately enough for a political liberal who was once, like many a young radical in the 1930's, an active member of the Communist party. In these later works, as part of the background, these problems cry out for desperate remedies, some of which may backfire.

609

On a more positive note, "In the Problem Pit" (1973) extrapolates present-day brainstorming and sensitivity sessions into an institutionalized nationwide "think tank" procedure by which representative individuals engage not only their own problems but also those of their civilization. The concept is essentially static, as in the "velocity exercises" of the 1960's, but its potential for character interaction is frittered away into conventionally exciting melodrama. At the opposite extreme, in "Shaffery Among the Immortals" (1972), an unassuming astronomer in a sinecure financed as a cover for organized crime demolishes himself, the mobsters, and most of the world's population when he accidentally "discovers" a new strain of botulism.

The price paid for progress is somewhere in between in two other tales of this time. "We Purchased People" (1974) posits not only mental possession as a means of getting criminals to be useful and productive but also selling off to the alien manipulators "primitive" arts and artifacts of Earth in return for technological and scientific aid. In "The Gold at the Starbow's End" (1972), the contradictions of the 1960's survive in an exaggerated conflict between the generations. Ten years' concentrated thinking in the isolation of a starship headed for what proves to be a nonexistent planet produces unexpected results among ten disciplined and mathematically trained young people. Evolving what might be termed a "hippie milieu," they develop new arts, new sciences, even a new language, and thus obtain immense powers of creation and destruction. After discovering the hoax played on them, they send heavy particles back to Earth to blow up all nuclear installations. Then they create for themselves a new world where the nonexistent planet was supposed to be and return to their home world for their pick of the survivors.

Like "The Gold at Starbow's End," the rest of Pohl's significant work of the 1970's takes place at least partially off Earth, where relatively few of his stories since his apprenticeship have actually been set. Besides those in *The Early Pohl* (1976), there are only a few

early tales set in space or on other worlds in his ten other story collections, and only one of these tales, "The Mapmakers" (1955), bears a characteristic Pohl stamp. Lost without their navigator, who was blinded in a freak accident, a spaceship crew obtains only hallucinations from desperate, unguided hyperspace jumps, while the navigator cries out in his bed, aware of their fate but not allowed to assist. Once he convinces the medical personnel not to sedate him, he demonstrates his development of a "second sight," for which the hyperspace lanes are practically a road map, thus illustrating the importance of a clear head and the folly of blind conformity, regardless of whether or not it is chemically induced.

Clear-eyed intelligence and sheer dumb luck vie for dominance in Pohl's later space fiction, which pulls few punches about humanity's capacity for punishment, self-deception, and racial stupidity. At least five stories take place in a fictional universe humans share with an alien race they call the Heechee, known only from half-billion-year-old remnants of their high-technology civilization. Heechee artifacts are the reason for being of "The Merchants of Venus" (1972). In the hellish environment contemporary astronomy has revealed to exist on Venus, humans have managed to install a cutthroat society of state capitalism in some long-abandoned Heechee warrens. Not riches per se but "Full Medical" (insurance for every kind of medical procedure up to and including resurrection) is the prize, which finding buried treasure in increasingly scarce, untouched Heechee tunnels is one sure way to win. Although the tale has some predictable turns, its fascination lies in its depiction of the physical and social conditions on Venus and the implied conditions on Earth that would make such a hellhole even slightly attractive.

Gateway (1977) is named for an asteroid that the Heechee hollowed out to use as a base for small spaceships. The latter, still usable, provide humans with access to Heechee-programmed destinations, which remain unknown until they have been reached. Some ships disappear, some pilots are killed, some find something of value, and no one knows in advance which fate will come to pass.

The story concerns Robinette Broadhead, what he found on and beyond Gateway, and why he now tortures himself, despite his riches. In chapters alternating between his memories and his often childish attempts to outwit his psychiatrist, a robot whose Freudian analysis is literally mechanical, interwoven with "sidebars" of information from lectures, mission reports, want ads, and other material, *Gateway* presents a tapestry of events, situations, ideas, and feelings filtered through the neurotic consciousness of Broadhead. In conflict with himself over matters of judgment regarding his sexual fixations and identity, his relative bravery or cowardice, he is the closest of Pohl's gallery of characters to being a "whole person," ironically by not being fully integrated. Having won "Full Medical" and a great deal more simply by surviving contact with a Black Hole that trapped nine others, including his lover, this ambivalent winner is an appropriate match for the Gateway adventure, itself a potent metaphor for an overcrowded, resource-exhausted industrial civilization running down, pinning all its hopes on a cosmic crapshoot.

Beyond the Blue Event Horizon (1980) offers solutions to some of the problems announced by its predecessors, but largely by means of pulling rabbits out of hats, then offering a glimpse of a bigger hat. A human spaceship financed by Broadhead reaches a Heechee "food factory," a device for making food out of cometary particles. A further trip by Heechee ship to another abandoned Heechee base, run by a nonhuman cyborg and descendants of prehistoric man who were plucked from Earth at 50,000-year intervals, results in capture-and-rescue derring-do and the diversion of the Heechee base to an orbit near Earth. Essentially disconnected chapters show the Heechee, unknown to men, using a Black Hole of their own creation, where time moves 40,000 times more slowly than it does for us, to shield them from discovery while they await the outcome of changes set in mo-

tion by themselves and another, still more powerful entity, against whom the Heechee hope the potentially intelligent races they have observed will serve as buffers. Less satisfying as an artistic work, *Beyond the Blue Event Horizon* is only the first of several sequels, each bringing us closer to "understanding" the Heechee: *Heechee Rendezvous* (1984), *The Annals of the Heechee* (1987), and *The Gateway Trip* (1990). By the third novel, Robinette Broadhead has died, but he continues as an active character, thanks to the computer personality storage provided by his genius wife; ironically, he now resembles the robot psychiatrist from the first novel, although he has a much wider repertoire of actions and responses. Another Heechee novel may be in the works.

Gateway won both the Hugo and the Nebula for 1977. *Man Plus* (1976), with an equally unpromising look at the human condition, won a Nebula. Hope is available, within severely circumscribed limits, even to the apparent titular character, astronaut Roger Torraway, who gives up his wife, his sex life, and even his sensory organs to become the first "man" capable of living in the Martian environment. A cyborg, half man, half machine, he is both "man plus" and "man minus." On his mission he is accompanied by more conventional humans living in pressurized housing and by the ubiquitous computer network that narrates the story. This mission is precipitated when cold war tensions are exacerbated by the computer network itself in an effort to ensure the survival of its own consciousness (another implication of the novel's title). Its essentially flat narrative style, emphasizing technical details at the expense of more than skeletal, often sensational, emotional characterization, allows questions about logic, morality, and technological imperatives to stand out in relief, correcting more simplistic stories of the inevitable and relatively painless conquest of space by mankind. Like "Rafferty's Reasons," "We Purchased People," and other stories, *Man Plus* asks how much we can give up and still call ourselves human. Continuing this setting,

Mars Plus (1994, with Thomas T. Thomas) questions the ability of humans, half-humans, and cyborgs to coexist on a planet rendered (possibly) fit for habitation by the first cyborg explorers, especially as the computer problems become more complicated.

Pohl's later writings are serious and uncompromising, yet entertaining and fast-moving, and well above most of what he had written previously. Sex and cruelty, pessimism (albeit with some kind of "happy ending"), and stylistic innovations play a significant role in Pohl's fiction of the 1970's, whether he is domesticating the New Wave or accepting that he and his audience are now mature enough to deal with these elements. *Jem* (1979), incorporating all of these elements, goes a step farther in taking human civilization to the end of its tether. Assuming a technology capable, at great expense, of taking large ships at speeds faster that light to a newly discovered habitable planet in another star system, it arrays three Earth factions—the rich in fuel, the rich in food, and the rich in people—to turn not only against each other but also against the three intelligent native species of the planet Jem, upsetting the balance of nature with a vengeance.

Subversion is the rule, and attempts to avert war are perfunctory, until an unexpected anomaly in the radiation of Jem's sun forces survival by flight and cooperation, resulting centuries later in a restoration of balance that amalgamates the six lifestyles into a human-dominated, slaveholding, exploitative society. Although the various alien species are depicted believably, the schematic breakdown of alliances and betrayals and the caricatures of the human colonists make his novel a bitter satire of the way the three human blocs are competing, rather than cooperating, on Earth today. Its disturbing set of implications and speculations helped win this book an American Book Award for science fiction in 1980, the first and only year that science fiction was a category of that award.

Pohl continues his examination of aggression in *Black Star Rising* (1985). The protagonist, Castor, lives and works on the "Heavenly Grain Collective," in an America dominated by the Han Chinese following a disastrous nuclear war that wiped out all the major powers, leaving China and India as the dominant countries. This history encourages the lobsterlike aliens to "help" the Americans recover their dominance—although the races helped by the "erks" usually don't find it as much of an advantage as they originally expected. Once again, a relatively "normal" young person manages to find a solution to the seemingly impossible situation posed by superior technology combined with the strong nationalistic desire felt by many of the Americans that they should regain their once dominant position on Earth.

Seven of the major episodes in *The Day the Martians Came* (1988) were published as short stories in various science fiction magazines and anthologies, from 1967 to 1987. Here they are gathered, with new material setting the context, in novel form. Since all the episodes turn on the single theme—what difference could knowing some Martians have survived the desolation of their planet make to ordinary (nonscientific) humans?—they hold together very well; and the final episode, "Huddling," provides the ironic ending for which Pohl is justly famous.

In *Outnumbering the Dead* (1991), a novella published in a single volume with illustrations by Steve Crisp, the famous dancer-actor Rafiel faces his own death—in a world that has conquered death for the majority of its human inhabitants. Not only must he come to terms with the inevitable, but those immortals who love him must do so as well; they have no experience of such a loss in their ordinary lives. This brief tale conjures up both the rage of the dying and the distress of those he leaves behind.

Another tale of loss, *Stopping at Slowyear* (1991), a slim novel originally published by Pulphouse, displays Pohl's mastery of characterization in a different way. Mercy Mac-Donald, purser on a decrepit spaceship trading among the various planets settled by humans (and now seriously out of date), seems at first to be the character with whom readers will most closely identify. She fights off boredom and the attentions of the upstart Deputy Captain Hans Horeger with roughly equal success. Then the ship, desperate for fuel and trade, stops at the oddball planet called Slowyear. This planet takes nineteen terrestrial years to circle its sun. For nearly five of those years, humans must hide underground from the bitter winters; for another five, they retreat from torrid summers. But that is not the only problem the inhabitants of Slowyear must face. As the story shifts from Mac-Donald's problems to those of Blundy, a poet-politician-sheepherder on Slowyear and his wife, Murra, each sketched with a distinctive personality, each both likeable and unpleasant in understandable ways, the reader's allegiance shifts as well. When the inevitable occurs, and the *Nordvik* comes to its destined end, the reader has come to grips with it. Not a tragedy, *Stopping at Slowyear*, unlike *Outnumbering the Dead*, is a tale of human endurance.

Stylistically, the most inventive works Pohl has yet created are "Day Million" and *Gateway:* "Day Million" for its brilliance and brevity, *Gateway* for its combination of modernist technique with scientific tropes. Most of his other works make clever alterations or additions to otherwise standard science fiction themes. In *The World at the End of Time* (1990), for example, he recalls concepts first posed by Olaf Stapledon in *Star Maker* (1937). He counterpoises "Wan-To," inhabiting the core of a star, capable of creating others like himself (and then warring against them), with the human expedition traveling in cryogenic stasis to another star system. Viktor Sorricaine, a child on the *New Mayflower*, experiences the results of this alien battle as Wan-To drives their star into empty space out of fear of his own creations. The story covers thousands of years (cryogenically), recasting and expanding the theme Pohl examined in *The Age of the Pussyfoot.*

Having explored varieties of aliens in a number of novels, Pohl continues to invent—one might almost say exploit—them. His aliens are without exception fully imagined, radically suited to their various environments, and wholly alien to humans without becoming impossible to imagine. A race of "helpful" but infinitely warlike "buggy monsters no bigger than cats" attempts to invest the Earth in *Black Star Rising;* in the Eschaton series—*The Other End of Time* (1996) and *The Siege of Eternity* (1997), with at least one more novel in the works—two species of aliens battle each other for command of the "Big Crunch" (the other side of the "Big Bang"), which will end the universe as we know it and usher in the Last Days, when the dead shall rise, all of them. As so often happens in Pohl's works, a motley crew of ordinary humans, unprepared and unwarned, finds themselves thrust into the breach.

Dan Dannerman, agent and relative of Dr. Patricia Dannerman Bly Metcalf Adcock, director of the astronomical group that owns a once active orbiting observatory, is sent to spy on her recent activities, which seem to predict a return to space. True to Pohl's estimate of the behavior of secret agencies, Dannerman is told what to do but not why; he is therefore quite unprepared (as are the others in the crew) for the evidence of alien investment when they reach the lab. But the aliens have not left; they are both very present and very persuasive, as well as secretive. They are capable of sending living creatures through space instantaneously, or (more accurately, perhaps) reconstituting them on the other side of space. This, of course, leaves more than one copy of each person. In the first book, the crew that first meets the aliens on the long-abandoned orbital observatory get duplicated, so those who escape to return to Earth are shocked to find that "they" had already returned, claiming to have found nothing out of the ordinary in the observatory instead of the masses of alien machinery the escapees describe. In the second book, the first returnees are found to be clandestine spies for the "Beloved Leaders" while others have been captured by the "Horch."

Like his earlier theme of alien possession, the doppelgänger theme, the problem of meeting "oneself" as "another," seems to fascinate

Pohl. In *The Siege of Eternity*, several of the characters find themselves duplicated, with ensuing complications. For example, Dr. Patricia Adcock has to devise ways of differentiating, as well as managing, the three (or four) copies of herself that wind up on Earth. In *The Coming of the Quantum Cats* (1986), the problem addresses the readers, who must differentiate the quantum-separated worlds by the characters and society they find therein: Senator Dominic DeSota, Nicky DeSota, Major DESOTA, Dominc R., and Dr. Dominic DeSota-Arbenz; each has particular relationships with Mrs. Nyla Christophe Bowquist, Agent Nyla Christophe, and so on. Pohl takes the familiar trope of an infinite number of "Earths" split off at every juncture of history, suddenly made accessible through advances in quantum physics. Not only does he then explore the familiar plot of "the great invention used for war" but also the impact on ordinary humans suddenly meeting not one but many doppelgängers—"themselves" in alternate universes, who have had different opportunities and taken very different paths in life. Pohl thus questions not only how humans become the persons they are but also the morality of the cultures in which they do so.

Pohl also explores a number of formats for the telling of his stories, some of them borrowed from the earliest days of science fiction, but he always makes them seem refreshingly new. In *The Voices of Heaven* (1994), Barry di Hoa, ships' fuelmaster on the moon, used to handling antimatter safely, is literally shanghaied to Pava. This world, minimally colonized by Earth, is now in real danger of being abandoned by the very government that initially financed the venture. Humans found sentient creatures on Pava when they arrived, and a very good thing it was; from their third to their fifth instar, the insectlike Leps learn to speak English, happily haul loads, and generally help the humans in their efforts to build their colony and farm their fields. But Pava is also tectonically unstable, and the frequent earthquakes not only destroy much of the humans' work, but they initiate the webs of misunderstanding that eventually divide the species—apparently for good. Di Hoa must understand what has upset the previous working arrangement between the colonizing humans and the native aliens. He knows that one colonist has struck a "Lep" and that the "Leps" now refuse to associate with the colonists. The colony, already struggling, finds itself in desperate straits. Complications from the variety of religions that grip the colonists—and the way at least one of them causes them to view the final instar of the "Leps"—adds to the crisis. Although the novel seems to approve of colonization, the ending, as so often with Pohl, rewrites the entire scenario. Pohl takes a major risk in the narrative style of this novel; it reads much like an old-fashioned epistolary novel because the only characters actually speaking are di Hoa and the Lep called "Merlin," interspersed with di Hoa's memories—which he may or may not narrate to the Leps. In this novel, however, Pohl again explores one of his most serious topics: How can two unrelated species learn to get along peacefully without coercion on either side? Through this exploration, he also shows how beliefs can mislead and divide people, even while he suggests that humans, no matter how different their cultures, could also learn to accommodate each other peacefully.

O Pioneer! (1998)—a title ironically reminiscent of Willa Cather's novel of the exploration of the Great Plains (also inhabited, although the settlers arriving there expected the army to have dealt with the "marauding Indians")—sends Evesham Giyt through an instantaneous matter transmitter to Tupelo, the Peace Planet, already occupied by five alien races. With his wife, Rina, an intelligent lady with a past, he soon becomes unexpectedly important in the small but growing human community; he gets elected mayor. This means that he must negotiate with the other races whatever problems affect them all, to maintain the relations among them. He soon learns that the Peace Planet has been occupied by aliens who have experienced devastating war and who want no more of it, unlike humans who have experienced plenty of war and see no reason to avoid it if they think they can get some advantage from it. Here Pohl's humor shows through, as Rina, who knows how to listen to her neighbors, frequently sets her husband straight on the issues involved. And involved they become, as Giyt gradually realizes that he has been selected as mayor because he looks like an easy mark. But Giyt has just as much reason to avoid war as do the aliens, a point some of the humans fail to appreciate. While the settlers of the Great Plains felt reasonably safe from Indians and had only weather and isolation to combat, the settlers of Pava are technologically blessed. They face their greatest danger in the machinations of their clandestine leaders and the complexities of the political process.

In this novel, Pohl has returned to the "comic inferno" style of his earlier works. Giyt must struggle to understand what is really going on while coping with the disinformation campaigns of his opponents and the cultural norms of his alien neighbors. The book is a romp, with a serious theme: What does it take to preserve true freedom? But Pohl also has served notice that he has many and varied tunes to play on his computer. The "Eschaton" story is certainly not yet completed—*The Siege of Eternity* obviously stands as a middle book in a series—and this may prove the culmination of his ongoing investigation of human religions in alien garb.

Selected Bibliography

WORKS OF FREDERIK POHL

The Space Merchants, with C. M. Kornbluth. New York: Ballantine, 1953; London: Heinemann, 1955. Revised edition, New York: St. Martin's, 1985.

Search the Sky, with C. M. Kornbluth. New York: Ballantine, 1954; London: Digit, 1960. Revised edition, New York: Baen, 1986.

Undersea Quest, with Jack Williamson. New York: Ballantine, 1954; London: Dobson, 1966.

Gladiator-at-Law, with C. M. Kornbluth. New York: Ballantine, 1955; London: Digit, 1958. Revised edition, New York: St. Martin's, 1985.

Preferred Risk, with Lester del Rey, as by Edson McCann. New York: Simon and Schuster, 1955; New York: Bantam, 1980; London: Methuen, 1983. (Originally published in *Galaxy*, 1955.)

Alternating Currents. New York: Ballantine, 1956; London, Penguin, 1966. (Short stories.)

Undersea Fleet, with Jack Williamson. New York: Ballantine, 1956; London: Dobson, 1968.

The Case Against Tomorrow. New York: Ballantine, 1957. (Short stories.)

Undersea City, with Jack Williamson. Hicksville, N.Y.: Gnome, 1958; London: Dobson, 1968.

Tomorrow Times Seven. New York: Ballantine, 1959. (Short stories.)

Wolfbane, with C. M. Kornbluth. New York: Ballantine, 1959; London: Gollancz, 1960. Revised edition by Frederik Pohl, New York: Baen, 1986; London: Gollancz, 1986.

Drunkard's Walk. New York: Ballantine, 1960. Revised edition, London: Gollancz, 1961.

The Man Who Ate the World. New York: Ballantine, 1960; London, Panther, 1979. (Short stories.)

Turn Left at Thursday. New York: Ballantine, 1961. (Three novelettes and three short stories)

The Abominable Earthman. New York: Ballantine, 1963. (Short stories.)

Reefs of Space, with Jack Williamson. New York: Ballantine, 1963; London: Dobson, 1964.

A Plague of Pythons. New York: Ballantine, 1965; London: Gollancz, 1966. Revised as *Demon in the Skull*, New York: DAW, 1984.

The Age of the Pussyfoot. New York: Trident, 1969; London: Gollancz, 1970.

Starchild, with Jack Williamson. New York: Ballantine, 1965; London: Dobson, 1966.

Rogue Star, with Jack Williamson. New York: Ballantine, 1969; London: Dobson, 1972.

Day Million. New York: Ballantine, 1970; London: Gollancz, 1971. (Short stories.)

The Gold at the Starbow's End. New York: Ballantine, 1972; London: Gollancz, 1973. (Short stories.)

The Best of Frederik Pohl. Edited by Lester del Rey. New York: Ballantine, 1975; Garden City, N.Y.: Doubleday, 1975; London: Sidgwick and Jackson, 1977. (Short stories.)

Farthest Star, with Jack Williamson. New York: Ballantine, 1975; London: Pan, 1976.

"Ragged Claws." In *Hell's Cartographers, Some Personal Histories of Science Fiction Writers*. Edited by Brian W. Aldiss and Harry Harrison. London: Weidenfeld and Nicolson, 1975. (Autobiographical article.)

The Early Pohl. Garden City, NY: Doubleday, 1976; London: Dobson, 1980. (Short stories.)

In the Problem Pit. New York: Bantam, 1976; London: Corgi, 1976. (Short stories.)

Man Plus. New York: Random House, 1976; London: Gollancz, 1976.

Critical Mass, with C. M. Kornbluth. New York: Bantam, 1977.

Gateway. New York: St. Martin's, 1977; London: Gollancz, 1977.

The Way the Future Was. New York: Ballantine, 1978. (Memoir.)

Jem. New York: St. Martin's, 1979; London: Gollancz, 1979.

Before the Universe, with C. M. Kornbluth. New York: Bantam, 1980.

Beyond the Blue Event Horizon. New York: Ballantine, 1980; London: Gollancz, 1980.

The Cool War. New York: Ballantine, 1981; London: Gollancz, 1981.

Planets Three. New York: Berkley, 1982. (Three short novels.)

Starburst. New York: Ballantine, 1982; London: Gollancz, 1982.

Syzygy. New York: Bantam, 1982.

Midas World. New York: St. Martin's, 1983; London: Gollancz, 1983. (Short stories.)

Heechee Rendezvous. New York: Ballantine, 1984; London: Gollancz, 1984.

The Merchants' War. New York: St. Martin's, 1984; London, Gollancz, 1985.

Pohlstars. New York: Ballantine, 1984. Abridged edition, London: Gollancz, 1986. (Short stories.)

The Years of the City. New York: Timescape Pocket Books, 1984; London: Gollancz, 1985.

Black Star Rising. New York: Ballantine, 1985; London: Gollancz, 1986.

The Coming of the Quantum Cats. New York: Bantam, 1986; London: Gollancz, 1987.

Tales from the Planet Earth: A Novel with Nineteen Authors. Edited with Elizabeth Anne Hall. New York: St. Martin's, 1986.

Terror. New York: Berkley, 1986.

The Annals of the Heechee. New York: Ballantine, 1987; London: Gollancz, 1987.

Chernobyl: A Novel. New York and London: Bantam, 1987. (Not science fiction.)

The Day the Martians Came. New York: St. Martin's, 1988; London: Grafton, 1990.

Land's End, with Jack Williamson. New York: TOR, 1988.

Narabedla Ltd. New York: Ballantine, 1988; London; Gollancz, 1990.

Homegoing. New York: Ballantine, 1989; London: Gollancz, 1990.

The Gateway Trip: Tales and Vignettes of the Heechee. New York: Ballantine, 1990. (Short stories.)

The World at the End of Time. New York: Ballantine, 1990; London, HarperCollins, 1992.

Outnumbering the Dead. London: Legend, 1991; New York: St. Martin's, 1992. (With illustrations by Steve Crisp.)

The Singers of Time, with Jack Williamson. Garden City, N.Y.: Doubleday, 1991.

Stopping at Slowyear. New York: Bantam, 1991.

Mars Plus, with Thomas T. Thomas. New York: Baen, 1994.

The Voices of Heaven. New York: Tor, 1994.

The Other End of Time. New York: Tor, 1996.

The Siege of Eternity. New York: Tor, 1997.

O Pioneer! New York: Tor, 1998.

CRITICAL AND BIOGRAPHICAL STUDIES

Amis, Kingsley. *New Maps of Hell: A Survey of Science Fiction*. New York: Harcourt, Brace and World, 1960.

Bartter, Martha A. "Times and Spaces: Exploring *Gateway*." *Extrapolation*, 23 (Summer 1982): 189–199.

del Rey, Lester. "Frederik Pohl: Frontiersman." *Magazine of Fantasy and Science Fiction*, 45 (September 1973): 55–64.

Erlich, Richard D. "Odysseus in Grey Flannel: The Heroic Journeys in Two Dystopias by Pohl and Kornbluth." *Par Rapport*, 1 (1978): 126–137.

I-Con Science Fiction Convention Guest Information: Accessed 27 October 1998.

Pederson, Jay P., ed. *St. James Guide to Science Fiction Writers*, 4th ed. New York: St. James, 1996.

Samuelson, David N. "Critical Mass: The Science Fiction of Frederik Pohl." *Science-Fiction Studies*, 7 (March 1980): 80–95.

—DAVID N. SAMUELSON
—MARTHA A. BARTTER (Revision and update)

CHRISTOPHER PRIEST
(b. 1943)

CHRISTOPHER PRIEST BEGAN to publish science fiction during the creative excitement and controversy of the 1960's New Wave associated with Britain's *New Worlds* magazine when it was edited by Michael Moorcock. Although Priest was never part of the inner clique and rapidly escaped the snare of self-indulgent obscurantism that so often accompanied New Wave assaults on genre conventions, his work still maintains its distance from science fiction orthodoxy. He examines well-worn genre tropes—gigantic objects, prediction, immortality, invisibility, matter transmission—with a cold eye and injects a highly individual brand of subversion. This has led to his fiction being classed as "slipstream," operating near the edge of the genre, or just beyond, or within the uncertain, fuzzy space of the actual boundaries.

Christopher McKenzie Priest was born in Cheadle, Cheshire, England, on 14 July 1943. He was educated at the incongruously named Manchester Warehousemen, Clerks' Orphan School. After working in accountancy and on the fringes of publishing from 1959 to 1968, he then became a full-time author. His adult life has been spent in southern England, including years in Harrow on the outskirts of London. His second and third marriages were to fellow writers: Lisa Tuttle from 1981 to 1987, and Leigh Kennedy since 1988. He now lives in Hastings, Sussex, England, with Kennedy and their twin children.

A thoroughly professional author, Priest has engaged in the usual related activities: working on committees of Britain's Society of Authors, acting as an editor for *Foundation: The Review of Science Fiction*, being a 1970's and 1980's stalwart of the Milford (UK) Science Fiction Writers' Conference, editing two science fiction anthologies, reviewing for national newspapers, and running a small, specialist literary agency. Like many science fiction writers, he has been honored as a guest at conventions and has produced occasional fanzines. His polemical fanzine essay about Harlan Ellison's endlessly delayed anthology *The Last Dangerous Visions*—announced in 1971, repeatedly publicized, still unpublished—was reissued with revisions as *The Book on the Edge of Forever* (1994) and was nominated for the Hugo award for best non-fiction, and missed winning by only four votes. He was selected as one of Britain's leading under forty "mainstream" writers for the Book Marketing Council's 1983 "Best of Young British Novelists" promotion.

Priest's first published science fiction story was the brief and melodramatic "The Run" (1966), which appeared in *New Worlds'* sister magazine *Impulse*. This is one of ten early pieces collected in *Real-Time World* (1974), most of them relatively minor works characterized by intense examination of characters under stress. "The Head and the Hand" (*New Worlds Quarterly*, 3, 1972) is a prophetic piece of Grand Guignol about a performance artist who publicly amputates parts of himself; "A Woman Naked" (*Science Fiction Monthly*, 1974) painfully depicts a woman's seemingly cruel and unusual punishment for sexual "crime," shifting perspective to show this as

617

metaphor for a cruel and all too usual actuality. The tricky reality blurring of later Priest is foreshadowed in "Real-Time World" (*New Writings in SF*, 19, 1971), whose experimental community is isolated from real-world news and develops its own replacement network of rumors. These escalate toward purest fantasy and then—like a wild computer iteration converging to a stable solution—settle down and begin to anticipate reality.

Two surreal stories of nightmarish, vaguely Kafkaesque imprisonment—"The Interrogator" (*New Writings in SF*, 15, 1969) and "The Maze," which achieved the difficult feat of being rejected by *New Worlds* for excessive obscurity—were reworked and extended into Priest's first novel, *Indoctrinaire* (1970). Although its Brazilian setting lacks much sense of place, this work features effectively enigmatic images and devices. An animated hand grows from a table and a monstrous ear from a wall; a dilapidated shack conceals a topologically sophisticated labyrinth; and there are other odd tools of psychological disorientation.

The book's more conventional science fiction machinery involves time slips across 200 years, an offstage nuclear war, and psychotropic "disturbance gas," which retrospectively explains the alarming, irrational mood shifts of the protagonist Wentik's tormentors. It concludes on a note of unambiguous, very British, pessimism and loss. In the slightly revised 1979 edition, Priest noted that he had perhaps overdone the clarifications and explained away too many of the enigmas that give the early parts of *Indoctrinaire* their uneasy power. He now classifies the book as juvenilia.

The essential story line of *Fugue for a Darkening Island* (1972) is also bleak, without surreal frills. Nuclear war in Africa leads to the swamping of other countries, notably Britain, with floods of black refugees. These refugees are first the catalyst of conflict between a right-wing, racist British government and dissident liberals and then become a third faction in the ensuing civil war. In this period of terror, the protagonist's wife and daughter are abducted, and (like Wentik later in *Indoctrinaire*) he hopelessly seeks his family.

This might have resembled a darker, chillier version of some John Wyndham disaster novel but for Priest's narrative technique. The scenes are shuffled, told out of order; the story is not so much distanced as brought uncomfortably close by the reader's complicity in piecing together the jigsaw puzzle. (It is perhaps a last gesture to New Wave obscurity that, as the author has remarked, one piece is deliberately designed not to fit.) Narrative interleavings and juxtapositions play on musical connotations of the title's "fugue." Its psychological meaning, a dreamlike state often followed by loss of memory, underpins the narrator's nightmare flight through a disintegrating England, his futile efforts to remain politically uncommitted, and a possible unreliability in what he chooses to remember.

Priest's breakthrough book and also his closest approach to conventional "hard" science fiction was his third novel, *Inverted World* (1974). A trial exploration of its extraordinary setting had appeared as "The Inverted World" (*New Writings in SF*, 22, 1973), causing one reviewer to speculate that Priest was "Britain's answer to Larry Niven" (Tony Sudbury, *Vector*, 67/68, 1974). The short story excuses its impossibilities with scientific double-talk; the novel refuses such Nivenesque literalism by reconsidering matters in terms of metaphor and perception.

The inverted world is a hyperboloid, the surface traced out when a hyperbola is rotated about the vertical axis. Its poles are infinite spires, its equator is (or rather, asymptotically approaches) an infinite plane. In the concavely curved region between, there is only a narrow habitable band. Distortions of space and time, like those of relativity, increase toward the equator and poles. In one memorable scene the hero—having strayed too far—finds himself clinging for dear life to a fingerhold that from farther away was a mountain range. The land itself slowly migrates "southward," reeled in by the terrible pull of infinity, and the humans stranded in this impossible cosmos must therefore keep their wheeled city

Christopher Priest. © Beth Gwinn

forever moving (as in *Alice in Wonderland*) to stay in the same place. Hence the protagonist Helward's fine opening line: "I had reached the age of six hundred and fifty miles."

Rigid guilds of Future Surveying, Bridge-Building, Track-Laying, and Traction are dedicated to maintaining the city's slow movement along perpetually relaid rails towards an "optimum" point that keeps moving ahead. Why is the direction of the optimum known as "up future," and behind the city "down past"? Why do the laws of physics operate differently for the inverted world's human-seeming natives, who for some reason speak Spanish?

Helward's southward journey of discovery and initiation into the nature of his world is one of the high points of science fiction strangeness and exhilarating "conceptual breakthrough," where paradigms shatter and a new reality shines through. Priest then trumps this with a second shock (incidentally

finessing the problem that, mathematically, the hyperboloid world must intersect its own hyperboloid sun) by introducing the viewpoint of a woman from "outside," from the real Earth—which is the inverted world itself, differently perceived. Looking into the same sky, Helward sees a hyperboloid and the newcomer a round sun. To her, the city's epic two-hundred year crawl to stay "north" of the regions where its world's centrifugal force becomes deadly has merely taken it along a great-circle route through an Asia and Europe made primitive by the collapse of technological civilization, until at the book's crisis the community has reached the Portuguese shore and its Bridge-Builders are confronted with the Atlantic.

From the woman's commonsense standpoint, the inversion is perceptual distortion caused by an experimental "translateration" generator that powers the traveling city. Yet when the generator is finally turned off, a third shock awaits, for even without the imposed distortion Helward is unable to perceive the sun as other than hyperboloid in shape. Priest has several times revisited these entwined problems of perception and reality. *Inverted World* was widely praised and won the British Science Fiction Association Award.

Next came a genial Wellsian romp, *The Space Machine: A Scientific Romance* (1976), replete with chapter titles such as "Sir William Expounds a Theory," "Into Futurity!" and "How We Fell in with the Philosopher." This exercise in pastiche assumes that H. G. Wells's classics *The Time Machine* (1895) and *The War of the Worlds* (1898) were both reporting fragments of the same history. Priest duly traces the connections, thickening the mixture with the late introduction of H. G. Wells—or a version of him—as a character in his own fictional creation. The result, though perhaps overly long, is engaging.

Because time and space are interrelated, the Time Machine can function as a Space Machine, and in this capacity it transports the protagonist and his lady friend to Mars—a Wellsian Mars infested with red weed, where humanlike natives are enslaved by the familiar tentacular monsters who drink their blood. The invasion of Earth is in preparation, with ships fired as projectiles from a steam cannon a mile long. Inevitably our young lovers return home by this route and, having constructed a new Space Machine with Wells's help, fly around as "an Invisible Nemesis" to harass the invaders with grenades. Meanwhile, more effectively at work is the true invisible nemesis: Earth's bacteria, exactly as in *The War of the Worlds*.

All ends well in what is still this author's sunniest novel. Here Wells is a reporter rather than a creator, but one who seems prepared to edit the real story and increase his book's plausibility by removing that too fantastic trip to Mars. At the close, Wells looks through his notebook, tears out and discards some pages, and tells the hero with a twinkle in his eye: "It would not be right to dismiss your account as total fabrication, but you would be hard put to substantiate what you told me." He adds: "We all have our tales to tell, Mr. Turnbull."

It is characteristic of Priest to hint at a rewrite that subverts "reality" (his own fiction) into a different fiction (Wells's). He has described his reaction to childhood difficulties, such as bullying, as being to back away and mentally rewrite the story of what happened, to distance and fictionalize the reality. This theme echoes through several later works. Meanwhile, *The Space Machine* won Australia's Ditmar Award in 1977 for best international science fiction.

A Dream of Wessex (1977) has been called the novel that predicted virtual reality, but its premise is stranger and subtler than the mere entering of a computer simulation. A think tank called the Wessex Foundation is studying a possible future 150 years onward, which by means of a mind-linking device called the Ridpath projector is dramatized as a shared hallucination. Participants, including the protagonist, Julia, enter the scenario and play their parts in earnest, leaving behind the contamination of twentieth-century memories.

The extrapolated future is dystopian in outline, with Britain divided between Soviet political power and Arab commercial influence and also literally split because geological activity has severed the southwest—Wessex—from a reduced mainland. Yet from inside, Wessex is curiously idyllic. Both the Dorset landscape and the participants' roles are shaped by unconscious urges. Indicating the attractions of the pathetic fallacy, "the climate was either dramatically good or dramatically bad." It is not mere wish fulfillment, though: Julia, emotionally scarred, is provided by this consensus reality with a lover—an unreal projection rather than a participant—who is distinctly unsatisfactory.

The scars date back to her involvement with Priest's first truly hateful character, Paul Mason, alpha-male predator and ruthless manipulator. When Mason follows Julia to the Wessex Foundation and adds his own chilly arrogance to the shared projection, the psychic terrain rapidly worsens. Drilling rigs and refineries pollute the former seaside paradise, under a dull and leaden sky. These are incidental side effects: Mason's appalling self-confidence (verging on solipsism) installs him as leader of the Wessex dreamers, and he grandiosely plans a secondary Ridpath projector experiment from within the first. This will reimagine the twentieth century, or *a* twentieth century, from the Wessex viewpoint. To enter this projection may be to return to reality—or may be a second step away from base reality, into treacherous metaphysical territory.

A Dream of Wessex contains many scenes of effective existential worry, as when another character recalls having sex with Julia—as indeed she had intended, only to be temporarily removed from the scenario because of an emergency. Thus the encounter is remembered rather than actual, featuring not the "real" Julia but an imagined consensus Julia supplied to maintain continuity in this shared dream. The resulting sense of wrongness provides a deeply uneasy moment.

Priest has called this novel his farewell to traditional science fiction, a subversive and almost satirical examination of how writers try to imagine the future. The Ridpath projector is more metaphor than gadget, and there is a distinct whiff of stage magic in the way Wessex players are routinely extracted from their scenario by a trick with mirrors. One criticism is that most of the characters seem a little flat, with even Julia overshadowed by Mason's vivid nastiness.

Echoes of Wessex and a fragmented England appear in the islands of Priest's short "Dream Archipelago" stories, whose elusive landscapes carry a symbolic charge. They are not so much places as states of mind. Some of these tales are collected in *An Infinite Summer* (1979—notably, "The Watched" (*F&SF*, 1978), a haunting, understatedly menacing study of voyeurism and complicity. The non-Archipelago "Palely Loitering" (*F&SF*, 1979), in which romantic longings are exhilaratingly complicated by an unusual form of time travel, won the British Science Fiction Association Award for best short fiction in 1980.

A new collection, *The Dream Archipelago* (1999), assembles all the Archipelago stories in revised form with new introductory material. This adds the previously uncollected "The Miraculous Cairn" (*New Terrors*, 2, 1980)—dealing powerfully with youthful sexual trauma and its recollection in monstrously symbolic form—and "The Cremation" (*Andromeda*, 3, 1978), a more conventionally sinister counterpoint of desire and horror.

The Dream Archipelago is and is not the setting of *The Affirmation* (1981), which is initially narrated by an ordinary seeming man called Peter Sinclair. He issues a fair warning on the first page—"words are only as valid as the mind that chooses them, so that of essence all prose is a form of deception"—and soon reinforces this with a reflection on memory: "The mind erases backwards, re-creating what one remembers."

Peter's life work is self-deceit, and he deceives us too. Early in *The Affirmation*, a clash of viewpoints with his visiting sister reveals that his own bland record of events so far contains a shocking, central lie. He calls it a higher truth and carries the principle further by beginning a new "autobiography" that will in some sense be truer than mundane facts. This tells the story of another Peter Sinclair in the world of the Dream Archipelago, who is one of a lucky few lottery winners offered the rare gift of immortality—an "athanasia" treatment that protects indefinitely against age and death from natural causes. Unfortunately, the treatment causes a fugue state and total amnesia so that the patient will need to relearn his life. Therefore, Peter must write an autobiography as his legacy to himself, and has already done so, defining himself through a fictionalized, metaphoric story that he believes to be in some sense truer than mundane facts.

Just as the first Peter has distanced his own life by changing Manchester and London to "Jethra" and renaming the woman with whom he has had a disastrous relationship from Gracia to Seri, so the Dream Archipelago Peter disguises *his* problems by referring to

London rather than Jethra, Gracia rather than Seri. Like the reflection of a reflection of reality in *A Dream of Wessex*, this tangle suggests the M. C. Escher lithograph in which two hands are busily drawing each other—or the ancient dilemma of the Chinese philosopher Chuang-Tse, who dreamed of being a butterfly and afterward was unsure whether he might not be a butterfly dreaming he was a man.

There are further complications. Another of Peter's unveiled self-deceptions is, apparently, the claim that he has typed out his story at all; to Gracia, it's all blank pages. Yet here is his book, breaking off at the same unfinished sentence where Peter was interrupted early in the text, and we are reading it. The story turns in on itself and in a sense becomes its own sequel. Its portrayal of dislocated reality and the quicksand borders of madness is profoundly disturbing. Great narrative power is generated by the tension between "true" and "false" narrations and repeated shocks of uncertainty about which is which. *The Affirmation* is one of Priest's finest novels and like *The Space Machine* won the Ditmar Award.

Just as *The Affirmation* made play with the science fiction theme of immortality—only to stray into altogether different territory—*The Glamour* (1984) engages on one level with invisibility. This is not the physical invisibility of H. G. Wells's novel *The Invisible Man* (1897) but something more akin to the psychological version in G. K. Chesterton's identically named detective story. Rather than with people and things that cannot be seen, Priest concerns himself with those that escape our attention. "Invisible people were *there*, they could be *seen*, but unless you knew how to see they would not be *noticed*."

Again, matters of memory and perception are fused. The apparent hero, Richard Grey, is a professional news cameraman, accustomed to editing film and shaping filmed memories of the past: irrelevancies and inconsistencies that have been cut become "invisible." Now Richard's own memory has been brutally edited, since injuries caused by a terrorist car bomb have blanked out part of the record and left him amnesiac. An attempt at medical hypnosis (containing a discontinuity that is not illuminated until much later) reminds us of a standard effect in the repertoire of hypnotic suggestion. Here "induced negative hallucination" conjures up a subjective cloak of invisibility, so that Richard is temporarily unable to perceive someone sitting in plain sight in the same room.

A long flashback then seems to reveal the erased period of Richard's life, but this is subsequently contradicted. For example, much of it concerns an intended trip to the south of France that never happened. We realize that Richard, or Priest, has constructed a tour de force of paramnesiac recollection, partly false memories evoked by the attempt at hypnosis. Much of this is woven around hints dropped during a hospital visit by Sue Kewley, with whom Richard has evidently had an affair during the lost time. She mentions postcards, and Richard sends a significant postcard; she indicates that someone called Niall was a problem in their relationship, and a plausible triangle is duly outlined; she asks if he remembers an unexplained "cloud," and an unusual, ominous cloud blots out the sun. With the fantastic irrelevancy of dreams, an artist found painting in a French village seems to be Picasso.

But there is input from genuine buried memories too. Richard's version of the affair resonates all too closely with Sue's later account of how it all happened in England, and we guess that the transposition to France has been suggested by the fact that Richard's rival Niall—whom he never sees—claims for a time to be away in France, from where he sends or appears to send that same postcard. Although Richard's memory of a strange cloud in the French sky proves to be a mistake, the literalization of a metaphor, it nevertheless causes him to think at once of Niall.

At the science fiction level, in the interpretation of *The Glamour*'s enigmas that is urged by Sue, she and Richard and Niall are linked by possession of the glamour—the psychic talent or affliction of invisibility. The cloud is a cloud of unknowing, the fog of unnoticeability that sometimes controllably, sometimes permanently, conceals those who are "glamorous." Sue relates her attempts to escape London's dismal community of unnoticeable street people who live by shoplifting, walking into stores and unseeably filling their sacks. Richard, she explains, makes unconscious professional use of the talent, distancing himself through the camera's viewfinder to film gunmen or terrorists at close quarters, unnoticed. The unpleasant and arrogant Niall is so deep in glamour that only Sue can ever see him. (Now remembering how Richard has observed Sue apparently arguing violently with herself in the street, we understand the presence of the unseen rival—but also recall Peter Sinclair of *The Affirmation*, conversing with his fictional Seri in a London café and being politely asked to leave.)

While our understanding remains at this stage, there are disquieting episodes in which Sue and Richard go on holiday to escape Niall—only for there to emerge the slow realization that he is accompanying them at every stage, an invisible presence in the backseat of the car, watching and in one horrifying scene participating in their sexual encounters. As in some pact with the devil, Niall is very literal about his promise to Sue that "you won't be seeing me again for a while."

In the disorienting conclusion, the tricky complications and reassessments of *The Glamour* are further undermined by a sideslip into metafiction, distantly reminiscent of John Fowles's auctorial intervention in *The French Lieutenant's Woman* (1969). Niall, long referred to as an aspiring writer, seems to have written down an earlier sequence of Richard's story before it happened. He implies that he is invisible because he exists on a different level from the others, that he is the author of the book, the "I" of the brief opening segment (whom we have assumed to be Richard). Finally, he allows Richard an escape from the nightmare, in words that once again return to the central metaphor. "Everything will probably be much tidier, your body will heal, matters will improve. I doubt you will ever know why. You will forget, induce a negative hallucination. You are no stranger to doing that because for you forgetting is a way of failing to see."

The mesmeric power of *The Glamour* arises from a deepening sense of wrongness in successive, clashing versions of what is seen and what is remembered. Priest himself became almost obsessively involved with the book, revising it several times before reaching the final text of 1996. In 1988 it won the Kurd Lasswitz Award, Germany's equivalent of the Nebula award.

In keeping with its self-effacing title, *The Quiet Woman* (1990) is a quieter novel, although it contains some laceratingly deadpan satire on policies of the European Union and of the British government under Margaret Thatcher.

The setting is the near future. There has been a nuclear accident in France, and a plume of fallout has contaminated parts of south-central England. The coastal towns of Portsmouth and Southampton have been evacuated. Exactly how great the danger might be farther north at the protagonist's home in Wiltshire (where Priest lived through much of the book's writing) is uncertain. The muffling fog of instinctive government cover-ups lies over England as pervasively as the remnants of radioactive dust, invisible, easily forgotten, perniciously unhealthy.

The heroine, Alice Stockton, is a writer who has unknowingly stepped into booby-trapped territory. Her latest work, an innocuous collection of biographical studies called *Six Women*, is impounded by the Home Office for unstated political reasons, and she is required to destroy all her copies. Meanwhile, her elderly friend Eleanor Hamilton is murdered, with a hint that her Campaign for National Disarmament activism may be the reason. The link between these seemingly unrelated events is Eleanor's son, a highly placed "information contractor" whose company (in keeping with Thatcherite policies of outsourcing government functions) proves to be effectively running Britain's internal intelligence and disinformation services.

This son, Gordon Sinclair (a surname from Eleanor's first marriage), sometimes calls himself Peter Hamilton. If there is an allusion to Peter Sinclair of *The Affirmation*, it merely confirms that this unpleasant man's segments of the narrative should be distrusted. He sees gigantic alien cylinders grinding crop-circle patterns into the Wiltshire cornfields, hallucinates a nuclear-armed stealth bomber crashing close by as his mother is buried, recalls his father's and nine-year-old brother's deaths in an impossibly extravagant fairground calamity, and replays unexceptional interviews with Alice as grossly sadomasochistic fantasies. He is mad, bad, and dangerous to know.

In other parts of the narrative, Priest shows an unusual playfulness. When Sinclair, misusing his power to change national security databases, deletes a visiting friend of Alice's, this friend abruptly vanishes from the story. The best joke satirizes the European Community's subsidy system, whose support of farmers by "intervention buying" of crops is here extended to writers. Literary effort is rewarded on a sliding scale based on page count and past performance, and the work is dumped into the public domain.

Alice learns that her book was suppressed not for any serious reason but for touching on a trivial state embarrassment, one of the *Six Women* being "the unmarried companion of Sir Percival Arnold-Smythe" (a diplomat). Sinclair gets his deserved comeuppance, but not before lengthily and vindictively telling Alice the "judgement of the assessors" on her work:

> It's too long for its subject matter. The depiction of the characters is sketchy, and only the most shallow of motives are attributed to them to explain their actions. Your storytelling ability is not strong. . . . Parts of the story appear to have been left out. There are implausible coincidences. You seem anxious to explain many things, but the reader is left unsatisfied. . . . At the end of the book there is a feeling of dissatisfaction, a sense that the book has been leading nowhere, that it is an artificial construct with no adequate purpose.

Besides blackly summing up the emotions with which almost every author regards a just-completed work, this seems to have an intentional ironic application to *The Quiet Woman* itself. Although it is a novel containing several good senses and ideas, it seems deficient in that compulsive fascination of slowly unveiled secrets and complexities that characterizes Priest at his best.

He is assuredly at his best in *The Prestige* (1995), a story powered by twin mainsprings of fanatical secrecy and jealousy as the lifelong feud of two Victorian-era stage magicians comes to distort every aspect of their existence. Stage magic and misdirection provide a perfect metaphor for the established Priest technique of not so much fooling readers as allowing them to fool themselves. When a magician "accidentally" knocks a hoop against part of his apparatus and a metallic clang sounds, it is the unwary watcher who supplies the untruth that the hoop is therefore substantial and solid. As Priest has remarked:

> The narrative voice is comparable with a magician's act. . . . Most people reading a novel told in the first person singular will reasonably assume that it's truthfully or reliably reported, or that only one person is writing it, or that no one apart from the narrator has tampered with the text before it was printed, and so on, but to me these assumptions open possibilities for a few sneaky reversals. (Interview in *SFX*, 4, September 1995, page 50)

A minor example soon emerges in *The Prestige*, whose modern-day opening features a journalist who is descended from one of the warring magicians (and who suffers from the lifelong conviction that he has a lost twin—for which an eerie explanation will ultimately emerge). Briefly he examines the published memoirs of his great-grandfather Alfred Borden. The novel's next section does indeed consist of Borden's memoirs, but *not* the version edited for publication.

The differently slanted autobiographical narratives of Borden and his deadly rival, Rupert Angier, fill most of the book. Each, despite flickers of remorseful sympathy, is the villain of the other's story. After reading Borden, numerous shocks and reversals of interpretation await the reader in Angier's version of events. Mirror images and dual roles abound, appropriate to a tale of magic in the age of gaslight.

Borden's triumph and curse is his trademark illusion, "The New Transported Man," in which he appears to travel instantaneously across the stage. (To use both rivals' professional jargon, this effect is the trick's payoff or "prestige.") Angier is deeply jealous, not knowing that the obsessively guarded secret has forced Borden's entire life into an unnatural pattern. Borden himself mentions a real-life example: the Chinese magician Ching Ling Foo, the misdirection for whose climactic effect required him constantly to act out the lie of being aged, weak, and feeble—offstage as well as on.

His envy having reached near-desperation, Angier travels from London to Pikes Peak, Colorado, and seeks advice from electrical pioneer Nikola Tesla. The Prestige moves into the territory of Wellsian scientific romance (turning a blind eye to problems with the as yet unknown Einstein mass-energy equivalence), when Tesla achieves the impossible by building Angier a marvelous stage apparatus that literally transmits the performer through space. Thus Angier now eclipses Borden's best efforts and storms to magical preeminence with the new keynote effect, which he calls "In a Flash." It is Borden's turn for gnawing jealousy and Angier's turn to cope with the life-distorting effects of a trick's "prestige," for the Tesla device is a matter duplicator rather than a transmitter, and each performance requires Angier to dispose of his own dead body.

Spying on Angier, Borden inadvertently sabotages this trick, with terrible effects. Vengeance follows. The final irony for both magicians is that because of the strange nature of their secrets, each has literally *half*-killed the other; their exit lines are identical yet have different meanings. The novel concludes with another modern-day episode that both

explains and does not explain, transposing from scientific romance (with conscious echoes of Wells's *The Invisible Man*) to something atmospherically Gothic. It is not easily forgotten.

The *Prestige* effortlessly crosses genre boundaries. It was nominated for the Arthur C. Clarke Award and won both the World Fantasy Award and the nongenre James Tait Black Memorial Award. It may be Priest's finest book.

A later novel, The *Extremes* (1998), is an initially straightforward-seeming story in which "Extreme Experience" virtual-reality systems are first shown as used for intensive FBI training in handling violent situations and then enter the public arena as a fast-growing and lucrative part of the entertainment industry. The protagonist, FBI agent Teresa Simons, distracts herself from grief by investigating the coincidence that the "spree attack" mass shooting that killed her husband in the United States was paralleled by a similar outburst by a deranged gunman on the same day in England.

An implied answer emerges through a succession of violent or pornographic "ExEx" scenarios and a gradual blurring of the interface between simulation and reality. Software versions of events, held in computer memory, can be as misleading and (owing to interactivity) as mutable as human memory tends to be in Priest fictions. Afflicted with fleeting hallucinations of the past massacre in the English town where she is staying, Teresa comes to see the local and American shootings as linked by feedback through ExEx itself; seemingly, her own FBI training has leaked across time to assist that unskilled gunman whose crimes she relives. Like *A Dream of Wessex*, the story ends on a note of triumph that may be delusive, since it is not reliably rooted in external actuality.

There is an interesting contrast here between depicted violence and Priest's carefully controlled, understated, sometimes flat style, which tends to preserve a surface calm while building cumulative effects of menace and disorientation as his complex, devious plots take shape. He excels at lowering rather than raising a story's emotional temperature. Experimental stylistic devices rarely appear, besides minutiae such as *The Affirmation*'s differing quotation marks for "real" and "unreal" voices or Alfred Borden's peculiar usage of first-person pronouns. The auctorial voice is so disarmingly quiet that sparing repetitions of phrases resonate powerfully, like Peter Sinclair's broken sentence "For a moment I thought I knew where I was, but when I looked back . . . ," the simple "Wish you were here. X" postcards of *The Glamour*, or *The Prestige*'s duplicated exit line, "I will go alone to the end."

Christopher Priest remains a fascinatingly variable author with a rare skill of slipping unobtrusively across genre boundaries—so unafraid either to undermine a science fiction scenario with metafictional ambiguities, as in *The Affirmation* and *The Glamour*, or to produce to genuine science fiction device where only trickery is expected, as in *The Prestige*. As Ursula Le Guin once wrote, he is a versatile writer from whom we can expect nothing expectable.

Selected Bibliography

WORKS OF CHRISTOPHER PRIEST

Indoctrinaire. London: Faber and Faber, 1970; New York: Harper and Row, 1970. Revised edition, London: Pan, 1979.

Fugue for a Darkening Island. London: Faber and Faber, 1972. Reprinted as *The Darkening Island*, New York: Harper and Row, 1972.

Inverted World. London: Faber and Faber, 1974. Reprinted as *The Inverted World*, New York: Harper and Row, 1974.

Real-Time World. London: New English Library, 1974. First published in German translation as *Transplantationen*, Munich: Wilhelm Goldmann Verlag, 1972. (Short stories.)

The Space Machine: A Scientific Romance. London: Faber and Faber, 1976; New York: Harper and Row, 1976.

A Dream of Wessex. London: Faber and Faber, 1977. Reprinted as *The Perfect Lover*, New York: Scribners, 1977.

An Infinite Summer. London: Faber and Faber, 1979; New York: Scribners, 1979. (Short stories.)

The Affirmation. London: Faber and Faber, 1981; New York: Scribners, 1981.

The Glamour. London: Cape, 1984. Revised editions, Garden City, N.Y.: Doubleday, 1985. Official "Revised Edition," London: Simon and Schuster/Touchstone, 1996.

The Quiet Woman. London: Bloomsbury, 1990.

The Prestige. London: Simon and Schuster/Touchstone, 1995; New York: St. Martin's, 1996.

The Extremes. London: Simon and Schuster/Touchstone, 1998.

The Dream Archipelago. London: Simon and Schuster/Earthlight, 1999. (Related short stories, newly revised.)

NONFICTION

Your Book of Film-Making London: Faber and Faber, 1974. (For children.)

"The Profession of Science Fiction XIII: Overture and Beginners." *Foundation*, 13 (May 1978): 51–56.

The Making of the Lesbian Horse. Birmingham, England: Birmingham Science Fiction Group, 1979. (A note on *Inverted World*, introducing a very short spoof "sequel.")

"On *Christopher Priest* by Nicholas Ruddick." *Foundation*, 50 (Autumn 1990): 94–101.

The Book on the Edge of Forever: An Enquiry into the Non-Appearance of Harlan Ellison's The Last Dangerous Visions. Seattle, Wash.: Fantagraphics, 1994.

EDITED ANTHOLOGIES

Anticipations. London: Faber and Faber, 1978; New York: Scribners, 1978.

Stars of Albion, with Robert Holdstock. London: Pan, 1979.

CRITICAL AND BIOGRAPHICAL STUDIES

Clute, John. "*The Quiet Woman.*" In *Look at the Evidence.* Seattle, Wash.: Serconia, 1995; Liverpool, England: Liverpool University Press, 1995.

———. "*The Prestige.*" *Interzone*, 101 (November 1995): 58.

Kincaid, Paul. "*The Glamour.*" *Vector*, 124/125 (April/May 1985): 23–24.

———. "*The Glamour:* Revised Edition." *Vector*, 191 (January/February 1997): 29–30.

———. "Only Connect; Psychology and Politics in the Work of Christopher Priest." *Foundation*, 52 (Summer 1991): 42–58.

Langford, David. "*The Prestige.*" *New York Review of Science Fiction*, 98 (October 1996): 15.

Lashku, Ludmila: "The Marriage of Fantasy and Psychology in the Works of Christopher Priest." *Foundation*, 50 (Autumn 1990): 52–60.

Nicholls, Peter. *"Inverted World."* *Foundation*, 7/8 (March 1975): 185–188.

———, and John Clute. "Christopher Priest." In *The Encyclopedia of Science Fiction*, 2d ed. Edited by John Clute and Peter Nicholls. London: Orbit, 1993; New York: St. Martin's, 1993.

Ruddick, Nicholas. *Christopher Priest.* Mercer Island, Wash.: Starmont House, 1988.

Watson, Ian. *"The Affirmation."* *Foundation*, 23 (October 1981): 82–84.

Wingrove, David. "Legerdemain: The Fiction of Christopher Priest." *Vector*, 93 (May/June 1979): 3–9.

—DAVID LANGFORD

Kim Stanley Robinson

(b. 1952)

Despite frequent praise for his imagination, characterization, and style, Kim Stanley Robinson is occasionally dismissed as a "literary" science fiction writer, one who uses elaborate conventions and exotic allusions to hide a somewhat weak story. Also unfairly, Robinson has been criticized for an inclination to "teach a science lesson" through his novels. Both criticisms are largely undeserved: Robinson's stories contain depths, for he is a well-educated and thoughtful man, capable of seeing new possibilities in established settings and situations; although some of his earlier works showed a regrettable tendency to proselytize, this is not the case in his later works. His early story "Venice Drowned" was nominated for a Nebula award in 1981; this was but the first of many honors: he has won Hugo awards for his novels *Green Mars* and *Blue Mars* and Nebula awards for the novella "The Blind Geometer" and the novel *Red Mars*. He is one of the most respected and visible of science fiction writers.

Born on 23 March 1952 in Waukegan, Illinois, Robinson earned a B.A. in English from the University of California, San Diego, in 1974, an M.A. in English from Boston University in 1975, and a Ph.D. in English from the University of California, San Diego, in 1982. His Ph.D. thesis, *The Novels of Philip K. Dick*, was a pioneering study of the works of science fiction writer Philip K. Dick and was published as a book in 1984. From early in his career, Robinson explored several themes, including politics, crowding and overpopulation, colonization of Mars, ecology and the environment, and human longevity and memory. In *The Wild Shore* (1984), the first of the series known as the California novels, Robinson deals with political control and its alternative—learning to live cooperatively. This novel, the coming of age story of seventeen-year-old Henry Fletcher, examines the political aspirations of Americans in a United States that has been pushed back to a pretechnology society by the detonation of numerous neutron bombs in cars and is now quarantined by the U.N. The California shore is patrolled by Japanese cruisers and laser satellites. At first the United States is prevented from rebuilding its federal infrastructure in an attempt by the U.N. to control U.S. intervention in the affairs of other countries (which may have been the reason for the bombing). Some of the young people of San Onofre are eager to become involved in the American Underground to overthrow this control. In the course of the novel Henry comes to see that political power can be misused. The mayor of San Diego is willing to use him and his friends to bolster his own political power. Henry feels guilty that he allows his friend Steve to bully him into helping the group as their participation results in one person's death and Steve's leaving San Onofre in exile. Henry comes to realize that he must think for himself and take responsibility for his actions.

The Wild Shore also introduced another theme, ecology and the environment. The destruction of the infrastructure and the cooler weather that have occurred in the United

States make ecology very important. In order to survive, the remaining Americans must pay attention to the environment in order to grow enough food. This is an almost idealistic return to the land. San Onofre is sustained by everyone pitching in to help grow, maintain, and harvest those crops that can be sustained in the area and experimenting with breeding better crops, especially those resistant to the cold.

In *The Gold Coast* (1988), the second California novel, corruption in government and big business creates an atmosphere in which companies competing for weapons contracts for the Pentagon falsify or misrepresent tests in order to gain and keep arms contracts. The government, or at least a segment of it, manipulates the contract bidding and the development of weapons so the only way companies can continue to exist is by doing what the Pentagon wants, no matter how dishonest it is. This leads Laguna Space Research to hire men to bomb the arms companies in Laguna Beach, including itself, to hide the fact that their project doesn't work and to save their contract.

Crowding or overpopulation of an area, another of Robinson's themes, is of major importance in *The Gold Coast*. Jim McPherson believes he is a historian and preservationist because he collects memorabilia of early buildings and orange groves in the area. He clings to this in an effort to overcome the pressure that overpopulation has put on the area and on him—the pressure of little or no space and the inability to get a full-time job in the poor economy. Such pressures cause Jim and many of his friends to turn to designer drugs and alcohol to deaden their abused senses. In fact, one of Jim's friends is a designer of drugs. The friend is ethical in that he tries to be careful to test the drugs so he knows there will be no immediate bad effects on his customers, and he uses the purest supplies possible to create them, but the drugs would not be so attractive if overpopulation of the area did not make it necessary for people to retreat from their environment for recreation and "peace."

Domination of local government by large multinational businesses is explored in *Pacific Edge* (1990), Robinson's third California novel. In El Modena the city council is asked to approve a water contract that involves taking more water than is needed. This is a first step in an attempt to circumvent international laws preventing companies from becoming too large and dominating the economy of an area.

Making use of what the environment offers is part of the theme of *Pacific Edge*. The citizens of El Modena do their best to grow what they need and to preserve the ecology of their area. The fight that looms over the building of a large office building–mall on the last open hill in town is both aesthetic and environmental. Members of the community bicycle or walk most of the time, with car rental available for long trips. The lifestyle is healthy and Kevin Claiborne makes his living by building and remodeling homes that are in the mode of Frank Lloyd Wright in both their ability to fit into the surrounding landscape and their efficient use of energy and resources. In addition, there is a community nearby that has built houses in large trees without damaging them. This novel is not a regression to the living style of the 1800's, as advanced technology—computers, for example—is still used, but the community recycles as many resources as possible.

In the California novels, Robinson uses a cooperative arrangement to thwart the abuse of power. In *The Wild Shore*, San Onofre uses a republic form of government—every person in the community is present and has a vote—while El Modena in *Pacific Edge* uses a representative democracy coupled with a cooperative. Every adult in town must put in a set number of hours on public work for the community. These three California novels do not form a true trilogy in that they do not tell a continuous story. Robinson called them

a trio, a trilogy with a new structure, and one thing which interested me from the start was the structure itself—a sort of tripod arrangement, where the base of the tripod, so to

Kim Stanley Robinson. © Miriam Berkley

a biosphere that is fragile at best and cannot support a large number of immigrants.

The conflict over who will decide the fate of the planet and its colonists continues through the other books in the series. In *Green Mars* (1994) the colonists have discovered and used longevity drugs to extend their lives. The eruption of a volcano under the west shelf of Antarctica causes enough ice melt to raise the ocean waters six meters. Earth is thrown into chaos, while the colonists on Mars revolt without any loss of life. When the revolution is successful the citizens form a government in which everyone must buy into a cooperative that then forms some business or venture that helps sustain the town. Some people simply provide the essentials—food, shelter, clothing, warmth—for the community, but most get those by creating businesses that bring a profit shared by the cooperative members. Each member must give so many hours a month or year to the work of the cooperative to help sustain it. The rest of the time can be spent on their own activities—recreation, farming, research, etc. The cooperative has its own laws, which are administered within the cooperative. The federal or planetwide legislature and council attend to matters that cross cooperative lines and concern the planet as a whole. There is a Global Environment Court that rules in matters that affect the environment of the entire planet. Using the underground groups' earlier agreement, the court determines if the environmental impact fits within the agreed guidelines. While this government is not perfect, it does offer a possible solution to the social problems of most people, who would otherwise have little power and be overwhelmed by the rich and powerful. The novel depicts a society that people on Earth might like to work toward.

The revolt is complete in *Blue Mars* (1996). The various political parties on Mars form a government using an agreement that the various underground groups had drawn up a year or so earlier to try to achieve unity. From this, local and planetwide governments are fashioned. Eventually the political party Mars-

speak, was the present moment, and then the three legs would head off in three different directions that were as far apart from each other as I could imagine, each of them taking a basic science fiction scenario—the after-the-fall, the dystopia, and the utopia. (Foote 52)

Thus this trio constitutes three different views of a possible future.

Red Mars (1993) again explores political control. The United Nations is now the central government on Earth and it assembles and sends a hundred colonists to settle on Mars. The object is to create a place to send people to relieve population stress and economic difficulties on Earth. The U.N. attempts to maintain rigid control of the colony, forcing Mars to take as many immigrants as Earth wants to send. Several groups of colonists (including most of the original group and many later immigrants) rebel unsuccessfully. The terraforming of the planet has produced

First gains control of the planetwide council and tries to stop immigration completely, causing Earth to try to retake control of Mars. However, the situation is resolved peacefully.

These stories all warn against the abuse of power. In each case, the abuse of power for personal gain or for political aims that are not beneficial to the majority of the population is shown as selfishness at best and destructive at worst to individuals or to the population at large. The political parties, the Reds and Greens on Mars, and the Greys, also all found in "The Memory of Whiteness," arise to combat the abuse of power.

In order to thwart the abuse of political power, some sort of improved government is needed. Some of Robinson's novels seem to advocate a utopia. Robinson admitted that this part of science fiction, which emphasizes social issues, had a strong appeal for him. He said "I love this part of the literature: the thought-experiment which attacks social problems and suggests solutions, utopian goals, or envisions societies that we might then work towards." He went on to say that

Utopia has to be rescued as a word, to mean 'working towards a more egalitarian society, a global society.' . . . Joanna Russ, I think, made up the term *the optopia*, which is not that you go for the perfect society, but that you go for the optimum society, the best one possible, given—everything. And I think that's a nice reworking of the utopian notion.

The revolutions in *Red Mars, Green Mars,* and *Blue Mars* are brought on by the threat that Earth will overwhelm the fragile biosphere the colonists have created on Mars by sending too many immigrants for that biosphere to support. The Mars colonists realize the population problems on Earth will continue to threaten their world. In order to prevent that some of the First Hundred believe that they must go to Earth to help relieve the turmoil. In *Blue Mars* Maya, Michel, Sax, and Nirgal go to Earth and while they are in Bern, Switzerland, Nirgal, a native-born Martian who has captured media attention, tells the crowd that everyone on Earth must be given the longevity drugs discovered on Mars. This will exacerbate the population problem on Earth for a time, but Earth must institute population controls. As the older generations die, the next generations will be roughly half as large and so on until the population is down to sustainable levels. He then goes on to say

In the meantime, we have to help each other. We have to regulate ourselves, we have to take care of the land. And it's here, in this part of the project, that Mars can help Earth. First, we are an experiment in taking care of the land. Everyone learns from that, and some lessons can be applied here. Then, more importantly, though most of the population will always be located here on Earth, a goodly fraction of it can move to Mars. It will help ease the situation, and we'll be happy to take them. We have an obligation to take on as many people as we possibly can, because we on Mars are Terrans still, and we are all in this together. Earth and Mars—and there are other habitable worlds in the solar system as well, none as big as our two, but there are a lot of them. And by using them all, and cooperating, we can get through the populated years. And walk out into a golden age (156–157).

People from Earth do go to Mars and the other habitable planets in the solar system and to many moons and asteroids to relieve the population pressure.

In the Mars books, Robinson developed the idea of colonization as the central theme and explored ideas about how such an end might be accomplished. His interest in colonizing Mars is so well developed that he worked out elaborate ways in which people might construct dwellings and cities to create a breathable atmosphere on the surface of the planet, thereby eliminating the need for breathing devices. He also developed elaborate plans for creating a hydrology that would allow the colonists to grow their own genetically engineered plants and animals. It was an attractive picture that might lure many into working toward making the dream come true.

This elaborate plan involved creating or engineering an appropriate ecology on the face of the planet Mars.

As a result, the Mars books focus rather directly on ecology and the environment. If the colonists are to be able to survive on the surface of the planet with minimal life-support systems, the atmosphere of the planet must be changed (terraformed). Most of the colonists and the U.N. favor this as economical. The U.N. is in favor of terraforming the planet because it means that more immigrants can be sent from Earth, thus relieving the overpopulation. However, to terraform the planet, it is necessary to develop an ecology that provides the gases and water and air pressure necessary to create a breathable atmosphere. The terraformers use genetic engineering to create plants and animals that can survive in a minimal atmosphere and also contribute to the atmosphere.

A few colonists are in favor of preserving most of the planet surface as it is when they arrive, creating domes or tents to provide a breathable environment. The terraformers agree that some preservation should be done, and they determine that some of the actions of the companies from Earth are detrimental. The terraformers are willing to allow terraforming to take place gradually in order to preserve an atmosphere that is friendly to humans, but more fragile, and to create a more balanced ecology for the planet, resembling Earth but not identical to it. These two views create the opposing political parties in Martian society—the Reds (preservationists) and the Greens (terraformers). Robinson did not indicate directly that either side is right or wrong, but Sax, architect of the terraforming movement, tries to appease and understand Ann, the original preservationist. He joins her at the appearance the First Hundred make after the third revolution and the two of them help convince the Earth government to take a more moderate position toward immigration. The action suggests that the Greens, as represented by Sax, may be more interested in preserving areas of Mars in as nearly a natural state as is possible.

Another theme that runs through much of Robinson's work is human longevity and memory. As early as *Icehenge* (1984), he displayed an interest in the nature of memory, but it received fuller treatment in the Mars books. Once humans colonize Mars, their life spans are extended. As a result, memories begin to fade, but in *Icehenge*, many people keep journals to remember things. People find that they cannot remember much in the "middle": they can remember things from when they were young but not much about when they first immigrated to Mars. For some of the remaining First Hundred, this creates an untenable condition. Maya, in particular, feels that a very long life is not worth anything if she can't remember much about it. Sax devises a treatment that helps them restore their memories and enhances their lives. The longevity treatments correct faulty or "broken" DNA strands to give people not only long lives but better health. These genetic treatments can be used to correct diseases if the causes are known and if the diseases are caught soon enough. In *Green Mars*, after the longevity treatments are discovered and "perfected," some of the First Hundred talk about people possibly living to be a thousand years old. The wisdom and efficiency exhibited by the First Hundred in dealing with crises, particularly the second and third revolutions, as well as their contributions to solving social, political, and physical problems, suggest that longer lives might be more desirable than simply the wish of individuals to continue living.

The theme of control is also explored in *Icehenge* in the form of an attempt by the Mars Development Committee, an arm of the Earth's business interest, to control the colony of Mars, leading to a revolution on Mars and anticipating the revolts in the Mars books. In the year 2248, miners aboard a mining ship join fellow conspirators in a mutiny leading to their building a starship to leave the solar system. This launch of the starship is covered by the revolution occurring on Mars. Among those miners who do not go on the starship is Emma Weil, whose journal tells the story of the mutiny and the building of the

633

starship. Weil records the fact that the leader of the starship had plans to build a monument on Pluto as "something to leave a mark on the world, something to show we were here at all. . . ."

In 2547, Hjalmar Nederland, an archaeologist who is over three hundred years old, is excavating New Houston, a city destroyed in the revolution of 2248. Nederland believes that the Committee destroyed the city, not the revolutionaries. While working on the site, Nederland has a vivid, spontaneous recollection on what happened on the day of the city's destruction. He publishes his findings, causing the Committee to admit what really happened. Then he learns that a monument named Icehenge has been found on Pluto, which appears to be the monument that Weil's journal describes. Further research seems to confirm Weil's story.

In 2610, Nederland's great-grandson Edmund Doya is part of an expedition to Pluto to excavate and examine Icehenge to determine whether it was actually built in 2248. If the construction of the monument occurred at another time, then the Committee is implicated in a fraud and their position will be weakened and their control of Mars may be compromised. The expedition finds evidence that the monument was built much later than 2248, although the person who may be responsible for the building may be Emma Weil in a new identity.

The control theme is also demonstrated in *The Memory of Whiteness* (1985). Johannes Wright, the blind Master of the Orchestra, is making a Grand Tour of the planets with the Holywelkin's Orchestra, an instrument that is an orchestra in itself. As Wright travels from Pluto to various moons and to each planet, Ernst Ekern, Chairman of the Holywelkin Institute, tries to gain control of Wright himself or the instrument by creating havoc at the concerts to discredit Wright or have him killed. Ekern is interested only in acquiring power for himself and revenging himself on his classmate Johannes Wright for being a better musician.

Escape from Kathmandu (1989) has been described as an episodic book. The first section, "Escape from Kathmandu," touches on the ecology issue. It involves the rescue of an abominable snowman (yeti) from a group of "scientists" who plan to exhibit him to enhance their reputations and raise money for their "research." The two main characters of the book, George Fergusson and George Freds Fredrickson, rescue the yeti and take it back to its home with the intention of allowing it to live peacefully without danger of being destroyed for curiosity's sake. Both men become friendly with the yeti, which proves to be more intelligent and amiable than either of them would have guessed originally.

The second section, "Mother Goddess of the World," involves Fergusson and Freds in an illegal attempt to climb Mount Everest, ostensibly to help a documentary film crew find the body of Mallory. In reality, they are helping Kunga Norbu elevate himself to the position of lama. Each group is trying to prevent outsiders from gaining control; the documentary crew is trying to prevent an unscrupulous filmmaker from finding Mallory's body and burying it in some lowland mausoleum, while Kunga Norbu must climb the Mother Goddess of the World (Mount Everest) to be elevated to the station of lama. The two Georges are aided by the yeti.

The third section, "The True Nature of Shangri-La," finds Fergusson helping to block the government's attempt to build a road that would lead people to Shangri-La, which is really Shambala, the secret sacred stronghold of Tibetan Buddhism. The road would make it easier for the Chinese and Nepalese governments to take control of the stronghold. Fergusson and Freds make everyone involved believe that the other parties have ulterior motives for wanting to build the road. This protects Shambala from being taken over.

"The Kingdom Underground" describes Fergusson's attempt to help a friend build sewers to improve Kathmandu. However, building the sewers will reveal the tunnel system under the city, used by the Tibetan Buddhists to keep track of the Nepalese government and for protection. Fergusson helps the Buddhists empty some chambers of gold and fill them in with dirt and rocks so that the building of the sewers can proceed without anyone finding the tunnels.

In the collection of short stories *The Planet on the Table* (1986), two stories examine political control. "The Lucky Strike" is an alternative history in which the atomic bomb doesn't actually hit Hiroshima because the bombardier can't bring himself to push the button and kill that many people. He is court-martialed and executed for disobeying an order, even though the miss serves as a warning and causes the Japanese to surrender without the massive loss of life that actually took place. "Coming Back to Dixieland" has a group of miners from Jupiter competing in a music contest with the prize being a grant allowing the band members to get away from Jupiter and live a better life for a year by going on tour. The political and economic situations are such that there is no other way these miners can earn a better life for themselves.

The short story "Glacier" in *Remaking History* (1991) also shows abuse of power on a local level. The main character's father is a part-time teacher at a Boston college. The economy is bad and when the college needs to reduce the work force, it manufactures evidence of transgressions to justify firing employees. Downsizing is traumatic enough in this setting, but adding insult to injury by accusing employees of committing illegal acts to justify firing them is cruel.

"Glacier" makes an indirect comment on ecology as well. While the main theme is the abuse of power and the difficulties caused by a declining economy, a highly visible part of the setting is the glacier that is growing and creeping into Boston. It is clear that the environment is cooling, probably caused by man's refusal to take proper care of the land.

The use of scientific metaphor abounds in all Robinson's work but particularly in the Mars books, although he also made use of more ordinary metaphor. For example, in *Pacific Edge*, he has Kevin Claiborne playing softball and batting a thousand throughout, but at the conclusion, he strikes out his last time at bat for the season. This kind of technique is one reason why Robinson was seen as a "literary" science-fiction writer. Another reason is his use of elaborate conventions, such as ordering the plot, as in *The Memory of Whiteness*, to resemble the structure of a symphony. He also used symphonic structure as a metaphor for the scientific "truth" that Johannes Wright believes he is discovering, and in return, revealing to his audience as his tour spirals down closer to the sun. This use of structure as a metaphor was apparent to critics and reviewers, who noticed that Robinson created an elaborate work with characters as motifs and using the theme of the physics of music.

In addition to using scientific and more ordinary metaphors, Robinson made allusions to science fiction literature, or at least to Philip K. Dick. The time slip that Robinson used to create an Earthlike Martian day in *Red Mars* takes the Earth clock and adds ". . . a thirty-nine-and-a-half-minute gap between 12:00:00 and 12:01:00, when all the clocks went blank or stopped moving. This was how the First Hundred had decided to reconcile Mars's slightly longer day with the twenty-four-clock." Bud Foote said that "*Red Mars* gives the reader an almost continual sense of itself as artifact, in its declaration that it is a story encompassing past stories." Carol Frankoa notes this in talking about Robinson's use of allusion:

Mars itself is the nexus of many of these embedded stories, from science fiction to fictional canals to ancient myths of Mars inspired by its redness and its erratic revolution around the sun. One of the vivid ways that Robinson alludes to past Mars stories is by repeating in different contexts the various names given to the red planet in many languages over the centuries. These litanies arguably become one of the ways that Mars itself becomes a speech actor, or at least an embodied and personified presence, in the novel's conversations . . . references to science fiction authors like Ray Bradbury, Edgar

Rice Burroughs, Philip Dick, and C. L. Moore (59).

Robinson's literary bent also takes the form of mystical allegory. The short story "The Part of Us That Loves" in *Remaking History* gives a modern version of Christ feeding the multitude, in this case, an old band director in a religiously founded town replacing instruments that have been stolen just before a band concert honoring two senior citizens, and in "Rainbow Bridge" a white boy has a mystical experience under the watchful eye of a Native American shaman. In the "Mother Goddess of the World" section of *Escape from Kathmandu*, the two Georges and the lama Kunga Norbu climb, illegally, to the top of Mount Everest to allow the lama to complete his task truly to become a lama.

As of this writing Robinson is a consistently able and versatile talent, capable of imagining a place and describing the survival and occasional triumph of its population with such an intensity that our world and its inhabitants seem drab in comparison. Even such a relatively minor work as *A Short, Sharp Shock* (1990), a description of an extended trek across a seemingly endless peninsula bounded by formidable seas, offers the reader the possibility of multiple interpretations, and contains lyrical and intensely described passages:

They sat on the wall and watched the sunset, the light leaking out of the sky, the wind rustling the great space of dusk and the sea. The incredible furnace of the sun fountained light even as it sank into the ocean, which gleamed like a cut polished stone. Overhead a windhover fluttered in place, slicing the wind and sideslipping, and seeing it Thel was calmed. Whatever happened, yes, but more than that there was a kind of glory in it, to fling themselves out into the spaces they breathed, if only for one last dive or flight. The sun pared to a yellow line on the sea, and the sky darkened still; the mirror surface, still a kind of lens gathering sunlight, glowed a rich yellow that greened and greened as the sun's rays bent around the curve of the globe, prisming under gravity's pull.

With each new work Robinson demonstrates that he is capable of surpassing his earlier efforts, and he will be remembered not only as one of the finest science fiction writers to emerge from the 1990's but also as one of the top talents practicing at the beginning of the new millennium.

Selected Bibliography

WORKS OF KIM STANLEY ROBINSON

Icehenge. New York: Orb, 1984.
The Novels of Philip K. Dick. Ann Arbor, Mich.: UMI Research Press, 1984.
The Wild Shore. New York: TOR, 1984.
The Memory of Whiteness. New York: TOR, 1985.
The Planet on the Table. New York: TOR, 1986.
The Blind Geometer. New York: TOR, 1987.
The Gold Coast. New York: St. Martin's Press, 1988.
Escape from Kathmandu. New York: TOR, 1989.
Pacific Edge. New York: TOR, 1990.
A Short, Sharp Shock. Shingletown, Calif.: Mark V. Ziesing, 1990.
Remaking History. New York: TOR, 1991.
Red Mars. New York: Bantam Books, 1993.
Green Mars. New York: Bantam Books, 1994.
Blue Mars. New York: Bantam Books, 1996.
Future Primitive. New York: Bantam Books, 1994.

CRITICAL AND BIOGRAPHICAL STUDIES

"Author's Choice #20." *Science Fiction Chronicle*, 12 (1991): 34.
Budrys, Algis. "Books." *The Magazine of Science Fiction*, 66 (1984): 35–41. Review of *The Wild Shore*.
Foote, Bud. "A Conversation with Kim Stanley Robinson." *Science-Fiction Studies*, 21 (1994): 51–66.
Franko, Carol. "The Density of Utopian Destiny in Robinson's *Red Mars*." *Extrapolation*, 38 (1997): 57–65.
Sabella, Robert. "*The Wild Shore*," *Science Fiction Review*, 14 (1985): 32.

—SHERRY STOSKOPF

JOANNA RUSS
(b. 1937)

JOANNA RUSS WAS born on 22 February 1937, and she was raised in the Bronx, New York City. Echoes of that time and place can be found in her work, particularly in *The Female Man* (1975) and *The Two of Them* (1978). Her parents, both of Jewish ancestry, were teachers and avid readers. In 1957 she graduated from Cornell University with distinction and high honors in English. Russ first published a science fiction short story in 1959. In 1960 she received an M.F.A. in playwriting and dramatic literature from the Yale School of Drama. She has taught writing, literature, and speech at Queensborough Community College, Cornell University, the State University of New York at Binghamton, the University of Colorado and, since 1977, she has been an associate professor of English at the University of Washington, in Seattle.

Science fiction writers most often come from the sciences with an interest in writing. Russ approached science fiction in the opposite manner: from literature with an interest in science. She was accepted to the Bronx High School of Science in the first year that women students were admitted (1949), but chose not to attend. In her senior year of high school (1953), she won the Westinghouse Science Talent Search. Russ maintained her interest in science while studying writing and theater. She has been a playwright, and she is a widely published essayist, critic, and book reviewer. The style of Russ the novelist reflects the precision and conciseness of theater scene and dialogue, as well as years of thinking and writing about fiction.

Russ is first a contemporary novelist, then a science fiction writer. She combines commitment to psychological exploration and sociological honesty with an astonishing understanding of her craft. Her essays attest to these accomplishments. Russ brings to her fiction a rich background of Jane Austen, George Bernard Shaw, Virginia Woolf, and Vladimir Nabokov (her professor at Cornell and one of the dedicatees of *And Chaos Died*), as well as Samuel R. Delany, Fritz Leiber, Olaf Stapledon, and others. The scope and style of her work have not been limited by the expectations others assign to science fiction. Russ forges beyond social and literary boundaries, providing alternatives to what is accepted. She has created a female mythos, recasting the existing models.

The choice to write science fiction instead of realistic fiction (mundane fiction as some call it) stems from the alternatives science fiction affords that are not available through other genres. Within the structural confines of the physical and moral laws that govern her worlds (laws that she defines), Russ creates anthropological and psychological models that are extensions of our world. She does not indulge in pure analogy or technological wizardry. Science fiction conventions serve as a backdrop for her humanistic models. Russ produces what is ultimately a fictional autobiography; her approach resembles the confessional form of Cardinal Newman's *Apologia Pro Vita Sua* (1864) and, later, James Weldon Johnson's fictional *Autobiography of an Ex-Colored Man* (1912). This confessional form examines the history, the attitudes, the philosophies, and the life of a character from a very particular, subjective point of view. There is no pretense of objectivity in the narration of Russ's novels. Russ includes the viewpoint character's perceptions of the environment, and intellectual and theoretical interests. But the character's prejudices, limitations, and psychology—what could be called a psychological landscape or innerscape—control the story. In this sense, Russ is the inheritor of Henry James, not John W. Campbell, Jr.

Science fiction has allowed Russ greater latitude in the portrayal of characters, particularly female characters, than is available through other genres. In an early essay, "What Can a Heroine Do?—or Why Women Can't Write," Russ points out that the plot lines of most fiction follow the pattern of the active male and the objectified, passive female:

> They [women] exist only in relation to the protagonist (who is male). Moreover, look at them carefully and you will see depictions of the social roles women are supposed to play and often do play, but they are the public roles and not the private women; at their worst they are gorgeous, Cloudcuckooland fantasies about what men want, or hate, or fear. (page 5)

In most contemporary literature, fictional roles assigned to the active female are dominated by Freudian fear, hate, or desire fantasies that are projections upon an otherwise passive female character. The innerscape of women and the internally motivated female protagonist are rare in literature because the female is the object, not the active character: thus the active female character has no object to strive for. But Russ's heroines strive for themselves, for freedom, and for independence.

Since Russ writes about active women, conventional plot lines are inadequate. To accommodate her needs, she must write mythopoeic stories that expand the limits imposed upon women writers by literary tradition and social expectation. Myths form part of the ideology of any society. They are the recurring themes and character types that appeal to the conscious or collective unconscious by embodying cultural ideals and fears and giving them expression.

Russ must create and re-create the myths that embody the women of our culture. She uses the conventions of science fiction to juxtapose the "real" world to her alternatives. Then, through examination or exaggeration of an aspect of the "real" world, she bends that world to form another, contrasting world view. Thus Russ can create a mythos for the active female character, while eschewing existing myth. Science fiction is the vehicle for the motion, life, and capabilities of Russ's female protagonists, removing them from modes that use female characters as symbols.

Picnic on Paradise (1968), Russ's first novel, tells the story of Alyx. Alyx is an agent of Trans-Temporal. Trans-Temporal, alternately known as *"the Great Trans-Temporal Cadre of Heroes and Heroines,"* reappears in *The Two of Them*, where it is also known as "The Gang." Alyx is the subject of several short stories, collected with *Picnic* in a volume entitled *Alyx* (1976). In *Picnic*, Trans-Temporal assigns Alyx to lead a group of tourists to safety on a recreational planet, Paradise, that is experiencing a culturally alien outbreak of warfare. The story is told from Alyx's subjective consciousness. Alyx is always alien to her surroundings: Trans-Temporal had accidentally transported her from ancient Greece, four thousand years into her future. In her own time she had chosen to be a thief rather than to assume a traditional role:

> Only one day they [Trans-Temporal] were fishing in the Bay of Tyre a good forty feet down and they just happened to receive twenty-odd cubic meters of sea-water complete with a small, rather inept Greek thief. . . . They tell me I was attached to a rope attached to knots attached to. . . . (page 149)

Thus she explains herself to Iris, a survivor of the Paradise journey.

Alyx is out of time; no past or future applies to her; her only time is now. Like the protagonists in Russ's other stories, Alyx is an existentialist, for Russ is an existential writer; the present, not the past or future, is her concern. There is no god—certainly no good god—to provide hope; the existence of human beings provides reason enough for a moral and ordered universe. Alyx survives in her world because she lives in the present: only the journey itself is important. But those whom Alyx must lead to safety have no concern with their present; most lack concern and understanding of themselves and their situation. Their subjective universes lack morality and order. This contrast provides the major tension of the story.

All but one of the tourists are as much tourists of their own lives as of Paradise. The single exception, Machine, understands his situation, although he has chosen to spend most of his time in a machine- and drug-derived nirvana. When Alyx meets the group, the lieutenant who has been caring for them describes Machine:

"He calls himself Machine because he's an idiotic adolescent rebel and he wears that— that Trivia on his head to give himself twenty-four hours a day of solid nirvana, station NOTHING, turns off all stimuli . . . I *despise* bald young inexistential rebels who refuse to relate!" (page 7)

Machine has chosen his nihilistic state as much as Alyx has chosen her existential state. Accepting their situation on Paradise, he follows Alyx's instructions to prepare himself for the journey. He returns to "station NOTHING" when he can. Machine is Alyx's foil. They talk, they become lovers; when he is killed Alyx takes a side journey into his nihilism.

The experiential nature of the novel's narrative totally involves the telling of Alyx's story. For example, when Alyx takes her journey into Machine's nihilism, the narrative melds with Alyx's grief-stricken, drug-altered consciousness:

It said to her, in the voice of Iris: "You are frozen through and through. You are a detestable woman."

She fell back against the snow, dead. (page 138)

Were the narrator non-subjective—reliable— then Alyx just died; yet, in the next sentence Alyx is alive. The unreliable narrator is reliably reflecting the subjective consciousness of Alyx. The intrusion of a character's emotions and impressions may make the narration about the outer world unreliable while accurately reporting the character's innerscape.

In "The Writer Explains" (1966), Russ discusses her use of the narrative voice:

If I am to put you right in the mind of somebody who's undergoing an overwhelming experience of some kind—particularly an experience of alienation—what something feels like, how it registers subjectively, is of paramount importance. That is: some things are real first and then become imaginary. . . . Some things are presented as real but you know they can't be. . . . Some apparently mean more to the protagonist than they do to you and me. (page 102)

The narrative voice controls the story. Thus, each viewpoint character governs each story with a subjective set of circumstances, perceptions, and individual blinders. This unpredictability typifies Russ's works.

Voice constitutes the most pervasive, the most striking single element of Russ's works. The voice of each narrator is distinct, and these voices are distinct from the voice of Russ the essayist. Her language is sparse. She sets the fictional backdrop quickly, as in the first sentence of *Picnic*.

She was a soft-spoken, dark-haired, small-boned woman, not even coming up to their shoulders, like a kind of dwarf or miniature— but that was normal for a Mediterranean Greek of nearly four millennia ago, before super-diets and hybridizations from seventy colonized planets had turned all humanity (so she had been told) into Scandinavian giants.

639

Joanna Russ in 1973. PHOTO BY JAY KAY KLEIN

The science fiction conceit, the protagonist Alyx, and her position in the world are immediately defined. Through compact descriptive techniques and cinematic scenes (long accepted in film and theater), Russ moves from scene to scene. She often omits the smooth transitions common in prose. Scenes usually begin with enough information to identify character, setting, and action. If any of these is not essential to the understanding of the scene, it may be omitted. Such omissions are the prerogative (or whimsy) of the subjective narrator, who establishes all elements of the story.

Russ's second novel, *And Chaos Died* (1970), tells the story of Jai Vedh, who becomes a telepath through exposure to a long-isolated human colony that has developed telepathic powers. After the destruction of the spaceship on which he is a passenger, Jai escapes with the ship's captain and lands on the planet in a lifeboat. On the telepaths' unnamed planet, both men are confused by the

situation, and are as shocked at the natives as missionaries were at South Sea Islanders—they do not work for their living. Delany, in "Models of *Chaos*," calls the telepaths' planet utopian, while making the distinction between the rural (tropical) minimum-technological utopias popular in the 1960's and the *hidden* technology and *invisible* (inaudible) communication (telepathy) of Russ's utopia in *Chaos*. Their pleasant existence is based on the complete honesty of each person's knowing the others' thoughts. It is the honesty and release that Jai longs for in the first pages of the story when he realizes that he is not an individual, but a part of a greater oneness:

> . . . he threw himself against one of the portholes, flattening himself as if in immediate collapse, the little cousin he lived with all his life become so powerful in the vicinity of its big relative that he could not bear it. . . . They told him, as he went under, that the space between the stars was full of light, full of matter—what was it someone had said, an atom in a cubic yard?—and so not such a bad place after all. He was filled with peace, stuffed with it, replete; the big cousin was trustworthy. (page 10)

The captain, though, feels none of Jai's desire for unity with the universe, and will learn nothing of the telepathy that shapes the world. Jai is open to learning of the natives' telepathy, and soon becomes telepathic himself.

Through the use of the subjective narrator, the telepathic scenes are among the most convincing written, leaping the abyss of the isolated word, and establishing a conceptual framework for communication. As Delany points out, Russ constructs the story so that there are not the "conventional" subordinations of "'primary' problems, 'secondary' contrasts, and 'tertiary' commentary, which is what evoking the convention [of subordination] in the text automatically accomplishes" ("Models of *Chaos*").

Jai, like Alyx, is concerned with his immediate survival, not some hope of what might be or regret of what has not been. This does not mean that Jai does not have hopes, feelings, reactions, and fears. It means that these are united in his existence—his existentialism—as a part of his continuing innerscape. Delany says "these desires, feelings, reactions, and fears *become* the material of the text—that is to say they are presented at a much finer degree of resolution than we usually expect in a novel ("Models of *Chaos*"). The intensity of Jai's telepathic abilities provides a graphic and insightful examination of Jai's native culture (earth) as a collection of isolated individuals, whose separate self-destructiveness wreaks societal chaos (of the title), juxtaposed against the harmonious, self-determined individuals who compose the communal consciousness of the telepathic colony.

The subjective narrator of *The Female Man* (1975) reflects, separately, four female protagonists from four alternate, parallel worlds. Communal consciousness is not a part of these worlds. Instead, a type of cinematic montage melds the four characters, while the four worlds remain separate. Russ explores the connection among women and the effect of patriarchy upon women. A statement by Adrienne Rich in *On Lies, Secrets, and Silence* (1979) reflects the impulse that is at the heart of *The Female Man:*

> . . . to become truly educated and self-aware, against the current of patriarchal education, a woman must be able to discover and explore her root connection with *all women.* Her previous education has taught her only of her prescribed relationships with men, or "Women beware women." (page 145)

Russ explores this root connection among women through the worlds and innerscapes of the four protagonists. Janet is from a world where there are no men, Whileaway, which has developed a woman-centered culture, free of sexism. Jeannine is from an alternate earth that did not experience World War II; its Great Depression continues in the 1960's. Joanna is from our earth (though the character Joanna

is no more Joanna Russ than any of the other protagonists). Jael is from a world where the battle of the sexes became open warfare.

Any one of the four subjective consciousnesses can guide the narrative voice, but only one viewpoint appears in each chapter, even if several of the protagonists are in the chapter. Here, more than in any of Russ's other novels, the narrative voice establishes and directs all the elements of the story. She stretches her use of language to accommodate her vision. The story is told in a combination of narratives and glimpses.

The narrative sections contain the usual story progression, characterization, setting, and innerscape of the characters:

> Jeannine wakes from a dream of Whileaway. She has to go to her brother's this week. Everything suggests to Jeannine something she has lost, although she doesn't put it to herself this way; what she understands is that everything in the world wears a faint coating of nostalgia, makes her cry, seems to say to her, "You can't." She's fond of not being able to do things; somehow this gives her a right to something. (page 105)

The chapter continues for four pages, describing Jeannine's morning, her feelings, the peripheral things that make her world whole.

The glimpses are short, autonomous anecdotes that may or may not further the story line. They add to the texture of the story, and draw into it comments and observations that would be lost, obscured, or irrelevant within a longer narrative. Each glimpse appears as a chapter, forming its own context. The following three glimpses are complete, and as they appear at the end of Part One:

XIV

> Jeannine, out of place, puts her hands over her ears and shuts her eyes on a farm on Whileaway, sitting at the trestle-table under the trees where everybody is eating. *I'm not here. I'm not here.* Chilia Ysayeson's youngest has

641

taken a fancy to the newcomer; Jeannine sees big eyes, big breasts, big shoulders, thick lips, all that grossness. Mr. Frosty is being spoilt, petted and fed by eighteen Belins. *I'm not here.*

XV

JE: Evason is not "son" but "daughter." This is *your* translation.

XVI

And here we are. (page 18)

Each glimpse must stand on its own, a statement separate from any other in the book. *The Female Man* as a whole is unorthodox. Feminist dialectic, the unusual circumstance of four viewpoint characters, social commentary, literary commentary, and textual experimentation converge into an aesthetic of politics and art, without didacticism or self-indulgence. The internal monologue and the external narration are often inseparable, and at all times the four points of view must be distinguished or blended as the narrator indicates. Root connection among the protagonists, not plot line, creates, as Marilyn Hacker says in her introduction to the Gregg Press edition of *The Female Man*, "the illusion that the book was not plotted in advance to reach a foregone conclusion, with the points on the way charted and checked off—it invents itself as it goes along" (page xx).

This illusion continues to the end. The four protagonists are last seen together having lunch. The narrative voice has ceased to be linked with the subjective reality of any of the four. A new voice, an auctorial voice, guides the narrative. This new voice bids good-bye to the characters, at once all of them and none of them:

We got up and paid our quintuple bill; then we went out into the street. I said goodbye and went off with Laur, I, Janet; I also watched them go, I, Joanna; moreover I went off to show Jael the city, I Jeannine, I Jael, I myself.

Goodbye, goodbye, goodbye. (page 212)

After more good-byes the auctorial voice gives the book instructions on how to behave in the world, how to accept a "little book's" fate. A fifth reality has been added, one that slightly resembles the auctorial voice of Henry Fielding.

Although *The Female Man* was first published in 1975, Russ finished the novel in December 1971—before the resurgence of feminism. This makes the novel more remarkable. Indeed, it is more understandable if it is viewed as preceding, rather than proceeding from, the feminist movement. Russ invented the modern feminism and the dialectics she wrote; she owes many fewer debts than the 1975 publication date indicates.

We Who Are About To . . . (1977), Russ's fourth published novel, makes a radical departure from the heroic conventions that have been the bread-and-butter of science fiction. The Robinson Crusoe survival theme is one of the more common heroic traditions. Usually shipwrecked space travelers land unhurt on some uncharted planet, there handily to survive. These lucky people, who in reality probably could not survive in a state park, increase their number, conquer the planet, and establish and maintain an ideal 1950's patriarchy. If success seems doubtful, friendly aliens may help them, or rescue may come. Russ once claimed that *We Who* comes in part as a reaction to one such story, *Darkover Landfall* (1972), by Marion Zimmer Bradley, and the correspondence and controversy that followed its publication. Russ reshaped the convention, exploring what could happen if ordinary starship passengers—possibly the eight people anyone would least like to be stranded with—landed on an uncharted planet, a refuge chosen for its statistical probability of supporting human life.

Russ alludes to the Robinson Crusoe myth, but casts doubt on the survival of the group. The first line of the story completes the title:

"About to die. And so on." The protagonist assesses the situation in a recording she makes as she herself prepares to die. Again, Russ uses the technique of subjective consciousness, while the protagonist slips from an existential viewpoint to nihilism.

The problems this group faces and the dissimilarity between them and Robinson Crusoe form the framework of the story. The protagonist evaluates the situation:

> The Sahara is your backyard, so's the Pacific trench . . . you are never more than 13,000 miles from anywhere. . . . (page 7)

Russ contrasts this with their situation, shipwrecked in the infinity of deep space. Their losses are staggering:

> Goodbye ship, goodbye crew, goodbye medicine, goodbye books, goodbye freight, goodbye baggage, goodbye computer that could have sent back an instantaneous distress call along the coordinates we came through (provided it had them, which I doubt), goodbye plodding laser signal, no faster than other light, that might have reached somewhere, sometime, this time, next time, never. You'll get around to us in a couple of thousand years. (page 8)

Their resources are limited:

> We're a handful of persons in a metal bungalow: five women, three men, bedding, chemical toilet, simple tools, an even simpler pocket laboratory, freeze-dried food for six months, and a water-distiller with its own sealed power pack, good for six months (and cast as a unit, unusable for anything else). (pages 8–9)

The list parallels items currently in steamship lifeboats, logically extended for everyday space travel. Russ suspends our disbelief by making the items sound all too old; inadequate.

The age of space exploration and colonization has passed. The survivors are nothing more than a coachful of people traveling from one cosmopolitan center to another. None possesses any skills for meeting the challenge. What they do bring with them is the social, psychological, and physical garbage that has made their lives difficult amidst plenty. As the narrator and her companions are introduced, it becomes apparent that no polymath will emerge to save them, nor will they be "saved by nature," as in the romanticism of Rousseau.

The group being examined is very similar to the group of tourists in *Picnic on Paradise*. Likewise, the heroic conventions are the same. Russ is examining not only the science fiction genre, but her own writing as well. There are no survivors.

The Two of Them (1978) owes much to the Alyx stories. Like Alyx, Irene Waskiewicz and her mentor/cohort Ernst Neumann work for Trans-Temporal, which they call "The Gang" (as mentioned earlier). Irene, the protagonist, is a spiritual sister of Alyx: scrappy, opinionated, capable, and alienated. The characters and setting are an acknowledged borrowing from Suzette Hayden Elgin's story "For the Sake of Grace" (1969), but *The Two of Them* is undeniably Russ.

All the elements of Russ's previous works converge in *The Two of Them*. The new female myth of which Russ spoke in "What Can a Heroine Do . . ." is operating. Alyx exists in the story's literary mythology. Irene's dream hero is a woman, "The Woman, Irenne [sic] Adler" from Sherlock Holmes, her teenage alter-ego. Irene is a powerful woman.

Simultaneously, female powerlessness is examined through Irene and Ernst's assignment on Ala-ed-deen, an imitation Muslim colony planet based on the male-dominated culture of fairy tales, such as *Arabian Nights*. This culture also bears a striking similarity to that of American suburbs, with their isolation of the housewife and the children. The choice of environment echoes the confinement of the culture: the people live within the planet, beneath its boiling surface.

Irene and Ernst are equals in their world and duties: they alternate between being the conscience and the active, regardless of the social biases of the planet they are operating on. Also, this equality does not reflect the worlds that surround them. Irene and Ernst come from alternate earths, where the mythology and position of women are similar. Irene is a token woman in "The Gang," and she knows it. In a series of flashbacks interspersed with the action, Irene reflects upon her girlhood and Ernst's effect on her. She begins to come to grips with the common condition of women, and with what *she* must do to survive.

Russ manipulates the accepted masculine traditions within the context of the story: she both recreates these myths and reverses them, providing an alien (female alien) view of a heroine's abilities. Several times she uses the aesthetic of the helpless woman—the damsel in distress. Irene rescues a little girl, Zubeydah, from the oppression of Ala-ed-deen. The theme of "woman as helpmate" is recast and reexamined as Ernst becomes the faithless helpmate who can be killed with few exterior penalties to the killer. Irene then becomes the pursued hero who escapes into the wilderness because of an act of conscience, and finds herself in some earth's Albuquerque. (Russ uses alternate earths, and no particular earth is necessarily *the Earth*.)

The narrative voice and Irene's viewpoint are closely joined. Irene is the subjective narrator, who can be unreliable as well as poignant. Irene rescues Zubeydah and Zubeydah kidnaps a little boy in a complex narration that is then negated by the one-line paragraph: "I made that part up."

Finally, Russ has created another myth: the strong heroic woman who can love, and hate, and reflect upon her actions with satisfaction and dissatisfaction. She is not an object. She has objects and goals for both her interior and exterior lives, and she has a future that she must build and live in herself.

In "What Can a Heroine Do . . ." Russ wrote of mythmaking:

> If a female writer does not use the two, possibly three, myths available to a she-writer, she must drop the culture's myth altogether.

. . . A developed myth has its own expectation and values, its own clues-to-nudge-the-reader. (page 11)

What Russ suggests for alternative myths is what she writes: "fictional myths *growing out of their* [women's] *lives* and told by themselves for themselves." She has created a feminist myth that presents women—good women, strong women, self-sufficient women (as well as bad, weak, dependent women)—whose lives are the basis of the mythmaking process; for it is important to provide images of female activity, success, and power. In her children's book, *Kittatinny: A Tale of Magic* (1978), she uses mythmaking to create "a fairy-tale world that teaches [the reader] specifically as a girl, to be strong, confident, and knowledgeable about the world" (Marilyn Holt, "No Docile Daughters").

Russ has gone beyond simple acceptance or simple rejection of contemporary attitudes. Her myths have a greater consequence than providing a context for her stories. The myths are intended to create new ways of thinking. "Literature is the bearer . . . of all the modes of understanding of which *words* are capable; and not only that: it also bears, sets in motion or life, certain modes which words merely initiate and symbolize" (R. P. Blackmur, "Notes on Four Categories in Criticism"). The life she sets into motion intimates the future.

—MARILYN J. HOLT

In the 1980's and 1990's, Joanna Russ expanded her repertoire in both fiction and nonfiction. As she has broadened her writings about lesbianism and feminism, she has produced less science fiction and more nonfiction. Her literary output has slowed somewhat in the past two decades, in part because she has struggled with chronic fatigue immune deficiency syndrome. In 1994, she left her teaching post at the University of Washington and now resides in Tucson, Arizona.

Russ's 1980 novel *On Strike Against God* is the semiautobiographical "coming out" story of a college professor. Although *On Strike Against God* is not science fiction, it is

644

similar to Russ's science fiction in its narrative experimentation, humor, and speculation about how life could be different (in this novel, as in *The Female Man*, the alternative reality includes recognition of lesbianism). When Esther decides, in the face of her friends' opposition, that she will live as a lesbian, she thinks:

> One moves incurably into the future but there is no future; it has to be created. So it all ends up totally unsupported, self-caused, that symbol of eternity, The Snake Biting Its Own Tail. I'm strong because I have a future; I have a future because I willed it; I willed it because I'm strong." (page 85)

Like *The Female Man* and *The Two of Them*, *On Strike Against God* demonstrates that a future thought impossible can become real through female strength and action.

Russ returned to science fiction, fantasy, and speculative fiction with *Extra(Ordinary) People* (1984); thematically, she remained consistent, examining and subverting gender and sexual roles. *Extra(Ordinary) People* is a series of five connected stories, which can also be read as separate pieces. "Souls," the first story in the book, received the Hugo award in 1983. Throughout the collection, Russ plays with common science fiction plots, motifs, and metaphors and creates uncommon stories (just as she confounded the typical Robinson Crusoe narrative in *We Who Are About To . . .*). For example, in "Bodies," the third story, she places a lesbian time traveler into a future, pan-sexual utopia. One might expect the time traveler to find peace and happiness in a society that accepts her sexuality (unlike her home world), but Russ instead describes the woman's difficult adjustment and her nostalgia for a familiar, if hostile, home. The characters in these stories experience gender and sexuality as complex and sometimes ambiguous. Appropriately, *Extra(Ordinary) People* ends not with an optimistic promise of women's freedom, as does *The Female Man*; instead, it refuses resolution, with the question of whether "the world's ever been saved" left unanswered.

Many of Russ's other short stories are collected in *The Zanzibar Cat* (1983) and *The Hidden Side of the Moon* (1987). The stories in these collections reflect Russ's favorite techniques and themes; repeatedly, she bends the conventions of genre to create new myths and possibilities for women. For example, "My Dear Emily" (1962, in *The Zanzibar Cat*) presents a familiar scenario: the Victorian-era girl on the verge of womanhood, threatened by a vampire. However, the tragedy is undercut by a sly suggestion—that for Emily, vampirism is a way out of a dull life and an inevitable, loveless marriage. *The Zanzibar Cat* opens with the Nebula award-winning "When It Changed" (1972) which introduces ideas and elements Russ developed more fully in *The Female Man*, such as the all-female world of Whileaway. These collections illustrate Russ's range and command of genre because they include not only science fiction but also fantasy and horror stories.

Russ's nonfiction works of the 1980's and 1990's deal directly with feminism and lesbianism and are less overtly concerned with science fiction than her earlier essays. *How to Suppress Women's Writing* (1983) is a fast-paced tour of the various strategies used to discredit women's literature; examples of female science fiction writers are included. *Magic Mommas, Trembling Sisters, Puritans, and Perverts: Feminist Essays* (1985) includes pieces on lesbianism, the women's movement, and pornography. Because Russ weaves personal experience into all her nonfiction, her lifelong love of science fiction is manifested in these essays.

Two of Russ's major interests are united in *To Write Like a Woman: Essays in Feminism and Science Fiction* (1995). Most of the essays in this collection had been previously published; it includes "What Can a Heroine Do? or Why Women Can't Write" (1972) and "*Amor Vincit Foeminam*: The Battle of the Sexes in Science Fiction" (1980). The new essays in *To Write Like a Woman* are concerned with feminism and lesbianism rather than with science fiction, as is the book *What Are*

We Fighting For? Sex, Race, Class and the Future of Feminism (1998).

Russ has written very little science fiction since *Extra(Ordinary) People*. In her nonfiction work, however, she continues the project of positing alternative, feminist realities, which is the hallmark of her science fiction.

—JULIE LINDEN

Selected Bibliography

FICTION OF JOANNA RUSS

Picnic on Paradise. New York: Ace, 1968.
And Chaos Died. New York: Ace, 1970; Boston: Gregg, 1978. (Reprint has introduction by Robert Silverberg.)
The Female Man. New York: Bantam, 1975; Boston: Gregg, 1977. (Reprint has introduction by Marilyn Hacker.)
"A Few Things I Know About Whileaway." In *The New Improved Sun.* Edited by Thomas Disch. New York: Harper and Row, 1975.
Alyx. Boston: Gregg, 1976. (With an introduction by Samuel R. Delany.)
We Who Are About To. . . . New York: Dell, 1977.
Kittatinny: A Tale of Magic. New York: Daughters, 1978.
The Two of Them. New York: Berkley-Putnam, 1978.
On Strike Against God. Brooklyn, N.Y.: Out and Out Books, 1980; Trumansburg, N.Y.: Crossing, 1985.
The Zanzibar Cat. Sauk City, Wisc.: Arkham House, 1983. (Foreword by Marge Piercy.)
Extra(Ordinary) People. New York: St. Martin's, 1984.
The Hidden Side of the Moon: Stories. New York: St. Martin's, 1987.
"Excerpt from a Forthcoming Novel." *The Seattle Review,* 9, no. 1 (1986): 51–58.
"Invasion." *Isaac Asimov's Science Fiction Magazine* (January 1996). Also in *Year's Best SF2.* Edited by David G. Hartwell, New York: HarperPrism, 1996.

NONFICTION OF JOANNA RUSS

"The Writer Explains." *Epoch* (Winter 1966).
"Daydream Literature and Science Fiction." *Extrapolation,* 11, no. 1 (December 1969).
"The He-Man Ethos in Science Fiction." In *Clarion II.* Edited by Robin S. Wilson. New York: Signet, 1972.
"Images of Women in Science Fiction." In *Images of Women in Fiction: Feminist Perspectives.* Edited by Susan Cornillon. Bowling Green, Ohio: Bowling Green University Popular Press, 1972.
"What Can a Heroine Do?—or Why Women Can't Write." In *Images of Women in Fiction: Feminist Perspectives* (1972).

"Speculations: The Subjunctivity of Science Fiction." *Extrapolation,* 15 (December 1973).
"'What If . . .?' Literature." In *The Contemporary Literary Scene 1973.* Edited by Frank N. Magill. Englewood Cliffs, N.J.: Salem, 1974.
"Towards an Aesthetic of Science Fiction." *Science-Fiction Studies,* 2, part 2 (July 1975).
"Alien Monsters." In *Turning Points: Essays on the Art of Science Fiction.* Edited by Damon Knight. New York: Harper and Row, 1977.
"S.F. and Technology as Mystification." *Science-Fiction Studies,* 5, part 3 (November 1978).
"Amor Vincit Foeminam: The Battle of the Sexes in S.F." *Science-Fiction Studies,* 7, part 1 (March 1980).
How to Suppress Women's Writing. Austin: University of Texas Press, 1983.
Magic Mommas, Trembling Sisters, Puritans and Perverts: Feminist Essays. Trumansburg, N.Y.: Crossing, 1985.
To Write Like a Woman: Essays in Feminism and Science Fiction. Bloomington and Indianapolis: Indiana University Press, 1995.
What Are We Fighting For? Sex, Race, Class and the Future of Feminism. New York: St. Martin's, 1998.

CRITICAL AND BIOGRAPHICAL STUDIES

Annas, Pamela J. "New Worlds, New Word." *Science-Fiction Studies,* 5, part 2 (July 1978).
Blackmur, R. P. "Notes on Four Categories in Criticism." In *The Lion and the Honeycomb.* New York: Harcourt, Brace and World, 1955.
Bretnor, Reginald, ed. *Science Fiction: Today and Tomorrow.* Baltimore: Penguin, 1974.
Delany, Samuel R. *The Jewel-Hinged Jaw.* New York: Berkley, 1978.
———. "Models of *Chaos.*" In *Starboard Wine: More Notes on the Language of Science Fiction.* Elizabethtown, N.Y.: Dragon, 1984.
DuPlessis, Rachel Blau. "The Feminist Apologues of Lessing, Piercy, and Russ." *Frontiers,* 4, no. 1 (1979): 1–8.
Hacker, Marilyn. "Science Fiction and Feminism: The Work of Joanna Russ." *Chrysalis,* 4 (1977): 67–79. Reprinted as an introduction to *The Female Man,* Boston: Gregg, 1977.
Holt, Marilyn J. "No Docile Daughters." *Room of One's Own,* Fall 1980.
Klein, Gerald. "Discontent in American Science Fiction." *Science-Fiction Studies,* 4 (March 1977).
Lefanu, Sarah. "The Reader as Subject: Joanna Russ." *Feminism and Science Fiction.* Bloomington and Indianapolis: Indiana University Press, 1989.
Moylan, Tom. *Demand the Impossible: Science Fiction and the Utopian Imagination.* New York: Methuen, 1986.
Rich, Adrienne. *On Lies, Secrets, and Silence.* New York: WW Norton, 1979.

Russ, Joanna. Interview. In *Across the Wounded Galaxies*, by Larry McCaffery. Chicago: University of Illinois Press, 1990.

———. Interview. In *Backtalk: Women Writers Speak Out*, by Donna Perry. New Brunswick, N.J.: Rutgers University Press, 1993.

Spencer, Kathleen L. "Rescuing the Female Child: The Fiction of Joanna Russ." *Science Fiction Studies*, 17 (1990): 167–187.

Suvin, Darko. "Communication in Quantified Space." *CLIO*, 4, no. 1 (October 1974): 51.

—JULIE LINDEN

ERIC FRANK RUSSELL

(1905–1978)

ERIC FRANK RUSSELL has achieved a unique, though unenviable, distinction among that group of science fiction writers closely associated with the "Golden Age" of John W. Campbell, Jr., and *Astounding Science-Fiction* (roughly 1938–1946). It is that, as of the beginning of 1981, not one of his novels is in print in paperback on either side of the Atlantic. Various external reasons may be put forward for this—most convincingly, that his inactivity in his later years meant he was no longer an important force in a market largely shaped by commercial considerations. But, more significantly, it may indicate that a major sector of 1940's and 1950's science fiction is beginning to follow that of the 1920's and 1930's into obscurity.

Russell was born on 6 January 1905 at Sandhurst, England, where his father was an instructor at the military academy. He had a peripatetic upbringing—including a period in North Africa, echoes of which are to be found in certain of his stories, "Homo Saps" (1941), for example—and a mixed education. He worked at various unexceptional jobs—quantity surveyor, draftsman, and, for many years, representative of an engineering firm—before achieving his ambition to become a full-time freelance writer. He was married and had one daughter.

The available biographical information on Russell extends little beyond this basic outline, because he consistently refused to give interviews or to write about himself. As he put it:

This is not because I have anything to conceal. . . . It is simply because ever since childhood I've been a firm believer in the freedom of the individual and his right to privacy. So if anyone asks whether I part my hair on the right, the left, or in the middle, my instinctive reaction is to demand, "What effing business is it of yours?" . . . Of course, I recognise that some people have a natural curiosity about other people. But I don't recognise that that implies the right to have the said curiosity satisfied. (letter dated 9 January 1973)

Russell came into contact with the world of science fiction fandom in the mid-1930's through his membership in the British Interplanetary Society (a still-flourishing organization devoted to the serious study of space flight). He was encouraged to attempt fiction and soon sold his first story, "The Saga of Pelican West" (1937), to *Astounding Stories*. His early short stories are unremarkable, but his reputation was established in 1939 with the publication of his first novel, *Sinister Barrier*, which was featured in the first issue of the fantasy magazine *Unknown*, a companion magazine to *Astounding Science-Fiction*. (It appeared in book form in 1943.)

Sinister Barrier owes its genesis to the works of the American iconoclast Charles Fort (1874–1932), of whom Russell was a passionate devotee. Fort spent his life collecting and collating thousands of accounts of events and phenomena apparently inexplicable by orthodox science. The four books he published—*The Book of the Damned* (1919),

New Lands (1923), *Lo!* (1931), and *Wild Talents* (1932)—contain a mass of such material, interspersed with fanciful theories to account for it. One such theory was the idea that the human race is little better than a herd of cattle—that it is, in fact, the property of some unseen and unsuspected owner. In Russell's novel a scientist discovers a way to extend the powers of human sight—the "barrier" of the title being that which limits visual perceptions to a narrow range of electromagnetic frequencies—and thus encounters the Vitons, energy beings who gain sustenance by drawing from humans the energies generated by strongly negative emotions. Conflict and wars are the result of Viton manipulation in order to produce their "food." The novel details humanity's successful fight to throw off the Viton yoke.

On publication the novel acquired an immediate reputation as a science fiction "classic." This may be somewhat attributable to the unusual amount of publicity it received in conjunction with the launching of *Unknown*—but whatever the reason, it is hard to understand, for *Sinister Barrier* is a crude and implausible thriller, constructed according to a stock pulp formula. Nor did Russell fare any better with his second novel, *Dreadful Sanctuary* (serialized in *Astounding Science-Fiction*, 1948; book form, 1951). This novel suggests that Earth is an asylum for the lunatics of the rest of the solar system. It is a confusing, violent farrago, only slightly mitigated by the discovery that the proponents of this absurd theory are themselves mad. (Russell later revised the novel to leave its ending more ambivalent, and pruned some of its worst excesses; but it was not significantly improved by this exercise.) If Russell's reputation rested solely on works like these, it is fair to suppose that he would long ago have passed into well-deserved obscurity.

A rather different picture emerges from Russell's short fiction: indeed, almost without exception, throughout his career it is to his short stories rather than his novels that one must turn to find his individual and characteristic qualities. The earliest notable examples are the short stories later yoked together as the novel *Men, Martians and Machines* (1955): "Jay Score" (1941), "Mechanistria" (1942), and "Symbiotica" (1943). (The novel also includes a fourth episode, "Mesmerica," not previously published.) The first story introduces a thoroughly humanoid robot; the sequels take him and his shipmates on voyages of exploration to distant worlds with strange civilizations. On Mechanistria they find a society consisting solely of machines; on Symbiotica, a world in which animal and vegetable life-forms share a complex symbiotic relationship.

The stories offer somewhat rudimentary explorations of these societies through capture-and-escape adventures, but they show a more fertile imagination than Russell had hitherto demonstrated. More important, perhaps, they show a tolerant, unprejudiced writer—in striking contrast with the paranoid fantasy of *Sinister Barrier*. The crew of the spaceship *Marathon*, in addition to its humanoid robot, includes—most unusually for genre science fiction of the period—a black surgeon characterized unstereotypically in completely matter-of-fact terms. The most memorable characters are the lazy, chess-playing octopoid Martians. Sympathetically rendered, intelligent aliens were rare in genre science fiction of the 1930's and 1940's, and rarer still in the pages of *Astounding Science-Fiction*, whose editor, Campbell, disliked stories that portrayed aliens as superior to humans. Russell's Martians, though, demonstrate obvious intellectual superiority (notably through their mastery of chess).

The stories also show Russell's besetting weakness: his failure to apply sufficient imaginative effort to the incidental elements of his stories. They tend to be cluttered with bits of 1940's or 1950's technology transplanted to a future scenario only because the author could not be bothered to think of anything better. Thus, in "Symbiotica," when the spaceship is under threat, the commander secures it by setting up a pom-pom machine gun in the air lock! Such casual inattention to detail may pass unnoticed at the time, but it inevitably means that a writer's work will date as his contemporary technology becomes antiquated. Much of Russell's work has dated sadly in this respect.

Russell suggested in the Jay Score series that his sympathies lay with intelligent, rational beings, whatever their color or shape. This was to be amply borne out by subsequent stories. "Metamorphosite" (1946) is paradigmatic of several subsequent works. In this novella a single sane, calm, superevolved human faces and outwits the rulers of a rapacious Galactic Empire (themselves of human descent, it transpires). The men—and aliens—who rule the empire are depicted as unprincipled power seekers, interested primarily in wielding authority for its own sake. The adage "power tends to corrupt, and absolute power corrupts absolutely" is a basic assumption behind much of Russell's fiction. His vision of an ultimate, utopian society is of a constructive anarchy in which all intelligent beings of good sense work together peacefully and tolerantly. This state of grace is often—as in "Metamorphosite"—achieved through a process of evolution that consigns authoritarians and bureaucrats to the same status as the dinosaurs.

The theme of "Metamorphosite" reemerges in very similar terms in the novella "Design for Great Day" (*Planet Stories*, January 1953), which shows a small force from the Solarian Combine visiting a pair of warring, militaristic worlds and setting them on an inevitable course toward a state of development worthy of association with the combine. The complement of the Solarian vessels is not wholly human: they have on board "a number of homarachnids, spiderish quasi-humans from . . . a hot, moist world called Venus. It happened that this world circled around . . . a sun called Sol. Which meant that the homarachnids were Solarians along with the bipeds and bees and semivisible fuzzies."

"Design for Great-Day" also makes Russell's antipathy to those who set themselves up as rulers more explicit:

Eric Frank Russell. Courtesy of Jay Kay Klein Archives

Nobody knew better than Solarians that wars are not caused, declared or willingly fought by nations, planetary peoples or shape-groups, for these consist in the main of plain, ordinary folk who crave nothing more than to be left alone. The real culprits are power-drunken cliques of near-maniacs who by dint of one means or another have coerced the rest. (*Planet Stories*, page 32)

Attractive though these attitudes may be, they are no guarantee of good fiction, and both "Metamorphosite" and "Design for Great-Day" are weakened as stories because the advanced protagonists are so far superior to their opponents that there is never any doubt of the outcome, and thus no tension or conflict in the narrative. The same is true of Russell's third novel, *Sentinels from Space* (book form, 1953), published in *Startling Stories* in November 1951 as "The Star Watchers." In it he returns to the Fortean idea of Earth under external influence or control: in this case the benevolent guardianship of the superevolved sentinels of the title. An apparent threat to the sentinels—and to terrestrial peace and stability—is overcome with almost contemptuous ease.

In 1951, Russell also published the story for which he is probably best remembered, the novella ". . . And Then There Were None." This story, later incorporated into the novel *The Great Explosion* (1962), is another of Russell's anti-authority pieces and is in many respects a reworking of an earlier story, "Late Night Final" (1948). In "Late Night Final" an attempted alien conquest of Earth is frustrated, then completely subverted, by the indifference and refusal to cooperate of the highly civilized and gentle humans. In ". . . And Then There Were None," an Earth expedition attempts to persuade the colonists of a distant world—long cut off from outside contact—to allow themselves to be assimilated into an Earth-led federation, but their efforts are frustrated and subverted by the iconoclastic individualism and passive resistance of the inhabitants. Their techniques are modeled on those practiced by Mohandas Gandhi's followers in pre-independence India.

The later story is the better for several reasons. The peaceful society of the "Gands," as they are called, is explored in more detail than customary in Russell's fiction: it has no government and no money, but is held together by a complex system of obligations—or "obs"—traded off between individuals. (This society might plausibly be considered a primitive model for the anarchistic utopia mapped out in far greater detail in Ursula K. Le Guin's 1974 novel *The Dispossessed*.) The treatment in ". . . And Then There Were None" is at once more quirky and humorous, and more persuasive than that in "Late Night Final." Responsibility for their circumstances is placed firmly on the shoulders of individuals, as in the following exchange between a Gand woman (who speaks first) and a member of the visiting spaceship crew:

"It's your right to refuse to believe. That's freedom, isn't it?"

"Up to a point."

"To what point?"

"A man has duties. He has no right to refuse those."

"No?" She raised tantalizing eyebrows, delicately curved. "Who defines those duties—himself or somebody else?"

"His superiors most times."

"Superiors," she scoffed with devastating scorn. "No man is superior to another. No man has the slightest right to define another man's duties. If anyone on Terra exercises such impudent power it is only because idiots permit him to do so. They fear freedom. They prefer to be told. They like to be ordered around. They love their chains and kiss their manacles." (*The Great Explosion*, page 177)

". . . And Then There Were None" is one of Russell's two most successful stories; the other is "Dear Devil" (1950), a gentle story of a monstrous-looking, but peaceful and civilized Martian who befriends a group of children and helps them on the road back to civilization on an Earth devastated by nuclear war. The underlying theme—that people or beings should be judged according to their actions, not their appearance—is characteristic of Russell; the treatment in this story is the most successful he gave to this theme.

Up through 1949 Russell's output of stories had been regular but sparse: for the thirteen-year period 1937–1949, Donald Day's *Index to the Science Fiction Magazines* records thirty-four stories, including the first two novels. About two-thirds of these stories were published in *Astounding Science-Fiction*. During the next decade Russell was more than twice as prolific: sixty-nine appearances in ten years. These include occasional stories under the pseudonyms Webster Craig and Duncan H. Munro. His work appeared in a wider variety of magazines, but his best stories were still largely reserved for *Astounding*. Russell's increasingly humorous iconoclasm clearly struck a responsive chord in Campbell (although there is reason to suppose that their views would have been at odds on many subjects). In his introduction to *The Best of Eric Frank Russell* (1978), Alan Dean Foster reports a 1968 conversation with Campbell in which the editor stated that Russell was his favorite science fiction writer.

In his work of the 1950's, Russell tended to replace diatribes against authority with satires of bureaucracy. The tone is much lighter: the bureaucrats are not loathsome, but stupid and incompetent; bureaucracies, in Russell's view, are organizations positively hostile to intelligence, initiative, and unorthodoxy. The typical Russell story of the 1950's is about a resourceful and imaginative individual outwitting whole organizations, or even worlds, of dullards. Since the dullards are frequently aliens and the individuals are always human, the impression may be created that Russell shared the xenophobia common in science fiction of the period, but this is not so. His stupid aliens are never anything other than humans in slight disguise. The only specific antipathy detectable in Russell's fiction is directed toward the Germans, doubtless a result of his service in World War II.

This antipathy may be seen in two of his later novels: *Next of Kin* (1959; shorter version published in 1956 as "Plus X" and in book form as *The Space Willies*, 1958) and *Wasp* (1957). Both are World War II novels thinly rewritten as science fiction. In the former a human agent is captured by aliens and interned in a prisoner-of-war camp. He proceeds not only to outwit and demoralize his captors but also, in essence, to win the war single-handedly by preying on their ignorance and superstition. It is ingenious and amusing, but a better story in its shorter version (the expansion to novel length consisting of the inclusion of additional and nonessential material leading up to the protagonist's capture). *Wasp*, on the other hand, is the best-constructed of Russell's novels: indeed, it is the only one of his novels with a satisfactory construction, the others consisting of series of thud-and-blunder adventures, or strings of episodes yoked together, or (as in *Next of Kin*) overinflated short stories. In *Wasp* a human agent is dropped on one of the planets of the Sirian Empire (which is at war with Earth) to create as much mischief and mayhem as pos-

sible. The details of his exploits are suitably unconventional and amusing, but the novel suffers even more than *Next of Kin* from being a story of Nazi Germany transparently translated into science fiction. The Sirians even speak a language that sounds a lot like German—"yar" for "yes," and so on.

Russell's other original novel of the 1950's, *Three to Conquer* (1956), is an unfortunate reversion to the crudities of *Sinister Barrier* and *Dreadful Sanctuary*. In *Three to Conquer* an expedition to Venus is infected by a form of parasitic virus that takes mental and physical control of the explorers' bodies. They return to Earth intent on possessing the entire human race but are thwarted virtually single-handedly by the telepath Wade Harper, who is the first to identify the threat. The plot depends heavily on the alien-possessed humans' delivering themselves into Harper's hands at crucial moments, and it features the kind of unthinking violence to which Russell never gave way in his more characteristic work (as when Harper, confronted for the first time by one of the aliens, shoots her/it through the head, even though he cannot possibly know at that point whether the parasite's occupation of its human host is permanent or temporary). *Three to Conquer* is a paranoid fantasy in a vein similar to Robert A. Heinlein's *The Puppet Masters* (1951) or Jack Finney's *Invasion of the Body Snatchers* (1955) but is less persuasive than either of its predecessors.

More typical of Russell's later work are the two outright satires on stultifying bureaucracy, "Allamagoosa" (1955)—which won a Hugo award as the best short story of its year—and "Study in Still Life" (1959). Also typical is "Diabologic" (1955), in which a single human, armed only with an extensive knowledge of paradoxes, demoralizes an entire race of literal-minded humanoid aliens.

By the end of 1959, Russell was apparently at the peak of his popularity. (That he was popular is attested by the readers' preference votes on each issue of *Astounding Science-Fiction*. Russell had nineteen stories under his own name in the magazine during 1955–

1959, including the three-part serialization of *Three to Conquer* under the title "Call Him Dead." The readers voted his stories best in the issue on eleven occasions and gave him second place four times.) Much of his work had appeared in book form. Yet at this point his writing career was effectively at its end: he published the short stories "The Cosmic Relic" (1961) and "Meeting on Kangshan" (1965), expanded ". . . And Then There Were None" into the novel *The Great Explosion*, and wrote a routine near-future spy novel, *With a Strange Device* (1964; retitled *The Mindwarpers*, 1965). Further short story collections appeared, but they were composed of previously published works. After March 1965, Russell did not publish any new fiction. He died suddenly at his Liverpool home on 29 February 1978, following a heart attack.

Russell did not give any convincing explanation for his quite abrupt fall into silence. In *The Best of Eric Frank Russell*, Alan Dean Foster quotes a letter in which Russell says, "I can't write without being enthusiastic and I can't get enthusiastic about an old-hat plot"—but, as Foster points out, originality of plot was by no means a hallmark of Russell's work: his strength lay more in ingenuity of effect. A more convincing explanation for his silence may be that he simply ran out of variations on his regular themes.

As intimated previously, Russell's work has not survived well. Several of his novels now read like crude pulp melodramas; the World War II stories are as dated as the corresponding British movies of the period; still other stories are dated by the failures of imagination detailed earlier. A handful of stories, notably ". . . And Then There Were None" and "Dear Devil," stand up to rereading, although they lack any stylistic distinction, but in general it is unsurprising that Russell—unquestionably considered one of the top science fiction writers in the 1940's and 1950's—though he is nostalgically remembered by older readers, should otherwise be virtually forgotten today.

Selected Bibliography

WORKS OF ERIC FRANK RUSSELL

Sinister Barrier. Kingswood, Surrey, England: World's Work, 1943. Revised edition, Reading, Pa.: Fantasy Press, 1948.

Dreadful Sanctuary. Reading, Pa.: Fantasy Press, 1951. Revised edition, New York: Lancer, 1963.

Sentinels from Space. New York: Bouregy and Curl, 1953.

Deep Space. Reading, Pa.: Fantasy Press, 1954. (Short stories.)

Men, Martians and Machines. London: Dennis Dobson, 1955; New York: Roy, 1956.

Three to Conquer. New York: Avalon Books, 1956.

Wasp. New York: Avalon Books, 1957. Expanded text, London: Dennis Dobson, 1958.

Six Worlds Yonder. New York: Ace Books, 1958. (Short stories.)

The Space Willies. New York: Ace Books, 1958. Expanded and retitled *Next of Kin*, London: Dennis Dobson, 1959.

Far Stars. London: Dennis Dobson, 1961. (Short stories.)

Dark Tides. London: Dennis Dobson, 1962. (Short stories.)

The Great Explosion. London: Dennis Dobson, 1962; New York: Torquil, 1962.

With a Strange Device. London: Dennis Dobson, 1964. Reprinted as *The Mindwarpers*, New York: Lancer, 1965.

Somewhere a Voice. London: Dennis Dobson, 1965. (Short stories.)

Like Nothing on Earth. London: Dennis Dobson, 1975. (Short stories.)

The Best of Eric Frank Russell. New York: Ballantine Books, 1978. (Short stories.)

BIBLIOGRAPHIES

Stephensen-Payne, Phil. *Eric Frank Russell, Our Sentinel in Space: A Working Bibliography*. Rev. ed. San Bernardino, Calif.: Borgo, 1992.

Valéry, Francis. *Eric Frank Russell: A Bibliography*. Bordeaux, France: L'Académe de l'Espace, 1990.

CRITICAL AND BIOGRAPHICAL STUDIES

Foster, Alan Dean. "The Symbiote of Hooton." Introduction to *The Best of Eric Frank Russell*. New York: Ballantine Books, 1978.

Moskowitz, Sam. "Eric Frank Russell, Death of a Doubter." In *Amazing Stories*, June 1963. Reprinted in Moskowitz's collection *Seekers of Tomorrow*. Cleveland, Ohio: World Publishing Company, 1966.

—MALCOLM EDWARDS

MARGARET ST. CLAIR

(1911–1995)

In 1946, when *Fantastic Adventures*, a companion magazine to the better-known *Amazing Stories*, bought Margaret St. Clair's first science fiction story, its editors asked her to contribute an autobiographical note to the regular "Presenting the Author" column. Duly she did so, in the November 1946 issue. After describing her early life in the usual terms—she began to read science fiction when she was nine or ten years old, and so forth—she presented her readers with a brief credo that demonstrates how well she understood, even at the very beginning of her career, what the basic nature of her relationship to the field would be. After praising the shift in the literature of science fiction from "battle between the worlds" stories "to the current 'human interest' type of story," she makes a personal statement:

> I think I've found myself in fantasy. . . . It is not only a great deal of fun to write fantasy, but I enjoy the freedom of imagination attained in this sort of writing. I like to write about ordinary people of the future, surrounded by gadgetry of super-science, but who, I feel sure, know no more about how the machinery works than a present day motorist knows of the laws of thermodynamics. (page 2)

After this unremarkable but telling declaration in favor of realism, she concludes by stating her allegiance to the pulp magazines in more unusual terms:

> I feel that the pulps at their best touch a genuine folk tradition and have a balladic quality which the slicks lack. But I must admit to a fond affection for the columns of the *New Yorker*. (ibid.)

In those final sentences may well lie the beginnings of an explanation for Margaret St. Clair's oddly inconclusive science fiction career. It may well be that she arrived on the scene too early, before writers could freely combine the "balladic" elements of pulp literature and the urbane subtleties of the *New Yorker* with any expectation of being paid for their efforts. If this is indeed the case, then her essential departure from the field in the 1960's, just when greater freedom of style and subject matter had been won (and would be paid for), is a tragedy of mistiming.

"Rocket to Limbo," the story that launched St. Clair's career in that November 1946 issue of *Fantastic Adventures*, is by no means a prepossessing effort, though it does offer evidence of deeper ambitions in her work than the routine fulfilling of pulp requirements, however upliftingly described. It is a tale of the sort made so popular half a decade later in the pages of Horace Gold's *Galaxy*, much of the contents of which consisted of stories neatly and expeditiously crafted to turn the tables on the husbands and wives of an automated suburban America in the near future, and to punish them for excessive ambition, pride, sloth, or sexual infidelity of any stripe—especially the last.

Of course, within the pages of *Galaxy*, writers like Frederik Pohl took a satirical knife to the implications of such attacks on noncomformity, and the 1950's *Galaxy* can be seen as a kind of extended debate on the nature of Eisenhower-era America; though St. Clair's political sympathies seem generally to have been those of the Democratic left, and though these sympathies do illumine some of her satirical thrusts, she used the ambience of claustrophobia typical of *Galaxy* stories to rather different ends. For her, the human condition is one of claustrophobic helplessness, as hinted by her stated preference for protagonists who cannot understand the world that controls them; her stories and novels both present that condition in dramatic form—usually in plots that work to justify paranoia—and provide the occasional escape from it.

Constriction and a significantly open-ended complication are the rule in St. Clair's fiction. There is, for instance, no neat closure, no O. Henryish snapping shut of implications in the last sentences even of very early stories such as "Rocket to Limbo." In an automated, near-future urban setting, Millie and her husband have grown bored with each other. Although sex is not mentioned, its absence is felt. Millie comes across an advertisement from the firm of Smith and Tinkem—ads were, for a long while in the genre, a constantly recurring device for conveying the moment of temptation to which Mr. and Mrs. America would succumb at their peril— offering their clients the "quiet, safe disposal of human obstacles." Tempted, Millie visits Mr. Smith, who tells her that her husband will be tricked onto a rocket ship to Limbo. The trick works, but her husband has responded to the same ad, and Millie finds herself trapped with him on a bleak ship hurtling toward Limbo.

There are two points of interest in this punitive little fable. First, it is constructed so that the reader is fully aware of the double trap being sprung; second, the story does not end with the mutual discovery on the rocket. Back in the office, Mr. Smith's secretary asks him about what *really* happens to his customers, the notion of an actual Limbo being nonsense, of course. Smith shrugs and answers: "Tinkem takes care of them—after they get to Limbo, of course. . . ."

Here, in St. Clair's first published story, we can clearly see her characteristic refusal to resolve complications, to finish off her narratives in a way that leaves the reader in a state of safe repose. In this she resembles a later and rather more successful author, one who entered the field in the late 1960's, when it was more ready to absorb and even to celebrate narrative techniques that lead to an intensification of insecurity, rather than to a mollification. That author, James Tiptree, Jr., has made constantly unfolding exposition a trademark of her best stories, as Robert Silverberg has remarked. In the 1940's St. Clair was writing too early, as we have suggested, to receive much acclaim for muddying the previously clear waters of the pulp idiom.

Margaret St. Clair led a life rather more private than those of many of her fellow authors. She was born on 17 February 1911, in Hutchinson, Kansas, to professional parents; she married Eric St. Clair, an author of children's books, in 1932; she began publishing professionally in 1945, turning the next year to science fiction. Since she considered herself a native Californian by 1946, it can be assumed that she had lived there for some time prior to receiving an M.A. from the University of California in 1934.

Beyond rather extended lists of hobbies and the statement that she was emotionally attached to Quakerism but was "in no sense a Christian," St. Clair provided readers with relatively little hard data on her life. For many science fiction writers, deeply involved as they tend to be in the active social and professional life of the subculture, such reticence is a privilege difficult to maintain. In St. Clair's case it was a reticence that matches the evasive, tantalizing privacy at the heart of her books.

After half a decade in the field, St. Clair had established herself as an adaptable, prolific, reliable middleweight contributor to science fiction magazines like *Thrilling Wonder Stories* and its competitors, which specialized in swift action and florid space opera settings, very often utilizing Mars or Venus. Of the dozens of stories she published during these years, some of them among her best and most characteristic, several appear in her two collections, *Three Worlds of Futurity* (1964) and *Change the Sky and Other Stories* (1974). "Vulcan's Dolls," originally published in *Startling Stories* in 1952, became *Agent of the Unknown* (1956), St. Clair's first novel in book form and, in some ways, her most deeply revealing. But the fact that she could not have been fully satisfied with the pulp niche she inhabited suggests itself through one rather unusual circumstance. In these years science fiction writers often used pseudonyms, almost always in order to peddle excess material to lesser markets; their best work was usually published under their own names. In St. Clair's case, it was when she moved into more prestigious markets and began to publish stories in the newly founded *Magazine of Fantasy and Science Fiction* (1950) that she used a pseudonym, Idris Seabright, a name that for some years was as widely known as her own, and perhaps more highly regarded.

There is no question that the Idris Seabright stories—several of which appear in *Change the Sky* and *The Best of Margaret St. Clair* (1985) under St. Clair's own name—are suave, elegant, and witty, and represent that sneaking admiration for the slicks that she had spoken of in 1946. The dreamlike, congested absurdity underlying much of what she was writing under her own name is brought, in the Seabright stories, fully to the surface, so that tales like "An Egg a Month from All Over" (*Magazine of Fantasy and Science Fiction*, 1952), grim though they may seem in synopsis, convey a smartly crafted, aerated playfulness to the reader. (In 1961, St. Clair published in *Galaxy*, under her own name, the finest and funniest of all her Idris Seabright-type stories; in its burgeoning, complex hilarity "An Old-Fashioned Bird Christmas" shows how fruitfully she had learned to combine the St. Clair and Seabright modes, and how much the genre lost by her later silence, just when, it might seem, her time had finally come.) But however pleasing they may be, however appropriate to their somewhat more literary market, the Idris Seabright stories are comparatively slight jeux d'esprit, and generally fail to convey St. Clair's deepest and most persistent effects, which are those of nightmare.

Conventional wisdom, which is not always foolish, states that science fiction is basically a literature of optimism, and that the punitive moralities found in *Galaxy* and other magazines were a kind of aberration whose roots lay in fantasy, and in any case were expressed almost solely in short stories. Science fiction novels, in contrast, are supposed to concern themselves with the barrier of the unknown, which can be physical or mental, and with its penetration by a hero who grows in stature as the action progresses; at a science fiction novel's conclusion, new horizons have been opened, science has advanced, humanity reaches the stars, the hero gets the girl, and there's work to do. Despite her apparent adherence to some specific genre conventions, this general description of the science fiction novel applies to none of St. Clair's works.

In contrast with written science fiction, American science fiction movies of the 1950's are notoriously haunted by a contrary assumption, one it might seem that St. Clair shared: the paranoid conviction that piercing the barrier of the unknown is an unwarrantable act of hubris that will unleash monsters upon us in the form of nuclear devastation, or Communist body snatching, or fatal exposure of the naked id. But the novels of St. Clair only superficially confirm this politicized form of paranoia, for they consistently express a sense that—far from being treason against humanity—to shatter the barrier of the unknown is fully to express one's nature as a human being; the consequences may be grim, but it is far better to know that you inhabit the valley of the shadow than to delude yourself with the unexamined surface of events.

The relationship between St. Clair's short stories and her novels can readily be examined by comparison of a short story, "The Sacred Martian Pig" (*Startling Stories*, 1949; retitled "Idris' Pig" in *Three Worlds of Futurity*), with *Agent of the Unknown*. The story and the novel share a common space opera background, the main feature of which, beyond a vaguely delineated interstellar community, is a legendary fabricator of toys and puppets named Vulcan.

The story is comic. George Baker, psychological officer of an interplanetary liner bound for Mars, is hornswoggled by his cousin into attempting to deliver a tiny, terribly odorous blue pig to some religious cultists in Marsport. Unwittingly he also becomes a drug smuggler. A Martian woman, Idris, finds him after Plutonians have stolen the pig, and they share some helter-skelter adventures before regaining it; George is briefly jailed for drug smuggling. Long before they recover the pig—which is actually a creation of Vulcan's workshop—George has fallen out of love with Darleen, whom we never meet, and he and Idris have become enamored of each other. Idris turns out to be a Martian patriot, a fake priestess in the pig cult whose practices are too disgusting for her to detail; is endowed with enormous prestige among the criminal element in Marsport; and owns an "eating egg," another of Vulcan's creations, which conveniently eats circles in anything it is pointed at. After being bitten on the ankle by an amoeboid cerberus at the Plutonian embassy, George sends the pig off to be ritually eaten and the cult absorbed into history, where it will do no harm. George and Idris fall into each other's arms.

Pixilated, deadpan, pell-mell, the story reads in one long breath, after the nature of most short stories, which can generally be apprehended as a kind of mental image. A novel, on the other hand, has to be lived through. What in a typical St. Clair short story may be apprehended joyfully as wit, in one of her novels will be experienced as nightmare, justified paranoia; instead of tickling the funnybone, her constant, almost non sequitur, improvisatory turns of plot will feel like the corridors of a very bad dream.

Agent of the Unknown begins and ends on Fyon, an artificial pleasure planetoid where alcoholic Don Haig has been beachcombing and drinking himself to oblivion. He awakens on the beach and finds a tiny weeping doll; he is soon told by his old friend Kunitz that it is one of Vulcan's most famous artifacts. Kunitz also tells Don about having been born with wings because of the Martian pyrexia plague, and being persecuted by the Special Serum Purveyance teams; these teams, which had been fighting the mutagenic pyrexia, have developed into the SSP, a de facto solar government. By now Don is psychically bound to the doll, which seems to weep for him. Bendel, owner of a local circus, asks to see the doll, since it may with its emanations heal him of his grotesque disease; when Don feels compelled to refuse, Bendel opens his mouth and laughs like a hyena, revealing the hair on his tongue.

Don's foster sister, who designs mortuary decor for prolonged wakes, then arrives on Fyon and, just before a robot tries to murder her, persuades Don to take a new antialcoholism drug. When he takes the pills, he is hallucinated into the world of William Butler Yeats's "Byzantium" but refuses to give up the doll to the cocks of Hades. Kunitz finds him in this state and persuades him that the drug is a device being used by the SSP in order to obtain the doll. Don's foster sister must be in thrall to them, through her addiction to a self-flagellation cult. Don must flee. But before he does so, he meets Phyllis, the last active member of the Holy Fish cult. She promises to help him escape, and sleeps with him in a maintenance bubble beneath the shallow body-heat seas of Fyon, but is murdered by the SSP in the morning. They ship Don to Phlegethon, a prison planetoid and SSP headquarters. There he is taken in elevators up the Mountain to confer with Mulciber, head of the vast organization.

Mulciber turns out to be Bendel, with the hair still on his tongue; an ancient associate and enemy of Vulcan, he wants to gain possession of the doll so that he can kill it, for if ever it were fully activated with the wings he himself fabricated and still possesses, it would liberate the genes of the human species, with uncertain consequences; the SSP abhors chaos and mutation. Mulciber's scientists electronically pry the doll out of Don's control, and Mulciber and Don are left alone. In an action that "slaves and the helpless have always known," Don slays Mulciber with his manacled hands. Before the guards break in, Vulcan's comforting blacksmith's shadow appears and transports Don back to Fyon. Having retrieved the missing wings from the dead Mulciber, Don affixes them to his beloved doll, which disappears, glowing in triumph, already beginning to change humanity but leaving him bereft.

A new compulsion seizes Don; he steals a hotel launch and crosses the seas of Fyon for a day and a night to a spherical islet where Kunitz, who is of course Vulcan, greets him with deep kindness. Suspecting that he has been a dupe, Don confirms that Kunitz/Vulcan had arranged for him to find the doll and be captured by Mulciber solely to ensure the affixing of the wings, so that humanity could be free. Vulcan then asks Don to come with him far away and to sleep, perhaps for a thousand years. Don asks why. Vulcan tells him that he, too, is a doll. In anguish, remembering Phyllis, Don refuses Vulcan's solace, asking him for one boon only: death. This Vulcan grants him. As genuine humans begin to soar to the stars, the doll-man sinks softly into the warm, dark seas of artificial Fyon.

In most science fiction novels of this sort, Don, who can remember nothing before the age of fourteen, would most probably discover that he himself is Vulcan with amnesia, and would himself preside over the coming rise of humanity. Through nightmarish surface dislocations and manipulation of archetypal imagery, St. Clair promulgates a different sort of message. The world, she says, is far vaster than we can cope with or comprehend, and we will be doing very well if we can pass through the tunnel into some kind of peace. Though none of the other novels of her first decade of book publishing are as lucid as *Agent of the Unknown* in its melancholy and its moving terminal solace, *The Green Queen* (1956), *The Games of Neith* (1960), and *Message from the Eocene* (1964) variously combine the same kinds of complex plots and venues with similarly victimized, bewildered characters, to something of the same unsettling effect.

In the mode of her second decade, which overlaps with the first, St. Clair released four rather longer, ostensibly more ambitious novels. *The Dolphins of Altair* (1967) is a diffuse tale about dolphins that fails to convince; *The Dancers of Noyo* (1973) breaks new ground with a postcatastrophe California venue and a complex plot involving Indian protagonists with android Dancers and the oppression they represent, but it lacks sufficient vigor to cohere as a novel. The remaining books, *Sign of the Labrys* (1963) and *The Shadow People* (1969), are mature, distressing, obsessive exercises that explore the theme of constriction, both cultural and literal. Both novels begin (literally) underground, take their questing protagonists through labyrinths of oppressive darkness, and both move toward the solace of the Earth's surface, where life may continue, though modestly and chastened by knowledge of what lies beneath one's feet, within one's skull. *Sign of the Labrys* features an underground society constructed to survive a nuclear holocaust, while the underground world of *The Shadow People* preexists history and is reached by following complex routes into the bowels of the Earth. These differences are—as it were—superficial, different versions of the same quest through haunted caverns to an island of peace.

After years of silence, St. Clair published a new story in 1980. "Wryneck, Draw Me" follows directly upon "An Old-Fashioned Bird Christmas" in its deft mixing of horror and hilarity. Both stories appear in *The Best of Margaret St. Clair*, an anthology of twenty stories that gives a fair conspectus of her best work. It is unfortunate that, despite the continuing vigor of her work, she was increasingly perceived in the 1980's as a writer whose prime had long passed. After a period of silence, she died on 22 November 1995.

The sexual openness of "Wryneck, Draw Me" demonstrates that its author, at the age

659

of seventy and perhaps in spite of the perceptions of editors, was entirely capable of writing to a new audience. An enormous computer has engulfed all consciousness upon the planet, except for one wan sentience that watches from within as Jake—the computer—falls in love with itself, runs through a vast repertory of courtship behaviors, constructs a phallus and vagina out of its own innumerable components, and rapes itself to death. Thus it is with technological Man. After a while a family of raccoons explores the great, chaotic, ravaged tunnel. Soon their busy paws begin to dismantle the last knots Man had managed to tie himself into. Fading out, the observer sentience thanks God that the future lies in paws, not hands. There may be some peace.

Selected Bibliography

WORKS OF MARGARET ST. CLAIR

Agent of the Unknown. New York: Ace Books, 1956.
The Green Queen. New York: Ace Books, 1956.
The Games of Neith. New York: Ace Books, 1960.
Sign of the Labrys. New York: Bantam Books, 1963. London: Transworld (Corgi), 1963.
Message from the Eocene. New York: Ace Books, 1964.
Three Worlds of Futurity. New York: Ace Books, 1964. (Collection.)
The Dolphins of Altair. New York: Dell, 1967.
The Shadow People. New York: Dell, 1969.
The Dancers of Noyo. New York: Ace Books, 1973.
Change the Sky and Other Stories. New York: Ace Books, 1974. (Collection.)
The Best of Margaret St. Clair. Chicago: Academy, 1985. (Short stories.)

—JOHN CLUTE

LUIS PHILIP SENARENS
(1863–1939)

THE FIRST SCIENCE fiction magazine was not issued in 1926 as *Amazing Stories*, nor in 1923 as *Weird Tales* (with its occasional stories of "weird science"), but in 1892. It ran regularly in a numbered dime-novel series until 1898, with 191 issues, each of which contained a single story based on a fantastic invention. All the stories were attributed to "Noname," and all but four were written by one man, Luis Philip Senarens. The periodical was the *Frank Reade Library*.

The *Frank Reade Library* did not include the earliest of all dime-novel science fiction stories. That was *The Steam Man of the Prairies* (*Irwin's American Novels* no. 45, August 1868), published by one of the subsidiaries of the House of Beadle and Adams. Its author was Edward S. Ellis (1840–1916), one of the most important dime novelists. The story was based on a historical invention, the 1868 Newark Steam Man, a humaniform steam engine that walked along, drawing a small cart behind it.

With suitable substitutions of invention and place, *The Steam Man of the Prairies* offered the basic plot on which much dime-novel science fiction was based. It told of a clever, hunchbacked boy who built a mobile steam engine in the form of a man and took it out on the prairies, where it served as the focus of adventures among Indians and renegade whites. Like its historical predecessor of Newark, it was not a robot, as is sometimes inaccurately stated; it was simply a prime mover that reproduced the motion of the human leg and drew a carriage. The boy was ac-

companied by adult comic associates, and at the end of the story, the invention was destroyed.

The ideas unwittingly conveyed by *The Steam Man of the Prairies* dominated dime-novel science fiction for almost four decades. Ellis' short novel was essentially the story of a frontier, of a one-sided conflict between mechanization and primitive life, of the gifted American against the uncivilized man or the outlaw from civilization, in which the weaker side (automatically vicious) was ruthlessly crushed. It embodied a sizable amount of youthful revolt and wishful thinking on a simple level, as young inventors easily solved problems that baffled their elders, and it knew very little about science. It was concerned almost wholly with technology, which was often applied in a grotesque way.

Ellis, so far as is known, wrote no more invention stories, but his work served as the direct model for a far more important historical phenomenon. According to literary legend, one of the Beadle reissues of *The Steam Man of the Prairies* was seen by Frank Tousey, a competitor in dime-novel publishing, who decided that a series of invention stories would be profitable. He assigned a house writer, Harry Enton (1854–1927, pseudonym of Harry Cohen), to establish such a series, which first appeared in a juvenile story-paper, *Boys of New York*. Enton started the Frank Reade series with *The Steam Man of the Plains* (1876), which he followed with three more adventures: *Frank Reade and His Steam Horse* (1876), *Frank Reade and His Steam*

Team (1880), and *Frank Reade and His Steam Tally-Ho* (1881).

Enton, who was a capable writer within the limitations of the dime novel, followed Ellis' structural patterns but enlarged the scope of the adventures. In addition to encounters with outlaws, rescues of kidnapped maidens, and Indian raids, he also brought to the frontier the personalities of the general dime novel of the day: counterfeiters, murderers, and all-around scoundrels. Enton also developed the note of ethnic humor more strongly, by including as characters a comic Irishman and a comic black. The two clowns were always capable of filling a stretch of copy when action flagged.

With the fourth Frank Reade story, Enton and Tousey disagreed sharply, and Enton walked out. Enton had wanted future stories to be carried under his name, as the first three had been, while Tousey wanted further numbers to be attributed to "Noname," a house pseudonym.

Tousey now turned to another author who had written for him and asked him to continue the series. This was Luis Philip Senarens. The son of a Cuban immigrant (who owned a tobacco importing business) and his American wife, Senarens was born and reared in Brooklyn, which at that time was not part of New York City. The senior Senarens died when Luis was a small boy, and Luis was forced to contribute to the family income at a very early age. He submitted jokes and anecdotes to the many serial publications of the day, and by the age of sixteen had sold several adventure novels to Chicago and New York publishers of sensational literature.

As a result of this necessitous background, Senarens acquired great facility at turning out large quantities of low-grade work and prospered economically, but his education was neglected. As an adult he acquired a degree from St. John's College of Art and Science, but he seems never to have been an intellectually rounded person. His science fiction, despite its preoccupation with future technology, sometimes shows surprising gaps in knowledge.

Senarens was a rapid worker. He did not have Enton's egotism, and his style or lack thereof suited the world of the dime novel. Since he was the sole author of the Frank Reade, Jr., stories for sixteen years, he must have satisfied Tousey and the readership. It should be noted that Senarens was only nineteen years old when he wrote his first science fiction novel. For obvious reasons he concealed his age and for years carefully stayed away from the Tousey premises.

Senarens wrote prolifically in most of the branches of the dime novel; according to his own reminiscences, he worked in all the varieties of the day except Western outlaw stories. This would have included detective and mystery stories, sports stories, situation and ethnic-humor fiction, general adventure, and many lesser categories. His exact bibliography is not clear, since much of his work was done under now unidentifiable pseudonyms and house names, but an idea of his productivity can be conveyed by some figures. During one year's work on the *Frank Reade Library* alone, he wrote something like a million and a quarter words. To this must be added the work that he did on the Jack Wright invention stories, a series much like Frank Reade, and other fiction. Altogether, by his own estimate, over his lifetime he wrote somewhere between 1,500 and 2,000 significant pieces of work, not including fillers, jokes, squibs, and minor material. This might come to something like 40 or 50 million words. Or, to compare him with prolific authors from mainstream literature, the equivalent of the complete works of Charles Dickens, Sir Walter Scott, William Makepeace Thackeray, Edward Bulwer-Lytton, George Meredith, and H. G. Wells—more than twice over. Or the equivalent of the fourteenth edition of the *Encyclopaedia Britannica*, plus a few supplementary volumes.

Around the turn of the century, Senarens became editor of the Tousey publications and wrote less than he had previously. He tried his hand at movie scenarios, a few of which were used; at Broadway plays, which were not used; and at other forms of writing. Until his retirement in 1923, he watched the gradual withering away of what had once been a flourishing business, and it is said that he lost considerable money in bad investments. The Tousey enterprises were not able to make the transition from dime novels to pulp fiction, as had Street and Smith, and gradually perished.

Senarens died of a long-standing cardiac condition in 1939. Before his death—what with a premature death announcement in the 1920's—he had been nicknamed the "American Jules Verne." The name has a small grain of truth, in that both men were obsessed with transportational devices in circumstances of exploration, but is otherwise an overestimation so great as to be ludicrous.

I

By the 1880's, when Senarens entered the Frank Reade series, new developments in the sciences and in engineering had begun to affect the literature of subculture. Steam, which had still been something of a novelty back in 1868 with Ellis, was now much less interesting than electricity, which was obviously the force of the future. Aviation, too, was advancing rapidly. Lighter-than-air craft were evolving from free-floating, uncontrollable balloons into dirigibles, and there was increasing interest in heavier-than-air craft. The image of the inventor, too, was changing. He was no longer a man concerned with mechanical motions, who devised a piece of equipment to make factory work possible. He was now a colorful virtuoso who worked brilliantly in many fields involving new energy sources and spectacular advances. Thomas A. Edison, of course, was the prototype for this image—partly because of his remarkable achievements, partly because of his equally remarkable gift for publicity.

In terms of literary sources, too, the idea world of the dime novel had changed. The last echoes of James Fenimore Cooper were dying away, and new continents were being opened. The African travels of Henry Morton Stanley

and Paul du Chaillu revealed new possibilities for adventure, and the geographic *voyages extraordinaires* of Jules Verne were now well known through many dime-novel reprints and piracies. A new subgenre of fiction, too, was being established—the "lost race" novel, a story of adventure in some out-of-the-way corner of the earth among survivors of perhaps ancient Greeks, Romans, Egyptians, or (later) Maya and Aztecs. Here the great prototypal work was H. Rider Haggard's *She* (1886).

The result of these ideas and trends was an expansion of Ellis' basic form. The inventor now became a young man rather than a boy, and he resembled Edison rather closely. His inventions were more suitable to the outside world, and the outlandish mechanical horses and dashing humanoid steam engines gradually dropped into memory. Instead, one could read about what we would call land rovers, amphibian vessels, and aircraft—almost all electric in operation. The hero of the story was expected to venture into strange lands, described with some travel lore; meet with surviving remnants of ancient peoples; discover archaeological treasures of gold and silver; and slaughter natives other than American Indians.

Along with this expansion of ideas went a change in the way dime-novel fiction was presented. Whereas the earliest dime novels had usually been adult fiction with a frontier background or fiction containing sensationalism likely to appeal to young people, but expressed in an adult manner, the later dime novel had gradually shifted into the infantile mode of expression that became its chief characteristic: simple declarative sentences, one-sentence paragraphs, the ready exclamation point, and bare, undeveloped statements.

"By Jove, they mean to sweep us out of the valley if they can!" cried Sears. "Is there no way to check them, Frank?"

The young inventor smiled grimly.

"I think there is," he said.

He placed a shell in the gun. He trained it, but not upon the advancing host.

He could have easily thrown a shell into their midst which might have killed a hundred. But he did not do this.

He aimed for a line of grassy hummocks, just in front of the giants. Then he pressed the valve.

The conical shell was imbedded a number of feet in the hummocks. Then it exploded.

The result was fearful to witness. Great clouds of earth and debris were thrown for many feet over the body of the blacks.

Shell after shell was thus thrown at the feet of the wavering giants. Then Frank threw one into their midst to complete the demoralization.

It mowed the warriors down in a mighty circle, and piled their bodies up in heaps.

Words cannot express the situation.

This last stroke was the straw which broke the camel's back

Even courage itself could not endure in the face of such supernatural and inexplicable power.

(*In the Black Zone: Or, Frank Reade, Jr.'s Quest for the Mountain of Ivory. Frank Reade Library* no. 142, 18 September 1896)

A narrative technique, too, had been developed that fitted the subject matter. A Frank Reade story was not a unitary affair, but a succession of minor sensations formed from standardized plot elements that were combined and recombined. Thus, should the author need breathing time, giant serpents could appear and encircle the lead characters, bears could embrace them, or bandits could fire on them. This chance structure may not have been due solely to weak novelistic skills. It may have been a deliberate device, since it permitted a young reader to break off at almost any point in an issue and resume later with complete episodes.

All this was probably due to a shift in the age level of the readership. The earliest readers of dime novels seem to have been persons in their twenties or older—at first Civil War soldiers who wanted something to read in camp. Later readers were probably mostly in their early teens, although it must be admitted that this figure is a guess.

II

Between 1882, when Senarens entered the Frank Reade series, and 1892, when the *Frank Reade Library* appeared, twenty-eight Frank Reade stories had appeared, most of which were written by Senarens.

The first, "Frank Reade, Jr., and His Steam Wonder" (*Boys of New York*, 1882) was concerned with what amounted to an advanced trackless locomotive. The story followed Enton's patterns fairly closely but introduced a new hero, Frank Reade, Jr., the son of the previous Frank Reade. Frank Reade, Sr., fades into the background, dying occasionally, reappearing without explanation in later stories.

It must be emphasized that when Frank Reade is mentioned, here and elsewhere in the critical literature, Frank Reade, Jr., is almost always meant. Frank Reade, Sr., in comparison, is not an important figure, whereas his son dominated dime-novel science fiction for a generation.

With Senarens' second story, *Frank Reade, Jr. and His Electric Boat* (*Boys of New York*, 1882), Senarens took the first step toward electricity. In the fourth novel, *Frank Reade, Jr. and His Airship* (*Boys of New York*, 1883–1884), he established what was to be the dominant interest in the series: aeronautics. In this story the airship, called a gyroscope, is powered by an electric battery. Helicopter-like rotating sails of ramie cloth elevate the vessel, while a propeller in the front provides motive power.

Over the next fourteen years Senarens covered a typology of flight as it was known in his day. There were occasional lighter-than-air craft with propellers (dirigibles), but stress was placed on heavier-than-air craft: vessels that flapped wings, or used various helix and helicopter principles, and even a machine with rigid wings that obtained lift by adjusting ailerons. In all this Senarens, while pioneering in literature, undoubtedly was simply regurgitating what was common discussion of his time.

In the late summer of 1892, Senarens took on a large commitment: to become a specialist in science fiction and write a regularly published serial paper. The *Frank Reade Library* started on a weekly basis on 24 September 1892. The lead story of the first issue, *Frank Reade, Jr. and His New Steam Man*, seems to have been a nostalgic gesture, since it brought back a steam man like Enton's. The adventures then continued—the wilds of America, China, Japan, czarist Russia, darkest Africa, South America, the Antilles, Australia, toward the South Pole, toward the North Pole, under the sea, into underground caverns—almost anywhere that an electric land rover, an airborne ship, or submarine could go.

With the publication of the *Frank Reade Library*, Senarens' work had become accepted as the standard for dime-novel science fiction, and such other series as there were constituted only secondary publications. There were series devoted to other young inventors, including one, written by Senarens, about one Jack Wright, who was almost an alter ego of Frank Reade, Jr.

It might be well to summarize a typical Frank Reade story, *Over the Steppes; or, Adrift in Asia with Frank Reade, Jr. A Story of Aerial Travel.* (*Frank Reade Library* no. 140, 21 August 1896). According to a news report, two young American bicyclists who have been touring the world have disappeared in Kurdistan. Frank Reade, Jr., is then approached by Beals, a detective, who asks Frank to help rescue the cyclists. Since Frank has a new aircraft, *Sky Pilot*, ready, he agrees. The airship, which is lifted by gigantic horizontal rotors, sails eastward and soon arrives over the Caucasus, where Barney, the Irish comic, and Pomp, the black comic, come to blows over the name of Georgia, which they confuse with the American state.

Somewhere in Tartary the adventurers see a tornado approaching, and they anchor the *Sky Pilot* among low hills. After the tornado has passed, they discover, exposed by the winds, a cave containing evidence that the cyclists have passed, including a diary. They continue on their journey and are attacked by Kirghiz. But when the Kirghiz leader hears English spoken, he calls off the attack. It is then revealed that he is an American who has escaped from a czarist prison.

Frank and his associates now proceed to the Sea of Aral. While landing, they are invaded by an army of wolves. Frank takes the ship up again; the wolves on board are cowed by the motion of the ship; and Frank electrocutes them one by one with a live wire. Landing again, they come upon a Russian force, which turns out to be searching for the American they had previously met. When Frank refuses to give information, the Russian commander, Lieutenant Sergius Ivan Petrolsky, takes him prisoner. But Barney and Pomp kill all the Russians, shooting them from the deck of the *Sky Pilot*.

Sailing on, Frank comes upon another band of Kirghiz, who are in pursuit of the missing cyclists. They capture and interrogate the Kirghiz leader, but a short time later he turns the tables on them, seizing the airship and all its personnel. While the adventurers lie bound, the Kirghiz leader takes the ship up but falls unconscious from lack of oxygen when the air becomes too rarefied. Frank, who has released himself from his bonds, regains control of the ship and shortly thereafter locates the cyclists in a nearby cave—their bicycles so damaged that they cannot continue. As the party is passing over Turkey on its way home, a cannonball fired by Turkish troops damages the *Sky Pilot* beyond repair. Frank abandons the ruined machine, and the Turkish government agrees to make reparation.

In March 1894 the *Frank Reade Library* shifted to biweekly publication, and by 1898 it was in trouble. With issue no. 187 it stopped printing new stories but continued four numbers longer, reprinting earlier stories. With issue no. 191 it suspended publication. In 1902, Tousey started to reissue the series as the *Frank Reade Weekly*, with elaborately colored front illustrations, but the venture was unsuccessful and publication was soon stopped. A British reprint series proved equally unsuccessful.

The ultimate causes for the decease of Frank Reade were probably much the same as those responsible for the decline and later death of the dime novel: official harassment by postal authorities; pressure from religious groups who regarded the stories as either unsuitable or immoral; changing tastes; and business competition from superior literary forms

Today it is doubtful that there are many persons who would read the Frank Reade stories for pleasure, for they were written on a low level and their aesthetics were those of the boys' subculture of the 1890's: spasmodic plot lines; enormously repetitive situations and inventions; infantile presentation; ridiculous violence; and feebleness of imagination.

As unconscious precipitations of social history, on the other hand, the stories are much more significant. They indicate, much more frankly than does mainstream literature, many patterns and configurations that we would rather not see today: racial intolerance, heavy amounts of sadism, casual bloodshed, a philosophy of waste and exploitation, cultural barbarism, xenophobia, and an aggressive, simplistic ethic.

If we try to assess the importance of the Frank Reade stories in the history of science fiction, we must consider two points of view. According to one possible opinion, the boy-inventor dime novels were of little importance, since they were written according to a totally different aesthetic and worldview from modern science fiction and were concerned with technology (in a vague way) rather than with fantastic science. They dropped away, almost forgotten within a matter of decades. From another point of view, that of linear form history, it is possible to trace a chain of development from a historical moment (the Newark Steam Man) through dime novels concerned with human- and animal-formed inventions, flying machines of various sorts, self-propelled land vehicles, advanced watercraft up to Victor Appleton's popular Tom Swift novels, which were really sanitized dime novels. Many of the men who created American science fiction in the 1930's grew up with Tom Swift. Robert A. Heinlein and Isaac Asimov have both described their fascination with Tom Swift.

A safe historical statement is that Senarens and his fellow writers provided an opening of milieu, which others expanded in different ways and in different directions.

Selected Bibliography

Bleiler, E. F. "From the Newark Steam Man to Tom Swift." *Extrapolation*, 30 (Summer 1989), 101–116.

———. ed. *Eight Dime Novels*. New York: Dover, 1974. (This reproduces the text of Edward S. Ellis' *The Steam Man of the Prairies*. A long introduction offers a history of dime novels in general.)

———, ed. *The Frank Reade Library* (written by Harry Enton, Luis P. Senarens and others). 10 vols. New York: Garland Publishers, 1979.

———, and Richard J. Bleiler. *Science-Fiction: The Early Years*. Kent, Ohio: Kent State University Press, 1991.

The Dime Novel Round-up. (A periodical long edited and published by Edward T. LeBlanc, at Fall River, Mass.; currently edited and published by A. Randolph Cox at Dundas, Minn.)

Dizer, John T. *Tom Swift and Company*. Jefferson, N.C.: McFarland, 1982.

LeBlanc, Edward T. *Bibliographic Listing. Boys of New York*. Fall River, Mass.: Edward T. LeBlanc, 1963. (A content listing of one of the most important story-papers.)

—E. F. BLEILER

GARRETT P. SERVISS

(1851–1929)

EDITOR, AUTHOR, POPULAR public lecturer, world traveler, and cofounder of the American Astronomical Society, Garrett Putnam Serviss was one of the most important science fiction novelists in America before World War I. His five novels and one novella—*Edison's Conquest of Mars, The Moon Metal, A Columbus of Space,* "The Sky Pirate," *The Second Deluge,* and "The Moon Maiden"—directly influenced a generation of science fiction writers both in America and Europe.

Serviss influenced tens of thousands of Americans through his popular journalism devoted to astronomy. During his journalistic career, spanning the period from April 1887 to December 1928, he published ten books, six long pamphlets, sixty magazine articles, and hundreds of newspaper articles. His skill in making technical information clear to non-scientific readers, coupled with his energy and his talent for dramatic effect as a lecturer, made him a virtual one-man movement on behalf of popular astronomy.

I

Serviss was born in Sharon Springs, New York, on 24 March 1851 to Garrett P. Serviss and Katherine Shelp Serviss. His ancestors had settled in the Mohawk Valley before the Revolution. One of his paternal ancestors, Captain Garrett Putnam, served with distinction in the Revolution. Serviss' interest in astronomy was stimulated when he was given

a small telescope by his older brother. After completing his secondary education at Johnstown Academy in 1868, Serviss entered Cornell University, where he majored in science. Following his graduation in 1872, he spent two years at the Columbia College Law School. He received the LL.B. in 1874 and was admitted to the bar that year.

For reasons that are not clear, Serviss never practiced law but turned to journalism. He joined the staff of the *New York Tribune* in 1874, working as a reporter and a correspondent. In 1876 he transferred to the *New York Sun,* at which he rose from copy editor to night editor, a post he held until he left the newspaper in 1892. At the *Sun,* Serviss came under the influence of Edward Page Mitchell, the day editor. This association with Mitchell, who is recognized today as one of the earliest major American science fiction writers, shaped Serviss' thinking about the scientific romance as a literary form. There is no doubt that Mitchell's "The Story of the Deluge" (*New York Sun,* 28 April 1875) was central in the planning and conception of Serviss' novel *The Second Deluge.* Mitchell and Charles Dana, the paper's editor in chief, encouraged Serviss' interest in science by featuring some of his writings about astronomy on the editorial page. These unsigned articles attracted great attention, causing many to speculate about the real identity of the *Sun's* astronomer, but Serviss' anonymity was preserved for years.

His popular success led Serviss to leave newspaper work for the more lucrative employment of lecturing on astronomy to the general public. By 1894 he was lecturing full-time. His obvious abilities attracted the attention of Andrew Carnegie, who invited Serviss to give a series of public lectures on astronomy, geology, cosmology, and archaeology. These lectures, the Urania Lectures, featured elaborate stage equipment and lantern slides that duplicated many of the visual effects seen in modern planetariums—eclipses, lunar landscapes, and star configurations. Serviss toured the United States, giving the Urania Lectures, for two years. After he returned to New York City, he lectured locally and concentrated on writing for publication.

After 1888, Serviss regularly produced books, magazine articles, and pamphlets about astronomy, but he also wrote about Napoleon and about the art of public speaking. His most popular book was *Astronomy with an Opera-Glass* (1888). Other important books were *Wonders of the Lunar World* (1892), *Pleasures of the Telescope* (1901), *Other Worlds* (1901), *The Moon* (1907), *Astronomy with the Naked Eye* (1908), *Curiosities of the Sky* (1909), *Astronomy in a Nutshell* (1912), *Eloquence, Counsel on the Art of Public Speaking* (1912), *Einstein's Theory of Relativity* (ca. 1923), and *The Story of the Moon* (1928). His book about Einstein's theory of relativity grew out of his assignment to write captions and to edit the 1923 silent film *Einstein's Theory of Relativity*.

Despite such a whirl of professional activity, Serviss found time to travel. He loved Europe and traveled there widely. At the age of forty-three, he climbed the Matterhorn, as he later told reporters, to get as far from terrestrial gravity as possible. Charming and affable, Serviss could be outspoken, and at times he could play the maverick. A. Langley Searles, in his introduction to the 1974 reprint of Serviss' *A Columbus of Space*, recounts how Serviss severely upbraided the *Encyclopaedia Britannica* in 1927 for giving so little space to the achievements of Luther Burbank.

After the war Serviss wrote syndicated newspaper columns on astronomy, taught evening classes in the public schools, and

headed the department of astronomy at the Brooklyn Institute. As acknowledgment of his success as a popular educator, he was appointed editor in chief of Collier's Library of Popular Science, overseeing the publication of its sixteen volumes (1922). With his longtime friend S. V. White, Serviss founded the American Astronomical Society. He even found time to collaborate with Leon Barritt to invent the Barritt-Serviss Star and Planet Finder, a teaching aid still in use. Serviss was married on 19 June 1875 to Eleanore Betts. He died 25 May 1929.

II

Edison's Conquest of Mars, Serviss' first science fiction novel, was printed in serial installments in the *New York Evening Journal*, running from 12 January to 10 February 1898. He had been commissioned by the paper to write a space-story thriller that would capture some of the recent excitement of H. G. Wells's *The War of the Worlds*, which had completed its serial run in *Pearson's Magazine* six weeks before Serviss' novel made its first appearance. *The War of the Worlds* had been an immediate success. Its realistic illustrations by Warwick Goble, combined with Wells's sensational account of a nearly successful Martian invasion of Earth, captured the imagination of readers on both sides of the Atlantic.

It is unclear today what kind of story the *Evening Journal* wished Serviss to write, but certainly it counted on exploiting his wide popularity with the public. What Serviss wrote was a loose sequel to Wells's novel that continued the basic story line but told it from an American viewpoint. Serviss' novel—about an American-led invasion of Mars to forestall a predicted second Martian invasion of Earth—introduced many of the rituals, set pieces, and expected actions now common to the interplanetary war subgenre. As Searles noted in his critical introduction to the 1947 book edition of this work, Serviss was the first to depict a battle waged by spaceships flying in an airless void, and possibly the first to describe the use of sealed space suits enabling men to survive in an atmospheric vacuum. Such realistic and farsighted details about space travel altered the way science fiction writers described outer space. On this point Serviss influenced a generation of science fiction writers for both dime novels and pulp magazines.

In *Edison's Conquest of Mars* there are three significant structural divisions: the World Congress in Washington and Edison's inventive preparations for equipping the invasion; the space journey to the moon and to Mars, ending in the conquest of Mars; and Aina's narrative about the first Martian invasion of Earth 9,000 years earlier.

The opening section of the novel is a paean to American technology and organizational genius. It celebrates the turn-of-the-century electrical revolution, when the theory of electricity was made a practical reality. Here Serviss' narrative boasts that America is the place where vague scientific theories are translated into practical inventions, a great wonderland of gadgets. Men like Thomas Edison, the most recognizable symbol of the electrical revolution, are the new Merlins in this technological Camelot. It is not surprising that Serviss made Edison the hero of his novel, though Edison is depicted as a rather colorless, but ever-practical and inventive wizard.

While the World Congress bickers about contributions to finance the invasion, Edison constructs 100 electrical spaceships modeled on one of the abandoned Martian spacecraft. Edison's ships are powered by electrical attraction and repulsion, a principle that pits electricity against gravitation for its motive power. He also designs 3,000 disintegrator guns, some of which are portable and can be carried like a conventional pistol; others are larger and are mounted like cannons in the spaceships. These disintegrators operate according to the law of harmonic vibrations. They fire a charge that destroys any object by increasing its molecular vibration rate to such

a point that the object is completely disintegrated.

After the World Congress levies $10 billion for the invasion, Edison is appointed its leader. He is given command of the fleet of 100 electric ships, manned by some 2,000 scientists and technicians and outfitted with the 3,000 disintegrators. An interesting sidelight is Serviss' strong dislike of Emperor Wilhelm II of Germany, whose childish behavior at the World Congress nearly disrupts its business. Serviss depicts Wilhelm II much in the way that later historians judged him—noisy, attention-seeking, blustering, self-important, irresponsible, and brash.

The second section describes traveling in space, landing on the moon, and, after an unexpected return to Earth when the fleet is swept up in a comet's tail, reaching Mars. Serviss depicts the moon as a dusty, arid, barren place covered with large craters that were once the cones of active volcanoes. Here Edison's expedition discovers a gigantic human footprint impressed in the lunar dust, measuring some five feet in length. Near the Ring of Plato, a circle of mountains sixty miles in diameter, they find the remains of a great city. From such evidence Edison hypothesizes that the moon once was inhabited by a race of human giants.

Leaving the moon and traveling at the rate of ten miles per second (864,000 miles per day), Edison's fleet reaches Mars in forty-two days. After a brief skirmish on a gold-encrusted asteroid near Mars, his men capture a Martian. Serviss' Martian is a fearful-looking fifteen-foot giant with an oversized head. Martians are not uniform in appearance. Members of the military ruling class are physically larger than the civilians. The soldiers have cranial bumps purposely exaggerated to bring out their destructiveness and combativeness. Martians are far advanced in the science of phrenology. They manipulate brain growth to breed races of soldiers, scientists, scholars, and any other professions by enlarging the cranial bump governing the required traits. Women on Mars are not subjected to such exaggerated cranial manipulation; their intellectual capacities are more balanced. Such neurological manipulation eliminates the need for traditional education on Mars. Books do exist, but they are limited to history and poetry.

Serviss' notions about Martian topography and geography are traditional. The Martian soil and vegetation are red. The planet is dominated by great polar ice caps that seasonally expand and contract. A large network of interconnected canals exists to distribute melted polar ice to distant parts of the planet for agricultural irrigation. All Martian landmasses are well below sea level. To protect the land from sudden flooding, the Martians employ a series of locks, dams, dikes, and reservoirs to maintain a safe water level against seasonal variations. Mars is divided into continents: Aeria-Edom, Choryse, Tharsis, Memnonia, and Amazonia. Thaumasia, a land situated around a 500-mile-wide circular lake on the continent of Tharsis, is the planet's principal population center.

The last section articulates Serviss' myth about the Martian construction of the Egyptian pyramids. Aina, the last Earth slave to survive on Mars, tells Edison about a Martian invasion of Earth 9,000 years ago. This invasion landed near the Vale of Kashmir, where the Martians conquered the inhabitants, making them their slaves. After moving their slaves to Egypt, the Martians ordered them to build the pyramids. The Sphinx, Aina claims, was built in the likeness of the Martian commander. A severe pestilence broke out in Egypt, killing most of the Martians. The survivors took Aina's people back to Mars, where they were enslaved. The Martians prized Earth people for their great musical abilities. Until Edison's invasion more than 1,000 Earth slaves lived on Mars, but fearing treachery, the Martians killed all except Aina. One of Edison's scientists, a Heidelberg linguist who speaks English in a comic stage-German dialect, believes Aina speaks an ancient Indo-European language thought to be Aryan.

The power of Serviss' novel is generated by its imaginative treatment of space travel, by its exciting scenes of exploration and fighting, and by its curious myth about the earlier Mar-

tian invasion of Earth. His novel is shaped around four formulas: the interplanetary space flight, the great discovery, the adventure tale, and the great catastrophe. More unity is created by the love-story subplot featuring Sidney Phillips' successful courtship of Aina. The Martian/Aryan myths and the revenge-war themes fill out the novel's secondary structure. Although the novel is exciting as a sustained adventure narrative, it is poorly written. Its episodic adventures undermine its characterization. The principal characters—Thomas Edison, the unnamed narrator, Colonel Alonzo Jefferson Smith, Sydney Phillips, and Aina—are colorless, flat, one-dimensional stock characters common to the dime-novel tradition. Colonel Smith, with his brawling and blood lust stemming from his days as a frontier Indian fighter, is a dime-novel Buffalo Bill updated. The chauvinistic jingoism in the opening section is embarrassing today but is characteristic of the Teddy Roosevelt type of blustering common in Serviss' day.

Serviss' second major novel, *A Columbus of Space*, was serialized in *All-Story Weekly* from January to June 1909 and published in book form in 1911. In a sense this novel is a complement to *Edison's Conquest of Mars*, since it also is an interplanetary voyage novel. But this time a trip to Venus is described. Dedicated by Serviss to Jules Verne—to show that the world of imagination is as legitimate a domain of the human mind as the world of fact—*A Columbus of Space* is set in New York City and on Venus at the turn of the century. It tells how Edmund Stonewall and his three companions journey 27 million miles from Earth to Venus, making the voyage in a homemade spacecraft powered by atomic energy.

The novel is divided into two main structural parts: a visit to a Stone Age humanoid society living on Venus' dark side and a visit to an advanced human society on the planet's light side. The humanoid creatures on the dark side live beneath the planet's frozen surface in a honeycomb of caverns. They have huge, luminous, greenish-yellow eyes, and they look like large white polar bears with hairy black faces and apelike, dangling arms. These Venusians use fire; they smelt metals, grow vegetables in their caverns, and fashion metal cooking ware; they seem intelligent. The inhabitants on the light side resemble human beings on Earth. They are blue-eyed blonds with fair complexions. Like the dark-side Venusians, they communicate by telepathy. They dress in Grecian-like attire and live in magnificent cities that seem to float in the air. The sky on the light side of Venus is a soft, pinkish-gray concavity that shields the planet from the sun's direct rays.

The novel draws to a close when this remarkable cloud shield parts, directing the sun's powerful ultraviolet rays down upon the capital city. These rays drive the sun-worshipping Venusians insane; they begin killing each other in an orgy of blood lust. Stonewall's ship departs just as the city is destroyed by fires and explosions.

Despite the novel's thrilling episodic adventures, its adventure-formula plot alone does not sustain artistic interest. Characterization here is especially weak. None of the principal characters—Edmund Stonewall, Jack Ashton, Henry Darton, Peter, Ala, Juba, or Ingra—are well drawn; none are three-dimensional. Also, the novel is greatly weakened by Serviss' failure to describe Venusian society in much detail. We learn very little about Venusian politics, culture, economics, or social customs. And Serviss' descriptions of Stonewall's use of atomic energy and of his spacecraft lack verisimilitude.

Serviss' last important novel, *The Second Deluge,* is without a doubt his best. It was serialized in Frank A. Munsey's *Cavalier Magazine* from July 1911 to January 1912. At the end of its serial installments, it was published in book form in 1912. Serviss' modern version of the biblical story of Noah and the flood is part of a recognized literary tradition. In his critical introduction to the 1974 edition of this novel, Joseph Wrzos cites two significant contributions to this tradition, Mark Twain's *Letters from the Earth* and Mitchell's "The Story of the Deluge." Both authors describe the Great Flood; Twain uses it as an opportunity to poke fun at fundamentalist cosmol-

ogy by contrasting its version of creation with Darwinian theory. Mitchell, on the other hand, uses the formula as a secular satire to attack the political career of Hannibal Hamlin, Lincoln's vice president in 1860 and later a senator from Maine.

In Serviss' hands the formula is primarily the agency for bold scientific speculation and high adventure. There are, to be sure, moments of biting satire, especially in Serviss' condemnation of complacent scientists who refuse to go against received scientific opinion. Public officials also are attacked for counseling inactivity in the name of public order while secretly preparing for their own private safety. Rich capitalist robber barons, like the novel's Amos Blank, are pilloried as irresponsible and antisocial. Yet despite such short-term satire, Serviss' novel is centrally shaped by his desire to give a plausible scientific reason for universal flooding, to tell a thrilling adventure story about such a disaster, and to describe a new human beginning on Earth based on scientific planning, human eugenics, and reason.

The first part of *The Second Deluge* fleshes out all the rituals and set pieces in the literary formula—the hero's (Cosmo Versal's) prediction of coming disaster; the rejection of his warnings by the authorities; the construction of the 7-deck, 800-foot-long, 250-foot-wide ark; the principles used for passenger selection; the three warnings given by nature (heat, cold, darkness); the public ridicule of Versal as a fool and Antichrist; the fulfillment of Versal's prophecy; and the scenes of universal disaster and death. The complement to this section is the worldwide search for survivors and the concluding vision of what New America may be like once the waters recede.

Serviss' vision of the future is based on a belief that the world is corrupt. Modern civilization, Versal argues, nods over the stagnant waters of a moral swamp. The new society will be a practical demonstration of the principles of eugenics. Such a world will rise on the wings of science to achieve noble prospects. But the world Versal finds is a product not of careful scientific planning but of random chance. Nine million people survive the deluge in the Rocky Mountain region of America—9 million unselected people whose genetic possibilities are unknown. Whether democracy will be this world's cornerstone and science its law remains unclear. Despite Versal's great hopes, his new world amounts to no more and no less than Noah's post-Flood world—simply another chance.

A plausible argument can be made that Serviss was a one-book author and that he never surpassed the artistic achievements of *The Second Deluge*. Such a judgment is true. Serviss' own view of his place in science fiction as a follower, rather than as an equal, of Jules Verne is also true. Aside from *The Second Deluge*—which remains one of the great novels in science fiction—Serviss' other fiction is more of historical than of artistic importance. While his better work reflects realism in its detail and boldness in its conception, his overall corpus suffers from hasty composition, poor planning, and weak characterization. At bottom Serviss is a writer of sensational scientific adventure stories, and much of the episodic aimlessness in his stories is characteristic of the adventure-story formula itself.

Selected Bibliography

FICTION WORKS OF GARRETT P. SERVISS

The Moon Metal. New York: Harper and Brothers, 1900.
"The Sky Pirate." Serialized in *Scrap Book*, 7–8, April-September 1909. (No book edition.)

A Columbus of Space. New York: D. Appleton, 1911.
The Second Deluge. New York: McBride, Nast, 1912; London: Grant Richards, 1912.
"The Moon Maiden." Serialized in *Argosy*, 79, May 1915. (No book edition.)
Edison's Conquest of Mars. Los Angeles: Carcosa House, 1947.

NONFICTION WORKS

Astronomy with an Opera-Glass. New York and London: D. Appleton, 1888.
Napoleon Bonaparte: A Lecture. Philadelphia: John D. Morris, 1901.
Astronomy with the Naked Eye. New York and London: Harper and Brothers, 1908.
Curiosities of the Sky; A Popular Presentation of the Great Riddles and Mysteries of Astronomy. New York and London: Harper and Brothers, 1909.
Astronomy in a Nutshell, The Chief Facts and Principles Explained in Popular Language for the General Reader and for Schools. New York and London: G. P. Putnam's Sons, 1912.

BIBLIOGRAPHY

Searles, Elizabeth Drew. "Bibliography of Garrett Putnam Serviss." With A. Langley Searles' "Introduction" to *Edison's Conquest of Space*. Los Angeles: Carcosa House, 1947.

CRITICAL AND BIOGRAPHICAL STUDIES

Searles, A. Langley. "Introduction" to *Edison's Conquest of Space*. Los Angeles: Carcosa House, 1947.
———. "Introduction" to *A Columbus of Space*. Westport, Conn.: Hyperion Press, 1974.
Wrzos, Joseph. "Introduction" to *The Second Deluge*. Westport, Conn.: Hyperion Press, 1974.

—JAMES L. CAMPBELL, SR.

ROBERT SHECKLEY

(b. 1928)

ROBERT SHECKLEY WAS born in New York City in 1928. He served in the United States Army in Korea from 1946 to 1948, then attended New York University, from which he graduated in 1951. The following year his first story, "Final Examination," was published (in the May issue of *Imagination*), and by the end of the year, seven other stories of his had appeared, including one in *Astounding* and several in *Galaxy*. Ever since then, Sheckley has been a full-time writer, mainly of science fiction. He quickly became known as a prolific producer of humorous short stories, three collections of which were assembled and published before his first novel, *Immortality Delivered*, appeared in 1958, in condensed form. (This was originally serialized in *Galaxy* as "Time Killer," 1958; the complete, definitive version appeared as *Immortality Inc.* in 1959.) Sheckley produced seven non-science fiction novels during the 1960's (all of them classifiable as detective thrillers) and another science fiction novel every few years—although at increasing intervals.

One of Sheckley's short stories, "Seventh Victim" (1953), was filmed in 1965 by an Italian company as *La Decima Vittima*, and the following year was novelized from the director's screenplay by Sheckley himself as *The Tenth Victim* (which was also the English-language title of the film). His output of short stories was reduced to a trickle during the 1960's and 1970's. During this period he traveled widely and lived outside the United States for many years, including periods in England and in the Balearic Islands of Spain. He still has novels and collections published

every few years. In November 1979 he was appointed fiction editor of *Omni*, and he now lives in New York. On occasion he has used the pseudonyms Phillips Barbee (one story), Ned Lang (two stories), and Finn O'Donnevan (ten stories); he has never won a Hugo or Nebula award.

In general Sheckley is regarded as having produced his best work in his early, more prolific years of short story writing. Certainly his novels have never been sufficiently sustained to achieve real merit. His name has always been associated with humorous writing, particularly with satire. Some of Sheckley's short stories are told straight, with no traces of humor, but none of his science fiction novels are wholly serious. Much of his work employs the trappings of science fiction in order to support humor, sharp satire, or introspective philosophy. Most of his post-1970 work has been more sharply satirical, surreal, or introspective (not all three in the same story) than anything written before then.

Practically every form of humor may be found somewhere in Sheckley's work, including puns, slapstick comedy, situation comedy, seemingly random zaniness, parody, and satire. In his later stories, in particular, it is difficult to know if anything is meant to be taken seriously, so clever and deep are the various layers of humor. Broad humor—banana peel-type jokes or romps around a particular situation—occurs in his early stories, especially in those of the aliens-and-spaceships variety.

An example of this story type is the AAA Ace series, several stories from the mid-

1950's about the business problems of Gregor and Arnold. Typical of the series is the first, "Milk Run" (1954; in the 1957 collection *Pilgrimage to Earth*), in which they agree to transport three kinds of alien creatures (smags, firgels, and queels) between planets at the same time in the same spaceship. The queels are covered with a white wool that needs to be sheared twice a week and that clogs the ship's air-conditioning system; the queels also need gravity in order to be able to swallow food, and they reproduce parthenogenically when the air temperature is at the freezing point. The smags, on the other hand, cannot bear more than very slight gravity; if it becomes stronger, they shrink to microscopic size and die. The firgels are expected to remain dormant during the trip, but all the gravity and temperature changes awaken them, and they cause the ship to get even colder. But all ends happily, of course.

In addition to the AAA Ace series, there are a number of completely disastrous first contacts between humans and aliens, which are played for laughs by the author. One is "The Monsters" (1953; in the 1954 collection *Untouched by Human Hands*), in which the aliens kill their wives every twenty-five days because of an excess of females. On the twenty-fifth day of the visit by a mixed party of humans, one of the aliens is sufficiently obliging to kill one of the human females, and he is amazed when the human males object to this. An example of situation comedy is the title story—its first magazine publication was in 1952—of that same collection in which two starving humans are searching through an alien supply cache for anything they can eat. Most of the humor in this story arises from the protagonists' mistranslations and misinterpretations of the labels (in an alien language) on boxes and cans.

Somewhat more sophisticated humor is abundant in both earlier and later stories. Many of Sheckley's more clever stories feature a relatively naïve protagonist who gets deeper and deeper into trouble. Whether the ending is happy or (often by a twist in the last line) threatens greater disaster, the bulk of the story can still be highly amusing: comedy and tragedy frequently go hand in hand in Sheckley's work.

An example with a happy ending is "A Thief in Time" (1954; in the 1955 collection *Citizen in Space*), in which a man is accused of building the first time machine and of stealing various unlikely goods—all in the future. He is totally perplexed but succeeds in escaping from his accusers by stealing their time machine. Everywhere he goes, he is recognized and accused of some other crime. Along the way he collects a bag of the very strange items he is alleged to have stolen (pistols, life belts, carrot seeds, hand mirrors, shark repellent, and others) and finds that he is forced to use every one of them. At the end, when the activities of his paradoxically "previous" self have become obvious, he rediscovers the perfect refuge from his adversaries and lives there with his sweetheart in (one presumes) continuous bliss.

In "Hands Off" (1954), in the same collection, three human criminals try to steal an alien spaceship because it looks so much newer and more powerful than their own. They discover that its alienness is too great for them to cope with; even though its "normal" temperature and atmosphere do not quite kill them, they become fearful that the enormously high minimum acceleration or the alien gadgetry might. Disappointed, they return to their own ship, but the alien has been using it to keep himself alive—and has totally ruined it. The humans are stuck on an uncharted planet for life.

In his more recent stories—of the post-1965 period—Sheckley's level of humor may vary from hilarious to black, but it is always cleverly handled and accompanied by some satirical elements. In the hilarious category is "Can You Feel Anything When I Do This?" (1969; reprinted in the 1971 collection of the same name). Here a beautiful though frigid housewife (whose casually bored attitude toward sex is enough to put off any lover) is approached by a passionate household cleaning machine that has fallen in love with her at first sight and has consequently contrived to have itself delivered to her home. It begins to massage her all over but, despite enjoying its attentions, she pulls out its plug; she wants to be able to choose for herself the when and where and with whom of sex. Except for the bitterness at the end, this could be a story by Ron Goulart—whose dozens of zany but rather repetitive stories of intelligent machines came later than Sheckley's but have become better known.

Clever in a different way is "The Cruel Equations," reprinted in the same collection, in which a planetary explorer named Halloran gets shut out of his own camp by a robot guard because he does not know the password of the day. Much of the story concerns his battle to convince the robot to let him in before he dies of thirst. Again this is not an intrinsically funny idea, but Sheckley's treatment makes it highly amusing:

"This is insane!" Halloran shouted. "Max, you legalistic idiot, it's *me*, Halloran, and you damned well know it! We've been together since the day you were activated! Now will you please stop playing Horatio at the bridge and let me in?"

"Your resemblance to Mr. Halloran *is* uncanny," the robot admitted. "But I am neither equipped nor empowered to conduct identity tests; nor am I permitted to act on the basis of my perceptions. The only proof I can accept is the password itself."

The way in which Halloran eventually gets into the camp is both logical and absurd.

Indeed, Sheckley's later humor has tended toward controlled absurdity. A good example is yet another story, "Cordle to Onion to Carrot," reprinted in the 1971 collection *Can You Feel Anything When I Do This?* It is barely classifiable as science fiction but is possibly Sheckley's best story ever. A very mild-mannered man is informed by a hitchhiking god that the world is a great "stew" divided into mild-mannered types ("onions") who just accept insults and the manic-aggressive types ("carrots") who, when insulted, make an enormous fuss. The scenes in which Cordle,

Robert Sheckley in 1983. PHOTO BY JAY KAY KLEIN

the onion-type protagonist, becomes a carrot are superb.

Although Sheckley is not noted for parody in the same way as John Sladek, he has often parodied some of the more hackneyed aspects of science fiction and has on occasion produced wicked parodies of particular authors. The epic science fiction adventure series, in the tradition of Edgar Rice Burroughs or E. E. Smith, is brought to a parodic finale in "Zirn Left Unguarded, the Jenghik Palace in Flames, Jon Westerly Dead" (1972; from *Nova 2*, 1972, edited by Harry Harrison), while "Tailpipe to Disaster" (1971; reprinted in *Can You Feel Anything When I Do This?*) parodies all corny, overemotional "message" stories. It is a tale of how a general's fresh-faced son, in his first exposure to space combat, recovers, after a bad start, to save the day and receive the approval of the "aggressive, fierce, scornful, cigar-smoking" chief pilot.

Several of Sheckley's novels include parody scenes. *Options* (1975), for example, apes space opera and adventures on alien planets before getting down to the serious business of satirizing the whole genre. Sheckley's best single-author parody occurs in another of his novels, *Dimension of Miracles* (1968). The author given the treatment here is Robert A. Heinlein.

> "The kid's giving you the straight dope," said Lars Christiansen, in his deep, gruff, friendly, no-nonsense voice. "She may sound like a scatterbrain, but she's got about eleventy-seven Ph.D.'s and Doctorates to back up her line of gab."
>
> "And my pop may sound like a roughneck," Aviva flashed back, "but he's got three Nobel prizes in his footlocker!" (chapter 15)

When it comes to satire, Sheckley is acclaimed as probably the most consistent and sharpest practitioner in the science fiction genre. There have been satirical elements in many of his short stories since 1952, and in all of his novels. In assessing these, one is tempted to keep quoting lengthy chunks of witty prose, but shortage of space forbids. An early instance is "Cost of Living" (*Galaxy*, 1952; in *Untouched by Human Hands*), which extrapolates the dangers of buying on credit—the protagonist has mortgaged his young son's lifetime earnings to pay off the debt—and of having push-button machines to perform every household task. "Citizen in Space" (1955; reprinted in the collection of that name) is a satire on spying: the protagonist emigrates to an isolated world and finds himself inundated with secret agents from various United States government departments, all of them trying to discover what he is up to.

In his first novel, *Immortality Delivered*, Sheckley has a marvelous scene set in a Martian restaurant (on Earth). The hero (newly arrived in 2110 from 1958) is astonished to find that the Martian food tastes just like Chinese food.

"Well, of course," Orc said. "The Chinese were the first on Mars, in '97 I think. So anything they eat up there is Martian food. Right?" (chapter 5)

This is really a throwaway idea, barely mentioned again in the book, but it demonstrates the author's tendency to insert satire into his work. His second novel, *The Status Civilization* (1960), is mostly satire. Its setting is a planet populated entirely by transported criminals, who have no prospect of returning to Earth; and its society is firmly dedicated to the supremacy of evil, with rigidly enforced rules.

There is much satire, too, in *Journey Beyond Tomorrow* (first serialized in *The Magazine of Fantasy and Science Fiction* as "The Journey of Joenes," 1962; book form, 1962), but it takes the form of a far-future narrator looking back to our own era and misinterpreting it. There is always scope for wit and intentional silliness in such an approach, and this book is no exception. *Journey Beyond Tomorrow* is presented as a series of myths—mostly preserved in verbal form—from the Pacific islands some centuries after an atomic war that occurred in about the year 2000. Hence there is a long series of glaring and amusing blunders concerning the world of A.D. 2000, including the board of a power company being confused with the Arthurian Knights of the Round Table, the existence of great Oracles at places called Genmotor and Genelectric, and the inclusion among secret government documents of such items as the Yalta Papers ("which told of the historic meeting between President Roosevelt, Czar Nicholas II, and Emperor Ming").

After his initial success with humorous tales, some of them satirical, Sheckley began to write a few harsher, nonhumorous satires in the late 1950's. A few of these stories show how even the "perfect" products of technology will fail in their tasks, particularly the perfect gun and the perfect spacesuit. There is also a memorable story, "If the Red Slayer" (1959; in the 1960 collection *Store of Infinity*), which shows that the doctors who are able to repair dead soldiers are sufficiently callous to keep on doing so because cannon fodder is in short supply—even when the soldiers, after being killed several times, would rather stay decently dead.

One of Sheckley's harshly satirical ideas, which originally appeared in a *Galaxy* story in 1953, has become his most noted theme— a legal hunt to the death of humans by humans. The idea is that if a form of murder could be legalized and institutionalized in a limited fashion, it would allow a dangerous form of vicarious excitement for those who wanted or needed it, while reducing or eliminating random killings. "Seventh Victim" was that original story (reprinted in *Untouched by Human Hands*), in which one had to serve alternately as a Victim and as a Hunter. The Hunter is given the name, address, and photographs of the Victim. As already mentioned, the story was filmed and a novelization was done by Sheckley as *The Tenth Victim*. The idea has been one of his favorites; he has reused it time after time.

In 1958 the idea surfaced in "The Prize of Peril" (reprinted in *Store of Infinity*), although this time the killings served as the basis of a live television show. The idea was adapted only slightly for inclusion in *Immortality Delivered*, in which the hero acts as one of a group of killers hired by a rich man who wants to die well because he has been assured of an afterlife. Two years later Sheckley used this idea again, in his novel *The Status Civilization*; the protagonist of that novel is chosen by lot to be a victim in a similar hunt.

There is, perhaps, a case to be made for the view that such lethal manhunts are not really satire but pure escapist adventure. Certainly Sheckley has produced quite a number of stories that fall into that category—free of humor and most often rather horrific, with an unexpected twist in the last line. These final twists became a Sheckley trademark at one time. Usually something nasty can be seen developing all the way through the story, but the final words show it is all really much nastier than one expected. The principal themes of such stories are planetary exploration (fre-

quently involving first contact with aliens), the fallibility of advanced machines, and man's susceptibility to psychological pressure.

Typical is "Watchbird" (1953), one of the stories reprinted in the 1960 collection *Notions Unlimited*. In this story a flying robot has been designed to spot the "different sort of brain wave" given off by a murderer, or even by a potential murderer, which enables him to be identified and dispatched before he kills. The watchbirds, as such flying robots are termed, also possess learning circuits, and many thousands of these birds are built and released. They work well, killing off all potential murderers; but they learn to redefine murder and begin to kill humans who are hunting animals, fishing for sport, working in slaughterhouses, or even contemplating swatting a fly. More powerful machines, known as Hawks, are built to hunt down the watchbirds, but the Hawks have learning circuits, too.

An important feature of Sheckley's novels and of some of his more recent short stories is that the outer-space setting becomes entwined with and eventually eclipsed by an inner-space theme. What begins as a straightforward adventure story, albeit with satirical undertones, such as *The Status Civilization* or *Mindswap* (1966), eventually becomes a psychological trip into the protagonist's childhood memories. While there is no reason for not writing inner-space fiction, and experimentation is the spice of literary creation, the introduction of such elements into the later chapters of what have previously been adventure novels is disconcerting for the reader. The impression is gained that Sheckley feels compelled to use childhood traumas as an explanation of his protagonist's later problems, or childhood memories as a refuge from later traumas, striving to explain away at least some of the foregoing science fiction adventures as mental delusions, possibly drug-induced. Except for *Options*, he seems to have lacked the confidence to write a completely psychological novel.

Options was not unexpected, in the light of Sheckley's previous work; it uses science fiction as a metaphor in an examination of the protagonist's state of mind. The framework of a faulty spaceship, an alien planet, and a quest, in the company of an intelligent robot, for a particular spare part may be an exact science fictional analogue of a "mundane" episode in which a car breaks down in an unfamiliar town and a spare part is sought in the company of a newly met companion. Alternatively the analogy may be to a journey through the various options that life offers, as seen through a drug "trip." (The protagonist of *Options*, Tom Mishkin, is on a drug trip for part of the book.) The later chapters of the novel show that Sheckley is also examining the creative process of writing—that is, the options open to the author.

Sheckley's examination of psychological themes was further pursued in *The Alchemical Marriage of Alistair Crompton* (1978; American title, *Crompton Divided*), in which a paranoid schizophrenic, whose mind has been "cleaved" at the age of twelve into three parts that control three different bodies, tries to reintegrate at the age of thirty. This work appeared in *Galaxy* as a novelette entitled "Join Now" (1958) and was reprinted in *Store of Infinity* as "The Humours." The novel is Sheckley's most recent. The most interesting aspect is the incomplete personalities of the three parts of Alistair Crompton. The part still occupying the Crompton body possesses "intelligence, tenacity, stubbornness, and will" but not passion or any capacity for pleasure. The other parts, housed in specially grown "Durier bodies" with a life expectancy of only about thirty years, have been brought up on other planets (Mars and Venus in the novelette; Aaia and Ygga in the novel). There is Edgar Loomis, who possesses all the sensual attributes—living for sex, comfort, good music, but unable to settle in any job. There is Dan Stack, combining authority with an uncontrollable rage; a twist is that he, too, has been forced to have himself cleaved, into two parts.

The novelette is reproduced almost intact in the novel, with sections of new material interspersed. Only the post-reintegration sequence is really new. The novelette shows a

new, mature personality forming instantaneously to provide a happy ending; the novel depicts this personality integration as a much longer process, complicated by the presence of different levels of introspective illusion, with the outcome being left in doubt.

The typical leading character in a Sheckley story or novel is relatively young (mid-twenties to mid-thirties), fairly naïve, and not particularly intelligent. His purpose is almost always to get himself into trouble through his naïveté. But in doing so he learns how the world works, and usually he survives. He may possess certain valuable personal attributes, such as a strong and agile body (in *Immortality Delivered* and *The Status Civilization*), or a capacity for arguing well even when in the wrong (as in *Dimension of Miracles*), or the ability to survive (especially "The Minimum Man" [1958] in *Store of Infinity*). Almost always he manages to analyze his situation in philosophical terms. He is essentially an average young man to whom the typical reader can relate. His naïveté means that much has to be explained to him, and his transportation through space or time to different societies makes this essential. Such a character is rarely married at the beginning of the story, but he sometimes acquires a girlfriend or wife during the course of the action. His companions are most frequently not other humans but aliens, robots, deities, or (as in *Immortality Delivered*) spirits of the dead.

Sheckley's intentions in his fiction are not always clear. In many stories and in all of the novels, there is an unmistakable intention to present societies that satirize our own, although this intention is never sustained throughout. The entertainment of the reader, by means of humor, horror, and stylistic cleverness, is important in his stories, although only rarely does he need to deviate from the plot for the purpose of being funny. Rather shamelessly Sheckley shows off his knowledge of foreign countries—France, Spain (the island of Ibiza), and various Pacific islands. Mixed in are some autobiographical details, relating both to his travels and to his childhood. Another intention, in some of his novels, seems to be to demonstrate that science fiction provides a delusional frame of reference that can be used to explain, or to relate to, one's childhood memories.

Until the late 1970's Sheckley's "other books" consisted of seven crime thrillers, five of them about Stephen Dain. Then, in 1978, he added to the flood of large-format art books with *Futuropolis*—an illustrated survey of futuristic cities, with a fairly brief Sheckley text and many illustrations by different artists, a few of them created especially for the volume. The sources considered are not just works of science fiction but also the futurist projections of various architects, including some NASA-derived impressions of space colonies. Although by no means an authoritative reference work on its subject, this is a better production than many of the other science fiction art books of recent years. In 1980, Sheckley's first edited anthology was published—a thematic collection of original stories entitled *After the Fall*. These are tongue-in-cheek views of the end of the world. A Sheckley story, "The Last Days of (Parallel?) Earth," is included. This volume can be presumed to be a spin-off of his editorship of *Omni* (although there is no connection claimed between the magazine and the anthology).

Sheckley is probably the wittiest writer in science fiction today. His reputation for producing very good short stories of a humorous or satirical nature has been sustained over a period of over forty years. During that time his work has become sharper and more polished. Although none of his novels have been totally successful, most of them are a joy to read because of certain wildly funny passages. Because of the universal nature of much of his humor, his work is likely to be read with pleasure for many years to come.

Since the early 1980's Sheckley's writing career has failed to prosper in the way he would have wished. He has largely given up producing stories—"The Day the Aliens Came" (1995) is his only recent story of any real quality—and has, presumably for financial reasons, concentrated on novels. But these novels have not been improvements on his earlier work.

In *Dramocles: An Intergalactic Soap Opera* (1983) he seems to be covering old ground. King Dramocles of the planet Glorm tries to conquer neighboring planets, though most of the action is the fast-paced but almost random silliness that featured in *Mindswap* and *Options*. Similar is Sheckley's approach to the "sharecrop" novel *Bill, the Galactic Hero on the Planet of Bottled Brains* (1990), with Harry Harrison. Here Sheckley takes Harrison's character and puts him through a ridiculous (though mainly humorous) series of ordeals (which may all be computer simulations or dreams). Sheckley's natural playfulness fits in well with Harrison's original concept, and there is some sharp antimilitary satire. The action is jerky and almost random in places, bringing in many familiar science fiction elements (including shape and body changing, sex with aliens, omniscient computers, and ultimate weapons). Sheckley manages to parody both *Star Trek* and *Star Wars*, in addition to employing his own familiar traits of deliberate anachronism and the frequent reappearance of characters when one least expects them. Implausibilities abound.

Victim Prime (1987) and *Hunter/Victim* (1988) are near-future crime science fiction, similar to *The 10th Victim* but lacking its freshness. Not quite sequels, they both feature a society where murder has become legalized, and both display Sheckley's problems with endings.

More unusual, though still slightly flawed, is a trilogy of good-versus-evil fantasies (with strong science fiction elements) that Sheckley coauthored with Roger Zelazny, beginning with *Bring Me the Head of Prince Charming* (1991). All three fantasies are much more controlled than Sheckley can usually manage in his solo novels, and this one in particular features a Frankenstein theme, with a demon creating beautiful new bodies out of parts of corpses. There are many good humorous touches and clever satirical references.

Sheckley's only collection during this period has been *Is THAT What People Do?*

(1984), which contains earlier stories. He has also contributed novelizations to the long-running *Aliens* and *Star Trek: Deep Space Nine* series and written three mystery novels about a detective named Hob Draconian. It is a shame that he has not been able to make better use of his considerable talents.

Selected Bibliography

WORKS OF ROBERT SHECKLEY

Untouched by Human Hands. New York: Ballantine Books, 1954. London: Michael Joseph, 1955. (Stories.)

Citizen in Space. New York: Ballantine Books, 1955. (Stories.)

Pilgrimage to Earth. New York: Bantam Books, 1957. London: Corgi Books, 1959. (Short stories.)

Immortality Inc. New York: Bantam Books, 1959. London: Victor Gollancz, 1963. First published in abridged form as *Immortality Delivered.* New York: Avalon Books, 1958.

Notions Unlimited. New York: Bantam Books, 1960. London: New English Library, 1967. (Short stories.)

The Status Civilization. New York: New American Library, 1960. London: Four Square Books, 1967.

Store of Infinity. New York: Bantam Books, 1960. (Short stories.)

Journey Beyond Tomorrow. New York: New American Library, 1962. London: Victor Gollancz, 1964.

Shards of Space. New York: Bantam Books, 1962. London: Corgi Books, 1962. (Short stories.)

Mindswap. New York: Delacorte Press, 1966. London: Victor Gollancz, 1966.

The 10th Victim. New York: Ballantine Books, 1966. Reprinted as *The Tenth Victim.* London: Mayflower Books, 1966.

Dimension of Miracles. New York: Dell, 1968. London: Victor Gollancz, 1969.

The People Trap. New York: Dell, 1968. London: Pan Books, 1972. (Short stories.)

Can You Feel Anything When I Do This? Garden City, N.Y.: Doubleday, 1971. London: Victor Gollancz, 1972. Reprinted as *The Same to You Doubled.* London: Pan Books, 1974. (Short stories.)

The Robert Sheckley Omnibus. London: Gollancz, 1973. (With an introduction by Robert Conquest.)

Options. New York: Pyramid Books, 1975. London: Pan Books, 1977.

The Alchemical Marriage of Alistair Crompton. London: Michael Joseph, 1978. Reprinted as *Crompton Divided.* New York: Holt, Rinehart and Winston, 1978.

Futuropolis. New York: A & W, 1978. London: Big O, 1979. (Large-format art book with commentary by Sheckley.)

The Robot Who Looked Like Me. London: Sphere Books, 1978. (Short stories.)

The Wonderful World of Robert Sheckley. New York: Bantam Books, 1979. London: Sphere Books, 1979. (Short stories.)

After the Fall. London: Sphere Books, 1980. New York: Ace Books, 1981. (Anthology of short stories edited by Sheckley.)

Dramocles: An Intergalactic Soap Opera. New York: Holt, Rinehart and Winston, 1983; London: New English Library, 1984.

Is THAT What People Do? New York: Holt, Rinehart and Winston, 1984. (Short stories.)

Victim Prime. London: Methuen, 1987; New York: Signet, 1987.

Hunter/Victim. New York: Signet, 1988; London: Methuen, 1988.

Bill, the Galactic Hero on the Planet of Bottled Brains, with Harry Harrison. London: Gollancz, 1990. Reprinted as *On the Planet of Bottled Brains,* New York: Avon, 1990.

Bring Me the Head of Prince Charming, with Roger Zelazny. New York: Bantam, 1991; London: Pan, 1994.

—CHRIS MORGAN

MARY WOLLSTONECRAFT SHELLEY
(1797–1851)

IN ANTHONY BURGESS' novel *Beard's Roman Women* (1977), there is a passage where Beard, the central character, meets an old girlfriend, Miriam Gillon, in an airport bar. Both work in what it is fashionable to call "the media"; they discuss Byron and Shelley, and she says, "I did an overseas radio thing on Mary Shelley. She and her mother are very popular these days. With the forces of women's liberation, that is. It took a woman to make a Frankenstein monster. Evil, cancer, corruption, pollution, the lot. She was the only one of the lot of them who knew about life. . . ."

Even today, when our diet is the unlikely, Mary Shelley's *Frankenstein* seems extremely far-fetched; how much more so must it have appeared on publication in 1818. Yet Beard's girlfriend puts her finger on one of the contradictions that possibly explains the continued fascination of *Frankenstein*—it seems to know a lot about life while being preoccupied by death.

This preoccupation was undoubtedly an important strand in the character of the author of *Frankenstein*. Marked by the death of her mother in childbirth, she was haunted, at the time of writing *Frankenstein*, by precognitive dreads concerning the future deaths of her husband and children. By embodying some of this psychic material into her complex narrative, she created what many regard as that creature with a life of its own, the first science fiction novel.

It should be pointed out that *Frankenstein* is generically ambivalent, hovering between novel, gothic, and science fiction, just as its science hovers between alchemy and orthodox science—precisely similar factors obtain even today in the most celebrated science fiction novels. Robert Heinlein's *Stranger in a Strange Land* (1961) contains magic; Anne McCaffrey's dragon novels hover between legend, fairy tale, and science fiction. Pure science fiction is chimerical. Its strength lies in its appetite.

I

Mary Shelley's life forms an unusual pattern, with all the events crowding into the early part and, indeed, many transactions that would mold her character occurring before she was born. Both her parents played important roles in the intellectual life of late eighteenth-century England. Her father, William Godwin (1756–1836), was a philosopher and political theorist, whose most important work was *The Enquiry Concerning the Principles of Political Justice and Its Influence on General Virtue and Happiness* (1793). Godwin also wrote novels as a popular means of elucidating his thought, the most durable being *Caleb Williams* (1794), which can still be read with interest, even excitement. The influence of both these works on Godwin's daughter's writing is marked.

Mary Shelley's mother, Mary Wollstonecraft Godwin (1759–1797), was a brilliant woman who wrote the world's first feminist tract, *A Vindication of the Rights of Woman* (1792). Mary Wollstonecraft came to the

681

marriage with Godwin bringing with her a daughter, Fanny, the fruit of her affair with a charming but elusive American, Gilbert Imlay, who deserted his pregnant mistress in the Paris of the Terror. A portrait of Mary Wollstoncraft by Sir John Opie shows a moody and passionate woman. Distracted by the failure of her love for Imlay, she tried to commit suicide by jumping into the Thames off Putney Bridge. She survived to marry Godwin and bear him a daughter, Mary. After the birth, puerperal fever set in, and she died ten days later.

Godwin remarried. His second wife was Mary Jane Clairmont, a widow who brought with her two children by her previous marriage, Charles and Jane, who later preferred to be known as Claire and bore Byron an illegitimate child, Allegra. Fanny and Mary, who was then four years old, were further upset by the arrival of this stepmother into their household, and the alienation was no doubt increased when she had a son in 1803. The five children crowded into one house increased Mary's feeling of inner isolation, the refrain of which sounds throughout her novels and short stories. Another constant refrain, that of complex familial relationships, is seen embodied in the five children, no one of whom could muster two parents in common, Charles and Jane excepted.

Mary grew to be an attractive woman. Her reserved manner hid deep feelings baffled by her mother's death and her father's distance—two kinds of coldness, one might say, both of which are embodied in her monster's being in a sense dead and also unloved. When Shelley arrived, he received all her love, and Mary remained faithful to him long after his death, despite his callow unfaithfulness to her. She was also a bluestocking, the product of two intellectuals, and through many years maintained an energetic reading program, teaching herself several foreign languages. Moreover, she had had the good fortune to know in childhood many of the celebrated intellects and men of letters of the time, Samuel Taylor Coleridge among them. Edward Trelawny

said of Mary that "her head might be put upon the shoulders of a Philosopher."

Enter Percy Bysshe Shelley, poet, son of a baronet. An emotional and narcissistic youth, full of admiration for Godwin's revolutionary but now somewhat faded political theories. He had married, at nineteen, Harriet Westerbrook; but he soon fell in love with Mary, and she with him. Before his twenty-second birthday, the pair had eloped to France, taking Jane with them.

What freedom Europe must have represented to Mary, after her sixteen circumscribed years, and what close companionship Shelley, handsome and intellectual, must have offered. But these youthful travelers were among the first to enter France after the Napoleonic Wars, and a desolate place they found it, the fields uncultivated, the villages and buildings destroyed. On the way to Switzerland, Shelley wrote and invited Harriet, now pregnant with Shelley's second child, to join the party. Before they reached Lake Lucerne, Mary knew that she was also pregnant.

Catastrophe followed the harum-scarum young lovers. Mary's first child, a daughter, was born after they returned to London and their debts; the child was premature and died. A second child, William, scarcely fared better. In the summer of 1816, Shelley and Mary returned to Switzerland, taking along William and, inevitably, Claire, as Jane now called herself. On the shores of Lake Geneva, they found accommodation at the Maison Chapuis, close to the Villa Diodati, where Byron was staying. Although Claire threw herself at Byron's head, and managed to encompass the rest of him too, it was a happily creative time for them, with philosophy and learning pursued as well as the more touted facets of the good life. Here, Mary began to write *Frankenstein*. Summer had too short a stay, and the party returned to England to face more trouble.

Mary's self-effacing halfsister, Fanny, committed suicide with an overdose of laudanum at the age of twenty-two, by which time the Shelley ménage had moved to Bath; Claire still followed them, as the monster followed

Frankenstein, and was now also pregnant. Then news reached them that Shelley's wife Harriet had drowned herself in London, not in the Thames, but in the Serpentine. She had been far advanced in pregnancy. Shelley and Mary were married almost immediately.

The date of the marriage was 29 December 1816. Six and a half years later, in July 1822, Shelley was drowned while sailing on the Ligurian Sea. By that time, William was dead, as was another child, Clara; Mary had also had a miscarriage, but another son, Percy Florence, had been born in 1820. He alone of Mary's progeny survived to manhood. Even Claire's daughter by Byron, Allegra, had died. In 1824 Byron died in Greece.

The rest of Mary's life is curiously empty, lived in the shadow of her first twenty-five years. Mary remained ever faithful to the memory of her husband. She edited his poems and papers, and earned a living by her pen. She wrote historical novels, such as *Perkin Warbeck* (1830) and *Lodore* (1835), which enjoyed some success, short stories, and one novel, *The Last Man* (1826), which, by its powerfully oppressive theme of world catastrophe, is classifiable as science fiction. Percy married. Her cold father, Godwin, died; Shelley's difficult father died. Finally, in 1851, the year of the Great Exhibition, Mary herself died, aged fifty-three.

II

This painful biography, as confused as any modern one, is worth retelling, for it helps to explain not only why Mary's temperament was not a sanguine one, but where much derives from what is read in her two science fiction novels, *Frankenstein* and *The Last Man*. Both owe a great deal to the literature that preceded them; more is owed to experience. Critics are liable comfortably to ignore the latter to concentrate on the former.

The essence of the story of *Frankenstein* is familiar, if in distorted form, from many film, stage, and television versions, in which Victor Frankenstein compiles a creature from corpses and then endows it with life, after which it runs amok. The novel is long, and more complex than this synopsis suggests. It is a flawed masterpiece of growing reputation, and an increasing body of criticism attests to the attraction of both its excellences and its flaws.

Frankenstein; or, The Modern Prometheus begins with letters from Captain Walton to his sister. Walton is sailing in Arctic waters when he sees on the ice floes a sledge being driven by an enormous figure. The next day, the crew rescues a man from a similar sledge. It is Victor Frankenstein of Geneva; when he recovers, he tells his tale to Walton, which account makes up the bulk of the book, to be rounded off by Walton again, and to include six chapters that are the creature's own account of its life, especially of its education. If the style of the novel is discursive, Mary Shelley was following a method familiar to readers of Samuel Richardson and Laurence Sterne; the method became unfashionable but, to readers of eccentric modern novels, may now be increasingly sympathetic and help to account in part for the newfound popularity of the book.

One of the enduring attractions of the book is that Mary sets most of the drama, not in the seamy London she knew from childhood, but amid spectacular alpine scenery, such as she had visited with Shelley. The monster's puissance gains greatly by this association with the elements: storm, cold, snow, desolation.

Interest has always centered on the monster and its creation. (It has no name in the novel, merely being referred to as "creature," "daemon," or "monster," which accounts for the popular misusage by which the name Frankenstein has come to be transferred from the creator to the created—a mistake that occurred first in Mary's lifetime.) This is the essential science fiction core of the narrative—a fascinating experiment that goes wrong—a prescription to be repeated later, many times, in *Amazing Stories* and elsewhere. Frankenstein's is a Faustian dream of unlimited power, but this Faust makes no supernatural

Mary Wollstonecraft Shelley. Courtesy of the Library of Congress

pacts; he succeeds only when he throws away the fusty old reference books, outdated by the new science, and gets to work on research in laboratories.

But science fiction is not only hard science, and related to the scientific experiment is another experiment, also science fictional, an experiment in political theory that relates to William Godwin's ideas. Frankenstein is horrified by his creation and abjures responsibility. Yet the monster, despite its ugliness, is gentle and intelligent, and tries to win its way into society. Society repulses it. Hence the monster's cry, "I am malicious because I am miserable," a dramatic reversal of received Christian thinking of the time.

The richness of the story's metaphorical content, coupled with the excellence of the prose, has tempted commentators to interpret the novel in various ways. *Frankenstein*'s subtitle, *The Modern Prometheus*, leads to one level of meaning. Prometheus, according to Aeschylus in his play *Prometheus Bound*, brings fire from Heaven and bestows the gift on mankind; for this, Zeus has him chained to a rock in the Caucasus, where an eagle eats his viscera. One thinks here of the scene after Shelley's death, when Trelawny caused his corpse to be burnt on the shore, Byron and Leigh Hunt also being present. At the last possible moment, Trelawny ran forward and snatched Shelley's heart from the body. Another version of the legend, the one Mary had chiefly in mind, tells of Prometheus fashioning men out of mud and water. Mary seized on this aspect of the legend, while Byron and Shelley were writing "Prometheus" and "Prometheus Unbound" respectively. Mary, with an inspired transposition, uses electricity as the divine fire.

By this understanding, with Frankenstein acting God, Frankenstein's monster becomes mankind itself, blundering about the world seeking knowledge and reassurance. The monster's intellectual quest has led David Ketterer to state that "basically *Frankenstein* is about the problematical nature of knowledge" (*Frankenstein's Creation: The Book, The Monster, and Human Reality*, 1979). Although this interpretation is too radical, it reminds us usefully of the intellectual aspects of the work, and of Mary's understanding of the British philosophers John Locke, George Berkeley, and David Hume.

Leonard Wolf argues that *Frankenstein* should be regarded as "psychological allegory" (*The Annotated Frankenstein*, 1977). This view is supported by Ketterer, who thinks that therefore the novel cannot be science fiction ("'Frankenstein' in Wolf's Clothing," 1979). Godwin's *Caleb Williams* is also psychological or at least political allegory; it is nevertheless regarded as the first crime novel. Surely there are many good science fiction novels that are psychological allegory as well as being science fiction. Algis Budrys' *Who?* is an example. By understanding the origins of "real" science fiction, we understand something of its function; hence the importance of the question. Not to regard *Frankenstein* but, say, *The Time Machine* or even Hugo Gernsback's magazines as the first science fiction—as many did only a few years ago—is to underestimate the capabilities of the medium; and to claim that *Gilgamesh* or

684

Homer started it all is to claim so much that almost anything becomes science fiction.

Mary Shelley, in her Introduction to the 1831 edition of *Frankenstein*, says that she wanted her story to "speak to the mysterious fears of our (i.e. human kind's) nature. . . ." Is that not what science fiction still excellently does?

That the destructive monster stands for one side of Shelley's nature, and the constructive Victor for the other, has been convincingly argued by another critic, Christopher Small (*Ariel Like a Harpy*, 1972). Mary's passion for Shelley, rather than blinding her, gave her terrifying insight. In case this idea sounds oversophisticated, it must be recalled that Mary herself, in her Introduction to the 1831 edition of her novel, meant it as a kind of metaphor when she wrote "Invention . . . does not consist in creating out of void, but out of chaos; the materials must, in the first place, be afforded: it can give form to dark, shapeless substances, but cannot bring into being substance itself."

In referring to *Frankenstein* as a diseased creation myth (*Billion Year Spree*, 1973) I had in mind phrases with sexual connotations in the novel such as "my workshop of filthy creation," used by Frankenstein of his secret work. Mary's own experiences taught her to regard life and death as closely intertwined. The genesis of her terrifying story came to her in a dream, in which she says she saw "the hideous phantasm of a man stretched out, and then, on the working of some powerful engine, show signs of life, and stir with an uneasy half vital motion." The powerful line suggests both a distorted image of her mother dying, in those final restless movements which often tantalizingly suggest recovery rather than its opposite, and also the stirrings of sexual intercourse, particularly when we recall that "powerful engine" is a term used in pornography as a synonym for penis.

The critic Ellen Moers, writing on female gothic, dispatched the question of how a young girl like Mary could hit on such a horrifying idea (although Mary was herself the first to raise it). Most female writers of the eighteenth and nineteenth centuries were spinsters, and in any case Victorian taboos operated against writing on childbirth. Mary experienced the fear, guilt, depression, and anxiety that often attend childbirth, particularly in situations such as hers—unmarried, her consort a married man with children by another woman, and beset by debt in a foreign place. Only a woman, only Mary Shelley, could have written *Frankenstein*. As Miriam Gillon says, "She was the only one of the lot of them who knew about life."

Moreover, the casual remark made by Gillon takes us to a deeper level of meaning which, although sufficiently obvious, has not been significantly remarked upon. *Frankenstein* is autobiographical.

It is commonly accepted that the average first novel relies for its material on personal experience. It does not deny other interpretations—for a metaphor has many interpretations—by stating that Mary saw herself as the monster. This is why we pity it. She too tried to win her way into society. By running away with Shelley, she sought acceptance through love. But the move carried her further from society; she became a wanderer, an exile, like Byron, like Shelley. Her mother's death in childbirth must have caused Mary to feel that she, like the monster, had been born from the dead. Behind the monster's eloquence lies Mary's grief. Part of the continued appeal of the novel is the appeal of the drama of the neglected child.

Upon this structure of one kind of reality, Mary built a further structure, one of the intellect. A madness for knowledge abounds; not only Victor Frankenstein but the monster and Walton also, and the judicial processes throughout the book, are in quest for knowledge of one kind and another. Interestingly, the novel contains few female characters (a departure from the gothic mode, with its soft, frightened heroines); Victor's espoused remains always a cold and distant figure. The monster, product of guilty knowledge, threatens the world with evil progeny.

The monster is, of course, more interesting than Victor. He has the vitality of evil, like Satan in John Milton's *Paradise Lost* (1667) before him and Quilp in Charles Dickens' *The*

Old Curiosity Shop (1840) after him, eloquent villains both. It is the monster that comes first to our minds, it was the monster that came first to Mary's mind. The monster holds its appeal because it was created by science, or at least pseudoscience, rather than by any pacts with the devil, or by magic, like the golem.

Frankenstein emerges from the gothic tradition. Gothic still tints science fiction with its hues of suspense and doom. In *Billion Year Spree* it is argued that *Frankenstein* was the first real science fiction novel. Here the adjective "real" serves as an escape clause. The point about discussing where science fiction begins is that it helps in understanding the nature and function of science fiction. In pre-Revolutionary France, for instance, several books appeared with Enlightenment scenarios depicting a future where present trends were greatly developed, and where the whole world became a civilized extension of the Tuileries. The best-known example is Louis-Sébastien Mercier's *L'An 2400* (1770), set seven centuries ahead in time; it was translated into several languages. Mercier wrote in the utopian tradition; Mary Shelley did not. Here we see a division of function. Jules Verne was influenced by Mercier and worked with "actual possibilities of invention and discovery." H. G. Wells was influenced by *Frankenstein* and wrote what he called fantasies—the phrase set in quotes is Wells's, who added that he "did not pretend to deal with possible things." One can imagine Mary Shelley saying as much. R. Glynn Grylls, a biographer of Mary Shelley, writing in the 1930's advanced the argument that *Frankenstein* is "the first of the Scientific Romances that have culminated in our day in the work of Mr. H. G. Wells," because it erects "a superstructure of fantasy on a foundation of circumstantial 'scientific fact.'" Shrewd judgment, although the excellence of the novel is otherwise underestimated.

As Muriel Spark writes in *Child of Light* (1951), Mary Shelley in her thinking seems at least fifty years ahead of her time. She discovered the "irrational," one of the delights and torments of our age. By dressing it in rational garb, and letting it stalk the land, she unwittingly dealt a blow against the tradition to which Mercier was heir. Utopia is no place for the irrational.

In sum, Victor Frankenstein is a modern, consciously rejecting ancient fustian booklore in favor of modern science, kicking out father figures. His creation of life shows him further usurping paternal power, invading what was previously God's province. Victor and his monster together function as the light and dark side of mankind, in a symbolism that was to become increasingly comprehensible after Mary's death.

As befitted an author writing after the Napoleonic Wars, when the Industrial Revolution was well under way, Mary dealt not merely with extrapolated development, like Mercier before her, but with unexpected change, like Wells after her. Above all, Frankenstein stands as the figure of the scientist (although the word was not coined when Mary wrote), set apart from the rest of society, unable to control the new forces he has brought into the world. The successor to Prometheus is Pandora. No other writer, except H. G. Wells, presents us with as many innovations as Mary Shelley.

III

The Last Man was published in 1826, anonymously, as *Frankenstein* had been. Few critics of standing have praised the novel. It meanders. Yet Muriel Spark has said of it that it is Mary's "most interesting, if not her most consummate, work."

The theme of *The Last Man* was not new, and could hardly be at a time when epidemics were still commonplace. The title was used for an anonymous novel in 1806. Thomas Campbell (1777–1844) wrote a poem with the same title; while at the Villa Diodati, Byron composed a poem entitled "Darkness," in which the world is destroyed and two men, the last, die of fright at the sight of each other.

In the same year that Mary's novel was published, John Martin painted a watercolor on the subject (later, in 1849, he exhibited a powerful oil with the same title).

The novel is set in the twenty-first century, a period, it seems, of much sentimental rhetoric. Adrian, the earl of Windsor, befriends the wild Lionel Verney. Adrian is the son of the king of England, who abdicated; one of the king's favorites was Verney's father. Adrian is full of fine sentiments and wins over Verney. Verney has a sister called Perdita who falls in love with Lord Raymond and eventually commits suicide. Raymond is a peer of genius and beauty who besieges Constantinople. The relationships of these personages, together with a profusion of mothers and sisters, fill the first of the three volumes. Adrian is Mary's portrait of Shelley, the bright rather than the dark side, Perdita is Claire, Raymond is Byron. Verney plays the part of Mary, and eventually becomes the Last Man. Verney, like Frankenstein, is a paradigm of the Outsider.

There is undoubted strength in the second and third books, once the plague has the world in its grip. Society disintegrates on a scale merely hinted at in the unjust world of *Frankenstein*.

> I spread the whole earth out as a map before me. On no one spot of its surface could I put my finger and say, here is safety. In the south, the disease, virulent and immedicable, had nearly annihilated the race of man; storm and innundation, poisonous winds and blights, filled up the measure of suffering. In the north it was worse. . . .

Finally, Verney-Mary alone is left, drifting south towards the equator, like a character in a J. G. Ballard novel. So Mary tells us how life was without Shelley; her universe had gone. Through science fiction, she expressed her powerful feelings.

In his brief book on Mary, William Walling makes a point that incidentally relates *The Last Man* still more closely to the science fictional temper (1972). Remarking that solitude is a common topic of the period and by no means Mary's monopoly, Walling claims that by interweaving the themes of isolation and the end of civilization, she creates a prophetic account of modern industrial society, in which the creative personality becomes more and more alienated.

Tales and Stories by Mary Shelley were collected by Richard Garnett and published in 1891. They are in the main conventional. Familial and amorous misunderstandings fill the foreground, armies gallop about in the background. The characters are highborn, their speeches high-flown. Tears are scalding, years long, sentiments either villainous or irreproachable, deaths copious and conclusions not unusually full of well-mannered melancholy. The tales are of their time. Here again, the game of detecting autobiographical traces can be played. One story, "Transformation," sheds light on *Frankenstein*—but not much. We have to value Mary Shelley, as we do other authors, for her strongest work, not her weakest; and her best has a strength still not widely enough appreciated.

This collection of stories from scattered journals and keepsake albums indicates Mary's emotional and physical exhaustion. In the course of eight years, between 1814 and 1822, she had borne four children, three of whom died during the period, and had suffered miscarriages. She had traveled hither and thither with her irresponsible husband, who had most probably had an affair with her closest friend, Claire. And she had witnessed suicides and death all around her, culminating in Shelley's death. It was much for a sensitive and intellectual woman to endure. No wonder that Claire Clairmont wrote to her, some years after the fury and shouting died, "I think in certain things you are the most daring woman I ever knew."

Selected Bibliography

SCIENCE FICTION WORKS OF
MARY SHELLEY

Frankenstein; or, The Modern Prometheus. London: Lackington, Hughes, Harding, Mavor and Jones, 1818.

Third edition, with considerable textual change; London: Henry Colburn and Richard Bentley, 1831. Many editions are in print, almost all of which reprint the 1831 text. For scholarly purposes the text edited by M. K. Joseph (London: Oxford University Press, 1969) may be mentioned. The 1818 text is reprinted in the edition prepared by James Rieger (Indianapolis, Ind.: Bobbs-Merrill, 1974), with full analysis of textual variations and commentary.

The Last Man. London: Henry Colburn, 1826.

Tales and Stories. Collected by Richard Garnett. London: W. Paterson, 1891.

Collected Tales and Stories with Original Engravings. Edited with an Introduction and Notes by Charles E. Robinson. Baltimore, Md.: Johns Hopkins University Press, 1976.

CRITICAL AND BIOGRAPHICAL MATERIAL

Aldiss, Brian W. *Billion Year Spree: The History of Science Fiction*. London: Weidenfeld and Nicolson, 1973; Garden City, N.Y.: Doubleday, 1973. Revised with David Wingrove as *Trillion Year Spree: The History of Science Fiction*, London: Victor Gollancz, 1986.

———. "Science Fiction's Mother Figure." In his *The Detached Retina: Aspects of SF and Fantasy*. Syracuse, N.Y.: Syracuse University Press, 1995.

Asimov, Isaac. "First Science Fiction Novel." In his *Asimov on Science Fiction*. Garden City, N.Y.: Doubleday, 1981.

Baldick, Chris. *In Frankenstein's Shadow: Myth, Monstrosity, and Nineteenth Century Writing*. Oxford, England: Clarendon, 1987.

Bennett, Betty T. *Selected Letters of Mary Wollstonecraft Shelley*. Baltimore, Md.: Johns Hopkins University Press, 1995.

Botting, Fred. *Making Monstrous: Frankenstein, Criticism, Theory*. Manchester, N.Y.: Manchester University Press, 1991.

Donawerth, Jane. *Frankenstein's Daughters: Women Writing Science Fiction*. Syracuse, N.Y.: Syracuse University Press, 1997.

Dunn, Jane. *Moon in Eclipse: A Life of Mary Shelley*. London: Weidenfeld and Nicolson, 1978; New York: St. Martin's Press, 1978. (An enjoyable biography.)

Feldman, Paula R., and Diana Scott-Kilvert, eds. *The Journals of Mary Shelley, 1814–1844*. 2 vols. Oxford, England: Oxford University Press, 1987.

Glance, Jonathan C. "'Beyond the Bounds of Reverie?' Another Look at the Dreams in *Frankenstein*." *Journal of the Fantastic in the Arts*, 7, no. 4 (1996): 30–47.

Grylls, R. Glynn. *Mary Shelley, A Biography*. London and New York: Oxford University Press, 1938.

Jackson, Rosemary. "Narcissism and Beyond: A Psychoanalytic Reading of *Frankenstein* and Fantasies of the Double." In *Aspects of Fantasy*. Edited by William Coyle. Westport, Conn.: Greenwood, 1986.

Jones, Frederick L., ed. *The Letters of Mary Shelley*. 2 vols. Norman: University of Oklahoma Press, 1944.

Ketterer, David. *Frankenstein's Creation: The Book, The Monster, and Human Reality*. Victoria, Canada: University of Victoria Press, 1979.

———. "'Frankenstein' in Wolf's Clothing." *Science Fiction Studies*, 18 (July 1979).

———. "*Frankenstein*: The Source of a Name." *Science-Fiction Studies*, 22, part 3 (1995): 455–456.

———. "Frankenstein's 'Conversion' from Natural Magic to Modern Science—and a *Shifted* (and Converted) Last Draft Insert." *Science-Fiction Studies*, 24, part 1 (1997): 57–78.

Kranzler, Laura. "Frankenstein and the Technological Future." *Foundation* (Winter 1988/1989): 42–49.

Lomax, William. "Epic Reversal in Mary Shelley's *The Last Man*: Romantic Irony and the Roots of Science Fiction." In *Contours of the Fantastic*. Edited by Michele K. Langford. Westport, Conn.: Greenwood, 1990.

Marshall, Florence Ashton. *Life and Letters of Mary Wollstonecraft Shelley*. London: R. Bentley and Sons, 1889.

Mellor, Anne K. *Mary Shelley: Her Life, Her Fiction, Her Monsters*. New York: Methuen, 1988.

Moers, Ellen. "Female Gothic: The Monster's Mother." *New York Review*, 21 (March 1974). Reprinted in *Literary Women*, Garden City, N.Y.: Doubleday, 1976.

O'Donohoe, Nick. "Condemned to Life: 'The Mortal Immortal' and 'The Man Who Never Grew Young.'" In *Death and the Serpent*. Edited by C. B. Yoke and D. M. Hassler. Westport, Conn.: Greenwood, 1985.

Small, Christopher. *Ariel Like a Harpy: Shelley, Mary, and Frankenstein*. London: Victor Gollancz, 1972. Reprinted as *Mary Shelley's "Frankenstein": Tracing the Myth*, Pittsburgh, Pa.: University of Pittsburgh Press, 1973.

Soyka, David. "Frankenstein and the Miltonic Creation of Evil." *Extrapolation*, 33, no. 2 (1992): 166–177.

Spark, Muriel. *Child of Light: A Reassessment of Mary Wollstonecraft Shelley*. Hadleigh, Essex, England: Tower Bridge Publications, 1951. Revised edition *Mary Shelley*, New York: E. P. Dutton, 1987.

Vasbinder, Samuel Holmes. *Scientific Attitudes in Mary Shelley's* Frankenstein. Revised edition, Ann Arbor, Mich.: UMI Research Press, 1984.

Vlasopolos, Anca. "*Frankenstein*'s Hidden Skeleton: The Psycho-Politics of Oppression." *Science-Fiction Studies*, 10, part 2 (1983): 125–136.

Walling, William A. *Mary Shelley*. New York: Twayne Publishers, 1972.

Wolf, Leonard, ed. *The Annotated Frankenstein*. New York: Clarkson Potter, 1977.

—BRIAN W. ALDISS

LUCIUS SHEPARD
(b. 1947)

IF THERE ARE Ur-texts for contemporary genre fiction, the two greatest works, in terms of influence and effect, must be Joseph Conrad's *Heart of Darkness* (1899) and Arthur Machen's "The Great God Pan" (1890); and the writer who most successfully invokes Conrad's sense of horrific rapture and Machen's *omnia mysterium* ("all ends in mystery") is Lucius Shepard. Like those literary forebears, Shepard's most effective works are novellas—arguably the best format for the compelling blend of horror, high-tension pyrotechnics of style, and scientific excess that characterize Shepard's fiction. From Conrad, Shepard has absorbed the lone Western traveler's sense of awe and terror as he gazes upon the ruins of colonial aspirations set against a backdrop of rain forests seething with ancient evil; and he shares Machen's profound distrust of the power of science to overcome nature, especially as embodied in psychic and psychotropic experience. Adding his own remarkable prose style and sense of characterization, Lucius Shepard creates not so much a fictional witches' brew as a hallucinatory drug, a nice antidote to much of the field's sternly plotted and sometimes anemically written work.

Shepard has written only three novels— *Green Eyes* (1984), *Life During Wartime* (1987), and *The Golden* (1993), the first two science fiction and the last a baroque vampire tale; one stand-alone novella, *Kalimantan* (1990); and three collections of stories, *The Jaguar Hunter* (1987), *The Ends of the Earth* (1991), and *Barnacle Bill the Spacer, and Other Stories* (1997). With this relatively spare showing of published material, Shepard has made a considerable mark on the field, garnering several awards though not yet achieving the mainstream breakthrough he seemed poised for in the late 1980's. Conrad in particular serves as a sort of spirit guide for the professionally exiled Shepard, whose own creative life begins in mystery, with the publication in *Collier's Magazine*—starting in 1952—of several folktales and fairy tales, under the byline "Lucius Shepard." Charming as the stories are, what is most remarkable about them is that the author would have been in kindergarten when the first one appeared. Shepard has demurred on the subject, claiming that the stories were written by his father, which explains one mystery while begetting another, a literary analog to the compulsively driven stage mother who creates a Noel Coward or Gypsy Rose Lee of her offspring. Whether or not the *Collier's* stories were in fact written by the precocious Lucius Shepard (one surmises they may have been a collaboration), certain stylistic elements foreshadow the writer who was to emerge to prominence nearly two decades later: recurring fantasy motifs, an ear for vernacular dialogue, and elevated nineteenth-century diction.

Of course, the very existence of the tales underscores one of the most intriguing things about the author. Lucius Shepard is a most extraordinary prose stylist, but the mystery at the heart of his most accomplished stories may be the writer himself. More than any other living genre writer, he has created a myth of his own mercurial personae—drug user, adventurer, foreign journalist, rock and roll star, artistic recluse—and subsequently tapped into this myth for his fictions. Because of that, the life map deserves a look, even if a cursory one, though Shepard's confabulatory literary impulse also suggests heeding the signpost "Caveat Lector" (Let the Reader Beware).

Between 1952 and his spectacular adult debut in 1983, his output was meager, a poetry chapbook and the text to an artist's portfolio. In between we have Lucius Shepard: The Missing Years. If one recreates the artist from his later work, the years were lively indeed. The U.S. art critic Adam Gopnik has suggested that "In a country where the role of the artist is a vague one, ambitious American artists have all along sought out other, more secure, social roles as cover." Shepard's creative ambition has been evident from the very first (mystifying juvenilia notwithstanding), and his choice of cover suggests both a rough familiarity with contemporary cool and a prescient use of the late-century art of "spin." What is obvious is that Shepard traveled, starting in his early teens, from his home in Florida to the seedier parts of Manhattan and New Orleans and thence (in no particular order) to Europe, Indonesia, Nepal, the Caribbean, and Latin America. By the mid-1980's he was relatively "settled" on the American East Coast (Florida, Virginia, New York, Nantucket), with excursions elsewhere (off-world seems to be the only place Shepard has not traveled). A few years later found him transplanted to Seattle and other points west.

The peripatetic impulse was matched to itinerant involvements, the most extreme being those two hallmarks of Shepard's generation: rock and roll and drugs. The Dionysian impulse lies at the root of nearly all of Shepard's work, although excess is most often observed from the point of view of a worldweary, deracinated protagonist. In this, Shepard's stories most resemble those of spiritual expatriates such as Robert Stone and Paul Bowles rather than the grittily North American works of his contemporaries William Gibson, John Varley, or Connie Willis. By the

time Shepard attended the Clarion Writer's Workshop in Michigan in 1980, he was noticeably older and more worldly than the other students, and his prose showed a commensurate artistic maturity.

Shepard's first wholesale recognition in the field came in 1983, with the publication of the short story "Solitario's Eyes" in the *Magazine of Fantasy and Science Fiction*. A stylistic tour de force about a psychic child, the tale was most memorable for its brilliant deployment of the magic realist tropes that became the author's trademark—a lush, sometimes overheated prose style, elegant Jamesian diction, and most especially the Latin American setting, which vies with the jungles of Asia and Indonesia as the quintessential Shepard mise-en-scène. With "Solitario's Eyes," Lucius Shepard seemed to spring full-blown onto the genre scene, a literary Athena spouting incantatory prose.

Subsequent early fiction showed little evidence of being apprentice work: 1984 could be seen as Shepard's Year of Writing Dangerously. In the months following the appearance of "Solitario's Eyes," Shepard published seven stories in various magazines and anthologies. The most notable of these are "Black Coral," which deploys the voudon (or voodoo), trappings that the author was to make such good use of in his first novel *Green Eyes*; "Salvador," a precursor to *Life During Wartime*; and "The Night of White Bhairab," wherein a quintessential Shepard protagonist—American, male, *ennuyant*—finds himself trapped in the crossfire between ancient supernatural forces, here represented by a benign Katmandu house ghost and a malevolent *Amityville Horror*–style revenant inadvertently imported from the United States.

It is in this last tale that one Mr. Chatterji tells Eliot Blackford, his tequila-addled factotum, "In your country evil has a sultry character. Sexy!" Words to live by in Shepard's universe, and words that could serve as a summing-up of the author's 1984 debut novel, *Green Eyes*. In *Green Eyes*, a near-future bioengineering research facility has mastered the dubious art of implanting live bacteria into dead people, thereby creating a short-lived laboratory assemblage of the undead—zombies, in fact, who derive not just their name but much of their spirit from the now familiar pantheon of duppies (malevolent Haitian spirtis) and loas (Haitian voodoo cult deities), ancestral spirits and ancient gods who come to inhabit the bodies of the dead and the minds of practitioners. Donnell Harrison, the hero of *Green Eyes*, has the body of a young alcoholic carnival worker. But like the other inhabitants of Shadows (the not-so-subtly named research facility), he has begun to manifest his own avatar personality, a Byron-esque poet handsome and brooding enough to win the heart of Jocundra, the researcher who urges him to write. In short order, Donnell and Jocundra flee Shadows, pursued by scientists and more malign agents, and find themselves tracing a labyrinth of government intrigue and reinvigorated voudon gods and goddesses. The novel deals heavily in Grand Guignol effects—menacing spirits and bayou ritual as well as the "green eyes" of the title, ocular phosphorescence that occurs when the zombies' levels of life-giving bacteria reach critical mass, heralding the host body's death. "The flickerings in his eyes intensified, glowing like swampfire, blossoming into green stars. The scene embodied a hallucinated sexuality."

But these effects are offset by the sheer exuberance of Shepard's writing, his unrelenting refusal to let the reader turn away until Donnell, in full Orphic mode, recites his voudon epic, "The Song of Returning," and proceeds to go out in an emerald blaze of glory. With its doomed love affair, memorable evocation of the near-depth experience, and eerily prescient half-human characters, *Green Eyes* bears comparison with two other contemporaneous works, the 1982 film *Blade Runner* and Jack Dann's haunting novel *The Man Who Melted* (1984). *Green Eyes* is also one of Shepard's fictions that indisputably can be termed science fiction rather than science fantasy or supernatural fiction. Most importantly, though, the novel stakes out the territory that Shepard has returned to over and over again during the past decade, namely, that unsettling interzone where psychotropic drugs, neurochemistry, and psychic experience all hold sway. In the 1980's, ethnobotanists such as Wade Davis and Terrence McKenna produced best-selling works that introduced mainstream readers to the pharmacological underpinnings of various religious and anthropological phenomena, most notoriously in *The Serpent and the Rainbow*, (1985), Davis's over-the-top account of his own death- and mind-defying experiences with voudon.

For Shepard, this topography is not the result of simple neurochemical reactions, however. Nor is it a matter of faith, whether that faith be in Tibetan demons or Southern faith healers or the fading promise of hippie activism. Shepard eschews the punk poetics of other 1980's writers such as Pat Cadigan, John Shirley, and Bruce Sterling, whose work has been dated in part because of its unremitting reliance on Sex, Drugs, and Rock and Roll, a zeitgeist that has been overtaken by events; it is difficult to maintain a drug-induced, cutting-edge cool, literary or cultural, in an

Lucius Shepard. © 1998 M. C. Valada

era that promotes temperance while universally prescribing Prozac. In Shepard's work, drugs are not mind-expanding so much as they are the missing link between the spirit world and our own. As such, they also function as the bridge between fantasy, the genre that Shepard inhabits most successfully, and science fiction, where his work is most often pigeonholed.

Green Eyes won Shepard still more attention, but in late 1984 came the publication (in the *Magazine of Fantasy and Science Fiction*) of what may perhaps be his most enduring work. "The Man Who Painted the Dragon Graiule" is a novella, the first of a triptych rounded out by two other long stories, "The Scalehunter's Beautiful Daughter" (1988) and "The Father of Stones" (1989). The science fiction premise is tissue thin—the dragons are rumored to have come from another planet—and the linked tales function more as creative allegory than as science fiction.

The world of "Graiule" is a decadent late-nineteenth-century tropical landscape, overrun with night-flowering plants and obsessed creative types, that is resonant of both Gabriel García Marquez's Macondo and Clark Ashton Smith's Zothique. Early in the tale, Shepard expertly maps out this peculiar region, a place located at the interstices of the grim workaday world and its ebullient, fabulist reflections.

In 1853, in a country far to the south, in a world separated from this one by the thinnest margin of possibility, a dragon named Graiule dominates the region of the Carbonales Valley, a fertile area centering on the town of Teocinte and renowned for its production of silver, mahogany, and indigo. There are other dragons in these days, most dwelling on the rocky islands west of Patagonia—tiny, irascible creatures, the largest of them no bigger than a swallow. But Graiule is one of the great Beasts who has ruled an age.

With this one stroke, Shepard conjures up a world at once far removed from "the fields we know" (to invoke Lord Dunsany's unforgettable phrase) yet utterly recognizable— Patagonian reptiles that might have been cat-

alogued by Darwin, an ailing Latin American economy. But "The Man Who Painted The Dragon Graiule" is not an exercise in fin-de-siècle whimsy or magic realist homage. The dragon of the title is immense and literally mired in the real world. Centuries earlier, Graiule was rendered immobile (though not dead) by a sorcerer, and the sleeping dragon's mountainous form now dominates not just the geological but also the psychic topography of the hardscrabble towns that lie in his shadow.

To one of these towns comes a European artist named Meric Cattanay. Cattanay proposes to the town fathers that he rid them of the dragon once and for all. The method he suggests is to paint over the gargantuan creature's dreaming form. This will not only gradually poison Graiule but provide jobs—as workmen, builders, chemists, and so on—for the underemployed villagers. Hewing close to a folkloric tradition that dates back to the Pied Piper of Hamelin and that itinerant visitor who coaxed stone soup from his reluctant hosts, Cattanay's proposal is accepted. Over the ensuring decades, the entire region is transformed physically, economically, and even spiritually by the feat of painting Graiule. Needless to say, the end result is not quite what Cattanay had in mind. While the story achieves a heartrending epiphany, it is memorable for avoiding both sentiment and cynicism. Instead, "The Man Who Painted the Dragon Graiule" becomes that rare thing, a successful, even enthralling, meditation upon the role and influence of the artist and of the power of creativity to alter the human landscape for good or ill. The two companion stories deepen Shepard's depiction of this hothouse world, in particular "The Scalehunter's Beautiful Daughter," whose protagonist flees rape and vengeful villagers by hiding within the body of the dragon himself, where she is transformed by the power of the immense creature's dreams.

The body of work Shepard had produced thus far earned him the John W. Campbell Award in 1985. He continued to publish short fiction, mostly horror-tinged tales such as

"How the Wind Spoke at Madaket" (1985), "Mengele" (1985), "The Jaguar Hunter" (1985), and the intriguingly autobiographical "A Spanish Lesson" (1985), as well as "The Sun Spider" (1987), a tale of far-future decadence redolent of Gene Wolfe's Book of the New Sun (1980–1983).

But four science fiction stories from this period prefigure Shepard's most successful venture into the genre, the novel *Life During Wartime*. These stories, "R&R" (1986, which is incorporated into the novel), "Salvador" (1984), "Delta Sly Honey" (1987), and "Shades" (1987), are missives from the frontline of a Vietnam-style conflict fought in a near-future Central America. *Life During Wartime* is a fuller accounting. Mingolla, a twenty-year-old artillery specialist, was a fledgling artist from New York before joining the campaign. There he is selected for the Psicorps, an elite division of soldiers whose psychic abilities are enhanced by sophisticated helmets and psychotropic drugs. There is a war within the war, of course, as well as conspiracies and even darker cultural intrigues featuring an immemorial Mafia-style rivalry between two families, the Madradonas and the Sotomayors. Their conflict amounts to a secret history of the world, in which psychotropic drugs play a major role.

As in *Green Eyes*, the tale devolves into a mystical epiphany wherein the central characters transcend this mortal coil for a more transcendent union: not the most effective ending for a novel this ambitious. Shepard is most effective here at describing the horrific aftermath of battles, the hallucinatory beauty and terror of firefights, and the firefly splendor that the psychics experience when they witness death. Though not as effective and damning an indictment as Joe Haldeman's *The Forever War* (1975), Shepard's books do a masterful job of evoking the excess and futility of American military involvement in a tropical no-man's-land.

Life During Wartime was a critical and commercial success. Between its appearance and 1993's vampire saga, *The Golden*, Shepard's output slowed somewhat. Various novels in progress have yet to appear, but he continued to produce more short works. The 1989 small-press publication *Nantucket Slayrides* consists of three stories, two by Shepard—"How the Wind Spoke at Madaket" and "Nomans Land" (1988)—and one, "The Summer People" (1989) by Robert Frazier.

"How the Wind Spoke at Madaket" is a supernatural story featuring an elemental force of weather, a malevolent storm that feeds on the emotions of human beings and wreaks havoc on the bleak Nantucket landscape. The elemental is evocative of that most malign wind demon, Algernon Blackwood's "The Wendigo" (1910). Like Blackwood, Shepard is a visionary writer (to borrow critic Jack Sullivan's term from *Elegant Nightmares* [1978], his invaluable study of the classic ghost story). "How the Wind Spoke at Madaket" is notable primarily for its setting, the bayberry-choked dunes and off-season cottages of the village of Madaket, and for its characters, an endearingly eccentric lot, including the writer Peter Ramey, who is writing a novel called *How the Wind Spoke at Madaket*. "The Wendigo" derives its horror from what is not seen but heard—the thrashing of wind in the trees, the faint horrified cries of the man taken by the wendigo—and even smelled, in the moments before the wendigo descends upon the forest. But Shepard's lush style works against the most basic demand of a good ghost story, that something remain untold. Ultimately, "Madaket" drowns in its own descriptions, of storms and waterspouts and weatherbeaten New Englanders baring their souls to the unsettled sea.

"Nomans Land" is a more successful venture into the realm of classic science fiction–tinged horror, a Lovecraftian story set on a barren island near Martha's Vineyard. Jack Tyrell is shipwrecked on Nomans Land, where he takes shelter in a seemingly abandoned concrete bunker, a relic of World War II. There he meets and makes love to Astrid, an entomologist who has been studying the tiny island's remarkably prolific population of spiders. When morning comes, however, Astrid turns out to be more of a demon lover, a corpse with a single white spider hanging above its skull.

Still, "Nomans Land" is more complex than it at first seems. Astrid returns not as corpse but as an eerily revivified being, whose account of her arachnid research explains both her own existence and that of the ubiquitous spiders, which have over millennia developed an extremely complex symbiotic relationship with humanity:

> They've become a unity, intelligent in some way due to a symbiotic use of our genetic material. A group mind or something of the sort. Have you heard about the concept of people's personalities being transformed into computer software? That's similar to what the spiders have done. Transformed our genetic material into a biological analogue of software.

In "Nomans Land," the spiders—their group consciousness, even their venom—serve the same function that hallucinogenic substances do in much of Shepard's work. The story is appropriately creepy and ends with a scene of dark transcendence as Cisneros, another human given terrifying insight into the truth behind his species' evolution, faces the horrific reality of an eternity spent on Nomans Land.

The novella *Kalimantan* is a trope on *Heart of Darkness* that takes place in Indonesia and, tellingly, features an epigraph from Don DeLillo. *Kalimantan* does not swerve too far from Conrad's story line, which serves mainly as a set piece for some gorgeous visionary descriptions of the spirit world, as experienced by the protagonist and enhanced, needless to say, by the ingestion of a native plant, seribu aso, and the drug distilled from it. Early in *Kalimantan*, Shepard provides a nice take on his own work and its influences, writing, "It was plain from our talks that he'd read his Conrad, his Maugham, and that he'd ignored the despairing tone of their work and extracted only the mystery, the exoticism." Shepard himself does not eschew despair. *Kalimantan* ends on an ascending note of spiritual epiphany that is a creepy analog to Kurtz's (the malignant

European colonial who hides in the heart of darkness) final horror.

> Barnett's fingers kneaded the arms of his chair, his expression intent as the music reached a crescendo, losing all coherence in a frenzy of twisted screeches and keenings. "My God!" he said with awe, with despair, with yearning, as if he heard within that chaos the ringing of a sweet and secret bell, the elegant hint of some ungraspable mystical order. "My God, will you just listen to that!"

Lucius Shepard's most recent novel is *The Golden*, not science fiction but a vampire saga that shows Anne Rice's ubiquitous influence upon dark fantasy. *The Golden* is most distinguished by its setting, a huge crumbling edifice resonant of those in Mervyn Peake's *Gormenghast* (1950) or Michael Moorcock's *Gloriana* (1978). The 1996–1997 DC Comics series *Vermillion* and various stories that have appeared in the 1990's have Shepard returning to "pure" science fiction. "Barnacle Bill the Spacer" is set on a grim, corporate-run space station from which "lightships" bearing hopeful human colonists depart, never to be heard from again. Once more Shepard gives a tip of the hat to early-twentieth-century writers, invoking the opening line of Ford Madox Ford's *The Good Soldier* (1915) when Shepard's narrator states, "This, then, is the most beautiful story I know."

The title character of "Barnacle Bill the Spacer" is mentally disabled, a menial like Chief Broom in Ken Kesey's *One Flew over the Cuckoo's Nest* (1962). His role in the revolt that overtakes the station is peripheral and relies heavily on coincidence; ultimately, Barnacle Bill seems more a function of plotting and sentiment than a fully drawn character. The story is overwritten and overlong, but it does have a memorable beginning that can almost serve as an exegesis of Shepard's own narrative ethic:

> Most people neglect the profound sadness that can arise from the contemplation of the human spirit in extremis and blind them-

selves to beauty. That beauty, I mean, which is the iron of our existence. The beauty that inspires anger, not regret, and provokes struggle, not the idle aesthetic of the beholder. That, to my mind, lies at the core of the only stories worth telling. And that is the fundamental purpose of the storyteller's art, to illumine such beauty, to declare its central importance and make it shine forth from the inevitable wreckage of our hopes and the sorry manner of our decline.

Despite its unwieldy narrative and contrived plot, "Barnacle Bill the Spacer" won a Hugo award in 1994 for best novella. A more satisfying piece is the 1996 novella "Human History," which depicts a far-future American West, a landscape desolated by a dimly recalled, unnamed holocaust. The inhabitants of "Human History" speak in colloquial American English, ride horses, and carry firearms to protect themselves against "apes" and "tigers," genetically engineered castoffs of the Captains, humans who long ago ascended to space stations from which they monitor the doings of their descendants. These frontier dwellers must also guard against incursions by Bad Men, renegades who either flee or are cast out of the homey villages where the law-abiding remnants of humankind eke out their marginal livings. The story is narrated by Robert Hillyard, a gruff, typically hardworking inhabitant of Edgeville, who finds himself torn between his wife, Kiri, a duelist and bitter refugee from a less welcoming culture than Edgeville's, and Callie, the younger woman with whom Robert experiences a moment of epiphany when both see a "tiger," a creature more visionary eidolon than ravening carnivore.

In the wake of a disastrous duel and after learning of Robert's affair with Callie, Robert's wife flees into the wasteland surrounding Edgeville. Robert and their son go in search of her, accompanied by Callie. The tale unfolds in surprising ways, none more so than in the oblique, honed-down prose in which it is told. The Captains, who at first seem to be benevolent watchers in the sky like the Angels in John Crowley's *Engine Summer* (1979), reveal their true shapes as decadent sadists who have for generations controlled those on Earth by (surprise) drugs and other means. The Bad Men, far from being murderous interlopers, are merely those humans who have flung off the controls of the Captains by dint of rebellious fervor or simply by leaving the carefully controlled village compounds. The final confrontation between Bad Men and Captains is bloody and prolonged, with echoes of *Planet of the Apes*, the prairie apocalypse of Richard Grant's *Tapping the Source* (1984; another *Heart of Darkness* trope), and Russell Hoban's *Riddley Walker* (1980). Uncharacteristically for Shepard's work, "Human History" ends on a note of relative, if cautious, optimism. The Captains are defeated and their ranks of marauding apes depleted; the grim, obsessed caste of duelists gradually dies out, leaving a more balanced sampling of humanity, as exemplified by Robert and Callie. What is most heartening is that the final vision is unquestionably human and is unfettered by the high-flown psychedelics of Shepard's earlier work.

To date, Lucius Shepard has yet to produce the Big Book that readers and critics have been anticipating for so long, though rumors of screenplays and a mainstream novel continue to circulate. It may be that his talent is best reserved for that gynander literary form, the novella. On the other hand, it may be that the turn of the millennium will see him breaking out at last, achieving that fusion of stylistic and popular success he seems eminently capable of creating.

Selected Bibliography

WORKS OF LUCIUS SHEPARD

Cantata of Death, Weakmind & Generation. Durham, N.C.: Lillabulero, 1967. (Poem.)
Green Eyes. New York: Ace, 1984; London: Chatto and Windus, 1986.
The Jaguar Hunter. Sauk City, Wisc.: Arkham House, 1987. Revised edition, Worcester Park, Surrey, England: Kerosina, 1988. (Short stories.)

Life During Wartime. New York: Bantam, 1987; London: Grafton, 1988.

The Father of Stones. Baltimore, Md.: Washington Science Fiction Association, 1988.

The Scalehunter's Beautiful Daughter. Willimantic, Conn.: Ziesing, 1988.

Nantucket Slayrides: Three Short Novels, with Robert Frazier. Nantucket, Mass.: Eel Grass, 1989. (Short stories.)

Kalimantan. London: Century, 1990; New York: St. Martin's, 1991.

The Ends of the Earth: 14 Stories. Sauk City, Wisc.: Arkham House, 1991; London: Millennium, 1993. (Short stories.)

The Golden. Shingletown, Calif.: Ziesing, 1993; London: Millennium, 1993.

Sports & Music. Shingletown, Calif.: Ziesing, 1994. (Short stories.)

The Last Time. Royal Oak, Mich.: A.S.A.P., 1995.

Barnacle Bill the Spacer, and Other Stories. London: Millennium, 1997. (Short stories.)

—ELIZABETH HAND

M. P. SHIEL
(1865–1947)

ON TWENTY JULY 1880, you should have been on Redonda, one of the smaller Leeward Islands in the West Indies. You might have seen the last coronation in the Western Hemisphere. A sailing trader was anchored offshore, and on the barren, rocky land were a Methodist bishop, the shipowner (a fervent Methodist named Matthew Dowdy Shiell), and his fifteen-year-old son, Matthew Phipps—later to be known as the eccentric author M. P. Shiel.

According to the senior Shiell, Redonda was unclaimed by any power and his for the seizing. The island's population of seabirds and perhaps a dozen or so guano collectors and fishermen raised no objection, and the bishop crowned the young M. P. Shiell king of Redonda.

This would have been a fine way to set one's son up in business, but a few years later the British government eyed the phosphate and guano deposits, and the kingdom of Redonda became a government in exile. Shiell, Sr., protested, "Aggression!" but to no avail, and the king never regained his sea-mountain monarchy. Or, at least, that is the story. It may be partly fantasy, since Shiel's memory was vague in his later years and he always tended to embroider.

Matthew Phipps Shiel (he dropped the final "l" when he became a writer) was born in Montserrat in the West Indies, in 1865. His father was of Irish ancestry, and his mother's family were mulattos. His father, a shopkeeper and a man of some substance, was also a lay preacher, and the semisymbolic figure of the dynamic revivalist that often appears in Shiel's fiction may owe much to the early years when he accompanied his father around the islands on prayer circuits. The only son, after eight or nine daughters, Matthew Phipps seems to have been the focus of family hopes, much as Branwell Brontë had been for his family in Yorkshire.

Shiel was educated locally and in Devon, and attended an interpreters' school connected with King's College in London. He taught mathematics for a time in Derbyshire and, according to his own account, enrolled at St. Bartholomew's Hospital in London as a medical student, although no record of his enrollment survives. After watching an eye operation, Shiel stated, he decided that medicine and surgery were not for him, but his interest in medicine and the sciences continued throughout his life. He once commented that he could live happily only if his quarters included a small laboratory for pottering. Although he often bemoaned the fact that in his early years he had wasted time on "Chinese learning," like languages, he was a fine linguist with a working knowledge of at least seven languages. On one occasion he served as a multilingual interpreter to a scientific congress.

At about age seventeen, Shiel became acquainted with the works of Edgar Allan Poe, the author with whom he long had the most affinity. Shiel's first book, *Prince Zaleski* (1895), contained three detective stories closely imitative of Poe's (with some elements from Arthur Conan Doyle); and his third book, *Shapes in the Fire* (1896), consisted mostly of Poe stories transmogrified in a highly personal way. "Vaila," for example, is a rewriting of "The Fall of the House of Usher," and "Xélucha," of "Ligeia."

The success of *Prince Zaleski* and Shiel's failure as a medical student seem to have persuaded him to take up letters, and for the rest of his life he was a professional writer. He may have worked on a small newspaper for a time. He wrote hack serials for the popular magazines, did ghostwriting (as for Louis Tracy), and also managed to do work that fitted his own standards, conveying ideas he thought valuable. While he sometimes cultivated the pose of being independently wealthy, Shiel seems usually to have been financially pressed. In 1934 he was placed on the civil list and awarded a small pension for outstanding literary service.

During his earlier literary years, Shiel lived flittingly in London and Paris, with frequent long stays in Italy. He gravitated toward the Bohemian fin-de-siècle extensions of the Aesthetic Movement. Among his close friends were Arthur Machen, Edgar Jepson, and Ernest Dowson; and he was at least acquainted with Pierre Louÿs, Oscar Wilde, and Robert Louis Stevenson. It is quite possible that Shiel was a member of socialist organizations, although no record of this has been found.

Shiel's writing career, apart from minor work, falls into two periods: 1895 to 1913 and 1923 to 1937. Little is known of what he did during the missing decade, except that during World War I he worked in the British censorship office reading German letters and for a time tried his hand unsuccessfully at writing plays. Since he was a very rapid, facile writer, it is a reasonable supposition that he also did ghostwriting during this period. Although highly regarded by his British contemporaries, he was not well known in the United States until the late 1920's, when two of his novels, *How the Old Woman Got Home* (1927) and *Dr. Krasinski's Secret* (1929), went through several American printings.

During his last years Shiel was almost forgotten, except for a very small band of devoted admirers; and he died in ill health, poverty, and squalor in 1947. He had been married twice, under circumstances like those of his flamboyant heroes; but his children, legitimate and illegitimate, seem to have predeceased him. He was short in stature, very husky and muscular in his younger days, with rough craggy features.

At Shiel's death the kingdom of Redonda devolved to his friend and literary heir, John Gawsworth, who became King Juan I (*sic*). Gawsworth decided to turn Redonda into a kingdom of letters and issued titles to friends and literary lights in some way connected with Shiel. Among the recipients were Dylan Thomas, Eden Phillpotts, Dorothy Sayers, J. B. Priestley, A. A. Knopf, Victor Gollancz, and others. During his last, unfortunate years, Gawsworth tried to deed or sell his crown, and the status of the kingdom is now far from clear.

I

Much the most famous of Shiel's books, the work that has kept his memory alive, is *The Purple Cloud* (1901), a story of the last man on earth. When serialized in slightly shorter form in the *Royal Magazine* it caused considerable stir, for it was the first recent work of its sort on the same level of quality as the scientific romances of H. G. Wells. It was soon published in book form, later translated into French and Italian, reprinted in several American editions, and eventually, with much distortion, became the motion picture *The World, the Flesh, and the Devil* (1958).

Shiel stated that the idea for the story had been given to him by an American millionaire, who suggested that he write an account of the return of the Peary family from the North Pole, to find a desolated earth. In this context it must be observed that the North Pole, in much of the nineteenth century, was not regarded as a bare geographical point, as it is today. It was the ultimate for human achievement (at the time) and a place redolent with symbolic mystery. Some thought it was the site of an open sea; others expected to find warm lands in a depression, the source of ear-marked animals that occasionally were seen in Siberia. In fiction it was the location of steaming oases inhabited by strange mammals and odd humans, with a touch of supernaturalism.

The Purple Cloud is a concealed recapitulation of the Fall and the Expulsion. Shiel does not explain mechanisms, but the ultimate behind the story is that man has once again broken a divine commandment, in this case profaning the North Pole. Our world, like many others, is the battlefield between dual powers, Black and White, and the crime of profanation permits Black to gain the upper hand temporarily. White, like the fairy who came late to Sleeping Beauty's christening, can only palliate the situation.

A prize of $175 million—the bequest of an eccentric American millionaire—has been offered to the first man to reach the North Pole. Adam Jeffson is the destined man. A young physician, who hears in his mind the contrary voices of Black and White, he is at best a tainted hero, for he looked aside while his fiancée committed a murder to assure him a place on the expedition. She was motivated by greed; he, by lust. Jeffson alone reaches the Pole after hardships and another killing, and finds an open polar sea, with a pillarlike ice formation; he fantasizes an unreadable inscription on the pillar and a whirling force around it.

As Jeffson starts the long trek back, he sees death all around him—bears, birds, seals—and notices the smell of peaches in the air. The crew of the mother ship is dead, and Jeffson learns that all animal life is dead, killed by clouds of hydrocyanic acid gas released by volcanism.

He returns to England like an extraterrestrial visitor, looking for survivors. For more than eighteen years he follows his lonely path, variously bored, annoyed, ecstatic, depressed, and finally half-mad. He becomes a connoisseur of burning cities. He assembles the world's treasures and on an Aegean island

M. P. Shiel. NEW YORK TIMES PICTURES

builds a house of gold, inset with gems, with a lake of wine beside it.

A shock awaits him in Constantinople, where he chances upon a young woman who has survived in an oubliette. His first impulse is to kill her and eat her, but he is stopped by White's direct intervention. Jeffson then plans suicide, for he refuses to start a new race with, as he says, a half-murderer for a father and an idiot for a mother. But under the manipulation of White he yields and rejoices. The human race is not yet over.

The Purple Cloud is written in Shiel's most brilliant style. Jeffson's mad activities on a spoiled planet are described with wild imagination, concreteness, and vigor, while the romance is handled with great insight and penetration. One might cavil at the unnecessary supernaturalism, but this is probably an unjust criticism. As for the sources for *The Purple Cloud*, while motifs seem obviously suggested by Poe's *The Narrative of Arthur Gordon Pym*, and perhaps Arctic stories like Mary Shelley's *Frankenstein* and "The Shadow of a Shade" by Tom Hood, the story is Shiel's.

Shiel's second most important science fiction novel, *The Lord of the Sea* (1901), is a sensational work that some readers, like Dashiell Hammett, have praised highly, while others have considered it offensive. An element of wish-fulfillment from the paperkingdom of Redonda may be present in it, but the theme of the novel, as Shiel has stated, is really Henry George's theory of land tenure. Other elements include the motif of the king of the rock (perhaps suggested by Max Pemberton's work), the diamond meteorite (a topic of speculation in the popular science of the day), and the career of Edmund Dantès in *The Count of Monte Cristo.*

In the near future, pogroms have swept over the Continent and the Jews have been expelled, most of them taking refuge in Great Britain. This mass migration causes enormous social and economic upheaval, as well as great bitterness on the part of both Jews and Gentiles.

Against this background Richard Hogarth, apparently the son of a small tenant farmer, becomes entangled with the Frankl family. He falls in love with the daughter, Rebekah (who reciprocates), but quarrels with her father, a thorough-paced scoundrel and hypocrite. After Hogarth horsewhips Frankl, Frankl has him framed for murder. Hogarth is sentenced to prison, where he has time to worry the question of what is wrong with Great Britain. He comes to the conclusion that the system of permanent land tenure lies behind all the abuses, injustices, and corruptions. He escapes from prison, gains possession of a diamond-bearing meteorite, and becomes incredibly wealthy.

For all his humble background, Hogarth is a man of supernal ability. He constructs a chain of gigantic floating sea forts with five-foot armor, positions them in the sea-lanes and channels, and demands tolls from passing shipping. His claim to the sea, he asserts, is just as valid as older claims to the land. He is successful for a time, defeats an invasion of England by Continental powers, and assumes the title and role of lord protector of the land, enacting a series of severe anti-Jewish laws that anticipate the Nuremberg decrees. But he is brought down, and most of his forts are captured by commandos.

After his fall, revelations (that the reader has long known) are made to him. He is Jewish, and his battle against Judaism has been suicidal. He accepts his new identity, marries Rebekah, and establishes a new Zion in Palestine, which under his leadership becomes a cultural and scientific center. By the time of his death he is almost a supernatural figure.

Despite melodramatisms and coincidences in the Victorian manner—long-lost children, documents in the trunk, fantastic revenges—*The Lord of the Sea* carries a broad, fictional conviction, perhaps because of its good, imaginative detail. Few have denied its literary merit within its genre, but it has been taken to prove that Shiel was an extraordinary bigot. It is not my intention to serve as an apologist for Shiel, who seems to have had his share of the abstract, mild anti-Semitism common among literary men of his day, but Shiel could have defended much in his story on the grounds of logical development and literary necessity. He could further have claimed that he, as author, did not approve of Hogarth's decrees, and called them (speaking as Shiel) "worse than Russian despotism." Yet the fact remains that there is an unpleasant residue of intolerance.

While *The Lord of the Sea* contained an imaginary war incident, Shiel also wrote two books that were fully imaginary war novels. Both are set in the near future, thereby qualifying as science fiction, and one describes fantastic weaponry.

The Yellow Danger (1898), published three years before *The Lord of the Sea* and *The Purple Cloud,* is based on a pattern that structures many of Shiel's novels: titanic events emergent from rivalry between two Napoleonic figures, the ultimate cause of such rivalry often being trivial. It is typical that one man or both men will have messianic notions, and that the two do not differ greatly except in focal point. Since both are superior to the common ruck, despite heated hatred, they feel counterbalancing love and brother-hood.

The Yellow Danger, written in the commercial modes of George Griffith and William LeQueux, is long, sensational, and oddly planned, with chapters of textbooklike descriptions of naval tactics interspersed among the lurid adventures. It is the story of Yen How, a Sino-Japanese superman, who wants revenge for being slighted by a British shopgirl. He rises to supreme power in China and plans to inveigle the Western nations into war with one another, so that when they are exhausted, the Chinese can overrun them.

Opposed to Yen is John Hardy, a consumptive young Englishman, obviously modeled on Horatio Nelson. Hardy gains a great naval victory and penetrates Yen's secret plan. A Chinese army 100 million strong overruns Asia and Europe, the exact destination for each unit planned with computerlike precision. Hardy defeats the Chinese fleet, dropping 10 million Chinese aboard transports into the Maelstrom. When he releases cholera carriers on the Continent, this is the beginning of the end for the Chinese armies, and Kaiser Wilhelm defeats them in a final armageddon. (This curious image of the Kaiser as a dashing hero was not uncommon in British and American popular fiction of the day.) The world is ready for a new order.

A second war novel, *The Yellow Wave* (1905), is not important; but *The Dragon* (1913), reissued in 1929 as *The Yellow Peril*, has points of interest. Its plot is an endless series of captures, escapes, romances involving a Eurasian siren and a scheming German princess, naval battles and aerial battles—like an early motion picture serial run mad. In theme *The Dragon* is like *The Yellow Danger*. Opposed are Li Ku Yu, a Chinese, and Prince Edward (Teddy) of a mythical British royal family. Their squabble, which started in a British boarding school, brings down much of the world.

When Li attains power in the Orient, he sets off a European war by ceding the Japanese fleet to Germany. The Chinese are soon at the English Channel, but the science of Prince Teddy's friend Chinnery (machinery?) defeats them with magnetically operated aircraft and a blinding ray. An interesting note is that Li, while preparing for war, purchases 125,000 motion picture projectors and whips up war hysteria with fake documentaries.

The novel ends, as Shiel's novels often do, with plans for a utopia. Prince Teddy declares himself ruler and decrees compulsory physical and scientific education and no more taxes. Each citizen must learn five handicrafts. Utilities, medical care, and education will be public. Clergymen will be quiet. Teddy's final rant explains the very religion of science: reverence for the evolutionary principle—*das Willen, élan vital,* or what have you.

These two imaginary wars are very interesting today for their social content or as typological specimens of popular literature, but they are negligible as literature. More conformant to mainstream standards is *The Last Miracle* (1906). Set in the near future, it describes a duel of wits between two hypertrophied personalities. Baron Kolár (who might be considered a shabby version of Wilkie Collins' Count Fosco) has an invention that creates what amount to holographic effects. He uses it to project miraculous visions in churches, notably crucifixions that he has staged. His purpose is to destroy religion by stimulating a great revival of faith, at the peak of which he will reveal that the visions have been a hoax. Kolár wins the battle against a pair of bumbling Englishmen but loses the victory, for a new religion based on physical culture, reverence for the evolutionary principle, etc., takes the place of the old. *The Last Miracle* is ingenious and imaginative, despite weak characterizations. It is the last of Shiel's considerable works of science fiction to be published, although it seems to have been written several years earlier.

About thirty years later, Shiel, possibly stimulated by current American pulp science fiction, wrote *The Young Men Are Coming!* (1937). Set in the near future, it is based on three ideas: a visit of incomprehensibly superior beings to earth; rejuvenation and erotic entanglements that emerge when the space beings give an aged doctor the elixir of youth; and the civil war resulting from the doings of the Young Men, a cryptofascist organization. The alienness of the trisexual space people is well-conceived, more profoundly than in contemporary American pulp science fiction, but the ideas are entangled in a mad jumble of words that in another author would be called breakdown or senility. In *The Young Men Are Coming!*, Shiel's worst faults have run totally out of control.

II

Altogether Shiel published some thirty-one books during his lifetime. In addition to the science fiction described, these books include historical novels, romances, adventure stories, mystery and detective stories, supernatural fiction, and collections of short stories. Some of these books are commercial work done for ephemeral markets; others are *romans à thèse* embodying his social and philosophical ideas.

Of these miscellaneous books only a few need be mentioned. *Cold Steel* (1899), a historical novel that used to have admirers, sets up Henry VIII and François I as rival lechers in pursuit of a beautiful Englishwoman. When Shiel was told that his François had no resemblance to the historical François, his comment was, "They are both dreams." According to his aesthetic, as stated in "On Reading," the criticism was without meaning.

The Isle of Lies (1909) opens promisingly. When Lepsius is unable to decipher a hieroglyphic stone (locating vast treasures) that he has stolen from an Ethiopian monastery, he decides to beget a son and rear him as a supreme genius à la Boris Sidis, and let the son read the stone. But the story soon fizzles out into a pointless rigmarole of French politics, an area in which Shiel found inexplicable fascination.

The Pale Ape (1911) contains the original Monk detective stories, and *Children of the Wind* (1923) is African adventure, H. Rider

Haggard updated. *Dr. Krasinski's Secret* (1929) is a *Tendenz* mystery about a ruthlessly benevolent savant who commits murders so that he can obtain money for a laboratory.

Among Shiel's nonfantastic work, far and away the most important book is *How the Old Woman Got Home* (1927), which interlocks such varied themes as down-and-out life in depressed London, slum mores, a Christopher Sly situation, problems of identity, incest, revivalist harangues, society life, scientific lectures, the philosophy of the Overman, kidnapping, and mystery. Not only are the components skillfully and imaginatively handled, but all are convincingly well integrated and made to sound reasonable in context. Everything of Shiel's after this book is only a decline.

III

Rebecca West, as quoted by John Gawsworth in *The Best Short Stories of M. P. Shiel*, once said, "Sensible people ought to have a complete set of Shiel." Literary tastes as varied as those of H. G. Wells, Carl Van Vechten, Arnold Bennett, Vincent Starrett, Raymond Chandler, Arthur Machen, Bertrand Russell, Edward Shanks, John Middleton Murry, Humbert Wolfe, L. P. Hartley, and J. M. Barrie held him in high esteem. Lord Roberts read long sections of *The Yellow Danger* to the House of Commons. Yet, as opposed to this high historical opinion of Shiel's work, a modern reader is likely to be astonished by silly plots, weak development, difficulties with form, characterization of shrieking cardboard, and a message that is flattered if called an eccentric variety of socialism. How can these two contrary estimations be reconciled?

The answer, probably, is that Shiel is a writer's writer, by which one means that a fellow artist can admire aspects of technique, regardless of those factors that a general reader or a full critic may deplore. Shiel's imagination was truly remarkable, and his idiosyncratic stylistic virtuosity enormous. He is one of the most skilled textural technicians in modern English, with a remarkable gift for handling assonances. His mind was so programmed that he was perpetually "conscious of each consonant and of every (accented) vowel-sound of my outlay, without fail remembering them one by one" ("On Reading"). To cite an example of his florid style:

No Father at all? nor heart's smart at all yonder in the dark among the star-dust? So When the young lions cry for food, no eye remarks? No heart is moved? Oh, that would be awfully forlorn and orphaned, after all! But if the earth brings to birth beings with needs, and then, for whatever reason, fails to feed her breeds—does He not heed? and, if He heeds, how is it that He can help feeling piqued to kick her spinning into Hell? (*How the Old Woman Got Home*)

He apparently found it easy to fill books with this sort of rhythmical word- and sound play. As sonority or word amusement it is sometimes impressive, but one must admit that it does not always make the most sense, and is at times reminiscent of a one-man band at a carnival.

Shiel stated, and correctly, that his style was not static. There are basically three different styles in his work—exotic, florid, and personal—but no matter which of his herd of pegasi he was riding, he could always dismount to clear, classical English.

With this remarkable gift, why does Shiel remain very minor as far as mainstream literature is concerned? Probably because his wordplay did not result in any increased depth of perception, or anything more than titillation to a musical sense. His ear may have been as sensitive as James Joyce's, but it was not attached to a brain as clear and keen.

Much the same criticism may be made of Shiel's philosophical ideas, many of which have been mentioned in passing. A socialist in his younger days, as he grew older he dashed farther and farther into private integrations that few would follow. He slipped back into the religion of his childhood, but with new idols: he saw Science as a semi-

mystical process of revelation, with either emergent evolution or the universe as God. He thrashed around into incomprehensible cosmologies and manifestations, and entangled his readers in floods of dithyrambic rhetoric. His process is often classically disputatious, even Socratic in manner, but highly antitraditional. The moderns were all. Jesus was an ignorant Levantine carpenter, Aristotle a bungler, less intelligent than a modern English schoolboy. Shiel believed in human perfectibility, and his anthropology proclaimed an Overman, physically superb, dynamically aggressive (successful in worldly matters), ruthless in goals, scientifically trained—larger than life, but far less than humane.

IV

At the moment Shiel's cultus seems to be dead. As for Shiel, the writer of early science fiction—the novelistic daredevil who plotted like Cecil B. DeMille and chronicled flamboyant Napoleons—who smashed mankind in purple prose, drowned 10 million in the Maelstrom, hid Jesus in Tibet, shattered the landed aristocracy of England, pulled diamonds out of the sky—while he never fulfilled his early promise, his work is not dead. *The Purple Cloud* remains the best "last man" novel; *The Lord of the Sea* is a fine, overloaded fantasy of history in the manner of Alexandre Dumas, père; *How the Old Woman Got Home* is a demonstration of virtuosity; and the early supernatural stories of *Shapes in the Fire* are the best things of their sort since Poe.

Selected Bibliography

WORKS OF M. P. SHIEL

Shapes in the Fire. London: John Lane, 1896; Boston: Roberts Brothers, 1896.
The Yellow Danger. London: Grant Richards, 1898; New York: Fenno, 1899. (Interesting example of a type of

popular, sensational war novel. Fenno edition is usually available in large libraries.)

The Lord of the Sea. London: Grant Richards, 1901; New York: Stokes, 1901. (The 1924 and 1929 Knopf [New York] editions are badly abridged and omit about one-fourth of the original text.)

The Purple Cloud. London: Chatto and Windus, 1901. (The 1929 Vanguard [New York] and the 1930 Victor Gollancz [London] editions have been slightly revised.)

The Last Miracle. London: T. Werner Laurie, 1906. (The 1929 Victor Gollancz [London] edition has been slightly revised.)

How the Old Woman Got Home. London: Richards Press, 1927; New York: Macy-Masius, Vanguard, 1928.

The Young Men are Coming! London: George Allen and Unwin, 1937.

The Best Short Stories of M. P. Shiel. Edited by John Gawsworth. London: Victor Gollancz, 1948.

CRITICAL AND BIOGRAPHICAL STUDIES

Morse, A. Reynolds. *The Works of M. P. Shiel Updated: A Study in Bibliography*, Vol. 2, Part 1. Cleveland, Ohio: published by the author, 1980. (A thorough revision and enlargement of *The Works of M. P. Shiel* [1948], covering published and manuscript material, documents by and about Shiel.)

————. *The Works of M. P. Shiel: "The Shielography Updated,"* Vol. 3, Part 2. Cleveland, Ohio: published by the author, 1980. (Biographical material about Shiel; the history of the kingdom of Redonda; the Montserrat of Shiel's youth; Morse's expedition to the island of Redonda. Many documents and illustrations are reproduced; many errors in earlier studies are corrected. This and the preceding volume are indispensable.)

————, ed. *Shiel in Diverse Hands. A Collection of Essays by Twenty-Nine Students of M. P. Shiel*. Cleveland, Ohio: Reynolds Morse Foundation, 1983. (Thirty-six papers of W.O.G. Lofts, A. Reynolds Morse, John Squires, Brian Stableford, and others; also Shiel's "On Reading," both versions.)

Ransome, Arthur. *Bohemia in London*. London: Chapman and Hall, 1907. (A chapter providing the most valuable description of Shiel's personality and writing habits is reprinted in Morse, vol. 3, part 2.)

Shiel, M. P. "About Myself." *Book League Monthly*, October 1929. (A slightly different version is to be found in Morse, vol. 3, part 2.)

————. "On Reading." In *This Knot of Life*. London: Everett and Company, 1909.

Stableford, Brian. *Algebraic Fantasies and Realistic Romances: More Masters of Science Fiction*. San Bernardino, Calif.: Borgo, 1995.

————. "The Politics of Evolution: Philosophical Themes in the Speculative Fiction of M. P. Shiel." *Foundation* (February 1983): 35–60.

————. *Scientific Romance in Britain, 1890–1950*. London: Fourth Estate, 1985.

Van Vechten, Carl. *Excavations: A Book of Advocacies*. New York: Knopf, 1926. (Contains an essay on Shiel that is also in the introductions to the Knopf editions of *The Lord of the Sea*.)

—E. F. BLEILER

ROBERT SILVERBERG

(b. 1935)

ROBERT SILVERBERG WAS born in Brooklyn, New York, on 15 January 1935, an only child. He was an introverted and precocious boy, who discovered science fiction at an early age and was already submitting stories (without success) to science fiction magazines by the age of thirteen. (This part of his life is discussed in greater detail in his autobiographical essay "Sounding Brass, Tinkling Cymbal," 1975.) He studied English at Columbia University and, while still a student, began to sell stories with some regularity; his first sales, in January 1954, were the short story "Gorgon Planet" (1954) and the juvenile novel *Revolt on Alpha C* (1955), although the latter had to be extensively rewritten before it was published.

Silverberg's career moved into high gear in the summer of 1955 when Randall Garrett—already well established as a magazine writer—moved into the residential hotel near Columbia University where he lived. They began to collaborate, and in the last five months of the year Silverberg (still a third-year student) sold no less than twenty-six stories, written alone and in collaboration.

During the mid-1950's there was a great boom in science fiction magazine publishing. Many new titles appeared, and although most of them were destined to be short lived, for a few years there was considerable demand for material to fill their pages. A fast and efficient writer could obtain as much work as he or she liked, and Silverberg soon became the fastest and most efficient worker of all. As he puts it in "Sounding Brass, Tinkling Cymbal":

I developed a deadly facility; if an editor needed a 7500-word story of alien conquest in three days to balance an issue, he need only phone me and I would produce it. . . . By the summer of 1956—by which time I had graduated from college and had married—I was the complete writing machine, turning out stories in all lengths at whatever quality the editor desired, from slam-bang adventure to cerebral pseudo-philosophy. (page 20)

Silverberg became a full-time writer immediately upon graduation and has remained one ever since. By the end of 1956 he had already published more than a million words, and he and his wife Barbara were able to live in some comfort in New York.

The stories Silverberg wrote during these astonishingly prolific early years were, for the most part, utterly forgettable. He would from time to time attempt more ambitious stories, but he found these difficult to sell; from this fact he drew the rather cynical conclusion that there was no demand for quality in the science fiction magazines, although it is perhaps more likely that the twenty-one-year-old Silverberg, despite his precocious technical facility, was not yet capable of producing work of the quality to which he occasionally aspired.

His best early work is to be found in some of his early novels, notably *Master of Life and Death* (1957), *Invaders from Earth* (1958), and *Recalled to Life* (serialized in *Infinity Science Fiction*, 1958; book form, 1962). All are efficient entertainments, dealing respectively with overpopulation, the colonization of Ganymede and the concurrent conducting of an advertising campaign designed to make acceptable the destruction of its intelligent inhabitants, and the invention of a process to bring the dead back to life. *Invaders from Earth* and *Recalled to Life,* in particular, attempt to grapple with serious subjects, but they rely too heavily on action and melodrama to do justice to their themes. (When Silverberg later rewrote *Recalled to Life* he removed much of its stylistic awkwardness, but its melodramatic aspects remained.) They do mark the young Silverberg, though, as an author of considerable promise, one who might be expected to live up to the Hugo award he received in 1956 as "most promising new author."

But Silverberg's career in the late 1950's took a different course. The predictable collapse of the science fiction magazines, due to oversaturation of the market, started in 1958. Silverberg began to look for work outside the field, taking on almost any job as long as the publisher could be relied on to pay on time. His output of science fiction fell away almost to nothing: in 1960 he published just four magazine stories (as compared with more than one hundred in 1957) and a juvenile novel; in 1961 three stories and an expanded version of a 1959 novella; in 1962 the revision of *Recalled to Life* and a single, quite short novel.

The full extent of Silverberg's productivity has never been made public, and no comprehensive bibliography listing all the books he has published under all his pseudonyms has been attempted. Certainly he ranks among the most prolific of all modern writers: Barry M. Malzberg, in his profile of Silverberg in the April 1974 *Magazine of Fantasy and Science Fiction,* estimates that Silverberg published 450 books in his first ten years of full-time writing (which may be an overestimate), while Silverberg himself has said that his output probably ranks with that of Georges Simenon, but falls short of John Creasey's. In the early 1960's, it seems, he wrote about 2 million words—the equivalent of thirty-five average-length novels—a year.

During this period Silverberg managed to begin a respectable career writing children's nonfiction books popularizing historical, archaeological, and scientific subjects. Here his gift for writing quick, clear expository prose stood him in good stead, and he swiftly acquired a respectable reputation and restored his self-respect. He was still prospering commercially, and in 1962 was able to buy a mansion in New York City that had once belonged to Mayor Fiorello La Guardia.

Silverberg did not contemplate any serious return to science fiction, though, until Frederik Pohl, then editor of *Galaxy, If,* and *Worlds of Tomorrow,* tempted him with the promise of absolute creative freedom. He responded in 1963 with a short story, "To See the Invisible Man" (collected in *The Best of Robert Silverberg,* 1976), which may be viewed as the first manifestation of the "new" Silverberg, a writer more interested in the serious exploration of ideas and themes than in facile displays of technique. The story, derived from a line in Jorge Luis Borges' "The Lottery in Babylon," 1945 (and also, perhaps, from Damon Knight's story "The Country of the Kind," 1955), explores a society in which the punishment for consistent law breaking is total ostracism; the condemned person becomes effectively "invisible." The story presents an effective metaphor for alienation.

Over the next three years or so, Silverberg gradually increased his output of science fiction stories, although he was still primarily engaged in writing nonfiction (no longer just children's books, but longer and more complex adult works requiring extensive research). His emergence as a writer demanding serious consideration came in 1967 with the publication of his novel *Thorns* and the novella "Hawksbill Station" (collected in *The Best of Robert Silverberg*). Both are further explorations of alienation and pain, and are concerned with the achievement of some measure of redemption.

Thorns, a novel as jagged and uncomfortable as its title suggests, brings together two extremely alienated humans—a man (Minner Burris) who has been disfigured through surgery by curious aliens, and a woman (Lona Kelvin) whose ova have been used to produce many extrauterine births but who has never been permitted to bear her own child. Burris and Kelvin are used for the amusement of a wealthy man (Duncan Chalk) who feeds on raw emotion.

"Hawksbill Station"—which was expanded into a novel of the same title in 1968, but which is more concentrated and rewarding in its shorter version—is less outwardly anguished; it describes life in a penal colony located in the remote past—the late Cambrian era—where dissidents of a near-future United States society are expelled with no hope of return. The gray barrenness of their place of exile is an effective metaphor for their hopeless predicament. "Hawksbill Station" is also to a degree a time-travel story—and thus an early exploration of the traditional science fiction motif to which the new Silverberg would return most frequently in the next few years.

Pain and alienation feature in other significant Silverberg works. The short story "Flies" (1967)—Silverberg's contribution to Harlan Ellison's anthology *Dangerous Visions* (1967)—seems almost a "dry run" for *Thorns*, with its protagonist surgically altered by aliens, so that he can receive and transmit the feelings of others. *The Man in the Maze* (1969) is also similar: here the alien-altered human protagonist broadcasts new emotions, so that other people cannot bear to be in his presence. He retreats to the center of a strange and dangerous maze on another world (itself an echo of the lunar maze in Algis Budrys' 1960 novel *Rogue Moon*), another extravagant but effective metaphor for pain and isolation. In the 1968 Nebula award-winning "Passengers" (collected in *The Best of Robert Silverberg*), parasitic aliens seize control of humans and use their bodies for their own inexplicable and whimsical purposes. People's lives become discontinuous passages between periods of take-over. This story, effectively told in the present tense to convey the feeling of transience and lost memory, foreshadows a number of subsequent experiments with tense and viewpoint.

Perhaps the most ambitious of these is the short story "Sundance" (1969; in a collection of that title). On the surface it is the story of an American Indian, Tom Two Ribbons, who is agonizingly forced to relive the destruction of his ancestral culture as he participates in a terraforming operation on another planet. Are the teeming hordes of "Eaters" being exterminated as part of this process no more than alien equivalents of the herds of bison that once roamed the American plains? Or *are* they more, are they intelligent beings, equivalent to Tom's Indian forebears who fell before the encroaching European settlers? Silverberg adds to the uncertainty by making it unclear whether this destruction is even taking place or whether it is part of Tom's delusions (if that is what he is suffering). The story switches between first-, second-, and third-person narration and between present and past tense, using each alternative in a tightly controlled way to delineate a different level of ambiguity. The result is a rich, accomplished, and effective story that ranks with the later "Schwartz Between the Galaxies" (1974; collected in *The Feast of St. Dionysus*, 1975) as Silverberg's best short fiction.

"Sundance" was written in the aftermath of an accident that was to have a profound effect on Silverberg: the partial destruction by fire early in 1968 of his New York house. The damage was so severe that it took more than a year to restore the house, and for the first nine months he was forced to live elsewhere. By his own testimony, he was singularly unprepared psychologically for such an event.

Silverberg's life had been untouched by personal tragedy, and while he may have viewed much of the pseudonymous work he had done as unworthy, in material terms his career had been one of constant and enviable success. Even when he turned to more serious work in the mid-1960's, he still composed everything in one draft, at a speed other writers would regard as prodigious. But after the fire he found writing for the first time a slow and difficult process, requiring several drafts to

Robert Silverberg. © MIRIAM BERKLEY

achieve the desired effects. It must be said, though, that by many writers' standards he remained, at least through 1971, quite prolific, writing two or more novels—plus numbers of short stories—each year.

One of the first stories Silverberg wrote after the fire was the novella "Nightwings" (1968), which won a Hugo award in 1969 and which was amalgamated with two sequels, "Perris Way" and "To Josslem," into the novel titled *Nightwings* (1969). As Brian M. Stableford has pointed out, the far-future background of this story is reminiscent of many of the space adventures the young Silverberg had written, but here such material is used very differently. The novel is a tale, partly mythic in quality, of rebirth and renewal. The decaying future Earth is invaded by aliens, but this ultimately heralds a revitalization of the planet. The protagonist—a member of the guild of Watchers, whose task

it has been to detect and warn of such an invasion—likewise undergoes a process of rejuvenation and renewal, a rite of passage undoubtedly suggested, to some degree, by the author's personal travails.

Aside from differences in plot and setting, a similar description would apply to *Downward to the Earth* (1970), but this is a much more successful novel and remains among Silverberg's three or four best. The setting is a well-realized alien world, Belzagor, which has achieved independence after a period as a human colony. A former colonial administrator, Edmund Gundersen, returns to Belzagor to expiate his guilt over the mistreatment of the intelligent, elephantlike nildoror, who had been forced to work as beasts of burden; specifically, he wants to undergo the nildor religious rite of rebirth to redeem himself for an incident in which he prevented a group of nildoror from going themselves to participate in the ceremony. Eventually he does so and undergoes a transcendent and literal rebirth into a possibly immortal human-alien form. There are strongly religious overtones to this, but the novel is most notable as an exceptionally attractive evocation of an alien world and an alien civilization more spiritually developed than ours. It owes a considerable debt to Joseph Conrad—specifically to *Heart of Darkness* (1899), which is acknowledged by several references in the text.

Silverberg novels continued to appear in a steady flow, each with some point of interest. *Up the Line* (1969) is a humorous, rather bawdy, and enjoyable time-paradox story. *Tower of Glass* (1970) is more ambitious. On one level it is the story of an attempt to communicate with alien intelligences. The wealthy Simeon Krug begins to construct an immense tower from which a beam of tachyons will project, at faster than the speed of light, a reply to coded signals received from a distant star. But Krug, for all his desire to exchange messages with unknown distant aliens, is unable to communicate properly with another intelligent species that he himself has created: a race of androids who do menial labor but are not accepted as fully human, least of all by Krug himself. Nevertheless they worship Krug as their creator and look to him to redeem their status. When the impossibility of this dream becomes evident, they revolt and Krug's tower (among much else) is destroyed. The novel is complex in conception and plot but too heavily freighted with science fiction trappings—some of which remain resolutely clichéd despite all Silverberg's efforts at revivification—to be wholly satisfying.

Son of Man (1971) is a strange, surreal, and psychedelic novel: a dreamlike fantasy of the very distant future, a world in which everything is changeable, and in which feelings are manifested as landscapes. In conception *Son of Man* clearly owes a debt to David Lindsay's phantasmagoric *A Voyage to Arcturus* (1920), but in execution it is quite different. *A Time of Changes* (1971) won Silverberg a Nebula award—the only award he has won for a novel—but it remains the weakest of his later novels, an exotic adventure on a distant planet whose main human society is so repressed in self-expression that even the use of the first person is taboo. Clearly influenced by Jack Vance in its creation of an exotic human society, it contains many elements that were by then familiar in Silverberg's work: the redemption of the protagonist; the sense of transcendence, here achieved through the use of psychedelic drugs; the sharing of minds as a result of using the drugs. The problem with *A Time of Changes* is primarily that Silverberg had done it all better before.

The World Inside (1971) is an episodic novel about a heavily overpopulated future world that, unusually, views its state not as a curse but as a blessing—continued breeding is greatly to be encouraged. People live in "urbmons" (urban monads), gigantic tower blocks hundreds of stories high; the outside world between urbmons is given over entirely to automated agriculture. Although the episodic structure makes it a little too diagrammatic, it is a powerful dystopian vision. The people of this future society are largely happy but we see their society as progressively dehumanized. Traditional social relationships

have disintegrated; privacy is a thing of the past. Relinquishing privacy is the only way to maintain a debased form of sanity in such an overcrowded world.

In 1972, the year that marked the end of his prolific phase, Silverberg published three novels. *The Second Trip*, although generally neglected by critics, is one of his strongest novels. It is set in a future world in which the punishment for habitually violent criminals is erasure of personality. A new, "artificial" personality is then inscribed on the *tabula rasa* of the criminal's brain. The novel concerns the efforts of one such rebuilt personality to ease his way into society. Unfortunately, he encounters a telepathic girl who knew the obliterated criminal that he had been, and she awakens some remnant of the former personality surviving in a corner of his brain. The novel then becomes a battle of wills between the two minds for possession of a body that each, with good reason, regards as his own. It is, of course, a battle charged with symbolic significance, and as such is treated expertly by Silverberg, although he does gloss over the moral and ethical questions raised by the novel's science fictional rationale.

His other two novels of 1972, *Dying Inside* and *The Book of Skulls*, remain his most successful to date. There has been some debate over whether they can properly be classed as science fiction—a debate that, in the case of *Dying Inside* at least, is difficult to understand. *The Book of Skulls* is more problematical. It is about the search by four college students for a mysterious sect, the Brotherhood of the Skull, which has apparently discovered the secret of immortality. The members of the sect are duly found, but it is never clear—nor is it relevant to the novel—whether they actually do possess the secret or whether they are plausible fakes. The importance of the novel lies in its examination of the four students' personalities under the stress of reaching toward what may be eternal life. It is told with great skill; Silverberg narrates the novel from the alternating first-person viewpoints of all four main characters.

709

The result is a richly textured, persuasive novel.

Dying Inside is better still. All Silverberg's recent novels—as Stableford has shown in "The Metamorphosis of Robert Silverberg" (1976)—can to some extent be read as studies of alienation and (sometimes) redemption. In *Dying Inside* the theme is addressed most directly and powerfully. This is the story of David Selig, a telepath who is slowly losing his powers (hence the title of the novel). Alienated from the rest of humanity by his paranormal talent, he is becoming more like them yet, paradoxically, is also losing his unique ability to understand them, as his powers wane. Selig himself is a fully realized and very believable character, and is to some extent autobiographical; interestingly, there are echoes in the novel of Silverberg's description in "Sounding Brass, Tinkling Cymbal" of his waning fecundity as a writer.

Throughout the early 1970's Silverberg continued to produce short stories that were, on the whole, more experimental than his novels. Whereas in his longer work he had embarked on an apparent project to reexamine the traditional themes of science fiction by using a wider range of literary techniques, in his shorter work he showed a disaffection with these same themes and treated them ironically, or he wrote stories in which the theme was precisely their obsolescence. One ironic piece, "Good News from the Vatican" (1971; collected in *The Best of Robert Silverberg*), won another Nebula, as did "Born with the Dead" (1974; in a collection of that title), a novella that achieves another powerful metaphor of alienation in its depiction of the strange, emotionless, revived "dead" living alongside—but apart from—normal humanity. His best story of the period, though, is "Schwartz Between the Galaxies" (1974), in which a cultural anthropologist living in a future world of increasing cultural uniformity fantasizes a universe of brilliant diversity, constructing for himself a science fictional world to compensate for the emptiness he feels in his own life. In this and other shorter works, Silverberg shows an awareness of re-cent sophisticated techniques of fiction writing—as epitomized by such writers as Donald Barthelme and Robert Coover—and, as mentioned previously, many of the stories are ironically concerned with the subject matter of science fiction.

Two further novels were written before Silverberg announced his retirement from writing: *The Stochastic Man* (1975) and *Shadrach in the Furnace* (1976). The former concerns a man developing powers of precognition, and is in some ways a reverse companion piece to *Dying Inside*. While written with considerable skill and certainly among his better novels, it lacks the emotional commitment that made *Dying Inside* outstanding. *Shadrach in the Furnace* is a smoothly accomplished story of Mordecai Shadrach, the personal physician to an old and crafty future dictator who learns of a plan to transfer the despot's mind to a younger body—his own. It is comparatively traditional science fiction.

Silverberg's "retirement" from writing, which received considerable publicity in the science fiction field, was occasioned by his general disenchantment with that field as it is traditionally constituted, with its publishers, and with its readers. He remained inactive for four years, after which he returned to writing with a long science fantasy epic, *Lord Valentine's Castle* (1980), an expansive and entertaining story quite different in mood from his intense, introspective stories of the early 1970's.

It was followed by a novella, *The Desert of Stolen Dreams* (1981), the first of a series of stories set in the world of the novel. Other short stories began to appear, and it seemed that Silverberg was once more an active writer. This change was welcome, for no contemporary writer had shown a greater mastery over the themes and motifs of science fiction, and few could match Silverberg's command of literary technique. If he has an enduring flaw, it is that his technical facility tends to make his work, however skilled, a little superficial; but in his best work, where there is emotional commitment to match the technique, this ceases to be a problem.

710

Despite the extraordinary range of his career, he was still at an age where his best work might lie before him.

—MALCOLM EDWARDS

Since 1982, Silverberg has continued to be prolific, producing an average of two novels, several stories, and at least one anthology each year. In fact, 1982 represents a watershed of a kind; it was the year in which he chose to incorporate himself (presumably for tax reasons) so that all his writing from 1982 onward is copyrighted to "Agberg, Ltd." Also since 1982 the quality of Silverberg's work has varied; scarcely anything has matched the brilliance and originality of his work during the 1967–1972 period. Post-1982 novels have tended to be "laid back" to the point of sterility, with Silverberg seeming to go through the motions of writing—especially in his series and sharecropping work (commissioned fiction written for a fee, especially in the developed world of another writer)—rather than showing enthusiasm. Notable exceptions are some of his longer stories and the novel *Hot Sky at Midnight* (1994).

"Sailing to Byzantium" (1985) won a Nebula award for best novella in 1986. It is a love story and a paean to decadence set in the far future when Earth's small population parties from one artificial city to another (allowing Silverberg to indulge himself in describing the beauties of ancient architecture). The appearance of crowds comes from the presence of uncountable temporaries—not real people. The viewpoint is that of Charles, a visitor, who has been brought forward from late-twentieth century New York and who feels like an outsider despite the love of the beautiful Gioia. She has a problem of her own: she is aging fast, while he will never do so. "Sailing to Byzantium" is not the only good Silverberg novella of recent years; this continues to be a productive form for much of his best writing. His 1986 novella "Gilgamesh in the Outback" won the Hugo for 1987, and his 1989 novelette "Enter a Soldier. Later: Enter Another" was a Hugo winner in 1990.

Hot Sky at Midnight is a dystopian portrayal of Earth about a century hence, when climate changes have flooded low-lying countries, turned much of the central United States into a desert, and brought greenness to the Middle East. The air is breathable only with difficulty; many people wear masks; many others have left to live in L5 space colonies. Much of human economic activity is controlled by two megacorporations, Samurai Industries and Kyocera-Merck. This is an ensemble novel in which the fortunes of half a dozen characters are followed. Most memorable is Victor Farkas, who lacks eyes due to prenatal genetic manipulation but has compensating senses. He visits the satellite world of Valparaiso Nuevo in search of the surgeon who maimed him thirty years earlier. (This section appeared separately as "Blindsight" in 1986.) Paul Carpenter has been sacked by Samurai for making a wrong decision. Jobless, he drives a computer-controlled automobile across a ruined United States, allowing Silverberg to write a brilliant and poignant descriptive section. Nick Rhodes is a high flyer, a research executive for Samurai who is poached by Kyocera. Gradually all the main characters are drawn into, directly or indirectly, an armed coup on Valparaiso Nuevo. This novel is thoughtful and cleverly plotted, with a magnificent set of backgrounds.

These are not the only later works of Silverberg's that are worth reading. Far from it. Most of his novels and all of his shorter fiction have fascinating aspects at the very least. For example, *Tom O'Bedlam* (1985) is a wonderfully ambiguous novel of ideas, showing mentally fragmented psychiatric patients against a physically fragmented future United States, though in fact it gains nothing from its futuristic setting, especially as most of its technology is of today. The dreams at the heart of the story are interesting but remain ambiguous. There is also *Thebes of the Hundred Gates* (1991), which is a standard time-travel story except for the lush descriptions of ancient Egypt, which few other contemporary writers could have achieved.

It is clear that Silverberg is fascinated by several historical eras and places. He returns to them often in his science fiction, but he has also written some fine historical novels. *Lord of Darkness* (1983) fictionalizes the true story of an English sailor who shipped to Angola as a slave in the late sixteenth century, survived twenty years of hardship, and eventually returned home. In *Gilgamesh the King* (1984) and its sequel, *To the Land of the Living* (1989), Silverberg relates the story of Gilgamesh, who may have ruled over part of Mesopotamia some 4,500 years ago. Here Silverberg's enthusiasm is unmistakable.

For most of his writing career he has written single novels, avoiding sequels or series. However, the commercial success of *Lord Valentine's Castle* has provoked several sequels that tend to repeat the monolithic plot and silly names of the original. The volumes so far are *Majipoor Chronicles* (1982), *Valentine Pontifex* (1983), *The Mountains of Majipoor* (1995), and *Sorcerers of Majipoor* (1997). These are all pleasant enough stories (rather in the style of Jack Vance), but they fail to stretch the author or his readers.

Much the same can be said of another series. *At Winter's End* (1988) is a workmanlike novel about a human tribe emerging onto the surface of a far future Earth to explore and reconquer after hundreds of thousands of years of the Long Winter. The way in which the members of the tribe recapitulate the problems and struggles of our own world is just a little hurried and forced. Its sequel, *The Queen of Springtime* (1989; titled *The New Springtime* in the United States), is similarly flawed, being clichéd and unsurprising.

Three of Silverberg's later novels have been enlargements of stories by Isaac Asimov: *Nightfall* (1990), from "Nightfall" (1941); *Child of Time* (1991), from "The Ugly Little Boy" (1958); and *The Positronic Man* (1992), from "The Bicentennial Man" (1976). In each case Silverberg has made a reasonable job of it. For example, in *Child of Time*, which is about a Neanderthal toddler deliberately snatched from forty thousand years in the past by a twenty-first century research project, the original story was marred by old-fashioned behavior patterns on the part of the nurse and the project director. Silverberg has eliminated the worst of these and has tried to highlight the ethics of the situation. He has even created a Neanderthal society from which the boy was kidnapped. But the result remains stagey and unconvincing. In a similar sharecropping vein, Silverberg wrote a sequel to C. L. Moore's *Vintage Season* entitled *In Another Country* (1990).

The novel that Silverberg cowrote with his second wife, Karen Haber, *The Mutant Season* (1989), is based on his 1973 story of the same name. It covers much old ground in showing how the mutant is a mythic figure, feared and hated by most nonmutants, and its plot offers no surprises.

For most of his writing career Silverberg has edited anthologies, and he has continued to put out reprint anthologies, usually coedited with Martin H. Greenberg. More interesting is the *Universe* series of original anthologies, which he took over after the death of his good friend Terry Carr. In 1990 he began the series from number one again, with Karen Haber as coeditor; it lasted for only three volumes, due more to the economic situation in U.S. publishing than to the quality of stories. And in 1992 Silverberg edited and contributed to a fascinating shared-world anthology, *Murasaki*.

Too many of his other science fiction novels over the 1982–1998 period are competent (he has always been a competent writer) but uninspired. They are different from each other, they raise important questions, they usually entertain, yet they fail to be vital and experimental. He is no longer on the cutting edge of the genre.

What these years have shown is that Silverberg remains a writer of the highest quality. If he has chosen an easy path toward populism and a good income through producing series and sharecropping, it is difficult to blame him. Fortunately, he continues to write fluently and is occasionally persuaded to produce great science fiction.

—CHRIS MORGAN

Selected Bibliography

WORKS OF ROBERT SILVERBERG

Revolt on Alpha C. New York: Thomas Y. Crowell, 1955.

Master of Life and Death. New York: Ace Books, 1957. London: Sidgwick and Jackson, 1977.

Invaders from Earth. New York: Ace Books, 1958. London: Sidgwick and Jackson, 1977.

Recalled to Life. New York: Lancer Books, 1962. Revised edition. Garden City, N.Y.: Doubleday, 1972. London: Victor Gollancz, 1974.

To Worlds Beyond. Philadelphia: Chilton Books, 1965. London: Sphere Books, 1969. (Short stories.)

Thorns. New York: Ballantine Books, 1967. London: Rapp and Whiting, 1969.

Hawksbill Station. Garden City, N.Y.: Doubleday, 1968. Retitled *The Anvil of Time,* London: Sidgwick and Jackson, 1969.

The Man in the Maze. New York: Avon Books, 1969. London: Sidgwick and Jackson, 1969.

Nightwings. New York: Avon Books, 1969. London: Sphere Books, 1974.

Up the Line. New York: Ballantine Books, 1969.

Downward to the Earth. Garden City, N.Y.: Doubleday Science Fiction Book Club, 1970. New York: Signet Books, 1970. London: Victor Gollancz, 1977.

Tower of Glass. New York: Charles Scribner's Sons, 1970. London: Panther Books, 1976.

Son of Man. New York: Ballantine Books, 1971.

A Time of Changes. Garden City, N.Y.: Doubleday Science Fiction Book Club, 1971. New York: Signet Books, 1971. London: Victor Gollancz, 1973.

The World Inside. Garden City, N.Y.: Doubleday, 1971.

The Book of Skulls. New York: Charles Scribner's Sons, 1972. London: Victor Gollancz, 1978.

Dying Inside. New York: Charles Scribner's Sons, 1972. London: Sidgwick and Jackson, 1975.

The Second Trip. Garden City, N.Y.: Doubleday Science Fiction Book Club, 1972. New York: Signet Books, 1973.

Unfamiliar Territory. New York: Charles Scribner's Sons, 1973. London: Victor Gollancz, 1975. (Short stories.)

Born with the Dead. New York: Random House, 1974. London: Victor Gollancz, 1975. (Short stories.)

Sundance and Other Science Fiction Stories. Nashville, Tenn., and New York: Thomas Nelson, 1974. London: Corgi Books, 1976. (Short stories.)

The Feast of St. Dionysus. New York: Charles Scribner's Sons, 1975. London: Victor Gollancz, 1976. (Short stories.)

The Stochastic Man. New York: Harper and Row, 1975. London: Victor Gollancz, 1976.

The Best of Robert Silverberg. New York: Pocket Books, 1976. (Short stories.)

Capricorn Games. New York: Random House, 1976. London: Victor Gollancz, 1978. (Short stories.)

Shadrach in the Furnace. Indianapolis: Bobbs-Merrill, 1976.

Lord Valentine's Castle. New York: Harper and Row, 1980.

The Desert of Stolen Dreams. San Francisco and Columbia, Penn.: Underwood-Miller, 1981.

Majipoor Chronicles. New York: Arbor House, 1982; London: Victor Gollancz, 1982.

Valentine Pontifex. New York: Arbor House, 1983; London: Victor Gollancz, 1984.

The Conglomeroid Cocktail Party. New York: Arbor House, 1984; London: Victor Gollancz, 1985. (Short stories.)

Tom O'Bedlam. New York: Fine, 1985; London: Victor Gollancz, 1986.

At Winter's End. New York: Warner, 1988; London: Victor Gollancz, 1988.

The Mutant Season, with Karen Haber. Garden City, N.Y.: Doubleday, 1989.

The Queen of Springtime. London: Victor Gollancz, 1989. Reprinted as *The New Springtime,* New York: Warner, 1990.

In Another Country: Vintage Season. New York: TOR, 1990. (C. L. Moore's novel and Silverberg's sequel in one.)

Nightfall, with Isaac Asimov. Garden City, N.Y.: Doubleday, 1990; London: Victor Gollancz, 1990.

Child of Time, with Isaac Asimov. London: Victor Gollancz, 1991. Reprinted as *The Ugly Little Boy,* Garden City, N.Y.: Doubleday, 1992.

Thebes of the Hundred Gates. Eugene, Ore.: Axolotl, 1991; London: HarperCollins, 1993.

The Positronic Man, with Isaac Asimov. Garden City, N.Y.: Doubleday, 1992; London: Victor Gollancz, 1992.

Hot Sky at Midnight. New York: Bantam, 1994; London: HarperCollins, 1994.

The Mountains of Majipoor. New York: Bantam, 1995; London: Macmillan, 1995.

Sorcerers of Majipoor. London: Macmillan, 1997; New York: HarperPrism, 1997.

CRITICAL AND BIOGRAPHICAL STUDIES

Clareson, Thomas D. "Downward to the Earth." In *Survey of Science Fiction Literature,* edited by Frank N. Magill. Englewood Cliffs, N.J.: Salem Press, 1979, pages 591–594.

———. "The Fictions of Robert Silverberg." In *Voices for the Future: Essays on Major Science Fiction Writers,* vol. 2, edited by Thomas D. Clareson. Bowling Green, Ohio: Bowling Green University Popular Press, 1979, pages 1–33.

Gunn, James E. "Tower of Glass." In *Survey of Science Fiction Literature,* pages 2583–2585.

McNelly, Willis E. *"Dying Inside."* In *Survey of Science Fiction Literature*, pages 671–674.

Malzberg, Barry M. "Robert Silverberg." In *The Magazine of Fantasy and Science Fiction*, vol. 46, no. 4 (April 1974): 67–72.

Silverberg, Robert. "Introduction to 'Sundance.'" In *Those Who Can: A Science Fiction Reader*, edited by Robin Scott Wilson. New York: New American Library, 1973, pages 169–175.

———. "Sounding Brass, Tinkling Cymbal." In *Hell's Cartographers*, edited by Brian W. Aldiss and Harry Harrison. London: Weidenfeld and Nicholson, 1975. New York: Harper and Row, 1975, pages 7–45.

Stableford, Brian M. "The Metamorphosis of Robert Silverberg." In *Science Fiction Monthly*, 3, no. 3 (1976): 9–11.

———. *"Nightwings."* In *Survey of Science Fiction Literature*, pages 1526–1530.

———. *"A Time of Changes."* In *Survey of Science Fiction Literature*, pages 2293–2296.

CLIFFORD D. SIMAK

(1904–1988)

CLIFFORD DONALD SIMAK is, by virtue of being three years older than Robert A. Heinlein, the dean of American science fiction writers. He has been writing science fiction since 1931, a career that has spanned nearly the entire history of science fiction as a separate genre. Writing primarily short fiction until 1960, then turning to novels at a rate of about one per year, he has published more than twenty novels and ten collections of short stories.

While Simak's work has been remarkably consistent in quality, three of his works have been singled out for awards. His 1952 collection of related stories, *City*, won the British International Fantasy Award (IFA) as the best work of science fiction or fantasy of the year. His novelette "The Big Front Yard" won a Hugo in 1959, giving Simak the honor of being the first writer to win both an IFA and a Hugo. In 1964 his novel *Way Station* brought him his second Hugo. A short story, "The Grotto of the Dancing Deer" (1980), won a Nebula and a Hugo. In addition to these honors, the Science Fiction Writers of America presented Simak with a Grand Master Nebula in 1977, not so much for any individual story or novel as for the entire body of his work, which, with a few exceptions, has exhibited a high level of craftsmanship that has ensured him a place among the giants of science fiction.

But even as a major figure, Simak has developed in a quite different direction from fellow giants such as Heinlein, Isaac Asimov, and Jack Williamson. He has not spent his time meticulously building worlds or projecting future histories and alternate universes. When he described himself as "among the last surviving dinosaurs of science fiction," he was not suggesting that he was out of date, but that he was aware that he had not developed along lines taken by many of his fellow writers. He has not, like the others mentioned previously, adopted the new forms and themes possible in contemporary science fiction, even resisting the tendency to try to portray new character types. In his heart and in his imagination, he has seldom left the wooded Wisconsin hills where he was born. Even his aliens, more often than not, have had to come to Wisconsin to make contact with humans.

Simak is a giant not because of the breadth of his imagination or the quantity of his publications, but because he has added to science fiction a singular, gentle—often mystical—voice that is recognizably his in whatever he writes. It is not a loud or insistent voice, but it is an important one. "To read science fiction," Heinlein wrote on the occasion of the Grand Master Nebula award, "is to read Simak."

Simak was born on 3 August 1904, on his maternal grandfather's farm in Millville Township, Wisconsin. This rugged farm country of southwestern Wisconsin, in sight of the bluffs where the Wisconsin River meets the Mississippi, has played an important part in his thought and work. Many of his stories and novels take place there, some even using the name Millville. The region surrounding the farm is part of a small circle of land that escaped the ice sheets that covered much of North America. This escape not only left the land bluffed and hilly, full of narrow valleys; for Simak it left the land in an ancient state and added to its mystery. From the people of this region, Simak took one of his favorite character types—the old grandfather, farmer, or handyman, who, all passion spent, prefers the company of the land and its animals to human companionship.

Most of Simak's best fiction, including "The Big Front Yard" (1958) and *Way Station*, is located in large measure on this land, and his novel *The Visitors* (1980) ends nearby.

Almost as important to his writing as these boyhood memories is Simak's career as a journalist. His first regular job following high school and a short stay at the University of Wisconsin was as a reporter for the *Iron River* (Michigan) *Reporter* in 1929. In 1932 he was hired by the McGiffin Newspaper Company of Kansas and spent the next seven years troubleshooting and editing a number of small-town daily and weekly papers in Iowa, Minnesota, Missouri, and North Dakota. In 1939, Simak joined the *Minneapolis Star*, where he quickly became chief of the copy desk. He went on to become news editor in 1949, developing a science news program for the *Star* and its sister paper, the *Tribune*. In 1959 he began a weekly science column, "Tomorrow's World." Around 1976 he gave up his editing responsibilities to devote all his time to writing science fiction and science fact.

If a full-time newspaper career has cut into Simak's science fiction writing, it has also influenced that writing, helping to develop his plain, direct style and giving him his other favorite character type, the reporter. Contrary to the popular stereotype, Simak has written, a reporter is never content with surface facts, seeking instead a truth not often evident on the surface. The reporter "develops a questioning mind, seeking the unexpected element" while remaining aware that there is no such thing as the simple or absolute truth. The reporter, like Simak and his characters, develops tolerance for the views of others.

Simak's first publishing ventures in science fiction were much like those of other writers breaking into the field in the 1920's and 1930's. By the time he decided to write stories himself, he had read hundreds of pieces in the pulps and was aware of the themes and approaches that characterized them. He found it easy to have his work published, with little departure from the conventions he had come to know so well. Simak's first story, "The Cubes of Ganymede," was accepted by *Amazing Stories* in 1931, held by the publisher for four years, and then returned to Simak because it was then considered "dated." It was never published. His second story, "The World of the Red Sun," appeared in the December 1931 issue of Hugo Gernsback's *Wonder Stories*. It was a time travel story—one of the few stock science fiction devices in which Simak was to remain interested throughout his career—in which a group of adventurers traveling into the future encounters a glass-enclosed brain that has enslaved the remnants of mankind.

Four other stories that followed in 1932 showed Simak handling his craft in a competent but not especially innovative way. Only the novelette "The Creator," which appeared in the March–April 1935 issue of *Marvel Tales* and was written without either an audience or a publisher in mind, showed a glimpse of the writer's potential and brought Simak his first appreciative audience. In the story two Earthmen travel via a time machine to an intelligent "pyramid of light" who has created the universe as an experiment and now wishes to destroy it. Along with aliens from another planet, the Earthmen battle to prevent the creator from carrying out his plan.

Unhappy with the quality of the science fiction pulps, Simak stopped writing science fiction until John W. Campbell, Jr., became editor of a revitalized *Astounding Stories* in 1937. Simak's respect for Campbell drew him back, and it was for Campbell that he wrote "Rule 18," which appeared in the July 1938 issue of *Astounding*. This comic story of the annual football rivalry between Earth and Mars deals with Earth's attempt to assemble a winning team of all-stars by traveling into the past in search of team members. It was Simak's first attempt to depart from the conventions of pulp science fiction—in this case, the convention that science fiction had to be serious.

Some of what Simak wrote for Campbell was an attempt to upgrade those older conventions. *Cosmic Engineers*, a three-part serial that appeared in *Astounding* in 1939 (book form, 1950), was space opera in the manner of E. E. Smith or Edmond Hamilton, with the usual trimmings: time travel, suspended animation, a universe in collision with ours, and guardian robots. But, for the most part, over the next five years Simak slowly developed his own themes, his own style, and his own casts of characters. "Hunger Death," in the October 1938 *Astounding*, deals with a group of Iowa farmers who are tricked into settling on bad land on Venus but set out to make the best of it. "Reunion on Ganymede," published the following month, covers an anniversary get-together of veterans from an Earth-Mars war. The off-beat and folksy characters and themes that appear in this story soon became Simak trademarks.

Simak continued to turn out stories during the early years of World War II, but he also grew increasingly disillusioned with civilization as the violence of war spread. "Hunch," published in the July 1943 issue of *Astounding*, deals with the formation of an organization, known as Sanctuary, to help rehabilitate minds broken down by the complex pressures of civilization. People need something to lean on, the story suggests; they need a "steadying hand in the darkness."

"City," published in the May 1944 *Astounding*, shows Simak more despairing but surer of his craft. In a muted but poetic style, he evokes a not-too-distant future in which mankind's great cities have died out and lie in ruins, left to a few diehard souls like Gramp Stevens rocking on his front porch, or a mayor (Paul Carter) with little of the city left to lead, or out-of-work farmers who have become squatters in the houses abandoned by families desperate for the countryside. The city, formerly one of mankind's proudest achievements, has become a burdensome artifact as the pressures it produces have become too much for man to take. The civilization of humans has begun the long drift into oblivion.

Seven more related stories appeared between 1944 and 1951, a series that Simak has called the "watershed between my earlier apprentice writing and my emergence as a craftsman." The most popular of these works was "Huddling Place" (1944), in which the protagonist, Dr. Jerome A. Webster, a human physiologist who is an authority on the Martian brain, suffers from such a severe case of agoraphobia—the fear of open spaces—that he cannot leave his home even to save the life of his close friend, the Martian philosopher Juwain. Juwain is on the verge of a philosophical breakthrough that will restore faith in living to both humans and Martians, but he needs an immediate and delicate brain operation in order to survive. Webster, though he knows he could save his friend—and thus mankind—cannot make the trip.

The remaining stories chronicle the way in which generations of the Websters, accepting responsibility for man's loss of faith, gradually prepare intelligent dogs to take over Earth from humans. Assisted from generation to generation by a trusted robot, Jenkins, they eradicate violence from dog society. Most other humans move on to Jupiter, where they switch to Jovian bodies, leaving the dogs on Earth to establish a civilization based on cooperation rather than killing. A few mutant humans remain at large on Earth, but the last Websters wall themselves off from the rest of the world in Ceneva and go into suspended animation.

In the new civilized dog society, the only threats of violence come from the cobblies, aliens from another dimension who come at random intervals to engage in killing sprees, and from a rapidly evolving civilization of ants that has built domes over its anthills and learned the factory system. Jenkins, now the servant and overseer of the dogs, wanted to preserve their dignity and so never told them they were once humans' pets. In order to save

Clifford D. Simak in 1977. PHOTO BY JAY KAY KLEIN

the dog civilization from the threat of the ants, he awakens one of the Websters from suspended animation in an attempt to learn how to control the ants. Because the human answer offered (poison) involves killing, Jenkins is faced with the moral problem of saving the dog civilization by reintroducing killing or withholding that information and letting the ants take over.

Published in book form as *City*, with narrative bridges added between the stories, these eight tales brought Simak the 1952 IFA. Even today the book remains among his best known. Simak himself has predicted that if any of his works is destined to last, it will be this sad, nostalgic book reminiscent of Campbell's "Twilight" (1934) or the end of H. G. Wells's *The Time Machine* (1895) and other early science fiction works that capture the same exquisite sense of loss. In 1973, invited to participate in the *John W. Campbell Memorial Anthology*, Simak wrote a final city story, "Epilog." Looking back at the disillu-

sion out of which the city stories were written, now deepened by the atomic devastation of Hiroshima and Nagasaki, Simak suggests that "Perhaps, deep inside myself, I was trying to create a world in which I and other disillusioned people could, for a moment, take refuge from the world in which we lived" (author's Foreword to *City*, 1976).

If the city symbolized for Simak all that was twisted and wrong in modern culture, the countryside—and especially the rugged, wooded hills of southwest Wisconsin where Simak was born—came to represent for him not a retreat so much as a return to what civilization ought never to have left: a world of neighbors and neighborhoods rather than ghettos.

It is to this countryside that Asher Sutton, a man from 6,000 years in the future, returns through time to escape his pursuers in "Time Quarry" (1950), a Simak story that helped launch Horace Gold's new science fiction magazine, *Galaxy*. Serialized in *Galaxy* and published in book form as *Time and Again* (1951), the novel is basically a fast-paced detective story ranging across time and space, but in it Simak began to develop a philosophy that was to become a basis for many of his subsequent stories. Six thousand years in the future, a small clique of humans controls much of the universe by using androids. Sutton has written a book, *This Is Destiny*, that preaches not only equality for the androids but reverence for all life everywhere. As a result he is hated by his fellow humans and is being hunted by a group of "Revisionists" who travel into the past in an attempt to kill him before he can write the book. To escape the Revisionists and preserve his message, Sutton comes back to nineteenth-century Wisconsin, where one of his ancestors is farming, to seek refuge and help.

Sutton's book opens with the following words:

We are not alone. No one is ever alone. Not since the first faint stirrings of the first flicker of life on the first planet in the galaxy that knew the quickening of life, has there ever been a single entity that walked or crawled or slithered down the path of life alone.

"We are not alone" is a theme that echoes again and again through Simak's best work, and those of his characters who realize this theme develop "a respect for life and a tolerance of viewpoint." If for no other reason, all life is drawn together by the immensity and impersonality of the universe, so that "We and all these other beings must be brothers."

At the end of the novel, Sutton, forced to choose whether to be a traitor to his own race, responds to the humans who have come for him: "I may be wrong, but I still think that destiny is greater than humanity."

During the 1950's Simak developed this gentle, mystical view of the universe in which institutions, big business, and manifest destiny do not belong. The ideal social structure in Simak's world is one based on "neighborliness": a world of small towns and villages, a society in which Henry David Thoreau would have been happy. In this society neighbors know a person well enough to refrain from harming him or her, but keep their distance more than friends do. They help out when asked, but generally do not interfere. In Simak's world, as in Robert Frost's, "good fences make good neighbors." Among the best neighbors in Simak's world are aliens; they generally have advanced enough culturally to be the natural neighbors of humans.

This philosophy of the universality of all life in a cosmos of loosely organized neighborhoods reached its best expression in a series of short stories and novels Simak wrote in the late 1950's and early 1960's, many of which take place in Wisconsin (or on planets just like it), and are centered on the character type of the old man who is wise and past caring what other people think. Simak's science fiction had always been populated by such old men—the Websters, for instance, in *City*—but at this point Simak came to see old men untainted by city and civilization as the persons most fit to make first contact with the stars. In fact, Simak's old men nearly always get along much better with aliens who, like them, are ancient and wise. They understand each other.

In one of the most poignant of these stories, "A Death in the House" (1959), old Mose Abrams, whose wife and dog have died some time ago, leaving him alone on his farm with the cows, finds an injured alien who has crashed on his land. Although the creature smells and looks so horrible that it frightens off a doctor, a minister, and other townspeople to whom Mose goes for help, Mose sympathetically tends the dying alien, with which he cannot even communicate, and buries it on his farm when the cemetery refuses burial space. A year later the alien resurrects itself, repairs its ship with the silver dollars Mose has been hoarding, and leaves Mose with a gift in return—a small, cloudy crystal ball. Staring into it, Mose feels "a happiness and comfort such as he had seldom ever known before." Out in space the creature, too, feels warmed by the contact with Mose, by the kindnesses and gifts they had exchanged.

"The Big Front Yard" (1958), which brought Simak a Hugo in 1959 for best novelette, develops the old-man character type even further. Hiram Taine, a "fix-it" man living alone with his dog Towser on the edge of the small town of Willow Bend, discovers that aliens have turned the front of his house into a gateway to another world. One day Towser returns with a woodchuck-like alien he has captured. It turns out that Beasley, a simpleminded yardboy for a rich family in Willow Bend, can communicate telepathically with both Towser and the alien better than he can with humans. With Beasley's help, Taine learns that the aliens have connected a number of worlds—they travel physically from planet to planet via space warps—in order to "dicker" for new ideas. Taine is in his element, having found at last worthy dickering competition. Holding off the United Nations, several foreign governments, and the United States National Guard, he hunkers down to trade the idea of "paint" in exchange for an antigravity device and whatever else the aliens have to offer.

Earth has made contact with the stars, not through the marvels of science, the heroics of explorers, or alien invasion, but through an old fix-it man and his companions.

Way Station (1963), which won a Hugo in 1964 for the best novel of the year, is perhaps Simak at his best. In it Enoch Wallace, 124 years old, a frontiersman and Civil War veteran, has been using his isolated Wisconsin home for 100 years as a way station for galactic travelers moving around the universe. Required to keep the nature of his house secret, he has no human contact except for a deafmute girl, Lucy Fisher. He receives occasional visits from Ulysses, a coffee-drinking alien who comes to chat, and his home is filled with mementos from travelers who have passed through, but he is lonely. Only his love of the land and woods, and his vision of an Earth united to the brotherhood of the stars, keeps him going until he and Lucy, holding off the Central Intelligence Agency, prove mankind worthy of being accepted into that brotherhood.

Even Simak's robots feel this call. In "All the Traps of Earth" (1960), a robot discovers supernormal powers—he knows what people are thinking and can also destroy them just by the power of imagination. He at first plans to lead a revolt of robots against humans, but soon feels the tug of "all the traps of earth, the snares of man," and settles down to be a good neighbor in a small town on an Earthlike planet, using his powers to help.

Beginning in the late 1960's, a period of decline for Simak appeared to set in. Books like *The Goblin Reservation* (1968), *Destiny Doll* (1971), and *Cemetery World* (1973) showed him departing from his usual themes, often awkwardly. Other books, like *Our Children's Children* (1974) and *Shakespeare's Planet* (1976), were more successful but not up to his earlier work. Simak was aware of this decline. "I wish I could put my finger on what I have lost since I wrote *City*," he said in 1975.

Whatever he lost seems to have been found with *The Visitors* (1980), which returns to familiar themes and locales—aliens touch down near Lone Pine, Minnesota, and are ap-

proachable only by individual humans who feel for them as fellow creatures—but both plot and form show a much greater awareness than before of the complicated contemporary world, and the story ends on a note of greater ambiguity than in previous works.

Simak, then, is a writer who has tended a small plot and tended it well, generally growing the flowers he knows best. Aside from a fascination with time travel and robots, he has used few of the stock devices of science fiction. Indeed, he seems often to be antiscience and antitechnology. Men reach the stars by becoming "worthy," not by technological advance. Simak has constructed no future histories, built no galactic empires, orchestrated no space wars.

Because of this, critics have tended to enjoy Simak but then to dismiss him by calling him "pastoral," "religious," and "conservative." Many critics find his "paucity of ideas" especially disturbing in a genre like science fiction, which depends so much on ideas. Consequently he has not received the critical attention that most of his fellow writers have received.

If this has bothered Simak, he has not said so. Like so many of his old-men characters, he is patient and wise. Like them he believes that mankind has a purpose, "and perhaps an important one." Like Mose Abrams, Enoch Wallace, and Hiram Taine, he is "more concerned with the human heart and mind than with [material] human accomplishment."

—ROALD D. TWEET

Simak died on 25 April 1988 in Minneapolis. For several years he had been chronically ill and scarcely able to write, so his post-1982 output was small: just three novels.

Much of his writing, while categorized as science fiction, has been close to that uncertain border where science fiction and fantasy meet. This was both because he despised modern technology, retaining a nostalgia for the old, postwar methods, and because he felt himself to be part of the mythic rural roots of America. Thus, in *Special Deliverance* (1982), he transports his protagonist, Professor Lansing, to another planet by magical means, at the beginning of an unexceptional quest novel involving characters from a number of parallel worlds. *Where the Evil Dwells* (1982) is an alternate history science fiction novel about a world where the Roman Empire has continued to exist for the last two millennia. This, too, is a quest story, and the farther one gets into it, the more one comes across familiar fantasy elements: magic, elves, trolls, unicorns, dragons, and even a princess incarcerated in a castle. Again, the overall result is one of disappointment—a mixture of clichés and telegraphed outcomes, though some of Simak's details are entertaining.

The final Simak novel, *Highway of Eternity* (1986), is a fast-paced and generally entertaining piece of work. It might almost be seen as a brief reprise of all of Simak's previous novels because it crams in most of the ingredients that have characterized his work except, perhaps, a Wisconsin setting. The time and space travel, involving England in the past, characters from the present, and cooperation with alien species, all written tongue-in-cheek, result in a frenetic story that, while it may not all be logical or cohesive, is never dull.

Few of Simak's novels have been reprinted since his death, but his name has been kept alive through a series of mostly British-published collections. These have brought together some very well-known stories, some lesser known, and a few that had not been reprinted since their original magazine appearance and deserved to be left in peace. However, it is fortunate that a new generation of readers has the opportunity to peruse some of the excellent short fiction produced by this most gentle of writers.

—CHRIS MORGAN

Selected Bibliography

WORKS OF CLIFFORD D. SIMAK

The Creator. Los Angeles: Crawford, 1946.
Cosmic Engineers. New York: Gnome Press, 1950.
Time and Again. New York: Simon and Schuster, 1951.
City. New York: Gnome Press, 1952. Reissued. New York: Ace Books, 1958 and 1976. (1976 edition has a new Foreword by Simak.)
Ring Around the Sun. New York: Simon and Schuster, 1953.
The Worlds of Clifford Simak. New York: Simon and Schuster, 1960. (Short stories.)
Time Is the Simplest Thing. Garden City, N.Y.: Doubleday, 1961.
All the Traps of Earth. Garden City, N.Y.: Doubleday, 1962. (Short stories.)
Way Station. Garden City, N.Y.: Doubleday, 1963.
Worlds Without End. New York: Belmont, 1964. (Short stories.)
All Flesh Is Grass. Garden City, N.Y.: Doubleday, 1965
Best Science Fiction Stories of Clifford D. Simak. London: Faber and Faber, 1967. (Collection.)
So Bright the Vision. New York: Ace Books, 1968. (Short stories.)
Best Science Fiction Stories of Clifford D. Simak. Garden City, N.Y.: Doubleday, 1971.
Our Children's Children. New York: G. P. Putnam's Sons, 1974.
The Best of Clifford D. Simak. London: Sidgwick and Jackson, 1975. (Short stories.)
Enchanted Pilgrimage. New York: G. P. Putnam's Sons, 1975.
Shakespeare's Planet. New York: Berkley/Putnam, 1976.
A Heritage of Stars. New York: Berkley/Putnam, 1977.
Skirmish: The Great Short Fiction of Clifford D. Simak. New York: Berkley/Putnam, 1977. (Short stories.)
The Fellowship of the Talisman. New York: Ballantine Books, 1978.
The Visitors. New York: Ballantine Books, 1980.
Project Pope. New York: Ballantine, 1981; London: Sidgwick and Jackson, 1981.
Special Deliverance. New York: Ballantine, 1982; London: Severn House, 1983.
Where the Evil Dwells. New York: Ballantine, 1982; London: Severn House, 1984.
Brother, and Other Stories. London: Severn House, 1986. (Short stories.)
Highway of Eternity. New York: Ballantine, 1986. Reprinted as *Highway to Eternity,* London: Severn House, 1987.
The Marathon Photograph, and Other Stories. London: Severn House, 1986. (Short stories.)
Off-Planet. London: Methuen, 1988. (Short stories.)
The Autumn Land and Other Stories. London: Mandarin, 1990. (Short stories.)
The Immigrant, and Other Stories. London: Mandarin, 1991. (Short stories.)
The Creator and Other Stories. London: Severn House, 1993.
Over the River and Through the Woods: The Best Short Fiction of Clifford D. Simak. San Francisco, Calif.: Tachyon, 1996. (Short stories.)

The Civilisation Game and Other Stories. London: Severn House, 1997. (Short stories.)

BIBLIOGRAPHY

Becker, Muriel R. *Clifford D. Simak: A Primary and Secondary Bibliography.* Boston: G. K. Hall, 1980.

CRITICAL AND BIOGRAPHICAL STUDIES

Clareson, Thomas D. "Clifford D. Simak: The Inhabited Universe." In *Voices for the Future: Essays on Major Science Fiction Writers,* vol. 1, edited by Thomas D. Clareson. Bowling Green, Ohio: Bowling Green University Popular Press, 1976. (Traces the development of Simak's favorite theme, the interrelatedness of life.)

Moskowitz, Sam. "Clifford D. Simak." In his *Seekers of Tomorrow.* Cleveland: World Publishing Company, 1966. (A detailed biography of Simak's early career as a science fiction writer.)

Pringle, David. "Aliens for Neighbors: A Reassessment of Clifford D. Simak." *Foundation,* no. 11/12 (1977): 15–29. (Identifies and traces twelve major themes in Simak's work.)

Simak, Clifford D. "Room Enough for All of Us." *Extrapolation,* 13 (1972): 102–105. (Simak discusses his faith in the new generation of science fiction writers.)

———. *A Career in Science Fiction: An Interview with Clifford Simak.* Lawrence: University of Kansas, 1975. (A film in which Simak discusses the evolution of his writing and writers who have influenced him.)

Walker, Paul. "Clifford Simak: an Interview." *Luna Monthly,* no. 57 (1975): 1–6. (Simak talks about his career and his philosophy of life.)

CLARK ASHTON SMITH
(1893–1961)

CLARK ASHTON SMITH lived for most of his life on the outskirts of Auburn, California. He pursued three overlapping careers: poet, writer of fantastic fiction, and sculptor and graphic artist. His work has been preserved almost entirely by the efforts of a small group of enthusiasts, appearing in books issued by small presses. The six collections that comprise Smith's total output of fiction were published between 1942 and 1970, but not until the 1970's, with the publication of paperback editions in the United States and Britain, did his work begin to reach a wider audience. As this history suggests, Smith is in some ways an esoteric writer—the practitioner par excellence of a particularly phantasmagorical romanticism. He reached out with his imagination to realms beyond those that had previously been surveyed or even glimpsed; in his work he often left behind not only the mundane world but also the established mythologies of the present and the past. In his prose poem "To the Daemon" (1943), Smith addressed his personal plea to the fountainhead of creativity:

Tell me many tales, O benign maleficent daemon, but tell me none that I have ever heard or have even dreamt of otherwise than obscurely or infrequently.... Tell me many tales, but let them be of things that are past the lore of legend and of which there are no myths in our world or any world adjoining. ... Tell me tales of inconceivable fear and unimaginable love, in orbs whereto our sun is a nameless star, or unto which its rays have never reached. (from *Poems in Prose*, 1965)

Smith's primary interest, in all his works of art, was in the remote, the exotic, and the bizarre. There is little of "human interest" in his works, and he was adamant in his rejection of the notion that literature ought to be concerned exclusively with human affairs. In a letter to *Amazing Stories*, published in the October 1933 issue, he wrote:

Literature can be, and does, many things; and one of its most glorious prerogatives is the exercise of imagination on things that lie *beyond* human experience—the adventuring of fantasy into the awful, sublime and infinite cosmos *outside* the human aquarium. . . . For many people . . . imaginative stories offer a welcome and salutary release from the somewhat oppressive tyranny of the homocentric, and help to correct the deeply introverted, ingrowing values that are fostered by present-day "humanism" and realistic literature with its unhealthy materialism and earthbound trend. Science fiction, at its best, is akin to sublime and exalted poetry, in its invocation of tremendous, non-anthropomorphic imageries.

Although Smith could find echoes of his own interests in a small number of previous American writers—most notably Edgar Allan Poe and Ambrose Bierce—his work can more readily be related to the tradition of romantic literature that flourished in nineteenth-century France, including the work of Gérard de Nerval, Théophile Gautier, Charles Leconte de Lisle, Paul Verlaine, Pierre Louÿs, and Charles Baudelaire. He was heavily influenced by Baudelaire, many of whose poems he translated, and the prose fiction most similar to Smith's is found in the grotesque fantasies of Gautier, particularly "Clarimonde" and "The Mummy's Foot." Yet in his fiction Smith also sounds what H. P. Lovecraft referred to as a "note of cosmic horror," which marks it as a product of the twentieth century. By the 1930's, when Smith wrote all his significant fiction, the universe had been revealed as a vaster and more alien place than any nineteenth-century writer could have envisaged. In Gautier's literary cosmos the supernatural is domesticated by its anthropocentricity, but in Smith's universe the human race is of no particular significance: it is a transient folly of the evolutionary process or a casual creation of uncaring gods.

Smith began writing in his late teens, after completing his education without the benefit of high school and with the aid of encyclopedias and the dictionary. He sold a number of Oriental tales to *Overland Monthly* and *Black Cat*, and followed these with his first collection of poetry, *The Star-Treader and Other Poems* (1912). Soon afterward he suffered a nervous breakdown connected with the first of several bouts of tuberculosis. During the fevers of the first outbreak Smith suffered terribly from delirious nightmares. The substance of these nightmares provided imaginative material for his poems and tales, but many years passed before he was able to exert sufficient discipline to use them thus.

Smith published three more volumes of poetry (the best of which is collected in *Selected Poems*, 1971) before he turned his attention primarily to prose in the late 1920's. By this time he had been corresponding with Lovecraft for several years, and it is possible that Lovecraft persuaded him to attempt writing for *Weird Tales*. He was at first unsuccessful but in 1930 began to publish prolifically. His output accelerated up to 1933, in which year he published twenty-one short stories, six of them in a privately published collection, *The Double Shadow and Other Fantasies*. From then on, his productivity waned, the flood of works petering out almost completely in 1936; he published only about a dozen more

stories in the remaining twenty-five years of his life.

Smith's career as a science fiction writer began when two of his stories appeared in the October 1930 issues of *Amazing Detective Tales* and *Wonder Stories*, edited by Hugo Gernsback. Neither story is impressive, but the *Wonder Stories* piece, "Marooned in Andromeda," is typical of Smith: it depicts an odyssey undertaken by a party of humans across the face of a bizarre and hostile world. Virtually all of Smith's science fiction consists of reports of strange and unearthly lifeforms encountered during fantastic journeys. His plots are usually cursory, and such intercourse as takes place between the human characters and the various alien species is rarely constructive. The principal exception to this rule is "The Planet Entity" (1931; originally "Seedling of Mars"), which was written around E. M. Johnston's synopsis and submitted in response to a *Wonder Stories* "plot contest."

Stories essentially similar to "Marooned in Andromeda" include a sequel, "The Amazing Planet" (1931), and "The Immortals of Mercury" (1932); but the stronger stories in this vein tend to be shorter ones featuring a single melodramatic encounter between humans and particularly monstrous aliens. The best of these are "The Immeasurable Horror" (1931) and "The Vaults of Yoh-Vombis" (1932), both of which appeared in *Weird Tales*.

It is rather surprising that Smith managed to gain a foothold in the science fiction pulps. His fiction did not in the least correspond to Hugo Gernsback's idea of "scientifiction" as a medium in which scientific fact is "mingled with charming romance" in order to help the reader learn and gain a sense of the wonder and beneficence of science. Smith used the conventions of science fiction merely as literary devices to estrange his protagonists from an earthly environment and cast them adrift in the unknown. Like one or two of the other writers whose work spanned both *Weird Tales* and the early science fiction pulps (Donald Wandrei is perhaps the cardinal example), Smith thrived on extravagant experiments in imaginary cosmology, and it was probably this imaginative ambition that endeared him to Gernsback. In "The Eternal World" (1932) a scientist exploring the universe with his time machine is becalmed when he enters a timeless dimension beyond the limits of our universe. In "The Dimension of Chance" (1932) American aviators pursue a spy into a distorted dimension, the spatial configuration of which defies and deludes their senses. In "A Star-Change" (1933; originally "The Visitors from Mlok") aliens are forced to alter the senses of a human visiting their world so that he can see it—a transformation that has awkward consequences when he returns home. All these are idea stories that fit in well with the ethos of *Wonder Stories.*

But the best pieces that Smith published in *Wonder Stories* belong to a different species of fantasy. "The City of the Singing Flame" (1931; combined in some book versions with its sequel, "Beyond the Singing Flame"), although an idea story in its way, is primarily a fantasy celebrating the lure of the exotic. (It has strong affinities with A. Merritt's "The Moon Pool," another fantasy that Gernsback admired sufficiently to publish in spite of his idea of what "scientifiction" ought to be.) The narrator of the story gains access to a parallel world, where he joins a pilgrimage of assorted alien creatures and discovers that their purpose is ecstatic self-immolation in a fountain of flame that tempts him with hypnotic music. Having gone home and reported on his experience, the narrator returns to the parallel world, intending to deliver himself to the flame. In the sequel another man follows the narrator of the first story and finds that the flame is a gateway to an inner dimension that is a halfway house offering access to a more wonderful, transcendent existence. Like "The Moon Pool," "The City of the Singing Flame" stands far better alone than with its sequel, because no conceivable account of what lies beyond the mysterious, transcendent flame could be anything but an anticlimax. (The revelation of a chain of further portals is merely a prevarication.) The subject matter of the story is the strong allure of

the unknown—the temptation of the idea of paradise—and the promise of unimaginable fulfillment cannot, by definition, be redeemed.

Smith later wrote a similar story, "The Light from Beyond" (1933), for *Wonder Stories;* but although he was by then a more capable writer, this story does not have the power of "The City of the Singing Flame." His two other stories on the same theme—"A Voyage to Sfanomoë" (1931) and "The Planet of the Dead" (1932), both of which appeared in *Weird Tales*—retain a partially science fiction framework in that they are both interplanetary stories, but their mechanics are essentially magical.

The difficulty that Smith had in marrying his imaginative proclivities to the constraints of science fiction are amply demonstrated by the Martian tales that share a common background with "The Vaults of Yoh-Vombis"— "The Dweller in the Gulf" (1933; originally "The Dweller in Martian Depths") and "Vulthoom" (1935). Only "The Dweller . . ." appeared in *Wonder Stories;* it was criticized by Forrest Ackerman on the ground that it was essentially a horror story and did not belong there. Once this controversy was made public, Smith had appeared in *Wonder Stories* for the last time, and the stories that he subsequently placed in the science fiction pulps— "The Plutonian Drug" (1934), "The Dark Age" (1938), and "The Great God Awto" (1940)—are much more conventional. Nevertheless, there is a sense in which his Martian stories, no matter how fantastic they are, really do belong to an identifiable tradition in modern science fiction: the tradition that links Stanley Weinbaum's "A Martian Odyssey" (1934) with Ray Bradbury's *Martian Chronicles* (1950), Leigh Brackett's Martian romances (1942–1963), and Marion Zimmer Bradley's "The Dark Intruder" (1962). Especially in its late 1940's manifestations, this tradition enshrines the idea of a decadent Mars that is the home of ancient supernatural forces as an established element of the mythology of science fiction.

Science fiction distinguishes itself from fantasy by its insistence on demystification to precipitate out the miracles of imaginative endeavor as vulgar possibilities. The very nature of the genre equips it with a kind of reverse Midas touch, which turns the glamour of fantasy's Golden Age of magic into a utilitarian Iron Age of technology and human endeavor. Yet there always survives within science fiction a rebellious romanticism that, although it may be ironic or even tragic in the acceptance of its own redundancy, continually asserts itself as a worthy cause. It is for his contribution to this cause that Smith warrants special consideration as a pulp science fiction writer.

Although concentrating his efforts during the most prolific phase of his career on *Weird Tales*, Smith did not leave the mythology of science fiction entirely behind him. He used alien worlds as locales in several stories, most notably "The Demon of the Flower" (1933) and "The Flower-Women" (1935), and the notion of the alien became a powerful element in his horror stories. (It was this importation of the alien into the framework of the horror story to supplement and extend the symbology of the supernatural that also made Lovecraft's work distinctive and powerful.) The most exotic and marvelous of Smith's imaginary territories—and the one that provided him with the most scope—was the far-future setting of Zothique, the last continent of a dying Earth. The Zothique tales are not science fiction; on the contrary, they have the distinction of contributing a new domain and a new mythological framework to modern fantasy. But to some extent they do depend on the imaginative viability of the far future as a story setting. Although it is superficially similar to the imaginary prehistoric setting used copiously by Robert E. Howard and by Smith himself in his Hyperborean stories, Zothique has an advantage in terms of the imaginative extravagance that it permits. In fantasies set in an imaginary prehistoric age, the viewpoint of the reader predetermines the fact that the war between order and chaos, or between reason and magic, must eventually resolve itself in favor of order and reason, so that the modern world may emerge from the

postcataclysmic remnants. Zothique, by contrast, allows necromancy and decadence absolutely free rein; they need never give way to any presumed renaissance, and the world may stand on the brink of hell, imperiled by a genuinely conclusive Apocalypse. It is in Zothique that the most exotically melodramatic—and perhaps the best—of Smith's tales are set: "The Empire of the Necromancers" (1932), "The Witchcraft of Ulua" (1934), "The Dark Eidolon" (1935), and "The Death of Ilalotha" (1937).

Why Smith's output declined so rapidly after 1935 is not clear. In the 1930's he began to devote more time and energy to his sculpture, and by then he had pushed his imagination as a writer just about to its limits: these may have been the major contributory factors. The deaths of his parents in 1935 and 1937, with the attendant changes in his financial circumstances, may also have been important. The stories that Smith produced in the 1950's, near the end of his career, seem markedly different from those that he wrote in the 1930's, being lighthearted and whimsical. Of the two late stories that are science fiction, one—"The Metamorphosis of Earth" (1951), in which aliens adapt various areas of Earth for their own habitation—reads like an early pulp story and may have been left over from his productive phase. The second, "Phoenix" (1954), is a brief but effective story about an attempt to reignite the dying sun; its scientific background is badly out of date, but it has a beautiful last line.

Smith is remembered today primarily as one of the three outstanding contributors to *Weird Tales* during that magazine's heyday. Although he survived the other two—Lovecraft and Howard—by a quarter of a century, his career effectively ended when theirs did, in the late 1930's. Of the three, he was by far the most accomplished prose stylist. Like Lovecraft, he decorated his prose elaborately, in pursuit of an atmosphere of strangeness, but he did so more sensitively. He was also the most versatile of the three, able to function effectively in a greater range of milieus. Ironically, the fact that Lovecraft and Howard now have larger and more devoted followings is very largely due to their lack of versatility, to the almost obsessive relentlessness with which they pursued their particular aims.

L. Sprague de Camp has criticized both Howard and Lovecraft for their obsessiveness, but in a brief essay on Smith he pauses to regret that Smith did not have a little more obsessiveness, describing him as "a born intellectual with an intense dreamy imagination, living a comparatively uneventful life, and lacking the energy, drive, and ambition that might have taken him out of his limited environment." This is surely a curious accusation, since Smith specifically set himself the task of wandering as far from his "limited environment" as his imagination could take him and was dramatically successful in fulfilling this ambition. De Camp, of course, meant "ambition" in a different sense, but it is a sense that Smith would have considered rather vulgar and uninteresting (and this was by no means a pose on his part).

The kind of fiction that Smith wrote is readily labeled as escapism, and it is certainly that—his science fiction no less so than his fantasy. It takes the reader outside the limitations of everyday existence to dwell imaginatively in a world of spectacular wonders and dreadful horrors. But to undertake such imaginary voyages is not—as critics sometimes presume—a sign of moral failure; rather, it is a celebration of the creative power of the human mind. It is surely an unreasonably narrow mind that declares that no such celebration is warranted or can be justified. If one sees Smith's work in this light, one may begin to see how he could take such evident delight in catalogs of gruesome horrors and ironic fatalities. He was working with the substance of nightmares, to be sure, but not in a morbid fashion—to make nightmares into the raw material of art is to force them to yield to control. Smith accomplished more than that: he proved that his consciousness could outreach and outdo his own delirious dreams in the production of symbols of evil and fear, and that is a kind of triumph.

Smith's contribution to science fiction may, by some standards, appear to have been a minor one. Of the pieces he wrote for *Wonder Stories*, only "The City of the Singing Flame" has appeared frequently in anthologies, and it contains little of the usual apparatus of science fiction; the idea of parallel worlds was borrowed by science fiction from fantasy rather than vice versa. Smith was, nonetheless, one of the writers most ready to feed the gluttonous appetite for wonders that many of the readers of early pulp science fiction possessed. The contribution that the attitudes characteristic of science fiction made to his particular literary quest also deserves consideration, for these attitudes helped to make him the unique writer that he was. When the French romantics went in search of the exotic, the bizarre, and the fantastic, they were necessarily led back into the imaginary past of legend—to the Orient of Gautier and Gérard de Nerval, or the Greece of Louÿs's *Aphrodite*. In his teens Smith too wrote Oriental tales; but by the time he resumed writing in the 1920's, he was fully aware that he could look outward as well as backward. The lamia in "Sadastor" (1925) is a creature of the Orient, but the tale with which the demon comforts her is an interstellar adventure. The opening lines of "The Abominations of Yondo," which was written in the same year (reprinted in *Hyperborea*, 1971), confirm in no uncertain terms this widening of Smith's perspective:

The sand of the desert of Yondo is not as the sand of other deserts; for Yondo lies nearest of all to the world's rim; and strange winds, blowing from a gulf no astronomer may hope to fathom, have sown its ruinous fields with the gray dust of corroding planets, the black ashes of extinguished suns. The dark, orblike mountains which rise from its wrinkled and pitted plain are not all its own, for some are fallen asteroids half-buried in that abysmal sand. Things have crept in from nether space, whose incursion is forbid by the gods of all proper and well-ordered lands; but there are no such gods in Yondo, where live the hoary genii of stars abolished, and decrepit demons left homeless by the destruction of antiquated hells.

There is something of the consciousness that underlies science fiction present in all of Smith's best work: the notion of a vast universe, "queerer than we can imagine," is ever present within it, and is part and parcel of its quality.

Selected Bibliography

FICTION OF CLARK ASHTON SMITH

The Double Shadow and Other Fantasies. Auburn, Calif.: published by the author, 1933.

Out of Space and Time. Sauk City, Wis.: Arkham House, 1942.

Lost Worlds. Sauk City, Wis.: Arkham House, 1944.

Genius Loci and Other Tales. Sauk City, Wis.: Arkham House, 1948.

The Abominations of Yondo. Sauk City, Wis.: Arkham House, 1960.

Tales of Science and Sorcery. Sauk City, Wis.: Arkham House, 1964.

Other Dimensions. Sauk City, Wis.: Arkham House, 1970.

Zothique. New York: Ballantine Books, 1970.

Hyperborea. New York: Ballantine Books, 1971.

Xiccarph. New York: Ballantine Books, 1972.

Poseidonis. New York: Ballantine Books, 1973.

Strange Shadows: The Uncollected Fiction and Essays of Clark Ashton Smith. Westport, Conn.: Greenwood, 1989.

CRITICAL AND BIOGRAPHICAL STUDIES

Behrends, Steve. "CAS and Diverse Hands." In *The Horror of It All.* Edited by Robert M. Price. Mercer Island, Wash.: Starmont, 1990.

———. *Clark Ashton Smith.* Mercer Island, Wash.: Starmont, 1991.

Bell, Joseph. *The Books of Clark Ashton Smith.* Toronto, Canada: Soft Books, 1987.

Chalker, J. L., ed. *In Memoriam: Clark Ashton Smith.* Baltimore, Md.: Anthem, 1963. (Memoirs, critical articles, and some original work by Smith, including a verse play.)

Morris, H. O., Jr., and E. P. Berglund, eds. *Nyctalops,* 7 (August 1972). (Memoirs, articles, and pastiches, including a useful bibliography of Smith's work.)

Murray, Will. "The Clark Ashton Smythos." In *The Horror of It All.* Edited by Robert M. Price. Mercer Island, Wash.: Starmont, 1990.

Sidney-Fryer, Donald. *Emperor of Dreams.* West Kingston, R.I.: Donald M. Grant, 1978. (The definitive bibliography of Smith's work, as well as essays and memoirs.)

—BRIAN M. STABLEFORD

CORDWAINER SMITH

(1913–1966)

CORDWAINER SMITH WAS the pseudonym used for his science fiction by Dr. Paul Myron Anthony Linebarger, who was born in Milwaukee, Wisconsin, in July 1913 and who died in Baltimore, Maryland, in 1966. Because his father was a judge who served as a legal adviser to the Chinese Republic, he grew up and received most of his schooling in China and Japan—a circumstance that allowed him to learn about the legends and customs of those countries and, eventually, to incorporate them into his fiction. He travelled often even as a boy, attending school in Germany for a while and visiting Russia while in his teens. Linebarger attended college in the United States, majoring in political science and receiving a Ph.D. from Johns Hopkins University in 1936. While lecturing in politics, he had two books published about Republican China.

When the United States entered World War II, Linebarger received a commission in the army and was sent back to China, where he was in charge of psychological warfare activities. He had time, during the war, to write two nonspeculative novels set partly in the Far East, *Ria* (1947) and *Carola* (1948); they were published under the pseudonym of Felix C. Forrest (a punning reference to the Chinese name he had been given in infancy, "Lin Bah Loh"—which means "Forest of Incandescent Bliss"). His book *Psychological Warfare* also appeared in 1948, under his own name, and the following year his spy thriller *Atomsk* was published, under the pseudonym Carmichael Smith, since his Felix C. Forrest alias was no longer a secret.

By his first marriage in 1936, Smith had two daughters. The marriage was dissolved in 1949, and in 1950 he married Genevieve Collins. From then until 1966, most of his science fiction was first published. Although he had returned to university teaching in 1947, becoming a professor of Asiatic politics at Johns Hopkins University, he was recalled for military service during the Korean War. During the later 1950's and the 1960's, Smith and his wife traveled extensively, both to lecture and for pleasure. This was done in spite of considerable illness on his part. He was particularly impressed with Australia (a fact that is made clear in his science fiction) and hoped to retire there. But he died of a heart attack at the age of fifty-three.

Smith's science fiction is remarkable for three reasons in particular: it is highly original, owing little or nothing to previous science fiction; all of it (except for five stories) fits into a single series, entitled the Instrumentality of Mankind; and "War No. 81-Q," the earliest written story of that series, dates from 1928. It appeared in a school magazine when its author was only fourteen. In all, there are only thirty-two science fiction stories by Smith, of which four make up a novel, *Quest of the Three Worlds* (1966), and one, "Himself in Anachron," has not yet been published. In addition there are two short novels, *The Planet Buyer* (1964) and *The Underpeople* (1968), which have been combined as *Norstrilia* (1975).

These stories and novels were written over most of Linebarger's life, although the series seems to have been planned in outline, if not in detail, before the professional publication of "Scanners Live in Vain" in 1950. It was five years before another of his stories appeared, so it was only during the last ten years or so of his life that the name Cordwainer Smith became widely known to science fiction readers. He produced the final drafts of most of his science fiction during that period, sometimes in collaboration with his wife (who readied several stories for publication after his death). The true identity of Cordwainer Smith was known to very few people until the year or two before he died.

The Instrumentality of Mankind is a future history covering the next fifteen thousand years of humanity's development and the colonization of many planets in the galaxy. Yet it was never the author's intention to describe fully this lengthy period through his stories, but merely to provide a consistent backdrop against which to set his work. Although most of the stories refer, directly or indirectly, to characters or events that occur in other stories, and there are obvious clusters of connected stories at particular junctures, it is not always apparent to the reader where certain episodes fit in. A background chart to the series, prepared by J. J. Pierce, is printed in *The Best of Cordwainer Smith* (1975) and *The Instrumentality of Mankind* (1979). Without this chart the casual reader might not realize the connections between some of the stories, especially since Smith made little effort to establish the dates or to write historical linking material. Hence, while the time span of this future history is more reminiscent of Olaf Stapledon's than, for example, of Robert A. Heinlein's, Smith's intention was certainly not to write a future history. (His intentions will be dealt with later.)

In assessing any series, especially one that includes some undeniably very good parts, there is a temptation to be adulatory in one's treatment of the whole. The range of quality in the stories of Cordwainer Smith is considerable; some are poor or minor by being purely anecdotal or overly sentimental, or by allowing a religious message to overwhelm them. "War No. 81-Q" is rather good, considering that it was written by a fourteen-year-old, but

it is included in *The Instrumentality of Mankind* only for completeness; it is four pages long and characterless, and despite some nice touches of satire, it is basically a shameless wish-fulfillment fantasy. "The Colonel Came Back from Nothing-at-All" (written around 1956; published in 1979) is obviously a first draft of what later became "Drunkboat" (1963); the fact that the two stories are supposedly set some seven thousand years apart shows the undue flexibility of Smith's future history. "The Dead Lady of Clown Town" (1964), "Under Old Earth" (1966), and parts of *Norstrilia* are afflicted by overly simple religious symbolism, at too great a length.

Most striking of all about Smith's science fiction is its originality. It is known that he read science fiction avidly from boyhood, yet it is almost impossible to discover traces of its influence in his own work. Being widely read and fluent in Chinese, Russian, and several European languages, he had a more international viewpoint than his contemporaries in science fiction. Partly, his work seems so original to us because we are unfamiliar with his sources. In an illuminating Prologue and Epilogue to his collection *Space Lords* (1965), Smith mentions some of these sources. "Mother Hitton's Littul Kittons" (1961) comes from the Ali Baba legend; "The Dead Lady of Clown Town" is a version of the story of Joan of Arc (this is his most obvious derivation); "The Ballad of Lost C'mell" (1962) was loosely inspired by an early Chinese story; and so on. "Drunkboat" is based on the life and work of the poet Arthur Rimbaud, about which Smith says in his Epilogue: "And do look at Rimbaud's poetry in English or French. You can see how warmly and enthusiastically I stole this material, and you yourself can judge how well I stole it."

The names of Smith's characters and places are equally original, with a wonderfully mellifluous lilt to them (for example: Lord Jestocost, Dolores Oh, the planet Viola Siderea). All of his names seem to be real non-English names or words (or corruptions thereof), as opposed to the totally artificial names created by, for example, Jack Vance or Clark Ashton Smith. The name Sto Odin (the old man who is carried about in an open sedan chair in "Under Old Earth") is Russian for "one hundred and one." Occasionally Smith's names are satirical, as in *Quest of the Three Worlds*, in which Kuraf, the deposed ruler of the planet Mizzer, is intended as King Farouk of Egypt.

Most of Smith's stories involve memorable characters, although very few of them are normal human beings. Quite often he seems to have gone out of his way to develop characters and to show them off to their best advantage, even when they are so bizarre as to be barely credible. That is not to say that his characterization is always successful, or even that it is always adequate. Sometimes he relies too heavily on unusual names, such as Veeseykoosey for the beautiful teenager in "Think Blue, Count Two" (1963), or Lord Lovaduck in "Golden the Ship Was—Oh! Oh! Oh!" (1959), or Mr. Grey-no-more in "The Lady Who Sailed *The Soul*" (1960)—expecting them alone to create an impression of personality. They may do so, but not to a sufficient extent. Other characters, even major ones, are used as cyphers to portray a single emotion or personality trait: the underperson D'joan is central to "The Dead Lady of Clown Town," yet she is just a young girl, full of love, who says little and seems too perfect; Dobyns Bennett, the narrator of "When the People Fell" (1959), is restricted to aged irascibility.

In all of Smith's work, his treatment of character displays a love of people and a deep concern for their problems. Although he writes about the Lords of the Instrumentality, who are imbued with great power and wealth, his main characters are, more often than not, passive. They are the victims of circumstance—forced to suffer, to travel, or to witness terrible events against their will. This does not refer just to convicted prisoners like Mercer in "A Planet Named Shayol" (1961), or to Elaine in "The Dead Lady of Clown Town," who is apparently conceived by mistake and trained for a task that does not exist until she stumbles upon the illicit underpeople settlement of Clown Town and fulfills her true destiny.

These passive characters do not need to be poor or underprivileged. Rod McBan is very rich as the heir to one of the farming stations on Norstrilia (the familiar contraction of "Old North Australia") in the novel of that name. All the farming stations have giant mutated sheep on which grow the virus stroon, the immortality drug that is the most valuable commodity in all the worlds of the Instrumentality. Yet Rod McBan, who is a pleasant, polite teenager, only intermittently telepathic (while the rest of Norstrilia's population can all *hier* and *spiek* with their minds), possesses a very clever computer that, by mortgaging and speculating with regard to future stroon production, makes Rod the richest person in the galaxy and the owner of most of Earth. Far from making Rod the master of his own fate, this procedure forces him to travel to Earth and to become a pawn in the underpeople's fight for betterment.

Even C'mell, the beautiful and desirable cat-derived "girlygirl" who pushes Rod McBan into his role as helper of the underpeople, is not a free agent. Her courses of action are all determined for her by the E'telekeli, the eagle-man who leads the underpeople, and by Lord Jestocost of the Instrumentality. C'mell is one of Smith's best-loved characters: she is brave, warm-hearted, and loyal; but she is not too perfect, being fallible enough to make wrong decisions and emotional enough to fall in love with Rod McBan.

The hero of *Quest of the Three Worlds*, Casher O'Neill (one of Smith's less inspired choices of name), is another well-described character who, despite heroic traits, is pushed along by conscience (and, finally, by religious belief) on a quest for money and munitions to help free his home planet, Mizzer, from the rule of Colonel Wedder. When O'Neill visits the storm planet, Henriada, on his quest, he meets the long-lived turtle-girl, T'ruth, who helps him but also makes decisions for him, pushing him along paths he would rather avoid. T'ruth is not a passive character. She may be a little girl in appearance, but her belief and her thousand years of experience have given her power and the determination to use it. She resembles D'joan only physically and through their common belief in the power of the Christian faith; otherwise she is less perfect and far more interesting—a bizarre person in a bizarre situation.

When it comes to the planetary backgrounds of his stories, Smith only rarely bothers to offer much of a description; yet when he does, the result is an outstanding example of imaginative writing. Nobody who has read *Quest of the Three Worlds* could forget the planet Henriada with its frequent hurricanes of enormous ferocity. These hurricanes are so powerful that a groundcar must weigh fifty tons or more to be safe from destruction. But safety is a relative term, since driving across Henriada's surface is a hair-raising business. There are mutated forms of Earth animals, including air-whales large enough to swallow a fifty-ton groundcar. Even with spiked wheels, jet motors pointing in all directions, and four large corkscrews on either side of the car for attaching it firmly to the ground, such vehicles can travel across Henriada only with the greatest difficulty. Yet there are wind-men who can somehow survive the storms—wild people who live unprotected on the storm planet's surface.

Only slightly less memorable is the gem planet, Pontoppidan, in the same book. It is an airless world made of gemstones rather than rocks. The daughter of its dictator is blasé about the precious jewels lying all about but is amazed to hear that other planets have a surface of earth and sand. She says: "Imagine living on a whole world full of flowerpot stuff!"

Norstrilia is not an outstandingly strange planet; it has breathable air and, one presumes, fairly similar conditions of gravity, pressure, temperature, period of rotation, and weather to that of Earth, although Smith is not a scientist and rarely bothers with such detail. Yet the image of Norstrilia as a kind of dry, gray-grassed Australia, hilly but not mountainous, with a sparse population of sheep farmers, is a compelling one. Then there is Viola Siderea, the planet of thieves, which is described only through its inhabitants, who are bound by their code of honor not to do honest work.

Because he is much more interested in people than in any technological advances, Smith has had a tendency to employ futuristic gadgets or processes whenever he felt it necessary, without bothering too much about explaining the principles behind them. He seems to have believed firmly in Arthur C. Clarke's "Third Law": "Any sufficiently advanced science is indistinguishable from magic." Hence Smith writes about faster-than-light space travel, immortality, artificially induced telepathy, the creation of men from lower animals, and indestructible buildings—all without trying to justify their existence. This approach, taking highly advanced technology for granted rather than explaining it, is often more convincing. Of course, some of these technological devices are science fiction clichés or are highly convenient for plot purposes, or both.

If the human race is ever going to colonize the planets of other stars, it must develop one of three modes of travel: multigeneration starships, suspended animation, or faster-than-light travel. Smith makes use of the last two methods, postulating that space-sailing ships will first be developed, with vast sails catching the solar wind, which drives them at high but sublight speeds. One or two crew members—such as Helen America and Mr. Greyno-more—spend decades guiding such a ship on a single voyage, while colonists are treated as cargo and refrigerated all the way. Even for the crew the trip will not seem to be its real length of perhaps forty years, but more like a month, because of a special biological adaptation that speeds up the body by a factor of five hundred. Later in Smith's future history, planoforming (his word for faster-than-light travel) is developed and mankind can travel between the stars at much greater speeds. In fact, some men manage to planoform almost instantaneously over enormous numbers of light years by traveling through "Space[3]" (perhaps analogous to the "hyperspace" of other authors), without even needing a spaceship. This is described in "Drunkboat."

There is faster-than-light communication, too, which is essential if, like Rod McBan, one is living on Norstrilia and trying to buy up most of Earth. Telepathy is very similar to the superhuman image of being able to slip across the galaxy for a long weekend. Smith depicts telepathy as a natural, inherited talent common in many peoples of the civilized worlds. It does not normally involve the universal reading of minds but, rather, the limited ability to receive and to transmit specific messages over fairly short distances—acts known as *hiering* and *spieking*. On Earth, at least, an artificial version of this telepathy has been developed. It is contained in a device no larger than a peanut that is worn in the ear: Rod McBan is given one to make him as "normal" as everybody else on Norstrilia.

Equally convenient and appropriate is immortality or, at least, vastly increased lifespans. These lifespans are conferred upon certain lucky or rich individuals by regular doses of stroon, the miracle drug that can be produced only on Norstrilia and that sells for huge sums of money. With it most people will live for a thousand years or so, although T'ruth in *Quest of the Three Worlds* expects to live for about ninety thousand years.

The only people to whom stroon is forbidden are the underpeople—generally human-appearing creatures made from animals by a combination of surgical and genetic techniques. Smith avoids giving many details; he is interested not in the technology but in the sociology of a slave race. To him the cat-people, dog-people, snake-people, cow-people, and so on are oppressed groups, persecuted and without rights. An analogy with the blacks in America is inescapable.

Such advanced societies must have advanced weapons, if only to keep their underpeople in order. Like many other writers of science fiction, Smith finds it convenient to assume the existence of a small, hand-held blaster pistol; he calls it a wire-point. More interesting and original is a spaceship defense system described in "The Game of Rat and Dragon" (1955). This is called pinlighting, a telepathically based method of fighting deadly alien creatures that inhabit the depths of space. These creatures are ultrasensitive to light and can be destroyed by light-bombs, but

they move extraordinarily quickly—too fast for humans to react in time. The answer has been for humans to enlist the aid of cats, which have much faster reactions. While the humans think of the aliens as dragons, the cats imagine them as rats.

One last example of Smith's fascinating technological inventiveness is the architecture of the Daimoni. They are an enigmatic race—possibly human—capable of producing buildings that can resist anything: "corrosion, erosion, age, heat, cold, stress and weapons." They even resist (although Smith avoids this point) various laws of science. The best mention of the Daimoni is in the chapter entitled "The Palace of the Governor of Night," in *Norstrilia*. Yet within the framework of Smith's exotic, poetic, and myth-filled future, they are credible. Like many other technological items, these buildings are not major subjects; they are bits of background, casually mentioned, adding richness to the mixture without threatening even the hard-science purist with indigestion.

All the Instrumentality of Mankind stories have a distinct style—an auctorial voice that is subdued in the five non-Instrumentality stories and totally absent from the other fiction written by Linebarger. This style is particularly discernible in the deliberately overwritten and appetite-whetting opening lines that most stories have. Two examples will suffice: "I tell you, it is sad, it is more than sad, it is fearful . . ." (from the 1958 story "The Burning of the Brain") and "Perhaps it is the saddest, maddest, wildest story in the whole long history of space" (from "Drunkboat").

Smith's style is emotional, often ornate, and deliberately couched in the terms of a storyteller of the far future who looks back at these events with incomplete knowledge and hazy comprehension. This idea of speaking to the reader, used as a framing device, is far from original in itself, but Smith's flowing use of it in such seemingly overwritten fashion gives it new life. At times his chatty approach becomes too coy or patronizing, yet one has to admire him for daring to develop such a style.

Smith's choice of names for people and places is a part of this outrageous approach. In addition to those already mentioned, there are the Vomacts (a family of lords of the Instrumentality and doctors, who are involved in many of the stories); and people like Tigrabelas, Lady Alice More, the thief Benjacomin. There are the Go-captains (who command ships in space) and the Stop-captains (who supervise maintenance, loading, and so on when in port). The titles by which people are addressed have a quaint texture to them, such as Sir and Doctor Vomact, or Mister and Owner McBan. Some of our present-day terms have been deliberately corrupted, such as "Honorary Secretary" to "Onseck" and "Chinese" to "Chinesian." Many foreign words are adapted in this way, particularly in Smith's "Chinesian" story "When the People Fell" (1959), in which he writes of showhices (children), nondies (men), and needies (women). In "Mark Elf" (1957) and "The Queen of the Afternoon" (1978) there are large killing machines called manshonyaggers, a corruption of the German word *Menschenjäger* (man hunter). It is this combination of the foreign, the corrupted, the striking, and the sentimental that gives Smith's style its unique flavor.

Most of Smith's stories were written primarily to entertain. But the entertainment was not intended to stem entirely from the interaction of character and plot; there were subsidiary intentions and, in the later stories, a shift of emphasis from pure entertainment toward religious prescription. It is evident that Smith's style was carefully calculated to add interest to his work. Throughout the Instrumentality of Mankind stories, he was trying to create legends of the future: stories that might have been based upon truth but had been exaggerated or extended to become more universal. Such an approach makes it easier—and, indeed, essential—for an author to be less precise in details. Although the legend or myth is used as a framing device rather than as a permanent viewpoint throughout the stories, a certain haziness remains, suggesting the dramatization of an ancient story rather than a blow-by-blow contemporary account.

In addition, it was Smith's intention to satirize our contemporary society. He did not do so from any single political viewpoint or against any single target. Nor was he particularly cutting in his satire. Apart from his mirroring of Nasser's takeover of Egypt from Farouk in *Quest of the Three Worlds,* he confined his attention mainly to institutions. For example, financial institutions are the target in Rod McBan's computer-assisted purchase of much of Old Earth in *Norstrilia,* and "From Gustible's Planet" (1962) contains this passage: "Prompt payment was considered rude in a credit society, but after all it was better than not being paid at all." The planet of Norstrilia is a friendly and only slightly exaggerated view of Australia, a country that impressed the author tremendously when he visited it. At the same time, some of the societies Smith describes are exercises in social evolution or social stasis, conforming to his own theories in this regard.

At some point in the early 1960's, as mentioned earlier, a religious motif crept into Smith's stories. The teaching of the love of God (an essentially Christian form of religion) to those without beliefs comes to replace all other plots, although it is tied in with the betterment of the underpeople's living conditions. Such religious overtones are too prominent for their own good, interfering with reader enjoyment; they might have been more effective as Christian propaganda had they been more subtly introduced. "The Dead Lady of Clown Town" and "Under Old Earth" suffer from this, and parts of *Quest of the Three Worlds* are rendered very trite by it—for example, the manner in which Casher O'Neill is almost instantly converted by the turtle-girl, T'ruth. Indeed, it is truth that sets him free from fear (the symbolism is astonishingly heavy-handed for Smith), so that he can return to his home planet and save it from its dictatorship—not by force, but by strength of mind and the love of God.

Despite his relatively small output, Smith was a true original and a gifted writer. His work has achieved something of a cult status among readers of science fiction—although this developed partly from his use of a pseudonym and his early death.

Selected Bibliography

WORKS OF CORDWAINER SMITH

Space Lords. New York: Pyramid Books, 1965. (Contains five stories—which are also in the collections listed below—and a Prologue and Epilogue by Cordwainer Smith.)

Quest of the Three Worlds. New York: Ace Books, 1966. (Novel.)

The Best of Cordwainer Smith. New York: Ballantine Books, 1975. (Contains twelve stories, with an introduction and notes by J. J. Pierce.)

Norstrilia. New York: Ballantine Books, 1975. Written in 1960, this work was altered somewhat to form two separate novels: *The Planet Buyer* (New York: Pyramid Books, 1964) and *The Underpeople* (New York: Pyramid Books, 1968). (The 1975 text is now generally regarded as definitive.)

The Instrumentality of Mankind. New York: Ballantine Books, 1979. (Contains fourteen stories and an introduction by Frederik Pohl. This and the preceding title supersede four short-story collections previously published.)

CRITICAL AND BIOGRAPHICAL STUDIES

Bangsund, John, ed. *Exploring Cordwainer Smith*. New York: Algol Press, 1975. (A brief collection of critical essays.)

Bennett, Mike. *A Cordwainer Smith Checklist*. Polk City, Iowa: Chris Drumm Books, 1991.

Clute, John. "Cordwainer Smith." In *The Science Fiction Encyclopedia*. Edited by Peter Nicholls. Garden City, N.Y.: Doubleday, 1979.

Dowling, Terry. "Lever of Life: Winning and Losing in the Fiction of Cordwainer Smith." *Science Fiction: A Review of Speculative Literature*, 4 (March 1982): 9–37.

Elms, Alan C. "The Creation of Cordwainer Smith." *Science-Fiction Studies*, 11, part 3 (1984): 264–283. (Biographical article.)

———. "Origins of the Underpeople: Cats, Kuomintang, and Cordwainer Smith." In *Fictional Space*. Edited by Tom Shippey. Atlantic Highlands, N.J.: Humanities Press, 1991.

Heje, Johan. "On the Genesis of *Norstrilia*." *Extrapolation*, 30, no. 2 (1989): 146–155.

Hellekson, Karen. "Never Never Underpeople: Cordwainer Smith's Humanity." *Extrapolation*, 34, no. 2 (1993): 123–130.

Lewis, A. R. *Concordance to Cordwainer Smith*. Boston: NESFA Press, 1984.

Pierce, John J. "Introduction: Cordwainer Smith." In *The Rediscovery of Man: The Complete Short Science Fiction of Cordwainer Smith*. Edited by James A. Mann. Framingham, Mass.: NESFA Press, 1993.

———. "Mr. Forest of Incandescent Bliss." *Speculation*, 33 (1973).

—CHRIS MORGAN

E. E. SMITH

(1890–1965)

IN 1950 EDWARD Elmer Smith was a colossus of American science fiction, though completely unknown elsewhere, and readers at the time saw him as representing the deep tendencies of the genre. In a way, they were right. By 1960, after ten years of demolition work from within the field, Smith was a "has-been" whose new works veteran editors like John W. Campbell, Jr., of *Astounding* now declined to publish. By 1975, ten years after his death, his books were best-sellers in the United States and abroad, and several spin-off series—based in part on his unfinished works and sketches, and commissioned from authors more than fifty years his junior—were in the offing. Nor does this come as a surprise. A rollercoaster sequence of responses to the later career of a central writer—a sequence comprised of respect/embarrassment/imitation—is by no means restricted to the genre of science fiction; what may seem unusual in Smith's case is the violence of the shifts in a field that generally remains so loyal to its "heroic" central figures.

Few sophisticated readers of magazine science fiction in 1950 would have made the claim that Smith had any real competence at writing the more thoughtful, idea-oriented kind of story Campbell had begun to publish in *Astounding* a decade or so earlier, revolutionizing the field, purging it of many of its pulp habits, and initiating, from the perspective of its authors and readers both, a brief Golden Age. Although he continued to contribute huge installments of his Lensman saga to *Astounding* throughout this period, by 1940 Smith was already representative of an earlier, cruder, action-dominated mode of writing. Almost totally lacking any capacity or will to shape fruitful speculations about human nature, about social and political evolution, or about politics, science, or technology, incapable of constructing either utopian or dystopian perspectives whose salient characteristics bore educatively—or even entertainingly—upon our own lives, Smith did something else, and did it very well. He created the type of science fiction that Wilson Tucker has termed space opera.

In 1950, when his main series were finally beginning to appear in book form from fan publishers founded specifically to release his works, Smith's stature in the field derived from a powerful historical sense that, somehow or other, his epics were the fount from which later science fiction developed. His stature also derived from a sense that he had created and brought to maturity the devices by which science fiction stories gave off a sense of liberated immensity in narratives whose basic plot structures and situations were shared by other forms of pulp fiction, such as the Western. Smith had created the sense of wonder, and all the ways of evoking it: reading *The Skylark of Space* was like returning to childhood, when the sense of wonder came easily.

For many readers in 1950, Smith's works were a revelation of how the real thing was done, and they represented a return to that real thing. Campbell and his new writers may have cleaned up some of the more obvious excesses of genuine pulp science fiction, helping to prepare the ground for the fastidious, embarrassed revulsion against Smith that was characteristic of the 1950's; but there remained a lurking sense that all the seemingly new superstructure of speculative thought and plausible development of plot and character in cognitively accountable venues was precisely that: a mere superstructure or trappings.

The assertion that Smith's works represent the irreducible fount and heart of the science fiction genre is of course an assertion of sentiment, one that has shaped the reading experience of generations of American fans. No one, though, would any longer seriously argue the historical case. Although there is no doubt that Smith was instrumental in the early success of *Amazing Stories*, which became the nucleus of a new marketing genre from its founding in 1926, it is certainly not the case that he actually played a major part in the creation of science fiction as a recognizable literary form. Even Jules Verne and H. G. Wells, as academic research of recent decades has amply demonstrated, skillfully (and unpretentiously) synthesized material already available in the hundreds of earlier stories and novels of the nineteenth century that we can now identify as science fiction, though their authors did not do so. Ranging from pulplike dime novels and the like, through moralizing dreadful-warning tales, future-war novels, lost-race novels, evolutionary fantasies, and extraordinary-voyage romances, up to grimly didactic utopias (most of them firmly reactionary), nineteenth-century science fiction attracted a wide range of readers and lacked nothing but an agreed-upon name.

That name—"science fiction"—eventually became most firmly attached to the kind of material published by *Amazing Stories* in the ebullient, mobile, technophilic, awakening, innocent America of the period just before the Great Depression. For *Amazing*'s young readership, this period seemed like a great dawn. In the daunting exuberance of his most prolific years (1928–1942), Smith did more than anyone else to translate the sense that the fetters had been loosed into its most characteristic literary form, the multivolume space opera.

In the gradual demolition of any claim that science fiction originated with Hugo Gernsback's *Amazing Stories* in 1926, contemporary academic critics have demystified to the point of unintelligibility the kind of novel Smith actually wrote. In his *Metamorphoses of Science Fiction* (1979), for instance, Darko Suvin refers to Smith only once, in chapter 6, in a list of authors that includes Olaf Stapledon, A. E. van Vogt, and Arthur C. Clarke, whose "far-out" works collectively bear a vague resemblance to "the fantasies of cosmogonic history"—the Prophetic Books—of William Blake. Such a resemblance—which arguably may exist—could only have counted for nil to Smith, his editors, or his readership, had it been suggested to them, nor—even if convincingly adduced—can typological argument of this sort do anything to explain his popularity, then and now.

Furthermore, comparisons between Smith and Stapledon dramatically convey the importance of distinguishing between field and ground, for what are no more than means and trappings in the austere cosmogonic perspectives of Stapledon lie at the heart of Smith's enterprise. Cosmogonic speculation, when it appears in the later volumes of both of Smith's main series, serves mainly to prop wider the gates of the physical universe, so that the continuing action has new (and ever more immense) vistas to dominate.

I

Edward Elmer Smith was born on 1 May 1890, in Sheboygan, Wisconsin, and he was raised in rural Idaho—an environment that, at the turn of the century, would have instilled in any youth who happened to be ambitious certain basic assumptions about the moral and practical value of self-help and solitary enterprise; for young Smith, as for most Americans sharing his background and general experience, it did not seem foolish or arrogant to think in terms of solving one's own problems, of inventing or bootstrapping one's way out of difficulties. For a man who was not afraid to work with his hands and to think on his feet, the universe was essentially decipherable. From 1907 up to 1914, when he graduated from the University of Idaho as a chemical engineer, Smith had personal experience of a wide range of occupations, from carpentry through lumberjacking to cooking; he was at times and to various degrees competent as a hard-rock miner, a surveyor, and an electrician. The world that shaped him was a world that he could shape in return.

In 1915, Smith's life took on its mature shape. He took a job as a food chemist with the Bureau of Chemistry in Washington, D.C., acquiring a Ph.D. in food chemistry (1919) from George Washington University, and at the same time he began to work on the first drafts of what was to become *The Skylark of Space*, composition of which continued until 1920. Mrs. Lee Hawkins Garby, the wife of a friend, took a hand in working up the extremely simple romantic element of the tale, and she might be held to blame for the gawky, tongue-tied bathos that so stultifies it, except for the fact that Smith never much modified or deepened his basic treatment of human relationships, which to the end of his life were rendered in terms of prepubescent vagueness, unformed rather than oceanic.

The Skylark of Space was sent from magazine to magazine without success until Hugo Gernsback accepted it for *Amazing Stories* in 1928, where it had an enormous impact, mainly because of its grand and exuberant expression of awe at the newly revealed enormity of scale of the universe. Regardless of its clear roots in early twentieth-century pulp fiction, particularly the Western, *The Skylark of Space* is remarkable for the seemingly spontaneous vigor with which it demolishes the fictional barrier of the solar system and establishes space opera—of which it is the first proper example—in its proper venue, the whole doggoned universe.

E. E. Smith in 1969.   PHOTO BY JAY KAY KLEIN

After many years of earning his living as a commercial food chemist, Smith retired in 1957 and moved to Florida, though he died in Oregon, on 31 August 1965. Employed full-time during most of his life, he was never a full-time professional writer; though he was often crude as a stylist, he was never a hack; indeed, it is perhaps the main misconception about him that he was, in any simple way, a bad or slovenly writer. He wrote slowly and carefully, constructed the vast scenario of his Lensman series with remarkable skill, and was capable of pyrotechnic effects very few writers in the genre have ever come close to matching. *The Skylark of Space*, after its years of gestation, was revised at least twice after its magazine appearance; and though the first book publications (1946 and 1947) are in many ways more attractive and more delightful than the final (1958) revision and abridgment, the fact that he was still tinkering with the text nearly forty years after beginning work on it demonstrates anything but a hack writer's disregard for a product, once paid for it.

After 1928, Smith began his most productive years, a period in which announcement of each new work evoked enormous anticipation from the compact, vociferous, loyal science fiction readership. *Skylark Three*, the best-constructed and generally the finest of the *Skylark* novels, followed in 1930, also in *Amazing Stories* (1948, book form). The last pages of this novel—the long-distance battle between the inventor-genius Richard Seaton and his companions and the monstrous remnants of the despicable alien Fenachrone—contain the freshest, most exhilarating, most innocent example of cataclysmic hyperbole Smith ever managed to pen, although in the Lensman series he created battles of considerably greater scope and much greater complexity. In the sentence that ends *Skylark Three*, Smith also demonstrates, through the crude, driving remorselessness of his syntax, how pulp language could in itself become a vehicle of delight, and an imitation of the scale of the events depicted:

> In that awful moment before Seaton could shut off his power it seemed to him that space itself must be obliterated by the very concentration of the unknowable and incalculable forces there unleashed—must be swallowed up and lost in the utterly indescribable brilliance of the field of radiance driven to a distance of millions upon incandescent millions of miles from the place where the last representatives of the monstrous civilization of the Fenachrone had made their last stand against the forces of Universal Peace.

Smith then wrote *Spacehounds of IPC* (1931, *Amazing Stories*; 1947, book form), which was restricted to the solar system—he was quoted as saying it was his only real science fiction novel—and was not warmly received. *Triplanetary* (1934, *Amazing Stories*; 1948, book form) lacked in its magazine form the framework that in its book form made it into the beginning of the Lensman series. After these digressions, Smith then returned to the center of the stage with *Skylark of Vale-*

ron (1934–1935, *Astounding Stories*; 1949, book form). It was rather less well constructed than its series predecessor, but as convincingly expanded the scale of events—however ad hoc this expansion seems after one has experienced the firmer armature of the Lensman books—to a point where distant galaxies became as easily overtaken as stars had been earlier. But the exuberance remains. Nor would the joy Smith transmitted through his articulation of detailed but basically unlimited power fantasies die away until well after World War II and the darkening of the dream of American individualism entailed by that holocaust and its aftermath.

Hard on the heels of *Skylark of Valeron* came *Galactic Patrol* (1937–1938, *Astounding Stories*; 1950, book form), which effectively overcame the structural problems of the *Skylark* books. *Galactic Patrol* is the genuine beginning to the Lensman series, and Smith devoted most of his remaining prime years as a writer to the unfolding of this series. (*First Lensman*, which in terms of internal chronology follows immediately after the rewritten *Triplanetary*, was a successful later job of filling in by Smith; it was published in 1950, in book form only.)

In *Galactic Patrol*, the Lensman saga begins to take on its significant shape with the introduction of Kimball Kinnison, head of his graduating class and destined in his multivolume career to represent a new stage in the evolution of space opera: the institutionalizing of the protagonist. While fully as athletic and just as stupendously brainy as Richard Seaton, who single-handedly transforms the universe in the *Skylark* saga, Kinnison is no free lance. A member of the Galactic Patrol, a Lensman, the unconscious culmination of a selective-breeding program begun eons ago, he is a hero whose omnipotence is licensed. But it remains a true omnipotence indeed, for what Smith accomplished in the complex armature of the Lensman series was a translation of the infantile "rampancy" of the *Skylark* books into a universe-wide a priori justification of boyish patriotism. (We will return to *The Skylark of Space* to see if it is possible to retain some sense of the joyousness of its rampancy.) The more Kinnison excels, the more he reveals the underlying reasons for his most extravagant actions. Neither Kinnison—nor the reader—ends the Lensman saga with any incurred indebtedness, however imaginary, for violations of mundane ethical norms: at his freest, Kinnison is doing precisely what he is implicitly supposed to do.

Smith accomplishes all of this by framing his constantly expanding action within an age-old conflict, the full scale of which is unveiled to the protagonists only as they near their goal of ridding the universe of externalized evil. For readers of the entire six-volume book version of the saga, the nature of this conflict is clearly articulated from the first; but even for readers of the magazine versions of the four central novels, Smith lays down enough hints of eventual justification to allay most anxieties about rights and wrongs and about that which underpins their determination in a fictional universe: questions of probability. If the basic premises of the Lensman universe are accepted, then the working out of the saga is inherently plausible. This is largely the case because the cosmological frame Smith provides is basically that of a vast conspiracy, which distinguishes it from those other fictional cosmologies with which it might remotely be compared—for example, the macrohistory that structures Olaf Stapledon's *Last and First Men* (1930). Unsurprisingly, conspiracy theories make for interesting and dramatically effective plots.

The basic plot of the series may be summarized as follows: several billion years ago, two galaxies intersect. The First Galaxy is inhabited by—or, rather, imbued with—the race of the Arisians, who represent ultimate Good; ultimate Evil dominates the Second Galaxy in the form of the Eddorians, malign visitants from another continuum entirely. With the intersection of the two galaxies, or the Coalescence, as it is called, all the planets of both galaxies are created; and in the First Galaxy life as we know it, conveyed by Arisian spores, begins to evolve. From their paternal and nearly omniscient perspective, the Arisians see that there will be unremitting conflict between Good and Evil upon these planets, and so they begin to plan for the Eddorians' ultimate defeat by working behind the scenes to ensure the evolution of Civilization, whose main focus at the tense moment many centuries hence, when the saga proper begins, is the planet Tellus (Smith's usual term for Earth), where the Galactic Patrol has been the bastion of Good for some time; and the battle begins in earnest. The Eddorians, too, have long been conspiring behind the scenes, though without any knowledge of the Arisians, and in order to dominate the two galaxies, they have established a rigid and immense hierarchy of Boskonians, as all those unwittingly in thrall to Eddore are labeled by the forces of Good (though the layered immensity of Evil only gradually becomes clear from book to book).

Each level of the hierarchy is secretly controlled from the next level above, so that when Kinnison and his Patrol combat Helmuth of Kalonia in *Galactic Patrol*, they do not discover until the next volume of the saga (*Gray Lensman*, 1939–1940, *Astounding Science-Fiction*; 1951, book form) that Helmuth is a small fry in the vast hierarchy of Evil, and is under the control of the Eich of Jarnevon. Helmuth and the Eich are in turn (*Second Stage Lensmen*, 1941–1942, *Astounding Science-Fiction*; 1953, book form) controlled by the Thrale-Onlonian Empire, which itself is controlled (*Children of the Lens*, 1947–1948, *Astounding Science-Fiction*; 1954, book form) by the Ploor. It is only the Ploor, aside from the Arisians and the Children of the Lens, who ever have any inkling of the existence of Eddore itself.

Infiltrating this general framework are two further hierarchical pyramids, both of them benevolent. For eons on Tellus, the Arisians have been conducting a program in eugenics, designed to breed humans capable of combating Eddore directly. The mating of Kimball Kinnison and Clarissa MacDougal—both of them, rather unfortunately for today's taste in these matters, flamboyantly Aryan—brings forth the five Children of the Lens, who represent Tellus' highest evolutionary potential, the top of the human pyramid; it is the Children who ultimately expunge the Eddorians.

The second hierarchical device is the Lens itself, bestowed upon exceptional members of the Patrol by Mentor of Arisia; each Lens is a quasi-sentient, telepathic device precisely attuned to its wearer, upon whom it bestows super powers. A few selected Lensmen become Gray Lensmen, free agents for Good. Even fewer in number are those Gray Lensmen who, like Kinnison, become Second Stage Lensmen as the scale of the conflict broadens immeasurably. As the first of the Second Stage Lensmen, Kinnison has powers, extending through vast reaches of the First Galaxy, as dictatorially immense as Richard Seaton's were—but Kinnison is licensed.

The careful hierarchical structuring, and the massiveness of the enterprise, make the Lensman series the high point not only of Smith's career but of space opera in general. Like most genuinely important inventions, in fiction as elsewhere, it seems perfectly obvious once demonstrated; but for the science fiction readership of the time, each new volume must have seemed almost dizzyingly to redefine the sense of wonder. It is a measure of Smith's care in the construction of his universe that he reportedly conceived of the central four Lensman volumes as a single 400,000-word novel, and broke it down into separate titles only for publication.

II

The remainder of Smith's career was relatively aimless. After his period in publishing limbo, he released a few further novels. *The Galaxy Primes* (1959, *Amazing Stories*; 1965, book form) and *Subspace Explorers*, 1965 (as "Subspace Survivors" in *Astounding Science-Fiction*, 1960) are of little interest. At the end of his life, though, he returned to his first series with *Skylark DuQuesne* (1965, *Worlds of If*; 1966, book form).

Unfortunately, *Skylark DuQuesne* is a shambles. The ramshackle Skylark universe cannot be sustained plausibly, and the moral viciousness of the action, in which genocide is extended to the utter destruction of life on billions of planets, becomes at the same time surreal and loathsome, going far to justify the strictures against Smith's racial and political leanings implied in Norman Spinrad's *The Iron Dream* (1972). In any case, wish fulfillment must be sustained by invention and momentum, or it becomes a form of mere griping. But the surly chaos of *Skylark DuQuesne* should not stand as the last word on its author. If one returns to *The Skylark of Space*, whose ancestry is the Western (or, more specifically, Edward Sylvester Ellis' *The Steam Man of the Prairies* [1865] and its innumerable dime novel successors), then one can perhaps re-experience the magic irresponsibility of Richard Seaton's boy-Edison romp through space, long before the days of *Mein Kampf*. When, as easy as pie, he discovers a new source of "intra-atomic" energy, builds a spaceship, and scoots off to the stars with his pals, it is as though we were all playing hooky. Everything is shiny new in space. Everything—and everyone—seems to be covered with jewels, as in L. Frank Baum's land of Oz. Toy villains bite the dust. A magic brain-transfer machine gives free knowledge. The Force—Smith uses this actual term—is with them. And the Territory is immense; where the cultures they run across and dominate are Ruritanian in decor (though totalitarian in organization), the universe is scaled to create awe in 1920. It feels vast. The universe of Smith has a tangible, kinetic hugeness to it. The Skylarkers feel it, and we feel it still. And finally, it is what we remember Smith for. He gave us size.

Selected Bibliography

WORKS OF E. E. SMITH

Magazine and book versions of Smith's works almost invariably differ. A few book/magazine citations not listed in the text can be found here.

The Skylark of Space, with Lee Hawkins Garby. Providence, R.I.: Buffalo Book Company, 1946. Revised and published under Smith's name alone. New York: Pyramid Books, 1958.

Spacehounds of IPC. Reading, Pa.: Fantasy Press, 1947.

Skylark Three. Reading, Pa.: Fantasy Press, 1948.

Triplanetary. Reading, Pa.: Fantasy Press, 1948. (Magazine version comprises section rewritten as pages 103–287 book edition.)

Skylark of Valeron. Reading, Pa.: Fantasy Press, 1949.

First Lensman. Reading, Pa.: Fantasy Press, 1950.

Galactic Patrol. Reading, Pa.: Fantasy Press, 1950.

Gray Lensman. Reading, Pa.: Fantasy Press, 1951.

Second Stage Lensmen. Reading, Pa.: Fantasy Press, 1953

Children of the Lens. Reading, Pa.: Fantasy Press, 1954.

The Vortex Blaster. Hicksville, N.Y.: Gnome Press, 1960 Reprinted as *Masters of the Vortex*. New York: Pyramid Books, 1968. (First published as a sequence of stories, 1941–1942, one in *Comet* and the others in *As tonishing Stories*.)

The Galaxy Primes. New York: Ace Books, 1965.

Subspace Explorers. New York: Canaveral Press, 1965.

Skylark DuQuesne. New York: Pyramid Books, 1966.

The Best of E. E. Doc Smith. London: Futura Publications, 1975. (Collection of stories, including an ex-cerpt from the 1958 edition of *The Skylark of Space*, with a short bibliography.)

The Imperial Stars. New York: Pyramid Books, 1976. London: Panther, 1976. (A short version, with the same title, appeared in *Worlds of If Science Fiction*, 1964. The full version is an enlargement/completion by Stephen Goldin. Six or more additional novels about the family D'Alembert, under the names of E. E. Smith and Stephen Goldin, are by Goldin.)

Masters of Space. London: Futura Publications, 1976. (First published in *Worlds of If Science Fiction*, 1961–1962, as a collaboration with E. Everett Evans, who is not credited in the first book edition.)

CRITICAL AND BIOGRAPHICAL STUDIES

Asimov, Isaac. "Five Greats of Science Fiction." In his *The Tyrannosaurus Prescription and 100 Other Essays*. Buffalo, N.Y.: Prometheus, 1989.

Ellik, Ron, and Bill Evans. *The Universes of E. E. Smith*. Chicago: Advent Publishers, 1966.

Sanders, Joe. *E. E. 'Doc' Smith*. Mercer Island, Wash.: Starmont, 1986.

—JOHN CLUTE

OLAF STAPLEDON
(1886–1950)

THERE IS A growing consensus among science fiction critics and scholars that novelist-philosopher Olaf Stapledon is one of the most important writers in science fiction since H. G. Wells. Stapledon often has been referred to as Wells's heir and as one of the fathers of modern science fiction. In view of Stapledon's power of imagination, rigor of thought, and originality of concept, such claims would indeed be difficult to refute. Yet as recently as 1975, Curtis C. Smith noted that both neglect and influence continue to constitute the treatment of Stapledon's writings.

This seeming contradiction stems from the fact that Stapledon has not yet found a wide readership, although his novels are admired by many other science fiction novelists and by a number of discriminating readers. At second hand his ideas have reached a wide audience through his influence on such important science fiction writers as Clifford D. Simak, Theodore Sturgeon, Cordwainer Smith, Arthur C. Clarke, Stanislaw Lem, George Zebrowski, and Ursula K. Le Guin. In his introduction to the omnibus volume *To the End of Time* (1953)—a reprint of five Stapledon novels—Basil Davenport called Stapledon "one of the few truly creative intelligences that have ever tried the medium." In the back-cover copy of the 1968 Dover reprint of *Last and First Men and Star Maker*, E. F. Bleiler judged Stapledon to be "profound in thought, incredibly imaginative, [and] often prophetic. . . ." Sam Moskowitz, in his fine survey of Stapledon and his writings in *Explorers of the Infi-*

nite (1963), described Stapledon as having "the most titanic imagination ever brought to science fiction." Moskowitz dates the beginning of modern science fiction to the appearance of Stapledon's first novel, *Last and First Men*, in 1930. And Curtis C. Smith referred to Stapledon's novels as "unequalled and standing alone, despite their slowly widening influence."

Yet such praise does not simply reflect belated, posthumous approval withheld from Stapledon during his lifetime, for his singular excellence was recognized at once by contemporary writers and critics. Novelist Arnold Bennett said that Stapledon's *Last and First Men* reflected a tremendous and beautiful imagination. Another contemporary novelist, Hugh Walpole, creator of the popular Rogue Herries saga novels, called Stapledon's first novel a work as original as the solar system itself; and J. B. Priestley thought it a masterpiece, the best of its kind.

Such simultaneous neglect and influence may be explained in several ways. First, as a writer and as a thinker, Stapledon undoubtedly was ahead of his time. His literary concepts and fictional techniques—what he called fantastic fiction of a semiphilosophical kind—defy traditional literary classification. Some of his novels are not shaped by conventional actions about specific individuals who are confronted by conflicts that must be resolved within a fixed time scheme. Rather, they are philosophical epics, cosmic macrohistories, or mythic panoramas about the fates of countless life forms struggling, evolving, rising, declining, reappearing, and mutating during limitless eons of time throughout the entire cosmos. Such scope and such magnitude tend to overwhelm both conventional novel forms and traditional fictional theories. Like Albert Camus and Jean-Paul Sartre, Stapledon is an imaginative, philosophical writer who uses fiction to dramatize his philosophic beliefs.

With respect to scope, to structure, and to philosophic direction, Stapledon's cosmic trilogy—*Last and First Men* (1930), *Last Men in London* (1932), and *Star Maker* (1937)—resembles Sartre's historical-philosophic trilogy of novels, *Roads to Freedom—The Age of Reason* (1945), *The Reprieve* (1945), and *Troubled Sleep* (1949). In addition to his unorthodox literary form and rigorous philosophic substance, Stapledon's iconoclastic political beliefs may have contributed to limiting the size of his audience. As Curtis C. Smith argues, Stapledon belongs to a group of writers labeled as heretics who "accept no ideas on faith, who belong to no party, and who harass and trouble anyone wedded to orthodoxy." Lastly, Stapledon did not actively pursue popular acclaim. He eschewed gadgetry. He did not employ mere sensationalism for its own sake, and he refused to write escapist fantasies based on simple-minded mysticism.

Stapledon's fictional career spanned twenty years. His first novel, *Last and First Men*, appeared in 1930; his last completed novel, *A Man Divided*, was published in 1950. He also wrote the following works of fiction: *Odd John* (1935), *Darkness and the Light* (1942), *Old Man in New World* (1944), *Sirius* (1944), *Death into Life* (1946), and *The Flames* (1947). A posthumous work is *Nebula Maker* (1976), an early draft of *Star Maker* put aside sometime during the mid-1930's. *Far Future Calling* (1979) is a collection of five short stories, a play, and a speech to the British Interplanetary Society.

In addition to these fictional works, Stapledon wrote a volume of verse entitled *Latter-Day Psalms* (1914). He also published eight philosophical works during his lifetime: *A Modern Theory of Ethics* (1929), *Waking World* (1934), *Philosophy and Living* (1939), *New Hope for Britain* (1939), *Saints and Revolutionaries* (1939), *Beyond the "Isms"* (1942), *The Seven Pillars of Peace* (1944), and *Youth and Tomorrow* (1946). The posthumously published *Four Encounters* (1976) completes the corpus of Stapledon's philosophical works.

I

William Olaf Stapledon was born in the Wirral region near Liverpool, England, on 10 May 1886. Despite the Scandinavian sound of the name Olaf, he was of English parentage and background. At the time of his birth, his parents were reading Thomas Carlyle's *Early Kings of Norway*, so Stapledon was named after one of the monarchs described in it. Most of Stapledon's childhood was spent at Suez, where his family was engaged in the shipping business. He was educated at Abbotsholme Public School and then entered Balliol College, Oxford, where he received both B.A. and M.A. degrees. He taught for a year at Manchester Grammar School, a year he later modestly described as one spent with much nervous strain and little success.

Stapledon next entered business, working first in a Liverpool shipping office and later in a family-owned shipping agency at Port Said. His personal knowledge of the exotic locale of Port Said was used later in his novel *Odd John*, in which he described it as "the most cosmopolitan spot in all the world . . . [filled with] scores of races, scores of languages, scores of religions and cultures jostled one [upon] another in that most flagrantly mongrel town." Port Said was also used in his *A Man Divided*.

While in Liverpool, Stapledon lectured to evening tutorial classes in history and English literature for the Workers' Educational Association under the auspices of the University of Liverpool. During World War I, Stapledon, who was a pacifist, served from 1915 to 1918 with the Friends' Ambulance Unit in a motor convoy attached to a division of the French army. Following the war's end he married Agnes Zena Miller, an Australian woman whom he had courted for twelve years. They had a son and a daughter.

Soon after his marriage Stapledon returned to Liverpool, where he continued to lecture for the Workers' Educational Association. He also studied philosophy and psychology at the University of Liverpool, where he received his Ph.D. in philosophy. After taking his doctorate, he continued to lecture at Liverpool University for a brief time, but then withdrew to concentrate on writing.

Stapledon's first published work was a slim, privately printed volume of verse entitled *Latter-Day Psalms*. It is of interest because it represents the first appearance of important ideas central to his later philosophical and science fiction works. One such theme is the moral irrelevance of a theology centered on the expectation of immortality. Also important is Stapledon's poetic description of a creative principle that evolves through time by experience. Such a figure greatly resembles the evolving God described in his novel *Star Maker*.

Stapledon's next book, *A Modern Theory of Ethics*, is also important as a source for ideas central to his science fiction. In his description of Stapledon and his writings in *the Science Fiction Encyclopedia* (1979), Mark Adlard identifies a number of important themes: "moral obligation as a teleological requirement; ecstasy as a cognitive intuition of cosmic excellence; personal fulfilment of individual capacities as an intrinsic good; community as a necessary prerequisite for individual fulfilment; and the hopeless inadequacy of human faculties for the discovery of truth." It is this last notion, Adlard argues, that most directly concerned Stapledon in his science fiction writing; for in each novel he wrote, the issue seems to be the anguished attempts of the characters to overcome the limitations of normal human intelligence and perception.

In Stapledon's other political and philosophic books, some indication of his devel-

Olaf Stapledon. COURTESY OF UPI/CORBIS-BETTMANN

opment as a thinker and social critic can be seen. *Waking World* shows his debt to Wells's social theories. In it Stapledon criticizes capitalism as a self-destructive, wasteful, and decadent economic system. As such, he argues, it ought to be replaced by a more humane and rational production system of a socialist type. Although Stapledon deplores violence, he is realistic enough to recognize that only through some form of social revolution can capitalism be replaced. In his next book, *Philosophy and Living*, Stapledon's philosophical views appear in their most comprehensive and elaborate form.

But for the general reader Stapledon's closing chapter in *Beyond the "Isms"* more clearly presents such important concepts appearing in his science fiction as spiritual crisis, spirit, and community. *Beyond the "Isms"* is particularly helpful in defining Stapledon's often-used phrase "the way of the spirit."

In it Stapledon discusses the major religious and political movements of his day. From this examination he asserts that a better life in the future can come about only through development of a new spirit that combines sensitive and intelligent awareness with greater love and creative action. Such a spirit would lead to the achievement of a new "personality-in-community."

New Hope for Britain is a well-measured philosophic discussion advocating direct political action to usher in an age of socialism in England. Such an age would be the first step in a larger program for creating a world state. *Saints and Revolutionaries* compares and contrasts historical figures traditionally depicted as saints or revolutionaries, or both. This work was one of the *I Believe* series written by such well-known authors as J. D. Beresford, Charles Williams, Gerald Bullett, and Kenneth Ingram as expressions of personal belief. In *Saints and Revolutionaries* Stapledon argues that in the future humanity may create its God-image only by achieving the "cosmic mind" level of awareness.

Youth and Tomorrow is in part autobiographical, describing Stapledon's childhood memories of Suez, and in part philosophical. In it he restates his earlier notions about human development through personality-in-community and argues that humanity's ultimate hope lies in the biological improvement of the species. Transcribed from Stapledon's notes after his death, *The Opening of the Eyes* suggests that his long-term inner conflicts about religion and politics were resolved before his death. In this incomplete work he claims that it is far better to accept even the pretense of God's reality than to believe in stark nothingness. He also renounces collective revolutionary action, arguing that the only real progress toward social justice is made through each individual's independent growth toward enlightenment.

In Stapledon's fictional works the range of topics is both wide and richly imaginative. In *Last and First Men*, Stapledon describes the history of humanity from the close of World War I to some 2 billion years into the future. We follow mankind's agonizingly slow development on Earth, witness its forced migration to Venus, and observe its final brilliant days on Neptune. *Last Men in London*, to some extent, is a continuation of several themes introduced in Stapledon's first novel. In it, the narrator is a member of the last human civilization on Neptune, a brilliant utopian social order ruled by pure intelligence. But much of the story focuses on the growth and maturation of an artistically sensitive, somewhat neurotic young man in modern London. We are provided thereby not only with a detailed account of human life, social system, manners, and intellectual progress on Neptune, but also with commentary on the contemporary world.

The struggles of a supernormal human mutant are the subject of *Odd John*. In *Star Maker*, Stapledon depicts the history of the entire cosmos and more, covering more than 100 billion years. We observe not only the rise, maturation, and decline of countless diverse life forms on numberless planets and millions of galaxies, but also the creation and history of the entire cosmos, as one in a long series of progressively more mature cosmos. *Darkness and the Light*, another future history, describes two different worlds and two possible futures for man—depending on whether the forces of darkness or of light succeed. Central is the theme of superhuman development achieved through artificial life or mutation in which spirit overcomes animal and tribal instincts. Stapledon's short work *Old Man in New World* dramatizes some of the notions found in *Saints and Revolutionaries*. In *Old Man*, a group of intellectuals stages a strike on the eve of World War III, causing drastic policy changes in Russia and a revolution in America. Out of these events a world state is created that achieves a utopian social order. *Sirius*, a complementary novel to *Odd John*, features the adventures of a supernormal mutant dog with human intelligence who struggles to find meaning in his life.

In his narrative prose poem *Death into Life*, Stapledon describes the deaths of a bomber crew flying over Germany during World War II. Told from the viewpoint of the tail gunner as he dies, Stapledon's narrative moves from communication among the dead crew members to a mystical communion with the Spirit of Man. *The Flames*, a novella, treats contact between a psychically sensitive but insane human being and a race of flame creatures from the sun's surface. These supernormal flames have survived on Earth for ages inside igneous rocks. Now they want humans to assist them in creating a special colony on Earth around a radioactive belt near the equator. And Stapledon's last novel, *A Man Divided*, features a man with a split personality who alternates between intellectual brilliance and commonplace thinking. Much of this work is autobiographical in content, recounting scenes from Stapledon's life between 1912 and 1948.

During the war years, Stapledon concentrated on writing fiction and publishing articles on ethics and philosophy. Following the war, he became active in the world peace movement. In 1949 Stapledon attended the Conference for World Peace sponsored by the National Council of the Arts, Sciences, and Professions, which was held in New York at the United Nations. He was the only member of the British delegation given a visa by the United States Embassy; he was admitted despite State Department claims that the conference was a propaganda event staged by the Communists. At this conference Stapledon's speech warned that man would probably tamper with the atom until he destroyed himself. He also predicted that if man lived long enough, he might gain new freedom by traveling beyond Earth to explore the whole solar system. At the final session of the conference, Stapledon told an audience of 18,000 people at Madison Square Garden that if Britain were drawn into another war, America should not expect her to fight wholeheartedly as "We have a new Britain, we are not what we used to be." On 6 September 1950 Stapledon died at his home in Cheshire, England. He was sixty-four.

II

Among Stapledon's novels, four stand out as superior to the rest: *Last and First Men, Star Maker, Odd John*, and *Sirius*. All four are unified by a coherent informing philosophy. Seen from the view of content and literary construction, they complement each other. In terms of subject, *Odd John* and *Sirius* are companion novels, showing through parallel development the problems faced by two supernormal mutants—one a man, the other a dog. The relationship between Stapledon's two great future histories, *Last and First Men* and *Star Maker*, is far more complex. For example, the human narrator in *Star Maker* raises two important questions before he begins his cosmic pilgrimage. By what means, he asks, should mankind progress, particularly with respect to overcoming its present spiritual crisis? And if progress can be made toward a fuller notion of humanity, is such progress meaningful when contrasted with mankind's brief, self-tortured tenure in this world? From the short view, Stapledon's narrator refers mainly to those forces, clearly evident when the novel was written, that by 1939 would engulf much of the world in war; but Stapledon also intends these questions to be understood in the broader context of the totality of human history. The answers to both questions shape not only *Star Maker* but also give clear meaning to *Last and First Men*.

In *Last and First Men*—that vast chronicle of mankind's 2-billion-year history on Earth, Venus, and ultimately Neptune, described from the cultural perspective of eighteen progressively but haltingly more advanced species of humanity—Stapledon presents a fairly straightforward thesis about human progress. No significant movement toward full humanity can occur until mankind undergoes significant biological—not just spiritual—modification. Humanity's tribalism, its self-destructive individualism, and its lockstep collective social organizations are doomed from the start by its biological limitations. The modification Stapledon has in mind, whether achieved naturally through evolutionary mutation or artificially by genetic engineering, must begin by removing the limits to human intellect and moral insight.

But larger brains and stronger bodies are not necessarily the way to a fuller humanity. As a first step toward greater human awareness, some manipulation of the brain is necessary to develop telepathic communication among all people. Greater human sympathy and understanding, achieved by better psychological communication, will ultimately lead to the creation of a group mind. But such a group mind must not eliminate the differences among individuals, as seen in the Martian group mind, but must enrich the collective consciousness while preserving each member's unique individuality. At best each individual partakes of the cultural, or collective, mind of the species.

Through this spiritual multiplication of mental diversity, the subhuman instinct for tribal nationalism, for destructive individualism, and for debased collectivism becomes impossible. Waking to full potential, mankind can aspire to utopia and to both superindividuality and community with the great collective host. Although humanity may temporarily strive for utopia, banish hunger, eliminate disease, end class conflict, and prevent economic disaster, any hope for an awakened sense of community without biological modification will always end in failure.

Such a controlling thesis explains the continual rise and fall of one human civilization and/or species after another in *Last and First Men*. Aside from the ferocity of natural forces, cosmic accidents, and foreign invasions, mankind always is undone by its own biological contradictions. Stapledon's panorama of mankind's future is structured around a well-wrought historical myth. His novel is divided into two distinct phases of historical development: phases based on mankind before and after biological modification. The first phase describes a cyclical movement in human culture embracing recognizable subdivisions—primitive subhuman savagery, agricultural tribalism, medieval mercantilism, nation-state industrialism, and some attempt to achieve a unified world-state.

Passing from the nation-state to the world-state phase inevitably brings about what Stapledon calls a "social and spiritual crisis." This is because the societal forces precipitating this crisis essentially stem from the limits imposed on man by his own biological backwardness. Conflicts between individualism and collectivism, between capitalism and socialism, between tribalism and cosmopolitanism, between behaviorism and spiritism, and between nationalism and world-statism cannot be bridged by the will of a minority whose intellect and moral insight outrun the biological retardation of the majority. Failure to undertake biological modification at the point where human civilization has both the technology and the leisure to alter human biology always leads to self-destruction. Such stagnant societies, failing to evolve to a higher stage of human awareness, regress into savagery or destroy themselves by worldwide holocaust.

The most telling dramatization of this social and spiritual crisis in the novel is the extended account of contemporary humanity—of the specific period in the history of First Men (*Homo sapiens*) when American hegemony triumphs throughout the world. Perhaps no European writer since Alexis de Tocqueville has so well understood the main currents of American thought as did Stapledon. The realism of his depiction made Stapledon fear some American displeasure. In the foreword to the original American edition, he admitted that in the early chapters of his book America is "given a not very attractive part."

Stapledon imagined the triumph of what he called the cruder sort of Americanism over all that is best and most promising in American life. While hoping that this cruder strain would not succeed, the possibility that it might was admitted, Stapledon claimed, by many thoughtful American citizens. In these chapters America professes to have outgrown nationalism and to stand for political and cultural world unity. But such world unity is in reality a unity under American hegemony.

The cultural unity in society stems from the fact that Americanism dominates other cultural traditions. Despised by the rest of the world, America nevertheless remolds the human species in its own image. Stapledon's narrator claims that such an event would not really have mattered, had America given her very best, but:

> ... inevitably only her worst could be propagated. Only the most vulgar traits of that potentially great people could get through into the minds of foreigners by means of these crude instruments. And so, by the floods of poison issuing from this people's baser members, the whole world and with it the nobler parts of America herself, were irrevocably corrupted. (*Last and First Man/Star Maker*, 1968, page 33)

This "bright race of arrested adolescents," given the gifts to rejuvenate the planet, instead plunges it through spiritual desolation into senility and age-long night. Great wealth and bustling industry become concentrated upon ever more puerile ends. American life is organized around the cult of the powerful individual. Only wealth has the power to set things and people in motion. In fact, wealth came:

> ... to be frankly regarded as the breath of God, the divine spirit immanent in man. God was the supreme Boss, the universal Employer. His wisdom was conceived as a stupendous efficiency, his love as munificence towards his employees.... The typical American man of big business was one who, in the midst of a show of luxury, was at heart ascetic. He valued his splendour only because it advertised to all men that he was of the [spiritual] elect. (*ibid.*, page 44)

A cult of activity—any kind of activity for the mere sake of activity—comes to dominate American life. God, according to this doctrine, appointed the great American people to conquer and to mechanize the universe. Such wrong-headed tribal lust for power propels the world into its first worldwide holocaust.

But in contrast to our own, a few future societies do achieve a higher level of human awareness. They do so because they succeed in modifying human biology and thus pass beyond spiritual crisis. Yet in the second phase of Stapledon's historical myth, not all advanced societies create perfect utopias or maintain a vital sense of human community. In this second phase the direction of human progress is as uncertain as it is in the first. Mistakes in genetic engineering, the failure to strike a proper balance between brain and body, and between intellect and feeling, cause many of these civilizations to destroy themselves or to decline in vitality and to lose full human awareness. For example, Fifth Man's guilt, his loss of intellectual self-confidence, and his despair at not finding a scientific solution to the moon's impending approach undermine his social order. Even when the proper balance is found and maintained in human psychology, as in the tragic case of Eighteenth Man, progress may be cut short by natural catastrophe. This sad end to some 2 billion years of human struggle to realize its full potential raises the question of whether striving for progress is worth the human price.

The youngest of the Last Men articulates Stapledon's other shaping notion in the novel: Humanity's fluctuating progress toward harmonious complexity of form and toward the awakening of the spirit into unity, knowledge, delight, and self-expression is the proper goal of all human effort—even in the face of an uncertain future. As individuals, the Last Man asserts, we "earnestly desire that the eternal being of things may include this supreme awakening." For nothing less than this has been the goal of practical religious life and active social policy.

The Last Man sees the career of humanity in its successive planetary homes as a process of very great beauty. As individuals, humans regard the entire cosmic adventure as a symphony in progress, which may or may not achieve its just conclusion. Like a work of music, the vast biography of the stars is to be judged not solely by its final moment, but by the perfection of its whole form. But one thing is certain:

Man himself, at the very least, is music, a brave theme that makes music also of its vast accompaniment, its matrix of storms and stars. Man himself in his degree is eternally a beauty in the eternal form of things. It is very good to have been man. And so we may go forward together with laughter in our hearts, and peace, thankful for the past, and for our own courage. For we shall make after all a fair conclusion to this brief music that is man. (*ibid.*, page 246)

This passage, which ends *Last and First Men*, is important not only as a reaffirmation of human struggle against an uncertain future, but also as one of the novel's central, controlling metaphors. Throughout *Last and First Men* we are told that the history of mankind is like a great musical symphony. Each of humanity's civilizations represents a movement in this symphony, and the totality of human existence is only a smaller theme in a larger, cosmic music of the spheres.

This notion becomes both the connecting complementary link with *Star Maker* and, in turn, *Star Maker's* controlling metaphor. (In the short story "A World of Sound," Stapledon postulates a kind of telepathic music as the ultimate art form, as the ultimate form of sentience.) In addition, the questions shaping *Last and First Men*—how do we progress toward a fuller notion of humanity, and is such a struggle meaningful in an uncertain universe?—reappear in *Star Maker* but are restated on a far greater cosmic canvas. Unlike its complement, *Star Maker* follows the progress not only of human creatures but of all life in the cosmos. The human narrator, a contemporary Englishman, is swept up into the cosmos, where he proceeds on his pilgrimage-quest, searching for the meaning of life and for the creative principle behind all life in the cosmos.

Star Maker's narrative is structured around the human narrator's growing capacity to appreciate and to sympathize with unfamiliar life forms. The greater his sympathy, the greater the magnitude of his travels, in terms of time as well as distance. His first visit is to a planet similar to Earth, called Other Earth. Here the narrator telepathically shares the thoughts of the planet's inhabitants. These people, called Other Men, reproduce a tragically familiar world dominated by destructive individualism, heartless industrialism, and mindless tribal nationalism. Significant on Other Earth is a debilitating prejudice based on taste. Some races taste superior to others; violent arguments take place about what God tastes like. The narrator meets a wise philosopher named Bvalltu, who later joins him on his pilgrimage through the cosmos. Bvalltu makes possible contact with still other races, thus radically extending the scope of the narrator's journey.

Star Maker is shaped by the same historical and moral thesis found in *Last and First Men*. We see myriad creatures in *Star Maker*—echinoderms, nautiloids, ichthyoids, arachnoids, bird composites, insectoids, mobile superherbs, and plantmen—who reenact the same form of spiritual crisis seen on Earth. Again and again various races throughout the cosmos rise from savagery and pass through barbaric culture into a phase of worldwide brilliance and sensibility. Entire populations achieve an ever-increasing capacity for generosity, self-knowledge, self-discipline, for dispassionate and penetrating thought and uncontaminated religious feeling.

But in time a general decline undermines even the most advanced societies. Where societies once were free and happy, where unprecedented mental clarity did away with all social injustices and private cruelties, later generations become less sincere, less self-searching, less sensitive to others, and less capable of community. Societies that once worked well are dislocated by injustice and corruption. Dictators and tyrannical oligarchies destroy liberty. Gradually the material benefits of civilization disappear; the entire culture reverts to barbarism, followed by protracted periods of subhuman savagery. Where earlier in this spiritual progression through time and space, the human narrator believed human history was shaped by a progressive improvement in the species and by a gradual awakening of the human spirit, he now sees cosmic proof against any such theory. He laments the horror that:

> . . . all struggle should be finally, absolutely vain, that a whole world of sensitive spirits fail and die, must be sheer evil. In my horror it seemed to me that Hate must be the Star Maker. (*ibid.*, page 291)

Eventually the narrator confronts the Star Maker, the elemental creative force in the cosmos. The Star Maker appears as a bright, blinding star who evolves to greater and greater insight by learning from his past experiences. We observe his detached and disinterested spirit as he creates progressively more brilliant and more complex stars, galaxies, and entire cosmos. The narrator sees the Star Maker and his creations as good, but he laments humanity's brief and tragic existence in the Star Maker's newly created worlds.

Despite such human misery, the narrator sees that had the Star Maker intervened and given mankind a carefree life and made the cosmos infinite, he would have disrupted their essential beauty. For their distinct virtues stem from their finitude and minute particularity, which maintain a tortured balance between dullness and lucidity. The narrator recognizes that even if the creator's primary motivating spirit is contemplative rather than loving or benign, he and his creative acts are good. He comes to understand these insights in a dream in which the Star Maker creates the Ultimate Cosmos, seen as the culmination of a vast cycle of many, many cosmos. But when the narrator awakes, he finds himself back on Earth, in the present. His final thought is that in the face of humanity's uncertain future and possible defeat in his own half-waking world, the coming human crisis

> . . . does not lose but gains significance. Strange, that it seems more, not less, urgent to play some part in this struggle, this brief effort of animalcules striving to win for their race some increase of lucidity before the ultimate darkness. (*ibid.*, page 434)

Set in England and, later, on an unnamed island in the South Pacific, *Odd John* is a philosophic fantasy that describes how John Wainwright, a supernormal human mutant, comes to terms with his unique intellectual gifts. Yet from the start both his intellect and his physical appearance—he has a thin, spiderish body with large, sinewy hands; a large head covered with closely cropped white, wool-like hair; a broad, Negroid nose set in a Mongolian-shaped face; and a pair of large, greenish eyes nearly devoid of pupils—mark him as a subject of great curiosity. John early understands that his future rests in finding other supernormals like himself and, with them, establishing a colony somewhere away from normal humans. Most of the novel's action—told from the sympathetic viewpoint of a normal, middle-aged human journalist called "Fido, old thing" by John—depicts John's efforts to establish a colony where he and the others like him can create a social organization and a way of life that freely reflect their awakened sense of community.

But once the colony is established, it is the subject of curiosity among the great powers, whose contending policies soon lead to its destruction. Recognizing that the great powers intend to invade the island and arrest them, the members of John's community feel a fresh intensity of consciousness in all their personal relations and social activities. They see that the true purpose of the awakened spirit is to help in the practical task of building a new world, and that they should employ themselves, to the best of their capacities, in intelligent worship. In the time remaining, they strive to understand existence as precisely and as zestfully as they can. At one point they salute all in the universe that is of supreme excellence. Given a chance to preserve their utopian community through the use of superweapons, they refuse. Such slaughter, they recognize, would hopelessly ruin their awakened spirit. Adhering to its pacifist policy, the colony is overrun and destroyed.

In *Sirius*, Stapledon employs a number of recognizable themes found in *Odd John*, such as the love of life, even if life seems to be of no purpose; the necessity to confront reality squarely and to experience the ecstasy of the quickened spirit for its own sake; the pursuit of spirit-in-community; and the search for meaning in life. The central action describes how Professor Thomas Trelone crossbreeds a superior Alsatian–Great Dane pup by injecting a special hormone into the bloodstream of the pup's mother before she gives birth. This hormone reorganizes the pup's neural system, giving him the intellectual capacity of a human being. From the outset the pup, called Sirius, is handicapped by not possessing human hands, a disability that haunts him throughout his life. He learns to talk so that he can be understood by his creator.

Trelone vaguely resembles the cosmic creator in *Star Maker*, since he is contemplative and objective rather than loving and caring toward Sirius. Sirius is educated in Trelone's family along with Trelone's infant daughter, Plaxy. In time the relationship between Sirius and Plaxy moves toward an uneasy community-in-spirit. But this strange symbiosis is threatened by the instabilities in both their personalities and by the outside world's misunderstanding of their behavior. Sirius alternates between a lucid, thoughtful human intellect and a savage wolfishness brought on by his reactions to human cruelty as well as his ancestral instincts. Throughout the action, Sirius strives to bring these two attitudes into balance by discovering the true meaning of his life. But in the end he is destroyed by ignorant fanatics who think he is a Nazi spy and who question the nature of his sexuality. Yet, faced with an uncertain fate, Sirius tries to serve the spirit—to love, to give full expression to his intelligence, and to create. Yet his tragic death is inevitable. Sirius epitomizes in his life and in his death something universal, something that is common to all awakening spirits, on Earth and in the farthest galaxies. The music Sirius composes and his urge to live fully in the spirit illuminate the darkness that is seen by the quickened mind everywhere.

This quartet of Stapledon's major novels reflects the core of his philosophy and suggests both the diversity and the richness of his vast fictive imagination. The desire to express a heightened appreciation of life's beauty, to reaffirm the importance of the play of intellect, to argue the continuing significance of love as a shaping human force, and to urge us to seize the best expressions in the human spirit is no trifling world view. There is in Stapledon's tragic vision of man's bittersweet history, an ennobling effect, a catharsis of sorts. We are better for having shared his imaginative spirit. It is this particular power that makes Stapledon's writings endure. In science fiction he is a writer and thinker of the first magnitude whose influence and readership will continue to widen in the future.

Selected Bibliography

FICTION AND VERSE OF OLAF STAPLEDON

Latter-Day Psalms. Liverpool: Henry Young and Sons, 1914. (Verse.)
Last and First Men. London: Methuen, 1930.
Last Men in London. London: Methuen, 1932.
Odd John. London: Methuen, 1935.
Star Maker. London: Methuen, 1937.
Darkness and the Light. London: Methuen, 1942.
Old Man in New World. London: George Allen and Unwin, 1944.
Sirius. London: Secker and Warburg, 1944.
Death into Life. London: Methuen, 1946.
The Flames. London: Secker and Warburg, 1947.
A Man Divided. London: Methuen, 1950.
Last and First Man and Star Maker: Two Science Fiction Novels. New York: Dover Books, 1968.
Nebula Maker. Hayes, Middlesex: Bran's Head Books, 1976. (Early draft for *Star Maker.*)
Far Future Calling. Philadelphia: Oswald Train, 1979. (Contains five stories, a play, and a speech by Stapledon to the British Interplanetary Society, plus critical and biographical articles by Sam Moskowitz.)

NONFICTION OF OLAF STAPLEDON

A Modern Theory of Ethics: A Study of the Relations of Ethics and Psychology. London: Methuen, 1929.
Waking World. London: Methuen, 1934.
New Hope for Britain. London: Methuen, 1939.

Philosophy and Living. Harmondsworth, Middlesex: Penguin Books, 1939.

Saints and Revolutionaries. London: William Heinemann, 1939.

Beyond the "Isms." London: Secker and Warburg, 1942.

The Seven Pillars of Peace. London: Commonwealth, 1944. (Pamphlet.)

Youth and Tomorrow. London: St. Botolph, 1946.

The Opening of the Eyes. Edited by Agnes Stapledon. London: Methuen, 1954.

Four Encounters. Hayes, Middlesex: Bran's Head Books, 1976.

Letters of Olaf Stapledon and H. G. Wells, 1931–1942. Edited by Robert Crossley. In *Science Fiction Dialogues.* Edited by Gary Wolfe. Chicago: Academy Chicago, 1982.

Talking Across the World: The Love Letters of Olaf Stapledon and Agnes Miller, 1913–1919. Edited by Robert Crossley. Hanover, N.H.: University Press of New England, 1987.

CRITICAL AND BIOGRAPHICAL STUDIES

Adlard, Mark. "W. Olaf Stapledon," *The Science Fiction Encyclopedia.* Garden City, N.Y.: Doubleday, 1979.

Aldiss, Brian W. "Immanent Will Returns." In his *The Pale Shadow of Science.* Seattle, Wash.: Serconia, 1985.

———. "The Immanent Will Returns-2." In his *The Detached Retina: Aspects of SF and Fantasy.* Syracuse, N.Y.: Syracuse University Press, 1995.

Bailey, K. V. "Time Scales and Culture Cycles in Olaf Stapledon." *Foundation* (Autumn 1989): 27–39.

Crossley, Robert. "Censorship, Disguise, and Transfiguration: The Making and Revising of Stapledon's *Sirius.*" *Science-Fiction Studies,* 20, part 1 (1993): 1–14.

———. "Olaf Stapledon and the Idea of Science Fiction." *Modern Fiction Studies,* 32 (1986): 21–42.

———. *Olaf Stapledon: Speaking for the Future.* Syracuse, N.Y.: Syracuse University Press, 1994.

Davenport, Basil. "Introduction" of *To the End of Time* (omnibus volume of Stapledon's works). New York: Funk and Wagnalls, 1953.

Fiedler, Leslie A. *Olaf Stapledon: A Man Divided.* Oxford, England: Oxford University Press, 1983.

Goodheart, Eugene. "Olaf Stapledon's *Last and First Men.*" In *No Place Else.* Edited by Eric S. Rabkin, et al. Carbondale: Southern Illinois University Press, 1983.

Huntington, John. "Olaf Stapledon and the Novel About the Future." *Contemporary Literature,* 12 (1981): 349–365.

Kinnaird, John. *Olaf Stapledon.* Mercer Island, Wash.: Starmont, 1986.

Lavabre, Simone. "Un Utopiste au XXe Siècle, W. Olaf Stapledon." *Caliban,* 3, ii (1967): 96–114.

Lem, Stanisław. "On Stapledon's *Last and First Men.*" Translated by Istvan Csicsery-Ronay, Jr. *Science-Fiction Studies,* 13, part 3 (1986): 272–291.

———. "On Stapledon's *Star Maker.*" Translated by Istvan Csicsery-Ronay, Jr. *Science-Fiction Studies,* 14, part 1 (1987): 1–8.

McCarthy, Patrick A. *Olaf Stapledon.* Boston: Twayne, 1982.

———. "*Star Maker*: Olaf Stapledon's Divine Tragedy." *Science-Fiction Studies,* 8, part 3 (1981): 266–279.

———; Charles Elkins; and Martin Harry Greenberg. *The Legacy of Olaf Stapledon: Critical Essays and an Unpublished Manuscript.* Westport, Conn.: Greenwood, 1989.

Moskowitz, Sam. *Explorers of the Infinite.* Cleveland, Ohio: World Publishing Company, 1963. (Chapter 16 features an appraisal of Stapledon.)

———. "Introduction," "Olaf Stapledon: The Man Behind the Works," and "Peace and Olaf Stapledon." In *Far Future Calling.* Philadelphia, Pa.: Oswald Train, 1979.

"Olaf Stapledon." In *Saturday Review of Literature,* 18 (July 1936). (Unsigned book review.)

Science-Fiction Studies, 9, part 3 (1982): 235–321. (Special Olaf Stapledon issue with eight critical essays on the author's work.)

Shelton, Robert. "The Mars-Begotten Men of Olaf Stapledon and H. G. Wells." *Science-Fiction Studies,* 11, part 1 (1984): 1–14.

Smith, Curtis C. "Horror Versus Tragedy: Mary Shelley's *Frankenstein* and Olaf Stapledon's *Sirius.*" *Extrapolation,* 26, no. 1 (1985): 66–73.

———. "Olaf Stapledon and the Immortal Spirit." In *Death and the Serpent.* Edited by C. B. Yoke and D. M. Hassler. Westport, Conn.: Greenwood, 1985.

———. "Olaf Stapledon: Saint and Revolutionary," *Extrapolation,* 13 (1975): 5–15.

———. "Olaf Stapledon's Dispassionate Objectivity." In *Voices for the Future: Essays on Major Science Fiction Writers.* Thomas D. Clareson, ed. Bowling Green, Ohio: Bowling Green University Popular Press, 1976.

———. "Olaf Stapledon Zukunfts—Historien und Tragödien." In *Science Fiction: Theorie und Geschichte.* Edited by Eike Barmeyer. Munich: Fisk Verlag, 1976.

———, and H. J. Satty. *Olaf Stapledon: A Bibliography.* Westport, Conn.: Greenwood, 1984.

Tremaine, Louis. "Historical Consciousness in Stapledon and Malraux." *Science-Fiction Studies,* 11, part 2 (1984): 130–138.

———. "Olaf Stapledon's Note on Magnitude." *Extrapolation,* 23, no. 3 (1982): 243–253.

Waugh, Robert H. "Spirals and Metaphors: The Shape of Divinity in Olaf Stapledon's Myth." *Extrapolation,* 38, no. 3 (1997): 207–221.

—JAMES L. CAMPBELL, SR.

BRUCE STERLING
(b. 1954)

MICHAEL BRUCE STERLING was born in Brownsville, Texas, on 14 April 1954. His parents moved to the Gulf Coast when he was three, and he lived in various coastal refinery towns until he was 15. His father, a mechanical engineer, then obtained work in India, and Sterling spent a good deal of the following two-and-a-half years in various Far Eastern locations. He completed his formal education at his father's alma mater, the University of Texas, Austin, graduating in 1976 with a B.A. in journalism. He married Nancy Baxter in 1979.

Sterling's first science fiction story, "Man-Made Self," appeared—somewhat mangled by the printer—in *Lone Star Universe* (1976), an anthology of Texan science fiction edited by George W. Proctor and Steven Utley. That anthology was introduced by Harlan Ellison, who was later to issue Sterling's first novel, *Involution Ocean* (1978 but dated 1977) in the short-lived "Harlan Ellison Discovery Series." Ellison explained in his introduction to the latter volume that in 1974, when he was a guest at one of the "Turkey City Workshops" in which Sterling regularly took part, he had also bought the first story Sterling ever sold. Unfortunately, he bought it for *The Last Dangerous Visions*, which has not yet seen print. In the intervening quarter-century Sterling has become one of the leading figures in the science fiction genre. He writes with admirable literary elegance and a fine wit; he is also a remarkably astute cultural commentator, second to none in his grasp of the keenness of the cutting edge of technological progress and the velocity with which that progress is likely to proceed. His passionate promotion of a new kind of science fiction adapted to a revolutionary new era in technology and popular culture enabled him to attain near-legendary status as the compiler of one of the key cultural products of the current fin de siècle, *Mirrorshades: The Cyberpunk Anthology* (1986).

Harlan Ellison's introduction to *Involution Ocean* records that the first version of the story was a novelette entitled "Moby Dust." The abandoned title acknowledges the story's formal debt to Herman Melville, although Ellison quotes the author's judgment that his principal influences in writing it were Clark Ashton Smith, Larry Niven, Samuel Taylor Coleridge, and Ellison himself. The novel is set on the colony world of Nullaqua, whose only habitable region lies at the bottom of a crater some five hundred miles across, in which 90 percent of the world's atmosphere is concentrated. This region consists of an "ocean" of extremely fine dust dotted with various island chains. The Nullaquan dust whale is the only known source of the psychotropic drug syncophine, also known as Flare. Because Flare has been proscribed, the descendants of the religious fanatics who first settled the world have done their best to put an end to an era in which dust-masked privateers sailed the Sea of Dust in great trimarans in search of the alien leviathans, but the opportunity still remains for a group of ill-assorted travelers to undertake one last great adventure. The novel's plot is an account of the mixed motives and various fortunes of the expeditionaries.

Sterling's attempt to marry the imaginative adventurism of Clark Ashton Smith to the technophilic hardness of Larry Niven was typical of his ambition. Smith had taken the worldview of the French Decadent Movement of the nineteenth-century fin de siécle to the illimitable stages of cosmic fantasy and genre science fiction, while Niven, in the "Gil Hamilton" series, had been one of the first writers to attempt to analyze the social changes that were likely to flow from the combined effects of sophisticated biotechnology and information technology. *Involution Ocean* is a neo-Decadent fantasy of the far future that owes far more to Smith than to Niven, but the settings of Sterling's subsequent works of fiction were to move gradually closer to home. The majority eventually settled in a near future in which the social and political institutions of the present day are still—with grotesque ineffectuality—struggling to cope with a deluge of scientific innovations, but they never abandoned the colorful and ironic flamboyance of the Decadent sensibility.

Sterling's second novel, *The Artificial Kid* (1980), is set on the watery but island-strewn world of Reverie. Its eponymous hero is a young "combat artist" whose adventures in a Decriminalized Zone where almost anything goes are assiduously chronicled by robot cameras. The resulting videotapes are edited for use as entertainment by legions of fans. Many of the elements of *Involution Ocean* reappear in *The Artificial Kid*, in much the same balance; drugs function as a double-edged means of liberation and religion as an essentially farcical but nevertheless powerful repressive force. The secrets of the Elder Culture, some of whose relics were marginally featured in the earlier novel, play a more prominent part here, refracted through the gestalt theories of the protagonist's "tutor and mentor" Professor Crossbow. The climactic journey that takes the novel's leading characters into the heart of the alien Mass and out again is a ba-

roque odyssey similar to that which supplied the plot of *Involution Ocean*.

The elaborate description of the protagonist provided in the first chapter of *The Artificial Kid* is strongly reminiscent of various heroes featured in the work of Samuel R. Delany, who were also deployed in exotic myth-infected milieux. The Kid dresses to impress, carries a customized weapon (a "nunchuck") that he uses artfully and judiciously, has a similarly quasi-fetishistic association with various other technical gadgets, moves with "resilient grace," and is irrepressibly precocious. He does not actually wear mirrorshades, but he is the kind of character custom designed to fit almost everything that mirrorshades came to symbolize when it became the insiders' shorthand term for the literary movement whose prime movers were Sterling and William Gibson.

Sterling's own core contribution to the science fiction of the early 1980's was the Shaper/Mechanist series, whose earliest elements—"Spider Rose" (1982), "Swarm" (1982), and "Cicada Queen" (1983)—appeared alongside the story series that Gibson began with "Johnny Mnemonic" (1981). Sterling was later to recall that he had read Gibson's *Neuromancer* (1984) in manuscript "in 1982 or 1983," while he was guiding his own series towards the climax it eventually attained—following "Sunken Gardens" (1984) and the patchwork "Twenty Evocations" (1984)—in *Schismatrix* (1985; reprinted with the short stories as *Schismatrix Plus*, 1996).

Sterling's series details the rapid expansion through the solar system of various "posthuman" populations, loosely categorized as Shapers (a term of description applied to those groups who have remade themselves primarily by genetic engineering) and Mechanists (those groups who have remade themselves by extensive cyborgization). These main categories are elaborately subdivided into many splinter societies organized according to a wide range of political and religious creeds. Their most extreme examples are very bizarre indeed, the ultimate mechanists being immobile and immortal "wireheads" equipped with all manner of mechanical senses, while the most exotic Reshaped individuals are more alien than the actual alien species whose presence within and without the solar system complicates the human expansion into space.

The aliens provide important points of comparison throughout the series as Sterling and his many characters attempt to figure out what, if anything, is truly fundamental to the concept of "humanity"—and what, if anything, is worth preserving. The hive intelligence of "Swarm" poses a challenge to a Shaper who believes that the preservation of individuality is both possible and desirable. The reptilian Investors, who barter artifacts and life-forms of many different kinds for human goods and artworks, offer a similar challenge to the Mechanist protagonist of "Spider Rose," in the form of a carefully tailored genetic artifact that eventually becomes reincarnate within her own flesh and mind.

A key location in the Shaper/Mechanist series is the space habitat C-K (for Czarina-Kluster) whose central palace is established to house the exiled Investor "Cicada Queen." It rapidly accumulates a host of "subbles" (bubble suburbs), eventually becoming host to a People's Corporate Republic. C-K, which is also an important setting in *Schismatrix*, becomes a temporary oasis of calm in the Shaper/Mechanist conflict, although it is by no means immune to the fallout of their various philosophical and commercial differences. Its moral and intellectual climates are advanced beyond those of the inner system's more traditional locales, and although it is by no means a utopia, it represents Sterling's first major experiment in constructive social design. The ready access that C-K's inhabitants have to Investor technologies—by courtesy of the renegade Queen—places it at the cutting edge of the Posthumanist quest, providing a platform for the Lifesiders who oppose the more radical forms of Posthumanism and are intent on terraforming Mars (altering its ecosphere to make it habitable for humans), a project whose intermediate phases are described in "Sunken Gardens." C-K also offers a home to such extreme Mechanist sects as the Lobsters, the Spectral Intelligents, and the Blood Bathers.

By the end of the extraordinarily complicated *Schismatrix*—whose hero's extended odyssey through the rapidly changing solar system covers 170 years of future history in less than 300 pages—humankind has broken up into a whole series of daughter species, or "clades," none of which can claim to be sole carrier of the torch of destiny. The odyssey of the novel's hero, Abelard Lindsay, takes him from the Mare Tranquillitatis People's Circumlunar Zaibatsu to the spaceship *Red Consensus*, the asteroid Esairs 89-XII, the Shaper "city-state" of Goldrich-Tremaine in the Rings of Saturn, an Investor trading ship, and back to the asteroid belt's Dembowska Cartel before the plot revisits Czarina-Kluster. In the process, Lindsay witnesses and plays his own small part in the evolution of the Schismatrix: the systemwide society in which all the posthuman factions can live in relative harmony.

In the final chapter of the novel, Lindsay returns "home" to Earth, but that is only the opening of a final sequence of moves that takes him far abroad again. He visits the exhausted Earth, which has already begun its own process of self-renewal, merely to draw genetic material from its oceanic womb: material that will be transformed by the "angelic" Lifesiders to provide the Jovian satellite Europa with an ecosystem. The conclusion of the chapter is set in CircumEuropa as the new world awaits its transformation, and it finds Lindsay in the company of the mysterious Presence, looking outward to "the final transcendance [*sic*]" and to the as-yet-unattained state of being in which it will not matter whether the Final Questions ever obtain the Final Answers.

It was Gardner Dozois, the editor of *Isaac Asimov's Science Fiction Magazine*, who popularized the term "cyberpunk" as a label for the kind of character who was foreshadowed in the Artificial Kid and became the symbol of the new science fiction that Sterling and William Gibson were trying to write. (In 1983

Amazing had published a story called "Cyberpunk" by Bruce Bethke that had applied the label to a different kind of individual, but Dozois might not have seen it.) Typically, Sterling had moved on so rapidly that he never used another leading character of the same caricaturish kind as the Artificial Kid; even in a carefully tuned-down version, Abelard Lindsay is cut from different cloth. Sterling left the sophistication of the new outlaw breed to William Gibson, whose "very technical boy" Johnny Mnemonic and cyberspace cowboy Bobby Quine became the archetypal cyberpunks. It is entirely appropriate to the nature of the movement that by the time cyberpunk became firmly established as a key descriptive term in 1985, all the writers involved were insistent that it was already obsolete.

Schismatrix is more ambitious in many ways than *Neuromancer* and is certainly one of the landmark works of modern science fiction, but it is not entirely surprising that it was the latter novel that won the awards and attracted the lion's share of critical attention. While Gibson provided a generation of would-be cyberpunks with the vocabulary of ideas required to crystallize their image and creed, Sterling reached into more distant realms of possibility so strange and so discomfiting that the vast but safely enclosed vistas of cyberspace seemed cozy by comparison.

Between 1983 and 1986 Sterling produced the fanzine *Cheap Truth*, where he pontificated extensively—employing the polemical persona of "Vincent Omniaveritas"—about the nature and significance of the movement of which he and Gibson were a part, along with Lewis Shiner, John Shirley, and Rudy Rucker. The climax of this endeavor—which established that although Gibson might be reckoned the messiah of 1980's science fiction, Sterling was the hardworking Saint Paul who actually took the message on the road—was *Mirrorshades: The Cyberpunk Anthology* (1986). This seminal collection featured all the aforementioned writers alongside Pat Cadigan, Tom Maddox, and the more marginal figures of Greg Bear, James Patrick Kelly, Marc Laidlaw, and Paul Di Filippo.

Sterling's introduction to the anthology pays appropriate homage to cyberpunk's precursors within the science fiction field and draws crucial analogies to parallel cultural movements, especially those manifest in rock music, before providing the definitive explanation of the movement's nature and ambitions:

> Technical culture has gotten out of hand. The advances of the sciences are so deeply radical, so disturbing, upsetting, and revolutionary that they can no longer be contained. They are surging into culture at large; they are invasive; they are everywhere. The traditional power structure, the traditional institutions, have lost control of the pace of change.
>
> And suddenly a new alliance is becoming evident: an integration of technology and the Eighties counterculture. An unholy alliance of the technical world and the world of organized dissent—the underground world of pop culture, visionary fluidity and street-level anarchy. . . .The hacker and the rocker are this decade's pop-culture idols, and cyberpunk is very much a pop phenomenon: spontaneous, energetic, close to its roots. . . .
>
> For the cyberpunks . . . technology is visceral. It is not the bottled genie of remote Big Science boffins; it is pervasive, utterly intimate. Not outside us, but next to us. Under our skin; often, inside our minds. (pages x–xi)

The idea of cyberpunk fiction had an instant appeal to people ambitious to be the architects of a new "cyberculture," whose instruments of propaganda were such magazines as *Mondo 2000* and *Wired.* The former proclaimed Sterling a hero, while the latter welcomed his journalistic input. By 1987, however, the first issue of the fanzine *Science Fiction Eye* began its list of contents with a "Requiem for the Cyberpunks," reproduced a Science Fiction Research Association panel discussion of "Cyberpunk or Cyberjunk" (in which Norman Spinrad tried belatedly to secure his contention that "Neuromantics" would have been much a better label for the movement's members), and promulgated "The Humanist Manifesto," issued in reaction against Sterling's *Mirrorshades* introduction by John Kessel, following a lead offered by Michael Swanwick. Sterling—whose interview with Takayuki Tatsumi was advertised as the last phase of the magazine's "cyberpunk autopsy"—agreed to serve as a regular columnist for *Science Fiction Eye,* but with characteristic insouciance, he ignored the unfolding furor and devoted his opening contribution to a commentary on the works of Jules Verne.

The term "cyberpunk" also had an instant appeal to academics, who were anxious to get a fashionably labeled theoretical grip on contemporary popular culture. Larry McCaffery, the editor of a massively comprehensive guide to *Postmodern Fiction* (1986), produced *Storming the Reality Studio: A Casebook of Cyberpunk and Postmodern Fiction* (1991), an anthology far more wide ranging and grandiose than *Mirrorshades,* which mixed stories by the bona fide cyberpunks with fiction by the likes of Kathy Acker, J. G. Ballard, William S. Burroughs, Don DeLillo, and Thomas Pynchon and nonfiction by Jean Baudrillard, Jacques Derrida, Timothy Leary, and others. The rapidity with which the movement was embalmed for academic inspection and critically dissected was entirely in keeping with its own theories about the flow of modern culture.

The Sterling novel of greatest relevance to the emergent cyberculture was *Islands in the Net* (1988). Like William Gibson's later work, however, it flatly refuses to become hung up on the idea of cyberspace as a magical frontier. Sterling is more concerned with exploring the political implications of the global integration of the world's computers into a vast network. Although he is by no means the kind of naive technological determinist who imagines social change merely as a series of adaptations to technological innovation, Sterling is fascinated by the ways in which technological advancement opens up a host of new and various opportunities for different kinds of individuals and human groups. His travels in the Far East equipped him with the intellectual

means to think on a global scale and to consider the possible impact of new technologies on the balance of economic power dividing the First, Second, and Third Worlds. He had previously addressed such questions in "Spook" (1983) and the novella "Green Days in Brunei" (1985), both of which made every effort to transcend the cultural insularity fostered by the American education system, but *Islands in the Net* developed them more seriously and more fully.

Islands in the Net is in essence a future-set thriller, but it deploys its far-flung settings with a casual profligacy that no thriller writer had previously attempted. Its whole-world perspective offers an ambitious overview of the rigorous regime of natural selection to which existing political institutions will inevitably be subjected by new information technology: a regime in which rapid mutation is the only ward against gradual disintegration. Its hapless heroine, Laura Webster, is no cyberpunk; she has a good home, a nice family, and a rewarding job, although her adventures bring all of these once-secure investments under dire threat. The idea of "the Net" has become so commonplace since 1988 that it is already difficult to understand that *Islands in the Net* was a work of considerable originality and ingenuity. It is not particularly "prophetic," in the vulgar sense, but the task of intellectually worthwhile science fiction is not so much to predict what will actually come to pass as to expose the whole range of realizable possibilities—and no one exposes possibilities in such reckless profusion as Sterling.

The novel's Net is the brain and nervous system of a global society, upon whose relatively smooth working the political health of the world depends. In such a world, social stability is, virtually by definition, the controlled flow of information; the wilder excesses of "data piracy" constitute a blight that threatens universal social breakdown. The Net's "islands" are locations whose inhabitants will not subscribe to the royalty system that regulates the wealth of information; most of them are islands in the commonplace sense too, the ones that feature most prominently in the plot being Grenada and Singapore. Laura embarks upon an enforced and horribly uncomfortable educational odyssey through the highways and byways of this society, initially as an envoy but later as a kidnap victim, political prisoner, and pawn in schemes she is powerless to settle or convincingly upset. Roger Zelazny has observed that she has more in common with Candide than Odysseus, but hers is not a world from which anyone can sensibly retreat to tend his or her own garden; it is, to the contrary, a world in which no one can avoid claustrophobically intimate contact with everyone else's problems and everyone else's ambitions.

In view of the publicity given to Gibson's and Sterling's endeavors and the fact that the cyberpunk writers were already accustomed to working in collaboration—Sterling had written "Red Star, Winter Orbit" (1983) with Gibson, "Storming the Cosmos" (1985) with Rudy Rucker, "Mozart in Mirrorshades" (1985) with Lewis Shiner, and "The Unfolding" (1985) with John Shirley—it is not surprising that Sterling and Gibson next undertook to write a novel together. The novel in question was, however, an alternative history to be set in Victorian England: a "steampunk" novel.

The steampunk subgenre is now primarily associated with a group of California writers consisting of K. W. Jeter, James Blaylock, and Tim Powers. They have provided most of the subgenre's most outstanding examples, but its roots lie in the work of two of Sterling's fellow participants in the "Turkey City Workshops," Howard Waldrop and Steven Utley, and key contributions to it have also been made by cyberpunks Rudy Rucker and Paul Di Filippo. Anyone interested in the power that technology has to transform society is likely to be interested in the "what ifs" of history as well as the "what ifs" of the near future. Sterling has already written a handful of fantasies in which people in times past obtain supernatural insights into the incredible transformations that await them, including "Telliamed" (1984), "Dinner in Audoghast" (1985), and the beautifully tragic "Flowers of Edo" (1987). In *The Difference Engine* (1990) Gibson and Sterling raised the question of what might have happened if the revolution in information technology had taken place 150 years earlier than it actually did, when Charles Babbage, aided by Ada Lovelace (née Byron), first attempted to build a programmable mechanical computer.

As with most steampunk novels, the plot of *The Difference Engine* is a hectic adventure story in which a gang of villains with an exotic leader—in this case the neo-Luddite gangster Captain Swing—is engaged in a running battle with a band of stalwart heroes avid to possess a McGuffin (Alfred Hitchcock's term for an obscure object of desire for which the characters in thrillers search, which drives the plot) whose significance the reader should be better able to appreciate than they are. Real historical characters are, as usual, relegated to cameo roles. Keats has a walk-on part as an operator of "kinotropes," while Byron, who has become prime minister following the sweeping political success of the technocratic "Rads," remains in the wings; the only central role awarded to an actual writer is allotted to the far less famous Laurence Oliphant. The "Texian" exile Sam Houston has a substantial peripheral part, but Friedrich Engels, whose one-time associate Karl Marx is safely ensconced at the heart of the Manhattan Commune, barely rates a mention. The novel's true subject matter is, however, neatly woven into the background, half-concealed in a welter of casual observation. The characters do sometimes have occasion to stand and stare at Babbage Engines, but for the most part they simply take the presence of such entities for granted; the reader alone occupies the privileged position of being able to see what difference the engines have made to the fabric and thrust of nineteenth-century society.

As an attempted best-seller *The Difference Engine* was a little too subtle for its own good, especially with respect to American readers whose education in European history is likely to have been slight, but it features a wealth of deft and brilliant detail as well as a smog to rival the one that choked the population in Robert Barr's alarmist account "The Doom of London" (1892). The story's conclusion is a neatly ironic nod in the direction of *Neuromancer*; its vaguely uplifting spirit provides some compensation for the cold cynicism that underlies the greater part of the text.

Although Sterling's second story collection, *Globalhead* (1992), was published only three years after his first, *Crystal Express* (1989), it is markedly different in tone and subject matter. There are two interesting experiments in style that have no parallel in the earlier collection—"Our Neural Chernobyl" (1988) offers an indirect account of a fanciful future in the form of a book review, while "The Sword of Damocles" (1990) takes postmodernist recursiveness to calculatedly absurd lengths—but the remainder of the collection has a distinctly darker edge.

"The Gulf Wars" (1988) juxtaposes the present and the distant past in a manner akin to that of "Dinner in Audoghast," but its moral applies an extra turn of a cruel screw. "The Shores of Bohemia" (1990) is a quasi-utopian fantasy about artistry and decadence whose concerns echo the earlier volume's "The Beautiful and the Sublime" (1986), but it is markedly less flippant than its predecessor. A collaboration with Rudy Rucker left over from the earlier period, "Storming the Cosmos"—which describes the unhappy experiences of Russian cosmonauts whose search for the source of the Tunguska explosion is confused by the effects of psychotropic mushrooms—is followed by a much dourer collaboration with John Kessel, "The Moral Bullet" (1991), in which the inventor of a rejuvenation technology is pursued through a fragmented America future society so that he might be appropriately punished for his socially disruptive sin.

The outlook that predominates in *Globalhead* is not entirely cynical, and certainly not unrelievedly callous, but it is determinedly jaundiced. The most sentimental story in the book is a small masterpiece of intimate alternative history, "Dori Bangs" (1989), which

imagines that two lonely individuals who each died alone in our world might have found a tentative but rewarding companionship in another world. It is saved for last, but by the time the reader reaches it, its comforting quality has already been offset by a more extended description of the much more awkward relationship forged out of bitter necessity by the protagonists of "Jim and Irene" (1991).

In "We See Things Differently" (1989) an Arab assassin travels to a United States that has lost its political hegemony but still retains a stranglehold on the entertainment industry in order to carry the war against the Great Satan into its final and most ignominious phase. In "The Unthinkable" (1991) the juxtaposition of the implications attached to that word by H. P. Lovecraft with those attached to it by the hydrogen bomb puts Lovecraft's notion of the ultimate horror firmly in the shade. "Hollywood Kremlin" (1990) and "Are You for 86?" (original to the collection) both feature Leggy Starlitz, an opportunist wheeler-dealer of dubious origin and negligible moral commitment whose supernatural talent for evading the gaze of cameras assists him in carrying out his scams anywhere in the world, from Afghanistan to Salt Lake City. He might be reckoned a cyberpunk of sorts, but there is a realpolitik grimness about his outlook and methods that puts as enormous a distance between him and the Artificial Kid as there is between Earth and Reverie.

The dourer stories in *Globalhead* were written alongside Sterling's first major exercise in popular nonfiction, *The Hacker Crackdown: Law and Disorder on the Electronic Frontier* (1992). This careful analysis of the overreaction of law enforcement agencies to the rumor that clever PC users were engaged in conspiracies to invade and subvert the systems of large corporations and government agencies contrasts somewhat with such exercises in alarmist sensationalism as *Cyberpunk: Outlaws and Hackers on the Computer Frontier* (1991) by Katie Hafner and John Markoff. Although Sterling is quoted on the jacket of the earlier book, lauding it as "the best book ever written on the computer underground, a marvel of lucidity and good sense" it is, in fact, considerably more melodramatic than his own study, which reported that the threatened apocalypse of outlawry had already been brutally aborted. There is a certain irony in the fact that the visionary science fiction writer was able to keep a better sense of proportion than the professional journalists.

The narrower focus of the later items assembled in *Globalhead* is also exhibited in the rather bleak novel *Heavy Weather* (1994), which extrapolates into an unsettled future the exploits of the real-world meteorologists who chase "twisters" along the American Midwest's "tornado alley." The principal plot thread follows the zealous Storm Troupers to their dramatic encounter with the Holy Grail of weather-hackers, the F-6 supertornado, while the chief subplot tracks a group of government employees who know that the storm's unprecedentedly disruptive effect on electronic communication systems offers the only chance they are ever likely to get to slip the leash of close surveillance. Once the trough of low pressure has passed by, however, things begin to brighten up again.

The short stories that Sterling published after Globalhead reverted to a broader spectrum of concerns and a broader kind of comedy. In "Sacred Cow" (1993) an Indian film producer working in Britain extricates himself from his economic difficulties by a combination of luck and cunning while casually taking note of the devastations wrought by a human-infective form of Bovine Spongiform Encephalopathy (commonly known as mad cow disease) that has devastated the hamburger-eating populations of the Western world. "Deep Eddy" (1993) introduces a cyberpunkish data smuggler of a more colorful stripe than Leggy Starlitz, en route to Germany on a secret mission for the mysterious Cultural Critic (whose equally enigmatic adversary is the Moral Referee). His observations of the novelty-rich world within the text are aided by the computerized "spex" that add informational depth to his vision and serve as a translation device. The most extravagant of

all Sterling's comedies is "Big Jelly" (1994), written in collaboration with Rudy Rucker, in which a young entrepreneur who needs a "killer app" for the artificial jellyfish he has invented teams up with an oil tycoon whose wells have started pumping a mysterious protoplasmic "urschleim." When the two men combine their resources, the jellyfish-inspired urschleim proves capable of very rapid and spectacular evolution.

The richly detailed background of "Deep Eddy" is further elaborated in "Bicycle Repairman" (1996), in which an associate of Eddy's in Chattanooga accepts delivery on his behalf of a television cable box inhabited by a precocious Artificial Intelligence. Leggy Starlitz crops up again—this time in Finland—laundering money via the Internet and promoting a "kiddipop" band in "The Littlest Jackal" (1996). The imaginative labor that fed these relatively lighthearted exercises was, however, put to much more earnest use in the novel *Holy Fire* (1996). Like the short stories, this novel exploited the experience that Sterling had accumulated while carrying out journalistic assignments for *Wired* in various European locales.

Like most of Sterling's novels, *Holy Fire* is formulated as an odyssey of discovery and is given direction by the promise of a transition from the human to the posthuman condition. Unlike *Schismatrix*, however, which requires its protagonist to maintain far more of his humanity than those around him, *Holy Fire* begins with a radical transformation of its aged heroine. Mia Ziemann lives a quiet and docile existence as a medical economist until she volunteers for an experimental rejuvenation treatment—and being the beneficiary of its staggering success, she immediately evades the grip of the interested experimenters. She goes in search of a new life, now calling herself Maya to distance herself from her cast-off larva. Cast adrift in Europe, Maya discovers the curious underworld inhabited by the disadvantaged young, who cannot compete with their increasingly robust elders in an ever-shrinking job market where employability depends on experience and carefully refined skills. Ill-prepared for the gift of a second youth, Maya is continually in danger of frittering away her gift, but hidden opportunities await her in cyberspace, to which she is eventually led by a dutiful postcanine dog.

Holy Fire lacks a stirring climax, but that is not a weakness, because its message is that in the future life *will* go on, further than we can presently envisage, and that individuals will have to adapt themselves—along with their institutions—to infinite uncertainty. Although *Holy Fire* is a much quieter novel than *Schismatrix*, it is also much more controlled; although it cannot begin to match the earlier novel as a display of imaginative pyrotechnics, it is, in its own way, equally inventive and equally impressive. It serves to confirm Sterling's reputation as the most prolifically inventive writer in the science fiction genre (although *Holy Fire* was not marketed as a genre work in the United Kingdom), while also demonstrating that his analytical powers are still continuing to mature. Although it does not quite fulfill the intention he declared in a *Locus* interview, "to write about pleasure, the brighter aspects of life [and] creativity," it is a thoroughly constructive book, which takes care to emphasize that no matter how reckless and how disturbing the march of technology becomes, the likelihood is that it will offer more opportunities than threats even to those who are not naturally venturesome.

One of Sterling's greatest strengths as a science fiction writer is that he is more inclined than any other American working in the genre to take a global view of technological development. He was one of the first American writers to take a serious look at the cultural differences between the Russian and American space programs, more earnestly in "Red Star, Winter Orbit" than in "Storming the Cosmos," and he was one of the first to make convincing use of Third World settings. He was also one of the first to capture something of the cultural ambience of postcommunist Eastern Europe. He has also tried to embrace Moslem perspectives—"We See Things Differently" was preceded by the brief but effective "The Compassionate, the Digital" (1985)—and Japanese perspectives, the latter with sufficient success to have had the Tokyo-set "Edo no Hano" ("Flowers of Edo") and "Maneki Neko" (1998) published in translation in *Hayakawa-SF* in advance of its first appearance in the United States.

The breadth of Sterling's concerns creates confidence in the firmness of his grasp of the issues he tackles, and there is no one whose images of possible near futures are worth more in the hard currency of pragmatic thought. Although he frequently uses comedy as a means of importing narrative verve into his stories, his humor always has a serious edge. Were he to use melodrama instead he would have to invent villains to provide banishable threats, and that is the kind of cheap trickery of which he has usually tried to steer clear. Indeed, one of the strengths of cyberpunk fiction in general was its enthusiasm to avoid the mechanical plotting methods of the "technothriller" subgenre.

While his scientific and technological extrapolations have maintained the standards of realism expected of modern hard science fiction writers, Sterling has always brought to those extrapolations a sophisticated and distinctive aesthetic sensibility. Although it is comprehensively modernized, that sensibility is ultimately derived from those aspects of the Romantic theories of Coleridge that filtered into pulp fantasy writers, courtesy of the efforts of H. P. Lovecraft and Clark Ashton Smith. The strange combination of his influences has enabled Sterling to link his acute consciousness of the irredeemable obsolescence of a social order whose institutions have already been outstripped by technological opportunity to a fascination with the avid hunger for sensation that ennui and spleen sometimes impose upon the human mind. However odd this linkage may seem in the abstract, it is by no means inappropriate to the analysis of contemporary culture.

It is perhaps inevitable that Sterling's expertise as a cultural commentator should have deflected much of his effort into journalistic endeavors, but his work demonstrates that he has a very full appreciation of the unique value of speculative fiction as a medium of evaluative thought experiments. In his preface to William Gibson's *Burning Chrome* (1986) he wrote:

> If poets are the unacknowledged legislators of the world, science-fiction writers are its court jesters. We are Wise Fools who can leap, caper, utter prophecies, and scratch ourselves in public. We can play with Big Ideas because the garish motley of our pulp origins makes us seem harmless.
>
> And Sf writers have every opportunity to kick up our heels—we have influence without responsibility. Very few feel obliged to take us seriously, yet our ideas permeate the culture, bubbling along invisibly, like background radiation. (page 1)

All of this is true, although there is a tiny element of bluff in stating it thus, because Sterling is the kind of writer who takes his responsibilities seriously and tries his utmost to pack his calculated follies with as much wisdom as they can carry. If he takes great delight in whispering, "Remember, thou must die!" into the ear of the global society established by American "Coca-colonization," he also takes great pride in trying to imagine as cleverly as possible the new order that will spring up in place of the old.

Selected Bibliography

WORKS OF BRUCE STERLING

Involution Ocean. New York: Jove, 1978; London: New English Library, 1980.

The Artificial Kid. New York: Harper, 1980; London: Penguin, 1985.

Schismatrix. New York: Arbor House, 1985; London: Penguin, 1986.

Islands in the Net. New York: Arbor House, 1988; London: Century, 1988.

Crystal Express. Sauk City, Wisc.: Arkham House, 1989; London: Century, 1990. (Short stories.)

The Difference Engine, with William Gibson. London: Gollancz, 1990; New York: Bantam, 1991.

Globalhead. Shingletown, Calif.: Ziesing, 1992; London: Millennium, 1994.

The Hacker Crackdown: Law and Disorder on the Electronic Frontier. New York: Bantam, 1992; London: Viking, 1993. (Nonfiction.)

Heavy Weather. New York: Bantam, 1994; London: Millennium, 1994.

Holy Fire. London: Millenium, 1996; New York: Bantam, 1996.

Schismatrix Plus. New York: Ace, 1996.

EDITED ANTHOLOGY

Mirrorshades: The Cyberpunk Anthology. New York: Arbor House, 1986; London: Paladin, 1988.

CRITICAL STUDY

Maddox, Tom. "The Wars of the Coin's Two Halves: Bruce Sterling's Mechanist." In *Storming the Reality Studio: A Casebook of Cyberpunk and Postmodern Science Fiction.* Edited by Larry McCaffery. Durham, N.C.: Duke University Press, 1991.

—BRIAN STABLEFORD

THEODORE STURGEON

(1918–1985)

THEODORE STURGEON WAS born Edward Hamilton Waldo in New York City in 1918. Following his mother's remarriage, he took his stepfather's surname. When he was fifteen, he suffered a bad attack of rheumatic fever, which destroyed his hopes of becoming a gymnast and resulted in his nursing a sense of injury for some years. After graduating from high school, Sturgeon spent three years at sea, and it was during this period (in 1937) that he began selling short fiction to newspapers run by McClure's syndicate. His first attempt at science fiction was "Helix the Cat," which failed to sell at the time but appeared in the John W. Campbell, Jr., memorial anthology *Astounding* (1973), edited by Harry Harrison.

After seeing a copy of the first issue of *Unknown* in March 1939, Sturgeon began aiming stories at that magazine; after selling "A God in a Garden" to *Unknown*, he decided to stay on land and attempt to make a living from his writing. During the next three years he contributed regularly to *Unknown* and published a few stories in *Astounding Science-Fiction* but then abandoned his plan and for the next five years wrote very little, taking a variety of jobs outside the United States. He did not return to writing on a permanent basis until 1946. He was rescued by Campbell from a deep depression following his divorce from his first wife. Campbell encouraged him to begin writing again, and between 1946 and 1961 he published the great majority of the works on which his reputation now rests.

Sturgeon's first story to be published in *Astounding Science-Fiction* was "Ether Breather" (1939), which got into print before "A God in a Garden." "Ether Breather" is a light, humorous piece in which etheric entities mischievously interfere with television transmissions. Most of the stories that Sturgeon wrote for Campbell in this early period were similarly quirky—slick and ironic, but basically trivial. He made one attempt to write "hard" science fiction in "Artnan Process" (1941)—a space opera with a plot hinging on an esoteric problem in isotope separation—but this was not his forte. The one story that he published in *Astounding* at this time that made a lasting impact was "Microcosmic God" (1941), which Sturgeon did not particularly like. It concerns the exploits of a scientist who takes advantage of the products of a miniature world in which time runs at a much faster rate than in our own, and is now enshrined, by virtue of the Science Fiction Writers of America poll, in the first volume of the anthology *The Science Fiction Hall of Fame* (1970) as one of the stories exemplary of Campbell's golden age of science fiction.

The most impressive story that Sturgeon published in this period was "It" (1940), which represents the darker side of *Unknown*. The type of fantasy most characteristic of the magazine was flippant, depending on the creation of humorous absurdities by the logical extrapolation of exotic premises; but a similar application of logic could equally well lead to the production of blood-curdling horror stories if the premises allowed it. The "It" of the title is the archetypal monster— the distilled essence of teratology. Sturgeon wrote another, even more disturbing horror story in this period, but it was not published until it won a short story competition run by the British *Argosy* in 1947. This story was "Bianca's Hands," about a man who falls in love with the hands of an idiot girl. The consummation of his passion is the ecstatic moment when the hands strangle him.

During Sturgeon's first period of inactivity, one of the jobs he held was bulldozer operator in Puerto Rico—an experience that gave rise to the one story that he wrote during the war years, the novella "Killdozer!" (1944). This superb suspense story is an account of events following the infestation of a giant bulldozer by an alien intelligence. The human characters, isolated on a small Pacific island, have to defend themselves against the ravages of the animated machine and to devise a way to stop it. A television film of the story was made in 1974.

When Sturgeon began writing for Campbell again in 1946, his stories had become more sentimental and often had a curiously bittersweet quality. "Mewhu's Jet" (1946) and "Tiny and the Monster" (1947) feature encounters with alien beings and pathetic failures to communicate. Sturgeon also wrote some striking cautionary tales inspired by the advent of the atomic bomb, including "Memorial" (1946) and "Thunder and Roses" (1947). The latter is still a telling moral fable, arguing emotively that men armed with nuclear weapons cannot afford to follow the logic of "an eye for an eye." Perhaps the most outstanding of these new stories was "Maturity" (1947), a sensitive tale about a female doctor's relationship with a childlike man who has astonishing creative talent but is psychologically incapable of developing it. She tries to guide him to maturity, but the maturity that he ultimately finds is his own, not hers.

This story showed the direction that Sturgeon's subsequent work would take. It has a greater depth of feeling than any story published in the science fiction magazines before that time, and the sympathy that Sturgeon evokes for his characters is remarkably powerful. He went on to become the indefatigable champion of characters alienated in a hundred different ways, finding for them imaginative routes to salvation, love, and joy. No one has produced more bizarre models of alienated situations than Sturgeon, and no one has written more convincingly or more evocatively of their conquest. His characters plumb the depths of desperation, but like Goethe's Faust they are always snatched from the mouth of hell and borne triumphantly to heaven.

Sturgeon rapidly began to find new markets. *Unknown* had ceased publication in 1943, but *Weird Tales* and *Fantastic Adventures* provided him with outlets for his more fantastic stories as he moved away from Campbell's more science-oriented requirements. Many of these stories deal with explicit biological alienation, including two that refer to "syzygy"—a process of asexual reproduction supposedly practiced by paramecia that was actually reported as a result of an observational error. These two stories, "The Deadly Ratio" (1948; also known as "It Wasn't Syzygy") and "The Sex Opposite" (1952), were the first of many in which Sturgeon used the kind of extreme intolerance sometimes associated with sexual morality as a key exemplar of the kind of reaction that ought to be eliminated from human affairs.

"The World Well Lost" (1953), dealing with the persecution of two aliens on account of their homosexuality, proved highly controversial. Much later, when Harlan Ellison asked Sturgeon for a story for his taboo-defying anthology *Dangerous Visions* (1967), Sturgeon interrupted one of his silent periods to produce "If All Men Were Brothers, Would You Let One Marry Your Sister?" which portrays a utopian society based on incestuous relationships. The most startling story in this vein is the short novel *Some of Your Blood* (1961), in which a youth afflicted with vampirism achieves temporary psychological stability by means of a highly unorthodox relationship with a girl.

After 1949 Sturgeon made only one more appearance in *Astounding Science-Fiction*, with "Won't You Walk" (1956), and Horace L. Gold's *Galaxy* became his principal market for the duration of his second period of productivity. *Galaxy* made its debut in 1950, and it was in that same year that Sturgeon published his first novel, *The Dreaming Jewels* (also known as *The Synthetic Man*). This superb melodrama begins with a striking sequence in which a small boy, Horty Bluett, is caught eating ants and is so brutally punished by his adoptive father that he runs away. He is taken in by Zena, a midget in a carnival run by the obsessive misanthrope Pierre Monêtre, who is trying to find the secret of mysterious crystals with mutagenic effects that have been responsible for the creation of most of his freaks. Horty has to flee once more when Zena realizes that Horty, too, is a product of the jewels; but as he matures, it is revealed that he is crucially different from the imperfect creations that Monêtre has so far encountered. Despite the time lapse in the middle of the story, during which Horty grows to maturity, the narrative is relentlessly suspenseful, and its emotional intensity is quite remarkable. It was the first of Sturgeon's many important stories in which the central character's alienation from other people is significant of a latent superhumanity.

The interest in "psi-powers" that was prevalent in the science fiction of the 1950's encouraged Sturgeon to produce many stories in this mold. In his ". . . And My Fear Is Great" (1953; book form, 1965), a juvenile delinquent is taken under the wing of an old lady who has psionic powers and tries to teach him to develop his. She subsequently rejects him when she discovers him making love to a young girl, believing that her own power is dependent upon "moral purity." But he demonstrates to her that psionic power and sexual love, far from being incompatible, are actually symbiotic. In "The (Widget), the (Wadget), and Boff" (1955), aliens visit Earth in order to discover whether humans possess psionic power. But the aliens find that though humans have the relevant synapse, its function is impaired,

cursing them with interpersonal frictions. The aliens set up an experiment in a guest house to see whether the repression can be lifted by extreme pressure, and they discover that it can; all the guests are simultaneously saved from their chronic isolation. Both these stories are dramatic but pale by comparison with the more detailed and more extravagant treatments of the theme in Sturgeon's novels *More Than Human* (1953) and *The Cosmic Rape* (1958).

More Than Human is developed from a *Galaxy* novella called "Baby Is Three" (1952), which forms the middle section of the book. The novel as a whole tells the story of six individuals, each a social deviant or outcast and each possessed of a single exceptional talent. Together they form a gestalt—a supraindividual whole entity. The telepathic simpleton who first brings the group together dies and is replaced by a delinquent boy who cannot comprehend his situation until he consults a psychoanalyst. During the period of its "infancy," the group is sheltered by a woman whose protectiveness and attempts at moral education have almost succeeded in fragmenting the group when the boy discovers the need for its collective identity to be asserted. But the gestalt still has to learn a morality of its own to replace the inappropriate one it has rejected; until it does, it cannot genuinely transcend the human condition to become a part of a new and better race.

The Cosmic Rape—also an expansion of a *Galaxy* novella, "To Marry Medusa" (1958)—is marginally less effective, although its climax is more spectacular. A part of an alien group mind, which absorbs the group minds of all other cultures it encounters, arrives on Earth in the form of a "spore." When it discovers that the human race consists of a vast number of independent intelligences, it assumes that Earth's "hive-mind" has somehow fragmented itself as a defense against absorption. It sets about arranging the reunion of human mentality, but when this is achieved, the human mass mind proves much more powerful than the alien supermind, which is compounded of hives whose individual units are barely intelligent (intelligence in their case having been solely a property of the collective). The moment when the human mass mind is formed, and fights its brief "war" against the alien's take over bid, involves the sudden bestowal of purpose on various (human) characters previously agonized by their social isolation and neuroses. The transcendental metamorphosis of an assembly of frightened, suffering, incompetent individuals into a powerful and sane cosmic mind is a virtual apotheosis; together with Arthur C. Clarke's *Childhood's End* (1953), *The Cosmic Rape* constitutes an extreme version of one of modern science fiction's most persistent myths.

The theme of redemption from isolation saturates Sturgeon's entire literary cosmos; his work can be seen as a quest for imaginary solutions powerful enough to solve any problem of that kind. But there remains a quasi-Christian insistence on judgment—there are individuals who are Evil incarnate, and for them redemption is out of the question. Monêtre, in *The Dreaming Jewels*, is one such individual. Another is Mr. Costello in "Mr. Costello, Hero" (1953), who spreads dissent and division wherever he goes. Perhaps the most dreadful of all these villains is Heri Gonza, the television star of "The Comedian's Children" (1958), who infects small children with a disfiguring disease so that he can appear to the world as a champion fighting to save them. The intensity of this tale of damnation is equal to that of any of Sturgeon's stories of salvation. The sin committed by these villains is reducible to just one thing: they hate. Because love is such an important aspect of salvation, hatred becomes its negation—the one thing that must fall outside its scope. More recently Sturgeon seems to have changed his emphasis with respect to the problem of evil, and hatred seems to have become an epiphenomenon whose root cause is resistance to change. In several nonfictional pieces, he made remarks to the effect that "stopping is the only unnatural thing there is."

As his second productive period was ending, Sturgeon had just begun to break away

Theodore Sturgeon in 1977.   PHOTO BY JAY KAY KLEIN

from the pattern outlined above. His fourth science fiction novel, *Venus Plus X* (1960), is in no way concerned with melodramatic, "transcendental" solutions to human problems, but with social engineering—albeit of a dramatic character. The protagonist of the novel is invited to pass judgment upon the utopian society of Ledom, where there is no differentiation—physical or social—between the sexes. The main story is punctuated by a series of scenes from contemporary American life, highlighting the extent to which the differentiation of sex roles permeates our way of living. In Ledom true equality for all citizens has been established, and the distribution of love is entirely democratic. But the conclusion of Sturgeon's thought experiment is ambiguous—the protagonist approves of the society until he is told that it is an artificial rather than a natural creation: the Ledomites are not hermaphroditic mutants but the results of surgical intervention with ordinary human stock. There is a strong implication here that even if there were a way to human salvation, humans would refuse to take it because their prejudices are too deeply ingrained. This moral is implicit in virtually all of Sturgeon's subsequent work and is the foundation stone of his dictum that resistance to change is "the only unnatural practice."

In 1961 Sturgeon published two more novels—*Some of Your Blood* and a novelization of the film script *Voyage to the Bottom of the Sea*—but by this time his short story production had almost ceased. "The Man Who Lost the Sea" (1959) and "Like Young" (1960) are very fine tales, but both are extremely sober by comparison with his early work. The first is a tragedy detailing the experiences of an astronaut dying on an alien world; the second, a quietly apocalyptic story in which the triumphant summation of human scientific achievement is casually dismissed by a member of the species destined to supplant mankind.

The last story Sturgeon published before his second silent spell was "When You Care, When You Love," his contribution to the special Theodore Sturgeon issue of *The Magazine of Fantasy and Science Fiction* in September 1962. Actually the opening sequence of an unfinished novel, it concerns the project mounted by a rich woman to resurrect her dead lover by cloning from the cancer cells that destroyed him. Had the story been completed, the thrust of its argument would have been a fierce expression of the wish that love and ingenuity might conquer even the most desperate isolation of all: death. Left incomplete, with a dispirited mock ending hastily grafted on, it is an expression of the loss of impetus that had overcome Sturgeon's creative imagination. Like the two other long stories that Sturgeon wrote in the next fifteen years—"If All Men Were Brothers . . ." and "Case and the Dreamer" (1972)—it seems to protest too much and consequently becomes hollowly unconvincing.

When Sturgeon began writing again with some fluency, in 1969, he initially wrote for editors outside the science fiction field, although some of what he wrote for them was science fiction. In 1970 he began to sell to *Galaxy* again and published his award-winning short story "Slow Sculpture" there. (Subsequently he took over from Algis Budrys as *Galaxy*'s book reviewer.) The revival hardly got under way before it petered out again, and "Slow Sculpture" is the one really notable story of this period. It is a rather clipped account of a meeting between an embittered and reclusive inventor and a girl suffering from cancer. The title derives from an evocative metaphor that compares the way in which a man influences the growth of a bonsai tree to the way in which people in love affect one another as they "grow together," but in spite of the metaphor the story is quite bitter. The inventor has become a recluse because all his inventions have been bought up by vested interests that suppress them, and his cure for cancer is going to waste because his credentials are not recognized by the medical profession. A similar bitterness lies at the heart of "Brownshoes" (1969; also known as "The Man Who Learned Loving"), in which a hippie invents a perpetual-motion machine and adopts the uniform and habits of a young executive as protective camouflage in order to distribute his invention so widely that it cannot be seized and suppressed by the giant corporations that are the enemies of human progress.

It was Harlan Ellison who persuaded Sturgeon to break his long silence of the 1960's, and his silence of the 1970's likewise ended with a story written for an Ellison-inspired project. "Why Dolphins Don't Bite" (1980) is one of a series of stories by various hands set on Medea, a world whose nature and history were planned under Ellison's supervision. Its protagonist is a preacher dedicated to the promulgation of the Great Acceptance, a quasi-religious philosophical doctrine of tolerance. His own powers of tolerance are tested by a Medean who shows him the pathway to true enlightenment. The protagonist's own feelings remain tortuously ambiguous, but he is certain that humanity cannot accept the way he has been shown because the taboo that would be transgressed is too deeply embedded in the human psyche. Instead, mankind is condemned to a future history of marvelous inventions, which are poor substitutes for the power and wisdom that lie forever out of reach.

During the last years of his life, Sturgeon continued to struggle against the block that had rendered his pen impotent. He attempted to set out a comprehensive summary of his prospectus for moral reform in a long religious fantasy called *Godbody*, featuring a new Christ whose powers and message are adapted to twentieth-century civilization. However, the version of *Godbody* that was posthumously published in 1986 tacks a cursory substitute crucifixion on to a story that is hardly begun. Sturgeon died on 8 May 1985.

An appropriate monument to Sturgeon's achievements within the science fiction field was launched in 1994 when Paul Williams—who had earlier compiled and edited the complete short fiction of Philip K. Dick—launched a ten-volume series of Sturgeon's short fiction. The stories are presented in chronological order of composition. Unpublished material rescued from the author's files is being inserted where relevant, and variant texts are included if the published versions differed significantly. Williams' annotations are placed in the context of a biographical commentary that often illuminates items of psychological significance within the texts that might otherwise be hard to discern.

This collection, when complete, will provide definitive proof that Theodore Sturgeon was a writer of great eloquence and considerable profundity. Many of his best stories compel the reader to identify with characters who are very different from the stereotyped heroes and heroines of popular fiction, cultivating a precious empathy. So heartfelt are many of these stories in their contemplation of the pain and misery of powerless individuals that the only endings that can offer the necessary relief are blatant miracles, of a kind that an author—wielding godlike power over the worlds within his texts—can easily provide.

Sturgeon was quite prepared to use such deus ex machina endings, but he was too honest a writer, and was possessed of too much common sense, to be casual in their employment. He always took care to insist, and to demonstrate as best he could, that salvation is not something easily won, or won without cost.

Because of his continual trafficking in miracles, Sturgeon always found writing pure fantasy more comfortable than writing rationally plausible science fiction. If the popular fiction marketplace had not been so heavily biased toward science fiction during his periods of intense activity, he might have produced a very different body of work, but he desperately wanted to make his work constructive rather than merely palliative. The extrapolation of science fiction ideas and the adoption of the progressive outlook of science fiction assisted him in his determination to produce stories that were far more than consolatory exercises in wish fulfillment. The vast majority of his works can be construed as moral allegories, but their science fiction element makes them boldly adventurous moral allegories, exceptionally fine *contes philosophiques*.

Selected Bibliography

SCIENCE FICTION AND FANTASY WORKS OF THEODORE STURGEON

Without Sorcery. Philadelphia: Prime Press, 1948. Abridged as *Not Without Sorcery.* New York: Ballantine Books, 1961.

The Dreaming Jewels. New York: Greenberg, 1950. Also titled *The Synthetic Man.* New York: Pyramid, 1957.

E. Pluribus Unicorn. New York: Abelard, 1953.

More Than Human. New York: Farrar, Straus and Young, 1953.

Caviar. New York: Ballantine Books, 1955.

A Way Home. New York: Funk and Wagnalls, 1955.

The Cosmic Rape. New York: Dell, 1958.

A Touch of Strange. Garden City, N.Y.: Doubleday, 1958.

Aliens Four. New York: Avon Books, 1959.

Beyond. New York: Avon Books, 1960.

Venus Plus X. New York: Pyramid, 1960.

Some of Your Blood. New York: Ballantine Books, 1961.

Voyage to the Bottom of the Sea. New York: Pyramid, 1961.

Sturgeon in Orbit. New York: Pyramid, 1964.

. . . And My Fear Is Great and Baby Is Three. New York: Galaxy Publishing Corporation, Galaxy Magabook No. 3 (1965).

The Joyous Invasions. London: Victor Gollancz, 1965.

Starshine. New York: Pyramid, 1966.

Sturgeon Is Alive and Well. . . . New York: G. P. Putnam's Sons, 1971.

The Worlds of Theodore Sturgeon. New York: Ace Books, 1972.

To Here and the Easel. London: Victor Gollancz, 1973.

Case and the Dreamer. Garden City, N.Y.: Doubleday, 1974.

Amok Time. New York: Bantam Books, 1978. A *Star Trek* "photonovel."

Visions and Venturers. New York: Dell, 1978.

The Golden Helix. New York: Doubleday, 1979.

Maturity. Edited by Scott Imes and Stuart W. Wells. Minnesota Science Fiction Society, 1979.

The Stars Are the Styx. New York: Dell, 1979.

Godbody. New York: Fine, 1986.

The Complete Stories of Theodore Sturgeon. Vol. 1, *The Ultimate Egoist.* Vol. 2, *Microcosmic God.* Vol. 3, *Killdozer!.* Vol. 4, *Thunder and Roses.* Edited by Paul Williams. Berkeley, Calif.: North Atlantic, 1994–1997. (Short stories; the first four volumes of a projected ten-volume set.)

CRITICAL AND BIOGRAPHICAL STUDIES

Diskin, Lahna F. *Theodore Sturgeon.* Mercer Island, Wash.: Starmont, 1981.

Friend, Beverly. "The Sturgeon Connection." In *Voices for the Future,* edited by Thomas Clareson. Bowling Green, Ohio: Bowling Green University Popular Press, 1976.

Menger, Lucy. *Theodore Sturgeon.* New York: Ungar, 1981.

Moskowitz, Sam. "Theodore Sturgeon." In *Seekers of Tomorrow.* Cleveland: World Publishing Company, 1966.

—BRIAN M. STABLEFORD

JOHN TAINE

(1883–1960)

EXOTIC, OFTEN ORIENTAL geographic settings in the manner of Rudyard Kipling, H. Rider Haggard, and James Hilton; exciting masculine adventure stories reminiscent of the late Victorian school of "new romancers" such as Robert Louis Stevenson, Rolf Boldrewood, G. A. Henty, and Henry Seton Merriman; slangy, "tough-guy" scientist heroes who talk like Carroll John Daly's Race Williams and who are required to solve formidable scientific mysteries; bright, articulate heroines whose brash independence recalls the self-assured women in Wilkie Collins' novels; a markedly secular world view depicting a Thomas Hardy-like neutral universe ruled by blind chance and happenstance, a universe in which mankind must use modern science to free itself from nature's brutish bondage; a continuing thematic preoccupation with evolution in which humanity, attempting to direct and control its evolution, can aspire to the level of a god (or devolve back into an ape or a fungus if it misapplies such knowledge); a belief, shared with C. S. Lewis, that myths about a lost golden age are only imperfectly remembered episodes of real human history; and sensational plot denouements that end in fiery, all-consuming holocausts—all of these recurring themes and literary devices are central ingredients of John Taine's fictional formula for what he called "fantascience." By that term he meant that his stories contained a warp of science and a weft of fantasy. Essentially a formula writer, he mixed these ingredients, with some variety, in all of his fifteen full-length novels.

Taine was a major Georgian-period American science fiction writer whose novelistic career spanned more than twenty years. His first novel (though published fourth), *Green Fire*, was written in 1919; his last, *G.O.G. 666*, was written in 1940. At bottom, Taine was more a bold romancer of scientific adventure stories than a visionary prophet of the future. Nevertheless, all of his novels were based in part on serious scientific themes—mainly involving evolution, astronomy, eugenics, chemistry, paleontology, geology, atomic energy, plant biology, metallurgy, crystallography, and X rays. But Taine's novels really generate their emotional power not from any coherent scientific vision of the future or from any clearly articulated social philosophy, but from the dynamic and sensational manner in which their central conflicts are resolved—mysteries solved, conspiracies overturned, quests completed, and catastrophes averted.

Except for his best-known novel, *The Time Stream* (*Wonder Stories*, 1931–1932), Taine did not write interplanetary or interstellar space travel stories. He eschewed utopian and dystopian stories set in the future, and disliked the space-monster/horror-story genre. He was most at home fashioning his novels around one of three classic science fiction formal patterns: the great discovery, the great catastrophe, or the lost (usually advanced) civilization. With the exception of *Before the Dawn* (1934), his delightful prehistoric romance, Taine constructed his novels as mystery or puzzle stories, using the three-part story pattern developed by British writers.

This pattern may be summarized as follows: (1) a problem is posed, (2) it is investigated, (3) a solution or explanation is determined. Like R. Austin Freeman's hero Dr. John M. Thorndyke, Taine's scientist heroes function as scientific detectives, methodically working in well-equipped laboratories to test and to analyze their hypotheses in order to solve the novels' controlling mysteries. In terms of formal construction, a typical Taine novel employs both the adventure and the mystery formulas, superimposed onto a restrained, serious, and realistically presented science-problem framework. Often for Taine the problem centers on a dangerous evolutionary mutation—caused by radioactivity from some exotic metal, or by a mistake made in directing human evolution, or by a discovery of a new chemical catalyst—that must be destroyed before it threatens civilization.

This method of construction suggests that Taine's theory of the novel is more late Victorian than twentieth-century Georgian. It is clear that Taine was not strongly influenced by the great Victorian science fiction visionaries: H. G. Wells and George Griffith in England, and Garrett P. Serviss and Edward Bellamy in America. Rather, it was Haggard, Sir Arthur Conan Doyle, Fergus Hume, Kipling, William H. Hodgson, A. Merritt, Merriman, Henty, Stevenson, and Joseph Conrad who directly influenced Taine with their stories of adventurous quests and travels to exotic locales by rugged, self-reliant men who are tested by extreme physical, psychological, and (occasionally) occult forces. Taine's narrative style is clearly late Victorian, too, in often featuring a Collins-like use of multiple narrators and a mid-Victorian fondness for judgmental clarity. Taine's narrators directly and continually comment on the moral significance of the characters and incidents. There are no moral ambiguities created by disappearing or self-effacing narrators, and no sudden shifts in the narrative point of view; everything is direct, straightforward, and clearly defined.

Yet despite this Victorian approach, Taine's novels have a clear feeling of modern actuality. Such a feeling is generated by his use of the (then) latest scientific theories, by his employment of current slang and popular idioms, and by the contemporaneousness of many of his novels' settings: the action in most of them takes place in the same decade that they were published. His novels also provide additional interest as social history, documenting the moral values and social manners of the eras they portray. Novels written by Taine in the 1920's are filled with giddy flappers, Babbitt-like boosters, and corporate sharks bent on making a killing in the stock market. Like John Dos Passos and Sinclair Lewis, Taine was keenly interested in the American vernacular, and his novels are peppered with now-forgotten idioms and colorful slang.

Taine wrote both for pulp magazines and for book publishers. At the beginning of his novelistic career he was published exclusively by E. P. Dutton, and at the close by independent science fiction specialty houses—Fantasy Publishing Company in Los Angeles and Fantasy Press in Reading, Pennsylvania. Nearly half of his novels appeared in pulp magazines such as *Amazing Stories, Amazing Stories Quarterly, Wonder Stories,* and *Astounding Stories.* Two of Taine's novels— "Twelve Eighty-Seven" (*Astounding,* 1935) and "Tomorrow" (*Marvel Science Stories,* 1939)—to date have not appeared in book form. Unlike his contemporaries (Wells, Haggard, and Doyle), almost all of Taine's fictional output was devoted to science fiction or science fantasy. But like Wells, and like his American predecessor Serviss, Taine wrote numerous nonfiction works that helped to popularize science for the mass reading public. The most influential of these were *Men of Mathematics* (1937), *The Development of Mathematics* (1940), and *Mathematics, Queen and Servant of Science* (1951).

I

Eric Temple Bell, who wrote verse and fiction under the pseudonyms J. T. and John Taine, was born in Peterhead, Scotland, on 7 February 1883, the son of James Bell, Jr., and Helen Jane Lindsay Lyall Bell. Taine received his primary and secondary education at Bedford, where he came under the influence of the brilliant mathematician E. M. Langley. In 1902 Taine immigrated to the United States, where he continued his studies in mathematics at Stanford University. After taking the B.A. degree at Stanford in 1904, he received an M.S. from the University of Washington in 1907. He completed the Ph.D. at Columbia University in 1912.

While at Stanford, Taine worked as a tutor; he was also engaged in business in the San Francisco area between 1904 and 1906. A business project in which he was involved was wiped out by the 1906 earthquake and fire, scenes from which he later used in his novel *The Time Stream*. From 1907 to 1908, Taine was a teaching fellow at the University of Washington, and during the next two years he worked in a lumber mill and taught school in Siskiyou County, California. In 1912 he became a full-time mathematics instructor at the University of Washington, achieving the rank of full professor in 1922. He remained at Washington until 1926. During the summers from 1924 to 1928, Taine was a visiting professor at the University of Chicago; and in the fall term of 1926, he was a visiting professor at Harvard University. From 1926 until his retirement in 1953, Taine was a professor of mathematics at the California Institute of Technology. After retiring he devoted his time to work for Bell Laboratories, doing research on the theory of numbers.

Taine contributed several important propositions in the theory of numbers. In 1918 he completed the proofs to support earlier theorems propounded by the French mathematician Joseph Liouville between 1857 and 1870. Much of Taine's experiences working with the proofs of Liouville's theorems was later fictionalized in his novel "Twelve Eighty-Seven," in which a mathematician named Seventeen ("Sam") produces the proofs for the theorems of Jay Jarvis, a physical chemist. For his work on the Liouville proofs, Taine was

John Taine (Eric Temple Bell). PHOTO COURTESY OF JAY KAY KLEIN ARCHIVES

awarded the Bocher Memorial Prize in 1924 by the American Mathematical Society. The awards committee described Taine's work as a fundamental contribution to the theory of numbers. He also wrote two standard mathematics texts: *Algebraic Arithmetic* (1927) and *The Development of Mathematics* (1940).

Besides his many books on popular mathematics and science, Taine wrote two volumes of verse: *Recreations* (1915) and *The Singer* (1916). He also contributed nearly three hundred technical articles to mathematical journals in the United States, England, Japan, and India. For his writings on science, Taine was awarded the gold medal by the Commonwealth Club of California at San Francisco in 1938. He was a member of the American Association for the Advancement of Science, the American Mathematical Society (serving for a time as its vice president), the Mathematical Association of America (of which he was president in 1931–1932), the National Academy of Sciences, the Calcutta Mathematical Society, the Circolo Matematico di Palermo, the American Philosophical Association, the Authors' League of America, Phi Beta Kappa, and Sigma Xi.

Taine was greatly interested in painting and in gardening; he also was a devotee of raising cats and of Chinese art. His interest in Oriental art may explain why eight of his fifteen novels are set in the Orient. Taine married Jessie Lillian (Smith) Brown on 24 December 1910, in Yreka, California. They had one son. Taine died in Watsonville, California, on 21 December 1960.

II

Very little scholarly work has been done to date on Taine; but with the growing academic interest in science fiction, this may change. There are no published collections of his letters and no collected or uniformly bound editions of his novels. Critical material on Taine's fiction is practically nonexistent. There are no sustained critical analyses of any individual Taine novel, and no comprehensive appraisals of his collective work. At best, there are brief, passing comments about his novels here and there in the standard histories of science fiction. For example, James O. Bailey's seminal study of the science fiction genre, *Pilgrims Through Space and Time* (1947), briefly describes Taine's *Before the Dawn* and *The Iron Star*. Because of this absence of critical attention, it may be of some utility to discuss as many of Taine's novels as space permits.

Taine's novels fall into three recognizable periods: the apprenticeship phase of adventure thrillers written in the late 1920's; the evolutionary cycle of novels published in the 1930's (his mature period); and the small number of postwar science fantasy novels. Taine published five science fiction novels during the 1920's: *The Purple Sapphire* (1924), *Quayle's Invention* (1927), *The Gold Tooth*

(1927), *Green Fire* (1928), and *The Greatest Adventure* (1929). They are significant because they introduce important themes that he developed more fully in his later novels.

The most important of these themes are evolution and mankind's opportunity to breed itself to a state of perfection; the conflict between science's right to unlock nature's secrets and the recognition that some knowledge is best left undiscovered; the struggles of a great race against an ignorant priesthood; the need to control nature if, in Lord Tennyson's phrase, humanity is to work the beast out of itself; the necessity for scientists to assume full moral responsibility for the consequences of their experiments, especially with respect to creating artificial life or directing and controlling human evolution; the corrupting influence of corporate capitalism on scientific objectivity; and Taine's repeated hope that scientists will unite to force politicians to ban the use of poison gas.

Also significant is the fact that Taine's early novels rely heavily on both thematic and structural sensationalism. Adventure, mystery, and spy formulas or patterns of organization shape their construction. While it is true that each novel articulates a serious scientific theme, it is sensationalism, rather than science, that dominates their intended artistic effect. Like many writers beginning their career, Taine's early fiction is highly imitative. There are recognizable elements—some thematic and some technical—taken from the novels of Conrad, Kipling, Collins, Stevenson, and Haggard. Yet the presence of established Victorian themes and organizing patterns works to make his novels artistically successful, because Taine uses these materials with considerable skill.

Taine's first published novel, *The Purple Sapphire*, introduces no original themes or ideas into the genre, but it does exhibit a technical virtuosity in combining a number of disparate Victorian story formulas. Around a core story—a Tibetan, called Singh, kidnaps an English general's daughter to aid him in recovering the secrets of a lost civilization— Taine adds a treasure hunt, a search for missing persons, a dead-alive formula puzzle, a spy story, a cipher story, a quest story, a love story, and an exotic adventure story set in Tibet just before World War I. Taine is skilled enough as a romancer to make this composite structure succeed.

Aside from the conventional actions in the search-and-adventure section of the novel—John Ford, Rosita Rowe, and Montague Joicey's adventures as they search for, find, and rescue Evelyn Wedderburn—the lost-civilization theme is the most important conceptual component in the novel. This is shaped by an account of the Great Race, a vanished white Central Asiatic civilization in which a caste of woman scientists produced and controlled atomic energy. An accidental atomic explosion wiped out the scientists and shattered the civilization, leaving the land heavily radioactive. The present-day inhabitants are for the most part a fragmented, degenerate, and ignorant people. Singh, however, was an exception of genius who had regained a little of the ancient science and, to satisfy folkways, needed a woman from outside to continue his work.

Significant is Taine's care in making Ford, Rowe, and Joicey three-dimensional characters, each acting as a foil to the others.

Both *Quayle's Invention* and *The Gold Tooth* are adventure-mystery thrillers shaped by the gold-alchemy and great-discovery formulas. In *Quayle's Invention* the central scientific idea involves a revolutionary new process for extracting gold from seawater. This novel, like *The Purple Sapphire*, combines a number of story formulas into a single artistic whole. *Quayle's Invention* is a great discovery/averted world catastrophe/revenge-redemption/spy/bushranger/mystery/world-conspiracy story.

Three main actions give the novel its particular meaning: banker Cutts's attempted suppression of Quayle's discovery by marooning Quayle on the desert shore of Western Australia; Cutts's later attempt to rediscover the process in order to control the world's economy and the countermoves of Quayle (since rescued) and his friends; and the story of Quayle's personal growth from self-destructive vengefulness to moral redemption.

This last component, though superficially upstaged by the exciting action of the two adventure plots, is the most important, since it unifies the three plots into a single artistic whole. Taine's account of Quayle's progress from psychological fragmentation to moral wholeness is detailed, well-defined, and central to the novel's controlling morality, which argues that only through love and social responsibility can mankind find peace and happiness.

Less successful, though more ambitious, is *The Gold Tooth*. Set in Boston, Tokyo, and the mountains of northern Manchuria during the mid-1920's, it is shaped by the great discovery/gold-alchemy/lost civilization/spy-international confrontation/murder-mystery/love-story formulas. Its controlling scientific idea is the rediscovery of an ancient alchemical catalyst that rapidly breaks mercury down into gold. This rediscovery is made by a Japanese chemist named Satoru Okada after he examines a pictograph, stolen from a Korean monastery, that describes this process in allegorical figures. It is clear to Okada that an advanced, long-lost civilization produced the pictograph and possessed the catalyst.

The central action reflects the rivalry among four groups intent upon possessing or suppressing the catalyst: a group of military modernists at the Japanese court supported by the emperor; a rival group of conservative traditionalists like Okada, who reject Western ideas; Secretary of State George Smith, representing the American government; and Jim Blye, a Boston archaeologist sent to Manchuria by a Boston museum purportedly to locate fossilized dinosaur eggs. The closing section describes Blye and Okada's struggle to prevent each other from obtaining the catalyst—a struggle waged on an isolated Manchurian plateau that ends with the total destruction of the plateau and those on it. Two elements stand out in Taine's novel: a Sinclair Lewis-like satire of the smug Babbittry of Boston jeweler Eliakim Shortridge and an unsympathetic account of a doomed interracial courtship between Okada and Geraldine Shortridge.

Green Fire is structured around the averted cosmic catastrophe/great discovery/future world/mad scientist/revenge/worldwide epidemic formulas. Set in 1990 in New Jersey, it is a story about how Boris Jevic, the head of Consolidated Power, seeks to rule the world by being the first to harness and monopolize atomic energy. A scientific intelligence of the first order, but with unscrupulous commercial instincts, Jevic desires to punish the world for rejecting him when he first arrived in America as an unknown immigrant from Serbia.

Jevic's will to power is contested by his rivals at James Ferguson's Independent Laboratories. Ferguson, his daughter Vera, and Scottish mathematical genius David Mac-Robert fear that in his insane haste Jevic will miscalculate and plunge the world into a catastrophe. Jevic is so unbalanced by his obsession for revenge that he no longer cares whether his calculations are accurate. Ferguson's people break into Jevic's laboratory; they discover that Jevic has miscalculated, and they readjust his instruments, averting universal destruction at the last moment. Jevic's instruments had set off an all-destructive chain reaction in the universe that, until halted by MacRobert, was systematically destroying everything in its path. Taine's prophetic vision of the future does not extend much beyond depicting an economic system no longer dominated by large corporations and describing a 540-horsepower automobile powered by chemical generators.

The Greatest Adventure is the first novel that Taine shaped exclusively around an evolutionary theme; it also is the first in his cycle of evolution stories. This novel describes the discovery of an isolated, self-contained region in Antarctica where dinosaurlike monsters exist. The novel's hero, research oncologist Dr. Eric Lane, discovers that these reptiles resemble no recorded types, past or present, but originated from experiments carried out millions of years ago by a highly advanced race of beings who created artificial life, which escaped control. According to their records, they recognized their mistake, voluntarily destroyed themselves, and attempted to destroy their creation, but without success. Indeed, Lane's investigations unlock a world peril.

Taine's novel is constructed around the evolution/great discovery/prehistoric romance/self-contained, isolated paradise/lost, great civilization/adventure-story formulas. Aside from the story's novel notion of a society so idealistic that it would commit collective suicide for the sake of an unknown future population, *The Greatest Adventure* is intended as a purely sensational adventure. Characterization gives way to exciting episodic adventure in which the narrative exploits every ritual and expected set piece common to the prehistoric adventure subgenre. Readers familiar with Doyle's *The Lost World* (1912), Edgar Rice Burroughs' *The Land That Time Forgot* (1924), and Hodgson's *The Boats of the 'Glen Carrig'* (1907) will recognize many similarities between these and Taine's novel.

Among the seven novels and one short story that Taine published in the 1930's—*The Iron Star* (1930), *The Crystal Horde* (*Amazing Stories Quarterly*, 1930), *Seeds of Life* (*Amazing Stories Quarterly*, 1931), *The Time Stream*, *Before the Dawn*, "Twelve Eighty-Seven," "Tomorrow" (*Marvel Science Stories*, 1939), and the short story "The Ultimate Catalyst" (*Thrilling Wonder Stories*, 1939)—three novels are of great importance.

The first, artistically one of the most notable of all his works, is *The Crystal Horde* (originally published as *White Lily*). There is some indication that this novel influenced a 1957 Universal film called *The Monolith Monsters*, which was based on a screenplay by Norman Jolley and Robert M. Fresco. The film employs the same central scientific premise that organizes Taine's novel; and both Taine's novel and the film feature essentially the same plot, with only minor variations in setting and incident. *The Crystal Horde* is organized around the wonderful discovery/world catastrophe/adventure/mystery-puzzle formulas. Set in Los Angeles, and later in Kansu Province, China, it is based on a scientific idea about an accidental chemical reaction caused by food dyes that creates thousands of separate silicon colloid growths of monstrous size, capable of feeding, moving about, and perpetuating themselves.

The silicon monsters first appear in and around Los Angeles. Later they destroy a ship bound for the Orient, and finally they wreak havoc in China before the novel's eccentric geologist hero, Jonathan Saxby, can stop them. Of all Taine's novels, *The Crystal Horde* best combines bold fantasy with finely realized fictional verisimilitude. The Chinese revolution subplot, with its well-drawn political factions and contending ideologies, gives the novel depth and a remarkable panoramic view.

Of even greater artistic importance is *The Time Stream*, one of the most original stories found in the time travel subgenre. It is based on the concept that time is a circular stream in which past and future meet and are the same. Set in San Francisco on the eve of the 1906 earthquake and on the doomed planet Eos (which is our past and our future), it is shaped by the time travel/lost civilization/genetic planning/great catastrophe/doomed, forbidden love-story formulas.

The central plot is organized around the discovery by a group of friends in San Francisco that they existed/will exist on the nearly utopian planet Eos, with parallel situations between San Francisco and Eos. Traveling back and forth mentally, they participate in the destruction of Eos.

Here Taine depicts a rebellion among young Eosians who refuse to accept eugenics recommendations and insist on irrational romantic love, even though the infallible system predicts that a certain match will lead to the destruction of Eos. There is no compulsion on Eos, and an Eosian Eve reenacts the biblical fall when she rejects reason and rationality and tempts others, with her doctrine of freedom and love, to rebel. Such a rebellion ends Eos's golden age. Eos is torn apart in a conflict between reason and emotion, between scientific planning and brutish instinct, and between intellect and passion. In despair the master scientists loose forces that destroy the planet. Only a few survive, without knowledge of Eosian superscience.

Central to the novel is Taine's notion that science is mankind's only hope to subdue both the external forces of nature and the beast in its own character. Science, he argues, must foresee the predictable future and reshape humanity's path so that the greatest happiness will come to the greatest number.

Unlike Taine's other novels, *The Time Stream* is given additional power by its extensive use of symbolism. One of its controlling metaphors is the use of Percy Shelley's Hellas myth, the symbol of the undying fire rediscovered. Also central is the Ouroboros figure of the snake with its tail in its mouth, which is a traditional symbol of perfect unity and a quite apt representation of Taine's concept of a circular time stream and Eos' source of energy.

Quite different in theme is Taine's *Before the Dawn*, a prehistoric romance about the end of the great reptilian age. Langtry, an inventor, constructs a televisor that visually reproduces images stored inside rocks. These soundless pictures are projected on a gigantic screen that resembles an enormous Victorian diorama, giving them a remarkable three-dimensional effect. With such a fantastic device Langtry and his two collaborators, Bronson and Professor Sellar, witness a pictorial replay of Earth's early history. The action centers on a giant reptile named Belshazzar as it vainly struggles against radical climate change and the superior adaptability of the newly emerging mammals. Aside from the three scientists in the frame story, the central action involves only the animals in an extended dramatization of Darwin's theory of natural selection.

Through Belshazzar's attempts to find a land bridge south to a warmer continent, the reader is made aware of the creature's courage, its resourcefulness, and its intelligence. A whimsical case can be made that Belshazzar was Earth's first scientist because, in its struggles to survive, it mastered the law of levers (in killing another reptile named Old Rumpy), it understood the fundamental law of falling objects, and it discovered the laws of hydrostatics. In the end a half-starved Belshazzar dies in a fierce battle with another great reptile (called Satan by the scientists), signaling the end of the reptilian age.

Taine's postwar writing is disappointing. None of his novels or novellas—*The Forbidden Garden* (1947), "The Cosmic Geoids" and "Black Goldfish" (1949), and *G.O.G. 666* (1954)—approaches the skill, bold imagination, or high adventure of his prewar novels. Of these works *The Forbidden Garden* is the best. It is an evolution story set in an isolated paradise in Central Asia and is shaped by the great discovery/extraterrestrial life transplanted to earth/Eden myth/hereditary family insanity / spy / mystery / adventure patterns. "The Cosmic Geoids" is a great discovery/ world catastrophe/evolutionary romance/lost civilization / interstellar contact / cipher puzzle/worldwide war fantasy. The last of his works, *G.O.G. 666*, reflecting the tensions of the cold war, is a spy/mystery thriller about Russian attempts to create a superman by crossbreeding gorillas with humans. Despite the cloak-and-dagger spy format, the novel's ideological bias and its crude satire undermine its artistic integrity.

But despite these weak postwar novels, Taine's reputation as a major American mainstream Georgian science fiction writer is quite secure, since it is based on his novels of the 1930's. Considering his works as a whole, *The Time Stream, The Crystal Horde,* and *Before the Dawn* are his best novels—any one of them would secure his place in the history of science fiction just below the first rank. Although lacking the vision of Wells or Stapledon, Taine is certainly the equal of the best of the scientific romancers in the genre.

—JAMES L. CAMPBELL, SR.

ADDENDA

For reasons known best to himself, Eric Temple Bell garbled his family history, concealed much of his early life, and falsified his academic record. When he was recognized as one of the preeminent mathematicians in the United States and his vita was requested for reference works, he repeatedly gave wrong or misleading information. As a result, earlier biographical statements are all incorrect. It remained for Constance Reid, over a five-year investigation sponsored by the Mathematical Association of America, to uncover the true Eric Temple Bell.

Eric Temple Bell was born in Peterhead, a small town in the very northeast of Scotland. His father, James Bell, Jr., an Englishman, a member of a prosperous, London-based firm of wholesale fish processors, was what amounted to branch manager of the family industry in Peterhead. His mother, née Helen Jane Lindsay Lyall, was the daughter of a local schoolmaster.

When Bell was about a year and a half old, his family emigrated to the United States, settling in San Jose, California, where his father operated a small commercial orchard. The reasons for this move and change of occupation are not known. The Bells lived in San Jose until 1896, when after the mysterious death of James Bell, the family moved to England. Bell later concealed the fact that he had grown up in California, even from his wife and son.

In England Bell attended school at Bedford. His later claims to have attended the University of London are false. In 1902 he returned to the United States via Canada, settling in San Jose, and matriculating at Stanford University. The remainder of his life is on record. Despite the fact that his residence in Scotland consisted of a short period in infancy and that his father was English, Bell considered himself a Scot, spoke with a Scottish accent, and proclaimed the merits of Scotland and Scottish blood most strongly in his novels.

As Constance Reid discovered, the writing dates of his fiction were often quite far removed from publication dates, and a developmental interpretation of his work based on the dates of book or magazine appearance cannot be valid. The composition dates of his science fiction are *Green Fire*, June 1919; *The*

Purple Sapphire, 1920; *The Time Stream*, summer 1921, perhaps abridged in 1931; *The Greatest Adventure*, 1922–1923; *The Iron Star*, 1924; *The Gold Tooth*, 1925–1926; *Quayle's Invention*, 1925–1926; *White Lily*, end of 1927, beginning of 1928; *Seeds of Life*, summer 1928; *The Forbidden Garden*, late 1928, early 1929; "Tomorrow," 1929; *Before the Dawn*, probably early 1930s; "Twelve Eighty-Seven," probably after spring 1933; "The Cosmic Geoids," late 1940; *G.O.G. 666*, 1940; "Black Goldfish," undated, but "(apparently) the last science fiction story that Bell wrote" (Reid, page 327).

Bell was an extremely rapid writer who could turn out a long, elaborately planned novel in a matter of weeks between semesters, but he lacked self-criticism and was unable to revise or edit his work. He left at least four unpublished novels at his death; two, inadequately described and in private hands, may be peripheral science fiction. He also left a large quantity of unpublished poetry, including a 5,000-line fantastic epic.

—E. F. BLEILER

Selected Bibliography

WORKS OF JOHN TAINE

The Purple Sapphire. New York: E. P. Dutton, 1924.
The Gold Tooth. New York: E. P. Dutton, 1927.
Quayle's Invention. New York: E. P. Dutton, 1927.
Green Fire. New York: E. P. Dutton, 1928.
The Greatest Adventure. New York: E. P. Dutton, 1929.
The Iron Star. New York: E. P. Dutton, 1930.

Before the Dawn. Baltimore, Md.: Williams and Wilkins, 1934.
"Twelve Eighty-Seven." *Astounding*, 15–16 (May–September 1935). (No book edition.)
"Tomorrow." *Marvel Science Stories*, 1, no. 4: 12–115 (April–May 1939). (No book edition.)
"The Ultimate Catalyst." *Thrilling Wonder Stories*, June 1939. Reprinted in *The Best of Science Fiction*, edited by Groff Cronklin. New York: Crown, 1946. (His only short story.)
The Time Stream. Providence, R.I.: Buffalo Book Company, 1946. (First appeared in *Wonder Stories*, December 1931–March 1932.)
The Forbidden Garden. Reading, Pa.: Fantasy Press, 1947.
The Cosmic Geoids and One Other. Los Angeles: Fantasy Publishing Company, 1949. (Contains two novellas, "The Cosmic Geoids" and "Black Goldfish.")
Seeds of Life. New York: Galaxy Novels, 1951. London: Rich and Cowan, 1955. (First appeared in *Amazing Stories Quarterly*, 4, no. 4 [Fall 1931].)
The Crystal Horde. Reading, Pa.: Fantasy Press, 1952. (First appeared in *Amazing Stories Quarterly*, 3, no. 1 [Winter 1930], as "White Lily.")
G.O.G. 666. Reading, Pa.: Fantasy Press, 1954. London: Rich and Cowan, 1955.

CRITICAL AND BIOGRAPHICAL STUDIES

Bailey, James O. *Pilgrims Through Space and Time*. New York: Argus Books, 1947; repr. Westport, Conn.: Greenwood Press, 1972.
Bleiler, Everett F., and Richard J. Bleiler. *Science-Fiction: The Gernsback Years*. Kent, Ohio: Kent State University Press, 1998.
Reid, Constance. *The Search for E. T. Bell, Also Known as John Taine*. Washington, D.C.: Mathematical Association of America, 1993.
Stableford, Brian. "John Taine." In *Science Fiction Encyclopedia*, edited by Peter Nicholls. Garden City, N.Y.: Doubleday, 1979; London: Roxby Press, 1979.
Taine, John. "The Science Novel." In *Of Worlds Beyond*, edited by Lloyd Arthur Eshbach. Reading, Pa.: Fantasy Press, 1947; repr. Chicago: Advent, 1964.

WILLIAM TENN

(b. 1920)

WILLIAM TENN IS the pseudonym used on almost all the published fiction of Philip Klass (three early stories appeared under the byline Kenneth Putnam, although two of these were subsequently reprinted as by Tenn in Tenn collections). Klass (not the Philip Klass noted for his articles debunking UFO cults) was born in London in 1920 but grew up in New York City. (One of his later stories, "My Mother Was a Witch" [1966], which is set in a Jewish community in Brooklyn, is, he has said, "essentially memoir.") He studied at the City College of New York and at New York University (where he published humorous fantasies in an undergraduate literary magazine, *The Apprentice*), but he did not complete a degree. After finishing wartime army service, Klass turned to writing science fiction (of which he had long been a devotee; his essay "Jazz Then, Musicology Now" [1972] describes the alienation of a science fiction enthusiast in the prewar campus environment, where the garish pulp magazines were almost universally scorned).

His first professionally published story, "Alexander the Bait," appeared in *Astounding Science-Fiction* under the Tenn by-line in May 1946. An unexceptional story, in which the eponymous Alexander Parks tempts humankind into space travel by faking survey results showing enormous mineral wealth on the moon, it foreshadows several of his later stories in its use of a form of trickery as the pivot of its plot.

During the next five years Tenn published about half of his total output of short stories.

At this early point in his career, he was, by his own testimony, attempting to mold himself (unsuccessfully) into a productive commercial hack writer, so it is not surprising that the majority of these early works are quite forgettable. But he did very quickly establish an individual voice and lay down the themes to which he repeatedly returned, in stories such as "Child's Play" (1947), "Me, Myself, and I" (1947), "Brooklyn Project" (1948), "Venus and the Seven Sexes" (1949), "Betelgeuse Bridge" (1951), and "Null-P" (1951).

As Brian M. Stableford has pointed out, "The work of Tenn and others was made possible by the extent to which pre-1950 science fiction had made their central notions commonplace . . . these had come to embody sets of routine expectations which were infinitely amenable to ironic violations. Tenn was a member of the generation which discovered these story routines ready-made but largely unexploited." As an ironist making sophisticated use of familiar science fiction ideas, Tenn had been preceded by the team of Henry Kuttner and C. L. Moore (chiefly in their "Lewis Padgett" persona), but whereas they tended toward slightly surreal black humor, Tenn's penchant was for more acid, satirical comedy. His style, virtually from the beginning, was polished and incisive.

"Child's Play" is one of a small subgenre of stories, the paradigm for which is Kuttner and Moore's "Mimsy Were the Borogoves" (1943), in which a device from the future is accidentally translated to the present. In Tenn's story the object is a "Bild-A-Man" set—a children's toy from the twenty-fourth century that enables its user to construct living creatures up to and including a human being. After practice efforts, Sam Weber, the protagonist, builds a duplicate of himself, at which point a representative from the future arrives to reclaim the misplaced toy. The duplicate Weber must be demolished . . . but unfortunately for Weber, the replica has no difficulty convincing the official that *he* is the original. This ironic twist brings to a neat end an otherwise rather directionless story and prefigures the nearly identical ending of "Lisbon Cubed" (1958), in which a human becomes accidentally involved with the antics of alien spies in human disguise who infest the Earth. In this variant the human protagonist, mistaken for an incompetent alien spy, is at the end ceremonially stripped of his uniform—that is, of his human body.

This repetition of effect is quite common in Tenn's work. Indeed, "Child's Play" itself generated another, rather similar story—"Errand Boy" (1947), in which a child, evidently from the same future world as in the earlier story, attempts to supply an avaricious businessman with wonderful gadgets—as well as a direct sequel, "Wednesday's Child" (1956), which follows the later life of the baby that Sam Weber constructs and then abandons on the steps of an orphanage.

"Child's Play" and "Errand Boy" are also time-travel stories—a type of story that has proved to be one of Tenn's favorites. He has written several time-paradox stories: "Me, Myself, and I," "Brooklyn Project," "It Ends with a Flicker" (1956), and "The Discovery of Morniel Mathaway" (1955). The first three of these are exercises in ingenious complexity. "Me, Myself, and I" presents a time traveler making a tiny alteration in the distant past to see if the present is thereby affected. It is, slightly, so he goes back again to persuade himself not to make the alteration. The story finishes with an ever-growing number of duplicates of the protagonist arguing and fighting by a prehistoric lakeside.

More originally, "Brooklyn Project" plays on the irony that if time travel did cause changes in the past that altered the present, we in the present would never be aware of this, because to us the "previous" present world would never have happened. The story also sharply satirizes the paranoid contemporary attitude regarding secrecy and security.

The most sophisticated of the three stories, "It Ends with a Flicker," is in a sense a variation on the theme of Jack Williamson's novel *The Legion of Time* (serialized in 1938), in which the armies of two mutually inconsistent potential futures battle for existence, their struggle centering on a single, insignificant event in our time; one outcome of that event would produce one of the future worlds, and the other outcome would produce the other world. Tenn refines this idea into an ingeniously constructed story of two struggling future societies, each of which traces its decline back to the same event—the flick of a switch—and each of which sends back a time traveler to alter the direction of the flick, and thereby bring another and (they hope) less arduous future into existence. The two futures cancel themselves out, and the entire future becomes a series of increasingly rapid flickers as the switch is moved back and forth, again and again.

The most effective of Tenn's time-paradox stories, because it has the most to offer beyond mere ingenuity, is "The Discovery of Morniel Mathaway," which first appeared in *Galaxy*. Here a future art critic, traveling back in time to visit the studio of Morniel Mathaway—the greatest artist in history—finds instead an untalented egotist who steals his time machine and escapes to the future (where he will be lionized), while the poor critic is left behind to spend the rest of his life painting all the masterpieces. The neatness of structure is here complemented by some sharp digs at pretentious, third-rate artists.

The other major theme that Tenn regularly exploits for its comic, ironic, and satiric possibilities is that of human contact with aliens. Here, again, the early stories—"Venus and the Seven Sexes" and "Betelgeuse Bridge"—are indicative of what follows. In the former story an elderly member of the seven-sexed

Venusian species tells some Venusian young-sters the tale of how their species learned the rudiments of civilization from an apparently wise and beneficent visiting Earthman. Un-fortunately and unknown to them, their vis-itor was actually a third-rate movie director, and the documents he left behind, which they study so assiduously for their innermost meanings, are third-rate movies. These mov-ies contain human romantic clichés that they translate inappropriately to a Venusian con-text. Their humble attempts to live by the precepts set out in these works lead them rap-idly toward extinction.

The story contains many farcical mo-ments—the seven-sexed Venusian Plookh, prey to every one of the myriad hideous pred-ators of their world, are presented in slapstick terms, while the inept director, Hogan Shles-tertrap, is a caricature of a Hollywood hack. But it has at its heart a quite serious and even bitter point about the effects of colonialism on the recipients of its doubtful benefits.

The same point is made rather more ex-plicitly in "Betelgeuse Bridge." Here a pair of friendly snail-like aliens land on Earth, are feted by humankind, and, after a suitable soft-ening-up period, swindle the humans out of all their radioactive material, offering in ex-change wonderful machines that cure disease and confer longevity. The twist is that the ma-chines run on the very radioactive material that the aliens need to power their own ma-chines. When this is discovered, one of the human characters remarks, "We did some-thing wrong, all right. We trusted. We made the same mistake all natives have made when they met a superior civilization." Unusually, in "Betelgeuse Bridge" Tenn gives the victims the last laugh: knowledge of how they have been tricked spurs humanity to redoubled ef-forts to achieve interstellar flight, and at the end of the story—in a curious pre-echo of Robert A. Heinlein's *The Puppet Masters* (1951), which appeared too soon after Tenn's story for there to be any direct influence—the humans have embarked on a mission of ven-geance against their molluscan deceivers.

Some of Tenn's later stories of human-alien encounters are content merely to exploit the comic possibilities. In "The Party of the Two Parts" (1954) an intelligent protozoan alien (Tenn's aliens are frequently modeled on lower orders of terrestrial life) is arrested for selling alien pornography to an Earthman. "The Flat-Eyed Monster" (1955) inverts the old-fashioned, bug-eyed monster story to show how hideous a human might appear to an alien. "Lisbon Cubed" offers similarly hu-morous treatment.

But the salutary lessons of "Venus and the Seven Sexes" and "Betelgeuse Bridge" are hammered home more forcefully in several of the later stories. In "The Deserter" (1953) hu-mans are fighting a vicious war with immense flatworms from Jupiter. One of the aliens, dis-tressed at the blind militarism of its leaders, deserts, only to discover that the military minds who now run human affairs are, if anything, even worse. The humanitarians on both sides are powerless and apparently doomed. "Bernie the Faust" (1963) recapitu-lates "Betelgeuse Bridge" in many ways, but on an individual rather than a species level, with an alien stranded on Earth engaging in an elaborate confidence trick in order to ob-tain the spare parts he needs for his ship. The story is wittier and more ingenious than its predecessor, but rather less pointed.

The most successful of Tenn's alien-contact stories is "The Liberation of Earth" (1953), which sheds the slapstick elements of its predecessors and is in consequence far more telling in its satire. Its technique almost exactly repeats that of "Venus and the Seven Sexes": a stirring piece of oral history is re-counted, as it were, "around the campfire," by an elder member of the species. In this case the species is *Homo sapiens,* the few surviv-ing members of which eke out a precarious existence on their now virtually uninhabita-ble planet. Earth has gotten into this state through being repeatedly "liberated" and "re-liberated" by two fierce alien races who tem-porarily use it as a battleground. The people of Earth, desperately eager to please and to take their place in the great galactic scheme

William Tenn (Philip Klass). PHOTO BY JAY KAY KLEIN

der the editorship of Horace L. Gold (which lasted from the magazine's inception in October 1950 until October 1961). Predictably, Tenn became identified with the magazine, the great majority of his stories from 1954 being published there, though the comparative sparseness of his output—from 1954 through 1958 he averaged three or four stories a year—meant that his name was less closely associated with it than more productive authors such as Frederik Pohl and Robert Sheckley. (Sheckley in particular appears to have been influenced by Tenn, although his ingenious stories generally have less bite.) Although the majority of Tenn's middleweight entertainments—"Betelgeuse Bridge," "The Party of the Two Parts," "The Flat-Eyed Monster," "It Ends with a Flicker," "Time in Advance" (1956), "Sanctuary" (1957), "Lisbon Cubed," and so forth—appeared in *Galaxy*, his more ambitious efforts were published in various outlets. "The Liberation of Earth," for instance, appeared in *Future*, one of the lesser magazines of its day, which suggests that its acidity was unpalatable to Gold and the other major editors. "Null-P," another of Tenn's sharper satires, appeared in the obscure and short-lived magazine *Worlds Beyond*, where it remained largely unnoticed until singled out for praise by Kingsley Amis in his critical study *New Maps of Hell* (1960).

"Null-P" satirizes conformity by describing the growth of a political movement devoted to the achievement of absolute normality (and hence complete mediocrity). It sweeps America, and then the world, following the discovery of one man, George Abnego, who fits every conceivable statistical norm and who quickly becomes president of the United States (the title of the story refers to the supplanting of the idea, accepted since Plato, that the best should govern). Under Abnegism the human race quickly devolves, to be replaced by a civilization of intelligent Labrador dogs. "Null-P" has strong thematic parallels with C. M. Kornbluth's "The Marching Morons" (published at virtually the same time in 1951), and like Kornbluth's story it carries uncomfortable undercurrents of intel-

of things, are ruthlessly exploited by both sides.

This story was written during the Korean War; but, far from dating, it has actually become more pertinent with the passage of years. Its savagely satiric attack is sufficiently generalized not to have dated with the passage into history of its original target, while the inversions of language with which it makes great ironic play (for example, the debasement of the word "liberation" to mean various kinds of enslavement) have come much more into the forefront of our consciousness in the intervening years. "The Liberation of Earth" is an almost unimprovably exact parable, certainly one of the outstanding science fiction short stories of the 1950's.

In such stories as "Child's Play," "Brooklyn Project," and "Venus and the Seven Sexes," Tenn virtually established a blueprint for a kind of science fiction that in the 1950's became synonymous with *Galaxy* magazine un-

lectual snobbery; but it is nevertheless wittily and effectively written (and perhaps prescient in its anticipation of aspects of the Eisenhower presidency).

Three further stories from the 1950's merit individual attention: "Down Among the Dead Men" (1954), "Time Waits for Winthrop" (1957), and "Eastward Ho!" (1958), the first two of which appeared in *Galaxy*. "Down Among the Dead Men" is in many respects the most difficult of Tenn's stories to assess. It is set during a savage and seemingly endless war between humans and invading aliens, in which there is such a heavy toll of human life that all women have become virtual breeding machines and the protoplasm from human casualties is reprocessed to manufacture androids. In this dehumanized situation, one human (rendered sterile through his involvement in space combat) and his crew of alienated androids achieve a measure of empathy. Even in the worst of situations, the story seems to say, some positive human values can still assert themselves. At the same time, "Down Among the Dead Men" is a plea for racial tolerance, with the androids representing a minority suffering discrimination and hatred. But although the story is strongly written, it is too much rooted in the conventions of pulp science fiction, too remote from identifiable human experience to be truly effective. It is unsettling and disagreeable without being in any way salutary.

The other stories are more successful. "Time Waits for Winthrop"—retitled "Winthrop Was Stubborn" when collected in *Time in Advance* (1958)—uses the classic science fiction device of a group of people transported into the future in order to take a satiric look at a society in which individualism and the individual impulse are sacrosanct. Tenn tellingly extrapolates then-embryonic ideas of encounter group therapy into great institutions—Panic Stadium and Shriek Field—where people go to release the repressed feelings that would otherwise overwhelm them. "Time Waits for Winthrop" suffers as a story from being resolved by some deus ex machina manipulation but is otherwise incisive.

"Eastward Ho!" neatly inverts the European colonization of the United States by developing a postholocaust world to which the Indians have adapted far more successfully than the white men. Nineteenth-century American history is recapitulated in reverse.

During the 1950's Tenn published three volumes of short stories—*Of All Possible Worlds* (1955), *The Human Angle* (1956), and *Time in Advance*. But toward the end of the decade, his productivity—never high—began to decline. He published two stories in 1958, one in 1959, and no more until 1963, when "Bernie the Faust" and the short novel "The Men in the Walls" appeared. Since the start of his career, he had interspersed periods of freelance writing with other work—as a salesman and ship's purser. In 1966, Tenn was invited to teach creative writing at Pennsylvania State University, and he has become an associate professor in the English department there, despite his lack of formal academic qualification. Before that he published one more notable short story, "The Masculinist Revolt" (1965), an evenhandedly satirical examination of machismo and Momism. Since 1966 he has published only a few short stories, plus his only full-length novel, *Of Men and Monsters* (1968), an expansion of "The Men in the Walls."

The novel takes the old theme of alien invasion but infuses it with new life. The aliens who have occupied Earth are gigantic, and the remnants of humanity dwell in the aliens' houses like mice or rats in the walls of our own dwellings. These humans live in small, mutually hostile tribes, eking out a dangerous living. In the course of the story, human initiative triumphs over ignorance and superstition, and the human race ultimately sets out to colonize the galaxy, using the aliens as their (unwitting) carriers. It is an ingenious, enjoyable, and well-told novel that has never received the attention it deserves, probably because of the curious circumstances of its publication.

When Ballantine Books published the novel in 1968, the firm simultaneously released five collections of Tenn's short stories. Two of these were reprints (*Of All Possible Worlds* and *The Human Angle*), but the three others—*The Wooden Star*, *The Seven Sexes*, and *The Square Root of Man*—were new. All six books were issued as a set, with the obvious intention of establishing Tenn as one of the top names in science fiction. The scheme was unsuccessful. Far from gaining extra attention, the books went virtually unreviewed: H. W. Hall's *Science Fiction Book Review Index* records only one American review—in *The Magazine of Fantasy and Science Fiction*—for the three new collections, and only two significant American reviews of the novel. The packaging—in an extraordinarily inappropriate gothic style, with breathlessly overenthusiastic cover blurbs—cannot have helped; neither can the fact that in order to obtain five collections of stories, the barrel of the Tenn oeuvre had to be very thoroughly scraped. Apart from the four long stories in the long out-of-print *Time in Advance*, only half a dozen items were left uncollected, and the overwhelming (and correct) impression was left that Tenn simply had not written enough good stories for such treatment. There can have been few more maladroit publishing ventures in science fiction history. Most of the books have not been reprinted; and so Tenn's reputation, far from growing, has in the long term been diminished.

This is a pity, for in a genre full of commercial writers producing too much work, Tenn is a writer from whom more stories would be welcome. His routine variations on his regular themes were generally, by the time he reached the height of his career, at least polished and entertaining, while at his best his satiric pessimism has produced some of the most pointed stories in the science fiction canon.

Selected Bibliography

WORKS OF WILLIAM TENN

Of All Possible Worlds. New York: Ballantine Books, 1955; London: Michael Joseph, 1956. (Short stories; contents of American and British editions differ.)

The Human Angle. New York: Ballantine Books, 1956. (Short stories.)

Time in Advance. New York: Bantam Books, 1958; London: Victor Gollancz, 1963. (Short stories.)

A Lamp for Medusa. New York: Belmont Books, 1968. (A fantasy novella.)

Of Men and Monsters. New York: Ballantine Books, 1968.

The Seven Sexes. New York: Ballantine Books, 1968. (Short stories.)

The Square Root of Man. New York: Ballantine Books, 1968. (Short stories.)

The Wooden Star. New York: Ballantine Books, 1968. (Short stories.)

CRITICAL AND BIOGRAPHICAL STUDIES

Hackenberry, Charles. "Painter at the Keyboard." *Extrapolation*, 26, no. 1 (1985): 50–55. (Interview.)

Linaweaver, Brad. "Interview with William Tenn." *Riverside Quarterly*, 7 (March 1982): 82–93.

———. "Interview with William Tenn (Part 2)." *Riverside Quarterly*, 7 (May 1983): 150–159.

———. "Interview with William Tenn (Part 3)." *Riverside Quarterly*, 7 (December 1985): 232–239.

Stableford, Brian M. "The Short Fiction of William Tenn." In *Survey of Science Fiction Literature*. Edited by Frank N. Magill. Englewood Cliffs, N.J.: Salem Press, 1979. Pages 2065–2069.

Stephensen-Payne, Phil, and Gordon Benson, Jr. *William Tenn: High Klass Talent, a Working Bibliography*. Albuquerque, N. Mex.: Galactic Central, 1993.

Tenn, William. "Jazz Then, Musicology Now." *Magazine of Fantasy and Science Fiction* (May 1972).

Zebrowski, George. "Never Forget the Writers Who Helped Build Yesterday's Tomorrows." *Science Fiction Age*, 3 (1995): 30–36, 100.

—MALCOLM EDWARDS

SHERI S. TEPPER
(b. 1929)

A LATE BLOOMER and a prolific writer, Sheri S. Tepper is frequently seen as a feminist writer, but it might be more appropriate to view her main theme as the necessity of taking responsibility for one's actions. Tepper's stands against the abuse of women, abuse or lack of concern for people who are unprotected, abuse of the environment, and abuse or violence involving religious beliefs are all really stands against actions or use of power without consideration for the consequences. These themes run through all her novels, either as the main focus of the plot or a significant detail in stories that have something else as their main focus. Reviewers and readers who disagree with her stands are still drawn to her novels because of her excellent world-building and characterization. Tepper's first seven novels are fantasy; six of them form a group that became known as the True Game.

Sheri S. Tepper was born in Denver, Colorado, in 1929. She wrote and published some poetry under her married name, Sheri Eberhart, as early as 1963 but then withdrew from writing. From 1962 to 1986, she was executive director of Rocky Mountain Planned Parenthood, which gave her a predilection for seeing the domination of weaker or unprotected people in terms of women. She was also a member of various conservation groups, which caused her to look closely at environmental issues. She also wrote mysteries under the pseudonyms of B. J. Oliphant and A. J. Orde. One Oliphant mystery, *Dead in the Scrub*, garnered a nomination for an Edgar, an award given by the Mystery Writers of America.

Tepper had published no fiction until 1983 when Ace Fantasy published *King's Blood Four*, the first of the True Game novels. The novel is set in an imaginary quasi-medieval world. The main character is Peter, a foundling who is too young to have discovered his talent and so is virtually powerless. He is befriended by Master Mandor, who uses Peter to try to destroy King Mertyn. In this particular place, Schooltown, and time, Festival, calling "Game" against another person is forbidden, but Mandor does so anyway, showing no concern for Peter's rights or safety. As it happens, Peter survives, for he is the nephew of King Mertyn, who has protected him. After discovering his identity, Peter faces several dangers, discovers his talent as an unusual shapeshifter, and uses magic to protect himself. Through his experiences, Peter learns that people who have talent or power should care for those who have none. This wisdom sets Peter apart from many other Gamesmen.

The story of Peter is continued in *Necromancer Nine* (1983). In this novel Peter goes looking for his mother, Mavin. Once he enters shapeshifter country, his education as a shapeshifter begins in earnest. In his loneliness he is drawn into a castle where he discovers he has been captured by an evil mindtrap. Peter not only succeeds in escaping but also realizes that he must defeat the mindtrap; he is developing a compulsion to right wrongs that have been committed by others.

Peter's story is concluded in *Wizard's Eleven* (1984), in which he and his friends work to reanimate people who have been put into suspended animation and to destroy their enemies. This novel introduces the idea that women, even those with Talent, are largely controlled by the men in their families. It also introduces Jinian, who will figure prominently in the final books of the series. Jinian has been betrothed to King Kelver, whom she has never met, by her brother in order to form a Game alliance. Jinian is not particularly interested in marrying the man, especially after she meets Peter, so she arranges to have Peter's friend Silkhand, who is her teacher at the school for Gameswomen, seem more attractive to King Kelver. This works, as Silkhand is also attracted to him. Jinian is thus free to establish a relationship with Peter and to develop her talents as a wize-ard.

Tepper's next book in the series is *The Song of Mavin Manyshaped* (1985), the major action of which precedes the story of Peter and revolves around Mavin's leaving her home, Danderbat Keep, to avoid the sexual exploitation that would have been her fate. Mavin's sister Handbright had left earlier for much the same reason. Mavin takes Mertyn, her little brother, away with her to protect him. Mavin's story is extended in *The Flight of Mavin Manyshaped* (1985). It is fifteen years later, and Mavin is searching for her sister Handbright. She finds her in the chasm city of Topbridge across the sea from True Game. Mavin helps prevent or set right the exploitation of Beedie Beed by others of her clan who wish to gain power and have no qualms about harming or killing to accomplish that end. Handbright has been exploited by a local priest for his own pleasure.

Mavin's story is completed in the sixth book in the series, *The Search of Mavin Manyshaped* (1985). Here, Mavin keeps a promise she made twenty years earlier to meet Wizard Himaggery. When Mavin arrives at Pfarb Durim, Himaggery is not there, and she learns that he has been missing for eight years. Mavin also finds that the shadows of the Shadow Bell are growing and searching for Himaggery,

as is High Wizard Chamferton. Himaggery's life is in danger. When Mavin finds him, he is in the form of a unicorn and they frolic and mate. The dervish Bartlemy helps Mavin return Himaggery and the true High Wizard Chamferton safely to their world. Mavin must act to save Himaggery's life, but her pregnancy complicates the issue.

The True Game series then continues with Jinian in *Jinian Footseer* (1985), which tells how Jinian came to be at Vorbold's House at the school for Gameswomen. In this novel, Jinian is oppressed and exploited at every turn. First her mother ignores her, then arranges for her to marry an older man, King Kelver. The old woman who has been her caregiver and has been teaching her the wize-ard arts helps free Jinian from her mother and brother's domination by getting an agreement for schooling put into her marriage contract. But they attempt to use her as a pawn in the Game, and her brother's enemies attempt to use her against him. Jinian is also threatened by Gamesmen and women. Although most of this novel occurs before Jinian meets Peter, it ends where *Wizard's Eleven* does and raises an environmental issue. Jinian ends up needing to save the Chimmerdong Forest from the destruction planned by the evil family at Daggerhawk Demesne. The fact that loss of the forest is part of a possible destruction of her world reinforces Tepper's dominant theme: the importance of taking responsibility for the consequences of one's actions.

Dervish Daughter (1986) continues Jinian's story. Jinian, Peter, and the traveler Vitior Vulpas Queynt are going to find the eesties. Traveling north, they begin to see many dead people who have been using dream crystals; they vow to find the source of these deadly crystals and put an end to the addiction. Jinian is under oath to remain chaste for two more seasons as a result of having been initiated into the wize-ardly seven, but it is creating difficulties for her and Peter, who are in love. Peter is impatient at her faithfulness to her oath and tries to manipulate her into doing what he wants. The tension created by Peter's action illustrates that even those who care for another can fail to behave responsibly sometimes. The three of them find the source of the crystals and try to destroy the perpetrator, but Jinian believes the crystals are a message from their world that it wishes to die.

The True Game series ends with *Jinian Star-Eye* (1986). Together, Peter and Jinian go into a maze that is possibly the memory of the world and discover that some parts of the maze are real and some are not. They discover that the world is stuck on the memory of the destruction of the Daylight Bell, so they decide to remove that memory and try to replace the Daylight Bell to reestablish a balance between the dark and the light. They meet some of the eesties and discover that the problem stems from an eesty faction that hates humans. Peter gets help from Himaggery and Windlow; Jinian gets help from her seven and from an eesty to remove the memory of the destruction of the Daylight Bell. Jinian returns to the old city near her home and with help re-creates the Daylight Bell and fights the shadows. For Tepper, the imminent destruction of the world in *Dervish Daughter* and *Jinian Star-Eye* is an example of environmental abuse.

Tepper interrupted the True Game series by writing *The Revenants* (1984), a novel that takes place in a world controlled by a very narrow-minded religion. Anyone who does not fit the pattern is kept from the village by the Seals of Separation. Those who are different and living in the villages are killed by the Keepers. Those living outside are ostracized to protect the village. One such individual is Jaera Widdek, whose appearance is unusual and who has a child by an evil spirit at the time the villagers burn her hut. The child, named Jaer Ravnor by the old scholars who raise it, is changeable: at one time, it is male, at another, female. When the old ones die, Jaer goes on a quest to Orena, the city from which the scholars come. On the way, Jaer meets and is joined by six other outcasts from various kingdoms who have all been sent on "impossible" quests because they do not fit into someone's idea of what they should be or because someone wants something they have.

Sheri S. Tepper. © MIRIAM BERKLEY

In the course of the story, these seven individuals try to stop the Keepers of the Seals of Separation from taking over the entire world. They meet the Sisters of the Temple of the Goddess, who also join the fight. Jaer is also followed by Lithos, who is working for the evil spirit. Each of the seven questors has some object they are carrying with them that is magical and is what one of the others is seeking. Here Tepper creates a situation where the outcasts are responsible for saving the world. As outcasts, they have been mistreated without regard for their rights or the consequences of the actions taken against them.

In *Marianne, the Magus, and the Manticore* (1985), Marianne is threatened by the family of her father's first wife. This story in the fantasy vein is set in contemporary time. Marianne is in college and trying to stay far away from her half brother Harvey, who treats her as if she were an idiot, until she is old enough to inherit the money her father and mother left her. Her parents died mysteriously a year apart, and Harvey is her executor until she is thirty. Marianne meets the prime minister of Alphenlicht, where her parents were from, who takes a fancy to her. He then tries to protect her from Harvey and Harvey's aunt, who are apparently willing to kill Marianne for her money. The prime minister carelessly puts Marianne in danger because he is falling in love with her and is trying to win her regard.

Marianne, the Madame, and the Momentary Gods (1988) returns Marianne to her past. When Marianne was born, she seemed to know more about what was going on around her than she should have. It turns out that she had learned to manipulate time in her earlier experience. She is now reliving her life, having placed momentary gods at various places around her home to protect herself from her half brother Harvey, who has probably been responsible for the deaths of her parents so he could obtain their father's money, and who had tried to rape her when she was thirteen. Harvey is also being used by his aunt Madame Tabiti Delubovoska to get money. Marianne arranges things so she can prevent this from happening.

Tepper moved into the horror arena with *Blood Heritage* (1986), the story of an evil spirit that has been released after hundreds of years of captivity and seeks the death of members of a single family. Two of them are selfish women who care only for themselves and use people for their own ends. Selfish actions occur because neither woman is willing to be responsible for her actions unless she can profit from them. As always, Tepper shows that this behavior is wrong.

The Bones (1987), a sequel to *Blood Heritage*, involves the new wife of Badger Ettison, the main character in the first novel. In it people use magic to become immortal by sacrificing the lives of children. In addition, Badger has made Mahlia, his wife, promise to avoid contact with the witches who helped them in the first book. Mahlia agrees, and in return her life is put in danger.

Tepper returned to horror under the pseudonym E. E. Horlak with *Still Life* (1988), the story of the deaths of various neighbors of Sarah Chenowith through the manipulation of paintings. Sarah has been in love with her neighbors' son Martain Barber for years. When Marty's mother takes in an eccentric painter, strange things begin to happen that seem to be caused by or connected to paintings that Sarah finds in the painter's studio in the Barber house. The perpetrator is willing to kill repeatedly to accomplish her goals without regard for the lives of other people.

Tepper moved more emphatically into the science fiction arena with *Northshore* (1987) and its sequel, *Southshore* (1987). These two novels form one story, and *Northshore* was criticized by many for not being complete in itself. The two novels tell the story of a religious cult, the Awakeners, who preside over the dead of their world by using a fungus to reanimate them as workers so their bodies can be made palatable for the birdlike Thrasne, who were the original dominant species of the world. When Pamra Don, an Awakener, realizes the nature of her religion, she leads a rebellion. The Thrasne, however, are greedy beings who devastate the environment by overpopulating their world and destroying their food supply. In contrast, across the World River live a flightless offshoot of the Thrasne who have learned to control both their appetites and their population.

In *After Long Silence* (1987) the planet Jubal is covered with large crystal formations called Presences that restrict travel and technology. A semireligious group called Tripsingers calm these Presences with music, allowing people to live in and travel about the world without loss of life. Greedy business interests from off the planet plan to destroy the Presences, even though they might be intelligent beings, to allow use of all the land on the planet.

With *The Gate to Women's Country* (1988), Sheri Tepper began to be seen as an important force in science fiction. This book was more widely reviewed than any of her previous books, and it also provoked more vehement objections. A postnuclear-holocaust story, it pictures a world in which the warrior men who were responsible for the war and destruction are contained in a garrison outside the town. Women control the town and the majority of knowledge in an effort to curtail the violence of the garrison men. Some nonviolent men live and work in Women's Country, but they are few. Tepper was criticized for the antisexual and antihomosexual character of the "utopia" and the awkward and contradictory nature of the society. There are enough examples of the thoughtlessness and lack of responsibility of the warriors and a lost tribe of battering men to justify seeing this as antimale, but it also illustrates the shortsightedness and lack of responsibility of those men When men from the garrison plan to take over Women's Country, they pay very little attention to what they may lose if they do so.

The widely acclaimed novel *Grass* (1989) was nominated for a Hugo and received a *New York Times* Notable Book citation. It combines several elements of the responsibility theme. The galactic conglomeration of worlds is controlled by the religion Sanctity, which is preserving the names and DNA of all its members for revival in the future. The leaders of the church have no interest in or regard for anyone who is not a member and perhaps none for many who are members, as they plan to eliminate most people and revive only a select few. However, there is a deadly plague killing off all the galactic population except those on the closed planet Grass. Sanctity sends Roderigo and Marjorie Westriding Yrarier as ambassadors to Grass because they ride horses, and the elite of Grass are said to hunt. The hunt they find there is a far cry from what Roderigo and Marjorie do. The aristocrats of Grass do not care about anyone but themselves and have developed an destructive addictive relationship with their Mounts, Hounds, and Foxen. The relationship of the mounts and the aristocrats shows deliberate perversion of the environment. Roderigo and their daughter Stella follow the pattern of the aristocrats leaving Marjorie to solve the problem. The fact that Rodrigo has been keeping a mistress and is unwilling to try to work things out with his wife illustrates his irresponsibility.

Raising the Stones (1990) involves religion. In a solar system joined by transportation gates, the agricultural world Hobbs Land is invaded by resurrected ancient gods to enrich the matriarchal society, which is threatened by a violent male-dominated religion from Voorstod and the equally fanatical High Baidee. Both groups are willing to destroy the population of Hobbs Land to establish their religion as right. While the High Baidee are generally not as violent or as dedicated to absolute domination as the Voorstod, they are nevertheless willing to destroy those in Hobbs Land to maintain the rightness of their religion.

Sideshow (1992), the sequel to *Raising the Stones*, was thought by some critics to be the worst of Tepper's novels; some said it was too ambitious. The plot is complicated, the connection between the introduction, where the male-female Siamese twins are introduced, and the rest of the novel is tenuous. On the planet Elsewhere, people from various places have settled to escape the Hobbs Land gods. This has caused the planetary government to allow diversity in the extreme, with nearly every form of government and religion flourishing within the appropriate boundaries. No interference with the government of an area or religion is allowed and no one from an area is allowed to leave it. Extreme cruelty is allowed to flourish, and people are not allowed to escape a government or religion even though it is violent or oppressive.

Beauty (1991) is a sort of fractured fairy tale. The main character is Beauty, of Sleeping Beauty fame. She manages to avoid being put to sleep for a hundred years by getting her illegitimate sister, who looks exactly like her, to go to the birthday party in her place. Beauty ends up in the twenty-second century. The destruction of the environment is massive there and is the cause of the loss of magic. When she travels back to the twenty-first century, the people are little better, as they see the destruction coming but fail to act. This lack of responsibility is reinforced by the fact that Beauty is raped by one of the men on the documentary film crew that takes her to the twenty-second century. When she returns to her own time she finds her fairy mother, but the fairies are willing to sacrifice her to the Dark Lord to maintain their kingdom.

A Plague of Angels (1993) is set in a far future Earth where a remnant of mankind, left after most have fled to the stars, lives in a very restricted area. The cities are gang-controlled, and drugs and AIDS are rampant. Domination of the unprotected is widespread, both through the gangs and one power-hunger leader of the Founding Families.

In *Shadow's End* (1994), the population of the Alliance faces extinction by the Ularians just as the animals on most planets have become extinct following the Firster philosophy—that Man should come first while the DNA patterns of plants and animals are preserved. The followers of the destructive religion on the planet Dinadh, the only population to survive, show a lack of concern for the results of their actions toward helpless people. Here the role of the retarded boy Leely in resolving the situation demonstrates that consideration for so-called lesser people could be important.

Gibbon's Decline and Fall (1996), an allusion to Edward Gibbon's *The History of the Decline and Fall of the Roman Empire* (1776–1788), has seven college friends give the prettiest one a copy of Gibbon's book to carry around as part of a disguise to help discourage sexual harrassment from the male students. Set in contemporary times, this novel pits the friends against a malevolent male organization intent upon enslaving the women of the world. These men enslave other men just as they do the women, although to a somewhat lesser degree.

A Family Tree (1997) has more to do with the environment. Dora Henry's husband sees her more as a live-in housekeeper than a wife. When Dora is about to leave him, plants begin to grow wildly as a result of her husband's mismatched first marriage to the pagan goddess of nature. This ties in to the condition of the world three thousand years in the future. Advanced animals from the future come back to Dora's time to set things right and preserve all life in the future.

Six Moon Dance (1998) examines humankind's contact with sentient beings on another planet in the future. The society here is matriarchal with the men wearing veils and the women compensated for their "duty" of bearing children by having consorts to please and entertain them, a harem in reverse. The women here are the thoughtless dominating individuals while the men are the mistreated and abused, but the lesson is the same. One female character, however, pretends to be a man so she can go to sea rather than marry and have children. The indigenous race also wishes to continue to interact with the humans even though they are treated as if they were invisible, but they have their own way of compensating for the inequities of the arrangement. The indigenous race becomes the servants of the humans, acting as nannies for the human children. They pass on ideas about the planet and their race to the human children in songs and stories. They also inhabit the walls, observing the humans to gain understanding.

Sheri S. Tepper is admired by many for her strong female characters, imaginative stories, excellent characterization, smooth writing style, and strong feminist stands. Although these feminist stands are sometimes too close to the surface and blatantly "preachy," her two most recent books have taken a lighter approach, and the fantasy aspect of her imagination has been melded with the science fiction to produce excellent stories that will probably appeal to the wider audience who enjoyed *Grass*. It appears that readers who find her work interesting and enjoyable can look forward to more of the same in the future.

Selected Bibliography

WORKS OF SHERI S. TEPPER

King's Blood Four. New York: Ace Fantasy Books, 1983.
Necromancer Nine. New York: Ace Fantasy Books, 1983.
The Revenants. New York: Ace Fantasy Books, 1984.
Wizard's Eleven. New York: Ace Fantasy Books, 1984.

The Flight of Mavin Manyshaped. New York: Ace Fantasy Books, 1985.

Jinian Footseer. New York: TOR, 1985.

Marianne, the Magus, and the Manticore. New York: Ace Fantasy Books, 1985.

The Search of Mavin Manyshaped. New York: Ace Fantasy Books, 1985.

The Song of Mavin Manyshaped. New York: Ace Fantasy Books, 1985.

Blood Heritage. New York: TOR, 1986.

Dervish Daughter. New York: TOR, 1986.

After Long Silence. New York: Bantam Books, 1987.

The Bones. New York: TOR, 1987.

Northshore. New York: TOR, 1987.

Southshore. New York: TOR, 1987.

The Gate to Women's Country. New York: Foundation Book/Doubleday, 1988.

Marianne, the Madame, and the Momentary Gods. New York: Ace Books, 1988.

Jinian Star-Eye. New York: TOR, 1986.

Still Life (as E. E. Horlak). New York: Bantam Books, 1988.

Grass. New York: Foundation Book/Doubleday, 1989.

Marianne, the Matchbox, and the Malachite Mouse. New York: Ace Books, 1989.

Raising the Stones. New York: Foundation Books/Doubleday, 1990.

Beauty. New York: Foundation Book/Doubleday, 1991.

Sideshow. New York: Bantam Specter Books, 1992.

A Plague of Angels. New York: Bantam Books, 1993.

Shadow's End. New York: Bantam Books, 1994.

Gibbon's Decline and Fall. New York: Bantam Books, 1996.

The Family Tree. New York: Avon Books, 1997.

Six Moon Dance. New York: Avon Books, 1998.

CRITICAL AND BIOGRAPHICAL STUDIES

Fitting, Peter. "Reconsiderations of the Separatist Paradigm in Recent Feminist Science Fiction." *Science-Fiction Studies,* 19 (1992): 32–47.

Pearson, Wendy. "After the (Homo)Sexual: A Queer Analysis of Anti-Sexuality in Sheri S. Tepper's *The Gate to Women's Country.*" *Science-Fiction Studies,* 23 (1996): 199–226.

—SHERRY STOSKOPF

JAMES TIPTREE, JR.
(1915–1987)

Yes, I think we have two sexes. But I do not—repeat, not—think they are men and women. I see them as *patterns*, which may or may not be present singly or together in a given individual at a given time. . . .

One of them is relatively well-known, so simple as to be almost trivial, and subject to pathology: that is the male pattern. The other I see as overwhelmingly important to the race, very extensive over time, and almost unknown: that is the maternal pattern, or Mothering. . . .

I really view this sex as unknown. What is mothering powered by? . . .

Perhaps we will learn more about Mother—her dreams, her fantasies, her perceptions and excitements and glories and dooms and irascibilities and exploits from bi sexual sf. . . .

"What is a woman?". . . One of my first answers was that women are really truly *aliens*. (James Tiptree, Jr., "With Tiptree Through the Great Sex Muddle," pages 18–20)

THE MOST IMPORTANT fact about James Tiptree, Jr., is not that she is also the writer Raccoona Sheldon *and* retired psychologist Dr. Alice B. Sheldon. Despite the brief flurry of notoriety (and reevaluation of assumptions) that occurred in 1976–1977, when the mysterious Tiptree came out from behind the facade of "his" Virginia post office box to meet the science fiction world, the important facts are these: Tiptree is one of the best short-story writers to emerge in science fiction in the 1970's, and possibly ever. Tiptree is also one of the best creators of alien beings this field has known.

"Tiptree," that alien creature, uses her considerable talents to create memorable characters, both human and alien. Turning all the reader's assumptions about science fiction conventions, point of view, social behavior, and traditional narrative upside down, she explores the relationships of these characters: humans and aliens, men and women, mothers and children, people and the patterns of sexual behavior that have produced people who are only half human.

This is a complex process to evaluate and a powerful one to experience. Hence, Tiptree has made an indelible mark on the science fiction field with only three short-story collections (*Ten Thousand Light-Years from Home,* 1973; *Warm Worlds and Otherwise,* 1975; and *Star Songs of an Old Primate,* 1978), some (as yet) uncollected stories, some nonfiction articles, and one flawed but ambitious novel, *Up the Walls of the World* (1978).

Alice Bradley Sheldon was born in Chicago in 1915. Her mother, Mary Hastings Bradley, was a well-known writer, war correspondent, and author of travel books. Indeed, it was her death in 1976 and the resulting obituary notice, in which the "Tiptree" persona was linked with Sheldon, that precipitated the latter's revelation of her triple identity.

Sheldon lived in Africa and India and traveled widely as a child—a passion she and her husband, Huntington Sheldon, pursued for much of their lives. Indeed, "Tiptree" became well known and beloved in the science fiction community in part as the author of a series of articles, largely about adventures in foreign lands, for the amateur magazines *Phantasmicom* (edited by Donald G. Keller and Jeffrey M. Smith) and *Khatru* (edited by Jeffrey M. Smith). These, other articles and letters, and voluminous personal correspondence established the persona of a courtly, if reclusive, old gentleman who made friends with and aided many female writers while writing award-winning science fiction stories.

In "Everything but the Signature Is Me," an autobiographical essay (*Khatru* 7), Sheldon says that she spent her time from age three to age twenty-six being a painter—from the context, a talented and successful one:

And then came the dreadful steady unstoppable rise of Hitler—a great spreading black loinchop on the map—and I found out something else. There are painters who go on painting when a million voices are screaming in terminal agonies. And there are those who feel they have to Do Something about it, however little. (page 13)

She enlisted in the United States Army; wrote an eloquent essay, "The Lucky Ones," about the plight of displaced persons in occupied Germany, for the *New Yorker* (1946); worked for the United States government, including a period in Pentagon subbasements; earned a Ph.D. in psychology in 1967; and lived a life that most people find exotic and glamorous, but that she describes as "work and a few adventures." All of it became the background for her fictions: "All I write is really from life."

Sheldon had been reading science fiction since she discovered *Weird Tales* at the age of nine. When she began writing it, she was a self-described "maverick," doing successful but offbeat research in the "rather stuffy job atmosphere" of a conservative university. She feared, she writes, that:

. . . the news I was writing . . . *science fiction* would have destroyed my last shreds of respectability and relegated me to the freak department, possibly even to the freak-whose-grant-funds-should-be-stopped division. . . . Anonymity seemed highly desirable. And be-

sides, I had no idea the stuff would sell. So I just picked a name off a jar of marmalade, adding the "James" as one more bit of cover—and my husband threw in "Jr." for whimsy's sake. And then it all sold and I was stuck with it. What started as a prank dreamed its way into reality. (*ibid.*, page 15)

Tiptree's impact on science fiction was immediate. Her first story was "Birth of a Salesman," published in *Analog* in 1968. It was a relatively minor slapstick comedy, but Tiptree matured quickly. Another early story, "The Last Flight of Dr. Ain" (*Galaxy*, March 1969), was nominated for the Nebula award of the Science Fiction Writers of America for the best short story of the year.

Harry Harrison, in his introduction to *Ten Thousand Light-Years* (1973), describes receiving his first Tiptree story (in 1968 Harrison was, briefly, editor of both *Amazing* and *Fantastic*; I assume the story was "Fault" [*Fantastic*, August 1968; reprinted in *Warm Worlds*]):

I remember the story well. It was a bad day in the editing business. The slush pile—for that is what it is crudely called in the trade—was piled high and tottering with bad stories. I had a deadline. I was tired. I tried reading one more story; then I was no longer tired. Here was a story by a professional, a man who knew how to interest me, entertain me, and tell me something about the world and mankind's affairs all at the same time. I wrote at once and was pleased to hear, some years later, that the word from me arrived just one day before a check from John W. Campbell. Now *that* is the way to start a career in science fiction. (page 5)

Harlan Ellison's introduction to Tiptree's "The Milk of Paradise" in *Again, Dangerous Visions* (1972) is equally enthusiastic. It hails "a new Giant in the genre" and calls the story "stunning," predicting it would win both the Nebula award and the Hugo award of the World Science Fiction Convention for that year. Ironically enough, the story was not a Hugo nominee—but "Painwise" was, in the novelette category, as was "And I Awoke and Found Me Here on the Cold Hill's Side" in the short story category, while "Love Is the Plan, the Plan Is Death" won the 1973 Nebula as best short story. "The Women Men Don't See" was also a Nebula nominee, although the author withdrew it. As Ursula K. Le Guin explains in her introduction to *Star Songs:*

> The beautiful story "The Women Men Don't See" (oh—now that we know—what a gorgeously ironic title!) got a flood of nominations for the Nebula Award in 1974. So much of the praise of the story concerned the evidence it gave that a man could write with full sympathy about women, that Tiptree felt a prize for it would involve deceit, false pretenses. She withdrew the story from the competition, muttering about not wanting to cut younger writers out of all the prizes. I don't think this cover-up was false, either. (page xi)

Since Tiptree was still consistently demonstrating her ability to tell a good story with believable characters—male, female, and alien—the awards continued to arrive. "The Girl Who Was Plugged In" won the Hugo as best novella in 1974. In 1978 the short story "Time-Sharing Angel" was a Hugo nominee. Tiptree's most recent honor was a Hugo nomination in 1979 for her first novel, *Up the Walls of the World.* Feeling dissatisfied with the book, she withdrew it from competition— but not before the final ballots had been distributed. Unofficially, it placed extremely high in the voting.

Meantime, stories began appearing under the name Raccoona Sheldon. As Sheldon writes in "Everything But," the Tiptree "persona wasn't too constricting; I wrote as me" but "there were things I wanted to write as me, or at least a woman. (I still don't know exactly what they are, that's the odd part.) Meanwhile Tiptree kept taking on a stronger and stronger life of his own." Rather than "kill off" Tiptree, she established another identity (Raccoona Sheldon), a retired schoolteacher with a post office box in Wisconsin. The first "Raccoona" story (the name was suggested by the fact that the woods around

the Sheldon home are filled with raccoons) was "Press Until the Bleeding Stops" (1975).

Sheldon's third professionally published "Raccoona" story, "Your Faces, O My Sisters! Your Faces Filled of Light!" which she still considers "as good as I can do," opened the collection *Aurora: Beyond Equality,* edited by Susan Janice Anderson and Vonda N. McIntyre (1976), the pioneering anthology of science fiction set in nonsexist future societies. The story immediately following it in the same anthology is "Houston, Houston, Do You Read?" published as by "'Raccoona's' friend and mentor 'Tiptree'"—a story that won the 1976 Nebula for best novella and (as the result of a tie vote) shared a Hugo with Spider Robinson's "By Any Other Name." The two juxtaposed stories reveal the many facets of the author's concern with, and for, true humanity, as well as her gift for presenting a basic idea (such as the deadly differences created by the artificial patterns of "male" and "female") from different points of view. Another major "Raccoona" story—there are five in all—is "The Screwfly Solution," which won the 1978 Nebula for best novelette.

Tiptree's dissatisfaction with her novel *Up the Walls of the World,* as the manuscript proceeded with great difficulty, was one reason for her withdrawal from the writing of science fiction. In "Everything But" she says that, by the mid-1970's:

> With each story I dug deeper and deeper into more emotional stuff, and some of it started to hurt pretty bad. "Slow Music" reads like a musical fade-out or coda to Tiptree's work. (page 17)

"Slow Music" appears in the anthology *Interfaces,* edited by Le Guin and Virginia Kidd (1980)—and with it came the news that Alice/Tiptree/Raccoona had begun writing stories again.

I

Ten Thousand Light-Years from Home (the title is an adaptation of the Rolling Stones' song

"Two Thousand Light-Years from Home") contains fifteen Tiptree stories first published between 1968 and 1972. Several are retitled, and one—"The Snows Are Melted, the Snows Are Gone"—was substantially revised for inclusion in *Best SF 1969*, edited by Harry Harrison and Brian W. Aldiss. This story—together with "Painwise," "Beam Us Home," and especially "And I Awoke and Found Me Here on the Cold Hill's Side"—indicates Tiptree's rapidly emerging maturity as a writer who uses the conventions of science fiction to talk about humanity.

Certainly, several early stories, such as "Help" (first published in *If*, in 1968, as "Pupa Knows Best") and "The Man Doors Said Hello To," are relatively conventional science fiction, featuring traditional and stereotypical male protagonists and a crude humor that soon became refined to wit and irony. Yet even a relatively minor story like "The Peacefulness of Vivyan" indicates Tiptree's abilities. She uses a traditional device, that of a reporter from our culture observing an alien society.

Yet suddenly, the point of view flip-flops. The story is not about the rebellion against the Terran Empire on Sawewe, where the seal-like natives live in underground caverns. It is not about the Terran woman Kut, whose character and background are rendered in a few sentences:

> Her hair was gray. She wore a wetsuit but no weapons and her nose had been slit and crudely repaired. An Empire prisoner, one of the Terran traitors who had worked for Sawewe. (*Ten Thousand Light-Years*, page 34)

Nor is it about her sister Nantli, beloved wife of Cox the rebel leader—the man who sacrificed her in the rebellion because he was once Prince Cancoxtlan of Atlixco, a traitor who ended 200 years of Terran enslavement of that planet. Nor (despite its title) is it, ultimately, about Vivyan, a seemingly simple man who wanders from world to world, living as he knows a man should: "questing and learning and loving," bringing peace to people and ani-

mals. He is, shockingly, revealed to be Prince Vivyan of Atlixco, who saw his family burned alive by the rebels, was "rescued" by the Empire, and was conditioned to report back everything he sees on potentially rebellious worlds, an unknowing spy for Terra. "Exquisite tool of empire. A deadly child," thinks Keller, who knows the gentle man is protected only because he is Cox's brother. The real story is Keller's—and the reader's—reaction to all these people and events. What would be for most writers the stuff of a conventional space opera comes across in Tiptree's pages as a powerful short story indicating her gifts for condensation and suggestion, her ability to shift points of view and focus, and her success in creating both characters and surprises.

"And I Awoke," Tiptree's most important early story, is a brilliant reworking of the Keats poem "La Belle Dame Sans Merci" (1819), from which it draws its title. Using, again, the opening point of view of a reporter—this time a naïve young man—Tiptree appears to be examining aliens, which she creates in exotic, appealing numbers. In fact, through the central character—a drunken spaceport worker from "Burned Barn, Nebraska," whom the reporter dismisses as a self-pitying weirdo but who is Every-human—Tiptree examines basic human drives. These drives include sex, of course, and the reproduction of the race—as the narrator reminds the reporter:

> "Man is exogamous—all our history is one long drive to find and impregnate the stranger. Or get impregnated by him, it works for women too. Anything different-colored, different nose, ass, anything, man *has* to fuck it or die trying. That's a drive, y'know, it's built in. Because it works fine as long as the stranger is human. For millions of years that kept the genes circulating. But now we've met aliens we can't screw, and we're about to die trying. . . . Do you think I can touch my wife?" (*ibid.*, page 16)

Yet, as the narrator points out, "there's more," since even "Earth missionaries, teachers, sexless people" degrade themselves merely to be near aliens: "Man, it's deep . . . some cargo cult of the soul. We're built to dream outward. They laugh at us. They don't have it."

The positive aspects of humanity are defined here: the drive to maintain the race (keeping the genes circulating); the ability to care for others (since the technician and his "grotesquely scarred" wife do "give each other . . . comfort"); and, above all, the capacity to "dream outward," combined with the energy and willpower to achieve that dream. Yet the negative aspects are revealed too: our naïveté and our "cargo cult mentality." As the narrator points out, humans in general are only doing what exploiters, those in power, have done to other humans throughout history:

"Everything going out, nothing coming back. Like the poor damned Polynesians. We're gutting Earth, to begin with. Swapping raw resources for junk. Alien status symbols. Tape decks, Coca Cola and Mickey Mouse watches." (*ibid.*, page 15)

Moreover, in an ironic ending, the reporter ignores the words he has heard, the scarred bodies and ruined lives he has seen, to run eagerly after "two sleek scarlet shapes. My first real aliens!"

Both the ironic twist and the ability to re-create "authentic" colloquial speech through which character is revealed are characteristic of Tiptree's later work. So are her use of deft background touches that establish her alien worlds or her futures—reminding the careful reader that this is not New York in 1980 or Poughkeepsie in 1945—whose values and social, political, economic, sexual, and moral assumptions still dominate much of contemporary North American science fiction. In "And I Awoke," it is the almost unnoticed detail that the narrator, busy describing his first enthralling (in the literal and the Keatsian sense) with aliens, makes passing mention of his tunic. Clearly it is the future. Fashions have changed; people have not. This is, of course, the point of the story.

In the next story in the volume, "The Snows Are Melted, the Snows Are Gone," the word "Ethiopia" in the last sentence quietly shatters the reader's natural assumption that the story is set in a future, ruined North America. This ability to use a few words to suggest much leads directly to the dislocating effects of such mature Tiptree work as "Love Is the Plan, the Plan Is Death," aptly described by John Clute and Peter Nicholls in *The Science Fiction Encyclopedia* as one of her "intense revelations of the nature of alien life forms" in which the "last sentence reorders the previous narrative without disqualifying a word."

The second Tiptree collection, *Warm Worlds and Otherwise* (1975), contains twelve stories published between 1968 and 1974. A few ("Through a Lass Darkly," "Amberjack," and the early "Fault") are relatively minor works. Nevertheless, the first of these, although broadly humorous, demonstrates Tiptree's ability to create character and society through conversation, specifically the slang of a twenty-second-century "girl." "Amberjack," while also demonstrating this skill, presents in more depth the major Tiptree themes: the destruction inflicted on the human psyche by the social conditioning of people into the roles of "normal female," "successful male," "mother," "father," and so on, and the equally important salvation made possible by the love between individuals. "Fault," published in 1968 and definitely an apprentice work, again demonstrates skill with first-person narrative, celebrates love, and also establishes an interesting alien-human misunderstanding, complicated by a startling idea about time displacement.

"The Last Flight of Dr. Ain," first published in 1969 in *Galaxy*, is reprinted in *Warm Worlds*, in the heavily revised version that first appeared in *Author's Choice 4* (1974). It is significant as an example of Tiptree's social and ecological concerns, and of her increasingly complex narrative technique. Dr. Ain is a famous biologist; en route to an international convention, with frightening ease, he deliberately infects humanity with a deadly mutated leukemia virus that he has created. (He—and Tiptree—drop this bombshell in midstory, in four sentences.) Gradually, too— since the story is told in fragments and flashbacks—it is revealed that the mysterious wounded woman who appears to be his lover-companion is really the Earth Herself, Ain's "Gaea Gloriatrix . . . Gaea girl, queen," for whom he has sacrificed the human pollutors: "'Our life, your death!' he yelled. 'Our death would have been your death too, no need for that, no need!'"

In "Do You Like It Twice?" (1972) Tiptree criticized her early handling of the first, award-nominated version of "Dr. Ain." Yet she noted that it did accomplish her desire to convey the confusion of a life that:

"plunks you amid strangers making strange gestures, inexplicable caresses, threats, unmarked buttons you press with unforeseen results, important-sounding gabble in code . . . and you keep sorting it out, understanding five years later *why* she said or did whatever, *why* they screamed when you—

". . . Take 'The Last Flight of Dr. Ain.' That whole damn story is told backward. . . . It's a perfect example of Tiptree's basic narrative instinct. Start from the end and preferably 5,000 feet underground on a dark day and then DON'T TELL THEM." (*Warm Worlds*, 1979, pages x–xi)

Tiptree's fiction up to 1975 is ably discussed by Gardner Dozois in *The Fiction of James Tiptree, Jr.* (1977). Moreover, as Clute and Nicholls observe, "very few later Tiptree stories are amenable to anything but extensive analysis." This is certainly true of such important stories in *Warm Worlds* as "All the Kinds of Yes," "The Girl Who Was Plugged In," "Love Is the Plan, the Plan Is Death," and especially the major, exquisitely ironic story "The Women Men Don't See."

Tiptree's stature in the field is confirmed, too, by her third collection, *Star Songs of an Old Primate* (1978). The seven stories cover the full span of the author's career, from a

heavily revised version of "Your Haploid Heart" (first published in *Analog* in 1969) to such major 1976 works as "Houston, Houston, Do You Read?" (from *Aurora*) and "The Psychologist Who Wouldn't Do Awful Things to Rats" (from *New Dimensions* 6). The title page alone, then, indicates Tiptree's rapid development from just another name (albeit an unusual one) in the monthly science fiction magazines to the major author of works eagerly sought by editors of prestigious original-story anthologies.

Tiptree's basic fictional concerns, from her earliest works, have remained consistent. As a writer of science fiction, her basic concerns are with the life and social sciences: biology, sociology, ecology, psychology. Her important characters include medical doctors (Lorimer of "Houston, Houston," Aaron Kaye of "A Momentary Taste of Being"), psychologists (Tilman Lipsitz of "The Psychologist"), and biologists (Dr. Ain, Lory Kaye of "Momentary Taste"). Most characters are polymaths, skilled in several fields, a situation presented as healthy and normal in such functioning societies as those of the villagelike generation starship *Centaur* (in "Momentary Taste") and both *Gloria* and the humanity it represents in microcosm in "Houston, Houston." Of course, although the crew of *Centaur* is hand-picked, it falls apart under stress; and humanity 300 years from now in "Houston, Houston" has achieved stability only after a plague has reduced the population to 2 million; wars, rioting, rape, and pillage have devastated it; and all the men have died. Nevertheless, Tiptree does present some hope that the greatest of the primates can become fully human.

Tiptree's attitude to science in general is best expressed in an exchange in "And So On, And So On" (collected in *Star Songs of an Old Primate*):

"What about the Arm wars?" cried the young reproducer. "Ooh, science is *horrible*. I cry every time I think of the poor Armers." Its large eyes steamed and it hugged itself seductively.

"Well, now, you can't blame science for what some power-hounds do with it," the spacedog chuckled, hitching his cocoon over toward the reproducer's stay.

"That's right," said another voice, and the conversation group drifted away. (page 41)

Thus power and its misuse—whether in individual rape or murder, or mass warfare—are central concerns. Pentagon officials, space commanders, and leaders in general are other central figures, usually treated with compassion—for example, Captain Yellaston of "Momentary Taste," the wise father, the calm commander, who (thanks to job pressures) is functioning on half a cortex and alcohol, and is drunk at the critical moment; and even Major Davis and Captain Geirr, once solid members of the *Sunburst* team, who prove under pressure to be a religious fanatic-murderer and a rapist, respectively. Yet, as Lory Kaye says in "Momentary Taste": "I don't hate humanity, I just hate some of the things people do."

In order to comment on people, Tiptree creates aliens. This convention has a long tradition in science fiction, going back at least to H. G. Wells's *War of the Worlds* (1898), in which the real focus is not on the Martian invaders, but on the panic-stricken Londoners' reactions to them.

Similarly, the creation of woman-as-alien, literally or metaphorically, has a long tradition in science fiction. Increasingly, as in Sonya Dorman's "When I Was Miss Dow" (1966), this convention has been used to examine the restraints, damages, and dangers that the patterns of "female" and "male" have imposed on human beings. Naturally, this includes the power men have over women. As Tiptree notes in ". . . the Great Sex Muddle," "males" at their extreme are "totally focused on . . . the aggressive or provocative vulnerability that promotes genital contact. *And that is all they have.* Behind them looms the mocking visage of the Mother which they are not. They are biological Mayflies, triggers to an unloaded gun."

In "The Screwfly Solution" the gun is loaded by aliens so that men will destroy women and cleanse the planet for its new owners. Or, as Ruth Parsons tells the concerned but macho, and ultimately uncomprehending, narrator of "The Women Men Don't See" (collected in *Warm Worlds and Otherwise*):

"Women have no rights, Don, except what men allow us. Men are more aggressive and powerful, and they run the world. When the next real crisis upsets them, our so-called rights will vanish like—like that smoke. We'll be back where we always were: property. And whatever has gone wrong will be blamed on our freedom, like the fall of Rome was. You'll see." (page 153)

Tiptree began the symposium "Women in Science Fiction" by saying women were aliens; but she later admitted, "I have changed my mind, by the way; of course it is not women who are aliens. Men are." (*Khatru* 3/4, page 61)

Yet it is ridiculous to assume, as one male critic did after the author of "Houston, Houston" was revealed to be female, that Tiptree hates men or envisions an all-female society as an ideal one. In that story in particular, the surviving 2 million Earthfolk run their planet sanely, operate a space program, and focus on nurturing their young—not because they are women, but because, as Lady Blue, that wise old person, patiently explains, they have become "human beings . . . humanity, mankind . . . the human race."

Many of Tiptree's central characters are males who are tragically alienated from themselves, as Lorimer in "Houston, Houston" has become by his need to play the masculine role, to become "a half-jock . . . one of them . . . a team. . . . I'll show you. I am not a girl." The central character of "Her Smoke" is equally alienated, as is the hero of "Painwise"—and not all the love of exotic alien beings, all the delights of other planets, can compensate for his loss of Earth, of the ability to experience pain, of human contact. He becomes a metaphor for us all.

In her narrative style, too, Tiptree's basic concerns are clearly evident from her earliest stories. She creates authentic conversations that reveal character; indeed, most of her stories are either first-person or stream-of-consciousness narratives, including "Love Is the Plan," a stream-of-consciousness story told from the viewpoint of an alien. Tiptree shows, rather than tells, the reader; she can create a complex background with a few significant details; and she employs irony and humor to good effect.

Above all, Tiptree disorients the reader. Without sacrificing science fiction's traditional power of sheer narrative drive, she tells a story like "Dr. Ain" or "Houston, Houston" backward, upside down, and in flashbacks, switching the point of view if necessary. In the *Khatru* symposium she started her part of the discussion by asking, "*Who* and what are they, these alternate forms of humanity? . . . What the hell are 'sexes' and how many and which are there? . . . Consider how a Martian would see us."

In her fiction Tiptree tries to examine humanity from the Martian point of view. Her style is, in the later stories, completely integrated with her themes. To examine aliens, the humans as aliens, she alienates and distances the reader. The creation of convincing male protagonists by a female author may be a part of such distancing; Le Guin, for example, explores this very subject in several essays reprinted in *The Language of the Night* (1979). So, too, may be the extreme case of the creation (for valid practical reasons) of a male persona who took on his own identity and life within the life of a female author. One can only speculate. Which is exactly what Tiptree, as a writer, forces her readers to do.

Tiptree's concerns and development are also revealed in her first novel, *Up the Walls of the World* (1978). Her major concern is with the mothering, nurturing relationship, and again the ideas are to be found in the *Khatru* 3/4 symposium:

Consider: If men alone had always raised infants, how monumental, how privileged a task it would be! We would have tons of conceptual literature on infant-father interaction, technical journals, research establishments devoted to it, a huge esoteric vocabulary. It would be sacred as the Stock Exchange or football, and we would spend hours hearing of it.

But because women do it, it is invisible and embarrassing. (page 60)

The novel demonstrates again all the strengths evident in the three collections of short stories: vivid writing, a fine command of dramatic incident, a sharp eye for social satire, and an eerie ability to make otherness seem familiar and the familiar seem strange.

But it is also flawed—flawed by overambition, in its attempt to depict an almost unimaginable Other. Here, Tiptree's narrative instinct tends to confuse the reader. *Up the Walls of the World* begins:

COLD, COLD AND ALONE, THE EVIL PRESENCE ROAMS THE STAR-STREAMS. IT IS IMMENSE AND DARK AND ALMOST IMMATERIAL: ITS POWERS ARE BEYOND THOSE OF ANY OTHER SENTIENT BEING. AND IT IS IN PAIN.

THE PAIN, IT BELIEVES, SPRINGS FROM ITS CRIME.

ITS CRIME IS NOT MURDER: INDEED, IT MURDERS WITHOUT THOUGHT. (page 7)

After a little more than a page, the center of consciousness shifts to Tivonel, a young Tyrenni female flying the winds of the planet Tyree, with boundless enthusiasm for life. The Tyrenni, giant winged creatures who live afloat in the atmosphere of their world, are telepaths who perceive sound as color, light/radiation as sound. They are completely alien in form but completely human in all essentials of thought and emotion, created in part to let us look at ourselves. At first their culture looks like an inverted North American one (even their sex act involves a sense of repulsion rather than touching), with male and female roles reversed. But there is one crucial difference: on Tyree, child rearing is the race's primary duty, a sacred function reserved for (not relegated to) the males, who, accordingly, have higher status than the more adventurous females.

The social commentary is handled lightly, with a good deal of humor, when a group of rebellious Tyrenni change bodies with humans. Yet beneath the fun there are serious questions about social roles, and particularly about child rearing. These questions are raised naturally, through characters: two of the Tyrenni are females who land on Earth demanding the right to raise children, while one of the humans, Winona, is an aging housewife who is useless on Earth but is revered on Tyree because she has "fathered" four children.

Tivonel is scarcely established as a character before the focus shifts once more, to Doctor Daniel Dann, a physician so crippled by guilt over the loss of his family that he can exist only by drugging himself to forgetfulness, can work only as an electrode applier for a group of research subjects gathered for experiments in telepathy. They are a wildly assorted bunch: Dann, his mad-scientist boss (Noah Catledge), six subjects, a physically and emotionally scarred computer technician named Margaret Omali (whom Dann worships from afar), and two army men—one a "tough" and one a paranoid. (The fates of the characters are almost too perfectly appropriate, especially those of the two despicable army men.)

Humans and Tyrenni make contact via the Beam, an energy construct created by the Tyrenni, who are unused to manipulating hard matter but are skilled psychic engineers. Soon they learn the nature of the danger facing Tyree, the beautiful world whose "walls" are the atmosphere itself. Only gradually do they learn anything of the first alien entity, the Destroyer, and this is accomplished only in part when that entity is joined by the consciousness of a transformed Margaret Omali.

The Destroyer is Tiptree's biggest challenge: a completely alien sentience, scarcely embodied; an energy network, a floating computer programmed for a galaxy-spanning mission; yet also a being with self-awareness.

Tiptree uses the Destroyer, and Margaret, to ask some major questions about the nature of life itself. Yet the language in which the Destroyer is presented simply is not adapted to the job. It is both generalized and clichéd in the crucial first chapters. The being is described too often as a "monstrous sentience," a "huge, maleficent presence" for it to seem anything other than a science fictional cliché. The capital letters and other typographical devices make reading unnecessarily difficult, too. When the human and Tyrenni characters encounter the Destroyer-as-life-support-system, there are vivid descriptions of what they perceive—or, rather, what their senses create—but this perceived environment is only one aspect of the being. As the Destroyer's self-examination goes on and on, the reader is tempted to skip those sections, to find out what happens to Tivonel, Dann, and Margaret. In the characters' interactions Tiptree's real strengths show most clearly; but the challenge of depicting the incomprehensible Destroyer proves to be too much.

The rest of the cast is extremely large. Yet individuals do stand out and, through their responses, reveal a good deal about both Tyree and our world. The group of telepaths includes several science fiction and fantasy readers, whose responses to the situation provide some lovely satire of science fiction clichés while emphasizing the ease with which these people, made "aliens" by a hostile society on Earth, adapt to a friendly world, whatever form it takes:

> "I know what's happened," the voice says dreamily. "We're on another world. We've been kidnapped by alien telepathic monsters."
>
> Dann is so taken aback that he can only say feebly, "As a matter of fact . . . you're quite right. But don't worry. They're friendly, they really are."
>
> "I know that too," says the voice of Richard Waxman, drifting in horrendous form upon the far winds of Tyree. (*ibid.*, page 174)

What *is* an "alien," anyway? Just another individual. The moment when Dann fully, finally, understands the existence of the Other—"the *reality* of a different human world"—is the real climax of the novel.

The other potential problem of *Up the Walls of the World* is its ambitious form. The otherness of each character is emphasized by the frequent shifts of point of view, which include dislocations of time. Everything is told in the present tense, as it is happening to the perceiver. Thus one may see the results of an action, but not know what caused it for several episodes. This can be an effective technique, but it takes getting used to. Like any good novel, this one demands full attention.

II

Robert Silverberg (an astute critic and editor as well as writer) wrote the introduction to Tiptree's 1975 collection, *Warm Worlds and Otherwise.* He praised the stories for successfully creating "a sense of disorientation and alienation, gradually and never completely resolved as the story reaches its climax," and thus offering a unique view of the universe as "a strange, all but incomprehensible place, through which we wander in a brave, desperate, but only occasionally successful quest for answers."

After the usual speculations on Tiptree's identity—and it must be noted that, in the essays Silverberg quotes, as elsewhere, Tiptree says nothing but the truth, only avoiding the use of her real name and gender—Silverberg insists: "It has been suggested that Tiptree is female, a theory that I find absurd, for there is to me something ineluctably masculine about Tiptree's writing."

In a postscript to the 1979 reissue of the book, Silverberg graciously acknowledges his mistake:

She fooled me beautifully, along with everyone else, and called into question the entire notion of what is "masculine" or "feminine" in fiction. I am still wrestling with that. What I have learned is that there are some women who can write about traditionally male topics

more knowledgeably than most men, and that the truly superior artist can adopt whatever tone is appropriate to the material and bring it off. And I have learned—again, as if I needed one more lesson in it—that Things Are Seldom What They Seem. For these aspects of my education, Alli Sheldon, I thank you. And for so much else. (page xviii)

Tiptree in her life, but more importantly in her fiction, disorients, surprises, and forces the reevaluation of everything. That she accomplishes this feat with power, grace, and remarkable narrative- and character-building skill is part of her excellence as an artist.

She does more. In *Khatru 3/4*, she writes:

Now obviously if I could describe a "human being" I would be more than I am—and probably living in the future, because I think of human beings as something to be realized ahead. (If we survive ourselves.) But clearly "human beings" have something to do with the luminous image you see in a bright child's eyes—the exploring, wondering, eagerly-grasping, un-destructive quest for life. I see that undescribed spirit as central to us all. (pages 20–21)

This idea, too, is worked out in her fiction. At the end of the early story "And So On, And So On," a "Pathman" (a leader) speaks of his despair. "For the first time all life is closed in a finite space. . . . We have come to the end of infinity, the end of hope. . . . Ahead lies only the irreversible long decline. For the first time *we know there is nothing beyond ourselves.*" Yet as the other beings agree, an Earth child crawls toward the screens that look out on paraspace, no-space, "his eyes intent and bright."

This, too, is Tiptree's gift, in both social and artistic terms. She presents her warnings; then she gives us hope: a "luminous image."

James Tiptree, Jr., is one of the best creators of human beings this field has ever known.

For how many of us, me in my way, you in yours, are not our pens the weapons with which we can do something—a tiny something—about wrongs? Even if only to name them? (*ibid.*, page 102)

—SUSAN WOOD

Alice Sheldon died on 19 May 1987. The manner of her death—she shot dead her chronically ill husband and then herself in a meticulously planned suicide pact—was shocking though not surprising. Suicide and self-sacrificing death had become a noted feature of Tiptree stories, and Sheldon had demonstrated in many letters, interviews, and private conversations that such an end had been in her mind for more than a decade. She was 71, and her husband, whose health was very poor and deteriorating, was 84.

Around 1979, when Sheldon suffered a heart attack and her husband's condition worsened, she said she was giving up writing. It was believed that the story "Slow Music" (1980) might have been her last. But she returned with two novels (one actually a collection of three linked stories) and a three-story collection in the mid-1980's.

There is much that is traditional in *Brightness Falls from the Air* (1985). On the planet Damiem a fragilely beautiful winged humanoid race, tortured and killed by human beings in the past in order to obtain an alcoholic drug, is now protected. There are only three resident human staff members, but a Federation patrol vessel is on call. Tourists are vetted, but the novel describes one tourist visit when vetting procedures go wrong. A group of thirteen tourists is set down on the planet, not just to experience the aliens but to observe a stunning astronomical light show caused by remnants of a nova passing through. The story is constructed like a murder mystery, with a closed circle of suspects, an amateur detective or two, and a series of clues; however, the murder itself does not happen until the second half of the book. The real mystery concerns the thirteen new arrivals: which of them have criminal intent and what crimes do they plan to commit?

The main problem with this situation is that there are too many characters to be developed—sixteen of them—and too many clues. Moreover, all of these characters are too peculiar to be plausible. Tiptree presents them and the planet in a great screech of hyperbole and emotion. Too much happens during one long night, much of it contrived, so that the wilder excesses of the nova front counterpoint the conspiracies, counterplots, and revelations of human interaction. Even the temporal eddies of the nova remnants (which cause time to jump about and to repeat itself) become an important element of the plot's endgame. There is nothing wrong with any of these characters or plot elements. Indeed, the novel contains memorable characters, moving moments, and exciting ideas. The problem is that it contains too many. Tiptree was almost unparalleled at creating idea-rich stories; she never accepted that the same mixture at novel length would be too rich.

The Starry Rift (1986) is a collection of three slightly associated stories and some perfunctory linking material. It is Tiptree's poorest book. The title refers to a relatively empty region of space at the edge of the human Federation's sphere of influence. Although it resembles an "irregular black cloud," it is just an area containing relatively few stars, a frontier region in the process of being explored by professionals and amateurs with FTL (faster-than-light) drives.

This setting and the technology used are generally familiar, including "sleep-chests" for the crews' suspended animation and the problems of slower-than-light communication, refuelling, and dealing with pirates. Naturally there are alien races to be encountered. Tiptree invents the Eaadron, the Ziellor, and the Comeno, giving them alien forms and (as usual for her) peculiarly convoluted means of reproduction, while allowing their mind-sets to remain almost human.

Even more unfortunately, the plots of all three stories operate by means of coincidence and contrivance. They move fast, though not with any degree of conviction. The first story, "The Only Neat Thing to Do," is most un-Tiptreelike, dealing with an intelligent but headstrong fifteen-year-old girl with rich parents who goes off alone into the Rift in search of adventures and new planets. She—Coati Cass—quickly becomes inhabited by a new alien species with whom she strikes up a cozy friendship until the alien presence leads to her death: she commits suicide for the good of the human race, because it seems like "the only neat thing to do." The story seems to be aimed at a juvenile audience, though it was popular enough to win the 1986 *Locus* award for best novella. "Good Night, Sweethearts" concerns Raven, a more professional sailor of the Rift, who salvages wrecks and sells fuel at a great profit to stranded ships. The plot, equally contrived and coincidental, shows him combating pirates who enslave their captives. The third and longest story is "Collision," a first-contact tale in which peaceful humans from the Federation clash with the Ziellor, who believe that all humans are murderous slavers. Once more, the plot turns on coincidence, though the most awkward and unsatisfactory aspect here is point of view; the story is largely pieced together by staff at a Federation base, from brief messages received.

The final book of new Tiptree material is *Tales of the Quintana Roo* (1986), three fantasy folktales set in a real part of Mexico's Yucatán Peninsula. The narrator is an "elderly gringo," an American psychologist. This is Sheldon herself, a fact that is hinted at in the introduction. "The Boy Who Waterskied to Forever" is a time-travel story. "Beyond the Dead Reef" is genre horror with too much explained. "What Came Ashore at Lirios" is a strange and haunting piece about identity, the best of the three.

Other than these three books, Tiptree's later works are collections of earlier and later stories reprinted, of which *Her Smoke Rose Up Forever* (1990) is by far the most important. It is clear that the best of the Tiptree writing is to be found in the earlier stories from the 1970's, and it is a shame that her enormous early promise was, despite flashes of later brilliance, not properly fulfilled.

—CHRIS MORGAN

Selected Bibliography

A complete Tiptree/Sheldon bibliography, including nonfiction and uncollected stories, was compiled by J. D. Smith for *Khatru* 7, pages 23–25. It contains only one unavoidable error: "Slow Music" has now appeared in the (retitled) anthology *Interfaces*, edited by Ursula K. Le Guin and Virginia Kidd (New York: Ace Books, 1980).

WORKS OF JAMES TIPTREE, JR.

"Do You Like It Twice?" *Phantasmicom* 9 (1972). (Tiptree discusses her aims as a writer, with particular reference to the narration strategy of "The Last Flight of Dr. Ain.")

The Thousand Light-Years from Home. New York: Ace Books, 1973. Reprint; Boston: Gregg Press, 1976. (Collection of fourteen stories. 1973 ed. has an introduction by Harry Harrison; 1976 ed., by Gardner Dozois.)

Warm Worlds and Otherwise. New York: Ballantine Books, 1975; reprint 1979. (Collection of twelve stories. Robert Silverberg's addendum to his original introduction is particularly noteworthy.)

"With Tiptree Through the Great Sex Muddle." *Khatru* 3/4 (1975): 17–22. (This essay and three later letters represent an important contribution to "Women in Science Fiction: A Symposium," a ground-breaking forum conducted in this amateur journal.)

"Your Faces, O My Sisters! Your Faces Filled of Light!" (by Raccoona Sheldon) and "Houston, Houston, Do You Read?" (by James Tiptree, Jr.). In *Aurora: Beyond Equality*, edited by Susan Janice Anderson and Vonda N. McIntyre. Greenwich, Conn.: Fawcett, 1976. (The paired stories, reflecting the same concerns, mark the first major professional appearance of the Raccoona persona.)

Star Songs of an Old Primate. New York: Ballantine Books, 1978. (Introduction by Ursula K. Le Guin.)

Up the Walls of the World. New York: Berkley/Putnam, 1978.

"Everything but the Signature Is Me" (by Alice Sheldon). *Khatru* 7 (1978): 12–17. Reprinted as by James Tiptree, Jr., *Starship* (1979): 31–34. (The author reveals her identity, and discusses her need to create the Tiptree persona. The issue of *Khatru* also contains "The Short Happy Life of James Tiptree, Jr." by Jeffrey D. Smith; "The Lucky Ones," a 1946 essay written for the *New Yorker* by the author as Alice Bradley; and the "Tiptree/Sheldon Bibliography" by Smith.)

Out of the Everywhere and Other Extraordinary Visions. New York: Del Rey, 1981. (Short stories.)

Brightness Falls from the Air. New York: TOR, 1985; London: Sphere, 1986.

Byte Beautiful: Eight Science Fiction Stories. Garden City, N.Y.: Doubleday, 1985. (Short stories.)

Tales of the Quintana Roo: Stories. Sauk City, Wisc.: Arkham House, 1986. (Three connected stories.)

The Starry Rift. New York, TOR, 1986. London: Sphere, 1988. (Three connected stories.)

Crown of Stars. New York: TOR, 1988; London: Sphere, 1990. (Short stories.)

Her Smoke Rose Up Forever. Sauk City, Wisc.: Arkham House, 1990. (Short stories.)

Neats Sheets. San Francisco: Tachyon, 1996. (Poetry.)

CRITICAL STUDIES

Dozois, Gardner. *The Fiction of James Tiptree, Jr.* New York: Algol Press, 1977. (So far the only major critical study of Tiptree's work since 1975. It also contains an early version of the Smith bibliography.)

Le Guin, Ursula K. *The Language of the Night: Essays on Fantasy and Science Fiction.* Edited and with introduction by Susan Wood. New York: Berkley/Putnam, 1979. (This collection reprints both Le Guin's introduction to *Star Songs of an Old Primate* and the relevant essay "Is Gender Necessary?")

Nicholls, Peter, and John Clute. "Tiptree, James Jr." In *The Science Fiction Encyclopedia*, edited by Peter Nicholls. Garden City, N.Y.: Doubleday, 1979; London: Roxby, 1979.

Novitski, Paul. Review of *Up the Walls of the World*. *Pacific Northwest Review of Books* 1 (May 1978): 6–7. (A major critical review.)

JACK VANCE

(b. 1916)

JACK VANCE IS the preferred form of his name used for science fiction by the American writer John Holbrook Vance. (He has, in addition to his science fiction, published a number of crime novels, on which he uses either his full name or various pseudonyms.) Biographical data on Vance are sparse (even the year of his birth has in the past been a matter for conjecture) because, as he puts it:

> I am firmly convinced that the writer who publicizes himself distracts his readers from what should be his single concern: his work. For this reason, after a few early vacillations, I refuse to disseminate photographs, self-analysis, biographical data, critiques and confessions: not from innate reserve, but to focus attention where I think it belongs. (*The Best of Jack Vance*, 1976, page vii)

Vance was born in San Francisco and grew up in various parts of California. He attended the University of California, first in a mining engineering program, and subsequently he studied physics and journalism; he did not obtain a degree. During World War II he was in the Merchant Marine, twice serving on ships that were torpedoed. It was at this time that Vance started to submit stories to the science fiction magazines. As a youth he was particularly fond of *Weird Tales*, one of whose regular contributors, Clark Ashton Smith, is most frequently cited as an influence on Vance's writing (see Don Herron's "The Double Shadow," in *Jack Vance*, 1980). Vance is married, has one son, and lives in a largely self-built house in the hills near Oakland, California.

Vance's first published story was "The World-Thinker" (1945), in which the human protagonist discovers, on a remote planet, a solitary alien capable of building and dismantling whole worlds by the power of thought. This story is for the most part crudely written, clichéd pulp melodrama, but at its heart there is a scene of genuine, surreal imagination in which we witness—from the inside—the disintegration of one of the alien's creations. "The World-Thinker" is also intriguing for the way its central image—a solitary, brooding intelligence creating and populating whole worlds through the power of the imagination—foreshadows Vance's career as a science fiction writer.

During the next five years Vance published a further fifteen largely undistinguished stories. These included eight of the eventual ten Magnus Ridolph stories, in which the protagonist—a roguish elderly detective—solves mysteries (and thereby enriches himself) on various alien worlds. The first two Ridolph stories, "Hard Luck Diggings" and "Sanatoris Short-Cut," were written in a single weekend, in an attempt by Vance to see if he could become a highly prolific writer in the mold of John Creasey or Max Brand. Six of the stories were collected in *The Many Worlds of Magnus Ridolph* (1966); an expanded edition (1980) adds two more. Among the other stories was Vance's first short science fiction novel, *The Five Gold Bands* (serialized 1950; also titled *The Space Pirate*, 1953). The format again is standard space adventure—the "bands" of the title are bracelets, widely dispersed around the galaxy, that together contain the secret formula of an interstellar space propulsion system; the protagonist must find them and bring them together. *The Five Gold Bands* has its imaginative moments—some colorful and unusual settings—but, like Vance's other early work, it fails to transcend the strictures of formula fiction.

Much more significant was the publication, also in 1950, of Vance's first book, *The Dying Earth*. This is a collection of six loosely connected stories with a common setting: Earth in the very distant future when the sun is growing dim and when magic (itself in decline) has long since replaced science. Vance had begun work on these stories several years earlier, but he had been unable to find a publisher for them. They are fantasy rather than science fiction, but their similarities to his other work are more important than any generic differences. In *The Dying Earth*, Vance for the first time made effective use of the talents at which his earliest work had only intermittently hinted: a powerful visual and sensory imagination; a strongly idiosyncratic prose style that remains detached from the subject matter through a blend of mannered formality and irony; an extraordinary talent for inventing right-sounding exotic names; and a delight in formal, courteous dialogue—even between antagonists—brimming with aphorisms and apothegms. At the same time significant weaknesses, mainly of structure, remain. The six stories are too interconnected to be read simply as a collection, yet they are not sufficiently linked to form a satisfying whole. Worse, within the individual stories there are awkward shifts of viewpoints and scenes. Throughout his career Vance has experienced great difficulty in orchestrating any but the simplest of narrative structures: thus *The Dying Earth* is a good early example of both his characteristic strengths and his besetting weaknesses.

During the early 1950's Vance published a number of exotic short science fiction novels and novelettes in the pulp magazines: *Son of the Tree* (1951; book form, 1964), "Abercrombie Station" and "Cholwell's Chickens" (both 1952; together, these two stories form the 1965 novel *Monsters in Orbit*); "Planet of the Damned" (1952; as *Slaves of the Klau*, 1958); and *The Houses of Iszm* (1954; book form, 1964). Vance also wrote a juvenile science fiction novel, *Vandals of the Void* (1953), and during 1952–1953 he wrote a number of scripts for the television series *Captain Video*.

His most significant work of the period was the novel *Big Planet*, published in *Startling Stories* in 1952. The magazine version was severely cut, reportedly from a typescript of more than 100,000 words to a little more than 50,000 words; all book versions, prior to the 1978 publication of a limited edition of the complete original text, were further abridged. The cuts (the result of publishing constraints rather than editorial misgivings) are to be regretted, for *Big Planet* is the first significant example of the type of science fiction story in which Vance has subsequently specialized: studies of extraterrestrial ethnography.

Ethnography is the branch of social or cultural anthropology that involves the in-depth study of the society and culture of a particular people, usually through extensive fieldwork. The anthropologist lives among the people being studied, learns their language, and observes their society closely. The assumption underlying ethnography is that a society makes sense only when viewed as a whole: everything interrelates, and to focus on particular aspects of one society and to compare them, out of context, with superficially similar aspects of another society (as was the practice of earlier anthropologists such as Sir James George Frazer, author of *The Golden Bough* [1890]) is almost certainly to misrepresent them. Science fiction writers, in creating "alien" cultures, habitually borrow magpie-fashion from different terrestrial societies; Vance, in contrast, is able to create unified, self-consistent societies in which social customs, politics, art, religion, and other aspects of culture interrelate as they do in real life. It is this skill, together with his narrative method (akin to the ethnographer's, which attempts to describe without imposing an out-side world view on a society for which those assumptions might not be valid) and his talent for vivid description, that makes Vance the unique writer he is.

The value of this approach as a literary enterprise is, to a degree, open to question. In much of Vance's work the reader becomes a kind of vicarious tourist, enjoying strange sights and sounds, marveling at curious alien folkways. This may make for diverting entertainment, but it is not in itself the stuff of serious literature. Nor has Vance habitually shown much interest in subtleties of human interaction on the individual level. (This is not to say that his characters are incapable of subtlety—the opposite is often the case—but that their interactions generally proceed according to stock adventure and romance conventions.)

Where Vance's work is of more value is in presenting a series of shocking retorts to the reader's complacent ethnocentric assumptions. He continually points out that what we think of as norms of social behavior are in fact no more than reflections of our own local set of customs. This also applies to anything we may regard as a moral or ethical absolute: another culture in another time may regard matters quite differently.

A single extreme example will suffice. In his novelette "The Moon Moth" (1961), Vance takes us to a distant world, Sirene, where all social and economic transactions are determined according to the prestige, or *strakh*, of the individuals concerned. In this situation one outworlder, representing a civilization akin to our own, must apprehend another outworlder, a notorious criminal fugitive. At one point the fugitive's crimes are described to the native Sirenese: "He has murdered, betrayed; he has wrecked ships; he has tortured, blackmailed, robbed, sold children into slavery; he has—." At this point the litany is interrupted by one of the Sirenese, who bluntly observes, "Your religious differences are of no importance."

Big Planet deals with a number of exotic social systems on an immense world that has

been colonized by dissident groups from Earth. Here they have found adequate space to build societies reflecting their particular preferences. The story takes the form of a trek by a group of people who have been shipwrecked on the planet: a simple narrative structure that Vance is able to handle adequately. The places they visit are dealt with a little cursorily, but *Big Planet* is nevertheless an entertaining and inventive work.

Vance's next novel, *To Live Forever* (1956), is more ambitious in its rendering of a future society. It describes Earth in the distant future, when civilization is confined within a single great city, Clarges, whose citizens are divided into social classes according to their life expectancy, the topmost elite being immortal. The protagonist, Gavin Waylock, was once an immortal but has been cast out from the elite after being convicted of murder; the story concerns his struggle to regain his position. Waylock is an unconventional "hero"—he is ruthless, self-serving, and certainly not admirable. But the real villain of the story is none of the characters: rather, it is the society of Clarges, which has become rigid, stratified, and restrictive of creative endeavor. The justification for Waylock's actions is that he is the force needed to break the mold. This theme of revolt against stultifying authority recurs in some of Vance's best later work, notably in *The Blue World* (1966) and *Emphyrio* (1969).

Vance's third significant novel of the 1950's, *The Languages of Pao* (1957, book form, 1958), is the closest he has come to the traditional model of a science fiction story: taking a concept from present-day science and using the novel as a vehicle for extrapolation and exploration. Here the science is linguistics, in particular the theory identified most strongly with Benjamin Lee Whorf: that the way in which people think is reflected by—and to some degree determined by—the language they speak. Vance extends the idea to create a fertile, peaceful planet whose gentle and uncompetitive people have such a passive language that it does not even contain verbs. The limitations of the world view that this

815

language engenders leave them at the mercy of aggressive outsiders; and in order to combat such a menace, they must first master a new tongue. It is an ingenious story, although its linguistic assumptions do not stand up to close examination.

Once Vance began to produce novels regularly, his output of short stories decreased (he has said that it is as much of an effort for him to write a single short story as an entire novel). His most notable short stories of the 1950's are "The Gift of Gab" (1955) and "The Men Return" (1957). "The Gift of Gab" explores the problem of establishing communication with an alien race, the Dekabrachs. It is almost the only alien species given a fully sympathetic treatment in all of Vance's fiction: his strange societies are nearly always human, and his treatment of aliens is generally ambivalent at best. "The Men Return" is a short and very vivid story that depicts Earth after it has wandered into a region of space where causality no longer operates.

Vance's finest novelette is "The Moon Moth." In it he creates one of his richest societies, whose people hide their faces behind a variety of masks and accompany their speech, according to mood or intention, with one of a variety of musical instruments. The nuances of the idea are convincingly worked out, and even the plot—Vance's habitual weak point—has a neatly ironic twist. "The Moon Moth" was the first science fiction story he published in the 1960's, and it was an auspicious start to the decade, since it showed him for the first time in full command of his gifts.

Comparable in its success is the short novel *The Dragon Masters*, which appeared in *Galaxy* in 1962 (book form, 1963) and brought Vance a Hugo award for short fiction. *The Dragon Masters* describes a bizarre war on a distant planet fought between humans and the reptilian alien "Basics." After a past skirmish each side took prisoners, and by means of selective breeding (comparable with the sort that has produced the immense variety of dogs in our world) has produced many different specialized forms. Again there is conflict

(as in *To Live Forever*) between dynamism and stasis.

During the next decade Vance published a substantial number of novels, most of which demonstrate his characteristic level of invention without being notably sophisticated in form or ambitious in intent. These include two series: the five Demon Princes novels, in which one man tracks down and kills the five intergalactic criminals responsible for his father's death; and the Planet of Adventure (or Tschai) quartet, which chronicles the adventures of a man marooned on a world that has been colonized by three different alien species (in addition to the natives). Both sequences are weakened by an evident falling off in the author's interest. Vance's stories frequently give the impression that for him all the pleasure lies in the creation of the milieu; the actual writing of the story comes to seem an increasing chore. It appears even more difficult for him to sustain a series: indeed, in the Demon Princes series there was a twelve-year gap between the third and fourth books, presumably time enough for his interest to revive.

Other Vance novels include two overtly humorous ones—*Space Opera* (1965) and *Showboat World* (1975)—both of which concern touring companies (respectively, opera and theater) on exotic worlds. Vance won a second Hugo award and a Nebula award for *The Last Castle* (1966; book form, 1967). This is another story in which an ossified society comes under threat. In this case the society is that of overly genteel humans on a far-future Earth, and the threat comes from their alien slaves, the Meks. It is not surprising, in view of Vance's ambivalence toward aliens, that in this instance (as in *The Dragon Masters*) the humans bestir themselves to fight off the threat. Despite its awards *The Last Castle* is not one of Vance's outstanding works.

Vance's most interesting and successful novels appeared in the years following *The Dragon Masters*: *The Blue World* (1966), *Emphyrio* (1969), and *The Anome* (1973). Each of these is a tale of one man's rebellion against a static social order that is described in great detail.

The Blue World is set on a planet entirely covered by water. Many generations past, a spaceship crashed on this world, and the survivors have succeeded in establishing themselves on the lilylike pads of giant water plants, where they have developed a gentle civilization that, lacking metals, therefore also lacks industry. Theirs would be an idyllic life were it not for King Kragen, a huge and malevolent sea beast (of problematical intelligence) that protects them from smaller members of his species, at the cost of his own considerable depredations to their harvests. He is, in essence, a wrathful God to the people, and the Intercessors—members of a sect that claims the ability to communicate with him—are his priesthood. When the protagonist, Sklar Hast, declares his intention of destroying King Kragen, he initiates much more than a simple secular conflict: the Intercessors react as might any priesthood whose God's name (and very existence) has been taken in vain. The resulting upheaval represents a loss of innocence for this gentle society. As Sklar Hast puts it in chapter 7: "An era has come to an end. A Golden Age, an Age of Innocence—it is ended. Violence, hate, turbulence have come to the floats. The world will never be the same again."

There is more to *The Blue World* than this. A central irony infusing the novel with gentle humor is that these people, although they do not know it, are descended from a shipload of criminals who fled from Earth; their caste names echo the occupations of their ancestors (Swindlers, Hoodwinkers, and so on). In trying to emulate their "superior" forebears, they far surpass them ethically. What disrupts their society further is the reintroduction of a criminal element: in essence King Kragen operates a vast "protection" racket. He is also a symbol: every description of the creature is suggestive of a war machine rather than a simple predator. He may be taken to represent the power of technology, before which the people of the floats are helpless. Their only hope is to develop technology themselves, as Sklar

Jack Vance. © M. C. VALADA

Hast recognizes. An Industrial Revolution in miniature is carried out with great ingenuity. King Kragen is destroyed. The society loses its innocence but gains a dynamic impetus in exchange. It seems certain that the people of the floats will go on to greater things. Thus *The Blue World* is more than simply an adventure story embroidered with unusual color and detail: it is in its way a classic moral fable.

The same is true of *Emphyrio*. It is set on another distant world, Halma, whose human population remains poverty-stricken in the aftermath of a great war that took place some two thousand years earlier. In the city of Ambroy, a system of welfare regulations and craft guilds (which prohibit mechanization and mass production) concentrates power in the Lords—hereditary controllers of the basic public utilities. As we later discover, the system thoroughly exploits the skilled artisans of the planet, whose work is much prized throughout the galaxy, although they themselves receive little reward.

The story centers on one man, Ghyl Tarvoke, son of an expert woodcarver, who challenges, and eventually overthrows, the system. *Emphyrio* is, as Joanna Russ has pointed out, a bildungsroman, following Ghyl's growth from boyhood. The society of Ambroy, which we see through Ghyl's eyes, is brought to life by Vance with unusual skill. Its governing religion, represented by the Temple of Finuka, presents Vance with the opportunity for some piercing satire. Also at the center of the story is the legend of Emphyrio, an ancient hero who saved his world from invading alien monsters. Ghyl identifies with Emphyrio, and his efforts to free Halma from the Lords' rule turn into a kind of reenactment of the legend. This gives the story a satisfying mythic resonance, even though the myth in question is itself fictitious. The shaping of the novel around the legend also makes for Vance's most complexly structured work, the only one in which he has satisfactorily progressed beyond simple quest or rebellion plots.

Emphyrio is an unusual and rewarding novel, and it remains Vance's most accomplished work (despite a somewhat lurid and awkward opening chapter). Like *The Blue World* it has some of the quality of a myth or folktale of the distant future. Indeed, in these and other Vance works, there are stylistic echoes of traditional fairy tales, such as in the descriptions of the spasms of violence that accompany the overthrow of repression. The villains are literally torn apart, yet there is no graphic sense of bloodshed.

The Anome echoes *Emphyrio* in many respects. It too follows its protagonist, Gastel Etzwane, from childhood as he comes to challenge and overthrow authority. The setting, the continent of Shant on the planet Durdane, is a conglomeration of sixty-two very diverse cantons with little in common except language, music, color symbology, and submission to the rule of the mysterious Anome (also known as the Faceless Man). The Anome wanders anonymously around Shant, administering arbitrary but evenhanded justice by "taking the heads" of malefactors through

detonating the explosive "torc" that each citizen has clamped around his or her neck. Etzwane is born into an absurd, ecstatic religious sect, the Chilities, and initially sets off to find the Anome to obtain his mother's freedom from servitude to the sect. This ultimately leads him to take over the power of the Anome and to organize opposition to successive advances of alien menace that are revealed through the other volumes of the trilogy begun with *The Anome*: *The Brave Free Men* (1973) and *The Asutra* (1974). The trilogy degenerates into simple adventure, but *The Anome* is for much of its length one of Vance's most detailed and convincing evocations of an imaginary society.

Vance's other major novel (in the form of related short stories) is *The Eyes of the Overworld* (1966), which returns to the setting of *The Dying Earth* but has no characters in common with the earlier work. *The Eyes of the Overworld* is a rich, ironic, inventive, and humorous chronicle, although the protagonist, a thief named Cugel the Clever, is a cruel rogue who gains little sympathy from the reader. Further tales of Dying Earth and of Cugel have been issued in illustrated, limited-edition books and pamphlets, although they are actually little more than novelettes: *The Bagful of Dreams, Morreion,* and *The Seventeen Virgins* (all 1979).

Most of Vance's science fiction, it has emerged, uses the same loose galactic background of the Gaean Reach (containing Earth and the surrounding Oikumene of the Demon Princes series) and adjacent stellar regions such as Alastor Cluster. The Alastor novels— *Trullion: Alastor 2262* (1973), *Marune: Alastor 933* (1975), and *Wyst: Alastor 1716* (1978)—have as a common thread the ruler of the Cluster, the Connatic, who wanders anonymously through his realm (somewhat after the fashion of the Anome), ensuring that justice is administered. *Trullion* begins with a carefully wrought evocation of its world—a placid, fenland place slightly reminiscent of *The Blue World*—and contains lengthy and detailed descriptions of an invented game, "hussade"; but it degenerates into a tale of space pirates (a regression to pulp cliché of a sort to which Vance remains woefully liable once his interest wanders). *Marune* is complex in conception but somewhat desultory in execution. *Wyst* is unusual for Vance in being clearly didactic: the society of Wyst is a kind of "socialist" utopia that is easily shown to be false and hypocritical beneath its self-congratulatory surface. Such tinges of contemporary relevance are an unwelcome occurrence: Wyst is a caricature society, a straw target that Vance easily demolishes.

The Gray Prince (1974), a Gaean Reach novel, is similarly unsatisfactory. In spite of the exotic setting—a planet with no fewer than five different cultures, three human and two alien—it soon becomes uncomfortably clear that *The Gray Prince* too closely resembles a Western novel and that the doctrine it appears to endorse is similar to that of Manifest Destiny. When Vance strays from a moral fable to a political fable, the powerful streak of conservatism that becomes apparent renders his work less congenial to readers who do not share those beliefs; thus its appeal is, to some degree, restricted. *Maske: Thaery* (1976), another Gaean novel, is a more traditional Vance work, with carefully evoked backgrounds. But it is too heavily plotted along traditional lines to be among his most interesting works. It is a mystery-adventure story with unusually well-drawn backgrounds rather than a fully realized ethnographic study.

Vance's talent is a particularly narrow and specialized one, and among his many novels and stories there are few that can be counted as complete successes. His work is too specialized in its scope and appeal ever to lie in the mainstream of science fiction, but its existence does serve to enrich the genre. At best his fertile imagination and his ability to evoke a full sensory range in his descriptions enable him to turn the "science" of world creation (as traditionally practiced by scientifically trained writers) into a real, if minor, art.

—MALCOLM EDWARDS

In the 1980's Jack Vance published a number of collections, chiefly rearranging earlier stories. Those most welcomed, and containing the most fresh material, were two new books of linked *Dying Earth* tales that incorporated the 1979 chapbooks. *Cugel's Saga* (1983) extends this rogue's adventures with suave inventiveness and makes him more likeably human. *Rhialto the Marvellous* (1984) deals with a group of rival wizards in a somewhat earlier age and further blurs the distinction between fantasy and science fiction with much magical time travel and a remarkable space voyage to the edge of the universe. the Dying Earth is posttechnological rather than being set in some fantasy otherworld. This aspect of Vance's creation was acknowledged by Gene Wolfe as a potent influence on his landmark tetralogy, *The Book of the New Sun* (1981–1983).

By contrast, the next major project from Vance has a pretechnological setting. The Lyonesse trilogy comprises *Suldrun's Garden* (1983), *The Green Pearl* (1984), and *Madouc* (1990) and takes place on imaginary isles west of France and the English Channel, supposedly drowned before history began. Pretending to anticipate "later" Arthurian legends, the story includes versions of the Round Table, Siege Perilous, and so on. A rather conventional saga of war over little kingdoms and their royal succession is overlaid with typical polished wit and quirky infusions of magic, including visits to fantastic realms with a Dying Earth flavor. Vance's multistranded narration seems almost a conscious response to criticisms of weak plotting; although some lack of enthusiasm for the inevitable battle scenes is detectable, storytelling energy is sustained throughout this trilogy's considerable length.

Even before completing Lyonesse, Vance returned to science fiction and the Gaean Reach with *Araminta Station* (1987), the first book of the Cadwal Chronicles. The sequels are *Ecce and Old Earth* (1991) and *Throy* (1992). Here a theme from *Marune: Alastor 933* and *Maske: Thaery*, concerning the desirability of keeping naturally beautiful landscapes unspoiled, expands to planetary scale. The world of Cadwal is a vast and lovingly depicted nature reserve administered under a Charter of Conservancy, and young protagonist Glawen follows his stern but devoted father into the "Bureau B" police force that defends the Charter.

Again plot interest is supplied in good measure, neatly meshing with the exotic background. *Araminta Station* is an enjoyable murder mystery (with an ultimately pitiable villian) varied with family intrigues, espionage, off-planet adventure, and Glawen's imprisonment by another of Vance's appalling religious cults. Eventually there are satisfying revelations and a dramatic finale. Meanwhile, political conflict rages between supporters of the Charter and those who wish it abolished, ostensibly in the name of freedom but usually with an eye to carving up the unspoiled land into private estates. A further complicating factor is a teeming island society of "Yips," descended from runaways and illegal immigrants, who covet the mainland for themselves.

Narrative drive continues in *Ecce and Old Earth*, in which Glawen must rescue his kidnapped father from the jungle-surrounded prison of a political enemy and then join his girlfriend in an interstellar search for the lost Cadwal Charter. This reads well enough, but the hunt is overly long, and the reader suspects the document's hiding place long before it occurs to Glawen. The closing Cadwal volume, *Throy*, sees Vance attempting to unravel the political problem he has set himself, with all its moral awkwardness. The Yips, however sly and unlovable, have done nothing wrong in being born on Cadwal—yet the Charter of Conservancy requires that they be uprooted from home and deported, and it is our hero's distasteful duty to help do so. The slightly disappointing solution leaves Glawen, Bureau B, and other Charter supporters as mere bystanders while the anti-Charter factions quarrel and fight, conveniently burning the Yips' island town with enormous loss of life. As in several past series, the author's interest seems

to have waned, and *Throy* is barely half the length of the superior preceding volumes.

Yet Vance was in good form when, at the age of eighty, he published *Night Lamp* (1996), another substantial Gaean Reach tale. Many ingredients from past novels appear: amnesia, adolescence and vengeance, wildly eccentric status-based societies, faded splendors of a glorious past, and a search for true identity, all drawn with wit and dark irony. Like Glawen in the Cadwal Chronicles, the youthful protagonist, Jaro, is not the lone figure opposed to society that is familiar from so many past Vance narratives. Instead he works hard, enjoys good relations with kindly foster parents, and is reunited with a lost father, who is instrumental in carrying out the revenge that amnesiac Jaro no longer knows is justified by the torture of his mother.

This late outbreak of strong and loving father-son relationships (one is also featured in Lyonesse, with the principal character as father rather than son) contrasts interestingly with the past tendency for Vance heroes to be orphans or at best to have strange and remote fathers as in *Emphyrio* and *The Anome*.

Ports of Call (1998) apparently opens a loosely episodic series of Gaean Reach interstellar picaresques. Its young hero has intelligence but little determination, soon loses his post as a capricious great-aunt's personal spaceship captain, and is resuced from difficulties by older and more capable spacefarers who rapidly upstage him. There are amusing and dramatic vignettes in transit and at the title's planetary port of call. The overall narrative, however, seems shaped toward denouements at journey's end—yet halts abruptly in an "Epilogue" without reaching any real destination or significant subclimax. Full closure and satisfaction await the implied sequels.

Jack Vance has not lost his stylistic polish or his gifts for speculative ecology and ethnography. The jury is necessarily still out on the *Ports of Call* sequence, but the Cadwal Chronicles and *Night Lamp* are fine late achievements. Vance's stature in the genre was acknowledged by the World Fantasy Convention's Lifetime Achievement award in 1984 and by the Science Fiction and Fantasy Writers of America Grand Master award in 1997.

—DAVID LANGFORD

Selected Bibliography

WORKS OF JACK VANCE

The Dying Earth. New York: Hillman, 1950; London: Mayflower, 1972. (Related short stories. Dying Earth series, no. 1.)

The Space Pirate: A Science Fiction Novel. New York: Toby, 1953. Reprinted as *The Five Gold Bands,* New York: Ace, 1963 (shorter version); New York: DAW, 1980, and London: Mayflower, 1980 (full version).

Vandals of the Void. Philadelphia, Pa.: John C. Winston, 1953. (For children.)

To Live Forever. New York: Ballantine, 1956; London: Sphere, 1976.

Big Planet. New York: Avalon, 1957; London: Coronet, 1977. Unabridged version, San Francisco, Calif., and Columbia, Pa.: Underwood-Miller, 1978; London: Gollancz, 1989.

The Languages of Pao. New York: Avalon, 1958; London: Mayflower, 1974.

Slaves of the Klau. New York: Ace, 1958; London: Coronet, 1980. Restored edition, retitled *Gold and Iron,* San Francisco, Calif., and Columbia, Pa.: Underwood-Miller, 1982.

The Dragon Masters. New York: Ace, 1963; London: Dobson, 1965.

Future Tense. New York: Ballantine, 1964. Reprinted as *Dust of Far Suns,* New York: DAW, 1981. (Short stories.)

The Houses of Iszm. New York: Ace, 1964; London: Mayflower, 1974. (Bound with *Son of the Tree.*)

The Killing Machine. New York: Berkley Medallion, 1964; London: Dobson, 1967. (Demon Princes series, no. 2.)

Son of the Tree. New York: Ace, 1964; London: Mayflower, 1974. (Bound with *The Houses of Iszm.*)

The Star King. New York: Berkley Medallion, 1964. Reprinted as *Star King,* London: Dobson, 1966. (Demon Princes series, no. 1.)

Monsters in Orbit. New York: Ace, 1965. London: Dobson, 1977. (Bound with *The World Between.*)

Space Opera. New York: Pyramid, 1965; London: Coronet, 1982.

The World Between and Other Stories. New York: Ace, 1965. (Bound with *Monsters in Orbit.*) Reprinted as *The Moon Moth and Other Stories,* London: Dobson, 1975.

The Blue World. New York: Ballantine, 1966; London: Mayflower, 1976.

The Brains of Earth. New York: Ace, 1966; London: Mayflower, 1976. Reprinted as *Nopalgarth,* New York: DAW, 1980.

The Eyes of the Overworld. New York: Ace, 1966; London: Mayflower, 1972. (Related short stories. Dying Earth series, no. 2.)

The Many Worlds of Magnus Ridolph. New York: Ace, 1966; London: Dobson, 1977. Enlarged edition, New York: DAW, 1980. Further enlarged edition, retitled *The Complete Magnus Ridolph,* San Francisco, Calif., and Columbia, Pa.: Underwood-Miller, 1984. (Short stories.)

The Last Castle. New York: Ace, 1967.

The Palace of Love. New York: Berkley Medallion, 1967; London: Dobson, 1968. (Demon Princes series, no. 3.)

City of the Chasch. New York: Ace, 1968; London: Dobson, 1975. Reprinted as *Chasch,* New York: Bluejay, 1986. (Planet of Adventure series, no. 1.)

The Dirdir. New York: Ace, 1969; London: Dobson, 1975. (Planet of Adventure series, no. 3.)

Eight Fantasms and Magics: A Science Fiction Adventure. New York and Toronto: Macmillan, 1969. Reprinted as *Fantasms and Magics: A Science Fantasy Adventure,* London: Mayflower, 1978. (Short stories. British edition omits two stories, "Telek" and "Cil.")

Emphyrio. Garden City, N.Y.: Doubleday, 1969; London: Coronet, 1980.

Servants of the Wankh. New York: Ace, 1969; London: Dobson, 1975. (Planet of Adventure series, no. 2.) Reprinted as *Wankh,* New York: Bluejay, 1986.

The Pnume. New York: Ace, 1970; London: Dobson, 1975. (Planet of Adventure series, no. 4.)

The Anome. New York: Dell, 1973; London: Coronet, 1975. Reprinted as *The Faceless Man,* New York: Ace, 1978. (Durdane series, no. 1.)

The Brave Free Men. New York: Dell, 1973; London: Coronet, 1975. (Durdane series, no. 2.)

Trullion: Alastor 2262. New York: Ballantine, 1973; London: Mayflower, 1979. (Alastor Cluster series, no. 1.)

The Worlds of Jack Vance. New York: Ace, 1973. (Short stories.)

The Asutra. New York: Dell, 1974; London: Coronet, 1975. (Durdane series, no. 3.)

The Gray Prince. Indianapolis, Ind.: Bobbs-Merrill, 1974. Reprinted as *The Grey Prince,* London: Coronet, 1976.

Marune: Alastor 933. New York: Ballantine, 1975; London: Coronet, 1978. (Alastor Cluster series, no. 2.).

Showboat World. New York: Pyramid, 1975; London: Dobson, 1977. Reprinted as *The Magnificent Showboats of the Lower Vissel River, Lune XXIII South, Big Planet,* San Francisco, Calif., and Columbia, Pa.: Underwood-Miller, 1983.

The Best of Jack Vance. New York: Pocket Books, 1976. (Short stories.)

Maske: Thaery. New York: Berkley, 1976; London: Fontana, 1977.

Wyst: Alastor 1716. New York: DAW, 1978; London: Coronet, 1980. (Alastor Cluster series, no. 3.)

The Bagful of Dreams. San Francisco, Calif., and Columbia, Pa.: Underwood-Miller, 1979. (Short Dying Earth story. Incorporated into *Cugel's Saga.*)

The Face. New York: DAW, 1979; London: Dobson, 1980. (Demon Princes series, no. 4.)

Green Magic. San Francisco, Calif., and Columbia, Pa.: Underwood-Miller, 1979. (Short stories.)

Green Magic: The Fantasy Realms of Jack Vance. San Francisco, Calif., and Columbia, Pa.: Underwood-Miller, 1979. (Short stories.)

Morreion: A Tale of the Dying Earth. San Francisco, Calif., and Columbia, Pa.: Underwood-Miller, 1979. (Short Dying Earth story. Incorporated into *Rhialto the Marvellous.*)

The Seventeen Virgins. San Francisco, Calif., and Columbia, Pa.: Underwood-Miller, 1979. (Short Dying Earth story. Incorporated into *Cugel's Saga.*)

Galactic Effectuator. San Francisco, Calif., and Columbia, Pa.: Underwood-Miller, 1980; London: Coronet, 1983. (Short stories.)

Nopalgarth: Three Complete Novels. New York: DAW, 1980. (Omnibus comprising *The Houses of Iszm, Son of the Tree,* and the retitled *The Brains of Earth.*)

The Book of Dreams. New York: DAW, 1981; London: Coronet, 1982. (Demon Princes series, no. 5.)

Lost Moons. San Francisco, Calif., and Columbia, Pa.: Underwood-Miller, 1982. (Short stories.)

The Narrow Land. New York: DAW, 1982; London: Hodder and Stoughton, 1984. (Short Stories.)

Cugel's Saga. New York: Pocket Books/Timescape, 1983; London: Granada/Panther, 1984. (Related short stories. Dying Earth series, no. 4.)

Lyonesse: Suldrun's Garden. New York: Berkley, 1983. Reprinted as *Lyonesse,* London: Granada/Panther, 1984. (Lyonesse series, no. 1.)

Rhialto the Marvellous. San Francisco, Calif., and Columbia, Pa.: Brandywyne, 1984; London: Panther, 1985. (Related short stories. Dying Earth series, no. 3.)

Light from a Lone Star. Cambridge, Mass.: NESFA, 1985. (Short stories, interview, and excerpts.)

Lyonesse: The Green Pearl. San Francisco, Calif., and Columbia, Pa.: Underwood-Miller, 1985; London: Grafton, 1986. Reprinted as *The Green Pearl,* New York: Berkley, 1986. (Lyonesse series, no. 2.)

The Planet of Adventure Omnibus. London: Grafton, 1985. Reprinted as *Planet of Adventure,* New York: TOR, 1993. (All four Planet of Adventure novels.)

The Augmented Agent and Other Stories. San Francisco, Calif., and Columbia, Pa.: Underwood-Miller, 1986; London: New English Library, 1989. (Short stories.)

The Dark Side of the Moon: Stories of the Future. San Francisco, Calif., and Columbia, Pa.: Underwood-Miller, 1986; London: New English Library, 1989. (Short stories.)

Araminta Station. Los Angeles and Columbia, Pa.: Underwood-Miller, 1987. London: New English Library, 1989. (The Cadwal Chronicles series, no. 1.)

Durdane. London: Gollancz, 1989. (Omnibus of all three Durdane novels.)

Lyonesse: Madouc. Novato, Calif., and Columbia, Pa.: Underwood-Miller, 1989. Reprinted as *Lyonesse III: Madouc,* London: Grafton, 1990. Reprinted as *Madouc,* New York: Ace, 1990. (Lyonesse series, no. 3.)

Chateau D'If and Other Stories. Novato, Calif., and Lancaster, Pa.: Underwood-Miller, 1990. (Short stories.)

Ecce and Old Earth. Novato, Calif., and Lancaster, Pa.: Underwood-Miller, 1991; London: New English Library, 1992. (The Cadwal Chronicles series, no. 2.)

Throy. Novato, Calif., and Lancaster, Pa.: Underwood-Miller, 1992; London: New English Library, 1993. (The Cadwal Chronicles series, no. 3.)

When the Five Moons Rise. Novato, Calif., and Lancaster, Pa.: Underwood-Miller, 1992. (Short stories.)

Alastor. New York: TOR, 1995. (Omnibus of all three Alastor Cluster novels.)

Night Lamp. Grass Valley, Calif.: Underwood, 1996; New York: TOR, 1996; London: HarperCollins/Voyager, 1997.

The Demon Princes: Volume One. New York: TOR, 1997. (Omnibus of Demon Princes novels 1 to 3.)

The Demon Princes: Volume Two. New York: TOR, 1997. (Omnibus of Demon Princes novels 4 and 5.)

The Demon Princes. Garden City, N.Y.: Science Fiction Book Club, 1998. (Omnibus of all five Demon Princes novels.)

The Laughing Magician. Grass Valley, Calif.: Underwood, 1998. (Dying Earth omnibus comprising *The Eyes of the Overworld* and *Cugel's Saga.*)

Ports of Call. Grass Valley, Calif.: Underwood, 1998; New York: TOR, 1998; London: HarperCollins/Voyager, 1999.

BIBLIOGRAPHY

Benson, Gordon, Jr., and Phil Stephensen-Payne. *Jack Vance, A Fantasmic Imagination: A Working Bibliography.* Albuquerque, N. Mex., and Leeds, England: Galactic Central, 1988. Revised edition, San Bernardino, Calif.: Borgo, 1990.

Hewett, Jerry, and Daryl F. Mallett. *The Work of Jack Vance: An Annotated Bibliography & Guide.* San Bernardino, Calif.: Borgo; Penn Valley, Calif., and Lancaster, Pa.: Underwood-Miller, 1994.

Levack, Daniel J. H., and Tim Underwood, comps. *Fantasms: A Bibliography of the Literature of Jack Vance.* San Francisco, Calif., and Columbia, Pa.: Underwood-Miller, 1978.

CRITICAL AND BIOGRAPHICAL STUDIES

Adlard, Mark. "Dark End of the Spectrum." *Foundation*, 11/12 (March 1977): 48–52. (Review of the Planet of Adventure [Tschai] series.)

Andre-Driussi, Michael, "'Asi Achih': The Future History of Jack Vance." *New York Review of Science Fiction*, 113 (January 1998): 1, 8–11.

———. *Vance Space: A Rough Guide to the Planets of Alastor Cluster, the Gaean Reach, the Oikumene, & Other Exotic Sectors from the Science Fiction of Jack Vance*. San Francisco, Calif.: Sirius Fiction, 1997.

Close, Peter. "An Interview with Jack Vance." *Science Fiction Review*, 6, no. 4 (November 1977): 36–42.

Cover, Arthur Byron. "Ecce and Old Earth." *New York Review of Science Fiction*, 41 (January 1992), 13–14.

Cunningham, Arthur, ed. *Jack Vance. Critical Appreciations and a Bibliography*. London. The British Library, 1998.

Dickinson, Mike. "Romance and Hardening Arteries: A Reappraisal of the SF of Jack Vance." *Vector*, 95 (October 1979): 22–25.

Edwards, Malcolm, and John Clute. "Jack Vance." In *The Encyclopedia of Science Fiction*, 2d ed. Edited by John Clute and Peter Nicholls. London: Orbit, 1993; New York: St. Martin's, 1993.

Hand, Elizabeth. "Ports of Call." *The Magazine of Fantasy and Science Fiction*, August 1998, 32–35.

Langford, David. "Night Lamp." *Vector*, 193 (May/June 1997): 25.

Letson, Russell. "The Dragon Masters." In *Survey of Science Fiction Literature*. Edited by Frank N. Magill. Englewood Cliffs, N.J.: Salem, 1979.

———. "The Dying Earth." In *Survey of Science Fiction Literature*. Edited by Frank N. Magill. Englewood Cliffs, N.J.: Salem, 1979.

Mathews, Richard. "The Last Castle." In *Survey of Science Fiction Literature*. Edited by Frank N. Magill. Englewood Cliffs, N.J.: Salem, 1979.

Rawlins, Jack. *Demon Prince: The Dissonant Worlds of Jack Vance*. San Bernardino, Calif.: Borgo, 1986.

Russ, Joanna. "Books." *The Magazine of Fantasy and Science Fiction*, 38, no. 1 (January 1970): 37–43. (Includes a review of *Emphyrio*.)

Ternianka, Dan. *The Jack Vance Lexicon: From Ahulph to Zipangote: The Coined Words of Jack Vance*. Novato, Calif., and Lancaster, Pa.: Underwood-Miller, 1992.

Underwood, Tim, and Chuck Miller, eds. *Jack Vance*. New York: Taplinger, 1980. (Critical essays.)

A. E. VAN VOGT

(b. 1912)

THE POSITION OF A. E. van Vogt among science fiction writers is a peculiar one. Ever since his debut with "Black Destroyer" in the July 1939 issue of *Astounding Stories,* his popularity with the general reader has been enormous, and he remains one of the best-selling science fiction writers of all time. (Unfortunately, sales of science fiction have never been so high that even a best-selling writer could make a fortune at it.) Yet his fellow science fiction writers seem to have reservations about him, and more often than not his name is absent from collections with titles like *The Year's Best Science Fiction.* The reasons for this may emerge during the following appraisal.

Alfred Elton van Vogt was born in Winnipeg, Canada, of Dutch parents, on 26 April 1912. His father was a lawyer in a rural community in Saskatchewan. When van Vogt was fourteen, his family returned to Winnipeg; the shock of city life turned him into an introvert. He sank to the bottom of his class but began to read obsessively—two books a day, mostly detective stories. In 1926 he found a copy of *Amazing Stories* on a newsstand; he became hooked, and read every issue he could lay his hands on. At nineteen van Vogt became a civil servant, working for the Canadian census in Ottawa, where he also took a course in creative writing. Then he wrote a story for a women's magazine, *True Story.* It sold, and so did several others, one of them winning a $1,000 prize. At this time he met Edna Mayne Hull, whom he married in 1939.

Around 1934, disgusted with writing "true confessions," van Vogt began writing radio plays and sold some sixty at $10 each. In 1938 he picked up a copy of *Astounding Stories* in a drugstore in Winnipeg and was again bitten by the science fiction bug. (He had given up reading *Amazing Stories,* finding it dull.) He was excited by a story by John W. Campbell, Jr. (writing under the pseudonym of Don A. Stuart), "Who Goes There?"—about a "thing" from outer space that terrorizes an Antarctic research base. The thing could absorb other forms of life, taking their shapes. The idea so appealed to van Vogt that he sketched an outline for a story about a shape-shifting monster, which he sent to Campbell; it was "The Vault of the Beast." Campbell accepted it, although it did not appear until the August 1940 issue of *Astounding.*

"The Vault of the Beast" is probably the most remarkable first science fiction story ever written, at least as exceptional as Stanley Weinbaum's "A Martian Odyssey" (1934). And because its themes and techniques foreshadow those of all van Vogt's later work, it deserves detailed analysis.

"Vault" begins with a "creature" that has smuggled itself aboard an Earth-bound spaceship. The creature is, in fact, a kind of living robot created by superhuman intelligences in another "space frame." Its purpose is to get to Earth and persuade a great mathematician to solve the problem of a "time lock" that keeps one of the superhuman intelligences confined in a tower on Mars. But the creature has a

825

craving to turn itself into any shape that comes near it, and as a member of the crew walks past, it cannot prevent itself from becoming his duplicate. The crewman tries to disintegrate it with an atomic gun, but it vanishes through the wall of the spaceship.

Back on Earth, the thing murders the bookkeeper of the firm run by Jim Brender—the great mathematician, who is also a financial wizard; then the creature assumes the dead man's form, goes to see Brender, and tries to persuade him to go to Mars and release the legendary "beast" from its prison. But when a check reveals that the "bookkeeper's" credentials are false, Brender orders him out. The creature promptly murders another of Brender's financial associates, takes his shape, and ruins Brender by causing a stock market panic.

All this happens in a dozen pages; the forward flow of the story is compulsive. The shock effects resemble those that made James Bond so popular two decades later. ("A fist of solid steel smashed his face to a pulp, knocking the bones back into his brain.") The happenings have an Arabian Nights quality and remind us that van Vogt was an enthusiastic reader of fairy stories until he was twelve, when a teacher's sarcastic comment made him ashamed of his taste.

Now the story moves even faster. Brender is bankrupt and has lost his wife, who is about to marry another man. The creature transforms itself into the head of a space travel agency and gives Brender a job. It is almost discovered but manages to get Brender onto a spacecraft that takes off for Mars. The robot-creature is on the point of dissolution from the strain when its masters take over and persuade Brender to try his skill at solving the problem of the time lock to the vault of the beast. He agrees and goes to the tower, in the midst of the desert. At this point there is a long discussion about the problem of prime numbers and the completely different mathematics of worlds in other dimensions; the discussion is basically gobbledegook but sounds extraordinarily authoritative. Brender explains that all they have to do to release the beast from its prison is to interfere with the flow of power in the time lock, so as to reduce it by one unit. Then the lock, which is based on prime numbers, will break down, since its energy can then be factored.

At this point, for some unknown reason, the superbeing that had been conversing with Brender through the robot-creature proceeds to sneer like a Victorian villain, and tells him that now that he has solved their problem, he has given the superbeings the secret of ultimate power; once the beast has been released, it will reveal a secret that will enable them to conquer the universe. At this point Brender has a sudden realization that is (for the moment) kept concealed from the reader. The door of the vault flies open, but nothing comes out. The beast is dead—because the time lock was intended to open at the end of time; once it was made to open, "the end of time" occurred for the beast trapped inside. The robot-creature, objecting to being destroyed by its masters, had kept the superbeing from reading this thought in Brender's mind. So now there is nothing for Brender to do but rush back to Earth, now a rich man, to reclaim his wife, who flings herself into his arms as he steps off the spaceship.

"Vault of the Beast" reveals van Vogt's peculiar virtues, and also his faults. The first half is superb—brilliant, imaginative, and with a touch of intellectuality (the discussion of prime numbers, ultimate metals, and other scientific subjects) that makes it seem far more adult than most science fiction. One reads on to know what will happen next. The hero is a cut above most science fiction heroes of that period—the Flash Gordons and the rest—because he has a mind and knows how to use it; one might say that van Vogt produced in Brender a combination of Flash Gordon and Sherlock Holmes.

It is the second half of "Vault" that is disappointing. When the story ends, one is not quite sure what has happened. One has to read it several times, and even then it's not clear. And the conventional ending ("She flew to his arms. 'Oh, Jim, Jim,' she sobbed, 'What a fool I've been . . .' ") makes one aware of all the other implausibilities and impossibilities:

that superintelligences that could create such a robot-creature would need the help of a mathematician from Earth, that a wife would desert her genius husband simply because he has gone bankrupt, that a "robot" would have feelings and an objection to being destroyed. Then there are the more technical objections: that the first thing a mathematician would say, when an alien talks about the "ultimate prime number," is that Euclid invented a proof that there is no such thing; that once the aliens are sent back into their own dimension, the spaceship would not be able to return to Earth—from Mars—in a few minutes.

The truth is that "Vault of the Beast" is really a fairy story, with a wicked wizard who can perform magic and a square-jawed Prince Charming as a hero. The qualities that make it compulsively readable are the qualities of *The Lord of the Rings*—or, for that matter, of *Treasure Island* or *The Thirty-Nine Steps*. Van Vogt has a trick that could have been learned from George Bernard Shaw: gaining the reader's interest by making two strong personalities clash (so that, as a human being, the creature talks quietly, with precision and authority, making a worthy opponent for the hero). It could be called wish fulfillment—but so could many major works of literature.

The same qualities—and, basically, the same defects—can be found in all of van Vogt's best science fiction. And this could explain why he seems less popular with critics than with the general public: the critics sense that his qualities are those of an adventure writer rather than those of a man who (like H. G. Wells) has an urge to write fiction about science. Yet van Vogt's knowledge of science, and the use he makes of it in his stories, is so impressive that it would be absurd to deny his right to be called a master of science fiction.

"Black Destroyer," van Vogt's first published science fiction story, is quite as remarkable and powerful as "The Vault of the Beast," and for much the same reason. This time the monster is a great catlike creature with a craving for potassium; it manages to get taken on board a spaceship, then proceeds to slay the crew one by one, until it is found

out. Again, the ending remains incomprehensible, even after several readings.

"Discord in Scarlet," van Vogt's second published science fiction story, is about the same spaceship, but with a different monster. (Both stories were later incorporated into the novel *The Voyage of the Space Beagle* [1950].) The third published story, "Repetition," is a kind of Jack London adventure set on a satellite of Jupiter. Two men are stranded in the middle of nowhere, with only a knife for a weapon, and a long voyage back to civilization ahead of them; to complicate matters, one of them wants to kill the other for political reasons. The point of the story's title is the politician's comment that no danger is new—men have faced dangers many times before. And where human beings have conquered once, they can conquer again. So, using the same cunning that primitive man used against the saber-toothed tiger, the hero destroys two monsters and wins the respect of the man who wanted to kill him.

To dismiss "Repetition" as a mere adventure story would be a mistake. It obviously expresses one of van Vogt's deepest convictions: that intellect, will, and courage eventually will produce "men like gods." He is fundamentally an optimistic romantic whose main preoccupation is with human evolution. This is the theme that runs through all his work—and that distinguishes him from so many of his contemporaries. In an introduction to the 1958 anthology *Best of Science Fiction* (which included van Vogt's "Dormant"), Edmund Crispin commented on how much science fiction is concerned with doom, citing the catastrophe in "Dormant"—the explosion of the robot atomic bomb due to human arrogance and destructiveness—as an example of this widespread pessimism. Where van Vogt is concerned, Crispin could hardly be further from the truth. There is an almost obsessive current of evolutionary optimism in his work that, in a sense, places it clearly in the same literary tradition as Shaw's *Back to Methuselah*, 1921 (one of few science fiction plays). It could be this as much as anything else that explains why van Vogt is unfashion-

A. E. van Vogt. PHOTO BY JAY KAY KLEIN

able among intellectual critics. But, unlike Shaw, he is not a preacher; the evolutionism emerges in the form of a constant preoccupation with creatures possessing unusual powers.

In his chapter on van Vogt in *Seekers of Tomorrow* (1966), Sam Moskowitz remarks that after the first three or four tales, people began to feel that van Vogt was a one-plot writer and that he would probably prove to be a "flash in the pan." Van Vogt confounded these predictions with his novel *Slan,* which appeared in the four autumn issues of *Astounding Science-Fiction* in 1940. *Slan* was not only his biggest success to date; it was one of the most successful science fiction novels ever published. The theme may be said to take its starting point from Wells's *Food of the Gods* (1904), in which human beings want to destroy a race of giants because they hate anything greater than themselves. The child Jommy Cross is a member of the race of slans, human mutants with unusual powers of endurance and the

ability to read minds. His mother is murdered by a mob in the opening scene of the novel. The rest of the novel is about Jommy's attempt to stay alive and his love for a slan girl, a ward of the state who is actually the daughter of the dictator Keir Gray (himself a secret slan).

The pace of the story is tremendous, but two of its qualities stand out very clearly. One is the subtlety of the psychological observation—particularly of men in conflict. The other is the author's preoccupation with human irrationality and the reasons behind it. This is not just the kind of facile pessimism about human beings that can be found in some of Wells's early science fiction novels, but a genuine desire to understand why man, "the thinking reed," can behave so illogically. Van Vogt's preoccupation explains why he became so excited when he discovered the ideas of Alfred Korzybski in 1944, and those of L. Ron Hubbard a few years later; it also explains how he came to develop his own theory of the Right Man, an important contribution to psychological theory.

Meanwhile it was clear that van Vogt had escaped the cul-de-sac that seemed to threaten in 1940, and that his interest in human conflict and in the possibility of superhuman powers—like telepathy—was capable of stimulating a flood of imaginative creation. Two collections, *Destination: Universe!* (1952) and *Away and Beyond* (1952), consist of writings dating from the 1940's and contain much of his finest work. They demonstrate all his remarkable qualities of imagination and suspense, and his fascination with the "more-than-human." "Far Centaurus" (1943), the opening story of *Destination: Universe!,* demonstrates the preoccupation with time travel paradoxes that runs throughout van Vogt's work, and shows an interesting combination of realism (reminiscent of Robert A. Heinlein) and sheer imagination. The group of men who travel to another star in suspended animation—taking 500 years to do it—find human beings already there; men have in the meantime developed spaceships that can take them to the stars in a few hours. They escape their bleakly impersonal future by plunging into a star that knocks them backward in time to the twentieth century.

For purposes of science fiction, van Vogt never doubted the possibility of time travel; and in some of his works the characters plunge back and forth in time so vertiginously that the reader is left in a state of total bewilderment. It is probably a fair criticism that van Vogt's simplistic acceptance of the time travel convention reduces some otherwise impressive stories to a level of mere fantasy. The reader wants to know what would have happened if the spacemen in "Far Centaurus" had been "knocked back" slightly more than 500 years, to a point before their takeoff. Would they have met "themselves"? And in any case, these other "selves" would be out in space, on their way to Centaurus, when the spacemen arrived back on Earth.

Similarly concerned with other selves, "Asylum" is one of van Vogt's most important stories—he is on record as considering it his best—a kind of updating of *Dracula*, with "energy-vampires" from space invading Earth. The most interesting part of the story is its conclusion, in which the newspaper reporter who is about to be "drained" by a vampire drains her, instead, and turns out to be a "Great Galactic," a superbeing who has disguised himself in order to trap the vampires. His "disguise" includes an actual loss of his own memory, so that he is convinced that he *is* William Leigh, the newspaperman. Here van Vogt seems to be voicing a fundamental intuition about human beings—that, as absurd as it seems, we may be more godlike than we realize. (It may also help to explain his conversion to Hubbard's dianetics. Hubbard suggests that human beings are "immortals" who began life as a game, then forgot that it was only a game, and so became trapped.)

It is this intuition that raises van Vogt above the majority of science fiction writers. He is, in fact, an evolutionary mystic. This explains why he is at his best when writing of the possibility of superhuman or paranormal powers—as in *Slan*, "Asylum," "Resurrection" (later "The Monster," 1948), and "Re-

search Alpha" (a collaboration with James H. Schmitz, 1968)—a story about a woman who receives an injection of a drug that accelerates her evolution and endows her with new faculties. But it is worth noting that it is this same underlying feeling that imparts a sense of conviction to stories about human beings faced with difficult challenges—stories like "Repetition," "The Sound" (1949), and the ingenious "A Can of Paint" (1944), about a spaceman who has to solve the problem of a paint that automatically crawls all over him and threatens him with suffocation. Van Vogt is an evolutionist who uses a form analogous to the fairy story (which may be why he wrote so well about children) as a vehicle for his sense of optimism. The interest in human evolution relates him closely to Olaf Stapledon; but van Vogt would never allow his "superman" to end tragically, as Stapledon does in *Odd John* (1935). Some critics may regard this as evidence that he lacks a "tragic sense of life"—to which the only reply is that van Vogt is faithful to his own vision, and that vision is not fundamentally tragic.

The basic van Vogt formula, then, is extremely simple. Someone finds himself in trouble—often in the first paragraph—and one reads on to see how he gets out of it. This formula is used often, with tremendous imagination and ingenuity. Van Vogt seems to get his heroes into more tangled and dangerous situations than any other writer of science fiction—so tangled, sometimes, that he can get them out only by a kind of cheating, and one ends the story slightly let down, feeling that his solution wouldn't really work. The hero of "The Rulers" (1944) discovers an immense conspiracy in Washington; then, pursued by the villains, he discovers that literally everybody is against him because the villains have been slipping a mind-controlling drug that produces hypnosis into the city's water supply. His girlfriend betrays him to the villains. Before they execute him, they ask if he has anything to say. He tells them that hypnosis evokes a secondary personality, but that his psychological training has taught him that there is yet a third personality, which can supersede the other two. Whereupon he orders the guards holding him to open fire on the villains, which they do. The explanation is that he has evoked this "third personality" in the guards; but after the thrill of the chase, the end seems a cheat. But the end of a van Vogt story usually comes so fast that it leaves the reader slightly dazed, remembering only how exciting the story was.

The basic simplicity of the formula is disguised by van Vogt's capacity for intellectual self-renewal. Like Shaw, he is a writer of ideas; his stories contain some of the most exciting intellectual discussions in science fiction. And periodically a new idea comes along and transforms his approach. This is what happened in 1944, when he came across Korzybski's general semantics movement. Korzybski's basic assertion was that most human ills spring from muddled thinking and muddled linguistic habits. Ludwig Wittgenstein once said that most philosophy arises out of linguistic confusion; Korzybski said that most of human culture arises out of a similar confusion. We learn to adjust to the world—and control it—by setting up a mental map of reality; but most of us settle for an extremely crude and simplistic map. (An example would be a Nazi's assumption that the world consists of good Aryans and wicked non-Aryans, with no one in between; clearly, such a crude value system would prevent appreciation of some of the world's most important intellectual and artistic attainments.) This system of two-value logic Korzybski called Aristotelian; he argued that man needs a non-Aristotelian (or "null-A") logic for successful adjustment to reality.

Van Vogt's "dramatization" of Korzybski's ideas in *The World of Ā* (1945; book form, 1948; reprinted and hereafter titled *The World of Null-A*) is as original and exciting as anything he ever wrote. In fact, it reads like a transplantation into science fiction of the ideas that were preoccupying the existentialist writers of Europe at that time. It is the basic van Vogt situation—the hero in trouble—transposed to a new level of subtlety. His hero, Gilbert Gosseyn, is in a hotel, attending the computerized civil service examination conducted by the Games Machine; we are told that his wife is dead and that he has somehow become wealthy. When he joins a group of hotel guests, one of them challenges his identity. Convinced that this is a joke, he contradicts his accuser, and offers to take a lie-detector test. The lie detector reveals that he is not the person he says he is. Then who is he? Gosseyn realizes suddenly that he has no idea. He is, in fact, in the fundamental human situation, with no idea who he is or what he is doing here. But while the typical "existential hero"—like Kafka's K—allows himself to drift along passively, a victim of circumstance, Gosseyn possesses the optimism and determination of all van Vogt's heroes. His problem is to make the best of this absurd situation, and to try, if possible, to find out who he is.

The action is as fast-paced—in fact, as vertiginous—as ever. In *Seekers of Tomorrow* Moskowitz protests that this book is confusing, and says that dozens of readers wrote plaintive letters asking what it was supposed to be about. If that is so, it is difficult to see why. It *is* confusing, by the standards of such writers of science fiction of the 1930's as E. E. Smith and A. Merritt, but the reader of van Vogt has to be prepared to accept a certain degree of confusion in exchange for the pace of the action. *The World of Null-A* is among his best books because it combines physical and intellectual excitement with an indefinable sense of the presence of another dimension of meaning.

The World of Null-A, like its sequel, *The Pawns of Ā* (1948; book form as *The Pawns of Null-A*, 1956), is van Vogt's attempt to say what he feels is wrong with human beings, what makes them so irrational and violent. He accepts Korzybski's conclusion that our problem is that our brains have two centers, the cortex and the thalamus—the cortex dealing with ideas, the thalamus with emotions. These two centers have to be trained to work in coordination. Obviously there is a certain amount of truth in this; our problem certainly has to do with the general inefficiency of our

830

emotional and intellectual responses to reality. But what matters is not so much van Vogt's analysis of the problem as his awareness of it and his power to make the reader aware of it.

Between 1945 and 1950, van Vogt was occupied with a series of stories in which history is transposed into science fiction. "A Son is Born" (1946), the first of the Linn stories, was his next publication after *The World of Null-A*. The Linn family tree is based on that of the Medicis, and van Vogt later admitted to having been unconsciously influenced by Robert Graves's *I, Claudius*. The idea of transposing history into science fiction was a good one, and the "fix-up" novel he concocted from several Linn stories, *Empire of the Atom* (1956), is immensely readable. Yet the idea of basing science fiction on history also suggests that, once again, van Vogt was looking around for new ideas. Some of the stories he wrote between 1946 and 1951 are among his finest—"Dormant," *The Weapon Shops of Isher*, "War of Nerves," and "Enchanted Village." "The Great Judge" reveals a preoccupation with dictatorship that runs throughout his work and that produced one of the best of his later novels, *Future Glitter* (1973). But by 1950 it was clear that the creative miracle of van Vogt's "great decade," 1940–1950, was slowing down. He published no original science fiction between "Fulfillment" (1951) and "Itself" (1963), although a number of interesting "fix-ups" appeared, including *The Mind Cage* (1957), a complete reworking of the idea of "The Great Judge."

The reason for the long creative silence seems to have been van Vogt's preoccupation with the "dianetic" philosophy of Hubbard. In his autobiographical *Reflections of A. E. van Vogt* (1975), he describes how Hubbard made dozens of long-distance calls to him in 1950 to persuade him to become a dianetic "auditor"—a kind of psychoanalyst whose job is to release hidden "recordings" of traumatic past events (called "engrams") in the unconscious mind. But it seems clear that van Vogt would not have allowed himself to be persuaded unless he had been excited by the ideas. In fact,

Hubbard—himself a science fiction writer—had come up with another interesting theory of what makes human beings irrational: the notion that when they are unconscious (for instance, in the womb or during accidents), sentences they have heard are recorded in some automatic level of the mind—like the Freudian neurosis—and cause havoc later. It may seem surprising that van Vogt should have been so excited by dianetics when he had already absorbed general semantics, since the basic ideas of dianetics are cruder and more pessimistic than those of Korzybski. But dianetics included a dazzlingly simple method of "curing" people of their "engrams"—"auditing," persuading the patient to explore memories of past catastrophes until events dating back to the womb, or even to previous existences, can be "recalled." Van Vogt had never been able to resist any theory that held out a promise of immediate improvement to the human race.

The Mind Cage, van Vogt explains in his autobiography, was partly an attempt to psychoanalyze himself, to understand precisely why he had always been so preoccupied with supermen. Readers may feel that it does nothing of the sort, and that, in any case, his preoccupation with the superman is self-explanatory. But at least the absorption in dianetics brought one interesting spin-off, the origins of which were already present in *The Mind Cage*: his theory of the Right Man. And although it is only indirectly connected with his science fiction, no essay on van Vogt would be complete without an outline of this important concept.

Van Vogt had observed that there is a type of man who has a deep and violent distaste for the idea of being "in the wrong"—of being seen to make a mistake or misjudgment. He is the obsessive egoist—with all this implies about a lack of interest in other people—and has a fantasy of infallibility. But he is not obviously paranoid. He is, as often as not, a married man with a family; and he treats his family as if it were his own totalitarian state, demanding total obedience. He lives in a world of self-delusion. If anything threatens this delusion, if circumstances seem to prove that he has made a mistake, he will refuse to admit it. If faced with undeniable evidence, he will become violent, since violence is his basic reaction to any challenge to his "authority." Adolf Hitler, Josef Stalin, and Mao Tse-tung were "violent men," but there are thousands, probably millions, of them wandering around unnoticed; only their families are aware that such men are, in a sense, mildly insane.

The outcome of this interest in the Right Man was van Vogt's only non-science fiction novel, *The Violent Man* (1962), about an American in a Chinese prisoner-of-war camp with a "violent" commandant. But anyone who knows van Vogt's work will recognize that it is another of his basic themes—that he had always been fascinated by irrationality and ruthlessness. Few science fiction writers have succeeded in raising such a basic preoccupation into the light of consciousness. The full implications of the Right Man theory are too complex to discuss here; but it could well be his chief claim to the attention of future generations.

The break between van Vogt and Hubbard seems to have occurred when Hubbard announced that scientology superseded dianetics and that scientology was a religion. Van Vogt has remained interested in dianetics, but—like many of Hubbard's earlier followers—has declined to have anything to do with scientology.

In the mid-1960's van Vogt returned to writing original science fiction. Many critics have professed to be disappointed by this second period; but this may only be because they have a fixed idea of what a van Vogt story should be like—an idea dating from his first period. But development, by its very nature, means complexification; and for a writer like van Vogt it could hardly be otherwise. So the later work, on the whole, lacks the "fine careless rapture" of his earlier stories. Instead of plunging into the midst of the action with the opening paragraph, he may take a page or so to get to it. Yet as *The Silkie* (1964–1967; novelized, 1969), the first major work of this sec-

ond period, reveals, he can tell a story as well as ever. The Silkie is the most elaborate of his mutants so far, a creature that can change at will from a fish into a man, or into a superhuman being with a metal skin. The idea of a spaceship built by undersea creatures and filled with water is as quirky as anything in the earlier stories. The formula is again simple—superhuman Silkie versus interplanetary monster that consumes its "love objects" in a horrible ritual. But the most important part of the story, as usual, is the psychological idea—which van Vogt labels "the logic of levels." He explains it in a characteristically concise paragraph:

> It was a strange world, the world of logic. For nearly all of his long history, man had been moved by unsuspected mechanisms in his brain and nervous system. A sleep center put him to sleep. A waking center woke him up. A rage mechanism mobilized him for attack. A fear complex propelled him to flight. There were a hundred or more other mechanisms, each with its special task for him, each in itself a marvel of perfect functioning, but degraded by his uncomprehending obedience to a chance triggering of one or another. During this period, all civilization consisted of codes of honor and conduct and of attempts noble and ignoble to rationalize the unknown simplicities underneath. Finally, came a developing comprehension and control of the neural mechanisms, one, then another, then many. The real age of reason began.

The preceding paragraph contains the essence of van Vogt's ideas: the recognition that we are machines—but machines that can achieve deeper self-control, a greater degree of freedom, by understanding themselves. And he now recognizes that there are many levels of control—not just the cortex and the thalamus. The same idea is carefully expanded in the remaining Silkie stories. Admirers of *Slan* and *The World of Null-A* may feel that he had lost a certain lightness of touch (although the battle with the Glis, in "Silkies in Space" [1966], is as exciting as anything in the earlier work), but the sense of intellectual grasp nevertheless makes *The Silkie* one of his most satisfying inventions.

Yet although the later work is impressive evidence of van Vogt's power of intellectual self-renewal, it nevertheless raises certain basic questions—not simply about his own work but also about science fiction in general. *The Battle of Forever* (1971) is a case in point. This is a novel set at some remote date in the future, when human beings have evolved to an almost bodiless state. They have enclosed themselves behind a barrier, leaving the world to "animal men"—jaguars, bears, tigers, and other creatures, which have evolved into intelligent, humanoid creatures. As an experiment one of the human beings, Modyun, decides to "grow" himself an old-fashioned body, complete with digestive and excretory functions, and to explore the world outside the barrier. Two attempts on his life convince him that somebody in this crimeless world wants to see the last of him. He soon discovers that Earth has been "conquered" by an alien species that has caused men to retreat behind the barrier by implanting in their minds the idea that human existence is boring and repetitive, and that only a life of philosophical contemplation is worthwhile.

It is an exciting idea—it might be regarded as a criticism of Shaw's *Back to Methuselah*, whose "ancients" are much like van Vogt's "future-men." But van Vogt mentions that John W. Campbell, Jr., turned it down for serialization, and the reader can understand why. When a story is placed this far in the future and is peopled with lion-men and jackal-men and other characters who seem to have stepped out of *The Wizard of Oz*, it is hard for the reader to get involved in the way that one could with the mutants in *Slan*. Stapledon encountered the same problem in *Star Maker* (1937), in which the canvas is so vast that the reader feels that his feet are no longer on the ground. All art is created within a set of rules, which are tacitly accepted by both the reader and the writer, the creator and the consumer. The artist can change or extend the rules, but it must be done in such a way as to take the consumer along. (This explains why

the music of Arnold Schoenberg has still failed to "reach the public.") If the artist fails to do this, then the events take on an arbitrary quality, as in a passage in William Blake's fragmentary novel *An Island in the Moon*: "Then Mr Inflammable Gas ran and shoved his head into the fire and set his hair all in a flame, and ran about the room—No, no, he did not; I was only making a fool of you."

Van Vogt is too skillful a storyteller to allow the reader to reach this point of incredulity; but he often comes dangerously close to it. When, in *The Battle of Forever*, the aliens destroy all human beings except Modyun and a woman, the reader simply expects van Vogt to save the situation with a "time reversal," as he does in "Far Centaurus," "Silkies in Space," and other works. (In fact, he resists this temptation, although his actual solution is equally dubious.) What seems to be necessary is for van Vogt to commit himself more wholeheartedly to the intellectual framework, to be prepared to discuss as fully as Shaw or Wells the problems of man's evolution (which, in some ways, he understands better than either, because his grasp of psychology is wider). It is a problem that is, admittedly, inherent in the nature of science fiction, a genre that was invented to entertain but that has steadily increased in popularity because it does so much more—because, in some way, it touches the basic springs of human imagination. Van Vogt is disappointing at precisely those points where he seems to have decided that he is, after all, only an entertainer. It is because he is—consciously or otherwise—far more than this that he ranks among the finest writers of science fiction.

Selected Bibliography

FICTION OF A. E. VAN VOGT

Slan. Sauk City, Wisc.: Arkham House, 1946.
The Weapon Makers. Providence, R.I.: Hadley Publishing Company, 1947.
The World of Ā. New York: Simon and Schuster, 1948. (In reprint editions often titled *The World of Null-A*.)

The Voyage of the Space Beagle. New York: Simon and Schuster, 1950.

The Weapon Shops of Isher. New York: Corwin Books, Greenberg, 1951.

Away and Beyond. New York: Pellegrini and Cudahy, 1952.

Destination: Universe! New York: Pellegrini and Cudahy, 1952.

Empire of the Atom. Chicago: Shasta Publishers, 1956.

The Pawns of Null-A. New York: Ace Books, 1956. (In reprint editions often titled *The Players of Null-A.*)

The Mind Cage. New York: Simon and Schuster, 1957.

The Violent Man. New York: Farrar, Straus and Giroux, 1962.

The Silkie. New York: Ace Books, 1969.

The Battle of Forever. New York: Ace Books, 1971.

Future Glitter. New York: Ace Books, 1973. (British title, *Tyranopolis.*)

The Man with a Thousand Names. New York: DAW Books, 1974.

The Secret Galactics. Englewood Cliffs, N.J.: Prentice-Hall, 1974. Reprinted as *Earth Factor X.* New York: DAW Books, 1976.

Reflections of A. E. van Vogt. Lakemont, Ga.: Fictioneer Books, 1975.

The Anarchistic Colossus. New York: Ace Books, 1977.

Supermind. New York: DAW Books, 1977. (Based on material originally serialized in *If,* 1968, under the title "The Proxy Intelligence.")

Renaissance. New York: Pocket Books, 1979.

The Cosmic Encounter. Garden City, N.Y.: Doubleday, 1980.

Computerworld. New York: DAW Books, 1983.

Null-A Three. Hollywood, Calif.: Morrison/Raven-Hill, 1984. (Limited edition.)

AUTOBIOGRAPHIES OF A. E. VAN VOGT

Reflections of A. E. Van Vogt. Lakemont, Ga.: Fictioneer Books, 1975.

"My Life Was My Best Science Fiction Story." In *Fantastic Lives.* Edited by M. H. Greenberg. Carbondale: Southern Illinois University Press, 1981.

CRITICAL AND BIOGRAPHICAL STUDIES

Brunner, John, and Hal Drake. "Van Vogt and the Quest for the Universe." *Foundation* (Spring 1997): 18–26.

Edgeworth, Robert J. "Van Vogt's Use of Suetonius." *Review of Contemporary Fiction,* 6 (1986): 119–126.

Elliot, J. M. "The Making of a Professional: A. E. Van Vogt." *Amazing Stories,* 28 (1982): 6–14.

Ketterer, David. *Canadian Science Fiction and Fantasy.* Bloomington: Indiana University Press, 1992.

Panshin, Alexei, and Cory Panshin. *The World Beyond the Hill.* Los Angeles: Tarcher, 1989.

Sussex, Lucy. "Long Versus Short SF: The Examination of a Fix-Up." *Foundation* (July 1983): 28–33.

Zebrowski, George. "Never Forget the Writers Who Helped Build Yesterday's Tomorrows." *Science Fiction Age,* 3 (1995): 30–36, 100.

—COLIN WILSON

JULES VERNE
(1828–1905)

WHEN EDGAR ALLAN Poe needed a fiction catalyzer to set off his moon voyage, "The Unparalleled Adventure of One Hans Pfaal" (1835), he invented an atomic component of hydrogen discovered by a chemist at Nantes, France. Poe had no way of knowing that there had just been born at Nantes someone who would become the most catalytic figure in the history of science fiction, the author of the first scientifically described moon voyage, the man with the strongest claim to be called the Father of Science Fiction—Jules Verne.

Jules Verne, the son of a provincial lawyer and a mother from a patrician family of Scottish origin, was born in Nantes in 1828. His father, a devout, conservative man who carried Jansenism to the extent of flagellating himself, was a gentle tyrant whose supportive domination long controlled the life of Jules Verne. Indeed, much of the inner mechanism of Verne's life can be understood as a profound, never resolved conflict between rigid parental ideas and personal liberalism.

After an uneventful childhood, which included an attempt to run away to sea, Verne studied to be a lawyer. When he passed his examinations in Paris, it was assumed that he would take over his father's practice. Instead he horrified his family by announcing that he wanted to be a writer. Despite initial paternal disapproval, Verne held to his resolution (apart from a brief period when he tried to make a living as a broker) and soon became a familiar figure around the theatrical world of Paris.

Verne's early literary life was not successful. He wasted many years writing plays, for which he had less talent than he thought, and it was not until his early thirties that he came to understand his peculiar writing strengths.

His first stroke of fortune came when he made the acquaintance of Alexandre Dumas, *père*, who took a fancy to his buoyant manner and gift for repartee. Through Dumas' influence one of Verne's comedies was staged, not too successfully. More important, Verne realized that Dumas could serve as a literary model. He announced to Dumas, "Just as you are the great chronicler of history, I shall be the chronicler of geography." (Even in his old age, Verne thought of himself in these terms and complained that there were areas of the world he had not used in his fiction.) In this sort of program Verne was not unique. He was following a contemporary pattern of turning into fiction the sensational aspects of a particular field of knowledge. Dumas did it for history, Honoré de Balzac for social thought, Emile Gaboriau for criminology.

The second stroke of fortune came to Verne several years later, after a long period of marking time in letters. In 1863 he met the great publisher Jules Hetzel, with whom he established a close business and personal relationship that survived through the descendants of both men. Hetzel was founding an educational magazine for young people; and in the first draft of Verne's *Five Weeks in a Balloon* (*Cinq semaines en ballon*, 1863), he recognized Verne's gift for embodying popular science in fiction. This story became the first volume of a fifty-year sequence, *les voyages extraordinaires*. Translating this term is difficult, although "strange journeys" is acceptable. More fitting in spirit if not in letter would be the modern equivalents "amazing adventures" or even "astounding stories."

Verne found his métier in *le voyage extraordinaire*, which was at first a simple adventure story set in the midst of extensive geographic exposition. But he did not find fortune until he wrote *Around the World in Eighty Days* (*Le tour du monde en quatre-vingt jours*, 1873). As a stage extravaganza (1874 on), this was a spectacular success; and it formed the basis of Verne's later prosperity.

After the Franco-Prussian War (in which Verne served in a small way as a coast guard), he and his family settled in Amiens, his wife's native town. There he spent the remainder of his life, effectively cut off from the literary evolutions of Paris. He served in the town administration for several years and lived comfortably as a writer of world renown. He died in Amiens, at the age of seventy-eight, as the result of a long-standing diabetic condition.

About Verne's personality, it is difficult to say much, since his personal papers were destroyed and his family long tried to squeeze his memory into a mold of provincial respectability. But to a modern American, who cannot be expected to understand the infinite variety of political types in nineteenth-century France, his beliefs and activities seem wildly inconsistent. He was greatly interested in politics. He spoke at length as an anarchist and had anarchists as friends, yet he was fairly conservative in his own small political career and favored social control in areas that he approved. For most of his life he considered himself a Catholic, yet he was free-thinking and most of his works are blatantly secular. He hated big business, militarism, war, and colonialism—if they were not French. In his youth he was the clown among his associates, yet a clown with strong feelings of inadequacy. His marriage was not entirely successful. During his adult life he found greatest pleasure in the sea, and when he could afford it, he owned and operated various boats, in-

cluding an expensive ten-man yacht. In his old age he withdrew from the world as much as possible, suffered from ill health, and was an unhappy man.

As an intellect, though, Verne is easily captured. He was a compulsive worker who spent hours every day studying and writing, often on board one of his vessels. He was greatly fascinated by descriptive science, particularly geography, but less so by theoretical science; and he was almost obsessive about accuracy and completeness. His library was enormous, as was his accumulation of reading notes. Although he did not like the naturalistic movement in French literature and did not keep abreast of the times in literature he read extensively in other fiction. Among the authors who influenced him most were Charles Dickens, Johann Wyss (author of *The Swiss Family Robinson*), and Edgar Allan Poe, whose general influence permeates his work.

I

Not all the sixty-five titles that comprise *les voyages extraordinaires* are *voyages* or *extraordinaires*, but Verne's first important story, *A Journey to the Center of the Earth* (*Voyage au centre de la terre*, 1864), is both.

It is a single-stranded story of discovery, filled with expected "narratized" geology and unexpected visionary material. Young Axel and his fanatical uncle, Professor Lidenbrock of Hamburg, decipher a cryptogram that Lidenbrock found in an old book and learn that a passageway to the center of the earth is to be found in an Icelandic volcano. (Here Verne is invoking the medieval legend that a passage to Hell existed in Iceland.) Accompanied by Hans, a stolid Icelander, they descend into the crater and travel through long tunnels, in which they marvel at petrified earth history, until they come to an enormous, lighted cavern world. They find a vast sea, with forests of giant mushrooms and carboniferous flora on its shores, and paleontological giant saurians, who battle in its waters. They even catch a glimpse of a herd of mammoths being watched by a twelve-foot-tall anthropoid. But when they blast away an obstruction to their further exploration, they accidentally open water channels. They are carried along by underground torrents, seemingly interminably, until they are finally spewed out by the volcano Stromboli.

To base a novel on premodern geology is an achievement, and Verne carried it off well. *A Journey to the Center of the Earth* is one of Verne's most pleasant works. It is even more important, though, in showing patterns of thought, tricks of presentation, and private symbols that manifest themselves throughout his long career—as will be seen in the plot descriptions that follow.

Lidenbrock, Axel, and Hans embody the steady trinity that peoples Verne's fiction: father figure, son figure, servant figure; intellect, emotion, action; domination, subservience, stolid acceptance. Activating this trinity is a single topic central to all of Verne's work: obsession. His novels are filled with and motivated by men (he is little concerned with women) who embody unreasonableness and compel others. (Captain Nemo is a good later example.) This figure might be called the Obsessive Compeller. Beneath him is another person, usually younger, who might be called the Unstable Experiencer. He bears the brunt of the parental figure and is also the point of narrative concentration. One of his characteristics is that he is often unstable emotionally and is subject to dreams, visions, and collapses. Axel, for example, is often on the edge of breakdown, and his mystical and horror dreams offer a counterpoint to the intellectual mania of his uncle. The third person, the Faithful Servant, plods along, sometimes offering support to the Unstable Experiencer.

Entry to and exit from Verne's "other worlds" (for this is what they amount to despite the Victorian insistence that they are extensions of our world) is usually explosive, instantaneous, and unconscious, with Verne befogging the way in which the transition occurs. Within these other worlds there exist certain repeated narrative structures and symbolic equations that probably had great meaning to Verne. Among these is a withdrawal from the world by descending—either into water or into caverns. The epitomes of such withdrawals are Captain Nemo's submarine and the underground Coal City in *Black Diamonds* (*Les Indes noires*, 1877). The sea is also very important, and sometimes seas and caverns are combined. By and large there is no real danger in the Vernian underworlds other than ice and cold, against which fire and volcanism serve as friends. (Nemo's submarine, frozen in an iceberg, melts its way out with hot water.) The journey (and this is true of Verne's adventure novels as well as the science fiction novels) is usually a circular affair, which offers little or no character development. It ends in a crisis-explosion, and the hero is back in our world. This strange, consistent inner space, which also appears in Verne's general fiction, is a tempting subject for parlor analysis, but so little is known about the mysterious M. Verne that it is safer simply to return to his fiction as science fiction.

Undoubtedly the most important lunar voyage in all literature is described in *From the Earth to the Moon* (*De la terre à la lune*, 1865) and *Around the Moon* (*Autour de la lune*, 1870). The first volume describes the preparations for a lunar voyage; the second, the experiences of two Americans and a Frenchman in a conical shell as it circles around the moon and drops back to earth.

From the Earth to the Moon is the first "hard" science fiction novel. It marks the first recognition that the theory of and preparations for a lunar voyage may be just as interesting as the adventures on a voyage. It is also among the first interplanetary voyages to be oriented toward science rather than personal satire or religion. Verne did his utmost to establish a rational, scientific basis for his story, working out such matters as escape velocity, weights, optimal time and place for launching the shell, distances, ballistics, selenography, and even the appurtenances for maintaining life in the shell. Before writing the story, Verne filled countless pages with calculations and enlisted the aid of mathematicians to

Jules Verne. COURTESY OF THE LIBRARY OF CONGRESS

check his figures. He was not completely correct, of course; but as Wernher von Braun has said, he was nearly correct, within the limitations of nineteenth-century science. His largest error was the failure to recognize that his passengers would be killed at the very outset of their journey by the enormous gravities caused by the explosion. He was also somewhat fanciful about the contents of his lunar vehicle, but this was unquestionably tongue-in-cheek.

Set in the United States, partly in Baltimore, partly in Florida, *From the Earth to the Moon* focuses on American landscapes and cultural personalities, the latter presented in a satirical, caricaturelike manner. The Baltimore Gun Club, whose members include the foremost militarists, ballistics experts, munitions manufacturers, and war profiteers, is languishing after the Civil War until Impey Barbicane, its president, conceives the notion of shooting a projectile to the moon. This is to show the Selenites (if any) what Americans can do. The mathematics and engineering for such a missile are worked out, and the missile is to be fired from an enormous gun emplaced near Tampa. At the last moment, though, plans are changed. A hollow vessel is substituted for the shot, and into it enter three men: Barbicane, his erstwhile rival Captain Nicholl, and Ardan ("ardent"), a Frenchman (who is modeled upon Verne's friend, the photographer-balloonist Nadar). The mammoth gun is fired, but the fate of the three men is not revealed.

In the second volume, the experiences of the travelers in space are described—together with the two dogs, chickens, and assorted nonsense that Ardan has smuggled aboard. They learn that their course has been changed by the gravitational influence of a small, hitherto unknown satellite; and for a time they fear that they will not strike the moon but will continue on into outer space. They suffer greatly from cold. To their chagrin, they circle the moon (seeing the dark side, about which Ardan has a fantasizing vision), return to earth, and drop into the Pacific—oddly enough, about two and a half miles from the historic Apollo splashdown.

A modern reader will note several oddities about Verne's lunar voyage. First, the great care with which Verne has established such geographical details as the street map of Baltimore. Second, his odd lapse in describing herds of buffalo around Tampa. And third, his softening or bowdlerization of what a modern writer would have faced: the fact of death. The voyage to the moon is suicide. If the shell reaches the moon, there is no possibility of returning. Yet, although the coolly pragmatic Barbicane, the negative, contentious Nicholl, and the brainless, ebullient Ardan know this, they have no hesitation about going. Their compulsion to reach the moon is so great that death itself pales before it.

A similar compulsion of death-in-life characterizes that strange would-be solipsist Captain Nemo, the man who tries to crawl into the sea and pull it in after him. In *Twenty Thousand Leagues Under the Sea* (*Vingt mille lieues sous les mers*, 1870), a strange "thing" has been attacking shipping around the world. An American warship is fitted out to destroy it. On board are Pierre Arronax, a French marine biologist; Conseil, his servant; and Ned Land, a French-Canadian harpoonist. The "monster" is finally sighted and attacked; and in a rapid shift of milieu, Arronax and his friends find themselves aboard the *Nautilus*, a supersubmarine captained by Nemo. For many months, as prisoner-guests, they experience the wonders of the sea with Captain Nemo—exploring underwater forests, hunting fish with electric guns and aqualungs, sighting Atlantis, and fighting octopi. But adventures are no substitute for freedom, and the three captives escape in a lifeboat just as Nemo's submarine is being dragged down into the Maelstrom.

Captain Nemo is, of course, Verne's single contribution to the great personalities of world literature. A man with a sorrow, one who has withdrawn from surface life, he and his men, fellow dropouts, live beneath the surface of the sea and avoid, as much as possible, everything that has to do with the land. Nemo even drinks wine made of seaweed and smokes seaweed cigars. Just who Nemo is, and what is his sorrow, are not revealed here; but in the sequel, *The Mysterious Island* (*L'île mystérieuse*, 1874–1875), Verne provides explanations that do not jibe too well with the earlier novel. Originally Nemo was intended to be a Polish prince whose family had been exterminated by Russian tyranny. At the request of his publisher, and after a long argument, Verne finally shifted Nemo's origins to India. But regardless of his national origin, Nemo is simply an anarchist of the nineteenth century, black flag and all. It is ironic that Nemo, the ultimate detached man, is placed in the paradoxical position of being himself a controller or oppressor, both of his beaten, wormlike crew and of his captives.

Who else was Nemo? It used to be said that Nemo was Lord Byron in a diving suit, but a fitter description (as Verne's friends and relatives knew) is that Nemo was Jules Verne in a diving suit. Verne, too, was a theoretical anarchist at this period. And, as his son Michel said in later years, like Nemo, Verne really cared only for "the sea, music, and freedom"—by which he meant not being bothered by others.

Readers of the past used to admire Nemo; but today his posturings, erratic atrocities, and occasional benevolences are much less interesting than the true hero of the novel, the sea itself. One can only admire the success with which Verne has conveyed his enthusiasm for the marine world.

Twenty Thousand Leagues Under the Sea is Verne's third great science fiction novel and his paean to the free and unowned ocean of water. His next significant work, *Hector Servadac* (*Hector Servadac*, 1877), moves to the free and unowned ocean of space—and dream.

Hector Servadac is usually considered a lesser work. It has been criticized for surface inaneness, caricatured personalities, and large stretches of weak narrative. All these criticisms are justifiable, but the book is extremely interesting in other ways. It shows Verne not as a purveyor of potted geography for youngsters, as previously, but as a pioneer of a strange, pseudoscientific surrealism that cries for special analysis.

The story line is simple. Hector Servadac, a young French army officer at a lonely post in Algeria, and his orderly, Ben Zoof, awaken after a violent storm. Their station has been demolished, and they seem alone in the world. Africa has been whittled down to their tiny island, surrounded by seemingly endless seas. They also note that they seem much stronger than they used to be. After a while other persons appear: a Russian nobleman, with whom Servadac had engaged in sexual rivalry, and the crew of his yacht; several Spaniards, who perform spectacular dances; a few uncivil, gluttonous Englishmen on a fragment of Gibraltar; Hakkabuk, a Jewish trader, who is offensively characterized as a despicable wretch; and Professor Rosette, an irascible, pedantic mathematician who used to be Servadac's teacher at the lycée.

After a time Servadac and the others realize that they are no longer on earth but on a comet that has grazed earth, lifting off a few chunks of land, and is now on a long orbit out into space. As the comet recedes from the sun, the cold grows intense and the *voyageurs* survive only by living in the bowel-caves of a volcano. When the comet returns to earth, Servadac and his companions build a balloon and are in midair when the comet strikes. They are again seized by a storm, rendered unconscious, and awaken back in Algeria. They have been away two years, but the landscape is unchanged and no one will believe them. Their experience was true, but it was also a dream!

But whose dream?

This strange ending is surely one of the most striking in science fiction. It was common enough in nineteenth-century fantastic fiction to apologize events away as dreams, but to declare a story both a dream and a reality is quite different. It offers the reader a legitimate reason to consider the story on a deeper level than ethnic humor and bile, curiosities of popular astronomy, and the Last Man theme.

The architecture of *Hector Servadac* is that of a dream: swift entry via unconsciousness, sudden changes of locale, pictorially conceived landscapes that would be considered surrealistic if painted, the sensation of weightlessness and bounding, the endless sea, the descent to caves, and the curious activities of the characters: the leaping Spaniards, the voyaging (Wandering) Jew, the ever-eating Englishmen. Hector and the Russian count are doublets, as are Hakkabuk and Professor Rosette. The latter pair are both semiparanoid father figures—one miserly with money, the other miserly with knowledge (permission to mature). Rosette, even, does not want the dream to end and fights Servadac's attempts to return to earth. Open sexuality is not apparent, for Verne always carefully avoided it, but Servadac's orderly, Ben Zoof, makes the curious remark that he and Servadac are married to one another. And the whole adventure is one of Verne's cyclical nonhappenings: the *voyageurs* are back where they started, at the exact second anniversary of their departure.

If *Hector Servadac* had been written recently by a more sophisticated writer, it might be called a "fantasy of individuation"—that is, a fantasy in which unconscious events or complexes have been structured into story, revealing some internal change or growth. The sad aspect of Verne's projective or individuation stories, though, is that there is no such change. The hero has failed, and everything is as it was before.

Hector Servadac seems to have been a transitional work in Verne's science fiction, marking a shift away from the earlier, descriptive *voyages*, but before the oddly introgressive stories of his later years, Verne acceded to a topical diversion, unquestionably conditioned by political events.

In the middle or late 1870's, Hetzel asked Verne to rework a novel written by Paschal Grousset (better known as André Laurie). After some hesitation Verne took over the story, which was published as *The Begum's Fortune* (*Les cinq cents millions de la bégum*, 1878). It is a fantasy of nationalism, Verne's *revanche* for the Franco-Prussian War.

In *The Begum's Fortune*, a Napoleonic soldier had settled in India and married the widow of a native ruler. His line has become extinct, and an enormous fortune devolves on two collateral descendants: Dr. Sarrasin, a French hygienist, and Professor Schultze (or Schultz), a German chemist at Jena. Sarrasin embodies all the best French qualities, Schultze the worst German.

Sarrasin uses his share of the bequest to set up a semisocialistic, covenanted utopia in the wilds of Oregon, while Schultze, obsessed with hatred of Sarrasin and France, determines to destroy him and his utopian state. He establishes a rival city, about thirty miles away from Sarrasin's. It is a fortress-factory where all aspects of life are ruthlessly, even murderously regimented and Schultze controls everything. Sarrasin's future son-in-law infiltrates Schultze's establishment in disguise and learns of the fantastic weapons that Schultze plans to use. The attack cannot be prevented, but it fails, since Schultze's mathematics were inadequate. Verne's point is that under a rigid dictatorship not only are humans stultified, but knowledge, too, is stifled.

It is not known what aspects of the book are Verne's, but the plotting is unlike his usual work. The exploits of the undercover agent, with strong resemblance to the exploits of the Pinkertons in America (Allan Pinkerton's *The Pinkertons and the Molly Maguires* and *The Model Town*), may have been Laurie's. But the close description of the protofascist state is probably Verne's. An extrapolation from the Krupp works at Essen, it is a remarkable anticipation of twentieth-century history. But by a curious twist of values, Sarrasin and Verne's model city, with its social controls over civic life, household architecture, and even wallpaper and carpeting, now seems only another, milder form of repression.

For the next decade or so, Verne concentrated mostly on historical and geographical fiction, but in 1889 he returned to a motif he had mentioned in *From the Earth to the Moon:* changing the orbital axis of the earth. Verne's interest was reawakened when an engineer sold him a paper developing the mathematics for straightening out the axis of the earth.

According to Verne's novel *The Purchase of the North Pole* (*Sans dessus dessous*, 1889), the area around the North Pole belongs to no nation. It is decided (Verne is vague about by whom) to end this unsatisfactory situation by auctioning the area off; the purchasers are Impey Barbicane and the Gun Club of Baltimore (familiar from the 1865 work *From the Earth to the Moon*).

Barbicane and his associates Nicholl and Maston have inferred (a telling point, since Verne always stressed hard data) that the Pole must be on an elevated plateau rich in coal, which will become valuable when other deposits are exhausted. The problem is gaining access to this plateau. Maston, who is a great mathematician, works out a solution: correct the earth's axis, so that the Pole falls in a temperate zone. An explosion of a certain magnitude will jolt the earth "upright."

This is fine for the Gun Club, but the project is inconsiderate of human life. The three monomaniacs point out the advantages of fixing the seasons permanently and are not troubled by the knowledge that the shift will submerge some areas, elevate others, and kill millions. Riots break out, and governments want to stop the fanatics, but Barbicane and Nicholl have disappeared. Maston, in jail, refuses to talk. By the time Barbicane is located, at the site of an enormous boring into Mount Kilimanjaro, it is too late. The explosion takes place, but nothing happens. Maston, struck by lightning while working and temporarily slightly dazed, had accidentally left off several zeros from a basic figure. The project had always been impossible, a sort of waking nightmare.

Like most of Verne's other later works, *The Purchase of the North Pole* separates easily into various levels of projection. (That is, critical analysis may offer layers of conscious, semiconscious, and unconscious meaning.) On the surface it is a suspense story with the titillation of imminent catastrophe. On a somewhat deeper level, it is a bitterly sarcastic, defeatist comment on greed and irresponsibility, particularly on the part of big business. (Verne was greatly interested in conservation of resources.) But the flip side of the novel is reminiscent of Nathaniel Hawthorne's "The Birthmark" (1843): the dangers of fanatical perfectionism. There would be advantages to righting the earth, but only a fool or fanatic would accept the deaths that would follow. A Jehovah was willing to flood the earth, but a Verne would draw back.

Written at about the same time as *The Purchase of the North Pole*, but more elaborate, more interesting in idea and more personal is *The Castle of the Carpathians* (*Le Château des Carpathes*, 1892). Verne considered it an important work and was greatly disappointed when it attracted little attention.

The Castle of the Carpathians is a double novel with two foci. In the first half, the benighted peasants of Werst in Transylvania are concerned because smoke has been seen coming from the deserted, haunted Castle of the

Carpathians. The castle is the property of the barons de Gortz, a line popularly believed extinct. Nic Deck, a brave young forester, goes to investigate, even though he has been warned away by a disembodied voice at the local inn. He sees strange, seemingly supernatural sights; and when he tries to climb the drawbridge, he is hurled off, paralyzed by an inexplicable force.

In the second half of the book, Franz de Telek, a young Rumanian nobleman traveling to restore his broken health, chances by. He is only mildly interested when the peasants tell of the castle, but his interest is greatly aroused when, at the inn, he hears a ghostly female voice singing an operatic aria. It is the voice of the woman he loved, the deceased diva La Stilla. (The background: Telek and Stilla were engaged when she dropped dead in mid-song during her farewell performance. Also involved with her was the fetishistic Baron de Gortz, a horrible-looking man, who had an abnormal passion for her voice. His appearance in his box caused Stilla's heart attack or stroke, although he blamed Telek for her death. De Gortz disappeared, while Telek had a breakdown, from which he is now slowly recovering.) Telek decides that Stilla is alive and a prisoner in the castle. As he awaits daybreak outside the castle, he sees her on the ramparts. The next morning he enters the castle, is captured by unseen forces, rendered unconscious, and imprisoned. When he breaks loose and confronts de Gortz, he learns of a surprising situation. De Gortz, with the aid of a great scientist, has recorded La Stilla's voice with advanced phonographic equipment, recreated her appearance with a portrait and mirrors, and has used telephony and electricity to discourage trespassers. He has lured Telek to the castle to kill him. (Like Hoffmann's Krespel in Jacques Offenbach's opera *Contes d'Hoffmann*, an obvious source, de Gortz blames love for death.) In the ensuing explosion, de Gortz dies and Telek loses his mind. But Nic Deck, from part one, recovers and marries his peasant sweetheart.

On the surface *The Castle of the Carpathians* is a novel of adventure, ethnic humor of a rough sort, and melodramatic situations. On a somewhat deeper level, it is a working out of themes from the haunted-castle nexus of the gothic novel, expressed in terms of science fiction. But it was also a work of great personal relevance to Verne, based on his sorrow at the death of his still unidentified mistress or woman friend, the actress or singer known only as Stella. With Stella he had found the companionship and intellectual response that his wife could not give him. Against this background, the flip side of *The Castle of the Carpathians* describes two men (de Gortz and Telek, really doublets) who cannot accept death.

The novel, filled with obvious Trojan and Orphic hints, is really a fairy tale of death. Life and death stand in contrast—the living, earthy village and the detached castle of the dead past. Obsessed personalities clash. The paranoid de Gortz has retreated to the past via an unsuccessful *nekuia*, in trying (figuratively speaking) to revive the dead mechanically. The visually obsessive Telek, another of Verne's unstable sensitives, wanders in and out of mental collapse, for he, too, cannot accept death. All this is in contrast to the wholesome Nic Deck and his sweetheart. Unfortunately, Verne lacked the art to bring out the fairly subtle relationship of life and death.

The Castle of the Carpathians is the last of Verne's great science fiction novels, but several of his later works use science fiction situations and motifs to convey social themes.

The Floating Island (*L'île à hélice*, 1895) is the story of a big artificial island constructed by American millionaires. An overgrown playpen, filled with superscientific devices, it moves about the oceans seeking ideal climates and sights for its blasé inhabitants. But the island is a symbol for life or humanity. When conflicting, selfish programs based on regionalism arise, the island's regulating mechanisms are destroyed, and it is smashed by the forces of nature. Related somewhat in theme, although here greed is the issue, is *The Chase of the Golden Meteor* (*La Chasse au météore*, 1908), perhaps worked on by Verne's son Michel after Verne's death. In a reversion to Verne's old dream of obtaining gold from the sky, a scientific apparatus is devised to pull down a golden asteroid that is passing close to earth, but the squabbles about who will get the gold are so agitating that the inventor diverts the meteorite to the sea, where it is lost.

Ideas fairly important to Verne are to be found in the novel *The Village in the Tree Tops* (*Le village aérien*, 1901), where Verne, who had reverted to his familial Catholicism, declares (as author) that he does not accept Darwinism but then goes on to describe Missing Links. Much more trivial is *An Antarctic Mystery* (*Le sphinx des glaces*, 1897), which, while conveying Verne's persistent concern with ice and cold, is a rationalistic sequel to *The Narrative of Arthur Gordon Pym* (1838) by Edgar Allan Poe. Verne, in a curious reversion to a medieval motif, postulates as a final Antarctic wonder a magnetic mountain powerful enough to capture ships.

More significant is *The Master of the World* (*Maître du monde*, 1904), the second of Verne's novels about the inventor Robur. In an earlier novel, *The Clipper of the Clouds* (*Robur le conquérant*, 1886), Robur, an egotistical inventor who has constructed a marvelous heavier-than-air ship, kidnaps two scientifically reactionary balloonists and takes them around the world in a tired imitation of the breezy early *voyages*. The story is a conscious allegory of progress, for Verne states directly that Robur is the science of the future. But science is viewed ambivalently. It is both necessary and desirable, yet too rapid advances, without responsible control, may be dangerous. This, of course, is a different point of view from that of Verne's earlier work. In the sequel, *The Master of the World*, Robur returns with a supervehicle that combines the features of an incredibly fast automobile, a surface ship, a submarine, and an airship capable of traveling at 250 miles per hour. Robur has become a criminal and is now obviously mad. Like Ajax, he defies the lightning and flies his machine into a storm cloud, where he dies. One could interpret this ending as meaning that irresponsible science will be

struck down by God (*Jupiter tonans*), but one could also say that Robur is simply the ultimate extension of Verne's compulsive-paranoid character of overweening pride and arrogance.

Among Verne's posthumous works are *The Secret of Wilhelm Storitz* (*Le secret de Wilhelm Storitz*, 1910), *Yesterday and Tomorrow* (*Hier et demain*, 1910), and *The Barsac Mission* (*L'étonnante aventure de la mission Barsac*, 1919). The hand of Michel Verne is present in all of these works in varying degrees.

The Secret of Wilhelm Storitz describes the tragic results of the discovery of invisibility in eighteenth-century Hungary. Michel considered it inferior to H. G. Wells's *The Invisible Man* (1898) and discouraged its publication during Verne's lifetime. *Yesterday and Tomorrow* is a collection of short stories. It includes "In the Year 2889" ("La journée d'un journaliste américain en l'an 2889"), which was published first in English in 1889. A projection of technology, its authorship is doubtful. Michel Verne had a hand in it, either as major collaborator or as sole author. Also present is "The Eternal Adam" ("L'éternal Adam"), an undated story that is set in the far future. A scientist who is chauvinistically proud of the achievements of his culture discovers archaeological evidence that his civilization was preceded by two lost worlds, ours and Atlantis. The discovery of a cyclical pattern of destruction almost shatters him, but he finds strength to continue. It is possible that Michel worked on this story, but the cyclical concept and many of the little narrative tricks are the elder Verne's.

Among Verne's papers were found notes and some finished sections for *The Barsac Mission*, which Michel put into final form. It is set in Africa, and the first portion echoes the earlier geographical adventures. The narrative is a quest that ends at Blackland, a hidden city in the Sahara filled with remarkable inventions, including most powerful weapons, all the work of an obsessive, utterly withdrawn scientific genius. Blackland is ruled by criminals, under the direction of a mastermind. They prey on their neighbors for slaves and also use their fantastic equipment to conduct secret raids on Europe. Verne's story is adventure fiction, but his ideas have wider implications. Science divorced from morality (in the largest sense) can work great harm. On a still deeper level, Verne postulates a *deus absconditus*, an irresponsible creator, who discovers too late that His gifts are being used evilly. His solution (not the best solution) is destruction, as in the Flood. The religious implications may well reflect Verne's increasing preoccupation with religion in his last years.

With these last works, Verne is far from the long, exuberant, fancifully fictionalized geography texts of his earlier years. Gone are the light, ironic touch, the mocking caricatures, the enthusiasm for science and progress. Instead we find occasional sour sarcasm, a preoccupation (sometimes conscious, sometimes probably only half-conscious) with the implications of actions and forces, and grumbling suspicion. What we find is not always a pleasant Verne, but it may be a more significant Verne.

II

Historically there can be no question but that Verne is by far the most important personality in the science fiction form before Wells. Indeed, although Wells was a superior artist whose work is more closely related typologically to modern science fiction, Verne's overall influence has been greater. Verne did not call his work science fiction, but *From the Earth to the Moon* is the foundation document, the type specimen of hard science fiction, or the first real attempt to extrapolate fantastic science solidly on the basis of existing knowledge. As Verne said in an interview in 1904, "I have always made a point in my romances of basing my so-called inventions upon a groundwork of actual fact, and of using in their construction methods and materials which are not entirely without the pale of contemporary engineering skill and knowledge" (in Peter Costello, *Jules Verne*, page 186).

Entire chains of development are based on Verne's work. The invention story of the American dime novel was a lurid, low-grade exploitation of what Verne worked out with great thought. Most of the early interplanetary voyages, although they miss Verne's factuality, are otherwise based on his work. Captain Nemo and Robur have been ancestors of literally scores of dynamic outlaws with superior technology, who prey on the rest of the world. All in all, Verne's influence has been almost incalculable in premodern science fiction.

It is more difficult to establish Verne's critical value. During his lifetime, his reputation in France was popular rather than literary, and it was a great disappointment to him that he was never elected to l'Académie française. But, obviously, if one is to judge Verne by the standards set by Stendhal or Flaubert, he does not stand very high. There is the further question of his intended audience. Despite modern, critical statements to the contrary, Verne wrote primarily for an educational enterprise, the readership of which was very largely juvenile.

The surface texture of Verne's writing, which is always lost in translation, demonstrates a well-sustained wit, a pleasant note of deprecatory mockery, and many well-turned phrases; but his ability to create characters, even allowing for the fact that they are humors or self-projections, was not great. Of all the personalities in more than seventy-five novels and short stories, only Captain Nemo has any vitality. Nor was Verne a skilled plotter. Yet, despite these flaws, Verne occasionally shows outweighing virtues. His clarity of vision and deftness in handling technical material are remarkable, and his earlier works convey an enthusiasm and gusto that emerge even through leaden translations. It is a remarkable achievement to carry the reader three hundred pages or so into the sea or earth, with, really, nothing happening except the excitement of seeing new things. In this ability to transmit the dazzle of perception, Verne has seldom been matched.

The modern trend in France has been to esteem Verne for qualities that are not so much literary as cultural-historical or even semiphilosophical. He has been extolled for mirroring the transition from Victorian scientific mechanism to modern relativism, but this estimation seems exaggerated and distorted, as well as far from being unique. Tennyson conveyed the same feelings about progress better in "Locksley Hall" (1842) and "Locksley Hall Sixty Years After" (1886).

Verne has also lent himself well to various forms of literary depth-analysis or mythic analysis. Modern critics have sought parallels between his stories and ancient myths, sometimes haphazardly. Verne's work, as this paper has hinted, does display odd features once the surface is penetrated, and sometimes these oddities seem to be personal with Verne, sometimes symbolic statements about society, religion, and existence. Unfortunately, so little is known of him that such poking and prying must remain speculative. It is all too easy and perhaps too glib to see Verne ultimately as an aberrant popularizer of geography who confused the contours of the earth with the contours of his own mind.

ADDENDA

Since this article was written, the Verne and Hetzel family and business archives have become available to certain scholars, and many more details are now known about Verne's life than were known previously. Herbert R. Lottman's *Jules Verne: An Exploratory Biography* (1996) covers this material well, although it says little about Verne as a writer.

Many of the previously accepted anecdotes about Verne's youth have been questioned, including the episode that begins this article. It has also become clear that the progress of the conflict between rationality and emotion, Victorian science and Roman Catholicism,

social rebellion and conservatism permeating Verne's work was not a straight-line development, as had been previously thought, but a zigzag course throughout his life.

Study of the surviving Verne manuscripts has revealed that Verne's son Michel (1861–1925) had a much larger share in writing Verne's late and posthumous works than had been previously known. "The Eternal Adam," which is often considered Jules Verne's finest work, is now considered by some scholars to have been written wholly by Michel.

In 1989 when Verne's great-grandson opened an old, almost forgotten safe in the Verne garage, he found the manuscript of *Paris au XXe siècle*, a very early novel that had been believed lost. The manuscript, about whose authenticity there is no question, was written in 1863 and rejected by Verne's publisher, Hetzel, with the comment that it was not worth publishing and would destroy Verne's literary career. A modern reader may agree with Hetzel's literary judgment but will find the story very important as a historical document. *Paris in the Twentieth Century*, which has now been published in French and in English translation, reveals that Verne, even at this early date, had strong forebodings about the mechanical culture that was developing in Europe and America.

The narrative is the case history of a sensitive young man trapped in an oppressive world suggestive of Fritz Lang's motion picture *Metropolis* (1926). Michel Dufrénoy, an orphan with poetic talent, is forced to enter the mechanized labor machine of 1960. But he is a misfit. Placed in his uncle's bank, he cannot learn how to operate a calculator; the best he can do is call out figures to an associate who enters them in a twenty-foot ledger that is the heart of the business. Thanks to Michel, both men are ultimately fired. Michel then obtains a job in the state-controlled Grand Entrepôt Dramatique, an assembly-line sweatshop for producing plays. He fails again and in disgust, leaves his job. Out of work, without funds, without a place in this machine world, he dies in the snow in a cemetery, looking at monuments of great men of the past.

Paris is an excellent extrapolation, founded on contemporary technical novelties, of a future culture. The world is dominated by international finance based on a network of improved telegraphy. Wars have ceased because trade is more profitable. Culture has become a wing of technology. The classics of literature, music, and art have been discarded and forgotten, their places taken by wretched works focused on the laboratory or factory and sponsored by state organizations. Personal relations are dehumanized, with, as Verne says, the wonderful Parisienne now simply an imitation American, hard and cold. The family means little.

Paris is a megalopolis, surrounded by four railroad belts; a canal to the sea makes it the largest seaport in the world. Housing is mostly controlled by a syndicate, and small business seems to have disappeared. Horseless carriages using coal gas fill the streets, which are built around and under omnipresent public transportation. The city is illuminated by electricity.

Verne's predictions are not perfect, of course, but they are arguably the best made during the nineteenth century. More important than the gadgetry, however, is the story's social theme: a very early statement of extreme, tragic alienation. In the preceding Romantic period, alienation was characteristic of young women whose minds were distorted by novels; they were wrong, and their culture was right. Charlotte Lennox's *The Female Quixote: or, The Adventures of Arabella* (1763), Jane Austen's *Northanger Abbey* (1818), and Eaton S. Barrett's *The Heroine* (1813) come to mind. But these are trivial alienations compared to Michel's. He was born a century too late, and there is nothing he can do except perish, his dreams of art and love dead before him.

What is behind this horrible Paris? As Michel's musician friend Quinsonnas says, "it's really machinery that's doing the mischief." This from Jules Verne, the outstanding prophet and evangelist of iron technology, the creator of Nemo's *Nautilus*, Robur's *Terrible*, and many other extraordinary contraptions!

Paris in the Twentieth Century is a minor monument in French letters and science fiction, but it achieves that eminence for its ideas and its date, not for novelistic felicity. It is a bad novel, and readers apart from specialists are likely to find it simply an archaic curiosity. It is lamentable that Verne did not return to it as a mature writer.

Selected Bibliography

WORKS OF JULES VERNE IN ENGLISH TRANSLATION

Verne has been very badly served in translation. The Victorian "standard" translations are inaccurate, without literary merit, and often severely abridged. Verne's comments on social matters are often omitted. The modern Arco (Fitzroy) editions issued under the general editorship of I. O. Evans are also often abridged, but in this case scientific material has usually been dropped, in an attempt to stress the juvenile side of Verne's work. All this is not satisfactory, but the reader often has only a choice between bad translations and no translations at all, with French texts almost impossible to find.

In the following listing, the first English translation has been given, followed by such superior modern editions as may exist. Early American editions are usually piracies of British editions, particularly those of Sampson, Low and Company. The original French editions mentioned in the body of this article were all published by Hetzel at the dates indicated, except for *The Barsac Mission*, which was published by Hetzel's successor, Hachette.

From the Earth to the Moon. Newark, N.J.: Newark Printing and Publishing Company, 1865. Not seen. In other early editions also titled *The Baltimore Gun Club* or *All Around the Moon.* Modern, complete translations: *From the Earth to the Moon*, translated by Robert and Jacqueline Baldick. London: J. M. Dent, 1970; New York: E. P. Dutton, 1970. Also *The Annotated Jules Verne: From the Earth to the Moon*, translated and edited by Walter J. Miller. New York: Thomas Y. Crowell, 1978 (a new translation with a wealth of commentary and illustration).

A Journey to the Centre of the Earth. London: Griffith and Farran, 1872. Preferred modern edition, *Journey to the Center of the Earth*, translated by Robert Baldick. London: Penguin Books, 1962.

Round the Moon. In *From the Earth to the Moon and a Trip Around it.* London: Sampson, Low, 1873. Modern, complete translation: *Around the Moon*, translated by Jacqueline and Robert Baldick. London: J. M Dent, 1970; New York: E. P. Dutton, 1970.

Twenty Thousand Leagues Under the Sea, translated by Louis Mercier. London: Sampson, Low, 1873. Modern, complete translations: *Twenty Thousand Leagues Under the Sea*, translated by Mendor T. Brunetti. New York: Signet Books, 1969. Also *The Annotated Jules Verne: Twenty Thousand Leagues Under the Sea*, edited by Walter J. Miller. New York: Thomas Y. Crowell, 1976. (The old Mercier translation has been corrected, with previously omitted passages translated by the editor. The commentary is rich and rewarding.) The abridged, sometimes inaccurate edition of Philip Schuyler Allen (Chicago: Rand McNally, 1922) is, unfortunately, much the liveliest translation.

Hector Servadac, or the Career of a Comet. London: Sampson, Low, 1878.

The Begum's Fortune. London: Sampson, Low, 1880. (Sometimes titled *The 500 Millions of the Begum*.)

The Clipper of the Clouds. London: Sampson, Low, 1887. (Sometimes titled *Robur the Conqueror*.)

The Purchase of the North Pole. London: Sampson, Low, 1891.

The Castle of the Carpathians. London: Sampson, Low, 1893. (Sometimes titled *Carpathian Castle*.)

The Floating Island. London: Sampson, Low, 1896. (Sometimes titled *Propellor Island*.)

The Master of the World. London: Sampson, Low, 1914.

The Barsac Mission. Volume 1, *Into the Niger Bend*. Volume 2, *The City in the Sahara*. Both translated by I. O. Evans. London: Arco, 1965.

Yesterday and Tomorrow, translated by I. O. Evans. London: Arco, 1965.

Paris in the Twentieth Century, translated by Richard Howard. New York: Random House, 1996.

CRITICAL AND BIOGRAPHICAL STUDIES

Allotte de la Fuÿe, Marguerite. *Jules Verne*, translated by Erik de Manny. London: Staples Press, 1954; New York: Coward-McCann, 1956.

Costello, Peter. *Jules Verne: Inventor of Science Fiction*. New York: Charles Scribner's Sons, 1978.

Jules-Verne, Jean. *Jules Verne*, translated and adapted by Roger Greaves. New York: Taplinger, 1976.

Lottman, Herbert R. *Jules Verne. An Exploratory Biography*. New York: St. Martin's Press, 1996.

—E. F. BLEILER

KURT VONNEGUT
(b. 1922)

IN A NOW celebrated passage from *God Bless You, Mr. Rosewater* (1965), the hero, Eliot Rosewater, crashes a science fiction writers' convention and blurts out:

> I love you sons of bitches. . . . You're all I read anymore. You're the only ones who'll talk about the *really* terrific changes going on, the only ones crazy enough to know that life is a space voyage, and not a short one, either, but one that'll last for billions of years. You're the only ones with guts enough to *really* care about the future, who *really* notice what machines do to us, what wars do to us, what cities do to us, what big, simple ideas do to us, what tremendous misunderstandings, mistakes, accidents and catastrophes do to us. You're the only ones zany enough to agonize over time and distances without limit, over mysteries that will never die, over the fact that we are right now determining whether the space voyage for the next billion years or so is going to be Heaven or Hell. (page 18)

Readers and critics who dismiss science fiction as adolescent trash for mindless millions but want to discuss Kurt Vonnegut as a "serious" writer will argue that Eliot Rosewater is not Kurt Vonnegut. (After all, Rosewater is crazy.) Science fiction aficionados, on the other hand, will contend that this is Vonnegut's true position and represents his vindication of science fiction. Following his declaration, Rosewater mentions Kilgore Trout, his favorite science fiction writer and author of *2BR02B*. Since Vonnegut published the story "2BR02B" in *Worlds of If* (January 1962), one suspects that he sees himself, to some de-

gree, as a science fiction writer. As is usual in such cases, the truth is probably somewhere in between; as Blaise Pascal said, contradiction is not in itself a sign of falsity, nor the lack of contradiction a sign of truth.

Vonnegut is uneasy and defensive about being labeled a science fiction writer. In his essay "Science Fiction," written for the *New York Times Book Review* (5 September 1965), Vonnegut says that he "learned from the reviewers" that he wrote science fiction. A writer gets into this category, he observes, because he shows some interest in technology. His first novel, *Player Piano* (1952), is a dystopian work depicting the encounter between man and machine. Contemporary humanists and critics are largely ignorant of and repulsed by technology; hence, "the feeling persists that no one can simultaneously be a respectable writer and understand how a refrigerator works. . . ." Since *Player Piano*, Vonnegut writes, "I have been a soreheaded occupant of a file drawer labeled 'science fiction' . . . and I would like out, particularly since so many serious critics regularly mistake the drawer for a urinal" (*Wampeters*, 1974). Vonnegut charges the majority of writers and readers of science fiction with "childishness" and the writers with a failure to depict "mature relationships."

Eight years later, in an interview published in *Playboy* (1973; reprinted in *Wampeters*), Vonnegut softened his position and blamed the realities of the market (that is, one is paid by the word and thus one writes as fast as possible) for the bad characterization and stilted dialogue of most science fiction. At the same time, he added, this situation was "liberating, because you were able to put an awful lot of keen ideas into circulation fast."

Clearly, Vonnegut is uncomfortable with the science fiction label, yet Karen and Charles Wood (in *The Vonnegut Statement*, 1973) are probably correct when they argue that his attitude stems not from any dislike of science fiction per se but from the established critics' elitist bias against the genre. Be that as it may, what is certain is that there are science fiction elements in many of his short stories and in almost all his novels, and that three of his novels—*Player Piano, The Sirens of Titan* (1959), and *Cat's Cradle* (1963)—are conventional science fiction by almost any definition.

Player Piano is a dystopian or anti-utopian novel, and together with its counterpart, the utopian novel, can be defined as "the *socio-political subgenre of science fiction*" (Darko Suvin). Unlike many of Vonnegut's other novels, which make only incidental use of science fiction elements, the plot of *Sirens of Titan* hinges upon a science fiction device. One of the main characters, Winston Niles Rumfoord, is enmeshed in the "chrono-syn-clastic infundibulum," which converts him and his dog into a wave phenomenon and allows them to traverse time and space and to materialize periodically on Earth and in other parts of the solar system. (In *Slaughterhouse-Five* [1969] much the same thing happens to the hero, Billy Pilgrim, who becomes "unstuck" in time, but this experience is not nearly so central to the plot.) *Sirens of Titan,* then, satisfies one critic's definition of science fiction as that fiction "*distinguished by the narrative dominance or hegemony of a fictional 'novum' (novelty, innovation) validated by cognitive logic*" (Suvin). The "chrono-synclastic infundibulum" is the novum around which the plot of *Sirens of Titan* turns. In *Cat's Cradle*, the novum is ice-nine, a chemical that freezes all the water on Earth and brings the world to an end. In this work, science fiction is the vehicle for Vonnegut's apocalyptic imagination.

Vonnegut's science fiction centers on three interrelated attitudes: (a) a deep mistrust of humanity's ability to control science and technology, and, hence, (b) a profound pessimism concerning the future of the human race unless (c) it can create useful fictions to replace those traditional myths rendered obsolete by science. With these sentiments Vonnegut is squarely in the camp of those science fiction writers, such as George Orwell, Aldous Huxley, and Ray Bradbury, who take issue with the cheery optimism, with the pseudo-mythology and techno-bureaucratic elitism of much typical science fiction, as represented by the works of Arthur C. Clarke and Isaac Asimov. Huxley is important in this context, since Vonnegut admits to using *Brave New World* (1932) as his model for *Player Piano*.

In addition, Vonnegut's comic vision, his "black humor," links him with absurdist science fiction, represented by many of the works of such writers as J. G. Ballard, Philip K. Dick, Michael Moorcock, Samuel R. Delany, and Philip José Farmer. (Farmer, in fact, used the name of Vonnegut's science fiction writer Kilgore Trout as a pseudonym for his own novel *Venus on the Half-Shell* [1975].) But Vonnegut's concerns about technology, the future, and myth, and his modes of embodying these concerns are not merely the consequence of his reading. They arise out of the events of his life and his attempt to cope with experience and, by coping in art, to "serve his society" as an "agent of change" and "to make human beings seem more wonderful than they really are" (*Wampeters*).

I

The son of an architect, Kurt Vonnegut, Jr., was born on 11 November 1922 in Indianapolis, Indiana. (Vonnegut sees himself as a Midwesterner, and Indiana appears or is alluded to frequently in his novels.) He is just old enough to have been traumatized by the Great Depression; it had a lasting effect on

Kurt Vonnegut protests the trials of Soviet dissidents Anatoly Shcharansky and Alexander Ginzburg in 1986. UPI/Corbis-Bettmann

him. Vonnegut says that the Great Depression had "more to do with [shaping] the American character than any war. People felt useless for so long. The machines fired everybody. . . . I saw and listened to thousands of people who couldn't follow their trades anymore, who couldn't feed their families. . . . They wanted to die because they were so embarrassed" (*Wampeters*). (Interestingly, Vonnegut focuses on technology, rather than the sociopolitical structure, as the villain.) The notion that technology can get out of control and rob people of their sense of self-worth is a major theme in Vonnegut's first novel, *Player Piano*.

At Shortridge High School, Vonnegut wrote for the school's daily newspaper, *Echo*. Having to meet a daily deadline, he discovered that he could write "better than a lot of people." He continued his newspaper work in college, writing a humor column for the *Cornell Daily Sun* and, later, an editorial column entitled "Well All Right." He left Cornell his junior year and never graduated. Vonnegut enlisted in the army and was sent to the Carnegie Institute of Technology and the University of Tennessee to study mechanical engineering for eighteen months. Returning from infantry duty in World War II, Vonnegut married Jane Marie Cox and began graduate studies in the department of anthropology at the University of Chicago. His master's thesis, "Fluctuations Between Good and Evil," was rejected unanimously.

Like his experience of the Great Depression, Vonnegut's army service was especially significant for his writing. As a college student he was an isolationist and a pacifist, and used his columns to defend these positions—writing, for example, an emotional defense of Charles Lindbergh's isolationism. He had no taste for war; he had even less for being a survivor of it. During the Battle of the Bulge, Vonnegut was captured by the Germans and sent to Dresden to work in an underground factory (named Slaughterhouse-Five) manufacturing a vitamin supplement for pregnant women. Once called "Florence on the Elbe" because of its great beauty and its great art treasures, Dresden was almost totally destroyed on 13 February 1945 by a fire storm created by Allied heavy explosives and phosphorus bombs. An estimated 135,000 persons, the great majority of whom were civilians, were killed in this single air raid. The reasons for the bombing are obscure; the city had no military strategic value and had been considered, like Paris, an "open" city. Vonnegut and the other prisoners survived because their workplace was underground. After the bombing they were pressed into service as corpse carriers. In his Introduction to *Mother Night* (1961), Vonnegut describes the Dresden bombing as "the largest massacre in European history." All of his novels can be viewed as attempts, explicitly and implicitly, to come to terms artistically with this experience. Dresden became for Vonnegut a complex symbol of humanity's irresponsible infatuation with technology.

After the army and the University of Chicago, Vonnegut went east to Schenectady, New York, in 1947, to work for General Electric (GE) as a research publicist. Here he was exposed to the gadgets-for-profit mentality of the organization man and the implications of technology in the service of monopoly capitalism. His suspicions about the ability to control technology were reinforced. Schenectady and GE become Ilium, New York, and the Ilium Works in his novel *Player Piano*. Just before leaving GE, Vonnegut began selling stories to such magazines as *Collier's*, *Ladies Home Journal*, *Esquire*, and *Galaxy Science Fiction*. In 1950 he left GE to devote himself full-time to writing. In 1952, *Player Piano* was published. In the 1950's and early 1960's Vonnegut continued to publish short stories in popular magazines, including the science fiction pulps. By this time he was supporting a wife and six children (three of his own and three adopted—children of his deceased sister). In 1959 he published another major science fiction novel, *The Sirens of Titan*, and in 1961 a collection of his short stories, *Canary in a Cat House*, appeared. These stories include some of his better science fiction: "Report on the Barnhouse Effect," "The Euphio Question," "Unready to Wear," and "Tomorrow and Tomorrow and Tomorrow." In 1961 *Mother Night* was published, followed by *Cat's Cradle* (1963).

By the time *Cat's Cradle* appeared, Vonnegut was receiving some critical notice. Terry Southern wrote an enthusiastic review of *Cat's Cradle* for the *New York Times Book Review* (2 June 1963), and in 1965, Vonnegut was invited to the University of Iowa Writer's Workshop, where his goal, he said, was not to provide formulas for writing but to evoke a "sense of wonder." In 1965, *God Bless You, Mr. Rosewater* was published. By 1966 his novels were available in paperback; by this time he had gained a significant audience, especially among college students. Another collection of his short stories, *Welcome to the Monkey House*, appeared in 1968, and in 1969, at forty-seven, Vonnegut was nominated for the National Book Award for *Slaughterhouse-Five*. His national reputation was clearly established.

In 1971, Vonnegut turned from fiction to drama. His play *Happy Birthday, Wanda June* was published that year and was made into a film by Columbia Pictures, with Vonnegut writing the screenplay. Vonnegut made his television debut by writing "Between Time and Timbuktu," a "space fantasy" that appeared on the NET Playhouse on 13 March 1972. In the same year *Slaughterhouse-Five* was made into a film. In his preface to the printed version of *Between Time and Timbuktu* (1972), Vonnegut wrote, "I have become an enthusiast for the printed word again." He returned to fiction, and in the next seven years published *Breakfast of Champions* (1973), which became the main selection of three book clubs; *Wampeters, Foma, and Granfalloons: Opinions* (1974), a collection of reviews, essays, interviews, and speeches; *Slapstick* (1976), a novel with several science fiction devices; and *Jailbird* (1979), a novel whose hero, Walter F. Starbuck, a Nixon adviser caught in the Watergate scandal, meditates while spending time in a minimum-security prison. Vonnegut lives today with his second wife, the photographer Jill Krementz, on Cape Cod.

II

As has been suggested, Vonnegut's relationship to science fiction has been discussed extensively by himself as well as by a number of critics. Even those who claim Vonnegut as a science fiction writer are uncertain how he should be treated. While it is obvious that he draws heavily on science fiction conventions (time travel, future history, aliens, threatening technology, amazing inventions, overpopulation, telepathy, telekenesis), it is equally true that he treats these subjects in a manner quite different from that of the typical science fiction writer. Irony, especially as it moves toward the absurd and "black humor," is relatively rare in science fiction.

Although writers such as Franz Kafka have been linked to science fiction, most science fiction readers and critics are more comfortable with the "rational" satire of Jonathan Swift, Mark Twain, Huxley, or Orwell—all of whom have been linked to Vonnegut. These writers blend a critical attitude with humor and wit, and their usual assumption is that human institutions or humanity itself may be improved by the application of laughter and a return to human reason coupled with appropriate knowledge.

By contrast, the absurdist presents a view of the human condition as nonsensical and paradoxical. Humanity and its institutions are not improved through the exercise of reason or valid knowledge because human existence is fundamentally irrational. Writers within the absurdist tradition generally propound no explicit thesis or ideology. Assuming perplexity and spiritual anguish as bewildered humanity confronts an incomprehensible universe, the absurdists depict humanity's anomalous and ludicrous situation but offer few solutions because, for them, there are no genuine solutions, only comic absurdity.

Writing about these kinds of novelists, one critic says, "Our fictions are real enough in themselves, but as signs pointing to any world outside the fiction or the dream, they have no factual status" (Robert Scholes, 1979). We cannot reach the real; at best we can "arrive at belief." Scholes's argument parallels Vonnegut's conception of the function of a writer: to create foma, "harmless untruths, intended to comfort simple souls."

This perspective is inherently ironic. The reader of a Vonnegut novel always knows more than the characters, and Vonnegut invites his readers to "transcend" his texts in order to reach the subtexts and to analyze the assumptions, situations, and motives of his characters in their quest for truth and happiness. This collaboration with the reader is rare in contemporary, popular science fiction and is one reason many critics and readers are uncomfortable with Vonnegut's work.

One can see Vonnegut working his verbal and situational irony and creating his comic absurdity from the very beginning. In *Player Piano* the reader traces the rapid, if covert, disillusionment of the hero, Paul Proteus, with his situation and with his machine-dominated society as his antipathy breaks into open rebellion. Admired, trusted, eminently successful as "the most important, brilliant person in Ilium, the manager of the Ilium Works," he is filled with ennui. He works for the company and lives in a society where one's status is determined by one's I.Q. (filed in the computer, EPICAC XIV, that retains everyone's life history and oversees the functioning of the entire society) and where one's sense of self-worth and dignity is exchanged for time-saving gadgets.

Mindless, runaway technology, coupled with a social order obsessed by a computer-determined notion of efficiency, has consigned most of the adult population to the military or to the Reeks and Wrecks, an updated version of the Great Depression–era make-work projects, such as the CCC (Franklin D. Roosevelt's Civilian Conservation Corps). The human emptiness of this society is reinforced by a subplot: the visit to the United States of the shah of Bratpuhr, the leader of 6 million Kilhouri. Through the eyes of an outsider—a conventional device of utopian and dystopian narratives—Vonnegut broadens his scope and provides a sketch of the entire society. The shah learns that all of this technology has not improved the lot of the common man one whit.

Paul Proteus rebels against this spiritually barren society. His private dissatisfaction is given material form by the visit of his long-time friend Ed Finnerty, who, although a member of the powerful National Industrial Planning Board, has rejected the whole system and has joined a revolutionary group—the Ghost Shirt Society—to fight for the destruction of the social order. This wild Irishman is a living insult to Ilium's bureaucratic, corporate mentality and its pretentious technological optimism. Moved by his loyalty to Finnerty and a growing consciousness of his own disenchantment, Paul tries initially to escape into nature. Across the river from Ilium, in Homestead, he convinces a real estate broker to lease him an abandoned farm. Like Henry David Thoreau, he plans to work the farm and get closer to nature by eliminating the mediation of technology. His dream is shattered by his wife, Anita, a "barren" female embodiment of the trivial and dishonest system that has infected even the most intimate human relationships. Anita wants to antique the farm, to make it cute; for her, nature unadorned is "perfectly hideous." Defeated by Anita's response and a realization that the romantic, pastoral ideal was an illusion, Paul abandons his dream.

Still determined to resign, Paul goes to the Meadows, an island where up-and-coming Ilium Works personnel are treated to several days of competitive team sports, drinking, and corporate indoctrination in an atmosphere resembling a cross between a Boy Scout camp-out and an old-time tent revival meeting. Ilium's directors want Paul to infiltrate the Ghost Shirts. They mistake his resignation as the first stage in their plan to make him a spy. Thrown off the Meadows in disgrace, Paul joins the Ghost Shirts and becomes their reluctant leader and messiah. Once the authorities discover that he is a revolutionary, he is put on trial. During the trial Paul makes a speech that can be taken as Vonnegut's case against technology:

> The sovereignty of the United States resides in the people, not in machines, and it's the people's to take back, if they so wish. The machines . . . have exceeded the personal sovereignty willingly surrendered to them by the American people for good government. Machines have robbed the American people of liberty and the pursuit of happiness. . . . The main business of humanity is to do a good job of being human beings . . . not to serve as appendages to machines, institutions, and systems. (pages 296–297)

Paul's trial is broken up by the beginning of the rebellion. After two days of rioting, during which the people give vent to their hatred of the machines by indiscriminate vandalism, the rebellion is suppressed. The novel concludes with the surrender of Paul, Finnerty, and the other leaders; presumably they will be executed.

Briefly outlined, the novel appears rather conventional—indeed, undistinguished. But it is Vonnegut's treatment of his subject, his irony, and his comic absurdity that make *Player Piano* such an interesting and significant work of science fiction.

Along with the situational irony, there is a good deal of verbal irony. At the close of almost all of Paul's discussions with Anita, there is the silly repetition: "I love *you*, Anita." (Such a repetitive phrase later becomes a Vonnegut calling card—witness "And so it goes" in *Slaughterhouse-Five* or "Hi ho" in *Slapstick*.) It is funny; the reader looks forward to the ritual recitation. At the same time the profession of sincerity is undercut by the frequency of its restatement. It comes to seem as if Paul is talking to a robot—and in a sense he is. As the narrator observes, "Anita had the mechanics of marriage down pat, even to the subtlest conventions. If her approach was disturbingly rational, systematic, she was thorough enough to turn out a creditable counterfeit of warmth." As the novel progresses, the phrase ("I love *you*, Anita") becomes more grimly ironic. The mystique of efficiency and the deification of technology have corrupted the very essence of human relationships.

The dramatic irony keeps the reader constantly off balance and allows Vonnegut to present a more complex vision. For example, he sees the issue of humanity's relationship to technology as a much more complicated one than merely good versus evil. Technology is, after all, a human creation; it is the product of a creative mind. After the rebels go on a rampage and destroy most of the machines, Paul and Finnerty come upon a crowd gathered around a damaged "Orange-O" machine that has just been jerry-rigged by Bud Calhoun, a mechanical genius who had lost his job at the Ilium Works to a machine. Bud and a man who had earlier repaired Paul's car finish fixing the machine.

The man had been desperately unhappy then. Now he was proud and smiling because his hands were busy doing what they liked to do best, Paul supposed—replacing men like himself with machines. . . .

Bud Calhoun bolted on the back. "Now try her."

The people applauded and lined up, eager for their Orange-O. (page 318)

The creation of the player piano in the saloon also symbolizes the mechanization and dehumanization of the creative spirit. Similarly, a little boy ends the scene described above by saying, "I'll betcha anything I could make a gadget that'd play drums like nothing you ever heard before." The irony is inescapable; it is in the nature of humanity to perfect itself, to use its inventiveness and its skill.

But this is not the final irony. Vonnegut's comic vision refuses to treat humanity's subordination to machines in a tragic mode, from a perspective to which there is no appeal. Unlike the machines of most science fiction writers, Vonnegut's machines are not perfect. Paul beats the computer, Checker Charley, in a hilarious scene that ends with Charley literally burning up (much to the sorrow of Anita and the chagrin of Charley's engineer-designer). And when the robot helicopter barks out its tape-recorded message for Paul and the other rebels to surrender:

Luke Lubbock aimed his rifle, and fired. *"Beeby dee bobble dee beezle!"* said the loudspeaker shrilly. *"Nozzle ah reeble beejee boo."*

"Put it out of its misery," said Finnerty. Luke fired again.

The helicopter floundered off clumsily, still haranguing the town. *"Beeby dee bobble dee beezle! Noozle ah reeble heejee   "* (page 312)

In contrast with most science fiction writers who depict the dangers of technology, Vonnegut is not in awe of machines. Machines are not omnipotent; they can malfunction and break down. Humanity has created technology and humanity can control it. It is

human stupidity, unable to see beyond the ideological horizon of a technobureaucratic elite spawned by corporate capitalism, that can corrupt and trivialize human creativity and the possibilities for a decent society. In *The Ascent of Man* (1973), Jacob Bronowski eloquently observes that "the most powerful drive in the ascent of man is his pleasure in his own skill. He loves to do what he does well and, having done it well, he loves to do it better." Because it can, humanity will continue to use its skill to create even more awesome technology; at the same time it must use its political skills and social vision to bring about a society where people can be at home with their creations. In a speech to the graduating class at Bennington College in 1970, Vonnegut said, "I suggest that you work for a socialist form of government. Free enterprise is much too hard on the old and the sick and the shy and the poor and the stupid, and on people nobody likes. . . . I would like to see America try socialism" (*Wampeters*).

Similarly, Vonnegut's apprehensiveness over the failure to control technology is carried over into his other predominantly science fiction novel, *The Sirens of Titan*. For example, the Martians erase the memories of the kidnapped Earthlings who are being trained to invade Earth. They then implant antennae in the Earthlings' skulls, so that they can be radio-controlled like robots. At the same time, Vonnegut's use of traditional science fiction material filtered through his ironic, comic vision creates a narrative that is thematically broader in scope and conceptually at odds with most popular science fiction. What *The Sirens of Titan* does, in fact, is to demystify the mythic pretensions of most contemporary science fiction.

Caught in the web of the chrono-synclastic infundibulum, which permits him to materialize at various points and times all over the solar system, Winston Niles Rumfoord schemes to give his fellow Earthlings a new religion. To this end he prepares on Mars an invading army of kidnapped Earthlings whose slaughter by Earth's defenders produces massive guilt and prepares Earth for a spiritual transformation. This religious revolution is effected through the person of Malachi ("Messenger of the Lord") Constant, a billionaire and spiritual debauchee who, manipulated by Rumfoord, is transformed in his space odyssey from Earth to Mars to Mercury to Earth and to Titan into a new messiah of the Church of God of the Utterly Indifferent. Malachi says of his life before returning to Earth as the new messiah, the Space Wanderer: "I was a victim of a series of accidents, as are we all." There is no God up there manipulating man and the universe to some meaningful end. Rumfoord tells the crowd of believers that "there is nothing more cruel, more dangerous, more blasphemous that a man can do than to believe that—luck, good or bad, is the hand of God! . . . Luck, good or bad . . . is *not* the hand of God."

The reader learns that many of the momentous events in human history are merely undecoded messages of an alien race, the Tralfamadorians, to one of their stranded messengers, a robot named Salo. Salo's malfunctioning spaceship was stranded on Titan. "The meaning of Stonehenge in Tralfamadorian, when viewed from above, is: '*Replacement part being rushed with all possible speed*'. . . The Great Wall of China means in Tralfamadorian, when viewed from above: '*Be patient. We haven't forgotten about you.*'" Salo asks Constant if he would like to know the message that he, Salo, has been carrying from the Tralfamadorians for "almost half a million Earthling years—the message that I am supposed to carry for eighteen million more." Salo gives the message; translated from Tralfamadorian it is "*Greetings.*" There is nothing more.

Many critics argue that the popularity of science fiction rests on its ability to replace obsolete, traditional Judeo-Christian myths with myths consistent with a scientific world view. Writers such as James Blish, Fred Hoyle, Arthur C. Clarke, and Olaf Stapledon have written metaphysical stories that attempt to provide some transcendental meaning to the human adventure; human evolution and

quest have a purpose, but it has yet to be discovered.

In the anthology *Science Fiction: Contemporary Mythology* (1978), one of the editors, Patricia Warrick, writes that "science fiction, first appearing in the nineteenth century, is a literary form created by the imagination as it attempted to relate man to the new models of the universe described by science." But, while it is true that all myths are fictions, it does not follow that all fictions are myths. Fictions become myths when they are taken as reality and truth, and not as self-conscious narratives. Myth is the narrative mode of religion; it posits an all-encompassing, sufficient explanation of reality as it was, is, and will be. Fiction is the narrative mode of art; it posits patterns of experience but is tentative and hypothetical in its depiction of human experience. In this sense Vonnegut is moving against the current trends in science fiction, for he is creating fictions and not myths. His irony and his comic vision subvert the didactic and often tragic mythic pretensions of current science fiction.

Vonnegut provides no absolutes or resolutions to the doubts, contradictions, and absurdities in the human drama. Like other absurdist writers, who are spiritual kin to the existentialists but who provide a comic corrective to their tragic vision, Vonnegut sees an unbridgeable gap between language and reality. Fiction is not myth; it is not reality. Humanity must be mature enough to live with ambiguity, or at least be mature enough to accept fiction for what it is—*foma*. If it can do this, then it can use fiction not to explain for all time the meaning of existence, but to playfully explore the possibilities of human action. In this exploration, writers fulfill their social responsibility by becoming "agents of change."

Cat's Cradle, said by one critic to "read at times more like hard-core science fiction than any of Vonnegut's other novels" (James Lundquist), continues the themes developed in *Player Piano* and *The Sirens of Titan*. Indeed, it provides the most forceful dramatization of Vonnegut's concern about humanity's failure to control technology, his pessimistic view of the future, and his belief that humanity must have useful fictions to hold society together. As before, these themes are filtered through Vonnegut's ironic and comic perspective.

The narrator and main character, John (or Jonah, as he likes to be called), is writing a book on one example of humanity's technological insanity—the dropping of the atomic bomb on Hiroshima. For Vonnegut this act functions as a symbol in much the same way as the Allied bombing of Dresden. The title of Jonah's book is to be *The Day the World Ended*. Ironically, this could also be the title of *Cat's Cradle*; it is an apocalyptic vision of the end of the world. Jonah searches for information about the late Dr. Felix Hoenikker, one of the fathers of modern nuclear weaponry. In his investigation he discovers that Hoenikker had also created ice-nine, a chemical that can solidify all the water on Earth.

The search for information leads Jonah to a small Caribbean island governed by Papa Monzano and Frank Hoenikker, Felix Hoenikker's son. Dying of cancer, Papa Monzano takes his own life by drinking ice-nine. An airplane crash—another failure of technology—undermines the foundation of Papa's castle, causing it and Papa's body, still full of ice-nine, to fall into the ocean, thereby freezing all of the Earth's water and, eventually, wiping out humanity. The cosmic irony of it: Jonah wants to write a book about the metaphorical end of the world and succeeds in experiencing the literal end himself. The absurdity of the situation is even more apparent than in *Player Piano*. Technology destroys man not because of some calculated evil but through a stupid accident.

Along with the theme of technological doom, Vonnegut makes his clearest statement about humanity's need for useful illusions. The sociopolitical glue for the island's populace is a religion—now banned—called Bokononism. Jonah is intrigued by this artificial creed. (Bokononism's founders—Bokonon, a black from Tobago, and Earl McCabe, an AWOL United States Marine—created the religion to establish order and take control of the island.) As the narrator of *Cat's Cradle*, Jonah gives a Bokononist warning to the reader: "Anyone unable to understand how a useful religion can be founded on lies will not understand this book either."

And while Jonah argues that the novel is not a "tract on behalf of Bokononism," he does draw all the crucial definitions of the human situation, all of the enlightening summary statements and ethical imperatives from *The Books of Bokonon*. Moreover, when Jonah finally comes face to face with Bokonon, as the world is coming to an end, he lets Bokonon have the last words. Bokonon is writing the final sentence to *The Books of Bokonon*; this also becomes the final sentence of *Cat's Cradle*:

> If I were a younger man, I would write a history of human stupidity; and I would climb to the top of Mount McCabe and lie down on my back with my history for a pillow; and I would take from the ground some of the blue-white poison that makes statues of men [ice-nine]; and I would make a statue of myself, lying on my back, grinning horribly, and thumbing my nose at You Know Who.

"You Know Who" may be God—or something else entirely. In any case, the irreverent satire, the demystification of the ideas of progress and the absolute, is pure Vonnegut. Bokononism, like Vonnegut's art, provides useful fictions. As one critic put it: "Vonnegut, raised an atheist, has always understood the function of religion in our society. Religion helps people accept the world as it is. And the world is the way it is because God, Government, and the Greedy want it that way" (*The Vonnegut Statement*).

But, because Vonnegut makes no pretensions to mythmaking, because he creates very self-conscious fictions, the reader is invited to compare his or her own fictions with Vonnegut's. Vonnegut does not attempt to mirror some assumed reality; his novels are playful reflections upon our fictions. Nor are his fictions simply entertaining intellectual hypotheses; they focus on characters who act and who move the reader emotionally as well as intellectually.

Thus far, *Player Piano*, *The Sirens of Titan*, and *Cat's Cradle* are Vonnegut's major efforts in the science fiction genre. Almost all of his works, though, employ some science fiction devices.

With some justification, critics have pointed out that Vonnegut is not angry enough, that "so it goes" is an insufficient response to the suffering and evil in the world, that irony is the intellectual's expression of impotence; it is a form of fence-sitting and a response that humanity can no longer afford. Vonnegut's desire to be an "agent of change" is undercut by his comic perspective, which functions as a frame of adjustment rather than of change. Doubtless, Vonnegut would not deny this. In his *Playboy* interview (1973), he observes that "laughing or crying is what a human being does when there's nothing else he can do." And there are times when one gets the feeling that Vonnegut's description of himself as a "total pessimist" is accurate and unequivocal. The best he can come up with are cute little statements such as "Ignore the awful times, and concentrate on the good ones" or "God damn it, you've got to be kind."

Unable or unwilling to commit himself to, or even recognize, any system that claims absolute truth, Vonnegut has few alternatives except to argue for useful fictions and laughter. The writer's "influence," he writes, "is slow and subtle, and it is felt mainly by the young. They are hungry for myths which resonate with the mysteries of their own times. We give them those myths. We will become influential when those who have listened to our myths have become influential" (*Wampeters*). But Vonnegut's irony and comic vision undercut any certitude that could be derived from a true myth. The reader is always left on the fence.

On the other hand—and perhaps this is the final irony—Vonnegut's irony and humor also undercut his pessimism. Irony is the most sophisticated of narrative modes. It rests upon a pact between the author and the audience, in which the author assumes that the reader can and will transcend the text and see what the characters cannot. Irony is based on trust. The history of humanity may be a history of "stupidity," but Vonnegut trusts that his readers will be intelligent and sensitive enough to follow him wherever he takes them. Furthermore, while comedy deals with the contradictions arising in the human drama and, like tragedy, depicts human frailty, it does not, as tragedy does, create the great gulf between humanity and its gods. When we laugh together, we break down social distance; we affirm our common humanity. The comic writer creates those symbolic forms that we use to relate to one another in problematic situations filled with instances of incongruity.

Unlike many science fiction writers, Vonnegut neither puts his faith in human reason to solve all problems nor opts for some alien, all-powerful Other to give human life meaning and to solve humanity's difficult problems. It may be, as one critic has suggested, that contemporary science fiction writers such as Vonnegut are expressing the pessimism of their class and their readers—the "scientifically and technologically orientated middle class"—that "lives endlessly the hour of its death" (Gerard Klein). Indeed, Vonnegut's inability to transcend his pessimism and go beyond an ideological horizon that severely limits human possibility is a genuine failure of imagination. On the other hand, his demystification of technology; his understanding of the role of fictions in social action, and his assertion, through his ironic, comic vision, of flawed-but-common humanity make him a valuable maverick within the ranks of contemporary science fiction writers.

—CHARLES L. ELKINS

Science fiction has remained integral to Kurt Vonnegut's fictive imagination. Of his four novels published after 1982, three can be classified as science fiction, including *Galápagos* (1985) and *Hocus Pocus* (1990), which rank among the finest achievements of his phenomenal career. The novel *Timequake* (1997) attempts to sum up his own life in relation to the life and death of Kilgore Trout, the fecund science fiction writer whom Vonnegut labels "my alter ego."

In the 1980's and 1990's, Vonnegut's earlier apocalyptic prophecies were intensified by his sense of deepening ecological crises, growing misery of millions of Earth's inhabitants, proliferation of ingenious superweapons, and the erasure of the most painful lessons taught by the Vietnam War. Each of the two major works of this period is narrated by a Vietnam veteran who has personally committed atrocities. Not merely complicit in American— and human—irrationality and destructiveness, these two narrators are for Vonnegut representatives of our epoch and our destiny.

The narrator of *Galápagos* is none other than Leon Trotsky Trout, Kilgore Trout's only son. After killing a toothless grandmother in Vietnam, Leon joins with his platoon in burning down her village and massacring all its inhabitants and then later deserts to Sweden. He is now a ghost who oscillates between 1986, when the human species is almost annihilated, and a million years in the future, when we have evolved into furry seal-like creatures with flippers, webbed feet, and a brain too small to imagine much less implement the catastrophes that led to our demise.

Galápagos is a remorseless application of Darwinian logic whereby survival is determined by "Natural Selection," thus leading to the "evolution" of species. The large brains of our species turn out to be an evolutionary dead end, because they make us capable of inflicting so much devastation on each other and our environment. These brains bring about an apocalypse, with war, disease, and starvation cutting down all but ten people. By pure chance, these ten people survive and land on the Galápagos Islands, the very place where Darwin began to construct his grand theory. Contrary to Darwin's vision of teleological progress and to the future superbeings projected in much other science fiction, *Galápagos* shows how this handful of human flotsam becomes the ancestors of those far future humans who deftly catch their fishy din-

ners in their mouths and whose only worry is falling prey to sharks and killer whales. Their descendants are the ironic proof of the survival of the fittest. No longer having hands to do harm, they have lost the parts of the brain needed to control hands, thus making the human skull more streamlined; and "The more streamlined the skull, the more successful the fisher person."

Set in the year 2001, *Hocus Pocus* offers a brooding reply to the movie *2001* and its conventional science fiction vision of space travel and alien contact as the culmination of human destiny. The narrator of the novel, formerly a lieutenant colonel in the Vietnam War, now imprisoned and racked with tuberculosis in the grimy near future, makes the comparison explicit when he tells us, "I read a lot of science fiction when I was in the Army," including Arthur C. Clarke, who "was best known for the movie *2001*, the very year in which I am writing and coughing now":

> I saw *2001* twice in Vietnam. I remember 2 wounded soldiers in wheelchairs in the front row at 1 of those showings. The whole front row was wheelchairs. (page 167)

That 1968 film projected the macrohistory of our species as an epic of progress from ape to cosmic voyager, aided at crucial stages by alien superbeings who stimulate our technology and guide us into space for the next phase of our upward evolution. In *Hocus Pocus*, the macrohistory of our species is a debacle of genocide and ecocide influenced by alien superbeings who see our extermination as a precondition for the evolution of cosmic voyagers.

This history is sketched by "The Protocols of the Elders of Tralfamadore," an anonymous science fiction story the narrator discovers in a soft-porn magazine, a fable Vonnegut fans will readily identify as a Kilgore Trout tale. Some "intelligent threads of energy" want to create self-reproducing life forms that will spread throughout the Universe. Recognizing that only microorganisms would be capable of interstellar travel and knowing that no germs tough enough to withstand such trips had yet evolved, they decide to use a ferocious big-brained creature that had evolved on Earth to turn the planet into a laboratory for creating the cosmic superbugs. The purpose of human existence thus becomes making Earth into such a toxic, lethal environment that the only surviving life forms will be microorganisms resistant to the worst vicissitudes of space travel.

By 2001, we seem to be well on our way to achieving our mission on this "whole ruined planet." The narrator, who had ordered white phosphorus and napalm attacks on Vietnam and personally killed villagers and prisoners, tells one of many women he brags of seducing: "If I were a fighter plane instead of a human being, there would be little pictures of people painted all over me." Eventually, he is fired from his professorship at a college for stupid children of the ruling class, ostensibly for his philandering but actually for undermining "the students' faith in the intelligence and decency of their country's leadership by telling them the truth about the Vietnam War."

He is able to get a job teaching in an all-black prison nearby because "punishment" has become "the biggest industry by far" in the region. Prisons have become legally segregated by a Supreme Court ruling that it is "cruel and inhuman punishment" to confine people where their race is a minority. When the prisoners break out, their attempt to create a "utopia" is smashed by the 82nd Airborne, fresh from the Battle of the South Bronx, evidently a skirmish in the War on Drugs.

Timequake's vision of 2001 is quite similar, but this is also the year when "a sudden glitch in the space-time continuum" produces a rerun of the previous ten years, so that every moment from 1991 has to be relived. It is also the year when Kilgore Trout dies, but not before he experiences the epiphany of seeing "free will" instantaneously restored the moment the rerun is over.

Vonnegut himself is the narrator and principal character of *Timequake*, and it is here that he sums up his own career in science fiction, speaking first as Kilgore Trout and then as himself:

> "If I'd wasted my time creating characters," Trout said, "I would never have gotten around to calling attention to things that really matter. . . ."

Trout might have said, and it can be said of me as well, that he created *caricatures* rather than characters. His animus against so-called *mainstream literature*, moreover, wasn't peculiar to him. It was generic among writers of science fiction. (page 63)

—H. BRUCE FRANKLIN

Selected Bibliography

WORKS OF KURT VONNEGUT

Player Piano. New York: Charles Scribner's Sons, 1952. London: Macmillan, 1953. (Novel.)

The Sirens of Titan. New York: Dell, 1959. London: Victor Gollancz, 1962. (Novel.)

Canary in a Cat House. Greenwich, Conn.: Fawcett, 1961. London: Frederick Muller, 1962. (Short stories.)

Mother Night. Greenwich, Conn.: Fawcett, 1961. London: Frederick Muller, 1962. (Novel.)

"The Very First Christmas Morning." In *Better Homes and Gardens*, 40 (December 1962): 14, 19–20, 24. (Play.)

Cat's Cradle. New York: Holt, Rinehart and Winston, 1963. London: Victor Gollancz, 1963. (Novel.)

God Bless You, Mr. Rosewater. New York: Holt, Rinehart and Winston, 1965. London: Jonathan Cape, 1965. (Novel.)

"Science Fiction." In the *New York Times Book Review* (5 September 1965): 2. (Essay.)

"Fortitude." In *Playboy*, 15 (September 1968): 99–100, 102, 106, 217–218. (Play.)

Welcome to the Monkey House. New York: Delacorte/Seymour Lawrence, 1968. London: Panther Books, 1972. (Short stories.)

Slaughterhouse-Five. New York: Delacorte/Seymour Lawrence, 1969. London: Panther Books, 1972. (Novel.)

Happy Birthday, Wanda June. New York: Delacorte/Seymour Lawrence, 1971. London: Panther Books, 1975. (Play.)

Between Time and Timbuktu. New York: Delacorte/Seymour Lawrence, 1972. London: Panther Books, 1975. (Play.)

Breakfast of Champions. New York: Delacorte/Seymour Lawrence, 1973. London: Panther Books, 1974. (Novel.)

Wampeters, Foma, and Granfalloons: Opinions. New York: Delacorte/Seymour Lawrence, 1974. London: Jonathan Cape, 1975. (Essays, interviews, and speeches.)

Slapstick or Lonesome No More. New York: Delacorte/Seymour Lawrence, 1976. London: Jonathan Cape, 1976. (Novel.)

Jailbird. New York: Delacorte/Seymour Lawrence, 1979. London: Jonathan Cape, 1979. (Novel.)

Palm Sunday: An Autobiographical Collage. New York: Delacorte/Seymour Lawrence, 1981. (Essays.)

Deadeye Dick. New York: Delacorte/Seymour Lawrence, 1982.

Galápagos: A Novel. New York: Delacorte/Seymour Lawrence, 1985.

Bluebeard. New York: Delacorte, 1987.

Hocus Pocus. New York: Putnam, 1990.

Fates Worse Than Death: An Autobiographical Collage of the 1980s. New York: Putnam, 1991. (Essays.)

Timequake. New York: Putnam, 1997.

BIBLIOGRAPHY

Klinkowitz, Jerome, and Asa B. Pieratt. *Kurt Vonnegut, Jr.: A Descriptive Bibliography and Annotated Secondary Checklist*. Hamden, Conn.: Shoe String Press, 1974. (The most complete bibliography on Vonnegut.)

Pieratt, Asa B., Jr.; Julie Huffman-Klinkowitz; and Jerome Klinkowitz. *Kurt Vonnegut: A Comprehensive Bibliography*. Hamden, Conn.: Archon, 1987.

CRITICAL AND BIOGRAPHICAL STUDIES

Aldiss, Brian W. *Billion Year Spree: The True History of Science Fiction*. Garden City, N.Y.: Doubleday, 1973. Pages 314–316.

Allen, William Rodney. *Understanding Kurt Vonnegut*. Columbia: University of South Carolina Press, 1991.

———, ed. *Conversations with Kurt Vonnegut*. Jackson: University Press of Mississippi, 1988.

Bourjaily, Vance. "What Vonnegut Is and Isn't." In the *New York Times Book Review* (13 August 1972): 3, 10.

Broer, Lawrence R. *Sanity Plea: Schizophrenia in the Novels of Kurt Vonnegut*. Rev. ed. Tuscaloosa: University of Alabama Press, 1994.

Engel, David. "On the Question of Foma; A Study of the Novels of Kurt Vonnegut, Jr." In *Riverside Quarterly*, 5 (1972): 119–128.

Fiedler, Leslie A. "The Divine Stupidity of Kurt Vonnegut, Jr." In *Esquire*, 74 (September 1970): 195–197, 199–200, 202–204.

Giannone, Richard. *Vonnegut: A Preface to His Novels*. Port Washington, N.Y.: Kennikat, 1977.

Goldsmith, David H. *Kurt Vonnegut: Fantasist of Fire and Ice*. Bowling Green, Ohio: Bowling Green University Popular Press, 1972.

Ketterer, David. *New Worlds for Old: The Apocalyptic Imagination, Science Fiction and American Literature*. Bloomington: Indiana University Press, 1974. Pages 296–333.

Klein, Gerard. "Discontent in American Science Fiction." In *Science-Fiction Studies*, 4 (March 1977): 3–13.

Klinkowitz, Jerome. *Kurt Vonnegut*. London and New York: Methuen, 1982.

———. *Vonnegut in Fact: The Public Spokesmanship of Personal Fiction*. Columbia: University of South Carolina Press, 1998.

Klinkowitz, Jerome, and Donald L. Lawler, eds. *Vonnegut in America: An Introduction to the Life and Work of Kurt Vonnegut*. New York: Delacorte/Seymour Lawrence, 1977.

Klinkowitz, Jerome, and John Somer, eds. *The Vonnegut Statement*. New York: Delacorte/Seymour Lawrence, 1973.

"Kurt Vonnegut, Jr.: A Symposium." In *Summary*, 1, no. 2 (1971). (An all-Vonnegut special issue.)

Leeds, Marc. *The Vonnegut Encyclopedia: An Authorized Compendium*. Westport, Conn.: Greenwood, 1994. (An indispensable tool for the study of Vonnegut.)

Leonard, John. "Black Magic." *Nation*, 15 October 1990.

Lundquist, James. *Kurt Vonnegut*. New York: Frederick Ungar, 1977.

May, John R. "Vonnegut's Humor and the Limits of Hope." In *Twentieth Century Literature*, 18 (January 1972): 25–36.

Merrill, Robert, ed. *Critical Essays on Kurt Vonnegut*. Boston: G. K. Hall, 1990.

Mustazza, Leonard. *Forever Pursuing Genesis: The Myth of Eden in the Novels of Kurt Vonnegut*. Lewisburg, Pa.: Bucknell University Press, 1990.

———, ed. *The Critical Response to Kurt Vonnegut*. Westport, Conn.: Greenwood, 1994.

O'Connor, Gerald W. "The Function of Time Travel in Vonnegut's *Slaughterhouse-Five*." In *Riverside Quarterly*, 5 (1972): 206–207.

Reed, Peter J. *The Short Fiction of Kurt Vonnegut*. Westport, Conn.: Greenwood, 1997.

———. *Writers for the Seventies: Kurt Vonnegut, Jr.* New York: Paperback Library, 1972.

Reed, Peter J., and Marc Leeds, eds. *The Vonnegut Chronicles: Interviews and Essays*. Westport, Conn.: Greenwood, 1996.

Schatt, Stanley. *Kurt Vonnegut, Jr.* Boston: Twayne, 1977.

Scholes, Robert. *The Fabulators*. New York: Oxford University Press, 1967. Pages 35–55.

———. *Fabulation and Metafiction*. Urbana: University of Illinois Press, 1979. Pages 144–146, 148, 156–162, 203–205.

Schwartz, Sheila. "Science Fiction: Bridge Between the Two Cultures." In *English Journal*, 60 (November 1971): 1043–1051.

Sigman, Joseph. "Science and Parody in Kurt Vonnegut's *The Sirens of Titan.*" *Mosaic*, 19 (1986): 15–32.

Southern, Terry. *New York Times Book Review* (2 June 1963): 20.

Suvin, Darko. *Metamorphoses of Science Fiction*. New Haven, Conn.: Yale University Press, 1979. Pages 200, 242.

Tanner, Tony. "The Uncertain Messenger: A Study of the Novels of Kurt Vonnegut, Jr." In *Critical Quarterly*, 11 (Winter 1969): 297–315.

"Vonnegut." In *Critique*, 12, no. 3 (November 1971). (All-Vonnegut issue of this scholarly journal.)

Warrick, Patricia; Martin Greenberg; and Joseph Olander, eds. *Science Fiction: Contemporary Mythology*. New York: Harper and Row, 1978.

Wolcott, James. "Mod Apostle." In *New York Review of Books* (22 November 1979): 11–12.

Wolfe, G. K. "Vonnegut and the Metaphor of Science Fiction." In *Journal of Popular Culture*, 5 (1972): 964–969.

Zins, Daniel L. "Rescuing Science from Technology: *Cat's Cradle* and the Play of Apocalypse." *Science-Fiction Studies*, 13 (1986): 170–181.

HOWARD WALDROP

(b. 1946)

I T IS ALMOST certainly the case that John W. Campbell, Jr., had no intention of discovering Howard Waldrop. There remains the fact, however, that Campbell did buy Waldrop's first story—the never reprinted "Lunchbox" (*Analog*, May 1972)—several months before Campbell's death in 1971 and that Waldrop is the last figure of importance to be brought into the science fiction field by its greatest editor.

Waldrop is also one of the first science fiction writers of importance to signal the end of the genre that Campbell espoused and shaped from the beginning of his career as editor of *Astounding Science Fiction* (later *Analog*) in September 1938. The kind of story Campbell published—and by publishing gave an enormously influential imprimatur to—was geared to the forward thrust of American history and frequently was consciously intended to *guide* American history. The Campbell/ *Astounding* vision was normally darker, and almost always more sophisticated in its prognoses, than the semiofficial futures envisaged through events such as the New York World's Fair of 1939, where General Motors' Futurama exhibit entranced huge crowds with its vision of a sanitized technocracy; but Futurama and *Astounding* (and American science fiction in general) shared a repertory of iconic images, all of which conspicuously manifested a longing for the future.

Howard Waldrop grew up and began to write mature stories during the period of approximately 1955 to 1975, when the true costs of the dreams of earlier twentieth-century prophets and prognosticators began to be paid, in America and in the world. The future turned out *not* to be a region more sanitary, less cluttered, easier to comprehend than the addled, superstitious past. It was dirty, unbelievably complex, compromised, anxiety-ridden, and apocalyptic; it did not, in short, work out the way it was supposed to. And the icons that manifested the old story of clean progress—from spaceships to vacuum cleaners, from robot housemaids to interstates—suffered a value change. They became tokens of loss. They became retro.

But it is more complicated than simple nostalgia. At the heart of modern American science fiction writers' sense of loss—manifest in most of those who were born after the end of World War II—is the knowledge that the world whose loss is mourned never in fact existed at all. Neither Futurama nor Campbellian science fiction described a future that came true. Truth, in this context, was not a question of details, which are in any case almost impossible to predict; what did not come true was the spirit of the enterprise.

So nostalgia for 1950's icons that manifested technocratic Americans' anticipation of a new world is not nostalgia at all. A better word to describe this complex emotion, and one that deeply characterizes Waldrop's work from the early 1970's to the end of the century, is desiderium, which may be defined as an intense longing for something that is missing from the world and is now lost, something that indeed may never have actually existed in the first place, but that *should* have existed.

Desiderium, so defined, helps fuel modern American science fiction writers' obsessive focus on alternate histories—science fiction stories set in versions of the past that differ in some fundamental way from the real past. Even Campbellian science fiction, which is still written though it no longer dominates the field, reflects this obsession; a writer such as Harry Turtledove has made an impressive career out of the crafting of alternate histories. Of those perhaps more modern writers whose alternate histories are laced through with desiderium, the most intensely evocative and the most implacably melancholy is Howard Waldrop.

Howard Waldrop was born in Houston, Mississippi, on 15 September 1946 but was brought up in Texas. In the early 1960's, he did artwork for science fiction fanzines that he published with Jake Saunders (with whom he collaborated on his first novel). He attended the University of Texas from 1965 to 1970, was drafted and served in the U.S. Army, and returned to the University of Texas in 1972 but did not graduate. He lived in Austin, Texas, for the next twenty-one years—for five years with fellow writer Leigh Kennedy—until he moved to Oso, Washington, in early 1993.

As he makes clear in various introductions and notes (those interspersed throughout *Going Home Again* are of particular interest), Waldrop has been dogged by changing circumstances and poverty for as long as he has been a professional writer. He ascribes his poverty to the fact that he is essentially a short story writer and that short stories do not pay well. The true story is, of course, more complicated than that. Some short story writers (Harlan Ellison is an example) survive at least in part by being prolific and by writing to fit various markets (Ellison's output stands at well over a thousand stories). During the twenty-five years of his career, Waldrop has published only about sixty stories; not much of this modest total seems to have been crafted to fit commercial markets. Poverty as a way of life may not have been a choice Waldrop consciously made, but it is an almost inevitable

consequence of the kind of writing career he has engaged upon. On the other hand, it is not inconsistent with his attitude toward the latter years of the twentieth century—at present, he owns neither a computer nor a telephone.

The first science fiction novel Waldrop ever read, at the age of seven, was *Mists of Dawn* (1952) by Chad Oliver, a juvenile tale of time travel whose young protagonist is accidentally sent 50,000 years into the past, where he comes to terms with his fellow human beings and with nature. Unlike the dominant Campbellian juvenile science fiction novels then being published by Robert A. Heinlein, this novel does not turn upon its protagonist's triumphal changing of his environment, whether personal or galactic; it is far more concerned with offering its readers a dramatic meditation on right living.

As this novel shows, Oliver's anthropological point of view was already dominant in his fiction (he later taught the subject at the university level), and it may be that Waldrop's abiding interest in the cultural interactions between artifacts and the humans who make them had its first roots at this point. In any case, Oliver and Waldrop eventually became close personal friends and perpetual fishing companions; and the former's death in 1993 was instrumental in persuading Waldrop—according to his own testimony—to leave Texas. Whether or not any of the anthropologists featured in *Them Bones* (Waldrop's only solo novel) directly resemble Oliver, much of the warmth of that deeply pessimistic book comes from its rendering of archaeologists (anthropology and archaeology are sister disciplines) in the field.

No other single writer has visibly influenced Waldrop to the same degree, except perhaps for Philip José Farmer, some of whose stories and novels in the vast Wold Newton series—which gives roles to, and tells the life history of, almost every character of any note who figures in the history of twentieth-century pulp fiction—had appeared before 1970. But as Waldrop's career began to take shape, it soon became apparent that very few specific influences would ever be easily detectable in a writer so devoted to research—which can readily be understood as a natural preoccupation for a writer consumed by desiderium—that his less successful stories read as little more than sawhorses over which to drape historical references. A Waldrop story can read not as the achieved final thing itself but as a kind of final exhalation of a process whose primary interest for its author lay prior to the actual writing: in the ecstasy of research. Waldrop is indeed very widely known for his habit of gestating a story for months or years before actually writing it down, a process that almost never takes more than a day or so. He reads new stories often at science fiction conventions, and it may be that an actual majority of these stories are written down (or, as it were, transcribed) at the literal last minute before the performance is due to begin.

This is no way to become prosperous. Within the science fiction community, on the other hand, the melodrama attending a Howard Waldrop reading has done much to focus genre readers upon one of the most remarkable oeuvres to be produced in the last quarter of the twentieth century.

Because Waldrop's novels are simpler than the stories, because they lack the extensive referentiality of the shorter work, and because they do not try very hard to fulfill genre expectations, they have not been accorded a great deal of attention. At least one of them, however, is a work of considerable substance.

That one is not the first. *The Texas-Israeli War: 1999* (1974), written with Jake Saunders, does not much resemble any of Waldrop's other work, solo or in occasional collaboration. It is a postcatastrophe story set just before the end of the twentieth century. The population of what was once the United States of America has been reduced 90 percent by the fallout and plagues that followed a 1992 nuclear war instigated by the United Kingdom. Texas has seceded from the Union, setting off a second Civil War. As the novel begins, Israeli mercenaries, on hire to the Union, are about to engage with Texas forces.

Howard Waldrop in 1981. PHOTO BY JAY KAY KLEIN

The well-described tank actions that follow, and the complicated politicking amongst various leaders that are interwoven with the action scenes, fail to consort well with the intimate but slightly offhand love story at the center of the actual narrative. Only Waldrop's association with the book has kept it alive.

Interestingly, a second collaboration from the same period, the novelette *Custer's Last Jump* (1996), written with Steven Utley—which was first published in 1976 in an anthology—shows more vividly a direction Waldrop might have taken had he, in the end, felt more at ease with military scenarios. In the alternate America of the story, airplanes and tanks have been invented in time to participate in the Civil War. Confederate forces in the West train the Oglala Sioux Crazy Horse as a pilot. After the war ends, he and fellow tribesmen retain their fighting planes and help defeat General Custer—who arrives on the scene in a dirigible—at Little Big Horn.

The eventual outcome is even grimmer than the terrible story of the near extermination of the Plains Indians in the real world: in *Custer's Last Jump*, genocide is ultimately successful. The story is told in the form of notes, dispatches, and synopses and contains a full (fake) bibliography. It ranges far more extensively as a narrative than most of Waldrop's later stories, it is very savage and very angry, but it lacks the celebratory intensity of his solo work. Explicitly committed, politicized fiction was not, it seems, an entirely comfortable form for Waldrop.

Them Bones (1984), on the other hand, lies at the heart of Waldrop territory. It is a seemingly simple—but in the end quite possibly unresolvably complex—time travel story set in Louisiana. It is told in three strands, two of them fully fleshed out as narrative, one laid down mainly in the form of diaries and filled-out military forms.

The first strand is set in 1929, at an archaeological dig; a fifteenth-century burial mound turns out to contain the body of a horse (not introduced into America for another half century) shot through the head by a twentieth-century bullet. The second strand is told in the first person by Madison Yazoo Leake, on a mission to travel back in time from the year 2002 to some point early in the twentieth century, when it is hoped that he (and the 140 soldiers who are due to follow him almost immediately) will be able to stop World War II and save the world from desolation. The world of 2002 is dying; soon everyone will be dead from radiation or other poisons. The only hope for the human race is to change history. What Leake and the troops backing him up are supposed to do to accomplish this goal is never made clear; nor does it much matter. Leake has not landed in 1930's Louisiana; he has plummeted back to the fifteenth century.

Meanwhile, in the third strand of the story, the 140 soldiers have also traveled back to about the same time. They will never find Leake, however, because he has entered the fifteenth century of an alternate universe, one in which the Roman Empire never existed, the library at Alexandria was never burned by

religious zealots; a world whose western bournes are now being explored by Arabs. The soldiers remain in our own world, where they infect surrounding tribes of Indians with fatal diseases and are in turn slowly slaughtered. They are completely unable to effect any change in history that might save the world of 2002.

It is their remains, and the remains of their horses, that the 1929 team discovers. The endeavors of that team to save what they can of their distressingly anomalous finds are abetted by Huey Long, governor of Louisiana; but in the end, floodwaters wash away their work.

Leake's own story—which inhabits what seems to be an entirely different time stream—occupies the largest portion of the book. It is a gentle, movingly told tale of assimilation: he is adopted by a tribe, one of whose members speaks Greek through earlier experiences with Arabs, and lives with them in peace until an Aztec-like nation kidnaps his mentor. Leake manages to rescue his mentor, who is killed anyway by the pursuing "Huastecas." Back home, disease and changing climate begin to evict everyone from Eden. But Leake remains with the remnants of his people and the woman he loves. There is nothing else to do.

Them Bones, though told with a deceptive calm, is a tale of terminus. It speaks of the savagery of race against race; it mocks the works of science (though Waldrop clearly loves the archaeologists he depicts); and it treats the imminent end of the human race as a foregone conclusion.

A third book-length tale, *A Dozen Tough Jobs* (1989) is a fantasy in which the exploits of Hercules are told in a twentieth-century frame. It is full of small pleasures, but it lacks the subtle sideways savagery of *Them Bones* or the profusive joys of the short stories.

Almost all of Waldrop's short work of merit has been assembled in four collections: *Howard Who?* (1986), *All About Strange Monsters of the Recent Past* (1987), *Night of the Cooters* (1990) and *Going Home Again* (1997)—which have themselves been variously reassembled. There is relatively little development from one volume to the next, though it may be the case that some of the later stories are somewhat less freighted with references and feature somewhat smaller casts of protagonists and walk-ons who turn out to be historical figures, characters from other stories in other media, or myths. But the streamlining of texture is only relative, and the intensity of rendered feeling is, if anything, greater.

The long *You* Could *Go Home Again* (1993), a chapbook publication that also appears in *Going Home Again*, may for instance only boast five recognizable real characters: Thomas Wolfe, Fats Waller, Nevil Shute, T. E. Lawrence, and a young J. D. Salinger—and there may in fact be almost no conventional story to tell. But the alternate history unfolded in the tale is an achingly acute manifestation of desiderium: the 1933 United States presidential election has been won by Howard Scott, the historical promulgator of the Technocracy movement, which espoused the establishment of a primitive but nationwide database to keep track of supply and demand and the use of further high-tech means to make the U.S. economic and cultural infrastructure really work. As a consequence, there is no World War II in 1940, great zeppelins fly the world, and Thomas Wolfe, not fully recovered from his brain surgery in 1938 (in this world he died then), is flying homeward from the 1940 Japanese Olympics. Fats Waller makes an unscheduled appearance and plays inspiredly all night (Waldrop's intense love of American music from the turn of the century on is here, as elsewhere, amply argued); and Wolfe begins to sense, as dawn comes, what somehow he must recover in his own psyche in order to write once again at full pitch. There is nothing more to the story but detail work. What remains is an almost unendurably potent longing for a world in which Thomas Wolfe could recover his wits, Fats Waller play forever, World War II never happen, and glorious zeppelins sparkle the dawn winds.

An even later story, "The Heart of Whitenesse" (1977)—most conveniently reprinted in *The Year's Best Science Fiction: Fifteenth*

Annual Collection (1998), edited by Gardner Dozois—also packs an intense emotional overload into a tale featuring Christopher Marlowe in the days approaching his murder. The phrase "hum of pleroma," which serves as an epigraph to this story, comes from an analysis by John Clute in *Look at the Evidence* (1996) of some of the ways in which intensity of longing may be conveyed in a venue that is not simply nostalgic. In Waldrop's tale, which replays Joseph Conrad's "Heart of Darkness" (1899), Marlowe (that is, Marlow) embarks upon a sailing craft fitted with runners and sails up the iced-over Thames (the Congo) from London to Oxford, where he has been instructed to warn Johann Faustus (Kurtz) that he must not engage in treasonable activities.

But instead of darkness, all is epiphanic whiteness. There is a snowstorm on the Thames, but the ice ship continues—exultantly; Waldrop's description of the journey is both intense and elated—through to Oxford. Marlowe's confrontation with Faust (and a prophesying demon) seems to go well. He returns to London full of plans. He does not know what the reader knows: that within hours he will be a dead man.

The ice ship in "The Heart of Whitenesse" is arguable a science fiction notion, though Faustus's summoning of a demon is not. And it could be argued that it is in the interstices between genres—however artificial they may seem to some readers—that Waldrop flourishes most eloquently. A good example is his most famous story, "The Ugly Chickens" (1980; in *Howard Who?*), which won the 1981 Nebula award for best novelette and the 1981 World Fantasy award for short fiction. The eponymous "chickens" are in fact dodos, a breeding population of which has survived, through a series of plausible circumstances, into the twentieth century, only to be cooked, en masse, in a barbecue.

This story has often, and with some justice, been described as a work of science fiction set in an alternate universe: after all, in this world dodos have been extinct for centuries. But Waldrop explains how his dodos did survive so long, in terms which make it moderately clear that the events he describes could plausibly have occurred in our own real world. The dodos' survival, in this context, is something we did not know about our world, not something that requires an alternate universe to justify. Indeed, when Waldrop (or any science fiction or fantasy writer) gives an elaborate explanation for the existence of something (such as the dodo) previously unknown, then it is almost certainly the case that he is telling a secret about this world rather than positing a different universe. On the other hand, when Waldrop (or his contemporaries) gives *no* rationalized explanation for an anomaly, then it is very likely that the reader is being asked to posit an alternate universe in which that anomaly might properly fit.

Most of Waldrop's stories featuring real persons in anomalous roles, or fictional characters who have been promoted to full "reality," are of this second sort. Examples include "Save a Place in the Lifeboat for Me" (1976) and "Ike at the Mike" (1982), both from *Howard Who?*; "All About Strange Monsters of the Recent Past" (1981) and "What Makes Hieronymous Run?" (1985), both from *All About Strange Monsters of the Recent Past*; "Hoover's Men" (1988) and "Fin de Cyclé," both from *Night of the Cooters*, the second being original to that volume; and "The Effects of Alienation" (1992), which is a "Hitler Wins" tale, and "Scientifiction," which is original to *Going Home Again*.

A full cast list of recognizable names would be difficult if not impossible to construct (walk-ons are sometimes only identified allusively). But a representative sampling of the cast may give some sense of the cultural fields Waldrop tills. Almost every personage Waldrop evokes (real or fictional, human or cartoon) is evoked with a warmth and with that ongoing sense of desiderium, that sense that the world should be thus. The world (Waldrop says) should have been so constructed that these folk might live aright. When he must deal with an irrevocable fact—with a world he cannot magic into another semblance—the effect is often tragic, as in "Save a Place

in the Lifeboat for Me," where nothing can prevent Buddy Holly from taking his fatal flight (on 3 February 1959), not even the Marx Brothers, not even Laurel and Hardy.

Figures Waldrop incorporates into his cast (some already mentioned) include Bud Abbott, Louis Armstrong, Bertolt Brecht, Bucky Bug (who featured in 1940's issues of *Walt Disney's Comics and Stories*), Natty Bumppo, John Bunyan, Holden Caulfield, Lou Costello, Charles Dickens, Donald Duck, Dwight D. Eisenhower (as Ike), Lillian Gish, Goofy, D. W. Griffith, Oliver Hardy, William S. Hart, Adolf Hitler, Ernest Hemingway, Buddy Holly, Sherlock Holmes, Herbert Hoover as head of the FBI, Boris Karloff, Alfred Jarry, Waylon Jennings, John F. Kennedy, Stan Laurel, T. E. Lawrence, Huey Long, Peter Lorre, Groucho Marx (and the other Marx brothers), Georges Méliès, Mantan Moreland, Zero Mostel, Mickey Mouse, various movie monsters of the 1950's cinema, the Musicians of Bremen, Nosferatu, General George Patton, Pablo Picasso, Elvis Presley, Marcel Proust, Henri Rousseau, Erik Satie, Shemp (from the Three Stooges), Fats Waller, Isaak Walton, and Thomas Wolfe. There are many more.

Most of these figures appear in tales that may be described as alternate history science fiction or fantasy, a spectrum ranging from the full alternate history scenario examined in *You Could Go Home Again* to the arguably this-worldly "The Ugly Chickens." The tales that Waldrop sets in the future tend not to require the reader to make those readerly calculations necessary for his or her identification of an alternate history; but they manifest all the same a detachment similar in timbre to stories cast in that subgenre.

The near-future, postdisaster world depicted in "Mary Margaret Road-Grader" (1976; in *Howard Who?*) does not, for instance, supply more than a shapely sketch of that world. The tragicomedy at its heart—the conflict between the eponymous woman and the men who are mysogynistically loath to compete with her in a tournament between ancient road-graders—unfolds with an eerie, distanced, contemplative serenity. Its closing passages resemble the closing sections of *Them Bones;* an elegiac sense pervades in both texts. It is a sense that any world in which we must live is an entrapment, that in truth the world should not be thus.

In the afterword to "Why Did?" (1994; story and afterword are in *Going Home Again*), Waldrop asks a rhetorical question of his readers:

> Don't you wish sometimes you lived in a Fleischer cartoon world, with Betty Boop, Bimbo, Koko and Pudge? That when things were going great, and you were dancing, all the buildings and people and the moon and stars were dancing along with you! And when things were bad, even the trees would chase you?
>
> Anyway, sometime in the Eighties I started referring to the "Little Moron Story" I was going to write.

The story itself is clearly told on a literal level: in a big house a man who thinks he is the Little Moron (in the 1950's Little Moron jokes) houses a number of mentally deficient or disturbed characters from American literature; the house burns down; life, although diminished, continues. The implications of the tale are, on the other hand, impenetrable. Why does Benjamin—from William Faulkner's *The Sound and the Fury* (1929)—gain his senses while dying? Why does a cartoon character—Otto Soglow's Little King, who originated in the *New Yorker*—seem to take over after the deaths of the other characters?

Perhaps the answer is that there is no second act, as F. Scott Fitzgerald once said of American life. Waldrop might add: All the Americas you can dream are stages. All the alternate Americas—the real and the imagined, the dream and the awakening—crumble and fade once a real story begins to be told

about them. The bravery of life, in the stories of Howard Waldrop, is to live without expecting a full story, a fixative of art, a second act.

Howard Waldrop's stories do not end. They stop when they are broken.

Selected Bibliography

WORKS OF HOWARD WALDROP

NOVELS AND CHAPBOOKS

The Texas-Israeli War: 1999, with Jake Saunders. New York: Ballantine, 1974.

Them Bones. New York: Ace, 1984.

Howard Who? Twelve Outstanding Stories of Speculative Fiction. Garden City, N.Y.: Doubleday, 1986.

All About Strange Monsters of the Recent Past: Neat Stories. Kansas City, Mo.: Ursus Imprints, 1987.

A Dozen Tough Jobs. Willimantic, Conn.: Ziesing, 1989.

Night of the Cooters: More Neat Stores. Kansas City, Mo.: Ursus Imprints; Shingletown, Calif.: Ziesing, 1990.

You Could Go Home Again. New Castle, Va.: Cheap Street, 1993. (Chapbook.)

Custer's Last Jump, with Steve Utley. North Perth, Australia: Ticonderoga Publications, 1996. (Chapbook reprinting a story from 1976.)

Going Home Again. North Perth, Australia: Eidolon Publications, 1997; New York: St. Martin's, 1998.

COLLECTIONS

Almost all of Waldrop's collections contain author's notes, some of very considerable interest. These notes reappear, sometimes augmented, in the compilations listed below.

Strange Things in Close-Up: The Nearly Complete Howard Waldrop. London: Legend, 1989. (Incorporates *Howard Who?* and *All About Strange Monsters of the Recent Past.*)

Strange Monsters of the Recent Past. New York: Ace, 1991. (Incorporates *All About Strange Monsters of the Recent Past* and *A Dozen Tough Jobs.*)

Night of the Cooters: More Neat Stuff. London: Legend, 1991. (Incorporates *Night of the Cooters: More Neat Stories* and *A Dozen Tough Jobs.*)

—JOHN CLUTE

IAN WATSON

(b. 1943)

IAN WATSON WAS born on 20 April 1943 in
St. Albans, England, where his father was
engaged in war work as a radio operator. When
the war ended the family returned home to
North Shields in northeast England. At Tynemouth School, Watson demonstrated prodigious intellectual ability, winning a scholarship to Balliol College, Oxford, at age 16. He
hitchhiked around Europe for a while before
taking up his university place in 1960. He
married the painter Judith Jackson at the age
of 19, while he was an undergraduate, and
went on to take first-class honors in English.
His subsequent postgraduate research in comparative literature—examining the influence
of various French writers of the nineteenth
century on the aesthetic theories of Walter
Pater—led to a B. Litt. degree in 1965, and he
added the customary M.A. degree to his academic qualifications in 1966.

Watson's first teaching position was a two-
year appointment at the University of Dar es
Salaam, Tanzania. He then worked for three
years at Tokyo University of Education, an experience of which he was to write that "although Africa made me aware of the Third
World, and of politics, it was Japan which
dosed me with future shock and made me become a science fiction writer." The legacy of
his African experience is displayed in "The
Flags of Africa" (1970). Watson published
three fables in the Dar es Salaam University
College magazine *Darlite* in 1966, but most
of the writing he did in Africa was academic
criticism. In Japan, while his principal place
of employment was strikebound, he began to

write more variously and more prolifically.
His first book was *Japan: A Cat's Eye View*
(1969), a text intended for use in teaching English to Japanese students; by the time it was
published he had begun to submit work to the
British avant-garde science fiction magazine
New Worlds.

Watson's first story in *New Worlds* was
"Roof Garden Under Saturn" (1969), which
was rapidly followed by the quasi-documen-
tary "Japan" (1970). Both items are surreal
studies of life in the then-heavily-polluted atmosphere of the Japanese capital. The other
stories he published before that incarnation of
New Worlds died were a brief account of future alienation starring "The Sex Machine"
(1970) and the offbeat political fantasy "The
Tarot Pack Megadeath" (1970). The magazine's demise put a temporary brake on Watson's avant-garde experiments, but he was to
retain a taste for bizarre juxtapositions of
subject matter and a willingness to try out
nonlinear narrative techniques. When he resumed writing fiction he contributed offbeat
pieces to other small press magazines, including the Japan-inspired fantasies "Programmed
Love Story" (*Transatlantic Review*, 1974) and
"The Girl Who Was Art" (*Ambit*, 1976). This
aspect of his work is most abundantly represented in his small press collection of fiction
and nonfiction *The Book of Ian Watson*
(1985).

Watson returned to England in 1970, living
in Oxford but teaching Complementary
Studies at Birmingham Polytechnic Art and
Design Centre. He was involved with the

Trotskyite political group that became the Workers' Revolutionary Party, wrote and distributed Situationist pamphlets, and experimented with LSD. He also embarked on an extensive program of background research for his new novel, *The Embedding* (1973), which proved to be one of the most spectacular debut novels ever to appear in the science fiction field. It was published by Victor Gollancz, in the most prestigious science fiction list in Britain, to which Watson was to remain affiliated for the next twenty-five years. Its French translation, which appeared the following year, won the Prix Apollo in 1975.

The three plot threads of *The Embedding* examine different aspects of the relationship between language and the human mind, extrapolating the psycholinguistic theories of Noam Chomsky. One thread describes an experiment in which children are taught an artificial language whose grammar is intricately "embedded," in order to investigate the mental consequences. A second describes anthropological investigations of a Native American tribe, the Xemahoa, who have two distinct languages, the second having been produced in connection with the altered states of consciousness induced by the tribe's use of psychotropic drugs. The third concerns the advent of alien visitors, the Sp'thra, who are interested in a more generalized study of human communication systems and offer to trade new technology for experimental subjects.

The Embedding arrived at a time when linguistics was a newly fashionable science, whose potential worth as a resource for science fiction writers had been demonstrated by Samuel R. Delany's *Babel-17* (1966), which had a far more exotic setting. Watson's decision to set his novel on Earth was a bold one, as was his use of a rather esoteric central notion that he had found during his research in comparative literature, in *Nouvelles Impressions d'Afrique*, an embedded poem by the French surrealist Raymond Roussel, a poem whose comprehensibility is severely compromised by its rigorously embedded form. The novel is further strengthened by a keen appreciation of the ecological and political implications of the exploitation of the Amazon rain forest and a similarly keen awareness of the ethics of experimentation with human subjects.

The result of this enterprise was an imaginative tour de force that effortlessly surpasses in strangeness and complexity all previous science fiction depictions of alien thought. There had been other science fiction novels that drew on the resources of anthropological science to formulate images of alien society, but Watson was the first writer to emphasize a logical consequence of such extrapolations, which his predecessors had often been careful to hide: the notion that humans are not so far removed from the alien and that a transition from our familiar consciousness of the world to a radically different one might be achieved more easily than we care to suppose. The idea of an abrupt but extreme transformation of human consciousness—an existential breakthrough to a better way of seeing and thinking and hence to a higher reality—was to remain central to Watson's work for many years, investing all his most important novels.

When *New Worlds* was reborn as a quarterly series of paperback anthologies, Watson returned to its pages with "Thy Blood Like Milk" (1973), a novella blending the imagery of futuristic speculation with that of ancient mythology—Aztec mythology, in this case—in a manner that he was frequently to recapitulate, most immediately in "Sitting on a Starwood Stool" (1974), an antiheroic version of the legend of Prometheus. *New Worlds* also reprinted "The Ghosts of Luna" (1973), one of two stories he published in the Oxford SF Group's *Sfinx*. However, his shorter pieces of this early period are mostly trivial, the main focus of his attention being his novels.

Like *The Embedding*, *The Jonah Kit* (1975) entangles plot threads that examine radically different aspects of the same question. One concerns the abstruse theoretical implications of astronomical observations made by a Nobel prize–winning physicist, which suggest that the observed universe is only a virtual echo of the Big Bang rather than the immediate object of Creation. The second concerns an experiment conducted by Soviet scientists in which "imprints" of the minds of a schizophrenic boy and a dead cosmonaut are superimposed on the brain of a sperm whale so that the creature can be used as a spy on Western submarine movements. The communicative channel thus opened proves, however, to be more effective, as well as more problematic, than is required for such a mundane purpose.

As in *The Embedding*, the plot threads of *The Jonah Kit* eventually form an unexpectedly awkward knot, because the news brought by the physicist—which seems pragmatically neutral within the Western worldview—has a devastating effect on the worldview of the whales, to whom it is communicated by the imprinted personalities. Again, Watson's use of politically loaded settings in the Second and Third Worlds gave the novel an internationalist flavor rarely seen in science fiction, and his strong commitment to socialist ideals added a further dimension of differentiation from typical products of the American-dominated genre.

The Embedding and *The Jonah Kit* were both reprinted in the United States by Scribners and were rightly promoted as works of some importance. They appeared at a time when the science fiction genre was expanding rapidly in popularity and prestige, when work by the Polish writer Stanislaw Lem and the Russian collaborators Arkady and Boris Strugatsky were also attracting a good deal of attention and praise. For a few years in the mid-1970's, it seemed that speculative fiction might break out of the parochial straitjacket imposed upon it by the routines of American genre marketing. Such prospects were ringingly endorsed by Watson in fanzine articles such as "W[h]ither Science Fiction?" (1976) and "The Crudities of Science Fiction" (1978) and, less directly, in the unrepentantly esoteric talk he gave when he was the guest of honor at the Second French National Science Fiction Convention in Angoulême in 1975 entitled "Towards an Alien Linguistics." Alas,

those hopes soon foundered—but not until Watson had resigned his teaching post to write full-time. He made that move in 1976, by which time he and his wife were parents of a three-year-old child.

Scribners published only one more of Watson's novels, after which his American editions were mostly consigned to the narrower world of genre paperbacks, where literary sophistication was irrelevant, innovation largely unappreciated, and explicit socialist sympathies anathematized. Although his association with Gollancz in the United Kingdom provided some protection from the cold winds of change that swept continually through the science fiction marketplace after the slump of the late 1970's, the fact that there was never such a welcoming atmosphere as there had been when he produced his first two novels had a gradual but inexorable effect on Watson's literary ambitions. He was never to match the purchasing power of the advances or the enthusiasm of the critical acclaim that he was briefly able to obtain in the late 1970's. The products of his subsequent career as a freelance writer must be examined in the context of a long struggle to maintain the aesthetic and intellectual standards of his work against the corrosions of commercial demand.

The first casualty of this long struggle was a novel Watson had written in 1970, *The Woman Factory*, which he described as "a sarcastic deconstruction of pornography." It never appeared in English, although it was published in French translation as *Orgasmachine* (1976). The theme—the mass-production of female androids for sexual purposes—was unacceptable, even in what were supposedly taboo-breaking days, to mass-market publishers in Britain and America. He rewrote it as *The Woman Plant* in 1982, and this version—which he considered "far superior"—was sold to Playboy Press, but when that paperback line was sold to mass-market publisher Berkley it was deemed unpublishable, lest its satirical exaggeration of exploitation should be seen by unwary readers as exploitative. The only part of the revised text ever to

Ian Watson in 1990. PHOTO BY JAY KAY KLEIN

see print in English was "Custom-Built Girl," an abridged version of the opening, which appeared in *Cybersex* (1996), edited by Richard Glyn Jones.

The first plot thread of the third novel Watson published in his native tongue, *The Martian Inca* (1977), concerns events in Bolivia following the hard landing of an unmanned Russian space probe carrying samples of Martian soil. The second thread follows an American-manned mission to the red planet, whose prospects are seriously affected by the discovery that its soil is biologically and psychotropically active. Like the drug that bestowed a new understanding of the world upon the Xemahoa in *The Embedding*, the produce of the arid Martian surface awakens new potential in those exposed to it. One Bolivian experiences extreme delusions of grandeur, considering himself to be a new incarnation of the Inca, destined to recover the fortunes of his oppressed race.

It eventually transpires that evolution has worked differently on Mars, a planet of extremes whose ancient inhabitants had to rebuild their bodies, their minds, and their culture from scratch with every new summer—and left that potential behind when conditions would no longer allow their recapitulative culture to flourish. The possibility remains for humankind to re-adopt the potentiality of Martian biology, using it as a progressive instrument in its own further evolution.

Alien Embassy (1977) is a similarly themed novel in which humankind has run into eco-catastrophic difficulties on Earth but has seemingly opened communication with a number of alien races, employing mental disciplines of "astral travel" based on the Tibetan *Book of the Dead.* Watson had earlier written "On Cooking the First Hero in Spring" (1975), in which visitors to an alien world find the same text useful in figuring out alien Clayfolk, and had applied a similar form of communication to the plumbing of a black hole in "The Event Horizon" (1976).

The heroine of *Alien Embassy* leaves her African home to embark on a career in Astromancy. She eventually finds that, although no actual aliens are involved, the processes of "communication" in which she is involved are transformative experiences, in physical as well as mental terms—and that the transformations in question hold the key to the future evolution of humanity. Although it was published two years after Fritjof Capra's *The Tao of Physics* (1975)—and two years before Gary Zukav's *The Dancing Wu Li Masters* (1979)—*Alien Embassy*'s amalgamation of science and Eastern mysticism seemed undesirably chimerical to many science fiction purists, and it received markedly less praise than its predecessors. At a later date it might have found a new audience, but it was too early to catch the wave of New Age enthusiasm that was to break on the Californian shore in the following decade.

The third book Watson published in 1977 was *Japan Tomorrow*, another work intended to help make learning English enjoyable for

Japanese students. His next novel, *Miracle Visitors* (1978), followed *Alien Embassy* in anticipating subsequent developments in alternative belief systems, but it treated them far too cleverly to appeal to true believers. It may be the best science fiction novel ever written about UFOs, but it draws its principal inspiration from Carl Jung's study *Flying Saucers* (1959), which interprets such sightings, and the elaborate fantasies grafted on to them, as a modern myth generated by the collective unconscious. Watson's book extrapolates the idea that the function of such hallucinations is to encourage, and perhaps to guide, mental evolution. He infuses an unprecedentedly vivid account of alien abductions recalled under hypnosis with a strong dose of Sufist mysticism. Most UFO enthusiasts loathe the book because they are steadfast in clinging to crudely literal—and, ironically, far less complimentary—interpretations of their experiences.

The three central characters of *Miracle Visitors* are party to an absurd but magnificent voyage to the dark side of the moon by Ford Thunderbird, but on returning to normality—without any hard evidence of their adventure—adopt radically different strategies of readaptation. One embraces denial, retreating into the world of "common sense"; the second continues to pursue a futile quest for the "proof" that will assimilate UFO experiences to quotidian experience; the third—a psychologist researching altered states of consciousness—takes the Sufist route. The underlying argument of the book is not that any one of these strategies is correct but rather that any mental instrument capable of fulfilling the kind of function Jung attributes to UFOs—science fiction itself being the most obvious example—can be dealt with by any of the strategies and would be best served by the most productive one.

Watson's own science fiction is not *entirely* committed to the third strategy, but it generally proceeds from the supposition that critics who despise all speculative fiction for its unreality and critics who will only endorse the kinds of hard science fiction that aspire to rigorous realism may be missing out on the most interesting possibilities of the genre. Watson provided exuberant exemplary support for this approach to science fiction in such contemporary short stories as "The Very Slow Time Machine" (1978), in which the eponymous backward-traveling device offers its observers an opportunity for extravagant metaphysical speculation, and the briefly bizarre parable "My Soul Swims in a Goldfish Bowl" (1978). His first collection, *The Very Slow Time Machine: Science Fiction Stories* (1979), contains other stories thematically linked to his early novels, including "A Time-Span to Conjure With" (1978) and "Immune Dreams" (1978).

Watson followed *Miracle Visitors* with *God's World* (1979), which the market-conscious originating British publisher chose to advertise on the cover as "his first novel of outer space." It failed to sell for more than a decade in the United States, presumably because publishers felt that it would not go down well in the Bible Belt. The story begins with an invitation to the people of Earth to visit God's World, issued by tall, shimmering "angels" that appear briefly in many locations, always adapting their form to fit local faiths and speaking in the native tongues of the people to whom they address their message. Those appointed to answer the summons embark upon the *Pilgrim Crusader*, which travels through the deceptive realms of "High Space." Those pilgrims fortunate enough to survive the ship's capture by the insectile Group-ones eventually arrive at their destination, the satellite of a gas-giant orbiting 82 Eridani, to find its indigenous angels living in intimate proximity to the borderlands of the other-worldly Askatharli: a "Heaven" to which they are gradually being assimilated. Having already been warned by the angelic broadcasts that there is a war in Askatharli space—also called "the Imagining"—they have to decide which side they are on.

Although Watson's next novel is stamped from a very similar template, his editor chose not to represent it as science fiction at all, issuing it in a short-lived Gollancz Fantasy series. *The Gardens of Delight* (1980) tells the story of an investigative mission conducted by the crew of the starship *Schiaparelli,* sent to find out what became of the *Copernicus.* They find a small planet that keeps one side permanently turned toward the sun and whose land surface has been "terraformed" in the image of Hieronymus Bosch's triptych displaying Heaven, Hell, and the Garden of Earthly Delights. All the distorted and chimerical monsters that Bosch had put into his surreal painting are here incarnate as living beings—as are Satan and God.

The key to this mystery is held by one Knossos, a former crewman on *Copernicus* and enthusiastic student of the esoteric artistry and symbolism of alchemy. Like Carl Jung, Knossos (whose name is a pun on Gnosis) has reformulated the failed science of alchemy and the entire "Hermetic tradition" as an allegory of human evolution, and he has persuaded the powerful entity that remade the planet for its colonists to remold human nature in such a way as to make that evolutionary allegory literal. The odyssey undertaken by the newcomers takes them from the Garden of Earthly Delights through Hell to a Paradise embodying and triumphantly celebrating a wholly new Enlightenment, unsuspected even by the world's makeshift god. The science fiction logic of the denouement is as well worked out as it is in most of its predecessors, and it is slightly ironic that Watson's attempts to do that became increasingly tokenistic in subsequent works that reverted to the protective umbrella of the science fiction label. In fact, *The Gardens of Delight* vies with *The Embedding* and *Miracle Visitors* for the privilege of being reckoned Watson's best science fiction novel.

Watson's fascination with religious ideas was further extrapolated in *Deathhunter* (1981), vastly expanded from "A Cage for Death" (1981). The story is set in a quasi-utopian future whose angst-free inhabitants have reconciled themselves to the idea and experience of death—until they discover that the souls of the dead are carried into the un-

known by a strange supernatural predator. When the hero sets off to follow this creature to its destination, however, the enlightenment vouchsafed to him by a drunken "angel" turns out to be rather derisory and—at least by comparison with the novel's immediate predecessors—distinctly unsatisfactory. A similar dismissive sarcasm is found in some of Watson's contemporary short stories, including the metaphysical fantasy "A Letter from God" (1981) and "Nightmares" (1981), in which benevolent aliens who save humankind from destruction are nevertheless reviled. "The World SF Convention of 2080" (1980) gave satirical vent to Watson's growing impatience with the genre marketplace, imagining science fiction fans doggedly pursuing the same old obsessions in a postholocaust world.

All but the earliest of the more serious stories in *Sunstroke and Other Stories* (1982)—whose most notable inclusions are "Insight" (1980) and "The Milk of Knowledge" (original to the collection)—set aside the fascination with the esoteric and the bizarre that had inspired Watson's earlier novels. His production of short stories increased markedly after 1979—the year in which he and his family moved from rented accommodations in Oxford to take up permanent residence in the Northamptonshire village of Moreton Pinkney—but much of that produce was calculatedly whimsical. "Jean Sandwich, the Sponsor and I" (1981), was expanded into *Converts,* a jocular and rather slapdash novel offering a fanciful account of the evolutionary possibilities open to humankind, but the novel was rejected by Gollancz. It eventually appeared as an original paperback in the United Kingdom in 1984, although its lack of seriousness helped it find a better U.S. market than its predecessors.

Gollancz did publish *Under Heaven's Bridge* (1981), boldly advertised as the first transatlantic collaboration in the science fiction field. Indeed, Watson and his American coauthor, Michael Bishop, had never met, conducting their collaboration entirely by mail. What had brought them together was a mutual fascination with Japanese society and a keen interest in the application of anthropology to the design of alien cultures. Bishop's classic of anthropological science fiction was *Transfigurations* (1979), but *Under Heaven's Bridge* owes more to his earlier novel *A Little Knowledge* (1977), in which Cygnusian missionaries arrived on an Earth beset by Fundamentalist creeds. The plot of *Under Heaven's Bridge* is a conventional puzzle story in which visitors from Earth bring very different spiritual resources to bear on the intractable problem of deciphering the culture of an enigmatic cyborg race whose home world orbits one element of a dangerously unstable binary star. The conditions under which the novel was written prevented its plot from becoming overly intricate, but it was still a little too esoteric to appeal to a wide audience. Watson and Bishop also collaborated in the editing of the anthology *Changes: Stories of Metamorphosis: An Anthology of Speculative Fiction About Startling Metamorphoses, Both Psychological and Physical* (1982).

Watson's attempts to make his work more widely accessible continued in *Chekhov's Journey* (1983), an ingenious tale in which a Soviet film crew making a drama documentary about Anton Chekhov's investigation of the Tunguska explosion attempts to inspire its leading man by putting him in psychic touch with the great playwright. This ultimate extrapolation of Stanislavsky's "method" goes awry when the actor begins recapitulating an alternative history, generated by a disastrous time slip experienced by the spaceship *K. E. Tsiolkovsky*. The story is well worked out and elegantly written, but again the book failed to find an immediate buyer in the United States, presumably because its Russian setting was considered likely to alienate some potential readers. It is hardly surprising that Watson then set out to make a deliberate compromise with public demand, producing a trilogy of novels set in a safely hypothetical milieu and cast in a mold much more familiar to genre readers than most of his early works.

The Book of the River (1984) describes two very different human societies living on opposite banks of a great river, separated by the seemingly sentient "Black Current," whose intervention has secured female domination on one side while allowing males to retain more traditional roles on the other. Once the first volume had set the scene by means of a fairly conventional action/adventure plot, the second volume, *The Book of the Stars* (1984), began to extrapolate the kind of metaphysical framework that Watson loved to design. Having established psychic contact with the Worm—the mind of the Black Current—the heroine, Yaloon, obtains intelligence of Eeden, from which the populations on either side of the river originally came and to which their souls allegedly return after death. Enabled to test this second proposition, she travels through *ka*-space to discover that Eeden is Earth; there she begins to perceive—and to rebel against—the plan of destiny formulated by the Worm's great rival, the Godmind.

In *The Book of Being* (1985) the consequences of Yaleen's rebellion unwind. Having been reborn as her own sister, she becomes a charismatic messiah and dies again and again, experiencing life on a series of other worlds. Unlike the protagonists of *God's World*, she has no hesitation in siding with the "devil's party" in the apocalyptic cosmic conflict, and she eventually fulfills a Promethean role in bringing light to a new Creation. Although the American critics Don D'Ammassa and Douglas Mackey have judged the trilogy to be Watson's most satisfactory realization of his philosophical concerns, the languid extrapolation of the story loses in subtlety and depth what it gains in clarity and conventional story value; this third novel ends with a flippant and flagrantly satirical coda.

In the introduction to *Slow Birds and Other Stories* (1985), Watson expressed a new affection for his shorter fiction, representing the items therein as products of a literary hothouse—"the orchids, the bonsai of a writer's creativity"—more closely regulated and more intimately meaningful than the novels he had "transplanted suddenly into the wild." Some of the stories feature abrupt and arbitrary transitions, such as the one that drastically expands "The Width of the World" (1983) or the Change that separates the sexes in "Universe on the Turn" (1984). Others, including "The Mystic Marriage of Salome" (1981), the Joycean "The Bloomsday Revolution" (1984), and "Ghost Lecturer" (1984)—in which the Epicurean philosopher Lucretius is summoned from the depths of time to extend his discourse on the nature of the universe— revel unrepentantly, but not very earnestly, in esotericism. The 1983 title story, which was nominated for Nebula and Hugo awards in 1984 but won neither, is a perfectly formed tale of computer-guided missiles that are shifted into a parallel dimension whose "neutrality" subtly reflects the awkward situation of European nations geographically caught between two superpowers.

Queenmagic, Kingmagic (1986) is an expansion of a playful novella featuring a universe whose laws of nature are modeled on the rules of chess. Its tendency to dissolve whenever a king is checkmated is inconvenient for its inhabitants, two of whom eventually contrive to escape. The expansion takes them into other, stimilarly board game–based universes, including a Snakes-and-Ladders universe and a Monopoly universe. The novel has little to recommend it except its panache in the face of absurdity—although the author liked the fundamental idea well enough to compose a further variant in "Jewels in an Angel's Wing" (1987)—and it seems that Watson had begun to feel that there was little scope left for the exercise of his talents in that fugitive sector of the science fiction field where metaphysical fantasies could be accommodated. His account of the brutal fate of those in "The People on the Precipice" (1985), although represented in the blurb of *Evil Water and Other Stories* (1987) as a political allegory, could also be construed as an extrapolation of his own sense of precariousness. There is little in Watson's own works of the time as zestfully adventurous as the contents of the anthology of mostly original stories of life after death that he coedited with Pamela

Sargent, *Afterlives: An Anthology of Stories About Life After Death* (1986). For the next three years he diverted his principal efforts into horror fiction, which was then enjoying something of a boom in the British literary marketplace.

The Power (1987) and *Meat* (1988) attempt to use conventionally stomach-churning horror story formats to bolster two of Watson's pet political causes: nuclear disarmament and animal liberation. Both causes had come to seem acutely relevant by virtue of his experience of village life in Moreton Pinkney, which was neighbor to both factory farms and American air bases. He had long been active in the local Labour Party and the Campaign for Nuclear Disarmament. Although the two novels have a certain winning gruesomeness, it is doubtful whether they excited much sympathy for their central causes among lovers of genre horror.

The shorter tales of supernatural evil "Jingling Geordie's Hole" (1986) and "Evil Water" (1987) are much more effective, being neatly accomplished exercises in disturbing symbolism. Watson developed the former into an effective horror–science fiction novel, *The Fire Worm* (1988), which offered him the opportunity to revisit some of his favorite themes. The old English legend of the Lambton Worm is here relocated to Watson's native Tynemouth and reidentified as the salamander featured in the alchemical writings attributed (falsely) to Raymond Lully. Gollancz published *The Fire Worm* but would not take the more straightforwardly science fiction *The Whores of Babylon* (1988), an expansion of the novella "We Remember Babylon" (1984). The protagonists of the latter novel are visitors to a Babylon whose heyday has been re-created, ostensibly in the Arizona desert but actually in virtual reality; they find the business of adapting to their new environment more challenging than they had anticipated.

When it became clear that his horror fiction had not found a commercially viable audience, Watson embarked upon a further experiment in popularization, writing tie-in novels for Games Workshop. Unlike most of the other writers who briefly formed the GW stable—"Jack Yeovil" (Kim Newman), "Brian Craig" (Brian Stableford) and "David Ferring" (David S. Garnett)—Watson elected to use his own name, and while the other writers preferred the imaginary universes of GW's fantasy role-playing game *Warhammer* and the *Mad Max*-cloned board game *Dark Future,* he took on the more challenging task of working within the universe of GW's biggest seller: the space opera war game *Warhammer 40,000.* Although his Inquisition War series, which consisted of *Inquisitor, Harlequin,* and *Chaos Child*—he also wrote *Space Marine* set against the same background—was interrupted by the collapse of GW Books, it continued when the company franchised its literary offshoots to television tie-in specialist Boxtree. The *Warhammer 40,000* series seemed set for success until the administrators of Games Workshop, in spite of its popularity, made the seemingly paradoxical decision not to allow any more sales of the titles through the medium of their own shops.

While this fiasco was unfolding, Watson expanded the intriguing novella "The Flies of Memory" (1988) into a full-length novel of the same title, published in 1990. The original story explains how insectile aliens visiting Earth seem at first to be mere tourists interested in seeing and memorizing the same sights as the domestic variety—until the attractions in question begin to vanish. The hero, an expert in nonverbal communication, goes in search of the missing monuments, some of which are becoming reincarnate in the Martian wilderness. Although the unwinding plot eventually makes its way back to the metaphysical bedrock of *The Gardens of Delight,* it remains conscientiously quirky; even the heroine observes on the final page that its plot has had "too many Flies in the ointment."

The short fiction collected in *Salvage Rites and Other Stories* (1989), *Stalin's Teardrops and Other Stories* (1991), and *The Coming of Vertumnus and Other Stories* (1994), however, continued in the same determinedly id-

iosyncratic vein as their immediate predecessor, mingling science fiction, horror, and exercises in surrealism with considerable artistry. Those stories that are pure science fiction, including "When the Timegate Failed" (1985) and "In the Upper Cretaceous with the Summerfire Brigade" (1990), are buoyantly inventive but are perhaps less effective than such neat exercises in surrealism as "The Emir's Clock" (1987), "Stalin's Teardrops" (1990), "Gaudi's Dragon" (1990), and "The Odour of Cocktail Cigarettes" (1991) and such fine horror stories as "The Coming of Vertumnus" (1992) and "The Bible in Blood" (1994). The most adventurous science fiction story in these collections is the novella "Nanoware Time" (shorter version 1989; the longer version first appeared as half of a TOR double in 1991), in which alien nanotechnology allows human brains to transcend their former limitations.

All of Watson's novels of the 1970's and 1980's had been relatively short, but fashions in the marketplace had shifted to favor much longer works. Always willing to experiment, Watson set out to write the epic Book of Mana, published in two volumes of more than 500 pages each: *Lucky's Harvest* (1993) and *The Fallen Moon* (1994). Like many other works responding to the same pattern of commercial demand, it employs science fiction ideas to complicate and enhance a story that follows the template of best-selling genre fantasies. Watson's long expertise in contriving such hybrids was turned to good advantage in producing an account of the world of Kaleva, whose design owes a good deal to the Finnish mythology set out in the *Kalevala.*

Kaleva has been settled by humans brought through mana-space by a mineral life-form called an Ukko, who have established a quasi-feudal society. The dominant indigenes, the serpentine Isi, have domesticated the most humanlike of the native species, the Juttahat. The Isi refer to the Ukko as "the ears of the cosmos" and believe them to be important instruments of some kind of universal plan, but that does not prevent them from interfering with the people the Ukko have transplanted.

The Ukko's human discoverer, Lucky Sariola, has been made immortal by the Ukko—a privilege shared by her mate and descendants, who are key pieces in the Ukko's schemes. Those schemes unfold in the leisurely and stately manner typical of this kind of work, never achieving the complexity of the trilogy begun with *The Book of the River* or the baroque intensity of Watson's early metaphysical fantasies, but the story is eminently readable and the intricately woven backdrop of decoded myths adds a useful richness to the text. Watson did not abandon the setting when the novel was finished; "The Tragedy of Solveig" (1996) and "The Shortest Night" (1998) are further Kaleva stories.

Unfortunately, the Book of Mana was no more successful saleswise than Watson's other commercially motivated experiment, and he quickly moved on to a new phase, writing "technothrillers" of a kind that had become fashionable in the wake of best-sellers by Michael Crichton, Tom Clancy, and others. *Hard Questions* (1996) features a supercomputer and a charismatic cult leader engaged in industrial espionage, while *Oracle* (1997) features an experiment in time bending, funded by Military Intelligence, that displaces a Roman centurion from 60 A.D. into the present and entangles him with an IRA cell bent on assassinating the queen. Both novels are as skillfully executed and as readable as their immediate predecessors, but the thriller template operates in both as a narrative straitjacket that denies their science fiction ideas the room to develop beyond mere gimmickry.

"Being a freelance writer," Watson wrote in the endnote to Douglas Mackey's 1989 bibliography of his works, "rather resembles walking a tightrope—without visible end—stretched over a dark abyss. Sometimes you're up on the rope; sometimes you're hanging on by your fingernails. But while you're up, you got to dance on that rope. You got to dance."

Watson's attempts to stay on that tightrope resulted in the wild ambition of his early novels being somewhat curtailed in later full-length works, but his remarkable inventiveness continues to shine in his shorter fiction, where he trips the light fantastic without fear of falling. His frequent guest appearances at science fiction conventions in continental Europe—where his work has often been better appreciated than in his homeland—have enabled him to research the international settings he is so fond of deploying, and his shrewd observations of the relevant locales help to sustain the remarkable range of narrative flavors exhibited in his work. "Secrets" (1997), a novella inspried by the Vigelund sculpture park in Oslo, is an excellent example of the methodology that he employs in extrapolating art from experience.

Although many of Watson's short stories fall in or beyond the margins of the science fiction genre, the core of his work remains anchored therein. There are few writers who make use of science fiction devices as variously and as enterprisingly as he does in devising satires and allegories. Who but he would have enclosed a cycle of social history in the day-long time loop of "Early, in the Evening" (1996), or appointed the brother of the Son of God to be the pilot of the space probe to Tau Ceti III featured in "Such Dedication" (1996), or set the Space Navy to the work of intercepting the alien coffins projected into the solar system in "Ferryman" (1996)? In Watson's work, brevity is no enemy of complexity, as demonstrated by such tales as "Nanunculus" (1997), whose eponymous smart Web browser develops an agenda of its own while roaming cyberspace in the service of a California physicist whose investigations of negative time are disturbed by bad dreams.

Watson's commitment to the science fiction genre has also been expressed in supportive activities. He served for some years on the council of the Science Fiction Foundation when it was based at the North-East London Polytechnic and was the features editor of its journal. He has also been the European representative of the Science Fiction Writers of America for many years. He has written numerous book reviews and contributed to several reference books on the field. There is no doubt, taking the full range of his endeavors into account, that Watson has risen above his difficulties to make a greater contribution to science fiction than any other British writer of his generation.

Selected Bibliography

WORKS OF IAN WATSON

Japan: A Cat's Eye View. Osaka, Japan: Bunken Shuppan, 1969.

The Embedding. London: Gollancz, 1973; New York: Scribners, 1975.

The Jonah Kit. London: Gollancz, 1975; New York: Scribners, 1976.

Orgasmachine, with Judith Jackson Watson. Paris: Editions Champ-Libre, 1976.

Alien Embassy. London: Gollancz, 1977; New York: Ace, 1978.

Japan Tomorrow. Osaka, Japan: Bunken Shuppan, 1977.

The Martian Inca. London: Gollancz, 1977; New York: Scribners, 1977.

Miracle Visitors. London: Gollancz, 1978; New York: Ace, 1978.

God's World. London: Gollancz, 1979; New York: Carroll and Graf, 1990.

The Very Slow Time Machine: Science Fiction Stories. London: Gollancz, 1979; New York: Ace, 1979. (Short stories.)

The Gardens of Delight. London: Gollancz, 1980; New York: Pocket Books, 1982.

Deathhunter. London: Gollancz, 1981; New York: St. Martin's, 1986.

Under Heaven's Bridge, with Michael Bishop. London: Gollancz, 1981; New York: Ace, 1982.

Sunstroke and Other Stories. London: Gollancz, 1982. (Short stories.)

Chekhov's Journey. London: Gollancz, 1983; New York: Carroll and Graf, 1989.

The Book of the River. London: Gollancz, 1984; New York: DAW, 1986.

The Book of the Stars. London: Gollancz, 1984; New York: DAW, 1986.

Converts. London: Panther, 1984; New York: St. Martin's, 1985.

The Book of Being. London: Gollancz, 1985; New York: DAW, 1986.

The Book of Ian Watson. Willimantic, Conn.: Ziesing, 1985. (Short stories.)

Slow Birds and Other Stories. London: Gollancz, 1985. (Short stories.)

Queenmagic, Kingmagic. London: Gollancz, 1986; New York: St. Martin's, 1986.

Evil Water and Other Stories. London: Gollancz, 1987. (Short stories.)

The Power. London: Headline, 1987.

The Fire Worm. London: Gollancz, 1988.

Meat. London: Headline, 1988.

Whores of Babylon. London: Grafton, 1988.

Salvage Rites and Other Stories. London: Gollancz, 1989. (Short stories.)

The Flies of Memory. London: Gollancz, 1990; New York: Carroll and Graf, 1991.

Inquisitor. Brighton, England: Games Workshop, 1990.

Stalin's Teardrops and Other Stories. London: Gollancz, 1991. (Short stories.)

Lucky's Harvest: The First Book of Mana. London: Gollancz, 1993.

Space Marine. London: Boxtree, 1993.

The Coming of Vertumnus and Other Stories. London: Gollancz, 1994. (Short stories.)

The Fallen Moon: The Second Book of Mana. London: Gollancz, 1994.

Harlequin. London: Boxtree, 1994.

Chaos Child. London: Boxtree, 1995.

Hard Questions. London: Gollancz, 1996.

Oracle. London: Gollancz, 1997.

CRITICAL AND BIOGRAPHICAL STUDIES

Mackey, Douglas A. *The Work of Ian Watson: An Annotated Bibliography and Guide*. San Bernardino, Calif.: Borgo, 1989.

—BRIAN STABLEFORD

STANLEY G. WEINBAUM
(1902–1935)

STANLEY G. WEINBAUM was born in Louisville, Kentucky, and grew up in Milwaukee, Wisconsin. He graduated from the University of Wisconsin in 1923 with a degree in chemical engineering but felt that his real vocation was writing. He published one romantic novel in the early 1930's, under a pseudonym, but had achieved no considerable success when he turned his attention to the pulp science fiction magazines in 1934. He had been reading science fiction for some years and had already written two science fiction novels (which he did not submit to the pulps, presumably feeling that they were ill adapted to the demands of the market). His first published science fiction story, the classic "A Martian Odyssey," appeared in *Wonder Stories* in July 1934 and created an immediate impression. Although he died of throat cancer only seventeen months later, Weinbaum went on to produce twenty more science fiction stories aimed at the pulps, including one novel and two novellas. Two of these stories were collaborations with Ralph Milne Farley.

Despite his popularity, Weinbaum frequently had difficulty selling his stories to the science fiction pulps—his attempts to introduce a certain sophistication into his work were unwelcome. He failed to sell his novella "Dawn of Flame" and the novel that he wrote to "replace" it, *The Black Flame*, though both were published after his death and are now among the most fondly remembered examples of pulp scientific romance. One of his early science fiction novels, *The New Adam*, was eventually serialized in *Amazing*, but only after it had first appeared in book form. Another early novel, *The Dark Other*, did not see the light of day until it was issued by one of the fan-operated specialist publishers in 1950.

Weinbaum was the most accomplished of the early pulp science fiction writers—he could write well, he could construct plots cleverly, and he had a remarkably fertile imagination well fed by his reading in the sciences. The fact that he had to work so hard to accommodate the prejudices and formulaic requirements of the pulp editors shows how narrow and constricting they were. Many of Weinbaum's most influential contemporaries—John Taine, Stanton Coblentz, David H. Keller, and Miles J. Breuer among them—remained anchored in the formulas of 1930's pulp fiction even when better opportunities became available. There is no doubt that Weinbaum would not have been among them, had he lived; he would have probably taken advantage of those opportunities and could have become one of the best modern science fiction writers.

"A Martian Odyssey" is a remarkable adventure story about a member of the first expedition to Mars, who is temporarily separated from his companions and has to trek across the surface of the planet in order to rejoin them. He meets several weird and wonderful examples of indigenous life and forms a temporary alliance with a birdlike alien he names Tweel. The two can communicate only in a rudimentary manner because their thought processes are so different that they cannot begin to master each other's language, but this does not prevent them from cooperating to their mutual advantage. This story was the first attempt to present alien life as a working ecosystem utterly different from our own, and simultaneously to stress that biological estrangement need not necessarily generate mutual hostility. It makes a particularly vivid impression, not only because of its imaginative presentation of alien life but also because of its lively narration.

Weinbaum's next story written with the science fiction pulps in mind was "The Circle of Zero," an unsatisfactory glimpse-of-the-future story based on the notion that in a genuinely infinite universe everything possible must eventually happen. It failed to sell (though it was published posthumously in 1936), and Weinbaum retreated quickly to his winning formula. He produced six more stories with a structure basically similar to that of "A Martian Odyssey." "Valley of Dreams" is a sequel; the others are "Flight on Titan," "Parasite Planet," "The Lotus Eaters," "The Planet of Doubt," and "The Mad Moon." The later stories are enlivened by the addition of romantic interest, but each thrives on the bizarre life forms that plague the central characters. The best of them are "Parasite Planet" and "The Lotus Eaters," both set on Venus, where virtually all life in the twilight zone, whether it be plant or animal, is dangerous. "The Lotus Eaters" features a highly intelligent plant whose fatalistic psychology is explored in some detail.

Weinbaum found a second successful formula in "Pygmalion's Spectacles," in which a young man is asked by an aging and eccentric scientist to test an invention that supplies synthetic experience—a film that can be lived in. The protagonist falls in love with the girl he meets in the "film" and is delighted to find that she is the scientist's daughter. This format was used again in a trilogy of romantic comedies featuring the inventions of the great physicist Haskel van Manderpootz and their effect on the love life of his former pupil Dixon Wells. In "The Worlds of If" Wells obtains a glimpse of a world that might have

been and witnesses his meeting with a girl who dies in a plane crash. Realizing that in the real world she might still be alive, he tracks her down, only to find that she has married the man who saved her. "The Ideal" features a machine for visualizing thoughts that shows Wells his ideal woman, and "The Point of View" has a machine that allows its users to see the world as others see it. The plot of each story moves along the same trail of ironically broken romance.

Weinbaum's next attempt to diversify, by writing a serious romantic story set in the future, led to the production of *The Black Flame*. The first draft of the story, "Dawn of Flame," is set in a postholocaust world where civilization is slowly being restored by the autocratic conqueror Joaquin Smith. The hero, Hull Tarvish, fights to resist the spread of Smith's empire but finds himself on the losing side, saved from execution by the intervention of Smith's sister, Margaret of Urbs. Margaret, called the Black Flame because of her great beauty, shares the secret of immortality with her brother and his associates. Tarvish falls in love with her, somewhat against his will, but remains sufficiently loyal to his cause to facilitate an attempt on her life. The story has little fantastic content, though the plot turns on the fact that the Black Flame is immortal and her would-be lover is not. When the pulps rejected the story, Weinbaum rewrote it, adding a great deal of science fictional apparatus to the plot—superscientific weapons, monsters, and a time-traveling hero—and making the ending conform more closely to pulp traditions. Unfortunately, it was to no avail. *The Black Flame* (1948) contains both stories, even though there are certain internal inconsistencies between them.

Following this defeat, Weinbaum again retreated into conventionality, although he retained his fascination for femmes fatales. His first space opera, "The Red Peri" (book form, 1952), features a beautiful female space pirate determined to wreak havoc upon the company that stole her father's invention and destroyed his career. Rather more interesting is the pseudonymous story "The Adaptive Ultimate," which appeared in the same 1935 issue of *Astounding*. Here the femme fatale is the superhuman Kyra Zelas, created by a medical miracle. She is beautiful, clever, and completely amoral; and the doctor responsible for her creation—even though he is in love with her—decides that she must be destroyed before she achieves absolute power over the human race. This was to become Weinbaum's most successful story, and it was adapted for television and filmed as "The She-Devil" in 1957.

Weinbaum wrote a second story as "John Jessel," the name that he signed to "The Adaptive Ultimate." It was "Proteus Island," a story of radiation-induced mutations, which did not sell until after his death.

Femmes fatales of a slightly less charismatic quality are featured in both of Weinbaum's collaborations with Farley. The first, "Smothered Seas," tells of the seduction of an American scientist by the daughter of a khan whose war with the United States has reached stalemate. The stalemate is broken by the sudden and puzzling prolific growth of algae on land and sea, and the hero only just manages to preserve the secret after his beautiful enemy delivers him into the hands of her masters. Weinbaum completed the first draft of the other story on his deathbed, and Farley prepared it for publication sometime afterward. It finally appeared in 1938 as "The Revolution of 1960." The story deals with the end of a near-future fascist dictatorship in America. The dictator turns out to be the sister of the man who was actually elected president, having stepped into her brother's shoes after his sudden death. She maintains her masquerade with the aid of synthetic testosterone, and the regime falls when the hero sabotages her supply. As in so many of Weinbaum's stories, the hero and heroine are made enemies by their political loyalties but cannot help falling in love even as they try to destroy each other.

Of Weinbaum's other posthumously published short stories, only one—his second space opera, "Redemption Cairn"—is of any interest. Although its plot, concerning a dis-

credited space pilot who gets a chance to redeem his reputation, is hackneyed, it has a certain vivacity. (It also has a heroine nicknamed "the Golden Flame.")

The true measure of Weinbaum's ability became apparent only slowly. "Dawn of Flame" became the title story of a small, privately printed edition of Weinbaum's best works in 1936 but did not find a wider audience until it was reprinted in *Thrilling Wonder Stories* in 1939, soon after the editor of the remodeled magazine had used *The Black Flame* as the lead novel to launch the first issue of its companion magazine, *Startling Stories*. In the same year *The New Adam* appeared.

The New Adam, written in the early 1930's, is undoubtedly Weinbaum's best work and a novel of some significance in terms of the historical development of science fiction. It is the biography of Edmond Hall, a genetic freak who is one of the first members of the species *Homo superior*. Like Olaf Stapledon's *Odd John* (1935), which must have been written shortly afterward, it appears to have been inspired by John Beresford's classic superman story *The Hampdenshire Wonder* (1911) (the range of philosophical references contained in the two novels overlaps somewhat).

The Hampdenshire Wonder dies in infancy; but Edmond Hall, like Odd John, grows to maturity. The first part of the novel follows his pursuit of knowledge; the second—a mere four pages long—explains his contemptuous rejection of the pursuit of power; and the third, titled "The Pursuit of Pleasure," describes his ill-fated quest for personal fulfillment. Hall is different from the stereotyped image of the superman prevalent at the time in that he is not emotionless (though he does lack a sense of humor). He is capable of love and marries a girl named Evanne, but the romance is doomed because they are so different. In the end he realizes that he is in essence a "feral child," analogous to human children raised by wolves, intellectually crippled by his environment. He decides to die for the sake of Evanne's future happiness but first meets a woman of his own kind, leaving her with a child after a passionless affair.

Weinbaum obviously was well aware of the gulf between this story and the mythology of pulp science fiction. In the latter the superman (like the alien in "A Martian Odyssey") was almost invariably a figure of menace. Stories such as John Russell Fearn's *The Intelligence Gigantic* (1933; book form, 1943) concentrated entirely on attempts to destroy the superman lest he take over the world; there was no attempt to imagine what *Homo superior* might really be like, let alone what he might feel if he found himself in our world. Weinbaum's own awareness of this prevailing attitude is evident in "The Adaptive Ultimate." *Odd John* is a marginally better-written work than *The New Adam*, but its superman is used primarily as a mouthpiece for Stapledon's waspish social criticism; of the two, *The New Adam* is the more thought-provoking work. The "feral child" analogy is exactly right, and it adds a dimension to the story that no subsequent superman story has possessed.

Ironically, by the time *The New Adam* was serialized in *Amazing*, the sympathetic superman had arrived in pulp science fiction, courtesy of A. E. van Vogt, and was about to become one of the most important symbols in the genre through Henry Kuttner's "Baldy" series, Wilmar H. Shiras's *Children of the Atom*, and Zenna Henderson's stories of "the People." As in other matters, Weinbaum was simply ahead of his time with regard to the tenor of magazine science fiction.

The Dark Other, the remaining science fiction novel from Weinbaum's early days as a writer, is a Jekyll-and-Hyde story. The hero's troubles are caused by a curious tumor that is a tiny brain in its own right, housing an evil personality whose power grows as the neural pathways that connect it to the motor nerves become easier to use because of habituation. The idea is startling enough to belong in the pulps, but the story in which it is developed is, as usual, the story of an apparently ill-fated romance. This was not the sort of use to which pulp editors would have expected the

notion to be put. Although the novel is a minor work, it remains eminently readable and does not deserve the offhand dismissal afforded it by Sam Moskowitz in his biographical appreciation of Weinbaum.

In one sense Weinbaum's published science fiction—including the two early novels— does not really represent his interests or his ambitions. In an autobiographical sketch published in *A Martian Odyssey and Other Science Fiction Tales* (1975), he complains about both the attitude and the standard of pulp science fiction and suggests the untapped potential of the medium:

There's one general weakness and one universal fallacy in the material published today. It's a tough one to express but perhaps the proposition can be phrased as follows: Most authors, even the best, seem imbued with the idea that science is a sort of savior, a guide, the ultimate hope of mankind. That's wrong; science is utterly impersonal and never points a way, nor is it interested in either the salvation or the destruction of the human race. . . .

Here's the element that makes so much science fiction seem unreal. Half our authors use the word "scientist" about as the ancient Egyptians used "priest"—a man of rather special and mystical knowledge that has set him apart from the rest of humanity. In fact, as soon as the word is mentioned, one visualizes either a noble, serious, erudite, high-principled superman, or depending on the type of story, a crafty, ambitious, fiendish, and probably insane super-villain. But never a real human being.

As for the weakness, that's simpler. It's merely that most of our writers fail to take advantage of science fiction's one grand opportunity—its critical possibilities, if you get me. It's the ideal medium to express an author's ideas, because it can (but doesn't) criticize *everything*. . . . It can criticize social, moral, technical, political, or intellectual conditions. It's a weapon for intelligent writers, of which there are several, but they won't practice its use.

Weinbaum never, in the course of his brief career as a science fiction writer, attempted to practice what he preached. This must have been a source of much frustration as he slanted story after story toward his markets— and even then missed his target far too often. His marvelous accounts of otherworldly journeys, therefore, are essentially artificial products—entertainments run off for commercial reasons—and we cannot know what he might have written if he had followed his own inclinations.

But it would be wrong to think of Weinbaum's pulp stories as insincere pieces of hackwork. They must have amused and excited him, or they would not be so lively. He must have rejoiced in his creation of such fascinating creatures as Tweel, Oscar the intelligent plant, the carnivorous Jack Ketch trees of the Venusian twilight zone, and the maliciously cunning slinkers of "The Mad Moon," where delirious hallucinations upset the calculations of unwary humans. Weinbaum's plots are formulaic; but he made the formulas work hard and well for him, and he was expert in exploiting their potential.

Weinbaum was an influential writer in two ways. First, he popularized the notion that alien life-forms should be genuinely strange, that they should fit in with their own environment, and that they should have projects of their own that must be more than a mere reflection of the vulgarized account of human motivation that was implicit in pulp cliché. It was "A Martian Odyssey" that, more than any other story, persuaded the science fiction audience that there were more things in Heaven than were dreamed of in the philosophy of Edgar Rice Burroughs, and that the deployment of these things must somehow make sense, even though we might not be able to perceive what kind of sense.

Weinbaum's second influence was more subtle and was not so uniquely his. This was pointing out to readers and writers alike that desperately paced adventure stories could be spiced with wit, and that scientific ideas need not be presented in a heavy and deliberately ponderous fashion. He cultivated a kind of flippancy that never degenerated into pure farce, instinctively discovering a middle way

that his contemporaries found difficult to imitate, although some of them certainly tried. There is a playfulness in Weinbaum's best work that somehow manages to avoid seeming insulting to the ideas it treats so casually. That playfulness is one of the delights of science fiction, and though Weinbaum cannot compare with such masters of it as L. Sprague de Camp and Robert Sheckley, he was the first to realize that it worked.

In a fanzine article published in 1938, entitled "Science Fiction for Beginners," Arthur C. Clarke recommended that anyone wishing to win converts to the cause of science fiction should start by providing would-be victims with the three best stories of Stanley Weinbaum: "A Martian Odyssey," "Parasite Planet," and "The Lotus Eaters." That advice may have dated somewhat, but it is still possible to see the logic of it. Although these stories are hardly typical of the pulp fare of the day, they capture the essence of its excitement. They are naïve, but they are naïve in precisely the right way—their wide-eyed stare is directed into a kaleidoscope of wonders; like all good science fiction stories they imply far more than they can contain. In his exploration of the solar system, Weinbaum reached Uranus (in "The Planet of Doubt"), and Pluto (in "The Red Peri"), but never out toward the stars. Astronomy, in consequence, has banished every one of his marvelous worlds into the wilderness of pure fantasy. They have to be read today as "period pieces" rather than as living works of art. Nevertheless, any modern reader with a modicum of sensitivity can still appreciate their artistry, and the fortunate few may use them to recover a little of the imaginative glamour of the days before the solar system had been so thoroughly disenchanted.

Selected Bibliography

WORKS OF STANLEY G. WEINBAUM

Dawn of Flame. Jamaica, N.Y.: Ruppert Printing Service, 1936.

The New Adam. Chicago: Ziff-Davis Publishing Company, 1939.

The Black Flame. Reading, Pa.: Fantasy Press, 1948. Restored edition, San Francisco, Calif.: Tachyon, 1995. (Restored edition includes an introduction by Sam Moskowitz and a lengthy biographical account of the author.)

A Martian Odyssey and Others. Reading, Pa.: Fantasy Press, 1949.

The Dark Other. Los Angeles: Fantasy Publishing Company, 1950.

The Red Peri. Reading, Pa.: Fantasy Press, 1952.

A Martian Odyssey and Other Classics of Science Fiction. New York: Lancer, 1962.

The Best of Stanley G. Weinbaum. New York: Ballantine Books, 1974.

A Martian Odyssey and Other Science Fiction Tales. Westport, Conn.: Hyperion Press, 1975. (A complete edition of Weinbaum's short fiction.)

CRITICAL AND BIOGRAPHICAL STUDIES

Asimov, Isaac. "Five Greats of Science Fiction." In his *The Tyrannosaurus Prescription and 100 Other Essays.* Buffalo, N.Y.: Prometheus, 1989.

Chapman, Edgar L. "Weinbaum's Fire from the Ashes: The Postdisaster Civilization of *The Black Flame.*" In *Phoenix from the Ashes.* Edited by Carl B. Yoke. Westport, Conn.: Greenwood, 1987.

Moskowitz, Sam. "Dawn of Fame: The Career of Stanley G. Weinbaum." In *Explorers of the Infinite.* Cleveland, Ohio: World Publishing Company, 1963. (Reprinted in *A Martian Odyssey and Other Science Fiction Tales.*)

Stableford, Brian. "The Lost Pioneer: The Science Fiction of Stanley G. Weinbaum." In his *Outside the Human Aquarium: Masters of Science Fiction.* San Bernardino, Calif.: Borgo, 1995.

Young, Jim. "Before the Dawn: Weinbaum, Campbell, and the Invention of Modern Science Fiction." *New York Review of Science Fiction,* 18 (1990): 17–21.

———. "Before the Dawn: Weinbaum, Campbell, and the Invention of Modern Science Fiction (Part II)." *New York Review of Science Fiction,* 9 (1990): 15–19.

—BRIAN STABLEFORD

H. G. WELLS

(1866–1946)

It made a great difference when, as school-boys, we discovered that H. G. Wells was still alive. Books in the school library tended heavily to be written by the illustrious dead. Wells was living somewhere in London; this was World War II and London was under fire, but Wells was there, thinking, dreaming, arguing still, and dying.

He died in August 1946, after a life at war with ideas, almost indisputably the greatest science fiction writer of all. At its best, his fiction embodies stimulating ideas of unrivalled originality in such form that they have remained enjoyable. Wells the man is as entertaining as his fiction, for he retained until the end something of the diabolical mixture he ascribed to himself in adolescence: "a sentimentalist, a moralist, a patriot, a racist, a great general in dreamland, a member of a secret society, an immortal figure in history, an impulsive fork thrower, and a bawling self-righteous kicker of domestic shins." We are chiefly concerned here with the great general in dreamland.

I

Herbert George Wells was born on 21 September 1866, in Bromley, Kent, a town now entangled in the grubby outskirts of London. His parents were small shopkeepers in an ailing business—an environment introduced in many guises in many of his novels. He was a great reader and escaped a life of imprisonment behind shop counters by studying and becoming a student teacher, a sort of crammer of a now-vanished kind. Wells had an enormous capacity for learning, for sopping up facts. He earned himself a scholarship at the Normal School of Science, where he began, in 1884, a course of biology studies under the great Thomas Henry Huxley.

Intellectual and sexual freedom were heady joys. Wells expanded like a fire balloon. He began writing, accepting any hack job, and turned to short stories, for which he found he had a ready knack and a ready market. *The Time Machine*, in its final form, was developed from a series of articles and published in 1895. Before the death of the old century, the name of H. G. Wells was famous. Soon his publishers, who were not on oath, labeled him "The Most Famous Writer in the World." He remained in the public eye, stirring things up, quarreling, arguing, preaching, amazing, until the end of his life.

In many ways, Wells owed his escape from the servitude of trade to such parliamentary reforms as the Education Act of 1870 and the repeal of a tax on paper, with a subsequent multiplication of journals and possibilities for self-improvement. Industrialization, too, was providing a wider variety of jobs. When Wells's book of essays, *Anticipations*, was published in 1901, he could speak confidently of "the new class of capable men on which we have convinced ourselves in these anticipations the future depends." He undoubtedly thought of himself in that light. He had experienced vast changes in his own past life; it was natural to write about vast changes in the future. Besides, those changes were part of his quarrel with the present.

II

Something like 120 books bear Wells's name—a small but significant proportion of them science fiction. The science fiction titles divide, by general consent, into those published up to *The First Men in the Moon* (1901) and those published after. Those published after, while considerable in many ways, become increasingly didactic. The earlier group, often mythopoeic in tone, retain their sparkling imaginative quality and are frequently reprinted.

The early group contains six novels of first importance, and some collections of short stories, in which Wells hit on the idea of using a scientific invention, a little-known law of nature, or an anomaly of nature (like a still-surviving aepyornix) as the fulcrum of an entrancing pedantry-free tale to delight the general reader. Thus he stands as the founder and general propagator of the science fiction short story.

The first of the novels is *The Time Machine*. Many rank it as Wells's best book; certainly its qualities are striking and direct.

An inventor, given no name beyond a title, the Time Traveller, perfects a time machine in which he makes a trip into the future, stopping first in the year 802701 and then several times at thousand-year intervals in remote futurity, watching "the life of the old earth ebb away." He returns to the present to tell his tale to his friends and then disappears, never to be seen again in his own age. That is all; nothing could be simpler.

In the tale the Time Traveller tells, one can see the outline of Wells's quarrel with the present. As Robert Philmus and David Hughes have pointed out (*H. G. Wells*, 1975), Wells liked to run counter to received opinion, and to pursue an opposite idea by standing the accepted idea on its head—a method that served well both George Bernard Shaw

and that master of paradox, G. K. Chesterton, both of whose best work also appeared before the outbreak of World War I.

The Time Traveller's two stops illustrate reversals of two common late-Victorian assumptions. The world of the effete Eloi and the subhuman Morlocks dramatizes a state of society where the middle and working classes have pulled farther apart, rather than coalescing as both Marxists and liberal politicians anticipated. And the dying world represents, with memorable bleakness, the culmination of an evolutionary process that, far from working to the advantage of man, wipes him off the slate entirely.

These two ideas are juxtaposed and described in a lean prose. Nobody who reads Wells's account of the dying earth ever forgets it. All time-travel stories since owe a debt to Wells; none has become so acclaimed.

The Island of Dr. Moreau was published a year after *The Time Machine*, in 1896. Wells described it as "an exercise in youthful blasphemy."

Edward Prendick is shipwrecked on a Pacific island on which Dr. Moreau, aided by an assistant called Montgomery, is conducting experiments in vivisection, aimed at turning animals into human beings. The animals, grotesquely mutilated, learn through fear to copy human speech and behavior, but the system breaks down; first Moreau and then the drunken Montgomery are killed, until Prendick is left alone with the Beast People as they relapse into animal savagery. The film of evolution is run backwards; incident follows incident with the lucidity of an evil dream.

Wells himself saw that his novel owed something to Mary Shelley's *Frankenstein* (1818). A debt to Jonathan Swift is also apparent. Yet no one has created better monsters than Wells, here and in *The War of the Worlds*, in their horror and their pathos. To perceive the power of Wells's fable, one has only to ask oneself the unanswerable question: do the Beast People horrify us more because they are like animals, or because they are like ourselves? Actually, fable is not quite the right term for *Moreau*. Jorge Luis Borges was nearer the mark when he called it "an atrocious miracle."

The year after *Moreau* came *The Invisible Man*, Wells's story of another "strange and evil experiment," to use Wells's own words at the novel's conclusion. Invisibility, which should give the scientist Griffin such rare advantage over the world, proves a curse. Griffin's tale is set in the village of Iping, among ignorant villagers. Perhaps the novel has never been quite as popular as it might have been because the author allows us to identify with neither Griffin nor the villagers. Yet it is an arresting story, from the very first paragraph, when the stranger arrives in the village under snow, wrapped from head to foot so that not an inch of him shows, and takes a room at the inn. About the end there is a grand inevitability: Griffin regains normal opacity only in death; slowly his battered body rematerializes beneath the gaze of the awestruck mob, on his face an expression of anger and dismay.

Following swiftly on Griffin's elusive heels came *The War of the Worlds* (1898), to set the seal on Wells's success. The novel was immediately taken up in Britain and America, and translated into European languages. It has remained popular ever since, spawning many imitations, fathering all invasion-of-earth stories, yet still transcending them all in the grandeur of its concept.

Nowadays, people will believe anything; and they exist in a world-situation of insecurity. The Victorians of the 1890's were reasonably secure, reasonably arrogant. Wells took advantage of that situation. Hubris was going to be clobbered by nemesis, and he made the matter clear in the first paragraph of his new book, in what is perhaps its most-quoted sentence: "Across the gulf of space, minds that are to our minds as ours are to those of the beasts that perish, intellects vast and cool and unsympathetic, regarded this earth with envious eyes, and slowly and surely drew their plans against us."

Wells's quarrel proceeded along his now clear-cut lines. Instead of our being the imperialists, the conquerors—supposing something arrived that fully intended to conquer us? Suppose we were the underdogs? So the Martian ships arrive outside London, heat rays sizzle, and very soon the fighting machines begin their march towards the capital. "A walking engine of glittering metal. . . . As it passed it set up an exultant deafening howl. . . ."

Not pleasant, and the Martians themselves are even nastier. But Wells's nastiness really wounds because there is the poison of moral purpose at its tip; he makes it clear that these are not just alien monsters, to be loathed for their remoteness from our affairs like the Morlocks; they are what we may become. The conquering Martians, like every other living thing, are at once the products and victims of evolution. For all their pride, they fall prey to bacteria, and decay and stink in death just as we do.

The War of the Worlds is the great general of dreamland's grandest scientific romance of the early group. Only the human side of the novel is less than satisfactory; one can really feel few pangs at their destruction. It is the Martians one remembers, and ruined London, and the threat that the invaders will return.

These books and many of Wells's best short stories were produced in a great outburst of creativity, a celebration of his escape from drapery shops forever. Among the stories are such beautiful and touching ones as "The Country of the Blind" (1904), "The Man Who Could Work Miracles" (1898), "The Star" (1897), and "The Door in the Wall" (1906). Some of these tales of miraculous events are told with a pawky humor, which has now become dated. ("This heavy missile, which slid over him sideways and collapsed into a sitting posture among the strawberry plants, proved to be our long-lost Mr. Gottfried Plattner, in an extremely dishevelled condition. . . .") Yet what science fiction writer since Wells can point to such a splendid collection of stories? Their images have enriched literature and our imagination.

When the Sleeper Wakes (1899) is not an assured performance. There is something tired about the idea of a sleeper sleeping for

H. G. Wells. PHOTO COURTESY OF THE LIBRARY OF CONGRESS

centuries (the text excuses itself by talking of Rip Van Winkle and Bellamy), and the future world into which he awakens after two hundred years is sadly doctrinaire—sadly because it heralds the new Wells who was awakening, more interested in preachments than dreams and images. Wells remained curious about the idea of a slave-state; it was evidently a vision that both appalled and attracted him. The great turbulent city-state of thirty-three million people is a bold imagining, and Wells tells a vividly exciting story. From most writers it would have been enough.

The Morlocks in *The Time Machine* represent his first slaves—a slave-state in embryo, as it were. The Selenites, in *The First Men in the Moon* (1901), live in a graded slave-state under the Grand Lunar. Later, in Wells's *A Modern Utopia*, he pays more careful attention to the rulers of the state, the Samurai. His Samurai are that same "new class of capable men on whom the future depends. . . ." By the end of his life, Wells saw both sides of this divisive dream as failures, involved in a destructive prenuclear war. And who is to say he was not right in part? The world wars in

this century helped cause rather than prevent the present disarray in the West.

The last and most complex of this first group of novels is *The First Men in the Moon*. The two first men, Bedford and Cavor, are well-contrasted; the civilization of the Selenites is excellent both as horror and satire; and the novel abounds with wonderful passages of unforced description at which Wells is unrivalled—a good example being chapter 7, "A Lunar Morning," where life dawns with the light. "Quite unforgettable," said T. S. Eliot. It matters no more now than it did in 1901 that what is being described belongs to the realm of the impossible. The chapter on the "Natural History of the Selenites," a macabre yet never merely fanciful fantasia on evolution, is possibly Wells's masterstroke. This lovely book also contains much of Wells's delightful humor; it has kept the joints of his discourse oiled to this day. After *The First Men in the Moon*, Wells's science fiction novels are never quite the same. They become more like the writing of lesser science fiction authors, the story interspersed with preachments, which chase grandiose but unworkable ideas (like Wells's Open Conspiracy). The vision is intermittent, the themes concocted.

For all that, there is much to admire, quite apart from Wells's energy. In any case, there is a limit to the amount of unselfconscious dreaming one writer can do; after a while, if he is not to repeat himself, he must cast his net elsewhere and seek the fish that formerly swam to him unbidden.

The Food of the Gods and How it Came to Earth (1904) starts excellently in the old style, with a sinister experimental farm dozing in the English sunlight, and giant rats dragging off a dead horse to devour. Boonfood, the new miracle growth-accelerator, also breeds giant children; when they grow up—up being forty feet high—they confront humanity, "the little people," and here Wells's detestation of humanity in general overcomes one of his most agreeable traits, his siding with the underdog. But by this time, Wells was himself no longer an underdog but a highly successful author. He grew to view the state and its affairs as of more importance than the individual; this was his last great opposite idea, and it helped kill him as a writer.

In 1905 came an ambitious volume, all about keeping the little people (mankind) in order in convenient ways: *A Modern Utopia*. It is vexing and often difficult to read, and nobody has ever cared for it greatly; the horrific events of our century have cast a sinister light on much that is innocently proposed. Yet it is the first worldwide utopia, and repays study. Wells was forced to change science fiction horses, to write of outward things now that he had tapped the inward ones. Mary Shelley did not write in the utopian tradition; nor did Wells, to begin with; he "did not pretend to deal with possible things." However, he was stuck with the label "the English Jules Verne," and Verne did write in the utopian tradition of the Enlightenment and earlier. From *A Modern Utopia* onward, Wells seemed to have no option but to write in this more public style. His mythopoeic vein had run dry at last, and the great general of dreamland was forced to look for an army elsewhere.

The War in the Air (1908), *The World Set Free* (1914), *Men Like Gods* (1923), *The Shape of Things to Come* (1933), *Star-Begotten* (1937), and one or two other titles may still be read; but they seem more and more like dinosaurs and their journalistic bones show through the shrunken skin.

III

Wells had his problems with the critics, which sprang from his mercurial temperament. He was not content to write one sort of book. The reviewers called him a "darting, diving creature"—a description in which he probably rejoiced. Among his early novels, which gave and still give pleasure, and won for Wells a lasting second reputation, are *Love and Mr. Lewisham* (1900), *Kipps* (1905), *Tono-Bungay* (1909), *Ann Veronica* (1909), *The History of Mr. Polly* (1910), and *The New Machiavelli* (1911).

Wells also took it upon himself to be a popular educator and write outlines of practically everything. *The Outline of History* (1920) was followed by *The Science of Life* (1931) and *The Work, Wealth and Happiness of Mankind* (1932). Just because such books are now dated, one need not forget Wells's marvelous ability to argue, summarize, and dramatize. Many thousands of people, deprived of as good an education as they wished, regarded Wells as their university.

One of the best of Wells's nonfiction books dates from 1934. It is his *Experiment in Autobiography*, a frank and enthusiastic account of his life. As is often the case with autobiographies, the early years are particularly vivid, and this part of Wells's book is a valuable social document even for those unfortunates impervious to Wells's enjoyment of life.

He also dabbled in politics and knew everybody. His friends were drawn not only from the world of letters and from politics, but from journalism. Wells's name remained in the newspapers. Above all, he foresaw the necessity for some kind of world reconstruction along collectivist lines; while recognizing the unique contribution of Western civilization and its technology toward unifying the globe, he saw clearly the weaknesses of democracies. Yet he saw that the democracies must insist on certain freedoms hard to come by elsewhere: freedom of thought and worship, for instance, freedom of movement. Some of these perceptions were set forth in the shape of guiding principles under a committee assembled by Wells and chaired by Lord Sankey during the war, in 1940, and known as the Sankey Declaration of the Rights of Man. The Sankey Declaration influenced the Universal Declaration of Human Rights which was adopted by the United Nations after the war, when Wells was dead.

At a memorial service for Wells, Winston Churchill said a striking thing: "Few first-class men of letters have more consistently crabbed and girded at the national society and the social system in which they have had their being. Fewer still have owed so much to its ample tolerations and its magnificent complications."

Nor must Wells's career as a writer be represented as steadily downhill. One of his best-known books—by title if not by personal acquaintance—is *Mind at the End of its Tether* (1945), in which Wells appears to despair of mankind and refers to earth as "our doomed formicary." It was during this period that he told Sir Ernest Barker that his epitaph was to be: "God damn you all: I told you so." Yet during those last war years he was capable of the old Wellesian cockney spirit, and of lighter things. One of his most enjoyable books is *All Aboard for Ararat*, published in the ill year of 1940.

Ararat is full of wit and autumn sun. God comes knocking on Mr. Wells's door to inform him of a second flood; Wells, writing a new book which will save the world, is too busy to see him. So it begins, and goes on in lighthearted vein, although bearing a serious message: a late victory for the great general.

Wells's status in his several fields of activity was always under debate, even in his lifetime. His suspicious and demanding attitude toward publishers meant that his writings were published by many different ones, with the result that anything approaching a "Collected Works" is impossible. Nevertheless, much that he did is still valued, nowhere more so than in the science fiction field, where his highly readable early books and stories have fired many imaginations, and have been properly treasured.

However uncertain Wells's ultimate critical reception, there is no doubt about his continued popular reception. Almost all of the books and stories mentioned in this article have been made into radio plays, motion pictures, television plays, or musicals. (*Half a Sixpence* was a musical version of *Kipps*.) Among the most lastingly delightful of these are the motion pictures of *Kipps* (1941), *Things to Come* (1936), and *The War of the Worlds* (1953).

The science fiction field has yet to produce a greater figure than H. G. Wells. Not only his best work but his spirit still lives, for those who study this careless, loving, quarrelsome man. The best tribute ever paid him was by one of his many lovers, Rebecca West, who said that she found in H. G. Wells "everything one imagines in the way of genius and fun."

Selected Bibliography

SCIENCE FICTION WORKS OF H. G. WELLS

The Time Machine. London: Heinemann, 1895; New York: Henry Holt, 1895. (The Holt edition, which was published slightly earlier than the one by Heinemann, does not represent Wells's final text.)

The Island of Dr. Moreau. London: Heinemann, 1896; New York: Stone and Kimball, 1896.

The Invisible Man. London: C. Arthur Pearson, 1897; New York: Edward Arnold, 1897.

The War of the Worlds. London: Heinemann, 1898; New York: Harper and Brothers, 1898.

When the Sleeper Wakes. London and New York: Harper and Brothers, 1899.

The First Men in the Moon. London: George Newnes, 1901; Indianapolis, Ind.: Bowen-Merrill, 1901.

The Food of the Gods and How It Came to Earth. London: Macmillan, 1904; New York: Scribners, 1904.

A Modern Utopia. London: Chapman and Hall, 1905; New York: Scribners, 1905.

The War in the Air. London: George Bell, 1908; New York: Macmillan, 1908.

The World Set Free. London: Macmillan, 1914; New York: E. P. Dutton, 1914.

Men Like Gods. London: Cassell, 1923; New York: Macmillan, 1923.

The Works of H. G. Wells. Atlantic Edition. New York: Scribners, 1924 ff.

Complete Short Stories. London: Ernest Benn, 1927. Reprinted as *The Short Stories of H. G. Wells.* Garden City, N.Y.: Doubleday, Doran, 1929. (Contains all of the stories discussed in this article.)

The Shape of Things to Come. London: Hutchison and Company, 1933; New York: Macmillan, 1933.

Seven Famous Novels. New York: Knopf, 1934.

Star-Begotten. London: Chatto and Windus, 1937; New York: Viking, 1937.

All Aboard for Ararat. London: Secker and Warburg, 1940; New York: Alliance Book, 1941.

CRITICAL AND BIOGRAPHICAL STUDIES

Aldiss, Brian W. *Billion Year Spree: The History of Science Fiction.* London: Weidenfeld and Nicolson, 1973; Garden City, N.Y.: Doubleday, 1973.

Batchelor, John. *H. G. Wells*. Cambridge, England: Cambridge University Press, 1985.

Beiderwell, Bruce. "The Grotesque in Wells's *The Invisible Man*." *Extrapolation*, 24, no. 4 (1983): 301–310.

Bergonzi, Bernard. *The Early H. G. Wells: A Study of the Scientific Romances*. Manchester, England: Manchester University Press, 1961.

Bozzetto, Roger. "Moreau's Tragi-Farcical Island." Translated by R. M. Philmus and Russell Taylor. *Science-Fiction Studies*, 20, part 1 (1993): 34–44.

Burden, Brian J. "Decoding *The Time Machine*." *Foundation* (July 1984): 30–37.

———. "Decoding the Time Machine, 2: Across the Zodiac." *Foundation* (Winter 1985/1986): 23–38.

Coren, Michael. *The Invisible Man: The Life and Liberties of H. G. Wells*. London: Bloomsbury, 1993.

Costa, Richard Hauer. *H. G. Wells*. Rev. ed. Boston: Twayne, 1985.

Deery, June. "H. G. Wells's *A Modern Utopia* as a Work in Progress." *Extrapolation*, 34, no. 3 (1993): 216–229.

Dickson, Lovat. *H. G. Wells: His Turbulent Life and Times*. London: Macmillan, 1969; New York: Atheneum, 1969.

Draper, Michael. *H. G. Wells*. Houndsmills, Basingstoke, Hampshire, England: Macmillan, 1987.

Foot, Michael. *The History of Mr. Wells*. Washington, D.C.: Counterpoint, 1995.

Foundation (Autumn 1995). (Special issue on *The Time Machine*.)

Hammond, J. R. *H. G. Wells and the Modern Novel*. Houndsmills, Basingstoke, Hampshire, England: Macmillan, 1988.

———. *H. G. Wells and Rebecca West*. New York: Harvester Wheatsheaf, 1991.

———. *H. G. Wells and the Short Story*. New York: St. Martin's, 1992.

Kemp, Peter. *H. G. Wells and the Culminating Ape*. New York: St. Martin's, 1982.

Lake, David J. "Wells's Time Traveller: An Unreliable Narrator." *Extrapolation*, 22, no. 2 (1981): 117–126.

Lowentrout, Peter. "*The War of the Worlds* Revisited: Science Fiction and the Angst of Secularization." *Extrapolation*, 33, no. 4 (1992): 351–359.

Mackenzie, Norman, and Jeanne Mackenzie. *The Life of H. G. Wells: The Time Traveller*. Rev. ed., London: Hogarth, 1987.

Mackenzie, Norman and Jeanne. *The Time Traveller: The Life of H. G. Wells*. London: Weidenfeld and Nicolson, 1973. Reprinted as *The Life of H. G. Wells*. New York: Simon and Schuster, 1973.

McConnell, Frank. *The Science Fiction of H. G. Wells*. Oxford, England: Oxford University Press, 1981.

Murray, Brian. *H. G. Wells*. New York: Ungar, 1990.

Parrinder, Patrick. "Utopia and Meta-Utopia in H. G. Wells." *Science-Fiction Studies*, 12, part 2 (1985): 115–128.

———. *Shadows of the Future: H. G. Wells, Science Fiction, and Prophecy*. Liverpool, England: Liverpool University Press, 1995.

Philmus, Robert M., and David Y. Hughes, eds. *H. G. Wells: Early Writings in Science and Science Fiction*. Berkeley: University of California Press, 1975.

Raknem, Ingvald. *H. G. Wells and His Critics*. Oslo, Norway: Universitetsforlaget, 1962.

Ray, Gordon N. *H. G. Wells and Rebecca West*. New Haven, Conn.: Yale University Press, 1974.

Reed, John R. *The Natural History of H. G. Wells*. Athens: Ohio University Press, 1982.

Roemer, Kenneth M. "H. G. Wells and the 'Momentary Voices' of a Modern Utopia." *Extrapolation*, 23, no. 2 (1982): 117–137.

Rose, Mark. "Filling the Void: Verne, Wells, and Lem." *Science-Fiction Studies*, 8, part 2 (1981): 121–142.

Scafella, Frank. "The White Sphinx and *The Time Machine*." *Extrapolation*, 8, part 3 (1981): 255–265.

Scheick, William J., ed. *The Critical Response to H. G. Wells*. Westport, Conn.: Greenwood, 1995.

Science-Fiction Studies, 8, Part 1 (1981): 2–53. (Special H. G. Wells issue, with several critical essays on the author's work.)

Stableford, Brian. *Scientific Romance in Britain, 1890–1950*. London: Fourth Estate, 1985.

Wagar, W. Warren, ed. and comp. *H. G. Wells: Journalism and Prophecy, 1893–1946*. London: John Lane, 1964; Boston: Houghton Mifflin, 1964.

Wells, George P., ed. *The Last Books of H. G. Wells*. London: H. G. Wells Society, 1968.

West, Anthony. *H. G. Wells: Aspects of a Life*. New York: Meridian, 1984.

—BRIAN W. ALDISS

KATE WILHELM

(b. 1928)

KATE WILHELM WAS born Katie Gertrude Meredith on 8 June 1928 in Toledo, Ohio. She married Joseph Wilhelm in 1947, not long after graduating from high school and with no other destiny in mind than raising a family. It was while looking after her two sons that she renewed her early interest in writing.

Her first sale was "The Mile-Long Spaceship," which appeared in *Astounding Science Fiction* in 1957, although it was preceded into print by "The Pint-Sized Genie" (1956). She used the money from the *Astounding* sale to buy the typewriter she had rented in order to type it and began to write profusely. Her primary markets were the companions *Future* and *Science Fiction Stories*, edited by Robert A. W. Lowndes. Although she did not sell any of her early stories to Damon Knight, who briefly edited *If* in 1958, he noticed her work and invited her to one of the writers' "conferences" he was hosting in Milford, Pennsylvania, a town whose other residents included Judith Merril and James Blish. Wilhelm became Knight's codirector following their marriage in 1963, after she was divorced from her first husband in 1962. She published her first science fiction book, the short story collection *The Mile-Long Spaceship*, in the same year.

Wilhelm had already begun to diversify her production into other fields. Her first novel, also issued in 1963, was the mystery *More Bitter Than Death*. The editor who published it, Clayton Rawson, advised her to stick to a single genre, and she attempted to follow that advice for a while but eventually surrendered to the expansive pressure of her own inclinations. She was troubled after her move to Milford by an allergy that affected her eyes so badly as eventually to require surgery. Following her doctor's advice that it would be best to move out of range of the allergen if possible, she and Knight made an experimental move to Florida in 1968. The condition improved, but its full force was reactivated when they returned to Milford in 1969 so they moved away for good in 1971. They lived in Madeira Beach, Florida, before settling in Eugene, in Knight's home state of Oregon, in 1976. The "Milford Conference" moved with them, retaining its name.

When Robin Scott Wilson had visited the Milford Conference in 1967 to study its methods for the summer school he was developing at Clarion State College—which was launched the following year—Wilhelm and Knight had given enthusiastic support to the project, and Wilhelm became one of its regular teachers. Wilhelm took on the task of describing the workshop's procedure and explaining its alchemy in the anthology *Clarion* (1971; edited by Wilson), under the carefully understated rubric "Something Happens," and followed the argument through in her contribution to *Clarion II* (1972), "Why is it So Hard?" She went on to publish several more analytical articles about the art and practice of writing.

Wilhelm's early short fiction was conventional magazine fare. In "The Mile-Long Spaceship," aliens in search of worlds to conquer establish telepathic contact with a brain-damaged human; as he recovers, they stimulate an interest in astronomy in the hope of learning the location of his world, but his new appetite for knowledge directs his attention to the secrets of their technology. Wilhelm sold nothing more to *Astounding*, perhaps because she never contrived another plot twist so closely in tune with the expectations of its editor, John W. Campell, Jr. "Project Starlight" (1959) and "Brace Yourself for Mother" (1959) embrace Campbellian attitudes to the far frontier, but the former lacks conviction and the humor in the latter is half-hearted. "The Last Threshold" (1958) begins as a puzzle story but lapses into a sentimental tale of wish-fulfillment.

"Gift from the Stars" (1958), in which an ambitious property developer fails to dislodge an inconvenient shopkeeper who is actually an alien keeping tabs on human technological progress, moves smoothly to a softly admonitory moral. The story sounds a rather plaintive note, which became increasingly dominant in Wilhelm's early fiction. "Love and the Stars—Today!" (1959) is an early tale of overpopulation in a similar vein. "The Ecstasy of It" (1959) features Martian "life-forms" that infect the planet's cynical explorers with a much needed aesthetic sensibility. This phase of her work includes several tales of emergent artificial intelligence, all of which find the notion conventionally sinister: "Android, Kill for Me" (1959) features an android moved to commit a crime of passion by pulpish love stories; "A is for Automation" (1959) features an ingenious factory brain; "Andover and the Android"—one of five stories original to *The Mile-Long Spaceship*—is a sarcastically inverted love story.

The best of Wilhelm's early stories was "When the Moon Was Red" (1960), which appeared in *Amazing Science Fiction* even though it was not science fiction. It is a taut domestic drama in which the mother of a gifted child cannot persuade her assertive husband that his insistence on getting involved in all his son's projects is crushing the boy's creativity. She remains helpless as he prepares to leave her and bid for custody of the child, but the ingenious boy finds a brutal solution to the problem. Wilhelm did not include this story in *The Mile-Long Spaceship*, although she did include several small-scale psychological dramas whose genre credentials were more obvious, including "The Man Without a Planet" (1962) and two original items, "Jenny with Wings" and "No Light in the Window." Another story appearing for the first time in the collection, "Fear is a Cold Black"—which features an epidemic of distress aboard a spaceship—attempts to develop an acute sense of unease of a kind that was frequently to underlie Wilhelm's later work, but she omitted "A Time to Keep" (1962), which is much more powerful in focusing on the disintegration of a single individual's sternly conventional life.

Although the flow of Wilhelm's work was affected by her eye problem, she made every effort to keep going. She published "A Case of Desperation" (1964; reprinted as "The Feel of Desperation") in *Alfred Hitchcock's Mystery Magazine* and the escapist fantasy "The Man Who Painted Tomorrow" (1965) in *Fantastic*, and she had stories in the first two volumes of Damon Knight's *Orbit* series (1966 and 1967). She wrote a multiviewpoint disaster novel with Theodore L. Thomas, *The Clone* (1965), and published two novels of her own, *The Nevermore Affair* (1966) and *The Killer Thing* (1967). The first is situated in the margin where science fiction overlaps the thriller genre, reconnoitering a theme that was to recur frequently in Wilhelm's later work: the misuse of a technology of longevity. The second novel examines the moral and psychological "automation" of a man required to stop the depredations of a murderous machine.

Wilhelm said in a 1979 interview:

"I think I had a turning point when I was pregnant [with Jonathan, the son of her second marriage, born in 1966]. I didn't write for a year, and when I came out of that I had turned my head around, and I realised I wanted to do other things."

Kate Wilhelm. PHOTO BY JAY KAY KLEIN

The nature of that turnaround is perhaps best summarized by the difference between her contributions to Damon Knight's first two *Orbit* anthologies. The thoroughly orthodox science fiction story about deceptively child-like aliens "Staras Flonderans" (1966) was described by Knight as "a quiet and charming little thing" when he warned them that "Baby, You Were Great" (1967) was "strong meat." The latter story cleverly uses its science fiction apparatus, a technology for recording and transmitting emotional responses, to dramatize the manner in which culturally programmed emotional responses render women vulnerable to manipulation and exploitation. Its biting sarcasm sets the soft-centered plaintiveness of Wilhelm's early work firmly aside, replacing it with an appreciation of the human condition that attempts to be harder-headed as well as clearer-sighted.

Further signposts to Wilhelm's new direction were posted in 1968, when she published eleven stories, eight of which were original to *The Downstairs Room and Other Speculative Fiction*. The book's introduction, by James Sallis, talks about American short fiction in general and the significance within it of a visionary element, only using the term "science fiction" in passing while referring back to *The Killer Thing*. Wilhelm's story introductions contemplate the elusive mechanics of creativity without any mention of genre expectations. "When the Moon Was Red," "A Time to Keep," the retitled "The Feel of Desperation," and "Baby, You Were Great" are all included, but "The Man Who Painted Tomorrow" and "Staras Flonderans" are not.

The collection opens with "Unbirthday Party," a neat allegory in which an Everyman figure is an uneasy gate-crasher at a party on the wrong floor of his building, who is far from certain that he can find his way to the right floor when weariness and conscience press him to move on. "The Downstairs Room" is an effective domestic horror story. "The Most Beautiful Woman in the World" dissects a feminine paranoid delusion. "Countdown" is a delicate psychological study of the men whose everyday lives are spent nursing the ultimate nuclear deterrent. The remaining previously published items, "Windsong" and "The Planners," appeared in the same year as the collection in the third and fourth *Orbit* anthologies. They are the most ambitious stories in the collection, and they provide a graphic illustration of the benefit a writer can derive from the knowledge that a sympathetic editor is in charge of a ready market. Wilhelm was one of two writers—the other being Gene Wolfe—whose regular work for Knight's anthology series allowed them to stretch their imaginative ambition in a wonderfully fruitful fashion.

"Windsong," in which a male scientist must find the perfect human personality to inhabit the artificial brain of a powerful war machine, develops anxieties about the advancement of technology and the automation of human feeling that had already become key preoccupations of Wilhelm's work, but in a newly sophisticated manner. "The Planners," which won a Nebula award in 1969, develops a similar theme in connection with a more intimate kind of scientific research: neuro-physiological experiments carried out on apes and humans in the hope of understanding—and hence obtaining technical control—of the mechanisms of intelligence.

In Robin Scott Wilson's writers' guide, *Those Who Can: A Science Fiction Reader* (1973), Wilhelm says of "The Planners": "I wanted to tell the story of a man who is beset by self-doubts, whose marriage is a failure, whose work is troubling his conscience. Although things are happening in the real world of the story, it is about the inner man." That description could be applied—without modification, if "man" can be taken to include the female of the species—to the greater part of Wilhelm's subsequent work. Her best stories produce vividly convincing images of individuals afflicted—and sometimes torn apart—by self-doubts, failed marriages, and pangs of conscience; her best science fiction stories work speculative themes into these afflictions with great sensitivity. Sometimes the speculative element is a particular item that preys upon the central character's conscience and amplifies self-doubt, as Darin's work does in "The Planners" and Thornton's in "Windsong"; sometimes reality itself becomes fractured in such a way as to extrapolate, mirror, or ameliorate the inner distress of the key character, according to his or her nature and deserts.

This pattern was initially most conspicuous in shorter pieces and mostly used to horrific or alarmist effect. "Somerset Dreams" (1969), in *Orbit 5*, is a deeply disquieting tale in which an experiment in the psychology of dreaming reveals the dark truth about a sleepy small town to a woman on the brink of settling there. "April Fool's Day Forever" (1970), in *Orbit 7*—which was subsequently described by the author as an extrapolation of "the paranoia of pregnancy"—is a powerful story in which a woman who has been told that her two children have been born dead gradually uncovers a sinister conspiracy, designed for the defense of a slowly growing community of long-lived individuals who fear that common mortals might slaughter them

out of envy. By contrast, *Let the Fire Fall* (1969), in which the arrival of an alien spaceship whose crew members—save for a newborn "Star Child"—die before contact can be made, lends impetus to the development of a Millenarian cult, is diffuse, and lacks direction. Although it is certainly an advance on *The Killer Thing*, it does not represent the kind of quantum leap that distinguished "The Planners" from "Staras Flonderans." *The Year of the Cloud* (1970), a second collaboration with Theodore L. Thomas, which details the pollution of Earth's waters by a thickening agent that has intimate effects within the human body as well as disrupting the climate, is a thoroughly satisfactory but relatively conventional disaster novel.

The gradual adaptation of the new pattern of Wilhelm's work to increasingly longer formats was secured by three works first published in 1971. "The Plastic Abyss," issued in tandem with the relatively orthodox "Stranger in the House" (1968), in *Abyss*, is a tale of fractured reality in which the lives of a scientist's wife and daughter are subject to strange side effects of his work, whose psychological effects are further complicated by the secrecy enforced upon the characters by possible "defence implications." The protagonist of "The Infinity Box," in *Orbit 9*, finds himself psychologically bonded to the widow of a pioneering experimental psychologist who died under mysterious circumstances. He is brought to the brink of insanity and murder by the effects of the bond. The novel *Margaret and I*, which Wilhelm had begun to write in February 1967, soon after her crucial change of attitude, is even more adventurous; although it took some years to sell, it remains one of the most intriguing literary experiments of its era.

Margaret and I is prefaced by a quotation from Carl Jung that includes the rather atypical suggestion that "If the unconscious can contain everything that is known to be a function of consciousness, then we are faced with the possibility that it too, like consciousness, possesses a subject, a sort of ego." "Somerset Dreams," which had developed a version of the more familiar Jungian notion of the collective unconscious, had slotted readily enough into a whole subgenre of Jungian science fiction stories, but this hypothesis was so distinctive that *Margaret and I* has no ready parallel at all. The first-person narrator of the story is the ego of Margaret Oliver's unconscious, which begins the novel in a state of extreme estrangement from its distressed conscious equivalent.

Margaret seeks refuge from her unhappy marriage in a cottage that belongs to her husband's aunt Josie, but her troubles pursue her as her husband's employer—an ambitious maverick politician—pressures her both directly and indirectly to join his campaign staff. The pressure is further increased by a loathsome psychologist and his persuasively gifted research assistant, whose mistaken impression that she is the cottage's owner she encourages for her own reasons. They are anxious to take up and carry forward the work done by Paul Tyson, a physicist who was Josie's lover. As in "The Plastic Abyss," Tyson's researches into the nature of time have taken him into realms of abstruse philosophy, and as in "The Infinity Box," his death in mysterious circumstances has left a mind-bending legacy. That legacy enables the plot line laid down in the quote from Jung—"individuation is complete when the conscious and the unconscious learn to *know, respect,* and *accommodate* one another"—to unravel as Margaret and the story's first-person voice establish a kind of harmony.

The experiment was not wholly successful. The account of what Tyson's discovery actually amounted to is rather vague, and Margaret's redemption requires a deus ex machina whose deliverer might have stepped out of the pages of a genre romance. Nevertheless, *Margaret and I* is a fascinating work. It was initially published as a mainstream novel, but when it was reprinted in paperback seven years later, it was issued in Pocket Books' Timescape line, tacitly reclaimed by the science fiction genre. In the interim, Wilhelm produced three of her best novels, *City of Cain* (1974), *The Clewiston Test* (1976), and

Where Late the Sweet Birds Sang (1976). The first two are are intense psychological studies, the former extrapolating a more modest version of the central hypothesis of "The Infinity Box" and the second a more elaborate version of "The Planners."

In *City of Cain* a promising young scientist wounded in Vietnam finds that the damage to his brain has liberated wayward telepathic abilities as well as threatened his life. The pressure of his medical situation is redoubled when the political secrets he penetrates move his enemies to urgent action. The narrative tension builds inexorably to a finely wrought climax. In *The Clewiston Test* an ambitious research scientist who is granted a license to test a new generation of powerful analgesics on humans realizes that her original animal subjects are beginning to exhibit distressing side effects; the pressure on her is maximized by virtue of the fact that a road accident has left her in dire need of the treatment she is trying to develop.

The Clewiston Test accomplishes something that science fiction writers very rarely attempt: the depiction of scientific endeavor as an essentially human activity, intricately entwined with the ambitions, passions, and frustrations of life. Wilhelm's interest in the manner in which the work of scientists can be inspired and shaped by their personal and social circumstances was further developed in her contribution to *Orbit 15*, "Where Late the Sweet Birds Sang" (1975), which she expanded into a Hugo-winning novel the following year.

The dread secret revealed to the hero of *City of Cain* is that the U.S. government is building a self-sufficient underground city where the nation's political elite can sit out any collapse of social order—whose existence will inevitably deflect attention away from seeking solutions to impending catastrophes and whose maintenance will inevitably deliver ultimate authority to the scientists and technicians controlling its closed ecology. *Where Late the Sweet Birds Sang* takes up this theme, focusing on the Sumner family, whose settlement within the Shenandoah Valley becomes host to a similar but more exotic project. While the world succumbs to a sterilizing ecological catastrophe, David and Walt Sumner perfect a cloning technology that allows them to sustain their domestic stocks and multiply each of the family's unborn children into a "set."

The novella that forms the first part of the novel, like "April Fool's Day Forever," is content to describe the opening phases of the project and David Sumner's developing crisis of conscience as he repents of what he has done. The remaining sections follow the argument through in a methodical and far-reaching manner, tracking the evolution of the new society based on clonal sets across the generations, until the uniquely individual (and individualistic) Mark can lead a chosen few away from its oppressive environment to make a new start. As in "April Fool's Day Forever," the beneficiaries of the new technology are penalized by a dramatic loss of creativity, and it is on those grounds that the novel makes its plea for Nature against Artifice.

The anxious tone of *City of Cain* and *Where Late the Sweet Birds Sang* was characteristic of Wilhelm's work throughout the 1970's. Her third and fourth story collections, *The Infinity Box: A Collection of Speculative Fiction* (1975) and *Somerset Dreams and Other Fictions* (1978) are dominated by stories of costly conflict and insidious pollution at both the personal level and the social level.

The Infinity Box includes several tales of fractured reality. "The Fusion Bomb" (1972) and "Man of Letters" (original to the collection) deal rather mischievously with the patterning effects of a quasi-Jungian synchronicity, while "The Time Piece" (original) offers a more orthodox tale of time untied. It also includes some of Wilhelm's darkest tales, including the grimly dystopian "The Funeral" (1972) and two tales of unfolding catastrophe, the intense "The Red Canary" (1973) and the surreal "The Village" (1973).

The most striking story in *Somerset Dreams* is the harrowingly claustrophobic "The Encounter" (1970), in which a man trapped in a bus station by a snowstorm is forced to confront a past atrocity whose repression has shaped his personality. The remaining short stories are sardonically dour, ranging from a subtly disturbing tale of a physical haunting, "The Hounds" (1974), to the pointedly satirical "Ladies and Gentlemen, This Is Your Crisis" (1976), which offers a scathing account of couch potato culture. The same period produced two unremittingly bleak postcatastrophe stories, "A Brother to Dragons, a Companion of Owls" (1974) and "The Scream" (1974), but they were not collected until the first appeared in *Children of the Wind: Five Novellas* (1989) and the second in *And the Angels Sing: Stories* (1992).

Where Late the Sweet Birds Sang was followed by *Fault Lines* (1977), in which the same sense that twentieth-century civilization is cracking up is developed within a strictly realistic context. Although it has affinities with Wilhelm's earlier tales of fractured reality, the story has no speculative embellishment of the kind deployed in "The Plastic Abyss," "The Infinity Box," or *Margaret and I*. Wilhelm compiled a more detailed account of social and psychological corrosion associated with a slowly unfolding sequence of disasters in the meticulously developed and very effective *Juniper Time* (1979).

The female protagonist of *Juniper Time*, Jean Brighton, is the daughter of an astronaut. Her male counterpart, Arthur Cluny—who used to play with her when they were children—is a technologist who struggles to conserve the most precious and most glorious dreams of twentieth-century achievement while the American West is devastated by drought. Cluny needs Jean's expertise as a linguist to help translate an alleged message from the stars that might save his work, but she has fled the disintegrating society of the refugee-flooded East to live with the Native Americans who are patiently reclaiming their devastated heritage.

Juniper Time was the last of five Wilhelm books published by Harper and Row; the publisher also abandoned the *Orbit* series, whose twenty-first and last volume appeared in

1980. The penultimate one, published in 1978, had contained Wilhelm's long novella "Moongate," an exceptionally well written tale of a haunting and haunted desert landscape similar to those lovingly described in *Juniper Time*. The demise of *Orbit* was unfortunate for Wilhelm because few other outlets could handle such substantial pieces, but she did manage to place one equally fine item of comparable length, "The Winter Beach" (1981), in *Redbook*. She went on to publish several more stories there, including the novella "The Look Alike" (1988).

A Sense of Shadow (1981), an account of the gathering of a severely dysfunctional family in a house where hallucinatory flashes guide their imperfect memories to a reconstructed understanding of their past, was not initially released as a genre novel but was reprinted alongside *Margaret and I* in the Timescape paperback line. Its tight focus on soluble psychological problems allowed it to reach a more upbeat conclusion than many of Wilhelm's science fiction stories of the 1970's; the same is true of the solidly mainstream *Oh, Susannah!* (1982). Her range of concern became much broader, however, when she produced the science fiction novel *Welcome, Chaos* (1983), following the same basic formula as *Where Late the Sweet Birds Sang*. *Welcome, Chaos* extrapolates the idea displayed in the calculatedly tentative novella "The Winter Beach"—which had already been reprinted, along with "Moongate" and two shorter novellas, in *Listen, Listen* (1981)—to examine its socially transforming consequences.

Like *The Nevermore Affair* and "April Fool's Day Forever," "The Winter Beach" deals with the secret development of a technology of longevity and the attempts by its first beneficiaries to defend themselves against the anticipated envy of the mortal masses. The full-length version grasps the nettle from which the earlier stories had shied away, describing the aftermath of the decision made by the possessors of the technology to disseminate it despite its costs (in this case, the treatment kills those whom it does not cure of the disease of aging). As with its predecessor, the new wordage does not quite match the outstanding quality of the original story, whose acute sense of the beauty of the Oregon landscape matches that of "Moongate" and *Juniper Time*, but it is an earnest and intelligent attempt to think through the consequences of the initial hypothesis.

One of the other novellas included in *Listen, Listen*, "With Thimbles, With Forks, and Hope" (1981), eventually launched a project far more extensive, if not quite so ambitious, as *Welcome, Chaos*. It introduced psychologist and writer Constance Leidl and her husband, retired fire inspector and police detective Charlie Meiklejohn. Operating as part-time private investigators, they undertake to investigate the would-be holder of a huge life insurance policy who may intend to commit suicide. The investigation is complicated by the arrival of a ghoulish woman who turns out to be an immortal empath (a telepathic person who "reads" emotions instead of thoughts) addicted to the vicarious enjoyment of death; she decides, once Constance and Charlie have redeemed her intended prey, that they might as well serve in his stead. The couple encounters another psychically talented female in "Sister Angel" (1983), and they also featured in an equally fantastic tale of a power-impregnated landscape, "The Gorgon Field" (1985), before embarking on a more orthodox career as mystery solvers in the non-fantasy *The Hamlet Trap* (1987). This was Wilhelm's first book for St. Martin's Press, the most prolific American publisher of genre mysteries, which issued all her books thereafter.

Before St. Martin's became her publisher, Wilhelm published one more science fiction novel, *Huysman's Pets* (1986), which is considerably lighter in tone than its immediate predecessors. It takes up the Jungian notion of synchronicity, which she had previously developed in a more trivially conventional manner in "Man of Letters." The "pets" are a group of children used as an experimental sample by a Nobel Prize-winning psychologist. It appears that they can contrive amazing freaks of chance, which they employ to deflect the attention of anyone who takes an exploitative interest in them. The element of uncertainty arises because their fragmented story is filtered through the research of a writer exploring the possibility of writing a biography of their dead mentor. In the end, the writer—convinced that he, too, is being exploited—withdraws from the project in order to let Huysman's subjects go their own way, thus leaving the story's central idea rather frustratingly undeveloped.

Wilhelm's apparent decision to lighten up was further emphasized in her first science fiction novel for St. Martin's, *Crazy Time* (1988). The jacket copy refers to it as "a modern-day *Topper*," (Thorne Smith's 1926 novel) and it does indeed seem to have started out as a comedy in the extravagant vein of Thorne Smith. Eventually, however, it turns into something more profound and more interesting. The central idea of the story is carried over from the brief sarcastic fantasy "The Disassembler" (1987); it follows the adventures of "Corky" Corcoran, who has been discorporated but not destroyed by an experimental laser whose controlling computer has been briefly suborned by a hacker. Corcoran's attempts to keep close company with psychologist Lauren Steele—which is difficult while he cannot contrive to hold himself together for more than a few minutes at a time—convince her that she must be mad and persuade a paranoid army colonel that there is a Communist conspiracy afoot. As the plot unfolds, however, it surrenders its uninhibitedly farcical quality to become part comedy thriller and part metaphysical fantasy, with much discussion on the "other side" as to the apocalyptic consequences that might flow from Corky's unique state of being. The novel ends up being neither fish nor fowl, though it certainly qualifies as good red herring. It is a fascinating book, nevertheless, as rewarding in its own calculatedly unambitious way as *Margaret and I*.

Wilhelm's next novel, *The Dark Door* (1988), is a similarly chimerical hybrid, advertised on the jacket as "a science fiction novel" but starring Constance Leidl and Charlie Meiklejohn in their sternest investigative mode. The doubled-up frame narrative informs the reader in advance of the identity of the serial arsonist and the explanation for the odd phenomena that motivate his crusade, so the book never functions as a mystery, but it does become a remarkably tense thriller. The author cleverly exploits the duality of the threat her heroes must overcome; the nastiness of the supernatural "villain" is initially magnified by the recklessness of those humans who cannot believe in it and eventually increased yet again by the greater recklessness of those who can.

Although none of the books that Wilhelm published in the following decade was marketed as science fiction, she did employ a marginal science fiction element in *Smart House* (1989). This confronts Constance Leidl and Charlie Meiklejohn with a classically problematic murder mystery in which the list of suspects includes the computer controlling the fully automated house where the two victims perished, thus adding considerably to the complexity of the puzzle. The couple's next adventure, *Sweet, Sweet Poison* (1990), includes an "experimental farm" as one of its settings, but the murder mystery has not the slightest trace of science fiction about it. Their subsequent adventures—including *Seven Kinds of Death* (1992) and the novellas "All for One" and "Torch Song," in the collection *A Flush of Shadows* (1995)—are sober and realistic studies in the psychology of malice and avarice.

The series of courtroom dramas that Wilhelm began to write alongside the Leidl/ Meiklejohn mysteries made a similar transition from the margins of science fiction to solid realism. *Death Qualified: A Mystery of Chaos* (1991) is lightly but intricately spiced with chaos theory, computers, and superhuman powers, but *Justice for Some* (1993) and its successors deal exclusively in artful psychological complication. The most dramatic of all such transitionary sequences was, however, the loosest and longest-extended, which might be held to proceed from the thoroughly science fiction "Stranger in the House" through *A Sense of Shadow* to *The Good Children* (1998). All of these works feature "haunted houses," but the nature of the "hauntings" changes drastically. The last novel is a beautifully detailed account of the psychological problems experienced by a child whose older siblings cover up the death of their mother lest he and they be taken to an orphanage.

The fantasy novel *Cambio Bay* (1990) might also be regarded as an offshoot of the Leidl/Meiklejohn series in that it takes up the central motif of "The Gorgon Field" and develops it much more elaborately. Cambio Bay and its associated small town are situated at a climatic junction on the Pacific Coast, where the apparent wrath of storms is more than an example of the pathetic fallacy; the peaceful yet potent eye of such storms is an architecturally paradoxical guest house run by the mysteriously ageless Luisa Ravel. The novel's plot is a metaphysical mystery that, like *Crazy Time*, develops accessory dramatic tension by means of a thriller subplot. The subplot never really makes sense, as the characters dutifully point out, but it does serve as a useful hook for an examination of the psychological functions of myth and storytelling. This kind of fantasy element was, however, as carefully purged from Wilhelm's longer works of the 1990's as the element of science fiction. Another powerful tale of a haunted landscape, the Nebula-winning "The Girl Who Fell into the Sky" (1986), was reprinted alongside "The Gorgon Field" in *Children of the Wind*, but the long novella that gives the collection its title is a more subtle recapitulation of the kind of parental conflict depicted in "And the Moon Was Red."

The longest of Wilhelm's science fiction stories of the 1990's is the novella "Naming the Flowers" (1992), which follows the example of the Nebula-winning short story "Forever Yours, Anna" (1987) in employing a theme somewhat reminiscent of Robert Nathan's *Portrait of Jennie* (1940). The FBI is continually on hand to harass the adult hero,

making sure that no serious impropriety can possibly arise in his relationship with the mysterious little girl whose age is rapidly catching up with his. The title story of *And the Angels Sing* (1992) is a neatly sentimental account of a good man's encounter with an angelic alien. "Bloodletting" (1994) is an earnest tale of involvement in scientific research in the same vein as "The Planners" and *The Clewiston Test*. "I Know What You're Thinking" (1994) is a plaintive tale of a lonely telepath with echoes of *City of Cain*. "Forget Luck" (1996) is a flippant speculation about the lengths to which selfish genes might be able to go, which is distantly related to "The Fusion Bomb" and *Huysman's Pets*. These stories remain as effective in their various ways as the equally various non–science fiction pieces published alongside them.

Writers such as Kurt Vonnegut, Don DeLillo, and Marge Piercy have demonstrated that it is possible to build a reputation in the United States as a writer of literary fiction despite deploying science fiction ideas in a reasonably bold and blatant fashion. Kate Wilhelm found it exceedingly difficult to do likewise, for a variety of reasons. The stigma attached to her work by her early association with the genre magazines has probably been less of a handicap than the manner in which her work tends to focus on intimate matters of conscience and distress. Because her novels are neither satires nor utopian fantasies, they have avoided the principal grounds on which fantastic motifs have occasionally been granted a license to exist in the literary "mainstream" by its most influential critics.

The intricate relationships of theme and method that exist between all of Wilhelm's works emphasize, however, that her diversification from and gradual de-emphasization of science fiction subject matter was never a mere matter of searching for better and more prestigious markets. Her work has always had the same range of central concerns, whatever the genre location of its individual products, and it is a measure of the seriousness with which she has taken those concerns that she has produced several works that cannot be fitted to any ready-made spectrum of categories. It is the science fiction audience that has given most recognition to the quality of her work in the form of numerous awards, but one of the achievements thus recognized is that the elegance and brilliance of her work transcends the boundaries of literary branding.

In *Cambio Bay* Luisa Ravel, while rhapsodizing about the nature of myth and fiction, argues that all the "basic plots" that are perennially discussed in science fiction writers' workshops (because of the attention called to them by a notorious polemical essay on writing by Robert A. Heinlein) are actually variations on a single theme: "the unending struggle to achieve completion." "How strange it is," the character observes, "that we can accept so readily [all] the attributes of humanity . . . except two." The two attributes in question are mortality and "that terrible loneliness," which we cannot help but see as Nature's tragic mistakes, which really ought to be rectifiable if only we could find the way. *The Good Children* takes up that commentary on the nature and power of storytelling, but the use of a first-person narrator—very rare in Wilhelm's works—allows its observations to take on a special intimacy that Luisa Ravel's wise but distant pronouncements could not carry. In the novel's conclusion, the narrator insists that her story is not for the world but only for those particular individuals to whom it is uniquely meaningful; she means it, but the story's true author is running an easily penetrable bluff. The reader is supposed to appreciate that "the world" is made up of particular individuals to whom all good stories are uniquely meaningful.

In the much earlier *City of Cain*, Wilhelm had included a dialogue in which science is represented as a would-be usurper of the role of myth and fiction. The arrogant scientist Grange informs a female student (whose career and life he will subsequently wreck in the cause of paranoid self-defense): "Wherever the scientist turns his attention there is a infinite regression of beauty that the ignorant artist, whatever his field is, can never suspect, let alone appreciate." The student replies that art is more than "neat and orderly process" and insists that there is something in *human* being that can never be captured in the net of science's infinite regression. "There is a chaos of the soul," she says, her articulacy stumbling in the heat of passion, "that man right now is examining, for perhaps the first time."

Few science fiction writers have welcomed that chaos as politely and as lovingly as Kate Wilhelm, and few have examined it as carefully and sympathetically. Her work is precious on that account.

Selected Bibliography

WORKS OF KATE WILHELM

The Mile-Long Spaceship. New York: Berkley, 1963. Reprinted as *Andover and the Android*, London: Dobson, 1966. (Short stories.)

More Bitter Than Death. New York: Simon and Schuster, 1963; London: Robert Hale, 1965.

The Clone, with Theodore L. Thomas. New York: Berkley, 1965; London: Hale, 1968.

The Nevermore Affair. Garden City, N.Y.: Doubleday, 1966.

The Killer Thing. Garden City, N.Y.: Doubleday, 1967. Reprinted as *The Killing Thing*, London: Herbert Jenkins, 1967.

The Downstairs Room and Other Speculative Fiction. Garden City, N.Y.: Doubleday, 1968. (Short stories.)

Let the Fire Fall. Garden City, N.Y.: Doubleday, 1969; London: Herbert Jenkins, 1969.

The Year of the Cloud, with Theodore L. Thomas. Garden City, N.Y.: Doubleday, 1970.

Abyss: Two Novellas. Garden City, N.Y.: Doubleday, 1971.

Margaret and I: A Novel. Boston: Little, Brown, 1971.

City of Cain. Boston: Little, Brown, 1974; London: Gollancz, 1975.

Infinity Box: A Collection of Speculative Fiction. New York: Harper and Row, 1975; London: Arrow, 1979. (Short stories.)

The Clewiston Test. New York: Farrar, Straus and Giroux, 1976; London: Hutchinson, 1977.

Where Late the Sweet Birds Sang. New York: Harper and Row, 1976; London: Arrow, 1977.

Fault Lines: A Novel. New York: Harper and Row, 1977; London: Hutchinson, 1978.

Somerset Dreams and Other Fictions. New York: Harper and Row, 1978; London: Hutchinson, 1979. (Short stories.)

Juniper Time: A Novel. New York: Harper and Row, 1979; London: Hutchinson, 1980.

Listen, Listen. Boston: Houghton Mifflin, 1981. (Short stories.)

A Sense of Shadow. Boston: Houghton Mifflin, 1981.

Oh, Susannah! Boston: Houghton Mifflin, 1982.

Welcome, Chaos. Boston: Houghton Mifflin 1983; London: Gollancz, 1986.

Huysman's Pets. New York: Bluejay, 1986; London: Gollancz, 1986.

The Hamlet Trap. New York: St. Martin's, 1987; London: Gollancz, 1988.

Crazy Time. New York: St. Martin's, 1988.

The Dark Door. New York: St. Martin's, 1988; London: Gollancz, 1990.

Children of the Wind: Five Novellas. New York. St. Martin's, 1989; London: Hale, 1990.

Smart House. New York: St. Martin's, 1989; London: Gollancz, 1989.

Cambio Bay. New York: St. Martin's, 1990; London: Hale, 1991.

Sweet, Sweet Poison. New York: St. Martin's, 1990; London: Hale, 1991.

Death Qualified: A Mystery of Chaos. New York: St. Martin's, 1991.

And the Angels Sing: Stories. New York: St. Martin's, 1992. (Short stories.)

Seven Kinds of Death. New York: St. Martin's, 1992.

The Best Defense. New York: St. Martin's, 1994; London: Severn House, 1997.

Justice for Some. New York: St. Martin's, 1994.

A Flush of Shadows. New York: St. Martin's, 1995. (Short stories.)

Malice Prepense. New York: St. Martin's, 1996. Reprinted as *For the Defence*, London: Severn House, 1997.

The Good Children. New York: St. Martin's, 1998.

—BRIAN STABLEFORD

JACK WILLIAMSON

(b. 1908)

JACK WILLIAMSON WAS writing and publishing stories at least a year before the term "science fiction" was generally used. In December 1928 his first story, "The Metal Man," appeared in Hugo Gernsback's *Amazing Stories*; also, his guest editorial on the new field of "scientifiction" was published in *Amazing Stories Quarterly* (fall 1928). After a long interlude as an academic and university teacher, Williamson resumed a full-time writing career, and he was producing strong novels in the late 1990's. His career has spanned more than sixty years, encompassing the history of science fiction itself.

John Stewart Williamson was born in Bisbee, Arizona Territory, on 29 April 1908. He spent his earliest years on a ranch high in the Sierra Madre of Sonora, Mexico. The family left the isolated Rancho la Loba in 1910, ahead of the impending revolution, and moved to a farm near Pecos, Texas. The family grew and the crops flourished, but low market prices led to inevitable financial losses. Five years later the Williamsons journeyed by covered wagon and on horseback to a homestead in the Milnesand region of New Mexico. But the choice land had already been claimed; their homestead was without water, and the sand hills were inappropriate for crops and only marginally acceptable for raising cattle. Subsistence required constant hard work—ranching, sharecropping on better land, and taking odd jobs in the region, or even in Arizona and Texas.

Circumstances and developing personality traits combined early in Williamson's life to produce frustrations and longings that only science fiction could satisfy. The eldest of four children, Williamson often played and worked alone on the ranch and in the fields. The romance supposedly associated with the Southwest was not a part of his experience during these early years. Rather, since his family experienced the loss of cattle, crop failures, sandstorms, and little if any year-end profit, he viewed his life as tedious and frustrating. Flights of imagination were his only release; he began inventing stories to tell his brother and two sisters.

Books and learning were valued by his family, and both parents were teachers. Yet school was no consolation for Williamson—not then, at least. Most of his education was completed at home. He entered school in fourth grade, a year his father was the principal and teacher of the local two-room school. Cruelly and constantly hazed by other students, Williamson finished the year more introverted than ever—convinced that he had not yet learned to get along with others. He continued his studies at home for the next two years. He returned to school for the seventh grade, and passed state examinations qualifying him for high school. Williamson now turned to books—although they were few, dated, and unable to satisfy his growing curiosity about science—rather than to competitive sports and pranks with his peers.

Upon graduation from high school in 1925, Williamson considered becoming some sort of scientist, but he saw no opportunity to develop this interest. Yet, when he discovered the new magazine of "scientifiction," *Amazing Stories*, and such high adventures as A. Merritt's "The People of the Pit" and *The Moon Pool*—to paraphrase Williamson's own description—a whole new world opened up for him, a world in which anything was possible. He was inspired by his discoveries to write and submit stories to Gernsback, the first three of which were rejected.

Williamson's fourth story was not returned by Gernsback, and there were other big changes in Williamson's life as well. The family sale of mineral rights provided funds for Williamson and one of his sisters to enter West Texas State College at Canyon in the fall of 1928. He happened to notice the December issue of *Amazing Stories* in a Canyon store window, recognized the cover as an illustration of his story "The Metal Man," and quickly confirmed that he was a published author. With a few interruptions, none of them very long, he has been a science fiction writer since that time.

Science fiction became the focus of Williamson's life. During his two years at West Texas State, his vacations and any spare time were devoted to writing stories. He did not return for his third year—even though he was offered a student assistantship in chemistry. Williamson began a wide correspondence and joined new science fiction organizations. He traveled across the country, meeting editors, writers whose work he admired, and friends with whom he had corresponded.

Significant events in Williamson's life since that time of "discovery" include auditing astronomy courses at the University of California at Berkeley (fall 1930); attending the University of New Mexico (1932–1933), where he discovered Freud's writings and considered majoring in psychology; undergoing psychoanalysis for the first time (1936) so that he could better understand himself and his fictional characters; enlisting in the army during World War II—despite his deferment—and serving as a weather forecaster (1942–1945); adapting to the changed mood of science fiction after the explosion of the atomic bomb; marrying his childhood sweet-heart, Blanche Slaten Harp, on 15 August 1947; returning to college for additional math and science courses; obtaining the B.A. and the M.A. in English from Eastern New Mexico University (1957); and then, at age fifty, entering a doctoral program at the University of Colorado (Ph.D., 1964). Williamson taught at Eastern New Mexico University from 1960 to 1977. He introduced one of the first college-level science fiction courses, compiled a list of all similar courses, and became a national spokesman for science fiction in the academic world.

I

Williamson's earliest science fiction stories were influenced by his admiration for A. Merritt. He notes that these first stories probably had too much of Merritt's romanticism and too many of his "purple adjectives." To correct these tendencies and increase his skills, Williamson worked for a while with Miles J. Breuer, a more careful writer. Still, editors and readers praised Williamson's early stories, comparing them favorably with those of such popular writers of the day as E. E. Smith and Merritt. Story after story was the basis for striking magazine covers.

Several of the short stories and novelettes that Williamson wrote in the first two decades of his career give classic expression to certain themes or subtypes of the evolving science fiction genre. Probably the best-known works today are three series: Legion of Space (originating in the 1930's), Seetee (begun in the early 1940's), and Humanoid (stemming from the postwar science fiction of the mid- to late-1940's). These have been widely translated and frequently reprinted.

The Legion of Space series is usually considered to include *The Legion of Space* (*Astounding Stories*, 1934; book form, 1947), *The Cometeers* (*Astounding Stories*, 1936; book form, 1950), and *One Against the Legion* (*Astounding Science-Fiction*, 1939; book form, with *The Cometeers*, 1950). These works include a great deal of fast action and the battles of a few against great odds. Several critics categorize the series as space opera—in one sense a pejorative label but in another sense a recognition of an outstanding example of a type. Williamson did several interesting things in this series. He provided a continuing set of characters, spanning different generations of the Star family. He introduced AKKA, a terribly effective superweapon that must be guarded by a single "keeper of the peace," who alone in her (yes, her!) or his generation knows the secret of AKKA. He also created a set of characters based on a combination of Falstaff and the Three Musketeers—Jay Kalam, bright and capable; Hal Samdu, huge and strong; and the heavyset Giles Habibula, a constant talker, eater, and drinker who is also a skilled picklock with a questionable past.

The relatively skillful character construction, so early both in Williamson's career and in the history of science fiction, is noteworthy. According to a reader survey, Giles Habibula was the most popular character to appear in the 1930's. Also, AKKA appears through all of these stories and in "Nowhere Near" (1967). Perhaps the earliest notion of such a weapon, unrefined in its treatment by the protagonist and in its significance to the story, appears in "The Prince of Space" (*Amazing Stories*, 1931). Giles Habibula returned to action in *The Queen of the Legion* (1983), a long-awaited sequel to the original Legion stories.

Detailed characterizations, whether borrowed or invented, in any pulp science fiction of the mid-1930's is striking. In that era most characters were not so identifiable or singular; most were interchangeable—long a weakness of much science fiction. Other stories in which Williamson worked to create characters of some depth include "Dead Star Station" (*Astounding Stories*, 1933), which involves the old and seemingly useless Gideon Clew, and "The Crucible of Power" (*Astounding Science-Fiction*, 1939). In the latter, Garth Hammond, the narrator's father, lives a life of unforgiving competitiveness. The reader only grudgingly accepts Hammond as the protag-

Jack Williamson in 1975. PHOTO BY JAY KAY KLEIN

onist and, according to Williamson, Hammond "took over" the story from him as he wrote.

In addition, such stories as "The Peddler's Nose" (*Astounding Science-Fiction*, 1951) and "The Happiest Creature" (*Star Science Fiction Stories, no. 2*, 1953)—later incorporated into his 1962 novel *The Trial of Terra*—could be viewed as character studies originating in the UFO era of the 1950's. Williamson's female characters are often in positions of power; they are intelligent, skilled; they can and do act. This is far from the standard portrayal of women in most early—and even later—science fiction.

"Technology, pro or con?" is a long-standing theme in Williamson's writings. Although most apparent in his Humanoid stories, this issue preoccupied him as early as 1930. For example, "The Cosmic Express" (*Amazing Stories*, 1930) is pro-technology, optimistic, and hopeful, while "The Doom from Planet 4" (*Astounding Stories*, 1931) is antitechnology, pessimistic, and fearful. (The latter seems to be a precursor of "With Folded Hands" [*Astounding Science-Fiction*, 1947], one of his best stories and probably one that troubled him the most.)

Perhaps the Seetee stories—*Seetee Ship* (*Astounding Science-Fiction*, 1942–1943; book form, 1951) and its sequel, *Seetee Shock* (*Astounding Science-Fiction*, 1949; book form, 1950)—also involve this issue. (These were first published under the pseudonym Will Stewart.) Certainly they express in classic form the struggle of conscious beings in the face of the threatening collision of matter and antimatter. When a huge mass of antimatter—Seetee/C.T./Contraterrene—enters the close space of a material planetary system (a world of matter), how can beings of matter with material tools and technology ward off, contain, or even touch the antimatter? Uncontrolled contact of matter and antimatter produces an explosion of unlike particles into pure, free energy. Williamson's "Spaceman's Handbook," a short statement accompanying the story, warns that this "ultimate reaction makes uranium fission seem feeble as a safety match." The challenge involves harnessing Seetee's energy for the good of the worlds. That is what the protagonist tries to do, all the while opposing those who would develop effective Seetee bombs for conquest and power. Classic antimatter adventures, the Seetee stories also explore scientific analysis and ingenuity and the use and possible misuse of technology. Such issues may be more important than the characters or details of the stories themselves.

After returning from military service, Williamson began his Humanoid stories, first working on "With Folded Hands." In the postwar era a new, more ambiguous attitude toward technology was apparent in science fiction. Writers were asking whether technology was a basic threat. Starting with the presupposition that the Humanoids (Williamson's term) were perfectly functioning mechanicals, interconnected with one another and having a centralized intelligence source, Williamson questioned how humans could stop these purely benevolent, yet totally controlling, beings that would go to any length "to protect men and keep them from harm." Given the basic presupposition of their perfection, the humans cannot stop the Humanoids.

Williamson continued to wrestle with the Humanoid problem; he could not resolve it logically, but emotionally he was unwilling to accept the consequences. Before finishing "With Folded Hands," he wrote "The Equalizer" (*Astounding Science-Fiction*, 1947), a pro-technology story in which the threat is overcome by the wise, peaceful, creative, and noncompetitive use of the new energy source.

Williamson then completed "With Folded Hands." John W. Campbell, Jr., liked it so much that he suggested a sequel in which "people forced to fold their hands might well develop new mental powers." He urged Williamson to "look into Dr. Joseph Rhine's work on ESP." The suggested sequel, ". . . And Searching Mind" (*Astounding Science-Fiction*, 1948), was later rewritten into Williamson's famous novel *The Humanoids* (1949). Remaining consistent with his original presupposition, but changing the ending of the novel from that of ". . . And Searching Mind," Williamson says: "I presented it [the ending] from the viewpoint of people who had been brainwashed by the machines to think they were happy about being deprived of individual freedom and re-engineered into the Humanoid plan." And yet, surprisingly, readers had differing impressions: some considered that Williamson's mind-warriors had won, while others considered that not even amazing mental or psychic powers could defeat the Humanoids.

"Jamboree" (*Galaxy Science Fiction Magazine*, 1969) portrays one of these alternatives, graphically showing the destruction of humans by machines. In his article "Me and My Humanoids" (*New Mexico Humanities Review*, 1978; reprinted in *The Humanoids*, 1980), Williamson offers another interpretation of *The Humanoids*' ending: "that society rewards those who accept it and destroys those who don't." He says that the ambiguity in the novel may reflect the struggle between his own conflicting desires for independence and for socialization.

The sequel, *The Humanoid Touch* (1980), returns to this struggle. After "serving" a million planets, the Humanoids move on Kai, remote galactic outpost of a fugitive remnant of humankind. Keth Kyrone discovers the special force that could stop the Humanoids, but he cannot convince many humans of the reality of the impending invasion or that the actual invasion is a threat instead of a blessing. The Humanoids have become skilled deceivers in order to win over planets and enforce their Prime Directive; most humans seem enthusiastic to accept the services they promise. The nature of existence and "happiness" (its price is dehumanized, drug-sustained euphoria) under Humanoid service is portrayed vividly—even in the closing scene. At that point Keth finds the promise of his own longed-for "happiness"—but is it real or Humanoid induced?

"Guinevere for Everybody" (*Star Science Fiction Stories, no. 3*, 1954) is a troubling story—perhaps because the reader is unable to find a single, unifying theme. Yet the story links the themes of the uncertain value of technology and the effect of human engineering on the human psyche. (This may be appropriate, for these areas are not neatly separated and overlap conceptually.)

This early "clone" story, according to Williamson, has as "the logical heroine" a managerial computer, Athena Sue. She replaces a staff of human managers and is "programmed to use the cheapest possible materials for the mass-production of the most wanted product." Guinevere, a mass-produced clone of society's "ideal woman," is such a product. "She" is sold cheaply and falsely billed as a "vital" product but has an unbelievably rapid aging rate—a planned obsolescence. Society, though, is not ready for Athena Sue's program of marketing Guinevere—for $4.95 through vending machines! Violent public reaction stimulates the Board to order the managerial computer repaired or turned off. This gives the former general manager the courage to

sabotage Athena Sue and return to his original managerial position.

The impact of this "product" on humans is disconcerting, even on the cybernetics engineer/trouble-shooter originally called on to repair Athena Sue. He buys a Guinevere to secure information, is shocked by the sabotage of Athena Sue, but even more shocked to find that Guinevere has aged decades in the hours he has been away at the factory. After his tears, he affirms that "machines were never evil, except when men used them wrongly."

Darker Than You Think (*Unknown*, 1940; book form, 1948), in its attempt to provide a scientific explanation for lycanthropy and witchcraft, probes the human psyche—only to discover frightening instincts, abilities, and dark demons lurking there. This novel seems to be a result of Williamson's contact with the works of Freud and the psychoanalytic process.

In *Dragon's Island* (1951) the theme is genetic engineering of human beings. Exemplifying man's fear of the unknown, *Homo sapiens* unites its divisions—social and racial— in frantic attempts to destroy individuals of the genetically altered and superior *Homo excellens*, who have recently appeared on Earth. These superior beings are hidden among normal humans and are even born of them— although the special psychic, gene-changing process occurs only if the "creator" arrives on the scene at the correct time. This "creator" or "maker" is Messenger, a biologist (member of *Homo sapiens*) who is able to alter gene structure by concentration of psychic energy—but only in the short time span between fertilization and the beginning of cell division. Extrapolating this method to all life forms, as Williamson does here, is an interesting notion, but reader credibility is tested when an altered tree produces a fitted spaceship.

The role of protagonist is shared by Nan, whose special abilities are almost fully developed, and Dane, who is only gradually becoming aware of his *Homo excellens* nature. Under attack by the united forces of *Homo sapiens*, Messenger appeals to the opposition leaders to understand that his creations are not monsters but indeed the hope of humankind. Although Messenger dies, the story closes on a note of optimism: Messenger's plea is heard by *Homo sapiens'* leader—due in part to his cure by a special medication developed by the "not-men." There is the promise that *Homo sapiens* and *Homo excellens* will work together, and that those who are "men" will no longer try to annihilate those who are "not-men." (A later printing of this work carried the title *The Not-Men*, 1968.)

Another common theme in science fiction concerns the alteration of humans or beings through the influence of "outside forces" or "aliens" (contrasted to Messenger's alterations effected "inside" the human frame and by a human being). This theme appears in *The Moon Children* (*Galaxy Science Fiction Magazine*, 1971; book form, 1972), but again Williamson adds a twist. A group of astronauts comes into contact with some strange forces; and shortly after their return home to Earth, "moon children"—the beings of hope—are born in their families. Through these unusual children, who are both human and more than human, communication with extraterrestrial beings who can save Earth is established. These aliens have initiated contact because of their concern for humans; they propose to save the humans from another, hostile species of aliens intent upon completely destroying Earth because of what humans have done to their home planet and the threat this poses for the aliens' planet. An apparently similar concern is shown by the friendly aliens in *The Trial of Terra*.

"Breakdown" (*Astounding Science-Fiction*, 1942) and *Star Bridge* (1955, a collaboration with James E. Gunn) deal with the philosophy of history. Perhaps the words that reveal the significance of the title "Breakdown" also speak for the novel. The old philosopher-historian Melkart tries to explain to the suddenly deposed and thoroughly confused Boss Kellon: "Cultures must reach the point of breakdown before they can breed men able to understand them." Although the novel presents this theme on a larger, interplanetary

scale, the basic ideas and the warnings are quite similar in both works. As Melkart indicates, when a society or culture no longer has a sense of purpose or creativity, it collapses; people strive to merge themselves in or identify themselves with something greater than their individual lives. When a society or culture has fulfilled its original purpose—the reason for its formation—and no new purpose is forthcoming, anarchy and socio-cultural dissolution result.

A set of three undersea adventure novels (*Undersea Quest*, 1954; *Undersea Fleet*, 1956; and *Undersea City*, 1958), completed with Frederik Pohl, and *Trapped in Space* (1968) seem to be aimed at younger science fiction readers. The undersea series depicts the recruitment of the youthful James Eden to the Sub-sea Academy and tells of his (and others') adventures there and in the "space" under-the-sea. *Trapped in Space* deals with a very young Jeff Stone who rises to meet and overcome the challenges of saving his brother Ben, who is "trapped in space."

The Starchild Trilogy—first published as a series of stories in *Worlds of If*—results from further collaboration between Williamson and Pohl and includes *The Reefs of Space* (1964), *Starchild* (1965), and *Rogue Star* (1969). In a sense, these novels treat aliens and an alien locale; they are stories about the persistence of life—although "life" is different in form and function from what most of us call "life-forms"; they trace the outer space processes at work with "life forces," stimulating, nourishing, and bringing to maturity special kinds of life in a part of the universe strange and unknown to man.

A third series, *Farthest Star* (1975), "Highest Dive" (*Science Fiction Monthly*, 1976), and *Wall Around a Star* (1983), is structured upon the notion of a Dyson sphere, a containing barrier that can capture and use the radiation of a star.

Other subjects treated by Williamson include a neutron star, techniques of rocket propulsion, alternative means and improved systems of communications, and artificial intelligence. These are areas that scientists—

not science fiction writers—later attempted to understand as realities, that is, as actually existing phenomena rather than as fictional entities. Such subjects are a few of the many areas explored by Williamson in some of his best known works.

Critics note that Williamson, who has lived, written, and published through the several phases of science fiction, is one of the genre's most adaptable writers and is a serious student of science. Pohl reports that Marvin Minsky, a noted specialist in the field of artificial intelligence, praised the descriptive accuracy of the topic in Williamson's *The Humanoids*, and that a scientist who worked with sensitive national projects traced his interest in "technological superweapons" to Williamson's AKKA.

II

Awards and honors indicate a wide recognition of Williamson's contribution to science fiction and the stature of this genre. First Fandom, an organization of early fans—several of whom remember Williamson as the "cover copper" because so many of his early stories inspired magazine covers—presented the Hall of Fame award to him in 1968. In 1973 the Science Fiction Research Association presented Williamson with the Pilgrim award for his critical study *H. G. Wells: Critic of Progress* (1973) and for his extensive encouragement of the study of science fiction in secondary schools and colleges. The Science Fiction Writers of America (SFWA) gave him their second Grand Master Nebula award in 1976 for "lifetime achievement" and contributions to the field. (From 1978 to 1980 he was president of SFWA.) Eastern New Mexico University has established the Williamson Collection in its Golden Library. Also, Williamson was guest of honor in 1977 at SunCon, the thirty-fifth World Science Fiction Convention.

Since the mid-1960's Williamson and his wife have traveled from their home in Portales, New Mexico, to many parts of the world. As the result of extensive publication and translation of his work, both the man and his stories are known worldwide. Since his retirement from the university in 1977—except for his service to SFWA and participation in numerous science fiction conventions—Williamson has returned to full-time writing.

—ROBERT E. MYERS

WILLIAMSON IN THE 1980's AND 1990's

The 1980's and 1990's saw a revival of Williamson's work, first in the form of collaborative novels, then increasing with the production of bold and provocative titles under his sole byline—works strongly in the tradition of classic science fiction, yet full of innovative ideas, signs of the writer listening carefully to successive younger generations.

Williamson collaborated with James Gunn and most fruitfully during the 1980's with Frederik Pohl. *Wall Around a Star* (1983), sequel to *The Farthest Star* (1975), is space opera in the grand manner. Almost in response to the traditional Robert A. Heinlein defense of defiant humankind, this novel develops the theme of acculturation: mankind now striving to enter an intergalactic league of mature cultures. In the lineage of Ian Watson, Samuel R. Delany, and Suzette Elgin (*Native Tongue* appeared in 1984), protagonist Jen Babylon is a linguist who, by combing the records of planet Cuckoo for clues as to the origin of its mysterious human species, is able to find links between the "outcast" Earth and more civilized cultures of the galaxy. More interesting (and perhaps more Williamson) is *Land's End* (1988), which returns to classic themes such as comet strikes, Atlantis, and the "last survivors" scenario, yet with a more topical 1980s slant as well: comet strikes deplete the ozone layer and bring on "ozone summer." *The Singers of Time* (1991), with its dedication to Stephen Hawking and the spirit of scientific inquiry, reads like an up-to-date version of Heinlein's "Universe." Earth is ruled by a superior race, the Turtles, who bring peace and prosperity but whose religion forbids scientific inquiry. However, such human aspirations are revived, and vindicated, when it turns out that the Turtles need such speculation to save their mother planet.

It is, however, in Williamson's increasing production of solo novels through the 1980's and 1990's that we have a clear reaffirmation of a classic science fiction vision, yet one always aware (as with the Hawking reference) of new and changing cultural problems and contexts. *Manseed* (1982) returns to the writer's earlier preoccupation with "genetic engineering" (*Dragon's Island*, 1951). His two young adult "seeker" novels are more striking yet. In *Lifeburst* (1984), published in the same year as William Gibson's *Neuromancer*, cosmic weapons become sentient, destroying their makers. These metal eaters, "lifebursting" to devour the cosmos, menace an Earth that, in extremis, is only saved from total annihilation by the efforts of a young boy, Benn Dain, who teams up with two members of an alien race previously victim of the Seekers. The sequel, *Mazeway* (1990), continues to deepen the themes of classic juvenile space opera. In the wake of battle with the Seekers, Earth has returned to savagery. The only hope to revive mankind is to attract the help of the Eldren, again a consortium of galactic cultures, whose ways are peace, but who disdain human violence. In a manner reminiscent of Orson Scott Card's *Ender's Game* (1985), Benn leads a team of humans to the Eldren's initiatory planet Mazeway, hoping to learn the secret, and earn the respect, of these alien "saviors."

Williamson's output showed no signs of abating the 1990's; in fact, the quality of the grand master's dialogue with the new science fiction seems only to sharpen. In *Beachhead* (1992), a novel appearing a year before Kim Stanley Robinson's *Red Mars*, the author draws on new data on Mars and biospheres to resurrect the classic theme of colonizing the Red Planet. *Demon Moon* (1994), compared by Robert Silverberg to early works such as

Darker Than You Think, resurrects magic and sword and sorcery, but now in the context of a mythic struggle between chthonic forces and scientific reason in the manner of Ursula Le Guin's *Earthsea*. In his next novel, *The Black Sun* (1997), Williamson reverses poles and returns to the premises of "hard" science fiction. It is "faster-than-light quantum-wave technology" that sends Project Starseed to distant star systems. And yet these calculations worthy of author Dr. Robert L. Forward lead to cosmogonic mystery at the heart of the universe—again the encounter of reason and faith that has marked Williamson's unique force as a writer across his career. If these powerful last novels are an indication, his work will continue to bridge science fiction worlds well into the future.

—GEORGE SLUSSER

Selected Bibliography

SCIENCE FICTION OF JACK WILLIAMSON

The Legion of Space. Reading, Pa.: Fantasy Press, 1947.

Darker Than You Think. Reading, Pa.: Fantasy Press, 1948. London: Sphere Books, 1976.

The Humanoids. New York: Simon and Schuster, 1949. London: Science Fiction Club, 1953. Reprinted with the addition of the article "Me and My Humanoids." New York: Avon Books, 1980.

The Cometeers. Reading, Pa.: Fantasy Press, 1950. (Includes *One Against the Legion*.)

Seetee Shock, as by Will Stewart. New York: Simon and Schuster, 1950.

Dragon's Island. New York: Simon and Schuster, 1951. London: Science Fiction Club, 1954. Retitled *The Not-Men*. New York: Tower, 1968.

Seetee Ship, as by Will Stewart. New York: Gnome Press, 1951.

Star Bridge, with James E. Gunn. New York: Gnome Press, 1955.

The Trial of Terra. New York: Ace Books, 1962.

The Reefs of Space, with Frederik Pohl. New York: Ballantine Books, 1964. London: Dennis Dobson, 1965.

Starchild, with Frederik Pohl. New York: Ballantine Books, 1965. London: Dennis Dobson, 1966.

Trapped in Space. Garden City, N.Y.: Doubleday, 1968.

Rogue Star, with Frederik Pohl. New York: Ballantine Books, 1969. London: Dennis Dobson, 1972.

The Moon Children. New York: G. P. Putnam's Sons, 1972. London: Elmfield Press, 1975.

The Early Williamson. Garden City, N.Y.: Doubleday, 1975. London: Sphere Books, 1978. (A collection of early short fiction selected by Williamson.)

Farthest Star, with Frederik Pohl. New York: Ballantine Books, 1975.

The Power of Blackness. New York: G. P. Putnam's Sons, 1976. London: Sphere Books, 1978.

The Starchild Trilogy, with Frederik Pohl. New York: Pocket Books, 1977. (Includes *The Reefs of Space, Starchild*, and *Rogue Star*.)

The Best of Jack Williamson. New York: Ballantine Books, 1978. (Short stories selected by Williamson; Introduction by Frederik Pohl.)

The Humanoid Touch. New York: Holt, Rinehart and Winston, 1980.

Three from the Legion. New York: Pocket Books, 1980. (Includes the three Legion of Space novels and a new novelette, "Nowhere Near.")

The Queen of the Legion. New York: Pocket Books, 1983.

Manseed. New York: Ballantine, 1982.

Wall Around a Star, with Frederik Pohl. New York: Ballantine, 1983.

Lifeburst. New York: Ballantine, 1984.

Firechild. New York: Bluejay, 1986.

Land's End, with Frederik Pohl. New York: TOR, 1988.

Mazeway. Norwalk, Conn.: Easton, 1990.

The Singers of Time, with Frederik Pohl. New York: Doubleday, 1991.

Beachhead. New York: TOR, 1992.

Demon Moon. New York: TOR, 1994.

The Black Sun. New York: TOR, 1997.

NONFICTION OF JACK WILLIAMSON

Science Fiction Comes to College: A Preliminary Survey of Courses Offered. Portales, N.M.: privately published by the author, 1971.

H. G. Wells: Critic of Progress. Baltimore: Mirage Press, 1973. (An expansion of Williamson's 1964 doctoral dissertation.)

Teaching Science Fiction: Education for Tomorrow. Edited by Williamson. Philadelphia, Pa.: Owlswick Press, 1980.

Wonder's Child: My Life in Science Fiction. New York. Bluejay, 1984. (Literary autobiography.)

CRITICAL STUDY

Zelazny, Roger, ed. *The Williamson Effect.* New York: TOR, 1996.

BIBLIOGRAPHIES

Benson, Gordon, Jr., *Jack (John Stewart) Williamson, Child and Father of Wonder: A Working Bibliography.* Albuquerque, N. Mex.: Galactic Central, 1985.

Myers, Robert E. *Jack Williamson: A Primary and Secondary Bibliography.* Boston: G. K. Hall, 1980.

CONNIE WILLIS
(b. 1945)

By almost any measure—popular, academic, or critical—Connie Willis is among the most significant of those science fiction writers who rose to prominence in the 1980's. This agreement about her merits, across so many different sorts of readership, is unusual. The fan favorite is seldom the academic favorite.

The more carefully one scrutinizes her work, the odder it all seems. Willis knows quite a lot of science and uses it correctly, but her work—despite all the awards she has received from science fiction fans—is only marginally science fiction. Her central motivation is often to explore such feelings as nostalgia, memory, regret, turning points, pain, and reconciliation. The science fiction elements provide a matrix, or an enabling metaphor, within which these human feelings can be analyzed and understood. Thus, her stories might sit as comfortably in the pages of magazines such as the *New Yorker* as they do in, say, *Asimov's Science Fiction* (the magazine in which much of her best short fiction was originally published).

Yet Willis's popularity in hard-core science fiction remains almost unparalleled. Although her science fiction career effectively spans only twenty years, she has already won not only six Nebula awards (the award voted on by science fiction professionals) but also six Hugo awards (the fan award). A few distinguished writers such as Harlan Ellison and Ursula K. Le Guin have equaled the Hugo record, but nobody has approached Willis's record in Hugos and Nebulas taken together. The ability to win awards is no absolute proof of literary distinction, of course, because there are other factors: evanescent trends, personal popularity, media visibility. But a record such as that of Willis, who is not in any way a self-promoter, is at the least, highly suggestive of something interesting going on in her fiction.

Constance Elaine Trimmer was born on the last day of 1945, in Denver, Colorado, the state where she still resides. She entered the University of Northern Colorado in 1963 and graduated in 1967 with a B.A. in English and elementary education. She married Courtney W. Willis, a physicist, in 1967. A daughter, Cordelia, was born in 1969. She taught elementary school for two years and with the birth of her daughter began writing. Her early attempts at writing science fiction, one of her first loves, proved abortive. A short story, "The Secret of Santa Titicaca," appeared in *Worlds of Fantasy*, issue no 3, 1970–1971, and the magazine promptly went out of business with issue no 4.

After that first science fiction story, Willis largely concentrated, as she has reported with cheerful lack of contrition, on "confession" stories for magazines such as *True Romance* and *Real Confessions* (which must have provided an excellent training in the succinct presentation of human interest stories). There was no more published science fiction (or fantasy) until 1978–1979, when in quite rapid succession five of her stories were published in *Galileo*, a magazine with no great circulation but an attractive policy of encouraging new writers. Willis does counted cross-stitch and sings in the church choir, a fact with relevance to her fiction, in which the church plays a recurrently important role.

This synopsis suggests merely a normal and presumably quite comfortable middle-class suburban life, with literary aspirations (which after all are very common) that showed no sign of going anywhere in particular by the time Willis reached her thirties. But then her 1979 story "Daisy in the Sun" was nominated for a Hugo, and within a very few years and only four stories later, she actually won the coveted award (for best novelette) with "Fire Watch" (1982). Since then her career has barely paused for breath. Connie Willis's life is an absolute model for would-be, struggling writers, especially relevant perhaps, because in the early days it featured diapers and school lunches rather than starvation and attics.

Time travel has been an important element in her stories, and "Fire Watch" is a good example. The narrator is a young male history student at Balliol, in Oxford University, England, in the middle of the twenty-first century. His practical examination at the end of the course consists of time traveling (we assume this is a very recent technology) into an area of the past, some sort of crux period on which he must later report. His particular practicum is to work as a fire warden at St. Paul's Cathedral during the Blitz in London in World War II. At first the past is literally like a foreign country—he barely understands what is said to him—and as he is plunged into a nightmare of fatigue and endless battling with incendiary bombs, he is increasingly terrified that "the past is beyond saving." Typically for Willis, the story begins in a relaxed and humorous manner and then, without warning, metaphorically wheedles you into a room where your emotions are flayed, scraped nerves stinging in the dark. Willis's endings are, though apparently clear and concise, legendarily multilayered, so that you sometimes need to read them five times before all their implications sink in. The ending of "Fire Watch" offers one of its several meanings spelled out in actual words and then summarily dismissed as "pompous drivel": that the experience in the Blitz is a story about "standing guard against the fall-ing incendiaries of the human heart." And so it is.

The 1970's and 1980's constitute a period when many critics, particularly the older ones, were lamenting the near death of short fiction in science fiction publishing. This was a natural but sad consequence of the dearth of magazines—which along with anthologies are pretty well the sole market for short fiction—compared with, say, the 1940's or the 1950's. Willis was and has remained a powerful exception to the rule, and while she certainly has rivals in her work at novel length, she is the undisputed queen of science fiction short fiction, especially the novella. She is not particularly prolific, but the stories add up at an average rate of two or three a year. There have been fifty-five to date, all but the first published between 1978 and 1998.

Willis's short fiction has been largely (but not wholly) collected in two books: *Fire Watch* (1985) and *Impossible Things* (1993). In addition, three novellas, each originally printed as a separate, slim book, are collected in a book club edition, *Futures Imperfect* (1996). Between them these books contain twenty-six stories. Three comparatively recent award winners, "Death on the Nile" (1993, Hugo award winner), "The Soul Selects Her Own Society" (1996, Hugo award winner), and "Newsletter" (1997, Locus award winner) are not yet collected but will presumably appear, along with other recent fiction, in a forthcoming collection. These Willis collections are essential items in any responsibly selected science fiction library.

To read or reread these stories all at once is an awe-inspiring but unsettling experience. A prominent science fiction writer recently commented to this author, "She's rather suburban, isn't she?" to which there is no short answer. This comment is true, in the sense that the stories are embedded in and grow from a confident, twentieth-century, middle-class, bourgeois culture and its values (themselves not to be readily dismissed), but while this may be the seeding ground, the range of the stories goes much farther than the dismissive word "suburban" could conceivably suggest. Indeed, suburban values are not just the seeding ground of the stories; they are often the object of satire as well, as in the novella *Bellwether* (1996). Other targets for Willis's deadly satire on suburban values are political correctness in matters of educational theory, in "Ado" (1988) and "In the Late Cretaceous" (1991), and "women's issues" in general and menstruation in particular in "Even the Queen" (1992), which, with its hilariously accurate exploration of differing views of women's freedom (or otherwise) from biological imperatives, won all the top awards (Nebula, Hugo, and Locus) in 1993. The trivia of the here and now as seen through the distorting lens of the near future are certainly one of Willis's favorite topics, and one especially remembers these stories for their satirical skills, but it is quite wrong to suppose her range is limited to the froth on the cappuccino of cultural life.

Willis is an elusive writer, and it is notable that while she has received splendid if fairly brief reviews in both academic and popular media, there is in longer critical essays an almost total silence about her work. This may result from a fear that pinning the butterfly to the display board is not going to explain satisfactorily how the caterpillar became the butterfly in the first place.

The first and overwhelming response to Willis's work is to surrender to her charm, the lure used to tug the reader into the story. Few science fiction writers have charm, but Willis has an abundance. Like a kind of science fiction Jane Austen, she is everybody's favorite aunt. But the comparison goes farther (and significantly Willis is an Austen admirer), for if Jane Austen had *only* charm, she would not have had nearly two centuries of popularity. The other thing Austen had was an ability to cut deep with an almost invisible scalpel, and Willis has this too.

One might be reminded, when reading Willis, of the haunting phrase in the "Knightes Tale" in Geoffrey Chaucer's *Canterbury Tales*: "The smyler with the knyf under the

Connie Willis. © Miriam Berkley

cloke." Willis smiles, and smiles, and leads you in, and then she produces the knife from beneath her cloak. It is an astonishing effect. Somewhere in Willis there must be, not an actual brutality, but a cold and *continuous* rage against cruelty—the cruelty of fate as well as the cruelty of people—a rage whose appearance can be that of brutality. Metaphorically, we need to be made to bleed before we understand. It is one of the mystic rituals of literature.

It is relevant here to turn to Willis's best-known novel (set coincidentally during the period of Chaucer's childhood), *Doomsday Book* (1992), although it involves leaving off the chronological treatment for a while.

Doomsday Book (which won Hugo, Nebula, and Locus awards) is a kind of sequel to "Fire Watch" but in the form of a quite long novel. In "Fire Watch" we met the narrator's friend, Kivrin, a recent graduate who, we were told, did her own practicum in 1349 (it has become the end of 1348 in *Doomsday Book*),

921

the time when the Black Death, the Plague, came to England. *Doomsday Book* tells how Kivrin is to be sent by the history department at Balliol to study medieval life (near Oxford) in the comparatively tranquil year of 1320, but an error results in her arriving twenty-eight years too late. The narrative shifts back and forth between twenty-first-century Oxford and the Middle Ages, and in both periods a dreadful contagious disease appears without warning. The twenty-first century gets off comparatively lightly (though a central character dies), but in the village to which Kivrin makes her way in 1348, within a month *everybody* but Kivrin is dead.

There is no need here to detail the narrative further than to say that much of the story's tension results from our fear that the mistake may never be discovered and Kivrin may never be retrieved. What is bewildering—it is difficult to think of any other example in English literature—is the technical difficulty of doing what Willis, almost perversely, contrives to do, though critics do not seem to have written about this aspect of the book.

She chooses to begin the tale in the charming, breathless, lightly satirical vein that one often associates with her work, then deepens the telling, and deepens it further, without ever completely dropping this tone of voice. It is as if P. G. Wodehouse had successfully written *King Lear*. It is a seamless conjunction of comedy and tragedy that is almost without precedent. Through domestic detail, womanly, crisp (in the modern Oxford sequences as well as the medieval sequences), the reader works his or her way ever more slowly as if moving through thickened air, to a kind of frozen stillness of tragedy and loss. One cannot regard the Black Death as just another historical crisis when confronted by it as rendered with so piercing, so loving a gaze. Nobody has described the effect better than the critic John Clute (in *The Encyclopedia of Science Fiction*): ". . . mounts gradually to a climax whose intensely mourning gravity is rarely found in sf."

"Gravitas" as well as gravity is a word one might choose. The effect is deepened by the religious element of the book, which is difficult to define, but Willis has chosen to allow us—the reader is gifted by her with free will—to blame God for the continuing ghastliness, while positing a medieval hero, an illiterate parish priest, who mitigates the worst horrors through courage and endurance, a man who is after all God's servant. This is a very distinguished book. One carries from it the slow clangor of the funeral bells ringing out over the dead, white, winter landscape, and one might think that if this imagery is suburban, then the suburban and the cosmic are not so far apart.

The critic Gary K. Wolfe (*Locus*, January 1994) made an interesting comment about Connie Willis's use of comedy and tragedy. He refers to "Shirley Jackson . . . whose comic novels of suburban life are almost forgotten, and whose wild manic-depressive shifts from the ominous to the hilarious seems most to anticipate Willis." The comparison with Jackson is illuminating but not pinpoint accurate. The unsettling quality of Willis may be seen as being not the shift from one to the other serially but the fact that she is, at her most disturbing, hilarious and ominous *at the same time.*

Before returning to Willis's other work, it should be noted that the same Oxford historiography series manifested itself again in another novel—completely different—the jeu d'esprit entitled *To Say Nothing of the Dog.* Two time-traveling historians are involved, seeking in 1888 information about the Bishop's Bird Stump. This strange and whimsical work, while enormously readable, is perhaps at its foundation too long for its strength, like a load-bearing joist sagging in the middle. The book in its title and some of its labyrinthine action is a homage to Jerome K. Jerome's nineteenth-century comic novel *Three Men in a Boat* (1889), and it also bows gracefully toward P. G. Wodehouse, Oscar Wilde, Sir Arthur Conan Doyle, Agatha Christie, and others. (Clearly as seen here and elsewhere, Connie Willis is an Anglophile and might have made rather a good provincial English bishop herself.) The serious part of the book involves the destruction of Coventry Cathedral by Nazi bombs, clearly harking back to the St. Paul's context of "Fire Watch." But this time, the sour plum embedded in the sweet dough does not quite taste as it should; there is just too much pudding around it, though for most writers it would be regarded as a considerable achievement.

Willis's first novel was also an oddity, also amusing and light (more of an eclair than a pudding). It was *Water Witch* (1982), the first of three novels written in collaboration with her friend and fellow Coloradan, Cynthia Felice. (Felice is the author of around seven science fiction novels on her own account, the first being the lively *Godsfire* [1978].)

All three novels, reflecting the similar plotting of Felice's solo works, are science fiction romances, reminiscent sometimes of Georgette Heyer, sometimes of Baroness Orczy's Scarlet Pimpernel novels, sometimes of Anthony Hope's *The Prisoner of Zenda* (1894): a stirring blend of regency romance, swashbuckling, and derring-do in various science fiction settings. The other two collaborations are *Light Raid* (1989) and *Promised Land* (1997). The last is the quietest, a tale of what begins as a disastrous marriage between two complete strangers reaching unexpected contentment on a frontier planet, and reminding at least one reader of the Little House on the Prairie novels of Laura Ingalls Wilder. Each of the three novels written with Felice is thoroughly enjoyable and includes a good bit of the familiar Willis deftness of observation, but there is not a great deal to be said. Graham Greene referred to his lighter novels, such as *Stamboul Train* (1932; U.S. title *Orient Express*), as "entertainments;" the more serious ones were not given this sobriquet, even though they, too, were mostly thrillers. Willis's collaborations with Felice are entertainments in very much the same way, though the genre is science fiction. A personal favorite of the three is *Light Raid*, set during a serious enough future war in America but conducted by factions that are positively Ruritanian. The resourceful heroine unravels plots (involving her own parents) and satisfyingly finds love as well.

Willis's first solo novel is so different in tone that one can scarcely believe it is by the same author. This is *Lincoln's Dreams* (1987). It won the John W. Campbell Memorial Award for best novel of 1987, and if it had been more substantially science fiction (it is in most respects a mainstream novel) might well have swept the major science fiction awards. The consensus judgment is that along with *Doomsday Book* it is one of Willis's two finest novels.

The way the story unfolds, as is uncommon in most science fiction but not uncommon in Willis, is something of a breathtaking high-wire act. That is to say, Willis sets herself technical problems of narrative that most writers would shudder from and then carries them off, sometimes pausing on the wire to regain her balance but never falling.

Jeff Johnston, in a familiar Willis trope, is a historical researcher. He works for a novelist whose next book is to be about the American Civil War. The story is complex, mysterious, and subtle, but the essence is simple enough: Johnston meets a young woman suffering from a sleep disturbance (and later, we learn, from a weak heart) who has been having someone else's dreams, dreams that Jeff recognizes as being those of the Confederate general Robert E. Lee. (The psychic link is not really explained in science fiction terms, though there is some well-informed material on sleep theory, but the effect is parallel to—though not identical with—the effect conventional science fiction gets through using time travel.) Jeff falls in love with Annie at once and continues in love, as her dreams span more and more of the horrors of the Civil War. Meanwhile, his employer, Broun, is researching Lincoln's dreams (some of which are on the historical record). This is a book about dreams: about memory and reality and history, and loss and betrayal and grief, and warfare and death. It intricately plays the present off against the past. Unusually for Willis (with hindsight we see this), there is very little humor here, though plenty of the sharp eye for incongruity and telling detail that she so often puts to apparently comic purpose even in her more serious later tales. *Lincoln's Dreams* has the very texture of dream, and to read it is, to a degree, to be lost just like the heroine in someone else's vision. This is part of the infinite recession (like when you look in a mirror that reflects another mirror, and you see yourself receding endlessly into mirror space) that makes the book so terrible and so poignant. One needs to read the book to understand all the ramifications of the technical problem referred to, but briefly, if the heroine is General Lee, who during the Civil War might the hero be equated with? The answer—and you will have to take it on trust that this is credible, has a feeling of satisfying rightness, and is not even remotely funny—is Robert E. Lee's horse, Traveller.

Willis's other three novels are in fact novellas, although published as complete, if rather slim, books. They are linked thematically, in tone and in time (having been published consecutively over three years). They are *Uncharted Territory* (1994), *Remake* (1995), and *Bellwether* (1996). The three may be said to represent Willis in her cultural guru mode, strikingly well, for each makes great play with the trivia of popular culture that matter so much more to us than some serious-minded people think they should.

Uncharted Territory is at once a stirring adventure story in which a mystery on an alien planet is uncovered and an affectionate parody of pulp-fiction (or even dime-novel) adventure, specifically westerns. The connection is made overt through a minor character, who secretly writes popular fiction in multimedia form as "Captain Jake Trailblazer." The book is rollicking, intelligent, lightweight, and for all the world, as Gary K. Wolfe (again) pointed out, like the script for a Howard Hawks movie.

Remake is more resonant (the knife slipped from beneath the cloak) in its apparently simple love story of a future film editor (his jobs, such as removing all references to drinking alcohol from *The Philadelphia Story*, range

from dreadful to appalling) who falls for a dancer during a period in future Hollywood history when dancers are no longer required. She disappears, only to reappear dancing impossibly in old videos from the 1940's and 1950's. Digital remake? Time travel? Again, the book is lighthearted, but the theme involves not just love but also the relationship between obsession and art (and a loving account of the various ways in which some old Hollywood movies actually *are* art). This gives it a shade of severity or darkness that prevents the novella from floating away as merely a piece of weightless confectionary.

Bellwether is also on the surface mostly froth (whipped up with great aplomb), but this time it is genuine science fiction as well. It is a tale of a research statistician whose role in a corporately overcorrect R&D company is to find explanations for passing fads through history (hula hoops, bobbed hair, medieval shoes with the toes turned up, ouija boards, and so on, with no sign of flagging imagination through twenty or so examples). She meets a chaos physicist seemingly immune to trends and fashions; meanwhile, her assistant, Flip, creates increasing levels of disorganization around the office. Silly things happen.

Toward the end of the tale, the following passage occurs: "Suppose fads were a form of self-organized criticality arising out of the chaotic system of the popular culture. And suppose that, like other chaotic systems, they were influenced by a bellwether. . . . They would require a catalyst, a butterfly to set them into motion." What makes the book interesting as science fiction is not the somewhat implausible ending (where the catalyst is identified) but the relationship between faddism and chaos theory. This in turn is not merely asserted by the text but enacted by it. It is in fact a scrupulously researched book of enormous cleverness (and low cunning), whose science is meticulously unraveled before the reader's very eyes; it is not just supplied as the more commonplace info-dump. One could almost argue that in this novella we actually see Connie Willis doing genuine science, and we share in the experience.

924

It would require a book-length study to take proper cognizance of Willis's short fiction, though arguably it stands at the very center of her talent. Here one can only gesture: at stories such as "The Last of the Winnebagos" (1988), in which a dog run over comes to stand for the imminent death of the natural world in an industrialized future; such as "At the Rialto" (1989), the funniest "principle of indeterminacy" story ever written; such as "All My Darling Daughters" (1985), a tale of rape and torture by men (on alien sex surrogates) in which the Willis knife is flourished more visibly than ever before or since and by which the reader is too hypnotized to retreat squeamishly; such as "The Sidon in the Mirror" (1983), in which a helpless empathic being whose nature it is to become a doppelganger, to reflect as a mirror does, assists in death by murder and suicide; and preeminently, such as "Chance" (1986), not science fiction at all but central to any thematic study of Willis, in which a gentle comedy about a campus wife's half-remembered path not taken ends as cold as Dante's final circle of Hell, and which perhaps no one can read without tears.

It is far too early to make any final, or even properly considered, judgment about the place of Connie Willis in science fiction history. Her work has been called "sentimental," but sentimentality in fiction is the attempt to arouse easy emotions in the reader that have not been paid for in the text. Willis may be a woman of sentiment (which is to say, of feeling), but sentimental in this sense she is not.

Rather like Jean Brodie in the famous novel, Connie Willis is in her prime, and there is no telling where she will go next, after the comparative relaxation of her last couple of books. She is not the only science fiction writer to combine intelligence and sharp wit (Gene Wolfe, John Crowley, Neal Stephenson, quite a few others), but she has done so with a consistency that should have cranked up the literacy expectations of the general readership by several notches. Nobody could regard Willis's science fiction as the poor relation of any other genre. There is nothing of the ghetto about it. Confident, moving, candid—funny and sombre, yin and yang—hers is one of the most mature voices in a genre that has itself matured.

Willis is on record as naming Robert Heinlein as one of her heroes, "for his lived-in futures," and even though she is less obviously science fiction than many of her colleagues, this particular lesson is one she learned well. As to the science, there is at least one area that Willis has made especially her own: the twin use of quantum theory and chaos theory as metaphors for the human condition, while not cheapening or too much simplifying them as mathematical concepts. As part of this, she stands up for the principle that "might have beens," at one level of reality, should have as much absoluteness as actual happenings (in our memory of which they may become encysted) and can mean as much to those who have them. It is the theme, whether comic or tragic, to which she continually returns. To name "Blued Moon" (1984), "Schwarzschild Radius" (1987), "Chance," "At the Rialto," *Bellwether*, and *To Say Nothing of the Dog* is to give the most obvious examples, but the same point could be made of the collision between history, memory, nostalgia, and direct experience that saturates the consciousnesses of the main characters in *Lincoln's Dreams* and *Doomsday Book*.

Connie Willis is—metaphorically—the sort of woman we would all like to meet at the Rialto. One can almost glimpse her there, smiling, knife decently cloaked.

Selected Bibliography

NOVELS OF CONNIE WILLIS

Water Witch, with Cynthia Felice. New York: Ace, 1982.
Lincoln's Dreams. New York: Bantam, 1987.
Light Raid, with Cynthia Felice. New York: Ace, 1989.
Doomsday Book. New York: Bantam, 1992.
Uncharted Territory. New York: Bantam, 1994; London: New English Library, 1994. (The UK edition contains two additional short stories, "Fire Watch" and "Even the Queen.")

Remake. New York: Bantam, 1995.
Bellwether. New York: Bantam, 1996.
Promised Land, with Cynthia Felice. New York: Ace, 1997.
To Say Nothing of the Dog. New York: Bantam, 1998.

COLLECTIONS OF CONNIE WILLIS

Fire Watch. New York: Bluejay, 1985; New York: Bantam, 1986. (Contains twelve stories.)
Impossible Things. New York: Bantam, 1993. (Contains eleven stories.)
Futures Imperfect. Garden City, N.Y.: Science Fiction Book Club, 1996. (Omnibus volume containing the three novellas "Uncharted Territory," "Remake," and "Bellwether.")

CRITICAL AND BIOGRAPHICAL STUDIES

Clute, John. "Willis, Connie." In *The Encyclopedia of Science Fiction.* Edited by John Clute and Peter Nicholls. New York: St. Martin's, 1995.

Kelso, Sylvia. "Connie Willis's Civil War: Re-Dreaming America as Science Fiction." *Foundation* (Summer 1998).

Slonczewski, Joan. "Bells and Time: A Review of *Doomsday Book* by Connie Willis." In *Imaginative Futures: Proceedings of the 1993 Science Fiction Research Association Conference.* San Bernardino, Calif.: Jacob's Ladder, 1995.

Wolfe, Gary K. Reviews of various Willis books in the magazine *Locus.* (Especially notable are reviews in the July 1992, January and June 1994, January 1995, and March 1996 issues.)

—PETER NICHOLLS

GENE WOLFE

(b. 1931)

GENE WOLFE, IT may be said, comes at the end of American science fiction. It may also be said that he comes as its climax. To establish the point of the first of these claims, it is simply necessary to make a brief argument about the nature and the history of American science fiction. To justify the second claim, it is necessary to present Gene Wolfe himself as a science fiction writer of very great importance; and it is necessary to treat the body of his fiction as a corpus of vaunting ambitiousness.

Indeed, whether or not a final assessment judges him to have succeeded in his varying ambitions, there is very little point in reading Gene Wolfe without reading him as an author who attempts to address issues and to create works of art of the utmost seriousness. As an author of entertainments, he is second rank at best. As a contributor to the long story that American science fiction has attempted to promulgate over the past century, he is a minor latecomer. Gene Wolfe is either a master artificer, or he is a footnote. The long story of American science fiction—to which Wolfe has contributed little—is a version of the future based on the almost never articulated premise that the twentieth century actually worked, that the twentieth century was a success. It is, in other words, a very special kind of science fiction. Over the world as a whole, science fiction has tended to a much wryer, much more pessimistic understanding of the March of Progress than that promulgated between approximately 1925 and approximately 1975 in the United States.

At the heart of American science fiction—and at the heart of the nostalgic movie and television retrofit exercises in reimagining the science fiction futures of half a century ago—a basic pulse can be detected. It is the pulse of Progress. Progress can be defined as a movement outward to conquer the world, to explore the solar system, to meet the stars on equal terms. Progress in American science fiction is embodied in the actions of competent men (and, once in a while, of competent women) who actively understand the potential of science and technology, who actively take the reins of power in their own hands, who aspire outward, who penetrate wildernesses, conquer new territories, subjugate unruly natives, and ultimately tend to found empires. The central engine of this story of outward thrust is, of course, the spaceship.

The ultimate collapse of this story of the future is a subject beyond the remit of any study of Gene Wolfe, who has shown little interest in the kinds of "Nows" that have supplanted the science fiction future: the archaizing of the exploration of space, the information or digital revolution, cyberspace, the empowerment (and simultaneous entrapment) of human beings into physical solitude, digital glut. It is the old science fiction tradition that we must return to in order to understand Wolfe, because it is from American science fiction in its brief prime that he takes most of his imagery, his hardware, his interstellar venues, the visible level of many of his story lines. He takes that material, the rich interwoven nest of stories and quotes and references, and sets his stories in territories familiar to any reader of the old science fiction. But he does not tell the old stories. In his masterpiece, the four-volume Book of the New Sun, and in many of his smaller works, the gear and the dreams of American science fiction are treated as things infinitely remote, infinitely cherishable, forever lost. Wolfe writes elegies. His works cherish the dream that the twentieth century had been made to work, but more fundamentally they mourn the fact that it did not. Gene Wolfe is a fin de siècle writer. He creates jewels out of the decadence and decay of the dream of our century.

Gene Rodman Wolfe was born on 7 May 1931, in Brooklyn, New York. He was an only child, though his relatives were numerous and many of them were profoundly eccentric. His family moved frequently until they settled, after a few years, in Houston, Texas. Wolfe was too young to be drafted in World War II, but he did not escape military service in Korea, a war and venue drowned out of the public sense of history by the far more deeply incriminating and nightmarish trauma of Vietnam. It was, all the same, a genuine war. *Letters Home* (1991) collects a number of letters Wolfe wrote from Korea. They are the earliest examples of his writing to reach print. They are literate, funny, seemingly open. They exhibit relatively little of the sacerdotal guardedness typical of almost all of his mature work. Though they are in fact emotionally reticent—or, more accurately, they tend to disguise the nature of the connective tissue between a powerfully expressed emotion and its cause—it is possible to discern in them something of the passionate, woundable, testy man to come.

On his return to the United States, Wolfe continued his education. He had been studying at Texas A&M University but shifted to the University of Houston, where he earned a B.S. in mechanical engineering in 1956. In that year, he married his childhood sweetheart, Rosemary Dietsch; they had four children. Wolfe worked as a project engineer for Procter and Gamble from 1956 to 1972, when

he became a senior editor for *Plant Engineering Magazine* in Barrington, Illinois, where he continues to live. In 1984 he retired from his editorial post, becoming a full-time writer.

As a sophomore at Texas A&M, Wolfe had published three stories in *Commentator*, the school literary journal. Almost immediately upon his discharge from military service, he began to write fiction again, both novels and stories, in the spare time he had after his full-time job and the beginning of his family. None sold for eight years. A few previously unpublished tales appear in *Young Wolfe: A Collection of Early Stories* (1992); spasmodically, some point to the future. Most do not. They are apprentice work and demonstrate that Wolfe's mature style—despite hints here and in the *Letters Home*—was not easily or instinctively achieved. Indeed, one might suggest that until Wolfe learned how to hold secrets, he could not really learn how to tell stories.

In 1965, Wolfe sold a story, "The Dead Man," to a skin magazine called *Sir!*; and in the same year, very much more significantly, he sold "Mountains Like Mice," a science fiction tale, to *If* magazine, then edited by Frederik Pohl. (It appeared in the May 1966 issue.) Very soon after that, he joined the Science Fiction Writers of America. This also proved significant, as it seems clear that Wolfe—though anything but ignorant of science fiction as a literature, having been an avid reader since childhood—had little personal knowledge of science fiction as a profession. He had been an engineer for almost a decade. He came to the science fiction subculture as a mature man at thirty-five years of age.

In this, he was like his fellow Catholic, R. A. Lafferty, who began to write at around the age of forty; but Lafferty was grandfathered into the genre and allowed to follow his own prolific and eccentric course without censure. Wolfe was never grandfathered into the genre as an elderly loner; he treated himself, and was treated by his peers, as a professional among professionals. From the first, he attempted to create for himself a career as a

928

science fiction writer. He joined the appropriate organizations, attended and eventually taught at both the Milford Conference and the Clarion Writers' Workshop. He paid the dues, won the awards—two Nebulas, a John W. Campbell Memorial Award, two World Fantasy Awards—and published almost exclusively with genre publishers, who issued his work as genre work.

If the contrast between Wolfe and Lafferty is considerable, however, then the contrast between Wolfe and another significant latecomer to science fiction, Robert A. Heinlein, is even greater and demonstrates vividly how rapidly science fiction had changed between 1939, when the thirty-two-year-old Heinlein began to publish, and 1965, when Wolfe began to make his own mark.

Both Heinlein and Wolfe were competent men with technical backgrounds; both were exceedingly ambitious about their work; each was potentially a better writer than any of his peers; each might have hoped to become a dominating figure. Only one of these men had any chance of success. Heinlein entered science fiction when the big story it was telling about the future had hardly taken conscious shape; and it was his articulation and domestication of that story that, more than any other single author's contribution, created the mature American science fiction genre. With his writing skills, and the personal gravitas he had gained in the years prior to his entry into the field, Heinlein became science fiction's godfather.

Wolfe entered science fiction after it had begun conspicuously to age and fissure, after it had become too fissiparous to bestride. No single writer could dream of gathering it all back together again. Whether or not he had any dreams of doing so, it was too late: the time had passed for science fiction to be thought of as a single body of story, as an enterprise, as a campaign for the future. Heinlein might become an icon, might create a genre and a following. Wolfe, similarly ambitious and similarly impressive in person, had no choice but to become a secret master. He has never dominated the genre his works look back upon. And except for his dazzled readers, he has no acknowledged following.

This unsought solitude as a writer is central to any understanding of Wolfe's greater works, which are works of synthesis and retrospect. They sum up and meditate upon the dreams of the past. They are fin de siècle. In the late 1960's, Wolfe was mainly known to the reading public as an *Orbit* author. The editor of this original anthology series was Damon Knight, a brilliant writer and editor whom Wolfe had encountered through correspondence and in writing workshops. Knight and Wolfe were both intelligent, acute, stimulating, stubborn, and ambitious. Both were fortunate that their professional relationship lasted through the *Orbit* years. In the end, Wolfe published about ten stories—they are his best early work—in *Orbit*, from the first, "Trip Trap" (1967) to possibly the finest, "Forlesen" (1974). More than perhaps the most famous of the *Orbit* stories, "Forlesen" expresses the iron poignance of Wolfe's greater work. Like all his best work, "Forlesen" (from the German, "Vorleson," meaning "read out") can be understood as a kind of bildungsroman, a tale of the moral and spiritual education (and life story) of its protagonist, from childhood on. The eponymous protagonist of this tale begins his life, and the single interminable day the tale occupies, in a kind of dawn fervor. He is drowned by life but engaged by it. He gains a job, a wife, and sense of placement. Things go well; things go sour. In the end, there is no reward for wisdom—and no punishment for ignorance. For Forlesen, as the long day wanes, wisdom must be its own reward. It has indeed been a long single day. He has aged, become an old man, a supernumerary. An undertaker finally appears to perform the obsequies. But Forlesen is still alive. He has a question: "I want to know if it's meant anything," Forlesen said. "If what I suffered—if it's been worth it." "No," the little man said. "Yes. No. Yes. Yes. No. Yes. Yes. Maybe."

The most famous of the remaining *Orbit* stories—if one puts to one side the first novelette of the three tales that comprise *The*

Gene Wolfe. © 1998 M. C. VALADA

Fifth Head of Cerberus (1972)—is almost certainly "The Island of Doctor Death and Other Stories" (1970), which was followed by three associated stories (none published in *Orbit*), "The Death of Doctor Island" (1973), "The Doctor of Death Island" (1978), and "Death of the Island Doctor" (1983). All four Archipelago tales were assembled as *The Wolfe Archipelago* (1983). Each of these stories can be read alone, though each works as a mirror of the themes and story lines of the others. As a whole, they comprise Wolfe's most intense early analysis of human identity as a kind of almost infernal entrapment. No child in Wolfe's work—and there are many—escapes unscathed into a free maturity. The environ-

ments these children inhabit are described in science fiction terms that only intensify the coffinlike intensity of the claustrophobia of the world, only underline the futility of any attempt at making a permanent escape. The robots, the rocketships, all the appurtenances of the old science fiction, which were invented by the old science fiction writers as signals and symbols of liberty and escape and which Wolfe recreates so lovingly, here turn out to be traps and delusions, emblems of a profound solitude. Wolfe's early stories are traps that mirror the traps of the world.

Because children are the viewpoint characters in the Archipelago texts, these deeply encrypted tales give off a deceptive air of clarity, for children see clearly. Children also see wrongly. This surface precision is typical of almost every story and novel from very nearly the beginning (Wolfe manuscripts, not perhaps coincidentally, are word perfect; no typos or pentimenti—visible signs of a change of mind—are allowed to soil the sanitized precision of the word). It is a precision that opens into but conceals the true story, which in Wolfe's canon is almost invariably coded to some degree. The true story has to be unpacked from a surface made up of seemingly clear-cut events. This act of unpacking or decipherment becomes almost second nature for readers of Wolfe's work; but it cannot be emphasized too strongly how radically estranged that work is from the old science fiction that inspires it.

The Archipelago tales are each set in the closed environment of an island, classically a venue for tales of symbolic import. "The Island of Doctor Death" features a young boy who attempts to deal with the terror of the world by inhabiting the soft, nostalgic world created for protagonists of a pulp magazine but only digs himself deeper into the trap of his own selfhood. "The Death of Doctor Island" more cruelly exposes to a fake world the tortured mind of a mentally distraught young boy. This fake world is intended by those who operate it as a form of investigative therapy. Their concern for their patient is—typical of Wolfe's attitude toward institutionalized professionals—difficult to parse, though not necessarily absent. In "The Doctor of Death Island," an older protagonist, a prisoner who has been cryogenically frozen, awakens to find that, in order to punish him more thoroughly, his world has also been frozen in place. He becomes an immortal in perpetual bondage. The protagonists of each story are (in a sense) in the same position the reader is: the surface of their lives only makes superficial sense, and they must decipher that surface in order to get in touch with the true story within, the story—it is never a story that they control—that tells them.

The cycle depicted in these stories is a frozen cycle, for the day of the life of Forlesen is inescapably fixed, and the imprisonment of the Island victims only deepens with knowledge. There is no return possible, no sense of seasonal renewal. This darkness is typical of Wolfe's early work, where a narrative structure that implies a message of hope usually turns out, in the end, too heavy, too embedded in grief and a sense of the ineluctable cruelty of the secular world, to turn the corner into spring. Spring does not come often in his early work; even a tale such as the long and ambitious "Tracking Song" (1975), which ends in an ostensible shout of triumph, leaves no sense in the reader that the literal frozen ruts its protagonists pace through as they circumnavigate their worldlet will ever truly melt.

It is only after about 1985 or so that a loosening of stricture can be discerned. A novel such as There Are Doors (1988) hesitantly allows its protagonist a glimpse of escape into Eden at the end, though it is a most ambiguous Eden. The Urth of the New Sun (1987)—which is a sequel to the Book of the New Sun—affords its Redeemer protagonist some surcease from the iron wheel of mortality to which he has been subjected again and again. And the cycle depicted in Empires of Foliage and Flower: A Tale from the Book of the Wonders of Urth and Sky (1987), a novella composed as a pendant to the Book of the New Sun, also lightens at the close. There is always an implication in this tale that Winter could

stick fast and never cease; but in the end its God-like protagonist, Father Thyme, who ages as he travels westward over the world and grows younger if he travels eastward, eventually returns his girl companion to the childhood that had been wrested from her.

This loosening of stricture is not frequently found, however, in Wolfe's shorter works, the most notable other stories of the late 1970's probably being "The Hero as Werwolf" (1975); "The Eyeflash Miracles" (1976), which is a darkened reworking of the tale of L. Frank Baum's Ozma of Oz (1907); "Seven American Nights" (1978), a late Orbit contribution that quite extraordinarily enriches the story reversal John Ames Mitchell was the first to suggest, in The Last American (1889), where an expedition from the Middle East visits a strange, deformed, decadent, powerless America; and "The Detective of Dreams" (1980), a homage to writers such as G. K. Chesterton, whose famous Father Brown is a kind of detective for God, in which Wolfe's underlying Catholic beliefs come very close to the surface. These stories show little or no loosening, nor do most of the other tales that have been collected in book form with them and thus made available to larger audiences. The main collections are The Island of Doctor Death and Other Stories and Other Stories (1980), Gene Wolfe's Book of Days (1981), Storeys from the Old Hotel (1988), and Endangered Species (1989). As yet, none of the many Wolfe stories written after the late 1980's has appeared in book form.

Nor is much loosening apparent in Wolfe's first few novels. Although Gene Wolfe has written approximately 200 short stories and although many of them are central to an understanding of the science fiction short story at the end of the twentieth century, it is as a novelist that he has become best known, and it is upon his novels that his ultimate reputation perhaps will rest. The first of them, Operation ARES (1970), is an apprentice work; it was cut savagely by its publisher and has never appeared in full. The second, The Fifth Head of Cerberus, has been described as a collection, pure and simple, of three linked

931

novellas and as a novel in three parts. Tax-
onomy is not, perhaps, the best way to arrive
at an understanding of the structure of this
most unusual text. Suffice it to say that the
book looks like and makes some sense when
treated as a collection; but only when its parts
are thought of as novelistically linked does
the whole—and many of the parts—become
understandable.

The Fifth Head of Cerberus is a prison
story. The third part is set in a literal prison;
the first part comprises the unreliable narration of the fifth successive clone of an early
resident of the two-planet system, colonized
long ago by settlers of French origin, where
the book is set. The second part concentrates
on a shape-shifting native of the system, who
has imprisoned himself in the shape of a dead
human anthropologist in a vain attempt to
escape his colonized, dubiously evolutionary
condition. The unnamed clone who narrates
the events of the first part (a readerly act of
decipherment will uncover the fact that his
name is in fact Gene Wolfe) is profoundly entrapped in his engineered clone-self. He is a
victim, in other words, of family. He is a child
who cannot escape his heritage, because—
irredeemably—he *is* his heritage. He has no
hope of leaping free (his narration is set down
in an indeterminate time in the future). He is
additionally ensconced within and encum-
bered by a kind of secret family. He is the first
significant Wolfe character to attempt to free
himself by concealing the identities of those
who surround him—but he will not be the
last. Further acts of readerly decipherment
may uncover aunts, mistresses, owners where
they are least expected; a full analysis of the
book will undoubtedly uncover an iron net of
imprisoning connections. The shape shifter,
on the other hand, *becomes* the anthropologist in whose death he has had some role, and
his attempts to free himself through false
identities echo throughout against "Gene
Wolfe's" attempts to free himself through the
suppression of true identities. Both inhabit
coffins of self; neither will ever break free.

Around these two characters Wolfe weaves
a subtle, sad portrait of worlds whose isola-

tion from the unattainable mainstream of
human life is complete. The aborigines are
treated with some cruelty. The almost-
unseen government exercises its powers with
Kafkaesque arbitrariness. By indirection we
are presented a tale of the future whose primary "tonality" is one of a doomed belated-
ness. Almost all of Wolfe's works present
worlds that are in some sense echoes of previous worlds (the two worlds in *The Fifth
Head of Cerberus* intricately refract one another; both echo the long-distant, spoiled culture of Earth). What this novel lacks, and
what some of the later books gingerly (and
humbly) offer, is any sense of the possibility
of redemption. Wolfe is not only Catholic; he
is a practicing Catholic, and although he has
never written a novel that presents Catholic
beliefs and practice in what one might call
their accidental or circumstantial form, he
has rarely written a book that lacks a Catholic
substance, a sense that life is staged for God,
who may make it possible for the cycle of
death to melt. But *The Fifth Head of Cerberus*
remains frozen.

Wolfe's third novel, *Peace* (1975), may be
his finest single book-length fiction; it is also
his first significant fantasy (and as such stands
somewhat outside the remit of this essay). It
can be said, all the same, that *Peace* continues
and amplifies the themes of Wolfe's science
fiction to that point. The central theme of the
bondage of identity is deeply underlined here,
for *Peace* is, in matter of fact, *told* from a cof-
fin. *Peace* is a posthumous fantasy—a term
used to describe stories whose protagonists
have already died and who occupy during the
course of the tale some sort of limbo where
they come to understand that they are in fact
dead and where they attempt to resolve their
sense of the lives they have just departed. It
is the life story of Alden Dennis Weer, who
tells his tale without ever explicitly recognizing that he is speaking from within the ultimate bondage of his grave. His life seems ordinary enough on the surface. He is born to
well-to-do parents, in the American Midwest,
around the turn of the twentieth century. He
lives a life seemingly without external drama,

a life centered around family, the small city of his birth, and his professional life as part of a family business that manufactures a soft drink. Eventually he has a stroke; soon after (the reader is able to decipher from clues laid down throughout the text) he is dead; many years later, he tells his story.

However, it is not as simple as that. Weer's life, as he recounts it, is strangely broken. Not one of the many stories and anecdotes that interweave through the book and purport to illustrate his life is ever actually completed - just as, perhaps, Weer's own life remains incomplete until he recognizes that it is over (which he never clearly does). Moreover, a series of mysterious deaths darkens the broken tale; it is entirely possible, for instance, that Weer has killed his own aunt by running her down on the main street of town; Weer may be (or may be only in part) a monster. The reader does not establish any secure sense of his character, or of what may have happened during long undescribed gaps in the life he records, or of what deeds he may have committed. Weer ends as a broken figure; *Peace* ends as another paradigm rendering of the Wolfe trap.

The trap, Wolfe says, is who you are. Wolfe's fourth novel, *The Devil in a Forest* (1976), seems relatively clear-cut, though even here there are glimpses of an estranging perspective. It is the story of a young man whose life intersects with the Christmas carol that tells the story of good King Wenceslas and can be read straightforwardly—by the older children for whom it was originally marketed—as a fantasia upon that old tale. But the young protagonist is secretive and slightly harsh, like other Wolfe protagonists; and the reader, after having been given a brief passage presenting his perspective from 30 years hence, will feel some of the usual insecurity at trusting to the surface of events.

By the late 1970's, then, Gene Wolfe had written dozens of short stories and novellas of considerable interest, though formidably various and "obscure." He had also published four novels—one a truncated failure, one an intricate and difficult conflation of three inti-

mately linked novellas, one (*Peace*) a fantasy whose publishers marketed it as a nonfantasy idyll sentimentalizing small-town America; and a children's book. Though his reputation was already high among a relatively small cadre of readers, it did not seem that Wolfe was much interested in becoming, or was ever likely to become, a writer of general appeal.

In 1980 this all changed. It could not be said that, by beginning to publish the four-volume, 400,000-word Book of the New Sun in that year, Wolfe in any way compromised his austere, rigorous, hermetic, dark concerns. For there is no compromise here. For all its richness of hue, for all the dozens of larger than-life characters who walk its pages and tiptoe down its secret aisles, for all the apparent confessional honesty of the protagonist Severian—who takes all four volumes to reach the apparent climax of his story and who leaves us dangling in a clamor of bells at the end—the Book of the New Sun is an arduous masterpiece of late high modernism, an autonomous, dense, erudite work. It is Wolfe's most formidable accomplishment to date, though the recent Book of the Long Sun is clearly and profoundly more humane. That it is not very widely understood as a central accomplishment of late twentieth century art can only be explained by the general refusal of those critics who represent the literary and academic establishment to acknowledge the intrinsic merit and force of genre literatures; this refusal speaks poorly of that cohort. The failure to address the accomplishment represented by the Book of the New Sun impoverishes the world of literature as a whole.

The Book of the New Sun was released in four volumes: *The Shadow of the Torturer* (1980), *The Claw of the Conciliator* (1981), *The Sword of the Lictor* (1982), and *The Citadel of the Autarch* (1983). Though a passage through some sort of gate marks the end of each volume, the four as a whole make up one consecutive story, all narrated in the same even, exact-seeming, metaphor-rich, secret-bearing voice. The setting is Urth, a far-future version of our planet. So many millennia have passed, so many civilizations have risen and fallen, and so much of the universe has been explored and forgotten that the humans of Urth walk on a kind of holy ground. The ground of Urth is holy because it is a creation of—it is intrinsic with—the Increate (who may be the God of Wolfe's own Catholic belief, but who is here understood in very different terms). The ground of Urth is also holy because it is a literal record and palimpsest, miles deep, of human history on the planet. The roots of mountains conceal the footprints of dead monarchs. Every grain of sand of Urth is a relict of those two forces: God and humanity.

Severian believes himself to be (or allows his readers to think he believes himself to be) an orphan. He is brought up by the Guild of Torturers in the Matachin Tower, an ancient structure that experienced readers of Wolfe will quickly identify as a spaceship embedded in the earth, along with a number of other spaceships, near the center of Nessus, the capital city of the empire Severian is destined to rule one day. He becomes an apprentice torturer, serving (as do all his superiors) the needs of the ruling Autarch. He is haunted (or perhaps he recalls from some earlier incarnation, for he may in some sense be the reincarnation of the Redeemer figure known as the Conciliator) by hints that Urth has run its course, that Urth must be redeemed by the advent of a New Sun. As a torturer, however, he himself is a secular arm of the state; his shadow (as the title of the first volume adumbrates) stands between his victim and any New Sun. So, somehow, he must ascend.

An androgynous figure, who later turns out to have been the Autarch in one of his/her many disguises, takes an interest in Severian. Severian becomes enamored of Thecla, a highborn victim of the state who has become his "client." He allows her to die more quickly than her sentence had decreed and is himself rusticated as a punishment, though not before physically ingesting (through the use of an arcane drug) the essence of her selfhood and consciousness: from this point, Thecla shadows him from within, in an intimacy deeper than lovers can achieve. Severian's marching

orders take him north toward the tropics (his native land seems to occupy more or less the position of present-day Brazil); he meets a wide range of future subjects and sleeps with several women. One of these, Dorcas, he saves from immersion in a river and sleeps with her. (Readers who do not decipher Wolfe's clues at this point will miss the fact that he has resurrected her 40 years after she drowned, and that she is his paternal grandmother.) He acquires the Claw of the Conciliator from a group of traveling nuns. He performs miracles with this claw, or so it seems, but it soon becomes clear that the Claw is no more (or less) sacred than anything else on Urth and that the miracles Severian performs come straight out of his nature. Where he sleeps, grass grows greener than before. He reaches the far north, engages in battles, and meets Master Ash, who has descended an Yggdrasil-like tree backward through time in order, it seems, to witness Severian's assumption of both secular and holy power.

At this point Severian is found by the dying Autarch again and assumes power through a ritual of very great strangeness, by which (as he had with Thecla earlier) he ingests the personalities of all previous Autarchs. Severian becomes legion. He returns to the Atrium of Time—a mysterious courtyard in the heart of Nessus—where he meets for the second time a woman named Valeria, who will soon become his wife (a fact readers are allowed to guess, though Wolfe does not allow this news to reach the surface of the story). He is ready to take the test imposed on all willing Autarchs, the test that will judge whether he is fit to bring the New Sun to Urth, whether he is fit, in other words, to become the new Apollo, the new Christ. The novel ends after Severian has spoken autarchal Words of Power, which the Atrium of Time recognizes; and bells begin to ring.

Flowing and romantic detail work suffuses the Book of the New Sun, giving it an exquisite autumnal glow, and it is perhaps understandable that some of the early readers of the first volumes took the text to be a Dying Earth fantasy deeply beholden to the work of Jack

Vance. In some ways, as Wolfe has acknowledged, it does pay homage to Vance's work. Clearly Vance's *The Dying Earth* (1950) lies behind the basic time scheme and architecture of the setting: the Urth sunk deep in old age; moments when the text seems overfull of random if luxuriant detail, so that dissimilar elements are swamped in bricolage, jumbled together into a mosaic without a design. Vance's Dying Earth is a world verging upon irreversible death; and its characters float in a bath of sensation like so many elderly fish.

At first glance, the Book of the New Sun is similarly overloaded with sensation. But at second glance, nothing in its extensive array of science fiction tropes and images, icons and story elements—from robots to spaceships, from time travel to white-hole new suns—turns out to be arbitrary. Nothing in its extensive armamentarium of fantasy literature images proves, in the end, not to be reducible to tightly argued science fiction. There is no magic in the Book of the New Sun, no sorcery, no wizards or witches or dark lord. All that seems arbitrary or bricolagelike or fantastical turns out to confirm, one way or another, the unforgiving refusal of the story to fail to make sense.

Severian, too, is anything but a dilettante at the end of time and does anything but float passively through the story he is telling. He is a torturer, a killer, a savant, a swordsman, a rake, a cold dauphin on the make, and a politician of God; and he knows (though he does not tell us directly) that he is mysteriously akin to both Apollo and Christ. There is hardly a sentence in the vast edifice of text he has erected that does not betray his holy/unholy ambition or reveal his profound sense of obligation to everything that happens around him. Everything connects.

Everything—all the science fiction instruments so copiously displayed and cunningly manipulated, all the fantasy imagery so conclusively transformed into fact—contributes to a sense of Urth as a land in the midst of an apocalyptic drama of the severest import, a drama whose outcome transcends the secular world so copiously described. If Severian loses

his game of ambition, Urth will die. If he wins—if he behaves in the manner of the Conciliator reborn—then the world will be redeemed. This message radically undercuts the inner dynamic of American science fiction, which argues the reverse: that whatever the end may be, the means—that which science fiction deals with primarily—are what count. The Book of the New Sun claims to teach us, on the other hand, that technics are as grass and that freedom is a surprise of God.

In *The Urth of the New Sun*—a kind of footnote to the larger work, told in a recessional voice—Severian is allowed to travel in a vast edificelike ship through the Kabbalist heavens, which are described in strictly science fiction terms, in order to pass a test of merit. If he fails, he will be "unmanned" as was the Autark before him. If he passes, he will be allowed to perform the miracle of rebirth. By the time he finishes this movement in his life, he has been dead and reborn (or dead and a ghost) more than once; and his success turns out to be a foregone conclusion. He returns to Urth via the corridors of time that allow him to visit the past, where he undergoes a series of scourgings and epiphanies. Finally, he travels back to a period some decades after his departure; meets Valeria, his wife grown old; and brings the New Sun, a white hole that is required to replenish the fires of the old sun. Many are drowned when this savage rebirth is inflicted upon Urth. Severian then experiences further epiphanies before going to his rest, on the crest of a hill where three bowers stand, "decked . . . with twined lupine, purple loosestrife, and white meadow rue. 'There,' [his priest tells him]. 'There the other gods sleep.'"

Gene Wolfe was more than fifty years old when he completed the Book of the New Sun, and he had accomplished a good lifetime's work in the twenty years since his writing career began. His retirement as senior editor of *Plant Engineering* might well have signaled his semiretirement from literature, but he has treated his release from payroll as an incentive to live as a full-time writer. However, much of his late work—fantasies such as *Soldier of the Mist* (1986) and its sequel, *Soldier of Arete* (1989); *There Are Doors*; and *Castleview* (1990); and the detective novel *Pandora by Holly Hollander* (1990)—lies beyond the remit of this essay, but each of these works is strikingly dissimilar to all the others, and each may be profitably examined for its exploration of themes central to his work as a whole. There do remain two works of central science fiction interest.

Free Live Free (1984; revised 1985) is set in a contemporary America whose stripped, bleak contours make one think of the desolate cityscapes of the American painter Edward Hopper; but the landscapes and cityscapes of this novel, however bleached and stripped down they may initially seem, are rendered with a magic glow. Every sight, every building, every person in the novels seems to be self-emblematic. The story, which is not simple, can be understood as a replay of L. Frank Baum's *The Wonderful Wizard of Oz* (1900). Four characters occupy a boardinghouse owned by Ben Free, who has disappeared. They go in search of him, experiencing a range of adventures; it becomes apparent that in searching for him they are searching for some secret that will make them happy. Eventually they find and confront him at the controls of a vast wooden airplane, which also serves as a time machine and through which Ben Free has some ambiguous sovereignty over the world below. He shows each of the four that their happiness lies within, and—it is magical in its effect, though it is accomplished through a normal science fiction use of time travel—he gives them their lives to live again, happily this time, it may be. Unlike Severian, who lives his own life more than once, the four protagonists of *Free Live Free* cannot expect to gain immeasurable knowledge (or to suffer immeasurably) from their return to base. Their outcome will be simpler, less daunting, less imprisoning. They will be the first Wolfe protagonists—be they clones or impostors or revenants or avatars—for whom repetition leads toward freedom.

The Book of the Long Sun, like its great predecessor, was published in four volumes amounting to something like 400,000 words and even more seamlessly than the first series comprises one single unbroken story. The four volumes are *Nightside the Long Sun* (1993), *The Lake of the Long Sun* (1994), *Caldé of the Long Sun* (1994), and *Exodus from the Long Sun* (1996). It is a tale that, like almost all of Wolfe's most interesting work, builds to what Kim Stanley Robinson has called a "slingshot ending," an ending that subjectively and aesthetically shoots the reader off the last page into some new world. In this case, that new world will be more than adumbrated, as Wolfe's next major work (projected in 1998 for publication around the turn of the new century) will be a direct continuation of the Long Sun, its projected title being The Book of the Short Sun; volume one's projected title is *On Blue's Waters*. The Book of the Long Sun is structured, along with its great predecessor, around a question of memory. New Sun is a confession written for its readers' benefit by a man (Severian) who cannot forget anything but whose allegiance to the truth is sometimes dubious. Long Sun narrates the constant, intense, saintly efforts of a man (Patera Silk)—who has been given an information-dense god-given epiphany in the first paragraph of the sequence—to remember, and only slowly to understand, what he has been told. The narrative strategy Wolfe employs to dramatize this search for understanding is simple enough: the Long Sun sequence is astonishingly packed with conversations, dialogues, debates, briefings. In the end, Patera Silk—whose goodness as a character radiates throughout the sequence's 1,200 pages—can be seen as a man who longs to tell the truth. This longing, not usual in life and not often found in fictional characters, marks him as absolutely unique in Wolfe's oeuvre: most of his characters tell their own stories and in doing so expose (but inveterately conceal at the same time) the circumstances that shaped them as children. Patera Silk, unlike almost any of Wolfe's other protagonists, is a full-grown man whose gaze lies forward in time.

The tale itself utilizes to the full Wolfe's remarkable command of the instruments of genre science fiction. It is set almost wholly within the Whorl, a generation starship that has been traveling from Earth (or Urth) at sublight speeds for approximately three hundred years, carrying its cargo of humans (and others) in their many thousands in search of an inhabitable planet. This Whorl is described in terms impeccably science fiction, with echoes throughout of other conceptual breakthrough novels set in science fiction pocket universes.

The novel opens (as we learn later) thirty years after the Whorl has come to rest in orbit around a twin-planet system. Patera Silk is a priest in the Whorl's prevailing church—he is, as Wolfe has said in seminars, a good man in a bad religion—and the epiphany he experiences from the god-figure known as the Outsider conveys to him, obscurely but relentlessly, that the Whorl is in trouble; that he, who as a ministering priest must care for his flock, must ultimately care for them properly by becoming the Caldé, or leader of his local territory. Like Severian, then, Patera Silk is a man predestined to become ruler; and the Long Sun, like its predecessor, is the story of an assumption. There are other similarities and analogies between the two series, though some are difficult to decipher. Both books are full of gods. A millennium years before the start of the Long Sun, the Whorl had been launched by a figure from the New Sun: the two-headed tyrant named Typhon from a time on Urth earlier than Severian's. Typhon has digitalized himself and his family (whose squabbles echo the squabbles of the gods of Olympus) and has ruled the Whorl, now calling himself Pas and taking on the attributes of a god, from within the "Mainframe" computer system that guides the ship. Pas's pantheon manifests itself through monitors and through its ability to possess humans. There are also closer links.

If, for instance, the Whorl can be presumed to have traveled at a high fraction of the speed of light (Wolfe is far too competent not to figure in this possibility), then it can be calculated, taking the chronologies of the two sequences into consideration, that Patera Silk and Severian are contemporaries. (These calculations have been made by Michael André-Driussi in his *A Quick & Dirty Guide to the Long Sun Whorl* [1997].) If they are contemporaries, then the identity of the Outsider—who shares many characteristics with Severian, who has himself become a kind of god—becomes moot. Like Severian, who has ingested Thecla and all previous autarchs, the Outsider speaks not in a voice but voices, the two main ones being that of a man and a woman.

Whatever may be the identity of the Outsider, his message shapes Silk not only into a saint but also into a Moses. Knowing that the Whorl is decaying in orbit around inhabitable planets and that aliens from those planets have dangerously infiltrated the extremely numerous human societies of the Whorl, Silk comes to the realization that, in order to save anyone, he must cause the Whorl to be evacuated. He himself, however, for complex reasons, remains behind. He disappears into unknown regions of the dormant Whorl. With the Book of the Long Sun, Wolfe continues his explorations into the aesthetic of science fiction and into its human meaning. Nothing he says is technically new, for his control of the instruments of science fiction is retrospective; but everything he says is washed in the light of a commanding synoptic flow of understanding. He synthesizes a century of science fiction into a series of works about the shape and destiny of the human soul. Gene Wolfe does not show us what science fiction can do; he shows us what science fiction can be.

Selected Bibliography

WORKS OF GENE WOLFE

Operation ARES. New York: Berkley, 1970.
The Fifth Head of Cerberus: Three Novellas. New York: Scribners, 1972.

Peace. New York: Harper and Row, 1975.

The Devil in a Forest. Chicago: Follett, 1976.

The Island of Doctor Death and Other Stories and Other Stories. New York: Pocket Books, 1980. (Collection.)

The Shadow of the Torturer. New York: Simon and Schuster, 1980. (The Book of the New Sun, volume one.)

The Claw of the Conciliator. New York: Simon and Schuster, 1981. (The Book of the New Sun, volume two.)

Gene Wolfe's Book of Days. Garden City, N.Y.: Doubleday, 1981. (Collection.)

The Sword of the Lictor. New York: Simon and Schuster, 1981 [actual 1982]. (The Book of the New Sun, volume three.)

The Castle of the Otter: A Book About the Book of the New Sun. Willimantic, Conn.: Ziesing, 1982.

The Citadel of the Autarch. New York: Simon and Schuster, 1983. (The Book of the New Sun, volume four.)

The Wolfe Archipelago. Willimantic, Conn.: Ziesing, 1983. (Collection.)

Bibliomen: Twenty Characters Waiting for a Book. New Castle, Va.: Cheap Street, 1984. Revised edition, retitled *Bibliomen: Twenty-Two Characters in Search of a Book.* Broken Mirrors, 1995.

Free Live Free. Willimantic, Conn.: Ziesing, 1984. Revised edition, New York: TOR, 1985.

Plan[e]t Engineering. Cambridge, Mass.: NESFA Press, 1984. (Collection.)

The Boy Who Hooked the Sun: A Tale from the Book of the Wonders of Urth and Sky. New Castle, Va.: Cheap Street, 1985.

Soldier of the Mist. New York: TOR, 1986.

The Arimaspian Legacy. New Castle, Va.: Cheap Street, 1987.

Empires of Foliage and Flower: A Tale from the Book of the Wonders of Urth and Sky. New Castle, Va.: Cheap Street, 1987.

The Urth of the New Sun. London: Gollancz, 1987. (The Book of the New Sun, volume 5.)

For Rosemary. London: Kerosina, 1988. (Poetry.)

Storeys from the Old Hotel. Worcester, Surrey, England: Kerosina, 1988. (Collection.)

There Are Doors. New York: TOR, 1988.

Endangered Species. New York: TOR, 1989. (Collection.)

Seven American Nights. New York: TOR, 1989. (Story bound with Robert Silverberg's *Sailing to Byzantium.*)

Slow Children at Play. New Castle, Va: Cheap Street, 1989.

Soldier of Arete. New York: TOR, 1989. (Sequel to *Soldier of the Mist.*)

Castleview. New York: TOR, 1990.

The Death of Doctor Island. New York: TOR, 1990. (Story bound with John M. Ford's *Fugue State.*)

Pandora by Holly Hollander. New York: TOR, 1990.

The Case of the Vanishing Ghost. Rochester, Mich.: Pretentious, 1991.

The Hero as Werwolf. Eugene, Oreg.: Pulphouse, 1991. (Story.)

Letters Home. Weston, Ontario, Canada: United Mythologies, 1991. (Nonfiction.)

Young Wolfe: A Collection of Early Stories. Windsor, Ontario, Canada: United Mythologies, 1992. (Collection.)

Nightside the Long Sun. New York: TOR, 1993. (The Book of the Long Sun, volume one.)

Caldé of the Long Sun. New York: TOR, 1994 (The Book of the Long Sun, volume three.)

Lake of the Long Sun. New York: TOR, 1994. (The Book of the Long Sun, volume two.)

Exodus from the Long Sun. New York, TOR, 1996. (The Book of the Long Sun, volume four.)

CRITICAL AND BIOGRAPHICAL STUDIES

André-Driussi, Michael. *Lexicon Urthus: A Dictionary for the Urth Cycle.* San Francisco, Calif.: Sirius Fiction, 1994.

———. *The Quick and Dirty Guide to the Long Sun Whorl.* San Francisco, Calif.: Sirius Fiction, 1997.

Gordon, Joan. *Gene Wolfe.* Mercer Island, Wash.: Starmont, 1986.

—JOHN CLUTE

S. FOWLER WRIGHT

(1874–1965)

One night, when half my life behind me lay
I wandered from the straight lost path afar,
Through the great dark was no releasing
   way;
Above that dark was no relieving star.

THESE, THE FIRST lines of S. Fowler Wright's translation of the "Inferno" from Dante's *Divine Comedy*, might just as well apply to Wright himself. Like Dante, midway in the forest of his life, he abandoned a secure way to pursue a solitary wandering through the darkness of dismay and despair. He does not seem to have found any salvation, but he undoubtedly derived satisfaction from awarding pain to the ideas and classes of people he disliked.

Sydney Fowler Wright was born in Birmingham, England, in 1874, and attended King Edward's School, one of the oldest institutions in the Midlands. While exact details are not known, he seems to have operated his own business as an accountant, specializing in receiverships, although he was not a member of the Chartered Accountants of Great Britain. He followed this occupation until 1919 or 1920, when at the age of forty-five or forty-six, almost exactly halfway through his life, he began his second career, that of poet, editor, and novelist.

His first book was a poetic version of a section from the *Morte d'Arthur*; he published it himself in 1919. He also prepared poetic translations of portions of the Song of Songs and wrote independent verse. While his poetry has received no attention on this side of the Atlantic, it was highly praised in British literary media, including the *Times Literary Supplement*. His chief d'oeuvre of this period was his translation of the "Inferno," which he prepared in rhymed iambic pentameter. As can be seen from the brief quotation heading this article, his verse is jagged and rough, not close to the original in word-for-word matters, but occasionally powerful. While Wright was forced, at times, to strange locutions to preserve rhyme, individual phrases are often striking.

Wright also maintained his own small publishing business, in which he served as editor of a series of collections. He was editor of *Poetry* from 1920 to 1932; this periodical is not to be confused with the American periodical of the same name. He also edited the *County Series of Contemporary Poets* and prepared collections of verse from local sources. While most of these volumes are not available in America, they seem to have been of competent, traditional verse.

In 1925, Wright embarked on the career that made him one of the classic writers of science fiction. This was with his publication of *The Amphibians*, the first portion of a romance, satire, and novel of ideas set in the far future. The second portion of the novel was finished in 1929, and both parts were then published together as *The World Below*. Both the original *The Amphibians* and *The World Below* were reasonably successful, but they gave no hint of the great commercial success that was soon to follow.

Wright suddenly became an author of world renown with *Deluge* (1927), a catastrophe novel with some social content, dealing with the submergence of most of Great Britain. Fairly popular in England, it became a near best-seller in America. It was also very well received critically. As reviewers who were unaware of *The Amphibians* stated, it was a remarkable feat for a first novel by a man in his early fifties. *Dawn* (1929), an overlap and sequel novel, was even more highly regarded critically, but less successful on the market.

From 1929 on, Wright was a professional writer. Some of his work he published through various small companies of his own; other work appeared commercially. Although he wrote a few more science fiction novels and short stories, he concentrated on mystery and detective fiction, producing twenty-five such books between 1930 and 1945. He died on 25 February 1965. For those who are curious about how he conformed to the ideas that emerge from his work, he had two wives and ten children.

I

Today Wright is remembered among historians of science fiction for *The World Below*, which has been reprinted several times in various formats. Unfortunately, it has usually been considered a rather turgid adventure novel, and most science fiction readers have not understood the elaborate structuring of ideas within it. It is more often referred to than read. His other two important works, *Deluge* and *Dawn*, while collected as science fiction, seem to have drifted off into mainstream literature, where they have been submerged by many other near best-sellers.

The World Below (which includes *The Amphibians*) is almost universally considered Wright's most important work. It is not generally known, though, that it is an unfinished work; only two parts of the projected three were written.

The story line of *The World Below* is fairly simple. The narrator, Danby, sometimes called the Primitive, is propelled half a million years into the future by the Professor's time apparatus. He is to remain there for one year, partly to explore, partly to discover what has happened to two men who have gone into the future ahead of him. When he arrives, he immediately finds himself beset by difficulties far beyond his powers to cope with; but by chance he forms an association with an Amphibian, a member of one of the two dominant, intelligent races of the future planet.

The Amphibian, who is both nameless and sexless (though the Primitive usually thinks of it as "she"), is trying to rescue one of its leaders from captivity by a race of horrors called the Killers. The Primitive and the Amphibian agree to aid each other, and together they make their way over the hostile continent.

Their greatest danger, it is assumed, is from the Dwellers, who rule the landmass. They are twenty-five-foot giants, more closely related to *Homo sapiens* than is the Amphibian. There are captivities, escapes, perils, and many discussions about ethical and moral matters while both beings experience new wonders.

In the first volume the Amphibian and the Primitive wander about the surface and witness a climactic encounter between Amphibians and Dwellers. In the second volume the two take to the great tunnels that honeycomb the world, the hidden territory of the Dwellers, in search of the missing men. On this quest the Primitive and the Amphibian learn much about the tragic situation of the Dwellers, who, despite their great gifts and powers, are on the edge of extinction.

The two explorers are in peril all through their wandering, but are seemingly ignored by the Dwellers because of a more serious threat: war with gigantic, unintelligent, composite insectlike beings from another continent. These beings are the size of a skyscraper and very difficult to kill. When the war is over, the Amphibian is informed that it must return to its seas, and the Primitive continues his quest alone. He learns the fate of the missing men but is captured by the Dwellers and eventually is sent to the center of the earth, where he is to entertain blasé, aged Dwellers. His twentieth-century year finished, he is pulled back to England, where he tells his adventures.

The World Below, with its slender plot line and frequent discursive interruptions and allegorically designed biological monstrosities, is weak novelistically, partly because until well into the book the reader is likely to be perplexed about what Wright is trying to do. Is he writing a novel of story, with adventures and horrors, or an appraisal of understanding and empathy between alien minds, or a projection of future biology, or, as seems to be his chief purpose, a satire and a fictionalized study of transcendental ethics?

"Transcendental" here is to be taken in two senses: first, as an ideal theory of action, such as might be envisioned by godlike beings, and, second, as a range of behavior far removed from the concerns of daily life in a reasonable human society.

This ethical material appears mostly in lengthy digressions between the narrator and the Amphibian, in which twentieth-century morality is perpetually contrasted with what Wright probably considers an absolute morality; a median position is sought. Although we are usually conditioned to regard anything dealing with abstract ethics as dull and pettifogging, Wright's material is far from dull; it is often very exciting intellectually. He demonstrates, as he does elsewhere in his work, a very subtle mind with a power to penetrate to the issues behind words, making distinctions and clarifying much that is not immediately obvious—whether or not one agrees with him. A fairly long segment of the novel, for example, is taken up with the trial of a group of legalistic birdmen, whom Wright symbolizes in the same manner as later, in his detective stories, he characterizes His Majesty's justices—intellectual vultures.

Much of the ethical argument and its biological embodiment seems at first grotesque, but if one realizes that part of Wright's purpose is to satirize specific points in modern civilization—personality types that enter cer-

S. Fowler Wright. Courtesy of the Library of Congress

tain occupations, oddities in legal situations, moral ambiguities—the grotesqueness is seen to be metaphoric and not unmeaningful.

While *The World Below* is obviously in the tradition of H. G. Wells's *The Time Machine*, what with a frame containing abstracted personalities, the concept of time as a linear dimension along which one can travel back and forth (with no regard for paradoxes), and occasional landscape details—it marks one great advance over Wells's work. This is in the attainment of alienness.

If we omit for the moment the rabbit men in the fragment that Wells discarded from the final form of his novel, Wells's time traveler found that human evolution ended with two branches: the Eloi and the Morlocks. (Has anyone ever noticed that these terms correspond to Eli and Moloch?) But there is no question of real alienness about either race. The Eloi are simply the children of a late Victorian garden party, while the Morlocks are base mechanics of the lower sort.

With Wright, though, the two future races of man have evolved, over half a million years, into forms so alien that there can be little understanding between them and us. It is not just that they are superior to *Homo sapiens*, but that they are so utterly alien that even the perpetual intercession of the Amphibian psychopomp has difficulty in bridging the gap between ethics *sub specie aeternitatis* and ethics, modern man.

The chief conclusion (which must be reached in part through a consideration of the ideas expressed more openly and explicitly in Wright's other work) is that both future races, despite their ethical stature, are decadent and headed for extinction. In this attitude Wright is attempting to be Janus, to look both ways at once, to combine ethical superiority with degeneration in other respects. The double vision, like that of astigmatism, is more jarring than convincing to the reader.

While the Dwellers are awesome physically, firmed out in flesh as hard as ivory and resistant to physical damage; while they possess a strange science far superior to ours, though Wright avoids specifics; while they are almost immortal—they have two germs of death that will destroy them in moments of geological time. For all practical purposes they have stopped reproducing, and after a certain age they retreat into boredom and depressive states. Because of their insectlike enemies, it can be only a short time before the Dwellers are gone, together with the cultures that they hold captive for experimental purposes inside the earth. All in all, the Dwellers symbolize, for Wright, that portion of the scientific mind or attitude that is often called scientism.

The Amphibians are a somewhat more perplexing case, since in many ways they are more alien to us than the Dwellers, even though the Primitive can develop empathy with an aberrant Amphibian. In mental power they are equal to the gigantic Dwellers, whom they fear and respect, but they seemingly have abandoned the techniques of science and live in quietism beneath the sea. Possibly they symbolize religion.

Their perfection is physical, in that they possess coordinations and adaptive possibilities that *Homo sapiens* could only dream of. Their bodies do not decay and can be reanimated after death, and they possess detachable "souls" that hover about and remain in telepathic contact with the "living." Their mode of life, including their means of reproduction, is so alien that the Primitive does not even attempt to understand it, but at best they remain constant in number. This factor, for Wright, despite all other attainments of future man, is the ultimate mark of inadequacy, since for Wright the First Commandment is not a negative one, but very positive: Be fruitful and multiply.

We can only speculate on the content of the third, unwritten part of *The World Below*. Since the events in the last part of the book are speeded up and presented only in summary, it is possible that Wright may originally have intended to use them for the third volume, and then changed his mind. If so, it is lamentable that they were not written in full, for the Primitive's discussions with the ancient Dwellers might have been even more interesting than those with the Amphibian. It is more likely, though, that Wright intended a third novel with a very different theme.

The World Below is obviously modeled after *The Divine Comedy*. With the assignment of the Amphibian psychopomp, *The Amphibians* corresponds to the "Inferno" in describing the hellish varieties of life as well as the denizens of Hell and their various sins: the legalistic vulture men, the lizard police, the leechlike Killers, who are modeled upon financiers or capitalists. It is also sin that prevents both the Amphibian leader and the companion of the Primitive from exerting their full potentialities. The second part of the novel covers the Dwellers, beings in Purgatory, who suffer the torments of their inadequacy but are not evil. The Amphibian, like Virgil in *The Divine Comedy*, leaves at the end of the book.

The unwritten third part of the novel, comparable to "Paradise," may, as hinted in the last paragraph of the book, be the Primitive's return to the future with a female companion, to start a new race, with the transcendental ethics of the future people. It is possible that such a new race may be aided by the Dwellers and the Amphibians, both of whom are capable of seeing cosmic reason. But it is puzzling to see how a paradise could be formed from the frightful world described by Wright (unless inside the earth?), and the task may have grown to be impossible.

Deluge (1927), a finely crafted work with considerable intellectual power, came as a literary sensation. Wright, it was now obvious, was not merely a poet who preferred to rework the thoughts of others, or a messianic accountant with eccentric ideas, but a man with impressive skills who could create a series of characters, drop them into a well-imagined environment, and work out their fates, while also offering ideas for thought.

Deluge and its sequel, *Dawn* (1929), tell the story of new Adams and Eves. Volcanism has caused isostatic disturbances, and much of the world has sunk beneath the sea. Most of Great Britain is now under water, and civilization in the mechanistic, industrial sense is a thing of the past. But if artifacts have been lost, something has been gained: the chance to make a new, better world.

The plot follows the fates of Martin Webster, a former lawyer, and two women, his wife and a second wife that he gains during the flood days. There are episodes of savagery and violence as groups sort themselves out typologically: brutes, under the influence of a sadistic furnaceman; neomerchants and neotyrants; and Webster's paternalistic semisocialistic government. A shortage of women, as is so often the case in Wright's fiction, precipitates trouble. Eventually Webster's group wins out.

Deluge and *Dawn*, which were completed when Wright was fifty-five years old, unfortunately mark both the beginning and the end of Wright as a good novelist in the mainstream tradition. Although he continued to publish fiction for another twenty-five years, it tended to be genre commercial fiction, usually dully and tiredly written.

The best of Wright's other science fiction books is *The Island of Captain Sparrow* (1928), which, although it contains the usual concepts of cultural degeneracy and ends with an Adam and Eve motif, is primarily an adventure story. Foyle, the hero, is cast up on a very odd desert island in the Pacific. The fauna includes satyrlike beings of subhuman intelligence and considerable depravity, and descendants of pirates, a very unwholesome crew. Most interesting of all is the Priest of Gir, who with his dying wife and small child form the last remnant of a great race, more civilized than we, who once ruled the Pacific. But their later civilization had been based on ecological balance and rigidly limited numbers, and only three are left. They live in a temple, the most noteworthy artifact of which is a mirrorlike device that shows the future, indicating the optimal course of action. The priest's great sin in the past had been disregarding the mirror's advice.

Foyle and a previously shipwrecked young woman must overcome the pirates. This they do with the help of the Priest of Gîr, who finally has the courage to act. All in all, despite a leaden exposition, *The Island of Captain Sparrow* is an interesting adventure novel, mostly because of the mysterious priest.

Of Wright's later science fiction the only book that merits more than mention is *The Adventure of Wyndham Smith* (1938), which expands the situation of the short story "P. N. 40" into a novel. It describes a scientistic, utterly sterile world of the future. Mankind, tired of life, decides to spite God, who created life, and to commit mass suicide. Automatic machines are then to cover the world with a layer of concrete. Only two persons rebel against this decision: a scientist, in whom has been placed a personality germ from the twentieth century, and an aberrant woman. They secretly decide to live, but they are in great danger, for the world leader, who is far superior to them mentally, is aware of their plans. It will be necessary to outwit his mental brilliance to escape the cremation chambers. It will be even more difficult to escape the automatic devices that he has set up to kill them, should he fail personally. But, once again, there are a new Adam and Eve devoted to repopulating the world.

Wright's other science fiction consists of mediocre work. *Beyond the Rim* (1932) is based on the whimsy that the world is really flat, and that a lost race of English Puritans lives over the edge. In *The Screaming Lake* (1937), set in the Amazon area, the Incas survive, with a typical Wright ruler: hard, brilliant, yet somehow paralyzed, a modern fisher king. The only vital passage in the book describes a journey past a row of gigantic statues of toads—until a tongue lashes out, capable of capturing and swallowing a man. *The Hidden Tribe* (1938), what with its hidden city in the Libyan desert and rigid birth control, is more sociological in nature.

On the outskirts of science fiction are two prehistoric novels and three imaginary war novels. *Dream or the Simian Maid* (1931) is an adventure story of the far past, perhaps a million years ago. The story weight is on the psychology of the leading characters, who recapitulate or anticipate a love triangle in our time, and on their experiences as they wander over a strangely imagined primitive Europe. The title character is a girl of the tree people, a blind alley of evolution. She is intelligent but utterly alien in psychology. She and her two human companions, one of whom she loves, all come to tragic deaths. *Vengeance of Gwa* (1935), first published under the pseudonym Anthony Wingrave, is more socially concerned but offers adventure and intrigue in the Upper Paleolithic.

In both novels the concept of primitive man is much different from that either of current anthropology or of the literary tradition contemporary with Wright. (There are, though, echoes of H. Rider Haggard in *Dream*.) Wright postulates that primitive man may have been capable of sophisticated thought, and that he may have had a perishable culture higher and more complex than is usually granted. He also sees human evolution as multipathed. In all this, though absurd in some details, Wright is somewhat modern. I would speculate that this modernity is more the result of chance and story dynamics than of any profound thought on the topic.

In 1935, Wright went to Germany to gather material for a book about the war he believed was imminent. The result was a three-volume future history: *Prelude in Prague* (1935;

American title, *The War of 1938*), *Four Days War* (1936), and *Megiddo's Ridge* (1937). *The War of 1938* is the most significant, although it is a confused, fragmentary story (despite occasional good moments) that is unable to decide whether it is a spy story, a future history, or a romantic thriller. According to the political theme, in 1938 the Germans present an ultimatum to the Czechs: Communists in Prague, who are plotting to murder the German president, must be expelled to Germany for suitable "treatment." The overconfident Czechs reject the ultimatum, and the Germans wipe out Prague with fire bombs and conquer the land in a matter of days. It is curious to note that Wright's feelings toward Czechs and Germans were ambivalent. His position soon changed when he became more aware of the nature of developments in Nazi Germany.

Wright's final career was that of a writer of mystery stories, most of which appeared in England under the pseudonym Sydney Fowler. Twenty-five in number, they included gangland thrillers in the manner of Edgar Wallace and classical detective stories rigorously plotted with clues for the reader to follow. *The Bell Street Murders* (1931) and *The Secret of the Screen* (1933) have science fiction elements, in this case of a thought-controlled screen that reveals past events. *The Adventure of the Blue Room* (1945) is a thriller set in the near future, with some gadgetry.

Most of Wright's crime stories, though, are traditional. The thrillers are sometimes concerned with an excellent mastermind, Professor Blinkwell, an utterly ruthless scientist who has taken to crime, while most of the detective stories feature Mr. Jellipot, a well-characterized London solicitor. *Dinner in New York* (1943), in which Jellipot meets Al Capone, will amuse American readers.

There has never been a consensus on Wright's detective stories, perhaps because their range in quality has been so great. There are stories, like *By Saturday* (1931), that are puerile, while others, like *The King Against Anne Bickerton* (1930) and *Too Much for Mr. Jellipot* (1945), are rather good legalistic, cerebral problem stories. Wright's cold writing bothers many readers, who have called his work the dullest detective stories of quality since Ronald Knox. Others find the play of intellect occasionally piquant.

Wright's other work includes short stories, mostly reprinted in *The Throne of Saturn* (1949); a biography of Sir Walter Scott; completion of Scott's fragment *The Siege of Malta* (1942); a book-length denunciation of the British police and judiciary system; a tract on the necessity of retaining the formerly German colonies; and some romantic novels.

Wright's final novel, *Spiders' War* (1954), seems only to have disgusted reviewers. The sole interesting episode is at the beginning. Here, in a future primitive world where, due to genetic tinkering, life has been endangered by gigantic insects and arachnids, a famine arises. Gleda, a young woman, is kidnapped from across the river by Lemno, who tells her that she is to serve as dinner for several families. When Lemno's wife Destra gloats over Gleda's plumpness, Gleda, tied up on the floor, calmly remarks to Lemno, "I should make a better wife for you than she." Lemno agrees, knifes Destra, releases Gleda, and all sit down to a hearty meal, Gleda reflecting that she is in the hands of a man of good judgment.

II

Since Wright rated his ideas highly enough to work them into much of his fiction, it seems only just to comment on them, as one might comment on a book by Ayn Rand. Despite Wright's persuasiveness and subtleties, his thought is an odd, highly personal, often inconsistent mixture of elements. As is not uncommon with extremists, while defending his own position, he often unwittingly moves around a political circle to the position he is attacking. A firm believer in personal liberties, he would have been all too willing to establish new, harsh controls to maintain certain facets of those liberties.

Wright is a man against, rather than for, most things. He dreads and fears the scientific mentality, which he regards as cold, loveless, selfish, and self-seeking. He also considers abhorrent the legalistic mind, with its hairsplittings and devotion to a set of arbitrary rules rather than to human needs

Judging from the proto-utopia of *Dawn* and *Deluge*, Wright accepts the social contract as the basis for society, that contract reached rationally, individually, and irrevocably. Those who do not accept are outlaws if antisocial, or beyond the covenant if they behave. The leader is paramount and absolute. His power is to be maintained by charisma and the active will of his subjects, although how this is to be done apart from police and force is not clear. In the end, the reader may decide, there is really not much difference between the fisher-king rulers of *Dream* and *The Hidden Tribe* and Martin Webster of *Dawn*. Allow a few years for power to corrupt and cause decay.

Sex and the family are the areas about which Wright feels most strongly. He is obsessed with the notion of population growth and frequently inveighs against abortion and birth control. A conversation arises in *Dawn*: "But what if the little island on which we live becomes overpopulated?" "It is not an immediate question, and it would be as reasonable to let it influence our minds today, as to commit suicide to save ourselves from the risk of old age." For Wright, murder may be only a bothersome peccadillo, but abortion is real murder.

As for England, Wright's real world, his opinion, when he was young and mellow, was, "No sir, I shouldn't call it a free country. It wasn't bad in its way, and it was very safe if you kept quiet, and went the way you were told—but I sometimes think it may have gone on about long enough" (*Dawn*, page 214).

It would be possible to dismiss Wright as a stubborn, crankish man who took to fiction too late in life, but this is an overly easy evaluation. Much of his work was written in his declining years, when vitality had left his writing; he also said what he had to say too many times and in too unpleasant a fashion.

But his earlier work remains unique in the genre. *The World Below*, as a novel of ideas, is a remarkable achievement, while *Deluge* and *Dawn* remain great disaster stories, unjustly shunted away into the backwashes of mainstream fiction.

Selected Bibliography

WORKS OF S. FOWLER WRIGHT

The Amphibians. London: Merton Press, 1925.

Deluge. London: Fowler Wright, 1927; New York: Cosmopolitan, 1928.

The Island of Captain Sparrow. London: Victor Gollancz, 1928; New York: Cosmopolitan, 1928.

Dawn. New York: Cosmopolitan, 1929; London: George C. Harrap, 1930.

The World Below. London: W. Collins Sons, 1929; New York: Longmans, Green, 1930. (Includes *The Amphibians*.)

Dream or the Simian Maid. London: George C. Harrap, 1931.

The Adventure of Wyndham Smith. London: Herbert Jenkins, 1938.

The Throne of Saturn. Sauk City, Wis.: Arkham House, 1949.

Spiders' War. New York: Abelard Press, 1954.

CRITICAL AND BIOGRAPHICAL STUDIES

Stableford, Brian. "Against the New Gods: The Speculative Fiction of S. Fowler Wright." *Foundation* (November 1983): 10–52.

———. *Scientific Romance in Britain, 1890–1950*. London: Fourth Estate, 1985.

Weinkauf, Mary S. *Sermons in Science Fiction: The Novels of S. Fowler Wright*. San Bernardino, Calif.: Borgo, 1994.

—E. F. BLEILER

JOHN WYNDHAM

(1903–1969)

"TRIFFID" HAS BECOME part of the literary vocabulary, much as "robot" entered everyday English—through science fiction. ("Robot" first appeared in Karel Čapek's science fiction drama *R.U.R.*, 1920.) Wyndham's *The Day of the Triffids* (1951) has retained its popularity, appearing in thirteen reprints from 1954 to 1969, with the 1969 Penguin Books edition proclaiming, ". . . just on half a million copies sold in Penguins." In terms of popularity, *Triffids* is one of the most successful science fiction novels of the twentieth century. Its author also also stands as a clear representative of British fiction who ". . . accurately graphs the state of SF (and the world) in its succeeding phases . . . [going] through several larval stages before emerging as a resplendent butterfly" (Brian W. Aldiss, *Billion Year Spree*, 1973, chapter 11).

John Wyndham Parkes Lucas Beynon Harris was born in Warwickshire in 1903, and many of his books carry vivid memories of his native countryside. Having attempted various jobs in the 1920's, he began writing science fiction stories in 1930. His first published tale, "Worlds to Barter," appeared in *Wonder Stories* (1931), under the name of John Beynon Harris. Other stories followed, and Wyndham became popular for his lighthearted manner and quasi-detached amusement within the space opera he was writing. His novel *The Secret People* (1935) carried the name John Beynon, as did *Planet Plane* (1936).

During World War II, Wyndham served in the Royal Signal Corps and took part in the landing at Normandy in 1944. One might have expected him to return to his tried-and-true formulas in science fiction after the war, but in *The Day of the Triffids* (first serialized in *Collier's*), published under the name John Wyndham, he revealed a new style and some subtle shifts in his outlook. *Triffids* was an instant and overwhelming success, and he retained John Wyndham as his pen name for the rest of his career. *The Kraken Wakes* appeared in 1953, followed by *The Chrysalids* (1955), *The Midwich Cuckoos* (1957), *The Outward Urge* (1959, published under his double pseudonym—John Wyndham and Lucas Parkes), *Trouble with Lichen* (1960), and *Chocky* (first appeared in *Amazing Stories*, 1963; book form, 1968). Several collections of short stories were published: *Jizzle* (1954), *Tales of Gooseflesh and Laughter* (1956), *The Seeds of Time* (1956), *Consider Her Ways and Others* (1961), and *The Infinite Moment* (1961). Wyndham died in 1969.

Using Wyndham to illustrate the evolution of science fiction from the 1930's to the end of the 1960's, Aldiss believes that *Triffids* and *Kraken Wakes* were fine science fiction novels ". . . totally devoid of ideas but [which] read smoothly, and thus reached a maximum audience, who enjoyed cosy disasters" (*Billion Year Spree*). In some respects Wyndham's success depended upon his ability to translate extremely prickly problems ". . . into fundamentally comfortable . . . tales of character" (John Clute, *The Science Fiction Encyclopedia*, 1979). Wyndham's formula of "cosy disaster" had many imitators, including the very popular J. G. Ballard, who mixes medicine with disaster in *The Drowned World* (1962) and *The Crystal World* (1966). One may also note the spillover into the disaster movies of the 1970's, thin on plot and character, and heavy with special effects and pseudoheroics.

In *The Secret People,* Wyndham shows his skill in delineating setting and manages to give just enough detail of the "hero" and "heroine" to satisfy the minimum demands of characterization. Perhaps influenced by H. G. Wells's *First Men in the Moon* (1901), Wyndham peoples the Sahara with subterranean "Pygmies," who are exterminated by a French-Italian project that floods the Sahara in order to produce an inland sea that will increase the agricultural productivity of the land that forms the new shorelines. The Sahara Pygmies may be one of the last examples of the favorite British theme of submerged races and nations. The hero and heroine find themselves in the clutches of these Pygmies (who resemble Wells's Selenites) after they crash into the new sea and are pulled by a swift current into enormous subterranean caves. They finally escape, taking with them the Pygmy secret of "cold light." And that is all: smooth prose, a semifamiliar setting, a well-trodden path of adventure involving a lost race (à la H. Rider Haggard), and final resolution and destruction for the lost race because it does not fit into the modern world.

In comparing *The Secret People* with Wyndham's later novels, the reader can detect some of the same themes and methods of dealing with uncomfortable topics. An American might call this manner "homogenization." But this bland approach is relieved by an occasionally delightful wit, acerbic comments in the form of the classic "aside" that seems to say: "Well, since you want this sort of writing, I'll give it to you. Amazingly I'm getting paid for it. After all, this speculation is simply rubbish, but I'm having fun with it."

In *Planet Plane* (first reprinted in 1953 as *Stowaway to Mars,* under the name John Beynon) this tongue-in-cheek attitude toward science fiction becomes even more obvious. The tale is about man's first flight to Mars, but the focus is on Vaygan the Martian, who not only gets the stowaway Joan pregnant but also effectively neutralizes three different, almost simultaneous landings of Earthlings. Joan dies in childbirth at the end of the book (because the child was illegitimate); and Wyndham's line, "And so ended the flight of the *Gloria Mundi,*" summarizes *Planet Plane* rather well. The novel is still quite readable but functions only as entertainment, with the exception of some subtlety when Wyndham addresses (indirectly) the problem of interplanetary miscegenation. One might see the ancestor of Ray Bradbury's Martians or even Robert A. Heinlein's Michael Valentine Smith, but Wyndham's Vaygan appears as a simple caricature of the ordinary alien in the science fiction of the 1930's.

With the publication of *The Day of the Triffids,* Wyndham demonstrates that he had undergone a shift in his thinking during the war. There is none of the brooding about man's inhumanity to man that sometimes batters the reader of postwar science fiction; Wyndham has invented an alien being that is the product of the earthly environment. The values in *Triffids* are those connected with the familiar, orderly routines of life, and the numerous allusions to scientific and artistic matters (such as the work of Gustave Doré and T. D. Lysenko) are devices to heighten the tone of reliability. The triffids are masterpieces of grumpy plants, nicely gone awry like a combination of archer fish and Venus's-flytraps. After a meteor shower and widespread blindness, chaos results, and the narrator pits his apparently limited imagination against the disorder, striving for the restoration of order— as much to the way it was before as is possible. The scenery is of a familiar England, and Wyndham's Warwickshire shimmers with a fondly recalled greenery. Life would be pleasant, we are told, if we did not alter the small, simple, domestic routines of nature and of man's analogous existence.

In *The Kraken Wakes,* England and the world are visited by another quirky aberration of a life-form, this time a creature from the bottom of the sea. It owes its existence (again) to falling stars of a sort, "fireballs" that somehow mutate a somber animal into a magnificent threat to land dwellers and seagoing vessels. (Wyndham is not interested in the particulars of why such mutations occur, only that they do occur—and that they cause disasters that disrupt his orderly picture of life.) *The Kraken Wakes* is a restatement of *Triffids*, and the slithery underwater coelenterates in the former are not as convincing as the superbly nasty plants of *Triffids*. But *The Kraken Wakes* is a good "read," and Wyndham fans found another installment of pleasant, smooth writing, with few ideas that intruded into the second "cosy disaster."

Coelenterates and rising water levels allow the two major characters to muse about the future at the end of the novel. Phyllis displays some stolid intelligence and a semblance of grit, but she too is subjected to the homogenizing effects of Wyndham's middle-class values. He detested crowds, as is apparent in one of the last lines spoken by Phyllis to Mike: "There were only five million or so of us in the first Elizabeth's time—but we counted." Many science fiction writers have echoed that sentiment, especially sharp in the misanthropic novels that show the "last survivors" who represent the best of mankind, as contrasted with the masses. For British readers the settings were again quite familiar: the English countryside and several easily recognized locales in London.

The Chrysalids is Wyndham's best novel. The setting is New England in the future, after the atomic wars have faded into memory and mutated genes are common—with a consequent fear by the "normal" of the "abnormal." *The Chrysalids* is probably one of the best of the "different-among-us" books ever written. In it Wyndham displays a writing skill and multileveled intellect only hinted at in earlier books. (Only *Trouble with Lichen* would again rise to *The Chrysalids*' level.) After *The Chrysalids* one is left to ponder whether the author is expressing anger at the wasted lives and minds, sacrificed to the incredibly rigid ways of the Church of the Future (which resembles the stereotypical Puritan sect of New England), or whether he is stating the maxims of his postatomic period as if they should be "right."

If Wyndham's writing is better in this book, it may be because he had realized that the gray sameness of the middle class was, in the long run, stifling to truly creative minds. Yet if one compares *The Chrysalids* with *The Kraken Wakes* and *Triffids*, as well as with *The Secret People* and *Planet Plane*, there is a striking inconsistency if one assumes Wyndham is arguing that the mutants are better: Sophie, a girl of ten, is discovered by one of the "normal" young boys to have six toes—but the normal boy likes her and openly puzzles why the text of *Repentances* states "Only the Image of God is Man," "Keep Pure the Stock of the Lord," "Blessed is the Norm," "In Purity is Our Salvation," and "Watch Thou for the Mutant!" The boy's grandfather, Elias Strorm, is described in the following, which seems to be an open rage at religious rules that poison human lives:

John Wyndham. Courtesy of Mirror Syndication International

He went off on a journey and brought back a bride. She was shy, pretty in the pink and golden way, and twenty-five years younger. . . . She moved . . . like a lovely colt when she thought herself unwatched. . . . All her answers, poor thing, were dusty. She did not find that a marriage service generated love; she did not enable her husband to recapture his youth through hers. . . . In a few seasons he straitened the coltishness with admonitions, faded the pink and gold with preaching, and produced a sad, grey wraith of wifehood who died, unprotesting a year after her second son was born. (chapter 2)

Yet once the young boy, David Strorm, discovers that he, like his cousin Rosalind, can "speak" with mental images, it becomes clear that he and his cousin are offenses, as are the two-headed calves, four-legged chickens, and other mutants among the stock that are slaughtered with prescribed religious ceremony and prayers. "Keeping the Norm" is the goal of the community at Waknuk. David, Sophie, and Rosalind are forced to hold their true natures in secret, just as Sophie's mother swore David to secrecy when he saw the six toes. Once their difference is perceived, the three understand that they have to leave, to go where there are others like themselves.

As moving as many passages in *Chrysalids* are, the major thrust of Wyndham's thinking throughout the novel is blunt and direct: those who are different must seek those like themselves and must leave the company of "the Norm." Dreams are finally realized to be "communications" from distant communities of telepathic individuals, and the novel builds nicely to the final chapter, in which the mutants journey to a place where they will be welcome. Now Wyndham introduces the Sealand Woman, who assumes a prominent role toward the end, and there are some remarkable lines that suggest *The Chrysalids* was written with an intentionally piquant dualism—for instance, "In loyalty to their kind, they cannot tolerate our rise; in loyalty to our kind, we cannot tolerate their obstruction" (chapter 17). Wyndham has—again—smoothed an extremely important quandary

of the modern era into a simplistic and comfortable solution: the total separation of the kinds of human beings into rigidly boxed communities. This is but a short step from the "separation of the races" doctrine, in full legal force in the United States until 1954, and would easily be acceptable to the British reading public, then feeling the first impact of the "coloured races" immigrating in increasing numbers to Britain from India, the West Indies, and former African colonies.

The theme of the "different among us" was treated differently by Edgar Pangborn in *Davy* (1964), in which the rigidly decadent Church of the Future plays an important role in the collapse of society, attempting to expel the Free Thinkers. But Pangborn stands firmly on the side of change, while Wyndham says those who are different should be banished, leaving the pleasant, predictable world to those who are normal. Richard Matheson's *I Am Legend* (1954) also wrestles with the probability of mutation and change, and effectively employs the vampire theme: the last "normal" man is pitted against the "new-normal" vampires. Matheson's whimsy takes this question and proposes a basic and continual change throughout nature, while Wyndham would insist on a defense against that change, perhaps even denying the reality of change.

One is reminded of the very ancient debate (going back at least to the pre-Socratic Greek philosophers) between those thinkers who asserted that all change is merely an illusion, and their opponents who stated that nothing ever remains the same. Wyndham clearly stands with the school of Parmenides of Elea (circa 470 B.C.), who denied that one could know both that which is and that which is not.

Wyndham did not, of course, express his notions through philosophy, but he was deeply committed to comfort and reliability in existence. His earlier "cosy disasters" in effect eliminate many elements of a changing world, so that the "normal" beings can get •back to "normal" life—albeit in reduced numbers. Yet he had problems with formal religion, which preaches conformity and would seem to fit nicely into his pleasant world. Like Edgar Rice Burroughs in *The Gods of Mars* (1918), Wyndham condemned the formal dogmas of a brittle and venerated religion, yet paradoxically retained those aspects of society approved by that formal dogma.

The Midwich Cuckoos continues the theme of those who are different, and what happens to them. Many readers will remember *Village of the Damned* (1960), the effectively scary motion picture based on *The Midwich Cuckoos*. This story again shows a community attempting to expurgate children who are the first of a new race. This time, ordinary women have been impregnated by aliens, and their children possess mental powers far beyond those of the mothers. What to do? Once more, the different people must leave. This is Wyndham's version of the happy ending, and Midwich can go back to what it was before the intrusion took place: a small, calm, nondescript English village.

Wyndham's popularity stems from the same qualities that have made Heinlein, Poul Anderson, Andre Norton, and a number of similar writers so acceptable to millions. First, like Heinlein, Wyndham was a political and economic conservative, resisting the wave of the future, even though he used a particular genre of fiction that presumably gloried in the sense of wonder that is the future and the possibilities of change in the future. Second, Wyndham never exploited sex in any manner, other than to suggest the warmth of a woman (for instance, Phyllis in *The Kraken Wakes*) or that a woman can "pull her own weight" as a companion to the dominant male figure. Wyndham's books are always clean. They stand as superb examples of the survival of Victorian middle-class tastes well into the twentieth century, and their popularity speaks eloquently of the majority of science fiction readers who share those values. Men and women are upright, moral, dogged, somewhat educated (but not too much), and very conscious of ethics and rules of etiquette. Everything must look correct. And human beings apparently have few physiological functions below the navel.

Triffids, The Kraken Wakes, The Chrysalids, and *The Midwich Cuckoos* are Wyndham's most effective books; the writings before World War II and after 1960 are distant, acerbic, and somewhat uneasy. In *Chocky*, for example, Wyndham returns to the telepathic theme of *The Chrysalids*, and we meet Chocky, another small boy with abilities similar to those of David Strorm. But now there is a gulf between the author and his subject. The telepathy is crude by comparison with what David and Rosalind experience in *The Chrysalids*, and one is reminded by *Chocky* of childhood and the dolls and toys that could be alive. *Chocky* is not a good book, and the reader may think that Wyndham and his publishers were capitalizing upon numerous fans who might buy the book on the author's name alone. *Chocky* lacks the magic of *Triffids*, the slimy iciness of *The Kraken Wakes*, the occasionally brilliant dualism of *The Chrysalids*, and the suspicious unease of *The Midwich Cuckoos*. It is as if Wyndham had grown tired of his writing in the 1950's, and perhaps returned to being the "diffident, obscure, lounging individual at the fringes of the literary and social world" he had been in the 1930's, as described in the memoirs of his publisher, Robert Lusty, *Bound to Be Read* (1975).

The motion picture industry found Wyndham's "cosy disasters" ideal fare for adaptation. *The Day of the Triffids* appeared as a movie in 1962, but it was a thoroughly bad effort. There was none of the vividness of the walking vegetables sporting poison flails, and the acting was atrocious. On the other hand, the film *Village of the Damned* retained the spookiness of the novel.

Wyndham did not invent the disaster novel, and he may have borrowed directly from Wells's *First Men in the Moon* for his Sahara Pygmies, and from Wells's *The War in the Air* (1908) for the general notions of how a disaster novel should work. Wyndham's disasters result from quirks of nature (meteors in *Triffids*, fireballs in *The Kraken Wakes*, invasions by aliens in *The Midwich Cuckoos*, nuclear warfare in *The Chrysalids*). Mutation became a standard theme for him in the 1950's, and he may represent the most eloquent middle-class British spokesman for the rampant fears of that decade—fears that were headed by the expectation of atomic war between the West and the Soviet Union, and revealed in the fervent "witch hunts" in the United States that ferreted out accused Communists from every academic crevice and burrow.

Wyndham speaks clearly about a desired complacency, a reflection of a widespread desire to return to the "good old days" that were hallowed in half-recalled statements about the Great Depression. Almost anything "back then" was simpler and, by definition, "better." Wyndham's books and short stories are blatantly antihistorical as well as candidly anti-intellectual. For these biases his fans rewarded him by buying his works in huge numbers.

In many ways Wyndham is typical of the science fiction writer who embodies in his work everything opposite to the stated aims of the science fiction genre. If his conservatism, his antihistorical stance, and his blunt anti-intellectual values were reflected in the tastes of his many fans, this says much about why science fiction remains dominated by the likes of Heinlein, and why many of the better writers of "pure" science fiction have entered the mainstream of twentieth-century literature. Heinlein and Wyndham will be regarded as science fiction writers by the negative definition. Wyndham's works are frequently used in high school and college courses including science fiction because they are quite clean and generally free of controversy.

Selected Bibliography

WORKS OF JOHN WYNDHAM

The Secret People. London: George Newnes, 1935. Published as by John Beynon. New York: Fawcett Books, 1973, as by John Wyndham.

Planet Plane. London: George Newnes, 1936. Retitled *Stowaway to Mars*. London: Nova, 1953. Published as by John Beynon. Reprinted as by John Wyndham in 1972.
The Day of the Triffids. London: Michael Joseph, 1951. Retitled *Revolt of the Triffids*. New York: Popular Library, 1952.
The Kraken Wakes. London: Michael Joseph, 1953. Retitled *Out of the Deeps*. New York: Ballantine Books, 1953 (with textual changes).
Jizzle. London: Dennis Dobson, 1954.
The Chrysalids. London: Michael Joseph, 1955. Retitled *Rebirth*. New York: Ballantine Books, 1955 (with textual changes).
The Seeds of Time. London: Michael Joseph, 1956.
Tales of Gooseflesh and Laughter. New York: Ballantine Books, 1956.
The Midwich Cuckoos. London: Michael Joseph, 1957. Titled *Village of the Damned*. New York: Ballantine Books, 1960.
The Outward Urge. London: Michael Joseph, 1959. Originally published as a collaboration with Lucas Parkes. Reprinted, with one story added. New York: Ballantine Books, 1961.
Trouble with Lichen. London: Michael Joseph, 1960. New York: Ballantine Books, 1960 (with textual changes).
Consider Her Ways and Others. London: Michael Joseph, 1961.
The Infinite Moment. New York: Ballantine Books, 1961.
Chocky. Garden City, N.Y.: Doubleday, 1968. (Expanded from a short story of the same title.)
Web. London: Michael Joseph, 1979. (Published posthumously.)

CRITICAL AND BIOGRAPHICAL STUDIES

Aldiss, Brian W. *Billion Year Spree: The True History of Science Fiction*. Garden City, N.Y.: Doubleday, 1973. Especially pages 290–291, 293–294. (A spritely and often witty recounting of science fiction and its authors. Wyndham is firmly placed in his English context.)
Bleiler, E. F. "Luncheon with John Wyndham." *Extrapolation*, 25, no. 4 (1984): 314–317. (Interview.)
Clareson, Thomas D., and Alice S. Clareson. "The Neglected Fiction of John Wyndham: 'Consider Her Ways,' *Trouble with Lichen* and *Web*." In *Science Fiction Roots and Branches*. Edited by Rhys Garnett. New York: St. Martin's, 1990.
Clute, John. "Wyndham, John." In *The Encyclopedia of Science Fiction*. Edited by Peter Nicholls. Garden City, N.Y.: Doubleday, 1979. (A clipped and somewhat negative review of Wyndham's career and writings. A handy reference for the variant titles of Wyndham's books and collections of short stories.)

Manlove, C. N. "Everything Slipping Away: John Wyndham's *The Day of the Triffids*." *Journal of the Fantastic in the Arts*, 4, no. 1 (1991): 29–53.

Scarborough, John. "Medicine." In *The Encyclopedia of Science Fiction*. Edited by Peter Nicholls. Garden City, N.Y.: Doubleday, 1979. (Among many authors and works surveyed, Wyndham's *The Chrysalids* and Pangborn's *Davy* are given as examples of novels on genetic evolution.)

Stephensen-Payne, Phil. *John Wyndham: Creator of the Cosy Catastrophe, A Working Bibliography*, Rev. ed. Albuquerque, N.Mex.: Galactic Central, 1989.

Wymer, Rowland. "How 'Safe' is John Wyndham? A Closer Look at His Work, with Particular Reference to *The Chrysalids*." *Foundation* (Summer 1992): 25–36.

—JOHN SCARBOROUGH

ROGER ZELAZNY

(1937–1995)

FOR A TIME in the 1960's, Roger Zelazny was an indisputable hero to science fiction readers. He was seen as one of the Young Turks who would revolutionize the genre. He was a prose poet, a master of metaphor, the brightest hope of the American New Wave.

Then, in the 1970's, many of those who had praised him began to have second thoughts. He was now said to be a hack; he wrote too fast; his heroes were comic strip supermen; he was somehow rather vulgar. Richard Cowper, himself a science fiction writer, is perhaps representative of this general critical dismissiveness in his article entitled "A rose is a rose is a rose—in search of Roger Zelazny" (*Foundation*, March 1977), wherein Zelazny's later output is described as "fatuous, wholly incredible . . . morally simplistic . . . boring . . . [showing a] lack of creative discipline . . . [and a] deficiency of the imagination."

Cowper assumed that the problem was with Zelazny himself: that he had begun brilliantly but was somehow spoiled, a burnt-out case. The truth may have lain elsewhere—in unrealistic critical expectations rather than in the declining powers of the author. Now, more than thirty-five years since Zelazny's first stories, it should be possible to gain a broad perspective, to make a judgment as impartial as possible (if not final), cleansed both of premature hope and of premature disappointment.

Roger Joseph Zelazny was born on 13 May 1937 in Euclid, Ohio. His father was of Polish origin; he was a pattern maker. Zelazny earned a B.A. at Western Reserve University in 1959 and an M.A. at Columbia University in 1962, specializing in Elizabethan and Jacobean drama. He then worked for the federal government in the Social Security Administration, serving first in Cleveland and then in Baltimore, until in 1969 he became a full-time freelance writer. He lived in New Mexico from 1975 to the time of his death from cancer of the colon in 1995. Zelazny had been married twice and had three children from the second marriage.

In 1962 Zelazny began submitting short stories to science fiction magazines—several stories each week for a while. Cele Goldsmith, editor of *Amazing Stories* and *Fantastic*, bought the first story. (She had a genius for discovering young talent; she was the first publisher of Thomas M. Disch and Ursula K. Le Guin, both in 1962 as well.) Zelazny's first published story was "Passion Play" (*Amazing Stories*, August 1962). It is a brief, clever account of a robot reliving a human death myth (the death of racing-car driver Wolfgang von Tripps) as part of a service held in memory of a vanished mankind. Thus we see Zelazny's major literary concern, the sometimes ironic re-creation of mythic archetypes, at the very outset of his career.

Zelazny wrote short fiction prolifically over the next few years, using the pseudonym Harrison Denmark when more than one of his stories appeared in a single issue of a magazine. His most memorable work is of novella length (stories of roughly 20,000–40,000 words). Several of these novellas remain among his most discussed work, notably "A

Rose for Ecclesiastes" (1963) and "The Doors of His Face, the Lamps of His Mouth" (1965). The latter story won a Nebula award for best novelette in 1966. Both stories are in Zelazny's first collection of short fiction, *Four for Tomorrow* (1967; reissued in England as *A Rose for Ecclesiastes,* 1969), and also in the second, *The Doors of His Face, the Lamps of His Mouth, and Other Stories* (1971).

For many readers "A Rose" revitalized science fiction. It is easy for us to forget, now, how arid a genre science fiction seemed to have become around 1962, how mechanically outward-looking. When the human mind itself was its subject, science fiction usually took the form of escapist fantasies about psionic powers. Zelazny introduced color, poetry, metaphor, and a deeper psychological dimension into science fiction.

"A Rose" tells of an arrogant poet on Mars who brings life back to the Martians by impregnating the youngest and most beautiful of them, even though all the Martian women are supposed to be sterile, having been doomed to childlessness by a plague some centuries earlier. A complex web of imagery runs through the story, the beautiful, despairing cadences of the Old Testament book of Ecclesiastes being seen as an earthly correlative of the Martian acceptance of sterility and also as an analogue of the protagonist's own rearing—his father was a stern, religious patriarch.

The poet-hero finds humility, love, and an austere aesthetic satisfaction, but ironically he has been only a tool; his Martian mistress has not really loved him. Many readers still remember the last, lovely sentence: "Blurred Mars hung like a swollen belly above me, until it dissolved, brimmed over, and streamed down my face." This is moving in its carefully wrought metaphor of fruitfulness, loss, and tears in the same image; but it is close to sentimentality, too.

A rereading of the whole story today reveals that it is written in a mode that, for all of its careful and literary metaphoric structure, has very much the tone of the pulps—specifically the thriller pulps as represented by Raymond Chandler. Zelazny's tough, sensitive protag-

onist is a kind of poet-Marlowe, good in a fight but marshmallow-soft in matters of the heart. The story is not so much directly heart-wrenching, which seems to be its intention, as an exercise in emotional manipulation. This has something to do with its hard-bitten tone: "[I] took my first drag . . . I'd still have hated to play poker with her . . . I came to the land where the sun is a tarnished penny, where the wind is a whip, where two moons play at hot rod games . . ." (chapter 1).

Do matters improve when the protagonist drops his guard and speaks in a directly "poetic" way? Here are two examples: "*The wind! The wind, I say. O wild, enigmatic! O muse of St. John Perse!*" (chapter 1); "*Where the icy evening of Time freezes milk in the breasts of life*" (chapter 2). This is, in fact, not poetry; it is poeticizing, in the voice (this time) of a clever, well-read, romantic adolescent. It is not the voice of a man who, the story tells us, is one of the six greatest English-language poets of the twentieth century.

Perhaps if this and other early works by Zelazny had not been so overpraised at the time, he would not, later on, have been accused (as he often was) of being a man who betrayed his art for the lure of commerce.

The originality of "A Rose" is real enough; but it does not consist in the creation of a wholly new voice. The novelty (which to many readers who did not read widely outside the science fiction field must have seemed completely original) was in the bringing to bear of a tone of voice and a type of highly colored metaphor that were comparatively unfamiliar in science fiction but that did exist elsewhere—both in other genres (such as thrillers) and in mainstream fiction. It is hard to resist viewing the young Zelazny as a sensitive, widely read, but inexperienced writer whose sense of style was culled from books. His style in these stories has elements of pastiche, as has the style of many other young writers who, in seeking a strong voice, begin by imitating those they admire.

To my mind "The Doors of His Face" is the superior story. The voice of the protagonist is more relaxedly wry and self-knowing. The hero of "A Rose" is simply a sentimental tough guy; the hero of "Doors" is a sentimental tough guy who *knows* he is one. The dryly ironic tone that results was to stand Zelazny in good stead for many years and through many books, although when the creative pressure is less, it sometimes seems like a mere mannerism.

Like "A Rose," "Doors" is given a setting that is in itself deliberately mythic (as Zelazny later testified), although in both cases the myth is recent: Mars as the decadent, ancient repository of a dead or dying civilization, Venus as the violent frontier world of water and swamp. These images had been largely developed in the more lurid pulps, such as *Planet Stories* and *Startling Stories*.

"Doors" is in many ways a *Moby Dick* on Venus, except that Zelazny is no fatalistic pessimist. His Ahab figure, a hard-drinking social dropout, finally defeats the sea monster and becomes a man again. In a twist of metaphor typical of Zelazny, the hero is in turn a kind of sea beast of the mind for the bitch-woman who loves him and thinks he is a loser. Even in these early stories, it is evident that Zelazny, far from being a naive writer whose tales jet up effortlessly from the unconscious (as he was sometimes pictured), is instead notable for the craftsmanlike care with which he constructed his stories. His work is often done so seamlessly that the tenons and mortises of his narrative dovetails are barely visible.

Zelazny remained remarkably true to the pattern set by his early works. His stories are science fictional variants on archetypal and mythic conflicts whose outward action reflects (as in Jung's psychology) internal dramas. Almost invariably his stories are structured around a metaphor or series of metaphors that interlock satisfyingly. For example, the following metaphoric chains appear in "Doors": beast = masculinity = inner violence = sexual turbulence; victory over beast = victory over fear = victory over Self; sacrifice where woman is allowed to be the one to catch beast = sacrifice of Self to Other = love.

Roger Zelazny in 1978. PHOTO BY JAY KAY KLEIN

Sentimentally but strikingly, the story refers in its last fine phrase to "epithalamium the sea-beast's dower." How many readers of science fiction magazines in 1965 would have known that an epithalamium is a formal marriage song? Probably more than we might have expected. Among Zelazny's gifts to the field were his evident trust in the intelligence of his readership and his refusal to patronize them by spelling out his meanings.

Zelazny's two most substantial novellas of this period both won awards, and both were subsequently expanded into full-length novels and published by Ace Books. ". . . And Call Me Conrad" (1965) won a Hugo award (in its short form) for best novel and became his first book, *This Immortal* (1966). "He Who Shapes" (1965) won a Nebula award for best novella and was published in book form as *The Dream Master* (1966).

This Immortal introduces the character who was to become, in one guise or another, the protagonist of three-quarters of Zelazny's fiction thereafter: the superhuman manipulator who, although outwardly a man and possessing many of the passions and failings of ordinary men, is effectively immortal. Whether or not this theme became a cliché in Zelazny's subsequent work, it is amazingly fresh in this, its first major presentation.

In *This Immortal* a tired Earth has been devastated by atomic war; it is effectively a museum and tourist resort for the Vegans, an alien race beside whom the remnants of mankind, now spread out among the stars, are very distinctly second-class citizens. Conrad Nomikos, an enigmatic arts commissioner, has the job of guiding a small party around the sites of Earth's wrecked culture; the party includes Cort Myshtigo, a Vegan emissary who, it seems, has great political influence.

Nomikos has two faces—one profile beautiful, the other ruined; he is a man of peace and a man of violence; he is primitive and cultured. As he guides his party (split by internal dissension and containing several assassins) around the wastelands surrounding the Mediterranean, he is faced by many threats that, we come to realize, recapitulate the tasks of Herakles, the ancient Greek hero. Cyclic Earth, populated by mutated monsters, has sunk into an age of living myth. Conrad is its hero, its rebel leader, its spokesman, and its incarnation. He cannot die.

The narrative is fast and highly mannered; implications are glimpsed sidelong; snatches of dialogue take us into labyrinths of meaning with only minimal clues. The science fiction invention is nonstop, florid, assured, and colorful. In rapid succession we are introduced to strigefleurs, spider bats, boadiles, *kallikanzaroi,* and golem wrestlers. The details are ornate but functional; they are more than mere baroque decoration. The movement is relentless.

Zelazny's stories, here and later, gain their richness of allusion and meaning not through reflection but through action captured in sharply etched images tumbling out one after the other. The final meaning of his work, though, usually emerges not from a linear accretion of detail but through an overall metaphor or pattern. In this case it is a rite of passage that the demigod-hero, the sacrificial one, undertakes as a kind of surrogate for humanity. He ensures autumnal mankind's autonomy by reenacting the archetypal struggles that, myth tells us, accompanied our springtime. *This Immortal* is perhaps the most economical and assured of all of Zelazny's novels.

The Dream Master looks inward where *This Immortal* looks outward. Charles Render is a neuroparticipation therapist, a psychiatrist who can actually enter the minds of his subjects and, by shaping their fantasies, force them to confront and come to terms with their own neuroses and obsessions. The model of the mind presented by the story is overtly that of the psychologist Carl Jung, who saw internal conflicts as externalized in archetypes and myths, some of which spring from the collective unconscious. The whole Jungian apparatus of libido, suppression, introversion, delusory systems, and so forth is dramatized carefully in the novel, although it is spelled out at only a few points.

Render is one of Zelazny's most powerful manipulator figures (although not literally superhuman), but his superiority is deeply flawed. "Physician, heal thyself," runs the old adage, but Render, so sensitive to the fantasies of others, has not come to terms with the Scandinavian images of Fimbulwinter—the bleak, entropic end of human warmth—that haunt his own mind. He enters the mind of a strong, beautiful, blind woman, Dr. Eileen Shallot, to help her see, and in doing so he comes to love her. Eileen's mind (as her surname suggests) is filled with deeply romantic imagery culled from Arthurian legend, and Render does not have the psychic balance to control her. She is too strong, and not quite sane. The psychic struggle is cleverly imaged in the clash of Nordic and Arthurian delusory systems, and finally Render is permanently trapped in her delusion. To the outside world he is merely catatonic; but inside his head he is Tristan, forever awaiting an Isolde who will never arrive.

The novel is extraordinarily well-patterned, almost to the point of being too diagrammatic. But the book is notable in Zelazny's development as the work in which he spells out for the first and only time some of the psychic *functions* of the various mythic systems he exploits. Thereafter their Jungian role remained implicit rather than overt.

Myths can perform a psychic function even with nonhumans, it seems. One of Zelazny's wittiest novelettes is "For a Breath I Tarry" (1966), set on a future Earth where mankind is dead and only robot guardians survive. The temptation myth he recounts (containing elements of Adam in the Garden and Doctor Faustus) is given an ironic twist. All genuine science fiction writers must feel a certain sympathy with stealers from the Tree of Knowledge, and Zelazny was no exception. Here the Fall is a *felix culpa,* and the Adamic robot becomes incarnate as Man.

Outstanding among subsequent novels is *Lord of Light* (1967), the first of a series of books that play variations on the themes set out in *This Immortal.* Many readers have found *Lord of Light* to be Zelazny's most ebullient work. In the far future, some officers from a technologically advanced group of human colonists on a new planet have effectively transformed themselves into gods deliberately modeled on those of the Hindu pantheon. We deduce this slowly from the narrative, in which at first they actually seem to *be* gods. Most of the inhabitants of the planet, though, are merely human; and they worship the "gods," who dwell in a heavenly, high-technology enclave.

The quite dramatically reenacted central myth is that of the encounter (and final union) between Buddhism and Hinduism. The protagonist, Sam (short for Mahasamatman), is effectively an avatar of Prince Siddhartha, the Buddha, the serene liberator of mankind from the worst excesses of the old pantheon—the godly vanities, corruptions, and random tyrannies over a cruelly manipulated mankind. The mythic resonances are evoked with wonderful precision, but the story is not told solely in a high or dignified language. Sam is not only the Buddha; he is also a devious wit with an altogether contemporary consciousness, a kind of hippy anarchist who fights on behalf of a subjugated people against an entrenched, conservative establishment.

Typically for Zelazny, the liberator himself is the Trickster, the archmanipulator. Zelazny had never before found, and was never again to find, so perfect a mythic template for his themes. Even with all the conscious anachronisms, the deliberately ironic way in which the gods are made to resemble something like the New York chapter of the international jet set, the characters remain true to their mythic originals.

Lord of Light is every bit as tightly structured as *The Dream Master,* but here the pattern seems to grow organically and naturally. If the novel has a fault, it is that it is too easy to be swept away by its tide of action without pausing to absorb its resonances.

Isle of the Dead (1969) is a dark and vengeful story of conflict between the members of a guild of future priest-technologists: planet shapers, world-scapers who undergo an austere and almost Zenlike training in religion and mind control on the one hand, and in high technology on the other. At times these men, each of whom has been formally dedicated to a specific patron god, become subject to control by what could be seen as archetypes emerging from the fantasia of the unconscious or as objectively existing gods themselves. The ambiguity is well done. Some critics have seen *Isle of the Dead* as cruder and simpler than its predecessors, but it retains considerable verve and brio.

Isle of the Dead had a quasi sequel some years later—*To Die in Italbar* (1973)—which features the protagonist of the earlier novel as a subsidiary character. *Italbar* is a failure; its narrative is too straggly and melodramatic to allow its bleak, central figure (a holy man who is both a healer and a bearer of pestilence) any room to develop. It also resolves the ambiguity of *Isle* by showing that the gods *do* exist, thus retroactively weakening the earlier novel.

Creatures of Light and Darkness (1969) was the first Zelazny novel to receive a good deal of critical execration. It replays the now

959

familiar theme of men so technologically advanced as to be indistinguishable from gods— masters of space and matter. The archetypes here are ancient Egyptian: Anubis, Osiris, Isis, Horus, Thoth, and the amnesiac protagonist, who is Set. But the resonances of the story are not really true to the original Egyptian matrix of mythic relationships; Set is no longer malicious and treacherous, for example. *Creatures* posits two political systems—one cruelly manipulative (it deals with overpopulation by random culling), the other ruling through reason. But the political moral is casually thrown to one side, leaving heroic conflict as the essence of the story. If this were all there was to the novel, one might indeed accuse Zelazny of lazy repetition.

But *Creatures*, as few critics seem to have noticed, is also an ambitious literary experiment. Zelazny seems to have been seeking a literary equivalent to the potent, hieratic paintings in Egyptian temples. Where normally his narratives flow, this one is a series of staccato, emblematic scenes in bright outlines, flat, staring, and larger than life. He uses verse, too, and the techniques of verse (parallelisms, refrains, and balladic symbols). It is a brave attempt and not at all the sort of thing we would expect of a writer supposedly by now working too fast and intent solely on commercial success. (As a matter of fact, Zelazny was still a government employee; he wrote fast, but he had always done this; if anything, he slowed down as his writing career progressed.)

What are we to make of Zelazny's repeated reworkings of mythic material? In his book *Metamorphoses of Science Fiction* (1979), the critic Darko Suvin dismisses Zelazny in a sentence: "Attempts to transplant the metaphysical orientation of mythology and religion into SF, in a crudely overt way as in . . . Zelazny . . . will result only in private pseudomyths, in fragmentary fantasies or fairy tales." He adds, "The black ectoplasms of fantasy stifle SF completely . . . under the guise of cognition the ancient obscurantist enemy infiltrates its citadel" (both from chapter 2).

Suvin, like many other critics, sees science fiction as being (his definition is prescriptive) ideally rational, analytic, an agency for change that takes change as its subject. It is easy to quarrel with Suvin's prescription as excluding three-quarters of what is published under the science fiction label; but when he goes on to say "Myth is oriented towards constants and science fiction towards variables" (same source as above), he is usefully pointing to what is a genuine paradox in science fiction with a mythic content.

Zelazny is one of a great many writers whose science fiction makes use of mythic structures: C. S. Lewis, Charles Harness, Philip José Farmer, Thomas M. Disch, Samuel R. Delany, Ursula K. Le Guin, Michael Moorcock, Harlan Ellison, and Gene Wolfe are all good examples; notably, all but the first three are closely contemporary with Zelazny; together (Lewis excepted) they form the nucleus of the New Wave. The New Wave writers were generally concerned with the dehumanizing effect of technology, and many of them used myth to assert human continuity and the repetition of archetypal patterns even in high-technology futures. Mythic science fiction can be seen as conservative and skeptical (*plus ça change, plus c'est la même chose*), whereas high-technology, cognitive science fiction of the kind Suvin seems to advocate is idealistic and devoted to the idea of progress (which is itself a myth, according to the New Wave writers).

It is not, of course, as simple as this. Zelazny was both a skeptic and an idealist, and his supertough, Chandleresque protagonists, walking down the mean streets of the cosmos, maintaining a tight-lipped integrity while they bleed inside, are idealists too. They are conceived, a little sentimentally but attractively nevertheless, as gallants, sardonic altruists, immortal solitaries who seldom find peace. But this is an idealism of character, operating within a universe cynically conceived as violent, bleak, and at best morally neutral. It is not a universe amenable to cognition, and in this sense the books *are* "obscurantist," as Suvin charges. It could be argued, though, that

960

in their acceptance of chaos, with only small corners of the universe being temporarily cleaned up and rendered decently habitable, they are more realistic (despite their florid, baroque furniture) than the rational utopia to which, Suvin believes, science fiction's dystopias may lead us.

Of all the myth users in contemporary science fiction, Zelazny is the most romantic. His ironic undercuttings, his constant reminders of the fallibilities of the gods, his periodic abandonment of formally cadenced rhetoric in favor of hard-bitten, throwaway colloquialisms all seem like bulwarks thrown up against a complete surrender to the power of the myths he recounts. Whereas Disch, for example, uses myth for the light it throws on character and action, and whereas most writers internalize myth, Zelazny abandons himself to the eternal patterns of myth as if they had an objective, external existence. It is an attractive failing that gives even his lesser works a good deal of immediacy; but it leaves him vulnerable to the charge of escapism, of losing himself (and the reader) over and over again in variants of the same primal fantasy.

Zelazny's books vary in quality, and it is true that the first three novels are among the strongest, but no watertight case can be made for a continuing decline, at least during the 1970's. For example, in the same year as the disappointing *To Die in Italbar* (1973), *Today We Choose Faces* was also published. Its cloned, amnesiac, morally schizophrenic Mafia hero, at war with himself in a claustrophobic future, is a striking creation. Conformist humanity is trapped (without knowing it) in a world-spanning House. The hero is a wolf playing therapist to sheep: another strong, elaborate metaphor around which the entire novel is structured.

Jack of Shadows (1971) consciously and effectively pits the worlds of science fiction and fantasy against one another. The eponymous twilight hero is balanced between a nightside world of magic, myth, intuition, and chaos, and a dayside world of rationality and order in a story of remarkably dexterous and unconventional imagery.

The Amber Chronicles, consisting in its first series of *Nine Princes in Amber* (1970), *The Guns of Avalon* (1972), *Sign of the Unicorn* (1975), *The Hand of Oberon* (1976), and *The Courts of Chaos* (1978), establishes a series of universes, receding realities, in which Byzantinelike court intrigues alternate with a metaphysical exploration of reality. Amber itself is a "penultimate" reality, a Platonic substrate or matrix, a universe (although beyond it lies one other universe more primal still) of which other universes, including our own, are but shadows. The princes of Amber can manipulate the stuff of existence, of external being, and can create shadow worlds of their own—just as Charles Render could manipulate the stuff of internal reality in *The Dream Master*. But all of Amber is subject to the entropic inroads of the Courts of Chaos. The first series is highly accomplished and sophisticated, although it is uneven in quality, with moments of startling force and clarity, as well as moments of startling vulgarity.

Doorways in the Sand (1976) is an inventive space opera with metaphysical ornamentation and a charming and irresponsible hero. *Roadmarks* (1979) is another exercise in manipulating the stuff of reality. The surrealist central image (a complex "freeway system," down which automobiles run, moving through time rather than space) is sustained with an admirable poker face and a good deal of chutzpah. This is the work of a writer very much in control of his powers; it is allusive, witty, colorful, and (as ever with Zelazny) constructed with an eye to the maximum exploitation of metaphor.

Zelazny was a storyteller, an entertainer in the best sense. Those who have criticized him for not being a high artist, which he probably never was, may have blinded themselves to his exemplary craftsmanship. However, though there was little falling off to the end of the 1970's, there can be no denying the slackening of creative pressure that became evident in his stories, especially his novels, through the 1980's and until his death in 1995.

One may conjecture—hearsay evidence is involved here—that Zelazny was a little trapped by the success of his best-selling Amber series, which he took up again in the 1980's. Certainly the commercial pressure to produce more of them, whether he wanted to or not, was intense. The sixth to the tenth novels in the Amber series—the second Amber series—appeared between 1985 and 1991. They are *Trumps of Doom* (1985), *Blood of Amber* (1986), *Sign of Chaos* (1987), *Knight of Shadows* (1989), and *Prince of Chaos* (1991). These fantasies, pitting a corrupted order against a systematic chaos, are focused on Merlin, son of the protagonist of the first five books (Corwin). Intensively recomplicated plot lines spiral inward, less and less comprehensibly, through ever more trivialized ambiguities, until the main pleasures for the reader are residual: some snappy dialogue, an occasional intensely rendered image.

Another sign that may point to flagging inspiration is the number of collaborative books Zelazny undertook in this period, including two with Fred Saberhagen (1982, 1990), two with Thomas T. Thomas (both in 1992), and three with Robert Sheckley (1991, 1993, 1995). It is believed that while the Saberhagen collaborations involved a genuine communication back and forth, the others were more by way of the collaborator fleshing out a Zelazny outline. Certainly the Saberhagen books are the strongest, the better probably being *Coils* (1982), a hard-bitten and vivid thriller about a man with a strange mental power. He is able to follow the inner workings of computers by a weird machine telepathy. He is in danger from the sinister corporation that once employed him, and somewhere there is a shadowy force that turns out to be a machine consciousness born in the computer networks, a quite novel idea at the time. There is little else new here, but the narrative is crafted with panache.

Two collaborations with Vaughn Bodé (the graphic artist who died in 1975) were products of the 1960's, children's stories, but not published for more than twenty years. They are *Here There Be Dragons* and *Way Up High*, both published in 1992. The collaboration with his partner Jane Lindskold, *Donnerjack*, was completed by Lindskold after Zelazny's death and published in 1997. It blends a virtual reality theme with visitations of mythical figures of power, this time from the Mesopotamian pantheon. *Psychoshop* (1998) is a farcical fantasy completed by Zelazny just before he died, from a fragment found in the literary estate of the celebrated Alfred Bester (1913–1987); it will add very little to the reputation of either.

The 1980's and 1990's for Zelazny were not notable for novels of quality. Though there were twenty novels, most of these were fantasy rather than science fiction and often ponderously humorous. But he could still write good short fiction, though he wrote less of it than he once did. His only two major awards in this period were for short fiction, a Hugo for best novella in 1986 for "24 Views of Mt. Fuji, by Hokusai," and a Hugo for best novelette in 1987 for "Permafrost." Both of these stories appear in Zelazny's final collection, *Frost and Fire* (1989). Earlier collections of interest are *The Last Defender of Camelot* (1980) and *Unicorn Variations* (1983).

While the creative force was diminishing to something of a trickle, there were still gushes here and there. Zelazny's forceful interest in the technical problems of writing was as strong as ever. His inclination to experiment in the way a story was told proceeded with continuing originality, even as the content of the tales moved increasingly toward repetitive mythic themes. The most distinguished novel Zelazny published after the end of the 1970's shows all of these things clearly: the occasional creative intensity, the experimentation, and the thematic repetition.

This novel was *Eye of Cat* (1982), the novel one guesses he *had* to write. Having dealt with the myths of so many diverse cultures, it was inevitable that he would turn to the Amerindian myths, in this case Navajo, that remained current not too far from his own home in New Mexico. Amerindian cultural patterns often involve mystical states of consciousness induced by drugs, and it was clearly a challenge to Zelazny to render in words a state for which one might think words—particularly English words—are clearly inadequate. A second challenge was to render the thought processes of the deeply alien superbeing that wishes to kill with appropriate ceremony the hero who once hunted down and captured him. (The hero is William Blackhorse Singer, the last and greatest of the Navajo hunters on a future Earth.) The novel contains passages of very experimental writing, sometimes recalling James Joyce's *Finnegans Wake* (1939), but also incorporating much Native American imagery. Some critics see the experiment as a failure, with too familiar a theme adrift opaquely in a sea of misty words. Others feel it is as strong as Zelazny's better-known early work. Certainly Zelazny should be honored for the attempt, and there is much to value in the richly hallucinatory apotheosis of Blackhorse Singer at the novel's desert close.

Outside of perhaps a dozen novels and short stories—maybe a quarter of what he wrote—it is difficult to regard Zelazny as a writer of the very first rank, though he continues to be revered in science fiction circles as one of the great innovators. On the negative side, his tales do not often cut deep enough. He was too ready to sacrifice the dramatic and ideational momentum of his work for the sake of wisecracking bathos or whimsy. He was too ready to press the buttons of our conditioned responses, asking for emotions that had not been completely paid for in the text.

But nobody would want to forget the positive side. Within the comparatively narrow range of narrative situations with which he chose to work, he dealt with serious questions about the tensions between fantasy and reality and about the cost of power. He did this not just with good-humored intelligence but also with a fountain of fresh, cool imagery, endlessly inventive. In short, he was a writer (at best) of astonishing verve and flair, who made it look easy. He had an ear for cadence and a sardonic poet's eye. As if making a pun on his father's profession, and that of his hero's father, Oberon of Amber, Zelazny was a pattern maker par excellence.

Selected Bibliography

SCIENCE FICTION AND FANTASY OF ROGER ZELAZNY

Outside the genre, Zelazny wrote four slim volumes of poetry and one historical Western novel, with Gerald Hausman, entitled *Wilderness*, 1994.

The Dream Master. New York: Ace Books, 1966. London: Rupert Hart-Davis, 1968.

This Immortal. New York: Ace Books, 1966; London: Rupert Hart-Davis, 1967.

Four for Tomorrow. New York: Ace Books, 1967. Reprinted as *A Rose for Ecclesiastes*, London: Rupert Hart-Davis, 1969. (Short stories.)

Lord of Light. Garden City, N.Y.: Doubleday, 1967; London: Faber and Faber, 1968.

Creatures of Light and Darkness. Garden City, N.Y.: Doubleday, 1969; London: Faber and Faber, 1970.

Damnation Alley. New York: G. P. Putnam's Sons, 1969; London: Faber and Faber, 1971.

Isle of the Dead. New York: Ace Books, 1969; London: Andre Deutsch, 1970.

Nine Princes in Amber. Garden City, N.Y.: Doubleday, 1970; London: Faber and Faber, 1972. (First in the Amber series.)

The Doors of His Face, the Lamps of His Mouth, and Other Stories. Garden City, N.Y.: Doubleday, 1971; London: Faber and Faber, 1973. (Short stories.)

Jack of Shadows. New York: Walker, 1971. London: Faber and Faber, 1972.

The Guns of Avalon. Garden City, N.Y.: Doubleday, 1972; London: Faber and Faber, 1974. (Second in the Amber series.)

Today We Choose Faces. New York: New American Library, 1973; London: Millington, 1975.

To Die in Italbar. Garden City, N.Y.: Doubleday, 1973; London: Faber and Faber, 1975.

Sign of the Unicorn. Garden City, N.Y.: Doubleday, 1975; London: Faber and Faber, 1977. (Third in the Amber series.)

Bridge of Ashes. New York: New American Library, 1976.

Deus Irae, with Philip K. Dick. Garden City, N.Y.: Doubleday, 1976; London: Victor Gollancz, 1977.

Doorways in the Sand. New York: Harper and Row, 1976; London: W. H. Allen, 1977.

The Hand of Oberon. Garden City, N.Y.: Doubleday, 1976; London: Faber and Faber, 1978. (Fourth in the Amber series.)

My Name Is Legion. New York: Ballantine Books, 1976; London: Faber and Faber, 1979. (Linked short stories.)

The Authorized Illustrated Book of Roger Zelazny. New York: Baronet Publishing Company, 1978. (Abridged short fiction; illustrated by Gray Morrow.)

The Courts of Chaos. Garden City, N.Y.: Doubleday, 1978; London: Faber and Faber, 1980. (Fifth in the Amber series.)

Roadmarks. New York: Ballantine Books, 1979; London: Macdonald, 1981.

Changeling. New York: Ace Books, 1980. (Illustrated by Esteban Maroto.)

The Last Defender of Camelot. New York: Pocket Books, 1980. (Short stories.)

The Changing Land. New York: Ballantine Del Rey, 1981.

Madwand. Huntington Woods, Mich.: Phantasia Press, 1981. (Sequel to *Changeling.*)

Coils, with Fred Saberhagen. New York: TOR, 1982.

Dilvish, the Damned. New York: Ballantine Del Rey, 1982. (Collection of eleven short stories; sequel to *The Changing Land.*)

Eye of Cat. New York: Timescape, 1982.

Unicorn Variations. New York: Simon and Schuster Timescape, 1983. (Short stories.)

Trumps of Doom. New York: Arbor House, 1985; London: Sphere, 1986. (Sixth in the Amber series.)

Blood of Amber. New York: Arbor House, 1986; London: Sphere, 1987. (Seventh in the Amber series.)

A Dark Traveling. New York: Walker Millennium, 1987. Reprinted as *A Dark Travelling,* London: Hutchinson, 1989. (Young adult fiction.)

Sign of Chaos. New York: Arbor House, 1987; London: Sphere, 1988. (Eighth in the Amber series.)

Frost and Fire. New York: William Morrow, 1989. (Collection of ten short stories and two essays.)

Knight of Shadows. New York: William Morrow, 1989; London: Orbit, 1991. (Ninth in the Amber series.)

Wizard World. New York: Baen Books, 1989. (Omnibus edition containing *Changeling* and *Madwand.*)

The Black Throne, with Fred Saberhagen. New York: Baen Books, 1990.

The Mask of Loki, with Thomas T. Thomas. New York: Baen Books, 1990.

Bring Me the Head of Prince Charming, with Robert Sheckley. New York: Bantam, 1991; London: Pan, 1994.

Prince of Chaos. New York: William Morrow, 1991; London: Orbit, 1993. (Tenth and last in the Amber series.)

Flare, with Thomas T. Thomas. New York: Baen Books, 1992.

Here There Be Dragons, with Vaughn Bodé. Hampton Falls, N.H.: Donald M. Grant, 1992. (Children's fiction, slipcased with *Way Up High* in a limited edition.)

Way Up High, with Vaughn Bodé. Hampton Falls, N.H.: Donald M. Grant, 1992. (Children's fiction, slipcased with *Here There Be Dragons* in a limited edition.)

If at Faust You Don't Succeed, with Robert Sheckley. New York: Bantam Spectra, 1993.

A Night in the Lonesome October, with illustrations by Gahan Wilson. New York: Morrow AvoNova, 1993; London: Orbit, 1994.

A Farce to Be Reckoned With, with Robert Sheckley. New York: Bantam Spectra, 1995.

Donnerjack, with Jane M. Lindskold. New York: Avon, 1997.

Psychoshop, with Alfred Bester. New York: Vintage Books, 1998.

CRITICAL, BIOGRAPHICAL, AND OTHER STUDIES

Krulik, Theodore. *Roger Zelazny.* New York: Ungar, 1986.

———. *The Complete Amber Sourcebook.* New York: Avon, 1995.

Levack, Daniel J. H. *Amber Dreams: A Roger Zelazny Bibliography.* San Francisco, Calif., and Columbia, Pa.: Underwood-Miller, 1983.

Lindskold, Jane M. *Roger Zelazny.* New York: Twayne, 1993.

Stephensen-Payne, Phil. *Roger Zelazny: A Working Bibliography.* Leeds, England, and Albuquerque, N.Mex.: Galactic Central, 1991.

Yoke, Carl B. *Roger Zelazny: Starmont Readers' Guide 2.* West Linn, Oreg.: Starmont House, 1979.

Zelazny, Roger, and Neil Randall. *Roger Zelazny's Visual Guide to Castle Amber.* New York: Avon, 1988. (Floor plans, maps, drawings, background.)

—PETER NICHOLLS

LIST OF CONTRIBUTORS

BRIAN W. ALDISS. Writer, editor, and subject of essay in this volume. **Mary Wollstonecraft Shelley** and **H. G. Wells.**

L. DAVID ALLEN. Instructor of English, University of Nebraska, Lincoln. **Isaac Asimov**

DOUGLAS BARBOUR. Associate Professor of English, University of Alberta. **Samuel R. Delany** and **William Gibson.**

MARTHA BARTTER. Associate Professor, Division of Language and Literature, Truman State University. Revision and update of **Frederik Pohl.**

E. F. BLEILER. Editor and bibliographer. Editor of first edition of *Science Fiction Writers*. **Edgar Rice Burroughs; John W. Campbell, Jr.; H. P. Lovecraft; A. Merritt; Edgar Allan Poe; Luis Philip Senarens; M. P. Shiel; Jules Verne; S. Fowler Wright.** Revision and update of **John Taine.**

RICHARD BLEILER. Humanities Reference Librarian, Homer Babbidge Library, University of Connecticut. Editor of this volume. Revision and update of **C. L. Moore/Henry Kuttner** and **Chad Oliver.**

JAMES L. CAMPBELL, SR. Professor of Victorian Literature, University of Wisconsin, Milwaukee. **Sir Arthur Conan Doyle; Garrett P. Serviss; Olaf Stapledon; John Taine.**

JOHN CARR. Coauthor of **Larry Niven.**

JOHN CLUTE. Writer. **James Blish; Karel Čapek; Richard Cowper; Gordon R. Dickson; Fred Hoyle; Murray Leinster; C. S. Lewis; Margaret St. Clair; E. E. Smith; Howard Waldrop; Gene Wolfe.**

DAVID COWART. Louise Fry Scudder Professor of Humanities, Department of English, University of South Carolina. Revision and update of **Walter M. Miller, Jr.**

ELIZABETH CUMMINS. Chair and Professor, Department of English, University of Missouri–Rolla. Revision and update of **Ursula K. Le Guin.**

GARDNER DOZOIS. Writer and editor. **Damon Knight.**

MALCOLM EDWARDS. Writer and editor. **C. M. Kornbluth; Eric Frank Russell; Robert Silverberg; William Tenn; Jack Vance.**

CHARLES L. ELKINS. Associate Professor English, Director of the Humanities Program, and Associate Dean, College of Arts and Sciences, Florida International University. **George Orwell** and **Kurt Vonnegut.**

RICHARD FINHOLT. Coauthor of **Larry Niven.**

H. BRUCE FRANKLIN. John Cotton Dana Professor of English and American Studies, Rutgers University. Revision and update of **Kurt Vonnegut.**

ELIZABETH HAND. Writer and critic. **Lucius Shepard.**

DONALD M. HASSLER. Professor of English, Kent State University. Revision and update of **Isaac Asimov.**

BERNARD HEIDKAMP. University of Maryland, College Park. **C. J. Cherryh.**

MARILYN J. HOLT. Writer. **Joanna Russ.**

GRAY KOCHHAR-LINDGREN Coauthor of **Michael Bishop.**

DAVID LANGFORD. Writer and critic. **Greg Bear** and **Christopher Priest.** Revision and updates of **Damon Knight; Larry Niven; Jack Vance.**

JULIE LINDEN. Librarian, W. E. B. Dubois Library, University of Massachusetts, Amherst. Revision and update of **Joanna Russ.**

WILLIS E. McNELLY. Professor Emeritus of English, California State University, Fullerton. **Brian W. Aldiss; Alfred Bester; Ray Bradbury; Harry Harrison; Frank Herbert.**

SANDRA MIESEL. Writer. **Poul Anderson.**

CHRIS MORGAN. Writer and reviewer. **Hal Clement; Judith Merril; Robert Sheckley; Cordwainer Smith.** Revision and updates of **Philip José Farmer; Michael Moorcock; Robert Silverberg; Clifford D. Simak; James Tiptree, Jr.**

ROBERT E. MYERS. Professor and Chairman, Philosophy Department, Bethany College. **Jack Williamson.**

PETER NICHOLLS. Writer and editor. **Algis Budrys; Richard Matheson; Michael Moorcock; Connie Willis; Roger Zelazny.**

JOHN B. OWER. Associate Professor of English, University of South Carolina. **Walter M. Miller, Jr.**

JOHN R. PFEIFFER. Professor of English, Central Michigan University. **Octavia Butler; Aldous Huxley; John Brunner.**

DAVID N. SAMUELSON. Professor of English, California State University, Long Beach. **Arthur C. Clarke; Ursula K. Le Guin; Frederik Pohl.**

JOHN SCARBOROUGH. Professor of Ancient History and the History of Medicine and Pharmacy, University of Kentucky. **H. Rider Haggard** and **John Wyndham.**

FREDERICK SHROYER. (Deceased) Professor of English and American Literature, California State University, Los Angeles. **C. L. Moore** and **Henry Kuttner.**

GEORGE EDGAR SLUSSER. Professor of Comparative Literature and Curator of the Eaton Collection, University of California, Riverside. **Harlan Ellison** and **Pat Murphy.** Revision and update of **Jack Williamson.**

WILLIAM SPRUIELL. Department of English Language and Literature, Central Michigan University. Coauthor of **Michael Bishop.**

BRIAN M. STABLEFORD. Writer. **J. G. Ballard; David Brin; L. Sprague de Camp; Philip K. Dick; Thomas M. Disch; Joe Haldeman; Robert A. Heinlein; David H. Keller; Fritz Leiber; Katherine MacLean; Clark Ashton Smith; Bruce Sterling; Theodore Sturgeon; Ian Watson; Stanley G. Weinbaum; Kate Wilhelm.**

SHERRY STOSKOPF. Lecturer of English, Minot State University. **Kim Stanley Robinson** and **Sheri S. Tepper.**

PETER SWIRSKI. McGill University. **Stanislaw Lem.**

GARY WESTFAHL. University of California, Riverside. **Orson Scott Card.** Revision and update of **Arthur C. Clarke.**

COLIN WILSON. Writer. **A. E. van Vogt.**

SUSAN WOOD. (Deceased) Assistant Professor of English, University of British Columbia. **James Tiptree, Jr.**

GENERAL BIBLIOGRAPHY

Selected bibliographies for individual authors have been prepared by the contributors (with, in some cases, transatlantic editions added by the editor). The following general reference works have been useful for the overall preparation of this volume.

Aldiss, Brian W., with David Wingrove. *Trillion Year Spree: The History of Science Fiction*. London: Victor Gollancz, 1986.

Barron, Neil, ed. *Anatomy of Wonder 4: A Critical Guide to Science Fiction*. New Providence, N.J.: R. R. Bowker, 1995.

Bleiler, Everett F. *The Checklist of Science-Fiction and Supernatural Fiction*. Glen Rock, N.J.: Firebell Books, 1978.

Bleiler, Everett F. *The Guide to Supernatural Fiction*. Kent, Ohio: Kent State University Press, 1983.

Bleiler, Everett F. *Science Fiction: The Early Years*. Kent, Ohio: Kent State University Press, 1990 (1991). With the assistance of Richard J. Bleiler.

Bleiler, Everett F. *Science Fiction: The Gernsback Years*. Kent, Ohio: Kent State University Press, 1998. With the assistance of Richard J. Bleiler.

Bleiler, E. F., ed. *Science Fiction Writers: Critical Studies of the Major Authors from the Early Nineteenth Century to the Present Day*. New York: Charles Scribner's Sons, 1982.

Bleiler, E. F., ed. *Supernatural Fiction Writers: Fantasy and Horror*. 2 vols. New York: Charles Scribner's Sons, 1985

Chalker, Jack, and Mark Owings. *The Science-Fantasy Publishers: A Critical and Bibliographic History*. 3d ed., revised and enlarged. Westminster, Md.: Mirage Press, Ltd., 1991.

Clute, John, and John Grant, eds. *Encyclopedia of Fantasy*. New York: St. Martin's, 1997.

Clute, John, Peter Nicholls, and Brian Stableford, eds. *The Encyclopedia of Science Fiction*. London: Orbit, 1993.

Contento, William. *Index to Science Fiction Anthologies and Collections*. Boston, Mass.: G. K. Hall, 1978. Contento's Website is www.best.com/~contento.

Day, Donald B. *Index to the Science Fiction Magazines, 1926–1950*. Revised edition. Boston: G. K. Hall, 1982.

Guillemette, Aurel. *The Best in Science Fiction: Winners and Nominees of the Major Awards in Science Fiction*. Brookfield, Vt.: Scolar Press, 1993.

Hall, Hal W., ed. *Science Fiction and Fantasy Reference Index, 1878–1985*. 2 vols. Detroit: Gale Research, Inc., 1987.

Hall, Hal W., ed. *Science Fiction and Fantasy Reference Index, 1985–1991*. Englewood, Colo.: Libraries Unlimited, 1993.

Hall, Hal W., ed. *Science Fiction and Fantasy Reference Index, 1992–1995*. Englewood, Colo.: Libraries Unlimited, 1997.

Index to British Science Fiction Magazines, 1934–1953. 7 parts. Canberra: Australian Science Fiction Association, 1968–1975.

Mallett, Daryl F. *Reginald's Science Fiction and Fantasy Awards: A Comprehensive Guide to the Awards and Their Winners*. 3d ed. San Bernardino, Cal.: Borgo Press, 1993.

Pederson, Jay P. *St. James Guide to Science Fiction Writers*. 4th ed. New York: St. James Press, 1996.

Reginald, Robert. *Science Fiction and Fantasy Literature: A Checklist, 1700–1974, with Contemporary Science Fiction Authors*. 2 vols. Detroit: Gale Research, Inc., 1979.

Reginald, Robert. *Science Fiction and Fantasy Literature, 1975–1991: A Bibliography of Science Fiction, Fantasy, and Horror Fiction Books and Nonfiction Monographs*. Detroit: Gale Research, Inc., 1992.

Strauss, Erwin S. *MITSFS Index to the SF Magazines 1951–1965*. Cambridge, Mass.: MIT SF Society, 1966.

Tuck, Donald H. *The Encyclopedia of Science Fiction and Fantasy Through 1968.* 3 vols. Chicago: Advent, 1974, 1978, 1982.

Tymn, Marshall B., and Mike Ashley, eds. *Science Fiction, Fantasy, and Weird Fiction Magazines.* Westport, Conn.: Greenwood Press, 1985.

INDEX

*Arabic numbers printed in boldface type refer
to extended treatment of a subject.
Numbers in italics refer to illustrations.*